PRINCIPLES OF
Economics

N. Gregory Mankiw
Harvard University

The Dryden Press
Harcourt Brace College Publishers

Fort Worth Philadelphia San Diego New York Orlando Austin San Antonio
Toronto Montreal London Sydney Tokyo

Publishers	Ted Buchholz, George Provol
Executive Editor	Emily Barrosse
Product Manager	Kathleen Sharp
Field Product Manager	David Theisen
Developmental Editors	Jane Tufts, Anita M. Fallon
Project Editor	Amy Schmidt
Production Manager	Eddie Dawson
Art Director	Jeanette Barber
Picture & Rights Editor	Annette Coolidge

Interior illustrations	© 1997 by Michael Steirnagle
Cover design	Didona Designs
Cover images	Alois Schonn (1826–1897) *Fruit Market in Vienna near Theresian Brucke,* Museum der Stadt Wien/ET Archive, London/Super Stock (painting, foreground); Howard Bjornson/Photonica (background)

About the cover The cover illustrates, as Alfred Marshall pointed out a century ago, that economics is "a study of mankind in the ordinary business of life." Alois Schonn's classic artwork was chosen by the author because of its beauty, elegance, simplicity, and friendly appeal. It overlays a modern financial report containing graphs and numbers. The contrast between the artwork and the financial report represents the art and science of economics.

About the interior illustrations The interior illustrations are the work of Michael Steirnagle. Each illustration brings to life the economic markets and activities associated with the chapter topics presented in the book. Steirnagle, an award-winning illustrator and artist, teaches at Palomar College in San Marcos, Calif. He has been awarded two gold medals from the Society of Illustrators and has recently illustrated a children's book.

Address for Orders
The Dryden Press
6277 Sea Harbor Drive
Orlando, FL 32887-6777
1-800-782-4479

Address for Editorial Correspondence
The Dryden Press
301 Commerce Street, Suite 3700
Fort Worth, TX 76102

ISBN: 0-03-098238-3

Derivative works in paperback are available for *Principles of Microeconomics* (0-03-024502-8) and *Principles of Macroeconomics* (0-03-024051-X).

Library of Congress Catalog Card Number: 96-71397

Printed in the United States of America

7 8 9 0 1 2 3 4 5 6   048   9 8 7 6 5 4 3 2 1

The Dryden Press
Harcourt Brace College Publishers

ABOUT THE AUTHOR

N. Gregory Mankiw is Professor of Economics at Harvard University. As a student, he studied economics at Princeton University and MIT. As a teacher, he has taught various courses, including macroeconomics, microeconomics, statistics, and principles of economics. He even spent one summer long ago as a sailing instructor on Long Beach Island.

Professor Mankiw is a prolific writer. His work has been published in academic journals, such as the *American Economic Review, Journal of Political Economy,* and *Quarterly Journal of Economics,* and in more popular forums, such as *The New York Times, Boston Globe,* and *The Wall Street Journal.* He is also the author of the best-selling textbook *Macroeconomics* (Worth Publishers). In addition to his teaching, research, and writing, Mankiw is Director of the Monetary Economics Program at the National Bureau of Economic Research, a nonprofit think tank in Cambridge, Mass., and an adviser to the Federal Reserve Bank of Boston and the Congressional Budget Office.

Professor Mankiw lives in Wellesley, Mass., with his wife, Deborah, their children, Catherine and Nicholas, and the family's border terrier, Keynes.

To Catherine and Nicholas,
my other contributions to the next generation

PREFACE: TO THE INSTRUCTOR

During my twenty-year career as a student, the course that excited me most was the two-semester sequence on the principles of economics I took during my freshman year in college. It is no exaggeration to say that it changed my life.

I had grown up in a family that often discussed politics over the dinner table. The pros and cons of various solutions to society's problems generated fervent debate. But, in school, I had been drawn to the sciences. Whereas politics seemed vague, rambling, and subjective, science was analytic, systematic, and objective. While political debate continued without end, science made progress.

My freshman course on the principles of economics opened my eyes to a new way of thinking. Economics combines the virtues of politics and science. It is, truly, a social science. Its subject matter is society—how people choose to lead their lives and how they interact with one another. But it approaches its subject with the dispassion of a science. By bringing the methods of science to the questions of politics, economics tries to make progress on the fundamental challenges that all societies face.

I was drawn to write this book in the hope that I could convey some of the excitement about economics that I felt as a student in my first economics course. Economics is a subject in which a little knowledge goes a long way. (The same cannot be said, for instance, of the study of physics or the Japanese language.) Economists have a unique way of viewing the world, much of which can be taught in one or two semesters. My goal in this book is to transmit this way of thinking to the widest possible audience and to convince readers that it illuminates much about the world around them.

I am a firm believer that everyone should study the fundamental ideas that economics has to offer. One of the purposes of general education is to make people more informed about the world in order to make them better citizens. The study of economics, as much as any discipline, serves this goal. Writing an economics textbook is, therefore, a great honor and a great responsibility. It is one way that economists can help promote better government and a more prosperous future. As the great economist Paul Samuelson put it, "I don't care who writes a nation's laws, or crafts its advanced treaties, if I can write its economics textbooks."

BREVITY

To reach a wide audience, I felt that one characteristic of this book would be especially important: its length. If you turn to the end of this book, you will find that it is hundreds of pages shorter than many of the standard texts used to teach the principles of economics. Moreover, the page count has not been reduced by cramming as much as possible on each page. As I requested, the designers of the book have given it an open, uncluttered, and friendly look. Instead, brevity has been achieved by trying to present the principles of economics in the fewest words possible.

To explain this choice, I must make a confession: I am a slow reader. As a student, I rarely finished the readings I was assigned. I relied on Cliff's Notes an embarrassing number of times. I groaned whenever a professor gave the class a 1,000-page tome to read (together, of course, with ancillary articles). I took some solace in the fact that my reaction was not unique. The Greek poet Callimachus put it succinctly: "Big book, big bore." Callimachus made that observation in 250 B.C., so he was probably not referring to an economics textbook. But today his sentiment is echoed around the world every semester in the first lecture of many economics courses.

When I decided to write a text for the first course in economics, I wanted to write a book that as a student I would like to have read. My first and foremost goal, therefore, was brevity. I kept in mind a dictum from the great novelist Robertson Davies: "One of the most important things about writing is to boil it down and not bore the hell out of everybody."

All textbooks on economics teach that resources are scarce, but few textbook writers remember that student time is one of those scarce resources. I have tried to respect that scarcity by avoiding the bells, whistles, and extraneous details that distract students from the key lessons. I hope this book lives up to the first word of its title, *Principles of Economics*.

ORIENTATION

To boil economics down to its essentials, I had to consider what is truly important for students to learn in their first course in economics. As a result, this book differs from others not only in its length but also in its orientation.

It is tempting for a professional economist writing a textbook to take the economist's point of view and to emphasize those topics that fascinate him and other economists. I have done my best to avoid that temptation. I have tried to put myself in the position of someone seeing economics for the first time. My goal is to emphasize the material that *students* should and do find interesting about the study of the economy.

One result is that more of this book is devoted to applications and policy, and less is devoted to formal economic theory, than is the case with many other books written for the principles course. For example, after students learn about the market forces of supply and demand in Chapters 4 through 6, they immediately apply these tools in Chapters 7 through 9 to consider three important questions facing our society: Why is the free market a good way to organize economic activity? How does taxation interfere with the market mechanism? Who are the winners and losers from international trade? These kinds of questions resonate with the concerns and interests that students hear about in the news and bring from their own lives.

Throughout this book I have tried to return to applications and policy questions as often as possible. Most chapters include "Case Studies" illustrating how the principles of economics are applied. In addition, "In the News" boxes offer excerpts of newspaper articles showing how economic ideas shed light on the current issues facing society. It is my hope that after students finish their first course in economics, they will think about news stories from a new perspective and with greater insight.

ORGANIZATION

To write a brief and student-friendly book, I had to consider new ways to organize the material. This book includes all the topics that are central to a first course in economics, but the topics are not always arranged in the traditional order.

What follows is a whirlwind tour of this text. This tour will, I hope, give instructors some sense of how the pieces fit together.

Chapter 1, "Ten Principles of Economics," introduces students to the economist's view of the world. It previews some of the big ideas that recur throughout economics, such as opportunity cost, marginal decisionmaking, the role of incentives, the gains from trade, and the efficiency of market allocations. Throughout the book, I refer regularly to the *Ten Principles of Economics* in Chapter 1 to remind students that these principles are the foundation for most economic analysis. A building-blocks icon in the margin calls attention to these references.

Chapter 2, "Thinking Like an Economist," examines how economists approach their field of study. It discusses the role of assumptions in developing a theory and introduces the concept of an economic model. It also discusses the role of economists in making policy. The appendix to this chapter offers a brief refresher course on how graphs are used and how they can be abused.

Chapter 3, "Interdependence and the Gains from Trade," presents the theory of comparative advantage. This theory explains why individuals trade with their neighbors, as well as why nations trade with other nations. Much of economics is about how market forces coordinate the many individual production and consumption decisions that take place in the economy. As a starting point for this analysis, students see in this chapter why specialization, interdependence, and trade can benefit everyone.

The next three chapters introduce the basic tools of supply and demand. Chapter 4, "The Market Forces of Supply and Demand," develops the supply curve, the demand curve, and the notion of market equilibrium. Chapter 5, "Elasticity and Its Application," introduces the concept of elasticity and uses it to analyze events in three different markets. Chapter 6, "Supply, Demand, and Government Policies," uses these tools to examine price controls, such as rent-control and minimum-wage laws, and tax incidence.

Chapter 7, "Consumers, Producers, and the Efficiency of Markets," extends the analysis of supply and demand using the concepts of consumer surplus and producer surplus. It begins by developing the link between consumers' willingness to pay and the demand curve and the link between producers' costs of production and the supply curve. It then shows that the market equilibrium maximizes the sum of the producer and consumer surplus. In this book, therefore, students learn early about the efficiency of market allocations.

The next two chapters apply the concepts of producer and consumer surplus to questions of policy. Chapter 8, "Application: The Costs of Taxation," shows why taxation results in deadweight losses and what determines the size of those losses. Chapter 9, "Application: International Trade," considers who wins and who loses from international trade and presents the debate over protectionist trade policies.

Having examined why market allocations are often desirable, the book then considers how the government can sometimes improve on market allocations. Chapter 10, "Externalities," explains how external effects such as pollution can render market outcomes inefficient. It also discusses the possible public and private solutions to those inefficiencies. Chapter 11, "Public Goods and Common Resources," considers the inefficiencies that arise when goods, such as national defense, have no market price. Chapter 12, "The Design of the Tax System," describes how the government raises the revenue necessary to pay for public goods. It presents some institutional background about the U.S. tax system and then discusses how the goals of efficiency and equity come into play in the design of a tax system.

The next five chapters examine firm behavior and industrial organization. Chapter 13, "The Costs of Production," discusses what to include in a firm's costs, and it introduces cost curves. Chapter 14, "Firms in Competitive Markets," analyzes the behavior of price-taking firms and derives the market supply curve. Chapter 15, "Monopoly," discusses the behavior of a firm that is the sole seller in its market. It discusses the inefficiency of monopoly pricing, the possible policy responses, and the attempts by monopolies to price discriminate. Chapter 16, "Oligopoly," covers markets in which there are only a few sellers and uses the prisoners' dilemma as the model for examining strategic interaction. Chapter 17, "Monopolistic Competition," looks at behavior in a market in which many sellers offer similar but differentiated products. It also discusses the debate over the effects of advertising.

The following three chapters present issues related to labor markets. Chapter 18, "The Markets for the Factors of Production," emphasizes the link between factor prices and marginal productivity. Chapter 19, "Earnings and Discrimination," discusses the determinants of equilibrium wages, including compensating differentials, human capital, and discrimination. Chapter 20, "The Distribution of Income," examines the degree of inequality in U.S. society, the alternative views about the government's role in changing the distribution of income, and the various policies aimed at helping society's poorest members.

Chapter 21, "The Theory of Consumer Choice," analyzes individual decisionmaking using budget constraints and indifference curves. It covers material that is somewhat more advanced than the rest of the book. Some instructors may want to skip this chapter, depending on the emphases of their courses and the interests of their students. Instructors who do cover this material may want to do so earlier, and I have written this chapter so that it can be covered anytime after the basics of supply and demand have been introduced.

Beginning in Chapter 22, the book turns to the topics of macroeconomics. This coverage starts with issues of measurement. Chapter 22, "Measuring a Nation's Income," discusses the meaning of gross domestic product and related statistics from the national income accounts. Chapter 23, "Measuring the Cost of Living," discusses the measurement and use of the consumer price index.

The next three chapters describe the behavior of the real economy in the long run over which wages and prices are flexible. Chapter 24, "Production and Growth," examines the determinants of the large variation in living standards over time and across countries. Chapter 25, "Saving, Investment, and the Financial System," discusses the types of financial institutions in our economy and examines the role of these institutions in allocating resources. Chapter 26, "The Natural Rate of Unemployment," considers the long-run determinants of the unemployment rate, including minimum-wage laws, the market power of unions, the role of efficiency wages, and the efficacy of job search.

Having described the long-run behavior of the real economy, the book then turns to the long-run behavior of money and prices. Chapter 27, "The Monetary System," introduces the economist's concept of money and the role of the central bank in controlling the quantity of money. Chapter 28, "Inflation: Its Causes and Costs," develops the link between money growth and inflation and discusses the social costs of inflation.

The next two chapters present the macroeconomics of open economies. Chapter 29, "Open-Economy Macroeconomics: Basic Concepts," explains the relationship among saving, investment, and the trade balance, the distinction between the nominal and real exchange rate, and the theory of purchasing-power parity. Chapter 30, "A Macroeconomic Theory of the Open Economy," presents a classical model of the international flow of goods and capital. The model sheds light on various issues, including the link between budget deficits and trade deficits and the macroeconomic effects of trade policies. Because instructors differ in how much they emphasize this material, these chapters were written so they could be used in different ways. Some instructors may choose to cover Chapter 29 but not Chapter 30; others may skip both chapters; and others may choose to defer the analysis of open-economy macroeconomics until the end of their courses.

After fully developing the long-run theory of the economy in Chapters 24 through 30, the book turns its attention to explaining short-run fluctuations around the long-run trend. This organization simplifies the teaching of the theory of short-run fluctuations because, at this point in the course, students have a good grounding in many basic macroeconomic concepts. Chapter 31, "Aggregate Demand and Aggregate Supply," begins with some facts about the business cycle and then introduces the model of aggregate demand and aggregate supply. Chapter 32, "The Influence of Monetary and Fiscal Policy on Aggregate Demand," explains how policymakers can use the tools at their disposal to shift the aggregate-demand curve. Chapter 33, "The Short-Run Tradeoff between Inflation and Unemployment," explains why policymakers who control aggregate demand face a tradeoff between inflation and unemployment. It examines why this tradeoff exists in the short run, why it shifts over time, and why it does not exist in the long run.

The book concludes with Chapter 34, "Five Debates over Macroeconomic Policy." This capstone chapter considers five controversial issues facing policymakers: the proper degree of policy activism in response to the business cycle, the choice between rules and discretion in the conduct of monetary policy, the desirability of reaching zero inflation, the importance of balancing the government's budget, and the need for tax reform to encourage saving. For each issue, the chapter presents both sides of the debate and encourages students to make their own judgments.

LEARNING TOOLS

The purpose of this book is to help students learn the fundamental lessons of economics and to show students how those lessons can be applied to the world in which they live. Toward that end, I have used various learning tools that recur throughout the book.

◆ **Chapter Objectives**   Every chapter begins with a list of the chapter's primary objectives to give students a sense of where the chapter is heading. Each list has been kept brief in order to help students stay focused on the four or five key lessons presented in that chapter.

◆ **Case Studies**   Economic theory is useful and interesting only if it can be applied to understand actual events and policies. This book, therefore, contains numerous case studies that apply the theory that has just been developed.

◆ **In the News Boxes**   One benefit from studying economics is that it gives students a new perspective and greater understanding about news from around the world. To highlight this benefit, I have included excerpts from many newspaper articles. These articles, together with my brief introductions, show how basic economic theory can be applied. Some of these articles are opinion columns written by prominent economists.

◆ **FYI Boxes**   These boxes provide additional material "for your information." Some of them give a glimpse into the history of economic thought. Others clarify difficult technical issues. Still others discuss supplementary topics that instructors might choose either to discuss or skip in their lectures.

◆ **Definitions of Key Concepts**   When key concepts are introduced in the chapter, they are presented in **bold** typeface. In addition, their definitions are placed in the margins. This treatment should aid students in learning and reviewing the material.

◆ **Quick Quizzes**   After each major section, students are offered a "quick quiz" to check their comprehension of what they have just learned. If students cannot readily answer these quizzes, they should stop and reread the material before continuing.

◆ **Chapter Summaries**   Each chapter ends with a brief summary that reminds students of the most important lessons that they have just learned. Later in their studying it offers them an efficient way to review for exams.

◆ **List of Key Concepts**   A list of key concepts at the end of each chapter allows students to test their understanding of the new terms that have been introduced. Page references are included so students can review the terms they do not understand.

◆ **Questions for Review**   At the end of each chapter are questions for review that test the chapter's primary lessons. Students can use these questions to check their comprehension after finishing a chapter and to prepare for exams.

◆ **Problems and Applications**   Each chapter also contains a variety of problems and applications that ask students to apply the material they have learned. Some professors may use these questions for homework assignments. Others may use them as a starting point for classroom discussions.

SUPPLEMENTS

The Dryden Press offers a variety of supplements for instructors and students who use this book. The goal of these ancillary resources is to provide an integrated package that makes teaching the principles of economics easy for the professor and learning them easy for the student. A. Andrew John (University of Virginia), an excellent economist and economics teacher, helped oversee the development of these materials.

The Dryden Press provides copies of these supplements free of charge to those instructors qualified under its adoption policy. Please contact your sales representative to learn how you may qualify, or call The Dryden Press at 1-800-237-2665.

For the Instructor

Teaching the principles of economics can be a demanding job. Often, classes are large and teaching assistants in short supply. The supplements designed for the instructor make that job less demanding and more fun.

- **Test Bank** Christopher Fawson and Dwight Israelsen (both of Utah State University) have prepared a test bank to accompany this text. The test bank contains 6,500 test questions consisting of multiple-choice questions and a large number of class-tested conceptual questions and problems. For the instructor's convenience, every question in the test bank is identified according to the chapter "Learning Objective" the question covers, the chapter section in which the material is covered, the level of difficulty, and the type of question (multiple-choice, true–false, short answer, critical thinking, definition, or graphical). Answers immediately follow each question.

- **Computerized Test Bank** The Dryden Press also offers a computerized version of the test bank (EXAMaster+) for IBM and Macintosh users. This software has many features that facilitate test preparation, scoring, and grade recording. It also offers great flexibility. The order of test questions can be altered to create different versions of any given test, and it is easy to modify questions and reproduce any of the graphing questions to meet the instructor's needs.

- **Instructor's Resource Manual with Adjunct & Teaching Assistant Guide** William T. Harris (University of Delaware) and Carolyn T. Bodkin (Trident Technical College) have written an instructor's manual aimed at helping both experienced and novice instructors prepare their lectures. Harris has written lecture notes for every chapter in this book. These notes briefly summarize the text material and provide additional examples and applications. Bodkin's adjunct and teaching assistant guide offers extensive outlines of every chapter, even more examples, and classroom warm-up activities to help introduce chapter topics.

- **Electronic Instructor's Resource Manual** The entire *Instructor's Resource Manual* is also available in an electronic format (for Windows). Using these electronic files, instructors can create their own lecture notes or incorporate parts of the *Instructor's Resource Manual* into their PowerPoint presentations.

- **Solutions Manual** Dean Croushore (Federal Reserve Bank of Philadelphia) has written a solutions manual that contains complete solutions for all the "Questions for Review" and "Problems and Applications" found in the text. The entire manual is three-hole punched and perforated to make it easier for the instructor to hand out solutions to students.

- **PowerPoint Presentation** Steve McGary (Ricks College) has developed a computer-based PowerPoint slide show that can save professors time as they prepare for class. This supplement covers all the essential topics presented in each chapter of this book. Graphs, tables, lists, and concepts are developed sequentially, much as one might develop them on a blackboard. Additional examples and applications, pulled from the *Instructor's Resource Manual*, are used to reinforce major lessons. The slides are crisp, clear, and colorful. Instructors may adapt or add slides to customize their lectures.

◆ **Web Site**   Robert Rycroft (Mary Washington College) has helped The Dryden Press develop a Web site to accompany this text. To appreciate this resource, we invite you to visit the site at http://www.dryden.com/econ. The ever-evolving Web site is both a teaching and economic research tool, with separate areas for students and instructors. Students visiting this page can learn from tutorials featuring interactive graphs, access a page of economic indicators, follow links relevant to each chapter, find out about career opportunities, and test their knowledge with our on-line quizzes. Instructors will be able to search a bank of news summaries and comprehension questions, download the instructor's resource material, and share ideas with others who are using this textbook.

◆ **Classroom Activities, Demonstrations, and Games for Principles of Economics**   Charles A. Stull (Kalamazoo College) has written a supplement that helps instructors interested in incorporating "cooperative learning" and "learning by experiment" exercises in their courses. This supplement contains over 50 games, classroom experiments, in-class demonstrations, and take-home and in-class assignments. Each activity is linked to a specific text chapter and lists the type of activity, topics covered, materials list, time required for completion, and classroom limitations. Thorough directions are provided for the instructor. For the instructor's convenience, the supplement is three-hole punched and perforated, and all pages are designed for easy overhead use and photocopying. The activities supplement is also available on the Web site.

◆ **The "Ten Principles" Video Set**   The Dryden Press has commissioned and produced ten video segments that illustrate the *Ten Principles of Economics* introduced in Chapter 1. Instructors can show these videos as an interesting and visually appealing introduction to topics. Questions for use with the videos will be available.

◆ **Overhead Transparencies**   For instructors who do not want to use PowerPoint presentations, overhead transparency acetates are available. These overhead transparencies consist of figures and tables from the text, allowing instructors to build text images into their lectures. Some of the more complex acetates are layered to show what happens graphically when curves shift.

For the Student

The Dryden Press makes supplements available for students who are studying the principles of economics. These supplements reinforce the basic lessons taught in this book and offer opportunities for additional practice and feedback.

◆ **Student Study Guide**   David R. Hakes (University of Northern Iowa) and Robert Harris (Indiana University–Purdue University at Indianapolis) have written a study guide that provides students with a useful summary and review of the important concepts presented in the text. Each study guide chapter includes a chapter overview, a chapter review, helpful hints, and definitions. Students can test their understanding of the material with practice problems and a chapter self-test. Solutions to all study guide problems follow each chapter.

◆ **TAG: Tutorial-Analytical-Graphical Student Software**   Andrew Foshee (McNeese State University) has customized for this book the award-winning educational software by Tod Porter and Teresa Riley (both of Youngstown State University). This software contains an extensive chapter-by-chapter tutorial, a hands-on graphic section in which students are required to draw curves (with key strokes or a mouse), and a practice exam for each section. Students receive immediate feedback on their answers. It is available in both DOS and Windows formats.

Supplement Accuracy

The accuracy of supplements is of critical importance for instructors and students. As a result, every supplement was thoroughly reviewed for accuracy and solid linkage to this text. I am grateful to the following team of "accuracy specialists" for helping to fine-tune the supplements:

Scott Benson, *Idaho State University*
Bob Beaudry, *Hesser College*
Jay Bhattacharya, *Okaloosa-Walton Community College*
Scott Bloom, *North Dakota State University*
Paula Bracy, *University of Toledo*
Mary Bumgarner, *Kennesaw State University*
Kevin Carey, *University of Miami*
Veree Ethridge, *College of St. Francis*
Frank Falero, *California State University at Bakersfield*
Richard Fenner, *Utica College*
Phil Forbus, *University of South Alabama*
Robert Francis, *Shoreline Community College*
W. E. Gentzel, *Pensacola Junior College*
Mehdi Haririan, *Bloomsburg University*
Mary Ann Hendryson, *Western Washington University*
C. Denise Hixson, *Midlands Technical College*
James Hubert, *Seattle Central Community College*

Herbert Kessel, *St. Michael's College*
Jim McGowen, *Belleville Area College*
Arthur W. Meyer, *Lincolnland Community College*
John Panagakis, *Onodaga Community College*
Robert Parks, *Washington University*
Timothy Perri, *Appalachian State University*
Reza Ramazani, *St. Michael's College*
Georges Rocourt, *Barry University*
Haideh Salehi-Esfahani, *University of Washington*
Rolando Santos, *Lakeland Community College*
Donald Schilling, *University of Missouri at Columbia*
Abu Selimuddin, *Berkshire Community College*
Bill Steen, *Santa Fe Community College*
Anthony Uremovic, *Joliet Junior College*
Ivan Weinel, *Park College*
Art Woolf, *University of Vermont*

Wall Street Journal Edition

One goal in teaching the principles of economics is to provide students a better understanding of the world around them. Many instructors, therefore, encourage students to read about economic issues in the newspaper as they take the course. Those instructors may want to consider the special *Wall Street Journal Edition* of this text. This edition is the same as the standard edition but includes a ten-week subscription to *The Wall Street Journal*. Students can activate their subscriptions simply by completing and mailing the business reply card found in the back of the book. Talk to your Dryden Press sales representative for more information, or call 1-800-237-2665.

ACKNOWLEDGMENTS

In writing this book, I had the benefit of the input from many talented people. Let me begin by thanking those economics professors who read and commented on portions of the manuscript. In some cases, these individuals read the manuscript several times as it was revised and (I hope) improved:

Ashraf Afifi, *Ferris State University*
Seemin Ahmad, *Dutchess Community College*
Terence Alexander, *Iowa State University*
Neil O. Alper, *Northeastern University*
Christine Amsler, *Michigan State University*
Lisa Anderson, *The American University*
Mahmoud P. Arya, *Edison Community College*
Aliakbar Ataiifar, *Delaware County Community College*
Leonardo Auernheimer, *Texas A&M University*
Paul Azrak, *Queensboro Community College*
Kevin Baird, *Montgomery County Community College*
Dru Barker, *Hollins College*
Klaus Becker, *Texas Technical University*
David Black, *University of Toledo*
Peter Boettke, *New York University*
Michael Boyd, *University of Vermont*
Chuck Britton, *University of Arkansas*
Doug Brown, *Georgetown University*
Oscar Brookins, *Northeastern University*
Mary Bumgarner, *Kennesaw State University*
Catherine Carey, *Western Kentucky University*
Michael Carter, *University of Massachusetts at Lowell*
Thomas Cate, *Northern Kentucky University*
Ken Chapman, *California State University at Northridge*
John Chilton, *University of South Carolina*
Joy Clark, *Auburn University at Montgomery*
Howard Cochran, *Belmont University*
Paul Comolli, *University of Kansas*
Joyce Cooper, *Boston University*
Doug Dalenberg, *University of Montana*
Patrick Dalendina, *Keene State College*
Mary E. Deily, *Lehigh University*
Stacy Dickert-Conlin, *University of Kentucky at Lexington*
Amy Diduch, *Mary Baldwin College*
Veda Doss, *Wingate College*
Mike Dowd, *University of Toledo*
Richard Easterlin, *University of Southern California*
John Edgren, *Eastern Michigan University*
Steffany Ellis, *University of Michigan at Dearborn*
S. Kirk Elwood, *James Madison University*
Amy Farmer, *University of Tennessee at Knoxville*
David Figlio, *University of Oregon*
Richard Fowles, *University of Utah*
Thomas Fox, *The Pennsylvania State University*
Jim Gapinski, *Florida State University*
Philip Gibbs, *College of William and Mary*

Kirk Gifford, *Ricks College*
J. Robert Gillette, *University of Kentucky*
Darrell Glenn, *Providence College*
Patrick Gormely, *Kansas State University*
Mark Paul Gius, *Quinnipiac College*
R. W. Hafer, *Southern Illinois University at Edwardsville*
David R. Hakes, *University of Northern Iowa*
Arne Hallam, *Iowa State University*
Andrew Hanssen, *Montana State University*
Richard Harper, *University of West Florida*
Robert Harris, *Indiana University–Purdue University at Indianapolis*
James Henderson, *Baylor University*
Jannett Highfill, *Bradley University*
Beth Ingram, *University of Iowa*
Dwight Israelsen, *Utah State University*
A. Andrew John, *University of Virginia*
Brad Kamp, *University of South Florida*
Demetri Kantarelis, *Assumption College*
Manfred Keil, *Northeastern University*
George Kelley, *Worcester State University*
Mark Killingsworth, *Rutgers University*
Philip King, *San Francisco State University*
Peter Klein, *University of Georgia*
Charles Klingensmith, *Miami-Dade Community College*
Morris Knapp, *Miami-Dade Community College*
Todd Knoop, *Northern Illinois University*
Marie Kratochvil, *Nassau Community College*
Rajaram Krishnan, *Northeastern University*
Mike Kupilik, *University of Montana*
Bob Lawson, *Shawnee State University*
Dan LeClair, *University of Tampa*
Luis Locay, *University of Miami*
Thomas Maloy, *Muskegon Community College*
Neela Manage, *Florida Atlantic University*
Mike Marlow, *California Polytechnic State University*
Don Matthews, *Brunswick College*
Bruce McClung, *Southwest Texas State University*
Rob Roy McGregor, *University of North Carolina at Charlotte*
Eugene McKibben, *Fullerton College*
Michael Meeropol, *Western New England College*
Deborah Merrigan, *Rockland Community College*
Charles Michalopoulos, *Virginia Polytechnic Institute and State University*
Jeffrey Miron, *Boston University*
Farzeen Nasri, *Ventura College*
Walter Nicholson, *Amherst College*
Stephen Nord, *Northern Illinois University*
Tony O'Brien, *Lehigh University*
John O'Connell, *College of the Holy Cross*

Ransford Palmer, *Howard University*

Tim Perri, *Appalachian State University*

Timothy Petry, *North Dakota State University*

Harmanna Poen, *Houston Community College*

William Rawson, *University of South Carolina*

Steve Robinson, *University of North Carolina at Wilmington*

Christina Romer, *University of California at Berkeley*

S. Scanlon Romer, *Delta College*

Leola Ross, *East Carolina University*

Rose Rubin, *University of Memphis*

Daniel Rupp, *Fort Hays State University*

Lynda Rush, *California Polytechnic State University*

Simran Sahi, *University of Minnesota at Minneapolis*

Jolyne Sanjak, *State University of New York at Albany*

Rolando Santos, *Lakeland Community College*

Sue Lynn Sasser, *University of South Dakota*

Edward Scahill, *University of Scranton*

Torsten Schmidt, *University of New Hampshire*

Bruce Seaman, *Georgia State University*

Stanley Sedo, *University of New Hampshire*

Mike Seelye, *San Joaquin Delta College*

Linda Shaffer, *California State University at Fresno*

Alden Shiers, *California Polytechnic State University*

David Shorow, *Richland College*

Mike Smitka, *Washington and Lee University*

John Sondey, *South Dakota State University*

Dennis Starleaf, *Iowa State University*

William Steen, *Santa Fe Community College*

E. Frank Stephenson, *University of North Carolina at Greensboro*

James L. Swofford, *University of South Alabama*

Bryan Taylor, *California State University at Los Angeles*

James Thornton, *University of Delaware*

Deborah Thorsen, *Palm Beach Community College*

Anthony Uremovic, *Joliet Junior College*

Sharmila Vishwasrao, *Florida Atlantic University*

Jack Wegman, *Santa Rosa Junior College*

James Wetzel, *Virginia Commonwealth University*

Steven L. Widener, *New Hampshire College*

William Wood, *James Madison University*

Joachim Zietz, *Middle Tennessee State University*

The accuracy of a textbook is critically important. Although I am, of course, responsible for any remaining errors, I am grateful to the following professors for reading through the final manuscript and page proofs with me:

Seemin Ahmad, *Dutchess Community College*

Dean Croushore, *Federal Reserve Bank of Philadelphia*

Patrick Dalendina, *Keene State College*

Deborah Merrigan, *Rockland Community College*

Linus Yamane, *Pitzer College*

As I developed this book, I felt that it was important not only to read instructors' comments but also to listen to their views and speak with them about their concerns. The six focus groups that Dryden organized were, therefore, invaluable to me. I want to thank those professors who took the time to meet with me or my editors and discuss the rough drafts of the manuscript:

Seemin Ahmad, *Dutchess Community College*

Aliakbar Ataiifar, *Delaware County Community College*

Peter Boettke, *New York University*

Doug Brown, *Georgetown University*

Catherine Carey, *Western Kentucky University*

Michael Carter, *University of Massachusetts at Lowell*

Joyce Cooper, *Boston University*

Mary E. Deily, *Lehigh University*

Amy Diduch, *Mary Baldwin College*

David R. Hakes, *University of Northern Iowa*

Dwight Israelsen, *Utah State University*

Demetri Kantarelis, *Assumption College*

Manfred Keil, *Northeastern University*

George Kelley, *Worcester State University*

Peter Klein, *University of Georgia*

Morris Knapp, *Miami-Dade Community College*

Marie Kratochvil, *Nassau Community College*

Rajaram Krishnan, *Northeastern University*

Dan LeClair, *University of Tampa*

Tom Maloy, *Muskegon Community College*

Mike Marlow, *California Polytechnic State University*

Don Matthews, *Brunswick College*
Michael Meeropol, *Western New England College*
John O'Connell, *College of the Holy Cross*
Ransford Palmer, *Howard University*

Torsten Schmidt, *University of New Hampshire*
David Shorow, *Richland College*
William Steen, *Santa Fe Community College*

Because writing a student-friendly text was one of my objectives, getting student feedback was of great importance. I want to thank the following students for taking time out of their weekends and school breaks to read my manuscript and then offer their input in focus groups:

Steven Burns, *Nassau Community College*
Nancy Dawson, *Delaware County Community College*
Edward Dougherty, *Nassau Community College*
William Ferrante, *Nassau Community College*
Barry Hallman, *Delaware County Community College*

Carl Hayden, *Delaware County Community College*
Patrice R. Mickle, *Delaware County Community College*
Brian J. Sherwood, *Delaware County Community College*
Farah Sodhi, *Nassau Community College*
Bill Sullivan, *Delaware County Community College*

I also want to thank the many students who served as class testers at Utah State University and Boston University and who took the time to fill out and send back our questionnaires.

I am grateful to the following professors from outside the United States, whose comments helped give this book a more international focus:

Robert Ackrill, *Leicester University, England*
Laurel Dawson, *Deakin University, Australia*
Lord Meghnad Desai of St. Clement Danes, *London School of Economics*
Robert Dixon, *University of Melbourne, Australia*
Paul Flatau, *Murdoch University, Australia*
John Freebairn, *University of Melbourne, Australia*
Mary Graham, *Deakin University, Australia*
Nigel Healey, *Manchester Metropolitan University, England*
John Hicks, *Charles Sturt University, Australia*
Andrew Hughes-Hallett, *University of Strathclyde, Scotland*
John Lodewijks, *University of New South Wales, Australia*
Rod Maddock, *La Trobe University, Australia*

Dermot McAleese, *Trinity College, Dublin, Ireland*
Jonathan Michie, *The Judge Institute, Cambridge University, England*
Alan Morris, *Victoria University of Technology, Australia*
David Owens, *Swinburne University of Technology, Australia*
Martin Shanahan, *University of South Australia*
Peter Sinclair, *University of Birmingham, England*
Lindsay Smyrk, *Victoria University of Technology, Australia*
Di Thomson, *Deakin University, Australia*
Neil Warren, *University of New South Wales, Australia*
Ed Wilson, *University of Wollongong, Australia*
Simon Wren-Lewis, *Exeter University, England*

A special thanks go to Karen Dynan and Douglas Elmendorf (both of the Federal Reserve Board). Karen and Doug read and commented on the entire manuscript and drafted many of the problems and applications presented at the end of each chapter. I am also grateful to the five Harvard students who worked with me as I refined the text: Niko Canner, Richard Johnson, Michael Rashes, David Sherwood, and Gabriella Skirnick. Yvonne Zinfon, my secretary at Harvard, as usual went beyond the call of duty and helped me proofread the entire book.

The team of editors that worked on this book improved it tremendously. Jane Tufts, freelance developmental editor, provided truly spectacular editing of at least three drafts of every chapter. Emily Barrosse, economics executive editor, did a splendid job of overseeing the many people involved in such a large project (including, at times, an irascible author). Anita M. Fallon, senior developmental editor, assembled an excellent team to write the supplements while beautifully managing thousands of related details. Eddie Dawson, senior production manager, and Amy Schmidt, senior project editor, had the patience and dedication necessary to turn my manuscript into this book. Melinda Welch and Jeanette Barber, senior art directors, gave this book its clean, friendly look. Michele Gitlin, copyeditor, refined my prose, and Alexandra Nickerson, indexer, prepared a careful and thorough index. Kathleen Sharp and Dave Theisen, product managers, worked long hours getting the word out to potential users of this book. The rest of The Dryden Press team was also consistently professional, enthusiastic, and dedicated: Jeanie Anirudhan, Donna Baum, Russ Boersma, Ted Buchholz, John Carey, Dave Chwalik, Ann Coburn, Annette Coolidge, Ben Eldred, Eunice Ferguson, Daryl Fox, Rick Hammonds, Roland Hernández, Lisé Johnson, Mary Jo Kovach, Jim Levy, Angus McDonald, Earl McPeek, Laura Miley, Michael Mueller, Pat Murphree, Brian Murphy, Gary Nelson, Jim Nye, George Provol, Dee Salisbury, Fritz Schanz, Paul Stewart, Scott Stewart, Stephanie Surfus, Lee Sutherlin, Annie Todd, Carl Tyson, Susan Van Buren, and Andrea Wright.

I must also thank my "in house" editor—Deborah Mankiw. As the first reader of the manuscript, she provided the right mix of criticism and encouragement. Just as important, her willingness to put up with a part-time husband for the past four years gave me the time I needed to write this book.

Finally, I am grateful to my children, Catherine and Nicholas, whose occasional and unpredictable visits to my study offered welcome relief from long spans of writing and rewriting. Although now they are only five and two years old, someday they will grow up and study the principles of economics. I hope this book provides its readers some of the education, entertainment, and enlightenment that I wish for my own children.

N. Gregory Mankiw
August 1997

PREFACE: TO THE STUDENT

"Economics is a study of mankind in the ordinary business of life." So wrote Alfred Marshall, the great nineteenth-century economist, in his textbook, *Principles of Economics.* Although we have learned much about the economy since Marshall's time, this definition of economics is as true today as it was in 1890, when the first edition of his text was published.

Why should you, as a student soon to enter the twenty-first century, embark on the study of economics? There are three reasons.

The first reason to study economics is that it will help you understand the world in which you live. There are many questions about the economy that might spark your curiosity. Why are apartments so hard to find in New York City? Why do airlines charge less for a round-trip ticket if the traveler stays over a Saturday night? Why is Jim Carrey paid so much to star in movies? Why are living standards so meager in many African countries? Why do some countries have high rates of inflation while others have stable prices? Why are jobs easy to find in some years and hard to find in others? These are just a few of the questions that a course in economics will help you answer.

The second reason to study economics is that it will make you a more astute participant in the economy. As you go about your life, you make many economic decisions. While you are a student, you decide how many years to stay in school. Once you take a job, you decide how much of your income to spend, how much to save, and how to invest your savings. Someday you may find yourself running a small business or a large corporation, and you will decide what prices to charge for your products. The insights developed in the coming chapters will give you a new perspective on how best to make these decisions. Studying economics will not by itself make you rich, but it will give you some tools that may help in that endeavor.

The third reason to study economics is that it will give you a better understanding of the potential and limits of economic policy. As a voter, you help choose the policies that guide the allocation of society's resources. When deciding which policies to support, you may find yourself asking various questions about economics. What are the burdens associated with alternative forms of taxation? What are the effects of free trade with other countries? What is the best way to protect the environment? How does a government budget deficit affect the economy? These and similar questions are always on the minds of policymakers in mayors' offices, governors' mansions, and the White House.

Thus, the principles of economics can be applied in many of life's situations. Whether the future finds you reading the newspaper, running a business, or sitting in the Oval Office, you will be glad that you studied economics.

N. Gregory Mankiw
August 1997

BRIEF TABLE OF CONTENTS

TABLE OF CONTENTS

PART II
SUPPLY AND DEMAND I: HOW MARKETS WORK   59

CHAPTER 6

SUPPLY, DEMAND, AND GOVERNMENT POLICIES   111

PART III
SUPPLY AND DEMAND II: MARKETS AND WELFARE   131

CHAPTER 7

CONSUMERS, PRODUCERS, AND THE EFFICIENCY OF MARKETS   133

PART IV
THE ECONOMICS OF THE PUBLIC SECTOR   197

CHAPTER 10
EXTERNALITIES   199

PART V
FIRM BEHAVIOR AND THE
ORGANIZATION OF INDUSTRY   261

CHAPTER 16

OLIGOPOLY   337

CHAPTER 17

MONOPOLISTIC COMPETITION   363

PART VI
THE ECONOMICS OF LABOR MARKETS   381

PART VII
ADVANCED TOPIC 445

CHAPTER 21
THE THEORY OF CONSUMER CHOICE 447

PART VIII
THE DATA OF MACROECONOMICS 475

CHAPTER 22
MEASURING A NATION'S INCOME 477

PART IX
THE REAL ECONOMY
IN THE LONG RUN   513

CHAPTER 24

PRODUCTION AND GROWTH   515

PART X
MONEY AND PRICES IN THE LONG RUN 589

CHAPTER 27

THE MONETARY SYSTEM 591

**PART XI
THE MACROECONOMICS
OF OPEN ECONOMIES   635**

**PART XII
SHORT-RUN ECONOMIC FLUCTUATIONS 679**

CHAPTER 31

AGGREGATE DEMAND AND AGGREGATE SUPPLY 681

PART XIII
FINAL THOUGHTS   757

CHAPTER 34
FIVE DEBATES OVER MACROECONOMIC POLICY   759

I

INTRODUCTION

1

TEN PRINCIPLES OF ECONOMICS

The word *economy* comes from the Greek word for "one who manages a household." At first, this origin might seem peculiar. But, in fact, households and economies have much in common.

A household faces many decisions. It must decide which members of the household do which tasks and what each member gets in return: Who cooks dinner? Who does the laundry? Who gets the extra dessert at dinner? Who gets to choose what TV show to watch? In short, the household must allocate its scarce resources among its various members, taking into account each member's abilities, efforts, and desires.

Like a household, a society faces many decisions. A society must decide what jobs will be done and who will do them. It needs some people to grow food, other people to make clothing, and still others to design computer software. Once society has allocated people (as well as land, buildings, and machines) to various jobs, it must also allocate the output of goods and services that they produce. It must decide who will eat caviar and who will eat potatoes. It must decide who will drive a Porsche and who will take the bus.

scarcity
the limited nature of society's resources

economics
the study of how society manages its scarce resources

The management of society's resources is important because resources are scarce. **Scarcity** means that society has less to offer than people wish to have. Just as a household cannot give every member everything he or she wants, a society cannot give every individual the highest standard of living to which he or she might aspire.

Economics is the study of how society manages its scarce resources. In most societies, resources are allocated not by a single central planner but through the combined actions of millions of households and firms. Economists therefore study how people make decisions: how much they work, what they buy, how much they save, and how they invest their savings. Economists also study how people interact with one another. For instance, they examine how the multitude of buyers and sellers of a good together determine the price at which the good is sold and the quantity that is sold. Finally, economists analyze forces and trends that affect the economy as a whole, including the growth in average income, the fraction of the population that cannot find work, and the rate at which prices are rising.

Although the study of economics has many facets, the field is unified by several central ideas. In the rest of this chapter, we look at *Ten Principles of Economics*. These principles recur throughout this book and are introduced here to give you an overview of what economics is all about.

HOW PEOPLE MAKE DECISIONS

There is no mystery to what an "economy" is. Whether we are talking about the economy of Los Angeles, of the United States, or of the whole world, an economy is just a group of people interacting with one another as they go about their lives. Because the behavior of an economy reflects the behavior of the individuals who make up the economy, we start our study of economics with four principles of individual decisionmaking.

PRINCIPLE #1: People Face Tradeoffs

The first lesson about making decisions is summarized in the adage: "There is no such thing as a free lunch." To get one thing that we like, we usually have to give up another thing that we like. Making decisions requires trading off one goal against another.

Consider a student who must decide how to allocate her most valuable resource—her time. She can spend all of her time studying economics; she can spend all her time studying psychology; or she can divide her time between the two fields. For every hour she studies one subject, she gives up an hour she could have used studying the other. And for every hour she spends studying, she gives up an hour that she could have spent napping, bike riding, watching TV, or working at her part-time job for some extra spending money.

Or consider parents deciding how to spend their family income. They can buy food, clothing, or a family vacation. Or they can save some of the family income for retirement or the children's college education. When they choose to spend an extra dollar on one of these goods, they have one less dollar to spend on some other good.

When people are grouped into societies, they face different kinds of trade-offs. The classic tradeoff is between "guns and butter." The more we spend on national defense to protect our shores from foreign aggressors (guns), the less we can spend on personal goods to raise our standard of living at home (butter). Also important in modern society is the tradeoff between a clean environment and a high level of income. Laws that require firms to reduce pollution raise the cost of producing goods and services. Because of the higher costs, these firms end up earning smaller profits, paying lower wages, charging higher prices, or some combination of these three. Thus, while pollution regulations give us the benefit of a cleaner environment and the improved health that comes with it, they have the cost of reducing the incomes of the firms' owners, workers, and customers.

Another tradeoff society faces is between efficiency and equity. **Efficiency** means that society is getting the most it can from its scarce resources. **Equity** means that the benefits of those resources are distributed fairly among society's members. In other words, efficiency refers to the size of the economic pie, and equity refers to how the pie is divided. Often, when government policies are being designed, these two goals conflict.

Consider, for instance, policies aimed at achieving a more equal distribution of economic well-being. Some of these policies, such as the welfare system or unemployment insurance, try to help those members of society who are most in need. Others, such as the individual income tax, ask the financially successful to contribute more than others to support the government. Although these policies have the benefit of achieving greater equity, they have a cost in terms of reduced efficiency. When the government redistributes income from the rich to the poor, it reduces the reward for working hard; as a result, people work less and produce fewer goods and services. In other words, when the government tries to cut the economic pie into more equal slices, the pie gets smaller.

Recognizing that people face tradeoffs does not by itself tell us what decisions they will or should make. A student should not abandon the study of psychology just because doing so would increase the time available for the study of economics. Society should not stop protecting the environment just because environmental regulations reduce our material standard of living. The poor should not be ignored just because helping them distorts work incentives. Nonetheless, acknowledging life's tradeoffs is important because people are likely to make good decisions only if they understand the options that they have available.

PRINCIPLE #2: The Cost of Something Is What You Give Up to Get It

Because people face tradeoffs, making decisions requires comparing the costs and benefits of alternative courses of action. In many cases, however, the cost of some action is not as obvious as it might first appear.

Consider, for example, the decision whether to go to college. The benefit is intellectual enrichment and a lifetime of better job opportunities. But what is the cost? To answer this question, you might be tempted to add up the money you spend on tuition, books, room, and board. Yet this total does not truly represent what you give up to spend a year in college.

efficiency
the property of society getting the most it can from its scarce resources

equity
the property of distributing economic prosperity fairly among the members of society

The first problem with this answer is that it includes some things that are not really costs of going to college. Even if you quit school, you would need a place to sleep and food to eat. Room and board are costs of going to college only to the extent that they are more expensive at college than elsewhere. Indeed, the cost of room and board at your school might be less than the rent and food expenses that you would pay living on your own. In this case, the savings on room and board are a benefit of going to college.

The second problem with this calculation of costs is that it ignores the largest cost of going to college—your time. When you spend a year listening to lectures, reading textbooks, and writing papers, you cannot spend that time working at a job. For most students, the wages given up to attend school are the largest single cost of their education.

opportunity cost
whatever must be given up to obtain some item

The **opportunity cost** of an item is what you give up to get that item. When making any decision, such as whether to attend college, decisionmakers should be aware of the opportunity costs that accompany each possible action. In fact, they usually are. College-age athletes who can earn millions if they drop out of school and play professional sports are well aware that their opportunity cost of college is very high. It is not surprising that they often decide that the benefit is not worth the cost.

PRINCIPLE #3: Rational People Think at the Margin

marginal changes
small incremental adjustments to a plan of action

Many decisions in life involve making small incremental adjustments to an existing plan of action. Economists call these **marginal changes**. In many situations, people will make the best decisions by thinking at the margin.

Suppose, for instance, that a friend asks your advice about how many years to stay in school. If you were to compare for him the lifestyle of a person with a Ph.D. to that of a grade school dropout, he might complain that this comparison is not helpful for his decision. Your friend is more likely to have some education already and to be deciding whether to spend an extra year or two in school. To make this decision, he needs to know the additional benefits that an extra year in school would offer and the additional costs that he would incur. By comparing these marginal benefits and marginal costs, he can evaluate whether the extra year is worthwhile.

As another example of how thinking at the margin helps decisionmaking, consider an airline deciding how much to charge passengers who fly standby. Suppose that flying a 200-seat plane across the country costs the airline $100,000. In this case, the average cost of each seat is $100,000/200, which is $500. One might be tempted to conclude that the airline should never sell a ticket for less than $500.

Yet the airline can raise its profits by thinking at the margin. Suppose that a plane is about to take off with ten empty seats. A standby passenger is waiting at the gate willing to pay $300 for a seat. Should the airline sell it to him? Of course it should. If the plane has empty seats, the cost of adding one more passenger is minuscule. Although the *average* cost of flying a passenger is $500, the *marginal* cost is merely the cost of the bag of peanuts and can of soda that the extra passenger will consume. As long as the standby passenger pays more than the marginal cost, selling him a ticket is profitable.

As these examples show, individuals and firms can make better decisions by thinking at the margin. A rational decisionmaker takes an action if and only if the marginal benefit of the action exceeds the marginal cost.

PRINCIPLE #4: People Respond to Incentives

Because people make decisions by comparing costs and benefits, their behavior may change when the costs or benefits change. That is, people respond to incentives. When the price of an apple rises, for instance, people decide to eat more pears and fewer apples, because the cost of buying an apple is higher. At the same time, apple orchards decide to hire more workers and harvest more apples, because the benefit of selling an apple is also higher.

The central role of incentives in determining behavior is important for those designing public policy. Public policies often alter the costs or benefits of private actions. When policymakers fail to consider how behavior might change as a result, their policies can have effects that they did not intend.

As an example of such unintended effects, consider public policy toward seat belts and auto safety. In the 1950s few cars had seat belts. Today all cars do, and the reason for the change is public policy. In the late 1960s, Ralph Nader's book *Unsafe at Any Speed* generated much public concern over auto safety. Congress responded with legislation requiring car companies to make various safety features, including seat belts, standard equipment on all new cars.

How does a seat belt law affect auto safety? The direct effect is obvious. With seat belts in all cars, more people wear seat belts, and the probability of surviving a major auto accident rises. In this sense, seat belts save lives. This direct impact of seat belts on safety is what motivated Congress to require seat belts.

Yet, to understand fully the effects of this law, one must recognize that people change their behavior in response to the incentives they face. In this case, the relevant behavior is the speed and care with which drivers operate their automobiles. Driving slowly and carefully is costly because it uses the driver's time and energy. When deciding how safely to drive, rational people compare the marginal benefit from safer driving to the marginal cost. They drive more slowly and carefully when the benefit of increased safety is high. This explains why people drive more slowly and carefully when roads are icy than when roads are clear.

Now consider how a seat belt law alters the cost–benefit calculation of a rational driver. Seat belts make accidents less costly for a driver because they reduce the probability of injury or death. Thus, a seat belt law reduces the benefits to slow and careful driving. People respond to seat belts as they would to an improvement in road conditions—by faster and less careful driving. The end result of a seat belt law, therefore, is a larger number of accidents.

How does the law affect the number of deaths from driving? Drivers who wear their seat belts are more likely to survive any given accident, but they are more likely to find themselves in an accident. The net effect is ambiguous. Moreover, the reduction in safe driving has a clear adverse impact on pedestrians (and on drivers who do not wear their seat belts). They are put in jeopardy by the law because they are more likely to find themselves in an accident but are not protected by a seat belt. Thus, a seat belt law tends to increase the number of pedestrian deaths.

At first, this discussion of incentives and seat belts might seem like idle speculation. Yet, in an article published in 1975, economist Sam Peltzman showed that the auto-safety laws have, in fact, had many of these effects. According to Peltzman's evidence, these laws produce both fewer deaths per accident and more accidents. The net result is little change in the number of driver deaths and an increase in the number of pedestrian deaths.

High school basketball star Kobe Bryant understands opportunity cost and incentives. Despite good grades and SAT scores, he decided to skip college and go straight to the NBA, where he is expected to earn about $10 million over four years.

Peltzman's analysis of auto safety is just one example of the general principle that people respond to incentives. Many of the incentives that economists study are more straightforward than those of the auto-safety laws. For example, no one is surprised that a tax on apples causes people to buy fewer apples. Yet, as the seat belt example shows, policies sometimes have effects that are not obvious in advance. In analyzing any policy, one must consider not only the direct effects but also the indirect effects that work through incentives. If the policy changes incentives, it will cause people to alter their behavior.

▌**QUICK QUIZ**   List and briefly explain the four principles of individual decisionmaking.

THE WALL STREET JOURNAL

ENGLEMAN.

"For $5 a week you can watch baseball without being nagged to cut the grass!"

HOW PEOPLE INTERACT

The first four principles discussed how individuals make decisions. As we go about our lives, many of our decisions affect not only ourselves but other people as well. The next three principles concern how people interact with one another.

PRINCIPLE #5: Trade Can Make Everyone Better Off

You have probably heard on the news that the Japanese are our competitors in the world economy. In some ways, this is true, for American and Japanese firms do produce many of the same goods. Ford and Toyota compete for the same customers in the market for automobiles. Compaq and Toshiba compete for the same customers in the market for personal computers.

Yet it is easy to be misled when thinking about competition among countries. Trade between the United States and Japan is not like a sports contest, where one side wins and the other side loses. In fact, the opposite is true: Trade between two countries can make each country better off.

To see why, consider how trade affects your family. When a member of your family looks for a job, he or she competes against members of other families who are looking for jobs. Families also compete against one another when they go shopping, because each family wants to buy the best goods at the lowest prices. So, in a sense, each family in the economy is competing with all other families.

Despite this competition, your family would not be better off isolating itself from all other families. If it did, your family would need to grow its own food, make its own clothes, and build its own home. Clearly, your family gains much from its ability to trade with others. Trade allows each person to specialize in the activities he or she does best, whether it is farming, sewing, or home building. By trading with others, people can buy a greater variety of goods and services at lower cost.

Countries as well as families benefit from the ability to trade with one another. Trade allows countries to specialize in what they do best and to enjoy a greater variety of goods and services. The Japanese, as well as the French and the Egyptians and the Brazilians, are as much our partners in the world economy as they are our competitors.

PRINCIPLE #6: Markets Are Usually a Good Way to Organize Economic Activity

The collapse of communism in the Soviet Union and Eastern Europe may be the most important change in the world during the past half century. Communist countries worked on the premise that central planners in the government were in the best position to guide economic activity. These planners decided what goods and services were produced, how much was produced, and who produced and consumed these goods and services. The theory behind central planning was that only the government could organize economic activity in a way that promoted economic well-being for the country as a whole.

Today, most countries that once had centrally planned economies have abandoned this system and are trying to develop market economies. In a **market economy,** the decisions of a central planner are replaced by the decisions of millions of firms and households. Firms decide whom to hire and what to make. Households decide which firms to work for and what to buy with their incomes. These firms and households interact in the marketplace, where prices and self-interest guide their decisions.

market economy
an economy that allocates resources through the decentralized decisions of many firms and households as they interact in markets for goods and services

At first glance, the success of market economies is puzzling. It might seem as if decentralized decisionmaking by millions of self-interested households and firms would result in chaos. Yet this is not the case. Market economies have proven remarkably successful in organizing economic activity in a way that promotes general economic well-being.

In his 1776 book *The Wealth of Nations*, economist Adam Smith made the most famous observation in all of economics: Households and firms interacting in markets act as if they are guided by an "invisible hand" that leads them to desirable market outcomes. One of our goals in this book is to understand how this invisible hand works its magic. As you study economics, you will learn that prices are the instrument with which the invisible hand directs economic activity. Prices reflect both the value of a good to society and the cost to society of making the good. Because households and firms look at prices when deciding what to buy and sell, they unknowingly take into account the social benefits and costs of their actions. As a result, prices guide these individual decisionmakers to reach outcomes that, in many cases, maximize the welfare of society as a whole.

There is an important corollary to the skill of the invisible hand in guiding economic activity: When the government prevents prices from adjusting naturally to supply and demand, it impedes the invisible hand's ability to coordinate the millions of households and firms that make up the economy. This corollary explains why taxes adversely affect the allocation of resources: Taxes distort prices and thus the decisions of households and firms. It also explains the even greater harm caused by policies that directly control prices, such as rent control. And it explains the failure of communism. In communist countries, prices were not determined in the marketplace but were dictated by central planners. These planners lacked the information that gets reflected in prices when prices are free to respond to market forces. Central planners failed because they tried to run the economy with one hand tied behind their backs—the invisible hand of the marketplace.

PRINCIPLE #7: Governments Can Sometimes Improve Market Outcomes

Although markets are usually a good way to organize economic activity, this rule has some important exceptions. There are two broad reasons for a government to intervene in the economy: to promote efficiency and to promote equity. That is, most policies aim either to enlarge the economic pie or to change how the pie is divided.

The invisible hand usually leads markets to allocate resources efficiently. Nonetheless, for various reasons, the invisible hand sometimes does not work. Economists use the term **market failure** to refer to a situation in which the market on its own fails to allocate resources efficiently.

One possible cause of market failure is an externality. An **externality** is the impact of one person's actions on the well-being of a bystander. Pollution is the classic example. If a chemical factory does not bear the entire cost of the smoke it emits, it will likely emit too much. In this case, the government can raise economic well-being through environmental regulation.

Another possible cause of market failure is market power. **Market power** refers to the ability of a single person (or small group of people) to unduly influence market prices. For example, suppose that everyone in town needs water but there is only one well. The owner of the well has market power—in this case a *monopoly*—over the sale of water. The well owner is not subject to the rigorous competition with which the invisible hand normally keeps self-interest in check. You will learn that, in this case, regulating the price that the monopolist charges can potentially enhance economic efficiency.

The invisible hand is even less able to ensure that economic prosperity is distributed fairly. A market economy rewards people according to their ability to produce things that other people are willing to pay for. The world's best basketball player earns more than the world's best chess player simply because people are willing to pay more to see basketball than chess. The invisible hand does not ensure that everyone has sufficient food, decent clothing, and adequate health care. A goal of many public policies, such as the income tax and the welfare system, is to achieve a more equitable distribution of economic well-being.

To say that the government *can* improve on market outcomes at times does not mean that it always *will*. Public policy is made not by angels but by a political process that is far from perfect. Sometimes policies are designed simply to reward the politically powerful. Sometimes they are made by well-intentioned leaders who are not fully informed. One goal of the study of economics is to help you judge when a government policy is justifiable to promote efficiency or equity and when it is not.

QUICK QUIZ   List and briefly explain the three principles concerning economic interactions.

market failure
a situation in which a market left on its own fails to allocate resources efficiently

externality
the impact of one person's actions on the well-being of a bystander

market power
the ability of a single economic actor (or small group of actors) to have a substantial influence on market prices

HOW THE ECONOMY AS A WHOLE WORKS

We started by discussing how individuals make decisions and then looked at how people interact with one another. All these decisions and interactions together make up "the economy." The last three principles concern the workings of the economy as a whole.

PRINCIPLE #8: A Country's Standard of Living Depends on Its Ability to Produce Goods and Services

The differences in living standards around the world are staggering. In 1993, the average American had an income of about $25,000. In the same year, the average Mexican earned $7,000, and the average Nigerian earned $1,500. Not surprisingly, this large variation in average income is reflected in various measures of the quality of life. Citizens of high-income countries have more TV sets, more cars, better nutrition, better health care, and longer life expectancy than citizens of low-income countries.

Changes in living standards over time are also large. In the United States, incomes have historically grown about 2 percent per year (after adjusting for changes in the cost of living). At this rate, average income doubles every 35 years. In some countries, economic growth has been even more rapid. In Japan, for instance, average income has doubled in the past 20 years, and in South Korea it has doubled in the past 10 years.

What explains these large differences in living standards among countries and over time? The answer is surprisingly simple. Almost all variation in living standards is attributable to differences in countries' **productivity**—that is, the amount of goods and services produced from each hour of a worker's time. In nations where workers can produce a large quantity of goods and services per unit of time, most people enjoy a high standard of living; in nations where workers are less productive, most people must endure a more meager existence. Similarly, the growth rate of a nation's productivity determines the growth rate of its average income.

productivity
the quantity of goods and services produced from each hour of a worker's time

The fundamental relationship between productivity and living standards is simple, but its implications are far-reaching. If productivity is the primary determinant of living standards, other explanations must be of secondary importance. For example, it might be tempting to credit labor unions or minimum-wage laws for the rise in living standards of American workers over the past century. Yet the real hero of American workers is their rising productivity. As another example, some commentators have claimed that increased competition from Japan and other countries explains slow growth in U.S. incomes in recent years. Yet the real villain is not competition from abroad but flagging productivity growth in the United States.

The relationship between productivity and living standards also has profound implications for public policy. When thinking about how any policy will affect living standards, the key question is how it will affect our ability to produce goods and services. To boost living standards, policymakers need to raise productivity by ensuring that workers are well educated, have the tools needed to produce goods and services, and have access to the best available technology.

Over the past decade, for example, much debate in the United States has centered on the government's budget deficit—the excess of government spending over government revenue. As we will see, concern over the budget deficit is based largely on its adverse impact on productivity. When the government needs to finance a budget deficit, it does so by borrowing in financial markets, much as a student might borrow to finance a college education or a firm might borrow to finance a new factory. As the government borrows to finance its deficit, therefore, it reduces the quantity of funds available for other borrowers. The budget deficit thereby reduces investment both in human capital (the student's education) and physical capital (the firm's factory). Because lower investment today means lower productivity in the future, budget deficits are generally thought to depress growth in living standards.

PRINCIPLE #9: Prices Rise When the Government Prints Too Much Money

inflation

an increase in the overall level of prices in the economy

In Germany in January 1921, a daily newspaper cost 0.30 marks. Less than two years later, in November 1922, the same newspaper cost 70,000,000 marks. All other prices in the economy rose by similar amounts. This episode is one of history's most spectacular examples of **inflation,** an increase in the overall level of prices in the economy.

Although the United States has never experienced inflation even close to that in Germany in the 1920s, inflation has at times been an economic problem. During the 1970s, for instance, the overall level of prices more than doubled, and President Gerald Ford called inflation "public enemy number one." By contrast, in the 1990s, inflation has been about 3 percent per year; at this rate it would take over 20 years for prices to double. Because high inflation imposes various costs on society, keeping inflation at a low level is a goal of economic policymakers around the world.

What causes inflation? In most cases of large or persistent inflation, the culprit turns out to be the same—growth in the quantity of money. When a government creates large quantities of the nation's money, the value of the money falls. In Germany in the early 1920s, when prices were on average tripling every month, the quantity of money was also tripling every month. Although less dramatic, the economic history of the United States points to a similar conclusion:

"WELL, IT MAY HAVE BEEN 68 CENTS WHEN YOU GOT IN LINE, BUT IT'S 74 CENTS NOW!"

The high inflation of the 1970s was associated with rapid growth in the quantity of money, and the low inflation of the 1990s has been associated with slow growth in the quantity of money.

PRINCIPLE #10: Society Faces a Short-Run Tradeoff between Inflation and Unemployment

If inflation is so easy to explain, why do policymakers sometimes have trouble ridding the economy of it? One reason is that reducing inflation is often thought to cause a temporary rise in unemployment. This tradeoff between inflation and unemployment is called the **Phillips curve,** after the economist who first examined this relationship.

Phillips curve
the short-run tradeoff between inflation and unemployment

The Phillips curve remains a controversial topic among economists, but most economists today accept the idea that there is a short-run tradeoff between inflation and unemployment. According to a common explanation, this tradeoff arises because some prices are slow to adjust. Suppose, for example, that the government reduces the quantity of money in the economy. In the long run, the only result of this policy change will be a fall in the overall level of prices. Yet not all prices will adjust immediately. It may take several years before all firms issue new catalogs, all unions make wage concessions, and all restaurants print new menus. That is, prices are said to be *sticky* in the short run.

Because prices are sticky, various types of government policy have short-run effects that differ from their long-run effects. When the government reduces the quantity of money, for instance, it reduces the amount that people spend. Lower spending, together with prices that are stuck too high, reduces the quantity of goods and services that firms sell. Lower sales, in turn, cause firms to lay off workers. Thus, the reduction in the quantity of money raises unemployment temporarily until prices have fully adjusted to the change.

The tradeoff between inflation and unemployment is only temporary, but it can last for several years. The Phillips curve is, therefore, crucial for understanding many developments in the economy. In particular, policymakers can exploit this tradeoff using various policy instruments. By changing the amount that the government spends, the amount it taxes, and the amount of money it prints, policymakers can, in the short run, influence the combination of inflation and unemployment that the economy experiences. Because these instruments of monetary and fiscal policy are potentially so powerful, how policymakers should use these instruments to control the economy, if at all, is a subject of continuing debate.

QUICK QUIZ List and briefly explain the three principles that describe how the economy as a whole works.

CONCLUSION

You now have a taste of what economics is all about. In the coming chapters we will develop many specific insights about people, markets, and economies. Mastering these insights will take some effort, but it is not an overwhelming task. The field of economics is based on a few basic ideas that can be applied in many different situations.

HOW PEOPLE MAKE DECISIONS	#1:	People Face Tradeoffs
	#2:	The Cost of Something Is What You Give Up to Get It
	#3:	Rational People Think at the Margin
	#4:	People Respond to Incentives
HOW PEOPLE INTERACT	#5:	Trade Can Make Everyone Better Off
	#6:	Markets Are Usually a Good Way to Organize Economic Activity
	#7:	Governments Can Sometimes Improve Market Outcomes
HOW THE ECONOMY AS A WHOLE WORKS	#8:	A Country's Standard of Living Depends on Its Ability to Produce Goods and Services
	#9:	Prices Rise When the Government Prints Too Much Money
	#10:	Society Faces a Short-Run Tradeoff between Inflation and Unemployment

Throughout this book we will refer back to the *Ten Principles of Economics* highlighted in this chapter and summarized in Table 1-1. Whenever we do so, a "building blocks" icon will show up in the margin, as it does now. But even when that icon is absent, you should keep these building blocks in mind. Even the most sophisticated economic analysis is built using the ten principles introduced here.

Summary

◆ The fundamental lessons about individual decisionmaking are that people face tradeoffs among alternative goals, that the cost of any action is measured in terms of forgone opportunities, that rational people make decisions by comparing marginal costs and marginal benefits, and that people change their behavior in response to the incentives they face.

◆ The fundamental lessons about interactions among people are that trade can be mutually beneficial, that

markets are usually a good way of coordinating trades among people, and that the government can potentially improve market outcomes if there is some market failure or if the market outcome is inequitable.

◆ The fundamental lessons about the economy as a whole are that productivity is the ultimate source of living standards, that money growth is the ultimate source of inflation, and that society faces a short-run tradeoff between inflation and unemployment.

Key Concepts

scarcity, p. 4
economics, p. 4
efficiency, p. 5
equity, p. 5
opportunity cost, p. 6

marginal changes, p. 6
market economy, p. 9
market failure, p. 10
externality, p. 10
market power, p. 10

productivity, p. 11
inflation, p. 12
Phillips curve, p. 13

Questions for Review

1. Give three examples of important tradeoffs that you face in your life.

2. What is the opportunity cost of seeing a movie?

3. Water is necessary for life. Is the marginal benefit of a glass of water large or small?

4. Why should policymakers think about incentives?

5. Why isn't trade among countries like a game with some winners and some losers?

6. What does the "invisible hand" of the marketplace do?

7. What are "efficiency" and "equity," and what do they have to do with government policy?

8. Why is productivity important?

9. What is inflation, and what causes it?

10. How are inflation and unemployment related in the short run?

Problems and Applications

1. Describe some of the tradeoffs faced by:
   a. a family deciding whether to buy a new car
   b. a member of Congress deciding whether to increase spending on national parks
   c. a company president deciding whether to open a new factory
   d. a professor deciding whether to prepare for class

2. You are trying to decide whether to take a vacation. Most of the costs of the vacation (airfare, hotel, forgone wages) are measured in dollars, but the benefits of the vacation are psychological. How can you compare the benefits to the costs?

3. You were planning to spend Saturday working at your part-time job, but a friend asks you to go skiing. What is the true cost of going skiing? Now suppose that you had been planning to spend the day studying at the library. What is the cost of going skiing in this case? Explain.

4. You win $100 in a basketball pool. You have a choice between spending the money now or putting it away for a year in a bank account that pays 5 percent interest. What is the opportunity cost of spending the $100 now?

5. The company that you manage has invested $5 million in developing a new product, but the development is not quite finished. At a recent meeting, your salespeople report that the introduction of competing products has reduced the expected sales of *your* new product to $3 million. If it would cost $1 million to finish development, should you go ahead and do so? What is the most that you should pay to complete development?

6. The Social Security system provides income for people over age 65. Recipients with more income from other sources receive smaller benefits (after taxes) than recipients with less income from other sources.
   a. How does the provision of Social Security affect people's incentive to save while working?
   b. How does the reduction in after-tax benefits associated with higher income affect people's incentive to work past age 65?

7. Some states have recently changed their laws so that welfare recipients who are able to work stop receiving benefits after two years.
   a. How do these changes in the laws affect the incentives for working?
   b. How might these changes represent a tradeoff between equity and efficiency?

8. Your roommate is a better cook than you are, but you can clean more quickly than your roommate can. If your roommate did all of the cooking and you did all of the cleaning, would your chores take you more or less time than if you divided each task evenly? Give a similar example of how specialization and trade can make two countries both better off.

9. Suppose the United States adopted central planning for its economy, and you became the chief planner. Among the millions of decisions that you need to make for next year are how many compact discs to produce, what artists to record, and who should receive the discs.
   a. To make these decisions intelligently, what information would you need about the compact disc industry? What information would you need about each person in the United States?
   b. How would your decisions about CDs affect some of your other decisions, such as how many CD players

to make or cassette tapes to produce? How might some of your other decisions about the economy change your views about CDs?

10. Explain whether each of the following government activities is motivated by a concern about equity or a concern about efficiency. In the case of efficiency, discuss the type of market failure involved.
    a. regulating cable-TV prices
    b. providing some poor people with vouchers that can be used to buy food
    c. prohibiting smoking in public places
    d. breaking up AT&T into several smaller phone companies
    e. imposing higher personal income tax rates on people with higher incomes
    f. instituting laws against driving while intoxicated

11. "Everyone in society should be guaranteed the best health care possible." Discuss this point of view from the standpoints of equity and efficiency.

12. In what ways is your standard of living different from that of your parents or grandparents when they were your age? Why have these changes occurred?

13. Suppose Americans decided to save more of their incomes. If banks lend this money to businesses, which use the money to build new factories, how might higher saving lead to faster productivity growth? Who do you suppose benefits from higher productivity? Is society getting a free lunch?

14. Suppose that when everyone wakes up tomorrow, they discover that the government has given them an additional amount of money equal to the amount they already had. Explain what effect this doubling of the money supply will likely have on:
    a. the total amount spent on goods and services
    b. the quantity of goods and services purchased if prices are sticky
    c. the prices of goods and services if prices can adjust

15. Imagine that you are a policymaker trying to decide whether to reduce the rate of inflation in the United States. To make an intelligent decision, what would you need to know about inflation, unemployment, and the tradeoff between them?

2

THINKING LIKE AN ECONOMIST

Every field of study has its own language and its own way of thinking. Mathematicians talk about axioms, integrals, and vector spaces. Psychologists talk about ego, id, and cognitive dissonance. Lawyers talk about venue, torts, and promissory estoppel.

Economics is no different. Supply, demand, elasticity, comparative advantage, consumer surplus, deadweight loss—these terms are part of the economist's language. In the coming chapters, you will encounter many new terms and some familiar words that economists use in specialized ways. At first, this new language may seem needlessly arcane. But, as you will see, its value lies in its ability to provide you a new and useful way of thinking about the world in which you live.

The single most important purpose of this book is to help you learn the economist's way of thinking. Of course, just as you cannot become a mathematician, psychologist, or lawyer overnight, learning to think like an economist will take some time. Yet with a combination of theory, case studies, and examples of economics in the news, this book will give you ample opportunity to develop and practice this skill.

Before delving into the substance and details of economics, it is helpful to have an overview of how economists approach the world. This chapter, therefore, discusses the field's methodology. What is distinctive about how economists confront a question? What does it mean to think like an economist?

THE ECONOMIST AS SCIENTIST

Economists try to address their subject with a scientist's objectivity. They approach the study of the economy in much the same way as a physicist approaches the study of matter and a biologist approaches the study of life: They devise theories, collect data, and then analyze these data in an attempt to verify or refute their theories.

To beginners, it can seem odd to claim that economics is a science. After all, economists do not work with test tubes or telescopes. The essence of science, however, is the *scientific method*—the dispassionate development and testing of theories about how the world works. This method of inquiry is as applicable to studying a nation's economy as it is to studying the earth's gravity or a species' evolution. As Albert Einstein once put it, "The whole of science is nothing more than the refinement of everyday thinking."

Although Einstein's comment is as true for social sciences such as economics as it is for natural sciences such as physics, most people are not accustomed to looking at society through the eyes of a scientist. Let's therefore discuss some of the ways in which economists apply the logic of science to examine how an economy works.

"I'm a social scientist, Michael. That means I can't explain electricity or anything like that, but if you ever want to know about people I'm your man."

THE SCIENTIFIC METHOD: OBSERVATION, THEORY, AND MORE OBSERVATION

Isaac Newton, the famous seventeenth-century scientist and mathematician, allegedly became intrigued one day when he saw an apple fall from an apple tree. This observation motivated Newton to develop a theory of gravity that applies not only to an apple falling to the earth but to any two objects in the universe. Subsequent testing of Newton's theory has shown that it works well in many circumstances (although, as Einstein would later emphasize, not in all circumstances). Because Newton's theory has been so successful at explaining observation, the theory is still taught today in undergraduate physics courses around the world.

This interplay between theory and observation also occurs in the field of economics. An economist might live in a country experiencing rapid increases in prices and be moved by this observation to develop a theory of inflation. The theory might assert that high inflation arises when the government prints too much money. (As you may recall, this was one of the *Ten Principles of Economics* in Chapter 1.) To test this theory, the economist could collect and analyze data on prices and money from many different countries. If growth in the quantity of money were not at all related to the rate at which prices are rising, the economist would start to doubt the validity of his theory of inflation. If money growth and inflation were strongly correlated in international data, as in fact they are, the economist would become more confident in his theory.

Although economists use theory and observation like other scientists, they do face an obstacle that makes their task especially challenging: Experiments are often difficult in economics. Physicists studying gravity can drop many objects in their laboratories to generate data to test their theories. By contrast, economists studying inflation are not allowed to control a nation's monetary policy simply to generate useful data. Economists, like astronomers and evolutionary biologists, usually have to make do with whatever data the world happens to give them.

To find a substitute for laboratory experiments, economists pay close attention to the natural experiments offered by history. When a war in the Middle East interrupts the flow of crude oil, for instance, oil prices skyrocket around the world. For consumers of oil and oil products, such an event depresses living standards. For economic policymakers, it poses a difficult choice about how best to respond. But for economic scientists, it provides an opportunity to study the effects of a key natural resource on the world's economies, and this opportunity persists long after the wartime increase in oil prices is over. Throughout this book, therefore, we consider many historical episodes. These episodes are valuable to study both because they give us insight into the economy of the past and, more important, because they allow us to illustrate and evaluate economic theories of the present.

THE ROLE OF ASSUMPTIONS

If you ask a physicist how long it would take for a marble to fall from the top of a ten-story building, she will answer the question by assuming that the marble falls in a vacuum. Of course, this assumption is false. In fact, the building is surrounded by air, which exerts friction on the falling marble and slows it down.

Yet the physicist will correctly point out that friction on the marble is so small that its effect is negligible. Assuming the marble falls in a vacuum greatly simplifies the problem without substantially affecting the answer.

Economists make assumptions for the same reason: Assumptions can make the world easier to understand. To study the effects of international trade, for example, we may assume that the world consists of only two countries and that each country produces only two goods. Of course, the real world consists of dozens of countries, each of which produces thousands of different types of goods. But by assuming two countries and two goods, we can focus our thinking. Once we understand international trade in an imaginary world with two countries and two goods, we are in a better position to understand international trade in the more complex world in which we live.

The art in scientific thinking—whether in physics, biology, or economics—is deciding which assumptions to make. Suppose, for instance, that we were dropping a beach ball rather than a marble from the top of the building. Our physicist would realize that the assumption of no friction is far less accurate in this case: Friction exerts a greater force on a beach ball than on a marble. The assumption that gravity works in a vacuum is reasonable for studying a falling marble but not for studying a falling beach ball.

Similarly, economists use different assumptions to answer different questions. Suppose that we want to study what happens to the economy when the government changes the number of dollars in circulation. An important piece of this analysis, it turns out, is how prices respond. Many prices in the economy change infrequently; the newsstand prices of magazines, for instance, are changed only every few years. Knowing this fact may lead us to make different assumptions when studying the effects of the policy change over different time horizons. For studying the short-run effects of the policy, we may assume that prices do not change much. We may even make the extreme and artificial assumption that all prices are completely fixed. For studying the long-run effects of the policy, however, we may assume that all prices are completely flexible. Just as a physicist uses different assumptions when studying falling marbles and falling beach balls, economists use different assumptions when studying the short-run and long-run effects of a change in the quantity of money.

ECONOMIC MODELS

High school biology teachers teach basic anatomy with plastic replicas of the human body. These models have all the major organs—the heart, the liver, the kidneys, and so on. The models allow teachers to show their students in a simple way how the important parts of the body fit together. Of course, these plastic models are not actual human bodies, and no one would mistake the model for a real person. These models are stylized, and they omit many details. Yet despite this lack of realism—indeed, because of this lack of realism—studying these models is useful for learning how the human body works.

Economists also use models to learn about the world, but instead of being made of plastic, they are most often composed of diagrams and equations. Like a biology teacher's plastic model, economic models omit many details to allow us to see what is truly important. Just as the biology teacher's model does not include all of the body's muscles and capillaries, an economist's model does not include every feature of the economy.

As we use models to examine various economic issues throughout this book, you will see that all the models are built with assumptions. Just as a physicist begins the analysis of a falling marble by assuming away the existence of friction, economists assume away many of the details of the economy that are irrelevant for studying the question at hand. All models—in physics, biology, or economics—simplify reality in order to improve our understanding of it.

OUR FIRST MODEL: THE CIRCULAR-FLOW DIAGRAM

The economy consists of millions of people engaged in many activities—buying, selling, working, hiring, manufacturing, and so on. To understand how the economy works, we must find some way to simplify our thinking about all these activities. In other words, we need a model that explains, in general terms, how the economy is organized.

Figure 2-1 presents a visual model of the economy, called a **circular-flow diagram.** In this model, the economy has two types of decisionmakers—households and firms. Firms produce goods and services using various inputs, such as labor,

circular-flow diagram
a visual model of the economy that shows how dollars flow through markets among households and firms

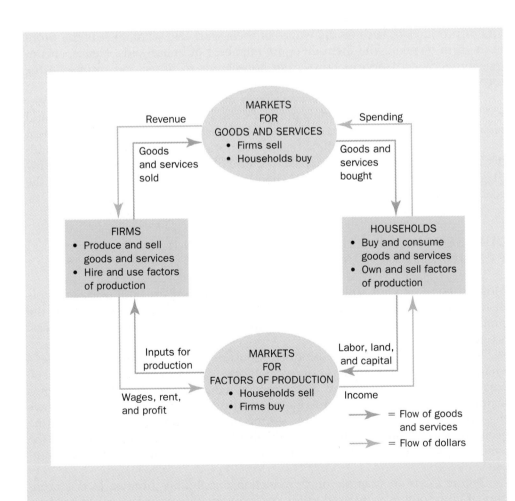

Figure 2-1

THE CIRCULAR FLOW. This diagram is a schematic representation of the organization of the economy. Decisions are made by households and firms. Households and firms interact in the markets for goods and services (where households are buyers and firms are sellers) and in the markets for the factors of production (where firms are buyers and households are sellers). The outer set of arrows shows the flow of dollars, and the inner set of arrows shows the corresponding flow of goods and services.

land, and capital (buildings and machines). These inputs are called the *factors of production*. Households own the factors of production and consume all the goods and services that the firms produce.

Households and firms interact in two types of markets. In the *markets for goods and services*, households are buyers, and firms are sellers. In particular, households buy the output of goods and services that firms produce. In the *markets for the factors of production*, households are sellers, and firms are buyers. In these markets, households provide firms the inputs that the firms use to produce goods and services. The circular-flow diagram offers a simple way of organizing all the economic transactions that occur between households and firms in the economy.

The inner loop of the circular-flow diagram represents the flows of goods and services between households and firms. The households sell the use of their labor, land, and capital to the firms in the markets for the factors of production. The firms then use these factors to produce goods and services, which in turn are sold to households in the markets for goods and services. Hence, the factors of production flow from households to firms, and goods and services flow from firms to households.

The outer loop of the circular-flow diagram represents the corresponding flow of dollars. The households spend money to buy goods and services from the firms. The firms use some of the revenue from these sales to pay for the factors of production, such as the wages of their workers. What's left is the profit of the firm owners, who themselves are members of households. Hence, spending on goods and services flows from households to firms, and income in the form of wages, rent, and profit flows from firms to households.

This circular-flow diagram is one simple model of the economy. It dispenses with various details that, for some purposes, are significant. A more complex and realistic circular-flow model would include, for instance, the roles of government and international trade. Yet these details are not crucial for a basic understanding of how the economy is organized. Because of its simplicity, this circular-flow diagram is useful to keep in mind when thinking about how the pieces of the economy fit together.

OUR SECOND MODEL: THE PRODUCTION POSSIBILITIES FRONTIER

Most economic models, unlike the circular-flow diagram, are built using the tools of mathematics. Here we consider one of the simplest such models, called the production possibilities frontier, and see how this model illustrates some basic economic ideas.

Although real economies produce thousands of goods and services, let's imagine an economy that produces only two goods—cars and computers. Together the car industry and the computer industry use all of the economy's factors of production. The **production possibilities frontier** is a graph that shows the various combinations of output—in this case, cars and computers—that the economy can possibly produce given the available factors of production and the available production technology that firms can use to turn these factors into output.

Figure 2-2 is an example of a production possibilities frontier. In this economy, if all resources were used in the car industry, the economy would produce

production possibilities frontier

a graph that shows the various combinations of output that the economy can possibly produce given the available factors of production and the available production technology

Figure 2-2

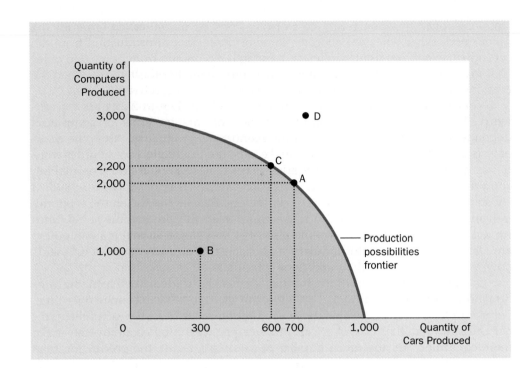

THE PRODUCTION POSSIBILITIES FRONTIER. The production possibilities frontier shows the combinations of output—in this case, cars and computers—that the economy can possibly produce. The economy can produce any combination on or inside the frontier. Points outside the frontier are not feasible given the economy's resources.

1,000 cars and no computers. If all resources were used in the computer industry, the economy would produce 3,000 computers and no cars. The two end points of the production possibilities frontier represent these extreme possibilities. If the economy were to divide its resources between the two industries, it could produce 700 cars and 2,000 computers, shown in the figure by point A. By contrast, point D is an infeasible outcome because the economy does not have the resources to support that level of production. In other words, the economy can produce at any point on or inside the production possibilities frontier, but it cannot produce at points outside the frontier.

An outcome is said to be *efficient* if the economy is getting all it can from the scarce resources it has available. Points on (rather than inside) the production possibilities frontier represent efficient levels of production. When the economy is producing at such a point, say point A, there is no way to produce more of one good without producing less of the other. Point B represents an *inefficient* outcome. For some reason, perhaps widespread unemployment, the economy is producing less than it could from the resources it has available: It is producing only 300 cars and 1,000 computers. If the source of the inefficiency were eliminated, the economy could move from point B to point A, increasing production of both cars (to 700) and computers (to 2,000).

One of the *Ten Principles of Economics* discussed in Chapter 1 is that people face tradeoffs. The production possibilities frontier shows one tradeoff that society faces. Once we have reached the efficient points on the frontier, the only way of getting more of one good is to get less of the other. When the economy moves from point A to point C, for instance, society produces more computers but at the expense of producing fewer cars.

Another of the *Ten Principles of Economics* is that the cost of something is what you give up to get it. This is called the *opportunity cost*. The production possibilities frontier shows the opportunity cost of one good as measured in terms of the other good. When society reallocates some of the factors of production from the car industry to the computer industry, moving the economy from point A to point C, it gives up 100 cars to get 200 additional computers. In other words, when the economy is at point A, the opportunity cost of 200 computers is 100 cars.

Notice that the production possibilities frontier in Figure 2-2 is bowed outward. This means that the opportunity cost of cars in terms of computers depends on how much of each good the economy is producing. When the economy is using most of its resources to make cars, the production possibilities frontier is quite steep. Because even workers and machines best suited to making computers are being used to make cars, each car the economy gives up yields a substantial increase in the number of computers. By contrast, when the economy is using most of its resources to make computers, the production possibilities frontier is quite flat. In this case, the resources best suited to making computers are already in the computer industry, and each car the economy gives up yields only a small increase in the number of computers.

The production possibilities frontier shows the tradeoff between the production of different goods at a given time, but the tradeoff can change over time. For example, if a technological advance in the computer industry raises the number of computers that a worker can produce per week, the economy can make more computers for any given number of cars. As a result, the production possibilities frontier shifts outward, as in Figure 2-3. Because of this economic

Figure 2-3

A SHIFT IN THE PRODUCTION POSSIBILITIES FRONTIER. An economic advance in the computer industry shifts the production possibilities frontier outward, increasing the number of cars and computers the economy can produce.

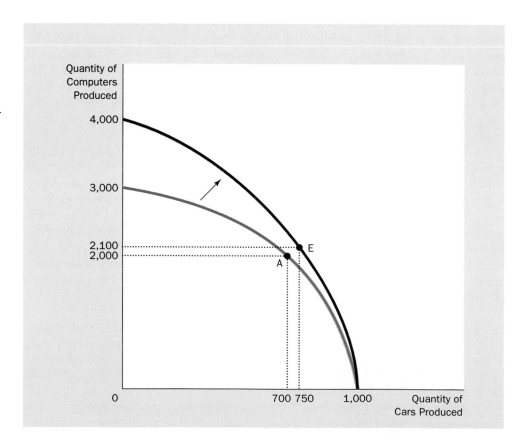

growth, society might move production from point A to point E, enjoying more computers and more cars.

The production possibilities frontier simplifies a complex economy in order to highlight and clarify some fundamental ideas. We have used it to illustrate some of the ideas mentioned briefly in Chapter 1: efficiency, tradeoffs, opportunity cost, and economic growth. As you study economics, these ideas will recur in various forms. The production possibilities frontier offers one simple way of thinking about them.

MICROECONOMICS AND MACROECONOMICS

Many subjects are studied on various levels. Consider biology, for example. Molecular biologists study the chemical compounds that make up living things. Cellular biologists study cells, which are made up of many chemical compounds and, at the same time, are themselves the building blocks of living organisms. Evolutionary biologists study the many varieties of animals and plants and how species change gradually over the centuries.

Economics is also studied on various levels. We can study the decisions of individual households and firms. Or we can study the interaction of households and firms in markets for specific goods and services. Or we can study the operation of the economy as a whole, which is just the sum of the activities of all these decisionmakers in all these markets.

The field of economics is traditionally divided into two broad subfields. **Microeconomics** is the study of how households and firms make decisions and how they interact in specific markets. **Macroeconomics** is the study of economy-wide phenomena. A microeconomist might study the effects of rent control on housing in New York City, the impact of foreign competition on the U.S. auto industry, or the effects of compulsory school attendance on workers' earnings. A macroeconomist might study the effects of borrowing by the federal government, the changes over time in the economy's rate of unemployment, or alternative policies to raise growth in national living standards.

Microeconomics and macroeconomics are closely intertwined. Because changes in the overall economy arise from the decisions of millions of individuals, it is impossible to understand macroeconomic developments without considering the associated microeconomic decisions. For example, a macroeconomist might study the effect of a cut in the federal income tax on the overall production of goods and services. To analyze this issue, he or she must consider how the tax cut affects the decisions of households about how much to spend on goods and services.

Despite the inherent link between microeconomics and macroeconomics, the two fields are distinct. In economics, as in biology, it may seem natural to begin with the smallest unit and build up. Yet doing so is neither necessary nor always the best way to proceed. Evolutionary biology is, in a sense, built upon molecular biology, since species are made up of molecules. Yet evolutionary biology and molecular biology are separate fields, each with its own questions and its own methods. Similarly, because microeconomics and macroeconomics address different questions, they sometimes take quite different approaches and are often taught in separate courses.

microeconomics
the study of how households and firms make decisions and how they interact in markets

macroeconomics
the study of economy-wide phenomena, including inflation, unemployment, and economic growth

▌ QUICK QUIZ   In what sense is economics like a science? ◆ Define *microeconomics* and *macroeconomics*.

THE ECONOMIST AS POLICYMAKER

Often economists are asked to explain the causes of economic events. Why, for example, is unemployment higher for teenagers than for older workers? Sometimes economists are asked to recommend policies to improve economic outcomes. What, for instance, should the government do to improve the economic well-being of teenagers? When economists are trying to explain the world, they are scientists. When they are trying to improve it, they are policymakers.

POSITIVE VERSUS NORMATIVE ANALYSIS

To help clarify the two roles that economists play, we begin by examining the use of language. Because scientists and policymakers have different goals, they use language in different ways.

For example, suppose that two people are discussing minimum-wage laws. Here are two statements you might hear:

POLLY: Minimum-wage laws cause unemployment.

NORMA: The government should raise the minimum wage.

Ignoring for now whether you agree with these statements, notice that Polly and Norma differ in what they are trying to do. Polly is speaking like a scientist: She is making a claim about how the world works. Norma is speaking like a policymaker: She is making a claim about how she would like to change the world.

In general, statements about the world are of two types. One type, such as Polly's, is positive. **Positive statements** are descriptive. They make a claim about how the world *is*. A second type of statement, such as Norma's, is normative. **Normative statements** are prescriptive. They make a claim about how the world *ought to be*.

A key difference between positive and normative statements is how we judge their validity. We can, in principle, confirm or refute positive statements by examining evidence. An economist might evaluate Polly's statement by analyzing data on changes in minimum wages and changes in unemployment over time. By contrast, evaluating normative statements involves values as well as facts. Norma's statement cannot be judged using data alone. Deciding what is good or bad policy is not merely a matter of science. It also involves our views on ethics, religion, and political philosophy.

Of course, positive and normative statements may be related. Our positive views about how the world works affect our normative views about what policies are desirable. Polly's claim that the minimum wage causes unemployment, if true, might lead us to reject Norma's conclusion that the government should raise the minimum wage. Yet our normative conclusions cannot come from positive analysis alone. Instead, they require both positive analysis and value judgments.

As you study economics, keep in mind the distinction between positive and normative statements. Much of economics just tries to explain how the economy works. Yet often the goal of economics is to improve how the economy works. When you hear economists making normative statements, you know they have crossed the line from scientist to policymaker.

positive statements
claims that attempt to describe the world as it is

normative statements
claims that attempt to prescribe how the world should be

ECONOMISTS IN WASHINGTON

President Harry Truman once said that he wanted to find a one-armed economist. When he asked his economists for advice, they always answered, "On the one hand, . . . On the other hand, . . ."

Truman was not alone in realizing that economists' advice is often equivocal. This tendency is rooted in one of the *Ten Principles of Economics* in Chapter 1: People face tradeoffs. Economists are aware that tradeoffs are involved in most policy decisions. A policy might increase efficiency at the cost of equity. It might help future generations but hurt current generations. An economist who says that all policy decisions are easy is an economist not to be trusted.

Truman was also not alone among presidents in relying on the advice of economists. Since 1946, the president of the United States has received guidance from the Council of Economic Advisers, which consists of three members and a staff of several dozen economists. The council, whose offices are just a few steps from the White House, has no duty other than to advise the president and to write the annual *Economic Report of the President*.

The president also receives input from economists in many administrative departments. Economists at the Department of Treasury help design tax policy. Economists at the Department of Labor analyze data on workers and those looking for work in order to help formulate labor-market policies. Economists at the Department of Justice help enforce the nation's antitrust laws.

Economists are also found outside the administrative branch of government. To obtain independent evaluations of policy proposals, Congress relies on the advice of the Congressional Budget Office, which is staffed by economists. The Federal Reserve, the quasi-governmental institution that sets the nation's monetary policy, employs hundreds of economists to analyze economic developments in the United States and throughout the world.

"Let's switch. I'll make the policy, you implement it, and he'll explain it."

The influence of economists on policy goes beyond their role as advisers and policymakers: Their research and writings often affect policy indirectly. Economist John Maynard Keynes offered this observation:

> The ideas of economists and political philosophers, both when they are right and when they are wrong, are more powerful than is commonly understood. Indeed, the world is ruled by little else. Practical men, who believe themselves to be quite exempt from intellectual influences, are usually the slaves of some defunct economist. Madmen in authority, who hear voices in the air, are distilling their frenzy from some academic scribbler of a few years back.

Although these words were written in 1935, they remain true today. Indeed, the "academic scribbler" now influencing public policy is often Keynes himself.

QUICK QUIZ   Give an example of a positive statement and an example of a normative statement. ◆ Name three parts of government that regularly rely on advice from economists.

WHY ECONOMISTS DISAGREE

"If all economists were laid end to end, they would not reach a conclusion." This quip from George Bernard Shaw is revealing. Economists as a group are often criticized for giving conflicting advice to policymakers. President Ronald Reagan once joked that if the game Trivial Pursuit were designed for economists, it would have 100 questions and 3,000 answers.

Why do economists so often appear to give conflicting advice to policymakers? There are three basic reasons:

◆ Economists may disagree about the validity of alternative positive theories about how the world works.

◆ Economists may have different values and, therefore, different normative views about what policy should try to accomplish.

◆ Economists may in fact agree, and yet the advice of charlatans or cranks obscures the consensus.

Let's discuss each of these reasons.

DIFFERENCES IN SCIENTIFIC JUDGMENTS

Several centuries ago, astronomers debated whether the earth or the sun was at the center of the solar system. More recently, meteorologists have debated whether the earth is experiencing "global warming." Science is a search for understanding about the world around us. It is not surprising that as the search continues, scientists can disagree about the direction in which truth lies.

Economists often disagree for the same reason. Economics is a young science, and there is still much to be learned. Economists sometimes disagree because they have different hunches about the validity of alternative theories or about the size of important parameters.

For example, economists disagree about whether the government should levy taxes based on a household's income or its consumption (spending). Advocates of a switch from the current income tax to a consumption tax believe that the change would encourage households to save more, because income that is saved would not be taxed. Higher saving, in turn, would lead to more rapid growth in productivity and living standards. Advocates of the current income tax believe that household saving would not respond much to a change in the tax laws. These two groups of economists hold different normative views about the tax system because they have different positive views about the responsiveness of saving to tax incentives.

DIFFERENCES IN VALUES

Suppose that Peter and Paul both take the same amount of water from the town well. To pay for maintaining the well, the town taxes its residents. Peter has income of $50,000 and is taxed $5,000, or 10 percent of his income. Paul has income of $10,000 and is taxed $2,000, or 20 percent of his income.

Is this policy fair? If not, who pays too much and who pays too little? Does it matter whether Paul's low income is due to a medical disability or to his decision to pursue a career in acting? Does it matter whether Peter's high income is due to a large inheritance or to his willingness to work long hours at a dreary job?

These are difficult questions on which people are likely to disagree. If the town hired two experts to study how the town should tax its residents to pay for the well, we would not be surprised if they offered conflicting advice.

This simple example shows why economists sometimes disagree about public policy. As we learned earlier in our discussion of normative and positive analysis, policies cannot be judged on scientific grounds alone. Economists give conflicting advice sometimes because they have different values. Perfecting the science of economics will not tell us whether it is Peter or Paul who pays too much.

CHARLATANS AND CRANKS

Fad diets are popular because they promise amazing results with minimal effort. Many people want to lose weight but are not eager to pay the price of eating fewer calories and exercising more regularly. These people are convinced all too easily by the reassuring words of some self-proclaimed expert selling a miraculous product. They *want* to believe that this new, easy-to-follow diet really will work.

Fad economics is also popular, for much the same reason. Anyone can adopt the title "economist" and claim discovery of some easy fix to the economy's troubles. These fads often tempt politicians, who are eager to find easy and novel solutions to hard and persistent problems. Some fads come from charlatans who use crazy theories to gain the limelight and promote their own interests. Others come from cranks who believe that their theories really are true.

An example of fad economics occurred in 1980, when a small group of economists advised presidential candidate Ronald Reagan that an across-the-board cut in income tax rates would raise tax revenue. They argued that if people could keep a higher fraction of their income, people would work harder to earn more income. Even though tax rates would be lower, income would rise by so much, they claimed, that tax revenue would rise. Almost all professional economists, including most of those who supported Reagan's proposal to cut taxes, viewed this outcome as far too optimistic. Lower tax rates might encourage people to work harder, and this extra effort would offset the direct effects of lower tax rates to some extent. But there was no credible evidence that work effort would rise by enough to cause tax revenues to rise in the face of lower tax rates. George Bush, also a presidential candidate in 1980, agreed with most of the professional economists: He called this idea "voodoo economics." Nonetheless, the argument was appealing to Reagan, and it shaped the 1980 presidential campaign and the economic policies of the 1980s.

People on fad diets put their health at risk but rarely achieve the permanent weight loss they desire. Similarly, when politicians rely on the advice of charlatans and cranks, they rarely get the desirable results they anticipate. After Reagan's election, Congress passed the cut in tax rates that Reagan advocated, but the tax cut did not cause tax revenue to rise. Instead, tax revenue fell, as most economists predicted it would, and the U.S. federal government began a long period of deficit spending, leading to the largest peacetime increase in the government debt in U.S. history.

Fads can make the experts seem less united than they actually are. It would be wrong to conclude that professional nutritionists are in disarray simply because fad diets are so popular. In fact, nutritionists have agreed on the basics of weight loss—exercise and a balanced low-fat diet—for many years. Similarly, when the economics profession appears in disarray, you should ask whether the disagreement is real or manufactured. It may be that some snake-oil salesman is trying to sell a miracle cure for what ails the economy.

PERCEPTION VERSUS REALITY

Because of differences in scientific judgments and differences in values, some disagreement among economists is inevitable. Yet one should not overstate the amount of disagreement. In many cases, economists do offer a united view.

Table 2-1 contains ten propositions about economic policy. In a survey of economists in business, government, and academia, these propositions were endorsed by an overwhelming majority of respondents. Most of these propositions would fail to command a similar consensus among the general public.

The first proposition in the table is about rent control. For reasons we will discuss in Chapter 6, almost all economists believe that rent control adversely affects the availability and quality of housing and is a very costly way of helping the most needy members of society. Nonetheless, many city governments choose to ignore the advice of economists and place ceilings on the rents that landlords may charge their tenants.

The second proposition in the table concerns tariffs and import quotas. For reasons we will discuss in Chapter 3 and more fully in Chapter 9, almost all economists oppose such barriers to free trade. Nonetheless, over the years, the president and Congress have chosen to restrict the import of certain goods. In 1993 the North American Free Trade Agreement, which reduced barriers to trade among the United States, Canada, and Mexico, passed Congress, but only by a

Table 2-1

TEN PROPOSITIONS ABOUT
WHICH MOST ECONOMISTS
AGREE

PROPOSITION AND PERCENTAGE OF ECONOMISTS WHO AGREE

1. A ceiling on rents reduces the quantity and quality of housing available. (93%)
2. Tariffs and import quotas usually reduce general economic welfare. (93%)
3. Flexible and floating exchange rates offer an effective international monetary arrangement. (90%)
4. Fiscal policy (e.g., tax cut and/or government expenditure increase) has a significant stimulative impact on a less than fully employed economy. (90%)
5. If the federal budget is to be balanced, it should be done over the business cycle rather than yearly. (85%)
6. Cash payments increase the welfare of recipients to a greater degree than do transfers-in-kind of equal cash value. (84%)
7. A large federal budget deficit has an adverse effect on the economy. (83%)
8. A minimum wage increases unemployment among young and unskilled workers. (79%)
9. The government should restructure the welfare system along the lines of a "negative income tax." (79%)
10. Effluent taxes and marketable pollution permits represent a better approach to pollution control than imposition of pollution ceilings. (78%)

SOURCE: Richard M. Alston, J. R. Kearl, and Michael B. Vaughn, "Is There Consensus among Economists in the 1990s?" *American Economic Review*, May 1992, 203–209.

narrow margin, despite overwhelming support from economists. In this case, economists did offer united advice, but many members of Congress chose to ignore it.

Why do policies such as rent control and import quotas persist if the experts are united in their opposition? The reason may be that economists have not yet convinced the general public that these policies are undesirable. One of the purposes of this book is to make you understand the economist's view of these and other subjects and, perhaps, to persuade you that it is the right one.

QUICK QUIZ Give three reasons why two economic advisers to the president might disagree about a question of policy.

LET'S GET GOING

The first two chapters of this book have introduced you to the ideas and methods of economics. We are now ready to get to work. In the next chapter we start learning in more detail the principles of economic behavior and economic policy.

As you proceed through this book, you will be asked to draw on many of your intellectual skills. You might find it helpful to keep in mind some advice from the great economist John Maynard Keynes:

The study of economics does not seem to require any specialized gifts of an unusually high order. Is it not . . . a very easy subject compared with the higher branches of philosophy or pure science? An easy subject, at which very few excel! The paradox finds its explanation, perhaps, in that the master-economist must possess a rare *combination* of gifts. He must be mathematician, historian, statesman, philosopher—in some degree. He must understand symbols and speak in words. He must contemplate the particular in terms of the general, and touch abstract and concrete in the same flight of thought. He must study the present in the light of the past for the purposes of the future. No part of man's nature or his institutions must lie entirely outside his regard. He must be purposeful and disinterested in a simultaneous mood; as aloof and incorruptible as an artist, yet sometimes as near the earth as a politician.

It is a tall order. But with practice, you will become more and more accustomed to thinking like an economist.

Summary

◆ Economists try to address their subject with a scientist's objectivity. Like all scientists, they make appropriate assumptions and build simplified models in order to understand the world around them.

◆ The field of economics is divided into two subfields: microeconomics and macroeconomics. Microeconomists study decisionmaking by households and firms and the interaction among households and firms in the market-place. Macroeconomists study the forces and trends that affect the economy as a whole.

◆ A positive statement is an assertion about how the world *is*. A normative statement is an assertion about how the world *ought to be*. When economists make normative statements, they are acting more as policymakers than scientists.

◆ Economists who advise policymakers offer conflicting advice either because of differences in scientific judgments or because of differences in values. Sometimes policymakers get conflicting advice because some charlatan is offering an unrealistically easy solution to a hard problem. At other times, economists are united in the advice they offer, but policymakers may choose to ignore it.

Key Concepts

circular-flow diagram, p. 21
production possibilities frontier, p. 22

microeconomics, p. 25
macroeconomics, p. 25

positive statements, p. 26
normative statements, p. 26

Questions for Review

1. How is economics like a science?

2. Why do economists make assumptions?

3. Should an economic model describe reality exactly?

4. Draw and explain a production possibilities frontier for an economy that produces milk and cookies. What happens to this frontier if a disease kills half of the economy's cow population?

5. What are the two subfields into which economics is divided? Explain what each subfield studies.

6. What is the difference between a positive and a normative statement? Give an example of each.

7. What is the Council of Economic Advisers?

8. Why do economists sometimes offer conflicting advice to policymakers?

Problems and Applications

1. Describe some unusual language used in one of the other fields that you are studying. Why are these special terms useful?

2. One common assumption in economics is that the products of different firms in the same industry are indistinguishable. For each of the following industries, discuss whether this is a reasonable assumption.
   a. steel
   b. novels
   c. wheat
   d. fast food

3. Draw a circular-flow diagram. Identify the parts of the model that correspond to the flow of goods and services and the flow of dollars for each of the following activities:
   a. Sam pays a storekeeper $1 for a quart of milk.
   b. Sally earns $4.50 per hour working at a fast-food restaurant.
   c. Serena spends $7 to see a movie.
   d. Stuart earns $10,000 from his 10 percent ownership of Acme Industrial.

4. What important features of the economy does the circular-flow model ignore? Can you think of some questions for which it is reasonable to ignore these features, and some questions for which it is not?

5. The first principle of economics discussed in Chapter 1 is that people face tradeoffs. Use a production possibilities frontier to illustrate society's tradeoff between a clean environment and high incomes. What do you suppose determines the shape and position of the frontier? Show what happens to the frontier if engineers develop an automobile engine with almost no emissions.

6. Classify the following topics as relating to microeconomics or macroeconomics:
   a. a family's decision about how much income to save
   b. the effect of government regulations on auto emissions
   c. the impact of higher saving on economic growth
   d. a firm's decision about how many workers to hire
   e. the relationship between the inflation rate and changes in the quantity of money

7. Classify each of the following statements as positive or normative. Explain.
   a. Society faces a short-run tradeoff between inflation and unemployment.
   b. A reduction in the rate of growth of money will reduce the rate of inflation.
   c. The Federal Reserve should reduce the rate of growth of money.
   d. Society ought to require welfare recipients to look for jobs.
   e. Lower tax rates encourage more work and more saving.

8. Classify each of the statements in Table 2-1 as positive, normative, or ambiguous. Explain.

9. If you were president, would you be more interested in your economic advisers' positive views or their normative views? Why?

10. The *Economic Report of the President* contains statistical information about the economy as well as the Council of Economic Advisers' analysis of current policy issues. Find a recent copy of this annual report at your library and read a chapter about an issue that interests you. Summarize the economic problem at hand and describe the council's recommended policy.

11. Who is the current chairman of the Federal Reserve? Who is the current chair of the Council of Economic Advisers? Who is the current secretary of the treasury?

12. Would you expect economists to disagree less about public policy as time goes on? Why or why not? Can their differences be completely eliminated? Why or why not?

13. The chapter tells a story about Peter and Paul and the town well.
   a. Do you think that the tax policy in the example is a fair one? Why?
   b. What additional information would you like to have about Peter and Paul before reaching a judgment?
   c. In light of your answer to part (b), do you think that complicated tax systems are more fair than simple tax systems? What other considerations should affect the complexity of our tax system?

APPENDIX

GRAPHING: A BRIEF REVIEW

Many of the concepts that economists study can be expressed with numbers—the price of bananas, the quantity of bananas sold, the cost of growing bananas, and so on. Often these economic variables are related to one another. When the price of bananas rises, people buy fewer bananas. One way of expressing the relationships among variables is with graphs.

Graphs serve two purposes. First, when developing economic theories, graphs offer a way to express visually ideas that might be less clear if described with equations or words. Second, when analyzing economic data, graphs provide a way of finding how variables are in fact related in the world. Whether we are working with theory or with data, graphs provide a lens through which a recognizable forest emerges from a multitude of trees.

Numerical information can be expressed graphically in many ways, just as a thought can be expressed in words in many ways. A good writer chooses words that will make an argument clear, a description pleasing, or a scene dramatic. An effective economist chooses the type of graph that best suits the purpose at hand.

In this appendix we discuss how economists use graphs to study the mathematical relationships among variables. We also discuss some of the pitfalls that can arise in the use of graphical methods.

GRAPHS OF A SINGLE VARIABLE

Three common graphs are shown in Figure 2A-1. The *pie chart* in panel (a) shows how health care expenditures are divided among individuals, their insurers, and the government. A slice of the pie represents each group's share of the total. The *bar graph* in panel (b) compares how much various large corporations are worth. The height of each bar represents the dollar value of each firm. The *time-series graph* in panel (c) traces the rising productivity of labor on American farms over time. The height of the line shows output per labor-hour in each year. You have probably seen similar graphs presented in newspapers and magazines.

GRAPHS OF TWO VARIABLES: THE COORDINATE SYSTEM

Although the three graphs in Figure 2A-1 are useful in showing how a variable changes over time or across individuals, such graphs are limited in how much they can tell us. These graphs display information only on a single variable. Economists are often concerned with the relationships between variables. Thus, they need to be able to display two variables on a single graph. The *coordinate system* makes this possible.

Suppose you want to examine the relationship between study time and grade point average. For each student in your class, you could record a pair of numbers: hours per week spent studying and grade point average. These numbers could then be placed in parentheses as an *ordered pair* and appear as a single

(a) Pie Chart

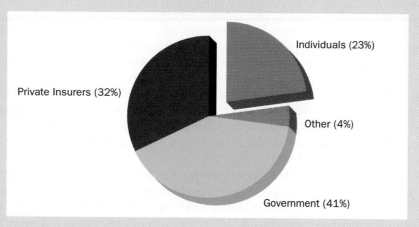

Individuals (23%)

Private Insurers (32%)

Other (4%)

Government (41%)

(b) Bar Graph

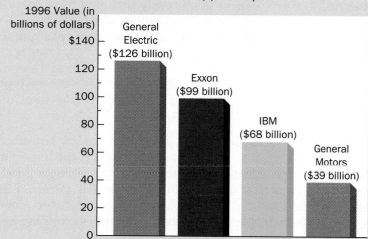

1996 Value (in billions of dollars)

General Electric ($126 billion)

Exxon ($99 billion)

IBM ($68 billion)

General Motors ($39 billion)

$140

120

100

80

60

40

20

0

(c) Time-Series Graph

Productivity Index (farm output per hour of labor, 1977 = 100)

160

140

120

100

80

60

40

20

0

1950   1960   1970   1980   1990

Figure 2A-1

TYPES OF GRAPHS. The pie chart in panel (a) shows how health care expenditures are divided up. The bar graph in panel (b) shows the market value of some of the world's largest corporations. The time-series graph in panel (c) shows the growth in the productivity of labor on American farms from 1950 to 1990.

SOURCES: (a) *Economic Report of the President*, 1993 (Health Care Financing Administration). Data from 1990. (b) *Business Week*, March 25, 1996. (c) *Economic Report of the President*, 1993.

point on the graph. Albert E., for instance, is represented by the ordered pair (25 hours/week, 3.5 GPA), while his "what-me-worry?" classmate Alfred E. is represented by the ordered pair (5 hours/week, 2.0 GPA).

We can graph these ordered pairs on a two-dimensional grid. The first number in each ordered pair, called the *x-coordinate*, tells us the horizontal location of the point. The second number, called the *y-coordinate*, tells us the vertical location of the point. The point with both an *x*-coordinate and a *y*-coordinate of zero is known as the *origin*. The two coordinates in the ordered pair tell us where the point is located in relation to the origin: *x* units to the right of the origin and *y* units above it.

Figure 2A-2 graphs grade point average against study time for Albert E., Alfred E., and their classmates. This type of graph is called a *scatterplot* because it plots scattered points. Looking at this graph, we immediately notice that points farther to the right also tend to be higher. Because higher study time is associated with higher grades, we say that these two variables have a *positive correlation*. By contrast, if we were to graph party time and grades, we would likely find that higher party time is associated with lower grades, and we would call this a *negative correlation*. In either case, the coordinate system makes the correlation between the two variables easy to see.

CURVES IN THE COORDINATE SYSTEM

Students who study more do tend to get higher grades, but other factors also influence a student's grade. Previous preparation is an important factor, for instance, as are talent, attention from teachers, even eating a good breakfast. A scatterplot like Figure 2A-2 does not attempt to isolate the effect that study has on grades from the effects of other variables. Often, however, economists prefer looking at how one variable affects another, holding everything else constant.

Figure 2A-2

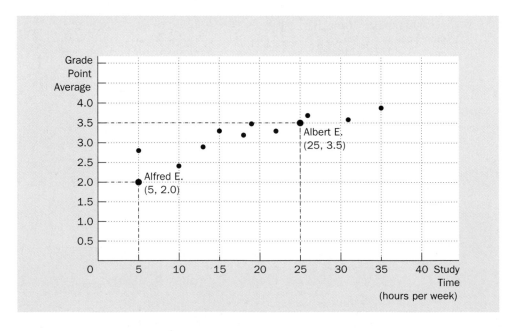

USING THE COORDINATE SYSTEM. Grade point average is measured on the vertical axis and study time on the horizontal axis. Albert E., Alfred E., and their classmates are represented by various points. We can see from the graph that students who study more tend to get higher grades.

One of the most important graphs in economics is the *demand curve*, which traces out the effect of a good's price on the quantity of the good consumers want to buy. Table 2A-1 shows how the number of novels that Emma B. buys depends on her income and on the price of novels. When novels are cheap, Emma buys them in large quantities. As they become more expensive, she borrows books from the library instead of buying them or chooses to go to the movies instead of reading. Similarly, at any given price, Emma buys more novels when she has a higher income. That is, when her income increases, she spends part of the additional income on novels and part on other goods.

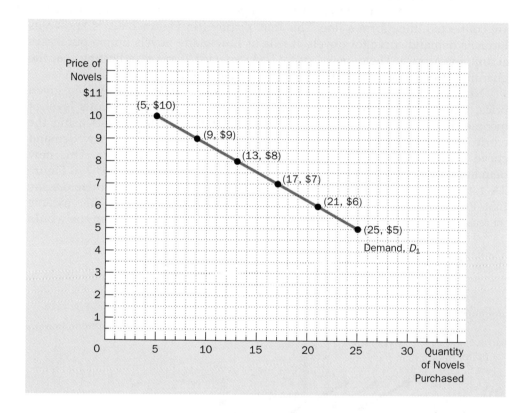

Figure 2A-3

DEMAND CURVE. The line D_1 shows how Emma's purchases of novels depend on the price of novels when her income is held constant. Because the price and the quantity demanded are negatively related, the demand curve slopes downward.

Table 2A-1

	INCOME		
PRICE	$20,000	$30,000	$40,000
$10	2 novels	5 novels	8 novels
9	6	9	12
8	10	13	16
7	14	17	20
6	18	21	24
5	22	25	28
	Demand curve, D_3	Demand curve, D_1	Demand curve, D_2

NOVELS PURCHASED BY EMMA B. This table shows the number of novels Emma B. buys at various incomes and prices. For any given level of income, the data on price and quantity demanded can be graphed to produce Emma's demand curve for novels.

We now have three variables—the price of novels, income, and the number of novels purchased—which is more than we can represent in two dimensions. To put the information from Table 2A-1 in graphical form, we need to hold one of the three variables constant and trace out the relationship between the other two. Because the demand curve represents the relationship between price and quantity demanded, we hold Emma's income constant and show how the number of novels she buys varies with the price of novels.

Suppose that Emma's income is $30,000 per year. If we place the number of novels Emma purchases on the x-axis and the price of novels on the y-axis, we can graphically represent the middle column of Table 2A-1. When the points that represent these entries from the table—(5 novels, $10), (9 novels, $9), and so on—are connected, they form a line. This line, pictured in Figure 2A-3, is known as Emma's demand curve for novels; it tells us how many novels Emma purchases at any given price. The demand curve is downward sloping, indicating that the quantity of novels demanded is negatively related to the price.

Now suppose that Emma's income rises to $40,000 per year. At any given price, Emma will purchase more novels than she did at her previous level of income. Just as earlier we drew Emma's demand curve for novels using the entries from the middle column of Table 2A-1, we now draw a new demand curve using the entries from the right-hand column of the table. This new demand curve (curve D_2) is pictured alongside the old one (curve D_1) in Figure 2A-4; the new curve is a similar line drawn farther to the right. We therefore say that Emma's demand curve for novels *shifts* to the right when her income increases. Likewise, if Emma's income were to fall to $20,000 per year, she would

Figure 2A-4

SHIFTING DEMAND CURVES. The location of Emma's demand curve for novels depends on how much income she earns. The more she earns, the more novels she will purchase at any given price, and the farther to the right her demand curve will lie. Curve D_1 represents Emma's original demand curve when her income is $30,000 per year. If her income rises to $40,000 per year, her demand curve shifts to D_2. If her income falls to $20,000 per year, her demand curve shifts to D_3.

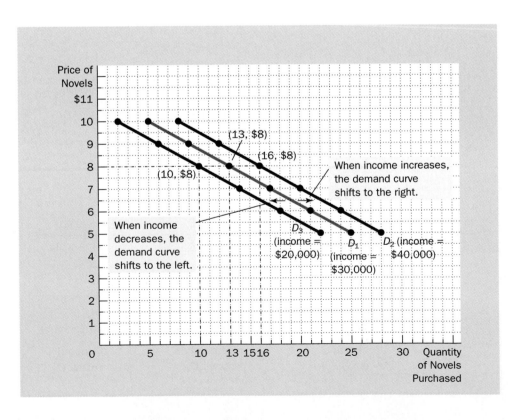

buy fewer novels at any given price and her demand curve would shift to the left (to curve D_3).

In economics, it is important to distinguish between *movements along a curve* and *shifts of a curve*. As we can see from Figure 2A-3, if Emma earns $30,000 per year and novels cost $8 apiece, she will purchase 13 novels per year. If the price of novels falls to $7, Emma will increase her purchases of novels to 17 per year. The demand curve, however, stays fixed in the same place. Emma still buys the same number of novels *at each price*, but as the price falls she moves along her demand curve from left to right. By contrast, if the price of novels remains fixed at $8 but her income rises to $40,000, Emma increases her purchases of novels from 13 to 16 per year. Because Emma buys more novels *at each price*, her demand curve shifts out, as shown in Figure 2A-4.

There is a simple way to tell when it is necessary to shift a curve. When a variable that is not named on either axis changes, the curve shifts. Income is on neither the x-axis nor the y-axis of the graph, so when Emma's income changes, her demand curve must shift. Any change that affects Emma's purchasing habits besides a change in the price of novels will result in a shift in her demand curve. If, for instance, the public library closes and Emma must buy all the books she wants to read, she will demand more novels at each price, and her demand curve will shift to the right. Or, if the price of movies falls and Emma spends more time at the movies and less time reading, she will demand fewer novels at each price, and her demand curve will shift to the left. By contrast, when a variable on an axis of the graph changes, the curve does not shift. We read the change as a movement along the curve.

SLOPE AND ELASTICITY

One question we might want to ask about Emma B. is how much her purchasing habits respond to price. Look at the demand curve pictured in Figure 2A-5. If this curve is very steep, Emma purchases nearly the same number of novels regardless of whether they are cheap or expensive. If this curve is much flatter, Emma purchases many fewer novels when the price rises. To answer questions about how much one variable responds to changes in another variable, we can use the concept of *slope*.

The slope of a line is the ratio of the vertical distance covered to the horizontal distance covered as we move along the line. This definition is usually written out in mathematical symbols as follows:

$$\text{slope} = \frac{\Delta y}{\Delta x},$$

where the Greek letter Δ (delta) stands for the change in a variable. In other words, the slope of a line is equal to the "rise" (change in y) divided by the "run" (change in x). The slope will be a small positive number for a fairly flat upward sloping line, a large positive number for a steep upward sloping line, and a negative number for a downward sloping line. A horizontal line has a slope of zero because in this case the y-variable never changes; a vertical line is defined to have an infinite slope because the y-variable can take any value without the x-variable changing at all.

What is the slope of Emma B.'s demand curve for novels? First of all, because the curve slopes down, we know the slope will be negative. To calculate a numerical value for the slope, we must choose two points on the line. With Emma's

Figure 2A-5

CALCULATING THE SLOPE OF A LINE. To calculate the slope of the demand curve, we can look at the changes in the *x*- and *y*-coordinates as we move from the point (21 novels, $6) to the point (13 novels, $8). The slope of the line is the ratio of the change in the *y*-coordinate (−2) to the change in the *x*-coordinate (+8), which equals −1/4.

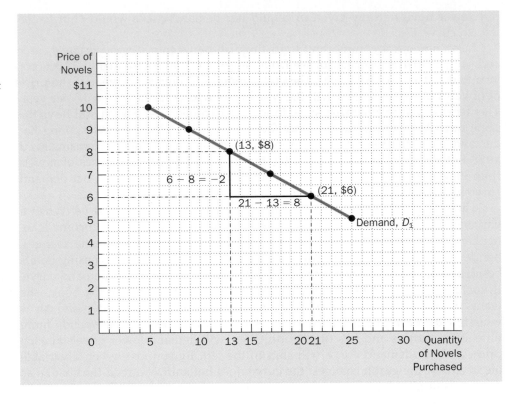

income at $30,000, she will purchase 21 novels at a price of $6 or 13 novels at a price of $8. When we apply the slope formula, we are concerned with the change between these two points; in other words, we are concerned with the difference between them, which lets us know that we will have to subtract one set of values from the other, as follows:

$$\text{slope} = \frac{\Delta y}{\Delta x} = \frac{\text{first } y\text{-coordinate} - \text{second } y\text{-coordinate}}{\text{first } x\text{-coordinate} - \text{second } x\text{-coordinate}} = \frac{6-8}{21-13} = \frac{-2}{8} = \frac{-1}{4}.$$

Figure 2A-5 shows graphically how this calculation works. Try computing the slope of Emma's demand curve using two different points. You should get exactly the same result, −1/4. One of the properties of a straight line is that it has the same slope everywhere. This is not true of other types of curves, which are steeper in some places than in others.

The slope of Emma's demand curve tells us something about how responsive her purchases are to changes in the price. A small slope (a number close to zero) means that Emma's demand curve is relatively flat; in this case, she adjusts the number of novels she buys substantially in response to a price change. A larger slope (a number farther from zero) means that Emma's demand curve is relatively steep; in this case, she adjusts the number of novels she buys only slightly in response to a price change.

The slope, however, is not a perfect measure of how much Emma responds to the price. The problem is that the slope depends on the units used to measure the variables on the *x* and *y* axes. If we measured the price of novels in pennies instead of dollars, we would find that Emma's demand curve has a slope of

−100/4 or −25, rather than −1/4 as we found originally. This is an equally valid calculation and tells us a useful fact—namely that Emma's demand for novels is less sensitive to a change in price of a certain number of pennies than a change of the same number of dollars. Yet if we try to compare the slope of Emma's demand curve for novels with the price measured in dollars to the slope of Don Q.'s demand curve with the price measured in pesos or to the slope of David C.'s demand curve with the price measured in pounds, great confusion will ensue. For this reason, economists often measure the sensitivity of one variable to changes in another variable not with slope but with *elasticity*, which uses the *percentage* change in a variable rather than the simple numerical magnitude of the change. A price decrease from $8 to $6 represents the same 25 percent drop as a price decrease from 800 pennies to 600 pennies. When we use elasticity, we no longer have to worry about whether variables are always expressed in the same units because percentage changes are the same no matter what units are used. We examine elasticities in more detail in Chapter 5.

CAUSE AND EFFECT

Economists often use graphs to advance an argument about how the economy works. In other words, they use graphs to argue about how one set of events *causes* another set of events. With a graph like the demand curve, there is no doubt about cause and effect. Because we are varying price and holding all other variables constant, we know that changes in the price of novels cause changes in the quantity Emma demands. Remember, however, that our demand curve came from a hypothetical example. When graphing data from the real world, it is often more difficult to establish how one variable affects another.

The first problem is that it is difficult to hold everything else constant when measuring how one variable affects another. If we are not able to hold variables constant, we might decide that one variable on our graph is causing changes in the other variable when actually those changes are caused by a third *omitted variable* not pictured on the graph. Even if we have identified the correct two variables to look at, we might run into a second problem—*reverse causality*. In other words, we might decide that A causes B when in fact B causes A. The omitted-variable and reverse-causality traps require us to proceed with caution when using graphs to draw conclusions about causes and effects.

Omitted Variables   To see how omitting a variable can lead to a deceptive graph, let's consider an example. Imagine that the government, spurred by public concern about the large number of deaths from cancer, commissions an exhaustive study from Big Brother Statistical Services, Inc. Big Brother examines many of the items found in people's homes to see which of them are associated with the risk of cancer. Big Brother reports a strong relationship between two variables: the number of cigarette lighters that a household owns and the probability that someone in the household will develop cancer. Figure 2A-6 shows this relationship.

What should we make of this result? Big Brother advises a quick policy response. It recommends that the government discourage the ownership of cigarette lighters by taxing their sale. It also recommends that the government require warning labels: "Big Brother has determined that this lighter is dangerous to your health."

Figure 2A-6

GRAPH WITH AN OMITTED VARIABLE. The upward sloping curve shows that households with more cigarette lighters are more likely to develop cancer. Yet we should not conclude that ownership of lighters causes cancer because the graph does not take into account the number of cigarettes smoked.

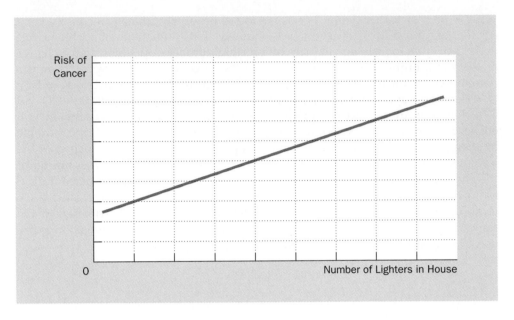

In judging the validity of Big Brother's analysis, one question is paramount: Has Big Brother held constant every relevant variable except the one under consideration? If the answer is no, the results are suspect. An easy explanation for Figure 2A-6 is that people who own more cigarette lighters are more likely to smoke cigarettes and that cigarettes, not lighters, cause cancer. If Figure 2A-6 does not hold constant the amount of smoking, it does not tell us the true effect of owning a cigarette lighter.

This story illustrates an important principle: When you see a graph being used to support an argument about cause and effect, it is important to ask whether the movements of an omitted variable could explain the results you see.

Reverse Causality   Economists can also make mistakes about causality by misreading its direction. To see how this is possible, suppose the Association of American Anarchists commissions a study of crime in America and arrives at Figure 2A-7, which plots the number of violent crimes per thousand people in major cities against the number of police officers per thousand people. The anarchists note the curve's upward slope and argue that since police increase rather than decrease the amount of urban violence, law enforcement should be abolished.

If we could run a controlled experiment, we would avoid the danger of reverse causality. To run an experiment, we would set the number of police officers in different cities randomly and then examine the correlation between police and crime. Figure 2A-7, however, is not based on such an experiment. We simply observe that more dangerous cities have more police officers. The explanation for this may be that more dangerous cities hire more police. In other words, rather than police causing crime, crime may cause police. Nothing in the graph itself allows us to establish the direction of causality.

It might seem that an easy way to determine the direction of causality is to examine which variable moves first. If we see crime increase and then the police force expand, we reach one conclusion. If we see the police force expand and then crime increase, we reach the other. Yet there is also a flaw with this approach: Often people change their behavior not in response to a change in

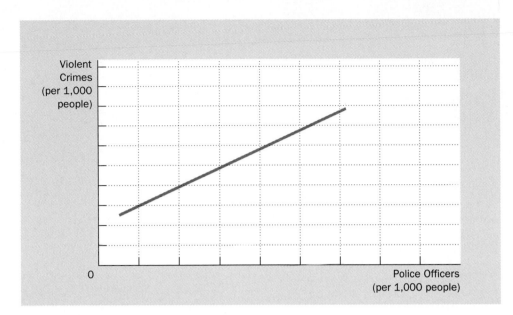

Figure 2A-7

GRAPH SUGGESTING REVERSE CAUSALITY. The upward sloping curve shows that cities with a higher concentration of police are more dangerous. Yet the graph does not tell us whether police cause crime or crime-plagued cities hire more police.

their present conditions but in response to a change in their *expectations* of future conditions. A city that expects a major crime wave in the future, for instance, might well hire more police now. This problem is even easier to see in the case of babies and station wagons. Couples often buy a station wagon in anticipation of the birth of a child. The station wagon comes before the baby, but we wouldn't want to conclude that the sale of station wagons causes the population to grow!

There is no exhaustive set of rules that specifies when it is appropriate to draw causal conclusions from graphs. Yet just keeping in mind that cigarette lighters don't cause cancer (omitted variable) and station wagons don't cause babies (reverse causality) will keep you from falling for many faulty economic arguments.

3

INTERDEPENDENCE AND THE GAINS FROM TRADE

IN THIS CHAPTER YOU WILL

Consider how everyone can benefit when people trade with one another

Learn the meaning of absolute advantage and comparative advantage

See how comparative advantage explains the gains from trade

Apply the theory of comparative advantage to everyday life and national policy

Consider your typical day. You wake up in the morning, and you pour yourself juice from oranges grown in Florida and coffee from beans grown in Brazil. Over breakfast, you watch a news program broadcast from New York on your television made in Japan. You get dressed in clothes made of cotton grown in Georgia and sewn in factories in Thailand. You drive to class in a car made of parts manufactured in more than a dozen countries around the world. Then you open up your economics textbook written by an author living in Massachusetts, published by a company located in Texas, and printed on paper made from trees grown in Oregon.

Every day you rely on many people from around the world, most of whom you do not know, to provide you with the goods and services that you enjoy. Such interdependence is possible because people trade with one another. Those people who provide you with goods and services are not acting out of generosity or concern for your welfare. Nor is some government agency directing them to make what you want and to give it to you. Instead, people provide you and other consumers with the goods and services they produce because they get something in return.

In subsequent chapters we will examine how our economy coordinates the activities of millions of people with varying tastes and abilities. As a starting point for this analysis, here we consider the reasons for economic interdependence. One of the *Ten Principles of Economics* highlighted in Chapter 1 is that trade can make everyone better off. This principle explains why people trade with their neighbors and why nations trade with other nations. In this chapter we examine this principle more closely. What exactly do people gain when they trade with one another? Why do people choose to become interdependent?

A PARABLE FOR THE MODERN ECONOMY

To understand why people choose to depend on others for goods and services and how this choice improves their lives, let's look at a simple economy. Imagine that there are two goods in the world—meat and potatoes. And there are two people in the world—a cattle rancher and a potato farmer—each of whom would like to eat both meat and potatoes.

The gains from trade are most obvious if the rancher can produce only meat and the farmer can produce only potatoes. In one scenario, the rancher and the farmer could choose to have nothing to do with each other. But after several months of eating beef roasted, boiled, broiled, and grilled, the rancher might decide that self-sufficiency is not all it's cracked up to be. The farmer, who has been eating potatoes mashed, fried, baked, and scalloped, would likely agree. It is easy to see that trade would allow them to enjoy greater variety: Each could then have a hamburger with french fries.

Although this scene illustrates most simply how everyone can benefit from trade, the gains would be similar if the rancher and the farmer were each capable of producing the other good, but only at great cost. Suppose, for example, that the potato farmer is able to raise cattle and produce meat, but that he is not very good at it. Similarly, suppose that the cattle rancher is able to grow potatoes, but that her land is not very well suited for it. In this case, it is easy to see that the farmer and the rancher can each benefit by specializing in what he or she does best and then trading with the other.

The gains from trade are less obvious, however, when one person is better at producing *every* good. For example, suppose that the rancher is better at raising cattle *and* better at growing potatoes than the farmer. In this case, should the rancher or farmer choose to remain self-sufficient? Or is there still reason for them to trade with each other? To answer this question, we need to look more closely at the factors that affect such a decision.

PRODUCTION POSSIBILITIES

Suppose that the farmer and the rancher each work 40 hours a week and can devote this time to growing potatoes, raising cattle, or a combination of the two. Table 3-1 shows the amount of time each person requires to produce 1 pound of each good. The farmer can produce a pound of potatoes in 10 hours and a pound of meat in 20 hours. The rancher, who is more productive in both activities, can produce a pound of potatoes in 8 hours and a pound of meat in 1 hour.

Panel (a) of Figure 3-1 illustrates the amounts of meat and potatoes that the farmer can produce. If the farmer devotes all 40 hours of his time to potatoes, he produces 4 pounds of potatoes and no meat. If he devotes all his time to meat, he produces 2 pounds of meat and no potatoes. If the farmer divides his time

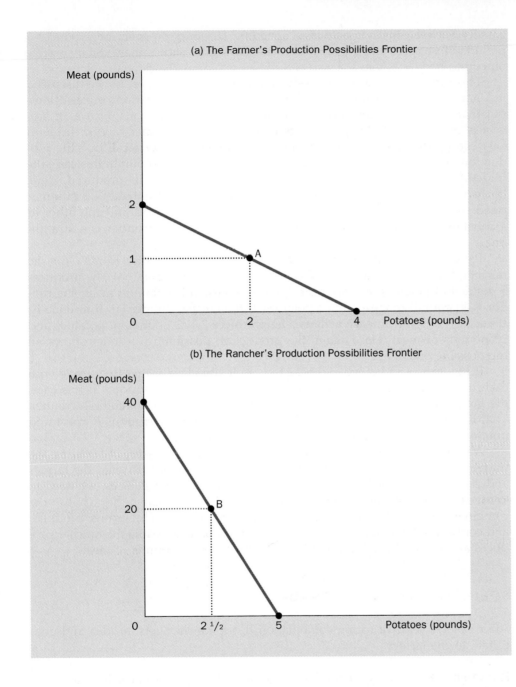

(a) The Farmer's Production Possibilities Frontier

(b) The Rancher's Production Possibilities Frontier

Figure 3-1

THE PRODUCTION POSSIBILITIES
FRONTIER. Panel (a) shows the
combinations of meat and potatoes that the farmer can produce.
Panel (b) shows the combinations
of meat and potatoes that the
rancher can produce. Both production possibilities frontiers are
derived from Table 3-1 and the
assumption that the farmer and
rancher each work 40 hours per
week.

Table 3-1

THE PRODUCTION OPPORTU-
NITIES OF THE FARMER
AND THE RANCHER

| | HOURS NEEDED TO MAKE 1 POUND OF: | | AMOUNT PRODUCED IN 40 HOURS (IN POUNDS): | |
	MEAT	POTATOES	MEAT	POTATOES
FARMER	20	10	2	4
RANCHER	1	8	40	5

equally between the two activities, spending 20 hours on each, he produces 2 pounds of potatoes and 1 pound of meat. The figure shows these three possible outcomes and all others in between.

This graph is the farmer's production possibilities frontier. As we discussed in Chapter 2, a production possibilities frontier shows the various mixes of output that an economy can produce. It illustrates one of the *Ten Principles of Economics* in Chapter 1: People face tradeoffs. Here the farmer faces a tradeoff between producing meat and producing potatoes. You may recall that the production possibilities frontier in Chapter 2 was drawn bowed out; in this case, the tradeoff between the two goods depends on the amounts being produced. Here, however, the farmer's technology for producing meat and potatoes (as summarized in Table 3-1) allows him to switch between one good and the other at a constant rate. In this case, the production possibilities frontier is a straight line.

Panel (b) of Figure 3-1 shows the production possibilities frontier for the rancher. If the rancher devotes all 40 hours of her time to potatoes, she produces 5 pounds of potatoes and no meat. If she devotes all her time to meat, she produces 40 pounds of meat and no potatoes. If the rancher divides her time equally, spending 20 hours on each activity, she produces 2 1/2 pounds of potatoes and 20 pounds of meat. Once again, the production possibilities frontier shows all the possible outcomes.

If the farmer and rancher choose to be self-sufficient, rather than trade with each other, then each consumes exactly what he or she produces. In this case, the production possibilities frontier is also the consumption possibilities frontier. That is, without trade, Figure 3-1 shows the possible combinations of meat and potatoes that the farmer and rancher can each consume.

Although these production possibilities frontiers are useful in showing the tradeoffs that the farmer and rancher face, they do not tell us what the farmer and rancher will actually choose to do. To determine their choices, we need to know the tastes of the farmer and the rancher. Let's suppose they choose the combinations identified by points A and B in Figure 3-1: The farmer produces and consumes 2 pounds of potatoes and 1 pound of meat, while the rancher produces and consumes 2 1/2 pounds of potatoes and 20 pounds of meat.

SPECIALIZATION AND TRADE

After several years of eating combination B, the rancher gets an idea and goes to talk to the farmer:

RANCHER: Farmer, my friend, have I got a deal for you! I know how to improve life for both of us. I think you should stop producing meat altogether and devote all your time to growing potatoes. According to my calculations, if you work 40 hours a week growing potatoes, you'll produce 4 pounds of potatoes. If you give me 1 of those 4 pounds, I'll give you 3 pounds of meat in return. In the end, you'll get to eat 3 pounds of potatoes and 3 pounds of meat every week, instead of the 2 pounds of potatoes and 1 pound of meat you now get. If you go along with my plan, you'll have more of *both* foods. [To illustrate her point, the rancher shows the farmer panel (a) of Figure 3-2.]

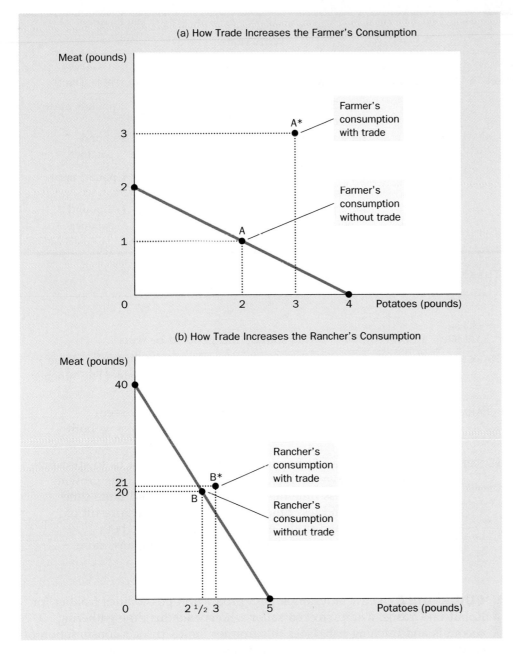

Figure 3-2

How Trade Expands the Set of Consumption Opportunities. The proposed trade between the farmer and the rancher offers each of them a combination of meat and potatoes that would be impossible in the absence of trade. In panel (a), the farmer gets to consume at point A* rather than point A. In panel (b), the rancher gets to consume at point B* rather than point B. Trade allows each to consume more meat and more potatoes.

FARMER: *(sounding skeptical)* That seems like a good deal for me. But I don't understand why you are offering it. If the deal is so good for me, it can't be good for you too.

RANCHER: Oh, but it is! If I spend 24 hours a week raising cattle and 16 hours growing potatoes, I'll produce 24 pounds of meat and 2 pounds of potatoes. After I give you 3 pounds of meat in exchange for 1 pound of potatoes, I'll have 21 pounds of meat and 3 pounds of potatoes. In the end, I will also get more of both foods than I have now. [She points out panel (b) of Figure 3-2.]

	WITHOUT TRADE:	WITH TRADE:			
	PRODUCTION AND CONSUMPTION	PRODUCTION	TRADE	CONSUMPTION	GAINS FROM TRADE
FARMER	1 pound meat	0 pounds meat	Gets 3 pounds meat	3 pounds meat	2 pounds meat
	2 pounds potatoes	4 pounds potatoes	for 1 pound potatoes	3 pounds potatoes	1 pound potatoes
RANCHER	20 pounds meat	24 pounds meat	Gives 3 pounds meat	21 pounds meat	1 pound meat
	2 1/2 pounds potatoes	2 pounds potatoes	for 1 pound potatoes	3 pounds potatoes	1/2 pound potatoes

Table 3-2   THE GAINS FROM TRADE: A SUMMARY

FARMER: I don't know. . . . This sounds too good to be true.

RANCHER: It's really not as complicated as it seems at first. Here—I have summarized my proposal for you in a simple table. [The rancher hands the farmer a copy of Table 3-2.]

FARMER: *(after pausing to study the table)* These calculations seem correct, but I am puzzled. How can this deal make us both better off?

RANCHER: We can both benefit because trade allows each of us to specialize in doing what we do best. You will spend more time growing potatoes and less time raising cattle. I will spend more time raising cattle and less time growing potatoes. As a result of specialization and trade, each of us can consume both more meat and more potatoes without working any more hours.

QUICK QUIZ   Draw an example of a production possibilities frontier for Robinson Crusoe, a shipwrecked sailor who spends his time gathering coconuts and catching fish. Does this frontier limit Crusoe's consumption of coconuts and fish if he lives by himself? Does he face the same limits if he can trade with natives on the island?

THE PRINCIPLE OF COMPARATIVE ADVANTAGE

The rancher's explanation of the gains from trade, though correct, poses a puzzle: If the rancher is better at both raising cattle and growing potatoes, how can the farmer ever specialize in doing what he does best? The farmer doesn't seem to do anything best. To solve this puzzle, we need to look at the principle of *comparative advantage*.

As a first step in developing this principle, consider the following question: In our example, who can produce potatoes at lower cost—the farmer or the rancher? There are two possible answers, and in these two answers lie both the solution to our puzzle and the key to understanding the gains from trade.

ABSOLUTE ADVANTAGE

One way to answer the question about the cost of producing potatoes is to compare the inputs required by the two producers. The rancher needs only 8 hours to produce a pound of potatoes, whereas the farmer needs 10 hours. Based on this information, one might conclude that the rancher has the lower cost of producing potatoes.

Economists use the term **absolute advantage** when comparing the productivity of one person, firm, or nation to that of another. The producer that requires a smaller quantity of inputs to produce a good is said to have an absolute advantage in producing that good. In our example, the rancher has an absolute advantage both in producing potatoes and in producing meat, because she requires less time than the farmer to produce a unit of either good.

absolute advantage
the comparison among producers of a good according to their productivity

OPPORTUNITY COST AND COMPARATIVE ADVANTAGE

There is another way to look at the cost of producing potatoes. Rather than comparing inputs required, we can compare the opportunity costs. Recall from Chapter 1 that the **opportunity cost** of some item is what we give up to get that item. In our example, we assumed that the farmer and the rancher each spend 40 hours a week working. Time spent producing potatoes, therefore, takes away from time available for producing meat. As the rancher and farmer change their allocations of time between producing the two goods, they move along their production possibility frontiers; in a sense, they are using one good to produce the other. The opportunity cost measures the tradeoff that each of them faces.

opportunity cost
whatever must be given up to obtain some item

Let's first consider the rancher's opportunity cost. Producing 1 pound of potatoes takes her 8 hours of work. When the rancher spends that 8 hours producing potatoes, she spends 8 hours less producing meat. Because the rancher needs only 1 hour to produce 1 pound of meat, 8 hours of work would yield 8 pounds of meat. Hence, the rancher's opportunity cost of 1 pound of potatoes is 8 pounds of meat. The rancher's production possibilities frontier reflects this opportunity cost: The downward-sloping line in panel (b) of Figure 3-1 has a slope ("rise over run") equal to 8.

Now consider the farmer's opportunity cost. Producing 1 pound of potatoes takes him 10 hours. Because he needs 20 hours to produce 1 pound of meat, 10 hours would yield 1/2 pound of meat. Hence, the farmer's opportunity cost of 1 pound of potatoes is 1/2 pound of meat. The farmer's production possibilities frontier in panel (a) of Figure 3-1 reflects this opportunity cost by having a slope of 1/2.

Table 3-3 shows the opportunity cost of meat and potatoes for the two producers. Notice that the opportunity cost of meat is the inverse of the opportunity cost of potatoes. Because 1 pound of potatoes costs the rancher 8 pounds of

Table 3-3

THE OPPORTUNITY COST OF
MEAT AND POTATOES

	OPPORTUNITY COST OF 1 POUND OF:	
	MEAT (IN TERMS OF POTATOES GIVEN UP)	POTATOES (IN TERMS OF MEAT GIVEN UP)
FARMER	2	1/2
RANCHER	1/8	8

Table 3-3

THE OPPORTUNITY COST OF
MEAT AND POTATOES

comparative advantage

the comparison among producers of a good according to their opportunity cost

meat, 1 pound of meat costs the rancher 1/8 pound of potatoes. Similarly, because 1 pound of potatoes costs the farmer 1/2 pound of meat, 1 pound of meat costs the farmer 2 pounds of potatoes.

Economists use the term **comparative advantage** when describing the opportunity cost of two producers. The producer who has the smaller opportunity cost of producing a good is said to have a comparative advantage in producing that good. In our example, the farmer has a lower opportunity cost of producing potatoes than the rancher (1/2 pound versus 8 pounds of meat). The rancher has a lower opportunity cost of producing meat than the farmer (1/8 pound versus 2 pounds of potatoes). Thus, the farmer has a comparative advantage in growing potatoes, and the rancher has a comparative advantage in producing meat.

Notice that it would be impossible for the same person to have a comparative advantage in both goods. Because the opportunity cost of one good is the inverse of the opportunity cost of the other, if a person's opportunity cost of one good is relatively high, his opportunity cost of the other good must be relatively low. Comparative advantage reflects the relative opportunity cost. Unless two people have exactly the same opportunity cost, one person will have a comparative advantage in one good, and the other person will have a comparative advantage in the other good.

COMPARATIVE ADVANTAGE AND TRADE

Differences in opportunity cost and comparative advantage create the gains from trade. When each person specializes in producing the good for which he or she has a comparative advantage, total production in the economy rises, and this increase in the size of the economic pie can be used to make everyone better off. In other words, as long as two people have different opportunity costs, each can benefit from trade by obtaining a good at a price lower than his or her opportunity cost of that good.

Consider the proposed deal from the viewpoint of the farmer. The farmer gets 3 pounds of meat in exchange for 1 pound of potatoes. In other words, the farmer buys each pound of meat for a price of 1/3 pound of potatoes. This price of meat is lower than his opportunity cost of meat, which is 2 pounds of potatoes. Thus, the farmer benefits from the deal because he gets to buy meat at a good price.

Now consider the deal from the rancher's viewpoint. The rancher buys a pound of potatoes for a price of 3 pounds of meat. This price of potatoes is lower than her opportunity cost of potatoes, which is 8 pounds of meat. Thus, the rancher benefits because she gets to buy potatoes at a good price.

These benefits arise because each person concentrates on the activity for which he or she has the lower opportunity cost: The farmer spends more time growing potatoes, and the rancher spends more time producing meat. As a result, the total production of potatoes and the total production of meat both rise, and the farmer and rancher share the benefits of this increased production. The moral of the story of the farmer and the rancher should now be clear: *Trade can benefit everyone in society because it allows people to specialize in activities in which they have a comparative advantage.*

QUICK QUIZ   Robinson Crusoe can gather 10 coconuts or catch 1 fish per hour. His friend Friday can gather 30 coconuts or catch 2 fish per hour. What is Crusoe's opportunity cost of catching one fish? What is Friday's? Who has an absolute advantage in catching fish? Who has a comparative advantage in catching fish?

APPLICATIONS OF COMPARATIVE ADVANTAGE

The principle of comparative advantage explains interdependence and the gains from trade. Because interdependence is so prevalent in the modern world, the principle of comparative advantage has many applications. Here are two examples, one fanciful and one of great practical importance.

SHOULD MICHAEL JORDAN MOW HIS OWN LAWN?

Michael Jordan is a great athlete. One of the best basketball players in the NBA, he can jump higher and shoot better than most other people. Most likely, he is better at other activities too. For example, Jordan can probably mow his lawn faster than anyone else. But just because he *can* mow his lawn fast, does this mean he *should*?

To answer this question, we can use the concepts of opportunity cost and comparative advantage. Let's say that Jordan can mow his lawn in 2 hours. In that same 2 hours, he could film a television commercial for athletic shoes and earn $10,000. By contrast, Jennifer, the girl next door, can mow Jordan's lawn in 4 hours. In that same 4 hours, she could work at McDonald's and earn $20.

In this example, Jordan's opportunity cost of mowing the lawn is $10,000, and Jennifer's opportunity cost is $20. Jordan has an absolute advantage in mowing lawns because he can do the work in less time. Yet Jennifer has a comparative advantage in mowing lawns because she has the lower opportunity cost.

The gains from trade in this example are tremendous. Rather than mowing his own lawn, Jordan should make the commercial and hire Jennifer to mow the lawn. As long as he pays her more than $20 and less than $10,000, both of them are better off.

SHOULD THE UNITED STATES TRADE WITH OTHER COUNTRIES?

imports

goods produced abroad and sold domestically

exports

goods produced domestically and sold abroad

Just as individuals can benefit from specialization and trade with one another, as the farmer and rancher did, so can populations of people in different countries. Many of the goods that Americans enjoy are produced abroad, and many of the goods produced in the United States are sold abroad. Goods produced abroad and sold domestically are called **imports.** Goods produced domestically and sold abroad are called **exports.**

To see how countries can benefit from trade, suppose there are two countries, the United States and Japan, and two goods, food and cars. Imagine that the two countries produce cars equally well: An American worker and a Japanese worker can each produce 1 car per month. By contrast, because the United States has more and better land, it is better at producing food: A U.S. worker can produce 2 tons of food per month, whereas a Japanese worker can produce only 1 ton of food per month.

The principle of comparative advantage states that each good should be produced by the country that has the smaller opportunity cost of producing that good. Because the opportunity cost of a car is 2 tons of food in the United

FYI

The Legacy of Adam Smith and David Ricardo

ECONOMISTS HAVE LONG UN-derstood the principle of comparative advantage. Here is how the great economist Adam Smith put the argument:

It is a maxim of every prudent master of a family, never to attempt to make at home what it will cost him more to make than to buy. The tailor does not attempt to make his own shoes, but buys them of the shoemaker. The shoemaker does not attempt to make his own clothes but employs a tailor. The farmer attempts to make neither the one nor the other, but employs those different artificers. All of them find it for their interest to employ their whole industry in a way in which they have some advantage over their neighbors, and to purchase with a part of its produce, or what is the same thing, with the price of part of it, whatever else they have occasion for.

This quotation is from Smith's 1776 book *An Inquiry into the Nature and Causes of the Wealth of Nations.* This book was a

landmark in the analysis of trade and economic interdependence. Many economists consider Smith to be the founder of modern economics.

Smith's book inspired David Ricardo, a millionaire stockbroker, to become an economist. In his 1817 book *Principles of Political Economy and Taxation*, Ricardo developed the principle of comparative advantage as we know it today. His defense of free trade was not a mere academic exercise. Ricardo put his economic beliefs to work as a member of the British Parliament, where he opposed the Corn Laws, which restricted the import of grain.

The conclusions of Adam Smith and David Ricardo on the gains from trade have held up well over time. Although economists often disagree on questions of policy, they are united in their support of free trade. Moreover, the central argument for free trade has not changed much in the past two centuries. Even though the field of economics has broadened its scope and refined its theories since the time of Smith and Ricardo, economists' opposition to trade restrictions is still based largely on the principle of comparative advantage.

DAVID RICARDO

States but only 1 ton of food in Japan, Japan has a comparative advantage in producing cars. Japan should produce more cars than it wants for its own use and export some of them to the United States. Similarly, because the opportunity cost of a ton of food is 1 car in Japan but only 1/2 car in the United States, the United States has a comparative advantage in producing food. The United States should produce more food than it wants to consume and export some of it to Japan. Through specialization and trade, both countries can have more food and more cars.

In reality, of course, the issues involved in trade among nations are more complex than this example suggests, as we will see in Chapter 9. Most important among these issues is that each country has many citizens with different interests. International trade can make some individuals worse off, even as it makes the country as a whole better off. When the United States exports food and imports cars, the impact on an American farmer is not the same as the impact on an American auto worker. Yet, contrary to the opinions sometimes voiced by politicians and political commentators, international trade is not like war, in which some countries win and others lose. Trade allows all countries to achieve greater prosperity.

QUICK QUIZ   Suppose that the world's fastest typist happens to be trained in brain surgery. Should he do his own typing or hire a secretary? Explain.

CONCLUSION

The principle of comparative advantage shows that trade can make everyone better off. You should now understand more fully the benefits of living in an interdependent economy. But having seen why interdependence is desirable, you might naturally ask how it is possible. How do free societies coordinate the diverse activities of all the people involved in their economies? What ensures that goods and services will get from those who should be producing them to those who should be consuming them?

In a world with only two people, such as the rancher and the farmer, the answer is simple: These two people can directly bargain and allocate resources between themselves. In the real world with millions of people, the answer is less obvious. We take up this issue in the next chapter, where we see that free societies allocate resources through the market forces of supply and demand.

Summary

◆ Each person consumes goods and services produced by many other people both in our country and around the world. Interdependence and trade are desirable because they allow everyone to enjoy a greater quantity and variety of goods and services.

◆ There are two ways to compare the ability of two people in producing a good. The person who can produce the good with the smaller quantity of inputs is said to have an *absolute advantage* in producing the good. The person who has the smaller opportunity cost of producing the good is said to have a *comparative advantage*. The gains from trade are based on comparative advantage, not absolute advantage.

◆   Trade makes everyone better off because it allows people to specialize in those activities in which they have a comparative advantage.

◆   The principle of comparative advantage applies to countries as well as to people. Economists use the principle of comparative advantage to advocate free trade among countries.

Key Concepts

absolute advantage, p. 51
opportunity cost, p. 51

comparative advantage, p. 52
imports, p. 54

exports, p. 54

Questions for Review

1.   Explain how absolute advantage and comparative advantage differ.

2.   Give an example in which one person has an absolute advantage in doing something but another person has a comparative advantage.

3.   Is absolute advantage or comparative advantage more important for trade? Explain your answer using the example in your answer to Question 2.

4.   Why do economists oppose policies that restrict trade among nations?

Problems and Applications

1.   Consider the farmer and the rancher from our example in this chapter. Explain why the farmer's opportunity cost of producing 1 pound of meat is 2 pounds of potatoes. Explain why the rancher's opportunity cost of producing 1 pound of meat is 1/8 pound of potatoes.

2.   Maria can read 20 pages of economics in an hour. She can also read 50 pages of sociology in an hour. She spends 5 hours per day studying.
     a.   Draw Maria's production possibilities frontier for reading economics and sociology.
     b.   What is Maria's opportunity cost of reading 100 pages of sociology?

3.   American and Japanese workers can each produce 4 cars a year. An American worker can produce 10 tons of grain a year, whereas a Japanese worker can produce 5 tons of grain a year. To keep things simple, assume that each country has 100 million workers.
     a.   For this situation, construct a table analogous to Table 3-1.
     b.   Graph the production possibilities frontier of the American and Japanese economies.

c.   For the United States, what is the opportunity cost of a car? Of grain? For Japan, what is the opportunity cost of a car? Of grain? Put this information in a table analogous to Table 3-3.
     d.   Which country has an absolute advantage in producing cars? In producing grain?
     e.   Which country has a comparative advantage in producing cars? In producing grain?
     f.   Without trade, half of each country's workers produce cars and half produce grain. What quantities of cars and grain does each country produce?
     g.   Starting from a position without trade, give an example in which trade makes each country better off.

4.   Pat and Kris are roommates. They spend most of their time studying (of course), but they leave some time for their favorite activities: making pizza and brewing root beer. Pat takes 4 hours to brew a gallon of root beer and 2 hours to make a pizza. Kris takes 6 hours to brew a gallon of root beer and 4 hours to make a pizza.
     a.   What is each roommate's opportunity cost of making a pizza? Who has the absolute advantage in making

pizza? Who has the comparative advantage in making pizza?

b. If Pat and Kris trade foods with each other, who will trade away pizza in exchange for root beer?

c. The price of pizza can be expressed in terms of gallons of root beer. What is the highest price at which pizza can be traded that would make both roommates better off? What is the lowest price? Explain.

5. Suppose that there are 10 million workers in Canada, and that each of these workers can produce either 2 cars or 30 bushels of wheat in a year.

a. What is the opportunity cost of producing a car in Canada? What is the opportunity cost of producing a bushel of wheat in Canada? Explain the relationship between the opportunity costs of the two goods.

b. Draw Canada's production possibilities frontier. If Canada chooses to consume 10 million cars, how much wheat can it consume without trade? Label this point on the production possibilities frontier.

c. Now suppose that the United States offers to buy 10 million cars from Canada in exchange for 20 bushels of wheat per car. If Canada continues to consume 10 million cars, how much wheat does this deal allow Canada to consume? Label this point on your diagram. Should Canada accept the deal?

6. Consider a professor who is writing a book. The professor can both write the chapters and gather the needed data faster than anyone else at his university. Still, he pays a student to collect data at the library. Is this sensible? Explain.

7. England and Scotland both produce scones and sweaters. Suppose that an English worker can produce 50 scones per hour or 1 sweater per hour. Suppose that a Scottish worker can produce 40 scones per hour or 2 sweaters per hour.

a. Which country has the absolute advantage in the production of each good? Which country has the comparative advantage?

b. If England and Scotland decide to trade, which commodity will Scotland trade to England? Explain.

c. If a Scottish worker could produce only 1 sweater per hour, would Scotland still gain from trade? Would England still gain from trade? Explain.

8. The following table describes the production possibilities of two cities in the country of Baseballia:

	Pairs of Red Socks per Worker per Hour	Pairs of White Socks per Worker per Hour
Boston	3	3
Chicago	2	1

a. Without trade, what is the price of white socks (in terms of red socks) in Boston? What is the price in Chicago?

b. Which city has an absolute advantage in the production of each color sock? Which city has a comparative advantage in the production of each color sock?

c. If the cities trade with each other, which color sock will each export?

d. What is the range of prices at which trade can occur?

9. Suppose that all goods can be produced with fewer worker hours in Germany than in France.

a. In what sense is the cost of all goods lower in Germany than in France?

b. In what sense is the cost of some goods lower in France?

c. If Germany and France traded with each other, would both countries be better off as a result? Explain in the context of your answers to parts (a) and (b).

10. Are the following statements true or false? Explain in each case.

a. "Two countries can achieve gains from trade even if one of the countries has an absolute advantage in the production of all goods."

b. "Certain very talented people have a comparative advantage in everything they do."

c. "If a certain trade is good for one person, it can't be good for the other one."

II

SUPPLY AND DEMAND I: HOW MARKETS WORK

4

THE MARKET FORCES OF SUPPLY AND DEMAND

**IN THIS CHAPTER
YOU WILL**

*Learn what a competitive
market is*

*Examine what determines
the demand for a good in
a competitive market*

*Examine what determines
the supply of a good in a
competitive market*

*See how supply and
demand together set the
price of a good and the
quantity sold*

*Consider the key role of
prices in allocating scarce
resources in market
economies*

When a cold snap hits Florida, the price of orange juice rises in supermarkets throughout the country. When the weather turns warm in New England every summer, the price of hotel rooms in the Caribbean plummets. When a war breaks out in the Middle East, the price of gasoline in the United States rises, and the price of a used Cadillac falls. What do these events have in common? They all show the workings of supply and demand.

Supply and *demand* are the two words that economists use most often—and for good reason. Supply and demand are the forces that make market economies work. They determine the quantity of each good produced and the price at which it is sold. If you want to know how any event or policy will affect the economy, you must think first about how it will affect supply and demand.

This chapter introduces the theory of supply and demand. It considers how buyers and sellers behave and how they interact with one another. It shows how supply and demand determine prices in a market economy and how prices, in turn, allocate the economy's scarce resources.

MARKETS AND COMPETITION

market

a group of buyers and sellers of a particular good or service

The terms *supply* and *demand* refer to the behavior of people as they interact with one another in markets. A **market** is a group of buyers and sellers of a particular good or service. The buyers as a group determine the demand for the product, and the sellers as a group determine the supply of the product. Before discussing how buyers and sellers behave, let's first consider more fully what we mean by a "market" and the various types of markets we observe in the economy.

COMPETITIVE MARKETS

Markets take many forms. Sometimes markets are highly organized, such as the markets for many agricultural commodities. In these markets, buyers and sellers meet at a specific time and place, where an auctioneer helps set prices and arrange sales.

More often, markets are less organized. For example, consider the market for ice cream in a particular town. Buyers of ice cream do not meet together at any one time. The sellers of ice cream are in different locations and offer somewhat different products. There is no auctioneer calling out the price of ice cream. Each seller posts a price for an ice-cream cone, and each buyer decides how much ice cream to buy at each store.

Even though it is not organized, the group of ice-cream buyers and ice-cream sellers forms a market. Each buyer knows that there are several sellers from which to choose, and each seller is aware that his product is similar to that offered by other sellers. The price of ice cream and the quantity of ice cream sold are not determined by any single buyer or seller. Rather, price and quantity are determined by all buyers and sellers as they interact in the marketplace.

competitive market

a market in which there are many buyers and many sellers so that each has a negligible impact on the market price

The market for ice cream, like most markets in the economy, is highly competitive. A **competitive market** is a market in which there are many buyers and many sellers so that each has a negligible impact on the market price. Each seller of ice cream has limited control over the price because other sellers are offering similar products. A seller has little reason to charge less than the going price, and if he or she charges more, buyers will make their purchases elsewhere. Similarly, no single buyer of ice cream can influence the price of ice cream because each buyer purchases only a small amount.

In this chapter we examine how buyers and sellers interact in competitive markets. We see how the forces of supply and demand determine both the quantity of the good sold and its price.

COMPETITION: PERFECT AND OTHERWISE

We assume in this chapter that markets are *perfectly competitive*. Perfectly competitive markets are defined by two primary characteristics: (1) the goods being offered for sale are all the same, and (2) the buyers and sellers are so numerous that no single buyer or seller can influence the market price. Because buyers and sellers in perfectly competitive markets must accept the price the market determines, they are said to be *price takers*.

There are some markets in which the assumption of perfect competition applies perfectly. In the wheat market, for example, there are thousands of farmers who sell wheat and millions of consumers who use wheat and wheat products. Because no single buyer or seller can influence the price of wheat, each takes the price as given.

The markets for many goods and services, however, are not perfectly competitive. Some markets have only one seller, and this seller sets the price. Such a seller is called a *monopoly*. Your local cable television company, for instance, may be a monopoly. Residents of your town probably have only one cable company from which to buy this service.

Some markets have only a few sellers, and these sellers do not always compete aggressively. This kind of market is called an *oligopoly*. For example, some airline routes are oligopolies. If a route between two cities is serviced by only two or three carriers, the carriers will likely try to avoid rigorous competition in order to keep prices high.

Some markets contain many sellers offering slightly different products. Because the products are not the same, each seller has some ability to set the price for its own product. Such a market is called *monopolistically competitive*. An example is the software industry. Many word processing programs compete with one another for users, but every program is different from every other and has its own price.

Despite the diversity of market types we find in the world, we begin by studying perfect competition. Perfectly competitive markets are the easiest to analyze. Moreover, because some degree of competition is present in most markets, many of the lessons that we learn by studying supply and demand under perfect competition apply in more complicated markets as well.

▌**QUICK QUIZ** What is a market? ◆ What does it mean for a market to be
▌competitive?

DEMAND

We begin our study of markets by examining the behavior of buyers. Here we consider what determines the **quantity demanded** of any good, which is the amount of the good that buyers are willing and able to purchase. To focus our thinking, let's keep in mind a particular good—ice cream.

quantity demanded
the amount of a good that buyers are willing and able to purchase

THE DETERMINANTS OF INDIVIDUAL DEMAND

Consider your own demand for ice cream. How do you decide how much ice cream to buy each month, and what factors affect your decision? Here are some of the answers you might give.

Price If the price of ice cream rose to $20 per scoop, you would buy less ice cream. You might buy frozen yogurt instead. If the price of ice cream fell to $0.20 per scoop, you would buy more. Because the quantity demanded falls as the price rises and rises as the price falls, we say that the quantity demanded is

law of demand

the claim that, other things being equal, the quantity demanded of a good falls when the price of the good rises

normal good

a good for which, other things being equal, an increase in income leads to an increase in quantity demanded

inferior good

a good for which, other things being equal, an increase in income leads to a decrease in quantity demanded

substitutes

two goods for which an increase in the price of one good leads to an increase in the demand for the other good

complements

two goods for which an increase in the price of one good leads to a decrease in the demand for the other good

negatively related to the price. This relationship between price and quantity demanded is true for most goods in the economy and, in fact, is so pervasive that economists call it the **law of demand:** Other things equal, when the price of a good rises, the quantity demanded of the good falls.

Income What would happen to your demand for ice cream if you lost your job one summer? Most likely, it would fall. A lower income means that you have less to spend in total, so you would have to spend less on some—and probably most—goods. If the demand for a good falls when income falls, the good is called a **normal good.**

Not all goods are normal goods. If the demand for a good rises when income falls, the good is called an **inferior good.** An example of an inferior good might be bus rides. As your income falls, you are less likely to buy a car or take a cab, and more likely to ride the bus.

Prices of Related Goods Suppose that the price of frozen yogurt falls. The law of demand says that you will buy more frozen yogurt. At the same time, you will probably buy less ice cream. Because ice cream and frozen yogurt are both cold, sweet, creamy desserts, they satisfy similar desires. When a fall in the price of one good reduces the demand for another good, the two goods are called **substitutes.** Other pairs of substitutes include hot dogs and hamburgers, sweaters and sweatshirts, and movie tickets and video rentals.

Now suppose that the price of hot fudge falls. According to the law of demand, you· will buy more hot fudge. Yet, in this case, you will buy more ice cream as well, since ice cream and hot fudge are often used together. When a fall in the price of one good raises the demand for another good, the two goods are called **complements.** Other pairs of complements include gasoline and automobiles, computers and software, and skis and ski lift tickets.

Tastes The most obvious determinant of your demand is your tastes. If you like ice cream, you buy more of it. Economists normally do not try to explain people's tastes because tastes are based on historical and 'psychological forces that are beyond the realm of economics. Economists do, however, examine what happens when tastes change.

Expectations Your expectations about the future may affect your demand for a good or service today. For example, if you expect to earn a higher income next month, you may be more willing to spend some of your current savings buying ice cream. As another example, if you expect the price of ice cream to fall tomorrow, you may be less willing to buy an ice-cream cone at today's price.

THE DEMAND SCHEDULE AND THE DEMAND CURVE

We have seen that there are many variables that determine the quantity of ice cream a person demands. Imagine for the moment that all these variables except price are held constant. Now let's consider how price affects quantity demanded.

Table 4-1 shows how many ice-cream cones Catherine buys each month at different prices of ice cream. If ice cream is free, Catherine eats 12 cones. At $0.50 per cone, Catherine buys 10 cones. As the price rises further, she demands fewer and fewer cones. When the price reaches $3.00, Catherine doesn't buy any ice cream at all. Table 4-1 is a **demand schedule,** a table that shows the relationship between the price of a good and the quantity demanded. (Economists use the term *schedule* because the table, with its parallel columns of numbers, resembles a train schedule.)

Figure 4-1 graphs the numbers in Table 4-1. By convention, the price of ice cream is on the vertical axis, and the quantity of ice cream demanded is on the horizontal axis. The downward-sloping line relating price and quantity demanded is called the **demand curve.**

demand schedule
a table that shows the relationship between the price of a good and the quantity demanded

demand curve
a graph of the relationship between the price of a good and the quantity demanded

Table 4-1

CATHERINE'S DEMAND SCHEDULE

PRICE OF ICE-CREAM CONE	QUANTITY OF CONES DEMANDED
$0.00	12
0.50	10
1.00	8
1.50	6
2.00	4
2.50	2
3.00	0

Figure 4-1

CATHERINE'S DEMAND CURVE. This demand curve, which graphs the demand schedule in Table 4-1, shows how the quantity demanded of the good changes as its price varies. Because a lower price increases the quantity demanded, the demand curve slopes downward.

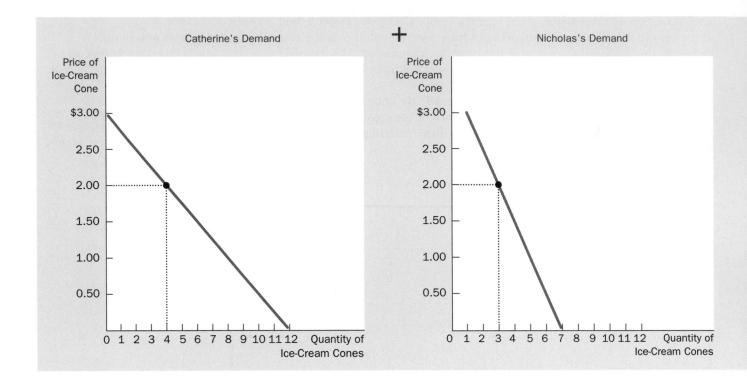

Catherine's Demand   +   Nicholas's Demand

CETERIS PARIBUS

ceteris paribus

a Latin phrase, translated as "other things being equal," used as a reminder that all variables other than the ones being studied are assumed to be constant

Whenever you see a demand curve, remember that it is drawn holding many things fixed. Catherine's demand curve in Figure 4-1 shows what happens to the quantity of ice cream Catherine demands when only the price of ice cream varies. The curve is drawn assuming that Catherine's income, tastes, expectations, and the prices of related products are not changing.

Economists use the term *ceteris paribus* to signify that all the relevant variables, except those being studied at that moment, are held constant. The Latin phrase literally means "other things being equal." The demand curve slopes downward because, *ceteris paribus*, lower prices mean a greater quantity demanded.

Although the term *ceteris paribus* refers to a hypothetical situation in which some variables are assumed to be constant, in the real world many things change at the same time. For this reason, when we use the tools of supply and demand to analyze events or policies, it is important to keep in mind what is being held fixed and what is not.

MARKET DEMAND VERSUS INDIVIDUAL DEMAND

So far we have talked about an individual's demand for a product. To analyze how markets work, we need to determine the *market demand*, which is the sum of all the individual demands for a particular good or service.

Table 4-2 shows the demand schedules for ice cream of two individuals—Catherine and Nicholas. At any price, Catherine's demand schedule tells us how much ice cream she buys, and Nicholas's demand schedule tells us how much

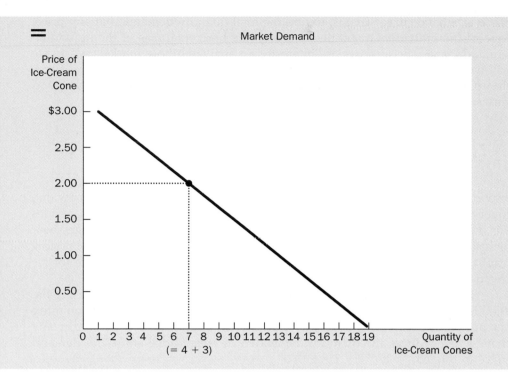

Market Demand

Figure 4-2

MARKET DEMAND AS THE SUM OF INDIVIDUAL DEMANDS. The market demand curve is found by adding horizontally the individual demand curves. At a price of $2, Catherine demands 4 ice-cream cones, and Nicholas demands 3 ice-cream cones. The quantity demanded in the market at this price is 7 cones.

Table 4-2

INDIVIDUAL AND MARKET DEMAND SCHEDULES

PRICE OF ICE-CREAM CONE	CATHERINE		NICHOLAS		MARKET
$0.00	12	+	7	=	19
0.50	10		6		16
1.00	8		5		13
1.50	6		4		10
2.00	4		3		7
2.50	2		2		4
3.00	0		1		1

ice cream he buys. The market demand is the sum of the two individual demands.

Because market demand is derived from individual demands, the quantity demanded in a market depends on those factors that determine the quantity demanded by individual buyers. Thus, the quantity demanded in a market depends not only on the price of the good but also on buyers' incomes, tastes, expectations, and the prices of related goods. It also depends on the number of buyers. (If more consumers were to join Catherine and Nicholas, the quantity demanded in the market would be higher at every price.) The demand schedules in Table 4-2 show what happens to quantity demanded as the price varies while all the other variables that determine quantity demanded are held constant.

Figure 4-2 shows the demand curves that correspond to these demand schedules. Notice that we sum the individual demand curves *horizontally* to obtain the market demand curve. That is, to find the total quantity demanded at any price, we add the individual quantities found on the horizontal axis of the individual demand curves. Because we are interested in analyzing how markets work, we will work most often with the market demand curve. The market demand curve shows how the total quantity demanded of a good varies as the price of the good varies.

SHIFTS IN THE DEMAND CURVE

Suppose that the American Medical Association suddenly announces a new discovery: People who regularly eat ice cream live longer, healthier lives. How does this announcement affect the market for ice cream? The discovery changes people's tastes and raises the demand for ice cream. At any given price, buyers now want to purchase a larger quantity of ice cream, and the demand curve for ice cream shifts to the right.

Whenever any determinant of demand changes, other than the price, the demand curve shifts. As Figure 4-3 shows, any change that increases the quantity demanded at every price shifts the demand curve to the right. Similarly, any change that reduces the quantity demanded at every price shifts the demand curve to the left.

Table 4-3 lists the variables that determine the quantity demanded in a market and how a change in the variable affects the demand curve. In summary, *the demand curve shows what happens to the quantity demanded of a good when its price*

Figure 4-3

Shifts in the Demand Curve. Any change that raises the quantity that buyers wish to purchase at a given price shifts the demand curve to the right. Any change that lowers the quantity that buyers wish to purchase at a given price shifts the demand curve to the left.

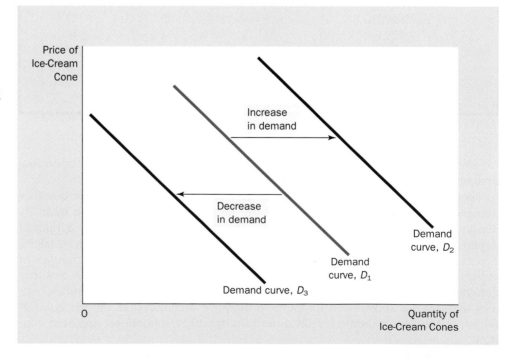

VARIABLES THAT AFFECT QUANTITY DEMANDED	A CHANGE IN THIS VARIABLE . . .
Price	Represents a movement along the demand curve
Income	Shifts the demand curve
Prices of related goods	Shifts the demand curve
Tastes	Shifts the demand curve
Expectations	Shifts the demand curve
Number of buyers	Shifts the demand curve

Table 4-3

THE DETERMINANTS OF DEMAND

varies, holding constant all other determinants of demand. When one of these other determinants changes, the demand curve shifts.

CASE STUDY   TWO WAYS TO REDUCE THE QUANTITY OF SMOKING DEMANDED

Public policymakers often want to reduce the amount that people smoke. There are two ways that policy can attempt to achieve this goal.

One way to reduce smoking is to shift the demand curve for cigarettes and other tobacco products. Public service announcements, mandatory health warnings on cigarette packages, and the prohibition of cigarette advertising on television are all policies aimed at reducing the quantity of cigarettes demanded at any given price. If successful, these policies shift the demand curve for cigarettes to the left, as in panel (a) of Figure 4-4.

Alternatively, policymakers can try to raise the price of cigarettes. If the government taxes the manufacture of cigarettes, for example, cigarette companies pass much of this tax on to consumers in the form of higher prices. A higher price encourages smokers to reduce the amount of cigarettes they smoke. In this case, the reduced amount of smoking does not represent a shift in the demand curve. Instead, it represents a movement along the same demand curve to a point with a higher price and lower quantity, as in panel (b) of Figure 4-4.

How much does the amount of smoking respond to changes in the price of cigarettes? Economists have attempted to answer this question by studying what happens when the tax on cigarettes changes. They have found that a 10 percent increase in the price causes a 4 percent reduction in the quantity demanded. Teenagers are found to be especially sensitive to the price of cigarettes: A 10 percent increase in the price causes a 12 percent drop in teenage smoking.

What is the best way to stop this?

QUICK QUIZ   List the determinants of the demand for pizza. ◆ Give an example of a demand schedule for pizza, and graph the implied demand curve. ◆ Give an example of something that would shift this demand curve. ◆ Would a change in the price of pizza shift this demand curve?

Figure 4-4

SHIFTS IN THE DEMAND CURVE
VERSUS MOVEMENTS ALONG
THE DEMAND CURVE. If warnings on cigarette packages convince smokers to smoke less, the
demand curve for cigarettes
shifts to the left. In panel (a), the
demand curve shifts from D_1 to
D_2. At a price of $2 per pack, the
quantity demanded falls from 20
to 10 cigarettes per day, as reflected by the shift from point A
to point B. By contrast, if a tax
raises the price of cigarettes, the
demand curve does not shift.
Instead, we observe a movement
to a different point on the demand curve. In panel (b), when
the price rises from $2 to $4, the
quantity demanded falls from 20
to 12 cigarettes per day, as reflected by the movement from
point A to point C.

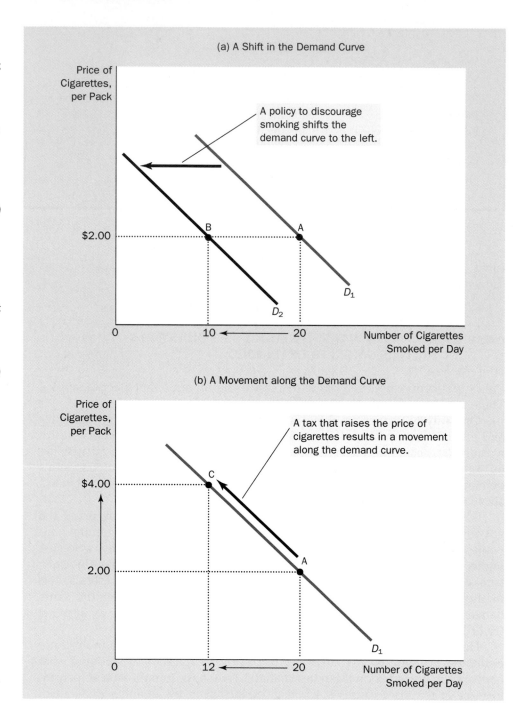

(a) A Shift in the Demand Curve

A policy to discourage smoking shifts the demand curve to the left.

(b) A Movement along the Demand Curve

A tax that raises the price of cigarettes results in a movement along the demand curve.

SUPPLY

quantity supplied

the amount of a good that sellers are willing and able to sell

We now turn to the other side of the market and examine the behavior of sellers. The **quantity supplied** of any good or service is the amount that sellers
are willing and able to sell. Once again, to focus our thinking, let's consider

the market for ice cream and look at the factors that determine the quantity supplied.

THE DETERMINANTS OF INDIVIDUAL SUPPLY

Imagine that you are running Student Sweets, a company that produces and sells ice cream. What determines the quantity of ice cream you are willing to produce and offer for sale? Here are some possible answers.

Price The price of ice cream is one determinant of the quantity supplied. When the price of ice cream is high, selling ice cream is profitable, and so the quantity supplied is large. As a seller of ice cream, you work long hours, buy many ice-cream machines, and hire many workers. By contrast, when the price of ice cream is low, your business is less profitable, and so you will produce less ice cream. At an even lower price, you may choose to go out of business altogether, and your quantity supplied falls to zero.

Because the quantity supplied rises as the price rises and falls as the price falls, we say that the quantity supplied is *positively related* to the price of the good. This relationship between price and quantity supplied is called the **law of supply:** Other things equal, when the price of a good rises, the quantity supplied of the good also rises.

law of supply
the claim that, other things being equal, the quantity supplied of a good rises when the price of the good rises

Input Prices To produce its output of ice cream, Student Sweets uses various inputs: cream, sugar, flavoring, ice-cream machines, the buildings in which the ice cream is made, and the labor of workers to mix the ingredients and operate the machines. When the price of one or more of these inputs rises, producing ice cream is less profitable, and your firm supplies less ice cream. If input prices rise substantially, you might shut down your firm and supply no ice cream at all. Thus, the quantity supplied of a good is negatively related to the price of the inputs used to make the good.

Technology The technology for turning the inputs into ice cream is yet another determinant of the quantity supplied. The invention of the mechanized ice-cream machine, for example, reduced the amount of labor necessary to make ice cream. By reducing firms' costs, the advance in technology raised the quantity of ice cream supplied.

Expectations The quantity of ice cream you supply today may depend on your expectations of the future. For example, if you expect the price of ice cream to rise in the future, you will put some of your current production into storage and supply less to the market today.

THE SUPPLY SCHEDULE AND THE SUPPLY CURVE

Consider how the quantity supplied varies with the price, holding input prices, technology, and expectations fixed. Table 4-4 shows the quantity supplied by Ben, an ice-cream seller, at various prices of ice cream. At a price below $1.00, Ben does not supply any ice cream at all. As the price rises, he supplies a greater and greater quantity. This table is called the **supply schedule.**

supply schedule
a table that shows the relationship between the price of a good and the quantity supplied

Table 4-4

BEN'S SUPPLY SCHEDULE

PRICE OF ICE-CREAM CONE	QUANTITY OF CONES SUPPLIED
$0.00	0
0.50	0
1.00	1
1.50	2
2.00	3
2.50	4
3.00	5

Figure 4-5

BEN'S SUPPLY CURVE. This supply curve, which graphs the supply schedule in Table 4-4, shows how the quantity supplied of the good changes as its price varies. Because a higher price increases the quantity supplied, the supply curve slopes upward.

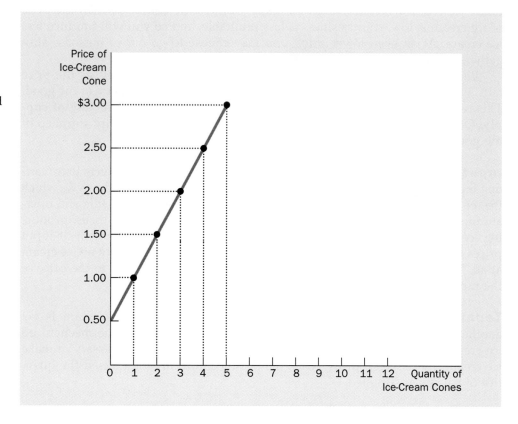

Figure 4-5 graphs the relationship between the quantity of ice cream supplied and the price. The curve relating price and quantity supplied is called the **supply curve.** The supply curve slopes upward because, *ceteris paribus*, a higher price means a greater quantity supplied.

supply curve

a graph of the relationship between the price of a good and the quantity supplied

MARKET SUPPLY VERSUS INDIVIDUAL SUPPLY

Just as market demand is the sum of the demands of all buyers, market supply is the sum of the supplies of all sellers. Table 4-5 shows the supply schedules for two ice-cream producers—Ben and Jerry. At any price, Ben's supply schedule

PRICE OF ICE-CREAM CONE	BEN		JERRY		MARKET
$0.00	0	+	0	=	0
0.50	0		0		0
1.00	1		0		1
1.50	2		2		4
2.00	3		4		7
2.50	4		6		10
3.00	5		8		13

Table 4-5

INDIVIDUAL AND MARKET
SUPPLY SCHEDULES

tells us how much ice cream Ben supplies, and Jerry's supply schedule tells us how much ice cream Jerry supplies. The market supply is the sum of the two individual supplies.

The quantity supplied in a market depends on those factors that determine quantity supplied by individual sellers: the price of the good, the prices of inputs used to produce the good, the available technology, and expectations. In addition, the quantity supplied in a market depends on the number of sellers. (If Ben or Jerry were to retire from the ice-cream business, the quantity supplied in the market would fall.) The supply schedules in Table 4-5 show what happens to quantity supplied as the price varies while all the other variables that determine quantity supplied are held constant.

Figure 4-6 shows the supply curves that correspond to the supply schedules in Table 4-5. As with demand curves, we sum the individual supply curves *horizontally* to obtain the market supply curve. That is, to find the total quantity supplied at any price, we add the individual quantities found on the horizontal axis of the individual supply curves. The market supply curve shows how the total quantity supplied varies as the price of the good varies.

SHIFTS IN THE SUPPLY CURVE

Suppose that the price of sugar falls. How does this change affect the supply of ice cream? Because sugar is an input into producing ice cream, the fall in the price of sugar makes selling ice cream more profitable. This raises the supply of ice cream: At any given price sellers are now willing to produce a larger quantity. Thus, the supply curve for ice cream shifts to the right.

Whenever any determinant of supply, other than the price, changes, the supply curve shifts. As Figure 4-7 shows, any change that raises quantity supplied at every price shifts the supply curve to the right. Similarly, any change that reduces the quantity supplied at every price shifts the supply curve to the left.

Table 4-6 lists the variables that determine the quantity supplied in a market and how a change in the variable affects the supply curve. In summary, *the supply curve shows what happens to the quantity supplied of a good when its price varies, holding constant all other determinants of supply. When one of these other determinants changes, the supply curve shifts.*

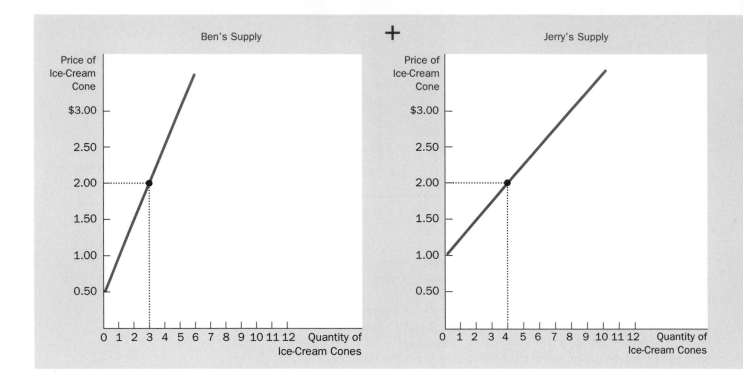

Table 4-6

THE DETERMINANTS OF SUPPLY

VARIABLES THAT AFFECT QUANTITY SUPPLIED	A CHANGE IN THIS VARIABLE . . .
Price	Represents a movement along the supply curve
Input prices	Shifts the supply curve
Technology	Shifts the supply curve
Expectations	Shifts the supply curve
Number of sellers	Shifts the supply curve

QUICK QUIZ   List the determinants of the supply of pizza. ◆ Give an example of a supply schedule for pizza, and graph the implied supply curve. ◆ Give an example of something that would shift this supply curve. ◆ Would a change in the price of pizza shift this supply curve?

SUPPLY AND DEMAND TOGETHER

Having analyzed supply and demand separately, we now combine them to see how they determine the quantity of a good sold in a market and its price.

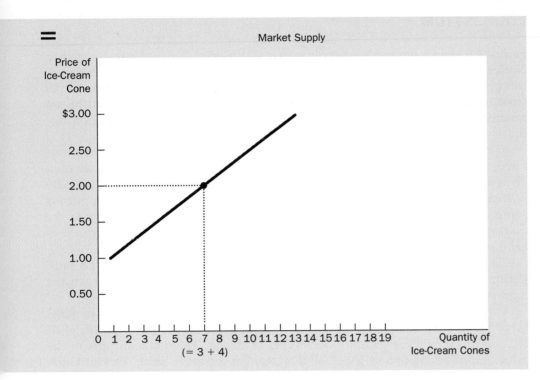

Figure 4-6

MARKET SUPPLY AS THE SUM OF INDIVIDUAL SUPPLIES. The market supply curve is found by adding horizontally the individual supply curves. At a price of $2, Ben supplies 3 ice-cream cones, and Jerry supplies 4 ice-cream cones. The quantity supplied in the market at this price is 7 cones.

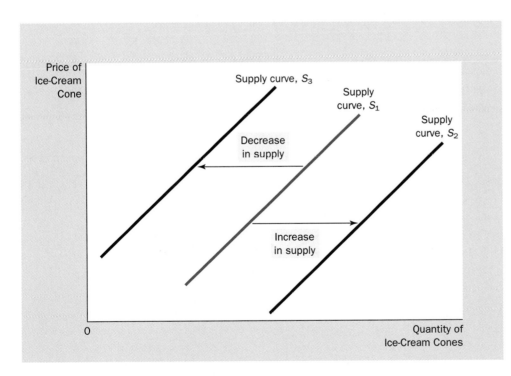

Figure 4-7

SHIFTS IN THE SUPPLY CURVE. Any change that raises the quantity that sellers wish to produce at a given price shifts the supply curve to the right. Any change that lowers the quantity that sellers wish to produce at a given price shifts the supply curve to the left.

EQUILIBRIUM

equilibrium

a situation in which supply and demand have been brought into balance

equilibrium price

the price that balances supply and demand

equilibrium quantity

the quantity supplied and the quantity demanded when the price has adjusted to balance supply and demand

excess supply

a situation in which quantity supplied is greater than quantity demanded

Figure 4-8 shows the market supply curve and market demand curve together. Notice that there is one point at which the supply and demand curves intersect; this point is called the market's **equilibrium.** The price at which these two curves cross is called the **equilibrium price,** and the quantity is called the **equilibrium quantity.** Here the equilibrium price is $2.00 per cone, and the equilibrium quantity is 7 ice-cream cones.

The dictionary defines the word *equilibrium* as a situation in which various forces are in balance—and this also describes a market's equilibrium. *At the equilibrium price, the quantity of the good that buyers are willing and able to buy exactly balances the quantity that sellers are willing and able to sell.* The equilibrium price is sometimes called the *market-clearing price* because, at this price, everyone in the market has been satisfied: Buyers have bought all they want to buy, and sellers have sold all they want to sell.

The actions of buyers and sellers naturally move markets toward the equilibrium of supply and demand. To see why, consider what happens when the market price is not equal to the equilibrium price.

Suppose first that the market price is above the equilibrium price, as in panel (a) of Figure 4-9. At a price of $2.50 per cone, the quantity of the good supplied (10 cones) exceeds the quantity demanded (4 cones). There is a surplus of the good: Suppliers are unable to sell all they want at the going price. This situation is called **excess supply.** When there is excess supply in the ice-cream market, for instance, sellers of ice cream find their freezers increasingly full of ice cream they

Figure 4-8

THE EQUILIBRIUM OF SUPPLY AND DEMAND. The equilibrium is found where the supply and demand curves intersect. At the equilibrium price, the quantity supplied equals the quantity demanded. Here the equilibrium price is $2: At this price, 7 ice-cream cones are supplied, and 7 ice-cream cones are demanded.

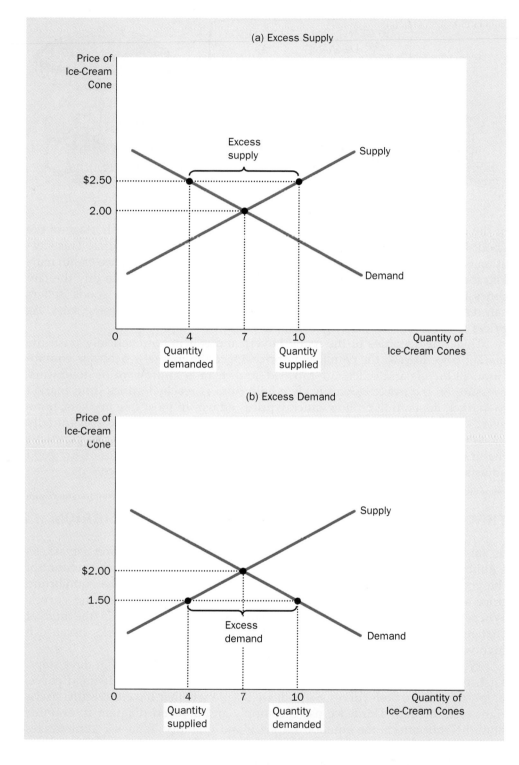

(a) Excess Supply

Figure 4-9

MARKETS NOT IN EQUILIBRIUM. In panel (a), there is excess supply. Because the market price of $2.50 is above the equilibrium price, the quantity supplied (10 cones) exceeds the quantity demanded (4 cones). Suppliers try to increase sales by cutting the price of a cone, and this moves the price toward its equilibrium level. In panel (b), there is excess demand. Because the market price of $1.50 is below the equilibrium price, the quantity demanded (10 cones) exceeds the quantity supplied (4 cones). Because too many buyers are chasing too few goods, suppliers can take advantage of the shortage by raising the price. Hence, in both cases, the price adjustment moves the market toward the equilibrium of supply and demand.

would like to sell but cannot. They respond to the excess supply by cutting their prices. Prices continue to fall until the market reaches the equilibrium.

Suppose now that the market price is below the equilibrium price, as in panel (b) of Figure 4-9. In this case, the price is $1.50 per cone, and the quantity of the good demanded exceeds the quantity supplied. There is a shortage of the good: Demanders are unable to buy all they want at the going price. This situation is called **excess demand.** When excess demand occurs in the ice-cream market, for instance, buyers have to wait in long lines for a chance to buy the few cones that are available. With too many buyers chasing too few goods, sellers can respond to excess demand by raising their prices without losing sales. As prices rise, the market once again moves toward the equilibrium.

excess demand

a situation in which quantity demanded is greater than quantity supplied

Thus, the activities of the many buyers and sellers automatically push the market price toward the equilibrium price. Once the market reaches its equilibrium, all buyers and sellers are satisfied, and there is no upward or downward pressure on the price. How quickly equilibrium is reached varies from market to market, depending on how quickly prices adjust. In most free markets, however, surpluses and shortages are only temporary because prices eventually move toward their equilibrium levels. Indeed, this phenomenon is so pervasive that it is sometimes called the **law of supply and demand:** The price of any good adjusts to bring the supply and demand for that good into balance.

law of supply and demand

the claim that the price of any good adjusts to bring the supply and demand for that good into balance

THREE STEPS TO ANALYZING CHANGES IN EQUILIBRIUM

So far we have seen how supply and demand together determine a market's equilibrium, which in turn determines the price of the good and the amount of the good that buyers purchase and sellers produce. Of course, the equilibrium price and quantity depend on the position of the supply and demand curves. When some event shifts one of these curves, the equilibrium in the market changes. The analysis of such a change is called *comparative statics* because it involves comparing an old equilibrium and a new equilibrium.

When analyzing how some event affects a market, we proceed in three steps. First, we decide whether the event shifts the supply curve, the demand curve, or, in some cases, both curves. Second, we decide whether the curve shifts to the right or to the left. Third, we use the supply-and-demand diagram to examine how the shift affects the equilibrium price and quantity. Table 4-7 summarizes these three steps. To see how this recipe is used, let's consider various events that might affect the market for ice cream.

Example: A Change in Demand   Suppose that one summer the weather is very hot. How does this event affect the market for ice cream? To answer this question, let's follow our three steps.

1. Decide whether the event shifts the supply or demand curve (or perhaps both).
2. Decide which direction the curve shifts.
3. Use the supply-and-demand diagram to see how the shift changes the equilibrium.

Table 4-7

A THREE-STEP PROGRAM FOR DOING COMPARATIVE STATICS

1. The hot weather affects the demand curve by changing people's taste for ice cream. That is, the weather changes the amount of ice cream that people want to buy at any given price. The supply curve is unchanged because the weather does not directly affect the firms that sell ice cream.

2. Because hot weather makes people want to eat more ice cream, the demand curve shifts to the right. Figure 4-10 shows this increase in demand as the shift in the demand curve from D_1 to D_2. This shift indicates that the quantity of ice cream demanded is higher at every price.

3. As Figure 4-10 shows, the increase in demand raises the equilibrium price from $2.00 to $2.50 and the equilibrium quantity from 7 to 10 cones. In other words, the hot weather increases the price of ice cream and the quantity of ice cream sold.

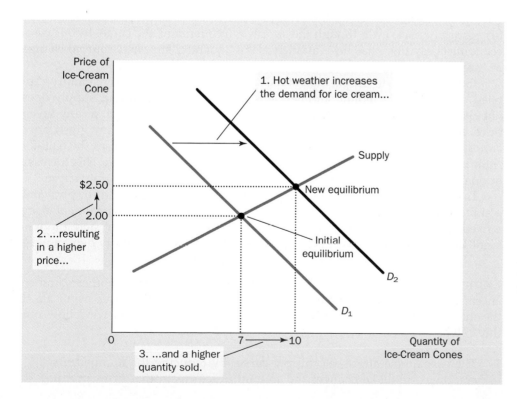

Figure 4-10

HOW AN INCREASE IN DEMAND AFFECTS THE EQUILIBRIUM. An event that raises quantity demanded at any given price shifts the demand curve to the right. The equilibrium price and the equilibrium quantity both rise. Here, an abnormally hot summer causes buyers to demand more ice cream. The demand curve shifts from D_1 to D_2, which causes the equilibrium price to rise from $2.00 to $2.50 and the equilibrium quantity to rise from 7 to 10 cones.

Figure 4-11

How a Decrease in Supply Affects the Equilibrium. An event that reduces quantity supplied at a given price shifts the supply curve to the left. The equilibrium price rises, and the equilibrium quantity falls. Here, an earthquake causes sellers to supply less ice cream. The supply curve shifts from S_1 to S_2, which causes the equilibrium price to rise from $2.00 to $2.50 and the equilibrium quantity to fall from 7 to 4 cones.

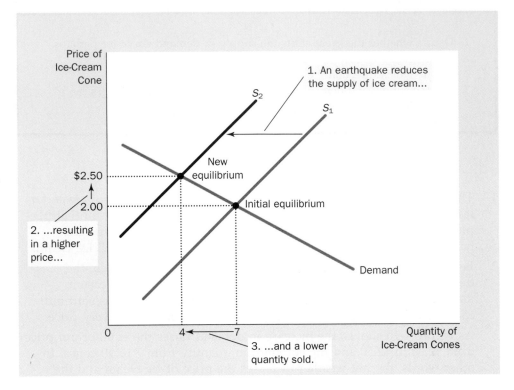

Shifts in Curves versus Movements along Curves   Notice that when hot weather drives up the price of ice cream, the amount of ice cream that firms supply rises, even though the supply curve remains the same. In this case, economists say there has been an increase in "quantity supplied" but no change in "supply."

"Supply" refers to the position of the supply curve, whereas the "quantity supplied" refers to the amount suppliers wish to sell. In this example, supply does not change because the weather does not alter firms' desire to sell at any given price. Instead, the hot weather alters consumers' desire to buy at any given price and thereby shifts the demand curve. The increase in demand causes the equilibrium price to rise. When the price rises, the quantity supplied rises. This increase in quantity supplied is represented by the movement along the supply curve.

To summarize, a shift *in* the supply curve is called a "change in supply," and a shift *in* the demand curve is called a "change in demand." A movement *along* a fixed supply curve is called a "change in the quantity supplied," and a movement *along* a fixed demand curve is called a "change in the quantity demanded."

Example: A Change in Supply   Suppose that, during another summer, an earthquake destroys several ice-cream factories. How does this event affect the market for ice cream? Once again, to answer this question, we follow our three steps.

1.   The earthquake affects the supply curve. By reducing the number of sellers, the earthquake changes the amount of ice cream that firms produce

and sell at any given price. The demand curve is unchanged because the earthquake does not directly change the amount of ice cream households wish to buy.

2. The supply curve shifts to the left because, at every price, the total amount that firms are willing and able to sell is reduced. Figure 4-11 illustrates this decrease in supply as a shift in the supply curve from S_1 to S_2.

3. As Figure 4-11 shows, the shift in the supply curve raises the equilibrium price from $2.00 to $2.50 and lowers the equilibrium quantity from 7 to 4 cones. As a result of the earthquake, the price of ice cream rises, and the quantity of ice cream sold falls.

Example: A Change in Both Supply and Demand   Now suppose that the hot weather and the earthquake occur at the same time. To analyze this combination of events, we again follow our three steps.

1. We determine that both curves must shift. The hot weather affects the demand curve because it alters the amount of ice cream that households want to buy at any given price. At the same time, the earthquake alters the supply curve because it changes the amount of ice cream that firms want to sell at any given price.

2. The curves shift in the same directions as they did in our previous analysis: The demand curve shifts to the right, and the supply curve shifts to the left. Figure 4-12 illustrates these shifts.

3. As Figure 4-12 shows, there are two possible outcomes that might result, depending on the relative size of the demand and supply shifts. In both cases, the equilibrium price rises. In panel (a), where demand increases substantially while supply falls just a little, the equilibrium quantity also rises. By contrast, in panel (b), where supply falls substantially while demand rises just a little, the equilibrium quantity falls. Thus, these events certainly raise the price of ice cream, but their impact on the amount of ice cream sold is ambiguous.

| **QUICK QUIZ**   Analyze what happens to the market for pizza if the price of tomatoes rises. ◆ Analyze what happens to the market for pizza if the price of hamburgers falls.

CONCLUSION: HOW PRICES ALLOCATE RESOURCES

This chapter has analyzed supply and demand in a single market. Although our discussion has centered around the market for ice cream, the lessons learned here apply in most other markets as well. Whenever you go to a store to buy something, you are contributing to the demand for that item. Whenever you look for a job, you are contributing to the supply of labor services. Because supply and

Figure 4-12

A SHIFT IN BOTH SUPPLY AND DEMAND. Here we observe a simultaneous increase in demand and decrease in supply. Two outcomes are possible. In panel (a), the equilibrium price rises from P_1 to P_2, and the equilibrium quantity rises from Q_1 to Q_2. In panel (b), the equilibrium price again rises from P_1 to P_2, but the equilibrium quantity falls from Q_1 to Q_2.

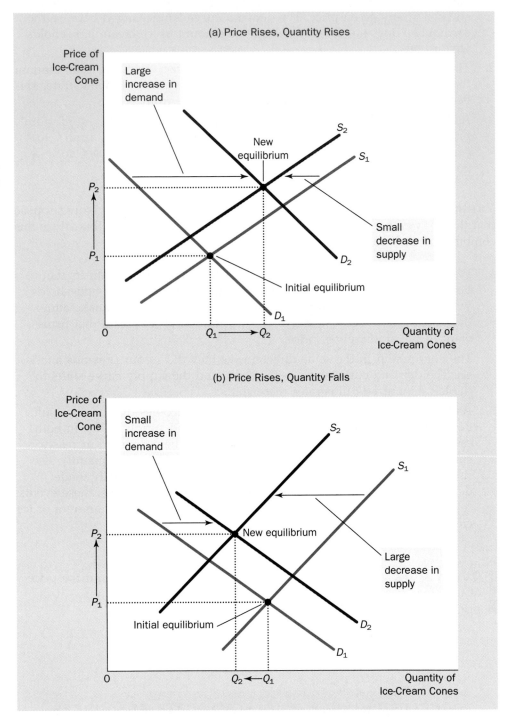

demand are such pervasive economic phenomena, the model of supply and demand is a powerful tool for analysis. We will be using this model repeatedly in the following chapters.

One of the *Ten Principles of Economics* discussed in Chapter 1 is that markets are usually a good way to organize economic activity. Although it is still too

IN THE NEWS

Supply, Demand,

and the Price

of Paper

THE FOLLOWING ARTICLE DESCRIBES DE-velopments in the paper market. As you read the article, try to identify shifts in the demand curve and shifts in the supply curve. Be careful to distin-guish between shifts *in* the curves and movements *along* the curves.

Pulp Reality

BY JERRY ACKERMAN

Look no farther than the newsstand or your grocery bag for evidence of the worldwide economic turnaround: Soar-ing demand for paper has pushed prices to near-record levels.

Virtually no type of paper is im-mune. Facial tissue, office paper, newsprint, even stock for cardboard car-tons—all today are ringing in at 25 to 40 percent more than in early 1994, and fur-

ther increases are expected, perhaps as soon as summer.

"The mills tell me that things are go-ing to be like this for the next six quar-ters," says Edward Rosenbloom, presi-dent of Empire Paper Co., a Boston office-paper distributor.

Supermarket shoppers now must speak up if they want paper bags instead of plastic. Office managers are trying to limit the number of photocopies being made. Printers are taking extra steps to reduce waste to keep customer prices down. And newspapers are sometimes trimming features while raising prices to make up for higher newsprint costs.

Not surprisingly, papermakers are happy, saying that their industry has been absorbing losses through years of reces-sion. Virgil Horton of the American Forest and Paper Association, a trade organiza-tion, says the papermaking industry has seen profits in only 3 of the past 14 years. . . .

All this comes after a five-year re-cession-induced slump that industry lead-ers say was one of the worst ever in a business accustomed to cycles. Across the Americas, Europe, and Asia, reduced advertising brought thinner newspapers and magazines, and product sales de-clines meant less packaging.

But papermakers, primed by the boom of the 1980s, already were build-ing new manufacturing capacity to meet

expected growth. According to the American Forest and Paper Association, five huge newsprint machines came on line in the United States in 1990 and 1991, costing nearly $2 billion and in-creasing production capacity by 9.5 per-cent. The story was much the same in Canada; between them, the two nations produce three-quarters of the world's newsprint supply.

With bills to pay on the new ma-chines, paper companies began running them even before deciding what to do with older units. The resulting paper glut pushed prices down. That is, until the economy turned around last year—not only in the United States but simultane-ously in Europe, Asia, and much of Latin America.

Now, with the once-excess older machines out of service, rising demand is pushing prices to near record highs. According to *Pulp & Paper*, a trade jour-nal, the average price of a metric ton of newsprint—a benchmark in the indus-try—rose from $445 at the end of 1993 to $515 in December. A separate survey by *The New York Times* pegged the price in January at $552, jumping to $600 at the beginning of March and due to hit $675 on May 1.

SOURCE: *Boston Globe*, March 20, 1995, p. 37.

early to judge whether market outcomes are good or bad, in this chapter we have begun to see how markets work. In any economic system, scarce resources have to be allocated among competing uses. Market economies harness the forces of supply and demand to serve that end. Supply and demand together determine the prices of the economy's many different goods and services; prices in turn are the signals that guide the allocation of resources.

For example, consider the allocation of beachfront land. Because the amount of this land is limited, not everyone can enjoy the luxury of living by the beach. Who gets this resource? The answer is, whoever is willing to pay the price. The price of beachfront land adjusts until the quantity of land demanded exactly

"Two dollars."   "—and seventy-five cents."

balances the quantity supplied. Thus, in market economies, prices are the mechanism for rationing scarce resources.

Similarly, prices determine who produces each good and how much is produced. For instance, consider farming. Because we need food to survive, it is crucial that some people work on farms. What determines who is a farmer and who is not? In a free society, there is no government planning agency making this decision and ensuring an adequate supply of food. Instead, the allocation of workers to farms is based on the job decisions of millions of workers. This decentralized system works well because these decisions depend on prices. The prices of food and the wages of farm workers (the price of their labor) adjust to ensure that enough people choose to be farmers.

If a person had never seen a market economy in action, the whole idea might seem preposterous. Economies are large groups of people engaged in many interdependent activities. What prevents decentralized decisionmaking from degenerating into chaos? What coordinates the actions of the millions of people with their varying abilities and desires? What ensures that what needs to get done does in fact get done? The answer, in a word, is *prices*.

Summary

◆ Economists use the model of supply and demand to analyze competitive markets. In a competitive market, there are many buyers and sellers, each of whom has little or no influence on the market price.

◆ The demand curve shows how the quantity of a good demanded depends on the price. According to the law of demand, as the price of a good falls, the quantity demanded rises. Therefore, the demand curve slopes downward.

◆ In addition to price, other determinants of the quantity demanded include income, tastes, expectations, and the prices of substitutes and complements. If one of these other determinants changes, the demand curve shifts.

◆ The supply curve shows how the quantity of a good supplied depends on the price. According to the law of supply, as the price of a good rises, the quantity supplied rises. Therefore, the supply curve slopes upward.

◆ In addition to price, other determinants of the quantity supplied include input prices, technology, and expectations. If one of these other determinants changes, the supply curve shifts.

◆ The intersection of the supply and demand curves determines the market equilibrium. At the equilibrium price, the quantity demanded equals the quantity supplied.

◆ The behavior of buyers and sellers naturally drives markets toward their equilibrium. When the market price is above the equilibrium price, there is excess supply, which causes the market price to fall. When the market price is below the equilibrium price, there is excess demand, which causes the market price to rise.

◆ To analyze how any event influences a market, we use the supply-and-demand diagram to examine how the event affects the equilibrium price and quantity. To do this we follow three steps. First, we decide whether the event shifts the supply curve or the demand curve.

Second, we decide which direction the curve shifts. Third, we compare the new equilibrium with the old equilibrium.

◆ In market economies, prices are the signals that guide economic decisions and thereby allocate scarce resources. For every good in the economy, the price ensures that supply and demand are in balance. The equilibrium price then determines how much of the good buyers choose to purchase and how much sellers choose to produce.

Key Concepts

market, p. 62
competitive market, p. 62
quantity demanded, p. 63
law of demand, p. 64
normal good, p. 64
inferior good, p. 64
substitutes, p. 64

complements, p. 64
demand schedule, p. 65
demand curve, p. 65
ceteris paribus, p. 66
quantity supplied, p. 70
law of supply, p. 71
supply schedule, p. 71

supply curve, p. 72
equilibrium, p. 76
equilibrium price, p. 76
equilibrium quantity, p. 76
excess supply, p. 76
excess demand, p. 78
law of supply and demand, p. 78

Questions for Review

1. What is a competitive market?

2. What determines the quantity of a good that buyers demand?

3. What are the demand schedule and the demand curve, and how are they related?

4. Why does the demand curve slope downward?

5. Does a change in consumers' tastes lead to a movement along the demand curve or a shift in the demand curve? Does a change in price lead to a movement along the demand curve or a shift in the demand curve?

6. What determines the quantity of a good that sellers supply?

7. What are the supply schedule and the supply curve, and how are they related?

8. Why does the supply curve slope upward?

9. Does a change in producers' technology lead to a movement along the supply curve or a shift in the supply curve? Does a change in price lead to a movement along the supply curve or a shift in the supply curve?

10. Define the equilibrium of a market. Describe the forces that move a market toward its equilibrium.

11. Beer and pizza are complements because they are often enjoyed together. When the price of beer rises, what happens to the supply, demand, quantity supplied, quantity demanded, and the price in the market for pizza?

12. Describe the role of prices in market economies.

Problems and Applications

1. Explain each of the following statements using supply-and-demand diagrams.
   a. When a cold snap hits Florida, the price of orange juice rises in supermarkets throughout the country.
   b. When the weather turns warm in New England every summer, the prices of hotel rooms in Caribbean resorts plummet.
   c. When a war breaks out in the Middle East, the price of gasoline rises, while the price of a used Cadillac falls.

2. "An increase in the demand for notebooks raises the quantity of notebooks demanded, but not the quantity supplied." Is this statement true or false? Explain.

3. Consider the market for minivans. For each of the events listed here, identify which of the determinants of demand or supply are affected. Also indicate whether demand or supply is increased or decreased.
   a. People decide to have more children.
   b. A strike by steelworkers raises steel prices.
   c. Engineers develop new automated machinery for the production of minivans.
   d. The price of station wagons rises.
   e. A stock-market crash lowers people's wealth.

4. Using supply-and-demand diagrams, show the effect of the following events on the market for sweatshirts:
   a. A hurricane in South Carolina damages the cotton crop.
   b. The price of leather jackets falls.
   c. All colleges require morning calisthenics in appropriate attire.
   d. New knitting machines are invented.

5. Suppose that in the year 2000 the number of births is temporarily high. How does this baby boom affect the price of baby-sitting services in 2005 and 2015? (Hint: Five-year-olds need baby-sitters, whereas fifteen-year-olds can be baby-sitters.)

6. The case study presented in the chapter discussed cigarette taxes as a way to reduce smoking. Now think about the markets for other tobacco products such as cigars and chewing tobacco.
   a. Are these goods substitutes or complements for cigarettes?
   b. Using a supply-and-demand diagram, show what happens in the markets for cigars and chewing tobacco if the tax on cigarettes is increased.
   c. If policymakers wanted to reduce total tobacco consumption, what policies could they combine with the cigarette tax?

7. The market for pizza has the following demand and supply schedules:

Price	Quantity Demanded	Quantity Supplied
$4	135	26
5	104	53
6	81	81
7	68	98
8	53	110
9	39	121

Graph the demand and supply curves. What is the equilibrium price and quantity in this market? If the actual price in this market were *above* the equilibrium price, what would drive the market toward the equilibrium? If the actual price in this market were *below* the equilibrium price, what would drive the market toward the equilibrium?

8. A technological breakthrough reduces the cost of producing computer chips. Using supply-and-demand diagrams, show the effect of this breakthrough on the equilibrium price and quantity in the following markets:
   a. the market for computers
   b. the market for computer software

9. Because bagels and cream cheese are often eaten together, they are complements.
   a. We observe that both the equilibrium price of cream cheese and the equilibrium quantity of bagels have risen. What could be responsible for this pattern—a fall in the price of flour or a fall in the price of milk? Illustrate and explain your answer.
   b. Suppose instead that the equilibrium price of cream cheese has risen but the equilibrium quantity of bagels has fallen. What could be responsible for this pattern—a rise in the price of flour or a rise in the price of milk? Illustrate and explain your answer.

10. Suppose that the price of basketball tickets at your college is determined by market forces. Currently, the demand and supply schedules are as follows:

Price	Quantity Demanded	Quantity Supplied
$4	10,000	8,000
8	8,000	8,000
12	6,000	8,000
16	4,000	8,000
20	2,000	8,000

   a. Draw the demand and supply curves. What is unusual about this supply curve? Why might this be true?
   b. What are the equilibrium price and quantity of tickets?
   c. Your college plans to increase total enrollment next year by 5,000 students. The additional students will have the following demand schedule:

PRICE	QUANTITY DEMANDED
$ 4	4,000
8	3,000
12	2,000
16	1,000
20	0

Now add the old demand schedule and the demand schedule for the new students to calculate the new demand schedule for the entire college. What will be the new equilibrium price and quantity?

11. An article in *The New York Times* (Oct. 18, 1990) described a successful marketing campaign by the French champagne industry. The article also noted that "many executives felt giddy about the stratospheric champagne prices. But they also feared that such sharp price increases would cause demand to decline, which would then cause prices to plunge." What mistake are the executives making in their analysis of the situation? Illustrate your answer with a graph.

12. "For a given increase in supply, the slopes of both the demand curve and the supply curve affect the change in equilibrium quantity." Is this statement true or false? Explain with diagrams.

13. (This question requires the use of high school algebra.) Market research has revealed the following information about the market for chocolate bars: The demand schedule can be represented by the equation $Q^D = 1,600 - 300P$, where Q^D is the quantity demanded and P is the price. The supply schedule can be represented by the equation $Q^S = 1,400 + 700P$, where Q^S is the quantity supplied. Calculate the equilibrium price and quantity in the market for chocolate bars.

14. What do we mean by a perfectly competitive market? Do you think that the example of ice cream used in this chapter fits this description? Is there another type of market that better characterizes the market for ice cream? Explain.

5

ELASTICITY AND
ITS APPLICATION

**IN THIS CHAPTER
YOU WILL**

*Learn the meaning of the
elasticity of demand*

*Examine what determines
the elasticity of demand*

*Learn the meaning of the
elasticity of supply*

*Examine what determines
the elasticity of supply*

*Apply the concept of
elasticity in three very
different markets*

Imagine yourself as a Kansas wheat farmer. Because you earn all your income from selling wheat, you devote much effort to making your land as productive as it can be. You monitor weather and soil conditions, check your fields for pests and disease, and study the latest advances in farm technology. You know that the more wheat you grow, the more you will have to sell after the harvest, and the higher will be your income and your standard of living.

One day Kansas State University announces a major discovery. Researchers in its agronomy department have devised a new hybrid of wheat that raises the amount farmers can produce from each acre of land by 20 percent. How should you react to this news? Should you use the new hybrid? Does this discovery make you better off or worse off than you were before? In this chapter we will see that these questions can have surprising answers. The surprise will come from applying the most basic tools of economics—supply and demand—to the market for wheat.

The previous chapter introduced supply and demand. In any competitive market, such as the market for wheat, the upward-sloping supply curve represents the behavior of sellers, and the downward-sloping demand curve represents the behavior of buyers. The price of the good adjusts to bring the quantity supplied and quantity demanded of the good into balance. To apply this basic analysis to understand the impact of the agronomists' discovery, we must first develop one more tool: the concept of elasticity. Elasticity, a measure of how much buyers and sellers respond to changes in market conditions, allows us to analyze supply and demand with greater precision.

89

THE ELASTICITY OF DEMAND

When we discussed the determinants of demand in Chapter 4, we noted that buyers usually demand more of a good when its price is lower, when their incomes are higher, when the prices of substitutes for the good are higher, or when the prices of complements of the good are lower. Our discussion of demand was qualitative, not quantitative. That is, we discussed the direction in which quantity demanded moves, but not the size of the change. To measure how much demand responds to changes in its determinants, economists use the concept of **elasticity.**

elasticity
a measure of the responsiveness of quantity demanded or quantity supplied to one of its determinants

THE PRICE ELASTICITY OF DEMAND AND ITS DETERMINANTS

The law of demand states that a fall in the price of a good raises the quantity demanded. The **price elasticity of demand** measures how much the quantity demanded responds to a change in price. Demand for a good is said to be *elastic* if the quantity demanded responds substantially to changes in the price. Demand is said to be *inelastic* if the quantity demanded responds only slightly to changes in the price.

price elasticity of demand
a measure of how much the quantity demanded of a good responds to a change in the price of that good, computed as the percentage change in quantity demanded divided by the percentage change in price

What determines whether the demand for a good is elastic or inelastic? Since the demand for any good depends on consumer preferences, the price elasticity of demand depends on the many economic, social, and psychological forces that shape individual desires. Based on experience, however, we can state some general rules about what determines the price elasticity of demand.

Necessities versus Luxuries Necessities tend to have inelastic demands, whereas luxuries have elastic demands. When the price of a visit to the doctor rises, people will not dramatically alter the number of times they go to the doctor, although they might go somewhat less often. By contrast, when the price of sailboats rises, the quantity of sailboats demanded falls substantially. The reason is that most people view doctor visits as a necessity and sailboats as a luxury. Of course, whether a good is a necessity or a luxury depends not on the intrinsic properties of the good but on the preferences of the buyer. For an avid sailor with little concern over his health, sailboats might be a necessity with inelastic demand and doctor visits a luxury with elastic demand.

Availability of Close Substitutes Goods with close substitutes tend to have more elastic demand because it is easier for consumers to switch from that good to others. For example, butter and margarine are easily substitutable. A small increase in the price of butter, assuming the price of margarine is held fixed, causes the quantity of butter sold to fall by a large amount. By contrast, because eggs are a food without a close substitute, the demand for eggs is probably less elastic than the demand for butter.

Definition of the Market The elasticity of demand in any market depends on how we draw the boundaries of the market. Narrowly defined markets tend to have more elastic demand than broadly defined markets, since it is easier to find close substitutes for narrowly defined goods. For example, food, a broad category, has a fairly inelastic demand because there are no good substitutes for food. Ice cream, a more narrow category, has a more elastic demand because it is easy to substitute other desserts for ice cream. Vanilla ice cream, a very narrow category, has a very elastic demand because other flavors of ice cream are almost perfect substitutes for vanilla.

Time Horizon Goods tend to have more elastic demand over longer time horizons. When the price of gasoline rises, the quantity of gasoline demanded falls only slightly in the first few months. Over time, however, people buy more fuel-efficient cars, switch to public transportation, and move closer to where they work. Within several years, the quantity of gasoline demanded falls substantially.

COMPUTING THE PRICE ELASTICITY OF DEMAND

Now that we have discussed the price elasticity of demand in general terms, let's be more precise about how it is measured. Economists compute the price elasticity of demand as the percentage change in the quantity demanded divided by the percentage change in the price. That is,

$$\text{Price elasticity of demand} = \frac{\text{Percentage change in quantity demanded}}{\text{Percentage change in price}}.$$

For example, suppose that an increase in the price of an ice-cream cone from \$2.00 to \$2.20 causes the amount of ice cream you buy to fall from 10 to 8 cones per month. We calculate the percentage change in price as

$$\text{Percentage change in price} = (2.20 - 2.00)/2.00 \times 100 = 10 \text{ percent.}$$

Similarly, we calculate the percentage change in quantity demanded as

$$\text{Percentage change in quantity demanded} = (10 - 8)/10 \times 100 = 20 \text{ percent.}$$

In this case, your elasticity of demand is

$$\text{Price elasticity of demand} = \frac{20 \text{ percent}}{10 \text{ percent}} = 2.$$

In this example, the elasticity is 2, reflecting that the change in the quantity demanded is proportionately twice as large as the change in the price.

Because the quantity demanded of a good is negatively related to its price, the percentage change in quantity will always have the opposite sign as the percentage change in price. In this example, the percentage change in price is a *positive* 10 percent (reflecting an increase), and the percentage change in quantity demanded is a *negative* 20 percent (reflecting a decrease). For this reason, price elasticities of demand are sometimes reported as negative numbers. In this book we follow the common practice of dropping the minus sign and reporting all price elasticities as positive numbers. (Mathematicians call this the *absolute value*.) With this convention, a larger price elasticity implies a greater responsiveness of quantity demanded to price.

FYI

Calculating

Elasticities

Using the

Midpoint Method

IF YOU TRY CALCULATING THE price elasticity of demand between two points on a demand curve, you will quickly notice an annoying problem: The elasticity from point A to point B seems different from the elasticity from point B to point A. For example, consider these numbers:

Point A: Price = $4,
Quantity = 120.
Point B: Price = $6,
Quantity = 80.

Going from point A to point B, the price rises by 50 percent, and the quantity falls by 33 percent, indicating that the price elasticity of demand is 33/50, or 0.66. By contrast, going from point B to point A, the price falls by 33 percent, and the quantity rises by 50 percent, indicating that the price elasticity of demand is 50/33, or 1.5.

One way to avoid this problem is to use the *midpoint method* for calculating elasticities. Rather than computing a percentage change using the standard way (by dividing the change by the initial level), the midpoint method computes a percentage change by dividing the change by the midpoint of the initial and final levels. For instance, $5 is the midpoint of $4 and $6. Therefore, according to the midpoint method, a change from $4 to $6 is considered a 40 percent rise. (Why? Because (6 − 4)/5 × 100 = 40.) Similarly, a change from $6 to $4 is considered a 40 percent fall.

Because the midpoint method gives the same answer regardless of the direction of change, it is often used when calculating the price elasticity of demand between two points. In our example, the midpoint between point A and point B is:

Midpoint: Price = $5, Quantity = 100.

According to the midpoint method, when going from point A to point B, the price rises by 40 percent, and the quantity falls by 40 percent. Similarly, when going from point B to point A, the price falls by 40 percent, and the quantity rises by 40 percent. In both directions, the price elasticity of demand equals 1.

If you ever need to calculate elasticities, you should keep the midpoint method in mind. Throughout this book, however, we only rarely need to perform such calculations. For our purposes, what elasticity represents—the responsiveness of quantity demanded to price—is more important than how it is calculated.

THE VARIETY OF DEMAND CURVES

Economists classify demand curves according to their elasticity. Demand is *elastic* when the elasticity is greater than 1, so that quantity moves proportionately more than the price. Demand is *inelastic* when the elasticity is less than 1, so that quantity moves proportionately less than the price. If the elasticity is exactly 1, so that quantity moves the same amount proportionately as price, demand is said to have *unit elasticity.*

Because the price elasticity of demand measures how much quantity demanded responds to the price, it is closely related to the slope of the demand curve. (For a discussion of slope and elasticity, see the appendix to Chapter 2.) The following rule of thumb is a useful guide: The flatter is the demand curve that passes through a given point, the greater is the price elasticity of demand. The steeper is the demand curve that passes through a given point, the smaller is the price elasticity of demand.

Figure 5-1 shows five cases. In the extreme case of a zero elasticity, demand is perfectly inelastic, and the demand curve is vertical. In this case, regardless of the price, the quantity demanded stays the same. As the elasticity rises, the demand curve gets flatter and flatter. At the opposite extreme is the case of per-

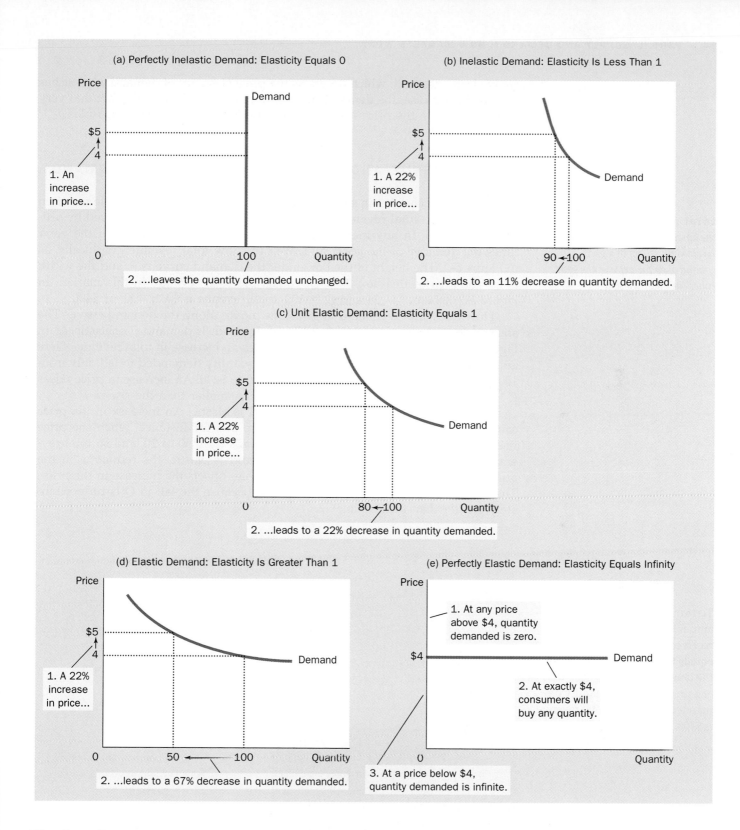

THE PRICE ELASTICITY OF DEMAND. The price elasticity of demand determines whether the demand curve is steep or flat. Note that all percentage changes are calculated using the midpoint method.

Figure 5-1

fectly elastic demand, which occurs as the price elasticity of demand approaches infinity. In this case, the demand curve is horizontal, reflecting the fact that very small changes in the price lead to huge changes in the quantity demanded.

TOTAL REVENUE AND THE PRICE ELASTICITY OF DEMAND

total revenue

the amount paid by buyers and received by sellers of a good, computed as the price of the good times the quantity sold

When studying changes in supply or demand in a market, one variable we often want to study is **total revenue,** the amount paid by buyers and received by sellers of the good. In any market, total revenue is $P \times Q$, the price of the good times the quantity of the good sold. We can show total revenue graphically, as in Figure 5-2. The height of the box under the demand curve is P, and the width is Q. The area of this box, $P \times Q$, equals the total revenue in this market. In Figure 5-2, where $P = \$4$ and $Q = 100$, total revenue is $\$4 \times 100$, or $\$400$.

How does total revenue change as one moves along the demand curve? The answer depends on the price elasticity of demand. If demand is inelastic, as in Figure 5-3, then an increase in the price causes an increase in total revenue. Here an increase in price from $1 to $3 causes the quantity demanded to fall only from 100 to 80, and so total revenue rises from $100 to $240. An increase in price raises $P \times Q$ because the fall in Q is proportionately smaller than the rise in P.

We obtain the opposite result if demand is elastic: An increase in the price causes a decrease in total revenue. In Figure 5-4, for instance, when the price rises from $4 to $5, the quantity demanded falls from 50 to 20, and so total revenue falls from $200 to $100. Because demand is elastic, the reduction in the quantity demanded is so great that it more than offsets the increase in the price. That is, an increase in price reduces $P \times Q$ because the fall in Q is proportionately greater than the rise in P.

Figure 5-2

TOTAL REVENUE. The total amount paid by buyers, and received as revenue by sellers, equals the area of the box under the demand curve, $P \times Q$. Here, at a price of $4, the quantity demanded is 100, and total revenue is $400.

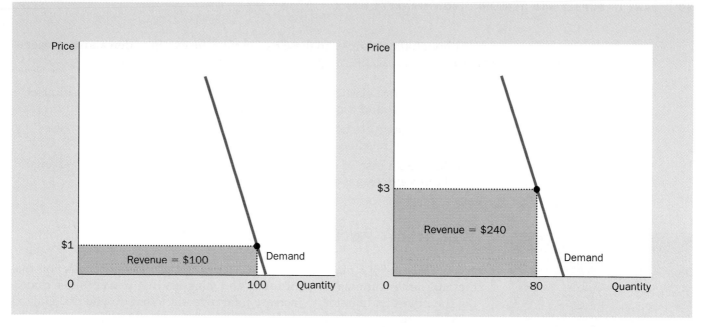

How Total Revenue Changes When Price Changes: Inelastic Demand. With an inelastic demand curve, an increase in the price leads to a decrease in quantity demanded that is proportionately smaller. Therefore, total revenue (the product of price and quantity) increases. Here, an increase in the price from $1 to $3 causes the quantity demanded to fall from 100 to 80, and total revenue rises from $100 to $240.

Figure 5-3

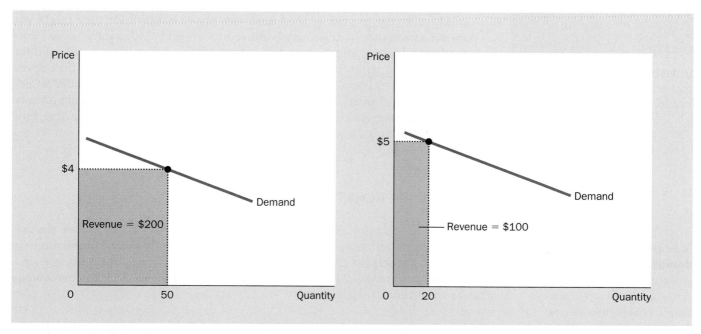

How Total Revenue Changes When Price Changes: Elastic Demand. With an elastic demand curve, an increase in the price leads to a decrease in quantity demanded that is proportionately larger. Therefore, total revenue (the product of price and quantity) decreases. Here, an increase in the price from $4 to $5 causes the quantity demanded to fall from 50 to 20, so total revenue falls from $200 to $100.

Figure 5-4

Although the examples in these two figures are extreme, they illustrate a general rule:

◆ When the price elasticity of demand is less than 1, a price increase raises total revenue, and a price decrease reduces total revenue.

◆ When the price elasticity of demand is greater than 1, a price increase reduces total revenue, and a price decrease raises total revenue.

◆ In the special case of demand with elasticity exactly equal to 1, a change in the price does not affect total revenue.

CASE STUDY PRICING ADMISSION TO A MUSEUM

You are curator of a major art museum. Your director of finance tells you that the museum is running short of funds and suggests that you consider changing the price of admission to increase total revenue. What do you do? Do you raise the price of admission, or do you lower it?

The answer depends on the elasticity of demand. If the demand for visits to the museum is inelastic, then an increase in the price of admission would increase total revenue. But if the demand is elastic, then an increase in price would cause the number of visitors to fall by so much that total revenue would decrease. In this case, you should cut the price. The number of visitors would rise by so much that total revenue would increase.

To estimate the price elasticity of demand, you would need to turn to your statisticians. They might use historical data to study how museum attendance varied from year to year as the admission price changed. Or they might use data on attendance at the various museums around the country to see how the admission price affects attendance. In studying either of these sets of data, the statisticians would need to take account of other factors that affect attendance—weather, population, size of collection, and so forth—in order to isolate the effect of price. In the end, such data analysis would provide an estimate of the price elasticity of demand, which you could use in deciding how to respond to your financial problem.

If the price of admission were higher, how much smaller would this crowd be?

THE INCOME ELASTICITY OF DEMAND

Income elasticity of demand

a measure of how much the quantity demanded of a good responds to a change in consumers' income, computed as the percentage change in quantity demanded divided by the percentage change in income

In addition to the price elasticity of demand, economists also use other elasticities. Most important, they use the **income elasticity of demand** to measure how the quantity demanded changes as consumer income changes. The income elasticity is the percentage change in quantity demanded divided by the percentage change in income. That is,

$$\text{Income elasticity of demand} = \frac{\text{Percentage change in quantity demanded}}{\text{Percentage change in income}}.$$

As we discussed in Chapter 4, most goods are *normal goods*: Higher income raises quantity demanded. Because quantity demanded and income move in the same

ALTHOUGH SOME DEMAND curves have an elasticity that is the same along the entire curve, that is not always the case. An example of a demand curve along which elasticity changes is a straight line, as shown in Figure 5-5. A linear demand curve has a constant slope. Recall that slope is defined as "rise over run," which here is the ratio of the change in price ("rise") to the change in quantity ("run"). In this case, the demand curve's slope is constant because each $1 increase in price causes the same 2-unit decrease in the quantity demanded.

Even though the slope of a linear demand curve is constant, the elasticity is not. The reason is that the slope is the ratio of *changes* in the two variables, whereas the elasticity is the ratio of *percentage changes* in the two variables. You can see this most easily by looking at Table 5-1. This table shows the demand schedule for the linear demand curve in Figure 5-5 and calculates the price elasticity of demand using the midpoint method discussed earlier. At points with low price and high quantity, the demand curve is inelastic. At points with a high price and low quantity, the demand curve is elastic.

Table 5-1 also presents total revenue at each point on the demand curve. These numbers illustrate the relationship between total revenue and elasticity. When the price is $1, for instance, demand is inelastic, and a price increase to $2 raises total revenue. When the price is $5, demand is elastic, and a price increase to $6 reduces total revenue. Between $3 and $4, demand is exactly unit elastic, and total revenue is the same at these two prices.

Figure 5-5

A LINEAR DEMAND CURVE. The slope of a linear demand curve is constant, but its elasticity is not.

PRICE	QUANTITY	TOTAL REVENUE (PRICE × QUANTITY)	PERCENT CHANGE IN PRICE	PERCENT CHANGE IN QUANTITY	ELASTICITY	DESCRIPTION
$0	14	$ 0				
			200%	15%	0.1	Inelastic
1	12	12				
			67	18	0.3	Inelastic
2	10	20				
			40	22	0.6	Inelastic
3	8	24				
			29	29	1.0	Unit elastic
4	6	24				
			22	40	1.8	Elastic
5	4	20				
			18	67	3.7	Elastic
6	2	12				
			15	200	13.0	Elastic
7	0	0				

Table 5-1

COMPUTING THE ELASTICITY OF A LINEAR DEMAND CURVE

NOTE: Elasticity is calculated here using the midpoint method.

IN THE NEWS

On the Road

with

Elasticity

HOW SHOULD A FIRM THAT OPERATES A private toll road set a price for its service? As the following article makes clear, answering this question requires an understanding of the demand curve and its elasticity.

For Whom the Booth Tolls, Price Really Does Matter

BY STEVEN PEARLSTEIN

All businesses face a similar question: What price for their product will generate the maximum profit?

The answer is not always obvious: Raising the price of something often has the effect of reducing sales as price-sensitive consumers seek alternatives or simply do without. For every product, the extent of that sensitivity is different. The trick is to find the point for each where the ideal tradeoff between profit margin and sales volume is achieved.

Right now, the developers of a new private toll road between Leesburg and Washington-Dulles International Airport are trying to discern the magic point. The group originally projected that it could charge nearly $2 for the 14-mile one-way trip, while attracting 34,000 trips on an average day from overcrowded public roads such as nearby Route 7. But after spending $350 million to build their much heralded "Greenway," they discovered to their dismay that only about a third that number of commuters were willing to pay that much to shave 20 minutes off their daily commute. . . .

It was only when the company, in desperation, lowered the toll to $1 that it came even close to attracting the expected traffic flows.

Although the Greenway still is losing money, it is clearly better off at this new point on the demand curve than it was when it first opened. Average daily revenue today is $22,000, compared with $14,875 when the "special introductory" price was $1.75. And with traffic still light even at rush hour, it is possible that the owners may lower tolls even further in search of higher revenue.

After all, when the price was lowered by 45 percent last spring, it generated a 200 percent increase in volume three months later. If the same ratio applies again, lowering the toll another 25 percent would drive the daily volume up to 38,000 trips, and daily revenue up to nearly $29,000.

The problem, of course, is that the same ratio usually does not apply at every price point, which is why this pricing business is so tricky. . . .

Clifford Winston of the Brookings Institution and John Calfee of the American Enterprise Institute have considered the toll road's dilemma. . . .

Last year, the economists conducted an elaborate market test with 1,170 people across the country who were each presented with a series of options in which they were, in effect, asked to make a personal tradeoff between less commuting time and higher tolls.

In the end, they concluded that the people who placed the highest value on reducing their commuting time already had done so by finding public transportation, living closer to their work, or selecting jobs that allowed them to commute at off-peak hours.

Conversely, those who commuted significant distances had a higher tolerance for traffic congestion and were willing to pay only 20 percent of their hourly pay to save an hour of their time.

Overall, the Winston/Calfee findings help explain why the Greenway's original toll and volume projections were too high: By their reckoning, only commuters who earned at least $30 an hour (about $60,000 a year) would be willing to pay $2 to save 20 minutes.

SOURCE: *The Washington Post,* October 24, 1996, p. E1.

direction, normal goods have positive income elasticities. A few goods, such as bus rides, are *inferior goods*: Higher income lowers the quantity demanded. Because quantity demanded and income move in opposite directions, inferior goods have negative income elasticities.

Even among normal goods, income elasticities vary substantially in size. Necessities, such as food and clothing, tend to have small income elasticities because consumers, regardless of how low their incomes, choose to buy some of these goods. Luxuries, such as caviar and furs, tend to have large income elasticities because consumers feel that they can do without these goods altogether if their income is too low.

QUICK QUIZ Define *price elasticity of demand.* ◆ Explain the relationship between total revenue and the price elasticity of demand.

THE ELASTICITY OF SUPPLY

When we discussed the determinants of supply in Chapter 4, we noted that sellers of a good increase the quantity supplied when the price of the good rises, when their input prices fall, or when their technology improves. To turn from qualitative to quantitative statements about supply, we once again use the concept of elasticity.

THE PRICE ELASTICITY OF SUPPLY AND ITS DETERMINANTS

The law of supply states that higher prices raise the quantity supplied. The **price elasticity of supply** measures how much the quantity supplied responds to changes in the price. Supply of a good is said to be *elastic* if the quantity supplied responds substantially to changes in the price. Supply is said to be *inelastic* if the quantity supplied responds only slightly to changes in the price.

The price elasticity of supply depends on the flexibility of sellers to change the amount of the good they produce. For example, beachfront land has an inelastic supply because it is almost impossible to produce more of it. By contrast, manufactured goods, such as books, cars, and televisions, have elastic supplies because the firms that produce them can run their factories longer in response to a higher price.

In most markets, a key determinant of the price elasticity of supply is the time period being considered. Supply is usually more elastic in the long run than in the short run. Over short periods of time, firms cannot easily change the size of their factories to make more or less of a good. Thus, in the short run, the quantity supplied is not very responsive to the price. By contrast, over longer periods, firms can build new factories or close old ones. In addition, new firms can enter a market, and old firms can shut down. Thus, in the long run, the quantity supplied can respond substantially to the price.

price elasticity of supply
a measure of how much the quantity supplied of a good responds to a change in the price of that good, computed as the percentage change in quantity supplied divided by the percentage change in price

COMPUTING THE PRICE ELASTICITY OF SUPPLY

Now that we have some idea about what the price elasticity of supply is, let's be more precise. Economists compute the price elasticity of supply as the percentage change in the quantity supplied divided by the percentage change in the price. That is,

$$\text{Price elasticity of supply} = \frac{\text{Percentage change in quantity supplied}}{\text{Percentage change in price}}.$$

For example, suppose that an increase in the price of milk from $3.00 to $3.30 a gallon raises the amount that dairy farmers produce from 10,000 to 11,500 gallons per month. We calculate the percentage change in price as

$$\text{Percentage change in price} = (3.30 - 3.00)/3.00 \times 100 = 10 \text{ percent}.$$

Similarly, we calculate the percentage change in quantity supplied as

$$\text{Percentage change in quantity supplied} = (11{,}500 - 10{,}000)/10{,}000 \times 100$$
$$= 15 \text{ percent}.$$

In this case, the price elasticity of supply is

$$\text{Price elasticity of supply} = \frac{15 \text{ percent}}{10 \text{ percent}} = 1.5.$$

In this example, the elasticity of 1.5 is greater than 1, which reflects the fact that the quantity supplied moves proportionately more than the price.

THE VARIETY OF SUPPLY CURVES

Because the price elasticity of supply measures the responsiveness of quantity supplied to the price, it is reflected in the appearance of the supply curve. Figure 5-6 shows five cases. In the extreme case of a zero elasticity, supply is perfectly inelastic, and the supply curve is vertical. In this case, the quantity supplied is the same regardless of the price. As the elasticity rises, the supply curve gets flatter, which shows that the quantity supplied responds more to changes in the price. At the opposite extreme is the case of perfectly elastic supply, which occurs as the price elasticity of supply approaches infinity. In this case, the supply curve is horizontal, reflecting the fact that very small changes in the price lead to very large changes in the quantity supplied.

In some markets, the elasticity of supply is not constant but varies over the supply curve. Figure 5-7 shows a typical case for an industry in which firms have factories with a limited capacity for production. For low levels of quantity supplied, the elasticity of supply is high, indicating that firms respond substantially to changes in the price. In this region, firms have capacity for production that is not being used, such as plants and equipment sitting idle for all or part of the day. Small increases in price make it profitable for firms to begin using this idle capacity. As the quantity supplied rises, firms begin to reach capacity. Once capacity is fully used, increasing production further requires the construction of new plants. To induce firms to incur this extra expense, the price must rise substantially, so supply becomes less elastic.

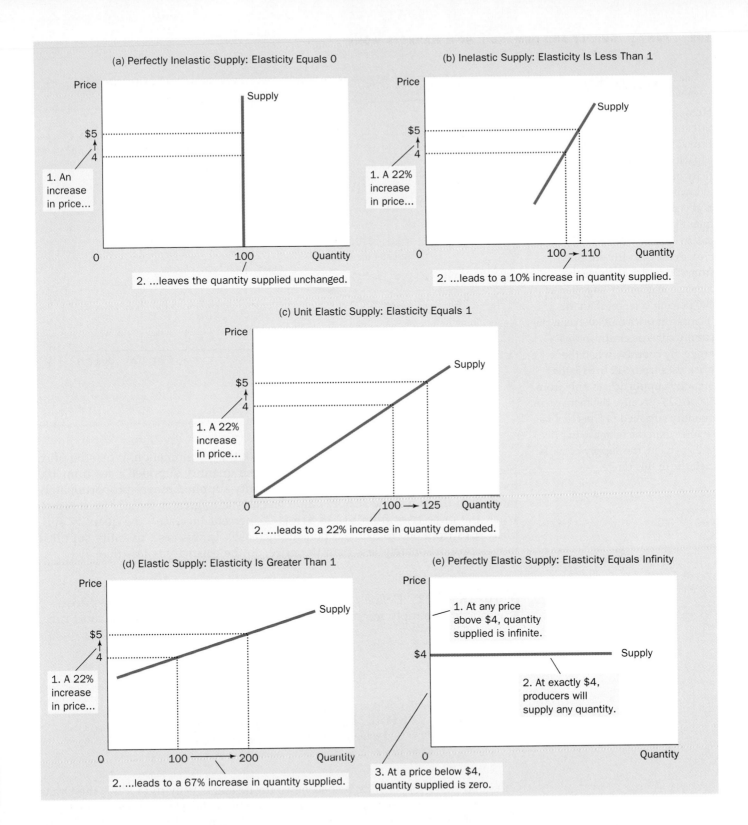

THE PRICE ELASTICITY OF SUPPLY. The price elasticity of supply determines whether the supply curve is steep or flat. Note that all percentage changes are calculated using the midpoint method.

Figure 5-6

Figure 5-7

How the Price Elasticity of Supply Can Vary. Because firms often have a maximum capacity for production, the elasticity of supply may be very high at low levels of quantity supplied and very low at high levels of quantity supplied. Here, an increase in price from $3 to $4 increases the quantity supplied from 100 to 200. Because the increase in quantity supplied of 100 percent is larger than the increase in price of 33 percent, the supply curve is elastic in this range. By contrast, when the price rises from $12 to $15, the quantity supplied rises only from 500 to 525. Because the increase in quantity supplied of 5 percent is smaller than the increase in price of 25 percent, the supply curve is inelastic in this range.

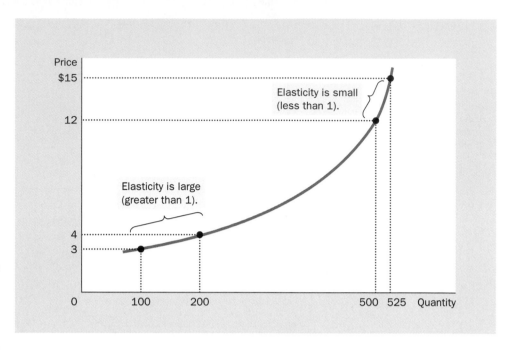

Figure 5-7 presents a numerical example of this phenomenon. When the price rises from $3 to $4 (a 33 percent increase), the quantity supplied rises from 100 to 200 (a 100 percent increase). Because quantity supplied moves proportionately more than the price, the supply curve has elasticity greater than 1. By contrast, when the price rises from $12 to $15 (a 25 percent increase), the quantity supplied rises from 500 to 525 (a 5 percent increase). In this case, quantity supplied moves proportionately less than the price, so the elasticity is less than 1.

QUICK QUIZ   Define *price elasticity of supply.* ◆ Explain why the price elasticity of supply might be different in the long run than in the short run.

THREE APPLICATIONS OF SUPPLY, DEMAND, AND ELASTICITY

Can good news for farming be bad news for farmers? Why did OPEC, the Organization of Petroleum Exporting Countries, fail to keep the price of oil high? Does drug interdiction increase or decrease drug-related crime? At first, these questions might seem to have little in common. Yet all three questions are about markets, and all markets are subject to the forces of supply and demand. Here we apply the versatile tools of supply, demand, and elasticity to answer these seemingly complex questions.

CAN GOOD NEWS FOR FARMING BE BAD NEWS FOR FARMERS?

Let's now return to the question posed at the beginning of this chapter: What happens to wheat farmers and the market for wheat when university agronomists discover a new wheat hybrid that is more productive than existing varieties? Recall from Chapter 4 that we answer such questions in three steps. First, we examine whether the supply or demand curve shifts. Second, we consider which direction the curve shifts. Third, we use the supply-and-demand diagram to see how the market equilibrium changes.

In this case, the discovery of the new hybrid affects the supply curve. Because the hybrid increases the amount of wheat that can be produced on each acre of land, farmers are now willing to supply more wheat at any given price. In other words, the supply curve shifts to the right. The demand curve remains the same because consumers' desire to buy wheat products at any given price is not affected by the introduction of a new hybrid. Figure 5-8 shows an example of such a change. When the supply curve shifts from S_1 to S_2, the quantity of wheat sold increases from 100 to 110, and the price of wheat falls from $3 to $2.

But does this discovery make farmers better off? As a first cut to answering this question, consider what happens to the total revenue received by farmers. Farmers' total revenue is $P \times Q$, the price of the wheat times the quantity sold. The discovery affects farmers in two conflicting ways. The hybrid allows farmers to produce more wheat (Q rises), but now each bushel of wheat sells for less (P falls).

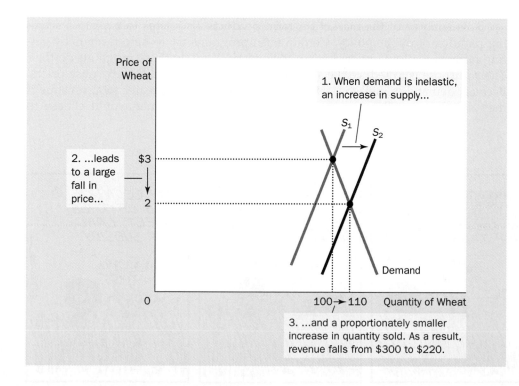

Figure 5-8

AN INCREASE IN SUPPLY IN THE MARKET FOR WHEAT. When an advance in farm technology increases the supply of wheat from S_1 to S_2, the price of wheat falls. Because the demand for wheat is inelastic, the increase in the quantity sold from 100 to 110 is proportionately smaller than the decrease in the price from $3 to $2. As a result, farmers' total revenue falls from $300 ($3 × 100) to $220 ($2 × 110).

Whether total revenue rises or falls depends on the elasticity of demand. In practice, the demand for basic foodstuffs such as wheat is usually inelastic, for these items are relatively inexpensive and have few good substitutes. When the demand curve is inelastic, as it is in Figure 5-8, a decrease in price causes total revenue to fall. You can see this in the figure: The price of wheat falls substantially, whereas the quantity of wheat sold rises only slightly. Total revenue falls from $300 to $220. Thus, the discovery of the new hybrid lowers the total revenue that farmers receive for the sale of their crops.

If farmers are made worse off by the discovery of this new hybrid, why do they adopt it? The answer to this question goes to the heart of how competitive markets work. Because each farmer is a small part of the market for wheat, he or she takes the price of wheat as given. For any given price of wheat, it is better to use the new hybrid in order to produce and sell more wheat. Yet when all farmers do this, the supply of wheat rises, the price falls, and farmers are worse off.

Although this example may at first seem only hypothetical, in fact it helps to explain a major change in the U.S. economy over the past century. A hundred years ago, most Americans lived on farms. Knowledge about farm methods was sufficiently primitive that most of us had to be farmers in order to produce enough food. Yet, over time, advances in farm technology increased the amount of food that each farmer could produce. This increase in food supply, together with inelastic food demand, caused farm revenues to fall, which in turn encouraged people to leave farming.

A few numbers show the magnitude of this historic change. As recently as 1948, there were 24 million people living on farms in the United States, representing 17 percent of the population. In 1993, less than 5 million people lived on farms, or 2 percent of the population. This change coincided with tremendous advances in farm productivity: Despite the 80 percent drop in the number of farmers, U.S. farms produced more than twice the output of crops and livestock in 1993 as they did in 1948.

This analysis of the market for farm products also helps to explain a seeming paradox of public policy: Certain farm programs try to help farmers by getting farmers to plow under some of their crops. Why do these programs do this? Their purpose is to reduce the supply of farm products and thereby raise prices. Because demand is inelastic, farmers as a group receive greater total revenue if they supply a smaller crop to the market. No single farmer would choose to destroy crops on his own, since each takes the market price as given. But if all farmers do so together, each of them can be better off.

When analyzing the effects of farm technology or farm policy, it is important to keep in mind that what is good for farmers is not necessarily good for society as a whole. Improvement in farm technology can be bad for farmers who become increasingly unnecessary, but it is surely good for consumers who pay less for food. Similarly, a policy aimed at reducing the supply of farm products may raise the incomes of farmers, but it does so at the expense of consumers.

WHY DID OPEC FAIL TO KEEP THE PRICE OF OIL HIGH?

Many of the most disruptive events for the world's economies over the past several decades have originated in the world market for oil. In the 1970s members of the Organization of Petroleum Exporting Countries (OPEC) decided to raise the world price of oil in order to increase their incomes. These countries accomplished this goal by jointly reducing the amount of oil they supplied. From 1973 to 1974, the price of oil (adjusted for overall inflation) rose more than 50 percent. Then, a few years later, OPEC did the same thing again. The price of oil rose 14 percent in 1979, followed by 34 percent in 1980, and 34 percent in 1981.

Yet OPEC found it difficult to maintain a high price. From 1982 to 1985, the price of oil steadily declined at about 10 percent per year. Dissatisfaction and disarray soon prevailed among the OPEC countries. In 1986 cooperation among OPEC members completely broke down, and the price of oil plunged 45 percent. In 1990 the price of oil (adjusted for overall inflation) was back to where it began in 1970, and it has stayed at that low level throughout most of the 1990s.

This episode shows how supply and demand can behave differently in the short run and in the long run. In the short run, both the supply and demand for oil are relatively inelastic. Supply is inelastic because the quantity of known oil reserves and the capacity for oil extraction cannot be changed quickly. Demand is inelastic because buying habits do not respond immediately to changes in price. Many drivers with old gas-guzzling cars, for instance, will just pay the higher price. Thus, as panel (a) of Figure 5-9 shows, the short-run supply and demand curves are steep. When the supply of oil shifts from S_1 to S_2, the price increase from P_1 to P_2 is large.

The situation is very different in the long run. Over long periods of time, producers of oil outside of OPEC respond to high prices by increasing oil exploration and by building new extraction capacity. Consumers respond with greater conservation, for instance by replacing old inefficient cars with newer efficient ones. Thus, as panel (b) of Figure 5-9 shows, the long-run supply and demand curves are more elastic. In the long run, the shift in the supply curve from S_1 to S_2 causes a much smaller increase in the price.

This analysis shows why OPEC succeeded in maintaining a high price of oil only in the short run. When OPEC countries agreed to reduce their production of oil, they shifted the supply curve to the left. Even though each OPEC member sold less oil, the price rose by so much in the short run that OPEC incomes rose. By contrast, in the long run when supply and demand are more elastic, the same reduction in supply, measured by the horizontal shift in the supply curve, caused a smaller increase in the price. Thus, OPEC's coordinated reduction in supply proved less profitable in the long run.

Figure 5-9

A REDUCTION IN SUPPLY IN THE WORLD MARKET FOR OIL. When the supply of oil falls, the response depends on the time horizon. In the short run, supply and demand are relatively inelastic, as in panel (a). Thus, when the supply curve shifts from S_1 to S_2, the price rises substantially. By contrast, in the long run, supply and demand are relatively elastic, as in panel (b). In this case, the same size shift in the supply curve (S_1 to S_2) causes a smaller increase in the price.

OPEC still exists today. You will occasionally hear in the news about meetings of officials from the OPEC countries. Cooperation among OPEC countries is now rare, however, in part because of the organization's past failure at maintaining a high price.

DOES DRUG INTERDICTION INCREASE OR DECREASE DRUG-RELATED CRIME?

A persistent problem facing our society is the use of illegal drugs, such as heroin, cocaine, and crack. Drug use has several adverse effects. One is that drug dependency can ruin the lives of drug users and their families. Another is that drug addicts often turn to robbery and other violent crimes to obtain the money needed to support their habit. To discourage the use of illegal drugs, the U.S. government devotes billions of dollars each year to reduce the flow of drugs into the country. Let's use the tools of supply and demand to examine this policy of drug interdiction.

Suppose the government increases the number of federal agents devoted to the war on drugs. What happens in the market for illegal drugs? As is usual, we answer this question in three steps. First, we consider whether the supply or demand curve shifts. Second, we consider the direction of the shift. Third, we see how the shift affects the equilibrium price and quantity.

Although the purpose of drug interdiction is to reduce drug use, its direct impact is on the sellers of drugs rather than the buyers. When the government stops some drugs from entering the country and arrests more smugglers, it raises the cost of selling drugs and, therefore, reduces the quantity of drugs supplied at any given price. The demand for drugs—the amount buyers want at any given price—is not changed. As panel (a) of Figure 5-10 shows, interdiction shifts the supply curve to the left from S_1 to S_2 and leaves the demand curve the same. The equilibrium price of drugs rises from P_1 to P_2, and the equilibrium quantity falls from Q_1 to Q_2. The fall in the equilibrium quantity shows that drug interdiction does reduce drug use.

But what about the amount of drug-related crime? To answer this question, consider the total amount that drug users pay for the drugs they buy. Because few drug addicts are likely to break their destructive habits in response to a higher price, it is likely that the demand for drugs is inelastic, as it is drawn in the figure. If demand is inelastic, then an increase in price raises total revenue in the drug market. That is, because drug interdiction raises the price of drugs proportionately more than it reduces drug use, it raises the total amount of money that drug users pay for drugs. Addicts who already had to steal to support their habits would have an even greater need for quick cash. Thus, drug interdiction could increase drug-related crime.

Because of this adverse effect of drug interdiction, some analysts argue for alternative approaches to the drug problem. Rather than trying to reduce the

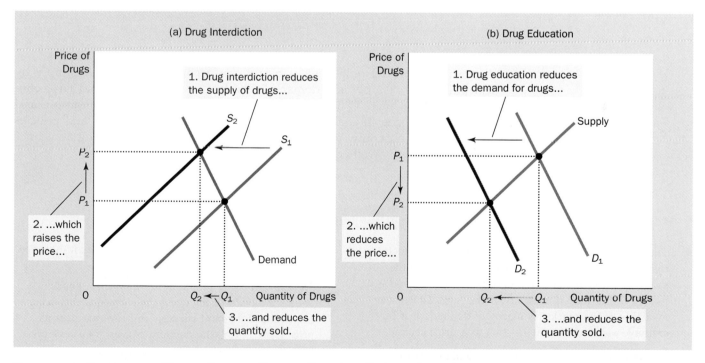

POLICIES TO REDUCE THE USE OF ILLEGAL DRUGS. Drug interdiction reduces the supply of drugs from S_1 to S_2, as in panel (a). If the demand for drugs is inelastic, then the total amount paid by drug users rises, even as the amount of drug use falls. By contrast, drug education reduces the demand for drugs from D_1 to D_2, as in panel (b). Because both price and quantity fall, the amount paid by drug users falls.

Figure 5-10

supply of drugs, policymakers might try to reduce the demand by pursuing a policy of drug education. Successful drug education has the effects shown in panel (b) of Figure 5-10. The demand curve shifts to the left from D_1 to D_2. As a result, the equilibrium quantity falls from Q_1 to Q_2, and the equilibrium price falls from P_1 to P_2. Total revenue, which is price times quantity, also falls. Thus, in contrast to drug interdiction, drug education can reduce both drug use and drug-related crime.

Advocates of drug interdiction might argue that the effects of this policy are different in the long run than in the short run, because the elasticity of demand may depend on the time horizon. The demand for drugs is probably inelastic over short periods of time because higher prices do not substantially affect drug use by established addicts. But demand may be more elastic over longer periods of time because higher prices would discourage experimentation with drugs among the young and, over time, lead to fewer drug addicts. In this case, drug interdiction would increase drug-related crime in the short run while decreasing it in the long run.

QUICK QUIZ   How might a drought that destroys half of all farm crops be good for farmers? If such a drought is good for farmers, why don't farmers destroy their own crops in the absence of a drought?

CONCLUSION

According to an old quip, even a parrot can become an economist simply by learning to say "supply and demand." The last two chapters should have convinced you that there is much truth in this statement. The tools of supply and demand allow you to analyze many of the most important events and policies that shape the economy. You are now well on your way to becoming an economist (or, at least, a well-educated parrot).

Summary

◆ The price elasticity of demand measures how much the quantity demanded responds to changes in the price. Demand tends to be more elastic if the good is a luxury rather than a necessity, if close substitutes are available, if the market is narrowly defined, or if buyers have substantial time to react to a price change.

◆ The price elasticity of demand is calculated as the percentage change in quantity demanded divided by the percentage change in price. If the elasticity is less than 1, so that quantity demanded moves proportionately less than the price, demand is said to be inelastic. If the elasticity is greater than 1, so that quantity

demanded moves proportionately more than the price, demand is said to be elastic.

◆ Total revenue, the total amount paid for a good, equals the price of the good times the quantity sold. For inelastic demand curves, total revenue rises as price rises. For elastic demand curves, total revenue falls as price rises.

◆ The income elasticity of demand measures how much the quantity demanded responds to changes in income. It is defined to be the percentage change in quantity demanded divided by the percentage change in income.

◆ The price elasticity of supply measures how much the quantity supplied responds to changes in the price. This elasticity often depends on the time horizon under consideration. In most markets, supply is more elastic in the long run than in the short run.

◆ The price elasticity of supply is calculated as the percentage change in quantity supplied divided by the percentage change in price. If the elasticity is less than 1, so that quantity supplied moves proportionately

less than the price, supply is said to be inelastic. If the elasticity is greater than 1, so that quantity supplied moves proportionately more than the price, supply is said to be elastic.

◆ The tools of supply and demand can be applied in many different kinds of markets. This chapter uses them to analyze the market for wheat, the market for oil, and the market for illegal drugs.

Key Concepts

elasticity, p. 90   total revenue, p. 94   price elasticity of supply, p. 99
price elasticity of demand, p. 90   income elasticity of demand, p. 96

Questions for Review

1. Define the price elasticity of demand and the income elasticity of demand.

2. List and explain some of the determinants of the price elasticity of demand.

3. If the elasticity is greater than 1, is demand elastic or inelastic? If the elasticity equals 0, is demand perfectly elastic or perfectly inelastic?

4. On a supply-and-demand diagram, show total spending by consumers. How does this compare to total revenue received by producers?

5. If demand is elastic, how will an increase in price change total revenue? Explain.

6. What do we call a good whose income elasticity is less than 0?

7. What is the formula for the price elasticity of supply? Explain what this measures.

8. What is the price elasticity of supply of Picasso paintings?

9. Is the price elasticity of supply usually larger in the short run or in the long run? Why?

10. In the 1970s, OPEC caused a dramatic increase in the price of oil. What prevented them from maintaining this high price through the 1980s?

Problems and Applications

1. For each of the following pairs of goods, which good would you expect to have more elastic demand and why?
   a. required textbooks or mystery novels
   b. Beethoven recordings or classical music recordings in general
   c. heating oil during the next six months or heating oil during the next five years
   d. root beer or water

2. Suppose that business travelers and vacationers have the following demand for airline tickets from New York to Boston:

PRICE	QUANTITY DEMANDED (BUSINESS TRAVELERS)	QUANTITY DEMANDED (VACATIONERS)
$150	2,100	1,000
200	2,000	800
250	1,900	600
300	1,800	400

   a. As the price of tickets rises from $200 to $250, what is the price elasticity of demand for (i) business travelers and (ii) vacationers?
   b. Why might vacationers have a different elasticity than business travelers?

3. Suppose that your demand schedule for compact discs is as follows:

PRICE	QUANTITY DEMANDED (INCOME = $10,000)	QUANTITY DEMANDED (INCOME = $12,000)
$ 8	40	50
10	32	45
12	24	30
14	16	20
16	8	12

   a. Calculate your price elasticity of demand as the price of compact discs increases from $8 to $10 if (i) your income is $10,000, and (ii) your income is $12,000.

   b. Calculate your income elasticity of demand as your income increases from $10,000 to $12,000 if (i) the price is $12, and (ii) the price is $16.

4. Emily has decided always to spend one-third of her income on clothing.

   a. What is her income elasticity of clothing demand?

   b. What is her price elasticity of clothing demand?

   c. If Emily's tastes change and she decides to spend only one-fourth of her income on clothing, how does her demand curve change? What is her income elasticity and price elasticity now?

5. *The New York Times* (Feb. 17, 1996) reported that subway ridership declined after a fare increase: "There were nearly four million fewer riders in December 1995, the first full month after the price of a token increased 25 cents to $1.50, than in the previous December, a 4.3 percent decline."

   a. Use these data to estimate the price elasticity of demand for subway rides.

   b. According to your estimate, what happens to the Transit Authority's revenue when the fare rises?

   c. Why might your estimate of the elasticity be unreliable?

6. Two drivers—Tom and Jerry—each drive up to a gas station. Before looking at the price, each places an order. Tom says, "I'd like 10 gallons of gas." Jerry says, "I'd like $10 of gas." What is each driver's price elasticity of demand?

7. Economists have observed that spending on restaurant meals declines more during economic downturns than does spending on food to be eaten at home. How might the concept of elasticity help to explain this phenomenon?

8. Consider public policy aimed at smoking.

   a. Studies indicate that the price elasticity of demand for cigarettes is about 0.4. If a pack of cigarettes currently costs $2 and the government wants to reduce smoking by 20 percent, by how much should it increase the price?

   b. If the government permanently increases the price of cigarettes, will the policy have a larger effect on smoking one year from now or five years from now?

   c. Studies also find that teenagers have a higher price elasticity than do adults. Why might this be true?

9. Would you expect the price elasticity of *supply* to be larger in the market for all ice cream or the market for vanilla ice cream? Explain.

10. In the summer of 1993, flooding along the Missouri and Mississippi rivers destroyed thousands of acres of wheat.

    a. Farmers whose crops were destroyed by the floods were much worse off, but farmers whose crops were not destroyed benefited from the floods. Why?

    b. What information would you need about the market for wheat in order to assess whether farmers as a group were hurt or helped by the floods?

11. Explain why the following might be true: A drought around the world raises the total revenue that farmers receive from the sale of grain, but a drought only in Kansas reduces the total revenue that Kansas farmers receive.

12. Because better weather makes farmland more productive, farmland in regions with good weather conditions is more expensive than farmland in regions with bad weather conditions. Over time, however, as advances in technology have made all farmland more productive, the price of farmland (adjusted for overall inflation) has fallen. Use the concept of elasticity to explain why productivity and farmland prices are positively related across space but negatively related over time.

13. In 1990 the U.S. Congress imposed a sales tax on the purchase of expensive cars. The revenue collected from the tax equals the tax rate multiplied by total spending on such cars. When the government needed more revenue several years later, it was suggested that this tax rate be increased. Would such an increase necessarily have raised tax revenue? Explain.

6

SUPPLY, DEMAND, AND GOVERNMENT POLICIES

IN THIS CHAPTER YOU WILL

Examine the effects of government policies that place a ceiling on prices

Examine the effects of government policies that put a floor under prices

Consider how a tax on a good affects the price of the good and the quantity sold

Learn that taxes levied on buyers and taxes levied on sellers are equivalent

See how the burden of a tax is split between buyers and sellers

Economists have two roles. As scientists, they develop and test theories to explain the world around them. As policymakers, they use their theories to try to change the world for the better. The focus of the past two chapters has been scientific. We have seen how supply and demand determine the price of a good and the quantity of the good sold. We have also seen how various events shift supply and demand and thereby change the equilibrium price and quantity.

This chapter offers our first look at policy. Here we analyze various types of government policy using only the tools of supply and demand. As you will see, the analysis yields some surprising insights. Policies often have effects that their architects did not intend or anticipate.

We begin by considering policies that directly control prices. For example, rent-control laws dictate a maximum rent that landlords may charge tenants. Minimum-wage laws dictate the lowest wage that firms may pay workers. Price controls are usually enacted when policymakers believe that the market price of a good or service is unfair to buyers or sellers. Yet, as we will see, these policies can generate inequities of their own.

After our discussion of price controls, we next consider the impact of taxes. Policymakers use taxes both to influence market outcomes and to raise revenue for public purposes. Although the prevalence of taxes in our economy is obvious, their effects are not. For example, when the government levies a tax on the amount that firms pay their workers, do the firms or the workers bear the burden of the tax? The answer is not at all clear—until we apply the powerful tools of supply and demand.

CONTROLS ON PRICES

To see how price controls affect market outcomes, let's look once again at the market for ice cream. As we saw in Chapter 4, if ice cream is sold in a competitive market free of government regulation, the price of ice cream adjusts to balance supply and demand: At the equilibrium price, the quantity of ice cream that buyers want to buy exactly equals the quantity that sellers want to sell. To be concrete, suppose the equilibrium price is $3 per cone.

Not everyone may be happy with the outcome of this free-market process. Let's say the American Association of Ice Cream Eaters complains that the $3 price is too high for everyone to enjoy a cone a day (their recommended diet). Meanwhile, the National Organization of Ice Cream Makers complains that the $3 price—the result of "cutthroat competition"—is depressing the incomes of its members. Each of these groups lobbies the government to pass laws that alter the market outcome by directly controlling prices.

Of course, because buyers of any good always want a lower price while sellers want a higher price, the interests of the two groups conflict. If the Ice Cream Eaters are successful in their lobbying, the government passes a legal maximum on the price at which ice cream can be sold, called a **price ceiling.** If the Ice Cream Makers are successful, the government passes a legal minimum on the price, called a **price floor.** Let us consider the effects of these policies in turn.

HOW PRICE CEILINGS AFFECT MARKET OUTCOMES

When the government, moved by the complaints of the Ice Cream Eaters, imposes a price ceiling on the market for ice cream, two outcomes are possible. In panel (a) of Figure 6-1, the government imposes a price ceiling of $4 per cone. In this case, because the price that balances supply and demand ($3) is below the ceiling, the price ceiling is *not binding*. Market forces naturally move the economy to the equilibrium, and the price ceiling has no effect.

Panel (b) of Figure 6-1 shows the other, more interesting, possibility. In this case, the government imposes a price ceiling of $2 per cone. Because the equilibrium price of $3 is above the price ceiling, the ceiling is a *binding constraint* on the market. The forces of supply and demand tend to move the price toward the equilibrium price, but when the market price hits the ceiling, it can rise no further. Thus, the market price equals the price ceiling. At this price, the quantity of ice cream demanded (125 cones in the figure) exceeds the quantity supplied (75 cones). There is a shortage of ice cream, so some people who want to buy ice cream at the going price are unable to.

When a shortage of ice cream develops because of this price ceiling, some mechanism for rationing ice cream will naturally develop. The mechanism could be long lines: Buyers who are willing to arrive early and wait in line get a cone, while those unwilling to wait do not. Alternatively, sellers could ration ice cream according to their own personal biases, selling it only to friends, relatives, or members of their own racial or ethnic group. Notice that even though the price ceiling was motivated by a desire to help buyers of ice cream, not all buyers benefit from the policy. Some buyers do get to pay a lower price, although they may have to wait in line to do so, but other buyers cannot get any ice cream at all.

price ceiling

a legal maximum on the price at which a good can be sold

price floor

a legal minimum on the price at which a good can be sold

A MARKET WITH A PRICE CEILING. In panel (a), the government imposes a price ceiling of $4. Because the price ceiling is above the equilibrium price of $3, the price ceiling has no effect, and the market can reach the equilibrium of supply and demand. In this equilibrium, quantity supplied and quantity demanded both equal 100 cones. In panel (b), the government imposes a price ceiling of $2. Because the price ceiling is below the equilibrium price of $3, the market price equals $2. At this price, 125 cones are demanded and only 75 are supplied, so there is a shortage of 50 cones.

Figure 6-1

This example in the market for ice cream shows a general result: *When the government imposes a binding price ceiling on a competitive market, a shortage of the good arises, and sellers must ration the scarce goods among the large number of potential buyers.* The rationing mechanisms that develop under price ceilings are rarely desirable. Long lines are inefficient, because they waste buyers' time. Discrimination according to seller bias is both inefficient (because the good does not go to the buyer who values it most highly) and potentially unfair. By contrast, the rationing mechanism in a free, competitive market is both efficient and impersonal. When the market for ice cream reaches its equilibrium, anyone who wants to pay the market price can get a cone. Free markets ration goods with prices.

CASE STUDY LINES AT THE GAS PUMP

As we discussed in the last chapter, in 1973 the Organization of Petroleum Exporting Countries (OPEC) raised the price of crude oil in world oil markets. Because crude oil is the major input used to make gasoline, the higher oil prices reduced the supply of gasoline. Long lines at gas stations became commonplace, and motorists often had to wait for hours to buy only a few gallons of gas.

What was responsible for the long gas lines? Most people blame OPEC. Surely, if OPEC had not raised the price of crude oil, the shortage of gasoline would not have occurred. Yet economists blame government regulations that limited the price oil companies could charge for gasoline.

Figure 6-2 shows what happened. As shown in panel (a), before OPEC raised the price of crude oil, the equilibrium price of gasoline, P_1, was below the price ceiling. The price regulation, therefore, had no effect. When the price of crude oil rose, however, the situation changed. The increase in the price of crude oil raised the cost of producing gasoline, and this reduced the supply of gasoline. As panel (b) shows, the supply curve shifted to the left from S_1 to S_2. In an unregulated market, this shift in supply would have raised the equilibrium price of gasoline from P_1 to P_2, and no shortage would have resulted. Instead, the price ceiling prevented the price from rising to the equilibrium level. At the price ceiling, producers were willing to sell Q_S, and consumers were willing to buy Q_D. Thus, the shift in supply caused a severe shortage at the regulated price.

Eventually, the laws regulating the price of gasoline were repealed. Lawmakers came to understand that they were partly responsible for the many hours Americans lost waiting in line to buy gasoline. Today, when the price of crude oil changes, the price of gasoline can adjust to bring supply and demand into equilibrium.

Figure 6-2

THE MARKET FOR GASOLINE WITH A PRICE CEILING. Panel (a) shows the gasoline market when the price ceiling is not binding because the equilibrium price, P_1, is below the ceiling. Panel (b) shows the gasoline market after an increase in the price of crude oil (an input into making gasoline) shifts the supply curve to the left from S_1 to S_2. In an unregulated market, the price would have risen from P_1 to P_2. The price ceiling, however, prevents this from happening. At the binding price ceiling, consumers are willing to buy Q_D, but producers of gasoline are willing to sell only Q_S. The difference between quantity demanded and quantity supplied, $Q_D - Q_S$, measures the gasoline shortage.

CASE STUDY RENT CONTROL IN THE SHORT RUN AND LONG RUN

One common example of a price ceiling is rent control. In many cities, the local government places a ceiling on rents that landlords may charge their tenants. The goal of this policy is to help the poor by making housing more affordable. Economists often criticize rent control, arguing that it is a highly inefficient way to help the poor raise their standard of living. One economist called rent control "the best way to destroy a city, other than bombing."

The adverse effects of rent control are less apparent to the general population because these effects occur over many years. In the short run, landlords have a fixed number of apartments to rent, and they cannot adjust this number quickly as market conditions change. Moreover, the number of people searching for housing in a city may not be highly responsive to rents in the short run because people take time to adjust their housing arrangements. Therefore, the short-run supply and demand for housing are relatively inelastic.

Panel (a) of Figure 6-3 shows the short-run effects of rent control on the housing market. As with any price ceiling, rent control causes a shortage. Yet because supply and demand are inelastic in the short run, the initial shortage caused by rent control is small. The primary effect in the short run is to reduce rents.

The long-run story is very different because the buyers and sellers of rental housing respond more to market conditions as time passes. On the supply side, landlords respond to low rents by not building new apartments and by failing to maintain existing ones. On the demand side, low rents encourage

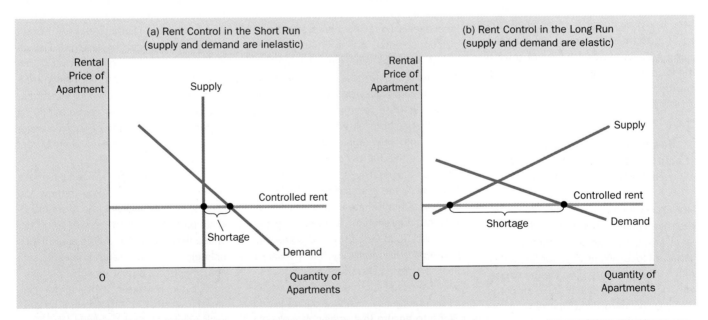

RENT CONTROL IN THE SHORT RUN AND IN THE LONG RUN. Panel (a) shows the short-run effects of rent control: Because the supply and demand for apartments are relatively inelastic, the price ceiling imposed by a rent-control law causes only a small shortage of housing. Panel (b) shows the long-run effects of rent control: Because the supply and demand for apartments are more elastic, rent control causes a large shortage.

Figure 6-3

people to find their own apartments (rather than living with their parents or sharing apartments with roommates) and induce more people to move into a city. Therefore, both supply and demand are more elastic in the long run.

Panel (b) of Figure 6-3 illustrates the housing market in the long run. When rent control depresses rents below the equilibrium level, the quantity of apartments supplied falls substantially, and the quantity of apartments demanded rises substantially. The result is a large shortage of housing.

IN THE NEWS

Rent Control in New York City

RENT CONTROL PLAYS A LARGE ROLE IN New York City, the largest city in the United States. Here is a description of how the policy works in practice. According to this 1994 article, local politicians will remove rent control only if the vacancy rate for apartments is high enough. What do you think about this decision?

Home Free: Some Rich and Famous of New York City Bask in Shelter of Rent Law

NEW YORK—Les Katz, a twenty-seven-year-old acting student and doorman, rents a small studio apartment in Manhattan's Upper West Side for $1,200—with two roommates. Two sleep in separate bedrooms in a loft built atop the kitchen, the third on a mattress in the main room.

Across town on Park Avenue, Paul Haberman, a private investor, and his wife live in a spacious, two-bedroom

apartment with a solarium and two terraces. The apartment in an elegant building on the prestigious avenue is worth at least $5,000 a month, real-estate professionals say. The couple pay around $350, according to rent records. (Mr. Haberman declines to discuss the amount.)

The reason for this disparity: New York rent regulation.

New York City is facing a $2.3 billion budget deficit and its worst fiscal crunch in 20 years. Meanwhile, the city, by various estimates, forfeits $100 million or more in property taxes annually because suppressed rents hold down the cash flow, and thus the assessed value, of residential buildings. Critics also say the restrictions deter construction of new rental buildings and force landlords—and, indirectly, taxpayers—to subsidize those tenants lucky enough to have one of the regulated apartments. . . .

People from all walks of life have lucked into rent-regulated apartments: actresses Mia Farrow and Cicely Tyson; Baroness Ingrid Thyssen; Sidney Biddle Barrows, the so-called Mayflower Madam; State Senate Democratic leader Manfred Ohrenstein; leveraged-buyout specialist Todd Goodwin; and some employees of the company that publishes this newspaper, Dow Jones & Co. . . .

Rent regulation in New York began as an emergency measure during World War II to ensure that transient, well-paid wartime workers didn't outbid local residents for the limited supply of apartments. After the war, city politicians retained rent regulation, ruling that as long as the vacancy rate remains below 5 percent, a housing emergency exists. The rate is now 3.4 percent. . . .

So how do tenants get these deals?

Some inherit them. Ms. Farrow pays about $2,900 a month for ten rooms on Central Park West, a fraction of the market value. The actress grew up in the apartment, which was the setting for one of her movies, *Hannah and Her Sisters*. Her mother, Maureen O'Sullivan, who also was in the Woody Allen film, first signed the lease 40 years ago.

Other rent-regulated tenants, like former New York Mayor David Dinkins and Manhattan District Attorney Robert Morgenthau, knew the landlord, in their case New York's Rudin family. "The Rudins like to cooperate in making rent-stabilized apartments available to former public officials," says Barbara Fife, a deputy mayor in charge of housing under Mr. Dinkins and a strong advocate of rent regulation. . . .

Other times, would-be tenants make payments, known as "key money," to prior tenants or to landlords. Some landlords prefer to rent to the well-to-do because they will spend on the apartment's upkeep. "We've rented inexpensive apartments to overly wealthy people," says Brian Edwards, a broker for Halstead Property Co. "That's who the landlords wanted in their buildings."

SOURCE: *The Wall Street Journal*, March 21, 1994, p. A1.

In cities with rent control, landlords use various mechanisms to ration housing. Some landlords keep long waiting lists. Others give a preference to tenants without children. Still others discriminate on the basis of race. Sometimes, apartments are allocated to those willing to offer under-the-table payments to building superintendents. In essence, these bribes bring the total price of an apartment (including the bribe) closer to the equilibrium price.

To understand fully the effects of rent control, we have to remember one of the *Ten Principles of Economics* from Chapter 1: People respond to incentives. In free markets, landlords try to keep their buildings clean and safe because desirable apartments command higher prices. By contrast, when rent control creates shortages and waiting lists, landlords lose their incentive to be responsive to tenants' concerns. Why should a landlord spend his money to maintain and improve his property when people are waiting to get in as it is? In the end, tenants get lower rents, but they also get lower quality housing.

Policymakers often react to the effects of rent control by imposing additional regulations. For example, there are laws that make racial discrimination in housing illegal and require landlords to provide minimally adequate living conditions. These laws, however, are difficult and costly to enforce. By contrast, when rent control is eliminated and a market for housing is regulated by the forces of competition, such laws are less necessary. In a free market, the price of housing adjusts to eliminate the shortages that give rise to undesirable landlord behavior.

HOW PRICE FLOORS AFFECT MARKET OUTCOMES

To examine the effects of another kind of government price control, let's return to the market for ice cream. Imagine now that the government is persuaded by the pleas of the National Organization of Ice Cream Makers. In this case, the government might institute a price floor. Price floors, like price ceilings, are an attempt by the government to maintain prices at other than equilibrium levels. Whereas a price ceiling places a legal maximum on prices, a price floor places a legal minimum.

When the government imposes a price floor on the ice-cream market, two outcomes are possible. If the government imposes a price floor of $2 per cone when the equilibrium price is $3, we obtain the outcome in panel (a) of Figure 6-4. In this case, because the equilibrium price is above the floor, the price floor is not binding. Market forces naturally move the economy to the equilibrium, and the price floor has no effect.

Panel (b) of Figure 6-4 shows what happens when the government imposes a price floor of $4 per cone. In this case, because the equilibrium price of $3 is below the floor, the price floor is a binding constraint on the market. The forces of supply and demand tend to move the price toward the equilibrium price, but when the market price hits the floor, it can fall no further. The market price equals the price floor. At this floor, the quantity of ice cream supplied (120 cones) exceeds the quantity demanded (80 cones). Some people who want to sell ice cream at the going price are unable to. Thus, *a binding price floor causes a surplus.*

Just as price ceilings and shortages can lead to undesirable rationing mechanisms, so can price floors and surpluses. In the case of a price floor, some sellers are unable to sell all they want at the market price. The sellers who appeal to the personal biases of the buyers, perhaps due to racial or familial ties, are

Figure 6-4

A MARKET WITH A PRICE FLOOR. In panel (a), the government imposes a price floor of $2. Because this is below the equilibrium price of $3, the price floor has no effect. The market price adjusts to balance supply and demand. At the equilibrium, quantity supplied and quantity demanded both equal 100 cones. In panel (b), the government imposes a price floor of $4, which is above the equilibrium price of $3. Therefore, the market price equals $4. Because 120 cones are supplied at this price and only 80 are demanded, there is a surplus of 40 cones.

better able to sell their goods than those who do not. By contrast, in a free market, the price serves as the rationing mechanism, and sellers can sell all they want at the equilibrium price.

CASE STUDY   THE MINIMUM WAGE

An important example of a price floor is the minimum wage. Minimum-wage laws dictate the lowest price for labor that any employer may pay. The U.S. Congress first instituted a minimum wage with the Fair Labor Standards Act of 1938 in order to ensure workers a minimally adequate standard of living. As of 1996, the minimum wage according to federal law is $4.75 per hour. Some states have laws that impose higher minimum wages.

To examine the effects of a minimum wage, we must consider the market for labor. Panel (a) of Figure 6-5 shows the labor market which, like all markets, is subject to the forces of supply and demand. Workers determine the supply of labor, and firms determine the demand. In the absence of government intervention, the wage adjusts to balance labor supply and labor demand.

Panel (b) of Figure 6-5 shows the labor market with a minimum wage. If the minimum wage is above the equilibrium level, as it is here, the quantity

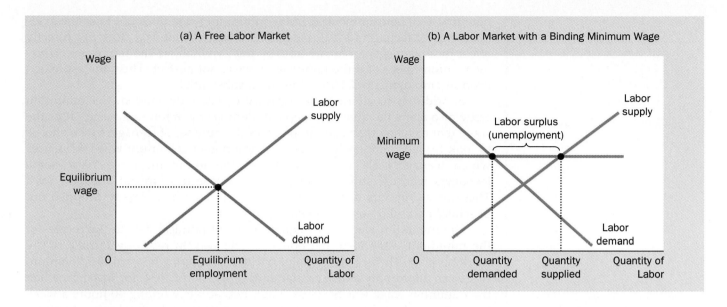

HOW THE MINIMUM WAGE AFFECTS THE LABOR MARKET. Panel (a) shows a labor market in which the wage adjusts to balance labor supply and labor demand. Panel (b) shows the impact of a binding minimum wage. Because the minimum wage is a price floor, it causes a surplus: The quantity of labor supplied exceeds the quantity demanded. The result is unemployment.

Figure 6-5

of labor supplied exceeds the quantity demanded. The result is unemployment. Thus, the minimum wage raises the incomes of those workers who have jobs, but it lowers the incomes of those workers who cannot find jobs.

To fully understand the minimum wage, it is important to keep in mind that the economy contains not a single labor market, but many labor markets for different types of workers. The impact of the minimum wage depends on the skill and experience of the worker. Workers with high skills and much experience are not affected, because their equilibrium wages are well above the minimum. For these workers, the minimum wage is not binding.

The minimum wage has its greatest impact on the market for teenage labor. The equilibrium wages of teenagers tend to be low because teenagers are among the least skilled and least experienced members of the labor force. In addition, teenagers are often willing to accept a lower wage in exchange for on-the-job training. (Indeed, some teenagers are willing to work as "interns" for no pay at all. Because internships pay nothing, however, the minimum wage does not apply to them. If it did, these jobs might not exist.) As a result, the minimum wage is more often binding for teenagers than for other members of the labor force.

Many economists have examined how minimum-wage laws affect the teenage labor market. These researchers compare the changes in the minimum wage over time with the changes in teenage employment. Although there is some debate about how much the minimum wage affects employment, the typical study finds that a 10 percent increase in the minimum wage depresses teenage employment between 1 and 3 percent. In interpreting this estimate, note that a 10 percent increase in the minimum wage does not raise the average wage of teenagers by 10 percent. A change in the law does not directly affect those teenagers who are already paid well above the minimum. Moreover, enforcement of minimum-wage laws is not perfect. Thus, the estimated drop in employment of 1 to 3 percent is substantial.

In addition to altering the quantity of labor demanded, the minimum wage also alters the quantity supplied. Because the minimum wage raises the wage that teenagers can earn, it increases the number of teenagers who choose to look for jobs. Studies have found that a higher minimum wage influences which teenagers are employed. When the minimum wage rises, some teenagers who are still attending school choose to drop out and take jobs. These new dropouts displace other teenagers who had already dropped out of school and who now become unemployed.

The minimum wage is a frequent topic of political debate. Advocates of the minimum wage view the policy as one way to raise the income of the working poor. They correctly point out that workers who earn the minimum wage can afford only a meager standard of living. In 1994, for instance, when the minimum wage was $4.25 per hour, two adults working 40 hours a week for every week of the year at minimum-wage jobs had a total annual income of only $17,680, which was less than half of the median family income. Many advocates of the minimum wage admit that it has some adverse effects, including unemployment, but they believe that these effects are small and that, all things considered, a higher minimum wage makes the poor better off.

Opponents of the minimum wage contend that it is not the best way to combat poverty. They note that a high minimum wage causes unemployment, encourages teenagers to drop out of school, and prevents some unskilled workers from getting the on-the-job training they need. Moreover, opponents of the minimum wage point out that the minimum wage is a poorly targeted policy. Not all minimum-wage workers are heads of households trying to help their families escape poverty. Many minimum-wage earners are teenagers from middle-class homes working at part-time jobs for extra spending money.

EVALUATING PRICE CONTROLS

One of the *Ten Principles of Economics* discussed in Chapter 1 is that markets are usually a good way to organize economic activity. This principle explains why economists almost always oppose price ceilings and price floors. To economists, prices are not the outcome of some haphazard process. Prices, they contend, are the result of the millions of business and consumer decisions that lie behind the supply and demand curves. Prices have the crucial job of balancing supply and demand and, thereby, coordinating economic activity. When policymakers set prices by legal decree, they obscure the signals that normally guide the allocation of society's resources.

Another one of the *Ten Principles of Economics* is that governments can sometimes improve market outcomes. Indeed, policymakers are led to control prices because they view the market's outcome as unfair. Price controls are often aimed at helping the poor. For instance, rent-control laws try to make housing affordable for everyone, and minimum-wage laws try to help people escape poverty.

Yet price controls often hurt those they are trying to help. Rent control may keep rents low, but it also discourages landlords from maintaining their buildings and makes housing hard to find. Minimum-wage laws may raise the incomes of some workers, but they also cause other workers to be unemployed.

Helping those in need can be accomplished in ways other than controlling prices. For instance, the government can make housing more affordable by paying a fraction of the rent for poor families. Unlike rent control, such rent subsidies do not reduce the quantity of housing supplied and, therefore, do not lead to housing shortages. Similarly, wage subsidies raise the living standards of the working poor without discouraging firms from hiring them. An example of a wage subsidy is the *earned income tax credit*, a government program that supplements the incomes of low-wage workers.

Although these alternative policies are often better than price controls, they are not perfect. Rent and wage subsidies cost the government money and, therefore, require higher taxes. As we see in the next section, taxation has costs of its own.

QUICK QUIZ Define *price ceiling* and *price floor*, and give an example of each. Which leads to a shortage? Which leads to a surplus? Why?

TAXES

All governments—from the federal government in Washington, D.C., to the local governments in small towns—use taxes to raise revenue for public purposes. Because taxes are such an important policy instrument, and because they affect our lives in many ways, the study of taxes is a topic to which we will return several times throughout this book. In this section we begin our study of how taxes affect the economy.

To set the stage for our analysis, imagine that a local government decides to hold an annual ice-cream celebration—with a parade, fireworks, and speeches by town officials. To raise revenue to pay for the event, it decides to place a $0.50 tax on the sale of ice-cream cones. When the plan is announced, our two lobbying groups swing into action. The National Organization of Ice Cream Makers claims that its members are struggling to survive in a competitive market, and it argues that *buyers* of ice cream should have to pay the tax. The American Association of Ice Cream Eaters claims that consumers of ice cream are having trouble making ends meet, and it argues that *sellers* of ice cream should pay the tax. The town mayor, hoping to reach a compromise, suggests that half the tax be paid by the buyers and half be paid by the sellers.

To analyze these proposals, we need to address a simple but subtle question: When the government levies a tax on a good, who bears the burden of the tax? The people buying the good? The people selling the good? Or, if buyers and sellers share the tax burden, what determines how the burden is divided? Can the government simply legislate the division of the burden, as the mayor is suggesting, or is the division determined by more fundamental forces in the economy? Economists use the term **tax incidence** to refer to these questions about the distribution of a tax burden. As we will see, we can learn some surprising lessons about tax incidence just by applying the tools of supply and demand.

tax incidence
the study of who bears the burden of taxation

HOW TAXES ON BUYERS AFFECT MARKET OUTCOMES

We first consider a tax levied on buyers of a good. Suppose, for instance, that our local government passes a law requiring buyers of ice-cream cones to send $0.50 to the government for each ice-cream cone they buy. How does this law affect the buyers and sellers of ice cream? To answer this question, we can follow the three steps in Chapter 4 for analyzing supply and demand: (1) We decide whether the law affects the supply or demand curve. (2) We decide which way the curve shifts. (3) We examine how the shift affects the equilibrium.

The initial impact of the tax is on the demand for ice cream. The supply curve is not affected because, for any given price of ice cream, sellers have the same incentive to provide ice cream to the market. By contrast, buyers now have to pay a tax to the government (as well as the price to the sellers) whenever they buy ice cream. Thus, the tax shifts the demand curve for ice cream.

The direction of the shift is easy to see. Because the tax on buyers makes buying ice cream less attractive, buyers demand a smaller quantity of ice cream at every price. As a result, the demand curve shifts to the left (or, equivalently, downward).

We can, in this case, be more precise about how much the curve shifts. Because of the $0.50 tax levied on buyers, the effective price to buyers is now $0.50 higher than the market price. For example, if the market price of a cone happened to be $2.00, the effective price to buyers would be $2.50. Because buyers look at their total cost including the tax, they demand a quantity of ice cream as if the market price were $0.50 higher than it actually is. In other words, to induce buyers to demand any given quantity, the market price must now be $0.50 lower to make up for the effect of the tax. Thus, as shown in Figure 6-6, the tax shifts the demand curve *downward* from D_1 to D_2 by exactly the size of the tax ($0.50).

Figure 6-6

A TAX ON BUYERS. When a tax of $0.50 is levied on buyers, the demand curve shifts down by $0.50 from D_1 to D_2. The equilibrium quantity falls from 100 to 90 cones. The price that sellers receive falls from $3.00 to $2.80. The price that buyers pay (including the tax) rises from $3.00 to $3.30. Even though the tax is levied on buyers, buyers and sellers share the burden of the tax.

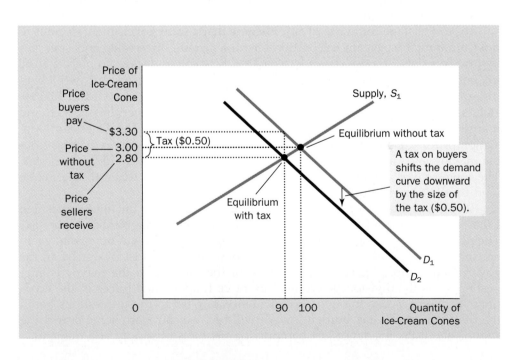

To see the effect of the tax, we compare the old equilibrium and the new equilibrium. You can see in the figure that the equilibrium price of ice cream falls from $3.00 to $2.80 and the equilibrium quantity falls from 100 to 90 cones. Because sellers sell less and buyers buy less in the new equilibrium, the tax on ice cream reduces the size of the ice-cream market.

Now let's return to the question of tax incidence: Who pays the tax? Although buyers send the entire tax to the government, buyers and sellers share the burden. Because the market price falls from $3.00 to $2.80 when the tax is introduced, sellers receive $0.20 less for each ice-cream cone than they did without the tax. Thus, the tax makes sellers worse off. Buyers pay sellers a lower price ($2.80), but the effective price including the tax rises from $3.00 before the tax to $3.30 with the tax ($2.80 + $0.50 = $3.30). Thus, the tax also makes buyers worse off.

To sum up, the analysis yields two general lessons:

◆ Taxes discourage market activity. When a good is taxed, the quantity of the good sold is smaller in the new equilibrium.

◆ Buyers and sellers share the burden of taxes. In the new equilibrium, buyers pay more for the good, and sellers receive less.

HOW TAXES ON SELLERS AFFECT MARKET OUTCOMES

Now consider a tax levied on sellers of a good. Suppose the local government passes a law requiring sellers of ice-cream cones to send $0.50 to the government for each cone they sell. What are the effects of this law?

In this case, the initial impact of the tax is on the supply of ice cream. Because the tax is not levied on buyers, the quantity of ice cream demanded at any given price is the same, so the demand curve does not change. By contrast, the tax on sellers raises the cost of selling ice cream, and this leads sellers to supply a smaller quantity at every price. The supply curve shifts to the left (or, equivalently, upward).

Once again, we can be precise about the magnitude of the shift. For any market price of ice cream, the effective price to sellers—the amount they get to keep after paying the tax—is $0.50 lower. For example, if the market price of a cone happened to be $2.00, the effective price received by sellers would be $1.50. Whatever the market price, sellers will supply a quantity of ice cream as if the price were $0.50 lower than it is. Put differently, to induce sellers to supply any given quantity, the market price must now be $0.50 higher to compensate for the effect of the tax. Thus, as shown in Figure 6-7, the supply curve shifts *upward* from S_1 to S_2 by exactly the size of the tax ($0.50).

When the market moves from the old to the new equilibrium, the equilibrium price of ice cream rises from $3.00 to $3.30, and the equilibrium quantity falls from 100 to 90 cones. Once again, the tax reduces the size of the ice-cream market. And once again, buyers and sellers share the burden of the tax. Because the market price rises, buyers pay $0.30 more for each cone than they did before the tax was enacted. Sellers receive a higher price than they did without the tax, but the effective price (after paying the tax) falls from $3.00 to $2.80.

Comparing Figures 6-6 and 6-7 leads to a surprising conclusion: *Taxes on buyers and taxes on sellers are equivalent.* In both cases, the tax places a wedge between the price that buyers pay and the price that sellers receive. The wedge between

Figure 6-7

A TAX ON SELLERS. When a tax of $0.50 is levied on sellers, the supply curve shifts up by $0.50 from S_1 to S_2. The equilibrium quantity falls from 100 to 90 cones. The price that buyers pay rises from $3.00 to $3.30. The price that sellers receive (after paying the tax) falls from $3.00 to $2.80. Even though the tax is levied on sellers, buyers and sellers share the burden of the tax.

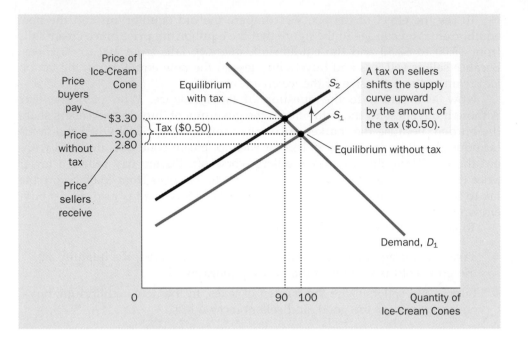

the buyers' price and the sellers' price is the same, regardless of whether the tax is levied on buyers or sellers. In either case, the wedge shifts the relative position of the supply and demand curves. In the new equilibrium, buyers and sellers share the burden of the tax. The only difference between taxes on buyers and taxes on sellers is who sends the money to the government.

The equivalence of these two taxes is perhaps easier to understand if we imagine that the government collects the $0.50 ice-cream tax in a bowl on the counter of each ice-cream store. When the government levies the tax on buyers, the buyer is required to place $0.50 in the bowl every time a cone is bought. When the government levies the tax on sellers, the seller is required to place $0.50 in the bowl after the sale of each cone. Whether the $0.50 goes directly from the buyer's pocket into the bowl, or indirectly from the buyer's pocket into the seller's hand and then into the bowl, does not matter. Once the market reaches its new equilibrium, buyers and sellers share the burden, regardless of how the tax is levied.

CASE STUDY   CAN CONGRESS DISTRIBUTE THE BURDEN OF A PAYROLL TAX?

If you have ever received a paycheck, you probably noticed that taxes were deducted from the amount you earned. One of these taxes is called FICA, an acronym for the Federal Insurance Contribution Act. The federal government uses the revenue from the FICA tax to pay for Social Security and Medicare, the income support and health care programs for the elderly. FICA is an example of a *payroll tax*, which is a tax on the wages that firms pay their workers. In 1995, the total FICA tax for the typical worker was 15.3 percent of earnings.

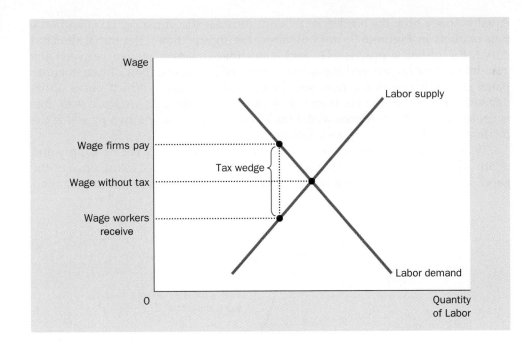

Figure 6-8

A PAYROLL TAX. A payroll tax places a wedge between the wage that workers receive and the wage that firms pay. Comparing wages with and without the tax, you can see that workers and firms share the tax burden. This division of the tax burden between workers and firms does not depend on whether the government levies the tax on workers, levies the tax on firms, or divides the tax equally between the two groups.

Who do you think bears the burden of this payroll tax—firms or workers? When Congress passed this legislation, it attempted to mandate a division of the tax burden. According to the law, half of the tax is paid by firms, and half is paid by workers. That is, half of the tax is paid out of firm revenue, and half is deducted from workers' paychecks. The amount that shows up as a deduction on your pay stub is the worker contribution.

Our analysis of tax incidence, however, shows that lawmakers cannot so easily distribute the burden of a tax. To illustrate, we can analyze a payroll tax as merely a tax on a good, where the good is labor and the price is the wage. The key feature of the payroll tax is that it places a wedge between the wage that firms pay and the wage that workers receive. Figure 6-8 shows the outcome. When a payroll tax is enacted, the wage received by workers falls, and the wage paid by firms rises. In the end, workers and firms share the burden of the tax, much as the legislation requires. Yet this division of the tax burden between workers and firms has nothing to do with the legislated division: The division of the burden in Figure 6-8 is not necessarily fifty-fifty, and the same outcome would prevail if the law levied the entire tax on workers or if it levied the entire tax on firms.

This example shows that the most basic lesson of tax incidence is often overlooked in public debate. Lawmakers can decide whether a tax comes from the buyer's pocket or from the seller's, but they cannot legislate the true burden of a tax. Rather, tax incidence depends on the forces of supply and demand.

ELASTICITY AND TAX INCIDENCE

When a good is taxed, buyers and sellers of the good share the burden of the tax. But how exactly is the tax burden divided? Only rarely will it be shared equally. To see how the burden is divided, consider the impact of taxation in the two markets in Figure 6-9. In both cases, the figure shows the initial demand curve, the initial supply curve, and a tax that drives a wedge between the amount paid by buyers and the amount received by sellers. (Not drawn in either panel of the figure is the new supply or demand curve. Which curve shifts depends on whether the tax is levied on buyers or sellers. As we have seen, this is irrelevant for the incidence of the tax.) The difference in the two panels is the relative elasticity of supply and demand.

Panel (a) of Figure 6-9 shows a tax in a market with very elastic supply and relatively inelastic demand. That is, sellers are very responsive to the price of the good, whereas buyers are not very responsive. When a tax is imposed on a mar-

Figure 6-9

How the Burden of a Tax Is Divided. In panel (a), the supply curve is elastic, and the demand curve is inelastic. In this case, the price received by sellers falls only slightly, while the price paid by buyers rises substantially. Thus, buyers bear most of the burden of the tax. In panel (b), the supply curve is inelastic, and the demand curve is elastic. In this case, the price received by sellers falls substantially, while the price paid by buyers rises only slightly. Thus, sellers bear most of the burden of the tax.

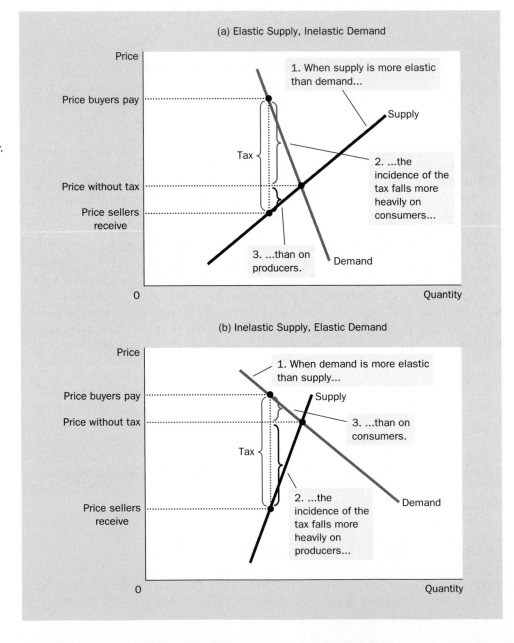

ket with these elasticities, the price received by sellers does not fall much, so sellers bear only a small burden. By contrast, the price paid by buyers rises substantially, indicating that buyers bear most of the burden of the tax.

Panel (b) of Figure 6-9 shows a tax in a market with relatively inelastic supply and very elastic demand. In this case, sellers are not very responsive to the price, while buyers are very responsive. The figure shows that when a tax is imposed, the price paid by buyers does not rise much, while the price received by sellers falls substantially. Thus, sellers bear most of the burden of the tax.

The two panels of Figure 6-9 show a general lesson about how the burden of a tax is divided: *A tax burden falls more heavily on the side of the market that is less elastic.* Why is this true? In essence, the elasticity measures the willingness of buyers or sellers to leave the market when conditions become unfavorable. A small elasticity of demand means that buyers do not have good alternatives to consuming this particular good. A small elasticity of supply means that sellers do not have good alternatives to producing this particular good. When the good is taxed, the side of the market with fewer good alternatives cannot easily leave the market and must, therefore, bear more of the burden of the tax.

CASE STUDY   WHO PAYS THE LUXURY TAX?

In 1990, Congress adopted a new luxury tax on items such as yachts, private airplanes, furs, jewelry, and expensive cars. The goal of the tax was to raise revenue from those who could most easily afford to pay. Because only the rich can afford to buy such extravagances, taxing luxuries seemed a logical way of taxing the rich.

Yet, when the forces of supply and demand took over, the outcome was quite different from what Congress intended. Consider, for example, the market for yachts. The demand for yachts is quite elastic. A millionaire can easily not buy a yacht; she can use the money to buy a bigger house, take a European vacation, or leave a larger bequest to her heirs. By contrast, the supply of yachts is relatively inelastic, at least in the short run. Yacht factories are not easily converted to alternative uses, and workers who build yachts are not eager to change careers in response to changing market conditions.

Our analysis makes a clear prediction in this case. With elastic demand and inelastic supply, the burden of a tax falls largely on the suppliers. That is, a tax on yachts places a burden largely on the firms and workers who build yachts because they end up getting a lower price for their product. The workers, however, are not wealthy. Thus, the burden of a luxury tax falls more on the middle class than on the rich.

"If this boat were any more expensive, we would be playing golf."

The mistaken assumptions about the incidence of the luxury tax quickly became apparent after the tax went into effect. Suppliers of luxuries made their congressional representatives well aware of the economic hardship they experienced, and Congress repealed most of the luxury tax in 1993.

> **QUICK QUIZ**   In a supply-and-demand diagram, show how a tax on car buyers of $1,000 per car affects the quantity of cars sold and the price of cars. In another diagram, show how a tax on car sellers of $1,000 per car affects the quantity of cars sold and the price of cars. In both of your diagrams, show the change in the price paid by car buyers and the change in price received by car sellers.

CONCLUSION

The economy is governed by two kinds of laws: the laws of supply and demand and the laws enacted by governments. In this chapter we have begun to see how these laws interact. Price controls and taxes are common in various markets in the economy, and their effects are frequently debated in the press and among policymakers. Even a little bit of economic knowledge can go a long way toward understanding and evaluating these policies.

In subsequent chapters we will analyze many government policies in greater detail. We will examine the effects of taxation more fully, and we will consider a broader range of policies than we considered here. Yet the basic lessons of this chapter will not change: When analyzing government policies, supply and demand are the first and most useful tools of analysis.

Summary

♦ A price ceiling is a legal maximum on the price of a good or service. An example is rent control. If the price ceiling is below the equilibrium price, the quantity demanded exceeds the quantity supplied. Because of the resulting shortage, sellers must in some way ration the good or service among buyers.

♦ A price floor is a legal minimum on the price of a good or service. An example is the minimum wage. If the price floor is above the equilibrium price, the quantity supplied exceeds the quantity demanded. Because of the resulting surplus, buyers' demands for the good or service must in some way be rationed among sellers.

♦ When the government levies a tax on a good, the equilibrium quantity of the good falls. That is, a tax on a market shrinks the size of the market.

♦ A tax on a good places a wedge between the price paid by buyers and the price received by sellers. When the market moves to the new equilibrium, buyers pay more for the good and sellers receive less for it. In this sense, buyers and sellers share the tax burden. The incidence of a tax does not depend on whether the tax is levied on buyers or sellers.

♦ The incidence of a tax depends on the price elasticities of supply and demand. The burden tends to fall on the side of the market that is less elastic because that side of the market can respond less easily to the tax by changing the quantity bought or sold.

Key Concepts

price ceiling, p. 112   price floor, p. 112   tax incidence, p. 121

Questions for Review

1. Give an example of a price ceiling and an example of a price floor.

2. Which causes a shortage of a good—a price ceiling or a price floor? Which causes a surplus?

3. Explain why economists usually oppose controls on prices.

4. What is the difference between a tax paid by buyers and a tax paid by sellers?

5. How does a tax on a good affect the price paid by buyers, the price received by sellers, and the quantity sold?

6. What determines how the burden of a tax is divided between buyers and sellers? Why?

Problems and Applications

1. Suppose the federal government requires beer drinkers to pay a $2 tax on each case of beer purchased. (In fact, both the federal and state governments impose beer taxes of some sort.)
   a. Draw a supply-and-demand diagram of the market for beer without the tax. Show the price paid by consumers, the price received by producers, and the quantity of beer sold. What is the difference between the price paid by consumers and the price received by producers?
   b. Now draw a supply-and-demand diagram for the beer market with the tax. Show the price paid by consumers, the price received by producers, and the quantity of beer sold. What is the difference between the price paid by consumers and the price received by producers? Has the quantity of beer sold increased or decreased?

2. The government has decided that the free-market price of cheese is too low.
   a. Suppose the government imposes a binding price floor in the cheese market. Use a supply-and-demand diagram to show the effect of this policy on the price of cheese and the quantity of cheese sold. Is there a shortage or surplus of cheese?
   b. Farmers complain that the price floor has reduced their total revenue. Is this possible? Explain.
   c. In response to farmers' complaints, the government agrees to purchase all of the surplus cheese at the price floor. Compared to the basic price floor, who benefits from this new policy? Who loses?

3. If the government places a $500 tax on luxury cars, will the price paid by consumers rise by more than $500, less than $500, or exactly $500? Explain.

4. A recent study found that the demand and supply schedules for frisbees are as follows:

Price per Frisbee	Quantity Demanded	Quantity Supplied
$11	1 million	15 million
10	2	12
9	4	9
8	6	6
7	8	3
6	10	1

   a. What are the equilibrium price and quantity of frisbees?

   b. Frisbee manufacturers persuade the government that frisbee production improves scientists' understanding of aerodynamics and thus is important for national security. A concerned Congress votes to impose a price floor $2 above the equilibrium price. What is the new market price? How many frisbees are sold?
   c. Irate college students march on Washington and demand a reduction in the price of frisbees. An even more concerned Congress votes to repeal the price floor and impose a price ceiling $1 below the former price floor. What is the new market price? How many frisbees are sold?

5. Congress and the president decide that the United States should reduce air pollution by reducing its use of gasoline. They impose a $0.50 tax for each gallon of gasoline sold.
   a. Should they impose this tax on producers or consumers? Explain carefully using a supply-and-demand diagram.
   b. If the demand for gasoline were more elastic, would this tax be more effective or less effective in reducing the quantity of gasoline consumed? Explain with both words and a diagram.
   c. Are consumers of gasoline helped or hurt by this tax? Why?
   d. Are workers in the oil industry helped or hurt by this tax? Why?

6. A case study in this chapter discusses the federal minimum-wage law.
   a. Suppose the minimum wage is above the equilibrium wage in the market for unskilled labor. Using a supply-and-demand diagram of the market for unskilled labor, show the market wage, the number of workers who are employed, and the number of workers who are unemployed. Also show the total wage payments to unskilled workers.
   b. Now suppose the secretary of labor proposes an increase in the minimum wage. What effect would this increase have on employment? Does the change in employment depend on the elasticity of demand, the elasticity of supply, both elasticities, or neither?
   c. What effect would this increase in the minimum wage have on unemployment? Does the change in unemployment depend on the elasticity of demand, the elasticity of supply, both elasticities, or neither?
   d. If the demand for unskilled labor were inelastic, would the proposed increase in the minimum wage

raise or lower total wage payments to unskilled workers? Would your answer change if the demand for unskilled labor were elastic?

7. Consider the following policies, each of which is aimed at reducing violent crime by reducing the use of guns. Illustrate each of these proposed policies in a supply-and-demand diagram of the gun market.
   a. a tax on gun buyers
   b. a tax on gun sellers
   c. a price floor on guns
   d. a tax on ammunition

8. The U.S. government administers two programs that affect the market for cigarettes. Media campaigns and labeling requirements are aimed at making the public aware of the dangers of cigarette smoking. At the same time, the Department of Agriculture maintains a price support program for tobacco farmers, which raises the price of tobacco above the equilibrium price.
   a. How do these two programs affect cigarette consumption? Use a graph of the cigarette market in your answer.
   b. What is the combined effect of these two programs on the price of cigarettes?
   c. Cigarettes are also heavily taxed. What effect does this tax have on cigarette consumption?

9. (This question requires the use of high school algebra.) The market for tickets to the symphony can be described by the following demand and supply curves:

$$Q^D = 20{,}000 - 90P \qquad Q^S = 10{,}000 + 110P$$

a. What are the equilibrium price and quantity in the ticket market?
b. Lovers of classical music persuade Congress to impose a price ceiling of $40 per ticket. How many tickets are now sold in the market? Does this policy get more or fewer people to attend classical music concerts?

10. (This question requires the use of high school algebra.) Suppose the demand curve for pizza can be represented by the equation $Q^D = 20 - 2P$, where Q^D is the quantity demanded and P is the price. The supply curve for pizza can be represented by the equation $Q^S = P - 1$, where Q^S is the quantity supplied. Suppose the government imposes a $3 tax per pizza. How much more will consumers now pay for a pizza? (Hint: The prices in the demand and supply equations are no longer equal. The price that determines quantity demanded now equals the price that determines quantity supplied plus $3.)

11. A subsidy is the opposite of a tax. With a $0.50 tax on the buyers of ice-cream cones, the government collects $0.50 for each cone purchased; with a $0.50 subsidy for the buyers of ice-cream cones, the government pays buyers $0.50 for each cone purchased.
   a. Show the effect of a $0.50 per cone subsidy on the demand curve for ice-cream cones, the effective price paid by consumers, the effective price received by sellers, and the quantity of cones sold.
   b. Do consumers gain or lose from this policy? Do producers gain or lose? Does the government gain or lose?

III

SUPPLY AND DEMAND II: MARKETS AND WELFARE

7

CONSUMERS, PRODUCERS, AND THE EFFICIENCY OF MARKETS

IN THIS CHAPTER YOU WILL

Examine the link between buyers' willingness to pay for a good and the demand curve

Learn how to define and measure consumer surplus

Examine the link between sellers' costs of producing a good and the supply curve

Learn how to define and measure producer surplus

See that the equilibrium of supply and demand maximizes total surplus in a market

When consumers go to grocery stores to buy their turkeys for Thanksgiving dinner, they may be disappointed that the price of turkey is as high as it is. At the same time, when farmers bring to market the turkeys they have raised, they wish the price of turkey were even higher. These views are not surprising: Buyers always want to pay less, and sellers always want to get paid more. But is there a "right price" for turkey from the standpoint of society as a whole?

In previous chapters we saw how, in market economies, the forces of supply and demand determine the prices of goods and services and the quantities sold. So far, however, we have described the way markets allocate scarce resources without directly addressing the question of whether these market allocations are desirable. In other words, our analysis has been *positive* (what is) rather than *normative* (what should be). We know that the price of turkey adjusts to ensure that the quantity of turkey supplied equals the quantity of turkey demanded. But, at this equilibrium, is the quantity of turkey produced and consumed too small, too large, or just right?

welfare economics
the study of how the allocation of resources affects economic well-being

In this chapter we take up the topic of **welfare economics,** the study of how the allocation of resources affects economic well-being. We begin by examining the benefits that buyers and sellers receive from taking part in a market. We then examine how society can make these benefits as large as possible. This analysis leads to a profound conclusion: The equilibrium of supply and demand in a market maximizes the total benefits received by buyers and sellers.

As you may recall from Chapter 1, one of the *Ten Principles of Economics* is that markets are usually a good way to organize economic activity. The study of welfare economics explains this principle more fully. It also answers our question about the right price of turkey: The price that balances the supply and demand for turkey is, in a particular sense, the best one because it maximizes the total welfare of turkey consumers and turkey producers.

CONSUMER SURPLUS

We begin our study of welfare economics by looking at the benefits buyers receive from participating in a market.

WILLINGNESS TO PAY

Imagine that you own a mint-condition recording of Elvis Presley's first album. Because you are not an Elvis Presley fan, you decide to sell it. One way to do so is to hold an auction.

Four Elvis fans show up for your auction: John, Paul, George, and Ringo. Each of them would like to own the album, but there is a limit to the amount that each is willing to pay for it. Table 7-1 shows the maximum price that each of the four possible buyers would pay. Each buyer's maximum is called his **willingness to pay,** and it measures how much that buyer values the good. Each buyer would be eager to buy the album at a price less than his willingness to pay, would refuse to buy the album at a price more than his willingness to pay, and would be indifferent about buying the album at a price exactly equal to his willingness to pay.

To sell your album, you begin the bidding at a low price, say $10. Because all four buyers are willing to pay much more, the price rises quickly. The bidding stops when John bids $80 (or slightly more). At this point, Paul, George,

willingness to pay
the maximum amount that a buyer will pay for a good

Table 7-1

FOUR POSSIBLE BUYERS'
WILLINGNESS TO PAY

BUYER	WILLINGNESS TO PAY
John	$100
Paul	80
George	70
Ringo	50

and Ringo have dropped out of the bidding, because they are unwilling to bid any more than $80. John pays you $80 and gets the album. Note that the album has gone to the buyer who values the album most highly.

What benefit does John receive from buying the Elvis Presley album? In a sense, John has found a real bargain: He is willing to pay $100 for the album but pays only $80 for it. We say that John receives *consumer surplus* of $20. **Consumer surplus** is the amount a buyer is willing to pay for a good minus the amount the buyer actually pays for it.

consumer surplus
a buyer's willingness to pay minus the amount the buyer actually pays

Consumer surplus measures the benefit to buyers of participating in a market. In this example, John receives a $20 benefit from participating in the auction because he pays only $80 for a good he values at $100. Paul, George, and Ringo get no consumer surplus from participating in the auction, because they left without the album and without paying anything.

Now consider a somewhat different example. Suppose that you had two identical Elvis Presley albums to sell. Again, you auction them off to the four possible buyers. To keep things simple, we assume that both albums are to be sold for the same price and that no buyer is interested in buying more than one album. Therefore, the price rises until two buyers are left.

In this case, the bidding stops when John and Paul bid $70 (or slightly higher). At this price, John and Paul are each happy to buy an album, and George and Ringo are not willing to bid any higher. John and Paul each receive consumer surplus equal to his willingness to pay minus the price. John's consumer surplus is $30, and Paul's is $10. John's consumer surplus is higher now than it was previously, because he gets the same album but pays less for it. The total consumer surplus in the market is $40.

USING THE DEMAND CURVE TO MEASURE CONSUMER SURPLUS

Consumer surplus is closely related to the demand curve for a product. To see how they are related, let's continue our example and consider the demand curve for this rare Elvis Presley album.

We begin by using the willingness to pay of the four possible buyers to find the demand schedule for the album. Table 7-2 shows the demand schedule that corresponds to Table 7-1. If the price is above $100, the quantity demanded in the market is 0, because no buyer is willing to pay that much. If the price is between $80 and $100, the quantity demanded is 1, because only John is willing to pay such a high price. If the price is between $70 and $80, the quantity

PRICE	BUYERS	QUANTITY DEMANDED
More than $100	None	0
$80 to $100	John	1
$70 to $80	John, Paul	2
$50 to $70	John, Paul, George	3
$50 or less	John, Paul, George, Ringo	4

Table 7-2

THE DEMAND SCHEDULE FOR THE BUYERS IN TABLE 7-1

Figure 7-1

THE DEMAND CURVE. This figure graphs the demand curve from the demand schedule in Table 7-2. Note that the height of the demand curve reflects buyers' willingness to pay.

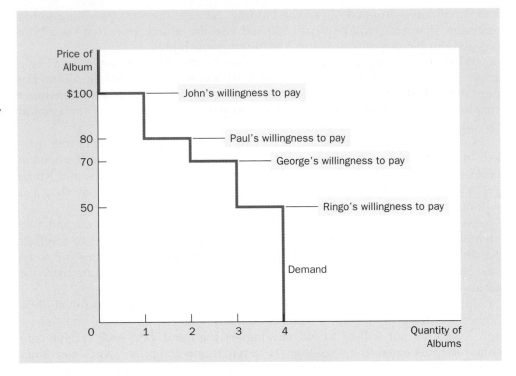

demanded is 2, because both John and Paul are willing to pay the price. We can continue this analysis for other prices as well. In this way, the demand schedule is derived from the willingness to pay of the four possible buyers.

Figure 7-1 graphs the demand curve that corresponds to this demand schedule. Note the relationship between the height of the demand curve and the buyers' willingness to pay. At any quantity, the price given by the demand curve shows the willingness to pay of the *marginal buyer*, the buyer who would leave the market first if the price were any higher. At a quantity of 4 albums, for instance, the demand curve has a height of $50, the price that Ringo (the marginal buyer) is willing to pay for an album. At a quantity of 3 albums, the demand curve has a height of $70, the price that George (who is now the marginal buyer) is willing to pay.

Because the demand curve reflects buyers' willingness to pay, we can also use it to measure consumer surplus. Figure 7-2 uses the demand curve to compute consumer surplus in our example. In panel (a), the price is $80 (or slightly above), and the quantity demanded is 1. Note that the area above the price and below the demand curve equals $20. This amount is exactly the consumer surplus we computed earlier when only 1 album is sold.

Panel (b) of Figure 7-2 shows consumer surplus when the price is $70 (or slightly above). In this case, the area above the price and below the demand curve equals the total area of the two rectangles: John's consumer surplus at this price is $30 and Paul's is $10. This area equals a total of $40. Once again, this amount is the consumer surplus we computed earlier.

The lesson from this example holds for all demand curves: *The area below the demand curve and above the price measures the consumer surplus in a market*. The reason is that the height of the demand curve measures the value buyers place on

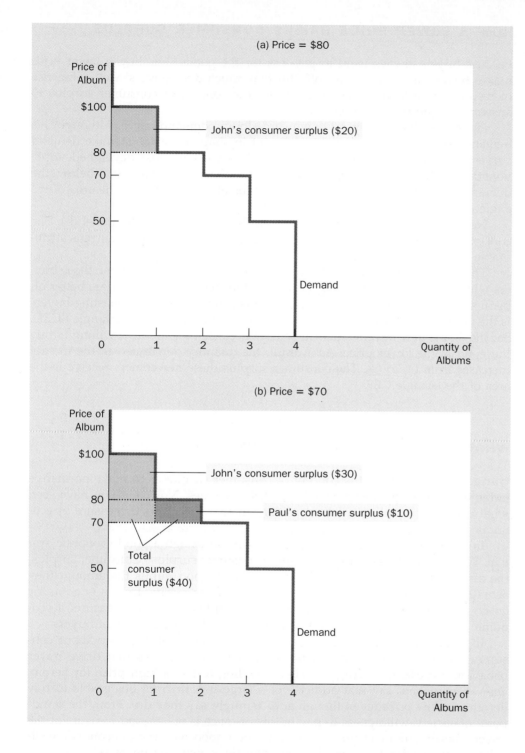

Figure 7-2

MEASURING CONSUMER
SURPLUS WITH THE DEMAND
CURVE. In panel (a), the price of
the good is $80, and the con-
sumer surplus is $20. In panel
(b), the price of the good is $70,
and the consumer surplus is $40.

the good, as measured by their willingness to pay for it. The difference between
this willingness to pay and the market price is each buyer's consumer surplus.
Thus, the total area below the demand curve and above the price is the sum of
the consumer surplus of all buyers in the market for a good or service.

HOW A LOWER PRICE RAISES CONSUMER SURPLUS

Because buyers always want to pay less for the goods they buy, a lower price makes buyers of a good better off. But how much does buyers' well-being rise in response to a lower price? We can use the concept of consumer surplus to answer this question precisely.

Figure 7-3 shows a typical downward-sloping demand curve. Although this demand curve appears somewhat different in shape from the steplike demand curves in our previous two figures, the ideas we have just developed apply nonetheless: Consumer surplus is the area above the price and below the demand curve. In panel (a), consumer surplus at a price of P_1 is the area of triangle ABC.

Now suppose that the price falls from P_1 to P_2, as shown in panel (b). The consumer surplus now equals area ADF. The increase in consumer surplus attributable to the lower price is the area BCFD.

This increase in consumer surplus is composed of two parts. First, those buyers who were already buying Q_1 of the good at the higher price P_1 are better off because they now pay less. The increase in consumer surplus of existing buyers is the reduction in the amount they pay; it equals the area of the rectangle BCED. Second, some new buyers enter the market because they are now willing to buy the good at the lower price. As a result, the quantity demanded in the market increases from Q_1 to Q_2. The consumer surplus these newcomers receive is the area of the triangle CEF.

WHAT DOES CONSUMER SURPLUS MEASURE?

Our goal in developing the concept of consumer surplus is to make normative judgments about the desirability of market outcomes. Now that you have seen what consumer surplus is, let's consider whether it is a good measure of economic well-being.

Imagine that you are a policymaker trying to design a good economic system. Would you care about the amount of consumer surplus? Consumer surplus, the amount that buyers are willing to pay for a good minus the amount they actually pay for it, measures the benefit that buyers receive from a good *as the buyers themselves perceive it*. Thus, consumer surplus is a good measure of economic well-being if policymakers want to respect the preferences of buyers.

In some circumstances, policymakers might choose not to care about consumer surplus because they do not respect the preferences that drive buyer behavior. For example, drug addicts are willing to pay a high price for heroin. Yet we would not say that addicts get a large benefit from being able to buy heroin at a low price (even though addicts might say they do). From the standpoint of society, willingness to pay in this instance is not a good measure of the buyers' benefit, and consumer surplus is not a good measure of economic well-being, because addicts are not looking after their own best interests.

In most markets, however, consumer surplus does reflect economic well-being. Economists normally presume that buyers are rational when they make decisions and that their preferences should be respected. In this case, consumers are the best judges of how much benefit they receive from the goods they buy.

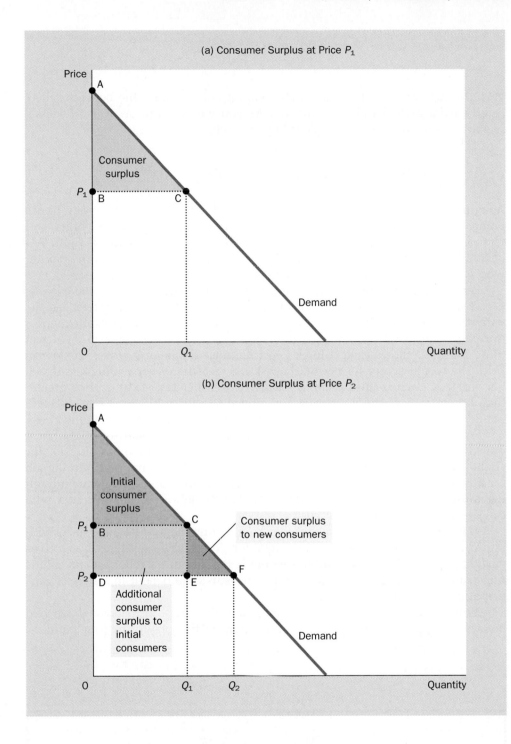

Figure 7-3

HOW THE PRICE AFFECTS CONSUMER SURPLUS. In panel (a), the price is P_1, the quantity demanded is Q_1, and consumer surplus equals the area of the triangle ABC. When the price falls from P_1 to P_2, as in panel (b), the quantity demanded rises from Q_1 to Q_2, and the consumer surplus rises to the area of the triangle ADF. The increase in consumer surplus (area BCFD) occurs in part because existing consumers now pay less (area BCED) and in part because new consumers enter the market at the lower price (area CEF).

QUICK QUIZ Draw a demand curve for turkey. In your diagram, show a price of turkey and the consumer surplus that results from that price. Explain in words what this consumer surplus measures.

PRODUCER SURPLUS

We now turn to the other side of the market and consider the benefits sellers receive from participating in a market. As you will see, our analysis of sellers' welfare is similar to our analysis of buyers' welfare.

COST AND THE WILLINGNESS TO SELL

Imagine now that you are a homeowner, and you need to get your house painted. You turn to four sellers of painting services: Mary, Louise, Georgia, and Grandma. Each painter is willing to do the work for you if the price is right. You decide to take bids from the four painters and auction off the job to the painter who will do the work for the lowest price.

cost

the value of everything a seller must give up to produce a good

Each painter is willing to take the job if the price she would receive exceeds her cost of doing the work. Here the term **cost** should be interpreted as the painters' opportunity cost: It includes both the painters' out-of-pocket expenses (for paint, brushes, and so on) and the value that the painters place on their own time. Table 7-3 shows each painter's cost. Because a painter's cost is the lowest price she would accept for her work, cost is a measure of her willingness to sell her services. Each painter would be eager to sell her service at a price greater than her cost, would refuse to sell her service at a price less than her cost, and would be indifferent about selling her service at a price exactly equal to her cost.

When you take bids from the painters, the price might start off high, but it quickly falls as the painters compete for the job. Once Grandma has bid $600 (or slightly less), she is the sole remaining bidder. Grandma is happy to do the job for this price, because her cost is only $500. Mary, Louise, and Georgia are unwilling to do the job for less than $600. Note that the job goes to the painter who can do the work at the lowest cost.

producer surplus

the amount a seller is paid for a good minus the seller's cost

What benefit does Grandma receive from getting the job? Because she is willing to do the work for $500 but gets $600 for doing it, we say that she receives *producer surplus* of $100. **Producer surplus** is the amount a seller is paid minus the cost of production. Producer surplus measures the benefit to sellers of participating in a market.

Now consider a somewhat different example. Suppose that you have two houses that need painting. Again, you auction off the jobs to the four painters.

Table 7-3

THE COSTS OF FOUR POSSIBLE SELLERS

SELLER	COST
Mary	$900
Louise	800
Georgia	600
Grandma	500

To keep things simple, let's assume that no painter is able to paint both houses and that you will pay the same amount to paint each house. Therefore, the price falls until two painters are left.

In this case, the bidding stops when Georgia and Grandma each offer to do the job for a price of $800 (or slightly less). At this price, Georgia and Grandma are willing to do the work, and Mary and Louise are not willing to bid a lower price. At a price of $800, Grandma receives producer surplus of $300, and Georgia receives producer surplus of $200. The total producer surplus in the market is $500.

USING THE SUPPLY CURVE TO MEASURE PRODUCER SURPLUS

Just as consumer surplus is closely related to the demand curve, producer surplus is closely related to the supply curve. To see how, let's continue our example.

We begin by using the costs of the four painters to find the supply schedule for painting services. Table 7-4 shows the supply schedule that corresponds to the costs in Table 7-3. If the price is below $500, none of the four painters is willing to do the job, so the quantity supplied is 0. If the price is between $500 and $600, only Grandma is willing to do the job, so the quantity supplied is 1. If the price is between $600 and $800, Grandma and Georgia are willing to do the job, so the quantity supplied is 2, and so on. Thus, the supply schedule is derived from the costs of the four painters.

Figure 7-4 graphs the supply curve that corresponds to this supply schedule. Note that the height of the supply curve is related to the sellers' costs. At any quantity, the price given by the supply curve shows the cost of the *marginal seller*, the seller who would leave the market first if the price were any lower. At a quantity of 4 houses, for instance, the supply curve has a height of $900, the cost that Mary (the marginal seller) incurs to provide her painting services. At a quantity of 3 houses, the supply curve has a height of $800, the cost that Louise (who is now the marginal seller) incurs.

Because the supply curve reflects sellers' costs, we can use it to measure producer surplus. Figure 7-5 uses the supply curve to compute producer surplus in our example. In panel (a), we assume that the price is $600. In this case, the quantity supplied is 1. Note that the area below the price and above the supply curve equals $100. This amount is exactly the producer surplus we computed earlier for Grandma.

Table 7-4

THE SUPPLY SCHEDULE FOR THE SELLERS IN TABLE 7-3

PRICE	SELLERS	QUANTITY SUPPLIED
$900 or more	Mary, Louise, Georgia, Grandma	4
$800 to $900	Louise, Georgia, Grandma	3
$600 to $800	Georgia, Grandma	2
$500 to $600	Grandma	1
Less than $500	None	0

Figure 7-4

THE SUPPLY CURVE. This figure graphs the supply curve from the supply schedule in Table 7-4. Note that the height of the supply curve reflects sellers' costs.

Figure 7-5

MEASURING PRODUCER SURPLUS WITH THE SUPPLY CURVE. In panel (a), the price of the good is $600, and the producer surplus is $100. In panel (b), the price of the good is $800, and the producer surplus is $500.

Panel (b) of Figure 7-5 shows producer surplus at a price of $800. In this case, the area below the price and above the supply curve equals the total area of the two rectangles. This area equals $500, the producer surplus we computed earlier for Georgia and Grandma when two houses needed painting.

The lesson from this example applies to all supply curves: *The area below the price and above the supply curve measures the producer surplus in a market.* The logic is straightforward: The height of the supply curve measures sellers' costs, and the difference between the price and the cost of production is each seller's producer surplus. Thus, the total area is the sum of the producer surplus of all sellers.

HOW A HIGHER PRICE RAISES PRODUCER SURPLUS

You will not be surprised to hear that sellers always want to receive a higher price for the goods they sell. But how much does sellers' well-being rise in response to a higher price? The concept of producer surplus offers a precise answer to this question.

Figure 7-6 shows a typical upward-sloping supply curve. Even though this supply curve differs in shape from the steplike supply curves in the previous figure, we measure producer surplus in the same way: Producer surplus is the area below the price and above the supply curve. In panel (a), the price is P_1, and producer surplus is the area of triangle ABC.

Panel (b) shows what happens when the price rises from P_1 to P_2. Producer surplus now equals area ADF. This increase in producer surplus has two parts. First, those sellers who were already selling Q_1 of the good at the lower price P_1

HOW THE PRICE AFFECTS PRODUCER SURPLUS. In panel (a), the price is P_1, the quantity demanded is Q_1, and producer surplus equals the area of the triangle ABC. When the price rises from P_1 to P_2, as in panel (b), the quantity supplied rises from Q_1 to Q_2, and the producer surplus rises to the area of the triangle ADF. The increase in producer surplus (area BCFD) occurs in part because existing producers now receive more (area BCED) and in part because new producers enter the market at the higher price (area CEF).

Figure 7-6

are better off because they now get more for what they sell. The increase in producer surplus for existing sellers equals the area of the rectangle BCED. Second, some new sellers enter the market because they are now willing to produce the good at the higher price, resulting in an increase in the quantity supplied from Q_1 to Q_2. The producer surplus of these newcomers is the area of the triangle CEF.

As this analysis shows, we use producer surplus to measure the well-being of sellers in much the same way as we use consumer surplus to measure the well-being of buyers. Because these two measures of economic welfare are so similar, it is natural to use them together. And, indeed, that is exactly what we do in the next section.

QUICK QUIZ   Draw a supply curve for turkey. In your diagram, show a price of turkey and the producer surplus that results from that price. Explain in words what this producer surplus measures.

MARKET EFFICIENCY

Consumer surplus and producer surplus are the basic tools that economists use to study the welfare of buyers and sellers in a market. These tools can help us address a fundamental economic question: Is the allocation of resources determined by free markets in any way desirable?

THE BENEVOLENT SOCIAL PLANNER

To evaluate market outcomes, we introduce into our analysis a new, hypothetical character, called the benevolent social planner. The benevolent social planner is an all-knowing, all-powerful, well-intentioned dictator. The planner wants to maximize the economic well-being of everyone in society. What do you suppose this planner should do? Should he just leave buyers and sellers at the equilibrium that they reach naturally on their own? Or can he increase economic well-being by altering the market outcome in some way?

To answer this question, the planner must first decide how to measure the economic well-being of a society. One possible measure is the sum of consumer and producer surplus, which we call *total surplus.* Consumer surplus is the benefit that buyers receive from participating in a market, and producer surplus is the benefit that sellers receive. It is therefore natural to use total surplus as a measure of society's economic well-being.

To better understand this measure of economic well-being, recall how we measure consumer and producer surplus. We define consumer surplus as

Consumer surplus = Value to buyers − Amount paid by buyers.

Similarly, we define producer surplus as

Producer surplus = Amount received by sellers − Costs of sellers.

FYI

The Invisible Hand of the Marketplace

THE EFFICIENCY OF FREE MARkets is, at first, a surprising idea. After all, no one is looking out for the general economic welfare. Free markets contain many buyers and sellers, and all of them are interested primarily in their own well-being. Yet, despite decentralized decisionmaking and self-interested decisionmakers, the result is not chaos but efficiency.

The virtue of free markets was well understood by the great economist Adam Smith. Here is what he wrote in his 1776 classic, *An Inquiry into the Nature and Causes of the Wealth of Nations*:

> Man has almost constant occasion for the help of his brethren, and it is vain for him to expect it from their benevolence only. He will be more likely to prevail if he can interest their self-love in his favor, and show them that it is for their own advantage to do for him what he requires of them. . . . It is not from the benevolence of the butcher, the brewer, or the baker that we expect our dinner, but from their regard to their own interest. . . .
>
> Every individual . . . neither intends to promote the public interest, nor knows how much he is promoting it. . . . He intends only his own gain, and he is in this, as in many other cases, led by an invisible hand to promote an end which was no part of his intention. Nor is it always the worse for the society that it was no part of it. By pursuing his own interest he frequently promotes that of the society more effectually than when he really intends to promote it.

ADAM SMITH

Smith is saying that participants in the economy are motivated by self-interest and that the "invisible hand" of the marketplace guides this self-interest into promoting general economic well-being.

Smith's insights remain true today. Indeed, our analysis in this chapter allows us to express Smith's view more precisely by showing that the equilibrium of supply and demand maximizes the sum of consumer and producer surplus.

When we add consumer and producer surplus together, we obtain

Total surplus = Value to buyers − Amount paid by buyers
+ Amount received by sellers − Costs of sellers.

The amount paid by buyers equals the amount received by sellers, so the middle two terms in this expression cancel each other. As a result, we can write total surplus as

Total surplus = Value to buyers − Costs of sellers.

Total surplus in a market is the total value to buyers of the goods, as measured by their willingness to pay, minus the costs to sellers of providing those goods. If an allocation of resources maximizes total surplus, we say that the allocation exhibits **efficiency.** If an allocation is not efficient, then some of the gains from trade among buyers and sellers are not being realized. For example, an allocation is inefficient if a good is not being produced by the sellers with lowest cost. In this case, moving production from a high-cost producer to a low-cost producer will lower the total costs of sellers and raise total surplus. Similarly, an allocation is inefficient if a good is not being consumed by the buyers who value

efficiency

the property of a resource allocation of maximizing the total surplus received by all members of society it most highly. In this case, moving consumption of the good from a buyer with a low valuation to a buyer with a high valuation will raise total surplus.

equity

the fairness of the distribution of well-being among the members of society

In addition to efficiency, the social planner might also care about **equity**—the fairness of the distribution of well-being among the various buyers and sellers. In essence, the gains from trade in a market are like a pie to be distributed among the market participants. The question of efficiency is whether the pie is as big as possible. The question of equity is whether the pie is divided fairly. Evaluating the equity of a market outcome is more difficult than evaluating the efficiency. Whereas efficiency is an objective goal that can be judged on strictly positive grounds, equity involves normative judgments that go beyond economics and enter into the realm of political philosophy.

In this chapter we concentrate on efficiency as the social planner's goal. Keep in mind, however, that real policymakers often care about equity as well. That is, they care about both the size of the economic pie and how the pie gets sliced and distributed among members of society.

EVALUATING THE MARKET EQUILIBRIUM

Figure 7-7 shows consumer and producer surplus when a market reaches the equilibrium of supply and demand. Recall that consumer surplus equals the area above the price and under the demand curve and producer surplus equals the area below the price and above the supply curve. Thus, the total area between the supply and demand curves up to the point of equilibrium represents the total surplus from this market.

Is this equilibrium allocation of resources efficient? Does it maximize total surplus? To answer these questions, keep in mind that when a market is in equi

---

Figure 7-7

CONSUMER AND PRODUCER SURPLUS IN THE MARKET EQUILIBRIUM. Total surplus—the sum of consumer and producer surplus—is the area between the supply and demand curves up to the equilibrium quantity.

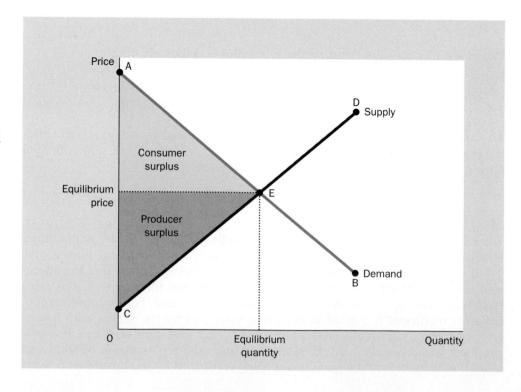

librium, the price determines which buyers and sellers participate in the market. Those buyers who value the good more than the price (represented by the segment AE on the demand curve) choose to buy the good; those buyers who value it less than the price (represented by the segment EB) do not. Similarly, those sellers whose costs are less than the price (represented by the segment CE on the supply curve) choose to produce and sell the good; those sellers whose costs are greater than the price (represented by the segment ED) do not.

These observations lead to two insights about market outcomes:

1. Free markets allocate the supply of goods to the buyers who value them most highly, as measured by their willingness to pay.

2. Free markets allocate the demand for goods to the sellers who can produce them at least cost.

Thus, given the quantity produced and sold in a market equilibrium, the social planner cannot increase economic well-being by changing the allocation of consumption among buyers or the allocation of production among sellers.

But can the social planner raise total economic well-being by increasing or decreasing the quantity of the good? The answer is no, as stated in this third insight about market outcomes:

3. Free markets produce the quantity of goods that maximizes the sum of consumer and producer surplus.

To see why this is true, consider Figure 7-8. Recall that the demand curve reflects the value to buyers and that the supply curve reflects the cost to sellers. At

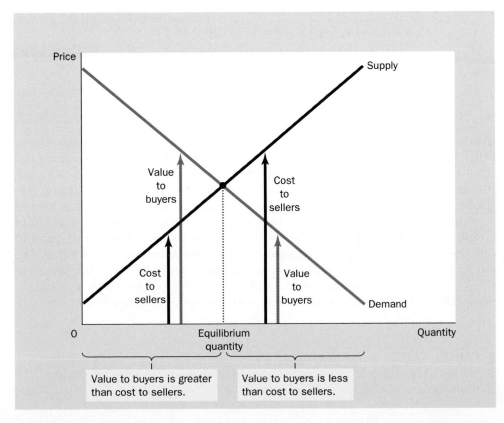

Figure 7-8

THE EFFICIENCY OF THE EQUILIBRIUM QUANTITY. At quantities less than the equilibrium quantity, the value to buyers exceeds the cost to sellers. At quantities greater than the equilibrium quantity, the cost to sellers exceeds the value to buyers. Therefore, the market equilibrium maximizes the sum of producer and consumer surplus.

IN THE NEWS

Ticket Scalping

IF AN ECONOMY IS TO ALLOCATE ITS scarce resources efficiently, goods must get to those consumers who value them most highly. Ticket scalping is one example of how markets reach efficient outcomes. Scalpers buy tickets to plays, concerts, and sports events and then sell the tickets at a price above their original cost. By charging the highest price the market will bear, scalpers help ensure that consumers with the greatest willingness to pay for the tickets actually do get them. As the following article describes, however, there is some debate over whether this market activity should be legal.

Tickets? Supply Meets Demand on Sidewalk

BY JOHN TIERNEY

Ticket scalping has been very good to Kevin Thomas, and he makes no apologies. He sees himself as a classic American entrepreneur: a high school dropout from the Bronx who taught himself a trade, works seven nights a week, earns $40,000 a year, and at age twenty-six has $75,000 in savings, all by providing a public service outside New York's theaters and sports arenas.

He has just one complaint. "I've been busted about 30 times in the last year," he said one recent evening, just after making $280 at a Knicks game. "You learn to deal with it—I give the cops a fake name, and I pay the fines when I have to, but I don't think it's fair. I look at scalping like working as a stockbroker, buying low and selling high. If people are willing to pay me the money, what kind of problem is that?"

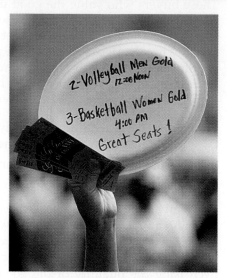

THE INVISIBLE HAND AT WORK DURING THE 1996 OLYMPICS

It is a significant problem to public officials in New York and New Jersey, who are cracking down on street scalpers like Mr. Thomas and on licensed ticket brokers. Undercover officers are enforcing new restrictions on reselling tickets

quantities below the equilibrium level, the value to buyers exceeds the cost to sellers. In this region, increasing the quantity raises total surplus, and it continues to do so until the quantity reaches the equilibrium level. Beyond the equilibrium quantity, however, the value to buyers is less than the cost to sellers. Producing more than the equilibrium quantity would, therefore, lower total surplus.

These three insights about market outcomes tell us that the equilibrium of supply and demand maximizes the sum of consumer and producer surplus. In other words, the equilibrium outcome is an efficient allocation of resources. The job of the benevolent social planner is, therefore, very easy: He can leave the market outcome just as he finds it. This conclusion explains why economists often advocate free markets as the best way to organize economic activity.

QUICK QUIZ   Draw the supply and demand for turkey. In the equilibrium, show producer and consumer surplus. Explain why producing more turkey would lower total surplus.

at marked-up prices, and the attorneys general of the two states are pressing well-publicized cases against more than a dozen ticket brokers.

But economists tend to see scalping from Mr. Thomas's perspective. To them, the governments' crusade makes about as much sense as the old campaigns by Communist authorities against "profiteering." Economists argue that the restrictions inconvenience the public, reduce the audience for cultural and sports events, waste the police's time, deprive New York City of tens of millions of dollars of tax revenue, and actually drive up the cost of many tickets.

"It is always good politics to pose as defender of the poor by declaring high prices illegal," says William J. Baumol, the director of the C. V. Starr Center for Applied Economics at New York University. "I expect politicians to try to solve the AIDS crisis by declaring AIDS illegal as well. That would be harmless, because nothing would happen, but when you outlaw high prices you create real problems."

Dr. Baumol was one of the economists who came up with the idea of selling same-day Broadway tickets for half price at the TKTS booth in Times Square, which theater owners thought dangerously radical when the booth opened in 1973. But the owners have profited by finding a new clientele for tickets that would have gone unsold, an illustration of the free-market tenet that both buyers and sellers ultimately benefit when price is adjusted to meet demand.

Economists see another illustration of that lesson at the Museum of Modern Art, where people wait in line for up to two hours to buy tickets for the Matisse exhibit. But there is an alternative on the sidewalk: Scalpers who evade the police have been selling the $12.50 tickets to the show at prices ranging from $20 to $50.

"You don't have to put a very high value on your time to pay $10 or $15 to avoid standing in line for two hours for a Matisse ticket," said Richard H. Thaler, an economist at Cornell University. "Some people think it's fairer to make everyone stand in line, but that forces everyone to engage in a totally unproductive activity, and it discriminates in favor of people who have the most free time. Scalping gives other people a chance, too. I can see no justification for outlawing it.". . .

Politicians commonly argue that without anti-scalping laws, tickets would become unaffordable to most people, but California has no laws against scalping, and ticket prices there are not notoriously high. And as much as scalpers would like to inflate prices, only a limited number of people are willing to pay $100 for a ticket. . . .

Legalizing scalping, however, would not necessarily be good news for everyone. Mr. Thomas, for instance, fears that the extra competition might put him out of business. But after 16 years—he started at age ten outside of Yankee Stadium—he is thinking it might be time for a change anyway.

SOURCE: *The New York Times*, December 26, 1992, p. A1.

CORPORATE LEADERS GATHER IN A FIELD OUTSIDE DARIEN, CONNECTICUT, WHERE ONE OF THEM CLAIMS TO HAVE SEEN THE INVISIBLE HAND OF THE MARKETPLACE.

CONCLUSION: MARKET EFFICIENCY AND MARKET FAILURE

This chapter introduced the basic tools of welfare economics—consumer and producer surplus—and used them to evaluate the efficiency of free markets. We showed that the forces of supply and demand allocate resources efficiently. That is, even though each buyer and seller in a market is concerned only about his or her own welfare, they are together led by an invisible hand to an equilibrium that maximizes the total benefits to buyers and sellers.

A word of warning is in order. To conclude that markets are efficient, we made several assumptions about how markets work. When these assumptions do not hold, our conclusion that the market equilibrium is efficient may no longer be true. As we close this chapter, let's consider briefly two of the most important of these assumptions.

First, our analysis assumed that markets are perfectly competitive. In the world, however, competition is sometimes far from perfect. In some markets, a single buyer or seller (or a small group of them) may be able to control market prices. This ability to influence prices is called *market power*. Market power can cause markets to be inefficient because it keeps the price and quantity away from the equilibrium of supply and demand.

Second, our analysis assumed that the outcome in a market matters only to the buyers and sellers in that market. Yet, in the world, the decisions of buyers and sellers sometimes affect people who are not participants in the market at all. Pollution is the classic example of a market outcome that affects people not in the market. Such side effects, called *externalities*, cause welfare in a market to depend on more than just the value to the buyers and the costs of the sellers. Because buyers and sellers do not take these side effects into account when deciding how much to consume and produce, the equilibrium in a market can be inefficient from the standpoint of society as a whole.

Market power and externalities are examples of a general phenomenon called *market failure*—the inability of some unregulated markets to allocate resources efficiently. When markets fail, public policy can potentially remedy the problem and increase economic efficiency. Microeconomists devote much effort to studying when market failure is likely and what sorts of policies are best at correcting market failures. As you continue your study of economics, you will see that the tools of welfare economics developed here are readily adapted to that endeavor.

Despite the possibility of market failure, the invisible hand of the marketplace is extraordinarily important. In many markets, the assumptions we made in this chapter work well, and the conclusion of market efficiency applies directly. Moreover, our analysis of welfare economics and market efficiency can be used to shed light on the effects of various government policies. In the next two chapters we apply the tools we have just developed to study two important policy issues—the welfare effects of taxation and of international trade.

Summary

◆ Consumer surplus equals buyers' willingness to pay for a good minus the amount they actually pay for it, and it measures the benefit buyers get from participating in a market. Consumer surplus can be computed by finding the area below the demand curve and above the price.

◆ Producer surplus equals the amount sellers receive for their goods minus their costs of production, and it measures the benefit sellers get from participating in a market. Producer surplus can be computed by finding the area below the price and above the supply curve.

◆ An allocation of resources that maximizes the sum of consumer and producer surplus is said to be efficient.

Policymakers are often concerned with the efficiency, as well as the equity, of economic outcomes.

◆ The equilibrium of supply and demand maximizes the sum of consumer and producer surplus. That is, the invisible hand of the marketplace leads buyers and sellers to allocate resources efficiently.

◆ Markets do not allocate resources efficiently in the presence of market failures such as market power or externalities.

Key Concepts

welfare economics, p. 134
willingness to pay, p. 134
consumer surplus, p. 135

cost, p. 140
producer surplus, p. 140

efficiency, p. 145
equity, p. 146

Questions for Review

1. Explain how buyers' willingness to pay, consumer surplus, and the demand curve are related.

2. Explain how sellers' costs, producer surplus, and the supply curve are related.

3. In a supply-and-demand diagram, show producer and consumer surplus in the market equilibrium.

4. What is efficiency? Is it the only goal of economic policymakers?

5. What does the invisible hand do?

6. Name two types of market failure. Explain why each may cause market outcomes to be inefficient.

Problems and Applications

1. An early freeze in California sours the lemon crop. What happens to consumer surplus in the market for lemons? What happens to consumer surplus in the market for lemonade? Illustrate your answers with diagrams.

2. Suppose the demand for French bread rises. What happens to producer surplus in the market for French bread? What happens to producer surplus in the market for flour? Illustrate your answer with diagrams.

3. It is a hot day, and Bert is very thirsty. Here is the value he places on a bottle of water:

Value of first bottle	$7
Value of second bottle	5
Value of third bottle	3
Value of fourth bottle	1

a. From this information, derive Bert's demand schedule. Graph his demand curve for bottled water.

b. If the price of a bottle of water is $4, how many bottles does Bert buy? How much consumer surplus does Bert get from his purchases? Show Bert's consumer surplus in your graph.

c. If the price falls to $2, how does quantity demanded change? How does Bert's consumer surplus change? Show these changes in your graph.

4. Ernie owns a water pump. Because pumping large amounts of water is harder than pumping small amounts, the cost of producing a bottle of water rises as he pumps more. Here is the cost he incurs to produce each bottle of water:

Cost of first bottle	$1
Cost of second bottle	3
Cost of third bottle	5
Cost of fourth bottle	7

   a. From this information, derive Ernie's supply schedule. Graph his supply curve for bottled water.
   b. If the price of a bottle of water is $4, how many bottles does Ernie produce and sell? How much producer surplus does Ernie get from these sales? Show Ernie's producer surplus in your graph.
   c. If the price rises to $6, how does quantity supplied change? How does Ernie's producer surplus change? Show these changes in your graph.

5. Consider a market in which Bert from Problem 3 is the buyer and Ernie from Problem 4 is the seller.
   a. Use Ernie's supply schedule and Bert's demand schedule to find the quantity supplied and quantity demanded at prices of $2, $4, and $6. Which of these prices brings supply and demand into equilibrium?
   b. What are consumer surplus, producer surplus, and total surplus in this equilibrium?
   c. If Ernie produced and Bert consumed one fewer bottle of water, what would happen to total surplus?
   d. If Ernie produced and Bert consumed one additional bottle of water, what would happen to total surplus?

6. The cost of producing computers has fallen substantially over the past decade. This question considers some implications of this fact.
   a. Use a supply-and-demand diagram to show the effect of falling production costs on the price and quantity of computers sold.
   b. In your diagram, show what happens to consumer surplus and producer surplus.
   c. Suppose the supply of computers is very elastic. Who benefits most from falling production costs—consumers or producers of computers?

7. There are four consumers willing to pay the following amounts for haircuts:

   Phil: $7   Oprah: $2   Sally Jessie: $8   Geraldo: $5

There are four haircutting businesses with the following costs:

   Firm A: $3   Firm B: $6   Firm C: $4   Firm D: $2

Each firm has the capacity to produce only one haircut.
   a. For efficiency, how many haircuts should be given? Which businesses should cut hair, and which consumers should have their hair cut? How large is the maximum possible total surplus?
   b. Suppose that firms A, C, and D are cutting hair, and that Phil, Oprah, and Geraldo are getting their hair cut. How might the allocation of haircuts be changed to increase total surplus?

8. A benevolent social planner discovers a market in which supply and demand are determining equilibrium price and quantity. On a diagram of this market, indicate the reduction in total surplus that would occur if the planner decided to reduce production of the good. Explain in words. On another diagram, indicate the reduction in total surplus that would occur if the planner decided to increase production of the good. Explain.

9. Consider how health insurance affects the quantity of health care services performed. Suppose that the typical medical procedure has a cost of $100, yet a person with health insurance pays only $20 out-of-pocket when she chooses to have an additional procedure performed. Her insurance company pays the remaining $80. (The insurance company will recoup the $80 through higher premiums for everybody, but the share paid by this individual is small.)
   a. Draw the demand curve in the market for medical care. (In your diagram, the horizontal axis should represent the number of medical procedures.) Show the quantity of procedures demanded if each procedure has a price of $100.
   b. On your diagram, show the quantity of procedures demanded if consumers pay only $20 per procedure. If the cost of each procedure to society is truly $100, and if individuals have health insurance as just described, will the number of procedures performed maximize total surplus? Explain.
   c. Economists often blame the health insurance system for excessive use of medical care. Given your analysis, why might the use of care be viewed as "excessive"?
   d. What sort of policies might prevent this excessive use?

10. Many parts of California experienced a severe drought in the late 1980s and early 1990s.
   a. Use a diagram of the water market to show the effects of the drought on the equilibrium price and quantity of water.

b. Many communities did not allow the price of water to change, however. What is the effect of this policy on the water market? Show on your diagram any surplus or shortage that arises.

c. A 1991 op-ed piece in *The Wall Street Journal* stated that "all Los Angeles residents are required to cut their water usage by 10 percent as of March 1 and another 5 percent starting May 1, based on their 1986 consumption levels." The author criticized this policy on both efficiency and equity grounds, saying "not only does such a policy reward families who 'wasted' more water back in 1986, it does little to encourage consumers who could make more drastic reductions, [and] . . . punishes consumers who cannot so readily reduce their water use." In what way is the Los Angeles system for allocating water inefficient? In what way does the system seem unfair?

d. Suppose instead that Los Angeles allowed the price of water to increase until the quantity demanded equaled the quantity supplied. Would the resulting allocation of water be more efficient? In your view, would it be more or less fair than the proportionate reductions in water use mentioned in the newspaper article? What could be done to make the market solution more fair?

11. What is the key assumption that justifies economists' use of consumer surplus as a measure of economic well-being? How might the existence of advertising affect our confidence in this assumption?

8

APPLICATION: THE COSTS
OF TAXATION

**IN THIS CHAPTER
YOU WILL**

*Examine how taxes
reduce consumer and
producer surplus*

*Learn the meaning and
causes of the deadweight
loss of a tax*

*Consider why some taxes
have larger deadweight
losses than others*

*Examine how tax revenue
and deadweight loss vary
with the size of a tax*

Taxes are often a source of heated political debate. In 1776 the anger of the American colonies over British taxes sparked the American Revolution. More than two centuries later Ronald Reagan was elected president on a platform of large cuts in personal income taxes, and during his eight years in the White House the top tax rate on income fell from 70 percent to 28 percent. In 1992 Bill Clinton was elected in part because incumbent George Bush had broken his 1988 campaign promise, "Read my lips: no new taxes."

We began our study of taxes in Chapter 6. There we saw how a tax on a good affects its price and the quantity sold and how the forces of supply and demand divide the burden of a tax between buyers and sellers. In this chapter we extend this analysis and look at how taxes affect welfare, the economic well-being of participants in a market.

The effects of taxes on welfare might at first seem obvious. The government enacts taxes to raise revenue, and that revenue must come out of someone's pocket. As we saw in Chapter 6, both buyers and sellers are worse off when a good is taxed: A tax raises the price buyers pay and lowers the price sellers receive. Yet to understand fully how taxes affect economic well-being, we must compare the reduced welfare of buyers and sellers to the amount of revenue the government raises. The tools of consumer and producer surplus allow us to make this comparison. The analysis will show that the costs of taxes to buyers and sellers exceeds the revenue raised by the government.

"You know, the idea of taxation with representation doesn't appeal to me very much, either."

THE DEADWEIGHT LOSS OF TAXATION

We begin by recalling one of the surprising lessons from Chapter 6: It does not matter whether a tax on a good is levied on buyers or sellers of the good. When a tax is levied on buyers, the demand curve shifts downward by the size of the tax; when it is levied on sellers, the supply curve shifts upward by that amount. In either case, when the tax is enacted, the price paid by buyers rises, and the price received by sellers falls. In the end, buyers and sellers share the burden of the tax, regardless of how it is levied.

Figure 8-1 shows these effects. To simplify our discussion, this figure does not show a shift in either the supply or demand curve, although one curve must shift. Which curve shifts depends on whether the tax is levied on sellers (the supply curve shifts) or buyers (the demand curve shifts). For our purposes here, however, we do not need to see the shift. The key result is that the tax places a wedge between the price buyers pay and the price sellers receive. Because of this tax wedge, the quantity sold falls below the level that would be sold without a tax. In other words, a tax on a good causes the size of the market for the good to shrink. These results should be familiar from Chapter 6.

HOW A TAX AFFECTS MARKET PARTICIPANTS

Now let's use the tools of welfare economics to measure the gains and losses from a tax on a good. To do this, we must take into account how the tax affects buyers, sellers, and the government. The benefit received by buyers in a market is measured by consumer surplus—the amount buyers are willing to pay for the good minus the amount they actually pay for it. The benefit received by sellers

Figure 8-1

THE EFFECTS OF A TAX. A tax on a good places a wedge between the price that buyers pay and the price that sellers receive. The quantity of the good sold falls.

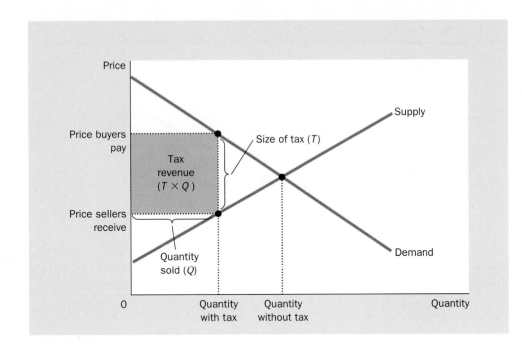

Figure 8-2

TAX REVENUE. The tax revenue that the government collects equals $T \times Q$, the size of the tax T times the quantity sold Q. Thus, tax revenue equals the area of the rectangle between the supply and demand curves.

in a market is measured by producer surplus—the amount sellers receive for the good minus their costs. These are precisely the measures of economic welfare we used in Chapter 7.

What about the third interested party, the government? If T is the size of the tax and Q is the quantity of the good sold, then the government gets total tax revenue of $T \times Q$. It can use this tax revenue to provide services, such as roads, police, and public education, or to help the needy. Therefore, to analyze how taxes affect economic well-being, we use tax revenue to measure the government's benefit from the tax. Keep in mind, however, that this benefit actually accrues not to government but to those on whom the revenue is spent.

Figure 8-2 shows that the government's tax revenue is represented by the rectangle between the supply and demand curves. The height of this rectangle is the size of the tax, T, and the width of the rectangle is the quantity of the good sold, Q. Because a rectangle's area is its height times its width, this rectangle's area is $T \times Q$, which equals the tax revenue.

Welfare without a Tax   To see how a tax affects welfare, we begin by considering welfare before the government has imposed a tax. Figure 8-3 shows the supply-and-demand diagram and marks the key areas with the letters A through F.

Without a tax, the price and quantity are found at the intersection of the supply and demand curves. The price is P_1, and the quantity sold is Q_1. Because the demand curve reflects buyers' willingness to pay, consumer surplus is the area between the demand curve and the price, A + B + C. Similarly, because the supply curve reflects sellers' costs, producer surplus is the area between the supply curve and the price, D + E + F. In this case, because there is no tax, tax revenue equals zero.

Total surplus, the sum of consumer and producer surplus, equals the area A + B + C + D + E + F. In other words, as we saw in Chapter 7, total surplus

Figure 8-3

HOW A TAX AFFECTS WELFARE.
A tax on a good reduces consumer surplus (by the area
B + C) and producer surplus (by
the area D + E). Because the fall
in producer and consumer surplus exceeds tax revenue (area
B + D), the tax is said to impose a
deadweight loss (area C + E).

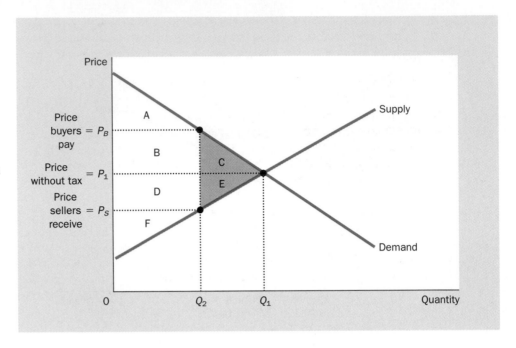

	WITHOUT TAX	WITH TAX	CHANGE
Consumer surplus	A + B + C	A	−(B + C)
Producer surplus	D + E + F	F	−(D + E)
Tax revenue	None	B + D	+(B + D)
Total surplus	A + B + C + D + E + F	A + B + D + F	−(C + E)

Table 8-1

CHANGES IN WELFARE FROM A TAX. This table refers to the areas marked in Figure
8-3 to show how a tax affects the welfare of buyers and sellers in a market.

is the area between the supply and demand curves up to the equilibrium quantity. The first column of Table 8-1 summarizes these conclusions.

Welfare with a Tax   Now consider welfare after the tax is enacted. The
price paid by buyers rises from P_1 to P_B, so consumer surplus now equals only
area A (the area below the demand curve and above the buyer's price). The price
received by sellers falls from P_1 to P_S, so producer surplus now equals only area
F (the area above the supply curve and below the seller's price). The quantity
sold falls from Q_1 to Q_2, and the government collects tax revenue equal to the
area B + D.

To compute total surplus with the tax, we add consumer surplus, producer
surplus, and tax revenue. Thus, we find that total surplus is area A + B + D + F.
The second column of Table 8-1 provides a summary.

Changes in Welfare   We can now see the effects of the tax by comparing
welfare before and after the tax is enacted. The third column in Table 8-1 shows

the changes. The tax causes consumer surplus to fall by the area B + C and producer surplus to fall by the area D + E. Tax revenue rises by the area B + D. Not surprisingly, the tax makes buyers and sellers worse off and the government better off.

The change in total welfare includes the change in consumer surplus (which is negative), the change in producer surplus (which is also negative), and the change in tax revenue (which is positive). When we add these three pieces together, we find that total surplus in the market falls by the area C + E. *Thus, the losses to buyers and sellers from a tax exceed the revenue raised by the government.* The reduction in total surplus that results from a tax is called the **deadweight loss.** The area C + E measures the size of the deadweight loss.

To understand why taxes impose deadweight losses, recall one of the *Ten Principles of Economics* in Chapter 1: People respond to incentives. In Chapter 7 we saw that markets normally allocate scarce resources efficiently. That is, the equilibrium of supply and demand maximizes the total surplus of buyers and sellers in a market. When a tax raises the price to buyers and lowers the price to sellers, however, it gives buyers an incentive to consume less and sellers an incentive to produce less than they otherwise would. As buyers and sellers respond to these incentives, the size of the market shrinks below its optimum. Thus, because taxes distort incentives, they cause markets to allocate resources inefficiently.

deadweight loss
the reduction in total surplus that results from a tax

DEADWEIGHT LOSSES AND THE GAINS FROM TRADE

To gain some intuition for why taxes result in deadweight losses, consider an example. Imagine that Joe cleans Jane's house each week for $100. The opportunity cost of Joe's time is $80, and the value of a clean house to Jane is $120. Thus, Joe and Jane each receive a $20 benefit from their deal. The total surplus of $40 measures the gains from trade in this particular transaction.

Now suppose that the government levies a $50 tax on the providers of cleaning services. There is now no price that Jane can pay Joe that will leave both of them better off after paying the tax. The most Jane would be willing to pay is $120, but then Joe would be left with only $70 after paying the tax, which is less than his $80 cost. Conversely, for Joe to receive his opportunity cost of $80, Jane would need to pay $130, which is above the $120 value she places on a clean house. As a result, Jane and Joe cancel their arrangement. Joe goes without the income, and Jane lives in a dirtier house.

The tax has made Joe and Jane worse off by a total of $40, because they have lost this amount of surplus. At the same time, the government collects no revenue from Joe and Jane because they decide to cancel their arrangement. The $40 is pure deadweight loss: It is a loss to buyers and sellers in a market not offset by an increase in government revenue. From this example, we can see the ultimate source of deadweight losses: *Taxes cause deadweight losses because they prevent buyers and sellers from realizing some of the gains from trade.*

The area of the triangle between the supply and demand curves (area C + E in Figure 8-3) measures these losses. This loss can be seen most easily in Figure 8-4 by recalling that the demand curve reflects the value of the good to consumers and that the supply curve reflects the costs of producers. When the tax raises the price to buyers to P_B and lowers the price to sellers to P_S, the marginal buyers and sellers leave the market, so the quantity sold falls from Q_1 to

Figure 8-4

THE DEADWEIGHT LOSS. When the government imposes a tax on a good, the quantity sold falls from Q_1 to Q_2. As a result, some of the potential gains from trade among buyers and sellers do not get realized. These lost gains from trade create the deadweight loss.

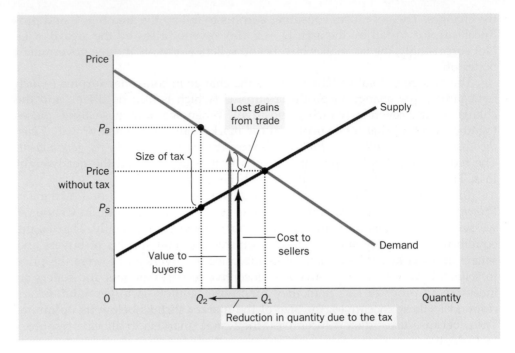

Q_2. Yet, as the figure shows, the value of the good to these buyers still exceeds the cost to these sellers. As in our example with Joe and Jane, the gains from trade—the difference between buyers' value and sellers' cost—is less than the tax. Thus, these trades do not get made once the tax is imposed. The deadweight loss is the surplus lost because the tax discourages these mutually advantageous trades.

QUICK QUIZ Draw the supply and demand curve for cookies. If the government imposes a tax on cookies, show what happens to the quantity sold, the price paid by buyers, and the price paid by sellers. In your diagram, show the deadweight loss from the tax. Explain the meaning of the deadweight loss.

THE DETERMINANTS OF THE DEADWEIGHT LOSS

What determines whether the deadweight loss from a tax is large or small? The answer is the price elasticities of supply and demand, which measure how much the quantity supplied and quantity demanded respond to changes in the price.

Let's consider first how the elasticity of supply affects the size of the deadweight loss. In the top two panels of Figure 8-5, the demand curve and the size of the tax are the same. The only difference in these figures is the elasticity of the supply curve. In panel (a), the supply curve is relatively inelastic: Quantity supplied responds only slightly to changes in the price. In panel (b), the supply curve is relatively elastic: Quantity supplied responds substantially to changes in

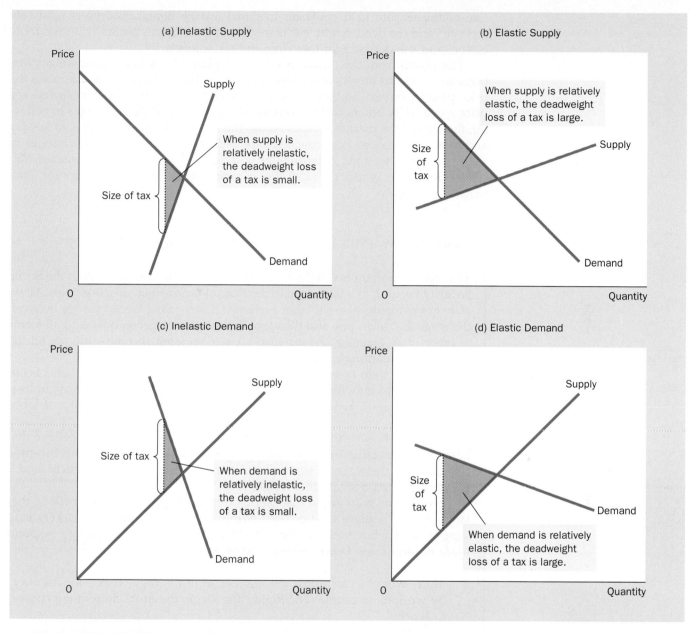

TAX DISTORTIONS AND ELASTICITIES. In panels (a) and (b), the demand curve and the size of the tax are the same, but the price elasticity of supply is different. Notice that the more elastic the supply curve, the larger the deadweight loss of the tax. In panels (c) and (d), the supply curve and the size of the tax are the same, but the price elasticity of demand is different. Notice that the more elastic the demand curve, the larger the deadweight loss of the tax.

Figure 8-5

the price. Notice that the deadweight loss, the area of the triangle between the supply and demand curves, is larger when the supply curve is more elastic.

Similarly, the bottom two panels of Figure 8-5 show how the elasticity of demand affects the size of the deadweight loss. Here the supply curve and the size of the tax are held constant. In panel (c) the demand curve is relatively inelastic, and the deadweight loss is small. In panel (d) the demand curve is more elastic, and the deadweight loss from the tax is larger.

The lesson from this figure is easy to explain. A tax has a deadweight loss because it induces buyers and sellers to change their behavior. The tax raises the price paid by buyers, so they consume less. At the same time, the tax lowers the price received by sellers, so they produce less. Because of these changes in behavior, the size of the market shrinks below the optimum. The elasticities of supply and demand measure how much sellers and buyers respond to the changes in the price and, therefore, determine how much the tax distorts the market outcome. Hence, *the greater the elasticities of supply and demand, the greater the deadweight loss of a tax.*

CASE STUDY THE DEADWEIGHT LOSS OF TAXES ON LABOR

The most important tax in the U.S. economy is the tax on labor. Both the Social Security tax and, to a large extent, the federal income tax are labor taxes. Many state governments also tax labor earnings. A labor tax places a wedge between the wage that firms pay and the wage that workers receive. If we add all forms of labor taxes together, the *marginal tax rate* on labor income—the tax on the last dollar of earnings—is almost 50 percent for many workers.

How much do taxes on labor distort the outcome in labor markets? Economists disagree on whether labor taxes have a large or small deadweight loss. The disagreement arises from different views about the elasticity of labor supply.

Economists who argue that labor taxes are not very distorting believe that labor supply is fairly inelastic. Most people, they claim, would work full-time regardless of the wage. If so, the labor supply curve is almost vertical, and a tax on labor has a small deadweight loss.

Economists who argue that labor taxes are highly distorting believe that labor supply is more elastic. They admit that some groups of workers may supply their labor inelastically but claim that many other groups respond more to incentives. Here are some examples:

◆ Many workers can adjust the number of hours they work—for instance, by working overtime. The higher the wage, the more hours they choose to work.

◆ Some families have second earners—often married women with children—with some discretion over whether to do unpaid work at home or paid work in the marketplace. When deciding whether to take a job, these second earners compare the benefits of being at home (including savings on the cost of child care) with the wages they could earn.

◆ Many of the elderly can choose when to retire, and their decisions are partly based on the wage. Once they are retired, the wage determines their incentive to work part-time.

◆ Some people consider engaging in illegal economic activity, such as the drug trade, or working at jobs that pay "under the table" to evade taxes. Economists call this the *underground economy*. In deciding whether to work in the underground economy or at a legitimate job, these potential criminals compare what they can earn by breaking the law with the wage they can earn legally.

In each of these cases, the quantity of labor supplied responds to the wage (the price of labor). Thus, the decisions of these workers are distorted when their labor earnings are taxed. Labor taxes encourage workers to work fewer hours, second earners to stay at home, the elderly to retire early, and the unscrupulous to enter the underground economy.

If tax rates were lower, would these Sun City residents still be retired?

CASE STUDY   HENRY GEORGE AND THE TAX ON LAND

Henry George was a nineteenth-century American economist and social philosopher. In his 1879 book *Progress and Poverty*, George argued that the government should raise all its revenue from a tax on land. This "single tax" was, he claimed, both equitable and efficient. George's ideas won him a sizable political following, and in 1886 he lost a close race for mayor of New York City (although he finished well ahead of Republican candidate Theodore Roosevelt).

George's proposal to tax land was motivated largely by a concern over the distribution of economic well-being. He deplored the "shocking contrast between monstrous wealth and debasing want" and thought landowners benefited more than they should from the rapid growth in the overall economy.

George's arguments for the land tax can be understood using the tools of modern economics. Consider first supply and demand in the market for renting land. As immigration causes the population to rise and technological progress causes incomes to grow, the demand for land rises over time. Yet since the amount of land is fixed, the supply is perfectly inelastic. Rapid increases in demand together with inelastic supply lead to large increases in the equilibrium rents on land, so that economic growth makes rich landowners even richer.

Now consider the incidence of a tax on land. As we first saw in Chapter 6, the burden of a tax falls more heavily on the side of the market that is less elastic. A tax on land takes this principle to an extreme. The suppliers of land—the landowners—have no better alternative than to supply all their

Henry George

land to the marketplace and obtain whatever they can for it. Thus, the elasticity of supply is zero, and the landowners bear the entire burden of the tax.

Consider next the question of efficiency. As we just discussed, the deadweight loss of a tax depends on the elasticities of supply and demand. Again, a tax on land is an extreme case. Since the elasticity of supply is zero, a tax on land does not alter the market allocation. Thus, there is no deadweight loss, and the government's tax revenue exactly equals the loss of the landowners.

Although taxing land may look attractive in theory, it is not as straightforward in practice as it may appear. For a tax on land not to distort economic incentives, it must be a tax on raw land. Yet the value of land often comes from improvements, such as clearing trees, providing sewers, and building roads. To see how important improvements are, compare an acre of land in Las Vegas to an acre of land in Death Valley. The raw land is similar in these two cases: Both acres are in the middle of deserts. Yet the acre in Las Vegas is more valuable because of the improvements that have been made to that acre and the surrounding land.

Unlike the supply of raw land, the supply of improvements has an elasticity greater than zero. If a land tax included improvements, it would distort incentives. Landowners would respond to the tax by devoting fewer resources to improving their land.

Today, few economists support George's proposal for a single tax on land. Not only is taxing improvements a potential problem, but the tax would not raise enough revenue to pay for the much larger government we have today. Yet many of George's arguments remain valid. Here is the assessment of the eminent economist Milton Friedman a century after George's book: "In my opinion, the least bad tax is the property tax on the unimproved value of land, the Henry George argument of many, many years ago."

QUICK QUIZ The demand for beer is more elastic than the demand for milk. Would a tax on beer or a tax on milk have larger deadweight loss? Why?

DEADWEIGHT LOSS AND TAX REVENUE AS TAXES VARY

Taxes rarely stay the same for long periods of time. Policymakers in local, state, and federal governments are always considering raising one tax or lowering another. Here we consider what happens to the deadweight loss and tax revenue when the size of a tax changes.

Figure 8-6 shows the effects of a small, medium, and large tax, holding constant the market's supply and demand curves. The deadweight loss—the reduction in total surplus that results when the tax reduces the size of a market below the optimum—equals the area of the triangle between the supply and demand curves. For the small tax in panel (a), the area of the deadweight loss triangle area is quite small. But as the size of a tax rises in panels (b) and (c), the deadweight loss grows larger and larger.

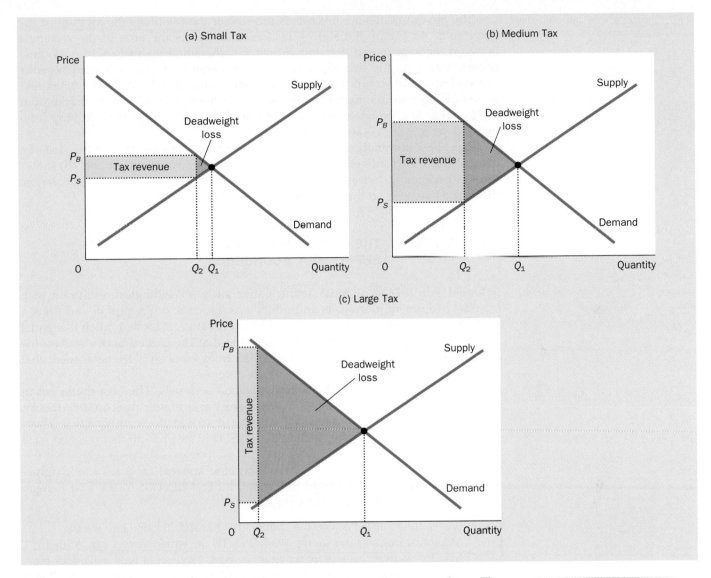

DEADWEIGHT LOSS AND TAX REVENUE FROM THREE TAXES OF DIFFERENT SIZE. The deadweight loss is the reduction in total surplus due to the tax. Tax revenue is the amount of the tax times the amount of the good sold. In panel (a), a small tax has a small deadweight loss and raises a small amount of revenue. In panel (b), a somewhat larger tax has a larger deadweight loss and raises a larger amount of revenue. In panel (c), a very large tax has a very large deadweight loss, but because it has reduced the size of the market so much, the tax raises only a small amount of revenue.

Figure 8-6

Indeed, the deadweight loss of a tax rises even more rapidly than the size of the tax. The reason is that the deadweight loss is an area of a triangle, and an area of a triangle depends on the *square* of its size. If we double the size of a tax, for instance, the base and height of the triangle double, so the deadweight loss rises by a factor of 4. If we triple the size of a tax, the base and height triple, so the deadweight loss rises by a factor of 9.

The government's tax revenue is the size of the tax times the amount of the good sold. As Figure 8-6 shows, tax revenue equals the area of the rectangle between the supply and demand curves. For the small tax in panel (a), tax revenue is small. As the size of a tax rises from panel (a) to panel (b), tax revenue grows. But as the size of the tax rises further from panel (b) to panel (c), tax revenue falls because the higher tax drastically reduces the size of the market. For a very large tax, no revenue would be raised, because people would stop buying and selling the good altogether.

Figure 8-7 summarizes these results. In panel (a) we see that as the size of a tax increases, its deadweight loss quickly gets larger. By contrast, panel (b) shows that tax revenue first rises with the size of the tax; but then, as the tax gets larger, the market shrinks so much that tax revenue starts to fall.

CASE STUDY   THE LAFFER CURVE AND
SUPPLY-SIDE ECONOMICS

One day in 1974, economist Arthur Laffer sat in a Washington restaurant with some prominent journalists and politicians. He took out a napkin and drew a figure on it to show how tax rates affect tax revenue. It looked much like panel (b) of our Figure 8-7. Laffer then suggested that the United States was on the downward-sloping side of this curve. Tax rates were so high, he argued, that reducing them would actually raise tax revenue.

Few economists took Laffer's suggestion seriously. The idea that a cut in tax rates could raise tax revenue was correct as a matter of economic theory, but there was more doubt about whether it would do so in practice. There was no evidence for Laffer's view that U.S. tax rates had in fact reached such extreme levels.

Nonetheless, the *Laffer curve* (as it became known) captured the imagination of Ronald Reagan. David Stockman, budget director in the first Reagan administration, offers the following story:

> [Reagan] had once been on the Laffer curve himself. "I came into the Big Money making pictures during World War II," he would always say. At that time the wartime income surtax hit 90 percent. "You could only make four pictures and then you were in the top bracket," he would continue. "So we all quit working after four pictures and went off to the country." High tax rates caused less work. Low tax rates caused more. His experience proved it.

When Reagan ran for president in 1980, he made cutting taxes part of his platform. Reagan argued that taxes were so high that they were discouraging hard work. He argued that lower taxes would give people the proper incentive to work, which would raise economic well-being and perhaps even tax revenue. Because the cut in tax rates was intended to encourage people to increase the quantity of labor they supplied, the views of Laffer and Reagan became known as *supply-side economics*.

Subsequent history failed to confirm Laffer's conjecture that lower tax rates would raise tax revenue. When Reagan cut taxes after he was elected, the result was less tax revenue, not more. Revenue from personal income taxes (per person, adjusted for inflation) fell by 9 percent from 1980 to 1984, even though average income (per person, adjusted for inflation) grew by 4 percent over this period. Yet once the policy was in place, it was hard to reverse. The

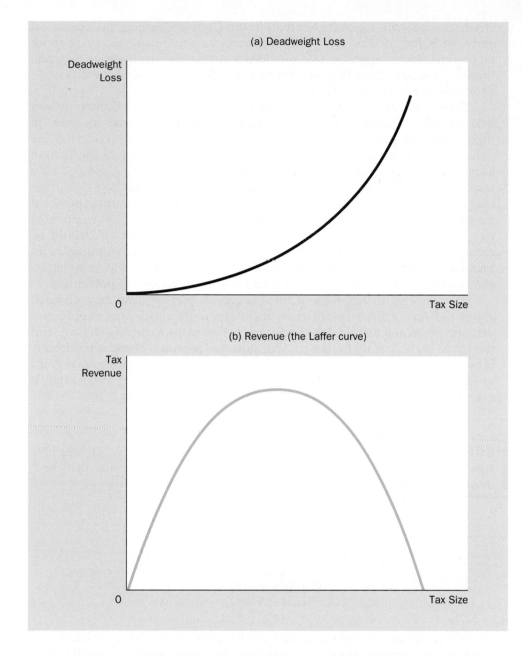

Figure 8-7

HOW DEADWEIGHT LOSS AND TAX REVENUE VARY WITH THE SIZE OF A TAX. Panel (a) shows that as the size of a tax grows larger, the deadweight loss grows larger. Panel (b) shows that tax revenue first rises, then falls. This relationship is sometimes called the Laffer curve.

tax cut helped begin a long period in which the government failed to collect enough tax revenue to pay for all its spending. Throughout Reagan's two terms in office, and for many years thereafter, the government ran large budget deficits.

Yet Laffer's argument is not completely without merit. Although an overall cut in tax rates does reduce revenue, there is evidence that *some* taxpayers may be on the wrong side of the Laffer curve. In the 1980s, tax revenue collected from the richest Americans, who face the highest tax rates, did rise when their taxes were cut. The idea that cutting taxes can raise revenue may be correct if applied to those taxpayers facing the highest tax rates. In addition, Laffer's argument may be more plausible when applied to other countries, where tax rates are much higher than in the United States. In Sweden in the early 1980s, for instance, the typical worker faced a marginal tax rate of about 80 percent. Such a high tax rate provides a substantial disincentive to work. Studies have suggested that Sweden would indeed have raised more tax revenue if it had lowered its tax rates.

These ideas arise frequently in political debate. When Bill Clinton moved into the White House in 1993, he increased the federal income tax rates on high-income taxpayers to about 40 percent. Some economists criticized the policy, arguing that the plan would not yield as much revenue as the Clinton administration estimated. They claimed that the administration did not fully take into account how taxes alter behavior. Conversely, when Bob Dole challenged Bill Clinton in the election of 1996, Dole proposed cutting personal income taxes. Although Dole rejected the idea that tax cuts would completely pay for themselves, he did claim that 28 percent of the tax cut would be recouped because lower tax rates would lead to more rapid economic growth. Economists debated whether Dole's 28 percent projection was reasonable, excessively optimistic, or (as Laffer might suggest) excessively pessimistic.

Policymakers disagree about these issues in part because they disagree about the size of the relevant elasticities. The more elastic that supply and demand are in any market, the more taxes in that market distort behavior, and the more likely it is that a tax cut will raise tax revenue. There is no debate, however, about the general lesson: How much revenue the government gains or loses from a tax change cannot be computed just by looking at tax rates. It also depends on how the tax change affects people's behavior.

QUICK QUIZ If the government doubles the tax on gasoline, can you be sure that revenue from the gasoline tax will rise? Can you be sure that the deadweight loss from the gasoline tax will rise? Explain.

CONCLUSION

Taxes, Oliver Wendell Holmes once said, are the price we pay for a civilized society. Indeed, our society cannot exist without some form of taxes. We all expect the government to provide us certain services, such as roads, parks, police, and national defense. These public services require tax revenue.

This chapter has shed some light on how high the price of civilized society can be. One of the *Ten Principles of Economics* discussed in Chapter 1 is that markets are usually a good way to organize economic activity. When the government imposes taxes on buyers or sellers of a good, however, society loses some of the benefits of market efficiency. Taxes are costly to market participants not only because taxes transfer resources from those participants to the government but also because they alter incentives and distort market outcomes.

IN THE NEWS

Should Ukraine Cut Tax Rates to Raise Tax Revenue?

THE HIGHER ARE TAXES, THE MORE likely an economy finds itself on the wrong side of the Laffer curve. According to the following article, Ukraine has recently been in exactly that position.

A Big Tax Cut to Lift the Economy—Not Here, in Ukraine

BY PETER PASSELL

Bob Dole's plan to speed growth by slashing taxes never played well with the American economics establishment— or, for that matter, with the deficit-wary electorate. But supply-siders are alive and well in the least likely of places: Ukraine.

Indeed, Ukraine's government is trying to convince its Western bankers at the International Monetary Fund and other institutions to countenance huge tax cuts to turn around the republic's benighted, post-Communist economy. And strikingly, it has the backing of some high-powered economists who rarely fraternize with the free-lunch crowd. "Ukraine may be the one country where lower tax rates really would produce more revenue," allows Jeffrey Sachs, director of the Harvard Institute for International Development.

As in the rest of the former Soviet empire, the collapse of Communism in Ukraine decentralized political power. But unlike what happened in, say, Poland or the Czech Republic, the government bureaucracy in Ukraine kept a heavy thumb on enterprises. To do business legally in Ukraine is to run a long gantlet of high taxes, heavy-handed regulations and very sticky palms.

It's no surprise, then, that once stripped of guaranteed markets at home and elsewhere in the old Soviet Union, the "official" economy imploded. Daniel Kaufmann, a visiting scholar at Harvard who formerly headed the World Bank's team in Ukraine, estimates that output from legal economic activities has shrunk by nearly two-thirds since 1989.

Shrinkage begets shrinkage, as an ever-smaller tax base is weighed down by the nation's heavy social obligations. Budget deficits make it increasingly difficult to contain inflation. Today, there is just one worker in the official economy to support each pensioner, and payroll taxes—by no means the only tax on enterprises—run an incredible 52 percent. "No business can survive in this environment," Mr. Sachs concludes.

But plenty do survive by operating out of reach of regulators and tax collectors. Using electricity consumption to estimate output because it is one of the few reliable indicators, Mr. Kaufmann estimates that the unofficial economy is now actually bigger than the official one.

That, of course, is bad news: An economy in which contact with the government is mostly under the table is hardly ready for prime time. But it is good news, too, since it implies that living standards are higher than the official statistics say. What's more, it suggests that given a little running room Ukrainians are no slouches at business.

The economic predicament is apparently understood by President Leonid Kuchma, Ukraine's most popular— and most skillful—politician. At least for the moment, free-market types led by Vice Prime Minister Viktor Pynzenyk are winning the internal battle with the old apparatchiks, who have saddled the country with the reputation of being the most corrupt of the former Soviet republics. Mr. Kuchma has signed on to bold reforms suggested by Western advisers. . . .

At the core of those reforms are sweeping cuts in taxes and deregulation designed to lure the underground economy to the surface. The 52 percent payroll tax would be cut to 15 percent, and the revenues would be entirely devoted to covering existing pension obligations. Employers would be obliged to collect an additional 10 percent in wages from workers, which would go into individual accounts managed by private international investment advisers—a plan not unlike Chile's privatized social security system.

There is reason for cautious optimism. A March 1996 survey conducted for Mr. Kaufmann suggested that roughly 40 percent of the underground economy would go legitimate within three years and another 40 percent within six years, provided the reforms proved "credible." Mr. Kaufmann emphasizes that credibility turns as much on deregulation as tax cuts, requiring an enduring commitment to preventing the paper-pushers from perpetuating the bad old ways.

SOURCE: *The New York Times,* November 14, 1996, p. D2.

Summary

◆ A tax on a good reduces the welfare of buyers and sellers of the good, and the reduction in consumer and producer surplus usually exceeds the revenue raised by the government. The fall in total surplus—the sum of consumer surplus, producer surplus, and tax revenue—is called the deadweight loss of the tax.

◆ Taxes have deadweight losses because they cause buyers to consume less and sellers to produce less, and this change in behavior shrinks the size of the market below the level that maximizes total surplus. Because the elasticities of supply and demand measure how much market participants respond to market conditions, larger elasticities imply larger deadweight losses.

◆ As a tax grows larger, it distorts incentives more, and its deadweight loss grows larger. Tax revenue first rises with the size of a tax. Eventually, however, a larger tax reduces tax revenue because it reduces the size of the market.

Key Concepts

deadweight loss, p. 159

Questions for Review

1. What happens to consumer and producer surplus when the sale of a good is taxed? How does the change in consumer and producer surplus compare to the tax revenue? Explain.

2. Draw a supply-and-demand diagram with a tax on the sale of the good. Show the deadweight loss. Show the tax revenue.

3. How do the elasticities of supply and demand affect the deadweight loss of a tax? Why do they have this effect?

4. What happens to the deadweight loss and tax revenue when a tax is increased?

Problems and Applications

1. The market for pizza is characterized by a downward-sloping demand curve and an upward-sloping supply curve.
   a. Draw the competitive market equilibrium. Label the price, quantity, consumer surplus, and producer surplus. Is there any deadweight loss? Explain.
   b. Suppose that the government forces each pizzeria to pay a $1 tax on each pizza sold. Illustrate the effect of this tax on the pizza market, being sure to label the consumer surplus, producer surplus, government revenue, and deadweight loss. How does each area compare to the pre-tax case?
   c. If the tax were removed, pizza eaters and sellers would be better off, but the government would lose tax revenue. Suppose that consumers and producers voluntarily transferred some of their gains to the government. Could all parties (including the government) be better off than they were with a tax? Explain using the labeled areas in your graph.

2. Evaluate the following two statements. Do you agree? Why or why not?
   a. "If the government taxes land, wealthy landowners will pass the tax on to their poorer renters."
   b. "If the government taxes apartment buildings, wealthy landlords will pass the tax on to their poorer renters."

3. Evaluate the following two statements. Do you agree? Why or why not?
   a. "A tax that has no deadweight loss cannot raise any revenue for the government."
   b. "A tax that raises no revenue for the government cannot have any deadweight loss."

4. Consider the market for rubber bands.
   a. If this market has very elastic supply and very inelastic demand, how would the burden of a tax on rubber bands be shared between consumers and producers? Use the tools of consumer surplus and producer surplus in your answer.
   b. If this market has very inelastic supply and very elastic demand, how would the burden of a tax on rubber bands be shared between consumers and producers? Contrast your answer with your answer to part (a).

5. Suppose that the government imposes a tax on heating oil.
   a. Would the deadweight loss from this tax likely be greater in the first year after it is imposed or in the fifth year? Explain.
   b. Would the revenue collected from this tax likely be greater in the first year after it is imposed or in the fifth year? Explain.

6. After economics class one day, your friend suggests that taxing food would be a good way to raise revenue because the demand for food is quite inelastic. In what sense is taxing food a "good" way to raise revenue? In what sense is it not a "good" way to raise revenue?

7. In November 1993 Senator Daniel Patrick Moynihan introduced a bill that would levy a 10,000 percent tax on certain hollow-tipped bullets.
   a. Do you expect that this tax would raise much revenue? Why or why not?
   b. Even if the tax would raise no revenue, what might be Senator Moynihan's reason for proposing it?

8. The government places a tax on the purchase of socks.
   a. Illustrate the effect of this tax on equilibrium price and quantity in the sock market. Identify the following areas both before and after the imposition of the tax: total spending by consumers, total revenue for producers, and government tax revenue.
   b. Does the price received by producers rise or fall? Can you tell whether total receipts for producers rise or fall? Explain.
   c. Does the price paid by consumers rise or fall? Can you tell whether total spending by consumers rises or falls? Explain carefully. (Hint: Think about elasticity.) If total consumer spending falls, does consumer surplus rise? Explain.

9. Suppose the government currently raises $100 million through a $0.01 tax on widgets, and another $100 million through a $0.10 tax on gadgets. If the tax rate on widgets was doubled and the tax on gadgets was eliminated, would the government raise more money than today, less money, or the same amount of money? Explain.

10. Most states tax the purchase of new cars. Suppose that New Jersey currently requires car dealers to pay the state $100 for each car sold, and plans to increase the tax to $150 per car next year.
    a. Illustrate the effect of this tax increase on the quantity of cars sold in New Jersey, the price paid by consumers, and the price received by producers.
    b. Create a table that shows the levels of consumer surplus, producer surplus, government revenue, and total surplus both before and after the tax increase.
    c. What is the change in government revenue? Is it positive or negative?
    d. What is the change in deadweight loss? Is it positive or negative?
    e. Give one reason why the demand for cars in New Jersey might be fairly elastic. Does this make the additional tax more or less likely to increase government revenue? How might states try to reduce the elasticity of demand?

11. Several years ago the British government imposed a "poll tax" that required each person to pay a flat amount to the government independent of his or her income or wealth. What is the effect of such a tax on economic efficiency? What is the effect on economic equity? Do you think this was a popular tax?

12. This chapter analyzed the welfare effects of a tax on a good. Consider now the opposite policy. Suppose that the government *subsidizes* a good: For each unit of the good sold, the government pays $2 to the buyer. How does the subsidy affect consumer surplus, producer surplus, tax revenue, and total surplus? Does a subsidy lead to a deadweight loss? Explain.

13. (This problem uses some high school algebra and is challenging.) Suppose that a market is described by the following supply and demand equations:

$$Q^S = 2P$$
$$Q^D = 300 - P$$

   a. Solve for the equilibrium price and the equilibrium quantity.
   b. Suppose that a tax of T is placed on buyers, so the new demand equation is

$$Q^D = 300 - (P + T).$$

Solve for the new equilibrium. What happens to the price received by sellers, the price paid by buyers, and the quantity sold?

c. Tax revenue is $T \times Q$. Use your answer to part (b) to solve for tax revenue as a function of T. Graph this relationship for T between 0 and 300.

d. The deadweight loss of a tax is the area of the triangle between the supply and demand curves. Recalling that the area of a triangle is $1/2 \times$ base $\times$ height,

solve for deadweight loss as a function of T. Graph this relationship for T between 0 and 300. (Hint: Looking sideways, the base of the deadweight loss triangle is T, and the height is the difference between the quantity sold with the tax and the quantity sold without the tax.)

e. The government now levies a tax on this good of $200 per unit. Is this a good policy? Why or why not? Can you propose a better policy?

9

APPLICATION: INTERNATIONAL TRADE

IN THIS CHAPTER
YOU WILL

Consider what determines whether a country imports or exports a good

Examine who wins and who loses from international trade

Learn that the gains to winners from international trade exceed the losses to losers

Analyze the welfare effects of tariffs and import quotas

Examine the arguments people use to advocate trade restrictions

If you check the labels on the clothes you are now wearing, you will probably find that some of your clothes were made in another country. A century ago the textiles and clothing industry was a major part of the U.S. economy, but that is no longer the case. Faced with foreign competitors that could produce quality goods at low cost, many U.S. firms found it increasingly difficult to produce and sell textiles and clothing at a profit. As a result, they laid off their workers and shut down their factories. Today, much of the textiles and clothing that Americans consume are imported from abroad.

The story of the textiles industry raises important questions for economic policy: How does international trade affect economic well-being? Who gains and who loses from free trade among countries, and how do the gains compare to the losses?

Chapter 3 introduced the study of international trade by applying the principle of comparative advantage. According to this principle, all countries can benefit from trading with one another because trade allows each country to specialize in doing what it does best. But the analysis in Chapter 3 was incomplete. It did not explain how the international marketplace achieves these gains from trade or how the gains are distributed among various economic actors.

We now return to the study of international trade and take up these questions. Over the past several chapters, we have developed many tools for analyzing how markets work: supply, demand, equilibrium, consumer surplus, producer surplus, and so on. With these tools we can learn more about the effects of international trade on economic well-being.

THE DETERMINANTS OF TRADE

Consider the market for steel. The steel market is well suited to examining the gains and losses from international trade: Steel is made in many countries around the world, and there is much world trade in steel. Moreover, the steel market is one in which policymakers often consider (and sometimes implement) trade restrictions in order to protect domestic steel producers from foreign competitors. We examine here the steel market in the imaginary country of Isoland.

THE EQUILIBRIUM WITHOUT TRADE

As our story begins, the Isolandian steel market is isolated from the rest of the world. By government decree, no one in Isoland is allowed to import or export steel, and the penalty for violating the decree is so large that no one dares try.

Because there is no international trade, the market for steel in Isoland consists of Isolandian buyers and sellers. As Figure 9-1 shows, the domestic price adjusts to balance the quantity supplied by domestic sellers and the quantity demanded by domestic buyers. The figure shows the consumer and producer surplus in the equilibrium without trade. The sum of consumer and producer surplus measures the total benefits that buyers and sellers receive from the steel market.

Now suppose that, in an election upset, Isoland elects a new president. The president campaigned on a platform of "change" and promised the voters bold

Figure 9-1

THE EQUILIBRIUM WITHOUT INTERNATIONAL TRADE. When an economy cannot trade in world markets, the price adjusts to balance domestic supply and demand. This figure shows consumer and producer surplus in an equilibrium without international trade for the steel market in the imaginary country of Isoland.

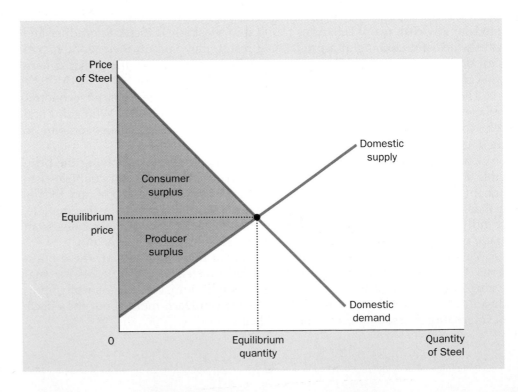

new ideas. Her first act is to assemble a team of economists to evaluate Isolandian trade policy. She asks them to report back on three questions:

◆ If the government allowed Isolandians to import and export steel, what would happen to the price of steel and the quantity of steel sold in the domestic steel market?

◆ Who would gain from free trade in steel and who would lose, and would the gains exceed the losses?

◆ Should a tariff (a tax on steel imports) or an import quota (a limit on steel imports) be part of the new trade policy?

After reviewing supply and demand in their favorite textbook (this one, of course), the Isolandian economics team begins its analysis.

THE WORLD PRICE AND COMPARATIVE ADVANTAGE

The first issue our economists take up is whether Isoland is likely to become a steel importer or a steel exporter. In other words, if free trade were allowed, would Isolandians end up buying or selling steel in world markets?

To answer this question, the economists compare the current Isolandian price of steel to the price of steel in other countries. We call the price prevailing in

---

FYI

*Comparing
Prices and
Comparative
Advantage*

WHEN COMPARING PRICES OF goods in different countries, it is important to pay attention to the units in which prices are quoted. One country may quote prices in dollars, whereas another quotes them in pesos. To compare prices, we need to measure them in terms of some item valued in both countries—ounces of gold, barrels of crude oil, or bushels of wheat. The price of a good measured in terms of another good is called a *relative price*. Because relative prices measure opportunity costs, they determine comparative advantage and patterns of trade.

Here is an example. In Isoland, the price of steel is $1,000 a ton, and the price of wheat is $200 a bushel. In Neighborland, the price of steel is 10,000 pesos a ton, and the price of wheat is 1,000 pesos a bushel. Now consider these questions: Which country has cheaper steel? Which country has cheaper wheat?

To answer these questions, we can express the price of steel in terms of wheat. This relative price gives us the amount of wheat that a person must give up to obtain one ton of steel. In Isoland, the price of a ton of steel is 5 bushels of wheat. In Neighborland, the price of a ton of steel is 10 bushels of wheat. Thus, the price of steel (measured in bushels of wheat) is lower in Isoland than in Neighborland, indicating that Isoland has a comparative advantage in producing steel.

We can similarly compare the price of wheat in the two countries. In Isoland, the price of a bushel of wheat is 1/5 ton of steel. In Neighborland, the price of a bushel of wheat is 1/10 ton of steel. The price of wheat (measured in tons of steel) is lower in Neighborland, indicating that Neighborland has a comparative advantage in producing wheat.

Notice that the price of wheat in terms of steel is the inverse of the price of steel in terms of wheat. If the price of steel is lower in one country, the price of wheat must be lower in the other. Thus, unless the prices are exactly the same, one country must have a comparative advantage in one good, and the other country must have a comparative advantage in the other good.

world price

the price of a good that prevails in the world market for that good

world markets the **world price.** If the world price of steel is higher than the domestic price, then Isoland would become an exporter of steel once trade is permitted. Isolandian steel producers would be eager to receive the higher prices available abroad and would start selling their steel to buyers in other countries. Conversely, if the world price of steel is lower than the domestic price, then Isoland would become an importer of steel. Because foreign sellers offer a better price, Isolandian steel consumers would quickly start buying steel from other countries.

In essence, comparing the world price and the domestic price before trade indicates whether Isoland has a comparative advantage in producing steel. The domestic price reflects the opportunity cost of steel: It tells us how much an Isolandian must give up to get one unit of steel. If the domestic price is low, the cost of producing steel in Isoland is low, suggesting that Isoland has a comparative advantage in producing steel relative to the rest of the world. If the domestic price is high, then the cost of producing steel in Isoland is high, suggesting that foreign countries have a comparative advantage in producing steel.

As we saw in Chapter 3, trade among nations is ultimately based on comparative advantage. That is, trade is beneficial because it allows each nation to specialize in doing what it does best. By comparing the world price and the domestic price before trade, we can determine whether Isoland is better or worse at producing steel than the rest of the world.

QUICK QUIZ   The country Autarka does not allow international trade. In Autarka, you can buy a wool suit for 3 ounces of gold. Meanwhile, in neighboring countries, you can buy the same suit for 2 ounces of gold. If Autarka were to allow free trade, would it import or export suits?

THE WINNERS AND LOSERS FROM TRADE

To analyze the welfare effects of free trade, the Isolandian economists begin with the assumption that Isoland is a small economy compared to the rest of the world so that its actions have negligible effect on world markets. The small-economy assumption has a specific implication for analyzing the steel market: If Isoland is a small economy, then the change in Isoland's trade policy will not affect the world price of steel. The Isolandians are said to be *price takers* in the world economy. That is, they take the world price of steel as given. They can sell steel at this price and be exporters or buy steel at this price and be importers.

The small-economy assumption is not necessary to analyze the gains and losses from international trade. But the Isolandian economists know from experience that this assumption greatly simplifies the analysis. They also know that the basic lessons do not change in the more complicated case of a large economy.

THE GAINS AND LOSSES OF AN EXPORTING COUNTRY

Figure 9-2 shows the Isolandian steel market when the domestic equilibrium price before trade is below the world price. Once free trade is allowed, the

Figure 9-2

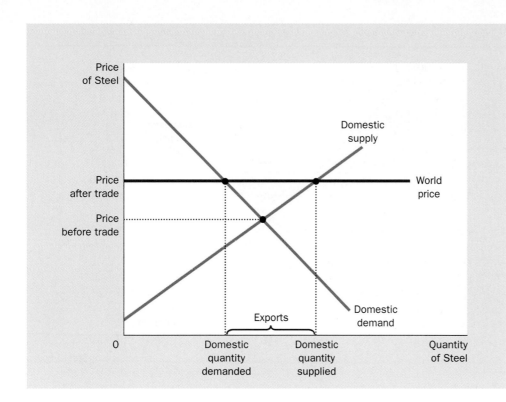

INTERNATIONAL TRADE IN AN EXPORTING COUNTRY. Once trade is allowed, the domestic price rises to equal the world price. The supply curve shows the quantity of steel produced domestically, and the demand curve shows the quantity consumed domestically. Exports from Isoland equal the difference between the domestic quantity supplied and the domestic quantity demanded at the world price.

domestic price rises to equal the world price. No seller of steel would accept less than the world price, and no buyer would pay more than the world price.

With the domestic price now equal to the world price, the domestic quantity supplied differs from the domestic quantity demanded. The supply curve shows the quantity of steel supplied by Isolandian sellers. The demand curve shows the quantity of steel demanded by Isolandian buyers. Because the domestic quantity supplied is greater than the domestic quantity demanded, Isoland sells steel to other countries. Thus, Isoland becomes a steel exporter.

Although domestic quantity supplied and domestic quantity demanded differ, the steel market is still in equilibrium because there is now another participant in the market: the rest of the world. One can view the horizontal line at the world price as representing the demand for steel from the rest of the world. This demand curve is perfectly elastic because Isoland, as a small economy, can sell as much steel as it wants at the world price.

Now consider the gains and losses from opening up trade. Clearly, not everyone benefits. Trade forces the domestic price to rise to the world price. Domestic producers of steel are better off because they can now sell steel at a higher price, but domestic consumers of steel are worse off because they have to buy steel at a higher price.

To measure these gains and losses, we look at the changes in consumer and producer surplus, which are shown in Figure 9-3 and summarized in Table 9-1. Before trade is allowed, the price of steel adjusts to balance domestic supply and domestic demand. Consumer surplus, the area between the demand curve and the before-trade price, is area A + B. Producer surplus, the area between the supply curve and the before-trade price, is area C. Total surplus before trade, the sum of consumer and producer surplus, is area A + B + C.

Figure 9-3

HOW FREE TRADE AFFECTS WELFARE IN AN EXPORTING COUNTRY. When the domestic price rises to equal the world price, sellers are better off (producer surplus rises from C to B + C + D), and buyers are worse off (consumer surplus falls from A + B to A). Total surplus rises by an amount equal to area D, indicating that trade raises the economic well-being of the country as a whole.

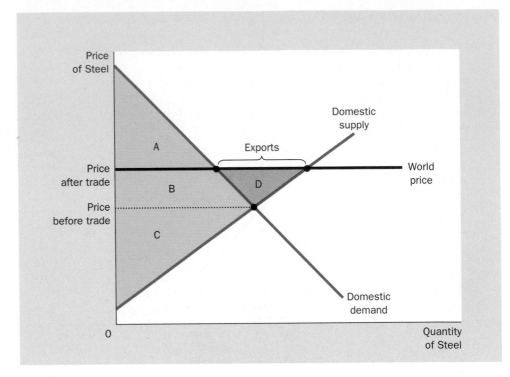

Table 9-1

CHANGES IN WELFARE FROM FREE TRADE: THE CASE OF AN EXPORTING COUNTRY. This table examines changes in economic welfare resulting from opening up a market to international trade. Letters refer to the regions marked in Figure 9-3.

	BEFORE TRADE	AFTER TRADE	CHANGE
Consumer surplus	A + B	A	−B
Producer surplus	C	B + C + D	+(B + D)
Total surplus	A + B + C	A + B + C + D	+D

After trade is allowed, the domestic price rises to the world price. Consumer surplus is area A (the area between the demand curve and the world price). Producer surplus is area B + C + D (the area between the supply curve and the world price). Thus, total surplus with trade is area A + B + C + D.

These welfare calculations show who wins and who loses from trade in an exporting country. Sellers benefit, since producer surplus increases by the area B + D. Buyers are worse off, since consumer surplus decreases by the area B. Because the gains of sellers exceed the losses of buyers by the area D, total surplus in Isoland increases.

This analysis of an exporting country yields two conclusions:

◆ When a country allows trade and becomes an exporter of a good, domestic producers of the good are better off, and domestic consumers of the good are worse off.

◆ Trade raises the economic well-being of a nation, for the gains of the winners exceed the losses of the losers.

THE GAINS AND LOSSES OF AN IMPORTING COUNTRY

Now suppose that the domestic price before trade is above the world price. Once again, after free trade is allowed, the domestic price must equal the world price. As Figure 9-4 shows, the domestic quantity supplied is less than the domestic quantity demanded. The difference between the domestic quantity demanded and the domestic quantity supplied is bought from other countries, and Isoland becomes a steel importer.

In this case, the horizontal line at the world price represents the supply of the rest of the world. This supply curve is perfectly elastic because Isoland is a small economy and, therefore, can buy as much steel as it wants at the world price.

Now consider the gains and losses from trade. Once again, not everyone benefits. When trade forces the domestic price to fall, domestic consumers are better off (they can now buy steel at a lower price), and domestic producers are worse off (they now have to sell steel at a lower price). Changes in consumer and producer surplus measure the size of the gains and losses, as shown in Figure 9-5 and Table 9-2. Before trade, consumer surplus is area A, producer surplus is area B + C, and total surplus is area A + B + C. After trade is allowed, consumer surplus is area A + B + D, producer surplus is area C, and total surplus is area A + B + C + D.

These welfare calculations show who wins and who loses from trade in an importing country. Buyers benefit because consumer surplus increases by the area B + D. Sellers are worse off because producer surplus falls by the area B. The gains of buyers exceed the losses of sellers, and total surplus increases by the area D.

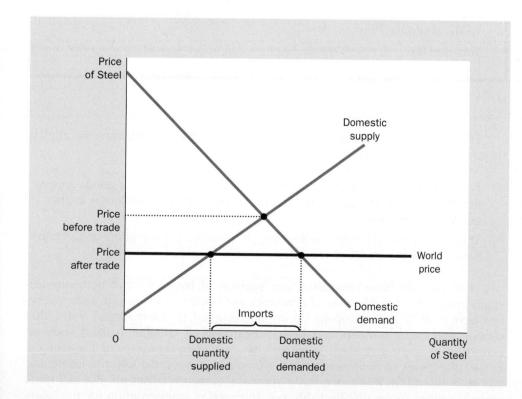

Figure 9-4

INTERNATIONAL TRADE IN AN IMPORTING COUNTRY. Once trade is allowed, the domestic price falls to equal the world price. The supply curve shows the amount produced domestically, and the demand curve shows the amount consumed domestically. Imports equal the difference between the domestic quantity demanded and the domestic quantity supplied at the world price.

Figure 9-5

HOW FREE TRADE AFFECTS
WELFARE IN AN IMPORTING
COUNTRY. When the domestic
price falls to equal the world
price, buyers are better off
(consumer surplus rises from A to
A + B + D), and sellers are worse
off (producer surplus falls from
B + C to C). Total surplus rises by
an amount equal to area D,
indicating that trade raises the
economic well-being of the
country as a whole.

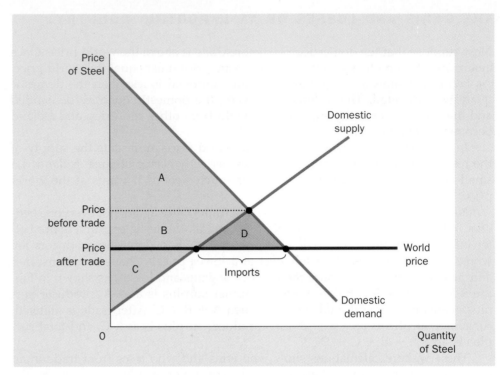

Table 9-2

CHANGES IN WELFARE FROM
FREE TRADE: THE CASE OF AN
IMPORTING COUNTRY. The table
examines changes in economic
welfare resulting from opening
up a market to international
trade. Letters refer to the regions
marked in Figure 9-5.

	BEFORE TRADE	AFTER TRADE	CHANGE
Consumer surplus	A	A + B + D	+(B + D)
Producer surplus	B + C	C	−B
Total surplus	A + B + C	A + B + C + D	+D

This analysis of an importing country yields two conclusions parallel to those for an exporting country:

◆   When a country allows trade and becomes an importer of a good, domestic consumers of the good are better off, and domestic producers of the good are worse off.

◆   Trade raises the economic well-being of a nation, for the gains of the winners exceed the losses of the losers.

Now that we have completed our analysis of trade, we can better understand one of the *Ten Principles of Economics* in Chapter 1: Trade can make everyone better off. If Isoland opens up its steel market to international trade, that change will create winners and losers, regardless of whether Isoland ends up exporting or importing steel. In either case, however, the gains of the winners exceed the losses of the losers, so the winners could compensate the losers and still be better off. In this sense, trade *can* make everyone better off. But *will* trade make everyone better off? Probably not. In practice, compensation for the losers from international trade is rare. Without such compensation, opening up to international trade is a policy that expands the size of the economic pie, while perhaps leaving some participants in the economy with a smaller slice.

THE EFFECTS OF A TARIFF

The Isolandian economists next consider the effects of a **tariff**—a tax on imported goods. The economists quickly realize that a tariff on steel will have no effect if Isoland becomes a steel exporter. If no one in Isoland is interested in importing steel, a tax on steel imports is irrelevant. The tariff matters only if Isoland becomes a steel importer. Concentrating their attention on this case, the economists compare welfare with and without the tariff.

Figure 9-6 shows the Isolandian market for steel. Under free trade, the domestic price equals the world price. A tariff raises the price of imported steel above the world price by the amount of the tariff. Domestic suppliers of steel, who compete with suppliers of imported steel, can now sell their steel for the world price plus the amount of the tariff. Thus, the price of steel—both imported and domestic—rises by the amount of the tariff and is, therefore, closer to the price that would prevail without trade.

The change in price affects the behavior of domestic buyers and sellers. Because the tariff raises the price of steel, it reduces the domestic quantity demanded from Q_1^D to Q_2^D and raises the domestic quantity supplied from Q_1^S to Q_2^S. Thus, *the tariff reduces the quantity of imports and moves the domestic market closer to its equilibrium without trade.*

Now consider the gains and losses from the tariff. Because the tariff raises the domestic price, domestic sellers are better off, and domestic buyers are worse off. In addition, the government raises revenue. To measure these gains and losses, we look at the changes in consumer surplus, producer surplus, and government revenue. These changes are summarized in Table 9-3.

Before the tariff, the domestic price equals the world price. Consumer surplus, the area between the demand curve and the world price, is area A + B + C + D + E + F. Producer surplus, the area between the supply curve and the world price, is area G. Government revenue equals zero. Total surplus, the sum of consumer surplus, producer surplus, and government revenue, is area A + B + C + D + E + F + G.

Once the government imposes a tariff, the domestic price exceeds the world price by the amount of the tariff. Consumer surplus is now area A + B. Producer surplus is area C + G. Government revenue, which is the quantity of after-tariff imports times the size of the tariff, is the area E. Thus, total surplus with the tariff is area A + B + C + E + G.

To determine the total welfare effects of the tariff, we add the change in consumer surplus (which is negative), the change in producer surplus (positive), and the change in government revenue (positive). We find that total surplus in the market decreases by the area D + F, which represents the deadweight loss of the tariff.

It is not surprising that a tariff causes a deadweight loss, for a tariff is a type of tax. Like any tax on the sale of a good, it distorts incentives and pushes the allocation of scarce resources away from the optimum. In this case, we can identify two effects. First, the tariff on steel raises the price of steel that domestic producers can charge above the world price and, as a result, encourages them to increase production of steel (from Q_1^S to Q_2^S). Second, the tariff raises the price

tariff

a tax on goods produced abroad and sold domestically

Figure 9-6

THE EFFECTS OF A TARIFF. A tariff reduces the quantity of imports and moves a market closer to the equilibrium that would exist without trade. Total surplus falls by an amount equal to area D + F. These two triangles represent the deadweight loss from the tariff.

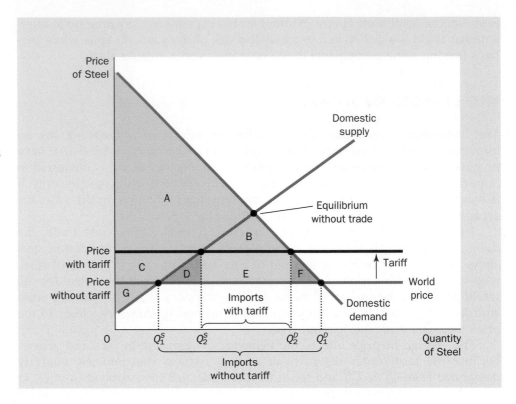

	BEFORE TARIFF	AFTER TARIFF	CHANGE
Consumer surplus	A + B + C + D + E + F	A + B	−(C + D + E + F)
Producer surplus	G	C + G	+C
Government revenue	None	E	+E
Total surplus	A + B + C + D + E + F + G	A + B + C + E + G	−(D + F)

Table 9-3

CHANGES IN WELFARE FROM A TARIFF. This table compares economic welfare when trade is unrestricted and when trade is restricted with a tariff. Letters refer to the regions marked in Figure 9-6.

that domestic steel buyers have to pay and, therefore, encourages them to reduce consumption of steel (from Q_1^D to Q_2^D). Area D represents the deadweight loss from the overproduction of steel, and area F represents the deadweight loss from the underconsumption. The total deadweight loss of the tariff is the sum of these two triangles.

THE EFFECTS OF AN IMPORT QUOTA

import quota

a limit on the quantity of a good that can be produced abroad and sold domestically

The Isolandian economists next consider the effects of an **import quota**—a limit on the quantity of imports. In particular, imagine that the Isolandian government distributes a limited number of import licenses. Each license gives the license holder the right to import one ton of steel into Isoland from abroad. The Isolandian economists want to compare welfare under a policy of free trade and welfare with the addition of this import quota.

Figure 9-7 shows how an import quota affects the Isolandian market for steel. Because the import quota prevents Isolandians from buying as much steel as they want from abroad, the supply of steel is no longer perfectly elastic at the world price. Instead, as long as the price of steel in Isoland is above the world price, the license holders import as much as they are permitted, and the total supply of steel in Isoland equals the domestic supply plus the quota amount.

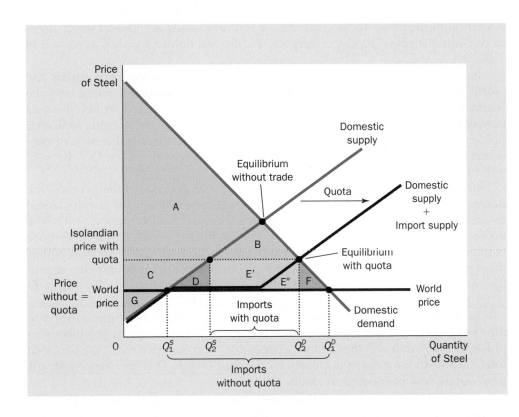

Figure 9-7

THE EFFECTS OF AN IMPORT QUOTA. An import quota, like a tariff, reduces the quantity of imports and moves a market closer to the equilibrium that would exist without trade. Total surplus falls by an amount equal to area D + F. These two triangles represent the deadweight loss from the quota. In addition, the import quota transfers E' + E" to whoever holds the import licenses.

	BEFORE QUOTA	AFTER QUOTA	CHANGE
Consumer surplus	A + B + C + D + E' + E" + F	A + B	−(C + D + E' + E" + F)
Producer surplus	G	C + G	+C
License-holder surplus	None	E' + E"	+(E' + E")
Total surplus	A + B + C + D + E' + E" + F + G	A + B + C + E' + E" + G	−(D + F)

CHANGES IN WELFARE FROM AN IMPORT QUOTA. The table compares economic welfare when trade is unrestricted and when trade is restricted with an import quota. Letters refer to the regions marked in Figure 9-7.

Table 9-4

That is, the supply curve above the world price is shifted to the right by exactly the amount of the quota. (The supply curve below the world price does not shift because, in this case, importing is not profitable for the license holders.)

The price of steel in Isoland adjusts to balance supply (domestic plus imported) and demand. As the figure shows, the quota causes the price of steel to rise above the world price. The domestic quantity demanded falls from Q_1^D to Q_2^D, and the domestic quantity supplied rises from Q_1^S to Q_2^S. Not surprisingly, the import quota reduces steel imports.

Now consider the gains and losses from the quota. Because the quota raises the domestic price above the world price, domestic sellers are better off, and domestic buyers are worse off. In addition, the license holders are better off because they make a profit from buying at the world price and selling at the higher domestic price. To measure these gains and losses, we look at the changes in consumer surplus, producer surplus, and license-holder surplus, as shown in Table 9-4.

Before the government imposes the quota, the domestic price equals the world price. Consumer surplus, the area between the demand curve and the world price, is area A + B + C + D + E' + E''+ F. Producer surplus, the area between the supply curve and the world price, is area G. The surplus of license holders equals zero because there are no licenses. Total surplus, the sum of consumer, producer, and license-holder surplus, is area A + B + C + D + E' + E'' + F + G.

After the government imposes the import quota and issues the licenses, the domestic price exceeds the world price. Domestic consumers get surplus equal to area A + B, and domestic producers get surplus equal to area C + G. The license holders make a profit on each unit imported equal to the difference between the Isolandian price of steel and the world price. Their surplus equals this price differential times the quantity of imports. Thus, it equals the area of the rectangle E' + E''. Total surplus with the quota is the area A + B + C + E' + E'' + G.

To see how total welfare changes with the imposition of the quota, we add the change in consumer surplus (which is negative), the change in producer surplus (positive), and the change in license-holder surplus (positive). We find that total surplus in the market decreases by the area D + F. This area represents the deadweight loss of the import quota.

This analysis should seem somewhat familiar. Indeed, if you compare the analysis of import quotas in Figure 9-7 with the analysis of tariffs in Figure 9-6, you will see that they are essentially identical. *Both tariffs and import quotas raise the domestic price of the good, reduce the welfare of domestic consumers, increase the welfare of domestic producers, and cause deadweight losses.* There is only one difference between these two types of trade restriction: A tariff raises revenue for the government (area E in Figure 9-6), whereas an import quota creates surplus for license holders (area E'+ E'' in Figure 9-7).

Tariffs and import quotas can be made to look even more similar. Suppose that the government tries to capture the license-holder surplus for itself by charging a fee for the licenses. A license to sell one ton of steel is worth exactly the difference between the Isolandian price of steel and the world price, and the government can set the license fee as high as this price differential. If the government does this, the license fee for imports works exactly like a tariff: Consumer surplus, producer surplus, and government revenue are exactly the same under the two policies.

In practice, however, countries that restrict trade with import quotas rarely do so by selling the import licenses. For example, the U.S. government has at times pressured Japan to "voluntarily" limit the sale of Japanese cars in the United States. In this case, the Japanese government allocates the import licenses to Japanese firms, and the surplus from these licenses (area E' + E'') accrues to those firms. This kind of import quota is, from the standpoint of U.S. welfare, strictly worse than a U.S. tariff on imported cars. Both a tariff and an import quota raise prices, restrict trade, and cause deadweight losses, but at least the tariff produces revenue for the U.S. government rather than for Japanese auto companies.

Although in our analysis so far import quotas and tariffs appear to cause similar deadweight losses, a quota can potentially cause an even larger deadweight loss, depending on the mechanism used to allocate the import licenses. Suppose that when Isoland imposes a quota, everyone understands that the licenses will go to those who spend the most resources lobbying the Isolandian government. In this case, there is an implicit license fee—the cost of lobbying. The revenues from this fee, however, rather than being collected by the government, are spent on lobbying expenses. The deadweight losses from this type of quota include not only the losses from overproduction (area D) and underconsumption (area F) but also whatever part of the license-holder surplus (area E' + E'') is wasted on the cost of lobbying.

THE LESSONS FOR TRADE POLICY

The team of Isolandian economists can now write to the new president:

Dear Madam President,

You asked us three questions about opening up trade. After much hard work, we have the answers.

Question: If the government allowed Isolandians to import and export steel, what would happen to the price of steel and the quantity of steel sold in the domestic steel market?

Answer: Once trade is allowed, the Isolandian price of steel would be driven to equal the price prevailing around the world.

If the world price is now higher than the Isolandian price, our price would rise. The higher price would reduce the amount of steel Isolandians consume and raise the amount of steel that Isolandians produce. Isoland would, therefore, become a steel exporter. This occurs because, in this case, Isoland would have a comparative advantage in producing steel.

Conversely, if the world price is now lower than the Isolandian price, our price would fall. The lower price would raise the amount of steel that Isolandians consume and lower the amount of steel that Isolandians produce. Isoland would, therefore, become a steel importer. This occurs because, in this case, other countries would have a comparative advantage in producing steel.

Question: Who would gain from free trade in steel and who would lose, and would the gains exceed the losses?

Answer: The answer depends on whether the price rises or falls when trade is allowed. If the price rises, producers of steel gain, and consumers of steel lose. If the price falls, consumers gain, and producers lose. In both cases, the gains are larger than the losses. Thus, free trade raises the total welfare of Isolandians.

Question: Should a tariff or an import quota be part of the new trade policy?

Answer: A tariff, like most taxes, has deadweight losses: The revenue raised would be smaller than the losses to the buyers and sellers. In this case, the deadweight losses occur because the tariff would move the economy closer to our current no-trade equilibrium. An import quota works much like a tariff and would cause similar deadweight losses. The best policy, from the standpoint of economic efficiency, would be to allow trade without a tariff or an import quota.

We hope you find these answers helpful as you decide on your new policy.

Your faithful servants,

Isolandian economics team

QUICK QUIZ   Draw the supply and demand curve for wool suits in the country of Autarka. When trade is allowed, the price of a suit falls from 3 to 2 ounces of gold. In your diagram, what is the change in consumer surplus, the change in producer surplus, and the change in total surplus? How would a tariff on suit imports alter these effects?

THE ARGUMENTS FOR RESTRICTING TRADE

The letter from the economics team persuades the new president of Isoland to consider opening up trade in steel. She notes that the domestic price is now high compared to the world price. Free trade would, therefore, cause the price of steel to fall and hurt domestic steel producers. Before implementing the new policy, she asks Isolandian steel companies to comment on the economists' advice.

Not surprisingly, the steel companies are opposed to free trade in steel. They believe that the government should protect the domestic steel industry from foreign competition. Let's consider some of the arguments they might give to support their position and how the economics team would respond.

THE JOBS ARGUMENT

Opponents of free trade often argue that trade with other countries destroys domestic jobs. In our example, free trade in steel would cause the price of steel to fall, reducing the quantity of steel produced in Isoland and thus reducing employment in the Isolandian steel industry. Some Isolandian steel workers would lose their jobs.

Yet free trade creates jobs at the same time that it destroys them. When Isolandians buy steel from other countries, other countries obtain the resources to buy other goods from Isoland. Isolandian workers would move from the steel industry to those industries in which Isoland has a comparative advantage. Although the transition may impose hardship on some workers in the short run, it allows Isolandians as a whole to enjoy a higher standard of living.

Opponents of trade are often skeptical that trade creates jobs. They might respond that *everything* can be produced more cheaply abroad. Under free trade, they might argue, Isolandians could not be profitably employed in any industry. As Chapter 3 explains, however, the gains from trade are based on comparative advantage, not absolute advantage. Even if one country is better than another country at producing everything, each country can still gain from trading with the other. Workers in each country will eventually find jobs in the industry in which that country has a comparative advantage.

Berry's World

"You like protectionism as a 'working man.' How about as a consumer?"

THE NATIONAL-SECURITY ARGUMENT

When an industry is threatened with competition from other countries, opponents of free trade often argue that the industry is vital for national security. In our example, Isolandian steel companies might point out that steel is used to make guns and tanks. Free trade would allow Isoland to become dependent on foreign countries to supply steel. If a war later broke out, Isoland might be unable to produce enough steel and weapons to defend itself.

Economists acknowledge that protecting key industries may be appropriate when there are legitimate concerns over national security. Yet they fear that this argument may be used too quickly by producers eager to gain at consumers' expense. The U.S. watchmaking industry, for instance, long argued that it was vital for national security, claiming that its skilled workers would be necessary in wartime. Certainly, it is tempting for those in an industry to exaggerate their role in national defense in order to obtain protection from foreign competition.

THE INFANT-INDUSTRY ARGUMENT

New industries sometimes argue for temporary trade restrictions in order to help them get started. After a period of protection, the argument goes, these industries will mature and be able to compete with foreign competitors. Similarly, older industries sometimes argue that they need temporary protection in order to help them adjust to new conditions. For example, General Motors chairman Roger Smith once argued for temporary protection "to give U.S. automakers turnaround time to get the domestic industry back on its feet."

Economists are often skeptical about such claims. The primary reason is that the infant-industry argument is difficult to implement in practice. To apply protection successfully, the government would need to decide which industries will eventually be profitable and decide whether the benefits of establishing these industries exceed the costs to consumers of protection. Yet "picking winners" is extraordinarily difficult. It is made even more difficult by the political process, which often awards protection to those industries that are politically powerful. And once a powerful industry is protected from foreign competition, the "temporary" policy is hard to remove.

IN THE NEWS

NAFTA
and
Mexican
Tomatoes

IN 1993 PRESIDENT CLINTON ADVOCATED and won passage of the North American Free Trade Agreement (NAFTA). Echoing the views of most economists, he argued that NAFTA would benefit all three parties to agreement—Canada, Mexico, and the United States. In 1996, however, when he was up for reelection, political arguments sometimes seemed more compelling than economic ones. For example, U.S. tomato growers were vocal in their demands for protection from Mexican competition. By contrast, U.S. tomato consumers, far more numerous but much less organized, were not nearly as effective at voicing their interests.

President Wins Tomato Accord for Floridians: Mexico Agrees to End Low-Price Shipments

BY DAVID E. SANGER

WASHINGTON—Defusing a major political issue in Florida just weeks before the election, the Clinton administration today pressured Mexico into an agreement that will set a minimum price for the tomatoes that it ships to the United States, greatly easing pressure on the growers.

The deal satisfies both growers and government officials in one of the most hotly contested states in the presidential election. For years Florida has been demanding protection from competition from roughly $800 million in tomatoes that come over the border annually.

Today's action, which seems likely to raise the price that consumers will pay this winter for tomatoes, was the latest in a series of efforts by the administration to sidestep trade problems that could prove politically troublesome.

Early this year, for example, it delayed an opening of the Mexican border to Mexican trucks under the North American Free Trade Agreement, contending that the trucks were unsafe and a conduit for drugs. It also limited lumber imports from Canada. Both countries have periodically accused the United States of not living up to the spirit of the North American Free Trade Agreement, and Mexico reiterated that complaint today.

The architect of these deals for the administration was also one of President Clinton's closest political confidants, Commerce Secretary Mickey Kantor. As Mr. Clinton's campaign manager in 1992—and, in recent weeks, his negotiator with Bob Dole's campaign over the ground rules for the presidential debates—Mr. Kantor is extraordinarily attuned to the politics of trade accords. . . .

Mr. Kantor was in Seattle today at a campaign appearance and could not be reached for comment. But in a statement released in Washington, he said: "The agreement will provide strong relief to the tomato growers in Florida and other states and help preserve jobs in the industry. Mexican growers will have continued access to the U.S. market, but only on fair terms."

Others in the administration put a harder political edge on Mr. Kantor's accomplishment. . . .

"The math was pretty simple," another official said. "Florida has 25 electoral votes, and Mexico doesn't."

SOURCE: *The New York Times*, October 12, 1996, p. A1.

In addition, many economists are skeptical about the infant-industry argument even in principle. Suppose, for instance, that the Isolandian steel industry is young and unable to compete profitably against foreign rivals. Yet there is reason to believe that the industry can be profitable in the long run. In this case, the owners of the firms should be willing to incur temporary losses in order to obtain the eventual profits. Protection is not necessary for an industry to grow. Firms in various industries—such as many biotechnology firms today—incur temporary losses in the hope of growing and becoming profitable in the future. And many of them succeed, even without protection from foreign competition.

THE UNFAIR-COMPETITION ARGUMENT

A common argument is that free trade is desirable only if all countries play by the same rules. If firms in different countries are subject to different laws and regulations, then it is unfair (the argument goes) to expect the firms to compete in the international marketplace. For instance, suppose that the government of Neighborland subsidizes its steel industry by giving steel companies large tax breaks. The Isolandian steel industry might argue that it should be protected from this foreign competition because Neighborland is not competing fairly.

Would it, in fact, hurt Isoland to buy steel from another country at a subsidized price? Certainly, Isolandian steel producers would suffer, but Isolandian steel consumers would benefit from the low price. Moreover, the case for free trade is no different: The gains of the consumers from buying at the low price would exceed the losses of the producers. Neighborland's subsidy to its steel industry may be a bad policy, but it is the taxpayers of Neighborland who bear the burden. Isoland can benefit from the opportunity to buy steel at a subsidized price.

THE PROTECTION-AS-A-BARGAINING-CHIP ARGUMENT

Another argument for trade restrictions concerns the strategy of bargaining. Many policymakers claim to support free trade but, at the same time, argue that trade restrictions can be useful when we bargain with our trading partners. They claim that the threat of a trade restriction can help remove a trade restriction already imposed by a foreign government. For example, Isoland might threaten to impose a tariff on steel unless Neighborland removes its tariff on wheat. If Neighborland responds to this threat by removing its tariff, the result can be freer trade.

The problem with this bargaining strategy is that the threat may not work. If it doesn't work, the country has a difficult choice. It can carry out its threat and implement the trade restriction, which would reduce its own economic welfare. Or it can back down from its threat, which would cause it to lose prestige in international affairs. Faced with this choice, the country would probably wish that it had never made the threat in the first place.

CASE STUDY   GATT AND THE MULTILATERAL APPROACH TO FREE TRADE

A country can take one of two approaches to achieving free trade. It can take a *unilateral* approach and remove its trade restrictions on its own. This is the approach that Great Britain took in the nineteenth century and that Chile and South Korea have taken in recent years. Alternatively, a country can take a *multilateral* approach and reduce its trade restrictions while other countries do the same. In other words, it can bargain with its trading partners in an attempt to reduce trade restrictions around the world.

IN THE NEWS

A Chicken Invasion

WHEN DOMESTIC PRODUCERS COMPLAIN about competition from abroad, they often assert that consumers are not well served by imperfect foreign products. The following article documents how Russian producers of chicken reacted to competition from the United States.

U.S. Chicken in Every Pot? Nyet! Russians Cry Foul

BY MICHAEL R. GORDON

MOSCOW—A nasty little skirmish between Russia and the United States is brewing here over a threatened trade barrier.

But this fight is not about manufactured consumer goods or high technology, but about American chicken, which has flooded the Russian market.

To the frustration, and considerable anxiety, of American companies, the Russian government has threatened to ban further American poultry sales effective March 19. . . .

The ostensible reason for the Russian government's warning is health—a seemingly strange concern in a country with a generally lax record in observing safety standards, where virtually every able-bodied man and woman smokes.

Today, no less an authority than the Veterinary Department of the Russian Agriculture and Food Ministry said the ban was needed to protect consumers here against infected poultry until the United States improved its standards.

But the real agenda, American producers contend, is old-fashioned protectionism.

Agitated Russian producers, whose birds, Russian consumers say, are no match for their American competition in terms of quality and price, have repeatedly complained that the United States is trying to destroy the Russian poultry industry and capture its market. And now American companies fear the Russian producers are striking back. . . .

The first big invasion of frozen poultry [into Russia] came during the Bush administration. . . . The export proved to be very popular with Russian consumers, who dubbed them Bush legs.

After the demise of the Soviet Union, American poultry exports continued to soar. Russian poultry production, meanwhile, fell 40 percent, the result of rising grain prices and declining subsidies.

Astoundingly, a third of all American exports to Russia is poultry, American officials say. . . .

If the confrontation continues, the United States has a number of possible

A THREAT TO RUSSIA?

recourses, including arguing that the Russian action is inconsistent with Moscow's bid to join the World Trade Organization.

Some experts, however, believe there is an important countervailing force here that may lead to a softening of the Russian position: namely Russian consumers.

Russian consumers favor the American birds, which despite the dire warnings of the Russian government, have come to symbolize quality. And they vote, too.

SOURCE: *The New York Times*, February 24, 1996, pp. 33, 34.

An important example of the multilateral approach is GATT, the General Agreement on Tariffs and Trade. GATT is a continuing series of negotiations among many of the world's countries with the goal of promoting free trade. The United States helped to found GATT after World War II. GATT was a response to the high tariffs imposed during the Great Depression of the 1930s. Many economists believe these tariffs contributed to the economic hardship during that period. GATT has successfully reduced the average tariff among member countries from about 40 percent after World War II to about 5 percent today.

What are the pros and cons of the multilateral approach to free trade? One advantage is that the multilateral approach has the potential to result in freer trade than a unilateral approach because it can reduce trade restrictions abroad as well as at home. At the same time, however, if international negotiations fail, the result could be more restricted trade than under a unilateral approach.

In addition, the multilateral approach may have a political advantage. In most markets, producers are fewer and better organized than consumers—and thus wield greater political influence. Reducing the Isolandian tariff on steel, for example, may be politically difficult if considered by itself. The steel companies would oppose free trade, and the users of steel who would benefit are so numerous that organizing their support would be difficult. Yet suppose that Neighborland promises to reduce its tariff on wheat at the same time that Isoland reduces its tariff on steel. In this case, the Isolandian wheat farmers, who are also politically powerful, would back the agreement. Thus, the multilateral approach to free trade can sometimes win political support when a unilateral reduction cannot.

QUICK QUIZ The textile industry of Autarka advocates a ban on the import of wool suits. Describe five arguments its lobbyists might make. Give a response to each of these arguments.

CONCLUSION

Economists and the general public often disagree about free trade. In 1993, for example, the United States faced the question of whether to ratify the North American Free Trade Agreement, which reduced trade restrictions among the United States, Canada, and Mexico. Opinion polls showed the general public in the United States about evenly split on the issue, and the agreement passed in Congress by a narrow margin. Opponents viewed free trade as a threat to job security and the American standard of living. By contrast, economists overwhelmingly supported the agreement. They viewed free trade as a way of allocating production efficiently and raising living standards in all three countries.

Economists view the United States as an ongoing experiment that confirms the virtues of free trade. Throughout its history, the United States has allowed unrestricted trade among the states, and the country as a whole has benefited from the specialization that trade allows. Florida grows oranges, Texas pumps oil, California makes wine, and so on. Americans would not enjoy the high standard of living they do today if people could consume only those goods and services produced in their own states. The world could similarly benefit from free trade among countries.

To better understand economists' view of trade, let's continue our parable. Suppose that the country of Isoland ignores the advice of its economics team and decides not to allow free trade in steel. The country remains in the equilibrium without international trade.

Then, one day, some Isolandian inventor discovers a new way to make steel at very low cost. The process is quite mysterious, however, and the inventor insists on keeping it a secret. What is odd is that the inventor doesn't need any workers or iron ore to make steel. The only input he requires is wheat.

The inventor is hailed as a genius. Because steel is used in so many products, the invention lowers the cost of many goods and allows all Isolandians to enjoy a higher standard of living. Workers who had previously produced steel do suffer when their factories close, but eventually they find work in other industries. Some become farmers and grow the wheat that the inventor turns into steel. Others enter new industries that emerge as a result of higher Isolandian living standards. Everyone understands that the displacement of these workers is an inevitable part of progress.

After several years, a newspaper reporter decides to investigate this mysterious new steel process. She sneaks into the inventor's factory and learns that the inventor is a fraud. The inventor has not been making steel at all. Instead, he has been illegally shipping wheat abroad and importing steel from other countries. The only thing that the inventor had discovered was the gains from international trade.

When the truth is finally revealed, the government shuts down the inventor's operation. The price of steel rises, and workers return to jobs in steel factories. Living standards in Isoland fall back to their former levels. The inventor is jailed and held up to public ridicule. After all, he was no inventor. He was just an economist.

Summary

◆ The effects of free trade can be determined by comparing the domestic price without trade to the world price. A low domestic price indicates that the country has a comparative advantage in producing the good and that the country will become an exporter. A high domestic price indicates that the rest of the world has a comparative advantage in producing the good and that the country will become an importer.

◆ When a country allows trade and becomes an exporter of a good, producers of the good are better off, and consumers of the good are worse off. When a country allows trade and becomes an importer of a good, consumers are better off, and producers are worse off. In both cases, the gains from trade exceed the losses.

◆ A tariff—a tax on imports—moves a market closer to the equilibrium that would exist without trade and,

therefore, reduces the gains from trade. Although domestic producers are better off and the government raises revenue, the losses to consumers exceed these gains.

◆ An import quota has effects that are similar to those of a tariff. Under a quota, however, the holders of the import licenses receive the revenue that the government would collect with a tariff.

◆ There are various arguments for restricting trade: protecting jobs, defending national security, helping infant industries, preventing unfair competition, and responding to foreign trade restrictions. Although some of these arguments have some merit in some cases, economists believe that free trade is usually the better policy.

Key Concepts

world price, p. 176   tariff, p. 181   import quota, p. 182

Questions for Review

1. What does the domestic price that prevails without international trade tell us about a nation's comparative advantage?

2. When does a country become an exporter of a good? An importer?

3. Draw the supply-and-demand diagram for an importing country. What is consumer surplus and producer surplus before trade is allowed? What is consumer surplus and producer surplus with free trade? What is the change in total surplus?

4. List five arguments often given to support trade restrictions. How do economists respond to these arguments?

Problems and Applications

1. The United States represents a small part of the world orange market.
   a. Draw a diagram depicting the equilibrium in the U.S. orange market without international trade. Identify the equilibrium price, equilibrium quantity, consumer surplus, and producer surplus.
   b. Suppose that the world orange price is below the U.S. price before trade, and that the U.S. orange market is now opened to trade. Identify the new equilibrium price, quantity consumed, quantity produced domestically, and quantity imported. Also show the change in the surplus of domestic consumers and producers. Has domestic total surplus increased or decreased?

2. The world price of wine is below the price that would prevail in the United States in the absence of trade.
   a. Assuming that American imports of wine are a small part of total world wine production, draw a graph for the U.S. market for wine under free trade. Identify consumer surplus, producer surplus, and total surplus in an appropriate table.
   b. Now suppose that an unusual shift of the Gulf Stream leads to an unseasonably cold summer in Europe, destroying much of the grape harvest there. What effect does this shock have on the world price of wine? Using your graph and table from part (a), show the effect on consumer surplus, producer surplus, and total surplus in the United States. Who are the winners and losers? Is the United States as a whole better or worse off?

3. The world price of cotton is below the no-trade price in Country A and above the no-trade price in Country B. Using supply-and-demand diagrams and welfare tables such as those in the chapter, show the gains from trade in each country. Compare your results for the two countries.

4. If the world price of a good is above the no-trade price in a country, what is the effect of a tariff on that good? If the world price is below the no-trade price, what is the effect of a tariff that exceeds the difference between those prices?

5. Suppose that Congress imposes a tariff on imported autos to protect the U.S. auto industry from foreign competition. Assuming that the U.S. is a price-taker in the world auto market, show on a diagram: the change in the quantity of imports, the loss to U.S. consumers, the gain to U.S. manufacturers, government revenue, and the deadweight loss associated with the tariff. The loss to consumers can be decomposed into three pieces: a transfer to domestic producers, a transfer to the government, and a deadweight loss. Use your diagram to identify these three pieces.

6. According to an article in *The New York Times* (Nov. 5, 1993), "many Midwest wheat farmers oppose the [North American] free trade agreement [NAFTA] as much as many corn farmers support it." For simplicity, assume that the United States is a small country in the markets for both corn and wheat, and that without the free trade agreement, the United States would not trade these commodities internationally. (Both of these assumptions are false, but they do not affect the qualitative responses to the following questions.)
   a. Based on this report, do you think the world wheat price is above or below the U.S. no-trade wheat price? Do you think the world corn price is above or below the U.S. no-trade corn price? Now analyze the welfare consequences of NAFTA in both markets.
   b. Considering both markets together, does NAFTA make U.S. farmers as a group better or worse off? Does it make U.S. consumers as a group better or worse off? Does it make the United States as a whole better or worse off?

7. The following table presents the demand and supply schedules for watches in the United States and Switzerland (which we assume are the only two countries in the world):

Price per Watch	Q^D in United States (thousands)	Q^S in United States (thousands)	Q^D in Switzerland (thousands)	Q^S in Switzerland (thousands)
$10	110	0	80	30
20	90	20	50	50
30	70	40	35	65
40	60	60	20	80
50	50	80	5	95
60	40	95	0	105
70	30	105	0	110
80	20	110	0	115

a. With no international trade, what are the equilibrium price and quantity in the U.S. watch market and in the Swiss watch market?

b. Now suppose that trade is opened between the United States and Switzerland only. What is the new equilibrium price in the world market for watches? How does it compare to the no-trade prices of watches in the two countries?

c. What is the total quantity of watch production at the new equilibrium in the two countries? Which country exports watches? How many?

d. When trade opens, what happens to the quantity of watches produced, and thus employment, in the U.S. watch industry? In the Swiss watch industry? Who benefits and who loses from the opening of trade?

8. Imagine that winemakers in the state of Washington petitioned the state government to tax wines imported from California. They argue that this tax would both raise tax revenue for the state government and raise employment in the Washington State wine industry. Do you agree with these claims? Is it a good policy?

9. In a letter to *The Wall Street Journal* (Aug. 27, 1990), Senator Ernest Hollings wrote that "consumers *do not* benefit from lower-priced imports. Glance through some mail-order catalogs and you'll see that consumers pay exactly the same price for clothing whether it is U.S.-made or imported." Comment.

10. When the government of Tradeland decides to impose an import quota on foreign cars, three proposals are suggested: (1) Sell the import licenses in an auction. (2) Distribute the licenses randomly in a lottery. (3) Let people wait in line and distribute the licenses on a first-

come, first-served basis. Compare the effects of these policies. Which policy do you think has the largest deadweight losses? Which policy has the smallest deadweight losses? Why? (Hint: The government's other ways of raising tax revenue all cause deadweight losses themselves.)

11. An article about sugar beet growers in *The Wall Street Journal* (June 26, 1990) explained that "the government props up domestic sugar prices by curtailing imports of lower-cost sugar. Producers are guaranteed a 'market stabilization price' of $0.22 a pound, about $0.09 higher than the current world market price." The government maintains the higher price by imposing an import quota.

a. Illustrate the effect of this quota on the U.S. sugar market. Label the relevant prices and quantities under free trade and under the quota.

b. Analyze the effects of the sugar quota using the tools of welfare analysis.

c. The article also comments that "critics of the sugar program say that [the quota] has deprived numerous sugar-producing nations in the Caribbean, Latin America, and Far East of export earnings, harmed their economies, and caused political instability, while increasing Third World demand for U.S. foreign aid." Our usual welfare analysis includes only gains and losses to U.S. consumers and producers. What role do you think the gains or losses to people in other countries should play in our economic policymaking?

d. The article continues that "at home, the sugar program has helped make possible the spectacular rise of the high-fructose corn syrup industry." Why has the sugar program had this effect? (Hint: Are sugar and corn syrup substitutes or complements?)

12. (This question is challenging.) Consider a small country that exports steel. Suppose that a "pro-trade" govern-

ment decides to subsidize the export of steel by paying a certain amount for each ton sold abroad. How does this export subsidy affect the domestic price of steel, the quantity of steel produced, the quantity of steel con-sumed, and the quantity of steel exported? How does it affect consumer surplus, producer surplus, government revenue, and total surplus? (Hint: The analysis of an export subsidy is similar to the analysis of a tariff.)

IV

THE ECONOMICS OF THE
PUBLIC SECTOR

10

EXTERNALITIES

*Learn what an
externality is*

*See why externalities can
make market outcomes
inefficient*

*Examine how people can
sometimes solve the
problem of externalities
on their own*

*Consider why private
solutions to externalities
sometimes do not work*

*Examine the various
government policies
aimed at solving the
problem of externalities*

Firms that make and sell paper also create, as a by-product of the manufacturing process, a chemical called dioxin. Scientists believe that once dioxin enters the environment, it raises the population's risk of cancer, birth defects, and other health problems.

Is the production and release of dioxin a problem for society? In Chapters 4 through 9 we examined how markets allocate scarce resources with the forces of supply and demand, and we saw that the equilibrium of supply and demand is typically an efficient allocation of resources. To use Adam Smith's famous metaphor, the "invisible hand" of the marketplace leads self-interested buyers and sellers in a market to maximize the total benefit that society derives from that market. This insight is the basis for one of the *Ten Principles of Economics* in Chapter 1: Markets are usually a good way to organize economic activity. Should we conclude, therefore, that the invisible hand prevents firms in the paper market from emitting too much dioxin?

Markets do many things well, but they do not do everything well. In this chapter we begin our study of another one of the *Ten Principles of Economics*:

Governments can sometimes improve market outcomes. We examine why markets sometimes fail to allocate resources efficiently, how government policies can potentially improve the market's allocation, and what kinds of policies are likely to work best.

externality

the impact of one person's actions on the well-being of a bystander

The market failures examined in this chapter fall under a general category called *externalities*. An **externality** is the impact of one person's actions on the well-being of a bystander. If the effect on the bystander is adverse, it is called a *negative externality*; if it is beneficial, it is called a *positive externality*. In the presence of externalities, society's interest in a market outcome extends beyond the well-being of buyers and sellers in the market; it also includes the well-being of bystanders who are affected. Because buyers and sellers neglect the external effects of their actions when deciding how much to demand or supply, the market equilibrium is not efficient in the presence of externalities. That is, the equilibrium fails to maximize the total benefit to society as a whole. The release of dioxin into the environment, for instance, is a negative externality. Self-interested paper firms will not consider the full cost of the pollution they create and, therefore, will emit too much unless the government prevents or discourages them from doing so.

Externalities come in many varieties, as do the policy responses that try to deal with the market failure. Here are some examples:

◆ The exhaust from automobiles is a negative externality because it creates smog that other people have to breathe. As a result of this externality, drivers tend to pollute too much. The federal government attempts to solve this problem by setting emission standards for cars. It also taxes gasoline in order to reduce the amount that people drive.

◆ Restored historic buildings convey a positive externality because people who walk or ride by them enjoy their beauty and the sense of history that these buildings provide. Building owners do not get the full benefit of restoration and, therefore, tend to discard older buildings too quickly. Many local governments respond to this problem by regulating the destruction of historic buildings and by providing tax breaks to owners who restore them.

◆ Barking dogs create a negative externality because neighbors are disturbed by the noise. Dog owners do not bear the full cost of the noise and, therefore, tend to take too few precautions to prevent their dogs from barking. Local governments address this problem by making it illegal to "disturb the peace."

◆ Research into new technologies provides a positive externality because it creates knowledge that other people can use. Because inventors cannot capture the full benefits of their inventions, they tend to devote too few resources to research. The federal government addresses this problem partially through the patent system, which gives inventors an exclusive use over their inventions for a period of time.

In each of the foregoing cases, some decisionmaker is failing to take account of the external effects of his or her behavior. The government responds by trying to influence this behavior in order to protect the interests of bystanders.

EXTERNALITIES AND MARKET INEFFICIENCY

In this section we use the tools from Chapter 7 to examine how externalities affect economic well-being. The analysis shows precisely why externalities cause markets to allocate resources inefficiently. Later in the chapter we examine various ways in which private actors and public policymakers may remedy this type of market failure.

WELFARE ECONOMICS: A RECAP

We begin by recalling the key lessons of welfare economics from Chapter 7. To make our analysis concrete, we will consider a specific market—the market for aluminum. Figure 10-1 shows the supply and demand curves in the market for aluminum.

As you should recall from Chapter 7, the supply and demand curves contain important information about costs and benefits. The demand curve for aluminum reflects the value of aluminum to consumers, as measured by the prices they are willing to pay. At any given quantity, the height of the demand curve shows the willingness to pay of the marginal buyer. In other words, it shows the value of the last unit of aluminum bought. Similarly, the supply curve reflects the costs of aluminum producers. At any given quantity, the height of the supply curve shows the cost of the marginal seller. In other words, it shows the cost of the last unit of aluminum sold.

In the absence of government intervention, the price of aluminum adjusts to balance the supply and demand for aluminum. The quantity produced and

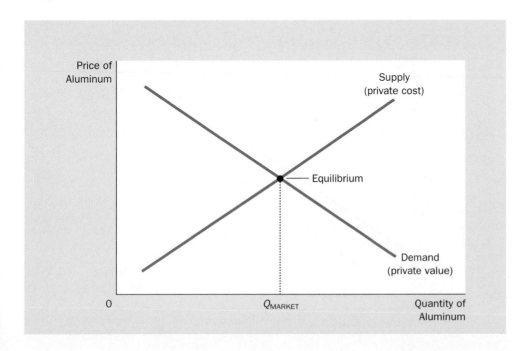

Figure 10-1

THE MARKET FOR ALUMINUM. The demand curve reflects the value to buyers, and the supply curve reflects the costs of sellers. The equilibrium quantity, Q_{MARKET}, maximizes the total value to buyers minus the total costs of sellers. In the absence of externalities, therefore, the market equilibrium is efficient.

consumed in the market equilibrium, shown as Q_{MARKET} in Figure 10-1, is efficient in the sense that it maximizes the sum of producer and consumer surplus. That is, the market allocates resources in a way that maximizes the total value to the consumers who buy and use aluminum minus the total costs to the producers who make and sell aluminum.

NEGATIVE EXTERNALITIES IN PRODUCTION

Now let's suppose that aluminum factories emit pollution: For each unit of aluminum produced, a certain amount of smoke enters the atmosphere. Because this smoke creates a health risk for those who breathe the air, it is a negative externality. How does this externality affect the efficiency of the market outcome?

Because of the externality, the cost to *society* of producing aluminum is larger than the cost to the aluminum producers. For each unit of aluminum produced, the *social cost* includes the private costs of the aluminum producers plus the costs to those bystanders adversely affected by the pollution. Figure 10-2 shows the social cost of producing aluminum. The social-cost curve is above the supply curve because it takes into account the external costs imposed on society by aluminum producers. The difference between these two curves reflects the cost of the pollution emitted.

What quantity of aluminum should be produced? To answer this question, we once again consider what a benevolent social planner would do. The planner wants to maximize the total surplus derived from the market—the value to consumers of aluminum minus the cost of producing aluminum. The planner understands, however, that the cost of producing aluminum includes the external costs of the pollution.

The planner would choose the level of aluminum production at which the demand curve crosses the social-cost curve. This intersection determines the opti-

Figure 10-2

POLLUTION AND THE SOCIAL OPTIMUM. In the presence of a negative externality to production, the social cost of producing aluminum exceeds the private cost. The optimal quantity of aluminum, $Q_{OPTIMUM}$, is therefore smaller than the equilibrium quantity, Q_{MARKET}.

"All I can say is that if being a leading manufacturer means being a leading polluter, so be it."

mal amount of aluminum from the standpoint of society as a whole. The planner reaches at least this level of production because, below this level, the value of the aluminum to consumers (as measured by the height of the demand curve) exceeds the social cost of producing it (as measured by the height of the social-cost curve). The planner does not produce more than this level because the social cost of producing additional aluminum exceeds the value to consumers.

Note that the equilibrium quantity of aluminum, Q_{MARKET}, is larger than the socially optimal quantity, $Q_{OPTIMUM}$. The reason for this inefficiency is that the market equilibrium reflects only the private costs of production. In the market equilibrium, the marginal consumer values aluminum at less than the social cost of producing it. That is, at Q_{MARKET} the demand curve lies below the social-cost curve. Thus, reducing aluminum production and consumption below the equilibrium level raises total economic well-being.

How can the social planner achieve this optimum? One way would be to tax aluminum producers for each ton of aluminum sold. The tax would shift the supply curve for aluminum upward by the size of the tax. If the tax accurately reflected the social cost of smoke released into the atmosphere, the new supply curve would coincide with the social-cost curve. In the new market equilibrium, aluminum producers would produce the socially optimal quantity of aluminum.

Such a tax is said to be **internalizing the externality** because it gives buyers and sellers in the market an incentive to take account of the external effects of their actions. Aluminum producers would, in essence, take the costs of pollution into account when deciding how much aluminum to supply because the tax now makes them pay for these external costs. Later in this chapter we consider other ways in which policymakers can deal with externalities.

internalizing an externality
altering incentives so that people take account of the external effects of their actions

POSITIVE EXTERNALITIES IN PRODUCTION

Although there are many markets in which the social cost of production exceeds the private cost, there are also some markets in which the opposite is the case.

Figure 10-3

TECHNOLOGY SPILLOVERS AND THE SOCIAL OPTIMUM. In the presence of a positive externality to production, the social cost of producing robots is less than the private cost. The optimal quantity of robots, $Q_{OPTIMUM}$, is therefore larger than the equilibrium quantity, Q_{MARKET}.

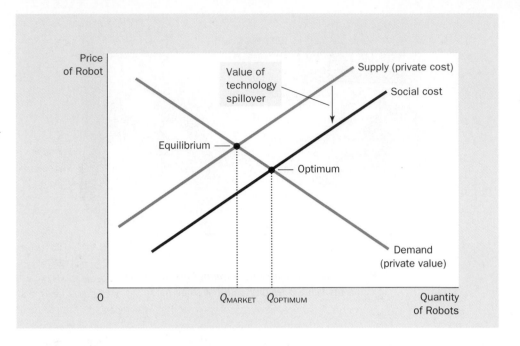

In these markets, the externality benefits bystanders, so the social cost of production is less than the private cost. One example is the market for industrial robots.

Robots are at the frontier of a rapidly changing technology. Whenever a firm builds a robot, there is some chance that it will discover a new and better design. This new design will benefit not only this firm but society as a whole because the design will enter society's pool of technological knowledge. This type of positive externality is called a *technology spillover*.

The analysis of positive externalities is similar to the analysis of negative externalities. Figure 10-3 shows the market for robots. Because of the technology spillover, the social cost of producing a robot is less than the private cost. Therefore, the social planner would choose to produce a larger quantity of robots than the private market does.

In this case, the government can internalize the externality by subsidizing the production of robots. If the government paid firms for each robot produced, the supply curve would shift down by the amount of the subsidy, and this shift would increase the equilibrium quantity of robots. To ensure that the market equilibrium equals the social optimum, the subsidy should equal the value of the technology spillover.

CASE STUDY   THE DEBATE OVER TECHNOLOGY POLICY

How large are technology spillovers, and what do they imply for public policy? This is an important question because technological progress is the key to why living standards rise from generation to generation. Yet it is also a difficult question on which economists often disagree.

Some economists believe that technology spillovers are pervasive and that the government should encourage those industries that yield the largest spillovers. For instance, these economists argue that if making computer chips yields greater spillovers than making potato chips, then the government should use the tax laws to encourage the production of computer chips relative to the production of potato chips. Government intervention in the economy that aims to promote technology-enhancing industries is called *technology policy*.

Other economists are skeptical about technology policy. Even if technology spillovers are common, the success of a technology policy requires that the government be able to measure the size of the spillovers from different markets. This measurement problem is difficult at best. Moreover, without precise measurements, the political system may end up subsidizing those industries with the most political clout, rather than those that yield the largest positive externalities.

One type of technology policy that most economists endorse is patent protection. The patent laws protect the rights of inventors by giving them exclusive use of their inventions for a period of time. When a firm makes a technological breakthrough, it can patent the idea and capture much of the economic benefit for itself. The patent is said to internalize the externality by giving the firm a *property right* over its invention. If other firms want to use the new technology, they would have to obtain permission from the inventing firm and pay it some royalty. Thus, the patent system gives firms a greater incentive to engage in research and other activities that advance technology.

Should the government subsidize this firm?

EXTERNALITIES IN CONSUMPTION

The externalities we have discussed so far are associated with the production of goods. Some externalities, however, are associated with consumption. The consumption of alcohol, for instance, yields negative externalities if consumers are more likely to drive under its influence and risk the lives of others. Similarly, the consumption of education yields positive externalities because a more educated population leads to better government, which benefits everyone.

The analysis of consumption externalities is similar to the analysis of production externalities. As Figure 10-4 shows, the demand curve no longer reflects the social value from the good. Panel (a) shows the case of a negative

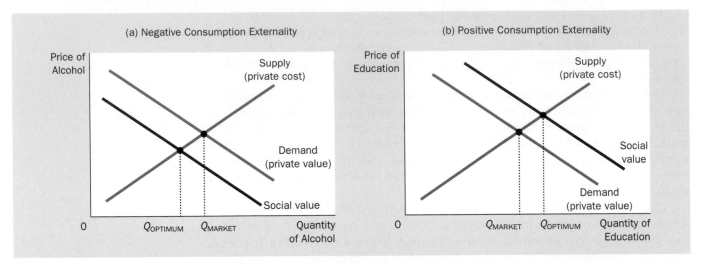

Figure 10-4

CONSUMPTION EXTERNALITIES. Panel (a) shows a market with a negative consumption externality, such as the market for alcoholic beverages. The curve representing social value is lower than the demand curve, and the socially optimal quantity, $Q_{OPTIMUM}$, is less than the equilibrium quantity, Q_{MARKET}. Panel (b) shows a market with a positive consumption externality, such as the market for education. The curve representing social value is above the demand curve, and the socially optimal quantity, $Q_{OPTIMUM}$, is greater than the equilibrium quantity, Q_{MARKET}.

consumption externality, such as that associated with alcohol. In this case, the social value is less than the private value, and the socially optimal quantity is smaller than the quantity determined by the private market. Panel (b) shows the case of a positive consumption externality, like that of education. In this case, the social value is greater than the private value, and the socially optimal quantity is greater than the quantity determined by the private market.

Once again, the government can correct the market failure by internalizing the externality. The appropriate response in the case of consumption externalities is similar to that in the case of production externalities. To move the market equilibrium closer to the social optimum, a negative externality requires a tax, and a positive externality requires a subsidy. In fact, that is exactly the policy the government follows: Alcoholic beverages are among the most highly taxed goods in our economy, and education is heavily subsidized through public schools and government scholarships.

As you may have noticed by now, these examples of externalities lead to some general lessons: Negative externalities in production or consumption lead markets to produce a larger quantity than is socially desirable. Positive externalities in production or consumption lead markets to produce a smaller quantity than is socially desirable. To remedy the problem, the government can internalize the externality by taxing goods that have negative externalities and subsidizing goods that have positive externalities.

QUICK QUIZ   Give an example of a negative externality and a positive externality. ◆ Explain why market outcomes are inefficient in the presence of externalities.

PRIVATE SOLUTIONS TO EXTERNALITIES

We have discussed why externalities lead markets to allocate resources inefficiently, but have mentioned only briefly how this inefficiency can be remedied. In practice, both private actors and public policymakers respond to externalities in various ways. All of the remedies share the goal of moving the allocation of resources closer to the social optimum. In this section we examine the variety of private solutions.

THE TYPES OF PRIVATE SOLUTIONS

Although externalities tend to cause markets to be inefficient, government action is not always needed to solve the problem. In some circumstances, people can develop private solutions.

Sometimes, the problem of externalities is solved with moral codes and social sanctions. Consider, for instance, why most people do not litter. Although there are laws against littering, these laws are not vigorously enforced. Most people do not litter just because it is the wrong thing to do. The Golden Rule taught to most children says, "Do unto others as you would have them do unto you." This moral injunction tells us to take account of how our actions affect other people. In economic terms, it tells us to internalize externalities.

Another private solution to externalities is charities, many of which are established to deal with externalities. For example, the Sierra Club, whose goal is to protect the environment, is a nonprofit organization funded with private donations. As another example, private colleges and universities receive gifts from alumni, corporations, and foundations in part because education has positive externalities for society.

The private market can often solve the problem of externalities by relying on the self-interest of the relevant parties. Sometimes the solution takes the form of integrating different types of business. For example, consider an apple grower and a beekeeper that are located next to each other. Each business confers a positive externality on the other: By pollinating the flowers on the trees, the bees help the orchard produce apples. At the same time, the bees use the nectar they get from the apple trees to produce honey. Nonetheless, when the apple grower is deciding how many trees to plant and the beekeeper is deciding how many bees to keep, they neglect the positive externality. As a result, the apple grower plants too few trees and the beekeeper keeps too few bees. These externalities could be internalized if the beekeeper bought the apple orchard or if the apple grower bought the beehive: Both activities would then take place within the same firm, and this single firm could choose the optimum number of trees and bees. Internalizing externalities is one reason that some firms are involved in different types of business.

Another way for the private market to deal with external effects is for the interested parties to enter into a contract. In the example above, a contract between the apple grower and the beekeeper can solve the problem of too few trees and too few bees. The contract can specify the number of trees, the number of bees, and perhaps a payment from one party to the other. By setting the right number of trees and bees, the contract can solve the inefficiency that normally arises from these externalities and make both parties better off.

IN THE NEWS

An Outraged Citizen Speaks Out

THE FOLLOWING LETTER TO THE EDITOR suggests a private solution to an externality. Do you think the proposed solution will work?

Smokers, Pick Up Your Butts

While citizens, politicians, and public health organizations have echoed calls to clean up the cigarette industry, we have forgotten to remind the smokers to clean up after themselves.

Daily, I witness inconsiderate smokers flicking their cigarettes onto sidewalks and streets, often within feet of ashtrays or refuse containers. Apparently many do not think there is anything wrong with this behavior. This is an outrage!

It is not right that I cannot enjoy an early-morning stretch on a park bench because the area is strewn with cigarette butts. These butts constitute litter. Nonsmokers and smokers who care should give these litterbugs friendly but firm reminders of how to dispose of their waste properly.

Howie Breinan
Cambridge, MA

SOURCE: *Boston Globe*, August 7, 1996, p. A14.

A NEGATIVE EXTERNALITY

THE COASE THEOREM

Coase theorem

the proposition that if private parties can bargain without cost over the allocation of resources, they can solve the problem of externalities on their own

How effective is the private market in dealing with externalities? A famous result, called the **Coase theorem** after economist Ronald Coase, suggests that it can be very effective in some circumstances. According to the Coase theorem, if private parties can bargain without cost over the allocation of resources, then the private market will always solve the problem of externalities and allocate resources efficiently.

To see how the Coase theorem works, consider an example. Suppose that Dick owns a dog named Spot. Spot barks and disturbs Jane, Dick's neighbor. Dick gets a benefit from owning the dog, but the dog confers a negative externality on Jane. Should Dick be forced to send Spot to the pound, or should Jane have to suffer sleepless nights because of Spot's barking?

Consider first what outcome is socially efficient. A social planner, considering the two alternatives, would compare the benefit that Dick gets from the dog to the cost that Jane bears from the barking. If the benefit exceeds the cost, it is efficient for Dick to keep the dog and for Jane to live with the barking. Yet if the cost exceeds the benefit, then Dick should get rid of the dog.

According to the Coase theorem, the private market will reach the efficient outcome on its own. How? Jane can simply offer to pay Dick to get rid of the dog. Dick will accept the deal if the amount of money Jane offers is greater than the benefit of keeping the dog.

By bargaining over the price, Dick and Jane can always reach the efficient outcome. For instance, suppose that Dick gets a $500 benefit from the dog and Jane bears an $800 cost from the barking. In this case, Jane can offer Dick $600 to get rid of the dog, and Dick will gladly accept. Both parties are better off than they were before, and the efficient outcome is reached.

It is possible, of course, that Jane would not be willing to offer any price that Dick would accept. For instance, suppose that Dick gets a $1,000 benefit from the dog and Jane bears an $800 cost from the barking. In this case, Dick would turn down any offer below $1,000, while Jane would not offer any amount above $800. Therefore, Dick ends up keeping the dog. Given these costs and benefits, however, this outcome is efficient.

So far, we have assumed that Dick has the legal right to keep a barking dog. In other words, we have assumed that Dick can keep Spot unless Jane pays him enough to induce him to give up the dog voluntarily. How different would the outcome be, on the other hand, if Jane had the legal right to peace and quiet?

According to the Coase theorem, the initial distribution of rights does not matter for the market's ability to reach the efficient outcome. For instance, suppose that Jane can legally compel Dick to get rid of the dog. Although having this right works to Jane's advantage, it probably will not change the outcome. In this case, Dick can offer to pay Jane to allow him to keep the dog. If the benefit of the dog to Dick exceeds the cost of the barking to Jane, then Dick and Jane will strike a bargain in which Dick keeps the dog.

Although Dick and Jane can reach the efficient outcome regardless of how rights are initially distributed, the distribution of rights is not irrelevant: It determines the distribution of economic well-being. Whether Dick has the right to a barking dog or Jane the right to peace and quiet determines who pays whom in the final bargain. But, in either case, the two parties can bargain with each other and solve the externality problem. Dick will end up keeping the dog only if the benefit exceeds the cost.

To sum up: *The Coase theorem says that private economic actors can solve the problem of externalities among themselves. Whatever the initial distribution of rights, the interested parties can always reach a bargain in which everyone is better off and the outcome is efficient.*

WHY PRIVATE SOLUTIONS DO NOT ALWAYS WORK

Despite the appealing logic of the Coase theorem, private actors on their own often fail to resolve the problems caused by externalities. The Coase theorem applies only when the interested parties have no trouble reaching and enforcing an agreement. In the world, however, bargaining does not always work, even when a mutually beneficial agreement is possible.

Sometimes the interested parties fail to solve an externality problem because of **transaction costs,** the costs that parties incur in the process of agreeing and following through on a bargain. In our example, imagine that Dick and Jane speak different languages so that, to reach an agreement, they will need to hire a translator. If the benefit of solving the barking problem is less than the cost of the translator, Dick and Jane might choose to leave the problem unsolved. In more realistic examples, the transaction costs are the expenses not of translators but of the lawyers required to draft and enforce contracts.

transaction costs
the costs that parties incur in the process of agreeing and following through on a bargain

Other times bargaining simply breaks down. The recurrence of wars and strikes shows that reaching agreement can be difficult and that failing to reach agreement can be costly. The problem is often that each party tries to hold out for a better deal. For example, suppose that Dick gets a $500 benefit from the dog, and Jane bears an $800 cost from the barking. Although it is efficient for Jane to pay Dick to get rid of the dog, there are many prices that could lead to this outcome. Dick might demand $750, and Jane might offer only $550. As they haggle over the price, the inefficient outcome with the barking dog persists.

Reaching an efficient bargain is especially difficult when the number of interested parties is large because coordinating everyone is costly. For example, consider a factory that pollutes the water of a nearby lake. The pollution confers a negative externality on the local fishermen. According to the Coase theorem, if the pollution is inefficient, then the factory and the fishermen could reach a bargain in which the fishermen pay the factory not to pollute. If there are many fishermen, however, trying to coordinate all of them in order to bargain with the factory may be almost impossible.

When private bargaining does not work, the government can sometimes play a role. The government is an institution designed for collective action. In this example, the government can act on behalf of the fishermen, even when it is impractical for the fishermen to act for themselves. In the next section, we examine how the government can try to remedy the problem of externalities.

QUICK QUIZ   Give an example of a private solution to an externality. ◆ What is the Coase theorem? ◆ Why are private economic actors sometimes unable to solve the problems caused by an externality?

PUBLIC POLICIES TOWARD EXTERNALITIES

When an externality causes a market to reach an inefficient allocation of resources, the government can respond in one of two ways. *Command-and-control* policies regulate behavior directly. *Market-based policies* provide incentives so that private decisionmakers will choose to solve the problem on their own.

REGULATION

The government can remedy an externality by making certain behaviors either required or forbidden. For example, it is a crime to dump poisonous chemicals into the water supply. In this case, the external costs to society far exceed the benefits to the polluter. The government therefore institutes a command-and-control policy that prohibits this act altogether.

In most cases of pollution, however, the situation is not this simple. Despite the stated goals of some environmentalists, it would be impossible to prohibit all polluting activity. For example, virtually all forms of transportation—even the horse—produce some undesirable polluting by-products. But it would not be sensible for the government to ban all transportation. Thus, instead of trying to eradicate pollution altogether, society has to weigh the costs and benefits in order to decide the kinds and quantities of pollution it will allow. In the United

States, the Environmental Protection Agency (EPA) is the government agency with the task of developing and enforcing regulations aimed at protecting the environment.

Environmental regulations can take many forms. Sometimes the EPA dictates a maximum level of pollution that a factory may emit. Other times the EPA requires that firms adopt a particular technology to reduce emissions. In all cases, to design good rules, the government regulators need to know the details about specific industries and about the alternative technologies that those industries could adopt. This information is often difficult for government regulators to obtain.

PIGOVIAN TAXES AND SUBSIDIES

Instead of regulating behavior in response to an externality, the government can use market-based policies to align private incentives with social efficiency. For instance, as we saw earlier, the government can internalize the externality by taxing activities that have negative externalities and subsidizing activities that have positive externalities. Taxes enacted to correct the effects of negative externalities are called **Pigovian taxes,** after economist Arthur Pigou (1877–1959), an early advocate of their use.

Pigovian tax
a tax enacted to correct the effects of a negative externality

Economists usually prefer Pigovian taxes over regulations as a way to deal with pollution because they can reduce pollution at a lower cost to society. To see why, let us consider an example. Suppose that two factories—a paper mill and a steel mill—are each dumping 500 tons of glop into a river each year. The EPA decides that it wants to reduce the amount of pollution. It considers two solutions:

◆ Regulation: The EPA could tell each factory to reduce its pollution to 300 tons of glop per year.
◆ Pigovian tax: The EPA could levy a tax on each factory of $50,000 for each ton of glop it emits.

The regulation would dictate a level of pollution, whereas the tax would give factory owners an economic incentive to reduce pollution. Which solution do you think is better?

Most economists would prefer the tax. They would first point out that a tax is just as effective as a regulation in reducing the overall level of pollution. The EPA can achieve whatever level of pollution it wants by setting the tax at the appropriate level. The higher the tax, the larger the reduction in pollution. Indeed, if the tax is high enough, the factories will close down altogether, reducing pollution to zero.

The reason why economists would prefer the tax is that it reduces pollution more efficiently. The regulation requires each factory to reduce pollution by the same amount, but an equal reduction is not necessarily the least expensive way to clean up the water. It is possible that the paper mill can reduce pollution at lower cost than the steel mill. If so, the paper mill would respond to the tax by reducing pollution substantially in order to avoid the tax, whereas the steel mill would respond by reducing pollution less and paying the tax.

In essence, the Pigovian tax places a price on the right to pollute. Just as markets allocate goods to those buyers who value them most highly, a Pigovian tax allocates pollution to those factories that face the highest cost of reducing it.

Whatever the level of pollution the EPA chooses, it can achieve this goal at the lowest total cost using a tax.

Economists also argue that Pigovian taxes are better for the environment. Under the command-and-control policy of regulation, the factories have no reason to reduce emission further once they have reached the target of 300 tons of glop. By contrast, the tax gives the factories an incentive to develop cleaner technologies, since a cleaner technology would reduce the amount of tax the factory has to pay.

Pigovian taxes are unlike most other taxes. As we discussed in Chapter 8, most taxes distort incentives and move the allocation of resources away from the social optimum. The reduction in economic well-being—that is, in consumer and producer surplus—exceeds the amount of revenue the government raises, resulting in a deadweight loss. By contrast, when externalities are present, society also cares about the well-being of the bystanders who are affected. Pigovian taxes correct incentives for the presence of externalities and thereby move the allocation of resources closer to the social optimum. Thus, while Pigovian taxes raise revenue for the government, they enhance economic efficiency.

TRADABLE POLLUTION PERMITS

Let us suppose that, despite the advice of its economists, the EPA adopts the regulation and requires each factory to reduce pollution to 300 tons of glop per year. Then one day, after the regulation is in place and both mills have complied, the two firms go to the EPA with a proposal. The steel mill wants to increase its emission of glop by 100 tons. The paper mill has agreed to reduce its emission by the same amount if the steel mill pays it $5 million. Should the EPA allow the two factories to make this deal?

From the standpoint of economic efficiency, allowing the deal is good policy. The deal must make the owners of the two factories better off, because they are voluntarily agreeing to it. Moreover, the deal does not have any external effects because the total amount of pollution remains the same. Thus, social welfare is enhanced by allowing the paper mill to sell its right to pollute to the steel mill.

The same logic applies to any voluntary transfer of the right to pollute from one firm to another. If the EPA allows firms to make these deals, it will, in essence, have created a new scarce resource: pollution permits. A market to trade these permits will eventually develop, and that market will be governed by the forces of supply and demand. The invisible hand will ensure that this new market efficiently allocates the right to pollute. The firms that can reduce pollution only at high cost will be willing to pay the most for the pollution permits. The firms that can reduce pollution at low cost will prefer to sell whatever permits they have.

One advantage of allowing a market for pollution permits is that the initial allocation of pollution permits among firms does not matter from the standpoint of economic efficiency. The logic behind this conclusion is similar to that behind the Coase theorem. Those firms that can reduce pollution most easily would be willing to sell whatever permits they get, and those firms that can reduce pollution only at high cost would be willing to buy whatever permits they need. As long as there is a free market for the pollution rights, the final allocation will be efficient whatever the initial allocation.

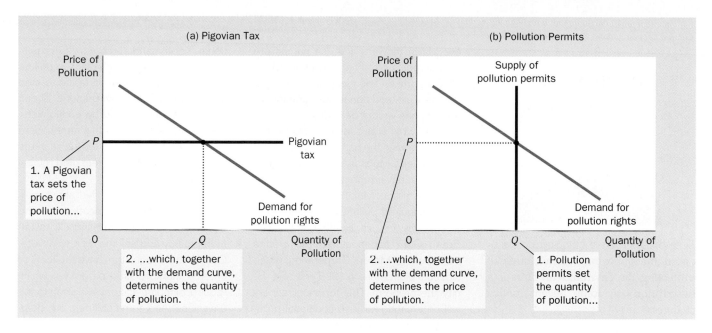

THE EQUIVALENCE OF PIGOVIAN TAXES AND POLLUTION PERMITS. In panel (a), the EPA sets a price on pollution by levying a Pigovian tax, and the demand curve determines the quantity of pollution. In panel (b), the EPA limits the quantity of pollution by limiting the number of pollution permits, and the demand curve determines the price of pollution. The price and quantity of pollution are the same in the two cases.

Figure 10-5

Although reducing pollution using pollution permits may seem quite different from using Pigovian taxes, in fact the two policies have much in common. In both cases, firms pay for their pollution. With Pigovian taxes, polluting firms must pay a tax to the government. With pollution permits, polluting firms must pay to buy the permit. (Even firms that already own permits must pay to pollute: The opportunity cost of polluting is what they could have received by selling their permits on the open market.) Both Pigovian taxes and pollution permits internalize the externality of pollution by making it costly for firms to pollute.

The similarity of the two policies can be seen by considering the market for pollution. Both panels in Figure 10-5 show the demand curve for the right to pollute. This curve shows that the lower the price of polluting, the more firms will choose to pollute. In panel (a), the EPA uses a Pigovian tax to set a price for pollution. In this case, the supply curve for pollution rights is perfectly elastic (because firms can pollute as much as they want by paying the tax), and the position of the demand curve determines the quantity of pollution. In panel (b), the EPA sets a quantity of pollution by issuing pollution permits. In this case, the supply curve for pollution rights is perfectly inelastic (because the quantity of pollution is fixed by the number of permits), and the position of the demand curve determines the price of pollution. Hence, for any given demand curve for pollution, the EPA can achieve any point on the demand curve either by setting a price with a Pigovian tax or by setting a quantity with pollution permits.

IN THE NEWS

Pollution Permits

in Action

ECONOMISTS HAVE INCREASINGLY INFLU-
enced the policymakers in charge of
protecting the environment. Here is a
description of some recent policy
changes.

Smog Swapping: New Rules Harness Power of Free Markets to Curb Air Pollution

BY JEFFREY TAYLOR

TORRANCE, CALIF.—In this tidy community of bungalows and palm trees, where
even lawn mowers and gas pumps are
strictly regulated to fight pollution, Mobil
Oil Corporation has just gained the right
to spew an additional 900 pounds of
noxious gas vapors each day.

So why aren't environmental activists storming the gates of the refinery?

Actually, Mobil is helping usher in a
new era in environmental protection. For
about $3 million, Mobil's refinery here re-
cently acquired pollution "credits" from
the nearby city of South Gate, Calif.
South Gate had acquired the credits
from General Motors Corporation, which
closed a plant there in 1985 and sold the
city the property. The Torrance refinery
will be emitting far less additional pollution than did General Motors.

Mobil bought the pollution rights under a rudimentary version of market-
based environmental regulation. The program has been around since the 1970s,
but its rules are so cumbersome that pollution "trades" like Mobil's are rare.

That will change soon. A growing
number of regulators believe conventional "command-and-control" regulation—which allows each plant to pollute
so much but no more—is failing to stop
destruction of the environment. These
authorities, encouraged by economists,
want to harness the Earth's atmosphere
to financial markets and let the markets
rid the world of acid rain and global
warming. . . .

Not everyone is thrilled about market-based regulation of the environment.
Some environmentalists think it is im-
moral to buy and sell the right to pollute.
Others doubt regulators have the tools to
enforce market-based programs, which
require pinpoint accuracy in monitoring
emissions. And some polluters are skeptical that regulators accustomed to com-
manding and controlling can give a market the freedom it needs to function.

Yet in Washington, California, and
elsewhere, proponents have won over
opposition by arguing that traditional regulation gives polluters no incentive to reduce emissions lower than what is allowed. Markets, they say, will create

---

In some circumstances, however, selling pollution permits may be better than
levying a Pigovian tax. Suppose the EPA wants no more than 600 tons of glop
to be dumped into the river. But, because the EPA does not know the demand
curve for pollution, it is not sure what size tax would achieve that goal. In this
case, it can simply auction off 600 pollution permits. The auction price would
yield the appropriate size of the Pigovian tax.

OBJECTIONS TO THE ECONOMIC ANALYSIS OF POLLUTION

"We cannot give anyone the option of polluting for a fee." This comment, made
by Senator Edmund Muskie in 1971, reflects the view of some environmentalists. Clean air and clean water, they argue, are fundamental human rights that
should not be debased by considering them in economic terms. How can you
put a price on clean air and clean water? The environment is so important, they
claim, that we should protect it as much as possible, regardless of the cost.

Economists have little sympathy with this type of argument. To economists,
good environmental policy begins by acknowledging the first of the *Ten Principles of Economics* in Chapter 1: People face tradeoffs. Certainly, clean air and clean

strong competition among companies to find the cheapest and most technologically advanced ways to cut pollution. . . .

The idea of turning pollutants into a marketable commodity isn't new. Early this century, a British professor named A. C. Pigou argued that a market price for cleaning air and water ought to be established and included among a polluter's expenses, like costs for labor and materials. It wasn't until 1975, however, that the U.S. Environmental Protection Agency created a limited pollution market by authorizing regional air-quality regulators to let companies buy and sell pollution credits. . . .

A broader plan [is now] being developed by southern California's Air Quality Management District.

In Los Angeles, strict emission limits have forced companies to spend billions of dollars to cut pollution, and the air quality is cleaner now than it was 15 years ago. Even so, pollution reached hazardous levels on 184 days last year, and the region, by state law, must re-

Los Angeles policymakers hope market forces will help people breathe easier.

duce emissions by 5 percent every year until 2010. Meanwhile, industry has begun fleeing southern California, in part because of high pollution-control costs.

After a year of hearings and feasibility studies, the AQMD board last month approved a shift to market-based regulation and told its staff to design markets for three of Los Angeles's most preva-

lent pollutants—sulfur oxide, nitrogen oxide, and reactive organic gas. The process has produced unprecedented cooperation among rival interest groups and changed many minds about market-based regulation.

Source: *The Wall Street Journal*, April 14, 1992, p. A1.

water have value. But their value must be compared to their opportunity cost—that is, to what one must give up to obtain them. Eliminating all pollution is impossible. Trying to eliminate all pollution would reverse many of the technological advances that allow us to enjoy a high standard of living. Few people would be willing to accept poor nutrition, inadequate medical care, or shoddy housing in order to make the environment as clean as possible.

Economists argue that some environmental activists hurt their own cause by not thinking in economic terms. A clean environment is a good like other goods. In fact, it is a luxury: Rich countries can afford a cleaner environment than poor ones and, therefore, usually have more rigorous environmental protection. Like the demands for other goods, the demand for clean air and water responds to the price. The lower the price of environmental protection, the more the public will want. The economic approach of using pollution permits and Pigovian taxes reduces the cost of environmental protection. It should, therefore, increase the public's demand for a clean environment.

QUICK QUIZ A glue factory and a steel mill emit smoke containing a chemical that is harmful if inhaled in large amounts. Describe three ways the town government might respond to this externality. What are the pros and cons of each of your solutions?

CONCLUSION

The invisible hand is powerful but not omnipotent. A market's equilibrium maximizes the sum of producer and consumer surplus. When the buyers and sellers in the market are the only interested parties, this outcome is efficient from the standpoint of society as a whole. But when there are external effects, such as pollution, evaluating a market outcome requires taking into account the well-being of third parties as well. In this case, the invisible hand of the marketplace may fail to allocate resources efficiently.

In some cases, people can solve the problem of externalities on their own. The Coase theorem suggests that the interested parties can bargain among themselves and agree on an efficient solution. Sometimes, however, an efficient outcome cannot be reached, perhaps because the large number of interested parties makes bargaining difficult.

When people cannot solve the problem of externalities privately, the government often steps in. Yet, even now, society should not abandon market forces entirely. Rather, the government can address the problem by requiring decisionmakers to bear the full costs of their actions. Pigovian taxes on emissions and pollution permits, for instance, are designed to internalize the externality of pollution. More and more, they are the policy of choice for those interested in protecting the environment. Market forces, properly redirected, are often the best remedy for market failure.

Summary

- When a transaction between a buyer and seller directly affects a third party, that effect is called an externality. Negative externalities, such as pollution, cause the socially optimal quantity in a market to be less than the equilibrium quantity. Positive externalities, such as technology spillovers, cause the socially optimal quantity to be greater than the equilibrium quantity.

- Those affected by externalities can sometimes solve the problem privately. For instance, when one business confers an externality on another business, the two businesses can internalize the externality by merging. Alternatively, the interested parties can solve the problem by signing a contract. According to the Coase theorem, if people can bargain without cost, then they can always reach an agreement in which resources are allocated efficiently. In many cases, however, reaching a bargain among the many interested parties is difficult, so the Coase theorem does not apply.

- When private parties cannot adequately deal with external effects, such as pollution, the government often steps in. Sometimes the government prevents socially inefficient activity by regulating behavior. Other times it internalizes an externality using Pigovian taxes. Another way to protect the environment is for the government to issue a limited number of pollution permits. The end result of this policy is largely the same as imposing Pigovian taxes on polluters.

Key Concepts

externality, p. 200   Coase theorem, p. 208   Pigovian tax, p. 211
internalizing an externality, p. 203   transaction costs, p. 209

Questions for Review

1. Use a supply-and-demand diagram to explain the effect of a negative externality in production.

2. List some of the ways that the problems caused by externalities can be solved without government intervention.

3. Imagine that you are a nonsmoker sharing a room with a smoker. According to the Coase theorem, what determines whether your roommate smokes in the room? Is this outcome efficient? How do you and your roommate reach this solution?

4. Why do economists prefer Pigovian taxes over regulations as a way to protect the environment from pollution?

Problems and Applications

1. Do you agree with the following statements? Why or why not?
   a. "The benefits of Pigovian taxes as a way to reduce pollution have to be weighed against the deadweight losses that these taxes cause."
   b. "A negative production externality calls for a Pigovian tax on producers, whereas a negative consumption externality calls for a Pigovian tax on consumers."

2. Consider the market for fire extinguishers.
   a. Why might fire extinguishers exhibit positive externalities in consumption?
   b. Draw a graph of the market for fire extinguishers, labeling the demand curve, the social-value curve, the supply curve, and the social-cost curve.
   c. Indicate the market equilibrium level of output and the efficient level of output. Give an intuitive explanation for why these quantities differ.
   d. If the external benefit is $10 per extinguisher, describe a government policy that would result in the efficient outcome.

3. Contributions to charitable organizations are deductible under the federal income tax. In what way does this government policy encourage private solutions to externalities?

4. It is rumored that the Swiss government subsidizes cattle farming, and that the subsidy is larger in areas with more tourist attractions. Can you think of a reason why this policy might be efficient?

5. Suppose a state is considering banning the use of studded snow tires because of the damage they cause to highways. In making this decision, the state cares only about efficiency. Use a graph to illustrate the situation in which the tires should be banned entirely. Now use a graph to illustrate the situation in which the use of studded snow tires should be reduced from the free-market level but not banned.

6. Both the use and production of aluminum cans may impose external costs.
   a. What might be the external costs of producing cans? Of using cans?
   b. Draw a diagram of the market for aluminum cans, indicating the demand curve, the supply curve, the social-value curve, and the social-cost curve. Label the quantity of cans that will be sold in a free market and the efficient quantity.

7. Greater consumption of alcohol leads to more motor vehicle accidents and, thus, imposes costs on people who do not drink and drive.
   a. Illustrate the market for alcohol, labeling the demand curve, the social-value curve, the supply curve, the social-cost curve, the market equilibrium level of output, and the efficient level of output.
   b. On your graph, shade the area corresponding to the deadweight loss of the market equilibrium. (Hint: The deadweight loss occurs because some units of alcohol are consumed for which the social cost exceeds the social value.) Explain.

8. Many observers believe that the levels of pollution in our economy are too high.
   a. If society wishes to reduce overall pollution by a certain amount, why is it efficient to have different amounts of reduction at different firms?
   b. Command-and-control approaches often rely on uniform reductions among firms. Why are these approaches generally unable to target the firms that should undertake bigger reductions?
   c. Economists argue that appropriate Pigovian taxes or tradable pollution rights will result in efficient

pollution reduction. How do these approaches target the firms that should undertake bigger reductions?

9. The Pristine River has two polluting firms on its banks. Acme Industrial and Creative Chemicals each dump 100 tons of glop into the river each year. The cost of reducing glop emissions per ton equals $10 for Acme and $100 for Creative. The local government wants to reduce overall pollution from 200 tons to 50 tons.

    a. If the government knew the cost of reduction for each firm, what reductions would it impose in order to reach its overall goal? What would be the cost to each firm and the total cost to the firms together?

    b. In a more typical situation, the government would not know the cost of pollution reduction at each firm. If the government decided to reach its overall goal by imposing uniform reductions on the firms, calculate the reduction made by each firm, the cost to each firm, and the total cost to the firms together.

    c. Compare the total cost of pollution reduction in parts (a) and (b). If the government does not know the cost of reduction for each firm, is there still some way for it to reduce pollution to 50 tons at the total cost you calculated in part (a)? Explain.

10. Figure 10-5 shows that for any given demand curve for the right to pollute, the government can achieve the same outcome either by setting a price with a Pigovian tax or by setting a quantity with pollution permits. Suppose there is a sharp improvement in the technology for controlling pollution.

    a. Using graphs similar to those in Figure 10-5, illustrate the effect of this development on the demand for pollution rights.

    b. What is the effect on the price and quantity of pollution under each regulatory system? Explain.

11. Suppose that the government decides to issue tradable permits for a certain form of pollution.

    a. Does it matter for economic efficiency whether the government distributes or auctions the permits? Does it matter in any other ways?

    b. If the government chooses to distribute the permits, does the allocation of permits among firms matter for efficiency? Does it matter in any other ways?

12. *The Wall Street Journal* article ("Smog Swapping") quoted in the text discusses the trading of pollution permits in southern California. What would be the primary advantage of allowing these permits to be traded throughout the entire West Coast? What would be the primary disadvantage?

13. The primary cause of global warming is carbon dioxide, which enters the atmosphere in varying amounts from different countries but is distributed equally around the globe within a year. In an article in the *Boston Globe* (July 3, 1990), Martin and Kathleen Feldstein argue that the correct approach to global warming is "not to ask individual countries to stabilize their emissions of carbon dioxide at current levels," as some have suggested. Instead, they argue that "carbon dioxide emissions should be reduced in countries where the costs are least, and the countries that bear that burden should be compensated by the rest of the world."

    a. Why is international cooperation necessary to reach an efficient outcome?

    b. Is it possible to devise a compensation scheme such that all countries would be better off than under a system of uniform emission reductions? Explain.

14. Some people object to market-based policies to reduce pollution, claiming that they place a dollar value on cleaning our air and water. Economists reply that society *implicitly* places a dollar value on environmental cleanup even under command-and-control policies. Discuss why this is true.

15. (This problem is challenging.) There are three industrial firms in Happy Valley.

FIRM	INITIAL POLLUTION LEVEL	COST OF REDUCING POLLUTION BY 1 UNIT
A	70 units	$ 20
B	80	25
C	50	10

The government wants to reduce pollution to 120 units, so it gives each firm 40 tradable pollution permits.

    a. Who sells permits and how many do they sell? Who buys permits and how many do they buy? Briefly explain why the sellers and buyers are each willing to do so. What is the total cost of pollution reduction in this situation?

    b. How much higher would the costs of pollution reduction be if the permits could not be traded?

11

PUBLIC GOODS AND COMMON RESOURCES

An old song lyric maintains that "the best things in life are free." A moment's thought reveals a long list of goods that the songwriter could have had in mind. Nature provides some of them, such as rivers, mountains, beaches, lakes, and oceans. The government provides others, such as playgrounds, parks, and parades. In each case, people do not pay a fee when they choose to enjoy the benefit of the good.

Free goods provide a special challenge for economic analysis. Most goods in our economy are allocated in markets, where buyers pay for what they receive and sellers are paid for what they provide. For these goods, prices are the signals that guide the decisions of buyers and sellers. When goods are available free of charge, however, the market forces that normally allocate resources in our economy are absent.

In this chapter we examine the problems that arise for goods without market prices. Our analysis will shed light on one of the *Ten Principles of Economics* in Chapter 1: Governments can sometimes improve market outcomes. When a good does not have a price attached to it, private markets cannot ensure that the good is produced and consumed in the proper amounts. In such cases, government policy can potentially remedy the market failure and raise economic well-being.

THE DIFFERENT KINDS OF GOODS

How well do markets work in providing the goods that people want? The answer to this question depends on the good being considered. As we discussed in Chapter 7, we can rely on the market to provide the efficient number of ice-cream cones: The price of ice-cream cones adjusts to balance supply and demand, and this equilibrium maximizes the sum of producer and consumer surplus. Yet, as we discussed in Chapter 10, we cannot rely on the market to prevent aluminum manufacturers from polluting the air we breathe: Buyers and sellers in a market typically do not take account of the external effects of their decisions. Thus, markets work well when the good is ice cream, but they work badly when the good is clean air.

In thinking about the various goods in the economy, it is useful to group them according to two characteristics:

excludability

the property of a good whereby a person can be prevented from using it

rivalness

the property of a good whereby one person's use diminishes other people's use

◆ Is the good **excludable?** Can people be prevented from using the good?
◆ Is the good **rival?** Does one person's use of the good diminish another person's enjoyment of it?

Using these two characteristics, Figure 11-1 divides goods into four categories:

private goods

goods that are both excludable and rival

1. **Private goods** are both excludable and rival. Consider an ice-cream cone, for example. An ice-cream cone is excludable because it is possible to prevent someone from eating an ice-cream cone—you just don't give it to him. An ice-cream cone is rival because if one person eats an ice-cream cone, another person cannot eat the same cone. Most goods in the economy are private goods like ice-cream cones. When we analyzed supply and demand in Chapters 4, 5, and 6 and the efficiency of markets in Chapters 7, 8, and 9, we implicitly assumed that goods were both excludable and rival.

public goods

goods that are neither excludable nor rival

2. **Public goods** are neither excludable nor rival. That is, people cannot be prevented from using a public good, and one person's enjoyment of a public good does not reduce another person's enjoyment of it. For example, national defense is a public good. Once the country is defended from foreign aggressors, it is impossible to prevent any single person from enjoying the benefit of this defense. Moreover, when one person enjoys the benefit of national defense, he does not reduce the benefit to anyone else.

common resources

goods that are rival but not excludable

3. **Common resources** are rival but not excludable. For example, fish in the ocean are a rival good: When one person catches fish, there are fewer fish for the next person to catch. Yet these fish are not an excludable good because it is almost impossible to charge fishermen for the fish that they catch.

4. When a good is excludable but not rival, there is said to be a *natural monopoly* for that good. For example, consider fire protection in a small town. It is easy to exclude people from enjoying this good: The fire department can just let their house burn down. Yet fire protection is not rival. Firefighters spend much of their time waiting for a fire, so protecting an

Figure 11-1

	Rival?	
	Yes	**No**
Excludable? **Yes**	Private Goods • Ice-cream cones • Clothing • Congested toll roads	Natural Monopolies • Fire protection • Cable TV • Uncongested toll roads
No	Common Resources • Fish in the ocean • The environment • Congested nontoll roads	Public Goods • National defense • Knowledge • Uncongested nontoll roads

FOUR TYPES OF GOODS. Goods can be grouped into four categories according to two questions: (1) Is the good excludable? That is, can people be prevented from using it? (2) Is the good rival? That is, does one person's use of the good diminish other people's use of it? This table gives examples of goods in each of the four categories.

additional household is unlikely to reduce the protection available to others. In other words, once a town has paid for the fire department, the extra cost of protecting one more household is small. We examine natural monopolies in Chapter 15.

In this chapter, we examine goods that are not excludable and, therefore, are available to everyone free of charge: public goods and common resources. As we will see, this topic is closely related to the study of externalities. For both public goods and common resources, externalities arise because something of value has no price attached to it. If one person were to provide a public good, such as national defense, other people would be better off, and yet they could not be charged for this benefit. Similarly, when one person uses a common resource, such as the fish in the ocean, other people are worse off, and yet they are not compensated for this loss. Because of these external effects, private decisions about consumption and production can lead to inefficient outcomes, and government intervention can potentially raise economic well-being.

QUICK QUIZ Define *public goods* and *common resources*, and give an example of each.

PUBLIC GOODS

To understand how public goods differ from other goods and what problems they present for society, let's consider an example: a fireworks display. This good is not excludable because it is impossible to prevent someone from seeing fireworks, and it is not rival because one person's enjoyment of fireworks does not reduce anyone else's enjoyment of them.

THE FREE-RIDER PROBLEM

The citizens of Smalltown, U.S.A., like seeing fireworks on the Fourth of July. Each of the town's 500 residents places a $10 value on the experience. The cost of putting on a fireworks display is $1,000. Because the $5,000 of benefits exceed the $1,000 of costs, it is efficient for Smalltown residents to see fireworks on the Fourth of July.

Would the private market produce the efficient outcome? Probably not. Imagine that Ellen, a Smalltown entrepreneur, decided to put on a fireworks display. Ellen would surely have trouble selling tickets to the event because her potential customers would quickly figure out that they could see the fireworks even without a ticket. Fireworks are not excludable, so people have an incentive to be free riders. A **free rider** is a person who receives the benefit of a good but avoids paying for it.

free rider
a person who receives the benefit of a good but avoids paying for it

One way to view this market failure is that it arises because of an externality. If Ellen did put on the fireworks display, she would confer an external benefit on those who saw the display without paying for it. When deciding whether to put on the display, Ellen ignores these external benefits. Even though a fireworks display is socially desirable, it is not privately profitable. As a result, Ellen makes the socially inefficient decision not to put on the display.

Although the private market fails to supply the fireworks display demanded by Smalltown residents, the solution to Smalltown's problem is obvious: The local government can sponsor a Fourth of July celebration. The town council can raise everyone's taxes by $2 and use the revenue to hire Ellen to produce the fireworks. Everyone in Smalltown is better off by $8—the $10 in value from the fireworks minus the $2 tax bill. Ellen can help Smalltown reach the efficient outcome as a public employee even though she could not do so as a private entrepreneur.

The story of Smalltown is stylized, but it is also realistic. In fact, many local governments in the United States do pay for fireworks on the Fourth of July. Moreover, the story shows a general lesson about public goods: Because public goods are not excludable, the free-rider problem prevents the private market from supplying them. The government, however, can potentially remedy the problem. If the government decides that the total benefits exceed the costs, it can provide the public good and pay for it with tax revenue, making everyone better off.

SOME IMPORTANT PUBLIC GOODS

There are many examples of public goods. Here we consider three of the most important.

National Defense   The defense of the country from foreign aggressors is a classic example of a public good. It is also one of the most expensive. In 1995 the U.S. federal government spent a total of $272 billion on national defense, or about $1,035 per person. People disagree about whether this amount is too small or too large, but almost no one doubts that some government spending for national defense is necessary. Even economists who advocate small government agree that the national defense is a public good the government should provide.

"I like the concept if we can do it with no new taxes."

Basic Research   The creation of knowledge is a public good. If a mathematician proves a new theorem, the theorem enters the general pool of knowledge that anyone can use without charge. Because knowledge is a public good, profit-seeking firms tend to free ride on the knowledge created by others and, as a result, devote too few resources to the creation of knowledge.

In evaluating the appropriate policy toward knowledge creation, it is important to distinguish general knowledge from specific, technological knowledge. Specific, technological knowledge, such as the invention of a better battery, can be patented. The inventor thus obtains much of the benefit of his invention, although certainly not all of it. By contrast, a mathematician cannot patent a theorem; such general knowledge is freely available to everyone. In other words, the patent system makes specific, technological knowledge excludable, whereas general knowledge is not excludable.

The government tries to provide the public good of general knowledge in various ways. Government agencies, such as the National Institutes of Health and the National Science Foundation, subsidize basic research in medicine, mathematics, physics, chemistry, biology, and even economics. Some people justify government funding of the space program on the grounds that it adds to society's pool of knowledge. Certainly, many private goods, including bullet-proof vests and the instant drink Tang, use materials that were first developed by scientists and engineers trying to land a man on the moon. Determining the appropriate level of governmental support for these endeavors is difficult because the benefits are hard to measure. Moreover, the members of Congress who appropriate funds for research usually have little expertise in science and, therefore, are not in the best position to judge what lines of research will produce the largest benefits.

Programs to Fight Poverty   Many government programs are aimed at helping the poor. Aid to Families with Dependent Children (AFDC), often called just "welfare," provides a meager income for some needy families. The Food Stamp program lowers the cost of food for those with low incomes. These poverty programs are financed by taxes on families that are financially more successful.

Economists disagree among themselves about what role the government should play in fighting poverty. Although we will discuss this debate more fully in Chapter 20, here we note one important argument: Advocates of antipoverty programs claim that fighting poverty is a public good.

Suppose that everyone prefers to live in a society without poverty. Even if this preference is widespread, fighting poverty is not a "good" that the private market can provide. No single individual can eliminate poverty because the problem is so large. Moreover, private charity is hard pressed to solve the problem: People who do not donate to charity can free ride on the generosity of others. In this case, taxing the wealthy to raise the living standards of the poor can make everyone better off. The poor are better off because they now enjoy a higher standard of living, and those paying the taxes are better off because they enjoy living in a society with less poverty.

CASE STUDY   ARE LIGHTHOUSES PUBLIC GOODS?

Some goods can switch between being public goods and being private goods depending on the circumstances. For example, a fireworks display is a public good if performed in a town with many residents. Yet if performed at a private amusement park, such as Walt Disney World, a fireworks display is more like a private good because visitors to the park pay for admission.

Another example is a lighthouse. Economists have long used lighthouses as an example of a public good. Lighthouses are used to mark specific locations so that passing ships can avoid treacherous waters. The benefit that the lighthouse provides to the ship captain is neither excludable nor rival, so each captain has an incentive to free ride by using the lighthouse to navigate without paying for the service. Because of this free-rider problem, private markets usually fail to provide the lighthouses that ship captains need. As a result, most lighthouses today are operated by the government.

In some cases, however, lighthouses may be closer to private goods. On the coast of England in the nineteenth century, some lighthouses were privately owned and operated. The owner of the local lighthouse did not try to

Use of the lighthouse is free to boat owners. Does this make the lighthouse a public good?

charge ship captains for the service but did charge the owner of the nearby port. If the port owner did not pay, the lighthouse owner turned off the light, and ships avoided that port.

In deciding whether something is a public good, one must determine the number of beneficiaries and whether these beneficiaries can be excluded from enjoying the good. A free-rider problem arises when the number of beneficiaries is large and exclusion of any one of them is impossible. If a lighthouse benefits many ship captains, it is a public good. Yet if it primarily benefits a single port owner, it is more like a private good.

THE DIFFICULT JOB OF COST–BENEFIT ANALYSIS

So far we have seen that the government provides public goods because the private market on its own will not produce an efficient quantity. Yet deciding that the government must play a role is only the first step. The government must then determine what kinds of public goods to provide and in what quantities.

Suppose that the government is considering a public project, such as building a new highway. To judge whether to build the highway, it must compare the total benefits of all those who would use it to the costs of building and maintaining it. To make this decision, the government might hire a team of economists and engineers to conduct a study, called a **cost–benefit analysis,** the goal of which is to estimate the total costs and benefits of the project to society as a whole.

cost–benefit analysis
a study that compares the costs and benefits to society of providing a public good

Cost–benefit analysts have a tough job. Because the highway will be available to everyone free of charge, there is no price with which to judge the value of the highway. Simply asking people how much they would value the highway is not reliable. First, quantifying benefits is difficult using the results from a questionnaire. Second, respondents have little incentive to tell the truth. Those who would use the highway have an incentive to exaggerate the benefit they receive in order to get the highway built. Those who would be harmed by the highway have an incentive to exaggerate the costs to them in order to prevent the highway from being built.

The efficient provision of public goods is, therefore, intrinsically more difficult than the efficient provision of private goods. Private goods are provided in the market. Buyers of a private good reveal the value they place on it by the prices they are willing to pay. Sellers reveal their costs by the prices they are willing to accept. By contrast, cost–benefit analysts do not observe any price signals when evaluating whether the government should provide a public good. Their findings on the costs and benefits of public projects are, therefore, rough approximations at best.

CASE STUDY   HOW MUCH IS A LIFE WORTH?

Imagine that you have been elected to serve as a member of your local town council. The town engineer comes to you with a proposal: The town can spend $10,000 to build and operate a traffic light at a town intersection that now has only a stop sign. The benefit of the traffic light is increased safety. The engineer estimates, based on data from similar intersections, that the traffic light would reduce the risk of a fatal traffic accident over the lifetime of the traffic light from 1.6 to 1.1 percent. Should you spend the money for the new light?

To answer this question, you turn to cost–benefit analysis. But you quickly run into an obstacle: The costs and benefits must be measured in the same units if you are to compare them meaningfully. The cost is measured in dollars, but the benefit—the possibility of saving a person's life—is not directly monetary. In order to make your decision, you have to put a dollar value on a human life.

At first, you may be tempted to conclude that a human life is priceless. After all, there is probably no amount of money that you could be paid to voluntarily give up your life or that of a loved one. This suggests that a human life has an infinite dollar value.

For the purposes of cost–benefit analysis, however, this answer leads to nonsensical results. If we truly placed an infinite value on human life, we should be placing traffic lights on every street corner. Similarly, we should all be driving large cars with all the latest safety features, instead of smaller ones with fewer safety features. Yet traffic lights are not at every corner, and people sometimes choose to buy small cars without side-impact air bags or antilock brakes. In both our public and private decisions, we are at times willing to risk our lives in order to save some money.

Once we have accepted the idea that a person's life does have an implicit dollar value, how can we determine what that value is? One approach, sometimes used by courts to award damages in wrongful-death suits, is to look at the total amount of money a person would have earned if he or she had lived. Economists are often critical of this approach. It has the bizarre implication that the life of a retired or disabled person has no value.

A better way to value human life is to look at the risks that people are voluntarily willing to take and how much they must be paid for taking them. Mortality risk varies across jobs, for example. Construction workers in high-rise buildings face greater risk of death than office workers. By comparing wages in risky and less risky occupations, controlling for education, experience, and other determinants of wages, economists can get some sense about what value people put on their own lives. Studies using this approach conclude that the value of a human life is about $10 million.

We can now return to our original example and respond to the town engineer. The traffic light reduces the risk of fatality by 0.5 percent. Thus, the expected benefit from having the traffic light is 0.005 × $10 million, or $50,000. This estimate of the benefit well exceeds the cost of $10,000, so you should approve the project.

Everyone would like to avoid the risk of this, but at what cost?

QUICK QUIZ   What is the *free-rider problem?* ◆ Why does the free-rider problem induce the government to provide public goods? ◆ How should the government decide whether to provide a public good?

COMMON RESOURCES

Common resources, like public goods, are not excludable: They are available free of charge to anyone who wants to use them. Common resources are, however, rival: One person's use of the common resource reduces other people's enjoyment of it. Thus, common resources give rise to a new problem. Once the good is provided, policymakers need to be concerned about how much it is used. This problem is best understood from the classic parable called the **Tragedy of the Commons.**

Tragedy of the Commons
a parable that illustrates why common resources get used more than is desirable from the standpoint of society as a whole

THE TRAGEDY OF THE COMMONS

Consider life in a small medieval town. Of the many economic activities that take place in the town, one of the most important is raising sheep. Many of the town's families own flocks of sheep and support themselves by selling the sheep's wool, which is used to make clothing.

As our story begins, the sheep spend much of their time grazing on the land surrounding the town, called the Town Common. No family owns the land. Instead, the town residents own the land collectively, and all the residents are allowed to graze their sheep on it. Collective ownership works well because land is plentiful. As long as everyone can get all the good grazing land they want, the Town Common is not a rival good, and allowing residents' sheep to graze for free causes no problems. Everyone in town is happy.

As the years pass, the population of the town grows, and so does the number of sheep grazing on the Town Common. With a growing number of sheep and a fixed amount of land, the land starts to lose its ability to replenish itself. Eventually, the land is grazed so heavily that it becomes barren. With no grass left on the Common, raising sheep is impossible, and the town's once prosperous wool industry disappears. Many families lose their source of livelihood.

What causes the tragedy? Why do the shepherds allow the sheep population to grow so large that it destroys the Town Common? The reason is that social and private incentives differ. Avoiding the destruction of the grazing land depends on the collective action of the shepherds. If the shepherds could act together, they would reduce the sheep population to a size that the Common can support. Yet no single family has an incentive to reduce the size of its own flock because each flock represents only a small part of the problem.

In essence, the Tragedy of the Commons arises because of an externality. When one family's flock grazes on the common land, it reduces the quality of the land available for other families. Because people neglect this negative externality when deciding how many sheep to own, the result is an excessive number of sheep.

If the tragedy had been foreseen, the town could have solved the problem in various ways. It could have regulated the number of sheep in each family's flock, internalized the externality by taxing sheep, or auctioned off a limited number of sheep-grazing permits. That is, the medieval town could have dealt with the problem of overgrazing in the way that modern society deals with the problem of pollution.

In the case of land, however, there is a simpler solution. The town can divide up the land among town families. Each family can enclose its parcel of land with a fence and then protect it from excessive grazing. In this way, the land becomes a private good rather than a common resource. This outcome in fact occurred during the enclosure movement in England in the seventeenth century.

The Tragedy of the Commons is a story with a general lesson: When one person uses a common resource, he diminishes other people's enjoyment of it. Because of this negative externality, common resources tend to be used excessively. The government can solve the problem by reducing use of the common resource through regulation or taxes. Alternatively, the government can sometimes turn the common resource into a private good.

This lesson has been known for thousands of years. The ancient Greek philosopher Aristotle pointed out the problem with common resources: "What is common to many is taken least care of, for all men have greater regard for what is their own than for what they possess in common with others."

CASE STUDY   CAPITALISM, COMMUNISM, AND COLLECTIVE RESOURCES

One of the *Ten Principles of Economics* in Chapter 1 is that markets are usually a good way to organize economic activity. Market economies work well, however, only when resources are owned privately; they work less well when resources are owned collectively. For this reason, the belief that markets are a good way to organize society is inextricably tied to the belief in private ownership. This view is sometimes called the political philosophy of *capitalism*.

Critics of capitalism often disapprove of private ownership. Private ownership allows wealth to be distributed unequally. Those who are lucky, talented, or shrewd often end up with more of society's resources than those who are not. Many critics of capitalism want to abolish private ownership as a step toward a classless society. Karl Marx, the philosophical father of *communism*, wanted society's resources to be distributed "from each according to his abilities, to each according to his needs." Collective ownership of all resources, Marx argued, would prevent the great inequities of capitalism.

Yet collective ownership has problems of its own. History has given little support to Marx's ideal of a classless society. In practice, communist countries are not as egalitarian as Marx had hoped. They merely replace the inequities of the private market with the inequities of the political system. In a capitalist economy, people get rich by supplying goods and services that other people are willing to pay for. In a communist economy, people get rich by gaining favor with the politically powerful.

Moreover, abolishing private ownership has a great cost in terms of economic efficiency. As we have seen, when people own resources collectively, they do not use them efficiently. Government decisionmaking can replace private decisionmaking in principle, but it rarely works well in practice. Central planning is just too difficult in a complex, modern economy. Indeed, the experiences of Russia and Eastern Europe before the collapse of communism are a testament to the virtues of decentralized decisionmaking and private ownership. The failure of communism can be viewed as the Tragedy of the Commons on a grand scale.

SOME IMPORTANT COMMON RESOURCES

There are many examples of common resources. In almost all cases, the same problem arises as in the Tragedy of the Commons: Private decisionmakers use the common resource too much. Governments often regulate behavior or impose fees in order to mitigate the problem of overuse.

Clean Air and Water   As we discussed in Chapter 10, markets do not adequately protect the environment. Pollution is a negative externality that can be remedied with regulations or with Pigovian taxes. One can view this market failure as an example of a common-resource problem. Clean air and clean water are common resources like open grazing land, and excessive pollution is like excessive grazing. Environmental degradation is a modern Tragedy of the Commons.

Oil Pools   Consider an underground pool of oil so large that it lies under many properties with different owners. Any of the owners can drill and extract the oil, but when one owner extracts oil, less is available for the others. The oil is a common resource.

Just as the number of sheep grazing on the Town Common was inefficiently large, the number of wells drawing from the oil pool will be inefficiently large. Because each owner who drills a well imposes a negative externality on the other owners, the benefit to society of drilling a well is less than the benefit to the owner who drills it. That is, drilling a well can be privately profitable even when it is socially undesirable. If owners of the properties decide individually how many oil wells to drill, they will drill too many.

To ensure that the oil is extracted at lowest cost, some type of joint action among the owners is necessary to solve the common-resource problem. The Coase theorem, which we discussed in Chapter 10, suggests that a private solution might be possible. The owners could reach an agreement among themselves about how to extract the oil and divide the profits. In essence, the owners would then act as if they were in a single business.

When there are many owners, however, a private solution is more difficult. In this case, government regulation could ensure that the oil is extracted efficiently.

Congested Roads   Roads can be either public goods or common resources. If a road is not congested, then one person's use does not affect anyone else. In this case, use is not rival, and the road is a public good. Yet if a road is congested, then use of that road yields a negative externality. When one person drives on the road, it becomes more crowded, and other people must drive more slowly. In this case, the road is a common resource.

One way for the government to address the problem of road congestion is to charge drivers a toll. A toll is, in essence, a Pigovian tax on the externality of congestion. Often, as in the case of local roads, tolls are not a practical solution because the cost of collecting them is too high.

TOLLS ARE A SIMPLE WAY TO SOLVE THE problem of road congestion and, according to some economists, are not used as much as they should be. In the following opinion column, economist Lester Thurow describes Singapore's success in dealing with congestion.

HOW CAN WE CLEAR THIS MARKET?

Economics of Road Pricing

BY LESTER C. THUROW

Start with a simple observational truth. No city has ever been able to solve its congestion and pollution problems by building more roads.

Some of the world's cities have built a lot of roads (Los Angeles) and some have very few (Shanghai only recently has had a lot of autos) but the degrees of congestion and pollution don't differ very much. More roads simply encourage more people to use their cars, to live farther away from work, and thus use more road space. . . . A recent analysis of congestion problems in London came to the conclusion that London could tear the entire central city down to make room for roads and would still have something approaching gridlock.

Economists have always had a theoretical answer for auto congestion and pollution problems—road pricing. Charge people for using roads based on

Sometimes congestion is a problem only at certain times of day. If a bridge is heavily traveled only during rush hour, for instance, the congestion externality is larger during this time than during other times of day. The efficient way to deal with these externalities is to charge higher tolls during rush hour. This toll would provide an incentive for drivers to alter their schedules in order to reduce traffic when congestion is greatest.

Another policy that responds to the problem of road congestion is the tax on gasoline. Gasoline is a complementary good to driving: An increase in the price of gasoline tends to reduce the quantity of driving demanded. Therefore, a gasoline tax reduces road congestion.

A gasoline tax, however, is an imperfect solution to road congestion. The problem is that the gasoline tax affects other decisions besides the amount of driving on congested roads. First, the gasoline tax discourages driving on non-congested roads, even though there is no congestion externality for these roads. Second, it encourages people to buy lighter-weight cars, which use less gasoline but are less safe. In these two ways, the gasoline tax distorts decisions and causes what roads they use, what time of day and year they use those roads, and the degree to which pollution problems exist at the time they are using those roads. Set prices at the levels that yield the optimal amounts of usage.

Until Singapore decided to try, no city had ever had the nerve to use road pricing. Many ideas seem good theoretically but have some hidden unexpected flaws. Singapore now has more than a decade of experience. The system works! There are no unexpected flaws. Singapore is the only city on the face of the earth without congestion and auto-induced pollution problems.

In Singapore a series of toll booths surrounds the central core of the city. To drive into the city, each car must pay a toll based on the roads being used, the time of day when the driving will occur, and that day's pollution problem. Prices are raised and lowered to get optimal usage.

In addition, Singapore calculates the maximum number of cars that can be supported without pollution outside of the central city and auctions off the rights to license new cars each month. Different types of plates allow different degrees of usage. A plate that allows one to use their car at any time is much more expensive than a plate that only allows one to use their car on weekends—a time when congestion problems are much less intense. Prices depend on supply and demand.

With this system Singapore ends up not wasting resources on infrastructure projects that won't cure congestion and pollution problems. The revenue collected from the system is used to lower other taxes.

If that is so, why then did London reject road pricing in its recent report on its auto congestion and pollution problems? They feared that such a system would be seen as too much interference from the heavy hand of government and that the public would not put up with a system that allows the rich to drive more than the poor.

Both arguments ignore the fact that we already have toll roads, but new technologies now also make it possible to avoid both problems.

Using bar codes and debit cards, a city can install bar code readers at different points around the city. As any car goes by each point a certain amount is deducted from the driver's debit card account depending upon weather, time of day, and location.

Inside the car, the driver has a meter that tells him how much he has been charged and how much remains in his debit card account. . . .

If one is an egalitarian and thinks that driving privileges should be distributed equally (i.e., not based upon income) then each auto can be given a specified debit card balance every year and those who are willing to drive less can sell their unused balances to those that want to drive more.

Instead of giving the city extra tax revenue, this system gives those who are willing to live near work or to use public transit an income supplement. Since poor people drive less than rich people, the system ends up being an egalitarian redistribution of income from the rich to the poor.

Source: *Boston Globe*, February 28, 1995, p. 40.

---

deadweight losses, which at least partly offset the efficiency gains from reduced congestion.

Fish, Whales, and Other Wildlife

Many species of animals are common resources. Fish and whales, for instance, have commercial value, and anyone can go to the ocean and catch whatever is available. Each person has little incentive to maintain the species for the next year. Just as excessive grazing can destroy the Town Common, excessive fishing and whaling can destroy commercially valuable marine populations.

The ocean remains one of the least regulated common resources. Two problems prevent an easy solution. First, many countries have access to the oceans, so any solution would require international cooperation among countries that hold different values. Second, because the oceans are so vast, enforcing any agreement is difficult. As a result, fishing rights have been a frequent source of international tension among normally friendly countries.

Within the United States, various laws aim to protect wildlife. For example, the government charges for fishing and hunting licenses, and it restricts the lengths of the fishing and hunting seasons. Fishermen are often required to throw back small fish, and hunters can kill only a limited number of animals. All these laws reduce the use of a common resource and help maintain animal populations.

CASE STUDY   WHY THE COW IS NOT EXTINCT

Throughout history, many species of animals have been threatened with extinction. When Europeans first arrived in North America, more than 60 million buffalo roamed the continent. Yet hunting the buffalo was so popular during the nineteenth century that by 1900 the animal's population fell to about

IN THE NEWS

Should Yellowstone Charge as Much as Disney World?

NATIONAL PARKS, LIKE ROADS, CAN BE either public goods or common resources. If congestion is not a problem, a visit to a park is not rival. Yet once a park becomes popular, it suffers from the same problem as the Town Common. In this opinion column from *The New York Times*, an economist argues for the use of higher entrance fees to solve the problem.

Save the Parks, and Make a Profit

BY ALLEN R. SANDERSON

It is common knowledge that our national parks are overcrowded, deteriorating, and broke. Some suggest that we ad-dress these problems by requiring reservations, closing some areas, or asking Congress to increase financing to the National Park Service. But to an economist, there is a more obvious solution: Raise the entrance fees.

When the National Park Service was established in 1916, the admission price to Yellowstone for a family of five arriving by car was $7.50; today, the price is only $10. Had the 1916 price been adjusted for inflation, the comparable 1995 fee would be $120 a day—about what that family would pay for a day of rides at Disney World, or to watch David Copperfield make someone disappear, or to see a professional football game.

No wonder our national parks are overrun and overtrampled. We are treating our natural and historical treasures as free goods when they are not. We are ignoring the costs of maintaining these places and rationing by congestion—when it gets too crowded, no more visitors are allowed—perhaps the most inefficient way to allocate scarce resources. The price of a family's day in a national park has not kept pace with most other forms of recreation. Systemwide, it barely averages a dollar a person. . . .

An increase in daily user fees to, say, $20 per person would either reduce the overcrowding and deterioration in our parks by cutting down on the number of visitors or it would substantially raise fee revenues for the Park Service (assuming that legislation was passed that would let the park system keep this money). Greater revenue is the more likely outcome. After spending several hundred dollars to reach Yellowstone Park, few people would be deterred by another $20.

The added revenues would bring more possibilities for outdoor recreation, both through expansion of the National Park Service and by encouraging private entrepreneurs to carve out and operate their own parks, something they cannot do alongside a public competitor giving away his product well below cost.

It is time to put our money where our Patagonia outfits are: Either we value the Grand Canyon and Yosemite and won't complain about paying a realistic entrance fee, or we don't really value them and shouldn't wring our hands over their present sorry state and likely sorrier fate.

SOURCE: *The New York Times*, September 30, 1995, p. 19.

400 before the government stepped in to protect the species. In some African countries today, the elephant faces a similar challenge, as poachers kill the animals for the ivory in their tusks.

Yet not all animals with commercial value face this threat. The cow, for example, is a valuable source of food, but no one worries that the cow will soon be extinct. Indeed, the great demand for beef seems to ensure that the species will continue to thrive.

Why is the commercial value of ivory a threat to the elephant, while the commercial value of beef is a guardian of the cow? The reason is that elephants are a common resource, whereas cows are a private good. Elephants roam freely without any owners. Each poacher has a strong incentive to kill as many elephants as he can find. Because poachers are numerous, each poacher has only a slight incentive to preserve the elephant population. By contrast, cows live on ranches that are privately owned. Each rancher takes great effort to maintain the cow population on his ranch because he reaps the benefit of these efforts.

Governments have tried to solve the elephant's problem in two ways. Some countries, such as Kenya, Tanzania, and Uganda, have made it illegal to kill elephants and sell their ivory. Yet these laws have been hard to enforce, and elephant populations have continued to dwindle. By contrast, other countries, such as Botswana, Malawi, Namibia, and Zimbabwe, have made elephants a private good by allowing people to kill elephants, but only those on their own property. Landowners now have an incentive to preserve the species on their own land, and as a result, elephant populations have started to rise. With private ownership and the profit motive now on its side, the African elephant might someday be as safe from extinction as the cow.

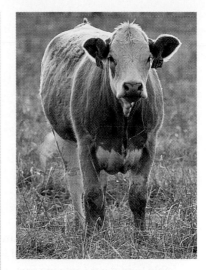
Will the market protect me?

QUICK QUIZ Why do governments try to limit the use of common resources?

CONCLUSION: THE IMPORTANCE OF PROPERTY RIGHTS

In this chapter and the previous one, we have seen there are some "goods" that the market does not provide adequately. Markets do not ensure that the air we breathe is clean or that our country is defended from foreign aggressors. Instead, societies rely on the government to protect the environment and to provide for the national defense.

Although the problems we considered in these chapters arise in many different markets, they share a common theme. In all cases, the market fails to allocate resources efficiently because *property rights* are not well established. That is, some item of value does not have an owner with the legal authority to control it. For example, although no one doubts that the "good" of clean air or national defense is valuable, no one has the right to attach a price to it and profit from its use. A factory pollutes too much because no one charges the factory for the pollution it emits. The market does not provide for national defense because no one can charge those who are defended for the benefit they receive.

When the absence of property rights causes a market failure, the government can potentially solve the problem. Sometimes, as in the sale of pollution permits, the solution is for the government to help define property rights and thereby unleash market forces. Other times, as in the restriction on hunting seasons, the solution is for the government to regulate private behavior. Still other times, as in the provision of national defense, the solution is for the government to supply a good that the market fails to supply. In all cases, if the policy is well planned and well run, it can make the allocation of resources more efficient and thus raise economic well-being.

Summary

◆ Goods differ in whether they are excludable and whether they are rival. A good is excludable if it is possible to prevent someone from using it. A good is rival if one person's enjoyment of the good prevents other people from enjoying the same good. Markets work best for private goods, which are both excludable and rival. Markets do not work as well for other types of goods.

◆ Public goods are neither rival nor excludable. Examples of public goods include fireworks displays, national defense, and the creation of fundamental knowledge. Because people are not charged for their use of the pub-

lic good, they have an incentive to free ride when the good is provided privately. Therefore, governments provide public goods, making their decision about the quantity based on cost–benefit analysis.

◆ Common resources are rival but not excludable. Examples include common grazing land, clean air, and congested roads. Because people are not charged for their use of common resources, they tend to use them excessively. Therefore, governments try to limit the use of common resources.

Key Concepts

excludability, p. 220
rivalness, p. 220
private goods, p. 220

public goods, p. 220
common resources, p. 220
free rider, p. 222

cost–benefit analysis, p. 225
Tragedy of the Commons, p. 227

Questions for Review

1. Explain what is meant by a good being "excludable." Explain what is meant by a good being "rival." Is a pizza excludable? Is it rival?

2. Define and give an example of a public good. Can the private market provide this good on its own? Explain.

3. Define and give an example of a common resource. Without government intervention, will people use this good too much or too little? Why?

Problems and Applications

1. The text says that both public goods and common resources involve externalities.
   a. Are the externalities associated with public goods generally positive or negative? Use examples in your

   answer. Is the free-market quantity of public goods generally greater or less than the efficient quantity?
   b. Are the externalities associated with common resources generally positive or negative? Use examples

in your answer. Is the free-market use of common resources generally greater or less than the efficient use?

2. Think about the goods and services provided by your local government.
   a. Using the classification in Figure 11-1, explain what category each of the following goods falls into:
      ◆ police protection
      ◆ snow plowing
      ◆ education
      ◆ rural roads
      ◆ city streets
   b. Why do you think the government provides items that are not public goods?

3. The text states that private firms will not undertake the efficient amount of basic scientific research.
   a. Explain why this is so. In your answer, classify basic research in one of the categories shown in Figure 11-1.
   b. What sort of policy has the United States adopted in response to this problem?
   c. It is often argued that this policy increases the technological capability of American producers relative to that of foreign firms. Is this argument consistent with your classification of basic research in part (a)? (Hint: Can excludability apply to some potential beneficiaries of a public good and not others?)

4. Why is there litter along most highways but rarely in people's yards?

5. The Washington, D.C., metro (subway) system charges higher fares during rush hours than during the rest of the day. Why might it do this?

6. Timber companies in the United States cut down many trees on publicly owned land and many trees on privately owned land. Discuss the likely efficiency of logging on each type of land in the absence of government regulation. How do you think the government should regulate logging on publicly owned lands? Should similar regulations apply to privately owned land?

7. An *Economist* article (Mar. 19, 1994) states: "In the past decade, most of the rich world's fisheries have been exploited to the point of near-exhaustion." The article continues with an analysis of the problem and a discussion of possible private and government solutions:
   a. "Do not blame fishermen for overfishing. They are behaving rationally, as they have always done." In what sense is "overfishing" rational for fishermen?
   b. "A community, held together by ties of obligation and mutual self-interest, can manage a common resource on its own." Explain how such management can work in principle, and what obstacles it faces in the real world.
   c. "Until 1976 most world fish stocks were open to all comers, making conservation almost impossible. Then an international agreement extended some aspects of [national] jurisdiction from 12 to 200 miles offshore." Using the concept of property rights, discuss how this agreement reduces the scope of the problem.
   d. The article notes that many governments come to the aid of suffering fishermen in ways that encourage increased fishing. How do such policies encourage a vicious cycle of overfishing?
   e. "Only when fishermen believe they are assured a long-term and exclusive right to a fishery are they likely to manage it in the same far-sighted way as good farmers manage their land." Defend this statement.
   f. What other policies to reduce overfishing might be considered?

8. In a market economy, information about the quality or function of goods and services is a valuable good in its own right. How does the private market provide this information? Can you think of any way in which the government plays a role in providing this information?

9. High-income people are willing to pay more than lower-income people to avoid the risk of death. For example, they are more likely to pay for safety features on cars. Do you think cost–benefit analysts should take this fact into account when evaluating public projects? Consider, for instance, a rich town and a poor town, both of which are considering the installation of a traffic light. Should the rich town use a higher dollar value for a human life in making this decision? Why or why not?

12

THE DESIGN OF THE TAX SYSTEM

**IN THIS CHAPTER
YOU WILL**

*Get an overview of how
the U.S. government
raises and spends money*

*Examine the efficiency
costs of taxes*

*Learn alternative ways
to judge the equity of
a tax system*

*See why studying tax
incidence is crucial for
evaluating tax equity*

*Consider the tradeoff
between efficiency and
equity in the design of
a tax system*

Al "Scarface" Capone, the notorious 1920s gangster and crime boss, was never convicted for his many violent crimes. Yet eventually he did go to jail—for tax evasion. He had neglected to heed Ben Franklin's advice that "in this world nothing is certain but death and taxes."

When Franklin made this claim in 1789, the average American paid less than 5 percent of his income in taxes, and that remained true for the next hundred years. Over the course of the twentieth century, however, taxes have become ever more important in the life of the typical person. Today, all taxes taken together—including personal income taxes, corporate income taxes, payroll taxes, sales taxes, and property taxes—use up about 35 percent of the average American's income.

Taxes are inevitable because we as citizens expect the government to provide us with various goods and services. The last two chapters have started to shed light on one of the *Ten Principles of Economics* from Chapter 1: The government can sometimes improve market outcomes. When the government remedies an externality (such as air pollution), provides a public good (such as national defense), or regulates the use of a common resource (such as fish in a public lake), it can raise economic well-being. Yet the benefits of government come with costs. For the government to perform these and its many other functions, it needs to raise revenue through taxation.

We began our study of taxation in previous chapters, where we saw how a tax on a good affects supply and demand for that good. In Chapter 6 we saw that a tax reduces the quantity sold in a market, and we examined how the burden of a tax is shared by buyers and sellers, depending on the elasticities of

237

supply and demand. In Chapter 8 we examined how taxes affect economic well-being. We learned that taxes cause *deadweight losses:* The reduction in consumer and producer surplus resulting from a tax exceeds the revenue raised by the government.

In this chapter we build on these lessons to discuss the design of a tax system. We begin with a financial overview of the U.S. government. When thinking about the tax system, it is useful to know some basic facts about how the U.S. government raises and spends money. We then consider the fundamental principles of taxation. Most people agree that taxes should impose as small a cost on society as possible and that the burden of taxes should be distributed fairly. That is, the tax system should be both *efficient* and *equitable.* As we will see, however, stating these goals is easier than achieving them.

A FINANCIAL OVERVIEW OF THE U.S. GOVERNMENT

How much of the nation's income does the government take as taxes? Figure 12-1 shows government revenue, including federal, state, and local governments, as a percentage of total income for the U.S. economy. It shows that, over time, the government has taken a larger and larger share of total income. In 1959, the government collected 27 percent of total income; in 1995, it collected 34 percent. In other words, the government has grown more quickly than the rest of the economy.

The overall size of government tells only part of the story. Behind the total lie thousands of individual decisions about taxes and spending. To understand the government's finances more fully, let's look at the breakdown of the total into some broad categories.

THE FEDERAL GOVERNMENT

The federal government collects about two-thirds of the taxes in our economy. It raises this money in a number of ways, and it finds even more ways to spend it.

Receipts Table 12-1 shows the receipts of the federal government in 1995. Total receipts in this year were $1,351 billion, a number so large that it is hard to comprehend. To bring this astronomical number down to earth, we can divide it by the size of the U.S. population, which was about 263 million in 1995. We then find that the average American paid $5,134 to the federal government. A typical family of four paid $20,528.

The largest source of revenue for the federal government is the individual income tax. As April 15 approaches, almost every American family fills out a tax form to determine how much income tax it owes the government. Each family is required to report its income from all sources: wages from working, interest on savings, dividends from corporations in which it owns shares, profits from any small businesses it operates, and so on. The family's *tax liability* (how much it owes) is then based on its total income.

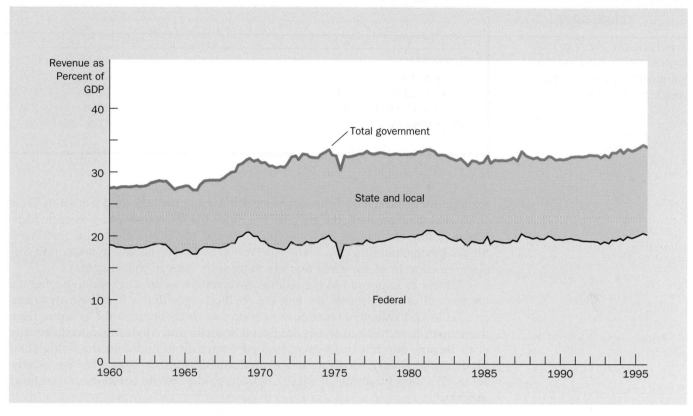

GOVERNMENT REVENUE AS A PERCENTAGE OF GDP. This figure shows revenue of the
federal government and of state and local governments as a percentage of gross domestic
product (GDP), which measures total income in the economy. The figure shows that the
government plays a large role in the U.S. economy and that its role has grown over time.

Figure 12-1

Table 12-1

RECEIPTS OF THE FEDERAL
GOVERNMENT: 1995

TAX	AMOUNT (BILLIONS)	AMOUNT PER PERSON	PERCENT OF RECEIPTS
Individual income taxes	$ 590	$2,243	44%
Social insurance taxes	485	1,842	36
Corporate income taxes	157	597	12
Excise taxes	58	219	4
Other	61	233	4
Total	$1,351	$5,134	100%

SOURCE: *Economic Report of the President,* 1996, Table B-77.

A family's income tax liability is not simply proportional to its income.
Instead, the law requires a more complicated calculation. Taxable income is computed by subtracting from total income the family's deductible expenses and also
an amount based on the number of dependents (primarily children). Then the

Table 12-2

THE FEDERAL INCOME TAX RATES: 1995. These are the marginal tax rates for a married couple filing jointly.

On Taxable Income ...	The Tax Rate Is ...
Up to $39,000	15.0%
From $39,000 to $94,250	28.0
From $94,250 to $143,600	31.0
From $143,600 to $256,500	36.0
Over $256,500	39.6

tax liability is calculated from taxable income using the schedule shown in Table 12-2. This table presents the *marginal tax rate*—the tax rate applied to each additional dollar of income. Because the marginal tax rate rises as income rises, higher-income families pay a larger percentage of their income in taxes. (We discuss the concept of marginal tax rate more fully later in this chapter.)

Almost as important to the federal government as the individual income tax are payroll taxes. A *payroll tax* is a tax on the wages that a firm pays its workers. Table 12-1 calls this revenue *social insurance taxes* because the revenue from these taxes is earmarked to pay for Social Security and Medicare. Social Security is an income support program, designed primarily to maintain the living standards of the elderly. Medicare is the government health program for the elderly. Table 12-1 shows that the average American paid $1,842 in social insurance taxes in 1995.

Next in magnitude is the corporate income tax. A *corporation* is a business that is set up as a separate legal entity. The government taxes each corporation based on its profit—the amount the corporation receives for the goods or services it sells minus the costs of producing those goods or services. Notice that corporate profits are, in essence, taxed twice. They are taxed once by the corporate income tax when the corporation earns the profits; they are taxed a second time by the individual income tax when the corporation uses its profits to pay dividends to the corporation's shareholders.

The last two categories in Table 12-1 each make up less than 5 percent of receipts. One is *excise taxes,* which are taxes on specific goods like gasoline, cigarettes, and alcoholic beverages. The "other" category includes various small items, such as estate taxes and customs duties. It also includes the interest the federal government earns from its deposits at the Federal Reserve, the central bank of the United States.

Spending   Table 12-3 shows the spending of the federal government in 1995. Total spending was $1,514 billion, or $5,757 per person. This table also shows how the federal government's spending was divided among major categories.

The largest category in Table 12-3 is Social Security, which represents mostly transfer payments to the elderly. (A *transfer payment* is a government payment not made in exchange for a good or service.) This category made up 22 percent of spending by the federal government in 1995 and is growing in importance. The reason for its growth is that increases in life expectancy and decreases in birthrates have caused the elderly population to grow more rapidly than the total population. Most analysts expect this trend to continue for many years into the future.

CATEGORY	AMOUNT (BILLIONS)	AMOUNT PER PERSON	PERCENT OF SPENDING
Social Security	$ 336	$1,277	22%
National defense	272	1,035	18
Net interest	232	883	15
Income security	220	837	14
Medicare	160	608	11
Health	115	436	8
Other	179	682	12
Total	$1,514	$5,757	100%

SOURCE: *Economic Report of the President, 1996*, Table B-77.

Table 12-3

SPENDING OF THE FEDERAL GOVERNMENT: 1995

The second largest category of spending is national defense. This includes both the salaries of military personnel and the purchases of military equipment such as guns, fighter jets, and warships. Spending on national defense fluctuates over time as international tensions and the political climate change. Not surprisingly, spending on national defense rises substantially during wars.

The third category of spending is net interest. When a person borrows from a bank, the bank requires the borrower to pay interest for the loan. The same is true when the government borrows from the public. The more indebted the government, the larger the amount it must spend in interest payments.

A bit smaller than net interest is the category of income security, which includes transfer payments to poor families. One program is Aid to Families with Dependent Children (AFDC), often called "welfare." Another is the Food Stamp program, which gives poor families vouchers that they can use to buy food. The federal government pays some of this money to state and local governments, which administer the programs under federal guidelines.

Medicare, the next category in Table 12-3, is the government's health plan for the elderly. Spending in this category has risen substantially over time for two reasons. First, the elderly population has grown more quickly than the overall population. Second, the cost of health care has risen more rapidly than the cost of other goods and services. The rapid growth of this budget item is one reason that President Clinton and others have proposed reforms of the health care system.

The next category is health spending other than Medicare. This includes Medicaid, the federal health program for the poor. It also includes spending on medical research, such as through the National Institutes of Health.

The "other" category in Table 12-3 consists of many less expensive functions of government. It includes, for example, the federal court system, the space program, and farm-support programs, as well as the salaries of Congress and the president.

You might have noticed that total spending of the federal government shown in Table 12-3 exceeds total receipts shown in Table 12-1 by $163 billion. Such a shortfall of receipts from spending is called a **budget deficit.** The government finances the budget deficit by borrowing from the public. If receipts exceed

budget deficit
an excess of government spending over government receipts

budget surplus

an excess of government receipts over government spending

spending, then the government is said to run a **budget surplus.** In this case, the government uses the excess receipts to reduce its outstanding debts.

STATE AND LOCAL GOVERNMENT

State and local governments collect about 40 percent of all taxes paid. Let's look at how they obtain tax revenue and how they spend it.

Receipts   Table 12-4 shows the receipts of the state and local governments in the United States. Total receipts in 1992 were $973 billion. Based on the 1992 population of about 255 million, this equals $3,811 per person. The table also shows how this total is broken down into different kinds of taxes.

The two most important taxes for state and local governments are sales taxes and property taxes. Sales taxes are levied as a percentage of the total amount spent at retail stores. Every time a customer buys something, he or she pays the storekeeper an extra amount that the storekeeper remits to the government. (Some states exclude certain items that are considered necessities, such as food and clothing.) Property taxes are levied as a percentage of the estimated value of land and structures, and are paid by property owners. Together these two taxes make up almost 40 percent of all receipts of state and local governments.

State and local governments also levy individual and corporate income taxes. In many cases, state and local income taxes are similar to federal income taxes. In other cases, they are quite different. For example, some states tax income from wages less heavily than income earned in the form of interest and dividends. Some states do not tax income at all.

State and local governments also receive some of their funds from the federal government. To some extent, the federal government's policy of sharing its revenue with state governments redistributes funds from high-income states (who pay more taxes) to low-income states (who receive more benefits). Often these funds are tied to specific programs that the federal government wants to subsidize.

Finally, state and local governments receive substantial receipts from various sources included in the "other" category in Table 12-4. These include fees for

Table 12-4

RECEIPTS OF STATE AND LOCAL GOVERNMENTS: 1992

TAX	AMOUNT (BILLIONS)	AMOUNT PER PERSON	PERCENT OF RECEIPTS
Sales taxes	$196	$ 769	20%
Property taxes	178	698	18
Individual income taxes	116	453	12
Corporate income taxes	24	93	2
From federal government	179	702	18
Other	280	1,096	29
Total	$973	$3,811	100%

SOURCE: *Economic Report of the President,* 1996, Table B-82.

Category	Amount (billions)	Amount per Person	Percent of Spending
Education	$326	$1,278	33%
Public welfare	158	619	16
Highways	67	261	7
Other	425	1,663	44
Total	$976	$3,820	100%

Source: *Economic Report of the President*, 1996, Table B-82.

Table 12-5

Spending of State and Local Governments: 1992

fishing and hunting licenses, tolls from roads and bridges, and fares for public buses and subways.

Spending   Table 12-5 shows the total spending of state and local governments in 1992 and its breakdown among the major categories.

By far the biggest single expenditure for state and local governments is education. Local governments pay for the public schools, which educate most students from kindergarten to high school. State governments contribute to the support of public universities. In 1992, education accounted for a third of the spending of state and local governments.

The second largest category of spending is for public welfare, which includes transfer payments to the poor. This category includes some federal programs that are administered by state and local governments. The next category is highways, which includes the building of new roads and the maintenance of existing ones. The "other" category in Table 12-5 includes the many other services provided by state and local governments, such as libraries, police, garbage removal, fire protection, park maintenance, and snow removal.

QUICK QUIZ   What are the two most important sources of tax revenue for the federal government? ◆ What are the two most important sources of tax revenue for state and local governments?

TAXES AND EFFICIENCY

Now that we have seen how the U.S. government at various levels raises and spends money, let's consider how one might evaluate its tax policy. Obviously, the aim of a tax system is to raise revenue for the government. But there are many ways to raise any given amount of money. In designing a tax system, policymakers have two objectives: efficiency and equity.

One tax system is more efficient than another if it raises the same amount of revenue at a smaller cost to taxpayers. What are the costs of taxes to taxpayers? The most obvious cost is the tax payment itself. This transfer of money from the taxpayer to the government is an inevitable feature of any tax system. Yet taxes also impose two other costs, which well-designed tax policy tries to avoid or, at least, minimize:

◆   The deadweight losses that result when taxes distort the decisions that people make.
◆   The administrative burdens that taxpayers bear as they comply with the tax laws.

An efficient tax system is one that imposes small deadweight losses and small administrative burdens.

DEADWEIGHT LOSSES

Taxes affect the decisions that people make. If the government taxes ice cream, people eat less ice cream and more frozen yogurt. If the government taxes housing, people live in smaller houses and spend more of their income on other things. If the government taxes labor earnings, people work less and enjoy more leisure.

Because taxes distort incentives, they entail deadweight losses. As we first discussed in Chapter 8, the deadweight loss of a tax is the reduction in economic well-being of taxpayers in excess of the amount of revenue raised by the government. The deadweight loss is the inefficiency that a tax creates as people allocate resources according to the tax incentive rather than the true costs and benefits of the goods and services that they buy and sell.

© 1977 by NEA, Inc.

"I was gonna fix the place up, but if I did the city would just raise my taxes!"

To recall how taxes cause deadweight losses, consider an example. Suppose that Joe places an $8 value on a pizza, and Jane places a $6 value on it. If there is no tax on pizza, the price of pizza will reflect the cost of making it. Let's suppose that the price of pizza is $5, so both Joe and Jane choose to buy one. Both consumers get some surplus of value over the amount paid. Joe gets consumer surplus of $3, and Jane gets consumer surplus of $1. Total surplus is $4.

Now suppose that the government levies a $2 tax on pizza and the price of pizza rises to $7. Joe still buys a pizza, but now he has consumer surplus of only $1. Jane now decides not to buy a pizza because its price is higher than its value to her. The government collects tax revenue of $2 on Joe's pizza. Total consumer surplus has fallen by $3 (from $4 to $1). Because total surplus has fallen by more than the tax revenue, the tax has a deadweight loss. In this case, the deadweight loss is $1.

Notice that the deadweight loss comes not from Joe, the person who pays the tax, but from Jane, the person who doesn't. The reduction in Joe's surplus of $2 exactly offsets the amount of revenue the government collects. The deadweight loss arises because the tax causes Jane to alter her behavior. When the tax raises the price of pizza, Jane is worse off, and yet there is no offsetting revenue to the government. This reduction in Jane's welfare is the deadweight loss of the tax.

CASE STUDY SHOULD INCOME OR CONSUMPTION BE TAXED?

Much government revenue comes from the individual income tax. One of the inefficiencies caused by this tax is that it discourages saving.

Consider a person twenty-five years old who is considering saving $100. If he puts this money in a savings account that earns 8 percent and leaves it

Spend?

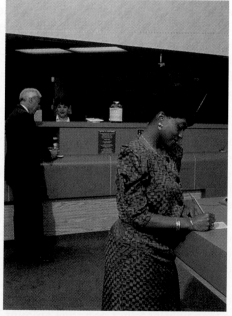

Or save?

there, he would have $2,172 when he retires at age sixty-five. Yet if the government taxes one-fourth of his interest income each year, the effective interest rate is only 6 percent. After 40 years of earning 6 percent, the $100 grows to only $1,029, less than half of what it would have been without taxation. Thus, because interest income is taxed, saving is much less attractive.

Some economists advocate eliminating the current tax system's disincentive toward saving by changing the basis of taxation. Rather than taxing the amount of income that people *earn*, the government could tax the amount that people *spend*. Under this proposal, all income that is saved would not be taxed until the saving is later spent. This alternative system, called a *consumption tax*, would not distort people's saving decisions.

This idea has some support from policymakers. Representative Bill Archer, who in 1995 became chairman of the powerful House Ways and Means Committee, has advocated replacing the current income tax system with a consumption tax. Moreover, various provisions of the current tax code already make the tax system a bit like a consumption tax. Taxpayers can put a limited amount of their saving into special accounts—such as Individual Retirement Accounts, Keogh plans, and 401(k) plans—that escape taxation until the money is withdrawn at retirement. For people who do most of their saving through these retirement accounts, their tax bill is, in effect, based on their consumption rather than their income.

ADMINISTRATIVE BURDEN

If you ask the typical person on April 15 for an opinion about the tax system, you might hear about the headache of filling out tax forms. The administrative burden of any tax system is part of the inefficiency it creates. This burden includes not only the time spent in early April filling out forms but also the time spent throughout the year keeping records for tax purposes and the resources the government has to use to enforce the tax laws.

Many taxpayers—especially those in higher tax brackets—hire tax lawyers and accountants to help them with their taxes. These experts in the complex tax laws fill out the tax forms for their clients and help their clients arrange their affairs in a way that reduces the amount of taxes owed. This behavior is legal tax avoidance, which is different from illegal tax evasion.

Critics of our tax system say that these advisers help their clients avoid taxes by abusing some of the detailed provisions of the tax code, often dubbed "loopholes." In some cases, loopholes are congressional mistakes: They arise from ambiguities or omissions in the tax laws. More often, they arise because Congress has chosen to give special treatment to specific types of behavior. For example, the U.S. federal tax code gives preferential treatment to investors in municipal bonds because Congress wanted to make it easier for state and local governments to borrow money. To some extent, this provision benefits states and localities; to some extent, it benefits high-income taxpayers. Most loopholes are well known by those in Congress who make tax policy, but what looks like a loophole to one taxpayer may look like a justifiable tax deduction to another.

The resources devoted to complying with the tax laws are a type of deadweight loss. The government gets only the amount of taxes paid. By contrast, the taxpayer loses not only this amount but also the time and money spent documenting, computing, and avoiding taxes.

The administrative burden of the tax system could be reduced by simplifying the tax laws. Yet simplification is often politically difficult. Most people are ready to simplify the tax code by eliminating the loopholes that benefit others, yet few are eager to give up the loopholes that they use. In the end, the

IN THE NEWS

Small Business and the Tax Laws

PEOPLE RUNNING SMALL BUSINESSES ARE most aware of the administrative burden of the tax system. Small firms must comply with many of the same laws as large ones. Yet, because of their size, compliance can take a much larger fraction of their revenue. According to one study, the administrative burden is ten times larger for small firms than for large firms. The following article describes some of these costs.

Obeying the Tax Laws: Small Business's Burden

BY ROBERT D. HERSHEY, JR.

In the grand scheme of a federal system that collects more than $1 trillion a year, Dante's Restaurant, Inc., a modest three-city chain in Pennsylvania, counts for little.

But to people like Lewis Kamin, Dante's controller, the Internal Revenue Code is a year-round headache. There are the biweekly remittances of Social Security and withheld income tax, quarterly reports of payroll and unemployment taxes, quarterly estimated corpo-

rate income taxes, and, of course, the maintaining of various records, including tips, W-4s for withholding, and I-9 citizenship forms.

All this doesn't count the ubiquitous state and local levies that in Dante's case are complicated because liquor-license considerations mean each of its ten restaurants must be separately incorporated.

"There is a lot to watch, a lot to worry about," Mr. Kamin grumbled. . . .

This is the real-world side of American taxation, the federal chunk of which is a system based on a monumentally complex set of laws and regulations that was just one-third its current size when Jimmy Carter called it "a disgrace to the human race."

The code is administered by a 115,000-member Internal Revenue Service army with a $7 billion budget. But that amount is dwarfed by what taxpayers themselves spend on meeting their obligations.

Estimates of what it costs American businesses to comply with federal tax law reach into the hundreds of billions of dollars a year. . . . Big companies are under almost continuous audit. The 1992 return for one giant company ran to 21,000 pages and 30 volumes. But the heaviest burden by far falls on small business.

In fact, according to Arthur P. Hall, a senior fellow at The Tax Foundation, the local hardware store, delicatessen, or gas station with assets of less than $1 million—a category embracing 90 percent of the nation's corporations—spends $390 for each $100 it sends to Washington. Put another way, the gov-

ernment got just $4.1 billion from these businesses in 1990, compared with the $15.9 billion they spent producing the basic corporate forms, the 1120 and 1120S.

"What this means is that the corporate income tax is a very inefficient revenue source for the federal government," Mr. Hall said. . . .

Although complaints about the tax system are often aimed at the I.R.S., businesspeople and policymakers generally contend that the real fault lies with Congress and its frequent, often well-intentioned tinkering with the law. The resulting complexity is taking an ever-mounting toll on respect for the system, and thereby undermines the willingness of even the best-intentioned taxpayer to figure out what he or she should pay. . . .

Since 1981, Washington has put ten major tax laws on the books, generating changes whose cumulative effect "is pretty staggering for the small businessperson," said Edward Koos, a tax-policy lawyer at the Small Business Administration.

Harold Apolinsky of the Small Business Council says 9,371 code sections have been amended since 1981, a total that owes much to the lobbying and campaign contributions of the powerful. "It appears to me that small business just has no clout," Mr. Apolinsky said. "Big business tolerates it," he added, referring to the resulting complexity. "Small business really can't."

SOURCE: *The New York Times*, January 30, 1994, Business section, p. 4.

complexity of the tax law results from the political process as various taxpayers with their own special interests lobby for their causes.

MARGINAL TAX RATES VERSUS AVERAGE TAX RATES

average tax rate

total taxes paid divided by total income

marginal tax rate

the extra taxes paid on an additional dollar of income

When discussing the efficiency and equity of income taxes, economists distinguish between two notions of the tax rate: the average and the marginal. The **average tax rate** is total taxes paid divided by total income. The **marginal tax rate** is the extra taxes paid on an additional dollar of income.

For example, suppose that the government taxes 20 percent of the first $50,000 of income and 50 percent of all income above $50,000. Under this tax, a person who makes $60,000 pays a tax of $15,000. (The tax equals $0.20 \times \$50,000$ plus $0.50 \times \$10,000$.) For this person, the average tax rate is $15,000/$60,000, or 25 percent. But the marginal tax rate is 50 percent because the amount of the tax would rise by $0.50 if the taxpayer earned an additional dollar.

The marginal and average tax rates each contain a useful piece of information. If we are trying to gauge the sacrifice made by a taxpayer, the average tax rate is more appropriate because it measures the fraction of income paid in taxes. By contrast, if we are trying to gauge how much the tax system distorts incentives, the marginal tax rate is more meaningful. One of the *Ten Principles of Economics* in Chapter 1 is that rational people think at the margin. A corollary to this principle is that the marginal tax rate measures how much the tax system discourages people from working hard. It is the marginal tax rate, therefore, that determines the deadweight loss of an income tax.

LUMP-SUM TAXES

lump-sum tax

a tax that is the same amount for every person

Suppose the government imposes a tax of $4,000 on everyone. That is, everyone owes the same amount, regardless of earnings or any actions that a person might take. Such a tax is called a **lump-sum tax.**

A lump-sum tax shows clearly the difference between average and marginal tax rates. For a taxpayer with income of $20,000, the average tax rate of a $4,000 lump-sum tax is 20 percent; for a taxpayer with income of $40,000, the average tax rate is 10 percent. For both taxpayers, the marginal tax rate is zero because an additional dollar of income would not change the amount of tax owed.

A lump-sum tax is the most efficient tax possible. Because a person's decisions do not alter the amount owed, the tax does not distort incentives and, therefore, does not cause deadweight losses. Because everyone can easily compute the amount owed and because there is no benefit to hiring tax lawyers and accountants, the lump-sum tax imposes a minimal administrative burden on taxpayers.

If lump-sum taxes are so efficient, why do we rarely observe them in the real world? The reason is that efficiency is only one goal of the tax system. A lump-sum tax would take the same amount from the poor and the rich, an outcome most people would view as unfair. To understand the tax systems that we observe, we must therefore consider the other major goal of tax policy: equity.

QUICK QUIZ   What is meant by the *efficiency* of a tax system?   ◆   What can make a tax system inefficient?

TAXES AND EQUITY

Since American colonists dumped imported tea into Boston harbor to protest high British taxes, tax policy has generated some of the most heated debates in American politics. The heat is rarely fueled by questions of efficiency. Instead, it arises from disagreements over how the tax burden should be distributed. Senator Russell Long once mimicked the public debate with this ditty:

> Don't tax you.
> Don't tax me.
> Tax that fella behind the tree.

Of course, if we are to rely on the government to provide some of the goods and services we want, taxes must fall on someone. In this section we consider the equity of a tax system. How should the burden of taxes be divided among the population? How do we evaluate whether a tax system is fair? Everyone agrees that the tax system should be equitable, but there is much disagreement about what equity means and how the equity of a tax system can be judged.

THE BENEFITS PRINCIPLE

One principle of taxation, called the **benefits principle,** states that people should pay taxes based on the benefits they receive from government services. This principle tries to make public goods similar to private goods. It seems fair that a person who often goes to the movies pays more in total for movie tickets than a person who rarely goes. Similarly, a person who gets great benefit from a public good should pay more for it than a person who gets little benefit.

benefits principle
the idea that people should pay taxes based on the benefits they receive from government services

The gasoline tax, for instance, is sometimes justified using the benefits principle. In some states, revenues from the gasoline tax are used to build and maintain roads. Because those who buy gasoline are the same people who use the roads, the gasoline tax might be viewed as a fair way to pay for this government service.

The benefits principle can also be used to argue that wealthy citizens should pay higher taxes than poorer ones. Why? Simply because the wealthy benefit more from public services. Consider, for example, the benefits of police protection from theft. Citizens with much to protect get greater benefit from police than do those with less to protect. Therefore, according to the benefits principle, the wealthy should contribute more than the poor to the cost of maintaining the police force. The same argument can be used for many other public services, such as fire protection, national defense, and the court system.

It is even possible to use the benefits principle to argue for antipoverty programs funded by taxes on the wealthy. As we discussed in Chapter 11, people prefer living in a society without poverty, suggesting that antipoverty programs are a public good. If the wealthy place a greater dollar value on this public good than the middle class do, perhaps just because they have more to spend, then, according to the benefits principle, they should be taxed more heavily to pay for these programs.

| INCOME | PROPORTIONAL TAX | | REGRESSIVE TAX | | PROGRESSIVE TAX | |
	AMOUNT OF TAX	PERCENT OF INCOME	AMOUNT OF TAX	PERCENT OF INCOME	AMOUNT OF TAX	PERCENT OF INCOME
$ 50,000	$12,500	25%	$15,000	30%	$10,000	20%
100,000	25,000	25	25,000	25	25,000	25
200,000	50,000	25	40,000	20	60,000	30

Table 12-6   THREE TAX SYSTEMS

THE ABILITY-TO-PAY PRINCIPLE

ability-to-pay principle
the idea that taxes should be levied on a person according to how well that person can shoulder the burden

Another way to evaluate the equity of a tax system is called the **ability-to-pay principle,** which states that taxes should be levied on a person according to how well that person can shoulder the burden. This principle is sometimes justified by the claim that all citizens should make an "equal sacrifice" to support the government. The magnitude of a person's sacrifice, however, depends not only on the size of his tax payment but also on his income and other circumstances. A $1,000 tax paid by a poor person may require a larger sacrifice than a $10,000 tax paid by a rich one.

The ability-to-pay principle leads to two corollary notions of equity: vertical equity and horizontal equity. **Vertical equity** states that taxpayers with a greater ability to pay taxes should contribute a larger amount. **Horizontal equity** states that taxpayers with similar abilities to pay should contribute the same amount. Although these notions of equity are widely accepted, applying them to evaluate a tax system is rarely straightforward.

vertical equity
the idea that taxpayers with a greater ability to pay taxes should pay larger amounts

horizontal equity
the idea that taxpayers with similar abilities to pay taxes should pay the same amount

Vertical Equity If taxes are based on ability to pay, then richer taxpayers should pay more than poorer taxpayers. But how much more should the rich pay? Much of the debate over tax policy concerns this question.

Consider the three tax systems in Table 12-6. In each case, taxpayers with higher incomes pay more. Yet the systems differ in how quickly taxes rise with income. The first system is called **proportional** because all taxpayers pay the same fraction of income. The second system is called **regressive** because high-income taxpayers pay a smaller fraction of their income, even though they pay a larger amount. The third system is called **progressive** because high-income taxpayers pay a larger fraction of their income.

Which of these three tax systems is most fair? There is no obvious answer, and economic theory does not offer any help in trying to find one. Equity, like beauty, is in the eye of the beholder.

proportional tax
a tax for which high-income and low-income taxpayers pay the same fraction of income

regressive tax
a tax for which high-income taxpayers pay a smaller fraction of their income than do low-income taxpayers

progressive tax
a tax for which high-income taxpayers pay a larger fraction of their income than do low-income taxpayers

CASE STUDY   HOW THE BURDEN OF TAXES IS DISTRIBUTED

Much of the debate over tax policy concerns whether the wealthy pay their fair share of taxes. There is no purely objective way to make this judgment.

Quintile	Average Income	Percent of All Income	Percent of All Taxes	Taxes as a Percent of Income	Taxes Minus Transfers as a Percent of Income
Lowest	$ 7,386	3.7%	1.4%	8.9%	−29.8%
Second	18,380	9.2	6.4	15.8	−2.1
Middle	29,849	14.5	12.5	19.5	9.5
Fourth	43,363	21.7	21.2	22.1	16.2
Highest	99,197	51.4	58.2	25.5	23.1

The Burden of Federal Taxes

Table 12-7

Source: *1993 Greenbook*, Committee on Ways and Means, U.S. House of Representatives, July 7, 1993. Data are for 1990.

In evaluating this issue for yourself, however, it is useful to know how much families of different incomes pay under the current tax system.

Table 12-7 shows how all federal taxes are distributed among income classes. To construct this table, families are ranked according to their income and placed into five groups of equal size, called *quintiles*. The second column of the table shows the average income of each group. The poorest one-fifth of families had average income of $7,386; the richest one-fifth had average income of $99,197.

The third and fourth columns compare the distribution of income and the distribution of taxes among these five groups. The poorest group receives 3.7 percent of all income and pays 1.4 percent of all taxes. The richest group receives 51.4 percent of all income and pays 58.2 percent of all taxes.

The next column of the table shows total taxes as a percent of income. As you can see, the U.S. federal tax system is progressive. The poorest families paid 8.9 percent of their incomes in taxes, and the richest paid 25.5 percent of their incomes.

These numbers on taxes paid give a somewhat misleading picture about the burden of government because they do not include the amount that families receive from the government. The last column in Table 12-7 shows taxes minus transfers as a percentage of income. Transfers include various programs, such as Social Security and welfare, under which the government supplements family incomes.

Including transfers substantially changes the distribution of the tax burden. The table shows that the richest group of families still pays about one-quarter of its income to the government, even after transfers are subtracted. By contrast, the two poorest groups receive more in transfers than they pay in taxes. The poorest group of families has income that is 29.8 percent higher than it would be without government taxes and transfers. Thus, to understand fully the progressivity of government policies, we must take account of both what people pay and what they receive.

Horizontal Equity   If taxes are based on ability to pay, then similar taxpayers should pay similar amounts of taxes. But what determines if two taxpayers are similar? Families differ in many ways. To evaluate whether a tax code is horizontally equitable, one must determine which differences are relevant for a family's ability to pay and which differences are not.

Suppose the Smith and Jones families each have income of $50,000. The Smiths have no children, but Mr. Smith has an illness that causes medical expenses of $20,000. The Joneses are in good health, but they have four children. Two of the Jones children are in college, generating tuition bills of $30,000. Would it be fair for these two families to pay the same tax because they have the same income? Would it be more fair to give the Smiths a tax break to help them offset their high medical expenses? Would it be more fair to give the Joneses a tax break to help them with their tuition expenses?

There are no easy answers to these questions. In practice, the U.S. income tax is filled with special provisions that alter a family's tax based on its specific circumstances.

CASE STUDY HORIZONTAL EQUITY AND THE MARRIAGE TAX

The treatment of marriage provides an important example of how difficult it is to achieve horizontal equity in practice. Consider two couples who are exactly the same except that one couple is married and the other couple is not. A peculiar feature of the U.S. income tax code is that these two couples pay different taxes. The reason that marriage affects the tax liability of a couple is that the tax law treats a married couple as a single taxpayer. When a man and woman get married, they stop paying taxes as individuals and start paying taxes as a family. If the man and woman have similar incomes, their total tax liability rises when they get married.

To see how this "marriage tax" works, consider the following example of a progressive income tax. Suppose that the government taxes 25 percent of all income above $10,000. Income below $10,000 is excluded from taxation. Let's see how this system treats two different couples.

Consider first Sam and Sally. Sam is a struggling poet and earns no income, whereas Sally is a lawyer and earns $100,000 a year. Before getting married, Sam pays no tax. Sally pays 25 percent of $90,000 ($100,000 minus the $10,000 exclusion), which is $22,500. After getting married, their tax bill is the same. In this case, the income tax neither encourages nor discourages marriage.

Now consider John and Joan, two college professors each earning $50,000 a year. Before getting married, they each pay a tax of $10,000 (25 percent of $40,000), or a total of $20,000. After getting married, they have a total income of $100,000, and so they owe a tax of 25 percent of $90,000, or $22,500. Thus, when John and Joan get married, their tax bill rises by $2,500. This increase is called the marriage tax.

We can fix the problem for John and Joan by raising the income exclusion from $10,000 to $20,000 for married couples. But this change would create another problem. In this case, Sam and Sally would pay a tax after getting married of only $20,000, which is $2,500 less than they paid when they were single. Eliminating the marriage tax for John and Joan would create a marriage subsidy for Sam and Sally.

This example illustrates a basic problem that has no simple solution. To see how fundamental the problem is, try designing an income tax with the following four properties:

"And do you promise to love, honor, and cherish each other, and to pay the United States government more in taxes as a married couple than you would have paid if you had just continued living together?"

◆ Two married couples with the same total income should pay the same tax.

◆ When two people get married, their total tax bill should not change.

◆ A person or family with no income should pay no taxes.

◆ High-income taxpayers should pay a higher fraction of their incomes than low-income taxpayers.

All four of these properties are appealing, yet it is impossible to satisfy all of them simultaneously. Any income tax that satisfies the first three must violate the fourth. The only income tax that satisfies the first three properties is a proportional tax.

Some economists have advocated abolishing the marriage penalty by making individuals rather than the family the taxpaying unit, a policy that many European countries follow. This alternative might seem more equitable because it would treat married and unmarried couples the same. Yet this change would give up on the first of these properties: Families with the same total income could end up paying different taxes. For example, if each married couple paid taxes as if they were not married, then Sam and Sally would pay $22,500, and John and Joan would pay $20,000, even though both couples have the same total income. Whether this alternative tax system is more or less fair than the current marriage tax is hard to say.

TAX INCIDENCE AND TAX EQUITY

Tax incidence—the study of who bears the burden of taxes—is central to evaluating tax equity. As we first saw in Chapter 6, the person who bears the burden of a tax is not always the person who gets the tax bill from the government. Because taxes alter supply and demand, they alter equilibrium prices. As a result, they affect people beyond those who, according to statute, actually pay the tax. When evaluating the vertical and horizontal equity of any tax, it is important to take account of these indirect effects.

Many discussions of tax equity ignore the indirect effects of taxes and are based on what economists derisively call the *flypaper theory* of tax incidence. According to this theory, the burden of a tax, like a fly on flypaper, sticks wherever it first lands. That assumption, however, is rarely valid.

For example, a person not trained in economics might argue that a tax on expensive fur coats is vertically equitable because most buyers of furs are wealthy. Yet if these buyers can easily substitute other luxuries for furs, then a tax on furs might only reduce the sale of furs. In the end, the burden of the tax will fall more on those who make and sell furs than on those who buy them. Because most workers who make furs are not wealthy, the equity of a fur tax could be quite different from what the flypaper theory indicates.

CASE STUDY WHO PAYS THE CORPORATE INCOME TAX?

The corporate income tax provides a good example of the importance of tax incidence for tax policy. The corporate tax is popular among voters. After all, corporations are not people. Voters are always eager to have their taxes reduced and have some impersonal corporation pick up the tab.

But before deciding that the corporate income tax is a good way for the government to raise revenue, we should consider who bears the burden of the corporate tax. This is a difficult question on which economists disagree, but one thing is certain: *People pay all taxes.* When the government levies a tax on a corporation, the corporation is more like a tax collector than a taxpayer. The burden of the tax ultimately falls on people—the owners, customers, or workers of the corporation.

Many economists believe that workers and customers bear much of the burden of the corporate income tax. To see why, consider an example. Suppose that the U.S. government decides to raise the tax on the income earned

These workers pay part of the corporate income tax.

by car companies. At first, this tax hurts the owners of the car companies, who receive less profit. But, over time, these owners will respond to the tax. Because producing cars is less profitable, they invest less in building new car factories. Instead, they invest their wealth in other ways—for example, by buying larger houses or by building factories in other industries or other countries. With fewer car factories, the supply of cars declines, as does the demand for auto workers. Thus, a tax on corporations making cars causes the price of cars to rise and the wages of auto workers to fall.

The corporate income tax shows how dangerous the flypaper theory of tax incidence can be. The corporate income tax is popular in part because it appears to be paid by rich corporations. Yet those who bear the ultimate burden of the tax—the customers and workers of corporations—are often not rich. If the true incidence of the corporate tax were more widely known, this tax might be less popular among voters.

CASE STUDY   THE FLAT TAX

A recurring topic of debate is whether the U.S. federal government should completely scrap the current tax system and replace it with a much simpler system called the *flat tax*. The flat tax was proposed in the early 1980s by economist Robert Hall and political scientist Alvin Rabushka. Since then, it has from time to time caught the attention of politicians on both the political left (such as Jerry Brown, former governor of California and onetime candidate in the Democratic presidential primaries) and the political right (such as Steve Forbes, multimillionaire publisher and onetime candidate in the Republican presidential primaries).

Although flat-tax advocates have proposed various plans that differ in detail, the essence of all the plans is a single, low tax rate that would apply to all income in the economy. If the tax rate were set at 19 percent, for example, then every taxpayer in the economy would face a marginal tax rate of 19 percent. Most of the plans allow a certain amount of income to be excluded from the tax. If the income exclusion were $10,000, for instance, then a person's tax bill would be

$$\text{Tax} = 0.19 \times (\text{Income} - \$10,000).$$

Because of the income exclusion, a flat tax can be progressive: Average tax rates rise with income, even though the marginal tax rate is constant. Some of the plans even allow a person with very low income (in this example, less than $10,000) to pay a "negative tax" by receiving a check from the government.

Because the flat-tax proposal calls for a major overhaul of the tax system, it raises almost every issue discussed in this chapter, especially the tradeoff between efficiency and equity. Here are some of the points made by flat-tax advocates:

◆ The flat tax would eliminate many of the deductions allowed under the current income tax, such as deductions for mortgage interest payments and charitable giving. By broadening the tax base in this way, the flat tax is able to reduce the marginal tax rates that most people face. Lower tax rates mean greater economic efficiency. Thus, flat-tax advocates claim that this change would expand the size of the economic pie.

◆ Because the flat tax is so simple, the administrative burden of taxation would be greatly reduced. Flat-tax advocates claim that many taxpayers could file their returns on a postcard. Because all taxpayers would pay the same low tax rate on all forms of income, people would have less incentive to hire tax lawyers and accountants to take advantage of loopholes.

◆ Because all taxpayers would face the same marginal tax rate, the tax could be collected at the source of income rather than from the person who receives the income. Income from corporate profit, for instance, would be taxed at the corporate level rather than at the personal level. This additional simplification also reduces administrative costs.

◆ The flat tax would replace both the personal income tax and the corporate income tax. All income, whether from working at a job or from owning shares in a corporation, would be taxed once at the same marginal rate. The flat tax would eliminate the current double taxation of corporate profits, which now discourages corporations from investing in new plants and equipment.

◆ In computing income for tax purposes, businesses would be allowed to deduct all legitimate business expenses, including expenses on new investment goods. This deduction for investment makes the flat tax more like a consumption tax than an income tax. As a result, a change to a flat tax would increase the incentive to save (or, more precisely, would eliminate the current tax system's disincentive to save).

In short, advocates of the flat tax claim that there is a strong efficiency argument for this dramatic tax reform.

Critics of the flat tax are sympathetic with the goal of a simpler and more efficient tax system, but they oppose the flat tax because they believe that it gives too little weight to the goal of vertical equity. They claim that a flat tax would be less progressive than the current tax system and, in particular, would shift some of the tax burden from the wealthy to the middle class. This concern may well be justified, but no one knows for sure. Our study of tax incidence shows that the burden of a tax is not necessarily borne by the person who sends the check to the government. If the flat tax did encourage greater saving, as advocates claim, it would lead to more rapid economic growth, which would benefit all taxpayers. No one can be certain, however, about how large the impact on economic growth would be.

QUICK QUIZ Explain the benefits principle and the ability-to-pay principle. ◆ What are vertical equity and horizontal equity? ◆ Why is studying tax incidence important for determining the equity of a tax system?

CONCLUSION: THE TRADEOFF BETWEEN EQUITY AND EFFICIENCY

Almost everyone agrees that equity and efficiency are the two most important goals of the tax system. But often these two goals conflict. Many proposed changes in the tax laws increase efficiency while reducing equity, or increase equity while reducing efficiency. People disagree about tax policy often because they attach different weights to these two goals.

The recent history of tax policy shows how political leaders differ in their views on equity and efficiency. When Ronald Reagan was elected president in 1980, the marginal tax rate on the earnings of the richest Americans was 50 percent. On interest income, the marginal tax rate was 70 percent. Reagan argued that such high tax rates greatly distorted economic incentives to work and save. In other words, he claimed that these high tax rates cost too much in terms of economic efficiency. Tax reform was, therefore, a high priority of his administration. Reagan signed into law large cuts in tax rates in 1981 and then again in 1986. When Reagan left office in 1989, the richest Americans faced a marginal tax rate of only 28 percent. During the four years of the Bush presidency, the top tax rate increased slightly to 31 percent.

When Bill Clinton ran for president in 1992, he argued that the rich were not paying their fair share of taxes. In other words, the low tax rates on the rich violated his view of vertical equity. One of President Clinton's first acts was to propose raising the tax rates on the highest levels of income. In 1993 the tax rates on the richest Americans became about 40 percent.

Economics alone cannot determine the best way to balance the goals of efficiency and equity. This issue involves political philosophy as well as economics. But economists do have an important role in the political debate over tax policy: They can shed light on the tradeoffs that society faces and can help us avoid policies that sacrifice efficiency without any benefit in terms of equity.

Summary

◆ The U.S. government raises revenue using various taxes. The most important taxes for the federal government are individual income taxes and payroll taxes for social insurance. The most important taxes for state and local governments are sales taxes and property taxes.

◆ The efficiency of a tax system refers to the costs it imposes on taxpayers. There are two costs of taxes beyond the transfer of resources from the taxpayer to the government. The first is the distortion in the allocation of resources that arises as taxes alter incentives and behavior. The second is the administrative burden of complying with the tax laws.

◆ The equity of a tax system concerns whether the tax burden is distributed fairly among the population.

According to the benefits principle, it is fair for people to pay taxes based on the benefits they receive from the government. According to the ability-to-pay principle, it is fair for people to pay taxes based on their capability to handle the financial burden. When evaluating the equity of a tax system, it is important to remember a lesson from the study of tax incidence: The distribution of tax burdens is not the same as the distribution of tax bills.

◆ When considering changes in the tax laws, policymakers often face a tradeoff between efficiency and equity. Much of the debate over tax policy arises because people give different weights to these two goals.

Key Concepts

budget deficit, p. 241
budget surplus, p. 242
average tax rate, p. 248
marginal tax rate, p. 248

lump-sum tax, p. 248
benefits principle, p. 249
ability-to-pay principle, p. 250
vertical equity, p. 250

horizontal equity, p. 250
proportional tax, p. 250
regressive tax, p. 250
progressive tax, p. 250

Questions for Review

1. Over the past several decades, has government grown more or less slowly than the rest of the economy?

2. What are the two most important sources of revenue for the U.S. federal government?

3. Explain how corporate profits are taxed twice.

4. Why is the burden of a tax to taxpayers greater than the revenue received by the government?

5. Why do some economists advocate taxing consumption rather than income?

6. Give two arguments why wealthy taxpayers should pay more taxes than poor taxpayers.

7. What is the concept of horizontal equity, and why is it hard to apply?

Problems and Applications

1. Some states exclude necessities, such as food and clothing, from their sales tax. Other states do not. Discuss the merits of this exclusion. Consider both efficiency and equity.

2. Government spending in the United States has grown as a share of national income over time. What changes in our economy and our society might explain this trend? Do you expect the trend to continue?

3. The information in many of the tables in this chapter is taken from the *Economic Report of the President*, which appears annually. Using a recent issue of the report at your library, answer the following questions and provide some numbers to support your answers.
   a. Figure 12-1 shows that government revenue as a percentage of total income has increased over time. Is this increase primarily attributable to changes in federal government revenue or in state and local government revenue?
   b. Looking at the combined revenue of the federal government and state and local governments, how has the composition of total revenue changed over time? Are personal income taxes more or less important? Social insurance taxes? Corporate profits taxes?
   c. Looking at the combined expenditures of the federal government and state and local governments, how

   have the relative shares of transfer payments and purchases of goods and services changed over time?

4. The chapter states that the elderly population in the United States is growing more rapidly than the total population. In particular, the number of workers is rising slowly, while the number of retirees is rising quickly. Concerned about the future of Social Security, some members of Congress propose a "freeze" on the program.
   a. If total expenditures were frozen, what would happen to benefits per retiree? To tax payments per worker? (Assume that Social Security taxes and receipts are balanced in each year.)
   b. If benefits per retiree were frozen, what would happen to total expenditures? To tax payments per worker?
   c. If tax payments per worker were frozen, what would happen to total expenditures? To benefits per retiree?
   d. What do your answers to parts (a), (b), and (c) imply about the difficult decisions faced by policymakers?

5. Explain how individuals' behavior is affected by the following features of the federal tax code.
   a. Contributions to charity are tax deductible.
   b. Sales of beer are taxed.
   c. Interest that a homeowner pays on a mortgage is tax deductible.

d. Realized capital gains are taxed, but accrued gains are not. (When someone owns a share of stock that rises in value, she has an "accrued" capital gain. If she sells the share, she has a "realized" gain.)

6. Suppose that your state raises its sales tax from 5 percent to 6 percent. The state revenue commissioner forecasts a 20 percent increase in sales tax revenue. Is this plausible? Explain.

7. Consider two of the income security programs in the United States: Aid to Families with Dependent Children (AFDC) and the Earned Income Tax Credit (EITC).
   a. When a woman with children and very low income earns an extra dollar, she receives less in AFDC benefits. What do you think is the effect of this feature of AFDC on the labor supply of low-income women? Explain.
   b. The EITC provides greater benefits as low-income workers earn more income (up to a point). What do you think is the effect of this program on the labor supply of low-income individuals? Explain.
   c. What are the disadvantages of eliminating AFDC and allocating the savings to the EITC?

8. The Tax Reform Act of 1986 eliminated the deductibility of interest payments on consumer debt (mostly credit cards and auto loans) but maintained the deductibility of interest payments on mortgages and home equity loans. What do you think happened to the relative amounts of borrowing through consumer debt and home equity debt?

9. Categorize each of the following funding schemes as examples of the benefits principle or the ability-to-pay principle.
   a. Visitors to many national parks pay an entrance fee.
   b. Local property taxes support elementary and secondary schools.
   c. An airport trust fund collects a tax on each plane ticket sold and uses the money to improve airports and the air traffic control system.

10. Federal payroll taxes equal 15.3 percent of earnings, up to a certain limit, after which the tax rate declines sharply.
    a. If there were no limit, would this tax be proportional, progressive, or regressive? With the limit, is the tax proportional, progressive, or regressive?
    b. The amount of Social Security benefits that a person receives depends on the amount of payroll taxes that he or she paid. Relative to people who had low earnings, people who had higher earnings and paid more taxes receive more benefits, but not proportionally more. Does this feature of the Social Security system make it more or less progressive than the payroll tax alone?

11. Any income tax schedule embodies two types of tax rates—average tax rates and marginal tax rates.
    a. The average tax rate is defined as total taxes paid divided by income. For the proportional tax system presented in Table 12-6, what are the average tax rates for people earning $50,000, $100,000, and $200,000? What are the corresponding average tax rates in the regressive and progressive tax systems?
    b. The marginal tax rate is defined as the extra taxes paid on additional income divided by the increase in income. Calculate the marginal tax rate for the proportional tax system as income rises from $50,000 to $100,000. Calculate the marginal tax rate as income rises from $100,000 to $200,000. Calculate the corresponding marginal tax rates for the regressive and progressive tax systems.
    c. Describe the relationship between average tax rates and marginal tax rates for each of these three systems. In general, which rate is relevant for someone deciding whether to accept a job that pays slightly more than her current job? Which rate is relevant for judging the vertical equity of a tax system?

12. What is the efficiency justification for taxing consumption rather than income? If the United States were to adopt a consumption tax, do you think that would make the U.S. tax system more or less progressive? Explain.

13. U.S. tax law says that one-half of social insurance taxes must be paid by employers and one-half by employees. Does this legal division of responsibility indicate the true incidence of these taxes? Explain.

14. If a salesman takes a client to lunch, part of the cost of the lunch is a deductible business expense for his company. Some members of Congress have argued that this feature of the tax code benefits relatively wealthy businesspeople and should be eliminated. Yet their arguments have been met with greater opposition from eating and drinking establishments than from companies themselves. Explain.

V

FIRM BEHAVIOR AND THE
ORGANIZATION OF INDUSTRY

13

THE COSTS OF PRODUCTION

The goods and services you enjoy every day are produced by firms. General Motors produces automobiles, General Electric produces lightbulbs, and General Mills produces breakfast cereals. The economy is made up of thousands of firms. Some firms, such as these three companies, are large; they employ thousands of workers and have thousands of stockholders who share in the firms' profits. Other firms, such as the local barbershop or candy store, are small; they employ only a few workers and are owned by a single person or family.

In previous chapters we used the supply curve to summarize firms' production decisions. According to the law of supply, firms are willing to produce and sell a greater quantity of a good when the price of the good is high, and this response leads to a supply curve that slopes upward. For analyzing many questions, the law of supply is all you need to know about firm behavior.

In this chapter and the ones that follow, we examine firm behavior in more detail. This topic will give you a better understanding of what decisions lie behind the supply curve in a market. In addition, it will introduce you to a part of economics called *industrial organization*—the study of how firms' decisions regarding prices and quantities depend on the market conditions they face. The town in which you live, for instance, may have several pizzerias but only one cable television company. How does this difference in the number of firms affect the prices in these markets and the efficiency of the market outcomes? The field of industrial organization addresses exactly this question.

As a starting point for the study of industrial organization, this chapter examines the costs of production. All firms, from Delta Air Lines to your local deli, incur costs as they make the goods and services that they sell. As we will see in the coming chapters, a firm's costs are a key determinant of its production and pricing decisions. Establishing what a firm's costs are, however, is not as straightforward as it might seem.

WHAT ARE COSTS?

We begin our discussion of costs at Hungry Helen's Cookie Factory. Helen, the owner of the firm, buys flour, sugar, flavorings, and other cookie ingredients. She also buys the mixers and ovens, and she hires workers to run this equipment. She then sells the resulting cookies to consumers. By examining some of the issues that Helen faces in her business, we can learn some lessons that apply to all firms in the economy, regardless of what market conditions they face.

TOTAL REVENUE, TOTAL COST, AND PROFIT

We begin with the firm's objective. To understand what decisions a firm makes, we must understand what it is trying to do. It is conceivable that Helen started her firm because of an altruistic desire to provide the world with cookies or, perhaps, out of love for the cookie business. More likely, however, Helen started her business to make money. Economists normally assume that the goal of a firm is to maximize profit, and they find that this assumption works well in most cases.

What is a firm's profit? The amount that the firm receives for the sale of its output (cookies) is called its **total revenue.** The amount that the firm pays to buy inputs (flour, sugar, workers, ovens, etc.) is called its **total cost.** Helen gets to keep any revenue that is not needed to cover costs. We define **profit** as a firm's total revenue minus its total cost. That is,

$$\text{Profit} = \text{Total revenue} - \text{Total cost.}$$

total revenue
the amount a firm receives for the sale of its output

total cost
the amount a firm pays to buy the inputs into production

profit
total revenue minus total cost

Helen's objective is to make her firm's profit as large as possible.

To see how a firm goes about maximizing profit, we must consider fully how to measure its total revenue and its total cost. Total revenue is the easy part: It equals the quantity of output the firm produces times the price at which it sells its output. If Helen produces 10,000 cookies and sells them at $2 a cookie, her total revenue is $20,000. By contrast, the measurement of a firm's total cost is more subtle.

COSTS AS OPPORTUNITY COSTS

When measuring costs at Hungry Helen's Cookie Factory or any other firm, it is important to keep in mind one of the *Ten Principles of Economics* from Chapter 1: The cost of something is what you give up to get it. Recall that the *opportunity cost* of an item refers to all those things that must be forgone to acquire that item. When economists speak of a firm's cost of production, they include all the opportunity costs of making its output of goods and services.

A firm's opportunity costs of production are sometimes obvious and sometimes less so. When Helen pays $1,000 for flour, that $1,000 is an opportunity cost because Helen can no longer use that $1,000 to buy something else. Similarly, when Helen hires workers to make the cookies, the wages she pays are part of the firm's costs. These costs are *explicit.* By contrast, some of a firm's opportunity costs are *implicit.* Imagine that Helen is skilled with computers and could earn $100 per hour working as a programmer. For every hour that Helen works at her cookie factory, she gives up $100 in income, and this forgone income is also part of her costs.

This distinction between explicit and implicit costs highlights an important difference between how economists and accountants analyze a business. Economists are interested in studying how firms make production and pricing decisions, so they include all opportunity costs when measuring costs. By contrast, accountants have the job of keeping track of the money that flows into and out of firms. As a result, they measure the explicit costs but often ignore the implicit costs.

The difference between economists and accountants is easy to see in the case of Hungry Helen's Cookie Factory. When Helen gives up the opportunity to earn money as a computer programmer, her accountant will not count this as a cost of her cookie business. Because no money flows out of the business to pay for this cost, it never shows up on the accountant's financial statements. An economist, however, will count the forgone income as a cost because it will affect the decisions that Helen makes in her cookie business. For example, if Helen's wage as a computer programmer rises from $100 to $500 per hour, she might decide that running her cookie business is too costly and choose to shut down the factory in order to become a full-time computer programmer.

THE COST OF CAPITAL AS AN OPPORTUNITY COST

An important implicit cost of almost every business is the opportunity cost of the financial capital that has been invested in the business. Suppose, for instance, that Helen used $300,000 of her savings to buy her cookie factory from the previous owner. If Helen had instead left this money deposited in a savings account that pays an interest rate of 5 percent, she would have earned $15,000 per year. To own her cookie factory, therefore, Helen has given up $15,000 a year in interest income. This $15,000 is one of the opportunity costs of Helen's business.

As we have already noted, economists and accountants treat costs differently, and this is especially true in their treatment of the cost of capital. An economist views the $15,000 in interest income that Helen gives up every year as a cost of her business, even though it is an implicit cost. Helen's accountant, however, will not show this $15,000 as a cost because no money flows out of the business to pay for it.

To explore further the difference between economists and accountants, let's change the example slightly. Suppose now that Helen did not have the entire $300,000 to buy the factory but, instead, used $100,000 of her own savings and borrowed $200,000 from a bank at an interest rate of 5 percent. Helen's accountant, who only measures explicit costs, will now count the $10,000 interest paid on the bank loan every year as a cost because this amount of money now flows out of the firm. By contrast, according to an economist, the opportunity cost of owning the business is still $15,000. The opportunity cost equals the interest on the bank loan (an explicit cost of $10,000) plus the forgone interest on savings (an implicit cost of $5,000).

ECONOMIC PROFIT VERSUS ACCOUNTING PROFIT

Now let's return to the firm's objective—profit. Because economists and accountants measure costs differently, they also measure profit differently. An economist measures a firm's *economic profit* as the firm's total revenue minus all the opportunity costs of producing the goods and services sold. An accountant measures the firm's *accounting profit* as the firm's total revenue minus only the firm's explicit costs.

Figure 13-1 summarizes this difference. Notice that because the accountant ignores the implicit costs, accounting profit is larger than economic profit. For a

Figure 13-1

ECONOMISTS VERSUS ACCOUNTANTS. Economists include all opportunity costs when analyzing a firm, whereas accountants measure only explicit costs. Therefore, economic profit is smaller than accounting profit.

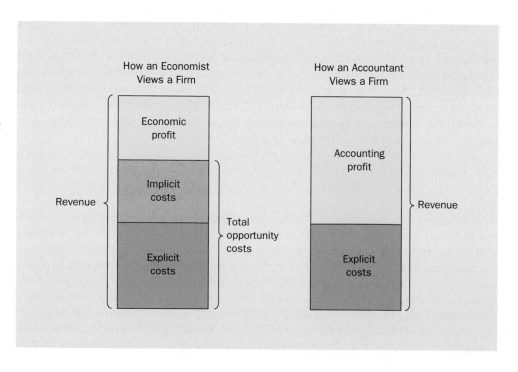

business to be profitable from an economist's standpoint, total revenue must cover all the opportunity costs, both explicit and implicit.

QUICK QUIZ Farmer McDonald gives banjo lessons for $20 an hour. One day, he spends 10 hours planting $100 worth of seeds on his farm. What opportunity cost has he incurred? What cost would his accountant measure? If these seeds will yield $200 worth of crops, does McDonald earn an accounting profit? Does he earn an economic profit?

PRODUCTION AND COSTS

Firms incur costs when they buy inputs to produce the goods and services that they plan to sell. In this section we examine this link between the firm's production process and its total cost. Once again, we consider Hungry Helen's Cookie Factory.

THE PRODUCTION FUNCTION

To simplify our analysis, let's assume that the size of Helen's factory is fixed and that Helen can vary the quantity of cookies produced only by changing the number of workers. Table 13-1 shows how the quantity of cookies Helen's factory produces per hour depends on the number of workers. If there are no workers in the factory, Helen produces no cookies. When there is 1 worker, she produces 50 cookies. When there are 2 workers, she produces 90 cookies, and so on.

Figure 13-2 presents a graph of these two columns of numbers. The number of workers is on the horizontal axis, and the number of cookies produced is on the vertical axis. This relationship between the quantity of inputs (workers) and quantity of output (cookies) is called the **production function.**

One of the *Ten Principles of Economics* introduced in Chapter 1 is that rational people think at the margin. As we will see in future chapters, this idea is the key to understanding how firms decide how many workers to hire and how much output to produce. To take a step toward these decisions, the third column in the table gives the marginal product of a worker. The **marginal product** of any input into production is the increase in the quantity of output obtained from an additional unit of that input. When the number of workers goes from 1 to 2, cookie production increases from 50 to 90, so the marginal product of the second worker is 40 cookies. And when the number of workers goes from 2 to 3, cookie production increases from 90 to 120, so the marginal product of the third worker is 30 cookies.

Notice that as the number of workers increases, the marginal product declines. The second worker has a marginal product of 40 cookies, the third worker has a marginal product of 30 cookies, and the fourth worker has a marginal product of 20 cookies. This property is called **diminishing marginal product.** At first, when only a few workers are hired, they have easy access to Helen's kitchen equipment. As the number of workers increases, additional workers have

production function
the relationship between quantity of inputs used to make a good and the quantity of output of that good

marginal product
the increase in output that arises from an additional unit of input

diminishing marginal product
the property whereby the marginal product of an input declines as the quantity of the input increases

to share equipment and work in more crowded conditions. Hence, as more and more workers are hired, each additional worker contributes less to the production of cookies.

Diminishing marginal product is also apparent in Figure 13-2. The production function's slope ("rise over run") tells us the change in Helen's output of

Number of Workers	Output (quantity of cookies produced per hour)	Marginal Product of Labor	Cost of Factory	Cost of Workers	Total Cost of Inputs (cost of factory + cost of workers)
0	0		$30	$ 0	$30
		50			
1	50		30	10	40
		40			
2	90		30	20	50
		30			
3	120		30	30	60
		20			
4	140		30	40	70
		10			
5	150		30	50	80

Table 13-1   A PRODUCTION FUNCTION AND TOTAL COST: HUNGRY HELEN'S COOKIE FACTORY

Figure 13-2

HUNGRY HELEN'S PRODUCTION FUNCTION. A production function shows the relationship between the number of workers hired and the quantity of output produced. Here the number of workers hired (on the horizontal axis) is from the first column in Table 13-1, and the quantity of output produced (on the vertical axis) is from the second column. The production function gets flatter as the number of workers increases, which reflects diminishing marginal product.

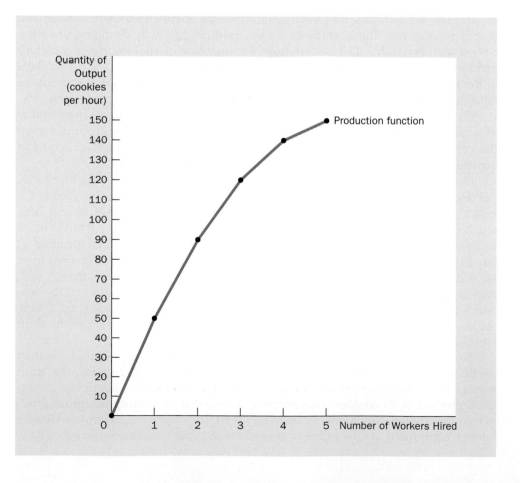

cookies ("rise") for each additional input of labor ("run"). That is, the slope of the production function measures the marginal product of a worker. As the number of workers increases, the marginal product declines, and the production function becomes flatter.

FROM THE PRODUCTION FUNCTION TO THE TOTAL-COST CURVE

The last three columns of Table 13-1 show Helen's cost of producing cookies. In this example, the cost of Helen's factory is $30 per hour, and the cost of a worker is $10 per hour. If she hires one worker, her total cost is $40. If she hires two workers, her total cost is $50, and so on. The information in this table shows how the number of workers Helen hires is related to the quantity of cookies she produces and to her total cost of production.

Our goal in the next several chapters is to study firms' production and pricing decisions. For this purpose, the most important relationship in Table 13-1 is between quantity produced (in the second column) and total costs (in the sixth column). Figure 13-3 graphs these two columns of data with the quantity produced on the horizontal axis and total cost on the vertical axis. This graph is called the *total-cost curve.*

Notice that the total cost gets steeper as the amount produced rises. The shape of the total-cost curve in this figure reflects the shape of the production

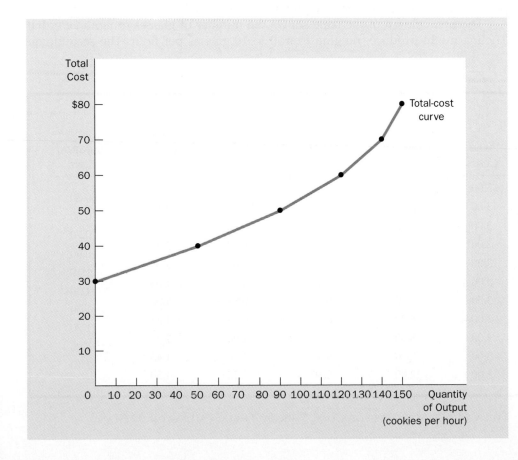

Figure 13-3

HUNGRY HELEN'S TOTAL-COST CURVE. A total-cost curve shows the relationship between the quantity of output produced and total cost of production. Here the quantity of output produced (on the horizontal axis) is from the second column in Table 13-1, and the total cost (on the vertical axis) is from the sixth column. The total-cost curve gets steeper as the quantity of output increases because of diminishing marginal product.

function in Figure 13-2. When Helen's kitchen gets crowded, each additional worker adds less to the production of cookies; this property of diminishing marginal product is reflected in the flattening of the production function as the number of workers rises. But now turn this logic around: When Helen is producing a large quantity of cookies, she must have hired many workers. Because her kitchen is already crowded, producing an additional cookie is quite costly. Thus, as the quantity produced rises, the total-cost curve becomes steeper.

QUICK QUIZ If Farmer Jones plants no seeds on his farm, he gets no harvest. If he plants 1 bag of seeds, he gets 3 bushels of wheat. If he plants 2 bags, he gets 5 bushels. If he plants 3 bags, he gets 6 bushels. A bag of seeds costs $100, and seeds are his only cost. Use these data to graph the farmer's production function and total-cost curve. Explain their shapes.

THE VARIOUS MEASURES OF COST

Our analysis of Hungry Helen's Cookie Factory demonstrated how a firm's total cost reflects its production function. From data on a firm's total cost, we can derive several related measures of cost, which will turn out to be useful when we analyze production and pricing decisions in future chapters. To see how these related measures are derived, we consider the example in Table 13-2. This table presents cost data on Helen's neighbor—Thirsty Thelma's Lemonade Stand.

The first column of the table shows the number of glasses of lemonade that Thelma might produce, ranging from 0 to 10 glasses per hour. The second col-

Quantity of Lemonade (Glasses per Hour)	Total Cost	Fixed Cost	Variable Cost	Average Fixed Cost	Average Variable Cost	Average Total Cost	Marginal Cost
0	$ 3.00	$3.00	$ 0.00	—	—	—	
1	3.30	3.00	0.30	$3.00	$0.30	$3.30	$0.30
2	3.80	3.00	0.80	1.50	0.40	1.90	0.50
3	4.50	3.00	1.50	1.00	0.50	1.50	0.70
4	5.40	3.00	2.40	0.75	0.60	1.35	0.90
5	6.50	3.00	3.50	0.60	0.70	1.30	1.10
6	7.80	3.00	4.80	0.50	0.80	1.30	1.30
7	9.30	3.00	6.30	0.43	0.90	1.33	1.50
8	11.00	3.00	8.00	0.38	1.00	1.38	1.70
9	12.90	3.00	9.90	0.33	1.10	1.43	1.90
10	15.00	3.00	12.00	0.30	1.20	1.50	2.10

Table 13-2   THE VARIOUS MEASURES OF COST: THIRSTY THELMA'S LEMONADE STAND

Figure 13-4

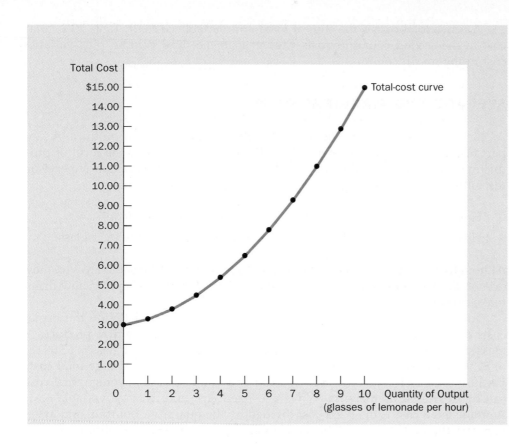

THIRSTY THELMA'S TOTAL-COST CURVE. Here the quantity of output produced (on the horizontal axis) is from the first column in Table 13-2, and the total cost (on the vertical axis) is from the second column. As in Figure 13-3, the total-cost curve gets steeper as the quantity of output increases because of diminishing marginal product.

umn shows Thelma's total cost of producing lemonade. Figure 13-4 plots Thelma's total-cost curve. The quantity of lemonade (from the first column) is on the horizontal axis, and total cost (from the second column) is on the vertical axis. Thirsty Thelma's total-cost curve has a shape similar to Hungry Helen's. In particular, it becomes steeper as the quantity produced rises, which (as we have discussed) reflects diminishing marginal product.

FIXED AND VARIABLE COSTS

Thelma's total cost can be divided into two types. Some costs, called **fixed costs,** do not vary with the quantity of output produced. Thelma's fixed costs include the rent she pays because this cost is the same regardless of how much lemonade Thelma produces. Similarly, if Thelma needs to hire a full-time bookkeeper to pay bills, regardless of the quantity of lemonade produced, the bookkeeper's salary is a fixed cost. The third column in Table 13-2 shows Thelma's fixed cost, which in this example is $3.00 per hour.

Some of the firm's costs, called **variable costs,** change as the firm alters the quantity of output produced. Thelma's variable costs include the cost of lemons and sugar: The more lemonade Thelma makes, the more lemons and sugar she needs to buy. Similarly, if Thelma has to hire more workers to make more lemonade, the salaries of these workers are variable costs. The fourth column of the table shows Thelma's variable cost. The variable cost is 0 if she produces nothing, $0.30 if she produces 1 glass of lemonade, $0.80 if she produces 2 glasses, and so on.

fixed costs
costs that do not vary with the quantity of output produced

variable costs
costs that do vary with the quantity of output produced

A firm's total cost is the sum of fixed and variable costs. In Table 13-2, total cost in the second column equals fixed cost in the third column plus variable cost in the fourth column.

AVERAGE AND MARGINAL COST

As the owner of her firm, Thelma has to decide how much to produce. A key part of this decision is how her costs will vary as she changes the level of production. In making this decision, Thelma might ask her production supervisor the following two questions about the cost of producing lemonade:

◆   How much does it cost to make the typical glass of lemonade?
◆   How much does it cost to increase production of lemonade by 1 glass?

Although at first these two questions might seem to have the same answer, they do not. Both answers will turn out to be important for understanding how firms make production decisions.

average total cost

total cost divided by the quantity of output

average fixed cost

fixed costs divided by the quantity of output

average variable cost

variable costs divided by the quantity of output

marginal cost

the increase in total cost that arises from an extra unit of production

To find the cost of the typical unit produced, we would divide the firm's costs by the quantity of output it produces. For example, if the firm produces 2 glasses per hour, its total cost is $3.80, and the cost of the typical glass is $3.80/2, or $1.90. Total cost divided by the quantity of output is called **average total cost.** Because total cost is just the sum of fixed and variable costs, average total cost can be expressed as the sum of average fixed cost and average variable cost. **Average fixed cost** is the fixed cost divided by the quantity of output, and **average variable cost** is the variable cost divided by the quantity of output.

Although average total cost tells us the cost of the typical unit, it does not tell us how much total cost will change as the firm alters its level of production. The last column in Table 13-2 shows the amount that total cost rises when the firm increases production by one unit of output. This number is called **marginal cost.** For example, if Thelma increases production from 2 to 3 glasses, total cost rises from $3.80 to $4.50, so the marginal cost of the third glass of lemonade is $4.50 − $3.80, or $0.70.

It may be helpful to express these definitions mathematically. If Q stands for quantity, TC total cost, ATC average total cost, and MC marginal cost, then we can then write:

$$ATC = \text{Total cost/Quantity} = TC/Q$$

and

$$MC = (\text{Change in total cost})/(\text{Change in quantity}) = \Delta TC/\Delta Q.$$

Here Δ, the Greek letter *delta,* represents the change in a variable. These equations show how average total cost and marginal cost are derived from total cost.

As we will see more fully in the next chapter, Thelma, our lemonade entrepreneur, will find the concepts of average total cost and marginal cost extremely useful when deciding how much lemonade to produce. Keep in mind, however, that these concepts do not actually give Thelma new information about her costs of production. Instead, average total cost and marginal cost express in a new way information that is already contained in her firm's total cost. *Average total cost tells us the cost of a typical unit of output if total cost is divided evenly over all the units produced. Marginal cost tells us the increase in total cost that arises from producing an additional unit of output.*

COST CURVES AND THEIR SHAPES

Just as in previous chapters we found graphs of supply and demand useful when analyzing the behavior of markets, we will find graphs of average and marginal cost useful when analyzing the behavior of firms. Figure 13-5 graphs Thelma's costs using the data from Table 13-2. The horizontal axis measures the quantity the firm produces, and the vertical axis measures marginal and average costs. The graph shows four curves: average total cost *(ATC)*, average fixed cost *(AFC)*, average variable cost *(AVC)*, and marginal cost *(MC)*.

The cost curves shown here for Thirsty Thelma's Lemonade Stand have shapes that are common to the cost curves of many firms in the economy. Let's examine three features of these curves in particular: the shape of marginal cost, the shape of average total cost, and the relationship between marginal and average total cost.

Rising Marginal Cost Thirsty Thelma's marginal cost rises with the quantity of output produced. This reflects the property of diminishing marginal product. When Thelma is producing a small quantity of lemonade, she has few workers, and much of her equipment is not being used. Because she can easily

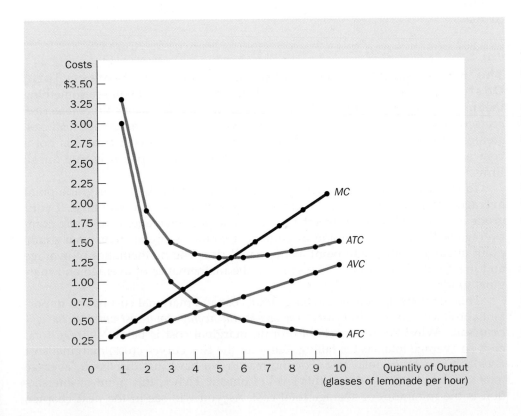

Figure 13-5

THIRSTY THELMA'S AVERAGE-COST AND MARGINAL-COST CURVES. This figure shows the average total cost *(ATC)*, average fixed cost *(AFC)*, average variable cost *(AVC)*, and marginal cost *(MC)* for Thirsty Thelma's Lemonade Stand. All of these curves are obtained by graphing the data in Table 13-2. These cost curves show three features that are considered common: (1) Marginal cost rises with the quantity of output. (2) The average-total-cost curve is U-shaped. (3) The marginal-cost curve crosses the average-total-cost curve at the minimum of average total cost.

put these idle resources to use, increasing production has a relatively small cost. By contrast, when Thelma is producing large quantities of lemonade, her stand is crowded with workers, and most of her equipment is fully utilized. Thelma can produce more lemonade by adding workers, but these new workers have to work in crowded conditions and may have to wait to use the equipment. Therefore, producing an extra glass of lemonade is more costly when the quantity being produced is already high.

U-Shaped Average Total Cost   Thirsty Thelma's average-total-cost curve is U-shaped. To understand why this is so, remember that average total cost is the sum of average fixed cost and average variable cost. Average fixed cost always declines as output rises because the fixed cost is getting spread over a larger number of units. Average variable cost typically rises as output increases because of diminishing marginal product. Average total cost reflects the shapes of both average fixed cost and average variable cost. At very low levels of output, such as 1 or 2 glasses per hour, average total cost is high because the fixed cost is spread over only a few units. Average total cost then declines as output increases until the firm's output reaches 5 glasses of lemonade per hour, when average total cost falls to $1.30 per glass. When the firm produces more than 6 glasses, average total cost starts rising again because average variable cost rises substantially.

The bottom of the U-shape occurs at the quantity that minimizes average total cost. This quantity is called the **efficient scale** of the firm. For Thirsty Thelma, the efficient scale is 5 or 6 glasses of lemonade. If she produces more or less than this amount, her average total cost rises above the minimum of $1.30.

The Relationship between Marginal Cost and Average Total Cost   If you look at Figure 13-5 (or back at Table 13-2), you will see something that may be surprising at first. *Whenever marginal cost is less than average total cost, average total cost is falling. Whenever marginal cost is greater than average total cost, average total cost is rising.* This feature of Thirsty Thelma's cost curves is not a coincidence from the particular numbers used in the example: It is true for all firms.

To see why, consider an analogy. Average total cost is like your grade point average. Marginal cost is like the grade in the next course you will take. If your grade in your next course is less than your grade point average, your grade point average will fall. If your grade in your next course is higher than your grade point average, your grade point average will rise. The mathematics of average and marginal costs is exactly the same as the mathematics of average and marginal grades.

This relationship between average total cost and marginal cost has an important corollary: *The marginal-cost curve crosses the average-total-cost curve at the efficient scale.* Why? At low levels of output, marginal cost is below average total cost, so average total cost is falling. But after the two curves cross, marginal cost rises above average total cost. For the reason we have just discussed, average total cost must start to rise at this level of output. Hence, this point of intersection is the minimum of average total cost. As you will see in the next chapter,

efficient scale
the quantity of output that minimizes average total cost

this point of minimum average total cost plays a key role in the analysis of competitive firms.

TYPICAL COST CURVES

In the examples we have examined so far, the firms exhibit diminishing marginal product and, therefore, rising marginal cost at all levels of output. In many firms, however, diminishing marginal product does not start to occur immediately after the first worker is hired. Depending on the production process, the second or third worker might have higher marginal product than the first because a team of workers can divide tasks and work more productively than a single worker. Such firms would first experience increasing marginal product for a while before diminishing marginal product sets in.

Table 13-3 shows the cost data for such a firm, called Big Bob's Bagel Bin. These data are graphed in Figure 13-6. Panel (a) shows how total cost (TC) depends on the quantity produced, and panel (b) shows average total cost (ATC), average fixed cost (AFC), average variable cost (AVC), and marginal cost (MC). In the range of output from 0 to 4 bagels per hour, the firm experiences increasing marginal product, and the marginal-cost curve falls. After 5 bagels per hour, the firm starts to experience diminishing marginal product, and the marginal-cost curve starts to rise. This combination of increasing and diminishing marginal product also makes the average-variable-cost curve U-shaped.

Quantity of Bagels (per hour)	Total Cost	Fixed Cost	Variable Cost	Average Fixed Cost	Average Variable Cost	Average Total Cost	Marginal Cost
0	$ 2.00	$2.00	$ 0.00	—	—	—	
1	3.00	2.00	1.00	$2.00	$1.00	$3.00	$1.00
2	3.80	2.00	1.80	1.00	0.90	1.90	0.80
3	4.40	2.00	2.40	0.67	0.80	1.47	0.60
4	4.80	2.00	2.80	0.50	0.70	1.20	0.40
5	5.20	2.00	3.20	0.40	0.64	1.04	0.40
6	5.80	2.00	3.80	0.33	0.63	0.96	0.60
7	6.60	2.00	4.60	0.29	0.66	0.95	0.80
8	7.60	2.00	5.60	0.25	0.70	0.95	1.00
9	8.80	2.00	6.80	0.22	0.76	0.98	1.20
10	10.20	2.00	8.20	0.20	0.82	1.02	1.40
11	11.80	2.00	9.80	0.18	0.89	1.07	1.60
12	13.60	2.00	11.60	0.17	0.97	1.14	1.80
13	15.60	2.00	13.60	0.15	1.05	1.20	2.00
14	17.80	2.00	15.80	0.14	1.13	1.27	2.20

THE VARIOUS MEASURES OF COST: BIG BOB'S BAGEL BIN

Table 13-3

Figure 13-6

BIG BOB'S COST CURVES. Many firms, like Big Bob's Bagel Bin, experience increasing marginal product before diminishing marginal product and, therefore, have cost curves like those in this figure. Panel (a) shows how total cost (TC) depends on the quantity produced. Panel (b) shows how average total cost (ATC), average fixed cost (AFC), average variable cost (AVC), and marginal cost (MC) depend on the quantity produced. These curves are derived by graphing the data from Table 13-3. Notice that marginal cost and average variable cost fall for a while before starting to rise.

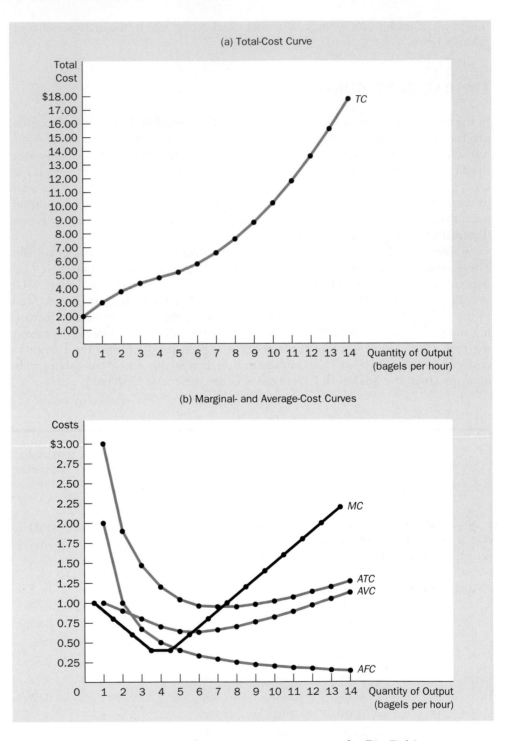

Despite these differences from our previous example, Big Bob's cost curves share the three properties that are most important to remember:

◆ Marginal cost eventually rises with the quantity of output.
◆ The average-total-cost curve is U-shaped.
◆ The marginal-cost curve crosses the average-total-cost curve at the minimum of average total cost.

> **QUICK QUIZ**   Suppose Honda's total cost of producing 4 cars is $225,000 and its total cost of producing 5 cars is $250,000. What is the average total cost of producing 5 cars? What is the marginal cost of the fifth car? ◆ Draw the marginal-cost curve and the average-total-cost curve for a typical firm, and explain why these curves cross where they do.

COSTS IN THE SHORT RUN AND IN THE LONG RUN

For many firms, the division of total costs between fixed and variable costs depends on the time horizon being considered. Consider, for instance, a car manufacturer, such as Ford Motor Company. Over a period of only a few months, Ford cannot adjust the number or sizes of its car factories. The only way it can produce additional cars is to hire more workers at the factories it already has. The cost of these factories is, therefore, a fixed cost in the short run. By contrast, over a period of several years, Ford can expand the size of its factories, build new factories, or close old ones. Thus, the cost of its factories is a variable cost in the long run.

Because many costs are fixed in the short run but variable in the long run, a firm's long-run cost curves differ from its short-run cost curves. Figure 13-7 shows an example. The figure presents three short-run average-total-cost curves—for a small, medium, and large factory. It also presents the long-run average-total cost curve. As the firm moves along the long-run curve, it is adjusting the size of the factory to the quantity of production.

This graph shows how short-run and long-run costs are related. The long-run average-total-cost curve is a much flatter U-shape than the short-run average-total-cost curve. In addition, the long-run curve lies below all of the

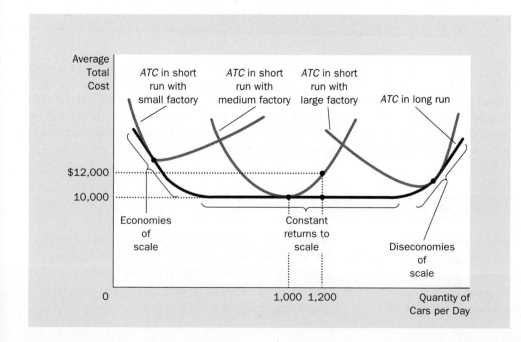

Figure 13-7

AVERAGE TOTAL COST IN THE SHORT AND LONG RUNS. Because fixed costs are variable in the long run, the average-total-cost curve in the short run differs from the average-total-cost curve in the long run.

short-run curves. These properties arise because of the greater flexibility firms have in the long run. When Ford wants to increase production from 1,000 to 1,200 cars per day, it has no choice in the short run but to hire more workers at its existing factories. Because of diminishing marginal product, average total cost rises from $10,000 to $12,000 per car. In the long run, however, Ford can expand both the size of the factory and its workforce, and average total cost remains at $10,000.

Although the long-run average-total-cost curve in Figure 13-7 is flatter than the short-run curves, it is still U-shaped. When long-run average total cost declines as output increases, there are said to be **economies of scale.** When long-run average total cost rises as output increases, there are said to be **diseconomies of scale.** When long-run average total cost does not vary with the level of output, there are said to be **constant returns to scale.** In this example, Ford has economies of scale at low levels of output, constant returns to scale at intermediate levels of output, and diseconomies of scale at high levels of output. Economies of scale might arise, for instance, because modern assembly-line production requires a large number of workers, each specializing in a particular task. If Ford were producing only a small quantity of cars, it could not take advantage of this approach and would have higher average total cost. Diseconomies of scale might arise, for instance, because it is difficult for firm managers to oversee a large organization. The larger the number of cars produced, the more stretched the management team becomes, and the less effective the managers become at keeping costs down.

economies of scale
the property whereby long-run average total cost falls as the quantity of output increases

diseconomies of scale
the property whereby long-run average total cost rises as the quantity of output increases

constant returns to scale
the property whereby long-run average total cost stays the same as the quantity of output changes

> **QUICK QUIZ**   If Boeing produces 9 jets per month, its long-run total cost is $9.0 million per month. If it produces 10 jets per month, its long-run total cost is $9.5 million per month. Does Boeing exhibit economies or diseconomies of scale?

CONCLUSION

The purpose of this chapter has been to develop some tools that we can use to study how firms make production and pricing decisions. You should now understand what economists mean by the term *costs* and how costs vary with the quantity of output a firm produces. By themselves, a firm's cost curves do not tell us what decisions the firm will make. But, as you will begin to see in the next chapter, they are an important component of that decision.

Summary

◆ The goal of firms is to maximize profit, which equals total revenue minus total cost.

◆ When analyzing a firm's behavior, it is important to include all the opportunity costs of production. Some of the opportunity costs, such as the wages a firm pays its

workers, are explicit. Other opportunity costs, such as the wages the firm owner gives up by working in the firm rather than taking another job, are implicit.

◆ A firm's costs reflect its production process. A typical firm's production function gets flatter as the quantity of an input increases, displaying the property of diminishing marginal product. As a result, a firm's total-cost curve gets steeper as the quantity produced rises.

♦ A firm's total costs can be divided between fixed costs and variable costs. Fixed costs are costs that do not change when the firm alters the quantity of output produced. Variable costs are costs that do change when the firm alters the quantity of output produced.

♦ From a firm's total cost, two related measures of cost are derived. Average total cost is total cost divided by the quantity of output. Marginal cost is the amount by which total cost would rise if output were increased by one unit.

♦ When analyzing firm behavior, it is often useful to graph average total cost and marginal cost. For a typical firm, marginal cost rises with the quantity of output. Average total cost first falls as output increases and then rises as output increases further. The marginal-cost curve always crosses the average-total-cost curve at the minimum of average total cost.

♦ A firm's costs often depend on the time horizon being considered. In particular, many costs are fixed in the short run but variable in the long run. As a result, when the firm changes its level of production, average total cost may rise more in the short run than in the long run.

Key Concepts

total revenue, p. 264
total cost, p. 264
profit, p. 264
production function, p. 267
marginal product, p. 267
diminishing marginal product, p. 267

fixed costs, p. 271
variable costs, p. 271
average total cost, p. 272
average fixed cost, p. 272
average variable cost, p. 272

marginal cost, p. 272
efficient scale, p. 274
economies of scale, p. 278
diseconomies of scale, p. 278
constant returns to scale, p. 278

Questions for Review

1. What is the relationship between a firm's total revenue, profit, and total cost?

2. Give an example of an opportunity cost that an accountant might not count as a cost. Why would the accountant ignore this cost?

3. Define total cost, average total cost, and marginal cost. How are they related?

4. Draw the marginal-cost and average-total-cost curves for a typical firm. Explain why the curves have the shapes that they do and why they cross where they do.

5. How and why does a firm's average-total-cost curve differ in the short run and in the long run?

Problems and Applications

1. This chapter discusses many types of costs: opportunity cost, total cost, fixed cost, variable cost, average total cost, and marginal cost. Fill in the type of cost that best completes the phrases below:
   a. The true cost of taking some action is its _____.
   b. _____ is falling when marginal cost is below it, and rising when marginal cost is above it.
   c. A cost that does not depend on the quantity produced is a _____.

   d. In the ice-cream industry in the short run, _____ includes the cost of cream and sugar, but not the cost of the factory.
   e. Profits equal total revenue less _____.
   f. The cost of producing an extra unit of output is _____.

2. Your aunt is thinking about opening a hardware store. She estimates that it would cost $500,000 per year to rent

the store and buy the stock. In addition, she would have to quit her $50,000 per year job as an accountant.

a. Define opportunity cost.

b. What is your aunt's opportunity cost of running a hardware store for a year? If your aunt thought she could sell $510,000 worth of merchandise in a year, should she open the store? Explain.

3. Suppose that your college charges you separately for tuition and for room and board.

a. What is a cost of attending college that is not an opportunity cost?

b. What is an explicit opportunity cost of attending college?

c. What is an implicit opportunity cost of attending college?

4. A commercial fisherman notices the following relationship between hours spent fishing and the quantity of fish caught:

HOURS	QUANTITY OF FISH (IN POUNDS)
0	0
1	10
2	18
3	24
4	28
5	30

a. What is the marginal product of each hour spent fishing?

b. Use these data to graph the fisherman's production function. Explain its shape.

c. The fisherman has a fixed cost of $10 (his pole). The opportunity cost of his time is $5 per hour. Graph the fisherman's total-cost curve. Explain its shape.

5. Suppose that you and your roommate have started a bagel delivery service on campus. List some of your fixed costs and describe why they are fixed. List some of your variable costs and describe why they are variable.

6. Consider the following cost information for a pizzeria:

Q (DOZENS)	TOTAL COST	VARIABLE COST
0	$300	$ 0
1	350	50
2	390	90
3	420	120
4	450	150
5	490	190
6	540	240

a. What is the pizzeria's fixed cost?

b. Construct a table in which you calculate the marginal cost per dozen pizzas using the information on total cost. Also calculate the marginal cost per dozen pizzas using the information on variable cost. What is the relationship between these sets of numbers? Comment.

7. You are thinking about setting up a lemonade stand. The stand itself costs $200. The ingredients for each cup of lemonade cost $0.50.

a. What is your fixed cost of doing business? What is your variable cost per cup?

b. Construct a table showing your total cost, average total cost, and marginal cost for output levels varying from 0 to 10 gallons. (Hint: There are 16 cups in a gallon.) Draw the three cost curves.

8. Your cousin Vinnie owns a painting company with a total fixed cost of $200 and the following schedule for total variable cost:

	QUANTITY OF HOUSES PAINTED PER MONTH						
	1	2	3	4	5	6	7
Total variable cost	$10	$20	$40	$80	$160	$320	$640

Calculate average fixed cost, average variable cost, and average total cost for each quantity. What is the efficient scale of the painting company?

9. Healthy Harry's Juice Bar has the following cost schedules:

Q (VATS)	VARIABLE COST	TOTAL COST
0	$ 0	$ 30
1	10	40
2	25	55
3	45	75
4	70	100
5	100	130
6	135	165

a. Calculate average variable cost, average total cost, and marginal cost for each quantity.

b. Graph all three curves. What is the relationship between the marginal-cost curve and the average-total-cost curve? Between the marginal-cost curve and the average-variable-cost curve? Explain.

10. Consider the following table of long-run total cost for three different firms:

	QUANTITY						
	1	2	3	4	5	6	7
Firm A	$60	$70	$80	$90	$100	$110	$120
Firm B	11	24	39	56	75	96	119
Firm C	21	34	49	66	85	106	129

Does each of these firms experience economies of scale or diseconomies of scale?

14

FIRMS IN COMPETITIVE MARKETS

If your local gas station raised the price it charges for gasoline by 20 percent, it would see a large drop in the amount of gasoline it sold. Its customers would quickly switch to buying their gasoline at other gas stations. By contrast, if your local water company raised the price of water by 20 percent, it would see only a small decrease in the amount of water it sold. People might water their lawns less often and buy more water-efficient shower heads, but they would be hard pressed to reduce water consumption greatly. The difference between the gasoline market and the water market is obvious: There are many firms pumping gasoline, but there is only one firm pumping water. As you might expect, this difference in market structure shapes the pricing and production decisions of the firms that operate in these markets.

In this chapter we examine the behavior of competitive firms, such as your local gas station. You may recall that a market is competitive if each buyer and seller is small compared to the size of the market and, therefore, has little ability to influence market prices. By contrast, if a firm can influence the market price of the good it sells, it is said to have *market power*. In the three chapters that follow this one, we examine the behavior of firms with market power, such as your local water company.

Our analysis of competitive firms in this chapter will shed light on the decisions that lie behind the supply curve in a competitive market. Not surprisingly, we will find that a market supply curve is tightly linked to firms' costs of production. (Indeed, this general insight should be familiar to you from our analysis in Chapter 7.) But among a firm's various costs—fixed, variable, average, and marginal—which ones are most relevant for its decision about the quantity to supply? We will see that all these measures of cost play important and interrelated roles.

WHAT IS A COMPETITIVE MARKET?

Our goal in this chapter is to examine how firms make production decisions in competitive markets. As a background for this analysis, we begin by considering what a competitive market is.

THE MEANING OF COMPETITION

competitive market
a market with many buyers and sellers trading identical products so that each buyer and seller is a price taker

Although we have already discussed the meaning of competition in Chapter 4, let's review the lesson briefly. A **competitive market,** sometimes called a *perfectly competitive market,* has two characteristics:

◆   There are many buyers and many sellers in the market.
◆   The goods offered by the various sellers are largely the same.

As a result of these conditions, the actions of any single buyer or seller in the market have a negligible impact on the market price. Each buyer and seller takes the market price as given.

An example is the market for milk. No single buyer of milk can influence the price of milk because each buyer purchases a small amount relative to the size of the market. Similarly, each seller of milk has limited control over the price because many other sellers are offering milk that is essentially identical. Because each seller can sell all he wants at the going price, he has little reason to charge less, and if he charges more, buyers will go elsewhere. Buyers and sellers in competitive markets must accept the price the market determines and, therefore, are said to be *price takers.*

In addition to the above two conditions for competition, there is a third condition sometimes thought to characterize perfectly competitive markets:

◆   Firms can freely enter or exit the market.

If, for instance, anyone can decide to start a dairy farm, and if any existing dairy farmer can decide to leave the dairy business, then the dairy industry would satisfy this condition. It should be noted that much of the analysis of competitive firms does not rely on the assumption of free entry and exit because this condition is not necessary for firms to be price takers. As we will see later in this chapter, however, when this third condition does hold, we can extend our analysis further and reach important additional conclusions.

THE REVENUE OF A COMPETITIVE FIRM

A firm in a competitive market, like most other firms in the economy, tries to maximize profit, which equals total revenue minus total cost. To see how it does this, we first consider the revenue of a competitive firm. To keep matters concrete, let's consider a specific firm: the Smith Family Dairy Farm.

The Smith Farm produces a quantity of milk Q and sells each unit at the market price P. The farm's total revenue is $P \times Q$. For example, if a gallon of milk sells for $6 and the farm sells 1,000 gallons, its total revenue is $6,000.

QUANTITY	PRICE	TOTAL REVENUE	AVERAGE REVENUE	MARGINAL REVENUE
(Q)	(P)	(TR = P × Q)	(AR = TR/Q)	(MR = ΔTR/ΔQ)
1 gallon	$6	$ 6	$6	
				$6
2	6	12	6	
				6
3	6	18	6	
				6
4	6	24	6	
				6
5	6	30	6	
				6
6	6	36	6	
				6
7	6	42	6	
				6
8	6	48	6	

TOTAL, AVERAGE, AND MARGINAL REVENUE FOR A COMPETITIVE FIRM

Table 14-1

Because the Smith Farm is small compared to the world market for milk, it takes the price as given by market conditions. This means, in particular, that the price of milk does not depend on the quantity of output that the Smith Farm produces and sells. If the Smiths double the amount of milk they produce, the price of milk remains the same, and their total revenue doubles. As a result, total revenue is proportional to the amount of output.

Table 14-1 shows the revenue for the Smith Family Dairy Farm. The first two columns show the amount of output the farm produces and the price at which it sells its output. The third column is the farm's total revenue. The table assumes that the price of milk is $6 a gallon, so total revenue is simply $6 times the number of gallons.

Just as the concepts of average and marginal were useful in the last chapter when analyzing costs, they are also useful when analyzing revenue. To see what these concepts tell us, consider these two questions:

◆   How much revenue does the farm receive for the typical gallon of milk?

◆   How much additional revenue does the farm receive if it increases production of milk by 1 gallon?

The next two columns in Table 14-1 answer these questions.

The fourth column in the table shows **average revenue,** which is total revenue (from the third column) divided by the amount of output (from the first column). Average revenue tells us how much revenue a firm receives for the typical unit sold. In Table 14-1, you can see that average revenue equals $6, the price of a gallon of milk. This illustrates a general lesson that applies not only to competitive firms but to other firms as well. Total revenue is the price times the quantity (P × Q), and average revenue is total revenue (P × Q) divided by the quantity (Q). Therefore, *for all firms, average revenue equals the price of the good.*

The fifth column shows **marginal revenue,** which is the change in total revenue from the sale of each additional unit of output. In Table 14-1, marginal revenue equals $6, the price of a gallon of milk. This result illustrates a lesson that

average revenue
total revenue divided by the quantity sold

marginal revenue
the change in total revenue from an additional unit sold

applies only to competitive firms. Total revenue is $P \times Q$, and P is fixed for a competitive firm. Therefore, when Q rises by one unit, total revenue rises by P dollars. *For competitive firms, marginal revenue equals the price of the good.*

▌**QUICK QUIZ**   When a competitive firm doubles the amount it sells, what happens to the price of its output and its total revenue?

PROFIT MAXIMIZATION AND THE COMPETITIVE FIRM'S SUPPLY CURVE

The goal of a competitive firm is to maximize profit, which equals total revenue minus total cost. We have just discussed the firm's revenue, and in the last chapter we discussed the firm's costs. We are now ready to examine how the firm maximizes profit and how that decision leads to its supply curve.

A SIMPLE EXAMPLE OF PROFIT MAXIMIZATION

Let's begin our analysis of the firm's supply decision with the example in Table 14-2. In the first column of the table is the number of gallons of milk the Smith Family Dairy Farm produces. The second column shows the farm's total revenue, which is $6 times the number of gallons. The third column shows the farm's total cost. Total cost includes fixed costs, which are $3 in this example, and variable costs, which depend on the quantity produced.

QUANTITY	TOTAL REVENUE	TOTAL COST	PROFIT	MARGINAL REVENUE	MARGINAL COST
(Q)	(TR)	(TC)	(TR − TC)	(MR = ΔTR/ΔQ)	(MC = ΔTC/ΔQ)
0 gallons	$ 0	$ 3	−$3		
				$6	$2
1	6	5	1		
				6	3
2	12	8	4		
				6	4
3	18	12	6		
				6	5
4	24	17	7		
				6	6
5	30	23	7		
				6	7
6	36	30	6		
				6	8
7	42	38	4		
				6	9
8	48	47	1		

Table 14-2   PROFIT MAXIMIZATION: A NUMERICAL EXAMPLE

The fourth column shows the farm's profit, which is computed by subtracting total cost from total revenue. If the farm produces nothing, it has a loss of $3. If it produces 1 gallon, it has a profit of $1. If it produces 2 gallons, it has a profit of $4, and so on. To maximize profit, the Smith Farm chooses the quantity that makes profit as large as possible. In this example, profit is maximized when the farm produces 4 or 5 gallons of milk, when the profit is $7.

There is another way to look at the Smith Farm's decision: The Smiths can find the profit-maximizing quantity by comparing the marginal revenue and marginal cost from each unit produced. The last two columns in Table 14-2 compute marginal revenue and marginal cost from total revenue and total cost. The first gallon of milk the farm produces has a marginal revenue of $6 and a marginal cost of $2; hence, producing that gallon increases profit by $4 (from −$3 to $1). The second gallon produced has a marginal revenue of $6 and a marginal cost of $3, so that gallon increases profit by $3 (from $1 to $4). As long as marginal revenue exceeds marginal cost, increasing the quantity raises profit. Once the Smith Farm has reached 5 gallons of milk, however, the situation is very different. The sixth gallon would have marginal revenue of $6 and marginal cost of $7, so producing it would reduce profit by $1 (from $7 to $6). As a result, the Smiths would not produce beyond 5 gallons.

One of the *Ten Principles of Economics* in Chapter 1 is that rational people think at the margin. We now see how the Smith Family Dairy Farm can apply this principle. If marginal revenue is greater than marginal cost—as it is at 1, 2, or 3 gallons—the Smiths should increase the production of milk. If marginal revenue is less than marginal cost—as it is at 6, 7, or 8 gallons—the Smiths should decrease production. If the Smiths think at the margin and make incremental adjustments to the level of production, they are naturally led to produce the profit-maximizing quantity.

THE MARGINAL-COST CURVE AND THE FIRM'S SUPPLY DECISION

To extend this analysis of profit maximization, consider the cost curves in Figure 14-1. These cost curves have the three features that, as we discussed in Chapter 13, are considered typical: The marginal-cost curve *(MC)* is upward sloping. The average-total-cost curve *(ATC)* is U-shaped. And the marginal-cost curve crosses the average-total-cost curve at the minimum of average total cost. The figure also shows a horizontal line at the market price *(P)* of the firm's output, which equals the firm's average revenue *(AR)* and its marginal revenue *(MR)*. The price line is horizontal because the firm is a price taker: The price is the same regardless of the quantity that the firm decides to produce.

We can use Figure 14-1 to find the quantity of output that maximizes profit. Imagine that the firm is producing at Q_1. At this level of output, marginal revenue is greater than marginal cost. That is, if the firm raised its level of production and sales by one unit, the additional revenue (MR_1) would exceed the additional costs (MC_1). Profit, which equals total revenue minus total cost, would increase. Hence, if marginal revenue is greater than marginal cost, as it is at Q_1, the firm can increase profit by raising production.

A similar argument applies when output is at Q_2. In this case, marginal cost is greater than marginal revenue. If the firm reduced production by one unit, the costs saved (MC_2) would exceed the revenue lost (MR_2). Therefore, if marginal

Figure 14-1

PROFIT MAXIMIZATION FOR A COMPETITIVE FIRM. This figure shows the marginal-cost curve (*MC*), the average-total-cost curve (*ATC*), and the average-variable-cost curve (*AVC*). It also shows the market price (*P*), which equals marginal revenue (*MR*) and average revenue (*AR*). At the quantity Q_1, marginal revenue MR_1 exceeds marginal cost MC_1, so raising production increases profit. At the quantity Q_2, marginal cost MC_2 is above marginal revenue MR_2, so reducing production increases profit. The profit-maximizing quantity Q_{MAX} is found where the horizontal price line intersects the marginal-cost curve.

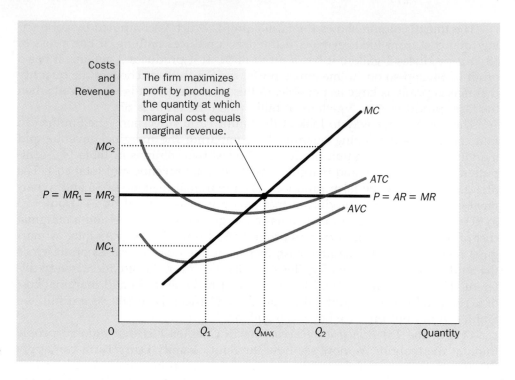

revenue is less than marginal cost, as it is at Q_2, the firm can increase profit by reducing production.

Where do these marginal adjustments to level of production end? Regardless of whether the firm begins with production at a low level (such as Q_1) or at a high level (such as Q_2), the firm will eventually adjust production until the quantity produced reaches Q_{MAX}. This analysis shows a general rule for profit maximization: *At the profit-maximizing level of output, marginal revenue and marginal cost are exactly equal.*

We can now see how the competitive firm decides the quantity of its good to supply to the market. Because a competitive firm is a price taker, its marginal revenue equals the market price. For any given price, the competitive firm's profit-maximizing quantity of output is found by looking at the intersection of the price with the marginal-cost curve. In Figure 14-1, that quantity is Q_{MAX}.

Figure 14-2 shows how a competitive firm responds to an increase in the price. When the price is P_1, the firm produces quantity Q_1, which is the quantity that equates marginal cost to the price. When the price rises to P_2, the firm finds that marginal revenue is now higher than marginal cost at the previous level of output, so the firm increases production. The new profit-maximizing quantity is Q_2, at which marginal cost equals the new higher price. *In essence, because the firm's marginal-cost curve determines how much the firm is willing to supply at any price, it is the competitive firm's supply curve.*

THE FIRM'S SHORT-RUN DECISION TO SHUT DOWN

So far we have been analyzing the question of how much a competitive firm will produce. In some circumstances, however, the firm will decide to shut down and not produce anything at all.

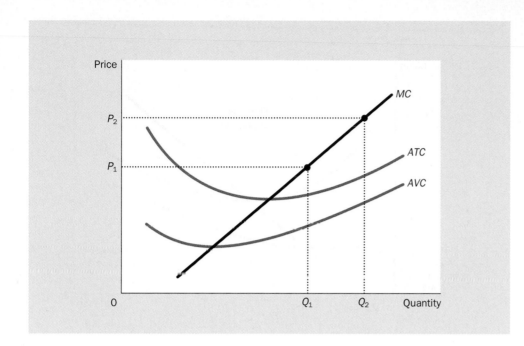

Figure 14-2

MARGINAL COST AS THE COMPETITIVE FIRM'S SUPPLY CURVE. An increase in the price from P_1 to P_2 leads to an increase in the firm's profit-maximizing quantity from Q_1 to Q_2. Because the marginal-cost curve shows the quantity supplied by the firm at any given price, it is the firm's supply curve.

Here we should distinguish between a temporary shutdown of a firm and the permanent exit of a firm from the market. A *shutdown* refers to a short-run decision not to produce anything during a specific period of time because of current market conditions. *Exit* refers to a long-run decision to leave the market. The long-run and short-run decisions differ because most firms cannot avoid their fixed costs in the short run but are able to do so in the long run. That is, a firm that shuts down temporarily still has to pay its fixed costs, whereas a firm that exits can save both its fixed and its variable costs.

For example, consider the production decision that a farmer faces. The cost of the land is one of the farmer's fixed costs. If the farmer decides not to produce any crops one season, the land lies fallow, and he cannot recover this cost. When making the short-run decision whether to shut down for a season, the fixed cost of land is said to be a *sunk cost*. By contrast, if the farmer decides to leave farming altogether, he can sell the land. When making the long-run decision whether to exit the market, the cost of land is not sunk.

Now let's consider what determines a firm's shutdown decision. If the firm shuts down, it loses all revenue from the sale of its product. At the same time, it saves the variable costs of making its product (but still pays the fixed costs). Thus, *the firm shuts down if the revenue that it would get from producing is less than the variable costs of production.*

A small bit of mathematics can make this shutdown criterion more useful. If *TR* stands for total revenue, and *VC* stands for variable costs, then the firm's decision can be written as

Shut down if $TR < VC$.

The firm shuts down if total revenue is less than variable cost. By dividing both sides of this inequality by the quantity Q, we can write it as

Shut down if $TR/Q < VC/Q$.

Figure 14-3

THE COMPETITIVE FIRM'S SHORT-RUN SUPPLY CURVE. In the short run, the competitive firm's supply curve is its marginal-cost curve *(MC)* above average variable cost *(AVC)*. If the price falls below average variable cost, the firm is better off shutting down.

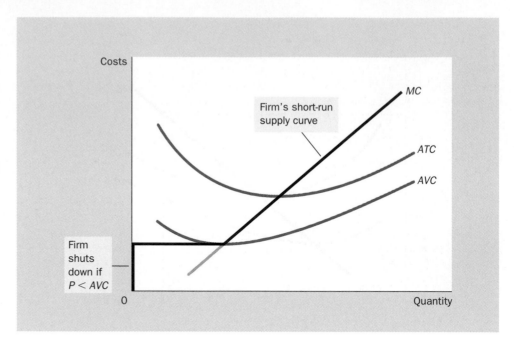

Notice that this can be further simplified. *TR/Q* is total revenue divided by quantity, which is average revenue. As we discussed previously, average revenue for any firm is simply the good's price *P*. Similarly, *VC/Q* is average variable cost *AVC*. Therefore, the firm's shutdown criterion is

$$\text{Shut down if } P < AVC.$$

That is, a firm chooses to shut down if the price of the good is less than the average variable cost of production. This criterion is intuitive: When choosing to produce, the firm compares the price it receives for the typical unit to the average variable cost that it must incur to produce the typical unit. If the price doesn't cover the average variable cost, the firm is better off stopping production altogether. The firm can reopen in the future if conditions change so that price exceeds average variable cost.

We now have a full description of a competitive firm's profit-maximizing strategy. If the firm produces anything, it produces the quantity at which marginal cost equals the price of the good. Yet if the price is less than average variable cost at that quantity, the firm is better off shutting down and not producing anything. These results are illustrated in Figure 14-3. *The competitive firm's short-run supply curve is the portion of its marginal-cost curve that lies above average variable cost.*

CASE STUDY NEAR-EMPTY RESTAURANTS AND OFF-SEASON MINIATURE GOLF

Have you ever walked into a restaurant for lunch and found it almost empty? Why, you might have asked, does the restaurant even bother to stay open? It might seem that the revenue from the few customers could not possibly cover the cost of running the restaurant.

In making the decision whether to open for lunch, a restaurant owner must keep in mind the distinction between fixed and variable costs. Many of a restaurant's costs—the rent, kitchen equipment, tables, plates, silverware, and so on—are fixed. Shutting down during lunch would not reduce these costs. When the owner is deciding whether to serve lunch, only the variable costs—the price of the additional food and the wages of the extra staff—are relevant. The owner shuts down the restaurant at lunchtime only if the revenue from the few lunchtime customers fails to cover the restaurant's variable costs.

An operator of a miniature-golf course in a summer resort community faces a similar decision. Because revenue varies substantially from season to season, the firm must decide when to open and when to close. Once again, the fixed costs—the costs of buying the land and building the course—are irrelevant. The miniature-golf course should be open for business only during those times of year when its revenue exceeds its variable costs.

Staying open can be profitable, even with many tables empty.

FYI

Spilt Milk and Sunk Costs

SOMETIME IN YOUR LIFE, YOU have probably been told, "Don't cry over spilt milk," or "Let bygones be bygones." These adages hold a deep truth about rational decision-making. Economists say that a cost is a *sunk cost* when it has already been committed and cannot be recovered. Once a cost is sunk, it is no longer an opportunity cost. Because nothing can be done about sunk costs, you can ignore them when making decisions about various aspects of life, including business strategy.

Our analysis of the firm's shutdown decision is one example of the irrelevance of sunk costs. We assume that the firm cannot recover its fixed costs by temporarily stopping production. As a result, the firm's fixed costs are sunk in the short run, and the firm can safely ignore these costs when deciding how much to produce. The firm's short-run supply curve is the part of the marginal-cost curve that lies above average variable cost, and the size of the fixed cost does not matter for this supply decision.

The irrelevance of sunk costs explains how real businesses make decisions. In the early 1990s, for instance, most of

the largest airlines reported large losses. American Airlines reported a loss in 1992 of $475 million, Delta a loss of $565 million, and USAir a loss of $601 million. Despite the losses, however, these airlines continued to sell tickets and fly passengers. At first, this decision might seem surprising: If the airlines were losing money flying planes, why didn't the owners of the airlines just shut down their businesses?

To understand this behavior, we must acknowledge that many of the airlines' costs are sunk in the short run. If an airline has bought a plane and cannot resell it, then the cost of the plane is sunk. The opportunity cost of a flight includes only the variable costs of fuel and the wages of pilots and flight attendants. As long as the total revenue from flying exceeds these variable costs, the airlines should continue operating. And, in fact, they did.

The irrelevance of sunk costs is also important for personal decisions. Imagine, for instance, that you place a $10 value on seeing a newly released movie. You buy a ticket for $7, but before entering the theater, you lose the ticket. Should you buy another ticket? Or should you now go home and refuse to pay a total of $14 to see the movie? The answer is that you should buy another ticket. The benefit of seeing the movie ($10) still exceeds the opportunity cost (the $7 for the second ticket). The $7 you paid for the lost ticket is a sunk cost. As with spilt milk, there is no point in crying about it.

THE FIRM'S LONG-RUN DECISION TO EXIT OR ENTER AN INDUSTRY

The firm's long-run decision to exit the industry is similar to its shutdown decision. If the firm exits, it again will lose all revenue from the sale of its product, but now it saves on both fixed and variable costs of production. Thus, *the firm exits if the revenue it would get from producing is less than its total costs.*

We can again make this criterion more useful by writing it mathematically. If *TR* stands for total revenue, and *TC* stands for total cost, then the firm's criterion can be written as

$$\text{Exit if } TR < TC.$$

The firm exits if total revenue is less than total cost. By dividing both sides of this inequality by quantity *Q*, we can write it as

$$\text{Exit if } TR/Q < TC/Q.$$

We can simplify this further by noting that *TR/Q* is average revenue, which equals the price *P*, and that *TC/Q* is average total cost *ATC*. Therefore, the firm's exit criterion is

$$\text{Exit if } P < ATC.$$

That is, a firm chooses to exit if the price of the good is less than the average total cost of production.

A parallel analysis applies to an entrepreneur who is considering starting a firm. The firm will enter the industry if such an action would be profitable, which occurs if the price of the good exceeds the average total cost of production. The entry criterion is

$$\text{Enter if } P > ATC.$$

The criterion for entry is exactly the opposite of the criterion for exit.

We can now describe a competitive firm's long-run profit-maximizing strategy. If the firm is in the market, it produces the quantity at which marginal cost equals the price of the good. Yet if the price is less than average total cost at that quantity, the firm chooses to exit (or not enter) the market. These results are illustrated in Figure 14-4. *The competitive firm's long-run supply curve is the portion of its marginal-cost curve that lies above average total cost.*

MEASURING PROFIT IN OUR GRAPH FOR THE COMPETITIVE FIRM

As we analyze exit and entry, it is useful to be able to analyze the firm's profit in more detail. Recall that profit equals total revenue *(TR)* minus total cost *(TC):*

$$\text{Profit} = TR - TC.$$

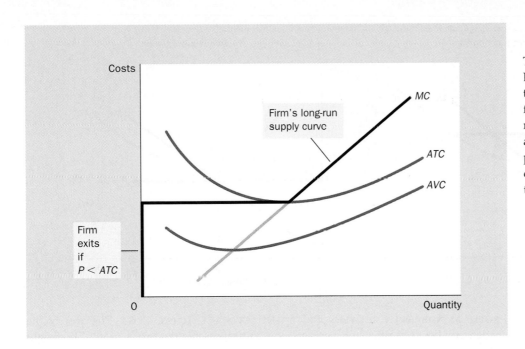

Figure 14-4

THE COMPETITIVE FIRM'S LONG-RUN SUPPLY CURVE. In the long run, the competitive firm's supply curve is its marginal-cost curve (MC) above average total cost (ATC). If the price falls below average total cost, the firm is better off exiting the market.

We can rewrite this definition by multiplying and dividing the right-hand side by Q:

$$\text{Profit} = (TR/Q - TC/Q) \times Q.$$

But note that TR/Q is average revenue, which is the price P, and TC/Q is average total cost ATC. Therefore,

$$\text{Profit} = (P - ATC) \times Q.$$

This way of expressing the firm's profit allows us to measure profit in our graphs.

Panel (a) of Figure 14-5 shows a firm earning positive profit. As we have already discussed, the firm maximizes profit by producing the quantity at which price equals marginal cost. Now look at the shaded rectangle. The height of the rectangle is $P - ATC$, the difference between price and average total cost. The width of the rectangle is Q, the quantity produced. Therefore, the area of the rectangle is $(P - ATC) \times Q$, which is the firm's profit.

Similarly, panel (b) of this figure shows a firm with losses (negative profit). In this case, maximizing profit means minimizing losses, a task accomplished once again by producing the quantity at which price equals marginal cost. Now consider the shaded rectangle. The height of the rectangle is $ATC - P$, and the width is Q. The area is $(ATC - P) \times Q$, which is the firm's loss. Because a firm in this situation is not making enough revenue to cover its average total cost, the firm would eventually choose to exit the market.

QUICK QUIZ How does the price faced by a profit-maximizing competitive firm compare to its marginal cost? Explain. ◆ When does a profit-maximizing competitive firm decide to shut down?

Figure 14-5

PROFIT AS THE AREA BETWEEN PRICE AND AVERAGE TOTAL COST. The area of the shaded box between price and average total cost represents the firm's profit. The height of this box is price minus average total cost $(P - ATC)$, and the width of the box is the quantity of output (Q). In panel (a), price is above average total cost, so the firm has positive profit. In panel (b), price is less than average total cost, so the firm has losses.

THE SUPPLY CURVE IN A COMPETITIVE MARKET

Now that we have examined the supply decision of a single firm, we can discuss the supply curve for a market. There are two cases to consider. First, we examine a market with a fixed number of firms. Second, we examine a market in which the number of firms can change as old firms exit the market and new firms enter. Both cases are important, for each applies over a specific time horizon. Over short periods of time, it is often difficult for firms to enter and exit, so the assumption of a fixed number of firms is appropriate. But over long periods of time, the number of firms can adjust to changing market conditions.

MARKET SUPPLY WITH A FIXED NUMBER OF FIRMS

Consider first a market with 1,000 identical firms. For any given price, each firm supplies a quantity of output so that its marginal cost equals the price, as shown in panel (a) of Figure 14-6. That is, as long as price is above average variable cost, each firm's marginal-cost curve is its supply curve. The quantity of output supplied to the market equals the sum of the quantities supplied by the individual firms. Thus, to derive the market supply curve, we add the quantity supplied by each firm in the market. As panel (b) of Figure 14-6 shows, because the firms are identical, the quantity supplied to the market is 1,000 times the quantity supplied by each firm.

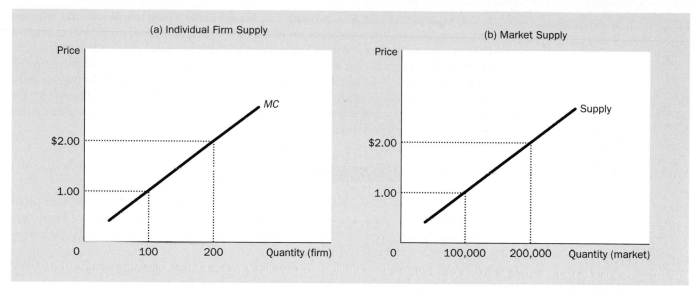

MARKET SUPPLY WITH A FIXED NUMBER OF FIRMS. When the number of firms in the market is fixed, the market supply curve, shown in panel (b), reflects the individual firms' marginal-cost curves, shown in panel (a). Here, in a market of 1,000 firms, the quantity of output supplied to the market is 1,000 times the quantity supplied by each firm.

Figure 14-6

MARKET SUPPLY WITH ENTRY AND EXIT

Now consider what happens if firms are able to enter or exit the market. Let's suppose that everyone has access to the same technology for producing the good and access to the same markets to buy the inputs into production. Therefore, all firms and all potential firms have the same cost curves.

Decisions about entry and exit in a market of this type depend on the incentives facing the owners of existing firms and the entrepreneurs who could start new firms. If firms already in the market are profitable, then new firms will have an incentive to enter the market. This entry will expand the number of firms, increase the quantity of the good supplied, and drive down prices and profits. Conversely, if firms in the market are making losses, then some existing firms will exit the market. Their exit will reduce the number of firms, decrease the quantity of the good supplied, and drive up prices and profits. *At the end of this process of entry and exit, firms that remain in the market must be making zero economic profit.* Recall that we can write a firm's profits as

$$\text{Profit} = (P - ATC) \times Q.$$

This equation shows that an operating firm has zero profit if and only if the price of the good equals the average total cost of producing that good. If price is above average total cost, profit is positive, which encourages new firms to enter. If price is less than average total cost, profit is negative, which encourages some firms to exit. *The process of entry and exit ends only when price and average total cost are driven to equality.*

This analysis has a surprising implication. We noted earlier in the chapter that competitive firms produce so that price equals marginal cost. We just noted that free entry and exit forces price to equal average total cost. But if price is to equal both marginal cost and average total cost, these two measures of cost must equal each other. Marginal cost and average total cost are equal, however, only when the firm is operating at the minimum of average total cost. Therefore, *the long-run equilibrium of a competitive market with free entry and exit must have firms operating at their efficient scale.*

FYI

Why Do Competitive Firms Stay in Business If They Make Zero Profit?

AT FIRST, IT MIGHT SEEM ODD that competitive firms earn zero profit in the long run. After all, people start businesses to make a profit. If entry eventually drives profit to zero, there might seem to be little reason to stay in business.

To understand the zero-profit condition more fully, recall that profit equals total revenue minus total cost, and that total cost includes all the opportunity costs of the firm. In particular, total cost includes the opportunity cost of the time and money that the firm owners devote to the business. In the zero-profit equilibrium, the firm's revenue must compensate the owners for the time and money that they expend to keep their business going.

For example, suppose that a farmer had to invest $1 million to open his farm and that he had to give up another job that would have paid $20,000 a year. Then the farmer's opportunity cost of farming includes both the interest he could have earned on the $1 million and the $20,000 of forgone wages. Even if his profit is driven to zero, his revenue from farming compensates him for these opportunity costs.

Keep in mind that accountants measure costs differently from the way economists do. As we discussed in Chapter 13, accountants keep track only of the money that flows into and out of firms and, therefore, do not include all the opportunity costs. In the zero-profit equilibrium, economic profit is zero, but accounting profit is positive.

"We're a nonprofit organization—we don't intend to be, but we are!"

(a) Firm's Zero-Profit Condition

(b) Market Supply

MARKET SUPPLY WITH ENTRY AND EXIT. Firms will enter or exit the market until profit is driven to zero. Thus, in the long run, price equals the minimum of average total cost, as shown in panel (a). The number of firms adjusts to ensure that all demand is satisfied at this price. The long-run market supply curve is horizontal at this price, as shown in panel (b).

Figure 14-7

Panel (a) of Figure 14-7 shows a firm in such a long-run equilibrium. In this figure, price P equals marginal cost MC, so the firm is profit-maximizing. Price also equals average total cost ATC, so profits are zero. New firms have no incentive to enter the market, and existing firms have no incentive to leave the market.

From this analysis of firm behavior, we can determine the long-run supply curve for the market. In a market with free entry and exit, there is only one price consistent with zero profit—the minimum of average total cost. As a result, the long-run market supply curve must be horizontal at this price, as in panel (b) of Figure 14-7. Any price above this level would generate profit, leading to entry and an increase in the total quantity supplied. Any price below this level would generate losses, leading to exit and a decrease in the total quantity supplied. Eventually, the number of firms in the market adjusts so that price equals the minimum of average total cost, and there are enough firms to satisfy all the demand at this price.

A SHIFT IN DEMAND IN THE SHORT RUN AND LONG RUN

Because firms can enter and exit a market in the long run but not in the short run, changes in demand have different effects over different time horizons. To see this, let's trace the effects of a shift in demand. This analysis will show how a market responds over time, and it will show how entry and exit drive a market to its long-run equilibrium.

Suppose the market for milk begins in long-run equilibrium. Firms are earning zero profit, so price equals the minimum of average total cost. Panel (a) of Figure 14-8 shows the situation. The long-run equilibrium is point A, the quantity sold in the market is Q_1, and the price is P_1.

Now suppose scientists discover that milk has miraculous health benefits. As a result, the demand curve for milk shifts outward from D_1 to D_2, as in panel (b). The short-run equilibrium moves from point A to point B; as a result, the quantity rises from Q_1 to Q_2, and the price rises from P_1 to P_2. All of the existing firms respond to the higher price by raising the amount produced. Because each firm's supply curve reflects its marginal-cost curve, how much they each increase production is determined by the marginal-cost curve. In the new, short-run equilibrium, the price of milk exceeds average total cost, so the firms are making positive profit.

Over time, the profit in this market encourages new firms to enter. Some farmers may switch to milk from other farm products, for example. As the number of firms grows, the short-run supply curve shifts to the right from S_1 to S_2, as in panel (c), and this shift causes the price of milk to fall. Eventually, the price is driven back down to the minimum of average total cost, profits are zero, and firms stop entering. Thus, the market reaches a new long-run equilibrium, point C. The price of milk has returned to P_1, but the quantity produced has risen to Q_3. Each firm is again producing at its efficient scale, but because more firms are in the dairy business, the quantity of milk produced and sold is higher.

WHY THE LONG-RUN SUPPLY CURVE MIGHT SLOPE UPWARD

So far we have seen that entry and exit can cause the long-run market supply curve to be horizontal. The essence of our analysis is that there are a large number of potential entrants, each of which faces the same costs. As a result, the long-run market supply curve is horizontal at the minimum of average total cost. When the demand for the good increases, the long-run result is an increase in the number of firms and in the total quantity supplied, without any change in the price.

There are, however, two reasons that the long-run market supply curve might slope upward. The first is that some resource used in production may be available only in limited quantities. For example, consider the market for farm products. Anyone can choose to buy land and start a farm, but the quantity of land is limited. As more people become farmers, the price of farmland is bid up, which raises the costs of all farmers in the market. Thus, an increase in demand for farm products cannot induce an increase in quantity supplied without also inducing a rise in farmers' costs, which in turn means a rise in price. The result is a long-run market supply curve that is upward sloping, even with free entry into farming.

A second reason for an upward-sloping supply curve is that firms may have different costs. For example, consider the market for painters. Anyone can enter the market for painting services, but not everyone has the same costs. Costs vary in part because some people work faster than others and in part because some people have better alternative uses of their time than others. For any given price, those with lower costs are more likely to enter than those with higher costs. To increase the quantity of painting services supplied, additional entrants must be encouraged to enter the market. Because these new entrants have higher costs,

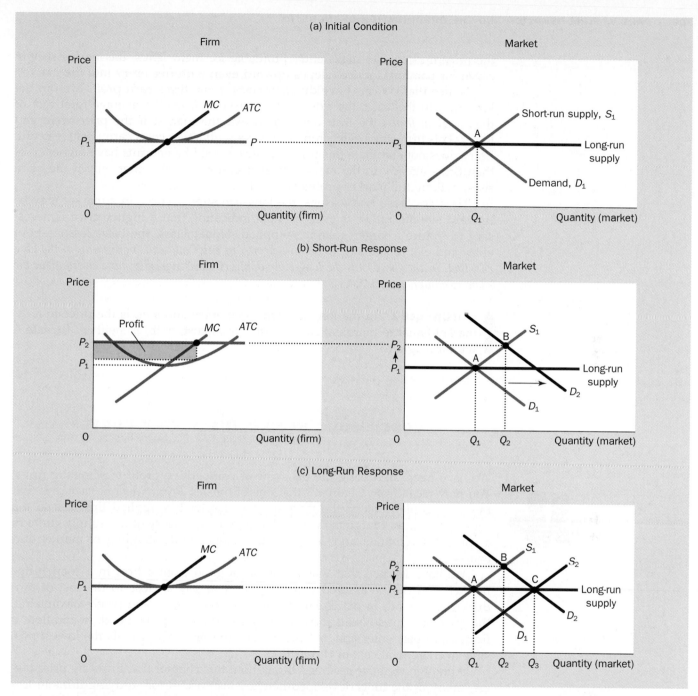

(a) Initial Condition

Firm

Market

(b) Short-Run Response

Firm

Market

(c) Long-Run Response

Firm

Market

AN INCREASE IN DEMAND IN THE SHORT RUN AND LONG RUN. The market starts in a long-run equilibrium, shown as point A in panel (a). In this equilibrium, each firm makes zero profit, and the price equals the minimum average total cost. Panel (b) shows what happens in the short run when demand rises from D_1 to D_2. The equilibrium goes from point A to point B, price rises from P_1 to P_2, and the quantity sold in the market rises from Q_1 to Q_2. Because price now exceeds average total cost, firms make profits, which over time encourage new firms to enter the market. This entry shifts the short-run supply curve to the right from S_1 to S_2, as shown in panel (c). In the new long-run equilibrium, point C, price has returned to P_1 but the quantity sold has increased to Q_3. Profits are again zero, price is back to the minimum of average total cost, but the market has more firms to satisfy the greater demand.

Figure 14-8

the price must rise to make entry profitable for them. Thus, the market supply curve for painting services slopes upward even with free entry into the market.

Notice that if firms have different costs, some firms earn profit even in the long run. In this case, the price in the market reflects the average total cost of the *marginal firm*—the firm that would exit the market if the price were any lower. This firm earns zero profit, but firms with lower costs earn positive profit. Entry does not eliminate this profit because would-be entrants have higher costs than firms already in the market. Higher-cost firms will enter only if the price rises, making the market profitable for them.

Thus, for these two reasons, the long-run supply curve in a market may be upward sloping rather than horizontal, indicating that a higher price is necessary to induce a larger quantity supplied. Nonetheless, the basic lesson about entry and exit remains true. *Because firms can enter and exit more easily in the long run than in the short run, the long-run supply curve is typically more elastic than the short-run supply curve.*

QUICK QUIZ In the long run with free entry and exit, is the price in a market equal to marginal cost, average total cost, both, or neither? Explain with a diagram.

CONCLUSION: BEHIND THE SUPPLY CURVE

We have been discussing the behavior of competitive profit-maximizing firms. You may recall from Chapter 1 that one of the *Ten Principles of Economics* is that rational people think at the margin. This chapter has applied this idea to the competitive firm. Marginal analysis has given us a theory of the supply curve in a competitive market and, as a result, a deeper understanding of market outcomes.

We have learned that when you buy a good from a firm in a competitive market, you can be assured that the price you pay is close to the cost of producing that good. In particular, if firms are competitive and profit-maximizing, the price of a good equals the marginal cost of making that good. In addition, if firms can freely enter and exit the market, the price also equals the lowest possible average total cost of production.

Although we have assumed throughout this chapter that firms are price takers, many of the tools developed here are also useful for studying firms in less competitive markets. In the next three chapters we will examine the behavior of firms with market power. Marginal analysis will again be useful in analyzing these firms, but it will have quite different implications.

Summary

◆ Because a competitive firm is a price taker, its revenue is proportional to the amount of output it produces. The price of the good equals both the firm's average revenue and its marginal revenue.

◆ To maximize profit, a firm chooses a quantity of output such that marginal revenue equals marginal cost. Because marginal revenue for a competitive firm equals the market price, the firm chooses quantity so that price equals marginal cost. Thus, the firm's marginal-cost curve is its supply curve.

◆ In the short run when a firm cannot recover its fixed costs, the firm will choose to shut down temporarily if the price of the good is less than average variable cost. In the long run when the firm can recover both fixed and variable costs, it will choose to exit if the price is less than average total cost.

◆ In a market with free entry and exit, profits are driven to zero in the long run. In this long-run equilibrium, all firms produce at the efficient scale, price equals the minimum of average total cost, and the number of firms adjusts to satisfy the quantity demanded at this price.

◆ Changes in demand have different effects over different time horizons. In the short run, an increase in demand raises prices and leads to profits, and a decrease in demand lowers prices and leads to losses. But if firms can freely enter and exit the market, then in the long run the number of firms adjusts to drive the market back to the zero-profit equilibrium.

Key Concepts

competitive market, p. 284   average revenue, p. 285   marginal revenue, p. 285

Questions for Review

1. What is meant by a competitive firm?

2. Draw the cost curves for a typical firm. For a given price, explain how the firm chooses the level of output that maximizes profit.

3. Under what conditions will a firm shut down temporarily? Explain.

4. Under what conditions will a firm exit a market? Explain.

5. Does a firm's price equal marginal cost in the short run, in the long run, or both? Explain.

6. Does a firm's price equal the minimum of average total cost in the short run, in the long run, or both? Explain.

Problems and Applications

1. What are the characteristics of a competitive market? Which of the following drinks do you think is best described by these characteristics? Why aren't the others?
   a. tap water
   b. bottled water
   c. cola
   d. beer

2. Your roommate's long hours in Chem lab finally paid off—she discovered a secret formula that lets people do an hour's worth of studying in 5 minutes. So far, she's sold 200 doses, and faces the following average-total-cost schedule:

Q	Average Total Cost
199	$199
200	200
201	201

If a new customer offers to pay her $300 for one dose, should she make one more? Explain.

3. The licorice industry is competitive. Each firm produces 2 million strings of licorice per year. The strings have an average total cost of $0.20 each, and they sell for $0.30.
   a. What is the marginal cost of a string?
   b. Is this industry in long-run equilibrium? Why or why not?

4. You go out to the best restaurant in town and order a lobster dinner for $40. After eating half of the lobster, you realize that you are quite full. Your date wants you to finish your dinner, because you can't take it home and because "you've already paid for it." What should you do? Relate your answer to the material in this chapter.

5. From *The Wall Street Journal* (July 23, 1991): "Since peaking in 1976, per capita beef consumption in the United

States has fallen by 28.6 percent . . . [and] the size of the U.S. cattle herd has shrunk to a 30-year low."

a. Using firm and industry diagrams, show the short-run effect of declining demand for beef. Label the diagram carefully and write out in words all of the changes you can identify.

b. On a new diagram, show the long-run effect of declining demand for beef. Explain in words.

6. "Strong prices traditionally cause expansion in an industry, eventually bringing an end to high prices and manufacturers' prosperity." Explain, using appropriate diagrams.

7. Many small boats are made of fiberglass, which is derived from petroleum. Suppose that the price of oil rises.

a. Using diagrams, show what happens to the cost curves of an individual boat-making firm and to the market supply curve.

b. What happens to the profits of boat makers in the short run? What happens to the number of boat makers in the long run?

8. Suppose that the U.S. textile industry is competitive, and there is no international trade in textiles. In long-run equilibrium, the price per unit of cloth is $30.

a. Describe the equilibrium using graphs for the entire market and for an individual producer.

Now suppose that textile producers in other countries are willing to sell large quantities of cloth in the United States for only $25 per unit.

b. Assuming that U.S. textile producers have large fixed costs, what is the short-run effect of these imports on the quantity produced by an individual producer? What is the short-run effect on profits? Illustrate your answer with a graph.

c. What is the long-run effect on the number of U.S. firms in the industry?

9. Suppose there are 1,000 hot pretzel stands operating in New York City. Each stand has the usual U-shaped average-total-cost curve. The market demand curve for pretzels slopes downward, and the market for pretzels is in long-run competitive equilibrium.

a. Draw the current equilibrium, using graphs for the entire market and for an individual pretzel stand.

b. Now the city decides to restrict the number of pretzel-stand licenses, reducing the number of stands to only 800. What effect will this action have on the market and on an individual stand that is still operating? Use graphs to illustrate your answer.

c. Suppose that the city decides to charge a license fee for the 800 licenses. How will this affect the number of pretzels sold by an individual stand, and the stand's profit? The city wants to raise as much revenue as possible and also wants to ensure that 800 pretzel stands remain in the city. By how much should the city increase the license fee? Show the answer on your graph.

10. Assume that the gold-mining industry is competitive.

a. Illustrate a long-run equilibrium using diagrams for the gold market and for a representative gold mine.

b. Suppose that an increase in jewelry demand induces a surge in the demand for gold. Using your diagrams, show what happens in the short run to the gold market and to each existing gold mine.

c. If the demand for gold remains high, what would happen to the price over time? Specifically, would the new long-run equilibrium price be above, below, or equal to the short-run equilibrium price in part (b)? Is it possible for the new long-run equilibrium price to be above the original long-run equilibrium price? Explain.

11. (This problem is challenging.) *The New York Times* (July 1, 1994) reported on a Clinton administration proposal to lift the ban on exporting oil from the North Slope of Alaska. According to the article, the administration said that "the chief effect of the ban has been to provide California refiners with crude oil cheaper than oil on the world market. . . . The ban created a subsidy for California refiners that had not been passed on to consumers." Let's use our analysis of firm behavior to analyze these claims.

a. Draw the cost curves for a California refiner and for a refiner in another part of the world. Assume that the California refiners have access to inexpensive Alaskan crude oil and that other refiners must buy more expensive crude oil from the Middle East.

b. All of the refiners produce gasoline for the world gasoline market, which has a single price. In the long-run equilibrium, will this price depend on the costs faced by California producers or the costs faced by other producers? Explain. (Hint: California cannot itself supply the entire world market.) Draw new graphs that illustrate the profits earned by a California refiner and another refiner.

c. In this model, is there a subsidy to California refiners? Is it passed on to consumers?

15

MONOPOLY

*Learn why some markets
have only one seller*

*Analyze how a monopoly
determines the quantity
to produce and the price
to charge*

*See how the monopoly's
decisions affect economic
well-being*

*Consider the various
public policies aimed at
solving the problem of
monopoly*

*See why monopolies try
to charge different prices
to different customers*

If you own a personal computer, it probably uses some version of Windows, the operating system sold by the Microsoft Corporation. When Microsoft first designed Windows many years ago, it applied for and received a copyright from the government. The copyright gives Microsoft the exclusive right to make and sell copies of the Windows operating system. So if a person wants to buy a copy of Windows, he or she has little choice but to give Microsoft the approximately $100 that the firm has decided to charge for its product. Microsoft is said to have a *monopoly* in the market for Windows.

Microsoft's business decisions are not well described by the model of firm behavior we developed in Chapter 14. In that chapter, we analyzed competitive markets, in which there are many firms offering essentially identical products, so each firm has little influence over the price it receives. By contrast, a monopoly such as Microsoft has no close competitors and, therefore, can influence the market price of its product. Whereas a competitive firm is a *price taker*, a monopoly firm is a *price maker*.

In this chapter we examine the implications of this market power. We will see that market power alters the relationship between a firm's price and its costs. A competitive firm takes the price of its output as given and then chooses the quantity supplied so that price equals marginal cost. By contrast, the price charged by a monopoly exceeds marginal cost. This result is clearly true in the case of Microsoft's Windows. The marginal cost of Windows—the extra cost that Microsoft would incur by printing one more copy of the program onto some floppy disks—is only a few dollars. The market price of Windows is many times marginal cost.

It is perhaps not surprising that monopolies charge high prices for their products. Customers of monopolies might seem to have little choice but to pay whatever the monopoly charges. But, if so, why does a copy of Windows not cost $1,000? Or $10,000? The reason, of course, is that if Microsoft set the price that high, fewer people would buy the product. People would buy fewer computers, switch to other operating systems, or make illegal copies. Monopolies cannot achieve any level of profit they want, because high prices reduce the amount that their customers buy. Although monopolies can control the prices of their goods, their profits are not unlimited.

As we examine the production and pricing decisions of monopolies, we also consider the implications of monopoly for society as a whole. Monopoly firms, like competitive firms, aim to maximize profit. But this goal has very different ramifications for competitive and monopoly firms. As we first saw in Chapter 7, self-interested buyers and sellers in competitive markets are unwittingly led by an invisible hand to promote general economic well-being. By contrast, because monopoly firms are unchecked by competition, the outcome in a market with a monopoly is often not in the best interest of society.

One of the *Ten Principles of Economics* in Chapter 1 is that governments can sometimes improve market outcomes. The analysis in this chapter will shed more light on this principle. As we examine the problems that monopolies raise for society, we will also discuss the various ways in which government policymakers might respond to these problems. The U.S. Department of Justice, for example, took notice when Microsoft announced in 1994 that it would buy Intuit, another software firm. Intuit held the copyright to Quicken, the leading program for personal finance. After months of investigation, the Justice Department decided that the combination of Microsoft and Intuit would lead to excessive market power concentrated in one firm. In a controversial move, it blocked the merger, and today Microsoft and Intuit remain separate companies.

WHY MONOPOLIES ARISE

monopoly
a firm that is the sole seller of a product without close substitutes

A firm is a **monopoly** if it is the sole seller of its product and if its product does not have close substitutes. The fundamental cause of monopoly is *barriers to entry*: A monopoly remains the only seller in its market because other firms cannot enter the market and compete with it. Barriers to entry, in turn, have three sources:

◆ A key resource is owned by a single firm.

◆ The government gives a single firm the exclusive right to produce some good.

◆ The costs of production make a single producer more efficient than a large number of producers.

Let's briefly discuss each of these.

MONOPOLY RESOURCES

The simplest way for a monopoly to arise is for a single firm to own a key resource. For example, consider the market for water in a small town in the Old West. If dozens of town residents have working wells, the competitive model discussed in Chapter 14 describes the behavior of sellers. As a result, the price of a gallon of water is driven to equal the marginal cost of pumping an extra gallon. But if there is only one well in town and it is impossible to get water from anywhere else, then the owner of the well has a monopoly on water. Not surprisingly, the monopolist has much greater market power than any single firm in a competitive market. In the case of a necessity like water, the monopolist could command quite a high price, even if the marginal cost is low.

Although exclusive ownership of a key resource is a potential cause of monopoly, in practice monopolies rarely arise for this reason. Actual economies are large, and resources are owned by many people. Indeed, because many goods are traded internationally, the natural scope of their markets is often worldwide. There are, therefore, few examples of firms that own a resource for which there are no close substitutes.

CASE STUDY   THE DEBEERS DIAMOND MONOPOLY

A classic example of a monopoly that arises from the ownership of a key resource is DeBeers, the South African diamond company. DeBeers controls about 80 percent of the world's production of diamonds. Although the firm's share of the market is not 100 percent, it is large enough to exert substantial influence over the market price of diamonds.

How much market power does DeBeers have? The answer depends in part on whether there are close substitutes for its product. If people view emeralds, rubies, and sapphires as good substitutes for diamonds, then DeBeers has relatively little market power. In this case, any attempt by DeBeers to raise the price of diamonds would cause people to switch to other gemstones. But if people view these other stones as very different from diamonds, then DeBeers can exert substantial influence over the price of its product.

DeBeers pays for large amounts of advertising. At first, this decision might seem surprising. If a monopoly is the sole seller of its product, why does it need to advertise? One goal of the DeBeers ads is to differentiate diamonds from other gems in the minds of consumers. When their slogan tells you that "a diamond is forever," you are meant to think that the same is not true of emeralds, rubies, and sapphires. If the ads are successful, consumers will view diamonds as unique, rather than as one among many gemstones, and this perception will give DeBeers greater market power.

GOVERNMENT-CREATED MONOPOLIES

In many cases, monopolies arise because the government has given one person or firm the exclusive right to sell some good or service. Sometimes the monopoly arises from the sheer political clout of the would-be monopolist. Kings, for example, once granted exclusive business licenses to their friends and allies. At other times, the government grants a monopoly because doing so is in the public interest.

Patent and copyright laws are one example of how the government creates a monopoly to serve the public interest. When a pharmaceutical company discovers a new drug, it can apply to the government for a patent. If the government deems the drug to be truly original, it approves the patent, which gives the company the exclusive right to manufacture and sell the drug for 17 years. Similarly, when a novelist finishes a book, she can copyright it. The copyright is a government guarantee that no one can print and sell the work without the author's permission. The copyright makes the novelist a monopolist in the sale of her novel.

The effects of patent and copyright laws are easy to see. Because these laws give one producer a monopoly, they lead to higher prices than would occur under competition. But by allowing these monopoly producers to charge higher prices and earn higher profits, the laws also encourage some desirable behavior. Drug companies are allowed to be monopolists in the drugs they discover in order to encourage research by these companies. Authors are allowed to be monopolists in the sale of their books in order to encourage them to write more and better books.

Thus, the laws governing patents and copyrights have both benefits and costs. The benefits of the patent and copyright laws are the increased incentive for creative activity. These benefits are offset, to some extent, by the costs of monopoly pricing, which we examine fully later in this chapter.

NATURAL MONOPOLIES

natural monopoly
a monopoly that arises because a single firm can supply a good or service to an entire market at a smaller cost than could two or more firms

An industry is a **natural monopoly** when a single firm can supply a good or service to an entire market at a smaller cost than could two or more firms. A natural monopoly arises when there are economies of scale over the relevant range of output. Figure 15-1 shows the average total costs of a firm with economies of scale. In this case, a single firm can produce any amount of output at least cost. That is, for any given amount of output, a larger number of firms leads to less output per firm and higher average total cost.

An example of a natural monopoly is the distribution of water. To provide water to residents of a town, a firm must build a network of pipes throughout the town. If two or more firms were to compete in the provision of this service, each firm would have to pay the fixed cost of building a network. Thus, the average total cost of water is lowest if a single firm serves the entire market.

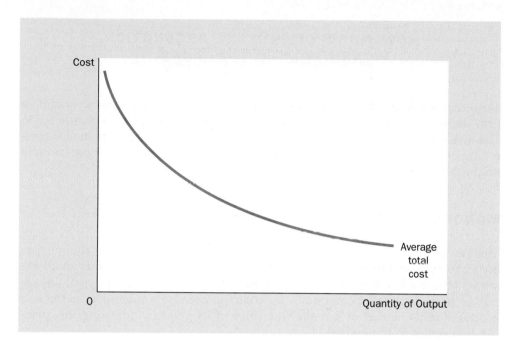

Figure 15-1

ECONOMIES OF SCALE AS A CAUSE OF MONOPOLY. When a firm's average-total-cost curve continually declines, the firm has what is called a natural monopoly. In this case, when production is divided among more firms, each firm produces less, and average total cost rises. As a result, a single firm can produce any given amount at the smallest cost.

We saw other examples of natural monopolies when we discussed public goods and common resources in Chapter 11. We noted in passing that some goods in the economy are excludable but not rival. An example is a bridge used so infrequently that it is never congested. The bridge is excludable because a toll collector can prevent someone from using it. The bridge is not rival because use of the bridge by one person does not diminish the ability of others to use it. Because there is a fixed cost of building the bridge and a negligible marginal cost of additional users, the average total cost of a trip across the bridge (the total cost divided by the number of trips) falls as the number of trips rises. Hence, the bridge is a natural monopoly.

When a firm is a natural monopoly, it is less concerned about new entrants eroding its monopoly power. Normally, a firm has trouble maintaining a monopoly position without ownership of a key resource or protection from the government. The monopolist's profit attracts entrants into the market, and these entrants make the market more competitive. By contrast, entering a market in which another firm has a natural monopoly is unattractive. Would-be entrants know that they cannot achieve the same low costs that the monopolist enjoys because, after entry, each firm would have a smaller piece of the market.

In some cases, the size of the market is one determinant of whether an industry is a natural monopoly. Consider a bridge across a river. When the population is small, the bridge may be a natural monopoly. A single bridge can satisfy the entire demand for trips across the river at lowest cost. Yet as the population grows and the bridge becomes congested, satisfying the entire demand may require two or more bridges across the same river. Thus, as a market expands, a natural monopoly can evolve into a competitive market.

QUICK QUIZ What are the three reasons that a market might have a monopoly? ◆ Give two examples of monopolies, and explain the reason for each.

HOW MONOPOLIES MAKE PRODUCTION AND PRICING DECISIONS

Now that we know how monopolies arise, we can consider how a monopoly firm decides how much of its product to make and what price to charge for it. The analysis of monopoly behavior in this section is the starting point for evaluating whether monopolies are desirable and what policies the government might pursue in monopoly markets.

MONOPOLY VERSUS COMPETITION

The key difference between a competitive firm and a monopoly is the monopoly's ability to influence the price of its output. A competitive firm is small relative to the market in which it operates and, therefore, takes the price of its output as given by market conditions. By contrast, because a monopoly is the sole producer in its market, it can alter the price of its good by adjusting the quantity it supplies to the market.

One way to view this difference between a competitive firm and a monopoly is to consider the demand curve that each firm faces. When we analyzed profit maximization by competitive firms in Chapter 14, we drew the market price as a horizontal line. Because a competitive firm can sell as much or as little as it wants at this price, the competitive firm faces a horizontal demand curve, as in panel (a) of Figure 15-2. In effect, because the competitive firm sells a product with many perfect substitutes (the products of all the other firms in its market), the demand curve that any one firm faces is perfectly elastic.

By contrast, because a monopoly is the sole producer in its market, its demand curve is the market demand curve. Thus, the monopolist's demand curve slopes downward for all the usual reasons, as in panel (b) of Figure 15-2. If the monopolist raises the price of its good, consumers buy less of it. Looked at another way, if the monopolist reduces the quantity of output it sells, the price of its output increases.

The market demand curve provides a constraint on a monopoly's ability to profit from its market power. A monopolist would prefer, if it were possible, to charge a high price and sell a large quantity at that high price. The market demand curve makes that outcome impossible. In particular, the market demand curve describes the combinations of price and quantity that are available to a monopoly firm. By adjusting the quantity produced (or, equivalently, the price charged), the monopolist can choose any point on the demand curve, but it cannot choose a point off the demand curve.

What point on the demand curve will the monopolist choose? As with competitive firms, we assume that the monopolist's goal is to maximize profit. Because the firm's profit is total revenue minus total costs, our next task in explaining monopoly behavior is to examine a monopolist's revenue.

A MONOPOLY'S REVENUE

Consider a town with a single producer of water. Table 15-1 shows how the monopoly's revenue might depend on the amount of water produced.

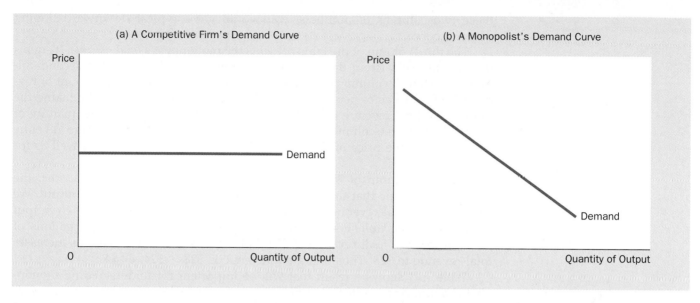

DEMAND CURVES FOR COMPETITIVE AND MONOPOLY FIRMS. Because competitive firms are price takers, they in effect face horizontal demand curves, as in panel (a). Because a monopoly firm is the sole producer in its market, it faces the downward-sloping market demand curve, as in panel (b). As a result, the monopoly has to accept a lower price if it wants to sell more output.

Figure 15-2

QUANTITY OF WATER	PRICE	TOTAL REVENUE	AVERAGE REVENUE	MARGINAL REVENUE
(Q)	(P)	(TR = P × Q)	(AR = TR/Q)	(MR = ΔTR/ΔQ)
0 gallons	$11	$ 0	—	
1	10	10	$10	$10
2	9	18	9	8
3	8	24	8	6
4	7	28	7	4
5	6	30	6	2
6	5	30	5	0
7	4	28	4	−2
8	3	24	3	−4

A MONOPOLY'S TOTAL, AVERAGE, AND MARGINAL REVENUE

Table 15-1

The first two columns show the monopolist's demand schedule. If the monopolist produces 1 gallon of water, it can sell that gallon for $10. If it produces 2 gallons, it must lower the price to $9 in order to sell both gallons. And if it produces 3 gallons, it must lower the price to $8. And so on. If you graphed these two columns of numbers, you would get a typical downward-sloping demand curve.

The third column of the table presents the monopolist's *total revenue*. It equals the quantity sold (from the first column) times the price (from the second column). The fourth column computes the firm's *average revenue*, the amount of revenue the firm receives per unit sold. We compute average revenue by taking the number for total revenue in the third column and dividing it by the quantity of output in the first column. As we discussed in Chapter 14, average revenue always equals the price of the good. This is true for monopolists as well as for competitive firms.

The last column of Table 15-1 computes the firm's *marginal revenue*, the amount of revenue that the firm receives for each additional unit of output. We compute marginal revenue by taking the change in total revenue when output increases by one unit. For example, when the firm is producing 3 gallons of water, it receives total revenue of $24. Raising production to 4 gallons increases total revenue to $28. Thus, marginal revenue is $28 − $24, or $4.

Table 15-1 shows a result that will be important for understanding monopoly behavior: *A monopolist's marginal revenue is always less than the price of its good.* For example, if the firm raises production of water from 3 to 4 gallons, it will increase total revenue by only $4, even though it will be able to sell each gallon for $7. For a monopoly, marginal revenue is lower than price because a monopoly faces a downward-sloping demand curve. To increase the amount sold, a monopoly firm must lower the price of its good. Hence, to sell the fourth gallon of water, the monopolist must get less revenue for each of the first three gallons.

Marginal revenue is very different for monopolies than it is for competitive firms. When a monopoly increases the amount it sells, it has two effects on total revenue ($P \times Q$):

◆ *The output effect:* More output is sold, so Q is higher.
◆ *The price effect:* The price falls, so P is lower.

Because a competitive firm can sell all it wants at the market price, there is no price effect. When it increases production by one unit, it receives the market price for that unit, and it does not receive any less for the amount it was already selling. That is, because the competitive firm is a price taker, its marginal revenue equals the price of its good. By contrast, when a monopoly increases production by one unit, it must reduce the price it charges for every unit it sells, and this cut in price reduces revenue on the units it was already selling. As a result, a monopoly's marginal revenue is less than its price.

Figure 15-3 graphs the demand curve and the marginal-revenue curve for a monopoly firm. (Since the firm's price equals its average revenue, the demand curve is also the average-revenue curve.) These two curves always start at the same point on the vertical axis because the marginal revenue of the first unit sold equals the price of the good. But, for the reason we just discussed, the monopolist's marginal revenue is less than the price of the good. Thus, a monopoly's marginal-revenue curve lies below its demand curve.

You can see in the figure (as well as in Table 15-1) that marginal revenue can even become negative. Marginal revenue is negative when the price effect on revenue is greater than the output effect. In this case, when the firm produces an extra unit of output, the price falls by enough to cause the firm's total revenue to decline, even though the firm is selling more units.

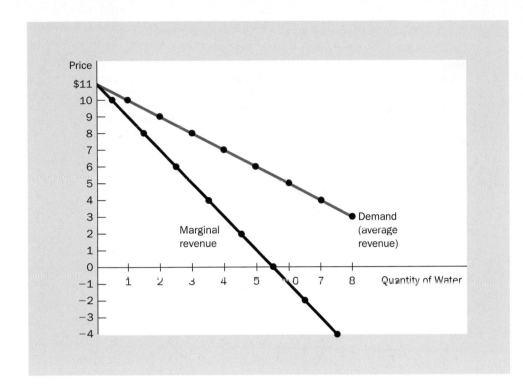

Figure 15-3

DEMAND AND MARGINAL-REVENUE CURVES FOR A MONOPOLY. The demand curve shows how the quantity affects the price of the good. The marginal-revenue curve shows how the firm's revenue changes when the quantity increases by one unit. Because the price on *all* units sold must fall if the monopoly increases production, marginal revenue is always less than the price.

PROFIT MAXIMIZATION

Now that we have considered the revenue of a monopoly firm, we are ready to examine how such a firm maximizes profit. Recall from Chapter 1 that one of the *Ten Principles of Economics* is that rational people think at the margin. This lesson is as true for monopolists as it is for competitive firms. Here we apply the logic of marginal analysis to the monopolist's problem of deciding how much to produce.

Figure 15-4 graphs the demand curve, the marginal-revenue curve, and the cost curves for a monopoly firm. All these curves should seem familiar: The demand and marginal-revenue curves are like those in Figure 15-3, and the cost curves are like those we introduced in Chapter 13 and used to analyze competitive firms in Chapter 14. These curves contain all the information we need to determine the level of output that a profit-maximizing monopolist will choose.

Suppose, first, that the firm is producing at a low level of output, such as Q_1. In this case, marginal cost is less than marginal revenue. If the firm increased production by one unit, the additional revenue would exceed the additional costs, and profit would rise. Thus, when marginal cost is less than marginal revenue, the firm can increase profit by producing more units.

A similar argument applies at high levels of output, such as Q_2. In this case, marginal cost is greater than marginal revenue. If the firm reduced production by one unit, the costs saved would exceed the revenue lost. Thus, if marginal cost is greater than marginal revenue, the firm can raise profit by reducing production.

In the end, the firm adjusts its level of production until the quantity reaches Q_{MAX}, at which marginal revenue equals marginal cost. Thus, *the monopolist's*

Figure 15-4

PROFIT-MAXIMIZATION FOR A
MONOPOLY. A monopoly
maximizes profit by choosing the
quantity at which marginal
revenue equals marginal cost
(point A). It then uses the
demand curve to find the price
that will induce consumers to
buy that quantity (point B).

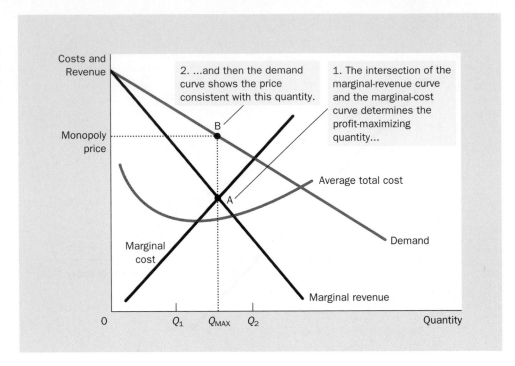

2. ...and then the demand
curve shows the price
consistent with this quantity.

1. The intersection of the
marginal-revenue curve
and the marginal-cost
curve determines the
profit-maximizing
quantity...

profit-maximizing quantity of output is determined by the intersection of the marginal-revenue curve and the marginal-cost curve. In Figure 15-4, this intersection occurs at point A.

You might recall from Chapter 14 that competitive firms also choose the quantity of output at which marginal revenue equals marginal cost. In following this rule for profit maximization, competitive firms and monopolies are alike. But there is also an important difference between these types of firm: The marginal revenue of a competitive firm equals its price, whereas the marginal revenue of a monopoly is less than its price. That is,

$$\text{For a competitive firm:} \quad P = MR = MC.$$
$$\text{For a monopoly firm:} \quad P > MR = MC.$$

The equality of marginal revenue and marginal cost at the profit-maximizing quantity is the same for both types of firm. What differs is the relationship of the price to marginal revenue and marginal cost.

How does the monopoly find the profit-maximizing price for its product? The demand curve answers this question, for the demand curve relates the amount that customers are willing to pay to the quantity sold. Thus, after the monopoly firm chooses the quantity of output that equates marginal revenue and marginal cost, it uses the demand curve to find the price consistent with that quantity. In Figure 15-4, the profit-maximizing price is found at point B.

We can now see a key difference between markets with competitive firms and markets with a monopoly firm: *In competitive markets, price equals marginal*

FYI

Why a Monopoly
Does Not Have a
Supply Curve

YOU MAY HAVE NOTICED THAT we have analyzed the price in a monopoly market using the market demand curve and the firm's cost curves. We have not made any mention of the market supply curve. By contrast, when we analyzed prices in competitive markets beginning in Chapter 4, the two most important words were always *supply* and *demand*.

What happened to the supply curve? Although monopoly firms make decisions about what quantity to supply (in the way we have just seen), a monopoly does not have a sup-

ply curve. A supply curve tells us the quantity that firms choose to supply at any given price. This concept makes sense when we are analyzing competitive firms, which are price takers. But a monopoly firm is a price maker, not a price taker. It is not meaningful to ask what such a firm would produce at any price because the firm sets the price at the same time it chooses the quantity to supply.

Indeed, the monopolist's decision about how much to supply is impossible to separate from the demand curve it faces. The shape of the demand curve determines the shape of the marginal-revenue curve, which in turn determines the monopolist's profit-maximizing quantity. In a competitive market, supply decisions can be analyzed without knowing the demand curve, but that is not true in a monopoly market. Therefore, we never talk about a monopoly's supply curve.

cost. In monopolized markets, price exceeds marginal cost. As we will see in a moment, this finding is crucial to understanding the social cost of monopoly.

A MONOPOLY'S PROFIT

How much profit does the monopoly make? To see the monopoly's profit, recall that profit equals total revenue (*TR*) minus total costs (*TC*):

$$\text{Profit} = TR - TC.$$

We can rewrite this as

$$\text{Profit} = (TR/Q - TC/Q) \times Q.$$

TR/Q is average revenue, which equals the price *P*, and *TC/Q* is average total cost *ATC*. Therefore,

$$\text{Profit} = (P - ATC) \times Q.$$

This equation for profit (which is the same as the profit equation for competitive firms) allows us to measure the monopolist's profit in our graph.

Consider the shaded box in Figure 15-5. The height of the box (the segment BC) is price minus average total cost, $P - ATC$, which is the profit on the typical unit sold. The width of the box (the segment DC) is the quantity sold Q_{MAX}. Therefore, the area of this box is the monopoly firm's total profit.

Figure 15-5

THE MONOPOLIST'S PROFIT.
The area of the box BCDE equals
the profit of the monopoly firm.
The height of the box (BC) is
price minus average total cost,
which equals profit per unit sold.
The width of the box (DC) is the
number of units sold.

Brand-name drugs compete with
generic products at Vons
supermarket.

CASE STUDY MONOPOLY DRUGS VERSUS GENERIC DRUGS

According to our analysis, prices are determined quite differently in monopolized markets from the way they are in competitive markets. A natural place
to test this theory is the market for pharmaceutical drugs because this market
takes on both market structures. When a firm discovers a new drug, patent
laws give the firm a monopoly on the sale of that drug. But eventually the
firm's patent runs out, and any company can make and sell the drug. At that
time, the market switches from being monopolistic to being competitive.

What should happen to the price of a drug when the patent runs out? Figure 15-6 shows the market for a typical drug. In this figure, the marginal cost
of producing the drug is constant. (This is approximately true for many
drugs.) During the life of the patent, the monopoly firm maximizes profit by
producing the quantity at which marginal revenue equals marginal cost and
charging a price well above marginal cost. But when the patent runs out, the
profit from making the drug should encourage new firms to enter the market. As the market becomes more competitive, the price should fall to equal
marginal cost.

Experience is, in fact, consistent with our theory. When the patent on a
drug expires, other companies quickly enter and begin selling so-called
generic products that are chemically identical to the former monopolist's
brand-name product. And just as our analysis predicts, the price of the competitively produced generic drug is well below the price that the monopolist
was charging.

The expiration of a patent, however, does not cause the monopolist to lose
all its market power. Some consumers remain loyal to the brand-name drug,
perhaps out of fear that the new generic drugs are not actually the same

Figure 15-6

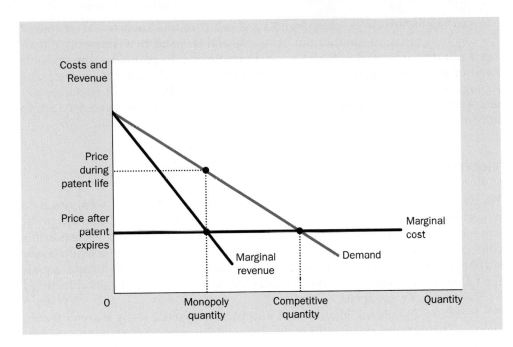

THE MARKET FOR DRUGS. When a patent gives a firm a monopoly over the sale of a drug, the firm charges the monopoly price, which is well above the marginal cost of making the drug. When the patent on a drug runs out, new firms enter the market, making it more competitive. As a result, the price falls from the monopoly price to marginal cost.

as the drug they have been using for years. As a result, the former monopolist can continue to charge a price at least somewhat above the price charged by its new competitors.

QUICK QUIZ Explain how a monopolist chooses the quantity of output to produce and the price to charge.

THE WELFARE COST OF MONOPOLY

Is monopoly a good way to organize a market? We have seen that a monopoly, in contrast to a competitive firm, charges a price above marginal cost. From the standpoint of consumers, this high price makes monopoly undesirable. At the same time, however, the monopoly is earning profit from charging this high price. From the standpoint of the owners of the firm, the high price makes monopoly very desirable. Is it possible that the benefits to the firm's owners exceed the costs imposed on consumers, making monopoly desirable from the standpoint of society as a whole?

We can answer this question using the type of analysis we first saw in Chapter 7. As in that chapter, we use total surplus as our measure of economic well-being. Recall that total surplus is the sum of consumer surplus and producer surplus. Consumer surplus is consumers' willingness to pay for a good minus the amount they actually pay for it. Producer surplus is the amount producers receive for a good minus their costs of producing it. In this case, there is a single producer—the monopolist.

You might already be able to guess the result of this analysis. In Chapter 7 we concluded that the equilibrium of supply and demand in a competitive market is not only a natural outcome but a desirable one. In particular, the invisible hand of the market leads to an allocation of resources that makes total surplus as large as it can be. Because a monopoly leads to an allocation of resources different from that in a competitive market, the outcome must, in some way, fail to maximize total economic well-being.

THE DEADWEIGHT LOSS

We begin by considering what the monopoly firm would do if it were run by a benevolent social planner. The social planner cares not only about the profit earned by the firm's owners but also about the benefits received by the firm's consumers. The planner tries to maximize total surplus, which equals producer surplus (profit) plus consumer surplus. Keep in mind that total surplus equals the value of the good to consumers minus the costs of making the good incurred by the monopoly producer.

Figure 15-7 analyzes what level of output a benevolent social planner would choose. The demand curve reflects the value of the good to consumers, as measured by their willingness to pay for it. The marginal-cost curve reflects the costs of the monopolist. Thus, *the socially efficient quantity is found where the demand curve and the marginal-cost curve intersect.* Below this quantity, the value to consumers exceeds the marginal cost of providing the good, so increasing output

Figure 15-7

THE EFFICIENT LEVEL OF OUTPUT. A benevolent social planner who wanted to maximize total surplus in the market would choose the level of output where the demand curve and marginal-cost curve intersect. Below this level, the value of the good to the marginal buyer (as reflected in the demand curve) exceeds the marginal cost of making the good. Above this level, the value to the marginal buyer is less than marginal cost.

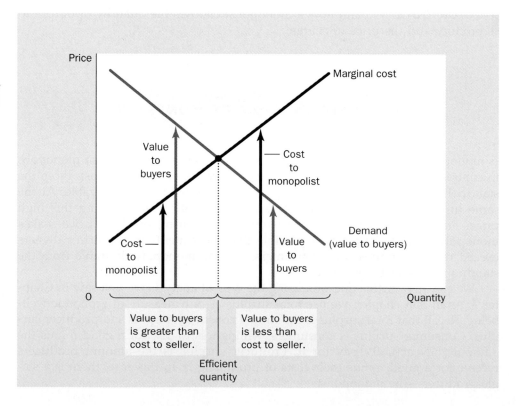

would raise total surplus. Above this quantity, the marginal cost exceeds the value to consumers, so decreasing output would raise total surplus.

If the social planner were running the monopoly, the firm could achieve this efficient outcome by charging the price found at the intersection of the demand and marginal-cost curves. Thus, like a competitive firm and unlike a profit-maximizing monopoly, a social planner would charge a price equal to marginal cost. Because this price would give consumers an accurate signal about the cost of producing the good, consumers would buy the efficient quantity.

We can evaluate the welfare effects of monopoly by comparing the level of output that the monopolist chooses to the level of output that a social planner would choose. As we have seen, the monopolist chooses to produce and sell the quantity of output at which the marginal-revenue and marginal-cost curves intersect; the social planner would choose the quantity at which the demand and marginal-cost curves intersect. Figure 15-8 shows the comparison. *The monopolist produces less than the socially efficient quantity of output.*

We can also view the inefficiency of monopoly in terms of the monopolist's price. Because the market demand curve describes a negative relationship between the price and quantity of the good, a quantity that is inefficiently low is equivalent to a price that is inefficiently high. When a monopolist charges a price above marginal cost, some potential consumers value the good at more than its marginal cost but less than the monopolist's price. These consumers do not end up buying the good. Because the value these consumers place on the good is greater than the cost of providing it to them, this result is inefficient. Thus, monopoly pricing prevents some mutually beneficial trades from taking place.

Just as we measured the inefficiency of taxes with the deadweight-loss triangle in Chapter 8, we can similarly measure the inefficiency of monopoly. Figure 15-8 shows the deadweight loss. Recall that the demand curve reflects the

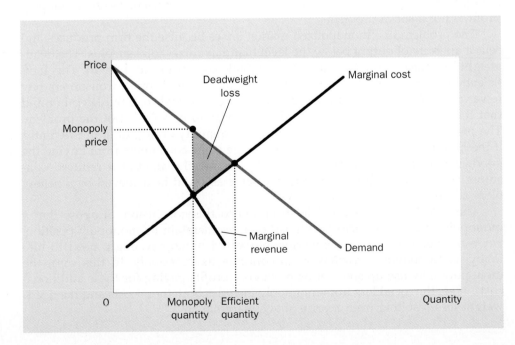

Figure 15-8

THE INEFFICIENCY OF MONOPOLY. Because a monopoly charges a price above marginal cost, not all consumers who value the good at more than its cost buy it. Thus, the quantity produced and sold by a monopoly is below the socially efficient level. The deadweight loss is represented by the area of the triangle between the demand curve (which reflects the value of the good to consumers) and the marginal-cost curve (which reflects the costs of the monopoly producer).

value to consumers and the marginal-cost curve reflects the costs to the monopoly producer. Thus, the area of the deadweight-loss triangle between the demand curve and the marginal-cost curve equals the total surplus lost because of monopoly pricing.

The deadweight loss caused by monopoly is similar to the deadweight loss caused by a tax. Indeed, a monopolist is like a private tax collector. As we saw in Chapter 8, a tax on a good places a wedge between consumers' willingness to pay (as reflected in the demand curve) and producers' costs (as reflected in the supply curve). Because a monopoly exerts its market power by charging a price above marginal cost, it places a similar wedge. In both cases, the wedge causes the quantity sold to fall short of the social optimum. The difference between the two cases is that the government gets the revenue from a tax, whereas a private firm gets the monopoly profit.

THE MONOPOLY'S PROFIT: A SOCIAL COST?

It is tempting to decry monopolies for "profiteering" at the expense of the public. And, indeed, a monopoly firm does earn a higher profit by virtue of its market power. According to the economic analysis of monopoly, however, the firm's profit is not in itself necessarily a problem for society.

Welfare in a monopolized market, like all markets, includes the welfare of both consumers and producers. Whenever a consumer pays an extra dollar to a producer because of a monopoly price, the consumer is worse off by a dollar, and the producer is better off by the same amount. This transfer from the consumers of the good to the owners of the monopoly does not affect the market's total surplus—the sum of consumer and producer surplus. In other words, the monopoly profit itself does not represent a shrinkage in the size of the economic pie; it merely represents a bigger slice for producers and a smaller slice for consumers. Unless consumers are for some reason more deserving than producers— a judgment that goes beyond the realm of economic efficiency—the monopoly profit is not a social problem.

The problem in a monopolized market arises because the firm produces and sells a quantity of output below the level that maximizes total surplus. The deadweight loss measures how much the economic pie shrinks as a result. This inefficiency is inextricably connected to the monopoly's high price: Consumers buy fewer units when the firm raises its price above marginal cost. But keep in mind that the profit earned on the units that continue to be sold is not the problem. The problem stems from the inefficiently low quantity of output. Put differently, if the high monopoly price did not discourage some consumers from buying the good, it would raise producer surplus by exactly the amount it reduced consumer surplus, leaving total surplus the same as could be achieved by a benevolent social planner.

There is, however, a possible exception to this conclusion. Suppose that a monopoly firm has to incur additional costs to maintain its monopoly position. For example, a firm with a government-created monopoly might need to hire lobbyists to convince lawmakers to continue its monopoly. In this case, the monopoly may use up some of its monopoly profits paying for these additional costs. If so, the social loss from monopoly includes both these costs and the deadweight loss resulting from a price above marginal cost.

QUICK QUIZ How does a monopolist's quantity of output compare to the quantity of output that maximizes total surplus?

PUBLIC POLICY TOWARD MONOPOLIES

We have seen that monopolies, in contrast to competitive markets, fail to allocate resources efficiently. Monopolies produce less than the socially desirable quantity of output and, as a result, charge prices above marginal cost. Policymakers in the government can respond to the problem of monopoly in one of four ways:

◆ By trying to make monopolized industries more competitive
◆ By regulating the behavior of the monopolies
◆ By turning some private monopolies into public enterprises
◆ By doing nothing at all.

INCREASING COMPETITION WITH ANTITRUST LAWS

If General Motors and Ford Motor Company wanted to merge, the deal would be closely examined by the federal government before it went into effect. The lawyers and economists in the Department of Justice might well decide that a merger between these two large car companies would make the U.S. car market substantially less competitive and, as a result, would reduce the economic well-being of the country as a whole. If so, the Justice Department would challenge the merger in court, and if the judge agreed, the two companies would not be allowed to merge. It is precisely this kind of challenge that prevented software giant Microsoft from buying Intuit in 1994.

The government derives this power over private industry from the antitrust laws, a collection of statutes aimed at curbing monopoly power. The first and most important of these laws was the Sherman Antitrust Act, which Congress passed in 1890 to reduce the market power of the large and powerful "trusts" that were viewed as dominating the economy at the time. The Clayton Act, passed in 1914, strengthened the government's powers and authorized private lawsuits. As the U.S. Supreme Court once put it, the antitrust laws are "a comprehensive charter of economic liberty aimed at preserving free and unfettered competition as the rule of trade."

The antitrust laws give the government various ways to promote competition. They allow the government to prevent mergers, such as our hypothetical merger between GM and Ford. They also allow the government to break up companies. For example, in 1984 the government split up the large telecommunications company, AT&T, into eight smaller companies. Finally, the antitrust laws prevent companies from coordinating their activities in ways that make markets less competitive; we will discuss some of these uses of the antitrust laws in Chapter 16.

"BUT IF WE DO MERGE WITH AMALGAMATED, WE'LL HAVE ENOUGH RESOURCES TO FIGHT THE ANTI-TRUST VIOLATION CAUSED BY THE MERGER."

Antitrust laws have costs as well as benefits. Sometimes companies merge not to reduce competition but to lower costs through more efficient joint production. These benefits from mergers are sometimes called *synergies*. For example, many U.S. banks have merged in recent years and, by combining operations, have been able to reduce administrative staff. If antitrust laws are to raise social welfare, the government must be able to determine which mergers are desirable and which are not. That is, it must be able to measure and compare the social benefit from synergies to the social costs of reduced competition. Critics of the antitrust laws are skeptical that the government can perform the necessary cost–benefit analysis with sufficient accuracy.

REGULATION

Another way in which the government deals with the problem of monopoly is by regulating the behavior of monopolists. This solution is common in the case of natural monopolies, such as water and electric companies. These companies are not allowed to charge any price they want. Instead, government agencies regulate their prices.

What price should the government set for a natural monopoly? This question is not as easy as it might at first appear. One might conclude that the price should equal the monopolist's marginal cost. If price equals marginal cost, customers will buy the quantity of the monopolist's output that maximizes total surplus, and the allocation of resources will be efficient.

IN THE NEWS

Boeing's Market Power

IN 1996 BOEING, THE WORLD'S LARGEST maker of commercial aircraft, proposed a merger with McDonnell Douglas, the second largest aircraft maker in the United States and the third largest in the world. Would this merger give Boeing too much market power, or would competition from Airbus, the European aircraft maker, be sufficient to keep Boeing's prices close to the costs of production? Before approving the merger, U.S. regulators had to ask themselves exactly this question. As the following article discusses, the buyers of aircraft—the airlines—did not oppose the merger, and this fact offers a clue about the answer.

Many Airlines Not Worried by Boeing-McDonnell Deal

BY ADAM BRYANT

Even though the proposed merger of the Boeing Company and the McDonnell Douglas Corporation would shrink the number of commercial jet aircraft makers to two from three, several airline executives said yesterday that they did not oppose the deal.

Their opinions matter because they are likely to be consulted by federal agencies scrutinizing the deal for potentially anticompetitive effects.

Robert L. Crandall, the chairman of American Airlines, which is one of the largest users of McDonnell Douglas aircraft, said yesterday that the marketplace lesson of the proposed merger was that the capital demands of the aircraft-building business were so great that there was no room for more than two big manufacturers, Boeing and Airbus Industries, the European consortium.

The merger, he added, would largely guarantee that American, a unit of the AMR Corporation, will have a steady supply of parts for its McDonnell Douglas planes, much better than McDonnell Douglas failing on its own.

"What's occurred is about as favorable a situation as you can have," he said. He added that he did not believe that prices of aircraft would, over the long term, rise as a result of the merger. "If you take the waste out of the system, and assume that the presence of two producers will continue to provide adequate price discipline, you may end up paying less," he said. . . .

"The No. 1 maker is Boeing and No. 2 is Airbus—that's where the main competitive arena is," Mark Abels, a spokesman for Trans World Airlines, said. "I wouldn't see this as a Coke and Pepsi merger."

SOURCE: *The New York Times*, December 19, 1996, p. D2.

There are, however, two practical problems with marginal-cost pricing as a regulatory system. The first is illustrated in Figure 15-9. Natural monopolies, by definition, have declining average total cost. As we discussed in Chapter 13, when average total cost is declining, marginal cost is less than average total cost. If regulators are to set price equal to marginal cost, that price will be less than the firm's average total cost, and the firm will lose money. Instead of charging such a low price, the monopoly firm would just exit the industry.

Regulators can respond to this problem in various ways, none of which is perfect. One way is to subsidize the monopolist. In essence, the government picks up the losses inherent in marginal-cost pricing. Yet to pay for the subsidy, the government needs to raise money through taxation, which involves its own deadweight losses. Alternatively, the regulators can allow the monopolist to charge a price higher than marginal cost. If the regulated price equals average total cost, the monopolist earns exactly zero profit. Yet average-cost pricing leads to deadweight losses, because the monopolist's price no longer reflects the marginal cost of producing the good. In essence, average-cost pricing is like a tax on the good the monopolist is selling.

Figure 15-9

MARGINAL-COST PRICING FOR
A NATURAL MONOPOLY.
Because a natural monopoly has
declining average total cost,
marginal cost is less than average
total cost. Therefore, if regulators
require a natural monopoly to
charge a price equal to marginal
cost, price will be below average
total cost, and the monopoly will
lose money.

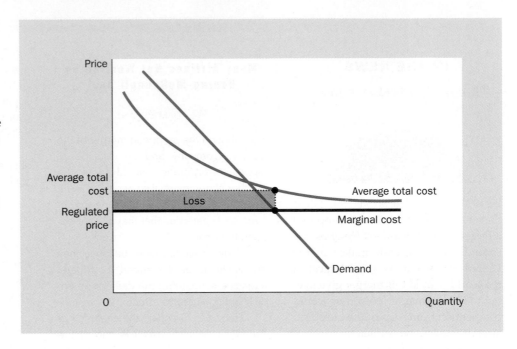

The second problem with marginal-cost pricing as a regulatory system (and
with average-cost pricing as well) is that it gives the monopolist no incentive to
reduce costs. Each firm in a competitive market tries to reduce its costs because
lower costs mean higher profits. But if a regulated monopolist knows that regulators will reduce prices whenever costs fall, the monopolist will not benefit
from lower costs. In practice, regulators deal with this problem by allowing
monopolists to keep some of the benefits from lower costs in the form of higher
profit, a practice that requires some departure from marginal-cost pricing.

PUBLIC OWNERSHIP

The third policy used by the government to deal with monopoly is public ownership. That is, rather than regulating a natural monopoly that is run by a private firm, the government can run the monopoly itself. This solution is common
in many European countries, where the government owns and operates utilities
such as the telephone, water, and electric companies. In the United States, the
government runs the Postal Service. The delivery of ordinary First Class mail is
often thought to be a natural monopoly.

Economists usually prefer private to public ownership of natural monopolies. The key issue is how the ownership of the firm affects the costs of production. Private owners have an incentive to minimize costs as long as they reap
part of the benefit in the form of higher profit. If the firm's managers are doing
a bad job of keeping costs down, the firm's owners will fire them. By contrast,
if the government bureaucrats who run a monopoly do a bad job, the losers are
the customers and taxpayers, whose only recourse is the political system. The
bureaucrats may become a special-interest group and attempt to block cost-
reducing reforms. Put simply, as a way of ensuring that firms are well run, the
voting booth is less reliable than the profit motive.

DOING NOTHING

Each of the foregoing policies aimed at reducing the problem of monopoly has drawbacks. As a result, some economists argue that it is often best for the government not to try to remedy the inefficiencies of monopoly pricing. Here is the assessment of economist George Stigler, who won the Nobel Prize for his work in industrial organization, writing in the *Fortune Encyclopedia of Economics*:

> A famous theorem in economics states that a competitive enterprise economy will produce the largest possible income from a given stock of resources. No real economy meets the exact conditions of the theorem, and all real economies will fall short of the ideal economy—a difference called "market failure." In my view, however, the degree of "market failure" for the American economy is much smaller than the "political failure" arising from the imperfections of economic policies found in real political systems.

As this quotation makes clear, determining the proper role of the government in the economy requires judgments about politics as well as economics.

QUICK QUIZ Describe the ways policymakers can respond to the inefficiencies caused by monopolies. List a potential problem with each of these policy responses.

PRICE DISCRIMINATION

So far we have been assuming that the monopoly firm charges the same price to all customers. Yet in many cases firms try to sell the same good to different customers for different prices. This practice is called **price discrimination.**

Before discussing the behavior of a price-discriminating monopolist, we should note that price discrimination is not possible when a good is sold in a competitive market. In a competitive market, there are many firms selling the same good at the market price. No firm is willing to charge a lower price to any customer because the firm can sell all it wants at the market price. And if any firm tried to charge a higher price to a customer, that customer would buy from another firm. For a firm to price discriminate, it must have some market power.

price discrimination
the business practice of selling the same good at different prices to different customers

A PARABLE ABOUT PRICING

To understand why a monopolist would want to price discriminate, let's consider a simple example. Imagine that you are the president of Readalot Publishing Company. Readalot's best-selling author has just written her latest novel. To keep things simple, let's imagine that you pay the author a flat $2 million for the exclusive rights to publish the book. Let's also assume that the cost of printing the book is zero. Readalot's profit, therefore, is the revenue it gets from selling the book minus the $2 million it has paid to the author. Given these assumptions, how would you, as Readalot's president, decide what price to charge for the book?

IN THE NEWS

*The Future
of Electricity*

FOR MANY YEARS THE COMPANIES THAT provide electricity in the United States have been regulated monopolies. The following article describes how that situation is changing.

The End of the Last Great Monopoly

BY JAMES DAO

Just as Americans were resigning themselves to the marketing schemes of the telephone companies, another industry is entering the competitive business of dinnertime phone pitches, discount rate packages, and rebate checks. Brace yourselves for the electric utilities.

From the days of Edison's first bulb, people have had virtually no choice as to who would supply their power. But at the urging of big customers, mainly manufacturers, many states have begun unfettering electric companies in the hopes that a hearty dose of competition will achieve what government regulators could not—namely, lower prices and improved service.

At least 41 states, including California, New York, and Texas, have adopted or are considering plans that would in most cases end utilities' monopolies, encouraging start-up companies and robust competition. Already, the federal government has ordered companies to open their wires to competing power suppliers so they can transmit low-cost electricity across state lines. . . .

What has prompted all this ferment in one of the last great American monopolies? The century-old industry has already been a natural for monopolization because only a few companies could raise the capital needed to build power plants and transmission lines. Over time,

larger companies gobbled up smaller ones, delivering what many economists thought were more efficient services.

But in recent years, lower fuel costs and new technologies have greatly reduced the cost of building and operating

Your first step in setting the price is to estimate what the demand for the book is likely to be. Readalot's marketing department tells you that the book will attract two types of readers. The book will appeal to the author's 100,000 die-hard fans. These fans will be willing to pay as much as $30 for the book. In addition, the book will appeal to about 400,000 less enthusiastic readers who will be willing to pay up to $5 for the book.

What price maximizes Readalot's profit? There are two natural prices to consider: $30 is the highest price Readalot can charge and still get the 100,000 die-hard fans, and $5 is the highest price it can charge and still get the entire market of 500,000 potential readers. It is a matter of simple arithmetic to solve Readalot's problem. At a price of $30, Readalot sells 100,000 copies, has revenue of $3 million, and makes profit of $1 million. At a price of $5, it sells 500,000 copies, has revenue of $2.5 million, and makes profit of $500,000. Thus, Readalot maximizes profit by charging $30 and forgoing the opportunity to sell to the 400,000 less enthusiastic readers.

power plants, enabling small start-up companies to produce power more cheaply than older utilities. And sophisticated buyers, aware of such developments, have begun demanding that they be allowed to purchase power from independent suppliers.

Though many power companies have resisted such demands, the high cost of power has become such a hot political issue in some regions—particularly the Northeast and California—that legislators and governors are rushing to deregulate the industry.

"Power will probably be cheaper," said Professor William W. Hogan at the Kennedy School of Government at Harvard. "But there will also be so much diversity in the way it is marketed that people will forget what it was like to have just one supplier."

As most regulators envision the new system, the existing network of high-voltage transmission lines would remain essentially unchanged, operated by state agencies or regulated companies. Those companies would be required to open their systems to competing suppliers, much the same way that local phone companies allow long-distance carriers to use their lines, for a price.

Where deregulation would refashion the industry would be at the two ends of the chain. Now, utilities control the flow of electrons from start to finish, building the generating plants, operating the transmission lines, and servicing the meters in every home. Under most states' plans, the process would be divided into three tiers involving three different sets of companies.

At one end would be the generating companies, which would compete to sell power on a spot market, much like a commodities exchange. At the other end, retail providers would buy power wholesale and market it to homeowners and businesses. In between would be the wire companies, which would charge wholesalers and retailers access fees to use their lines. Prices at the wholesale and retail levels would be set by market forces, not government regulators, except perhaps in areas that cannot attract competition. Free-market advocates say competition will force utilities to abandon or modernize inefficient power plants and cut prices for everyone. . . .

One thing seems certain: Deregulation is likely to unleash the feverish fight for customers that the telecommunications industry witnessed after the breakup of AT&T.

New Hampshire offers a glimpse of the future. There, two dozen companies are participating in a pilot program to sell power to a small number of businesses and homeowners.

So far, the results could only warm a capitalist's heart. Companies are bombarding potential buyers with advertisements, solicitation calls, and gifts. One offered $25 rebate checks to potential customers, only to see a competitor up the ante with a $50 offer. Suppliers have given out free showerheads, spruce trees, and almanacs—even to people who refused their business. Several companies are marketing environmentally "clean" power produced by hydroelectric plants. And one is planning to package electric service with credit card and long-distance telephone services.

SOURCE: *The New York Times*, August 4, 1996, Week in Review, p. 5.

Notice that Readalot's decision causes a deadweight loss. There are 400,000 readers willing to pay $5 for the book, and the marginal cost of providing it to them is zero. Thus, $2 million of total surplus is lost when Readalot charges the higher price. This deadweight loss is the usual inefficiency that arises whenever a monopolist charges a price above marginal cost.

Now suppose that Readalot's marketing department makes an important discovery: These two groups of readers are in separate markets. All the die-hard fans live in Australia, and all the other readers live in the United States. Moreover, it is difficult for readers in one country to buy books in the other. How does this discovery affect Readalot's marketing strategy?

In this case, the company can make even more profit. To the 100,000 Australian readers, it can charge $30 for the book. To the 400,000 American readers, it can charge $5 for the book. In this case, revenue is $3 million in Australia and $2 million in the United States, for a total of $5 million. Profit is then $3 million, which is substantially greater than the $1 million the company could earn charging the same $30 price to all customers. Not surprisingly, Readalot chooses to follow this strategy of price discrimination.

Although the story of Readalot Publishing is hypothetical, it describes accurately the business practice of many publishing companies. Textbooks, for example, are often sold at a lower price in Europe than in the United States. Even more important is the price differential between hardcover books and paperbacks. When a publisher has a new novel, it initially releases an expensive hardcover edition and later releases a cheaper paperback edition. The difference in price between these two editions far exceeds the difference in printing costs. The publisher's goal is just as in our example. By selling the hardcover to die-hard fans and the paperback to less enthusiastic readers, the publisher price discriminates and raises its profit.

THE MORAL OF THE STORY

Like any parable, the story of Readalot Publishing is stylized. Yet, also like any parable, it teaches some important and general lessons. In this case, there are three lessons to be learned about price discrimination.

The first and most obvious lesson is that price discrimination is a rational strategy for a profit-maximizing monopolist. In other words, by charging different prices to different customers, a monopolist can increase its profit. In essence, a price-discriminating monopolist charges each customer a price closer to his or her willingness to pay than is possible with a single price.

The second lesson is that price discrimination requires the ability to separate customers according to their willingness to pay. In our example, customers were separated geographically. But sometimes monopolists choose other differences, such as age or income, to distinguish among customers.

A corollary to this second lesson is that certain market forces can prevent firms from price discriminating. In particular, one such force is *arbitrage*, the process of buying a good in one market at a low price and selling it in another market at a higher price in order to profit from the price difference. In our example, suppose that Australian bookstores could buy the book in the United States and resell it to Australian readers. This arbitrage would prevent Readalot from price discriminating because no Australian would buy the book at the higher price.

The third lesson from our parable is perhaps the most surprising: Price discrimination can raise economic welfare. Recall that a deadweight loss arises when Readalot charges a single $30 price, because the 400,000 less enthusiastic readers do not end up with the book, even though they value it at more than its marginal cost of production. By contrast, when Readalot price discriminates, all readers end up with the book, and the outcome is efficient. Thus, price discrimination can eliminate the inefficiency inherent in monopoly pricing.

Note that the increase in welfare from price discrimination shows up as higher producer surplus rather than higher consumer surplus. In our example, consumers are no better off for having bought the book, because the price they pay exactly equals the value they place on the book. The entire increase in total surplus from price discrimination accrues to Readalot Publishing in the form of higher profit.

THE ANALYTICS OF PRICE DISCRIMINATION

Let's consider a bit more formally how price discrimination affects economic welfare. We begin by assuming that the monopolist can price discriminate perfectly. *Perfect price discrimination* describes a situation in which the monopolist knows exactly the willingness to pay of each customer and can charge each customer a different price. In this case, the monopolist charges each customer exactly his willingness to pay, and the monopolist gets the entire surplus in every transaction.

Figure 15-10 shows producer and consumer surplus with and without price discrimination. Without price discrimination, the firm charges a single price above marginal cost, as shown in panel (a). Because some potential customers who value the good at more than marginal cost do not buy it at this high price, the monopoly causes a deadweight loss. Yet when a firm can perfectly price discriminate, as shown in panel (b), each customer who values the good at more than marginal cost buys the good and is charged his willingness to pay. All mutually beneficial trades take place, there is no deadweight loss, and the entire surplus derived from the market goes to the monopoly producer in the form of profit.

In the world, of course, price discrimination is not perfect. Customers do not walk into stores with signs displaying their willingness to pay. Instead, firms price discriminate by dividing customers into groups: young versus old, weekday versus weekend shoppers, Americans versus Australians, and so on. Unlike

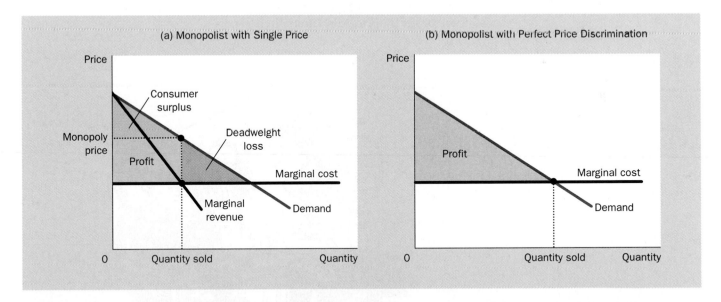

WELFARE WITH AND WITHOUT PRICE DISCRIMINATION. Panel (a) shows a monopolist that charges the same price to all customers. Total surplus in this market equals the sum of profit (producer surplus) and consumer surplus. Panel (b) shows a monopolist that can perfectly price discriminate. Because consumer surplus equals zero, total surplus now equals the firm's profit. Comparing these two panels, you can see that perfect price discrimination raises profit, raises total surplus, and lowers consumer surplus.

Figure 15-10

those in our parable of Readalot Publishing, customers within each group differ in their willingness to pay for the product, making perfect price discrimination impossible.

How does this imperfect price discrimination affect welfare? The analysis of these pricing schemes is quite complicated, and it turns out that there is no general answer to this question. Compared to the monopoly outcome with a single price, imperfect price discrimination can raise, lower, or leave unchanged total surplus in a market. The only certain conclusion is that price discrimination raises the monopoly's profit—otherwise the firm would choose to charge all customers the same price.

EXAMPLES OF PRICE DISCRIMINATION

Firms in our economy use various business strategies aimed at charging different prices to different customers. Now that we understand the economics of price discrimination, let's consider some examples.

Movie Tickets   Many movie theaters charge a lower price for children and senior citizens than for other patrons. This fact is hard to explain in a competitive market. In a competitive market, price equals marginal cost, and the marginal cost of providing a seat for a child or senior citizen is the same as the marginal cost of providing a seat for anyone else. Yet this fact is easily explained if movie theaters have some local monopoly power and if children and senior citizens have a lower willingness to pay for a ticket. In this case, movie theaters raise their profit by price discriminating.

Would it bother you to hear how little I paid for this flight?

Airline Prices   Seats on airplanes are sold at many different prices. Most airlines charge a lower price for a round-trip ticket between two cities if the traveler stays over a Saturday night. At first this seems odd. Why should it matter to the airline whether a passenger stays over a Saturday night? The reason is that this rule provides a way to separate business travelers and personal travelers. A passenger on a business trip has a high willingness to pay and, most likely, does not want to stay over a Saturday night. By contrast, a passenger traveling for personal reasons has a lower willingness to pay and is more likely to be willing to stay over a Saturday night. Thus, the airlines can successfully price discriminate by charging a lower price for passengers who stay over a Saturday night.

Discount Coupons   Many companies offer discount coupons to the public in newspapers and magazines. A buyer simply has to clip out the coupon in order to get $0.50 off his next purchase. Why do companies offer these coupons? Why don't they just cut the price of the product by $0.50?

The answer is that coupons allow companies to price discriminate. Companies know that not all customers are willing to spend the time to clip out coupons. Moreover, the willingness to clip coupons is related to the customer's willingness to pay for the good. A rich and busy executive is unlikely to spend her time clipping discount coupons out of the newspaper, and she is probably willing to pay a higher price for many goods. A person who is unemployed is more likely to clip coupons and has a lower willingness to pay. Thus, by charging a lower price only to those customers who clip coupons, firms can successfully price discriminate.

Financial Aid   Many colleges and universities give financial aid to needy students. One can view this policy as a type of price discrimination. Wealthy students have greater financial resources and, therefore, a higher willingness to pay than needy students. By charging high tuition and selectively offering financial aid, schools in effect charge prices to customers based on the value they place on going to that school. This behavior is similar to that of any price-discriminating monopolist.

Quantity Discounts   So far in our examples of price discrimination, the monopolist charges different prices to different customers. Sometimes, however, monopolists price discriminate by charging different prices to the same customer for different units that the customer buys. For example, many firms offer lower prices to customers who buy large quantities. A bakery might charge $0.50 for each donut, but $5 for a dozen. This is a form of price discrimination because the customer pays a higher price for the first unit bought than for the twelfth. Quantity discounts are often a successful way of price discriminating because a customer's willingness to pay for an additional unit declines as the customer buys more units.

QUICK QUIZ   Give two examples of price discrimination. ◆ How does perfect price discrimination affect consumer surplus, producer surplus, and total surplus?

Competing

to Be

the Best

Monopolist

WHAT ORGANIZATION IN OUR ECONOMY is most successful at exerting market power and keeping prices away from their competitive levels? Robert Barro, a Harvard University economics professor and *Wall Street Journal* columnist, reports on the first (and only) annual competition to find the most successful monopoly.

Let's Play Monopoly

BY ROBERT J. BARRO

It's almost the end of summer and time for the first annual contest to choose the best operating monopoly in America. The contestants, selected by a panel of Harvard economists, are as follows:

1. The U.S. Postal Service
2. OPEC [Organization of Petroleum Exporting Countries]
3. Almost any cable TV company
4. The Ivy League universities (for administering financial aid to students)

5. The NCAA [National Collegiate Athletic Association] (for administering payments to student-athletes).

Some other worthy candidates, which just missed the cut, are the National Football League, the American Medical Association, and the U.S. Departments of Agriculture and Defense.

Each contestant exhibits fine monopolistic characteristics and is worthy of serious consideration for the award. The U.S. Postal Service claims to be the longest-running monopoly in America and has the distinction of having its control over First Class mail prescribed (perhaps) by the Constitution. The monopoly has preserved large flows of revenues and high wage rates despite studies showing that private companies could carry the mail more efficiently at much lower cost.

On the other hand, the position of the Postal Service has been eroded: first, by successful competition on package delivery; second, by the recent entry of express delivery services; and third, and potentially most damaging, by the introduction of the fax machine. Since faxes are bound to supplant a substantial fraction of First Class letters, the failure to get Congress to classify a fax as First Class mail and, hence, the exclusive domain of the post office shows a remarkable loss of political muscle. Thus, despite past glories, it is hard to be sanguine about the long-term prospects of the post office as a flourishing monopoly.

OPEC was impressive in generating billions of dollars for its members from 1973 to the early 1980s. To understand the functioning of this cartel it is impor-

IS THE NCAA THE BEST MONOPOLIST?

tant to sort out the good guys from the bad guys.

The good guys, like Saudi Arabia and Kuwait, are the ones who have typically held oil production below capacity and thereby kept prices above the competitive level. The bad guys, like Libya and Iraq (when Iraq was allowed to produce oil), are the ones who have produced as much as they could and thereby kept prices low.

The good guys were responsible for the vast expansion of oil revenues during the blissful period after 1973. (Hence, they were responsible for the considerable difficulties endured by oil consumers.) But, unfortunately, these countries could not keep the other OPEC members in line and were also unable to exclude new producers or prevent conservation by consumers. Thus, oil prices plummeted in 1986. . . .

In any event, it is unclear that OPEC qualifies for the contest: It is not really American, and its members would probably be arrested for price-fixing if they ever held an official meeting in America.

Most cable TV companies have government-issued licenses that keep competitors out. Thus, this business supports the hypothesis (offered, I think, by George Stigler) that private monopolies are not sustainable for long unless they have the weight of government behind them.

The rapid escalation of prices and the limitations on services seem, however, to be getting customers and their congressional representatives progressively more annoyed. Thus, it would not be surprising if legislative action leads soon to a deterioration of the cable companies' monopoly power . . . . This fear about the future diminishes the claim of this otherwise worthy contestant for the first annual prize.

Officials of Ivy League universities have been able to meet in semi-public forums to set rules that determine prices of admission (tuition less financial aid) as a function of applicant characteristics, especially financial resources. In some cases, the schools pooled information to agree in advance on the right price to charge a specific customer. Airlines and other industries that wish to price discriminate can only dream about this kind of setup.

Moreover, the universities have more or less successfully applied a high moral tone to the process: Rich applicants—especially smart rich applicants—are charged more than the competitive price for schooling in order to subsidize the smart poor, but it is unclear why this subsidy should come from the smart rich rather than from taxpayers in general.

In any event, the universities' enviable cartel position has been damaged by the unenlightened Justice Department, which argued that the price-setting meetings were a violation of antitrust laws. Since most of the universities involved have agreed to stop these practices, it may be that future prices for private higher education will come closer to being competitively determined. . . .

The final contestant, the NCAA, has been remarkably successful in holding down "salaries" paid to college athletes. It would be one thing merely to collude to determine price ceilings (for example, to restrict payments so that they not exceed tuition plus room and board and some minor additional amount), but the NCAA has also managed to monopolize all the moral arguments.

Consider a poor ghetto resident who can play basketball well, but not well enough to make it to the NBA. If there were no NCAA, this player might be able legitimately to accumulate a significant amount of cash during a four-year career. But the NCAA ensures that the player will remain poor after four years and, moreover, has convinced most observers that it would be morally wrong for the college to pay the player a competitively determined wage for his or her services.

For many economists, this interference with competition—in a setting that has no obvious reasons for market failure—is itself morally repugnant. But the outrage is compounded here because the transfer is clearly from poor ghetto residents to rich colleges. Compare the situation of contestant number 4, the Ivy League universities, in which the transfer from rich to poor students can readily be supported on Robin Hood grounds.

The NCAA has the much more difficult task of defending a policy that prevents many poor individuals from earning money. Incredibly, this defense has been so successful that it has even allowed the organization to maintain the moral high ground. When the NCAA maintains its cartel by punishing schools that violate the rules (by paying too much), almost no one doubts that the evil entities are the schools or people who paid the athletes, rather than the cartel enforcers who prevented the athletes from getting paid. Given this extraordinary balancing act, the decision of the panelists was straightforward and the NCAA is the clear and deserving winner of the first annual prize for best monopoly in America.

The panel of economists also considered briefly an award for the least efficient monopoly in America. This choice was, however, too easy. It goes to the American Economic Association, which has been a dismal failure at establishing licensing requirements or other restrictions on entry into the economics profession. It is a sad state of affairs when almost anyone can assume the title of economist.

SOURCE: *The Wall Street Journal*, August 27, 1991, p. A12.

CONCLUSION: THE PREVALENCE OF MONOPOLY

This chapter has discussed the behavior of firms who have control over the prices they charge. We have seen that because monopolists produce less than the socially efficient quantity and charge prices above marginal cost, they cause deadweight losses. These inefficiencies can be mitigated through prudent public policies or, in some cases, through price discrimination by the monopolist.

How prevalent are the problems of monopoly? There are two answers to this question.

In one sense, monopolies are common. Most firms have some control over the prices they charge. They are not forced to charge the market price for their goods, because their goods are not exactly the same as those offered by other firms. A Ford Mustang is not the same as a Chevy Corvette. Ben and Jerry's ice cream is not the same as Breyer's. Each of these goods has a downward-sloping demand curve, which gives each producer some degree of monopoly power.

Yet firms with substantial monopoly power are quite rare. Few goods are truly unique. Most have substitutes that, even if not exactly the same, are very similar. Ben and Jerry can raise the price of their ice cream a little without losing all their sales; but if they raise it very much, sales will fall substantially.

In the end, monopoly power is a matter of degree. It is true that many firms have some monopoly power. It is also true that their monopoly power is usually quite limited. In these cases, we will not go far wrong assuming that firms operate in competitive markets, even if that is not precisely the case.

Summary

♦ A monopoly is a firm that is the sole seller in its market. A monopoly arises when a single firm owns a key resource, when the government gives a firm the exclusive right to produce a good, or when a single firm can supply the entire market at a smaller cost than many firms could.

♦ Because a monopoly is the sole producer in its market, it faces a downward-sloping demand curve for its product. When a monopoly increases production by one unit, it causes the price of its good to fall, which reduces the amount of revenue earned on all units produced. As a result, a monopoly's marginal revenue is always below the price of its good.

♦ Like a competitive firm, a monopoly firm maximizes profit by producing the quantity at which marginal revenue equals marginal cost. The monopoly then chooses the price at which that quantity is demanded. Unlike a competitive firm, a monopoly firm's price exceeds its marginal revenue, so its price exceeds marginal cost.

♦ A monopolist's profit-maximizing level of output is below the level that maximizes the sum of consumer and producer surplus. That is, when the monopoly charges a price above marginal cost, some consumers who value the good more than its cost of production do not buy it. As a result, monopoly causes deadweight losses similar to the deadweight losses caused by taxes.

♦ Policymakers can respond to the inefficiency of monopoly behavior in four ways. They can use the antitrust laws to try to make the industry more competitive. They can regulate the prices that the monopoly charges. They can turn the monopolist into a government-run enterprise. Or, if the market failure is deemed small compared to the inevitable imperfections of policies, they can do nothing at all.

♦ Monopolists often can raise their profits by charging different prices for the same good based on a buyer's willingness to pay. This practice of price discrimination can raise economic welfare by getting the good to some consumers who otherwise would not buy it. In the extreme case of perfect price discrimination, the dead-weight losses of monopoly are completely eliminated. More generally, when price discrimination is imperfect, it can either raise or lower welfare compared to the outcome with a single monopoly price.

Key Concepts

monopoly, p. 304

natural monopoly, p. 306

price discrimination, p. 323

Questions for Review

1. Give an example of a government-created monopoly. Is creating this monopoly necessarily bad public policy? Explain.

2. Define natural monopoly. What does the size of a market have to do with whether an industry is a natural monopoly?

3. Why is a monopolist's marginal revenue less than the price of its good?

4. Draw the demand, marginal-revenue, and marginal-cost curves for a monopolist. Show the profit-maximizing level of output. Show the profit-maximizing price.

5. In your diagram from the previous question, show the level of output that maximizes total surplus. Show the deadweight loss from the monopoly. Explain your answer.

6. What gives the government the power to regulate mergers between firms? From the standpoint of the welfare of society, give a good reason and a bad reason that two firms might want to merge.

7. Describe the two problems that arise when regulators tell a natural monopoly that it must set a price equal to marginal cost.

8. Give two examples of price discrimination. In each case, explain why the monopolist chooses to follow this business strategy.

Problems and Applications

1. Define a firm's marginal revenue. If the price of a good is always greater than zero, can a monopolist's marginal revenue ever be negative? Explain.

2. Does a monopolist or a competitive firm face a more elastic demand curve? What characteristic of the good being sold leads to a larger elasticity? Explain.

3. Suppose that a natural monopolist were required by law to charge average total cost. On a diagram, label the price charged and the deadweight loss to society relative to marginal-cost pricing.

4. Consider the delivery of mail. In general, what is the shape of the average-total-cost curve? How might the shape differ between isolated rural areas and densely populated urban areas? How might the shape have changed over time? Explain.

5. Suppose the Clean Springs Water Company has a monopoly on bottled water sales in California. If the price of tap water increases, what is the change in Clean Springs' profit-maximizing levels of output, price, and profit? Explain in words and with a graph.

6. A small town is served by many competing supermarkets, which have constant marginal cost.
   a. Using a diagram of the market for groceries, show the consumer surplus, producer surplus, and total surplus.
   b. Now suppose that the independent supermarkets combine into one chain. Using a new diagram, show the new consumer surplus, producer surplus, and total surplus. Relative to the competitive market, what is the transfer from consumers to producers? What is the deadweight loss?

7. Johnny Rockabilly has just finished recording his latest CD. His record company's marketing department determines that the demand for the CD is as follows:

PRICE	NUMBER OF CDs
$24	10,000
22	20,000
20	30,000
18	40,000
16	50,000
14	60,000

The company can produce the CD with no fixed cost and a variable cost of $5 per CD.

a. Find total revenue for quantity equal to 10,000, 20,000, and so on. What is the marginal revenue for each 10,000 increase in the quantity sold?

b. What quantity of CDs would maximize profit? What would the price be? What would the profit be?

c. If you were Johnny's agent, what recording fee would you advise Johnny to demand from the record company? Why?

8. In 1969 the government charged IBM with monopolizing the computer market. The government argued (correctly) that a very large share of all mainframe computers sold in the United States were produced by IBM. IBM argued (correctly) that a much smaller share of the market for *all* types of computers consisted of IBM products. Based on these facts, do you think that the government should have brought suit against IBM for violating the antitrust laws? Explain.

9. A company is considering building a bridge across a river. The bridge would cost $2 million to build and nothing to maintain. The following table shows the company's anticipated demand over the lifetime of the bridge:

P (PER CROSSING)	Q (NUMBER OF CROSSINGS, IN THOUSANDS)
$8	0
7	100
6	200
5	300
4	400
3	500
2	600
1	700
0	800

a. If the company were to build the bridge, what would be its profit-maximizing price? Would that be the efficient level of output? Why or why not?

b. If the company is interested in maximizing profit, should it build the bridge? What would be its profit or loss?

c. If the government were to build the bridge, what price should it charge?

d. Should the government build the bridge? Explain.

10. The Placebo Drug Company holds a patent on one of its discoveries.

a. Assuming that the production of the drug involves rising marginal cost, illustrate Placebo's profit-maximizing price and quantity. Also show Placebo's profits.

b. Now suppose that the government imposes a tax on each bottle of the drug produced. On a new diagram, illustrate Placebo's new price and quantity. How does each compare to your answer in part (a)?

c. Although it is not easy to see in your diagrams, the tax reduces Placebo's profit. Explain why this must be true.

d. Instead of the tax per bottle, suppose that the government imposes a tax on Placebo of $10,000 regardless of how many bottles are produced. How does this tax affect Placebo's price, quantity, and profits? Explain.

11. Larry, Curly, and Moe run the only saloon in town. Larry wants to sell as many drinks as possible without losing money. Curly wants the saloon to bring in as much revenue as possible. Moe wants to make the largest possible profits. Using a single diagram of the saloon's demand curve and cost curves, show the price and quantity combinations favored by each of the three partners. Explain.

12. For many years AT&T was a regulated monopoly, providing both local and long-distance telephone service.

a. Explain why long-distance phone service was originally a natural monopoly.

b. Over the past two decades, many companies have launched communication satellites, each of which can transmit a limited number of calls. How did the growing role of satellites change the cost structure of long-distance phone service?

After a lengthy legal battle with the government, AT&T agreed to compete with other companies in the long-distance market. It also agreed to spin off its local phone service into the "Baby Bells," which remain highly regulated.

c. Why might it be efficient to have competition in long-distance phone service and regulated monopolies in local phone service?

13. The Best Computer Company just developed a new computer chip, on which it immediately acquires a patent.

   a. Draw a diagram that shows the consumer surplus, producer surplus, and total surplus in the market for this new chip.

   b. What happens to these three measures of surplus if the firm can perfectly price discriminate? What is the change in deadweight loss? What transfers occur?

14. Explain why a monopolist will always produce a quantity at which the demand curve is elastic. (Hint: If demand is inelastic and the firm raises its price, what happens to total revenue and total costs?)

15. The "Big Three" American car companies are GM, Ford, and Chrysler. If these were the only car companies in the world, they would have much more monopoly power. What action could the U.S. government take to create monopoly power for these companies? (Hint: The government took such an action in the 1980s.)

16. The rock singer Rod Stewart has a monopoly over a scarce resource: himself. He is the only person who can produce a Rod Stewart concert. Does this fact imply that the government should regulate the prices of his concerts? Why or why not?

17. Many schemes for price discriminating involve some cost. For example, discount coupons take up time and resources from both the buyer and the seller. This question considers the implications of costly price discrimi-nation. To keep things simple, let's assume that our monopolist's production costs are simply proportional to output, so that average total cost and marginal cost are constant and equal to each other.

   a. Draw the cost, demand, and marginal-revenue curves for the monopolist. Show the price the monopolist would charge without price discrimination.

   b. In your diagram, mark the area equal to the monopolist's profit and call it X. Mark the area equal to consumer surplus and call it Y. Mark the area equal to the deadweight loss and call it Z.

   c. Now suppose that the monopolist can perfectly price discriminate. What is the monopolist's profit? (Give your answer in terms of X, Y, and Z.)

   d. What is the change in the monopolist's profit from price discrimination? What is the change in total surplus from price discrimination? Which change is larger? Explain. (Give your answer in terms of X, Y, and Z.)

   e. Now suppose that there is some cost of price discrimination. To model this cost, let's assume that the monopolist has to pay a fixed cost C in order to price discriminate. How would a monopolist make the decision whether to pay this fixed cost? (Give your answer in terms of X, Y, Z, and C.)

   f. How would a benevolent social planner, who cares about total surplus, decide whether the monopolist should price discriminate? (Give your answer in terms of X, Y, Z, and C.)

   g. Compare your answers to parts (e) and (f). How does the monopolist's incentive to price discriminate differ from the social planner's? Is it possible that the monopolist will price discriminate even though it is not socially desirable?

16

OLIGOPOLY

*See what market
structures lie between
monopoly and
competition*

*Examine what outcomes
are possible when a
market is an oligopoly*

*Learn about the
prisoners' dilemma and
how it applies to
oligopoly and other issues*

*Consider how the
antitrust laws try to
foster competition in
oligopolistic markets*

If you go to a store to buy tennis balls, it is likely that you will come home with one of four brands: Wilson, Penn, Dunlop, or Spalding. These four companies make almost all of the tennis balls sold in the United States. Together these firms determine the quantity of tennis balls produced and, given the market demand curve, the price at which tennis balls are sold.

How can we describe the market for tennis balls? The previous two chapters discussed two types of market structure. In a competitive market, each firm is so small compared to the market that it cannot influence the price of its product and, therefore, takes the price as given by market conditions. In a monopolized market, a single firm supplies the entire market for a good, and that firm can choose any price and quantity on the market demand curve.

The market for tennis balls fits neither the competitive nor the monopoly model. Competition and monopoly are extreme forms of market structure. Competition occurs when there are many firms in a market offering essentially identical products; monopoly occurs when there is only one firm in a market. It is natural to start the study of industrial organization with these polar cases, for they are the easiest cases to understand. Yet many industries, including the tennis ball industry, fall somewhere between these two extremes. Firms in these industries have competitors but, at the same time, do not face so much competition that they are price takers. Economists call this situation *imperfect competition*.

In this chapter we discuss the types of imperfect competition and examine a particular type called *oligopoly*. The essence of an oligopolistic market is that there are only a few sellers. As a result, the actions of any one seller in the market can have a large impact on the profits of all the other sellers. That is, oligopolistic firms are interdependent in a way that competitive firms are not. Our goal in this chapter is to see how this interdependence shapes the firms' behavior and what problems it raises for public policy.

BETWEEN MONOPOLY AND PERFECT COMPETITION

The previous two chapters analyzed markets with many competitive firms and markets with a single monopoly firm. In Chapter 14, we saw that the price in a perfectly competitive market always equals the marginal cost of production. We also saw that, in the long run, entry and exit drive economic profit to zero, so the price also equals average total cost. In Chapter 15, we saw how firms with market power can use that power to keep prices above marginal cost, leading to a positive economic profit for the firm and a deadweight loss for society.

The cases of perfect competition and monopoly illustrate some important ideas about how markets work. Most markets in the economy, however, include elements of both these cases and, therefore, are not completely described by either of them. The typical firm in the economy faces competition, but the competition is not so rigorous as to make the firm exactly described by the price-taking firm analyzed in Chapter 14. The typical firm also has some degree of market power, but its market power is not so great that the firm can be exactly described by the monopoly firm analyzed in Chapter 15. In other words, the typical firm in our economy is imperfectly competitive.

oligopoly

a market structure in which only a few sellers offer similar or identical products

monopolistic competition

a market structure in which many firms sell products that are similar but not identical

There are two types of imperfectly competitive markets. An **oligopoly** is a market with only a few sellers, each offering a product similar or identical to the others. One example is the market for tennis balls. Another is the world market for crude oil: A few countries in the Middle East control much of the world's oil reserves. **Monopolistic competition** describes a market structure in which there are many firms selling products that are similar but not identical. Examples include the markets for novels, movies, CDs, and computer games. In a monopolistically competitive market, each firm has a monopoly over the product it makes, but many other firms make similar products that compete for the same customers.

Figure 16-1 summarizes the four types of market structure. The first question to ask about any market is how many firms there are. If there is only one firm, the market is a monopoly. If there are only a few firms, the market is an oligopoly. If there are many firms, we need to ask another question: Do the firms sell identical or differentiated products? If the many firms sell differentiated products, the market is monopolistically competitive. If the many firms sell identical products, the market is perfectly competitive.

Reality, of course, is never as clear-cut as theory. In some cases, you may find it hard to decide what structure best describes a market. There is, for instance, no magic number that separates "few" from "many" when counting the num-

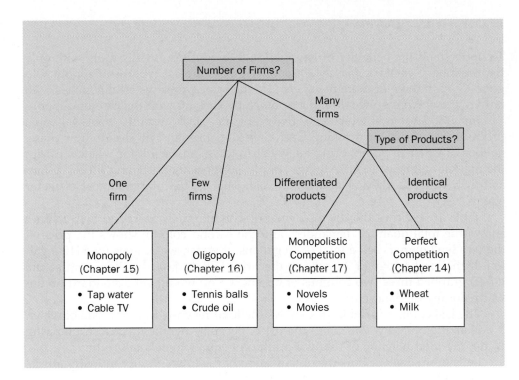

Figure 16-1

THE FOUR TYPES OF MARKET STRUCTURE. Economists who study industrial organization divide markets into four types—monopoly, oligopoly, monopolistic competition, and perfect competition.

ber of firms. (Do the approximately dozen companies that now sell cars in the United States make this market an oligopoly or more competitive? The answer is open to debate.) Similarly, there is no sure way to determine when products are differentiated and when they are identical. (Are different brands of milk really the same? Again, the answer is debatable.) When analyzing actual markets, economists have to keep in mind the lessons learned from studying all types of market structure and then apply each lesson as it seems appropriate.

Now that we understand how economists define the various types of market structure, we can continue our analysis of them. In the next chapter we analyze monopolistic competition. In this chapter we examine oligopoly.

QUICK QUIZ Define *oligopoly* and *monopolistic competition* and give an example of each.

MARKETS WITH ONLY A FEW SELLERS

Because an oligopolistic market has only a small group of sellers, a key feature of oligopoly is the tension between cooperation and self-interest. The group of oligopolists is best off cooperating and acting like a monopolist—producing a small quantity of output and charging a price above marginal cost. Yet because each oligopolist cares about only its own profit, there are powerful incentives at work that hinder a group of firms from maintaining the monopoly outcome.

A DUOPOLY EXAMPLE

To understand the behavior of oligopolies, let's consider an oligopoly with only two members, called a *duopoly*. Duopoly is the simplest type of oligopoly. Oligopolies with three or more members face the same problems as oligopolies with only two members, so we do not lose much by starting with the case of duopoly.

Imagine a town in which only two residents—Jack and Jill—own wells that produce water safe for drinking. Each Saturday, Jack and Jill decide how many gallons of water to pump, bring the water to town, and sell it for whatever price the market will bear. To keep things simple, suppose that Jack and Jill can pump as much water as they want without cost. That is, the marginal cost of water equals zero.

Table 16-1 shows the town's demand schedule for water. The first column shows the total quantity demanded, and the second column shows the price. If the two well owners sell a total of 10 gallons of water, water goes for $110 a gallon. If they sell a total of 20 gallons, the price falls to $100 a gallon. And so on. If you graphed these two columns of numbers, you would get a standard downward-sloping demand curve.

The last column in Table 16-1 shows the total revenue from the sale of water. It equals the quantity sold times the price. Because there is no cost to pumping water, the total revenue of the two producers equals their total profit.

Let's now consider how the organization of the town's water industry affects the price of water and the quantity of water sold.

COMPETITION, MONOPOLIES, AND CARTELS

Before considering the price and quantity of water that would result from the duopoly of Jack and Jill, let's discuss briefly the two market structures we already understand: competition and monopoly.

Table 16-1

THE DEMAND SCHEDULE FOR WATER

QUANTITY (IN GALLONS)	PRICE	TOTAL REVENUE (AND TOTAL PROFIT)
0	$120	$ 0
10	110	1,100
20	100	2,000
30	90	2,700
40	80	3,200
50	70	3,500
60	60	3,600
70	50	3,500
80	40	3,200
90	30	2,700
100	20	2,000
110	10	1,100
120	0	0

Consider first what would happen if the market for water were perfectly competitive. In a competitive market, the production decisions of each firm drive price equal to marginal cost. In the market for water, marginal cost is zero. Thus, under competition, the equilibrium price of water would be zero, and the equilibrium quantity would be 120 gallons. The price of water would reflect the cost of producing it, and the efficient quantity of water would be produced and consumed.

Now consider how a monopoly would behave. Table 16-1 shows that total profit is maximized at a quantity of 60 gallons and a price of $60 a gallon. A profit-maximizing monopolist, therefore, would produce this quantity and charge this price. As is standard for monopolies, price would exceed marginal cost. The result would be inefficient, for the quantity of water produced and consumed would fall short of the socially efficient level of 120 gallons.

What outcome should we expect from our duopolists? One possibility is that Jack and Jill get together and agree on the quantity of water to produce and the price to charge for it. Such an agreement among firms over production and price is called **collusion**, and the group of firms acting in unison is called a **cartel**. Once a cartel is formed, the market is in effect served by a monopoly, and we can apply our analysis from Chapter 15. That is, if Jack and Jill were to collude, they would agree on the monopoly outcome because that outcome maximizes the total profit that the producers can get from the market. Our two producers would produce a total of 60 gallons, which would be sold at a price of $60 a gallon. Once again, price exceeds marginal cost, and the outcome is socially inefficient.

A cartel must agree not only on the total level of production but also on the amount produced by each member. In our case, Jack and Jill must agree how to split between themselves the monopoly production of 60 gallons. Each member of the cartel will want a larger share of the market because a larger market share means larger profit. If Jack and Jill agreed to split the market equally, each would produce 30 gallons, the price would be $60 a gallon, and each would get a profit of $1,800.

collusion
an agreement among firms in a market about quantities to produce or prices to charge

cartel
a group of firms acting in unison

THE EQUILIBRIUM FOR AN OLIGOPOLY

Although oligopolists would like to form cartels and earn monopoly profits, often that is not possible. As we discuss later in this chapter, antitrust laws prohibit explicit agreements among oligopolists as a matter of public policy. In addition, sometimes squabbling among cartel members over how to divide the profit in the market makes agreement among them impossible. Let's therefore consider what happens if Jack and Jill decide separately how much water to produce.

At first, one might expect Jack and Jill to reach the monopoly outcome on their own, for this outcome maximizes their joint profit. In the absence of a binding agreement, however, the monopoly outcome is unlikely. To see why, imagine that Jack expects Jill to produce only 30 gallons (half of the monopoly quantity). Jack would reason as follows:

"I could produce 30 gallons as well. In this case, a total of 60 gallons of water would be sold at a price of $60 a gallon. My profit would be $1,800 (30 gallons × $60 a gallon). Alternatively, I could produce 40 gallons. In this case, a total of 70 gallons of water would be sold at a price of $50 a gallon. My profit would be $2,000 (40 gallons × $50 a gallon). Even though total profit in the market would fall, my profit would be higher, because I would have a larger share of the market."

Of course, Jill might reason the same way. If so, Jack and Jill would each bring 40 gallons to town. Total sales would be 80 gallons, and the price would fall to $40. Thus, if the duopolists individually pursue their own self-interest when deciding how much to produce, they produce a total quantity greater than the monopoly quantity, charge a price lower than the monopoly price, and earn total profit less than the monopoly profit.

Although the logic of self-interest increases the duopoly's output above the monopoly level, it does not push the duopolists to reach the competitive allocation. Consider what happens when each duopolist is producing 40 gallons. The price is $40, and each duopolist makes a profit of $1,600. In this case, Jack's self-interested logic leads to a different conclusion:

"Right now, my profit is $1,600. Suppose I increase my production to 50 gallons. In this case, a total of 90 gallons of water would be sold, and the price would be $30 a gallon. Then my profit would be only $1,500. Rather than increasing production and driving down the price, I am better off keeping my production at 40 gallons."

The outcome in which Jack and Jill each produce 40 gallons looks like some sort of equilibrium. In fact, this outcome is called a *Nash equilibrium* (named after economic theorist John Nash). A **Nash equilibrium** is a situation in which economic actors interacting with one another each choose their best strategy given the strategies the others have chosen. In this case, given that Jill is producing 40 gallons, the best strategy for Jack is to produce 40 gallons. Similarly, given that Jack is producing 40 gallons, the best strategy for Jill is to produce 40 gallons. Once they reach this Nash equilibrium, neither Jack nor Jill has an incentive to make a different decision.

Nash equilibrium

a situation in which economic actors interacting with one another each choose their best strategy given the strategies that all the other actors have chosen

This example illustrates the tension between cooperation and self-interest. Oligopolists would be better off cooperating and reaching the monopoly outcome. Yet because they pursue their own self-interest, they do not end up reaching the monopoly outcome and maximizing their joint profit. Each oligopolist is tempted to raise production and capture a larger share of the market. As each of them tries to do this, total production rises, and the price falls.

At the same time, self-interest does not drive the market all the way to the competitive outcome. Like monopolists, oligopolists are aware that increases in the amount they produce reduce the price of their product. Therefore, they stop short of following the competitive firm's rule of producing up to the point where price equals marginal cost.

In summary, *when firms in an oligopoly individually choose production to maximize profit, they produce a quantity of output greater than the level produced by monopoly and less than the level produced by competition. The oligopoly price is less than the monopoly price but greater than the competitive price (which equals marginal cost).*

HOW THE SIZE OF AN OLIGOPOLY AFFECTS THE MARKET OUTCOME

We can use the insights from this analysis of duopoly to discuss how the size of an oligopoly is likely to affect the outcome in a market. Suppose, for instance, that John and Joan suddenly discover water sources on their property and join Jack and Jill in the water oligopoly. The demand schedule in Table 16-1 remains the same, but now more producers are available to satisfy this demand. How would an increase in the number of sellers from two to four affect the price and quantity of water in the town?

If the sellers of water could form a cartel, they would once again try to maximize total profit by producing the monopoly quantity and charging the monopoly price. Just as when there were only two sellers, the members of the cartel would need to agree on production levels for each member and find some way to enforce the agreement. As the cartel grows larger, however, this outcome is less likely. Reaching and enforcing an agreement becomes more difficult as the size of the group increases.

If the oligopolists do not form a cartel—perhaps because the antitrust laws prohibit it—they must each decide on their own how much water to produce. To see how the increase in the number of sellers affects the outcome, consider the decision facing each seller. At any time, each well owner has the option to raise production by 1 gallon. In making this decision, the well owner weighs two effects:

◆ *The output effect:* Because price is above marginal cost, selling 1 more gallon of water at the going price will raise profit.

◆ *The price effect:* Raising production will increase the total amount sold, which will lower the price of water and lower the profit on all the other gallons sold.

If the output effect is larger than the price effect, the well owner will increase production. If the price effect is larger than the output effect, the owner will not raise production. (In fact, in this case, it is profitable to reduce production.) Each oligopolist continues to increase production until these two marginal effects exactly balance, taking the other firms' production as given.

Now consider how the number of firms in the industry affects the marginal analysis of each oligopolist. The larger the number of sellers, the less concerned each seller is about its own impact on the market price. That is, as the oligopoly grows in size, the magnitude of the price effect falls. When the oligopoly grows very large, the price effect disappears altogether, leaving only the output effect. In this extreme case, each firm in the oligopoly increases production as long as price is above marginal cost.

We can now see that a large oligopoly is essentially a group of competitive firms. A competitive firm considers only the output effect when deciding how much to produce: Because a competitive firm is a price taker, the price effect is absent. Thus, *as the number of sellers in an oligopoly grows larger, an oligopolistic market looks more and more like a competitive market. The price approaches marginal cost, and the quantity produced approaches the socially efficient level.*

This analysis of oligopoly offers a new perspective on the effects of international trade. Imagine that Toyota and Honda are the only automakers in Japan, Volkswagen and Mercedes-Benz are the only automakers in Germany, and Ford and General Motors are the only automakers in the United States. If these nations prohibited trade in autos, each would have an auto oligopoly with only two members, and the market outcome would likely depart substantially from the competitive ideal. With international trade, however, the car market is a world market, and the oligopoly in this example has six members. Allowing free trade increases the number of producers from which each consumer can choose, and this increased competition keeps prices closer to marginal cost. Thus, the theory of oligopoly provides another reason, in addition to the theory of comparative advantage discussed in Chapter 3, why all countries can benefit from free trade.

CASE STUDY   OPEC AND THE WORLD OIL MARKET

Our story about the town's market for water is fictional, but if we change water to crude oil, and Jack and Jill to Iran and Iraq, the story is quite close to being true. Much of the world's oil is produced by a few countries, mostly in the Middle East. These countries together make up an oligopoly. Their decisions about how much oil to pump are much the same as Jack and Jill's decisions about how much water to pump.

The countries that produce most of the world's oil have formed a cartel, called the Organization of Petroleum Exporting Countries (OPEC). As originally formed in 1960, OPEC included Iran, Iraq, Kuwait, Saudi Arabia, and Venezuela. By 1973, eight other nations had joined: Qatar, Indonesia, Libya, the United Arab Emirates, Algeria, Nigeria, Ecuador, and Gabon. These countries control about three-fourths of the world's oil reserves. Like any cartel, OPEC tries to raise the price of its product through a coordinated reduction in quantity produced. OPEC tries to set production levels for each of the member countries.

The problem that OPEC faces is much the same as the problem that Jack and Jill face in our story. The OPEC countries would like to maintain a high price of oil. But each member of the cartel is tempted to increase production in order to get a larger share of the total profit. OPEC members frequently agree to reduce production but then cheat on their agreements.

OPEC was most successful at maintaining cooperation and high prices in the period from 1973 to 1985. The price of crude oil rose from $2.64 a barrel in 1972 to $11.17 in 1974 and then to $35.10 in 1981. But in the early 1980s member countries began arguing about production levels, and OPEC became ineffective at maintaining cooperation. By 1986 the price of crude oil had fallen back to $12.52 a barrel.

Today, the members of OPEC continue to meet about twice a year, but the cartel is no longer successful at reaching or enforcing agreement. (See the accompanying In the News box.) As a result, the members of OPEC make production decisions largely independently of one another, and the world market for oil is fairly competitive. The price of crude oil, adjusted for overall inflation, is about the same today as it was before OPEC was formed.

OPEC: A not very cooperative cartel

IN THE NEWS

Squabbling

in OPEC

LIKE MOST CARTELS, OPEC HAS TROUBLE reaching and enforcing agreement among its members. The following article describes the problems OPEC was having in 1996, when the United Nations started to allow Iraq back into the world oil market.

OPEC Is Expected to Delay Action on New Oil Output by Iraq

BY YOUSSEF M. IBRAHIM

VIENNA—The Organization of Petroleum Exporting Countries, meeting here, appeared paralyzed today, stuck between a certainty of lower oil prices if it failed to reduce its 11 members' output, but stymied by its members' refusal to cut their current market shares.

As a result, OPEC was headed for an inconclusive resolution that would authorize Iraq to pump some 800,000 barrels of oil a day without any offsetting cuts. A United Nations resolution in May allowed Iraqi exports, which had been halted following the Persian Gulf War, to resume soon.

Saudi Arabia and Venezuela, two of the largest producers, with 8.4 million barrels a day and nearly 3 million barrels a day respectively, made it clear they would not cut back, despite demands by other OPEC members that they do so. . . .

The Saudis seemed to be taking a new hard-line attitude, regarding as permanent the increase of 3 million barrels a day they added to their exports in 1990 to replace Iraqi output after Baghdad came under United Nations sanctions— even as Iraq works its way up to its old output.

Iraq's oil minister, Amer Mohammad Rashid, said his country would sign its first sales contract within ten days. Iraq vowed to double and eventually triple its oil output.

Mr. Rashid forecast rapid sales growth acceleration. Indeed, a number of oil company executives were holding talks with his aides.

Briefing reporters, Mr. Rashid, a former general in the Iraqi Air Force, said exports could reach 1.2 million barrels a day within three months—far higher than the OPEC projection of 700,000 to 800,000 barrels a day. If he is right, the extra output could add to downward pressure on prices, perhaps by as much as $3 a barrel.

Mr. Rashid also said he assumed the United Nations resolution was "a bridge" to a complete lifting of the embargo within six months. Then, he asserted, Iraqi production could reach its prewar level of 3 million barrels a day. Two Security Council members, France and Russia, are known to support a total lifting of sanctions.

That development would be a bonanza for Iraq and for consumers around the world, but a catastrophe for hard-pressed OPEC countries like Venezuela, which is in the midst of a severe economic crisis.

SOURCE: *The New York Times,* June 7, 1996, p. D3.

QUICK QUIZ If the members of an oligopoly could agree on a total quantity to produce, what quantity would they choose? ◆ If the oligopolists do not act together but instead make production decisions individually, do they produce a total quantity more or less than in your answer to the previous question? Why?

GAME THEORY AND THE ECONOMICS OF COOPERATION

As we have seen, oligopolies would like to reach the monopoly outcome, but doing so requires cooperation, which at times is difficult to maintain. In this section we look more closely at the problems that people face when cooperation is

game theory
the study of how people behave in strategic situations

prisoners' dilemma
a particular "game" between two captured prisoners that illustrates why cooperation is difficult to maintain even when it is mutually beneficial

dominant strategy
a strategy that is best for a player in a game regardless of the strategies chosen by the other players

desirable but difficult. To analyze the economics of cooperation, we need to learn a little about game theory.

Game theory is the study of how people behave in strategic situations. By "strategic" we mean a situation in which each person, in deciding what actions to take, must consider how others might respond to that action. Because the number of firms in an oligopolistic market is small, each firm must act strategically. Each firm knows that its profit depends not only on how much it produces but also on how much the other firms produce. In making its production decision, each firm in an oligopoly should consider how its decision might affect the production decisions of all the other firms.

Game theory is not necessary for understanding competitive or monopoly markets. In a competitive market, each firm is so small compared to the market that strategic interactions with other firms are not important. In a monopolized market, strategic interactions are absent because the market has only one firm. But, as we will see, game theory is quite useful for understanding the behavior of oligopolies.

A particularly important "game" is called the **prisoners' dilemma.** This game provides insight into the difficulty of maintaining cooperation. Many times in life, people fail to cooperate with one another even when cooperation would make them all better off. An oligopoly is just one example. The story of the prisoners' dilemma contains a general lesson that applies to any group trying to maintain cooperation among its members.

THE PRISONERS' DILEMMA

The prisoners' dilemma is a story about two criminals who have been captured by the police. Let's call them Bonnie and Clyde. The police have enough evidence to convict Bonnie and Clyde of the minor crime of carrying an unregistered gun, so that each would spend a year in jail. The police also suspect that the two criminals have committed a bank robbery together, but they lack hard evidence to convict them of this major crime. The police question Bonnie and Clyde in separate rooms, and they offer each of them the following deal:

"Right now, we can lock you up for 1 year. If you confess to the bank robbery and implicate your partner, however, we'll give you immunity, and you can go free. Your partner will get 20 years in jail. But if you both confess to the crime, we won't need your testimony and we can avoid the cost of a trial, so you will each get an intermediate sentence of 8 years."

If Bonnie and Clyde, heartless bank robbers that they are, care only about their own sentences, what would you expect them to do? Would they confess or remain silent? Figure 16-2 shows their choices. Each prisoner has two strategies: confess or remain silent. The sentence each prisoner gets depends on the strategy he or she chooses and the strategy chosen by his or her partner in crime.

Consider first Bonnie's decision. She reasons as follows: "I don't know what Clyde is going to do. If he remains silent, my best strategy is to confess, since then I'll go free rather than spending a year in jail. If he confesses, my best strategy is still to confess, since then I'll spend 8 years in jail rather than 20. So, regardless of what Clyde does, I am better off confessing."

In the language of game theory, a strategy is called a **dominant strategy** if it is the best strategy for a player to follow regardless of the strategies pursued by other players. In this case, confessing is a dominant strategy for Bonnie. She

Bonnie's Decision

	Confess	Remain Silent
Confess	• 8 years for each	• Bonnie gets 20 years • Clyde goes free
Remain Silent	• Bonnie goes free • Clyde gets 20 years	• 1 year for each

Clyde's Decision

Figure 16-2

THE PRISONERS' DILEMMA. In this game between two criminals suspected of committing a crime, the sentence that each receives depends both on the criminal's decision to either confess or remain silent and on the decision made by the other criminal.

spends less time in jail if she confesses, regardless of whether Clyde confesses or remains silent.

Now consider Clyde's decision. He faces exactly the same choices as Bonnie, and he reasons in much the same way. Regardless of what Bonnie does, Clyde can reduce his time in jail by confessing. In other words, confessing is also a dominant strategy for Clyde.

In the end, both Bonnie and Clyde confess, and both spend 8 years in jail. Yet, from their standpoint, this is a terrible outcome. If they had *both* remained silent, both of them would have been better off, spending only 1 year in jail on the gun charge. By each pursuing his or her own interests, the two prisoners together reach an outcome that is worse for each of them.

To see how difficult it is to maintain cooperation, imagine that, before the police captured Bonnie and Clyde, the two criminals had made a pact not to confess. Clearly, this agreement would make them both better off *if* they both live up to it, because they would each spend only 1 year in jail. But would the two criminals in fact remain silent, simply because they had agreed to? Once they are being questioned separately, the logic of self-interest takes over and leads them to confess. Cooperation between the two prisoners is difficult to maintain, because cooperation is individually irrational.

OLIGOPOLIES AS A PRISONERS' DILEMMA

What does the prisoners' dilemma have to do with markets and imperfect competition? It turns out that the game that oligopolists play in trying to reach the monopoly outcome is similar to the game that the two prisoners play in the prisoners' dilemma.

Consider an oligopoly with two members, called Iran and Iraq. Both countries sell crude oil. After prolonged negotiation, the countries agree to keep production of oil low in order to keep the world price of oil high. After they agree on production levels, each country must decide whether to cooperate and live up to this agreement or to ignore it and produce at a higher level. Figure 16-3 shows how the profits of the two countries depend on the strategies they choose.

Figure 16-3

AN OLIGOPOLY GAME. In this game between members of an oligopoly, the profit that each earns depends both on the member's production decision and on the production decision made by the other member.

		Iraq's Decision	
		High Production	**Low Production**
Iran's Decision	**High Production**	• $40 billion for each	• Iraq gets $30 billion • Iran gets $60 billion
	Low Production	• Iraq gets $60 billion • Iran gets $30 billion	• $50 billion for each

Suppose you are the president of Iraq. You might reason as follows: "I could keep production low as we agreed, or I could raise my production and sell more oil on world markets. If Iran lives up to the agreement and keeps its production low, then my country earns profit of $60 billion with high production and $50 billion with low production. In this case, Iraq is better off with high production. If Iran fails to live up to the agreement and produces at a high level, then my country earns $40 billion with high production and $30 billion with low production. Once again, Iraq is better off with high production. So, regardless of what Iran chooses to do, my country is better off reneging on our agreement and producing at a high level."

Producing at a high level is a dominant strategy for Iraq. Of course, Iran reasons in exactly the same way, and so both countries produce at a high level. The result is the inferior outcome (from Iran and Iraq's standpoint) with low profits for each country.

This example illustrates why oligopolies have trouble maintaining monopoly profits. The monopoly outcome is jointly rational for the oligopoly, but each oligopolist has an incentive to cheat. Just as self-interest drives the prisoners in the prisoners' dilemma to confess, self-interest makes it difficult for the oligopoly to maintain the cooperative outcome with low production, high prices, and monopoly profits.

OTHER EXAMPLES OF THE PRISONERS' DILEMMA

We have seen how the prisoners' dilemma can be used to understand the problem facing oligopolies. The same logic applies to many other situations as well. Here we consider three examples in which self-interest prevents cooperation and leads to an inferior outcome for the parties involved.

Arms Races An arms race is much like the prisoners' dilemma. To see this, consider the decisions of two countries—the United States and the Soviet Union—about whether to build new weapons or to disarm. Each country prefers

IN THE NEWS

Modern Pirates

OCEAN SHIPPING FIRMS, WHICH IN THE past have managed to run a successful cartel, are now having trouble maintaining this cooperative and profitable outcome.

Ocean Shippers Break Ranks on Pricing

BY ANNA WILDE MATTHEWS

There's a new battle on the high seas these days: price wars.

After operating a little-noticed but legalized price cartel for years, the world's ocean shipping lines have started rebelling against one another, dropping rates as much as 10 percent on some trade lanes—the largest decline in a decade. In the U.S. alone, $460 billion a year in trade could be affected, including everything from VCRs from Japan to mineral water from France.

The rates are "finally starting to reflect supply and demand," says Bud LaLonde, professor emeritus of transportation at Ohio State University, which he expects will become a "windfall" for consumers if retailers pass on the savings.

For the industry, however, the change is a sharp break from tradition. Since the days of the vast British Empire in the nineteenth century, many of the major shipping lines have held so-called rate conferences to decide fee schedules. Today, these conferences still meet—as often as twice a week. Executives from more than a dozen lines, including such giants as Sea-Land Service, Inc., a unit of CSX Corporation, and Tokyo-based Nippon Yusen Kaisha Line, attend them, setting rates on literally thousands of consumer-good categories.

Such price fixing is legal because U.S. laws still allow ocean shipping lines to cooperate to set rates. Though not as powerful as they once were, the cartels still control rates on as much as 60 percent of the world's containerized ocean cargo. . . .

But the shipping industry is in the midst of a potential disaster in overbuilding, which is already breaking down the cartels. During a boom a few years ago in cargo business, nearly every major shipping line went on a building spree. Over the next three years, 653 new vessels are expected to come on line. . . .

"It's a classic case of the lemming effect," says James Winchester, a transportation analyst at Lazard Freres & Company. "All of the shipping lines jumped for the same golden hoop, and now they're coming crashing downward."

The cartel also has been undermined by a group of renegade shipping lines from Asia that set their own prices. By improving their service and offering lower rates, these lines have taken business from the cartels, forcing some conference members to break ranks and cut their rates. "As soon as one little rate action happens, boom, boom, boom, everything else kicks in," says Theodore Prince, a senior vice president of operations for "K" Line America, a conference member. "It's kind of hard to hold the line."

Already, most U.S. retailers are noticing the change. For them, transportation fees can account for 5 to 10 percent of their total costs. . . . The change has made a big difference at Emerson Electric Co., an electronics and motor concern in St. Louis, which spends about $10 million a year to ship and receive goods over the ocean. Sinking rates will be "a major contribution" to cost-cutting efforts, said Robert D. White, global transportation manager there.

But shipping lines—itself an $80 billion-a-year industry—aren't rejoicing. Even with lower rates, most lines have still reported profits this year, but they are scrambling to contend with overcapacity. The Transpacific Stabilization Agreement, an alliance of 15 major shipping lines, for example, has announced a plan to intentionally keep some ship space empty—to help drive up rates. The industry has tried this before, with limited success.

SOURCE: *The Wall Street Journal*, October 29, 1996, p. A2.

to have more arms than the other because a larger arsenal gives it more influence in world affairs. But each country also prefers to live in a world safe from the other country's weapons.

Figure 16-4 shows the deadly game. If the Soviet Union chooses to arm, the United States is better off doing the same to prevent the loss of power. If the Soviet Union chooses to disarm, the United States is better off arming because

Figure 16-4

AN ARMS-RACE GAME. In this game between two countries, the safety and power of each depends both on the country's decision whether to arm and on the decision made by the other country.

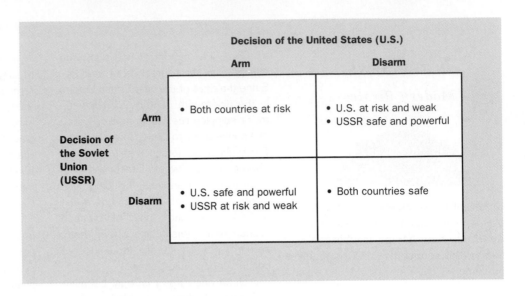

doing so would make it more powerful. For each country, arming is a dominant strategy. Thus, each country chooses to continue the arms race, resulting in the inferior outcome in which both countries are at risk.

Throughout the era of the Cold War, the United States and the Soviet Union attempted to solve this problem through negotiation and agreements over arms control. The problems that the two countries faced were similar to those that oligopolists encounter in trying to maintain a cartel. Just as oligopolists argue over production levels, the United States and the Soviet Union argued over the amount of arms that each country would be allowed. And just as cartels have trouble enforcing production levels, the United States and the Soviet Union each feared that the other country would cheat on any agreement. In both arms races and oligopolies, the relentless logic of self-interest drives the participants toward a noncooperative outcome that is worse for each party.

Advertising   When two firms advertise to attract the same customers, they face a problem similar to the prisoners' dilemma. For example, consider the decisions facing two cigarette companies, Marlboro and Camel. If neither company advertises, the two companies split the market. If both advertise, they again split the market, but profits are lower, since each company must bear the cost of advertising. Yet if one company advertises while the other does not, the one that advertises attracts customers from the other.

Figure 16-5 shows how the profits of the two companies depend on their actions. You can see that advertising is a dominant strategy for each firm. Thus, both firms choose to advertise, even though both firms would be better off if neither firm advertised.

A test of this theory of advertising occurred in 1971, when Congress passed a law banning cigarette advertisements on television. To the surprise of many observers, cigarette companies did not use their considerable political clout to oppose the law. When the law went into effect, cigarette advertising fell, and the profits of cigarette companies rose. The law did for the cigarette companies what they could not do on their own: It solved the prisoners' dilemma by enforcing the cooperative outcome with low advertising and high profit.

Figure 16-5

An Advertising Game. In this game between firms selling similar products, the profit that each earns depends both on the firm's advertising decision and on the advertising decision of the other firm.

Marlboro's Decision

	Advertise	Don't Advertise
Advertise	• $3 billion profit for each	• Marlboro gets $2 billion profit • Camel gets $5 billion profit
Don't Advertise	• Marlboro gets $5 billion profit • Camel gets $2 billion profit	• $4 billion profit for each

Camel's Decision

Common Resources In Chapter 11 we saw that people tend to overuse common resources. One can view this problem as an example of the prisoners' dilemma.

Imagine that two oil companies—Exxon and Arco—own adjacent oil fields. Under the fields is a common pool of oil worth $12 million. Drilling a well to recover the oil costs $1 million. If each company drills one well, each will get half of the oil and earn a $5 million profit ($6 million in revenue minus $1 million in costs).

Because the pool of oil is a common resource, the companies will not use it efficiently. Suppose that either company could drill a second well. If one company has two of the three wells, that company gets two-thirds of the oil, which yields a profit of $6 million. Yet if each company drills a second well, the two companies again split the oil. In this case, each bears the cost of a second well, so profit is only $4 million for each company.

Figure 16-6 shows the game. Drilling two wells is a dominant strategy for each company. Once again, the self-interest of the two players leads them to an inferior outcome.

THE PRISONERS' DILEMMA AND THE WELFARE OF SOCIETY

The prisoners' dilemma describes many of life's situations, and it shows that cooperation can be difficult to maintain, even when cooperation would make both players in the game better off. Clearly, this lack of cooperation is a problem for those involved in these situations. But is lack of cooperation a problem from the standpoint of society as a whole? The answer depends on the circumstances.

In some cases, the noncooperative equilibrium is bad for society as well as the players. In the arms-race game in Figure 16-4, both the United States and the Soviet Union end up at risk. In the common-resources game in Figure 16-6, the extra wells dug by Arco and Exxon are pure waste. In both cases, society would be better off if the two players could reach the cooperative outcome.

Figure 16-6

A COMMON-RESOURCES GAME. In this game between firms pumping oil from a common pool, the profit that each earns depends both on the number of wells the firm drills and on the number of wells drilled by the other firm.

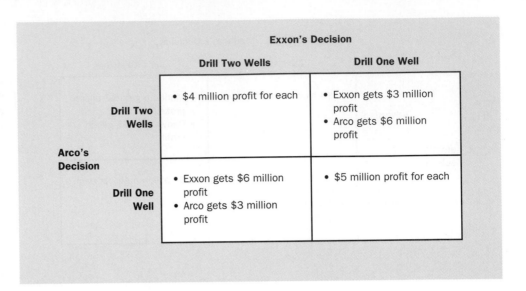

By contrast, in the case of oligopolists trying to maintain monopoly profits, lack of cooperation is desirable from the standpoint of society as a whole. The monopoly outcome is good for the oligopolists, but it is bad for the consumers of the product. As we first saw in Chapter 7, the competitive outcome is best for society because it maximizes total surplus. When oligopolists fail to cooperate, the quantity they produce is closer to this optimal level. Put differently, the invisible hand guides markets to allocate resources efficiently only when markets are competitive, and markets are competitive only when firms in the market fail to cooperate with one another.

Similarly, consider the case of the police questioning two suspects. Lack of cooperation between the suspects is desirable, for it allows the police to convict more criminals. The prisoners' dilemma is a dilemma for the prisoners, but it can be a boon to everyone else.

WHY PEOPLE SOMETIMES COOPERATE

The prisoners' dilemma shows that cooperation is difficult. But is it impossible? Not all prisoners, when questioned by the police, decide to turn in their partners in crime. Cartels sometimes do manage to maintain collusive arrangements, despite the incentive for individual members to defect. Very often, the reason that players can solve the prisoners' dilemma is that they play the game not once but many times.

To see why cooperation is easier to enforce in repeated games, let's return to our duopolists, Jack and Jill. Recall that Jack and Jill would like to maintain the monopoly outcome in which each produces 30 gallons, but self-interest drives them to an equilibrium in which each produces 40 gallons. Figure 16-7 shows the game they play. Producing 40 gallons is a dominant strategy for each player in this game.

Imagine that Jack and Jill try to form a cartel. To maximize total profit, they would agree to the cooperative outcome in which each produces 30 gallons. Yet, if Jack and Jill are to play this game only once, neither has any incentive to live

Figure 16-7

JACK AND JILL'S OLIGOPOLY GAME. In this game between Jack and Jill, the profit that each earns from selling water depends both on the quantity he or she chooses to sell and on the quantity the other chooses to sell.

up to this agreement. Self-interest drives each of them to renege and produce 40 gallons.

Now suppose that Jack and Jill know that they will play the same game every week. When they make their initial agreement to keep production low, they can also specify what happens if one party reneges. They might agree, for instance, that once one of them reneges and produces 40 gallons, both of them will produce 40 gallons forever after. This penalty is easy to enforce, for if one party is producing at a high level, the other has every reason to do the same.

The threat of this penalty may be all that is needed to maintain cooperation. Each person knows that defecting would raise his or her profit from $1,800 to $2,000. But this benefit would last for only one week. Thereafter, profit would fall to $1,600 and stay there. As long as the players care enough about future profits, they will choose to forgo the one-time gain from defection. Thus, in a game of repeated prisoners' dilemma, the two players may well be able to reach the cooperative outcome.

CASE STUDY   THE PRISONERS' DILEMMA TOURNAMENT

Imagine that you are playing a game of prisoners' dilemma with a person being "questioned" in a separate room. Moreover, imagine that you are going to play not once but many times. Your score at the end of the game is the total number of years in jail. You would like to make this score as small as possible. What strategy would you play? Would you begin by confessing or remaining silent? How would the other player's actions affect your subsequent decisions about confessing?

Repeated prisoners' dilemma is quite a complicated game. To encourage cooperation, players must penalize each other for not cooperating. Yet the strategy described earlier for Jack and Jill's water cartel—defect forever as soon as the other player defects—is not very forgiving. In a game repeated many times, a strategy that allows players to return to the cooperative outcome after a period of noncooperation may be preferable.

To see what strategies work best, political scientist Robert Axelrod held a tournament. People entered by sending computer programs designed to play repeated prisoners' dilemma. Each program then played the game against all the other programs. The "winner" was the program that received the fewest total years in jail.

The winner turned out to be a simple strategy called *tit-for-tat*. According to tit-for-tat, a player should start by cooperating and then do whatever the other player did last time. Thus, a tit-for-tat player cooperates until the other player defects; he then defects until the other player cooperates again. In other words, this strategy starts out friendly, penalizes unfriendly players, and forgives them if warranted. To Axelrod's surprise, this simple strategy did better than all the more complicated strategies that people had sent in.

The tit-for-tat strategy has a long history. It is essentially the biblical strategy of "an eye for an eye, a tooth for a tooth." The prisoners' dilemma tournament suggests that this may be a good rule of thumb for playing some of the games of life.

QUICK QUIZ Tell the story of the prisoners' dilemma. Write down a table showing the prisoners' choices and explain what outcome is likely. ◆ What does the prisoners' dilemma teach us about oligopolies?

PUBLIC POLICY TOWARD OLIGOPOLIES

One of the *Ten Principles of Economics* in Chapter 1 is that governments can sometimes improve market outcomes. The application of this principle to oligopolistic markets is, as a general matter, straightforward. As we have seen, cooperation among oligopolists is undesirable from the standpoint of society as a whole, because it leads to production that is too low and prices that are too high. To move the allocation of resources closer to the social optimum, policymakers should try to induce firms in an oligopoly to compete rather than cooperate. Let's consider how policymakers do this and then examine the controversies that arise in this area of public policy.

RESTRAINT OF TRADE AND THE ANTITRUST LAWS

One way that policy discourages cooperation is through the common law. Normally, freedom of contract is an essential part of a market economy. Businesses and households use contracts to arrange mutually advantageous trades. In doing this, they rely on the court system to enforce contracts. Yet, for many centuries, judges in England and the United States have deemed agreements among competitors to reduce quantities and raise prices to be contrary to the public good. They therefore refused to enforce such agreements.

The Sherman Antitrust Act of 1890 codified and reinforced this policy:

> Every contract, combination in the form of trust or otherwise, or conspiracy, in restraint of trade or commerce among the several States, or with foreign

nations, is declared to be illegal. . . . Every person who shall monopolize, or attempt to monopolize, or combine or conspire with any person or persons to monopolize any part of the trade or commerce among the several States, or with foreign nations, shall be deemed guilty of a misdemeanor, and on conviction therefor, shall be punished by fine not exceeding fifty thousand dollars, or by imprisonment not exceeding one year, or by both said punishments, in the discretion of the court.

The Sherman Act elevated agreements among oligopolists from an unenforceable contract to a criminal conspiracy.

The Clayton Act of 1914 further strengthened the antitrust laws. According to this law, if a person could prove that he was damaged by an illegal arrangement to restrain trade, that person could sue and recover three times the damages he sustained. The purpose of this unusual rule of triple damages is to encourage private lawsuits against conspiring oligopolists.

Today, both the U.S. Justice Department and private parties have the authority to bring legal suits to enforce the antitrust laws. As we discussed in Chapter 14, these laws are used to prevent mergers that would lead to excessive market power in any single firm. In addition, these laws are used to prevent oligopolists from acting together in ways that would make their markets less competitive.

CASE STUDY AN ILLEGAL PHONE CALL

Firms in oligopolies have a strong incentive to collude in order to reduce production, raise price, and increase profit. The great eighteenth-century economist Adam Smith was well aware of this potential market failure. In *The Wealth of Nations* he wrote, "People of the same trade seldom meet together, but the conversation ends in a conspiracy against the public, or in some diversion to raise prices."

To see a modern example of Smith's observation, consider the following excerpt of a phone conversation between two airline executives in the early 1980s. The call was reported in *The New York Times* on February 24, 1983. Robert Crandall was president of American Airlines, and Howard Putnam was president of Braniff Airways.

CRANDALL: I think it's dumb as hell for Christ's sake, all right, to sit here and pound the @#$% out of each other and neither one of us making a #$%& dime.

PUTNAM: Do you have a suggestion for me?

CRANDALL: Yes, I have a suggestion for you. Raise your $%*& fares 20 percent. I'll raise mine the next morning.

PUTNAM: Robert, we . . .

CRANDALL: You'll make more money, and I will, too.

PUTNAM: We can't talk about pricing!

CRANDALL: Oh @#$%, Howard. We can talk about any &*#@ thing we want to talk about.

Putnam was right: The Sherman Antitrust Act prohibits competing executives from even talking about fixing prices. When Putnam gave a tape of this conversation to the Justice Department, the Justice Department filed suit against Mr. Crandall.

Two years later, Crandall and the Justice Department reached a settlement in which Crandall agreed to various restrictions on his business activities, including his contacts with officials at other airlines. The Justice Department said that the terms of settlement would "protect competition in the airline industry, by preventing American and Crandall from any further attempts to monopolize passenger airline service on any route through discussions with competitors about the prices of airline services."

CONTROVERSIES OVER ANTITRUST POLICY

Over time, much controversy has centered on the question of what kinds of behavior the antitrust laws should prohibit. Most commentators agree that price-fixing agreements among competing firms should be illegal. Yet the antitrust laws have been used to condemn some business practices whose effects are not obvious. Here we consider two examples.

Resale Price Maintenance One example of a controversial business practice is *resale price maintenance*, also called *fair trade*. Imagine that Superduper Electronics sells VCRs to retail stores for $300. If Superduper requires the retailers to charge customers $350, it is said to engage in resale price maintenance. Any retailer that charged less than $350 would have violated its contract with Superduper.

At first, resale price maintenance might seem anticompetitive and, therefore, detrimental to society. Like an agreement among members of a cartel, it prevents the retailers from competing on price. For this reason, the courts have often viewed resale price maintenance as a violation of the antitrust laws.

Yet some economists have defended resale price maintenance on two grounds. First, they deny that it is aimed at reducing competition. To the extent that Superduper Electronics has any market power, it can exert that power through the wholesale price, rather than through resale price maintenance. Moreover, Superduper has no incentive to discourage competition among its retailers. Indeed, because a cartel of retailers sells less than a group of competitive retailers, Superduper would be worse off if its retailers were a cartel.

Second, economists have argued that resale price maintenance has a legitimate goal. Superduper may want its retailers to provide customers a pleasant showroom and a knowledgeable sales force. Yet, without resale price maintenance, some customers would take advantage of one store's service to learn about the VCR's special features and then buy the VCR at a discount retailer that does not provide this service. To some extent, good service is a public good among the retailers that sell Superduper VCRs. As we discussed in Chapter 11, when one person provides a public good, others are able to enjoy it without paying for it. In this case, discount retailers would free ride on the service provided by other retailers, leading to less service than is desirable. Resale price maintenance is one way for Superduper to solve this free-rider problem.

The example of resale price maintenance illustrates an important principle: *Business practices that appear to reduce competition may in fact have legitimate purposes.* This principle makes the application of the antitrust laws all the more

IN THE NEWS

Anticompetitive

"R" Us?

APPLYING THE NATION'S ANTITRUST LAWS is not easy. What to one person looks like an attempt to suppress competition may to another look like a reasonable business practice. The following article describes a recent controversy surrounding Toys "R" Us. Discount retailers claim that Toys "R" Us is exerting its market power to try to exclude them from the retail toy market. Toys "R" Us claims that the discount retailers are trying to free ride on the advertising it has done.

Toys "R" Us Is Expecting U.S. Charges of Antitrust

BY JENNIFER STEINHAUER

Toys "R" Us, the country's largest toy retailer, said yesterday that it expected that the Federal Trade Commission would bring antitrust charges against it today, and that the company would vigorously contest any action challenging its buying practices. . . .

At the heart of the civil litigation, which began as part of a broad look at the toy industry, is whether Toys "R" Us violated the antitrust laws by telling manufacturers like Mattel and Hasbro that it would not buy their products unless they refused to sell to warehouse clubs that Toys "R" Us says undercut it on prices. Warehouse clubs sell merchandise, typi-

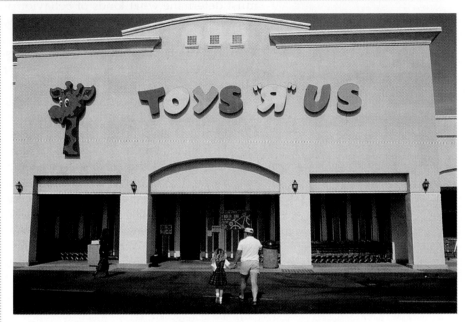

"Daddy, could we get a better deal at Wal-Mart?"

cally at cut-rate prices, to customers who pay a membership fee.

Although a retailer has the right to refuse to buy from anyone, an issue can arise over whether a retailer is using its size and marketing power to pressure a group of manufacturers to freeze out competitors. In the case of Toys "R" Us, which has annual revenue of $8.8 billion and accounts for more than 20 percent of toy sales in the United States, that size and marketing power is formidable. . . .

The investigation began with complaints from warehouse clubs that large toy manufacturers were refusing to sell them many products and that the manufacturing firms said they were doing so because of Toys "R" Us. . . .

Toys "R" Us has said its practices are justified because it faces fierce competition not just from the warehouse clubs but also from regular discount chains like Wal-Mart and Target.

"We are frankly astounded that the F.T.C. would bring a case against Toys 'R' Us," Michael Goldstein, the company's chief executive, said yesterday in a statement.

Saying that Toys "R" Us spends millions of dollars throughout the year to promote toys, he added, "The warehouse clubs then come along during the six weeks before Christmas, without making any such investment, and select the few hottest-selling items, selling them at or below cost to create customer traffic.

"Given that behavior, and Toys 'R' Us's contribution to the industry, we have told manufacturers that we reserve our unquestionable right to refuse to carry the same items as warehouse clubs. This is central to our ability to compete."

SOURCE: *The New York Times*, May 22, 1996, pp. D1, D7.

difficult. The economists, lawyers, and judges in charge of enforcing these laws must determine what kinds of behavior public policy should prohibit as impeding competition and reducing economic well-being. Often that job is not easy.

Tying   Another example of a controversial business practice is *tying.* Suppose that Makemoney Movies produces two new films—*Star Wars* and *Hamlet.* If Makemoney offers theaters the two films together at a single price, rather than separately, the studio is said to be tying its two products.

When the practice of tying movies was challenged in the courts, the Supreme Court banned the practice. The court reasoned as follows: Imagine that *Star Wars* is a blockbuster, whereas *Hamlet* is an unprofitable art film. Then the studio could use the high demand for *Star Wars* to force theaters to buy *Hamlet.* It seemed that the studio could use tying as a mechanism for expanding its market power.

Economists have been skeptical of this argument. Imagine that theaters are willing to pay $20,000 for *Star Wars* and nothing for *Hamlet.* Then the most that a theater would pay for the two movies together is $20,000—the same as it would pay for *Star Wars* by itself. Forcing the theater to accept a worthless movie as part of the deal does not increase the theater's willingness to pay. Makemoney cannot increase its market power simply by bundling the two movies together.

Why, then, does tying exist? One possibility is that it is a form of price discrimination. Suppose there are two theaters. City Theater is willing to pay $16,000 for *Star Wars* and $5,000 for *Hamlet.* Country Theater is willing to pay $14,000 for *Star Wars* and $6,000 for *Hamlet.* If Makemoney charges separate prices for the two films, its best strategy is to charge $14,000 for *Star Wars* and $5,000 for *Hamlet,* for a total of $19,000 from each theater. Yet if Makemoney offers the two movies as a bundle, it can charge each theater $20,000 for the movies. Thus, if different theaters value the films differently, tying allows the studio to increase profit by charging a combined price closer to the buyers' total willingness to pay.

Tying remains a controversial business practice. The Supreme Court's argument that tying allows a firm to extend its market power to other goods is not well founded, at least in its simplest form. Yet economists have proposed more elaborate theories for how tying can impede competition. Given our current economic knowledge, it is unclear whether tying has adverse effects for society as a whole.

In recent years, the debate over tying has become increasingly important. As noted in Chapter 15, the Microsoft Corporation has a near monopoly in operating systems for personal computers. Almost all personal computers use Microsoft's DOS, Windows, or Windows 95. Other software companies have claimed that Microsoft is trying to extend its market power by including unrelated software, such as Internet browsers, as part of its operating systems. These claims are the subject of continuing investigations by the U.S. Justice Department.

■ **QUICK QUIZ**   What kind of agreement is illegal for businesses to make?
■ ◆ Why are the antitrust laws controversial?

CONCLUSION

Oligopolies would like to act like monopolies, but self-interest drives them closer to competition. Thus, oligopolies can end up looking either more like monopolies or more like competitive markets, depending on the number of firms in the oligopoly and how cooperative the firms are. The story of the prisoners' dilemma shows why oligopolies can fail to maintain cooperation, even when cooperation is in their best interest.

Policymakers regulate the behavior of oligopolists through the antitrust laws. The proper scope of these laws is the subject of ongoing debate. Although price fixing among competing firms clearly reduces economic welfare and should be illegal, some business practices that appear to reduce competition may have legitimate if subtle purposes. As a result, policymakers need to be careful when using the substantial powers of the antitrust laws to place limits on firm behavior.

Summary

◆ Oligopolists maximize their total profits by forming a cartel and acting like a monopolist. Yet, if oligopolists make decisions about production levels individually, the result is a greater quantity and a lower price than under the monopoly outcome. The larger the number of firms in the oligopoly, the closer the quantity and price will be to the levels that would prevail under competition.

◆ The prisoners' dilemma shows that self-interest can prevent people from maintaining cooperation, even when cooperation is in their mutual interest. The logic of the prisoners' dilemma applies in many situations, including arms races, advertising, common-resource problems, and oligopolies.

◆ Policymakers use the antitrust laws to prevent oligopolies from engaging in behavior that reduces competition. The application of these laws can be controversial, because some behavior that may seem to reduce competition may in fact have legitimate business purposes.

Key Concepts

oligopoly, p. 338
monopolistic competition, p. 338
collusion, p. 341

cartel, p. 341
Nash equilibrium, p. 342
game theory, p. 346

prisoners' dilemma, p. 346
dominant strategy, p. 346

Questions for Review

1. If a group of sellers could form a cartel, what quantity and price would they try to set?

2. Compare the quantity and price of an oligopoly to those of a monopoly.

3. Compare the quantity and price of an oligopoly to those of a competitive market.

4. How does the number of firms in an oligopoly affect the outcome in its market?

5. What is the prisoners' dilemma, and what does it have to do with oligopoly?

6. Give two examples other than oligopoly to show how the prisoners' dilemma helps to explain behavior.

7. What kinds of behavior do the antitrust laws prohibit?

8. What is resale price maintenance, and why is it controversial?

Problems and Applications

1. *The New York Times* (Nov. 30, 1993) reported that "the inability of OPEC to agree last week to cut production has sent the oil market into turmoil . . . [leading to] the lowest price for domestic crude oil since June 1990."

   a. Why were the members of OPEC trying to agree to cut production?

   b. Why do you suppose OPEC was unable to agree on cutting production? Why did the oil market go into "turmoil" as a result?

   c. The newspaper also noted OPEC's view "that producing nations outside the organization, like Norway and Britain, should do their share and cut production." What does the phrase "do their share" suggest about OPEC's desired relationship with Norway and Britain?

2. A large share of the world supply of diamonds comes from Russia and South Africa. Suppose that the marginal cost of mining diamonds is $1,000 per diamond, and the demand for diamonds is described by the following schedule:

Price	Quantity
$8,000	5,000
7,000	6,000
6,000	7,000
5,000	8,000
4,000	9,000
3,000	10,000
2,000	11,000
1,000	12,000

   a. If there were many suppliers of diamonds, what would be the price and quantity?

   b. If there were only one supplier of diamonds, what would be the price and quantity?

   c. If Russia and South Africa formed a cartel, what would be the price and quantity? If the countries split the market evenly, what would be South Africa's production and profit? What would happen to South Africa's profit if it increased its production by 1,000 while Russia stuck to the cartel agreement?

   d. Use your answer to part (c) to explain why cartel agreements are often not successful.

3. This chapter discusses companies that are oligopolists in the market for the goods they sell. Many of the same ideas apply to companies that are oligopolists in the market for the inputs they buy.

   a. If sellers who are oligopolists try to increase the price of goods they sell, what is the goal of buyers who are oligopolists?

   b. Major league baseball team owners have an oligopoly in the market for baseball players. What is the owners' goal regarding players' salaries? Why is this goal difficult to achieve?

   c. Baseball players went on strike in 1994 because they would not accept the salary cap that the owners wanted to impose. If the owners were already colluding over salaries, why did the owners feel the need for a salary cap?

4. Why is game theory helpful for understanding markets with a few firms, but not markets with many firms?

5. Describe several activities in your life in which game theory could be useful. What is the common link among these activities?

6. Consider trade relations between the United States and Mexico. Assume that the leaders of the two countries believe the payoffs to alternative trade policies are as follows:

   | | | United States' Decision | |
		Low Tariffs	High Tariffs
Mexico's Decision	Low Tariffs	• U.S. gains $25 billion • Mexico gains $25 billion	• U.S. gains $30 billion • Mexico gains $10 billion
	High Tariffs	• U.S. gains $10 billion • Mexico gains $30 billion	• U.S. gains $20 billion • Mexico gains $20 billion

   a. What is the dominant strategy for the United States? For Mexico? Explain.

   b. Define *Nash equilibrium*. What is the Nash equilibrium for trade policy?

   c. In 1993 the U.S. Congress ratified the North American Free Trade Agreement, in which the United States and Mexico agreed to reduce trade barriers simultaneously. Do the perceived payoffs as shown here justify this approach to trade policy?

   d. Based on your understanding of the gains from trade (discussed in Chapters 3 and 9), do you think that these payoffs actually reflect a nation's welfare under the four possible outcomes?

7. Suppose that you and a classmate are assigned a project on which you will receive one combined grade. You

each want to receive a good grade, but you also want to do as little work as possible. The decision box and pay-offs are as follows:

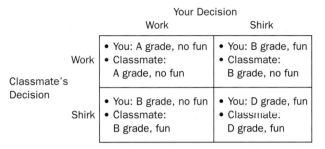

Your Decision

		Work	Shirk

Classmate's Decision	Work	• You: A grade, no fun
		• Classmate:
		  A grade, no fun
			• You: B grade, fun
			• Classmate:
			  B grade, no fun

	Shirk	• You: B grade, no fun
		• Classmate:
		  B grade, fun
			• You: D grade, fun
			• Classmate:
			  D grade, fun

Assume that having fun is your normal state, but having no fun is as unpleasant as receiving a grade that is two letters lower.

a. Write out the decision box that combines the letter grade and the amount of fun you have into a single payoff for each outcome.

b. If neither you nor your classmate knows how much work the other person is doing, what is the likely outcome? Does it matter whether you are likely to work with this person again? Explain your answer.

8. The chapter states that the ban on cigarette advertising on television in 1971 increased the profits of cigarette companies. Could the ban still be good public policy? Explain your answer.

9. A case study in the chapter describes a phone conversation between the presidents of American Airlines and Braniff Airways. Let's analyze the game between the two companies. Suppose that each company can charge either a high price for tickets or a low price. If one company charges $100, it earns low profits if the other company charges $100 also, and high profits if the other company charges $200. On the other hand, if the company charges $200, it earns very low profits if the other company charges $100, and medium profits if the other company charges $200 also.

a. Draw the decision box for this game.

b. What is the Nash equilibrium in this game? Explain.

c. Is there an outcome that would be better than the Nash equilibrium for both airlines? How could it be achieved? Who would lose if it were achieved?

10. Farmer Jones and Farmer Smith graze their cattle on the same field. If there are 20 cows grazing in the field, each cow produces $4,000 of milk over its lifetime. If there are more cows in the field, then each cow can eat less grass, and its milk production falls. With 30 cows on the field, each produces $3,000 of milk; with 40 cows, each produces $2,000 of milk. Cows cost $1,000 apiece.

a. Assume that Farmer Jones and Farmer Smith can each purchase either 10 or 20 cows, but that neither knows how many the other is buying when she makes her purchase. Calculate the payoffs of each outcome.

b. What is the likely outcome of this game? What would be the best outcome? Explain.

c. There used to be more common fields than there are today. Why? (For more discussion of this topic, reread Chapter 11.)

17

MONOPOLISTIC COMPETITION

You walk into a bookstore to buy a book to read during your next vacation. On the store's shelves you find a John Grisham mystery, a Stephen King thriller, a Danielle Steel romance, a Dennis Rodman autobiography, and many other choices. When you pick out a book and buy it, what kind of market are you participating in?

On the one hand, the market for books seems quite competitive. As you look over the shelves at your bookstore, you find many authors and many publishers vying for your attention. A buyer in this market has thousands of competing products from which to choose. And because anyone can enter the industry by writing and publishing a book, the book business is not very profitable. For every highly paid novelist, there are hundreds of struggling ones.

On the other hand, the market for books seems quite monopolistic. Because each book is unique, publishers have some latitude in choosing what price to charge. The sellers in this market are price makers rather than price takers. And, indeed, the price of books greatly exceeds marginal cost. The price of a typical hardcover novel, for instance, is about $25, whereas the cost of printing one additional copy of the novel is less than $5.

monopolistic competition
a market structure in which many firms sell products that are similar but not identical

In this chapter we examine markets that have some features of competition and some features of monopoly. This market structure is called **monopolistic competition.** Monopolistic competition describes a market with the following attributes:

◆ *Many sellers:* There are many firms competing for the same group of customers.

◆ *Product differentiation:* Each firm produces a product that is at least slightly different from those of other firms. Thus, rather than being a price taker, each firm faces a downward-sloping demand curve.

◆ *Free entry:* Firms can enter (or exit) the market without restriction. Thus, the number of firms in the market adjusts until economic profits are driven to zero.

A moment's thought reveals a long list of markets with these attributes: books, CDs, movies, computer games, restaurants, piano lessons, cookies, furniture, and so on.

Monopolistic competition, like oligopoly, is a market structure that lies between the extreme cases of competition and monopoly. But oligopoly and monopolistic competition are quite different. Oligopoly departs from the perfectly competitive ideal of Chapter 14 because there are only a few sellers in the market. The small number of sellers makes rigorous competition less likely, and it makes strategic interactions among them vitally important. By contrast, under monopolistic competition, there are many sellers, each of which is small compared to the market. A monopolistically competitive market departs from the perfectly competitive ideal because each of the sellers offers a somewhat different product.

COMPETITION WITH DIFFERENTIATED PRODUCTS

To understand monopolistically competitive markets, we first consider the decisions facing an individual firm. We then examine what happens in the long run as firms enter and exit the industry. Next, we compare the equilibrium under monopolistic competition to the equilibrium under perfect competition that we examined in Chapter 14. Finally, we consider whether the outcome in a monopolistically competitive market is desirable from the standpoint of society as a whole.

THE MONOPOLISTICALLY COMPETITIVE FIRM IN THE SHORT RUN

Each firm in a monopolistically competitive market is, in many ways, like a monopoly. Because its product is different from those offered by other firms, it

MONOPOLISTIC COMPETITORS IN THE SHORT RUN. Monopolistic competitors, like monopolists, maximize profit by producing the quantity at which marginal revenue equals marginal cost. The firm in panel (a) makes a profit because, at this quantity, price is above average total cost. The firm in panel (b) makes losses because, at this quantity, price is less than average total cost.

Figure 17-1

faces a downward-sloping demand curve. (By contrast, a perfectly competitive firm faces a horizontal demand curve at the market price.) Thus, the monopolistically competitive firm follows a monopolist's rule for profit maximization: It chooses the quantity at which marginal revenue equals marginal cost and then uses its demand curve to find the price consistent with that quantity.

Figure 17-1 shows the cost, demand, and marginal-revenue curves for two typical firms, each in a different monopolistically competitive industry. In both panels of this figure, the profit-maximizing quantity is found at the intersection of the marginal-revenue and marginal-cost curves. The two panels in this figure show different outcomes for the firm's profit. In panel (a), price exceeds average total cost, so the firm makes a profit. In panel (b), price is below average total cost. In this case, the firm is unable to make a positive profit, so the best the firm can do is to minimize its losses.

All this should seem familiar. A monopolistically competitive firm chooses its quantity and price just as a monopoly does. In the short run, these two types of market structure are similar.

THE LONG-RUN EQUILIBRIUM

The situations depicted in Figure 17-1 do not last long. When firms are making profits, as in panel (a), new firms have an incentive to enter the market. This

"GIVEN THE DOWNWARD SLOPE OF OUR DEMAND CURVE, AND THE EASE WITH WHICH OTHER FIRMS CAN ENTER THE INDUSTRY, WE CAN STRENGTHEN OUR PROFIT POSITION ONLY BY EQUATING MARGINAL COST AND MARGINAL REVENUE. ORDER MORE JELLY BEANS."

entry increases the number of products from which customers can choose and, therefore, reduces the demand faced by each firm already in the market. In other words, profit encourages entry, and entry shifts the demand curves faced by the incumbent firms to the left. As the demand for incumbent firms' products fall, these firms experience declining profit.

Conversely, when firms are making losses, as in panel (b), firms in the market have an incentive to exit. As firms exit, customers have fewer products from which to choose. This decrease in the number of firms expands the demand faced by those firms that stay in the market. In other words, losses encourage exit, and exit shifts the demand curves of the remaining firms to the right. As the demand for the remaining firms' products rises, these firms experience rising profit (that is, declining losses).

This process of entry and exit continues until the firms in the market are making exactly zero economic profit. Figure 17-2 depicts the long-run equilibrium. Once the market reaches this equilibrium, new firms have no incentive to enter, and existing firms have no incentive to exit.

Notice that the demand curve in this figure just barely touches the average-total-cost curve. Mathematically, we say the two curves are *tangent* to each other.

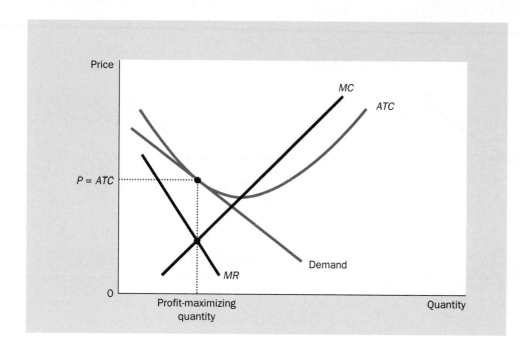

Figure 17-2

A MONOPOLISTIC COMPETITOR IN THE LONG RUN. In a monopolistically competitive market, if firms are making profit, new firms enter, and the demand curves for the incumbent firms shift to the left. Similarly, if firms are making losses, old firms exit, and the demand curves of the remaining firms shift to the right. Because of these shifts in demand, a monopolistically competitive firm eventually finds itself in the long-run equilibrium shown here. In this long-run equilibrium, price equals average total cost, and the firm earns zero profit.

These two curves must be tangent once entry and exit have driven profit to zero. Because profit per unit sold is the difference between price (found on the demand curve) and average total cost, the maximum profit is zero only if these two curves touch each other without crossing.

To sum up, two characteristics describe the long-run equilibrium in a monopolistically competitive market:

◆ As in a monopoly market, price exceeds marginal cost. This conclusion arises because profit maximization requires marginal revenue to equal marginal cost and because the downward-sloping demand curve makes marginal revenue less than the price.

◆ As in a competitive market, price equals average total cost. This conclusion arises because free entry and exit drive economic profit to zero.

The second characteristic shows how monopolistic competition differs from monopoly. Because a monopoly is the sole seller of a product without close substitutes, it can earn positive economic profit, even in the long run. By contrast, because there is free entry into a monopolistically competitive market, the economic profit of a firm in this type of market is driven to zero.

MONOPOLISTIC VERSUS PERFECT COMPETITION

Figure 17-3 compares the long-run equilibrium under monopolistic competition to the long-run equilibrium under perfect competition. (Chapter 14 discussed the equilibrium with perfect competition.) There are two noteworthy differences between monopolistic and perfect competition—excess capacity and the markup.

Figure 17-3

MONOPOLISTIC VERSUS PERFECT COMPETITION. Panel (a) shows the long-run equilibrium in a monopolistically competitive market, and panel (b) shows the long-run equilibrium in a perfectly competitive market. Two differences are notable. (1) The perfectly competitive firm produces at the efficient scale, where average total cost is minimized. By contrast, the monopolistically competitive firm produces at less than the efficient scale. (2) Price equals marginal cost under perfect competition, but price is above marginal cost under monopolistic competition.

Excess Capacity   As we have just seen, entry and exit drive each firm in a monopolistically competitive market to a point of tangency between its demand and average-total-cost curves. Panel (a) of Figure 17-3 shows that the quantity of output at this point is smaller than the quantity that minimizes average total cost. Thus, under monopolistic competition, firms produce on the downward-sloping portion of their average-total-cost curves. In this way, monopolistic competition contrasts starkly with perfect competition. As panel (b) of Figure 17-3 shows, free entry in competitive markets drives firms to produce at the minimum of average total cost.

The quantity that minimizes average total cost is called the *efficient scale* of the firm. In the long run, perfectly competitive firms produce at the efficient scale, whereas monopolistically competitive firms produce below this level. Firms are said to have *excess capacity* under monopolistic competition. In other words, a monopolistically competitive firm, unlike a perfectly competitive firm, could increase the quantity it produces and lower the average total cost of production.

Markup over Marginal Cost   A second difference between perfect competition and monopolistic competition is the relationship between price and marginal cost. For a competitive firm, such as that shown in panel (b) of Figure 17-3, price equals marginal cost. For a monopolistically competitive firm, such as that shown in panel (a), price exceeds marginal cost, because the firm always has some market power.

How is this markup over marginal cost consistent with free entry and zero profit? The zero-profit condition ensures only that price equals average total cost. It does *not* ensure that price equals marginal cost. Indeed, in the long-run equilibrium, monopolistically competitive firms operate on the declining portion of their average-total-cost curves, so marginal cost is below average total cost. Thus, for price to equal average total cost, price must be above marginal cost.

In this relationship between price and marginal cost, we see a key behavioral difference between perfect competitors and monopolistic competitors. Imagine that you were to ask a firm the following question: "Would you like to see another customer come through your door ready to buy from you at your current price?" A perfectly competitive firm would answer that it didn't care. Because price exactly equals marginal cost, the profit from an extra unit sold is zero. By contrast, a monopolistically competitive firm is always eager to get another customer. Because its price exceeds marginal cost, an extra unit sold at the posted price means more profit. According to an old quip, monopolistically competitive markets are those in which sellers send Christmas cards to the buyers.

MONOPOLISTIC COMPETITION AND THE WELFARE OF SOCIETY

Is the outcome in a monopolistically competitive market desirable from the standpoint of society as a whole? Can policymakers improve on the market outcome? There are no simple answers to these questions.

One source of inefficiency is the markup of price over marginal cost. Because of the markup, some consumers who value the good at more than the marginal cost of production (but less than the price) will be deterred from buying it. Thus, a monopolistically competitive market has the normal deadweight loss of monopoly pricing. We first saw this type of inefficiency when we discussed monopoly in Chapter 15.

Although this outcome is clearly undesirable compared to the first-best outcome of price equal to marginal cost, there is no easy way for policymakers to fix the problem. To enforce marginal-cost pricing, policymakers would need to regulate all firms that produce differentiated products. Because such products are so common in the economy, the administrative burden of such regulation would be overwhelming.

Moreover, regulating monopolistic competitors would entail all the problems of regulating natural monopolies. In particular, because monopolistic competitors are making zero profits already, requiring them to lower their prices to equal marginal cost would cause them to make losses. To keep these firms in business, the government would need to help them cover these losses. Rather than raising taxes to pay for these subsidies, policymakers may decide it is better to live with the inefficiency of monopolistic pricing.

Another way in which monopolistic competition may be socially inefficient is that the number of firms in the market may not be the "ideal" one. That is, there may be too much or too little entry. One way to think about this problem is in terms of the externalities associated with entry. Whenever a new firm considers entering the market with a new product, it considers only the profit it would make. Yet its entry would also have two external effects:

◆ *The product-variety externality:* Because consumers get some consumer surplus from the introduction of a new product, there is a positive externality associated with entry.

◆ *The business-stealing externality:* Because other firms lose customers and profits from the entry of a new competitor, there is a negative externality associated with entry.

Thus, in a monopolistically competitive market, there are both positive and negative externalities associated with the entry of new firms. Depending on which externality is larger, a monopolistically competitive market could have either too few or too many products.

Both of these externalities are closely related to the conditions for monopolistic competition. The product-variety externality arises because a new firm would offer a product different from those of the existing firms. The business-stealing externality arises because firms post a price above marginal cost and, therefore, are always eager to sell additional units. Conversely, because perfectly competitive firms produce identical goods and charge a price equal to marginal cost, neither of these externalities exists under perfect competition.

In the end, we can conclude only that monopolistically competitive markets do not have all the desirable welfare properties of perfectly competitive markets. That is, the invisible hand does not ensure that total surplus is maximized under monopolistic competition. Yet because the inefficiencies are subtle, hard to measure, and hard to fix, there is no easy way for public policy to improve the market outcome.

QUICK QUIZ   List the three key attributes of monopolistic competition. ◆ Draw and explain a diagram to show the long-run equilibrium in a monopolistically competitive market. How does this equilibrium differ from that in a perfectly competitive market?

FYI

Is Excess Capacity a Social Problem?

AS WE HAVE SEEN, MONOPOLISTICALLY competitive firms produce a quantity of output below the level that minimizes average total cost. By contrast, firms in perfectly competitive markets are driven to produce at the quantity that minimizes average total cost. This comparison between perfect and monopolistic competition has led some economists in the past to argue that the excess capacity of monopolistic competitors was a source of inefficiency.

Today economists understand that the excess capacity of monopolistic competitors is not directly relevant for evaluating economic welfare. There is no reason that society should want all firms to produce at the minimum of average total cost. For example, consider a publishing firm. Producing a novel might take a fixed cost of $50,000 (the author's time) and variable costs of $5 per book (the cost of printing). In this case, the average total cost of a book declines as the number of books increases because the fixed cost gets spread over more and more units. The average total cost is minimized by printing an infinite number of books. But in no sense is infinity the right number of books for society to produce.

In short, monopolistic competitors do have excess capacity, but this fact tells us little about the desirability of the market outcome.

ADVERTISING

It is nearly impossible to go through a typical day in a modern economy without being bombarded with advertising. Whether you are reading a newspaper, watching television, or driving down the highway, some firm will try to convince you to buy its product. Such behavior is a natural feature of monopolistic competition. When firms sell differentiated products and charge prices above marginal cost, each firm has an incentive to advertise in order to attract more buyers to its particular product.

The amount of advertising varies substantially across products. Firms that sell highly differentiated consumer goods, such as over-the-counter drugs, perfumes, soft drinks, razor blades, breakfast cereals, and dog food, typically spend between 10 and 20 percent of revenue for advertising. Firms that sell industrial products, such as drill presses and communications satellites, typically spend very little on advertising. And firms that sell homogeneous products, such as wheat, peanuts, or crude oil, spend nothing at all. For the economy as a whole, spending on advertising comprises about 2 percent of total firm revenue, or more than $100 billion.

Advertising takes many forms. About one-half of advertising spending is for space in newspapers and magazines, and about one-third is for commercials on television and radio. The rest is spent on various other ways of reaching customers, such as direct mail, billboards, and the Goodyear blimp.

THE DEBATE OVER ADVERTISING

Is society wasting the resources it devotes to advertising? Or does advertising serve a valuable purpose? Assessing the social value of advertising is difficult and often generates heated argument among economists. Let's consider both sides of the debate.

The Critique of Advertising Critics of advertising argue that firms advertise in order to manipulate people's tastes. Much advertising is psychological rather than informational. Consider, for example, the typical television commercial for some brand of soft drink. The commercial most likely does not tell the viewer about the product's price or quality. Instead, it might show a group of happy people at a party on a beach on a beautiful sunny day. In their hands are cans of the soft drink. The goal of the commercial is to convey a subconscious (if not subtle) message, "You too can have many friends and be happy, if only you drink our product." Critics of advertising argue that such a commercial creates a desire that otherwise might not exist.

Critics also argue that advertising impedes competition. Advertising often tries to convince consumers that products are more different than they truly are. By increasing the perception of product differentiation and fostering brand loyalty, advertising makes buyers less concerned with price differences among similar goods. With a less elastic demand curve, each firm charges a larger markup over marginal cost.

The Defense of Advertising Defenders of advertising argue that firms use advertising to provide information to customers. Advertising conveys the prices of the goods being offered for sale, the existence of new products, and the locations of retail outlets. This information allows customers to make better choices about what to buy and, thus, enhances the ability of markets to allocate resources efficiently.

Defenders also argue that advertising fosters competition. Because advertising allows customers to be more fully informed about all the firms in the market, customers can more easily take advantage of price differentials. Thus, each firm has less market power. In addition, advertising allows new firms to enter more easily, because it gives entrants a means to attract customers from existing firms.

Over time, policymakers have come to accept the view that advertising can make markets more competitive. One important example is the regulation of certain professions, such as lawyers, doctors, and pharmacists. In the past, these groups have succeeded in getting state governments to prohibit advertising in their fields on the grounds that advertising was "unprofessional." In recent years, however, the courts have concluded that the primary effect of these restrictions on advertising was to curtail competition. They have, therefore, overturned many of the laws that prohibit advertising.

CASE STUDY   ADVERTISING AND THE PRICE OF EYEGLASSES

What effect does advertising have on the price of a good? On the one hand, advertising might make consumers view products as being more different than they otherwise would. If so, it would make markets less competitive and firms' demand curves less elastic, and this would lead firms to charge higher prices. On the other hand, advertising might make it easier for consumers to find the firms offering the best prices. In this case, it would make markets more competitive and firms' demand curves more elastic, and this would lead to lower prices.

In an article published in the *Journal of Law and Economics* in 1972, economist Lee Benham tested these two views of advertising. In the United States during the 1960s, the various state governments had vastly different rules about advertising by optometrists. Some states allowed advertising for eyeglasses and eye examinations. Many states, however, prohibited it. For example, the Florida law read as follows:

> It is unlawful for any person, firm, or corporation to . . . advertise either
> directly or indirectly by any means whatsoever any definite or indefinite
> price or credit terms on prescriptive or corrective lens, frames, complete
> prescriptive or corrective glasses, or any optometric service. . . . This section
> is passed in the interest of public health, safety, and welfare, and its provi-
> sions shall be liberally construed to carry out its objects and purposes.

Professional optometrists enthusiastically endorsed these restrictions on advertising.

Benham used the differences in state law as a natural experiment to test the two views of advertising. The results were striking. In those states that prohibited advertising, the average price paid for a pair of eyeglasses was $33. (This number is not as low as it seems, for this price is from 1963, when all prices were much lower than they are today. To convert 1963 prices into today's dollars, you can multiply them by five.) In those states that did not restrict advertising, the average price was $26. Thus, advertising reduced average prices by more than 20 percent. In the market for eyeglasses, and probably in many other markets as well, advertising fosters competition and leads to lower prices for consumers.

ADVERTISING AS A SIGNAL OF QUALITY

Many types of advertising contain little apparent information about the product being advertised. Consider a firm introducing a new breakfast cereal. A typical advertisement might have some highly paid actor eating the cereal and exclaiming how wonderful it tastes. How much information does the advertisement really provide?

The answer is: more than you might think. Defenders of advertising argue that even advertising that appears to contain little hard information may in fact tell consumers something about product quality. The willingness of the firm to spend a large amount of money on advertising can itself be a *signal* to consumers about the quality of the product being offered.

Consider the problem facing two firms—Post and Kellogg. Each company has just come up with a recipe for a new cereal, which it would sell for $3 a box. To keep things simple, let's assume that the marginal cost of making cereal is zero, so the $3 is all profit. Each company knows that if it spends $10 million on advertising, it will get 1 million consumers to try its new cereal. And each company knows that if consumers like the cereal, they will buy it not once but many times.

Consider first Post's decision. Based on market research, Post knows that its cereal is only mediocre. Although advertising would sell one box to each of 1 million consumers, the consumers would quickly learn that the cereal is not very good and stop buying it. Post decides it is not worth paying $10 million in advertising to get only $3 million in sales. So it does not bother to advertise. It sends its cooks back to the drawing board to find another recipe.

Kellogg, on the other hand, knows that its cereal is great. Each person who tries it will buy a box a month for the next year. Thus, the $10 million in advertising will bring in $36 million in sales. Advertising is profitable here because Kellogg has a good product that consumers will buy repeatedly. Thus, Kellogg chooses to advertise.

Now that we have considered the behavior of the two firms, let's consider the behavior of consumers. We began by asserting that consumers are inclined to try a new cereal that they see advertised. But is this behavior rational? Should a consumer try a new cereal just because the seller has chosen to advertise it?

In fact, it may be completely rational for consumers to try new products that they see advertised. In our story, consumers decide to try Kellogg's new cereal because Kellogg advertises. Kellogg chooses to advertise because it knows that its cereal is quite good, while Post chooses not to advertise because it knows that its cereal is only mediocre. By its willingness to spend money on advertising, Kellogg signals to consumers the quality of its cereal. Each consumer thinks, quite sensibly, "Boy, if the Kellogg Company is willing to spend so much money advertising this new cereal, it must be really good."

What is most surprising about this theory of advertising is that the content of the advertisement is irrelevant. Kellogg signals the quality of its product by its willingness to spend money on advertising. What the advertisements say is not as important as the fact that consumers know ads are expensive. By contrast, cheap advertising cannot be effective at signaling quality to consumers. In our example, if an advertising campaign cost less than $3 million, both Post and Kellogg would use it to market their new cereals. Because both good and mediocre cereals would be advertised, consumers could not infer the quality of a new cereal from the fact that it is advertised. Over time, consumers would learn to ignore such cheap advertising.

This theory can explain why firms pay famous actors large amounts of money to make advertisements that, on the surface, appear to convey no information at all. The information is not in the advertisement's content, but simply in its existence and expense.

BRAND NAMES

Advertising is closely related to the existence of brand names. In many markets, there are two types of firms. Some firms sell products with widely recognized brand names, while other firms sell generic substitutes. For example, in a typical drugstore, you can find Bayer aspirin on the shelf next to a generic aspirin. In a typical grocery store, you can find Pepsi next to less familiar colas. Most often, the firm with the brand name spends more on advertising and charges a higher price for its product.

Just as there is disagreement about the economics of advertising, there is disagreement about the economics of brand names. Let's consider both sides of the debate.

Critics of brand names argue that brand names cause consumers to perceive differences that do not really exist. In many cases, the generic good is almost indistinguishable from the brand-name good. Consumers' willingness to pay more for the brand-name good, these critics assert, is a form of irrationality fostered by advertising. Economist Edward Chamberlin, one of the early developers of the theory of monopolistic competition, concluded from this argument that brand names were bad for the economy. He proposed that the government discourage their use by refusing to enforce the exclusive trademarks that companies use to identify their products.

More recently, economists have defended brand names as a useful way for consumers to ensure that the goods they buy are of high quality. There are two related arguments. First, brand names provide consumers *information* about quality when quality cannot be easily judged in advance of purchase. Second, brand names give firms an *incentive* to maintain high quality, since firms have a financial stake in maintaining the reputation of their brand names.

To see how these arguments work in practice, consider a famous brand name: McDonald's hamburgers. Imagine that you are driving through an unfamiliar town and want to stop for lunch. You see a McDonald's and a local restaurant next to it. Which do you choose? The local restaurant may in fact offer better food at lower prices, but you have no way of knowing that. By contrast, McDonald's offers a consistent product across many cities. Its brand name is useful to you as a way of judging the quality of what you are about to buy.

The McDonald's brand name also ensures that the company has an incentive to maintain quality. For example, if some customers were to become ill from bad food sold at a McDonald's, the news would be disastrous for the company. McDonald's would lose much of the valuable reputation that it has built up with years of expensive advertising. As a result, it would lose sales and profit not just in the outlet that sold the bad food but in its many outlets throughout the country. By contrast, if some customers were to become ill from bad food at a local restaurant, that restaurant might have to close down, but the lost profits would be much smaller. Hence, McDonald's has a greater incentive to ensure that its food is safe.

The debate over brand names thus centers on the question of whether consumers are rational in preferring brand names over generic substitutes. Critics of brand names argue that brand names are the result of an irrational consumer response to advertising. Defenders of brand names argue that consumers have good reason to pay more for brand-name products because they can be more confident in the quality of these products.

CASE STUDY   BRAND NAMES UNDER COMMUNISM

Defenders of brand names get some support for their view from experiences in the former Soviet Union. When the Soviet Union adhered to the principles of communism, central planners in the government replaced the invisible hand of the marketplace. Yet, just like consumers living in an economy with free markets, Soviet central planners learned that brand names were useful in helping to ensure product quality.

In an article published in the *Journal of Political Economy* in 1960, Marshall Goldman, an expert on the Soviet economy, described the Soviet experience:

> In the Soviet Union, production goals have been set almost solely in quantitative or value terms, with the result that, in order to meet the plan, quality is often sacrificed. . . . Among the methods adopted by the Soviets to deal with this problem, one is of particular interest to us—intentional product differentiation. . . . In order to distinguish one firm from similar firms in the same industry or ministry, each firm has its own name. Whenever it is physically possible, it is obligatory that the firm identify itself on the good or packaging with a "production mark."

Goldman quotes the analysis of a Soviet marketing expert:

> This [trademark] makes it easy to establish the actual producer of the product in case it is necessary to call him to account for the poor quality of his goods. For this reason, it is one of the most effective weapons in the battle for the quality of products. . . . The trademark makes it possible for the consumer to select the good which he likes. . . . This forces other firms to undertake measures to improve the quality of their own product in harmony with the demands of the consumer.

Goldman notes that "these arguments are clear enough and sound as if they might have been written by a bourgeois apologist."

IN THE NEWS

TV Networks as Brand Names

BRAND NAMES CONVEY INFORMATION TO consumers about the goods that firms are offering. Establishing a brand name—and ensuring that it conveys the right information—is an important strategy for many businesses, including TV networks.

A TV Season When Image Is Everything

BY STUART ELLIOTT

A marketing blitz to promote fall television programming, estimated at a record $400 million to $500 million, has been inundating America with a barrage of branding.

Branding is a shorthand term along Madison Avenue for attempts to create or burnish an identity or image, just as Coca-Cola seeks to distinguish itself from Pepsi-Cola. For the 1996-1997 prime-time broadcast television season,

which officially began this week, viewers have been swamped by the torrent of teasing practically since the 1995–1996 season ended in May.

At the center of those efforts is the most ambitious push ever by the broadcast networks to brand themselves and many of the blocks of programming they offer—a marked departure from the past, when they would promote only specific shows.

"The perception was that people watched shows, not networks," said Bob Bibb, who with Lewis Goldstein jointly heads marketing for WB, a fledgling network owned by Time Warner, Inc., and based in Burbank, California.

"But that was when there were only three networks, three choices," Mr. Bibb added, "and it was easy to find the shows you liked."

WB has been presenting a sassy singing cartoon character named Michigan J. Frog as its "spokesphibian," personifying the entire lineup of the "Dubba-dubba-WB"—as he insists upon calling the network.

"It's not a frog, it's an attitude," Mr. Bibb said, "a consistency from show to show."

In television, an intrinsic part of branding is selecting shows that seem related and might appeal to a certain audience segment. It means "developing an overall packaging of the network to

AN ATTITUDE, NOT JUST A FROG

build a relationship with viewers, so they will come to expect certain things from us," said Alan Cohen, executive vice president for the ABC-TV unit of the Walt Disney Company in New York.

That, he said, means defining the network so that "when you're watching ABC, you'll *know* you're watching ABC"—and to accomplish it in a way that appeals to the primary ABC audience of youngish urbanites and families with children.

SOURCE: *The New York Times*, September 20, 1996, p. D1.

QUICK QUIZ   How might advertising make markets less competitive? How might it make markets more competitive? ◆ Give the arguments for and against brand names.

CONCLUSION

Monopolistic competition is true to its name: It is a hybrid of monopoly and competition. Like a monopoly, each monopolistic competitor faces a downward-sloping demand curve and, as a result, charges a price above marginal cost. As in a competitive market, however, there are many firms, and entry and exit drive the profit of each monopolistic competitor toward zero.

Because monopolistically competitive firms produce differentiated products, each firm advertises in order to attract customers to its own brand. To some extent, advertising manipulates consumers' tastes, promotes irrational brand loyalty, and impedes competition. To a larger extent, advertising provides information, establishes brand names of reliable quality, and fosters competition.

The theory of monopolistic competition seems to describe many markets in the economy. It is somewhat disappointing, therefore, that the theory does not yield simple and compelling advice for public policy. From the standpoint of the economic theorist, the allocation of resources in monopolistically competitive markets is not perfect. Yet, from the standpoint of a practical policymaker, there may be little that can be done to improve it.

Summary

◆ A monopolistically competitive market is characterized by three attributes: many firms, differentiated products, and free entry.

◆ The equilibrium in a monopolistically competitive market differs from that in a perfectly competitive market in two related ways. First, each firm has excess capacity. That is, it operates on the downward-sloping portion of the average-total-cost curve. Second, each firm charges a price above marginal cost.

◆ Monopolistic competition does not have all the desirable properties of perfect competition. There is the standard deadweight loss of monopoly caused by the markup of price over marginal cost. In addition, the number of firms (and thus the variety of products) can be too large or too small. In practice, the ability of policymakers to correct these inefficiencies is limited.

◆ The product differentiation inherent in monopolistic competition leads to the use of advertising and brand names. Critics of advertising and brand names argue that firms use them to take advantage of consumer irrationality and to reduce competition. Defenders of advertising and brand names argue that firms use them to inform consumers and to compete more vigorously on price and product quality.

Key Concepts

monopolistic competition, p. 364

Questions for Review

1. Describe the three attributes of monopolistic competition. How is monopolistic competition like monopoly? How is it like perfect competition?

2. Draw a diagram of the long-run equilibrium in a monopolistically competitive market. How is price related to average total cost? How is price related to marginal cost?

3. Does a monopolistic competitor produce too much or too little output compared to the most efficient level?

What practical considerations make it difficult for policymakers to solve this problem?

4. How might advertising reduce economic well-being? How might advertising increase economic well-being?

5. How might advertising with no apparent informational content in fact convey information to consumers?

6. Explain two benefits that might arise from the existence of brand names.

Problems and Applications

1. Classify the following markets as perfectly competitive, monopolistic, or monopolistically competitive, and explain your answer.
   a. wooden #2 pencils
   b. bottled water
   c. copper
   d. local telephone service
   e. peanut butter
   f. lipstick

2. What feature of the product being sold distinguishes a monopolistically competitive firm from a monopolistic firm?

3. The chapter states that monopolistically competitive firms could increase the quantity they produce and lower the average total cost of production. Why don't they do so?

4. Sparkle is one firm of many in the market for toothpaste, which is in long-run equilibrium.

   a. Draw a diagram showing Sparkle's demand curve, marginal-revenue curve, average-total-cost curve, and marginal-cost curve. Label Sparkle's profit-maximizing output and price.
   b. What is Sparkle's profit? Explain.
   c. On your diagram, show the consumer surplus derived from the purchase of Sparkle toothpaste. Also show the deadweight loss relative to the efficient level of output.
   d. If the government forced Sparkle to produce the efficient level of output, what would happen to the firm? What would happen to Sparkle's customers?

5. Do monopolistically competitive markets typically have the optimal number of products? Explain.

6. Complete the following table by filling in YES, NO, or MAYBE for each type of market structure.

Do Firms:	Perfect Competition	Monopolistic Competition	Monopoly
Make differentiated products?			
Have excess capacity?			
Advertise?			
Pick Q so that $MR = MC$?			
Pick Q so that $P = MC$?			
Earn economic profits in long-run equilibrium?			
Face a downward-sloping demand curve?			
Have MR less than price?			
Face the entry of other firms?			
Exit in the long run if profits are less than zero?			

7. The chapter says that monopolistically competitive firms may send Christmas cards to their customers. What do they accomplish by this? Explain in words and with a diagram.

8. If you were thinking of entering the ice-cream business, would you try to make ice cream that is just like one of the existing brands? Explain your decision using the ideas of this chapter.

9. Describe three commercials that you have seen on TV. In what ways, if any, were each of these commercials socially useful? In what ways were they socially wasteful? Did the commercials affect the likelihood of your buying the product, and why?

10. For each of the following pairs of firms, explain which firm would be more likely to engage in advertising:
   a. a family-owned farm or a family-owned restaurant
   b. a manufacturer of forklifts or a manufacturer of cars
   c. a company that invented a very reliable watch or a company that invented a less reliable watch that costs the same amount to make

11. Twenty years ago the market for chicken was perfectly competitive. Then Frank Perdue began marketing chicken under his name.
   a. How do you suppose Perdue created a brand name for chicken? What did he gain from doing so?
   b. What did society gain from having brand-name chicken? What did society lose?

12. The makers of Tylenol pain reliever do a lot of advertising and have very loyal customers. In contrast, the makers of generic acetaminophen do no advertising, and their customers shop only for the lowest price. Assume that the marginal costs of Tylenol and generic acetaminophen are the same and constant.
   a. Draw a diagram showing Tylenol's demand, marginal-revenue, and marginal-cost curves. Label Tylenol's price and markup over marginal cost.
   b. Repeat part (a) for a producer of generic acetaminophen. How do the diagrams differ? Which company has the bigger markup? Explain.
   c. Which company has the bigger incentive for careful quality control? Why?

VI

THE ECONOMICS OF
LABOR MARKETS

18

THE MARKETS FOR THE
FACTORS OF PRODUCTION

When you finish school, your income will be determined largely by what kind of job you take. If you become a computer programmer, you will earn more than if you become a gas station attendant. This fact is not surprising, but it is not obvious why it is true. No law requires that computer programmers be paid more than gas station attendants. No ethical principle says that programmers are more deserving. What then determines which job will pay you the higher wage?

Your income, of course, is a small piece of a larger economic picture. In 1995 the total income of all U.S. residents was about $7 trillion. People earned this income in various ways. Workers earned about three-fourths of it in the form of wages and fringe benefits. The rest went to landowners and to the owners of *capital*—the economy's stock of equipment and structures—in the form of rent, profit, and interest. What determines how much goes to workers? To landowners? To the owners of capital? Why do some workers earn higher wages than others, some landowners higher rental income than others, and some capital owners greater profit than others? Why, in particular, do computer programmers earn more than gas station attendants?

The answer to these questions, like most in economics, hinges on supply and demand. The supply and demand for labor, land, and capital determine the prices paid to workers, landowners, and capital owners. To understand why some people have higher incomes than others, therefore, we need to look more deeply at the markets for the services they provide. That is our job in this and the next two chapters.

This chapter provides the basic theory for the analysis of factor markets. As you may recall from Chapter 2, the **factors of production** are the inputs used to produce goods and services. Labor, land, and capital are the three most important factors of production. When a computer firm produces a new software program, it uses programmers' time (labor), the physical space on which its offices sit (land), and an office building and computer equipment (capital). Similarly, when a gas station sells gas, it uses attendants' time (labor), the physical space (land), and the gas tanks and pumps (capital).

Although in many ways factor markets resemble the goods markets we have analyzed in previous chapters, they are different in one important way: The demand for a factor of production is a *derived demand*. That is, a firm's demand for a factor of production is derived from its decision to supply a good in another market. The demand for computer programmers is inextricably tied to the supply of computer software, and the demand for gas station attendants is inextricably tied to the supply of gasoline.

In this chapter we analyze factor demand by considering how a competitive, profit-maximizing firm decides how much of any factor to buy. We begin our analysis by examining the demand for labor. Labor is the most important factor of production, for workers receive most of the total income earned in the U.S. economy. Later in the chapter, we see that the lessons we learn about the labor market apply directly to the markets for the other factors of production.

The basic theory of factor markets developed in this chapter takes a large step toward explaining how the income of the U.S. economy is distributed among workers, landowners, and owners of capital. Chapter 19 will build on this analysis to examine in more detail why some workers earn more than others. Chapter 20 will examine how much inequality results from this process and then consider what role the government should and does play in altering the distribution of income.

factors of production

the inputs used to produce goods and services

A FIRM'S DEMAND FOR LABOR

Labor markets, like other markets in the economy, are governed by the forces of supply and demand. This is illustrated in Figure 18-1. In panel (a) the supply and demand for apples determine the price of apples. In panel (b) the supply and demand for apple pickers determine the price, or wage, of apple pickers.

As we have already noted, however, labor markets are different from most other markets because labor demand is a derived demand. Most labor services, rather than being final goods ready to be enjoyed by consumers, are inputs into the production of other goods. To understand labor demand, we need to focus on the firms that hire the labor and use it to produce goods for sale. By examining the link between the production of goods and the demand for labor, we gain insight into the determination of equilibrium wages.

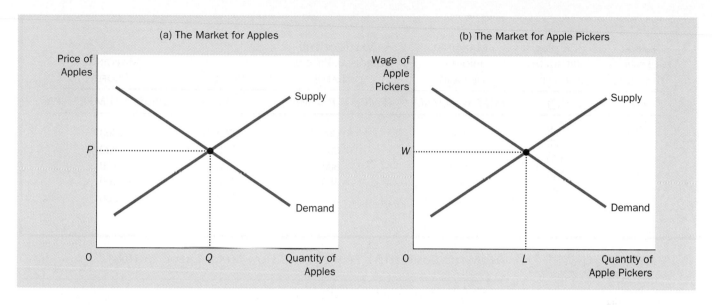

(a) The Market for Apples

(b) The Market for Apple Pickers

THE VERSATILITY OF SUPPLY AND DEMAND. The basic tools of supply and demand apply to goods and to labor services. Panel (a) shows how the supply and demand for apples determine the price of apples. Panel (b) shows how the supply and demand for apple pickers determine the wage of apple pickers.

Figure 18-1

THE COMPETITIVE PROFIT-MAXIMIZING FIRM

Let's look at how a typical firm, such as an apple producer, decides the quantity of labor to demand. The firm owns an apple orchard and each week must decide how many apple pickers to hire to harvest its crop. After the firm makes its hiring decision, the workers pick as many apples as they can. The firm then sells the apples, pays the workers, and keeps what is left as profit.

We make two assumptions about our firm. First, we assume that our firm is *competitive* both in the market for apples (where the firm is a seller) and in the market for apple pickers (where the firm is a buyer). Recall from Chapter 14 that a competitive firm is a price taker. Because there are many other firms selling apples and hiring apple pickers, a single firm has little influence over the price it gets for apples or the wage it pays apple pickers. The firm takes the price and the wage as given by market conditions. It only has to decide how many workers to hire and how many apples to sell.

Second, we assume that the firm is *profit-maximizing*. Thus, the firm does not directly care about the number of workers it has or the number of apples it produces. It cares only about profit, which equals the total revenue from the sale of apples minus the total cost of producing them. The firm's supply of apples and its demand for workers are derived from its primary goal of maximizing profit.

THE PRODUCTION FUNCTION AND THE MARGINAL PRODUCT OF LABOR

To make its hiring decision, the firm must consider how the size of its workforce affects the amount of output produced. In other words, it must consider how the

LABOR (NUMBER OF WORKERS)	OUTPUT (BUSHELS PER WEEK)	MARGINAL PRODUCT OF LABOR	VALUE OF THE MARGINAL PRODUCT OF LABOR	WAGE	MARGINAL PROFIT
(L)	(Q)	$(MPL = \Delta Q / \Delta L)$	$(VMPL = P \times MPL)$	(W)	$(\Delta Profit = VMPL - W)$
0	0				
		100	$1,000	$500	$500
1	100				
		80	800	500	300
2	180				
		60	600	500	100
3	240				
		40	400	500	−100
4	280				
		20	200	500	−300
5	300				

Table 18-1   HOW THE COMPETITIVE FIRM DECIDES HOW MUCH LABOR TO HIRE

production function

the relationship between quantity of inputs used to make a good and the quantity of output of that good

marginal product of labor

the increase in the amount of output from an additional unit of labor

diminishing marginal product

the property whereby the marginal product of an input declines as the quantity of the input increases

number of apple pickers affects the quantity of apples it can harvest and sell. Table 18-1 gives a numerical example. In the first column is the number of workers. In the second column is the quantity of apples the workers harvest each week.

These two columns of numbers describe the firm's ability to produce. As we noted in Chapter 13, economists use the term **production function** to describe the relationship between the quantity of the inputs used in production and the quantity of output from production. Here the "input" is the apple pickers and the "output" is the apples. The other inputs—the trees themselves, the land, the firm's trucks and tractors, and so on—are held fixed for now. This firm's production function shows that if the firm hires 1 worker, that worker will pick 100 bushels of apples per week. If the firm hires 2 workers, the two workers together will pick 180 bushels per week, and so on.

Figure 18-2 graphs the data on labor and output presented in Table 18-1. The number of workers is on the horizontal axis, and the amount of output is on the vertical axis. This figure illustrates the production function.

One of the *Ten Principles of Economics* introduced in Chapter 1 is that rational people think at the margin. This idea is the key to understanding how firms decide what quantity of labor to hire. To take a step toward this decision, the third column in Table 18-1 gives the **marginal product of labor,** the increase in the amount of output from an additional unit of labor. When the firm increases the number of workers from 1 to 2, for example, the amount of apples produced rises from 100 to 180 bushels. Therefore, the marginal product of the second worker is 80 bushels.

Notice that as the number of workers increases, the marginal product of labor declines. As you may recall from Chapter 13, this property is called **diminishing marginal product.** At first, when only a few workers are hired, they pick apples from the best trees in the orchard. As the number of workers increases, additional workers have to pick from the trees with fewer apples. Hence, as more and more workers are hired, each additional worker contributes less to the production of apples. For this reason, the production function in Figure 18-2 becomes flatter as the number of workers rises.

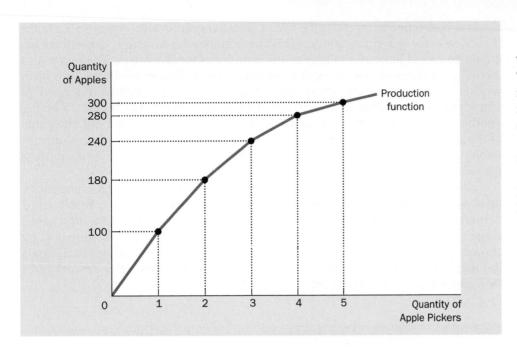

Figure 18-2

THE PRODUCTION FUNCTION.
The production function is the
relationship between the inputs
into production (apple pickers)
and the output from production
(apples). As the quantity of the
input increases, the production
function gets flatter, reflecting the
property of diminishing marginal
product.

THE VALUE OF THE MARGINAL PRODUCT
AND THE DEMAND FOR LABOR

Our profit-maximizing firm is concerned more with money than with apples. As
a result, when deciding how many workers to hire, the firm considers how much
profit each worker would bring in. Because profit is total revenue minus total
cost, the profit from an additional worker is the worker's contribution to revenue minus the worker's wage.

To find the worker's contribution to revenue, we must convert the marginal
product of labor (which is measured in bushels of apples) into the *value* of the
marginal product (which is measured in dollars). We do this using the price of
apples. To continue our example, if a bushel of apples sells for $10 and if an
additional worker produces 80 bushels of apples, then the worker produces $800
of revenue.

The **value of the marginal product** of any input is the marginal product of
that input multiplied by the market price of the output. The fourth column in
Table 18-1 shows the value of the marginal product of labor in our example,
assuming the price of apples is $10 per bushel. Because the market price is con-
stant for a competitive firm, the value of the marginal product (like the marginal
product itself) diminishes as the number of workers rises.

Now consider how many workers the firm will hire. Suppose that the market wage for apple pickers is $500 per week. In this case, the first worker that
the firm hires is profitable: The first worker yields $1,000 in revenue, or $500 in
profit. Similarly, the second worker yields $800 in additional revenue, or $300 in
profit. The third worker produces $600 in additional revenue, or $100 in profit.
After the third worker, however, hiring workers is unprofitable. The fourth
worker would yield only $400 of additional revenue. Because the worker's wage
is $500, hiring the fourth worker would mean a $100 reduction in profit. Thus,
the firm hires only three workers.

**value of the marginal
product**
*the marginal product of an input
times the price of the output*

It is instructive to consider the firm's decision graphically. Figure 18-3 graphs the value of the marginal product. This curve slopes downward because the marginal product of labor diminishes as the number of workers rises. The figure also includes a horizontal line at the market wage. To maximize profit, the firm hires workers up to the point where these two curves cross. Below this level of employment, the value of the marginal product exceeds the wage, so hiring another worker would increase profit. Above this level of employment, the value of the marginal product is less than the wage, so the marginal worker is unprofitable. Thus, *a competitive, profit-maximizing firm hires workers up to the point where the value of the marginal product of labor equals the wage.*

Having explained the profit-maximizing hiring strategy for a competitive firm, we can now offer a theory of labor demand. Recall that a firm's labor demand curve tells us the quantity of labor that a firm demands at any given wage. We have just seen in Figure 18-3 that the firm makes that decision by choosing the quantity of labor at which the value of the marginal product equals the wage. As a result, *the value-of-marginal-product curve is the labor demand curve for a competitive, profit-maximizing firm.*

FYI

Input Demand and Output Supply: Two Sides of the Same Coin

IN CHAPTER 14 WE SAW HOW A competitive, profit-maximizing firm decides how much of its output to sell: It chooses the quantity of output at which the price of the good equals the marginal cost of production. We have just seen how such a firm decides how much labor to hire: It chooses the quantity of labor at which the wage equals the value of the marginal product. Because the production function links the quantity of inputs to the quantity of output, you should not be surprised to learn that the firm's decision about input demand is closely linked to its decision about output supply. In fact, these two decisions are two sides of the same coin.

To see this relationship more fully, let's consider how the marginal product of labor (*MPL*) and marginal cost (*MC*) are related. Suppose an additional worker costs $500 and has a marginal product of 50 bushels of apples. In this case, producing 50 more bushels costs $500; the marginal cost of a bushel is $500/50, or $10. More generally, if *W* is the wage, and an extra unit of labor produces *MPL* units of output, then the marginal cost of a unit of output is $MC = W/MPL$.

This analysis shows that diminishing marginal product is closely related to increasing marginal cost. When our apple orchard grows crowded with workers, each additional worker adds less to the production of apples (*MPL* falls). Similarly, when the apple firm is producing a large quantity of apples, the orchard is already crowded with workers, so it is more costly to produce an additional bushel of apples (*MC* rises).

Now consider our criterion for profit maximization. We determined earlier that a profit-maximizing firm chooses the quantity of labor so that the value of the marginal product ($P \times MPL$) equals the wage (*W*). We can write this mathematically as

$$P \times MPL = W.$$

If we divide both sides of this equation by *MPL*, we obtain

$$P = W/MPL.$$

We just noted that W/MPL equals marginal cost *MC*. Therefore, we can substitute to obtain

$$P = MC.$$

This equation states that the price of the firm's output is equal to the marginal cost of producing a unit of output. Thus, *when a competitive firm hires labor up to the point at which the value of the marginal product equals the wage, it also produces up to the point at which the price equals marginal cost.* Our analysis of labor demand in this chapter is just another way of looking at the production decision we first saw in Chapter 14.

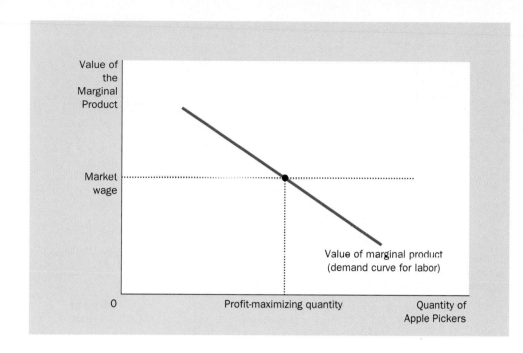

Figure 18-3

THE VALUE OF THE MARGINAL PRODUCT OF LABOR. This figure shows how the value of the marginal product (the marginal product times the price of the output) depends on the number of workers. The curve slopes downward because of diminishing marginal product. For a competitive, profit-maximizing firm, this value-of-marginal-product curve is also the firm's labor demand curve.

QUICK QUIZ Define *marginal product of labor* and *value of the marginal product of labor.* ◆ Describe how a competitive, profit-maximizing firm decides how many workers to hire.

LABOR-MARKET EQUILIBRIUM

Having considered the hiring decision of the typical competitive, profit-maximizing firm, let's return to the larger market for labor in which this firm is one of many buyers.

MARGINAL PRODUCTIVITY IN EQUILIBRIUM

So far we have established two facts about how wages are determined in competitive labor markets:

◆   The wage adjusts to balance the supply and demand for labor.
◆   The wage equals the value of the marginal product of labor.

At first, it might seem surprising that the wage can do both these things at once. In fact, there is no real puzzle here, but understanding why there is no puzzle is an important step to understanding wage determination.

Figure 18-4 shows the labor market in equilibrium. The wage and the quantity of labor have adjusted to balance supply and demand. When the market is

Figure 18-4

EQUILIBRIUM IN A LABOR MAR-
KET. Like all prices, the price of
labor (the wage) depends on
supply and demand. Because the
demand curve reflects the value
of the marginal product of labor,
in equilibrium workers receive
the value of their marginal contribution to the production of goods
and services.

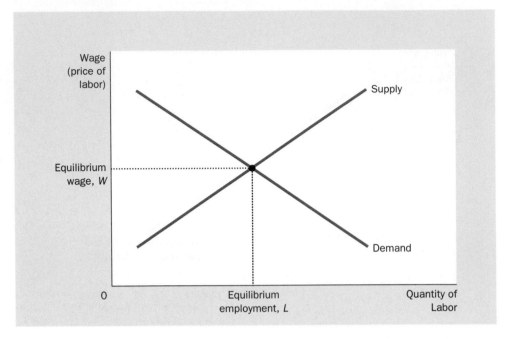

in this equilibrium, each firm has bought as much labor as it finds profitable at
the equilibrium wage. That is, each firm has followed the rule for profit maximization: It has hired workers until the value of the marginal product equals the
wage. Hence, the wage must equal the value of marginal product of labor once
it has brought supply and demand into equilibrium.

This brings us to an important lesson: *Any event that changes the supply or
demand for labor must change the equilibrium wage and the value of the marginal product by the same amount, because these must always be equal.* To see how this works,
let's consider some events that shift these curves.

SHIFTS IN LABOR SUPPLY

Suppose that immigration increases the number of workers willing to pick
apples. As Figure 18-5 shows, the supply of labor shifts to the right from S_1 to
S_2. At the initial wage W_1, the quantity of labor supplied now exceeds the quantity demanded. This surplus of labor puts downward pressure on the wage of
apple pickers, and the fall in the wage in turn makes it profitable for firms to
hire more workers. As the number of workers employed in each apple orchard
rises, the marginal product of a worker falls, and so does the value of the marginal product. In the new equilibrium, both the wage and the value of the marginal product of labor are lower than they were before the influx of new workers.

An episode from Israel illustrates how a shift in labor supply can alter the
equilibrium in a labor market. During most of the 1980s, many thousands of
Palestinians regularly commuted from their homes in the Israeli-occupied West
Bank and Gaza Strip to jobs in Israel, primarily in the construction and agriculture industries. In 1988, however, political unrest in these occupied areas induced

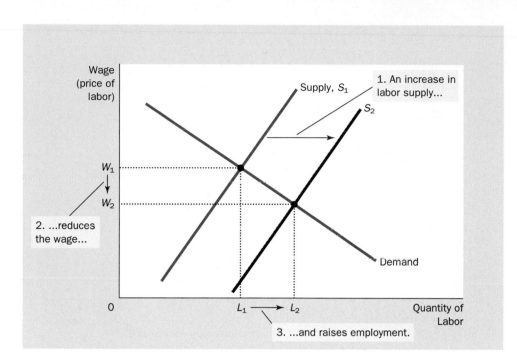

Figure 18-5

A SHIFT IN LABOR SUPPLY. When labor supply increases from S_1 to S_2, perhaps because of an immigration of new workers, the equilibrium wage falls from W_1 to W_2. At this lower wage, firms hire more labor, so employment rises from L_1 to L_2. The change in the wage reflects a change in the value of the marginal product of labor: With more workers, the added output from an extra worker is smaller.

the Israeli government to take steps that, as a by-product, reduced this supply of workers. Curfews were imposed, work permits were checked more thoroughly, and a ban on overnight stays of Palestinians in Israel was enforced more rigorously. The economic impact of these steps was exactly as theory predicts: The number of Palestinians with jobs in Israel fell by half, while those that continued to work in Israel enjoyed wage increases of about 50 percent. With a reduced number of Palestinian workers in Israel, the value of the marginal product of the remaining workers was much higher.

SHIFTS IN LABOR DEMAND

Now suppose that an increase in the popularity of apples causes their price to rise. This price increase does not change the marginal product of labor for any given number of workers, but it does raise the *value* of the marginal product. With a higher price of apples, hiring more apple pickers is now profitable. As Figure 18-6 shows, when the demand for labor shifts to the right from D_1 to D_2, the equilibrium wage rises from W_1 to W_2, and equilibrium employment rises from L_1 to L_2. Once again, the wage and the value of the marginal product of labor move together.

This analysis shows that prosperity for firms in an industry is often linked to prosperity for workers in that industry. When the price of apples rises, apple producers make greater profit, and apple pickers earn higher wages. When the price of apples falls, apple producers earn smaller profit, and apple pickers earn lower wages. This lesson is well known to workers in industries with highly volatile prices. Workers in oil fields, for instance, know from experience that their earnings are closely linked to the world price of crude oil.

Figure 18-6

A Shift in Labor Demand. When labor demand increases from D_1 to D_2, perhaps because of an increase in the price of the firms' output, the equilibrium wage rises from W_1 to W_2, and employment rises from L_1 to L_2. Again, the change in the wage reflects a change in the value of the marginal product of labor: With a higher output price, the added output from an extra worker is more valuable.

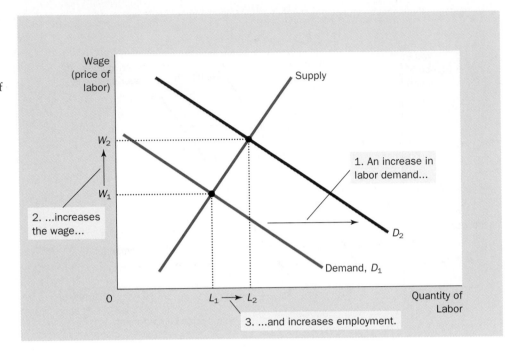

From these examples, you should now have a good understanding of how wages are set in competitive labor markets. Labor supply and labor demand together determine the equilibrium wage, and shifts in the supply or demand curve for labor cause the equilibrium wage to change. At the same time, profit maximization by the firms that demand labor ensures that the equilibrium wage always equals the value of the marginal product of labor.

CASE STUDY PRODUCTIVITY AND WAGES

One of the *Ten Principles of Economics* in Chapter 1 is that our standard of living depends on our ability to produce goods and services. We can now see how this principle works in the market for labor. In particular, our analysis of labor demand shows that wages equal productivity as measured by the value of the marginal product of labor. Put simply, highly productive workers are highly paid, and less productive workers are less highly paid.

This lesson is key to understanding why workers today are better off than workers in previous generations. Table 18-2 presents some data on growth in productivity and growth in wages (adjusted for inflation). From 1959 to 1994, productivity as measured by output per hour of work grew about 1.8 percent per year; at this rate, productivity doubles about every 40 years. Over this period, wages grew at a similar (but somewhat slower) rate of 1.2 percent per year.

Table 18-2 also shows that growth in productivity slowed around 1973 from 2.9 to 1.0 percent per year. This 1.9 percentage-point slowdown in productivity coincided with a slowdown in wage growth of 2.1 percentage points. Because of this productivity slowdown, young workers today cannot expect the same rapid growth in living standards that their parents enjoyed. A slow-

Table 18-2

PRODUCTIVITY AND WAGE
GROWTH IN THE UNITED STATES

TIME PERIOD	GROWTH RATE OF PRODUCTIVITY	GROWTH RATE OF WAGES
1959–1994	1.8	1.2
1959–1973	2.9	2.4
1973–1994	1.0	0.3

SOURCE: *Economic Report of the President 1996,* Table B-45, p. 332. Growth in productivity is measured here as the annualized rate of change in output per hour in the nonfarm business sector. Growth in wages is measured as the annualized change in real compensation per hour in the nonfarm business sector. These productivity data measure average productivity—the quantity of output divided by the quantity of labor—rather than marginal productivity, but average and marginal productivity are thought to move closely together.

Table 18-3

PRODUCTIVITY AND WAGE
GROWTH AROUND THE WORLD

COUNTRY	GROWTH RATE OF PRODUCTIVITY	GROWTH RATE OF WAGES
South Korea	8.5	7.9
Hong Kong	5.5	4.9
Singapore	5.3	5.0
Indonesia	4.0	4.4
Japan	3.6	2.0
India	3.1	3.4
United Kingdom	2.4	2.4
United States	1.7	0.5
Brazil	0.4	−2.4
Mexico	−0.2	−3.0
Argentina	−0.9	−1.3
Iran	−1.4	−7.9

SOURCE: *World Development Report 1994,* Table 1, pp. 162–163, and Table 7, pp. 174–175. Growth in productivity is measured here as the annualized rate of change in gross national product per person from 1980 to 1992. Growth in wages is measured as the annualized change in earnings per employee in manufacturing from 1980 to 1991.

down of 1.9 percentage points might not seem large, but accumulated over many years, even a small change in a growth rate is significant. If productivity and wages had grown at the same rate since 1973 as they did previously, workers' earnings would now be about 50 percent higher than they are.

The link between productivity and wages also sheds light on international experience. Table 18-3 presents some data on productivity growth and wage growth for a representative group of countries, ranked in order of their productivity growth. Although these international data are far from precise, a close link between the two variables is apparent. In South Korea, Hong Kong, and Singapore, productivity has grown rapidly, and so have wages. In Mexico, Argentina, and Iran, productivity has fallen, and so have wages. The United States falls in the middle of the distribution: By international standards,

U.S. productivity growth and wage growth have been neither exceptionally bad nor exceptionally good.

What causes productivity and wages to vary so much over time and across countries? A complete answer to this question requires an analysis of long-run economic growth, a topic beyond the scope of this chapter. We can, however, briefly note three key determinants of productivity:

◆ *Physical capital:* When workers work with a larger quantity of equipment and structures, they produce more.

◆ *Human capital:* When workers are more educated, they produce more.

◆ *Technological knowledge:* When workers have access to more sophisticated technologies, they produce more.

Physical capital, human capital, and technological knowledge are the ultimate sources of most of the differences in productivity, wages, and standards of living.

QUICK QUIZ How does an immigration of workers affect labor supply, labor demand, the marginal product of labor, and the equilibrium wage?

THE OTHER FACTORS OF PRODUCTION: LAND AND CAPITAL

We have seen how firms decide how much labor to hire and how these decisions determine workers' wages. At the same time that firms are hiring workers, they are also deciding about other inputs to production. For example, our apple-producing firm might have to choose the size of its apple orchard and the number of ladders to make available to its apple pickers. We can think of the firm's factors of production as falling into three categories: labor, land, and capital.

The meaning of the terms *labor* and *land* is clear, but the definition of *capital* is somewhat tricky. Economists use the term **capital** to refer to the stock of equipment and structures used for production. That is, the economy's capital represents the accumulation of goods produced in the past that are being used in the present to produce new goods and services. For our apple firm, the capital stock includes the ladders used to climb the trees, the trucks used to transport the apples, the buildings used to store the apples, and even the trees themselves.

capital
the equipment and structures used to produce goods and services

EQUILIBRIUM IN THE MARKETS FOR LAND AND CAPITAL

What determines how much the owners of land and capital earn for their contribution to the production process? Before answering this question, we need to distinguish between two prices: the purchase price and the rental price. The *purchase price* of land or capital is the price a person pays to own that factor of production indefinitely. The *rental price* is the price a person pays to use that factor for a limited period of time. It is important to keep this distinction in mind

THE MARKETS FOR LAND AND CAPITAL. Supply and demand determine the compensation paid to the owners of land, as shown in panel (a), and the compensation paid to the owners of capital, as shown in panel (b). The demand for each factor, in turn, depends on the value of the marginal product of that factor.

Figure 18-7

because, as we will see, these prices are determined by somewhat different economic forces.

Having defined these terms, we can now apply the theory of factor demand we developed for the labor market to the markets for land and capital. The wage is, after all, simply the rental price of labor. Therefore, much of what we have learned about wage determination applies also to the rental prices of land and capital. As Figure 18-7 illustrates, the rental price of land, shown in panel (a), and the rental price of capital, shown in panel (b), are determined by supply and demand. Moreover, the demand for land and capital is determined just like the demand for labor. That is, when our apple-producing firm is deciding how much land and how many ladders to rent, it follows the same logic as when deciding how many workers to hire. For both land and capital, the firm increases the quantity hired until the value of the factor's marginal product equals the factor's price. Thus, the demand curve for each factor reflects the marginal productivity of that factor.

We can now explain how much income goes to labor, how much goes to landowners, and how much goes to the owners of capital. As long as the firms using the factors of production are competitive and profit-maximizing, each factor's rental price must equal the value of the marginal product for that factor. *Labor, land, and capital each earn the value of their marginal contribution to the production process.*

Now consider the purchase price of land and capital. The rental price and the purchase price are obviously related: Buyers are willing to pay more to buy a piece of land or capital if it produces a valuable stream of rental income. And, as we have just seen, the equilibrium rental income at any point in time equals the value of that factor's marginal product. Therefore, the equilibrium purchase

FYI

The Various
Forms of Capital
Income

WHEN DISCUSSING THE IN-come earned by the owners of capital, we have been implicitly assuming that households own capital and rent it to the firms that use it. This assumption simplified our analysis of how capital owners are compensated, but it is not entirely realistic. In fact, firms usually own the capital they use and, therefore, they receive the earnings from this capital.

These earnings eventually get paid from firms to households in various ways. Some of it gets paid in the form of interest to those households who have lent money to firms. Bondholders and bank depositors are two examples of recipients of interest. Thus, when you receive interest on your bank account, that income is part of the economy's capital income.

In addition, some of the earnings from capital are paid to households in the form of dividends. Dividends are payments by a firm to the firm's stockholders. A stockholder is a person who has bought a share in the ownership of the firm and, therefore, is entitled to share in the firm's profits.

A firm does not have to pay out all of its earnings to households in the form of interest and dividends. Instead, it can retain some earnings within the firm and use these earnings to buy additional capital. Although these retained earnings do not get paid to the firm's stockholders, the stockholders benefit from them nonetheless. Because retained earnings increase the amount of capital the firm owns, they tend to increase future earnings and, thereby, the value of the firm's stock.

These institutional details are interesting and important, but they do not alter our conclusion about the income earned by the owners of capital. Capital is paid according to the value of its marginal product, regardless of whether this income gets transmitted to households in the form of interest or dividends or whether it is kept within firms as retained earnings.

price of a piece of land or capital depends on both the current value of the marginal product and the value of the marginal product expected to prevail in the future.

LINKAGES AMONG THE FACTORS OF PRODUCTION

We have seen that the price paid to any factor of production—labor, land, or capital—equals the value of the marginal product of that factor. The marginal product of any factor, in turn, depends on the quantity of that factor that is available. Because of diminishing returns, a factor in abundant supply has a low marginal product and thus a low price, and a factor in scarce supply has a high marginal product and a high price. As a result, when the supply of a factor falls, its equilibrium factor price rises.

When the supply of any factor changes, however, the effects are not limited to the market for that factor. In most situations, factors of production are used together in a way that makes the productivity of each factor dependent on the quantities of the other factors available to be used in the production process. As a result, a change in the supply of any one factor alters the earnings of all the factors.

For example, suppose that a hurricane destroys many of the ladders that workers use to pick apples from the orchards. What happens to the earnings of the various factors of production? Most obviously, the supply of ladders falls and, therefore, the equilibrium rental price of ladders rises. Those owners who were lucky enough to avoid damage to their ladders now earn a higher return when they rent out their ladders to the firms that produce apples.

Yet the effects of this event do not stop at the ladder market. Because there are fewer ladders with which to work, the workers who pick apples have a smaller marginal product. Thus, the reduction in the supply of ladders reduces the demand for apple pickers, and this causes the equilibrium wage to fall.

This story shows a general lesson: An event that changes the supply of any factor of production can alter the earnings of all the factors. The change in earnings of any factor can be found by analyzing the impact of the event on the value of the marginal product of that factor.

CASE STUDY THE ECONOMICS OF THE BLACK DEATH

In fourteenth century Europe, the bubonic plague wiped out about one-third of the population within a few years. This event, called the *Black Death*, provides a grisly natural experiment to test the theory of factor markets that we have just developed. Consider the effects of the Black Death on those who were lucky enough to survive. What do you think happened to the wages earned by workers and the rents earned by landowners?

To answer this question, let's examine the effects of a reduced population on the marginal product of labor and the marginal product of land. With a smaller supply of workers, the marginal product of labor rises. (This is simply diminishing marginal product working in reverse.) Thus, we would expect the Black Death to raise wages.

Because land and labor are used together in production, a smaller supply of workers also affects the market for land, the other major factor of production in medieval Europe. With fewer workers available to farm the land, an additional unit of land produced less additional output. In other words, the marginal product of land fell. Thus, we would expect the Black Death to lower rents.

In fact, both predictions are consistent with the historical evidence. Wages approximately doubled during this period, and rents declined 50 percent or more. The Black Death led to economic prosperity for the peasant classes and reduced incomes for the landed classes.

The surviving workers were lucky in more ways than one.

QUICK QUIZ What determines the income of the owners of land and capital? ◆ How would an increase in the quantity of capital affect the incomes of those who already own capital? How would it affect the incomes of workers?

CONCLUSION

This chapter explained how labor, land, and capital are compensated for the roles they play in the production process. The theory developed here is called the *neoclassical theory of distribution*. According to the neoclassical theory, the amount paid to each factor of production depends on the supply and demand for that factor. The demand, in turn, depends on that particular factor's marginal productivity. In equilibrium, each factor of production earns the value of its marginal contribution to the production of goods and services.

The neoclassical theory of distribution is widely accepted. Most economists begin with the neoclassical theory when trying to explain how the U.S. economy's $7 trillion of income is distributed among the economy's various members. In the following two chapters, we consider the distribution of income in more detail. As you will see, the neoclassical theory provides the framework for this discussion.

Even at this point you can use the theory to answer the question that began this chapter: Why are computer programmers paid more than gas station attendants? It is because programmers can produce a good of greater market value than can a gas station attendant. People are willing to pay dearly for a good computer game, but they are willing to pay little to have their gas pumped and their windshield washed. The wages of these workers reflect the market prices of the goods they produce. If people suddenly got tired of using computers and decided to spend more time driving, the prices of these goods would change, and so would the equilibrium wages of these two groups of workers.

Summary

◆ The economy's income is distributed in the markets for the factors of production. The three most important factors of production are labor, land, and capital.

◆ The demand for factors is a derived demand that comes from firms that use the factors to produce goods and services. Competitive, profit-maximizing firms hire each factor up to the point at which the value of the marginal product of the factor equals its price.

◆ The price paid to each factor adjusts to balance the supply and demand for that factor. Because factor demand

reflects the value of the marginal product of that factor, in equilibrium each factor is compensated according to its marginal contribution to the production of goods and services.

◆ Because factors of production are used together, the marginal product of any one factor depends on the quantities of all factors that are available. As a result, a change in the supply of one factor alters the equilibrium earnings of all the factors.

Key Concepts

factors of production, p. 384
production function, p. 386

marginal product of labor, p. 386
diminishing marginal product, p. 386

value of the marginal product, p. 387
capital, p. 394

Questions for Review

1. Explain how a firm's production function is related to its marginal product of labor.

2. Explain how a firm's marginal product of labor is related to the value of its marginal product.

3. Explain how a firm's value of marginal product is related to its demand for labor.

4. If the population of the United States suddenly grew because of a large immigration, what would happen to wages? What would happen to the rents earned by the owners of land and capital?

Problems and Applications

1. Suppose that the president proposes a new law aimed at reducing heath care costs: All Americans are to be required to eat one apple daily.
    a. How would this apple-a-day law affect the demand and equilibrium price of apples?
    b. How would the law affect the marginal product and the value of the marginal product of apple pickers?
    c. How would the law affect the demand and equilibrium wage for apple pickers?

2. Henry Ford once said: "It is not the employer who pays wages—he only handles the money. It is the product that pays wages." Explain.

3. Show the effect of each of the following events on the market for labor in the computer manufacturing industry:
    a. Congress buys personal computers for all American college students.
    b. More college students major in engineering and computer science.
    c. Computer firms build new manufacturing plants.

4. Explain why a profit-maximizing firm hires a factor of production up to the point at which the factor's value of marginal product equals its price, rather than hiring a smaller amount that would have a much higher value of marginal product.

5. Your enterprising uncle opens a sandwich shop that employs 7 people. The employees are paid $6 per hour,

and a sandwich sells for $3. If your uncle is maximizing his profit, what is the value of the marginal product of the last worker he hired? What is that worker's marginal product?

6. During the 1980s the United States experienced a significant inflow of capital from other countries. For example, Toyota, BMW, and other foreign car companies built auto plants in the United States.
    a. Using a diagram of the U.S. capital market, show the effect of this inflow on the rental price of capital in the United States and on the quantity of capital in use.
    b. Using a diagram of the U.S. labor market, show the effect of the capital inflow on the average wage paid to U.S. workers.

7. Suppose that labor is the only input used by a perfectly competitive firm that can hire workers for $50 per day. The firm's production function is as follows:

DAYS OF LABOR	UNITS OF OUTPUT
0	0
1	7
2	13
3	19
4	25
5	28
6	29

Each unit of output sells for $10. Plot the firm's demand for labor. How many days of labor should the firm hire? Show this point on your graph.

8. (This question is challenging.) In recent years some policymakers have proposed requiring firms to give workers certain fringe benefits. For example, in 1993, President Clinton proposed requiring firms to provide health insurance to their workers. Let's consider the effects of such a policy on the labor market.

    a. Suppose that a law required firms to give each worker $3 of fringe benefits for every hour that the worker is employed by the firm. How does this law affect the marginal profit that a firm earns from each worker? How does the law affect the demand curve for labor? Draw your answer on a graph with the cash wage on the vertical axis.

    b. If there is no change in labor supply, how would this law affect employment and wages?

    c. Why might the labor supply curve shift in response to this law? Would this shift in labor supply raise or lower the impact of the law on wages and employment?

    d. As Chapter 6 discussed, the wages of some workers, particularly the unskilled and inexperienced, are kept above the equilibrium level by minimum-wage laws. What effect would a fringe-benefit mandate have for these workers?

9. (This question is challenging.) This chapter has assumed that labor is supplied by individual workers acting competitively. In some markets, however, the supply of labor is determined by a union of workers.

    a. Explain why the situation faced by a labor union may resemble the situation faced by a monopoly firm.

    b. The goal of a monopoly firm is to maximize profits. Is there an analogous goal for labor unions?

    c. Now extend the analogy between monopoly firms and unions. How do you suppose that the wage set by a union compares to the wage in a competitive market? How do you suppose employment differs in the two cases?

    d. What other goals might unions have that make unions different from monopoly firms?

19

EARNINGS AND
DISCRIMINATION

In 1994, the average baseball player in the major leagues earned $1.2 million, the average physician earned $177,000, and the average factory worker earned $22,000. These three examples illustrate the large differences in earnings that are so common in our economy. These differences explain why some people live in mansions, ride in limousines, and vacation on the French Riviera, while other people live in small apartments, ride the bus, and vacation in their own backyards.

What causes earnings to vary so much from person to person? Chapter 18, which developed the basic neoclassical theory of the labor market, offers an answer to this question. There we saw that wages are governed by labor supply and labor demand. Labor demand, in turn, reflects the marginal productivity of labor. In equilibrium, each worker is paid the value of his or her marginal contribution to the economy's production of goods and services.

This theory of the labor market, though widely accepted by economists, is only the beginning of the story. To understand the wide variation in earnings that we observe, we must go beyond this general framework and examine more precisely what determines the supply and demand for different types of labor. That is our goal in this chapter.

SOME DETERMINANTS OF EQUILIBRIUM WAGES

Workers differ from one another in many ways. Jobs also have differing characteristics—both in terms of the wage they pay and in terms of their nonmonetary attributes. In this section we consider how the characteristics of workers and jobs affect labor supply, labor demand, and equilibrium wages.

COMPENSATING DIFFERENTIALS

When a worker is deciding whether to take a job, the wage is only one of many job attributes that the worker takes into account. Some jobs are easy, fun, and safe; others are hard, dull, and dangerous. The better the job as gauged by these nonmonetary characteristics, the more people there are who are willing to do the job at any given wage. In other words, the supply of labor for easy, fun, and safe jobs is greater than the supply of labor for hard, dull, and dangerous jobs. As a result, "good" jobs will tend to have lower equilibrium wages than "bad" jobs.

For example, imagine you are looking for a summer job in the local beach community. Two kinds of jobs are available. You can take a job as a beach-badge checker, or you can take a job as a garbage collector. The beach-badge checkers take leisurely strolls along the beach during the day and check to make sure the

"On the one hand, I know I could make more money if I left public service for the private sector, but, on the other hand, I couldn't chop off heads."

tourists have bought the required beach permits. The garbage collectors wake up before dawn to drive dirty, noisy trucks around town to pick up garbage. Which job would you want? Most people would prefer the beach job if the wages were the same. In order to get people to become garbage collectors, the town has to offer higher wages to garbage collectors than to beach-badge checkers.

Economists use the term **compensating differential** to refer to a difference in wages that arises from nonmonetary characteristics of different jobs. Compensating differentials are prevalent in the economy. Here are some examples:

compensating differential
a difference in wages that arises to offset the nonmonetary characteristics of different jobs

♦ Coal miners are paid more than other workers with similar levels of education. Their higher wage compensates them for the dirty and dangerous nature of coal mining, as well as the long-term health problems that coal miners experience.

♦ Workers who work the night shift at factories are paid more than similar workers who work the day shift. The higher wage compensates them for having to work at night and sleep during the day, a lifestyle that most people find undesirable.

♦ Professors are paid less than lawyers and doctors, who have similar amounts of education. Professors' lower wages compensate them for the great intellectual and personal satisfaction that their jobs offer. (Indeed, teaching economics is so much fun that it is surprising that economics professors get paid anything at all!)

HUMAN CAPITAL

As we discussed in the previous chapter, the word *capital* usually refers to the economy's stock of equipment and structures. The capital stock includes the farmer's tractor, the manufacturer's factory, and the teacher's blackboard. The essence of capital is that it is a factor of production that itself has been produced.

There is another type of capital that, while less tangible than physical capital, is just as important to the economy's production. **Human capital** is the accumulation of investments in people. The most important type of human capital is education. Like all forms of capital, education represents an expenditure of resources at one point in time to raise productivity in the future. But, unlike an investment in other forms of capital, an investment in education is tied to a specific person, and this linkage is what makes it human capital.

human capital
the accumulation of investments in people, such as education and on-the-job training

Not surprisingly, workers with more human capital on average earn more than those with less human capital. College graduates in the United States, for example, earn about 65 percent more than those workers who end their education with a high school diploma. This large difference has been documented in many countries around the world. It tends to be even larger in less developed countries, where educated workers are in scarce supply.

It is easy to see why education raises wages from the perspective of supply and demand. Firms—the demanders of labor—are willing to pay more for the highly educated because highly educated workers have higher marginal products. Workers—the suppliers of labor—are willing to pay the cost of becoming educated only if there is a reward for doing so. In essence, the difference in wages between highly educated workers and less educated workers may be considered a compensating differential for the cost of becoming educated.

CASE STUDY   THE INCREASING VALUE OF SKILLS

"The rich get richer, and the poor get poorer." Like many adages, this one is not always true, but recently it has been. Many studies have documented that the earnings gap between workers with high skills and workers with low skills has increased over the past two decades.

Figure 19-1 shows the ratio of the earnings of the typical college graduate to the earnings of the typical high school graduate without any additional education. The figure shows the gradual increase in this ratio over time. In 1976, college graduates earned on average 55 percent more than high school graduates; in 1994, they earned 84 percent more. The economic incentive to stay in school is as great today as it has ever been.

Why has the gap in earnings between skilled and unskilled workers risen in recent years? No one knows for sure, but economists have proposed two hypotheses to explain this trend. Both hypotheses suggest that the demand for skilled labor has risen over time relative to the demand for unskilled labor. The shift in demand has led to a corresponding change in wages, which in turn has led to greater inequality.

The first hypothesis is that international trade has altered the relative demand for skilled and unskilled labor. In recent years, the amount of trade with other countries has increased substantially. Imports into the United States have risen from 5 percent of total U.S. production in 1970 to 13 percent in 1995. Exports from the United States have risen from 6 percent in 1970 to 11 percent in 1995. Because unskilled labor is plentiful and cheap in many foreign countries, the United States tends to import goods produced with unskilled labor and export goods produced with skilled labor. Thus, when international trade expands, the domestic demand for skilled labor rises, and the domestic demand for unskilled labor falls.

Figure 19-1

The Ratio of the Earnings of College Graduates to the Earnings of High School Graduates. This figure shows that over the past 20 years, the gap in earnings between highly skilled workers and less skilled workers has increased substantially.

Source: Department of Labor and author's calculations.

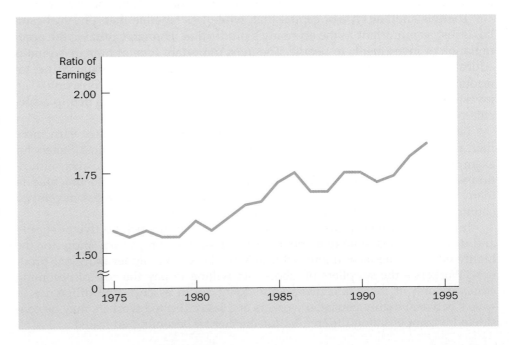

The second hypothesis is that changes in technology have altered the relative demand for skilled and unskilled labor. Consider, for instance, the introduction of computers. Computers raise the demand for skilled workers who can use the new machines and reduce the demand for the unskilled workers whose jobs are replaced by the computers. For example, many companies now rely more on computer databases, and less on filing cabinets, to keep business records. This change raises the demand for computer programmers and reduces the demand for filing clerks. Thus, as more firms begin to use computers, the demand for skilled labor rises, and the demand for unskilled labor falls.

Economists have found it difficult to gauge the validity of these two hypotheses. It is possible, of course, that both are true: Increasing international trade and technological change may share responsibility for the increasing inequality we have observed in recent decades.

ABILITY, EFFORT, AND CHANCE

Why do major league baseball players get paid more than minor league players? Certainly, the higher wage is not a compensating differential. Playing in the major leagues is not a less pleasant task than playing in the minor leagues; in fact, the opposite is true. The major leagues do not require more years of schooling or more experience. To a large extent, players in the major leagues earn more just because they have greater natural ability.

Natural ability is important for workers in all occupations. Because of heredity and upbringing, people differ in their physical and mental attributes. Some people are strong, others weak. Some people are smart, others less so. Some people are outgoing, others awkward in social situations. These and many other personal characteristics determine how productive workers are and, therefore, play a role in determining the wages they earn.

Closely related to ability is effort. Some people work hard, others are lazy. We should not be surprised to find that those who work hard are more productive and earn higher wages. To some extent, firms reward workers directly by paying people on the basis of what they produce. Salespeople, for instance, are often paid as a percentage of the sales they make. At other times, hard work is rewarded less directly in the form of a higher annual salary or a bonus.

Chance also plays a role in determining wages. If a person attended a trade school to learn how to repair televisions with vacuum tubes and then found this skill made obsolete by the invention of solid-state electronics, he or she would end up earning a low wage compared to others with similar years of training. The low wage of this worker is due to chance—a phenomenon that economists recognize but do not shed much light on.

How important are ability, effort, and chance in determining wages? It is hard to say, because ability, effort, and chance are hard to measure. But indirect evidence suggests that they are very important. When labor economists study wages, they relate a worker's wage to those variables that can be measured—years of schooling, years of experience, age, and job characteristics. Although all of these measured variables affect a worker's wage as theory predicts, they account for less than half of the variation in wages in our economy. Because so much of the variation in wages is left unexplained, omitted variables, including ability, effort, and chance, must play an important role.

Good looks pay.

CASE STUDY   THE BENEFITS OF BEAUTY

People differ in many ways. One difference is in how attractive they are. The actor Mel Gibson, for instance, is a handsome man. In part for this reason, his movies attract large audiences. Not surprisingly, the large audiences mean a large income for Mr. Gibson.

How prevalent are the economic benefits of beauty? Labor economists Daniel Hamermesh and Jeff Biddle tried to answer this question in a study published in the December 1994 issue of the *American Economic Review.* Hamermesh and Biddle examined data from surveys of individuals in the United States and Canada. The interviewers who conducted the survey were asked to rate each respondent's physical appearance. Hamermesh and Biddle then examined how much the wages of the respondents depended on the standard determinants—education, experience, and so on—and how much they depended on physical appearance.

Hamermesh and Biddle found that beauty pays. People who are deemed to be more attractive than average earn 5 percent more than people of average looks. People of average looks earn 5 to 10 percent more than people considered less attractive than average. Similar results were found for men and women.

What explains these differences in wages? There are several ways to interpret the "beauty premium."

One interpretation is that good looks are themselves a type of innate ability determining productivity and wages. Some people are born with the attributes of a movie star; other people are not. Good looks are useful in any job in which workers present themselves to the public—such as acting, sales, and waiting on tables. In this case, an attractive worker is more valuable to the firm than an unattractive worker. The firm's willingness to pay more to attractive workers reflects its customers' preferences.

A second interpretation is that reported beauty is an indirect measure of other types of ability. How attractive a person appears depends on more than just heredity. It also depends on dress, hairstyle, personal demeanor, and other attributes that a person can control. Perhaps a person who successfully projects an attractive image in a survey interview is more likely to be an intelligent person who succeeds at other tasks as well.

A third interpretation is that the beauty premium is a type of discrimination, a topic to which we return later.

AN ALTERNATIVE VIEW OF EDUCATION: SIGNALING

Earlier we discussed the human-capital view of education, according to which schooling raises workers' wages because it makes them more productive. Although this view is widely accepted, some economists have proposed an alternative theory, which emphasizes that firms use educational attainment as a way of sorting between high-ability and low-ability workers. According to this alternative view, when people earn a college degree, for instance, they do not become more productive, but they do *signal* their high ability to prospective employers. Because it is easier for high-ability people to earn a college degree than it is for low-ability people, more high-ability people get college degrees. As a result, it is rational for firms to interpret a college degree as a signal of ability.

The human-capital and signaling views of education have important similarities and important differences. Both views can explain why more-educated workers tend to earn more than less-educated workers. According to the human-capital view, education makes workers more productive; according to the signaling view, education is correlated with natural ability. But the two views have radically different predictions for the effects of policies that aim to increase educational attainment. According to the human-capital view, increasing educational levels for all workers would raise all workers' productivity and thereby their wages. According to the signaling view, education does not enhance productivity, so raising all workers' educational levels would not affect wages.

Skeptics of the signaling view of education point out that education is a very costly way for firms to sort job applicants by ability. If signaling were the only benefit from going to college, firms could devise better ways to hire high-ability applicants. Ability tests and trial periods, for example, are less costly than requiring people to spend four years in college just to establish their innate ability. Because firms continue to rely on a college degree to screen workers, rather than these cheaper alternatives, it seems that college itself must have at least some beneficial impact on workers' productivity.

CASE STUDY HUMAN CAPITAL, NATURAL ABILITY, AND COMPULSORY SCHOOL ATTENDANCE

Does attending school increase wages because it increases productivity, or does it only appear to increase productivity because high-ability people are more likely to stay in school? This question is important both for judging the various theories of education and for evaluating alternative education policies.

If economists could conduct controlled experiments like laboratory scientists, it would be easy to answer this question. We could choose some experimental subjects from the school-age population and then randomly divide them into various groups. For each group we could require a different amount of school attendance. By comparing the difference in the educational attainment and the difference in subsequent wages of the various groups, we could see whether education does in fact increase productivity. Because the groups would be chosen randomly, we could be sure that the difference in wages was not attributable to a difference in natural ability.

Although conducting such an experiment might seem difficult, the laws of the United States inadvertently provide a natural experiment that is quite similar. All students in the United States are required by law to attend school, but the laws vary from state to state. Some states allow students to drop out at age sixteen, while others require attendance until age seventeen or eighteen. Moreover, the laws have changed over time. Between 1970 and 1980, for instance, Wyoming reduced the school-attendance age from seventeen to sixteen, while Washington raised it from sixteen to eighteen. This variation across states and over time provides data with which to study the effects of compulsory school attendance.

Even within a state, school-attendance laws have different effects on different people. Students start attending school at different ages, depending on the month of the year in which they were born. Yet all students can drop out as soon as they reach the minimum legal age; they are not required to finish out the school year. As a result, those who start school at a relatively young age are required to spend more time in school than those who start school at a relatively old age. This variation across students within a state also provides a way to study the effects of compulsory attendance.

In an article published in the November 1991 issue of the *Quarterly Journal of Economics,* labor economists Joshua Angrist and Alan Krueger used this natural experiment to study the relationship between schooling and wages. Because the duration of each student's compulsory schooling depends on his or her state of residence and month of birth, and not on natural ability, it was possible to isolate the productivity-enhancing effect of education from the ability-signaling effect. According to Angrist and Krueger's research, those students who were required to finish more school did earn significantly higher subsequent wages than those with lower requirements. This finding indicates that education does raise a worker's productivity, as the human-capital theory suggests.

Although establishing the benefits of compulsory schooling is useful, it does not by itself tell us whether these laws are desirable. That policy judgment requires a more complete analysis of the costs and benefits. At the very least, we would need to compare the benefits of schooling to the opportunity cost—the wages that the student could have earned by dropping out. In addition, requiring a student to stay in school may have external effects on others in society. On the one hand, compulsory school attendance may reduce crime rates, for young dropouts are at high risk of engaging in criminal activity. On the other hand, students who stay in school only because they are required to do so may interfere with the learning of other students who are more committed to their educations.

"When can I drop out? Should I?"

THE SUPERSTAR PHENOMENON

Although most actors earn very little and often have to take jobs as waiters to support themselves, actor Jim Carrey earned $29 million in 1995. Similarly, while most people who play basketball do it for free as a hobby, Shaquille O'Neal plays for the L.A. Lakers at an annual salary of $17 million. Jim Carrey and Shaquille O'Neal are superstars in their fields, and their great public appeal is reflected in astronomical incomes.

Why do Jim Carrey and Shaquille O'Neal earn so much? It is not surprising that there are differences in incomes within occupations. Good carpenters earn more than mediocre carpenters, and good plumbers earn more than mediocre plumbers. People vary in ability and effort, and these differences lead to differences in income. Yet the best carpenters and plumbers do not earn the many millions that are common among the best actors and athletes. What explains the difference?

To understand the tremendous incomes of Jim Carrey and Shaquille O'Neal, we must examine the special features of the markets in which they sell their services. Superstars arise in markets that have two characteristics:

◆ Every customer in the market wants to enjoy the good supplied by the best producer.

◆ The good is produced with a technology that makes it possible for the best producer to supply every customer at low cost.

If Jim Carrey is the funniest actor around, then everyone will want to see his next movie; seeing twice as many movies by an actor half as funny is not a good substitute. Moreover, it is *possible* for everyone to enjoy the comedy of Jim Carrey. Because it is easy to make multiple copies of a film, Jim Carrey can provide his service to millions of people simultaneously. Similarly, because Lakers games are broadcast on television, millions of fans can enjoy the extraordinary athletic skills of Shaquille O'Neal.

We can now see why there are no superstar carpenters and plumbers. Other things equal, everyone may prefer to employ the best carpenter, but a carpenter, unlike a movie actor, can provide his services to only a limited number of customers. Although the best carpenter will be able to command a somewhat higher wage than the average carpenter, the average carpenter will still be able to earn a good living.

QUICK QUIZ   Define *compensating differential* and give an example. ◆ Give two reasons why more-educated workers earn more than less-educated workers.

THE ECONOMICS OF DISCRIMINATION

Another source of differences in wages is discrimination. **Discrimination** occurs when the marketplace offers different opportunities to similar individuals who differ only by race, ethnic group, sex, age, or other personal characteristics. Discrimination reflects some people's prejudice against certain groups in society. Although discrimination is an emotionally charged topic that often generates heated debate, economists try to study the topic objectively in order to separate myth from reality.

discrimination
the offering of different opportunities to similar individuals who differ only by race, ethnic group, sex, age, or other personal characteristics

MEASURING LABOR-MARKET DISCRIMINATION

How much does discrimination in labor markets affect the earnings of different groups of workers? This question is important, but answering it is not easy.

It might seem natural to gauge the amount of discrimination in labor markets by looking at the average wages of different groups. For instance, in recent years the wage of the average black worker in the United States has been about 20 percent less than the wage of the average white worker. The wage of the average female worker has been about 30 percent less than the wage of the average male worker. These wage differentials are sometimes presented in political debate as evidence that many employers discriminate against blacks and women.

Yet there is an obvious problem with this approach. Even in a labor market free of discrimination, different people have different wages. People differ in the amount of human capital they have and in the kinds of work they are able and willing to do. The wage differences we observe in the economy are, to a large extent, attributable to the determinants of equilibrium wages we discussed in the last section. Simply observing differences in wages among broad groups—whites and blacks, men and women—says little about the prevalence of discrimination.

Consider, for example, the role of human capital. About 80 percent of white male workers have a high school diploma, and 25 percent have a college degree. By contrast, only 67 percent of black male workers have a high school diploma, and only 12 percent have a college degree. Thus, at least some of the difference between the wages of whites and the wages of blacks can be traced to differences in educational attainment. Similarly, among white workers, 25 percent of men have a college degree, whereas only 19 percent of women have a college degree, indicating that some of the difference between the wages of men and women is attributable to educational attainment.

In fact, human capital is probably even more important in explaining wage differentials than the foregoing numbers suggest. For many years, public schools in predominantly black areas have been of lower quality—as measured by expenditure, class size, and so on—than public schools in predominantly white areas. Similarly, for many years, schools directed girls away from science and math courses, even though these subjects may have had greater value in the marketplace than some of the alternatives. If we could measure the quality as well as the quantity of education, the differences in human capital among these groups would seem even larger.

Human capital acquired in the form of job experience can also help explain wage differences. In particular, women tend to have less job experience on average than men. One reason is that female labor-force participation has increased over the past several decades. Because of this historic change, the average female worker today is younger than the average male worker. In addition, women are more likely to interrupt their careers to raise children. For both reasons, the experience of the average female worker is less than the experience of the average male worker.

Yet another source of wage differences is compensating differentials. Some analysts have suggested that women take more pleasant jobs on average than men and that this fact explains some of the earnings differential between men and women. For example, women are more likely to be secretaries, and men are more likely to be truck drivers. The relative wages of secretaries and truck drivers depend in part on the working conditions of each job. Because these non-monetary aspects are hard to measure, it is difficult to gauge the practical importance of compensating differentials in explaining the wage differences that we observe.

In the end, the study of wage differences among groups does not establish any clear conclusion about the prevalence of discrimination in U.S. labor markets. Most economists believe that some of the observed wage differentials are attributable to discrimination, but there is no consensus about how much. The only conclusion about which economists are in consensus is a negative one: *Because the differences in average wages among groups in part reflect differences in human capital and job characteristics, they do not by themselves say anything about how much discrimination there is in the labor market.*

Of course, differences in human capital among groups of workers may themselves reflect discrimination. The inferior schools historically available to black students, for instance, may be traced to prejudice on the part of city councils and school boards. But this kind of discrimination occurs long before the worker enters the labor market. In this case, the disease is political, even if the symptom is economic.

DISCRIMINATION BY EMPLOYERS

Let's now turn from measurement to the economic forces that lie behind discrimination in labor markets. If one group in society receives a lower wage than another group, even after controlling for human capital and job characteristics, who is to blame for this differential?

The answer is not obvious. It might seem natural to blame employers for discriminatory wage differences. After all, employers make the hiring decisions that determine labor demand and wages. If some groups of workers earn lower wages than they should, then it seems that employers are responsible. Yet many economists are skeptical of this easy answer. They believe that competitive, market economies provide a natural antidote to employer discrimination. That antidote is called the profit motive.

Imagine an economy in which workers are differentiated by their hair color. Blondes and brunettes have the same skills, experience, and work ethic. Yet, because of discrimination, employers prefer not to hire workers with blonde hair. Thus, the demand for blondes is lower than it otherwise would be. As a result, blondes earn a lower wage than brunettes.

How long can this wage differential persist? In this economy, there is an easy way for a firm to beat out its competitors: It can hire blonde workers. By hiring blondes, a firm pays lower wages and thus has lower costs than firms that hire brunettes. Over time, more and more "blonde" firms enter the market to take advantage of this cost advantage. The existing "brunette" firms have higher costs and, therefore, begin to lose money when faced with the new competitors. These losses induce the brunette firms to go out of business. Eventually, the entry of blonde firms and the exit of brunette firms cause the demand for blonde workers to rise and the demand for brunette workers to fall. This process continues until the wage differential disappears.

Put simply, business owners who care only about making money are at an advantage when competing against those who also care about discriminating. As a result, firms that do not discriminate tend to replace those that do. In this way, competitive markets have a natural remedy for employer discrimination.

CASE STUDY SEGREGATED STREETCARS AND THE PROFIT MOTIVE

In the early twentieth century, streetcars in many southern cities were segregated by race. White passengers sat in the front of the streetcars, and black passengers sat in the back. What do you suppose caused and maintained this discriminatory practice? And how was this practice viewed by the firms that ran the streetcars?

In a 1986 article in the *Journal of Economic History,* economic historian Jennifer Roback looked at these questions. Roback found that the segregation of races on streetcars was the result of laws that required such segregation. Before these laws were passed, racial discrimination in seating was rare. It was far more common to segregate smokers and nonsmokers.

Moreover, the firms that ran the streetcars often opposed the laws requiring racial segregation. Providing separate seating for different races raised the firms' costs and reduced their profit. One railroad company manager complained to the city council that, under the segregation laws, "the company has to haul around a good deal of empty space."

Here is how Roback describes the situation in one southern city:

> The railroad company did not initiate the segregation policy and was not at all eager to abide by it. State legislation, public agitation, and a threat to arrest the president of the railroad were all required to induce them to separate the races on their cars. . . . There is no indication that the management was motivated by belief in civil rights or racial equality. The evidence indicates their primary motives were economic; separation was costly. . . . Officials of the company may or may not have disliked blacks, but they were not willing to forgo the profits necessary to indulge such prejudice.

The story of southern streetcars illustrates a general lesson: Business owners are usually more interested in making profit than in discriminating against a particular group. When firms engage in discriminatory practices, the ultimate source of the discrimination often lies not with the firms themselves but elsewhere. In this particular case, the streetcar companies segregated whites and blacks because discriminatory laws, which the companies opposed, required them to do so.

DISCRIMINATION BY CUSTOMERS AND GOVERNMENTS

Although the profit motive is a strong force acting to eliminate discriminatory wage differentials, there are limits to its corrective abilities. Here we consider two of the most important limits: *customer preferences* and *government policies.*

To see how customer preferences for discrimination can affect wages, consider again our imaginary economy with blondes and brunettes. Suppose that restaurant owners discriminate against blondes when hiring waiters. As a result, blonde waiters earn lower wages than brunette waiters. In this case, a restaurant could open up with blonde waiters and charge lower prices. If customers only cared about the quality and price of their meals, the discriminatory firms would be driven out of business, and the wage differential would disappear.

On the other hand, it is possible that customers prefer being served by brunette waiters. If this preference for discrimination is strong, the entry of blonde restaurants need not succeed in eliminating the wage differential between brunettes and blondes. That is, if customers have discriminatory preferences, a competitive market is consistent with a discriminatory wage differential. An economy with such discrimination would contain two types of restaurants. Blonde restaurants hire blondes, have lower costs, and charge lower prices. Brunette restaurants hire brunettes, have higher costs, and charge higher prices. Customers who did not care about the hair color of their waiters would be attracted to the lower prices at the blonde restaurants. Bigoted customers would go to the brunette restaurants. They would pay for their discriminatory preference in the form of higher prices.

Another way for discrimination to persist in competitive markets is for the government to mandate discriminatory practices. If, for instance, the government passed a law stating that blondes could wash dishes in restaurants but could not work as waiters, then a wage differential could persist in a competitive market. The example of segregated streetcars in the foregoing case study is one example of government-mandated discrimination. More recently, before South Africa abandoned its system of apartheid, blacks were prohibited from working in some jobs. Discriminatory governments pass such laws in order to suppress the normal equalizing force of free and competitive markets.

To sum up: *Competitive markets contain a natural remedy for employer discrimination. The entry of firms that care only about profit tends to eliminate discriminatory wage differentials. These wage differentials persist in competitive markets only when customers are willing to pay to maintain the discriminatory practice or when the government mandates it.*

CASE STUDY DISCRIMINATION IN SPORTS

As we have seen, measuring discrimination is often difficult. To determine whether one group of workers is discriminated against, a researcher must correct for differences in the productivity between that group and other workers in the economy. Yet, in most firms, it is difficult to measure a particular worker's contribution to the production of goods and services.

One type of firm in which such corrections are easier is the sports team. Professional teams have many objective measures of productivity. In baseball, for instance, we can measure a player's batting average, the frequency of home runs, the number of stolen bases, and so on.

Studies of sports teams suggest that racial discrimination is, in fact, common and that much of the blame lies with customers. One study, published in the *Journal of Labor Economics* in 1988, examined the salaries of basketball players. It found that black players earned 20 percent less than white players of comparable ability. The study also found that attendance at basketball games was larger for teams with a greater proportion of white players. One interpretation of these facts is that customer discrimination makes black players less profitable than white players for team owners. In the presence of such customer discrimination, a discriminatory wage gap can persist, even if team owners care only about profit.

A similar situation once existed for baseball players. A study using data from the late 1960s showed that black players earned less than comparable

IN THE NEWS

Men, Women,

and Wages

WHY DOES THE AVERAGE FEMALE worker earn less than the average male worker? In the following article, economist June O'Neill offers some answers to this question. When this article was written, O'Neill was a professor of economics. Now she holds the powerful position of Director of the Congressional Budget Office.

The Shrinking Pay Gap

BY JUNE ELLENOFF O'NEILL

"Fifty-nine cents," the popular button said, a symbol of the stubborn fact that throughout the post-World War II period, women's wages hovered at around 60 percent of men's, despite an increasing proportion of women working outside the home. This gender gap did not de-

cline through the 1960s and the 1970s despite the rise of the feminist movement, equal pay and employment legislation, and affirmative action.

But starting in the Reagan years, the gender gap in wages began to decline dramatically. By some measures the ratio of women's earnings to men's rose to nearly 80 percent; and even this number, I believe, overstates the gender gap between men and women with similar skills and training. Why did this dramatic narrowing in relative wages happen?

The answer has less to do with politics or protests than with the realities of the labor market. Although basic skills are acquired in school, it is in the labor market where specialized skills are developed that bring higher wages. During the three decades following World War II women entered the labor market in record numbers. But many of the new entrants had been out of the labor force for considerable periods of time, raising their children. These women diluted the skill level of the rapidly expanding group of employed women. This was the main reason why the gender gap in pay did not narrow during the postwar years.

Today's working women, particularly those younger than forty, are much more nearly equal to men in work experience

JUNE O'NEILL: DIRECTOR OF THE CONGRESSIONAL BUDGET OFFICE

than were their mothers. Through delayed marriage, low fertility, and an increasing tendency for mothers of young children to work, women have acquired many more years of continuous work experience than was true in the past. (Close to 60 percent of married women with children under age six are now in the labor force; in 1960, the proportion was only 19 percent.)

And the work experience gained by these younger women is likely to have an even greater impact on their future earn-

white players. Moreover, fewer fans attended games pitched by blacks than games pitched by whites, even though black pitchers had better records than white pitchers. Studies of more recent salaries in baseball, however, have found no evidence of discriminatory wage differentials.

Another study, published in the *Quarterly Journal of Economics* in 1990, examined the market prices of old baseball cards. This study found similar evidence of discrimination. The cards of black hitters sold for 10 percent less than the cards of comparable white hitters. The cards of black pitchers sold for 13 percent less than the cards of comparable white pitchers. These results suggest customer discrimination among baseball fans.

ings because their work experience has been more correctly anticipated. Many investment choices affecting careers are made at younger ages: years of schooling, subjects in school, other professional training. In the past, women were much less likely than men to invest in lengthy training because they assumed they would not be working enough years to justify it.

In fact, the National Longitudinal Surveys found that even in the late 1960s less than 30 percent of young women anticipated that they would be working at age thirty-five, yet when this group actually reached thirty-five, more than 70 percent of them were in the labor force. Their underestimation of future work activity surely influenced their early career preparations (or lack thereof). More recent survey data show a dramatic change in expectations. The vast majority of young women now report an intention to work at age thirty-five.

Those changing work expectations are reflected in rising female enrollments in higher education. In 1960, women received 35 percent of all bachelor's degrees in the U.S.; by the 1980s, they received somewhat more than half of them. In 1968, women received 8 percent of the medical degrees, 3 percent of the MBAs, and 4 percent of the law degrees granted that year. In 1986, they received 31 percent of the medical degrees and MBAs and 39 percent of the law degrees. This recent trend in schooling is likely to reinforce the rise in work experience and contribute to continuing increases in the relative earnings of women workers. . . .

Despite the advances of the past decade, women still earn less than men. The hourly earnings of women were 74 percent of the earnings of men in 1992 when ages twenty-five to sixty-four are considered, up from 62 percent in 1979. At ages twenty-five to thirty-four, where women's skills have increased the most, the ratio is 87 percent.

Economist Barbara Bergmann and others attribute the pay gap to "widespread, severe, ongoing discrimination by employers and fellow workers." But discrimination cannot be directly measured. Instead, researchers estimate the extent to which differences in productivity appear to explain the gap and then attribute the rest to discrimination. Such a conclusion is premature, however, when productivity differences are not accurately measured, which is usually the case.

For example, data are seldom available on lifetime patterns of work experi-ence, and even less material is available on factors bearing on work expectations and the intensity and nature of work investments. As these are still the key sources of skill differences between men and women, there is considerable room for interpretation and disagreement.

When earnings comparisons are restricted to men and women more similar in their experience and life situations, the measured earnings differentials are typically quite small. For example, among people twenty-seven to thirty-three who have never had a child, the earnings of women in the National Longitudinal Survey of Youth are close to 98 percent of men's. . . .

It is true that women and men still do not have the same earnings. But I believe that the differential is largely due to continuing gender differences in the priority placed on market work vs. family responsibilities. Until family roles are more equal, women are not likely to have the same pattern of market work and earnings as men. Technology has reduced the burden of housework, but child care remains a responsibility that is harder to shift to the market.

SOURCE: *The Wall Street Journal,* Friday, October 7, 1994, p. A10.

THE DEBATE OVER COMPARABLE WORTH

Should engineers get paid more than librarians? This question is at the heart of the debate over **comparable worth,** a doctrine according to which jobs deemed comparable should be paid the same wage.

Advocates of comparable worth point out that traditionally male occupations have higher wages than traditionally female occupations. They believe that these occupational differences are discriminatory against women. Even if women were paid the same as men for the same type of work, the gender gap in wages would persist until comparable occupations were paid similar wages. Comparable-worth

comparable worth
a doctrine according to which jobs deemed comparable should be paid the same wage

advocates want jobs rated according to a set of impartial criteria—education, experience, responsibility, working conditions, and so on. Under this system, comparably rated jobs would pay the same wage. A librarian with a master's degree, ten years of experience, and a forty-hour workweek, for instance, would be paid the same as an engineer with a master's degree, ten years of experience, and a forty-hour workweek.

Most economists are critical of comparable-worth proposals. They argue that a competitive market is the best mechanism for setting wages. It would be nearly impossible, they claim, to measure all of the factors that are relevant for determining the right wage for any job. Moreover, the fact that traditionally female occupations pay less than traditionally male occupations is not by itself evidence of discrimination. Women have in the past spent more time than men raising children. Women are, therefore, more likely to choose occupations that offer flexible hours and other working conditions compatible with childrearing. To some extent, the gender gap in wages is a compensating differential.

Economists also point out that comparable-worth proposals would have an important unintended side effect. Comparable-worth advocates want the wages in traditionally female occupations to be raised by legal decree. Such a policy would have many of the effects of a minimum wage, which we first discussed in Chapter 6. In particular, when the wage is forced to rise above the equilibrium level, the quantity of labor supplied to these occupations would rise, and the quantity demanded would fall. The result would be higher unemployment in traditionally female occupations. In this way, a comparable-worth law could adversely affect some members of groups that the policy is aimed at helping.

The debate over comparable worth continues. The courts have usually rejected the claim that occupational wage differences are discriminatory. Nonetheless, the comparable-worth movement has had some political success. For example, in 1985, a government employees union sued the state of Washington for discrimination using a comparable-worth argument. The case came before Circuit Court Judge Anthony Kennedy, who later became a justice on the U.S. Supreme Court. Kennedy decided against comparable worth, writing that "neither law nor logic deems the free market system a suspect enterprise." Despite their defeat in the courts, however, the advocates of comparable worth ultimately got what they wanted. The state of Washington eventually succumbed to political pressure and adopted a comparable-worth system for paying state employees.

QUICK QUIZ Why is it hard to establish whether a group of workers is being discriminated against? ◆ Explain how profit-maximizing firms tend to eliminate discriminatory wage differentials. ◆ How might a discriminatory wage differential persist?

CONCLUSION

In competitive markets, workers earn a wage equal to the value of their marginal contribution to the production of goods and services. There are, however, many things that affect the value of the marginal product. Firms pay more for workers who are more talented, more diligent, more experienced, and more educated because these workers are more productive. Firms pay less to those workers against whom customers discriminate because these workers contribute less to revenue.

The theory of the labor market we have developed in the last two chapters explains why some workers earn higher wages than other workers. The theory does not say that the resulting distribution of income is equal, fair, or desirable in any way. That is the topic we take up in Chapter 20.

Summary

- Workers earn different wages for many reasons. To some extent, wage differentials compensate workers for job attributes. Other things equal, workers in hard, unpleasant jobs get paid more than workers in easy, pleasant jobs.

- Workers with more human capital get paid more than workers with less human capital. The return to accumulating human capital is high and has increased over the past decade.

- Although years of education, experience, and job characteristics affect earnings as theory predicts, there is much variation in earnings that cannot be explained by things that economists can measure. The unexplained variation in earnings is largely attributable to natural ability, effort, and chance.

- Some economists have suggested that more-educated workers earn higher wages not because education raises productivity but because workers with high natural ability use education as a way to signal their high ability

to employers. If this signaling theory were correct, then increasing the educational attainment of all workers would not raise the overall level of wages.

- Some differences in earnings are attributable to discrimination on the basis of race, sex, or other factors. Measuring the amount of discrimination is difficult, however, because one must correct for differences in human capital and job characteristics.

- Competitive markets tend to limit the impact of discrimination on wages. If the wages of a group of workers are lower than those of another group for reasons not related to marginal productivity, then nondiscriminatory firms will be more profitable than discriminatory firms. Profit-maximizing behavior, therefore, can act to reduce discriminatory wage differentials. Discrimination can persist in competitive markets if customers are willing to pay more to discriminatory firms or if the government passes laws requiring firms to discriminate.

Key Concepts

compensating differential, p. 403
human capital, p. 403

discrimination, p. 409

comparable worth, p. 415

Questions for Review

1. Why do coal miners get paid more than other workers with similar amounts of education?

2. In what sense is education a type of capital?

3. How might education raise a worker's wage without raising the worker's productivity?

4. What difficulties arise in deciding whether a group of workers has a lower wage because of discrimination?

5. Do the forces of economic competition tend to exacerbate or ameliorate discrimination on the basis of race?

6. Give an example of how discrimination might persist in a competitive market.

Problems and Applications

1. College students sometimes work as summer interns for private firms or the government. Many of these positions pay little or nothing.
   a. What is the opportunity cost of taking such a job?
   b. Explain why students are willing to take these jobs.
   c. If you were to compare the earnings later in life of workers who had worked as interns and those who had taken summer jobs that paid more, what would you expect to find?

2. As explained in Chapter 6, a minimum-wage law distorts the market for low-wage labor. To reduce this distortion, some economists advocate a two-tiered minimum-wage system, with a regular minimum wage for adult workers and a lower, "sub-minimum" wage for teenage workers. Give two reasons why a single minimum wage might distort the labor market for teenage workers more than it would the market for adult workers.

3. A basic finding of labor economics is that workers who have more experience in the labor force are paid more than workers who have less experience but the same amount of formal education. Why might this be so? Some studies have also found that experience at the same job (called "job tenure") has an extra positive influence on wages. Explain.

4. The wages of college-educated workers were stagnant during the 1970s and then rose during the 1980s. Yet economists believe that the demand for college-educated workers increased fairly steadily during this whole period. What could explain the pattern of wage changes?

5. Relative to the industrialized countries, developing countries have more unskilled workers and fewer skilled workers. Would you expect the value of skills to be relatively higher or lower in developing countries than in industrialized countries? Explain.

6. *The New York Times* (Dec. 13, 1993) reported that the Clinton administration intended to propose "a larger job-retraining plan for laid-off workers [with obsolete skills], a new apprenticeship program to provide special skills for young people not bound for college and a loan program to enable more low-income youths to afford college." The administration argued that these programs would reduce income inequality. Assess the administration's argument using supply-and-demand diagrams of the markets for skilled and unskilled labor.

7. At some colleges and universities, economics professors receive higher salaries than professors in some other fields.
   a. Why might this be true?
   b. Some other colleges and universities have a policy of paying equal salaries to professors in all fields. At some of these schools, economics professors have lighter teaching loads than professors in some other fields. What role do the differences in teaching loads play?

8. When recording devices were first invented almost 100 years ago, musicians could suddenly supply their music to large audiences at low cost. How do you suppose this event affected the income of the best musicians? How do you suppose it affected the income of average musicians?

9. Alan runs an economic consulting firm. He hires primarily female economists because, he says, "they will work for less than comparable men because women have fewer job options." Is Alan's behavior admirable or despicable? If more employers were like Alan, what would happen to the wage differential between men and women?

10. Suppose that it were true (which it is not) that all of the difference in earnings between black workers and white workers could be attributed to the difference in years of schooling and school quality. Would this imply that discrimination plays no role in the difference in earnings across racial groups? Why or why not?

11. A case study in this chapter described how customer discrimination in sports seems to have an important effect on players' earnings. Note that this is possible because sports fans know the players' characteristics, including their race. Why is this knowledge important for the existence of discrimination? Give some specific examples of industries where customer discrimination is and is not likely to influence wages.

12. Suppose that all young women were channeled into careers as secretaries, nurses, and teachers; at the same time, young men were encouraged to consider these three careers and many others as well.
   a. Draw a diagram showing the combined labor market for secretaries, nurses, and teachers. Draw a diagram showing the combined labor market for all other fields. In which market is the wage higher? Do men or women receive higher wages on average?

b. Now suppose that society changed and encouraged both young women and young men to consider a wide range of careers. Over time, what effect would this change have on the wages in the two markets you illustrated in part (a)? What effect would the change have on the average wages of men and women?

13. Economist June O'Neill argues that "until family roles are more equal, women are not likely to have the same pattern of market work and earnings as men." What does she mean by the "pattern" of market work? How do these characteristics of jobs and careers affect earnings?

14. This chapter considers the economics of discrimination by employers, customers, and governments. Now consider discrimination by workers. Suppose that some brunette workers did not like working with blonde workers. Do you think this worker discrimination could explain lower wages for blonde workers? If such a wage differential existed, what would a profit-maximizing entrepreneur do? If there were many such entrepreneurs, what would happen over time?

20

THE DISTRIBUTION OF INCOME

"The only difference between the rich and other people," Mary Colum once said to Ernest Hemingway, "is that the rich have more money." Maybe so. But this claim leaves many questions unanswered. The gap between rich and poor is a fascinating and important topic of study—for the comfortable rich, for the struggling poor, and for the aspiring and worried middle class.

From the previous two chapters you should have some understanding about why different people have different incomes. A person's earnings depend on the supply and demand for that person's labor, which in turn depend on natural ability, human capital, compensating differentials, discrimination, and so on. Because labor earnings make up about three-fourths of the total income in the U.S. economy, the factors that determine wages are also largely responsible for determining how the economy's total income is distributed among the various members of society. In other words, they determine who is rich and who is poor.

In this chapter we discuss the distribution of income. As we shall see, this topic raises some fundamental questions about the role of economic policy. One of the *Ten Principles of Economics* in Chapter 1 is that governments can sometimes improve market outcomes. This possibility is particularly important when considering the distribution of income. The invisible hand of the marketplace acts to allocate resources efficiently, but it does not necessarily ensure that resources are allocated fairly. As a result, many economists—though not all—believe that the government should redistribute income to achieve greater equality. In doing so, however, the government runs into another of the *Ten Principles of Economics*: People face tradeoffs. When the government enacts policies to make the distribution of income more equitable, it distorts incentives, alters behavior, and makes the allocation of resources less efficient.

Our discussion of the distribution of income proceeds in three steps. First, we assess how much inequality there is in our society. Second, we consider some different views about what role the government should play in altering the distribution of income. Third, we discuss various public policies aimed at helping society's poorest members.

THE MEASUREMENT OF INEQUALITY

We begin our study of the distribution of income by addressing four questions of measurement:

◆ How much inequality is there in our society?

◆ How many people live in poverty?

◆ What problems arise in measuring the amount of inequality?

◆ How often do people move among income classes?

These measurement questions are the natural starting point from which to discuss public policies aimed at changing the distribution of income.

U.S. INCOME INEQUALITY

There are various ways to describe the distribution of income in the economy. Table 20-1 presents a particularly simple way. It shows the percentage of fami-

"As far as I'm concerned, they can do what they want with the minimum wage, just as long as they keep their hands off the maximum wage."

ANNUAL FAMILY INCOME	PERCENT OF FAMILIES
Under $10,000	8.7%
$10,000–$14,999	6.9
$15,000–$24,999	15.0
$25,000 $34,999	14.3
$35,000–$49,999	18.0
$50,000–$74,999	19.9
$75,000 and over	17.2

SOURCE: U.S. Bureau of the Census.

Table 20-1

THE DISTRIBUTION OF INCOME IN THE UNITED STATES: 1994

lies that fall into each of seven income categories. You can use this table to find where your family lies in the income distribution.

For examining differences in the income distribution over time or across countries, economists find it more useful to present the income data as in Table 20-2. To see how to interpret this table, consider the following thought experiment. Imagine that you lined up all the families in the economy according to their annual income. Then you divided the families into five equal groups: the bottom fifth, the second fifth, the middle fifth, the fourth fifth, and the top fifth. Next you computed the share of total income that each group of families received. In this way, you could produce the numbers in Table 20-2.

These numbers give us a way of gauging how the economy's total income is distributed. If income were equally distributed across all families, each one-fifth of families would receive one-fifth (20 percent) of income. If all income were concentrated among just a few families, the top fifth would receive 100 percent,

YEAR	BOTTOM FIFTH	SECOND FIFTH	MIDDLE FIFTH	FOURTH FIFTH	TOP FIFTH	TOP 5 PERCENT
1994	4.2%	10.0%	15.7%	23.3%	46.9%	20.1%
1990	4.6	10.8	16.6	23.8	44.3	17.4
1980	5.2	11.5	17.5	24.3	41.5	15.3
1970	5.5	12.2	17.6	23.8	40.9	15.6
1960	4.8	12.2	17.8	24.0	41.3	15.9
1950	4.5	12.0	17.4	23.4	42.7	17.3
1935	4.1	9.2	14.1	20.9	51.7	26.5

INCOME INEQUALITY IN THE UNITED STATES. This table shows the percent of total before-tax income received by families in each fifth of the income distribution and by those families in the top 5 percent.

SOURCE: U.S. Bureau of the Census.

Table 20-2

and the other fifths would receive 0 percent. The actual economy, of course, is between these two extremes. The table shows that in 1994 the bottom fifth of all families received 4.2 percent of all income, and the top fifth of all families received 46.9 percent of all income. In other words, even though the top and bottom fifths include the same number of families, the top fifth has about ten times as much income as the bottom fifth.

The last column in Table 20-2 shows the share of total income received by the very richest families. In 1994, the top 5 percent of families received 20.1 percent of total income. Thus, the total income of the richest 5 percent of families was greater than the total income of the poorest 40 percent.

Table 20-2 also shows the distribution of income in various years beginning in 1935. At first glance, the distribution of income appears to have been remarkably stable over time. Throughout the past several decades, the bottom fifth of families has received about 4 to 5 percent of income, while the top fifth has received about 40 to 50 percent of income. Closer inspection of the table reveals some trends in the degree of inequality. From 1935 to 1970, the distribution gradually became more equal. The share of the bottom fifth rose from 4.1 to 5.5 percent, and the share of the top fifth fell from 51.7 percent to 40.9 percent. In more recent years, this trend has reversed itself. From 1970 to 1994, the share of the bottom fifth fell from 5.5 percent to 4.2 percent, and the share of the top fifth rose from 40.9 to 46.9 percent.

In Chapter 19 we discussed some of the reasons for this recent increase in inequality. Increases in international trade with low-wage countries and changes in technology have tended to reduce the demand for unskilled labor and raise the demand for skilled labor. As a result, the wages of unskilled workers have fallen relative to the wages of skilled workers, and this change in relative wages has increased inequality in family incomes.

CASE STUDY THE WOMEN'S MOVEMENT AND THE INCOME DISTRIBUTION

Over the past several decades, there has been a dramatic change in women's role in the economy. The percentage of women who hold jobs has risen from about 32 percent in the 1950s to about 54 percent in the 1990s. As full-time homemakers have become less common, a woman's earnings have become a more important determinant of the total income of a typical family.

While the women's movement has led to more equality between men and women in access to education and jobs, it has also led to less equality in family incomes. The reason is that the rise in women's labor-force participation has not been the same across all income groups. In particular, the women's movement has had its greatest impact on women from high-income households. Women from low-income households have long had high rates of participation in the labor force, even in the 1950s, and their behavior has changed much less.

In essence, the women's movement has changed the behavior of the wives of high-income men. In the 1950s, a male executive or physician was likely to marry a woman who would stay at home and raise the children. Today, the wife of a male executive or physician is more likely to be an executive or physician herself. The result is that rich households have become even richer, a pattern that raises inequality in family incomes.

As this example shows, there are social as well as economic determinants of the distribution of income. Moreover, the simplistic view that "income inequality is bad" can be misleading. Increasing the opportunities available to women was surely a good change for society, even if one effect was greater inequality in family incomes. When evaluating any change in the distribution of income, policymakers must look at the reasons for that change before deciding whether it presents a problem for society.

Equality for women has meant less equality for family incomes.

CASE STUDY   INCOME INEQUALITY AROUND THE WORLD

How does the amount of income inequality in the United States compare to that in other countries? This question is interesting, but answering it is problematic. Not every country in the world collects data in the same way; for example, some countries collect data on individual incomes, whereas other countries collect data on family incomes. As a result, data from one country may not be strictly comparable with data from another. Whenever we find a difference between two countries, we can never be sure whether it reflects a true difference in the economies or merely a difference in the way data are collected.

With this warning in mind, consider Table 20-3, which compares the income distribution of the United States to that of six other major countries.

COUNTRY	BOTTOM FIFTH	SECOND FIFTH	MIDDLE FIFTH	FOURTH FIFTH	TOP FIFTH
Japan	8.7%	13.2%	17.5%	23.1%	37.5%
South Korea	7.4	12.3	16.3	21.8	42.2
China	6.4	11.0	16.4	24.4	41.8
United States	4.7	11.0	17.4	25.0	41.9
United Kingdom	4.6	10.0	16.8	24.3	44.3
Mexico	4.1	7.8	12.3	19.9	55.9
Brazil	2.1	4.9	8.9	16.8	67.5

INCOME INEQUALITY AROUND THE WORLD. This table shows the percent of total before-tax income received by families in each fifth of the income distribution.

Table 20-3

SOURCE: *World Development Report: 1994*, pp. 220–221.

The countries are ranked from the most equal to the most unequal. On the top of the list is Japan, where the richest fifth of the population has income only about 4 times that of the poorest fifth. On the bottom of the list is Brazil, where the richest fifth has income more than 30 times that of the poorest fifth. Although all countries have substantial inequality in income, the degree of inequality is not the same everywhere.

When countries are ranked by inequality, the United States ends up in the middle of the pack. The poorest fifth of the U.S. population earns 4.7 percent of total income, compared to 8.7 percent in Japan and 2.1 percent in Brazil. The income distribution in the United States is almost the same as the income distribution in the United Kingdom. The similarity in the economic systems of these two countries is reflected in a similar distribution of income.

THE POVERTY RATE

poverty rate

the percentage of the population whose family income falls below an absolute level called the poverty line

poverty line

an absolute level of income set by the federal government for each family size below which a family is deemed to be in poverty

A commonly used gauge of the distribution of income is the poverty rate. The **poverty rate** is the percentage of the population whose family income falls below an absolute level called the **poverty line.** The poverty line is set by the federal government at roughly three times the cost of providing an adequate diet. This line is adjusted every year to account for changes in the level of prices, and it depends on family size.

To get some idea about what the poverty rate tells us, consider the data for 1994. In that year, the typical family had an income of about $39,000, and the poverty line for a family of four was $15,141. The poverty rate was 14.5 percent. In other words, 14.5 percent of the population were members of families with incomes below the poverty line for their family size.

Figure 20-1 shows the poverty rate since 1959, when the official data begin. You can see that the poverty rate fell from 22.4 percent in 1959 to a low of 11.1 percent in 1973. This decline is not surprising, for average income in the econ-

Figure 20-1

THE POVERTY RATE. The poverty rate shows the percentage of the population with incomes below an absolute level called the poverty line.

SOURCE: U.S. Bureau of the Census.

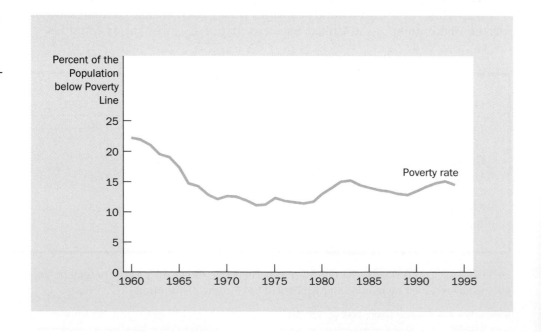

GROUP	POVERTY RATE
All persons	14.5%
White	11.7
Black	30.6
Hispanic	30.7
Children (under age 18)	21.8
Elderly (over age 64)	11.7
Female household, no husband present	38.6

SOURCE: U.S. Bureau of the Census. Data are for 1994.

Table 20-4

WHO IS POOR?

omy (adjusted for inflation) rose more than 50 percent during this period. Because the poverty line is an absolute rather than a relative standard, more families are pushed above the poverty line as economic growth pushes the entire income distribution upward. As John F. Kennedy once put it, a rising tide lifts all boats.

Since the early 1970s, however, the economy's rising tide has left some boats behind. Despite continued (although somewhat slower) growth in average income, the poverty rate has not declined and, in fact, has drifted upward to some extent. This lack of progress in reducing poverty in recent years is closely related to the increasing inequality we saw in Table 20-2. Although economic growth has raised the income of the typical family, the increase in inequality has prevented the poorest families from sharing in this greater economic prosperity.

Poverty is an economic malady that affects all groups within the population, but it does not affect all groups with equal frequency. Table 20-4 shows the poverty rates for several groups, and it reveals three striking facts:

◆ Poverty is correlated with race. Blacks and Hispanics are about three times more likely to live in poverty than are whites.

◆ Poverty is correlated with age. Children are more likely than average to be members of poor families, and the elderly are less likely than average to be poor.

◆ Poverty is correlated with family composition. Families headed by a female adult and without a husband present are more than twice as likely to live in poverty as the average family.

These three facts have described U.S. society for many years, and they show which people are most likely to be poor. These effects also work together: Among black and Hispanic children in female-headed households, more than half live in poverty.

PROBLEMS IN MEASURING INEQUALITY

Although data on the income distribution and the poverty rate help to give us some idea about the degree of inequality in our society, interpreting these data is not as straightforward as it might first appear. The data are based on households' annual incomes. What people care about, however, is not their incomes but their ability to maintain a good standard of living. For various reasons, data on the income distribution and the poverty rate give an incomplete picture of inequality in living standards. We examine these reasons below.

In-Kind Transfers   Measurements of the distribution of income and the poverty rate are based on families' *money* income. Through various government programs, however, the poor receive many nonmonetary items, including food stamps, housing vouchers, and medical services. Transfers to the poor given in the form of goods and services rather than cash are called **in-kind transfers.** Standard measurements of the degree of inequality do not take account of these in-kind transfers.

Because in-kind transfers are received mostly by the poorest members of society, the failure to include in-kind transfers as part of income greatly affects the measured poverty rate. According to a study by the Census Bureau, if in-kind transfers were included in income at their market value, the number of families living in poverty would be about 10 percent lower than the standard data indicate.

The important role of in-kind transfers makes evaluating changes in poverty more difficult. Over time, as public policies to help the poor evolve, the composition of assistance between cash and in-kind transfers changes. Some of the fluctuations in the measured poverty rate, therefore, reflect the form of government assistance rather than the true extent of economic deprivation.

The Economic Life Cycle   Incomes vary predictably over people's lives. A young worker, especially one in school, has a low income. Income rises as the worker gains maturity and experience, peaks at around age 50, and then falls sharply when the worker retires at around age 65. This regular pattern of income variation is called the **life cycle.**

Because people can borrow and save to smooth out life cycle changes in income, their standard of living in any year depends more on lifetime income than on that year's income. The young often borrow, perhaps to go to school or to buy a house, and then repay these loans later when their incomes rise. People have their highest saving rates when they are middle-aged. Because people can save in anticipation of retirement, the large declines in incomes at retirement need not lead to similar declines in the standard of living.

This normal life cycle pattern causes inequality in the distribution of annual income, but it does not represent true inequality in living standards. To gauge the inequality of living standards in our society, the distribution of lifetime incomes is more relevant than the distribution of annual incomes. Unfortunately, data on lifetime incomes are not readily available. When looking at any data on inequality, however, it is important to keep the life cycle in mind. Because a person's lifetime income smooths out the highs and lows of the life cycle, lifetime incomes are surely more equally distributed across the population than are annual incomes.

Transitory versus Permanent Income   Incomes vary over people's lives not only because of predictable life cycle variation but also because of random and transitory forces. One year a frost kills off the Florida orange crop, and

in-kind transfers

transfers to the poor given in the form of goods and services rather than cash

life cycle

the regular pattern of income variation over a person's life

IN THE NEWS

Is the Poverty

Rate Correctly

Measured?

THE POVERTY RATE IS A VERY CLOSELY watched economic statistic. Yet, as the following article makes clear, it has many critics.

Old Flaws Undermine New Poverty-Level Data

BY DANA MILBANK

There are lies, damned lies, and statistics. Then, there are the annual poverty figures.

This morning, reporters will crowd into the Commerce Department in Washington to hear the Census Bureau declare the number of Americans living in poverty. The bureau will also release household-income statistics that will tell us whether the rich are still getting richer and the poor poorer. Politicians will argue about the numbers. Interest groups will twist them. Bureaucrats will use them to fix eligibility for 27 federal programs, including food stamps, Medicaid, Head Start, and school lunches.

Footnote: The statistics are suspect.

Conservatives think so. The Heritage Foundation calls the report a "Soviet-style disinformation campaign" and the Census Bureau a "Potemkin village."

Liberals think so, too. The bureau is using data that are "completely outdated, with a technique that makes no sense," says Rebecca Blank, a poverty specialist at Northwestern University.

Even the Census Bureau concedes there is a problem. "The current measure is flawed," says Daniel Weinberg, the bureau's division chief who will introduce the numbers today. "I've made that point for many years."

The principal problem: The methodology behind the income and poverty data dates back to 1963 and ignores the vast changes in poverty programs. Why not bring it up to date? A committee of 13 academics, commissioned by the 1988 Family Support Act, spent $1 million and issued a 500-page report in May recommending an overhaul of the methodology. So far, nothing has happened.

The Office of Management and Budget uses the census figures to determine poverty standards, but with a redistribution of handouts to the states at stake, Congress would want a say, too. "You have a big political rock in the middle of the road," says Douglas Besharov of the American Enterprise Institute, a conservative think tank.

The methodology was questionable even back in 1963, when the poverty line was drawn by Mollie Orshansky, a civil

servant in what is now the Department of Health and Human Services. Ms. Orshansky, now retired, says her calculation was intended solely for a survey of the aged but was misappropriated by President Johnson, who was looking for a national poverty measure.

That measure, still in use today, is based on an Agriculture Department estimate of how much money is needed for food annually, a number that is multiplied by three to account for all other expenses and is adjusted to reflect family size.

But the poverty line measures pre-tax income only, with no mention of in-kind benefits like food stamps and credits like the Earned Income Tax Credit. Including these would decrease poverty significantly. It also makes no allowance for child care and transportation expenses, thus understating the number of working poor. It doesn't consider regional cost-of-living differences, even though a rural Mississippian would pay far less for housing than a Manhattanite, a quirk that understates urban poor and overstates rural poor. . . .

Indeed, whatever their political leanings, poverty analysts say the poverty-level and income measures have become so distorted that trends may be masked. Prof. Blank says it's "very possible" that reported trends of rising poverty and greater inequality over time could actually be the opposite.

SOURCE: *The Wall Street Journal*, October 5, 1995, p. B1.

Florida orange growers see their incomes fall temporarily. At the same time, the Florida frost drives up the price of oranges, and California orange growers see their incomes temporarily rise. The next year the reverse might happen.

Just as people can borrow and lend to smooth out life cycle variation in income, they can also borrow and lend to smooth out transitory variation in income. When California orange growers experience a good year, they would be foolish to spend all of their additional income. Instead, they save some of it, knowing that their good fortune is unlikely to persist. Similarly, the Florida orange growers respond to their temporarily low incomes by drawing down their savings or by borrowing. To the extent that a family saves and borrows to buffer itself from transitory changes in income, these changes do not affect its standard of living. A family's ability to buy goods and services depends largely on its **permanent income,** which is its normal, or average, income.

permanent income

a person's normal income

To gauge inequality of living standards, the distribution of permanent income is more relevant than the distribution of annual income. Although permanent income is hard to measure, it is an important concept. Because permanent income excludes transitory changes in income, permanent income is more equally distributed than is current income.

ECONOMIC MOBILITY

People sometimes speak of "the rich" and "the poor" as if these groups consisted of the same families year after year. In fact, this is not at all the case. Economic mobility, the movement of people among income classes, is substantial in the U.S. economy. Movements up the income ladder can be due to good luck or hard work, and movements down the ladder can be due to bad luck or laziness. Some of this mobility reflects transitory variation in income, while some reflects more persistent changes in income.

Because economic mobility is so great, many of those below the poverty line are there only temporarily. Poverty is a long-term problem for relatively few families. In a typical ten-year period, about one in four families falls below the poverty line in at least one year. Yet fewer than 3 percent of families are poor for eight or more years. Because it is likely that the temporarily poor and the persistently poor face different problems, policies that aim to combat poverty need to distinguish between these groups.

Another way to gauge economic mobility is the persistence of economic success from generation to generation. Economists who have studied this topic find substantial mobility. If a father earns 20 percent above his generation's average income, his son will most likely earn 8 percent above his generation's average income. There is almost no correlation between the income of a grandfather and the income of a grandson. There is much truth to the old saying, "From shirtsleeves to shirtsleeves in three generations."

One result of this great economic mobility is that the U.S. economy is filled with self-made millionaires (as well as with heirs who squandered the fortunes they inherited). According to estimates for 1996, about 2.7 million households in the United States had net worth (assets minus debts) that exceeded $1 million. These households represented the richest 2.8 percent of the population. About four out of five of these millionaires made their money on their own, such as by starting and building a business or by climbing the corporate ladder. Only one in five millionaires inherited their fortunes.

▌ QUICK QUIZ What does the poverty rate measure? ◆ Describe three potential problems in interpreting the measured poverty rate.

THE POLITICAL PHILOSOPHY OF REDISTRIBUTING INCOME

We have just seen how the economy's income is distributed and have discussed some of the problems encountered in interpreting measured inequality. We now turn to the policy question: What should the government do about economic inequality?

This question is not just about economics. Economic analysis alone cannot tell us whether policymakers should try to make our society more egalitarian. Our views on this question are, to a large extent, a matter of political philosophy. Yet because the government's role in redistributing income is central to so many debates over economic policy, here we digress from economic science to consider a bit of political philosophy.

UTILITARIANISM

A prominent school of thought in political philosophy is **utilitarianism.** The founders of utilitarianism are the English philosophers Jeremy Bentham (1748–1832) and John Stuart Mill (1806–1873). To a large extent, the goal of utilitarians is to apply the logic of individual decisionmaking to questions concerning morality and public policy.

The starting point of utilitarianism is the notion of **utility**—the level of happiness or satisfaction that a person receives from his or her circumstances. Utility is a measure of well-being and, according to utilitarians, is the ultimate objective of all public and private actions. The proper goal of the government, they claim, is to maximize the sum of utility of everyone in society.

The utilitarian case for redistributing income is based on the assumption of *diminishing marginal utility*. It seems reasonable that an extra dollar of income to a poor person provides that person with more additional utility than does an extra dollar to a rich person. In other words, as a person's income rises, the extra well-being derived from an additional dollar of income falls. This plausible assumption, together with the utilitarian goal of maximizing total utility, implies that the government should try to achieve a more equal distribution of income.

The argument is simple. Imagine that Peter and Paul are the same, except that Peter earns $80,000 and Paul earns $20,000. In this case, taking a dollar from Peter to pay Paul will reduce Peter's utility and raise Paul's utility. But, because of diminishing marginal utility, Peter's utility falls by less than Paul's utility rises. Thus, this redistribution of income raises total utility, which is the utilitarian's objective.

At first, this utilitarian argument might seem to imply that the government should continue to redistribute income until everyone in society has exactly the same income. Indeed, that would be the case if the total amount of income—$100,000 in our example—were fixed. But, in fact, it is not. Utilitarians reject complete equalization of incomes because they accept one of the *Ten Principles of Economics* presented in Chapter 1: People respond to incentives.

To take from Peter to pay Paul, the government must pursue policies that redistribute income, such as the U.S. federal income tax and welfare system.

utilitarianism
the political philosophy according to which the government should choose policies to maximize the total utility of everyone in society

utility
a measure of happiness or satisfaction

Under these policies, people with high incomes pay high taxes, and people with low incomes receive income transfers. Yet, as we have seen in Chapters 8 and 12, taxes distort incentives and cause deadweight losses. If the government takes away additional income a person might earn through higher income taxes or reduced transfers, both Peter and Paul have less incentive to work hard. As they work less, society's income falls, and so does total utility. The utilitarian government has to balance the gains from greater equality against the losses from distorted incentives. To maximize total utility, therefore, the government stops short of making society fully egalitarian.

A famous parable sheds light on the utilitarian's logic. Imagine that Peter and Paul are thirsty travelers trapped at different places in the desert. Peter's oasis has much water; Paul's has little. If the government could transfer water from one oasis to the other without cost, it would maximize total utility from water by equalizing the amount in the two places. But suppose that the government has only a leaky bucket. As it tries to move water from one place to the other, some of the water is lost in transit. In this case, a utilitarian government might still try to move some water from Peter to Paul, depending on how thirsty Paul is and how leaky the bucket is. But, with only a leaky bucket at its disposal, a utilitarian government will not try to reach complete equality.

LIBERALISM

liberalism

the political philosophy according to which the government should choose policies deemed to be just, as evaluated by an impartial observer behind a "veil of ignorance"

A second way of thinking about inequality might be called **liberalism.** Philosopher John Rawls develops this view in his book *A Theory of Justice.* This book was first published in 1971, and it quickly became a classic in political philosophy.

Rawls begins with the premise that a society's institutions, laws, and policies should be just. He then takes up the natural question: How can we, the members of society, ever agree on what justice means? It might seem that every person's point of view is inevitably based on his or her particular circumstances—whether he or she is talented or less talented, diligent or lazy, educated or less educated, born to a wealthy family or a poor one. Could we ever *objectively* determine what a just society would be?

To answer this question, Rawls proposes the following thought experiment. Imagine that before any of us is born, we all get together for a meeting to design the rules that govern society. At this point, we are all ignorant about the station in life each of us will end up filling. In Rawls's words, we are sitting in an "original position" behind a "veil of ignorance." In this original position, Rawls argued, we can choose a just set of rules for society because we must consider how those rules will affect every person. As Rawls puts it, "Since all are similarly situated and no one is able to design principles to favor his particular conditions, the principles of justice are the result of fair agreement or bargain." Designing public policies and institutions in this way allows us to be objective about what policies are just.

Rawls then considers what public policy designed behind this veil of ignorance would try to achieve. In particular, he considers what income distribution a person would consider just if that person did not know whether he or she would end up at the top, bottom, or middle of the distribution. Rawls argues that a person in the original position would be especially concerned about the possibility of being at the *bottom* of the income distribution. In designing public policies, therefore, we should aim to raise the welfare of the worst-off person in society. That is, rather than maximizing the sum of everyone's utility, as a utilitarian would do, Rawls would maximize the minimum utility. Rawls's rule is called the **maximin criterion.**

Because the maximin criterion emphasizes the least fortunate person in society, it justifies public policies aimed at equalizing the distribution of income. By transferring income from the rich to the poor, society raises the well-being of the least fortunate. The maximin criterion would not, however, lead to a completely egalitarian society. If the government promised to equalize incomes completely, people would have no incentive to work hard, society's total income would fall substantially, and the least fortunate person would be worse off. Thus, the maximin criterion still allows disparities in income, because such disparities can improve incentives and thereby raise society's ability to help the poor. Nonetheless, because Rawls's philosophy puts weight on only the least fortunate members of society, it calls for more income redistribution than does utilitarianism.

Rawls's views are controversial, but the thought experiment he proposes has much appeal. In particular, this thought experiment allows us to consider the redistribution of income as a form of *social insurance.* That is, from the perspective of the original position behind the veil of ignorance, income redistribution is like an insurance policy. Homeowners buy fire insurance to protect themselves from the risk of their housing burning down. Similarly, when we as a society choose policies that tax the rich to supplement the incomes of the poor, we are all insuring ourselves against the possibility that we might have been a member of a poor family. Because people dislike risk, we should be happy to have been born into a society that provides us this insurance.

It is not at all clear, however, that rational people behind the veil of ignorance would truly be so averse to risk as to follow the maximin criterion. Indeed, because a person in the original position might end up anywhere in the distribution of outcomes, he or she might treat all possible outcomes equally when designing public policies. In this case, the best policy behind the veil of ignorance would be to maximize the average utility of members of society, and the resulting notion of justice would be more utilitarian than Rawlsian.

LIBERTARIANISM

A third view of inequality is called **libertarianism.** The two views we have considered so far—utilitarianism and liberalism—both view the total income of society as a shared resource that a social planner can freely redistribute to achieve some social goal. By contrast, libertarians argue that society itself earns no income—only individual members of society earn income. According to libertarians, the government should not take from some individuals and give to others in order to achieve any particular distribution of income.

For instance, philosopher Robert Nozick writes the following in his famous 1974 book, *Anarchy, State and Utopia:*

> We are not in the position of children who have been given portions of pie by someone who now makes last minute adjustments to rectify careless cutting. There is no *central* distribution, no person or group entitled to control all the resources, jointly deciding how they are to be doled out. What each person gets, he gets from others who give to him in exchange for something, or as a

maximin criterion
the claim that the government should aim to maximize the well-being of the worst-off person in society

libertarianism
the political philosophy according to which the government should punish crimes and enforce voluntary agreements but not redistribute income

gift. In a free society, diverse persons control different resources, and new holdings arise out of the voluntary exchanges and actions of persons.

Whereas utilitarians and liberals try to judge what amount of inequality is desirable in a society, Nozick denies the validity of this very question.

The libertarian alternative to evaluating economic *outcomes* is to evaluate the *process* by which these outcomes arise. When the distribution of income is achieved unfairly—for instance, when one person steals from another—the government has the right and duty to remedy the problem. But, as long as the process determining the distribution of income is just, the resulting distribution is fair, no matter how unequal.

Nozick criticizes Rawls's liberalism by drawing an analogy between the distribution of income in society and the distribution of grades in a course. Suppose you were asked to judge the fairness of the grades in the economics course you are now taking. Would you imagine yourself behind a veil of ignorance and choose a grade distribution without knowing the talents and efforts of each student? Or would you ensure that the process of assigning grades to students is fair without regard for whether the resulting distribution is equal or unequal? For the case of grades at least, the libertarian emphasis on process over outcomes is compelling.

Libertarians conclude that equality of opportunities is more important than equality of incomes. They believe that the government should enforce individual rights to ensure that everyone has the same opportunity to use his or her talents and achieve success. Once these rules of the game are established, the government has no reason to alter the resulting distribution of income.

QUICK QUIZ   Pam earns more than Pauline. Someone proposes taxing Pam in order to supplement Pauline's income. How would a utilitarian, a liberal, and a libertarian evaluate this proposal?

POLICIES TO REDUCE POVERTY

As we have just seen, political philosophers hold various views about what role the government should take in altering the distribution of income. Political debate among the larger population of voters reflects a similar disagreement. Despite these continuing debates, however, most people believe that, at the very least, the government should try to help those most in need. According to a popular metaphor, the government should provide a "safety net" to prevent any citizen from falling too far.

Poverty is one of the most difficult problems that policymakers face. Poor families are more likely than the overall population to experience homelessness, drug dependency, domestic violence, health problems, teenage pregnancy, illiteracy, unemployment, and low educational attainment. Members of poor families are both more likely to commit crimes and more likely to be victims of crimes. Although it is hard to separate the causes of poverty from the effects, there is no doubt that poverty is associated with various economic and social ills.

Suppose that you were a policymaker in the government, and your goal was to reduce the number of people living in poverty. How would you achieve this goal? Here we consider some of the policy options that you might consider. As we shall see, although each of these options does help some people escape poverty, none of them is perfect, and deciding which is best is not easy.

MINIMUM-WAGE LAWS

Laws setting a minimum wage that employers can pay workers are a perennial source of debate. Advocates view the minimum wage as a way of helping the working poor without any cost to the government. Critics view it as hurting those it is intended to help.

The minimum wage is easily understood using the tools of supply and demand, as we first saw in Chapter 6. For workers with low levels of skill and experience, a high minimum wage forces the wage above the level that balances supply and demand. It therefore raises the cost of labor to firms and reduces the quantity of labor that those firms demand. The result is higher unemployment among those groups of workers affected by the minimum wage. Although those workers who remain employed benefit from a higher wage, those who might have been employed at a lower wage are worse off.

The magnitude of these effects depends crucially on the elasticity of demand. Advocates of a high minimum wage argue that the demand for unskilled labor is relatively inelastic, so that a high minimum wage depresses employment only slightly. Critics of the minimum wage argue that labor demand is more elastic, especially in the long run when firms can adjust employment and production more fully. They also note that many minimum-wage workers are teenagers from middle-class families, so that a high minimum wage is imperfectly targeted as a policy for helping the poor.

WELFARE

One way to raise the living standards of the poor is for the government to supplement their incomes. The primary way in which the government does this is through the welfare system. **Welfare** is a broad term that encompasses various government programs. Aid to Families with Dependent Children (AFDC) has been a program that assists families where there are children but no adult able to support the family. In a typical AFDC family, the father is absent, and the mother is at home raising small children. (In 1996 a welfare reform bill, discussed in the accompanying In the News box, initiated major changes in the AFDC program.) Another welfare program is Supplemental Security Income (SSI), which provides assistance to the poor who are sick or disabled. Note that for both of these welfare programs, a poor person cannot qualify for assistance simply by having a low income. He or she must also establish some additional "need," such as small children or a disability.

A common criticism of welfare programs is that they create incentives for people to become "needy." For example, these programs may encourage families to break up, for many families qualify for financial assistance only if the father is absent. The programs may also encourage illegitimate births, for many poor, single women qualify for assistance only if they have children. Because

welfare
government programs that supplement the incomes of the needy

IN 1996 PRESIDENT CLINTON SIGNED into law a major reform of the U.S. welfare system. In the following opinion column, economist Gary Becker presents the case for this welfare bill.

What Makes the Welfare Bill a Winner

BY GARY S. BECKER

The welfare reform bill passed by Congress and signed into law by President Clinton does not cut welfare spending sharply. Nevertheless, it is revolutionary because it establishes the principle that individuals and families are no longer automatically entitled to government support just because they are poor.

Although most families on welfare use the benefits only to tide them over temporary difficulties, about 40 percent stay for more than two years. Unfortunately, the evidence is clear that the longer a family has been on welfare, the harder it is to get off.

That's why limiting the time families can be on welfare is one of the most important provisions of the new law. These limits prevent families from using welfare as a permanent crutch: They stipulate that recipients must give up most of the benefits unless the family head begins to work within two years. Families can spend more than one spell on welfare, but lifetime benefits are limited to five years—although states can waive that requirement for up to 20 percent of their families.

The termination of benefits after the allotted period has been sharply criticized. In my view, however, it is an important step in the right direction. Time limits are desirable not only because they reduce government outlays but also because long periods on welfare erode work skills and entrench the habit of depending on the government for handouts. This destroys earning power, individual initiative, and self-confidence.

Democrats in Congress who voted against the bill argue that many children will become innocent victims if their mothers are forced off the welfare rolls. (But note that 50 percent of House Democrats and more than half of those in the Senate supported it—along with practically all Republican members.) I agree that the effect of welfare reform on children should be the main consideration. But critics are comparing the new sys-

poor, single mothers are such an important part of the poverty problem and because welfare programs seem to raise the number of poor, single mothers, critics of the welfare system assert that these policies exacerbate the very problems they are supposed to cure.

How severe are these potential problems with the welfare system? No one knows for sure. Proponents of the welfare system point out that being a poor, single mother on welfare is a difficult existence at best, and they are skeptical that many people would be encouraged to pursue such a life if it were not thrust upon them. Moreover, trends over time do not support the view that the decline of the two-parent family is largely a symptom of the welfare system, as the system's critics sometimes claim. Since the early 1970s, welfare benefits (adjusted for inflation) have declined, yet the percentage of children living with only one parent has risen.

NEGATIVE INCOME TAX

Whenever the government chooses a system to collect taxes, it affects the distribution of income. This is clearly true in the case of a progressive income tax, whereby high-income families pay a larger percentage of their income in taxes than do low-income families. As we discussed in Chapter 12, equity across income groups is an important criterion in the design of a tax system.

tem with an ideal standard, not with the failed approach being replaced. New approaches to poverty and welfare are long overdue.

In the past 50 years, more than $5 trillion has been spent on means-tested government programs for the poor. The number of families on welfare grew from less than 8 million in 1970 to almost 15 million in the 1990s. Yet mistreatment, neglect, and other abuses of poor children continue to worsen. I do not know of evidence that shows that children in welfare families do even as well as those in the many equally poor eligible families that forgo welfare benefits.

Prolonged exposure to welfare severely harms many children, despite the monetary benefits, mainly because it corrupts their values. Children in families that spend long periods on welfare begin to accept that it is more normal to be supported by the government than to be financially and psychologically indepen-

dent. This is why even five years of benefits is often too long. Forcing welfare parents to get even modest jobs can contribute to giving new hope and motivation to their children.

The new law decentralizes welfare policy through federal lump-sum grants to state governments that are free to operate their own welfare programs—subject to federally imposed time limits and other restrictions. Opponents of this devolution of power argue that many states will neglect poor blacks and other minorities. Some may develop weak programs—but it is more difficult now to discriminate against minorities than it was before civil-rights and related federal laws were enacted.

Moreover, practically all the innovative approaches to welfare during the past decade, including major provisions of the federal law, were first begun or proposed by California, Michigan, New Jersey, Wisconsin, and other states.

Many others will copy these innovators, which is why I expect most states to spend their welfare grants with less bureaucracy and more effectiveness than the federal government has.

The welfare law is not perfect. For example, it is doubtful whether the best way to deter immigrants is to make legal aliens ineligible for many welfare benefits. The law is, however, a significant step toward recognizing a basic lesson of economics: that government benefits greatly affect incentives, behavior, and values.

Welfare reform should be followed by similar reforms of Social Security, Medicare, and other so-called entitlement programs to incorporate much more powerful incentives for families to help themselves. The result would be higher savings for old age, greater economies in spending on medical care, and a society with much better values.

SOURCE: *Business Week*, September 23, 1996, p. 22.

Many economists have advocated supplementing the income of the poor using a **negative income tax**. According to this policy, every family would report its income to the government. High-income families would pay a tax based on their incomes. Low-income families would receive a subsidy. In other words, they would "pay" a "negative tax."

For example, suppose the government used the following formula to compute a family's tax liability:

$$\text{Taxes owed} = (1/3 \text{ of Income}) - \$10,000.$$

In this case, a family that earned $60,000 would pay $10,000 in taxes, and a family that earned $90,000 would pay $20,000 in taxes. A family that earned $30,000 would owe nothing. And a family that earned $15,000 would "owe" −$5,000. In other words, the government would send this family a check for $5,000.

Under a negative income tax, poor families would receive financial assistance without having to demonstrate need. The only qualification required to receive assistance would be a low income. Depending on one's point of view, this feature can be either an advantage or a disadvantage. On the one hand, a negative income tax does not encourage illegitimate births and the breakup of families, as critics of the welfare system believe current policy does. On the other hand, a negative income tax would subsidize those who are just lazy and, in some people's eyes, undeserving of government support.

negative income tax
a tax system that collects revenue from high-income households and gives transfers to low-income households

One actual tax provision that works much like a negative income tax is the Earned Income Tax Credit. This credit allows poor working families to receive income tax refunds greater than the taxes they paid during the year. Because the Earned Income Tax Credit applies only to the working poor, it does not discourage recipients from working, as other antipoverty programs are claimed to do. For the same reason, however, it also does not help alleviate poverty due to unemployment, sickness, or other inability to work.

IN-KIND TRANSFERS

Another way to help the poor is to provide them directly with some of the goods and services they need to raise their living standards. For example, charities provide the needy with food, shelter, and toys at Christmas. The government gives poor families *food stamps*, which are government vouchers that can be used to buy food at stores; the stores then redeem these vouchers for money. The government also gives many poor people health care through a program called *Medicaid*.

Is it better to help the poor with these in-kind transfers or with direct cash payments? There is no clear answer.

Advocates of in-kind transfers argue that such transfers ensure that the poor get what they need most. Among the poorest members of society, alcohol and drug addiction is more common than it is in society as a whole. By providing the poor with food and shelter, society can be more confident that it is not helping to support such addictions. This is one reason that in-kind transfers are more politically popular than cash payments to the poor.

Advocates of cash payments argue that in-kind transfers are inefficient and disrespectful. The government does not know what goods and services the poor need most. Many of the poor are ordinary people down on their luck. Despite their misfortune, they are in the best position to decide how to raise their own living standards. Rather than giving the poor in-kind transfers of goods and services that they may not want, it may be better to give them cash and allow them to buy what they think they need most.

ANTIPOVERTY PROGRAMS AND WORK INCENTIVES

Many policies aimed at helping the poor can have the unintended effect of discouraging the poor from escaping poverty on their own. To see why, consider the following example. Suppose that a family needs an income of $15,000 to maintain a reasonable standard of living. And suppose that, out of concern for the poor, the government promises to guarantee every family that income. Whatever a family earns, the government makes up the difference between that income and $15,000. What effect would you expect this policy to have?

The incentive effects of this policy are obvious: Any person who would make under $15,000 by working has no incentive to find and keep a job. For every dollar that the person would earn, the government would reduce the income supplement by a dollar. In effect, the government taxes 100 percent of additional earnings. An effective marginal tax rate of 100 percent is surely a policy with a large deadweight loss.

IN THE NEWS

Saving and Welfare

PROGRAMS AIMED AT HELPING THE POOR have many unintended side effects. One is that they discourage the poor from saving. The following article describes what happened to one mother on welfare when she tried to put something away for a rainy day.

For Welfare Parents, Scrimping Is Legal, but Saving Is Out

BY ROBERT L. ROSE

A penny saved is a penny earned. Usually.

Take the case of Grace Capetillo, a thirty-six-year-old mother with a true talent for parsimony. To save on clothing, Ms. Capetillo dresses herself plainly in thrift-store finds. To cut her grocery bill, she stocks up on 67-cent boxes of saltines and 39-cent cans of chicken soup.

When Ms. Capetillo's five-year-old daughter, Michelle, asked for "Li'l Miss Makeup" for Christmas, her mother bypassed Toys "R" Us, where the doll retails for $19.99. Instead, she found one at Goodwill—for $1.89. She cleaned it up and tied a pink ribbon in its hair before giving the doll to Michelle. Ms. Capetillo found the popular Mr. Potato Head at Goodwill, too, assembling the plastic toy one piece at a time from the used toy bin. It cost her 79 cents, and saved $3.18.

Ms. Capetillo's stingy strategies helped her build a savings account of more than $3,000 in the last four years. Her goal was to put away enough to buy a new washing machine and maybe one day help send Michelle to college. To some, this might make her an example of virtue in her gritty North Side neighborhood, known more for boarded up houses than high aspirations. But there was one catch: Ms. Capetillo is on welfare—$440 a month, plus $60 in food stamps—and saving that much money on public aid is against the law. When welfare officials found out about it, they were quick to act. Ms. Capetillo, they charged, was saving at the expense of taxpayers.

Last month, the Milwaukee County Department of Social Services took her to court, charged her with fraud and demanded she return the savings—and thousands more for a total of $15,545. Ms. Capetillo says she didn't know it, but under the federal program Aid to Families with Dependent Children, she was ineligible for assistance the day in 1985 when her savings eclipsed $1,000.

Uncle Sam wanted the money back.

"Tax dollars are going to support a person's basic needs on the AFDC program," says Robert Davis, associate director of the Milwaukee social services department. Federal rules, and the spirit of the program, don't intend for "people to take the money and put it in a savings account.". . .

After the law caught up with her, Ms. Capetillo reduced her savings to avoid having her welfare checks cut off. She bought her new washing machine, a used stove to replace her hotplate, a $40 refrigerator, and a new bedroom set for Michelle. But that didn't resolve the charge of fraud.

Finally, her day in court arrived. At first, Circuit Judge Charles B. Schudson had trouble figuring out Ms. Capetillo's crime. To him, welfare fraud meant double dipping: collecting full benefits and holding a job at the same time.

After the lawyers explained the rules about saving money, he made it clear he didn't think much of the rules. "I don't know how much more powerfully we could say it to the poor in our society: Don't try to save," he said. Judge Schudson said it was "ironic" that the case came as President Bush promotes his plan for Family Savings Accounts. "Apparently, that's an incentive that this country would only give to the rich."

Others differ. County welfare worker Sophia Partipilo says Ms. Capetillo's savings raise the question of whether she needed a welfare check at all. "We're not a savings and loan," says Ms. Partipilo, who handled the case. "We don't hand out toasters at the end of the month. We're here to get you over the rough times."

Ms. Capetillo could have fought the charge. Her lawyer and even the judge said later that there was a good chance a jury would have sided with the welfare mother. Even the prosecutor admits that had she simply spent the money, rather than saving it, she could have avoided a run-in with the law.

But for Ms. Capetillo, going to court once was enough. She was so frightened and her throat so dry that the judge could barely hear her speak. She pleaded guilty to "failure to report change in circumstances." The judge sentenced her to one-year probation and ordered her to repay $1,000.

SOURCE: *The Wall Street Journal,* February 6, 1990, pp. 1, 11.

The adverse effects of this high effective tax rate can persist over time. A person discouraged from working loses the on-the-job training that a job might offer. In addition, his or her children miss the lessons learned by observing a parent with a full-time job, and this may adversely affect their own ability to find and hold a job.

Although the antipoverty program we have been discussing is hypothetical, it is not as unrealistic as it might first appear. Welfare, Medicaid, food stamps, and the Earned Income Tax Credit are all programs aimed at helping the poor, and they are all tied to family income. As a family's income rises, the family becomes ineligible for these programs. When all these programs are taken together, it is common for families to face effective marginal tax rates that are very high. Sometimes the effective marginal tax rates even exceed 100 percent, so that poor families are worse off when they earn more. By trying to help the poor, the government discourages those families from working. According to critics of antipoverty programs, these programs alter work attitudes and create a "culture of poverty."

It might seem that there is an easy solution to this problem: Reduce benefits to poor families more gradually as their incomes rise. For example, if a poor family loses 30 cents of benefits for every dollar it earns, then it faces an effective marginal tax rate of 30 percent. This effective tax reduces work effort to some extent, but it does not eliminate the incentive to work completely.

The problem with this solution is that it greatly increases the cost of programs to combat poverty. If benefits are phased out gradually as a poor family's income rises, then families just above the poverty level will also be eligible for substantial benefits. The more gradual is the phase-out, the more families are eligible, and the greater is the cost of the program. Thus, policymakers face a trade-off between burdening the poor with high effective marginal tax rates and burdening taxpayers with costly programs to reduce poverty.

In 1996 the Republican-controlled Congress passed a major welfare reform bill aimed at solving this problem. The bill limits the number of years that any person can collect welfare. Advocates of the bill argued that it would reduce the adverse incentive effects of permanent welfare. Critics argued that it would push many families with children well below the poverty line. President Clinton, who had promised in the 1992 election to "end welfare as we know it," signed the bill over the objections of many in his party.

▌ QUICK QUIZ List three policies aimed at helping the poor, and discuss the pros and cons of each.

CONCLUSION

People have long reflected on the distribution of income in society. Plato, the ancient Greek philosopher, concluded that in an ideal society the income of the richest person would be no more than four times the income of the poorest person. Although the measurement of inequality is difficult, it is clear that our society has much more inequality than Plato recommended.

One of the *Ten Principles of Economics* discussed in Chapter 1 is that governments can sometimes improve market outcomes. There is little consensus, however, about how this principle should be applied to the distribution of income. Philosophers and policymakers today do not agree on how much income inequality is desirable, or even whether public policy should aim to alter the distribution of income. Much of public debate reflects this disagreement. Whenever taxes are raised, for instance, lawmakers argue over how much of the tax hike should fall on the rich, the middle class, and the poor.

Another of the *Ten Principles of Economics* is that people face tradeoffs. This principle is important to keep in mind when thinking about economic inequality. Policies that penalize the successful and reward the unsuccessful reduce the incentive to succeed. Thus, policymakers face a tradeoff between equality and efficiency. The more equally the pie is divided, the smaller the pie becomes. This is the one lesson concerning the distribution of income about which almost everyone agrees.

Summary

◆ Data on the distribution of income show wide disparity in our society. The richest fifth of families earns about ten times as much income as the poorest fifth.

◆ Because in-kind transfers, the economic life cycle, transitory income, and economic mobility are so important for understanding variation in income, it is difficult to gauge the degree of inequality in our society using data on the distribution of income in a single year. When these factors are taken into account, they tend to suggest that economic well-being is more equally distributed than is annual income.

◆ Political philosophers differ in their views about the role of government in altering the distribution of income. Utilitarians (such as John Stuart Mill) would choose the distribution of income to maximize the sum of utility of everyone in society. Liberals (such as John Rawls) would determine the distribution of income as if we were behind a "veil of ignorance" that prevented us from knowing our own stations in life. Libertarians (such as Robert Nozick) would have the government enforce individual rights to ensure a fair process but then not be concerned about inequality in the resulting distribution of income.

◆ Various policies aim to help the poor—minimum-wage laws, welfare, negative income taxes, and in-kind transfers. Although each of these policies helps some families escape poverty, they also have unintended side effects. Because financial assistance declines as income rises, the poor often face effective marginal tax rates that are very high. Such high effective tax rates discourage poor families from escaping poverty on their own.

Key Concepts

poverty rate, p. 426
poverty line, p. 426
in-kind transfers, p. 428
life cycle, p. 428

permanent income, p. 430
utilitarianism, p. 431
utility, p. 431
liberalism, p. 432

maximin criterion, p. 433
libertarianism, p. 433
welfare, p. 435
negative income tax, p. 437

Questions for Review

1. Does the richest fifth of the U.S. population earn two, four, or ten times the income of the poorest fifth?

2. What groups in the population are most likely to live in poverty?

3. When gauging the amount of inequality, why do transitory and life cycle variations in income cause difficulties?

4. How would a utilitarian, a liberal, and a libertarian determine how much income inequality is permissible?

5. What are the pros and cons of in-kind (rather than cash) transfers to the poor?

Problems and Applications

1. Table 20-2 shows that income inequality in the United States has increased during the past 20 years. Some factors contributing to this increase were discussed in Chapter 19. What are they?

2. The share of total income received by the top fifth of the population was especially high in 1935, according to Table 20-2. Can you think of a reason why this might have occurred?

3. Table 20-4 shows that the percentage of children in families with income below the poverty line is almost twice the percentage of the elderly in such families. How might the allocation of government money across different social programs have contributed to this phenomenon? (Hint: See Chapter 12.)

4. Economists often view life cycle variation in income as one form of transitory variation in income around people's lifetime, or permanent, income. In this sense, how does your current income compare to your permanent income? Do you think your current income accurately reflects your standard of living?

5. The chapter suggests that people can use saving and borrowing to smooth out transitory variation in income in order to maintain steady consumption.
   a. What obstacles might prevent such smoothing?
   b. What does this tell you about whether it is appropriate to base measures of income inequality purely on permanent income?

6. The chapter discusses the importance of economic mobility.
   a. What policies might the government pursue to increase economic mobility *within* a generation?
   b. What policies might the government pursue to increase economic mobility *across* generations?
   c. Do you think we should reduce spending on current welfare programs in order to increase spending on programs that enhance economic mobility? What are some of the advantages and disadvantages of doing so?

7. Consider two communities. In one community, ten families have incomes of $100 each and ten families have incomes of $20 each. In the other community, ten families have incomes of $200 each and ten families have incomes of $22 each.
   a. In which community is the distribution of income more unequal? In which community is the problem of poverty likely to be worse?
   b. Which distribution of income would Rawls prefer? Explain.
   c. Which distribution of income do you prefer? Explain.

8. The chapter uses the analogy of a "leaky bucket" to explain one constraint on the redistribution of income.
   a. What elements of the U.S. system for redistributing income create the leaks in the bucket? Be specific.
   b. Do you think that Republicans or Democrats generally believe that the bucket used for redistributing income is more leaky? How does that belief affect their views about the amount of income redistribution that the government should undertake?

9. Suppose there are two possible income distributions in a society of ten people. In the first distribution, nine people have incomes of $30,000 and one person has an income of $10,000. In the second distribution, all ten people have incomes of $25,000.
   a. If the society had the first income distribution, what would be the utilitarian argument for redistributing income?
   b. Which income distribution would Rawls consider more equitable? Explain.
   c. Which income distribution would Nozick consider more equitable? Explain.

10. Do you think a person who believes that the government should help poor children but not poor adults would be more likely to advocate cash welfare payments or in-kind transfers?

11. The poverty rate would be substantially lower if the market value of in-kind transfers were added to family

income. The government spends more money on Medicaid than on any other in-kind transfer, with expenditures per recipient family amounting to roughly $5,000 annually.

a. If the government gave each recipient family a check for this amount instead of enrolling them in the Medicaid program, do you think that most of these families would spend that much to purchase health insurance? (Recall that the poverty line is below $15,000 for a family of four.) Why?

b. How does your answer to part (a) affect your view about whether we should determine the poverty rate by valuing in-kind transfers at the price the government pays for them? Explain.

c. How does your answer to part (a) affect your view about whether we should provide assistance to the poor in the form of cash transfers or in-kind transfers? Explain.

12. Suppose that a family's tax liability equaled its income multiplied by one-half, minus $10,000. Under this system, some families would pay taxes to the government, and some families would receive money from the government through a "negative income tax."

a. Consider families with pre-tax incomes of $0, $10,000, $20,000, $30,000, and $40,000. Make a table showing pre-tax income, taxes paid to the government or money received from the government, and after-tax income for each family.

b. What is the marginal tax rate in this system? (See Chapter 12 if you need to review the definition of marginal tax rate.) What is the maximum amount of income at which a family *receives* money from the government?

c. Now suppose that the tax schedule is changed, so that a family's tax liability equals its income multiplied by one-quarter, minus $10,000. What is the marginal tax rate in this new system? What is the maximum amount of income at which a family receives money from the government?

d. What is the main advantage of each of the tax schedules discussed here?

13. John and Jeremy are both utilitarians. John believes that labor supply is highly elastic, whereas Jeremy believes that labor supply is quite inelastic. How do you suppose their views about income redistribution differ?

14. Consider each of the following statements. Do you agree or disagree? What do your views imply for public policies, such as taxes on inheritance?

a. "Every parent has the right to work hard and save in order to give his or her children a better life."

b. "No child should be disadvantaged by the sloth or bad luck of his or her parents."

VII

ADVANCED TOPIC

21

THE THEORY OF
CONSUMER CHOICE

*See how a budget
constraint represents
the choices a consumer
can afford*

*Learn how indifference
curves can be used to
represent a consumer's
preferences*

*Analyze how a
consumer's optimal
choices are determined*

*See how a consumer
responds to changes
in income and changes
in prices*

*Decompose the impact of
a price change into an
income effect and a
substitution effect*

*Apply the theory of
consumer choice to
four questions about
household behavior*

When you walk into a store, you are confronted with thousands of goods that you might buy. Of course, because your financial resources are limited, you cannot buy everything that you want. You therefore consider the prices of the various goods being offered for sale and buy a bundle of goods that, given your resources, best suits your needs and desires.

In this chapter we develop the theory that describes how consumers make decisions about what to buy. So far throughout this book, we have summarized consumers' decisions with the demand curve. As we discussed in Chapters 4 through 7, the demand curve for a good reflects consumers' willingness to pay for it. When the price of a good rises, consumers are willing to pay for fewer units, so the quantity demanded falls. We now look more deeply at the decisions that lie behind the demand curve. The theory of consumer choice presented in this chapter provides a more complete understanding of demand, just as the theory of the competitive firm in Chapter 14 provides a more complete understanding of supply.

One of the *Ten Principles of Economics* discussed in Chapter 1 is that people face tradeoffs. The theory of consumer choice examines the tradeoffs that people face in their role as consumers. When a consumer buys more of one good, he can afford less of other goods. When he spends more time enjoying leisure and less time working, he has lower income and can afford less consumption. When he spends more of his income in the present and saves less of it, he must accept a lower level of consumption in the future. The theory of consumer choice examines how consumers facing these tradeoffs make decisions and how they respond to changes in their environment.

After developing the basic theory of consumer choice, we apply it to several questions about household decisions. In particular, we ask:

◆ Do all demand curves slope downward?
◆ How do wages affect labor supply?
◆ How do interest rates affect household saving?
◆ Do the poor prefer to receive cash or in-kind transfers?

At first, these questions might seem unrelated. But, as we will see, we can use the theory of consumer choice to address each of them.

THE BUDGET CONSTRAINT: WHAT THE CONSUMER CAN AFFORD

Most people would like to increase the quantity or quality of the goods they consume—to take longer vacations, drive fancier cars, or eat at better restaurants. People consume less than they desire because their spending is *constrained*, or limited, by their income. We begin our study of consumer choice by examining this link between income and spending.

To keep things simple, we examine the decision facing a consumer who buys only two goods: Pepsi and pizza. Of course, real people buy thousands of different kinds of goods. Yet assuming there are only two goods greatly simplifies the problem without altering the basic insights about consumer choice.

We first consider how the consumer's income constrains the amount he spends on Pepsi and pizza. Suppose that the consumer has an income of $1,000 per month and that he spends his entire income each month on Pepsi and pizza. The price of a pint of Pepsi is $2, and the price of a pizza is $10.

Table 21-1 shows some of the many combinations of Pepsi and pizza that the consumer can buy. The first line in the table shows that if the consumer spends all his income on pizza, he can eat 100 pizzas during the month, but he would not be able to buy any Pepsi at all. The second line shows another possible consumption bundle: 90 pizzas and 50 pints of Pepsi. And so on. Each consumption bundle in the table costs exactly $1,000.

Figure 21-1 graphs the consumption bundles that the consumer can choose. The vertical axis measures the number of pints of Pepsi, and the horizontal axis measures the number of pizzas. Three points are marked on this figure. At point A, the consumer buys no Pepsi and consumes 100 pizzas. At point B, the con-

PINTS OF PEPSI	NUMBER OF PIZZAS	SPENDING ON PEPSI	SPENDING ON PIZZA	TOTAL SPENDING
0	100	$ 0	$1,000	$1,000
50	90	100	900	1,000
100	80	200	800	1,000
150	70	300	700	1,000
200	60	400	600	1,000
250	50	500	500	1,000
300	40	600	400	1,000
350	30	700	300	1,000
400	20	800	200	1,000
450	10	900	100	1,000
500	0	1,000	0	1,000

Table 21-1

THE CONSUMER'S OPPORTUNITIES. This table shows what the consumer can afford if his income is $1,000, the price of Pepsi is $2, and the price of pizza is $10.

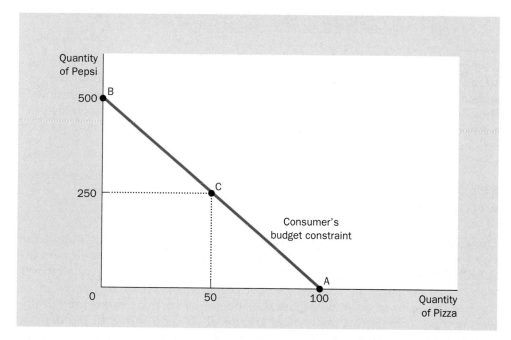

Figure 21-1

THE CONSUMER'S BUDGET CONSTRAINT. The budget constraint shows the various bundles of goods that the consumer can afford for a given income. Here the consumer buys bundles of Pepsi and pizza. The more Pepsi he buys, the less pizza he can afford.

sumer buys no pizza and consumes 500 pints of Pepsi. At point C, the consumer buys 50 pizzas and 250 pints of Pepsi. Point C, which is exactly at the middle of the line from A to B, is the point at which the consumer spends an equal amount ($500) on Pepsi and pizza. Of course, these are only three of the many combinations of Pepsi and pizza that the consumer can choose. All the points on the line from A to B are possible. This line, which is called the **budget constraint,** shows the consumption bundles that the consumer can afford. In this case, it shows the consumer's tradeoff between Pepsi and pizza.

The slope of the budget constraint measures the rate at which the consumer can trade one good for the other. Recall from the Appendix to Chapter 2 that the slope between two points is calculated as the change in the vertical distance

budget constraint
the limit on the consumption bundles that a consumer can afford

divided by the change in the horizontal distance ("rise over run"). From point A to point B, the vertical distance is 500 pints, and the horizontal distance is 100 pizzas. Thus, the slope is 5 pints per pizza. (Actually, because the budget constraint slopes downward, the slope is a negative number. But for our purposes we can ignore the minus sign.)

Notice that the slope of the budget constraint equals the *relative price* of the two goods—the price of one good compared to the price of the other. A pizza costs 5 times as much as a pint of Pepsi. Thus, the consumer can trade 1 pizza for 5 pints. This tradeoff is reflected in a budget constraint with a slope of 5.

QUICK QUIZ Draw the budget constraint for a person with income of $1,000 if the price of Pepsi is $5 and the price of pizza is $10. What is the slope of this budget constraint?

PREFERENCES: WHAT THE CONSUMER WANTS

Our goal in this chapter is to see how consumers make choices. The budget constraint is one piece of the analysis: It shows what combination of goods the consumer can afford given his income and the prices of the goods. The consumer's choices, however, depend not only on his budget constraint but also on his preferences over goods. Therefore, the consumer's preferences are the next piece of our analysis.

REPRESENTING PREFERENCES WITH INDIFFERENCE CURVES

indifference curve
a curve that shows consumption bundles that give the consumer the same level of satisfaction

The consumer's preferences allow him to choose among different bundles of Pepsi and pizza. If you offer the consumer two different bundles, he chooses the bundle that best suits his tastes. If the two bundles suit his tastes equally well, we say that the consumer is *indifferent* between the two bundles.

Just as we have represented the consumer's budget constraint graphically, we can also represent his preferences graphically. We do this with indifference curves. An **indifference curve** shows the bundles of consumption that make the consumer equally happy. In this case, the indifference curves show the combinations of Pepsi and pizza with which the consumer is equally satisfied.

Figure 21-2 shows two of the consumer's many indifference curves. The consumer is indifferent among combinations A, B, and C, because they are all on the same curve. Not surprisingly, if the consumer's consumption of pizza is reduced, say from point A to point B, consumption of Pepsi must increase to keep him equally happy. If consumption of pizza is reduced again, from point B to point C, the amount of Pepsi consumed must increase yet again.

marginal rate of substitution
the rate at which a consumer is willing to trade one good for another

The slope at any point on an indifference curve equals the rate at which the consumer is willing to substitute one good for the other. This rate is called the **marginal rate of substitution** (MRS). In this case, the marginal rate of substitution measures how much Pepsi the consumer requires in order to be compen-

Figure 21-2

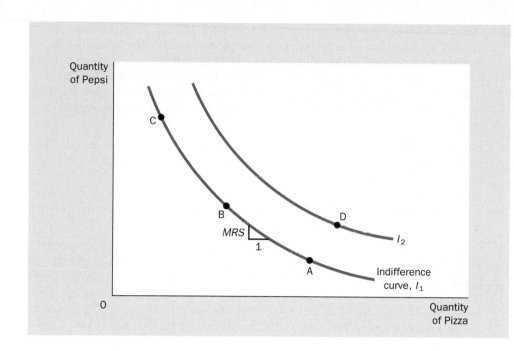

THE CONSUMER'S PREFER-
ENCES. The consumer's preferences are represented with
indifference curves, which show
the combinations of Pepsi and
pizza that make the consumer
equally satisfied. Because the
consumer prefers more of a good,
points on a higher indifference
curve (I_2 here) are preferred to
points on a lower indifference
curve (I_1). The marginal rate of
substitution *(MRS)* shows the
rate at which the consumer is
willing to trade Pepsi for pizza.

sated for a one-unit reduction in pizza consumption. Notice that because the indifference curves are not straight lines, the marginal rate of substitution is not the same at all points on a given indifference curve. The rate at which a consumer is willing to trade one good for the other depends on the amounts of the goods he is already consuming. That is, the rate at which a consumer is willing to trade pizza for Pepsi depends on whether he is more hungry or more thirsty, which in turn depends on how much pizza and Pepsi he has.

The consumer is equally happy at all points on any given indifference curve, but he prefers some indifference curves to others. Because he prefers more consumption to less, higher indifference curves are preferred to lower ones. In Figure 21-2, any point on curve I_2 is preferred to any point on curve I_1.

A consumer's set of indifference curves gives a complete ranking of the consumer's preferences. That is, we can use the indifference curves to rank any two bundles of goods. For example, the indifference curves tell us that point D is preferred to point A because point D is on a higher indifference curve than point A. (That conclusion may be obvious, however, because point D offers the consumer both more pizza and more Pepsi.) The indifference curves also tell us that point D is preferred to point C because point D is on a higher indifference curve. Even though point D has less Pepsi than point C, it has more than enough extra pizza to make the consumer prefer it. By seeing which point is on the higher indifference curve, we can use the set of indifference curves to rank any combinations of Pepsi and pizza.

FOUR PROPERTIES OF INDIFFERENCE CURVES

Because indifference curves represent a consumer's preferences, they have certain properties that reflect those preferences. Here we consider four properties that describe most indifference curves:

◆ *Property 1: Higher indifference curves are preferred to lower ones.* Consumers usually prefer more of something to less of it. (That is why we call this something a "good" rather than a "bad.") This preference for greater quantities is reflected in the indifference curves. As Figure 21-2 shows, higher indifference curves represent larger quantities of goods than lower indifference curves. Thus, the consumer prefers being on higher indifference curves.

◆ *Property 2: Indifference curves are downward sloping.* The slope of an indifference curve reflects the rate at which the consumer is willing to substitute one good for the other. In most cases, the consumer likes both goods. Therefore, if the quantity of one good is reduced, the quantity of the other good must increase in order for the consumer to be equally happy. For this reason, most indifference curves slope downward.

◆ *Property 3: Indifference curves do not cross.* To see why this is true, suppose that two indifference curves did cross, as in Figure 21-3. Then, because point A is on the same indifference curve as point B, the two points would make the consumer equally happy. In addition, because point B is on the same indifference curve as point C, these two points would make the consumer equally happy. But these conclusions imply that points A and C would also make the consumer equally happy, even though point C has more of both goods. This contradicts our assumption that the consumer always prefers more of both goods to less. Thus, indifference curves cannot cross.

◆ *Property 4: Indifference curves are bowed inward.* The slope of an indifference curve is the marginal rate of substitution—the rate at which the consumer is willing to trade off one good for the other. The marginal rate of substitution (MRS) usually depends on the amount of each good the consumer is currently consuming. In particular, because people are more willing to

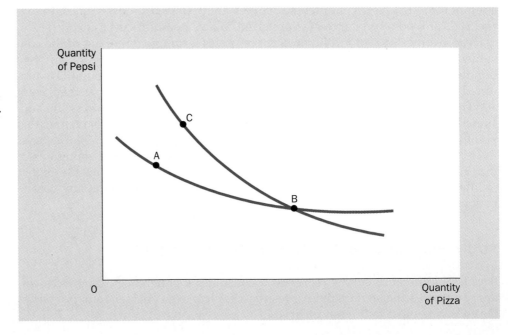

Figure 21-3

THE IMPOSSIBILITY OF INTERSECTING INDIFFERENCE CURVES. A situation like this can never happen. According to these indifference curves, the consumer would be equally satisfied at points A, B, and C, even though point C has more of both goods than point A.

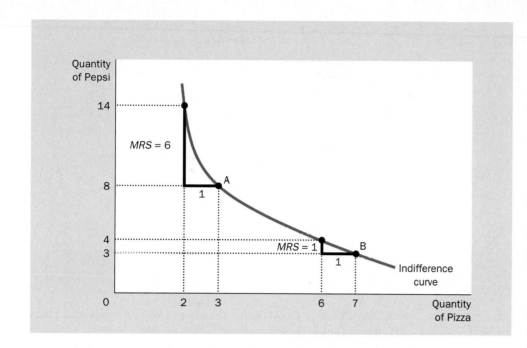

Figure 21-4

BOWED INDIFFERENCE CURVES. Indifference curves are usually bowed inward. This shape implies that the marginal rate of substitution *(MRS)* depends on the quantity of the two goods the consumer is consuming. At point A, the consumer has little pizza and much Pepsi, so he requires a lot of extra Pepsi to induce him to give up one of the pizzas: The marginal rate of substitution is 6 pints of Pepsi per pizza. At point B, the consumer has much pizza and little Pepsi, so he requires only a little extra Pepsi to induce him to give up one of the pizzas: The marginal rate of substitution is 1 pint of Pepsi per pizza.

trade away goods that they have in abundance and less willing to trade away goods of which they have little, the indifference curves are bowed inward. As an example, consider Figure 21-4. At point A, because the consumer has a lot of Pepsi and only a little pizza, he is very hungry but not very thirsty. To induce the consumer to give up 1 pizza, the consumer has to be given 6 pints of Pepsi: The marginal rate of substitution is 6 pints per pizza. By contrast, at point B, the consumer has little Pepsi and a lot of pizza, so he is very thirsty but not very hungry. At this point, he would be willing to give up 1 pizza to get 1 pint of Pepsi: The marginal rate of substitution is 1 pint per pizza. Thus, the bowed shape of the indifference curve reflects the consumer's greater willingness to give up a good that he already has in large quantity.

TWO EXTREME EXAMPLES OF INDIFFERENCE CURVES

The shape of an indifference curve tells us about the consumer's willingness to trade one good for the other. When the goods are easy to substitute for each other, the indifference curves are less bowed; when the goods are hard to substitute, the indifference curves are very bowed. To see why this is true, let's consider the extreme cases.

Perfect Substitutes Suppose that someone offered you bundles of nickels and dimes. How would you rank the different bundles?

Most likely, you would care only about the total monetary value of each bundle. If so, you would judge a bundle based on the number of nickels plus twice the number of dimes. In other words, you would always be willing to trade 1 dime for 2 nickels, regardless of the number of nickels and dimes in the bundle.

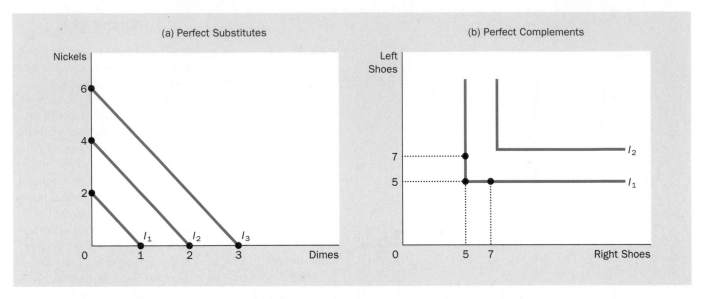

Figure 21-5

PERFECT SUBSTITUTES AND PERFECT COMPLEMENTS. When two goods are easily substitutable, such as nickels and dimes, the indifference curves are straight lines, as shown in panel (a). When two goods are strongly complementary, such as left shoes and right shoes, the indifference curves are right angles, as shown in panel (b).

Your marginal rate of substitution between nickels and dimes would be a fixed number—2.

We can represent your preferences over nickels and dimes with the indifference curves in panel (a) of Figure 21-5. Because the marginal rate of substitution is constant, the indifference curves are straight lines. In this extreme case of straight indifference curves, we say that the two goods are **perfect substitutes.**

perfect substitutes

two goods with straight-line indifference curves

Perfect Complements   Suppose now that someone offered you bundles of shoes. Some of the shoes fit your left foot, others your right foot. How would you rank these different bundles?

In this case, you might care only about the number of pairs of shoes. In other words, you would judge a bundle based on the number of pairs you could assemble from it. A bundle of 5 left shoes and 7 right shoes yields only 5 pairs. Getting 1 more right shoe has no value if there is no left shoe to go with it.

We can represent your preferences for right and left shoes with the indifference curves in panel (b) of Figure 21-5. In this case, a bundle with 5 left shoes and 5 right shoes is just as good as a bundle with 5 left shoes and 7 right shoes. It is also just as good as a bundle with 7 left shoes and 5 right shoes. The indifference curves, therefore, are right angles. In this extreme case of right-angle indifference curves, we say that the two goods are **perfect complements.**

perfect complements

two goods with right-angle indifference curves

In the real world, of course, most goods are neither perfect substitutes (like nickels and dimes) nor perfect complements (like right shoes and left shoes). More typically, the indifference curves are bowed inward, but not so bowed as to become right angles.

❚ **QUICK QUIZ** Draw some indifference curves for Pepsi and pizza. Explain the four properties of these indifference curves.

FYI

Utility: An Alternative Way to Represent a Consumer's Preferences

WE HAVE USED INDIFFERENCE curves to represent the consumer's preferences. Another common way to represent preferences is with the concept of *utility*. Utility is an abstract measure of the satisfaction or happiness that a consumer receives from a bundle of goods. Economists say that a consumer prefers one bundle of goods to another if the first provides more utility than the second.

Indifference curves and utility are closely related. Because the consumer prefers points on higher indifference curves, bundles of goods on higher indifference curves provide higher utility. Because the consumer is equally happy with all points on the same indifference curve, all these bundles provide the same utility. Indeed, you can think of an indifference curve as an "equal-utility" curve. The slope of the indifference curve (the marginal rate of substitution) reflects the marginal utility generated by one good compared to the marginal utility generated by the other good.

When economists discuss the theory of consumer choice, they might express the theory using different words. One economist might say that the goal of the consumer is to maximize utility. Another might say that the goal of the consumer is to end up on the highest possible indifference curve. In essence, these are two ways of saying the same thing.

OPTIMIZATION: WHAT THE CONSUMER CHOOSES

The goal of this chapter is to understand how a consumer makes choices. We have the two pieces necessary for this analysis: the consumer's budget constraint and the consumer's preferences. Now we put these two pieces together and consider the consumer's decision about what to buy.

THE CONSUMER'S OPTIMAL CHOICES

Consider once again our Pepsi and pizza example. The consumer would like to end up with the best possible combination of Pepsi and pizza—that is, the combination on the highest possible indifference curve. But the consumer must also end up on or below his budget constraint, which measures the total resources available to him.

Figure 21-6 shows the consumer's budget constraint and three of his many indifference curves. The highest indifference curve that the consumer can reach (I_2 in the figure) is the one that just barely touches the budget constraint. The point at which this indifference curve and the budget constraint touch is called the *optimum*. The consumer would prefer point A, but he cannot afford that point because it lies above his budget constraint. The consumer can afford point B, but that point is on a lower indifference curve and, therefore, provides the consumer less satisfaction. The optimum point represents the best combination of consumption of Pepsi and pizza available to the consumer.

Notice that, at the optimum, the slope of the indifference curve equals the slope of the budget constraint. We say that the indifference curve is *tangent* to the budget constraint. The slope of the indifference curve is the marginal rate of

Figure 21-6

THE CONSUMER'S OPTIMUM. The consumer chooses the point on his budget constraint that lies on the highest indifference curve. At this point, called the optimum, the marginal rate of substitution equals the relative price of the two goods. Here the highest indifference curve the consumer can reach is I_2. The consumer prefers point A, which lies on indifference curve I_3, but the consumer cannot afford this bundle of Pepsi and pizza. By contrast, point B is affordable, but because it lies on a lower indifference curve, the consumer does not prefer it.

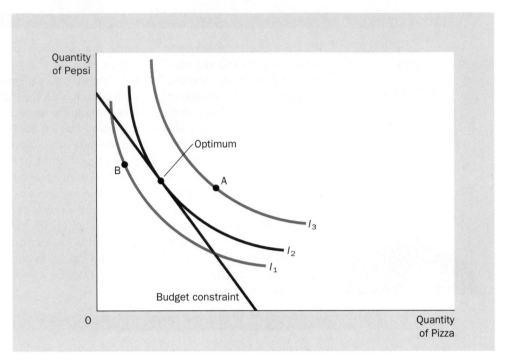

substitution between Pepsi and pizza, and the slope of the budget constraint is the relative price of Pepsi and pizza. Thus, *the consumer chooses consumption of the two goods so that the marginal rate of substitution equals the relative price.*

In Chapter 7 we saw how market prices reflect the marginal value that consumers place on goods. This analysis of consumer choice shows the same result in another way. In making his consumption choices, the consumer takes as given the relative price of the two goods and then chooses an optimum at which his marginal rate of substitution equals this relative price. The relative price is the rate at which the *market* is willing to trade one good for the other, whereas the marginal rate of substitution is the rate at which the *consumer* is willing to trade one good for the other. At the consumer's optimum, the consumer's valuation of the two goods (as measured by the marginal rate of substitution) equals the market's valuation (as measured by the relative price). As a result of this consumer optimization, market prices of different goods reflect the value that consumers place on those goods.

HOW CHANGES IN INCOME AFFECT THE CONSUMER'S CHOICES

Now that we have seen how the consumer makes the consumption decision, let's examine how consumption responds to changes in income. To be specific, suppose that income increases. With higher income, the consumer can afford more of both goods. The increase in income, therefore, shifts the budget constraint outward, as in Figure 21-7. Because the relative price of the two goods has not changed, the slope of the new budget constraint is the same as the slope of the initial budget constraint. That is, an increase in income leads to a parallel shift in the budget constraint.

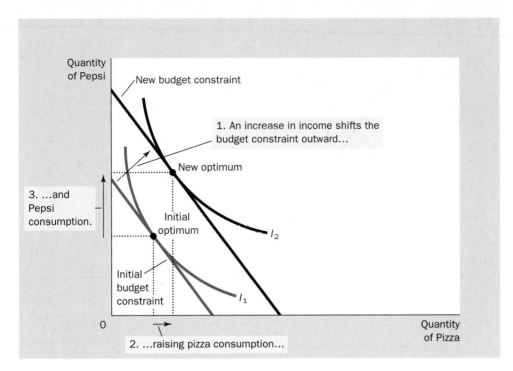

Figure 21-7

AN INCREASE IN INCOME. When the consumer's income rises, the budget constraint shifts out. If both goods are normal goods, the consumer responds to the increase in income by buying more of both of them. Here the consumer buys more pizza and more Pepsi.

The expanded budget constraint allows the consumer to choose a better combination of Pepsi and pizza. In other words, the consumer can now reach a higher indifference curve. Given the shift in the budget constraint and the consumer's preferences as represented by his indifference curves, the consumer's optimum moves from the point labeled "initial optimum" to the point labeled "new optimum."

Notice that, in Figure 21-7, the consumer chooses to consume more Pepsi and more pizza. Although the logic of the model does not require increased consumption of both goods in response to increased income, this situation is the most common one. As you may recall from Chapter 4, if a consumer wants more of a good when his income rises, economists call it a **normal good.** The indifference curves in Figure 21-7 are drawn under the assumption that both Pepsi and pizza are normal goods.

Figure 21-8 shows an example in which an increase in income induces the consumer to buy more pizza but less Pepsi. If a consumer buys less of a good when his income rises, economists call it an **inferior good.** Figure 21-8 is drawn under the assumption that pizza is a normal good and Pepsi is an inferior good.

Although most goods are normal goods, there are some inferior goods in the world. One example is bus rides. High-income consumers are more likely to own cars and less likely to ride the bus than low-income consumers. Bus rides, therefore, are an inferior good.

normal good
a good for which an increase in income raises the quantity demanded

inferior good
a good for which an increase in income reduces the quantity demanded

HOW CHANGES IN PRICES AFFECT THE CONSUMER'S CHOICES

Let's now use this model of consumer choice to consider how a change in the price of one of the goods alters the consumer's choices. Suppose, in particular,

Figure 21-8

AN INFERIOR GOOD. A good is an inferior good if the consumer buys less of it when his income rises. Here Pepsi is an inferior good: When the consumer's income increases and the budget constraint shifts outward, the consumer buys more pizza but less Pepsi.

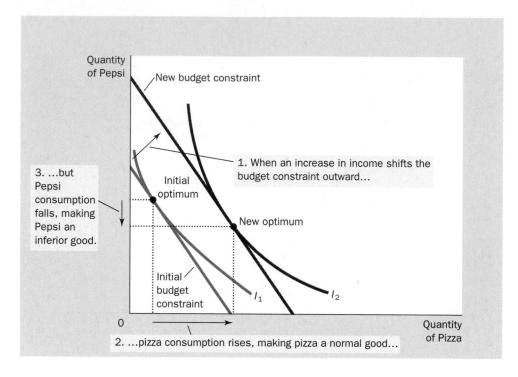

that the price of Pepsi falls from $2 to $1 a pint. It is no surprise that the lower price expands the consumer's set of buying opportunities. In other words, a fall in the price of any good shifts the budget constraint outward.

Figure 21-9 considers more specifically how the fall in price affects the budget constraint. If the consumer spends his entire $1,000 income on pizza, then the price of Pepsi is irrelevant. Thus, point A in the figure stays the same. Yet if the consumer spends his entire income of $1,000 on Pepsi, he can now buy 1,000 rather than only 500 pints. Thus, the end point of the budget constraint moves from point B to point D.

Notice that in this case the outward shift in the budget constraint changes the slope of the budget constraint. (This differs from what happened previously when prices stayed the same but the consumer's income changed.) As we have discussed, the slope of the budget constraint reflects the relative price of Pepsi and pizza. Because the price of Pepsi has fallen to $1 from $2, while the price of pizza has remained $10, the consumer can now trade a pizza for 10 rather than 5 pints of Pepsi. As a result, the new budget constraint is more steeply sloped.

How such a change in the budget constraint alters the consumption of both goods depends on the consumer's preferences. For the indifference curves drawn in this figure, the consumer buys more Pepsi and less pizza.

income effect

the change in consumption that results when a price change moves the consumer to a higher or lower indifference curve

substitution effect

the change in consumption that results when a price change moves the consumer along a given indifference curve to a point with a new marginal rate of substitution

INCOME AND SUBSTITUTION EFFECTS

The impact of a change in the price of a good on consumption can be decomposed into two effects: an **income effect** and a **substitution effect.** To see what these two effects are, consider how our consumer might respond when he learns that the price of Pepsi has fallen. He might reason in the following ways:

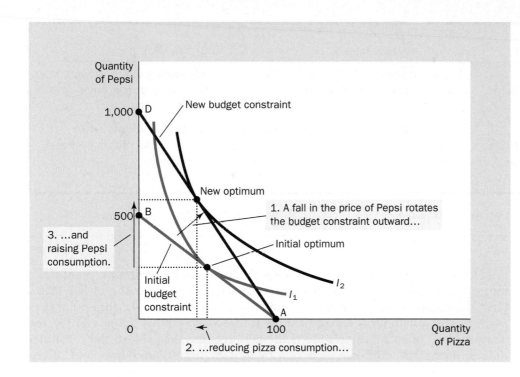

Figure 21-9

A CHANGE IN PRICE. When the price of Pepsi falls, the consumer's budget constraint shifts outward and changes slope. The consumer moves from the initial optimum to the new optimum, which changes his purchases of both Pepsi and pizza. In this case, the quantity of Pepsi consumed rises, and the quantity of pizza consumed falls.

◆ "Great news! Now that Pepsi is cheaper, my income has greater purchasing power. I am, in effect, richer than I was. Because I am richer, I can buy both more Pepsi and more pizza." (This is the income effect.)

◆ "Now that the price of Pepsi has fallen, I get more pints of Pepsi for every pizza that I give up. Because pizza is now relatively more expensive, I should buy less pizza and more Pepsi." (This is the substitution effect.)

Which statement do you find more compelling?

In fact, both of these statements make sense. The decrease in the price of Pepsi makes the consumer better off. If Pepsi and pizza are both normal goods, the consumer will want to spread this improvement in his purchasing power over both goods. This income effect tends to make the consumer buy more pizza and more Pepsi. Yet, at the same time, consumption of Pepsi has become less expensive relative to consumption of pizza. This substitution effect tends to make the consumer choose more Pepsi and less pizza.

Now consider the end result of these two effects. The consumer certainly buys more Pepsi, because the income and substitution effects both act to raise purchases of Pepsi. But it is ambiguous whether the consumer buys more pizza, because the income and substitution effects work in opposite directions. This conclusion is summarized in Table 21-2.

We can interpret the income and substitution effects using indifference curves. *The income effect is the change in consumption that results from the movement to a higher indifference curve. The substitution effect is the change in consumption that results from being at a point on an indifference curve with a different marginal rate of substitution.*

Figure 21-10 shows graphically how to decompose the change in the consumer's decision into the income effect and the substitution effect. When the

GOOD	INCOME EFFECT	SUBSTITUTION EFFECT	TOTAL EFFECT
Pepsi	Consumer is richer, so he buys more Pepsi.	Pepsi is relatively cheaper, so consumer buys more Pepsi.	Income and substitution effects act in same direction, so consumer buys more Pepsi.
Pizza	Consumer is richer, so he buys more pizza.	Pizza is relatively more expensive, so consumer buys less pizza.	Income and substitution effects act in opposite directions, so the total effect on pizza is ambiguous.

Table 21-2   INCOME AND SUBSTITUTION EFFECTS WHEN THE PRICE OF PEPSI FALLS

price of Pepsi falls, the consumer moves from the initial optimum, point A, to the new optimum, point C. We can view this change as occurring in two steps. First, the consumer moves *along* the initial indifference curve I_1 from point A to point B. The consumer is equally happy at these two points, but at point B, the marginal rate of substitution reflects the new relative price. Next, the consumer *shifts* to the higher indifference curve I_2 by moving from point B to point C. Even though point B and point C are on different indifference curves, they have the same marginal rate of substitution. That is, the slope of the indifference curve I_1 at point B equals the slope of the indifference curve I_2 at point C.

Although the consumer never actually chooses point B, this hypothetical point is useful to clarify the two effects that determine the consumer's decision.

Figure 21-10

INCOME AND SUBSTITUTION EFFECTS. The effect of a change in price can be broken down into an income effect and a substitution effect. The substitution effect—the movement along an indifference curve to a point with a different marginal rate of substitution—is shown here as the change from point A to point B along indifference curve I_1. The income effect—the shift to a higher indifference curve—is shown here as the change from point B on indifference curve I_1 to point C on indifference curve I_2.

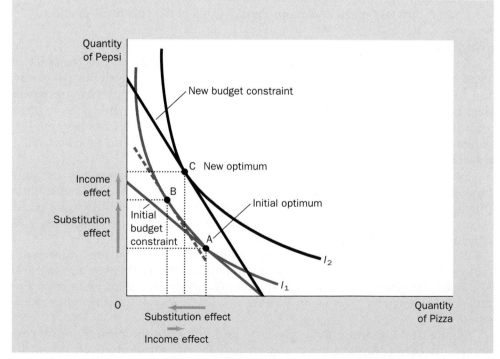

Notice that the change from point A to point B represents a pure change in the marginal rate of substitution without any change in the consumer's welfare. Similarly, the change from point B to point C represents a pure change in welfare without any change in the marginal rate of substitution. Thus, the movement from A to B shows the substitution effect, and the movement from B to C shows the income effect.

DERIVING THE DEMAND CURVE

We have just seen how changes in the price of a good alter the consumer's budget constraint and, therefore, the quantities of the two goods that he chooses to buy. The demand curve for any good reflects these consumption decisions. As you should recall, a demand curve shows how the price of a good affects the quantity demanded. We can view a consumer's demand curve as a summary of the optimal decisions that arise from his budget constraint and indifference curves.

For example, Figure 21-11 considers the demand for Pepsi. Panel (a) shows that when the price of a pint falls from $2 to $1, the consumer's budget constraint shifts outward. Because of both income and substitution effects, the consumer increases his purchases of Pepsi from 50 to 150 pints. Panel (b) shows the demand curve that results from this consumer's decisions. In this way, the theory of consumer choice provides the theoretical foundation for the consumer's demand curve, which we first introduced in Chapter 4.

Although it is comforting to know that the demand curve arises naturally from the theory of consumer choice, this exercise by itself does not justify

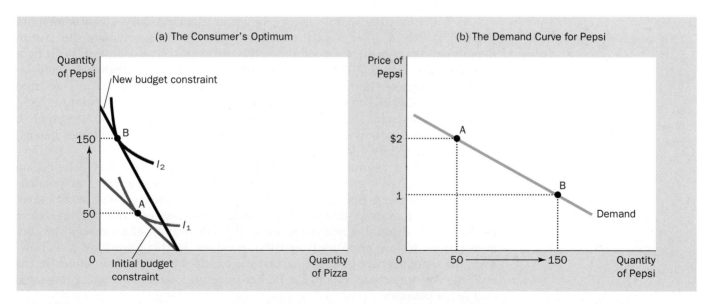

DERIVING THE DEMAND CURVE. Panel (a) shows that when the price of Pepsi falls from $2 to $1, the consumer's optimum moves from point A to point B, and the quantity of Pepsi consumed rises from 50 to 150 pints. The demand curve in panel (b) reflects this relationship between the price and the quantity demanded.

Figure 21-11

developing the theory. There is no need for a rigorous, analytic framework just to establish that people respond to changes in prices. The theory of consumer choice is, however, very useful. As we see in the next section, we can use the theory to delve more deeply into the determinants of household behavior.

QUICK QUIZ   Draw a budget constraint and indifference curves for Pepsi and pizza. Show what happens to the budget constraint and the consumer's optimum when the price of pizza rises. In your diagram, decompose the change into an income effect and a substitution effect.

FOUR APPLICATIONS

Now that we have developed the basic theory of consumer choice, let's use it to shed light on four questions about how the economy works. These four questions might at first seem unrelated. But because each question involves household decisionmaking, we can address it with the model of consumer behavior we have just developed.

DO ALL DEMAND CURVES SLOPE DOWNWARD?

Normally, when the price of a good rises, people buy less of it. Chapter 4 called this usual behavior the *law of demand*. This law is reflected in the downward slope of the demand curve.

As a matter of economic theory, however, demand curves can sometimes slope upward. In other words, consumers can sometimes violate the law of demand and buy *more* of a good when the price rises. To see how this can happen, consider Figure 21-12. In this example, the consumer buys two goods—meat and potatoes. Initially, the consumer's budget constraint is the line from point A to point B. The optimum is point C. When the price of potatoes rises, the budget constraint shifts inward and is now the line from point A to point D. The optimum is now point E. Notice that a rise in the price of potatoes has led the consumer to buy a larger quantity of potatoes.

Why is the consumer responding in a seemingly perverse way? The reason is that potatoes here are a strongly inferior good. When the price of potatoes rises, the consumer is poorer. The income effect makes the consumer want to buy less meat and more potatoes. At the same time, because the potatoes have become more expensive relative to meat, the substitution effect makes the consumer want to buy more meat and less potatoes. In this particular case, however, the income effect is so strong that it exceeds the substitution effect. In the end, the consumer responds to the higher price of potatoes by buying less meat and more potatoes.

Giffen good

a good for which an increase in the price raises the quantity demanded

Economists use the term **Giffen good** to describe a good that violates the law of demand. (The term is named for economist Robert Giffen, who first noted this possibility.) In this example, potatoes are a Giffen good. Giffen goods are inferior goods for which the income effect dominates the substitution effect. Therefore, they have demand curves that slope upward.

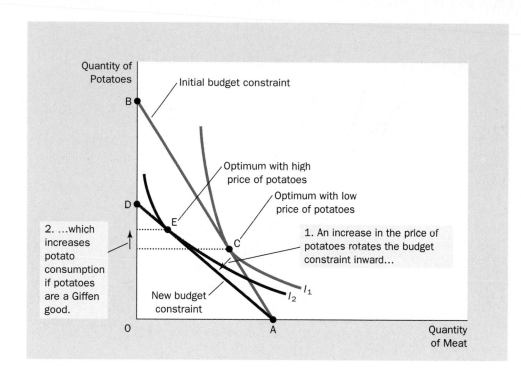

Figure 21-12

A GIFFEN GOOD. In this example, when the price of potatoes rises, the consumer's optimum shifts from point C to point E. In this case, the consumer responds to a higher price of potatoes by buying less meat and more potatoes.

Economists disagree about whether any Giffen good has ever been discovered. Some historians suggest that potatoes were in fact a Giffen good during the Irish potato famine of the nineteenth century. Potatoes were such a large part of people's diet that when the price of potatoes rose, it had a large income effect. People responded to their reduced living standard by cutting back on the luxury of meat and buying more of the staple food of potatoes. Thus, it is argued that a higher price of potatoes actually raised the quantity of potatoes demanded.

Whether or not this historical account is true, it is safe to say that Giffen goods are very rare. The theory of consumer choice does allow demand curves to slope upward. Yet such occurrences are so unusual that the law of demand is as reliable a law as any in economics.

HOW DO WAGES AFFECT LABOR SUPPLY?

So far we have used the theory of consumer choice to analyze how a person decides how to allocate his income between two goods. We can use the same theory to analyze how a person decides to allocate his time between work and leisure.

Consider the decision facing Sally, a freelance software designer. Sally is awake for 100 hours per week. She spends some of this time enjoying leisure—riding her bike, watching television, studying economics, and so on. She spends the rest of this time at her computer developing software. For every hour she spends developing software, she earns $50, which she spends on consumption goods. Thus, her wage ($50) reflects the tradeoff Sally faces between leisure and consumption. For every hour of leisure she gives up, she works one more hour and gets $50 of consumption.

Figure 21-13

THE WORK-LEISURE DECISION. This figure shows Sally's budget constraint for deciding how much to work, her indifference curves for consumption and leisure, and her optimum.

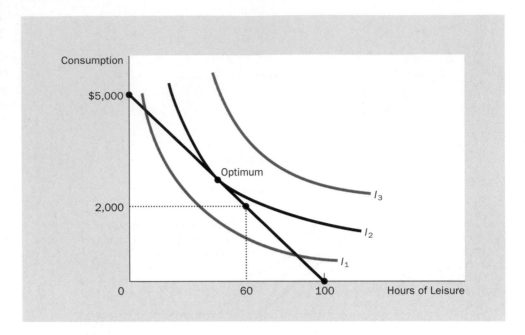

Figure 21-13 shows Sally's budget constraint. If she spends all 100 hours enjoying leisure, she has no consumption. If she spends all 100 hours working, she earns a weekly consumption of $5,000 but has no time for leisure. If she works a normal 40-hour week, she enjoys 60 hours of leisure and has weekly consumption of $2,000.

Figure 21-13 uses indifference curves to represent Sally's preferences for consumption and leisure. Here consumption and leisure are the two "goods" that Sally is choosing between. Because Sally always prefers more leisure and more consumption, she prefers points on higher indifference curves to points on lower ones. At a wage of $50 per hour, Sally chooses a combination of consumption and leisure represented by the point labeled "optimum." This is the point on the budget constraint that is on the highest possible indifference curve, which is curve I_2.

Now consider what happens when Sally's wage increases from $50 to $60 per hour. Figure 21-14 shows two possible outcomes. In each case, the budget constraint, shown in the left-hand graph, shifts outward from BC_1 to BC_2. In the process, the budget constraint becomes steeper, reflecting the change in relative price: At the higher wage, Sally gets more consumption for every hour of leisure that she gives up.

Sally's preferences, as represented by her indifference curves, determine the resulting responses of consumption and leisure to the higher wage. In both panels, consumption rises. Yet the response of leisure to the change in the wage is different in the two cases. In panel (a), Sally responds to the higher wage by enjoying less leisure. In panel (b), Sally responds by enjoying more leisure.

Sally's decision between leisure and consumption determines her supply of labor, for the more leisure she enjoys the less time she has left to work. In each panel, the right-hand graph in Figure 21-14 shows the labor supply curve implied by Sally's decision. In panel (a), a higher wage induces Sally to enjoy less leisure and work more, so the labor supply curve slopes upward. In panel (b), a higher wage induces Sally to enjoy more leisure and work less, so the labor supply curve slopes "backward."

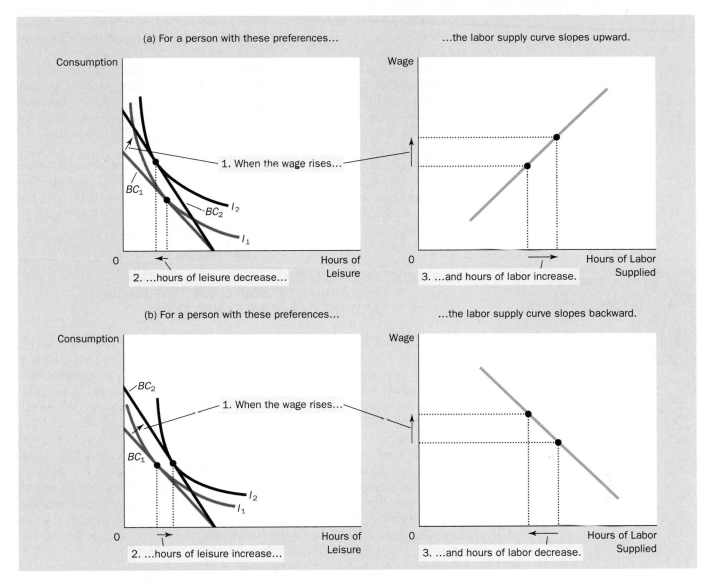

(a) For a person with these preferences...   ...the labor supply curve slopes upward.

1. When the wage rises...

BC_1 BC_2 I_2 I_1

2. ...hours of leisure decrease...   3. ...and hours of labor increase.

(b) For a person with these preferences...   ...the labor supply curve slopes backward.

1. When the wage rises...

BC_2 BC_1 I_2 I_1

2. ...hours of leisure increase...   3. ...and hours of labor decrease.

AN INCREASE IN THE WAGE. The two panels of this figure show how a person might respond to an increase in the wage. The graphs on the left show the consumer's initial budget constraint BC_1 and new budget constraint BC_2, as well as the consumer's optimal choices over consumption and leisure. The graphs on the right show the resulting labor supply curve. Because hours worked equal total hours available minus hours of leisure, any change in leisure implies an opposite change in the quantity of labor supplied. In panel (a), when the wage rises, consumption rises and leisure falls, resulting in a labor supply curve that slopes upward. In panel (b), when the wage rises, both consumption and leisure rise, resulting in a labor supply curve that slopes backward.

Figure 21-14

At first, the backward-sloping labor supply curve is puzzling. Why would a person respond to a higher wage by working less? The answer comes from considering the income and substitution effects of a higher wage.

Consider first the substitution effect. When Sally's wage rises, leisure becomes more costly relative to consumption, and this encourages Sally to substitute consumption for leisure. In other words, the substitution effect induces Sally to work harder in response to higher wages, which tends to make the labor supply curve slope upward.

Now consider the income effect. When Sally's wage rises, she moves to a higher indifference curve. She is now better off than she was. As long as consumption and leisure are both normal goods, she tends to want to use this increase in well-being to enjoy both higher consumption and greater leisure. In other words, the income effect induces her to work less, which tends to make the labor supply curve slope backward.

In the end, economic theory does not give a clear prediction about whether an increase in the wage induces Sally to work more or less. If the substitution effect is greater than the income effect for Sally, she works more. If the income effect is greater than the substitution effect, she works less. The labor supply curve, therefore, could be either upward or backward sloping.

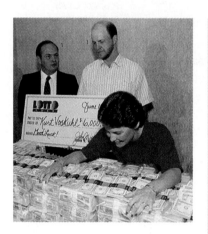

"No more 9 to 5 for me."

CASE STUDY   INCOME EFFECTS ON LABOR SUPPLY: HISTORICAL TRENDS, LOTTERY WINNERS, AND THE CARNEGIE CONJECTURE

The idea of a backward-sloping labor supply curve might at first seem like a mere theoretical curiosity, but in fact it is not. Evidence indicates that the labor supply curve, considered over long periods of time, does in fact slope backward. A hundred years ago many people worked six days a week. Today five-day workweeks are the norm. At the same time that the length of the workweek has been falling, the wage of the typical worker (adjusted for inflation) has been rising.

Here is how economists explain this historical pattern: Over time, advances in technology raise workers' productivity and, thereby, the demand for labor. The increase in labor demand raises equilibrium wages. As wages rise, so does the reward for working. Yet rather than responding to this increased incentive by working more, most workers choose to take part of their greater prosperity in the form of more leisure. In other words, the income effect of higher wages dominates the substitution effect.

Further evidence that the income effect on labor supply is strong comes from a very different kind of data: winners of lotteries. Winners of large prizes in the lottery see large increases in their incomes and, as a result, large outward shifts in their budget constraints. Because the winners' wages have not changed, however, the *slopes* of their budget constraints remain the same. There is, therefore, no substitution effect. By examining the behavior of lottery winners, we can isolate the income effect on labor supply.

The results from studies of lottery winners are striking. Of those winners who win more than a total of $50,000, almost 25 percent quit working within a year, and another 9 percent reduce the number of hours they work. Of those winners who win than $1 million, almost 40 percent stop working. The income effect on labor supply of winning such a large prize is substantial.

Similar results were found in a recent study, published in the May 1993 issue of the *Quarterly Journal of Economics,* of how receiving a bequest affects a person's labor supply. The study found that a single person who inherits more than $150,000 is four times as likely to stop working as a single person who inherits less than $25,000. This finding would not have surprised the nineteenth-century industrialist Andrew Carnegie. Carnegie warned that "the parent who leaves his son enormous wealth generally deadens the talents and energies of the son, and tempts him to lead a less useful and less worthy life than he otherwise would." That is, Carnegie viewed the income effect on labor supply to be substantial and, from his paternalistic perspective, regrettable. During his life and at his death, Carnegie gave much of his vast fortune to charity.

HOW DO INTEREST RATES AFFECT HOUSEHOLD SAVING?

An important decision that every person faces is how much income to consume today and how much to save for the future. We can use the theory of consumer choice to analyze how people make this decision and how the amount they save depends on the interest rate their savings will earn.

Consider the decision facing Sam, a worker planning ahead for retirement. To keep things simple, let's divide Sam's life into two periods. In the first period, Sam is young and working. In the second period, he is old and retired. When young, Sam earns $100,000. He divides this income between current consumption and saving. When he is old, Sam will consume what he has saved, including the interest that his savings have earned.

Suppose that the interest rate is 10 percent. Then for every dollar that Sam saves when young, he can consume $1.10 when old. We can view "consumption when young" and "consumption when old" as the two goods that Sam must choose between. The interest rate determines the relative price of these two goods.

Figure 21-15 shows Sam's budget constraint. If he saves nothing, he consumes $100,000 when young and nothing when old. If he saves everything, he consumes nothing when young and $110,000 when old. The budget constraint shows these and all the intermediate possibilities.

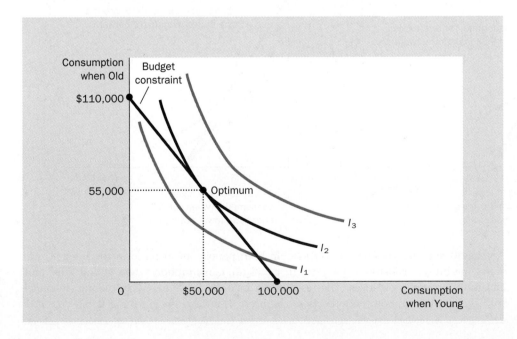

Figure 21-15

THE CONSUMPTION-SAVING DECISION. This figure shows the budget constraint for a person deciding how much to consume in the two periods of his life, the indifference curves representing his preferences, and the optimum.

Figure 21-15 uses indifference curves to represent Sam's preferences for consumption in the two periods. Because Sam prefers more consumption in both periods, he prefers points on higher indifference curves to points on lower ones. Given his preferences, Sam chooses the optimal combination of consumption in both periods of life, which is the point on the budget constraint that is on the highest possible indifference curve. At this optimum, Sam consumes $50,000 when young and $55,000 when old.

Now consider what happens when the interest rate increases from 10 percent to 20 percent. Figure 21-16 shows two possible outcomes. In both cases, the budget constraint shifts outward and becomes steeper. At the new higher interest rate, Sam gets more consumption when old for every dollar of consumption that he gives up when young.

The two panels show different preferences for Sam and the resulting response to the higher interest rate. In both cases, consumption when old rises. Yet the response of consumption when young to the change in the interest rate is different in the two cases. In panel (a), Sam responds to the higher interest rate by consuming less when young. In panel (b), Sam responds by consuming more when young.

Sam's saving, of course, is his income when young minus the amount he consumes when young. In panel (a), consumption when young falls when the interest rate rises, so saving must rise. In panel (b), Sam consumes more when young, so saving must fall.

The case shown in panel (b) might at first seem odd: Sam responds to an increase in the return to saving by saving less. Yet this behavior is not as pecu-

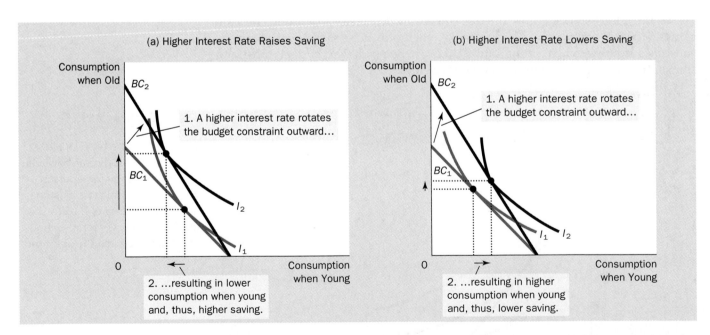

Figure 21-16   AN INCREASE IN THE INTEREST RATE. In both panels, an increase in the interest rate shifts the budget constraint outward. In panel (a), consumption when young falls, and consumption when old rises. The result is an increase in saving when young. In panel (b), consumption in both periods rises. The result is a decrease in saving when young.

liar as it might seem. We can understand it by considering the income and sub-stitution effects of a higher interest rate.

Consider first the substitution effect. When the interest rate rises, consumption when old becomes less costly relative to consumption when young. Therefore, the substitution effect induces Sam to consume more when old and less when young. In other words, the substitution effect induces Sam to save more.

Now consider the income effect. When the interest rate rises, Sam moves to a higher indifference curve. He is now better off than he was. As long as consumption in both periods consists of normal goods, he tends to want to use this increase in well-being to enjoy higher consumption in both periods. In other words, the income effect induces him to save less.

The end result, of course, depends on both the income and substitution effects. If the substitution effect of a higher interest rate is greater than the income effect, Sam saves more. If the income effect is greater than the substitution effect, Sam saves less. Thus, the theory of consumer choice says that an increase in the interest rate could either encourage or discourage saving.

Although this ambiguous result is interesting from the standpoint of economic theory, it is disappointing from the standpoint of economic policy. It turns out that an important issue in tax policy hinges in part on how saving responds to interest rates. Some economists have advocated reducing the taxation of interest and other capital income, arguing that such a policy change would raise the after-tax interest rate that savers can earn and would thereby encourage people to save more. Other economists have argued that because of offsetting income and substitution effects, such a tax change might not increase saving and could even reduce it. Unfortunately, research has not led to a consensus about how interest rates affect saving. As a result, there remains disagreement among economists about whether changes in tax policy aimed to encourage saving would, in fact, have the intended effect.

DO THE POOR PREFER TO RECEIVE CASH OR IN-KIND TRANSFERS?

Paul is a pauper. Because of his low income, he has a meager standard of living. The government wants to help. It can either give Paul $1,000 worth of food (perhaps by issuing him food stamps) or simply give him $1,000 in cash. What does the theory of consumer choice have to say about the comparison between these two policy options?

Figure 21-17 shows how the two options might work. If the government gives Paul cash, then the budget constraint shifts outward. He can divide the extra cash between food and nonfood consumption however he pleases. By contrast, if the government gives Paul an in-kind transfer of food, then his new budget constraint is more complicated. The budget constraint has again shifted out. But now the budget constraint has a kink at $1,000 of food, for Paul must consume at least that amount in food. That is, even if Paul spends all his money on nonfood consumption, he still consumes $1,000 in food.

The ultimate comparison between the cash transfer and in-kind transfer depends on Paul's preferences. In panel (a), Paul would choose to spend at least $1,000 on food even if he receives a cash transfer. Therefore, the constraint imposed by the in-kind transfer is not binding. In this case, his consumption moves from point A to point B regardless of the type of transfer. That is, Paul's

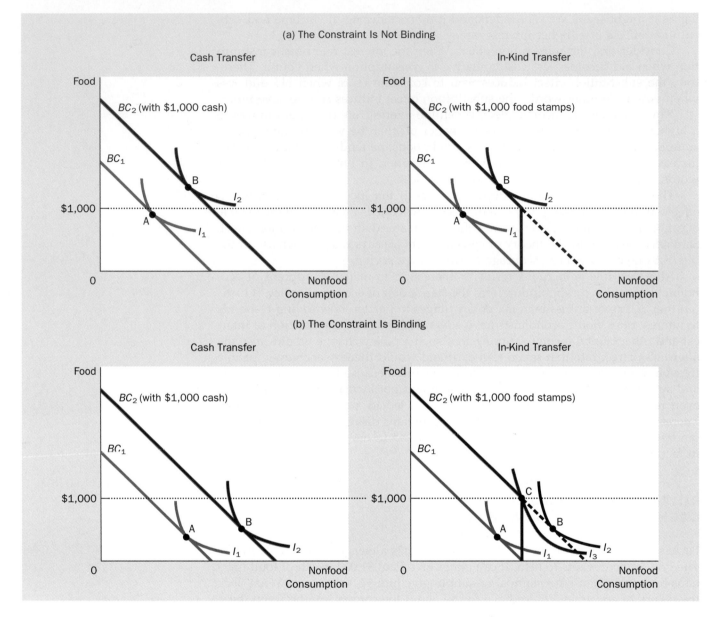

(a) The Constraint Is Not Binding

Figure 21-17

CASH VERSUS IN-KIND TRANSFERS. Both panels compare a cash transfer and a similar in-kind transfer of food. In panel (a), the in-kind transfer does not impose a binding constraint, and the consumer ends up on the same indifference curve under the two policies. In panel (b), the in-kind transfer imposes a binding constraint, and the consumer ends up on a lower indifference curve with the in-kind transfer than with the cash transfer.

choice between food and nonfood consumption is the same under the two policies.

In panel (b), however, the story is very different. In this case, Paul would prefer to spend less than $1,000 on food and spend more on nonfood consumption. The cash transfer allows him discretion to spend the money as he pleases, and he consumes at point B. By contrast, the in-kind transfer imposes the binding constraint that he consume at least $1,000 of food. His optimum allocation is at the kink, point C. Compared to the cash transfer, the in-kind transfer induces Paul to consume more food and less of other goods. The in-kind transfer also forces Paul to end up on a lower (and thus less preferred) indifference curve. Paul is worse off than if he had the cash transfer.

Thus, the theory of consumer choice teaches a simple lesson about cash versus in-kind transfers. If an in-kind transfer of a good forces the recipient to consume more of the good than he would on his own, then the recipient prefers the cash transfer. If the in-kind transfer does not force the recipient to consume more of the good than he would on his own, then the cash and in-kind transfer have exactly the same effect on the consumption and welfare of the recipient.

QUICK QUIZ   Explain how an increase in the wage can potentially decrease the amount that a person wants to work.

CONCLUSION: DO PEOPLE REALLY THINK THIS WAY?

The theory of consumer choice describes how people make decisions. As we have seen, it has broad applicability. It can explain how a person chooses between Pepsi and pizza, work and leisure, consumption and saving, and on and on.

At this point, however, you might be tempted to treat the theory of consumer choice with some skepticism. After all, you are a consumer. You decide what to buy every time you walk into a store. And you know that you do not decide by writing down budget constraints and indifference curves. Doesn't this knowledge about your own decisionmaking provide evidence against the theory?

The answer is no. The theory of consumer choice does not try to present a literal account of how people make decisions. It is a model. And, as we first discussed in Chapter 2, models are not intended to be completely realistic.

The best way to view the theory of consumer choice is as a metaphor for how consumers make decisions. No consumer (except an occasional economist) goes through the explicit optimization envisioned in the theory. Yet consumers are aware that their choices are constrained by their financial resources. And, given those constraints, they do the best they can to achieve the highest level of satisfaction. The theory of consumer choice tries to describe this implicit, psychological process in a way that permits explicit, economic analysis.

The proof of the pudding is in the eating. And the test of a theory is in its applications. In the last section of this chapter we applied the theory of consumer choice to four practical issues about the economy. If you take more advanced courses in economics, you will see that this theory provides the framework for much additional analysis.

Summary

◆   A consumer's budget constraint shows the possible combinations of different goods he can buy given his income and the prices of the goods. The slope of the budget constraint equals the relative price of the goods.

◆   The consumer's indifference curves represent his preferences. An indifference curve shows the various bundles of goods that make the consumer equally happy. Points on higher indifference curves are preferred to points on lower indifference curves. The slope of an indifference curve at any point is the consumer's marginal rate of substitution—the rate at which the consumer is willing to trade one good for the other.

◆ The consumer optimizes by choosing the point on his budget constraint that lies on the highest indifference curve. At this point, the slope of the indifference curve (the marginal rate of substitution between the goods) equals the slope of the budget constraint (the relative price of the goods).

◆ When the price of a good falls, the impact on the consumer's choices can be broken down into an income effect and a substitution effect. The income effect is the change in consumption that arises because a lower price makes the consumer better off. The substitution effect is the change in consumption that arises because a price change encourages greater consumption of the good that has become relatively cheaper. The income effect is reflected in the movement from a lower to a higher indifference curve, whereas the substitution effect is reflected by a movement along an indifference curve to a point with a different slope.

◆ The theory of consumer choice can be applied in many situations. It can explain why demand curves can potentially slope upward, why higher wages could either increase or decrease the quantity of labor supplied, why higher interest rates could either increase or decrease saving, and why the poor prefer cash to in-kind transfers.

Key Concepts

budget constraint, p. 449
indifference curve, p. 450
marginal rate of substitution, p. 450
perfect substitutes, p. 454

perfect complements, p. 454
normal good, p. 457
inferior good, p. 457
income effect, p. 458

substitution effect, p. 458
Giffen good, p. 462

Questions for Review

1. A consumer has income of $3,000. Wine costs $3 a glass, and cheese costs $6 a pound. Draw the consumer's budget constraint. What is the slope of this budget constraint?

2. Draw a consumer's indifference curves for wine and cheese. Describe and explain four properties of these indifference curves.

3. Pick a point on an indifference curve for wine and cheese and show the marginal rate of substitution. What does the marginal rate of substitution tell us?

4. Show a consumer's budget constraint and indifference curves for wine and cheese. Show the optimum consumption choice. If the price of wine is $3 a glass and the price of cheese is $6 a pound, what is the marginal rate of substitution at this optimum?

5. A person who consumes wine and cheese gets a raise, so his income increases from $3,000 to $4,000. Show what happens if both wine and cheese are normal goods. Now show what happens if cheese is an inferior good.

6. The price of cheese rises from $6 to $10 a pound, while the price of wine remains $3 a glass. For a consumer with a constant income of $3,000, show what happens to consumption of wine and cheese. Decompose the change into income and substitution effects.

7. Can an increase in the price of cheese possibly induce a consumer to buy more cheese? Explain.

Problems and Applications

1. Jennifer divides her income between coffee and croissants. An early frost in Brazil causes a large increase in the price of coffee in the United States.
   a. Show the effect of the frost on Jennifer's budget constraint.

   b. Show the effect of the frost on Jennifer's optimal consumption bundle assuming that the substitution effect outweighs the income effect for croissants.
   c. Show the effect of the frost on Jennifer's optimal consumption bundle assuming that the income effect outweighs the substitution effect for croissants.

2. Compare the following two pairs of goods:
   ◆ Coke and Pepsi
   ◆ Skis and ski bindings

   In which case do you expect the indifference curves to be fairly straight, and in which case do you expect the indifference curves to be very bowed? In which case will the consumer respond more to a change in the relative price of the two goods?

3. Mario consumes only cheese and crackers.
   a. Could cheese and crackers both be inferior goods for Mario? Explain.
   b. Suppose that cheese is a normal good for Mario while crackers are an inferior good. If the price of cheese falls, what happens to Mario's consumption of crackers? What happens to his consumption of cheese? Explain.

4. Jim buys only milk and cookies.
   a. In 1997, Jim earns $100, milk costs $2 per quart, and cookies cost $4 per dozen. Draw Jim's budget constraint.
   b. Now suppose that all prices increase by 10 percent in 1998 and that Jim's salary increases by 10 percent as well. Draw Jim's new budget constraint. How would Jim's optimal combination of milk and cookies in 1998 compare to his optimal combination in 1997?

5. Consider your decision about how many hours to work.
   a. Draw your budget constraint assuming that you pay no taxes on your income. On the same diagram, draw another budget constraint assuming that you pay a 15 percent tax.
   b. Show how the tax might lead to more hours of work, fewer hours, or the same number of hours. Explain.

6. Sarah is awake for 100 hours per week. Using one diagram, show Sarah's budget constraints if she earns $6 per hour, $8 per hour, and $10 per hour. Now draw indifference curves such that Sarah's labor supply curve is upward sloping when the wage is between $6 and $8 per hour, and backward sloping when the wage is between $8 and $10 per hour.

7. Draw the indifference curve for someone deciding how much to work. Suppose the wage increases. Is it possible that the person's consumption would fall? Is this plausible? Discuss. (Hint: Think about income and substitution effects.)

8. The labor-force participation rate of married women has more than doubled over the past 50 years. One economic influence on this rate was the increase in women's wages over this period. Another economic influence was the increase in men's wages, which raised the standard of living for most married women.
   a. Using an indifference-curve diagram, show and then explain how a rise in the income of a husband can lead to a fall in the number of hours worked by his wife. What assumption do you need to make about leisure to get this result?
   b. Using another indifference-curve diagram, show and then explain how a rise in female wages affects a woman's decision of how many hours to work.

9. Suppose you take a job that pays $30,000 and set some of this income aside in a savings account that pays an annual interest rate of 5 percent. Use a diagram with a budget constraint and indifference curves to show how your consumption changes in each of the following situations. To keep things simple, assume that you pay no taxes on your income.
   a. Your salary increases to $40,000.
   b. The interest rate on your bank account rises to 8 percent.

10. As discussed in the text, we can divide an individual's life into two hypothetical periods: "young" and "old." Suppose that the individual earns income only when young and saves some of that income to consume when old. If the interest rate on savings falls, can you tell what happens to consumption when young? Can you tell what happens to consumption when old? Explain.

11. Suppose that your state gives each town $5 million in aid per year. The way in which the money is spent is currently unrestricted, but the governor has proposed that towns be required to spend the entire $5 million on education. You can illustrate the effect of this proposal on your town's spending on education using a budget constraint and indifference-curve diagram. The two goods are education and noneducation spending.
   a. Draw your town's budget constraint under the existing policy, assuming that your town's only source of revenue besides the state aid is a property tax that yields $10 million. On the same diagram, draw the budget constraint under the governor's proposal.
   b. Would your town spend more on education under the governor's proposal than under the existing policy? Explain.
   c. Now compare two towns—Youngsville and Oldsville—with the same revenue and the same state aid. Youngsville has a large school-age population, and Oldsville has a large elderly population. In which town is the governor's proposal most likely to increase education spending? Explain.

12. (This problem is challenging.) The welfare system provides income to some needy families. Typically, the

maximum payment goes to families that earn no income; then, as families begin to earn income, the welfare payment declines gradually and eventually disappears. Let's consider the possible effects of this program on a family's labor supply.

a. Draw a budget constraint for a family assuming that the welfare system did not exist. On the same diagram, draw a budget constraint that reflects the existence of the welfare system.

b. Adding indifference curves to your diagram, show how the welfare system could reduce the number of hours worked by the family. Explain, with reference to both the income and substitution effects.

c. Using your diagram from part (b), show the effect of the welfare system on the well-being of the family.

13. (This problem is challenging.) Suppose that an individual owed no taxes on the first $10,000 she earned and 15 percent of any income she earned over $10,000. (This is a simplified version of the actual U.S. income tax.) Now suppose that Congress is considering two ways to reduce the tax burden: a reduction in the tax rate and an increase in the amount on which no tax is owed.

a. What effect would a reduction in the tax rate have on the individual's labor supply if she earned $30,000 to start? Explain in words using the income and substitution effects. You do not need to use a diagram.

b. What effect would an increase in the amount on which no tax is owed have on the individual's labor supply? Again, explain in words using the income and substitution effects.

14. (This problem is challenging.) Consider a person deciding how much to consume and how much to save for retirement. This person has particular preferences: Her lifetime utility depends on the lowest level of consumption during the two periods of her life. That is,

Utility = Minimum {consumption when young, consumption when old}.

a. Draw this person's indifference curves. (Hint: Recall that indifference curves show the combinations of consumption in the two periods that yield the same level of utility.)

b. Draw the budget constraint and the optimum.

c. When the interest rate increases, does this person save more or less? Explain your answer using income and substitution effects.

VIII

THE DATA OF MACROECONOMICS

22

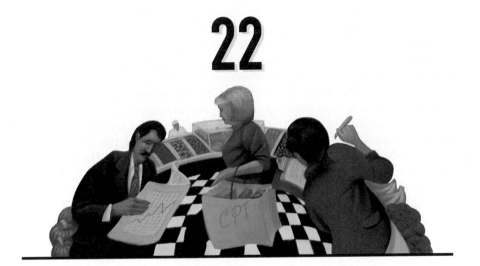

MEASURING A NATION'S
INCOME

When you finish school and start looking for a full-time job, your experience will, to a large extent, be shaped by prevailing economic conditions. In some years, firms throughout the economy are expanding their production of goods and services, employment is rising, and jobs are easy to find. In other years, firms are cutting back on production, employment is declining, and finding a good job takes a long time. Not surprisingly, any college graduate would rather enter the labor force in a year of economic expansion than in a year of economic contraction.

Because the condition of the overall economy profoundly affects all of us, changes in economic conditions are widely reported by the media. Indeed, it is hard to pick up a newspaper without seeing some newly reported statistic about the economy. The statistic might measure the total income of everyone in the economy (GDP), the rate at which average prices are rising (inflation), the percentage of the labor force that is out of work (unemployment), total spending at stores (retail sales), or the imbalance of trade between the United States and the rest of the world (the trade deficit). All these statistics are *macroeconomic*. Rather than telling us about a particular household or firm, they tell us something about the entire economy.

microeconomics
the study of how households and firms make decisions and how they interact in markets

macroeconomics
the study of economy-wide phenomena, including inflation, unemployment, and economic growth

As you may recall from Chapter 2, economics is divided into two branches: microeconomics and macroconomics. **Microeconomics** is the study of how individual households and firms make decisions and how they interact with one another in markets. **Macroeconomics** is the study of the economy as a whole. The goal of macroeconomics is to explain the economic changes that affect many households, firms, and markets at once. Macroeconomists address diverse questions: Why is average income high in some countries while it is low in others? Why do prices rise rapidly in some periods of time while they are more stable in other periods? Why do production and employment expand in some years and contract in others? These diverse questions are all macroeconomic because they concern the workings of the entire economy.

Because the economy as a whole is just a collection of many households and many firms interacting in many markets, microeconomics and macroeconomics are closely linked. The basic tools of supply and demand, for instance, are as central to macroeconomic analysis as they are to microeconomic analysis. Yet studying the economy in its entirety raises some new and intriguing challenges.

In this chapter and the next one, we discuss some of the data that economists and policymakers use to monitor the overall economy. These data reflect the economic changes that macroeconomists try to explain. This chapter considers *gross domestic product,* or simply GDP, which measures the total income of a nation. GDP is the most closely watched economic statistic because it is thought to be the best single measure of a society's economic well-being.

THE ECONOMY'S INCOME AND EXPENDITURE

If you were to judge how a person is doing economically, you might first look at his or her income. A person with a high income can more easily afford life's necessities and luxuries. It is no surprise that people with higher incomes enjoy higher standards of living—better housing, better health care, fancier cars, more opulent vacations, and so on.

The same logic applies to a nation's overall economy. When judging whether the economy is doing well or poorly, it is natural to look at the total income that everyone in the economy is earning. That is the task of gross domestic product (GDP).

GDP measures two things at once: the total income of everyone in the economy and the total expenditure on the economy's output of goods and services. The reason that GDP can perform the trick of measuring both total income and total expenditure is that these two things are really the same. *For an economy as a whole, income must equal expenditure.*

Why is this true? The reason that an economy's income is the same as its expenditure is simply that every transaction has two parties: a buyer and a seller. Every dollar of spending by some buyer is a dollar of income for some seller. Suppose, for instance, that Karen pays Doug $100 to mow her lawn. In this case, Doug is a seller of a service, and Karen is a buyer. Doug earns $100, and Karen spends $100. Thus, the transaction contributes equally to the economy's income and to its expenditure. GDP, whether measured as total income or total expenditure, rises by $100.

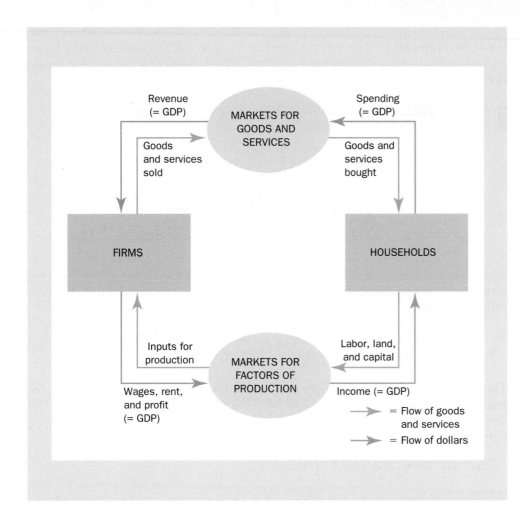

Figure 22-1

THE CIRCULAR-FLOW DIAGRAM. Households buy goods and services from firms, and firms use their revenue from sales to pay wages to workers, rent to landowners, and profit to firm owners. GDP equals the total amount spent by households in the market for goods and services. It also equals the total wages, rent, and profit paid by firms in the markets for the factors of production.

Another way to see the equality of income and expenditure is with the circular-flow diagram in Figure 22-1. (You may recall this circular-flow diagram from Chapter 2.) This diagram describes all the transactions between households and firms in a simple economy. In this economy, households buy goods and services from firms; these expenditures flow through the markets for goods and services. The firms in turn use the money they receive from sales to pay workers' wages, landowners' rent, and firm owners' profit; this income flows through the markets for the factors of production. In this economy, money continuously flows from households to firms and then back to households.

We can compute GDP for this economy in one of two ways: by adding up the total expenditure by households or by adding up the total income (wages, rent, and profit) paid by firms. Because all expenditure in the economy ends up as someone's income, GDP is the same regardless of how we compute it.

The real economy is, of course, more complicated than the one illustrated in Figure 22-1. In particular, households do not spend all of their income. Households pay some of their income to the government in taxes, and they save and invest some of their income for use in the future. In addition, households do not buy all goods and services produced in the economy. Some goods and services are bought by governments, and some are bought by firms that plan to use them in the future to produce their own output. Yet, regardless of whether a household, government, or firm buys a good or service, the transaction has a buyer and seller. Thus, for the economy as a whole, expenditure and income are always the same.

QUICK QUIZ What two things does gross domestic product measure? How can it measure two things at once?

THE MEASUREMENT OF GROSS DOMESTIC PRODUCT

Now that we have discussed the meaning of gross domestic product in general terms, let's be more precise about how this statistic is measured. Here is a definition of GDP:

gross domestic product (GDP)

the market value of all final goods and services produced within a country in a given period of time

◆ **Gross domestic product (GDP)** is the market value of all final goods and services produced within a country in a given period of time.

This definition might seem simple enough. But, in fact, many subtle issues arise when computing an economy's GDP. Let's therefore consider each phrase in this definition with some care.

"GDP IS THE MARKET VALUE . . ."

You have probably heard the adage, "You can't compare apples and oranges." Yet GDP does exactly that. GDP adds together many different kinds of products into a single measure of the value of economic activity. To do this, it uses market prices. Because market prices measure the amount people are willing to pay for different goods, they reflect the value of those goods. If the price of an apple is twice the price of an orange, then an apple contributes twice as much to GDP as does an orange.

". . . OF ALL . . ."

GDP tries to be comprehensive. It includes all items produced in the economy and sold legally in markets. GDP measures the market value of not just apples and oranges, but also pears and grapefruit, books and movies, haircuts and health care, and on and on.

GDP also includes the market value of the housing services provided by the economy's stock of housing. For rental housing, this value is easy to calculate—the rent equals both the tenant's expenditure and the landlord's income. Yet many people own the place where they live and, therefore, do not pay rent. The government includes this owner-occupied housing in GDP by estimating its rental value. In essence, GDP is based on the assumption that the owner pays himself this imputed rent, so the rent is included both in his expenditure and in his income.

There are some products, however, that GDP excludes because measurement of them is so difficult. GDP excludes items produced and sold illicitly, such as illegal drugs. It also excludes most items that are produced and consumed at home and, therefore, never enter the marketplace. Vegetables you buy at the grocery store are part of GDP; vegetables you grow in your garden are not.

These exclusions from GDP can at times lead to paradoxical results. For example, when Karen pays Doug to mow her lawn, that transaction is part of GDP. If Karen were to marry Doug, the situation would change. Even though Doug may continue to mow Karen's lawn, the value of the mowing is now left out of GDP because Doug's service is no longer sold in a market. Thus, when Karen and Doug marry, GDP falls.

" . . . FINAL . . ."

When International Paper makes paper, which Hallmark uses to make a greeting card, the paper is called an *intermediate good,* and the card is called a *final good.* GDP includes only the value of final goods. The reason is that the value of intermediate goods is already included in the prices of the final goods. Adding the market value of the paper to the market value of the card would be double counting. That is, it would (incorrectly) count the paper twice.

An important exception to this principle arises when an intermediate good is produced and, rather than being used, is added to a firm's inventory to be used or sold at a later date. In this case, the intermediate good is taken to be "final" for the moment, and its value as inventory investment is added to GDP. When the inventory of the intermediate good is later used or sold, the firm's inventory investment is negative, and GDP for the later period is reduced accordingly.

" . . . GOODS AND SERVICES . . ."

GDP includes both tangible goods (food, clothing, cars) and intangible services (haircuts, housecleaning, doctor visits). When you buy a CD by your favorite singing group, you are buying a good, and the purchase price is part of GDP. When you pay to hear a concert by the same group, you are buying a service, and the ticket price is also part of GDP.

" . . . PRODUCED . . ."

GDP includes goods and services currently produced. It does not include transactions involving items produced in the past. When General Motors produces and sells a new car, the value of the car is included in GDP. When one person sells a used car to another person, the value of the used car is not included in GDP.

" . . . WITHIN A COUNTRY . . ."

GDP measures the value of production within the geographic confines of a country. When a Canadian citizen works temporarily in the United States, his

gross national product (GNP)

the market value of all final goods and services produced by permanent residents of a nation within a given period of time

production is part of U.S. GDP. When an American citizen owns a factory in Haiti, the production at his factory is not part of U.S. GDP. (It is part of Haiti's GDP.) Thus, items are included in a nation's GDP if they are produced domestically, regardless of the nationality of the producer.

Another statistic, called **gross national product (GNP),** takes a different approach to dealing with the goods and services produced by foreigners. GNP is the value of the production of a nation's permanent residents. When a Canadian citizen works temporarily in the United States, his production is not part of U.S. GNP. (It is part of Canada's GNP.) When an American citizen owns a factory in Haiti, the profit from production at his factory is part of U.S. GNP. Thus, income is included in a nation's GNP if it is earned by the nation's permanent residents (called *nationals*), regardless of where they earn it.

Throughout this book, we follow the standard practice of using GDP to measure the value of economic activity. For most purposes, however, the distinction between GDP and GNP is not very important. In the United States and most other countries, domestic residents are responsible for most domestic production, so GDP and GNP are quite close.

" . . . IN A GIVEN PERIOD OF TIME."

GDP measures the value of production that takes place within a specific interval of time. Usually that interval is a year or a quarter (three months). GDP measures the economy's flow of income and expenditure during that interval.

When the government reports the GDP for a quarter, it usually presents GDP "at an annual rate." This means that the figure reported for quarterly GDP is the amount of income and expenditure during the quarter multiplied by four. The government uses this convention so that quarterly and annual figures on GDP can be compared more easily.

In addition, when the government reports quarterly GDP, it presents the data after they have been modified by a statistical procedure called *seasonal adjustment.* The unadjusted data show clearly that the economy produces more goods and services during some times of the year than during others. (As you might guess, December's Christmas shopping season is a high point.) When monitoring the condition of the economy, economists and policymakers often want to look beyond these regular seasonal changes. Therefore, government statisticians adjust the quarterly data to take out the seasonal cycle. The GDP data reported in the news are always seasonally adjusted.

Now let's repeat the definition of GDP:

◆ Gross domestic product (GDP) is the market value of all final goods and services produced within a country in a given period of time.

It should now be apparent that GDP is a sophisticated measure of the value of economic activity. In advanced courses in macroeconomics, you will learn more of the subtleties that arise in its calculation. But even now you can see that each phrase in this definition is packed with meaning.

QUICK QUIZ   Which contributes more to GDP—the production of a pound of hamburger or the production of a pound of caviar? Why?

FYI

Three Other

Measures of

Income

WHEN THE U.S. DEPARTMENT of Commerce computes the nation's GDP every three months, it also computes various other measures of income for the economy. These other measures differ from GDP by excluding or including certain categories of income. What follows is a brief description of three of the most important of these income measures.

◆ *Net National Product (NNP)* is total income of the residents of a nation after subtracting losses from depreciation. *Depreciation* is the wear and tear on the economy's stock of equipment and structures, such as trucks rusting and lightbulbs burning out. In the national income accounts prepared by the Department of Commerce, depreciation is called the "consumption of fixed capital."

◆ *Personal income* is the income that households and noncorporate businesses receive. Unlike GDP and NNP, it excludes *retained earnings*, which is income that corporations have earned but have not paid out to their owners in the form of dividends. Also unlike GDP and NNP, personal income includes the interest income that households receive from their holdings of government debt and the income that households receive from government transfer programs, such as welfare and Social Security.

◆ *Disposable personal income* is the income that households and noncorporate businesses have left after satisfying their obligations to the government. It equals personal income minus taxes and certain nontax payments (such as traffic tickets).

Although the various measures of income differ in detail, they almost always tell the same story about economic conditions. When GDP is growing rapidly, these other measures of income are usually growing rapidly. And when GDP is falling, these other measures are usually falling as well. For monitoring fluctuations in the overall economy, it does not matter much which measure of income we use.

THE COMPONENTS OF GDP

Spending in the economy takes many forms. At any moment, the Smith family may be having lunch at Burger King; General Motors may be building a car factory; the Navy may be procuring a submarine; and British Airways may be buying an airplane from Boeing. GDP includes all of these various forms of spending on domestically produced goods and services.

To understand how the economy is using its scarce resources, economists are often interested in studying the composition of GDP among various types of spending. To do this, GDP (which we denote as Y) is divided into four components: consumption (C), investment (I), government purchases (G), and net exports (NX):

$$Y = C + I + G + NX.$$

This equation is an *identity*—an equation that must be true by the way the variables in the equation are defined. In this case, because each dollar of expenditure included in GDP is placed into one of the four components of GDP, the total of the four components must be equal to GDP.

consumption

spending by households on goods and services, with the exception of purchases of new housing

investment

spending on capital equipment, inventories, and structures, including household purchases of new housing

government purchases

spending on goods and services by local, state, and federal governments

net exports

spending on domestically produced goods by foreigners (exports) minus spending on foreign goods by domestic residents (imports)

We have just seen an example of each component. **Consumption** is spending by households on goods and services, such as the Smiths' lunch at Burger King. **Investment** is the purchase of capital equipment, inventories, and structures, such as the General Motors factory. Investment also includes expenditure on new housing. (By convention, expenditure on new housing is the one form of household spending categorized as investment rather than consumption.) **Government purchases** include spending on goods and services by local, state, and federal governments, such as the Navy's purchase of a submarine. **Net exports** equal the purchases of domestically produced goods by foreigners (exports) minus the domestic purchases of foreign goods (imports). A domestic firm's sale to a buyer in another country, such as the Boeing sale to British Airways, increases net exports.

The "net" in "net exports" refers to the fact that imports are subtracted from exports. This subtraction is made because imports of goods and services are included in other components of GDP. For example, suppose that a household buys a $30,000 car from Volvo, the Swedish car maker. That transaction increases consumption by $30,000 because car purchases are part of consumer spending. It also reduces net exports by $30,000 because the car is an import. In other words, net exports include goods and services produced abroad (with a minus sign) because these goods and services are included in consumption, investment, and government purchases (with a plus sign). Thus, when a domestic household, firm, or government buys a good or service from abroad, the purchase reduces net exports—but because it also raises consumption, investment, or government purchases, it does not affect GDP.

The meaning of "government purchases" also requires a bit of clarification. When the government pays the salary of an Army general, that salary is part of government purchases. But what happens when the government pays a Social Security benefit to one of the elderly? Such government spending is called a *transfer payment* because it is not made in exchange for a currently produced good or service. From a macroeconomic standpoint, transfer payments are like a tax rebate. Like taxes, transfer payments alter household income, but they do not reflect the economy's production. Because GDP is intended to measure the income from (and expenditure on) the production of goods and services, transfer payments are not counted as part of government purchases.

Table 22-1

GDP AND ITS COMPONENTS. This table shows total GDP for the U.S. economy in 1996 and the breakdown of GDP among its four components.

	TOTAL (IN BILLIONS OF DOLLARS)	PER PERSON (IN DOLLARS)	PERCENT OF TOTAL
Gross domestic product	$7,576	$28,589	100%
Consumption	5,152	19,441	68
Investment	1,116	4,211	15
Government purchases	1,407	5,309	19
Net exports	−99	−373	−1

SOURCE: U.S. Department of Commerce.

Table 22-1 shows the composition of U.S. GDP in 1996. In this year, the GDP of the United States was about $7.5 trillion. If we divide this number by the 1996 U.S. population of 265 million, we find that GDP per person—the amount of expenditure for the average American—was $28,589. Consumption made up about two-thirds of GDP, or $19,441 per person. Investment was $4,211 per person. Government purchases were $5,309 per person. Net exports were −$373 per person. This number is negative because Americans earned less from selling to foreigners than we spent on foreign goods.

QUICK QUIZ List the four components of expenditure. Which is the largest?

REAL VERSUS NOMINAL GDP

As we have seen, GDP measures the total spending on goods and services in all markets in the economy. If total spending rises from one year to the next, one of two things must be true: (1) the economy is producing a larger output of goods and services, or (2) goods and services are being sold at higher prices. When studying changes in the economy over time, economists want to separate these two effects. In particular, they want a measure of the total quantity of goods and services the economy is producing that is not affected by changes in the prices of those goods and services.

To do this, economists use a measure called *real GDP*. Real GDP answers a hypothetical question: What would be the value of the goods and services produced this year if we valued these goods and services at the prices that prevailed in some specific year in the past? By evaluating current production using prices that are fixed at past levels, real GDP shows how the economy's overall production of goods and services changes over time.

To see more precisely how real GDP is constructed, let's consider an example.

A NUMERICAL EXAMPLE

Table 22-2 shows some data for an economy that produces only two goods—hot dogs and hamburgers. The table shows the quantities of the two goods produced and their prices in the years 2001, 2002, and 2003.

To compute total spending in this economy, we would multiply the quantities of hot dogs and hamburgers by their prices. In the year 2001, 100 hot dogs are sold at a price of $1 per hot dog, so expenditure on hot dogs equals $100. In the same year, 50 hamburgers are sold for $2 per hamburger, so expenditure on hamburgers also equals $100. Total expenditure in the economy—the sum of expenditure on hot dogs and expenditure on hamburgers—is $200. This amount, the production of goods and services valued at current prices, is called **nominal GDP.**

The table shows the calculation of nominal GDP for these three years. Total spending rises from $200 in 2001 to $600 in 2002 and then to $1,200 in 2003. Part of this rise is attributable to the increase in the quantities of hot dogs and

nominal GDP
the production of goods and services valued at current prices

	PRICE AND QUANTITIES			
YEAR	PRICE OF HOT DOGS	QUANTITY OF HOT DOGS	PRICE OF HAMBURGERS	QUANTITY OF HAMBURGERS
2001	$1	100	$2	50
2002	2	150	3	100
2003	3	200	4	150
YEAR	CALCULATING NOMINAL GDP			
2001	($1 per hot dog × 100 hot dogs) + ($2 per hamburger × 50 hamburgers) = $200			
2002	($2 per hot dog × 150 hot dogs) + ($3 per hamburger × 100 hamburgers) = $600			
2003	($3 per hot dog × 200 hot dogs) + ($4 per hamburger × 150 hamburgers) = $1,200			
YEAR	CALCULATING REAL GDP (BASE YEAR 2001)			
2001	($1 per hot dog × 100 hot dogs) + ($2 per hamburger × 50 hamburgers) = $200			
2002	($1 per hot dog × 150 hot dogs) + ($2 per hamburger × 100 hamburgers) = $350			
2003	($1 per hot dog × 200 hot dogs) + ($2 per hamburger × 150 hamburgers) = $500			
YEAR	CALCULATING THE GDP DEFLATOR			
2001	($200/$200) × 100 = 100			
2002	($600/$350) × 100 = 171			
2003	($1,200/$500) × 100 = 240			

Table 22-2

REAL AND NOMINAL GDP. This table shows how to calculate real GDP, nominal GDP, and the GDP deflator for a hypothetical economy that produces only hot dogs and hamburgers.

real GDP

the production of goods and services valued at constant prices

hamburgers, and part is attributable to the increase in the prices of hot dogs and hamburgers.

To obtain a measure of the amount produced that is not affected by changes in prices, we use **real GDP**, which is the production of goods and services valued at constant prices. We calculate real GDP by first choosing one year as a *base year*. We then use the prices of hot dogs and hamburgers in the base year to compute the value of goods and services in all of the years. In other words, the prices in the base year provide the basis for comparing quantities in different years.

Suppose that we choose 2001 to be the base year in our example. We can then use the prices of hot dogs and hamburgers in 2001 to compute the value of goods and services produced in 2001, 2002, and 2003. Table 22-2 shows these calculations. To compute real GDP for 2001, we use the prices of hot dogs and hamburgers in 2001 (the base year) and the quantities of hot dogs and hamburgers produced in 2001. (Thus, for the base year, real GDP always equals nominal GDP.) To compute real GDP for 2002, we use the prices of hot dogs and hamburgers in 2001 (the base year) and the quantities of hot dogs and hamburgers produced in 2002. Similarly, to compute real GDP for 2003, we use the prices in 2001 and the quantities in 2003. When we find that real GDP has risen from $200 in 2001 to $350 in 2002 and then to $500 in 2003, we know that the increase is attributable to an increase in the quantities produced, because the prices are being held fixed at base-year levels.

To sum up: *Nominal GDP uses current prices to place a value on the economy's production of goods and services. Real GDP uses constant base-year prices to place a value on the economy's production of goods and services.* Because real GDP is not affected by changes in prices, changes in real GDP reflect only changes in the amounts being produced. Thus, real GDP is a measure of the economy's production of goods and services.

Our goal in computing GDP is to gauge how well the overall economy is performing. Because real GDP measures the economy's production of goods and services, it reflects the economy's ability to satisfy people's needs and desires. Thus, real GDP is a better gauge of economic well-being than is nominal GDP. When economists talk about the economy's GDP, they usually mean real rather than nominal GDP. And when they talk about growth in the economy, they measure that growth with the percentage change in real GDP from an earlier period.

THE GDP DEFLATOR

From nominal GDP and real GDP, we can compute a third useful statistic: the GDP deflator. The GDP deflator measures the current level of prices relative to the level of prices in the base year. In other words, the GDP deflator tells us the rise in nominal GDP that is attributable to a rise in prices rather than a rise in the quantities produced.

The **GDP deflator** is calculated as follows:

$$\text{GDP deflator} = \frac{\text{Nominal GDP}}{\text{Real GDP}} \times 100.$$

GDP deflator
a measure of the price level calculated as the ratio of nominal GDP to real GDP times 100

This formula shows why the GDP deflator measures the level of prices in the economy. A change in the price of some good or service, without any change in the quantity produced, affects nominal GDP but not real GDP. This price change, therefore, is reflected in the GDP deflator.

The GDP deflator in our example is computed at the bottom of Table 22-2. For year 2001, nominal GDP is $200, and real GDP is $200, so the GDP deflator is 100. (The GDP deflator is always 100 in the base year.) For the year 2002, nominal GDP is $600, and real GDP is $350, so the GDP deflator is 171. Because the GDP deflator rose in year 2002 from 100 to 171, we can say that the price level increased by 71 percent.

The GDP deflator is one measure that economists use to monitor the average level of prices in the economy. We examine another—the consumer price index—in the next chapter.

CASE STUDY REAL GDP OVER RECENT HISTORY

Now that we know how real GDP is defined and measured, let's look at what this macroeconomic variable tells us about the recent history of the United States. Figure 22-2 shows quarterly data on real GDP for the U.S. economy since 1970.

Figure 22-2

REAL GDP IN THE UNITED STATES. This figure shows quarterly data on real GDP for the U.S. economy since 1970. Recessions—periods of falling real GDP—are marked with the shaded vertical bars.

SOURCE: U.S. Department of Commerce.

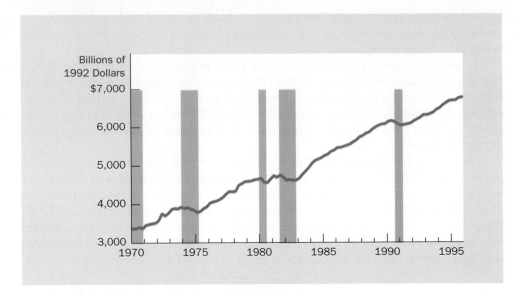

The most obvious feature of these data is that real GDP grows over time. The real GDP of the U.S. economy in 1995 was almost twice its level in 1970. Put differently, the output of goods and services produced in the United States has grown on average about 3 percent per year. This continued growth in real GDP enables the typical American to enjoy greater economic prosperity than his or her parents and grandparents did.

A second feature of the GDP data is that growth is not steady. The upward climb of real GDP is occasionally interrupted by periods of decline, called *recessions*. Figure 22-2 marks recessions with shaded vertical bars. Recessions are associated not only with lower incomes but also with other forms of economic distress: rising unemployment, falling profits, increased bankruptcies, and so on.

Much of macroeconomics is aimed at explaining the long-run growth and short-run fluctuations in real GDP. As we will see in the coming chapters, we need different models for these two purposes. Because the short-run fluctuations represent deviations from the long-run trend, we first examine the behavior of the economy in the long run. In particular, Chapters 24 through 30 examine how key macroeconomic variables, including real GDP, are determined in the long run. We then build on this analysis to explain short-run fluctuations in Chapters 31 through 33.

QUICK QUIZ   Define real and nominal GDP. Which is a better measure of economic well-being? Why?

GDP AND ECONOMIC WELL-BEING

Earlier in this chapter, GDP was called the best single measure of the economic well-being of a society. Now that we know what GDP is, we can evaluate this claim.

As we have seen, GDP measures both the economy's total income and the economy's total expenditure on goods and services. Thus, GDP per person tells us the income and expenditure of the average person in the economy. Because most people would prefer to receive higher income and enjoy higher expenditure, GDP per person seems a natural measure of the economic well-being of the average individual.

Yet some people dispute the validity of GDP as a measure of welfare. Senator Robert Kennedy, when he was running for president in 1968, gave a moving critique of such economic measures:

> [Gross domestic product] does not allow for the health of our children, the quality of their education, or the joy of their play. It does not include the beauty of our poetry or the strength of our marriages, the intelligence of our public debate or the integrity of our public officials. It measures neither our courage, nor our wisdom, nor our devotion to our country. It measures everything, in short, except that which makes life worthwhile, and it can tell us everything about America except why we are proud that we are Americans.

Much of what Robert Kennedy said is correct. Why then do we care about GDP?

The answer is that a large GDP does in fact help us to lead a good life. GDP does not measure the health of our children, but nations with larger GDP can afford better health care for their children. GDP does not measure the quality of their education, but nations with larger GDP can afford better educational systems. GDP does not measure the beauty of our poetry, but nations with larger GDP can afford to teach more of their citizens to read and to enjoy poetry. GDP does not take account of our intelligence, integrity, courage, wisdom, or devotion to country, but all of these laudable attributes are easier to foster when people are less concerned about affording the material necessities of life. In short, GDP does not directly measure those things that make life worthwhile, but it does measure our ability to obtain the inputs into a worthwhile life.

GDP is not, however, a perfect measure of well-being. Some things that contribute to a good life are left out of GDP. One is leisure. Suppose, for instance, that everyone in the economy suddenly started working every day of the week, rather than enjoying leisure on weekends. More goods and services would be produced, and GDP would rise. Yet, despite the increase in GDP, we should not conclude that everyone would be better off. The welfare loss from reduced leisure would offset the welfare gain from producing and consuming a greater quantity of goods and services.

Another thing that GDP excludes is the quality of the environment. Imagine that the government eliminated all environmental regulations. Firms could then produce goods and services without considering the pollution they create, and GDP might rise. Yet well-being would most likely fall. The deterioration in the quality of air and water would more than offset the welfare gain from greater production.

Because GDP uses market prices to value goods and services, it also excludes the value of almost all activity that takes place outside of markets. Child-rearing and volunteer work, for instance, contribute to the well-being of those in society, but GDP does not reflect these contributions. If parents decided to spend fewer hours at their jobs in order to spend more time with their children, the economy would produce fewer goods and services, and GDP would fall, but that change would not necessarily reflect a lower quality of life.

In the end, we can conclude that GDP is a good measure of welfare for most—but not all—purposes. It is important to keep in mind what GDP includes and what it leaves out.

CASE STUDY   INTERNATIONAL DIFFERENCES IN GDP AND THE QUALITY OF LIFE

One way to gauge the usefulness of GDP as a measure of economic well-being is to examine international data. Rich and poor countries have vastly different levels of GDP per person. If a large GDP leads to a higher standard of living, then we should observe GDP to be strongly correlated with measures of the quality of life. And, in fact, we do.

Table 22-3 shows 12 of the world's most populous countries ranked in order of GDP per person. The table also shows life expectancy (the expected life span at birth) and literacy (the percentage of the adult population that can read). These data show a clear pattern. In rich countries, such as the United States, Japan, and Germany, people can expect to live well into their seventies, and almost all of the population can read. In poor countries, such as Nigeria, Bangladesh, and India, people typically live only into their fifties, and only about half of the population is literate.

Although data on other aspects of the quality of life are less complete, they tell a similar story. Countries with low GDP per person tend to have more infants with low birth weight, higher rates of infant mortality, higher rates of maternal mortality, higher rates of child malnutrition, and less common access to safe drinking water. In countries with low GDP per person, fewer school-age children are in fact in school, and those who are in school must learn with fewer teachers per student. These countries also tend to have fewer radios,

---

Table 22-3

GDP, LIFE EXPECTANCY, AND ILLITERACY. The table shows GDP per person and two measures of the quality of life for 12 major countries.

COUNTRY	REAL GDP PER PERSON (1993)	LIFE EXPECTANCY	ADULT LITERACY
United States	$24,680	76 years	99%
Japan	20,660	80	99
Germany	18,840	76	99
Mexico	7,010	71	89
Brazil	5,500	67	82
Russia	4,760	67	99
Indonesia	3,270	63	83
China	2,330	69	80
Pakistan	2,160	62	36
Nigeria	1,540	51	54
Bangladesh	1,290	56	37
India	1,240	61	51

SOURCE: *Human Development Report 1996*, United Nations.

fewer televisions, fewer telephones, fewer paved roads, and fewer households with electricity. International data leave no doubt that a nation's GDP is closely associated with its citizens' standard of living.

■ **QUICK QUIZ** Why should policymakers care about GDP?

CONCLUSION

This chapter has discussed how economists measure the total income of a nation. Measurement is, of course, only a starting point. Much of macroeconomics is aimed at revealing the long-run and short-run determinants of a nation's gross domestic product. Why, for example, is GDP higher in the United States and Japan than in India and Nigeria? What can the governments of the poorest countries do to promote more rapid growth in GDP? Why does GDP in the United States rise rapidly in some years and fall in others? What can U.S. policymakers do to reduce the severity of these fluctuations in GDP? These are the questions we will take up shortly.

At this point, it is important to acknowledge the importance of just measuring GDP. We all get some sense of how the economy is doing as we go about our lives. But the economists who study changes in the economy and the policymakers who formulate economic policies need more than this vague sense— they need concrete data on which to base their judgments. Quantifying the behavior of the economy with statistics such as GDP is, therefore, the first step to developing a science of macroeconomics.

Summary

♦ Because every transaction has a buyer and a seller, the total expenditure in the economy must equal the total income in the economy.

♦ Gross domestic product (GDP) measures an economy's total expenditure on newly produced goods and services and the total income earned from the production of these goods and services. More precisely, GDP is the market value of all final goods and services produced within a country in a given period of time.

♦ GDP is divided among four components of expenditure: consumption, investment, government purchases, and net exports. Consumption includes spending on goods and services by households, with the exception of purchases of new housing. Investment includes spending on new equipment and structures, including households' purchases of new housing. Government purchases include spending on goods and services by local,

state, and federal governments. Net exports equal the value of goods and services produced domestically and sold abroad (exports) minus the value of goods and services produced abroad and sold domestically (imports).

♦ Nominal GDP uses current prices to value the economy's production of goods and services. Real GDP uses constant base-year prices to value the economy's production of goods and services. The GDP deflator— calculated from the ratio of nominal to real GDP— measures the level of prices in the economy.

♦ GDP is a good measure of economic well-being because people prefer higher to lower incomes. But it is not a perfect measure of well-being. For example, GDP excludes the value of leisure and the value of a clean environment.

Key Concepts

microeconomics, p. 478
macroeconomics, p. 478
gross domestic product (GDP), p. 480
gross national product (GNP), p. 482

consumption, p. 484
investment, p. 484
government purchases, p. 484
net exports, p. 484

nominal GDP, p. 485
real GDP, p. 486
GDP deflator, p. 487

Questions for Review

1. Explain why an economy's income must equal its expenditure.

2. Which contributes more to GDP—the production of an economy car or the production of a luxury car? Why?

3. A farmer sells wheat to a baker for $2. The baker uses the wheat to make bread, which is sold for $3. What is the contribution to GDP?

4. Many years ago Peggy paid $500 to put together a record collection. Today she sold her albums at a garage sale for $100. How does this sale affect current GDP?

5. List the four components of GDP. Give an example of each.

6. In the year 2001, the economy produces 100 loaves of bread that sell for $2 each. In the year 2002, the economy produces 200 loaves of bread that sell for $3 each. Calculate nominal GDP, real GDP, and the GDP deflator for each year. (Use 2001 as the base year.) By what percentage does each of these three statistics rise from one year to the next?

7. Why is it desirable for a country to have a large GDP? Give an example of something that would raise GDP and yet be undesirable.

Problems and Applications

1. What components of GDP (if any) would each of the following transactions affect? Explain.
   a. A family buys a new refrigerator.
   b. Aunt Jane buys a new house.
   c. Ford sells a Thunderbird from its inventory.
   d. You buy a pizza.
   e. California repaves Highway 101.
   f. Your parents buy a bottle of French wine.
   g. Honda expands its factory in Marysville, Ohio.

2. The "government purchases" component of GDP does not include spending on transfer payments such as Social Security. Thinking about the definition of GDP, explain why transfer payments are excluded.

3. Why do you think households' purchases of new housing are included in the investment component of GDP rather than the consumption component? Can you think of a reason why households' purchases of new cars should also be included in investment rather than in consumption? To what other consumption goods might this logic apply?

4. As the chapter states, GDP does not include the value of used goods that are resold. Why would including such transactions make GDP a less informative measure of economic well-being?

5. What is the advantage of measuring GDP using the prices, rather than the sizes or weights, of different goods?

6. Consider the following data on U.S. GDP:

Year	Nominal GDP (in billions)	GDP Deflator (base year 1987)
1993	$6,343	124
1994	6,738	126

   a. What was the growth rate of nominal income between 1993 and 1994? (Note: The growth rate is the percentage change from one period to the next.)
   b. What was the growth rate of the GDP deflator between 1993 and 1994?
   c. What was real income in 1993 measured in 1987 prices?

d. What was real income in 1994 measured in 1987 prices?

e. What was the growth rate of real income between 1993 and 1994?

f. Was the growth rate of nominal income higher or lower than the growth rate of real income? Explain.

7. If prices rise, people's income from selling goods increases. The growth of real GDP ignores this gain, however. Why, then, do economists prefer real GDP as a measure of economic well-being?

8. Revised estimates of U.S. GDP are usually released by the government near the end of each month. Go to a library and find a newspaper article that reports on the most recent release. Discuss the recent changes in real and nominal GDP and in the components of GDP.

9. If a farmer sells the same amount of corn as last year, but at a higher price per ear, her income has increased. Can you tell whether she is better off? Explain.

10. A friend tells you that the GDP of China is three times the GDP of Sweden. Does this imply that China is better off economically than Sweden? Why or why not?

11. Goods and services that are not sold in markets, such as food produced and consumed at home, are generally not included in GDP. Can you think of how this might cause the numbers in the second column of Table 22-3 to be misleading in a comparison of the economic well-being of the United States and India? Explain.

12. Until the early 1990s, the U.S. government emphasized GNP rather than GDP as a measure of economic well-being. Which measure should the government prefer if it cares about the total income of Americans? Which measure should it prefer if it cares about the total amount of economic activity occurring in the United States?

13. The participation of women in the U.S. labor force has risen dramatically since 1970.

a. How do you think this rise affected GDP?

b. Now imagine a measure of well-being that includes time spent working in the home and taking leisure. How would the change in this measure of well-being compare to the change in GDP?

c. Can you think of other aspects of well-being that are associated with the rise in women's labor-force participation? Would it be practical to construct a measure of well-being that includes these aspects?

23

MEASURING THE
COST OF LIVING

In 1931, as the U.S. economy was suffering through the Great Depression, famed baseball player Babe Ruth earned $80,000. At the time, this salary was extraordinary, even among the stars of baseball. According to one story, a reporter asked Ruth whether he thought it was right that he made more than President Herbert Hoover, who had a salary of only $75,000. Ruth replied, "I had a better year."

Today the average baseball player earns more than ten times Ruth's 1931 salary, and the best players can earn 100 times as much. At first, this fact might lead you to think that baseball has become much more lucrative over the past six decades. But, as everyone knows, the prices of goods and services have also risen. In 1931, a nickel would buy an ice-cream cone, and a quarter would buy a ticket at the local movie theater. Because prices were so much lower in Babe Ruth's day than they are in ours, it is not clear whether Ruth enjoyed a higher or lower standard of living than today's players.

In the preceding chapter we looked at how economists use gross domestic product (GDP) to measure the quantity of goods and services that the economy is producing. This chapter examines how economists measure the overall cost of living. To compare Babe Ruth's salary of $80,000 to salaries from today, we need to find some way of turning dollar figures into meaningful measures of purchasing power. That is exactly the job of a statistic called the *consumer price index*. After seeing how the consumer price index is constructed, we discuss how we can use such a price index to compare dollar figures from different points in time.

The consumer price index is used to monitor changes in the cost of living over time. When the consumer price index rises, the typical family has to spend more dollars to maintain the same standard of living. Economists use the term *inflation* to describe a situation in which the economy's overall price level is rising. The *inflation rate* is the percentage change in the price level from the previous period. As we will see in the coming chapters, inflation is a closely watched aspect of macroeconomic performance and is a key variable guiding macroeconomic policy. This chapter provides the background for that analysis by showing how economists measure the inflation rate using the consumer price index.

THE CONSUMER PRICE INDEX

consumer price index (CPI)
a measure of the overall cost of the goods and services bought by a typical consumer

The **consumer price index (CPI)** is a measure of the overall cost of the goods and services bought by a typical consumer. Each month the Bureau of Labor Statistics, which is part of the Department of Labor, computes and reports the consumer price index. In this section we discuss how the consumer price index is calculated and what problems arise in its measurement. We also consider how this index compares to the GDP deflator, another measure of the overall level of prices, which we examined in the last chapter.

HOW THE CONSUMER PRICE INDEX IS CALCULATED

When the Bureau of Labor Statistics calculates the consumer price index and the inflation rate, it uses data on the prices of thousands of goods and services. To see exactly how these statistics are constructed, let's consider a simple economy in which consumers buy only two goods—hot dogs and hamburgers. Table 23-1 shows the five steps that the Bureau of Labor Statistics follows.

1. *Fix the Basket.* The first step in computing the consumer price index is to determine which prices are most important to the typical consumer. If the typical consumer buys more hot dogs than hamburgers, then the price of hot dogs is more important than the price of hamburgers and, therefore, should be given greater weight in measuring the cost of living. The Bureau of Labor Statistics sets these weights by surveying consumers and finding the basket of goods and services that the typical consumer buys. In the example in the table, the typical consumer buys a basket of 4 hot dogs and 2 hamburgers.

2. *Find the Prices.* The second step in computing the consumer price index is to find the prices of each of the goods and services in the basket for each point in time. The table shows the prices of hot dogs and hamburgers for three different years.

3. *Compute the Basket's Cost.* The third step is to use the data on prices to calculate the cost of the basket of goods and services at different times. The table shows this calculation for each of the three years. Notice that only the prices in this calculation change. By keeping the basket of goods the same (4 hot dogs and 2 hamburgers), we are isolating the effects of

Table 23-1

STEP 1: SURVEY CONSUMERS TO DETERMINE A FIXED BASKET OF GOODS

4 hot dogs, 2 hamburgers

STEP 2: FIND THE PRICE OF EACH GOOD IN EACH YEAR

YEAR	PRICE OF HOT DOGS	PRICE OF HAMBURGERS
2001	$1	$2
2002	2	3
2003	3	4

STEP 3: COMPUTE THE COST OF THE BASKET OF GOODS IN EACH YEAR

YEAR	COST OF BASKET
2001	($1 per hot dog × 4 hot dogs) + ($2 per hamburger × 2 hamburgers) = $8
2002	($2 per hot dog × 4 hot dogs) + ($3 per hamburger × 2 hamburgers) = $14
2003	($3 per hot dog × 4 hot dogs) + ($4 per hamburger × 2 hamburgers) = $20

STEP 4: CHOOSE ONE YEAR AS A BASE YEAR (2001) AND COMPUTE THE CONSUMER PRICE INDEX IN EACH YEAR

YEAR	CONSUMER PRICE INDEX
2001	($8/$8) × 100 = 100
2002	($14/$8) × 100 = 175
2003	($20/$8) × 100 = 250

STEP 5: USE THE CONSUMER PRICE INDEX TO COMPUTE THE INFLATION RATE FROM PREVIOUS YEAR

YEAR	INFLATION RATE
2002	(175 − 100)/100 × 100 = 75%
2003	(250 − 175)/175 × 100 = 43%

CALCULATING THE CONSUMER PRICE INDEX AND THE INFLATION RATE: AN EXAMPLE. This table shows how to calculate the consumer price index and the inflation rate for a hypothetical economy in which consumers buy only hot dogs and hamburgers.

price changes from the effect of any quantity changes that might be occurring at the same time.

4. *Choose a Base Year and Compute the Index.* The fourth step is to designate one year as the base year, which is the benchmark against which other years are compared. To calculate the index, the price of the basket of goods and services in each year is divided by the price of the basket in the base year, and this ratio is then multiplied by 100. The resulting number is the consumer price index.

In the example in the table, the year 2001 is the base year. In this year, the basket of hot dogs and hamburgers costs $8. Therefore, the price of the basket in all years is divided by $8 and multiplied by 100. The consumer price index is 100 in 2001. (The index is always 100 in the base year.) The consumer price index is 175 in 2002. This means that the price of the basket in 2002 is 175 percent of its price in the base year. Put differently, a basket of goods that costs $100 in the base year costs $175 in 2002. Similarly, the consumer price index is 250 in 2003, indicating that the price level in 2003 is 250 percent of the price level in the base year.

FYI

What Is in the CPI's Basket?

WHEN CONSTRUCTING THE consumer price index, the Bureau of Labor Statistics tries to include all the goods and services that the typical consumer buys. Moreover, it tries to weight these goods and services according to how much consumers buy of each item.

Figure 23-1 shows the breakdown of consumer spending into the major categories of goods and services. By far the largest category is housing, which makes up 41 percent of the typical consumer's budget. This category includes the cost of shelter (28 percent), fuel and other utilities (7 percent), and household furnishings and operation (6 percent). The next largest category at 17 percent is food and beverages; this includes food at home (10 percent), food away from home (6 percent), and alcoholic beverages (2 percent). The next category, also at 17 percent, is transportation, which includes spending on cars, gasoline, buses, subways, and so on. Next are medical care at 7 percent, apparel and upkeep at 6 percent, and entertainment at 4 percent.

The last category in the figure, at 8 percent of spending, comprises other goods and services. This category is a catchall for things consumers buy that do not naturally fit into the other categories. Your purchase of this book, for example, falls into this category. (Although books and supplies for school may be a large part of your spending, they make up only one-quarter of 1 percent of the spending of the typical consumer.)

Figure 23-1

THE BASKET OF GOODS AND SERVICES. This figure shows how the typical consumer divides his spending among various categories of goods and services. The Bureau of Labor Statistics calls each percentage the "relative importance" of the category.

SOURCE: Bureau of Labor Statistics.

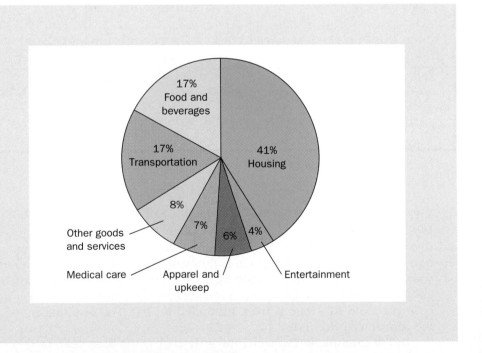

5. *Compute the Inflation Rate.* The fifth and final step is to use the consumer price index to calculate the **inflation rate,** which is the percentage change in the price index from the preceding period. In our example, the consumer price index rose by 75 percent from 2001 to 2002 and by 43 percent from 2002 to 2003. The inflation rate is said to be 75 percent in 2002 and 43 percent in 2003.

inflation rate
the percentage change in the price index from the preceding period

Although this example simplifies the real world by including only two goods, it shows how the Bureau of Labor Statistics computes the consumer price index and the inflation rate. The Bureau collects and processes data on the prices of thousands of goods and services every month and, by following the five foregoing steps, determines how quickly the cost of living for the typical consumer is rising. When the Bureau makes its monthly announcement of the consumer price index, you can usually hear the number on the evening television news or see it in the next day's newspaper.

In addition to the consumer price index for the overall economy, the Bureau of Labor Statistics calculates several other price indexes. It reports the index for regions within the country (such as Boston, New York, and Los Angeles) and for some narrow categories of goods and services (such as food, clothing, and energy). It also calculates the **producer price index,** which measures the cost of a basket of goods and services bought by firms rather than consumers. Because firms eventually pass on their costs to consumers in the form of higher consumer prices, changes in the producer price index are often thought to be useful in predicting changes in the consumer price index.

producer price index
a measure of the cost of a basket of goods and services bought by firms

PROBLEMS IN MEASURING THE COST OF LIVING

The goal of the consumer price index is to measure changes in the cost of living. In other words, the consumer price index tries to gauge how much incomes must rise in order to maintain a constant standard of living. The consumer price index, however, is not a perfect measure of the cost of living. Three problems with the index are widely acknowledged but difficult to solve.

The first problem is called *substitution bias.* When prices change from one year to the next, they do not all change proportionately: Some prices rise by more than others. Consumers respond to these differing price changes by buying less of the goods whose prices have risen by large amounts and by buying more of the goods whose prices have risen less or even have fallen. That is, consumers substitute toward goods that have become relatively less expensive. Yet the consumer price index is computed assuming a fixed basket of goods. By not taking into account the possibility of consumer substitution, the index overstates the increase in the cost of living from one year to the next.

Let's consider a simple example. Imagine that in the base year, apples are cheaper than pears, and so consumers buy more apples than pears. When the Bureau of Labor Statistics constructs the basket of goods, it will include more apples than pears. Suppose that next year pears are cheaper than apples. Consumers will naturally respond to the price changes by buying more pears and fewer apples. Yet, when computing the consumer price index, the Bureau uses a fixed basket, which in essence assumes that consumers continue buying the now-expensive apples in the same quantities as before. For this reason, the index will measure a much larger increase in the cost of living than consumers actually perceive.

IN THE NEWS

Shopping for

the CPI

BEHIND EVERY MACROECONOMIC STATIStic are thousands of individual pieces of data on the economy. The following article follows some of the people who collect these data.

Is the CPI Accurate? Ask the Federal Sleuths Who Get the Numbers

BY CHRISTINA DUFF

TRENTON, N.J.—The hospital's finance director is relentlessly unhelpful, but she is still no match for Sabina Bloom, government gumshoe.

Mrs. Bloom wants to know the exact prices of some hospital services. "Nothing's changed," the woman says.

"Well, do you have the ledger?" Mrs. Bloom asks. "We *haven't* changed any prices," the woman insists. Mrs. Bloom's fast talk finally pries the woman from behind her desk, and she gets the numbers. It turns out that a semiprivate surgery recovery room now costs $753.80 a day— or $0.04 less than a month ago.

Chalk up another small success for Mrs. Bloom, one of about 300 Bureau of Labor Statistics employees who gather the information that is fed into the monthly Consumer Price Index. . . .

Mrs. Bloom's travails sometimes read like a detective novel. Each month, she covers 900 miles in her beat-up Geo Prizm (three accidents in the past 18 months) to visit about 150 sites. Her mission: to record the prices of certain items, time and again. If prices change, she needs to find out why. Each month, some 90,000 prices are shipped to Washington, plugged into a computer, scrutinized, aggregated, adjusted for seasonal ups or downs, and then spit out as the monthly CPI report.

Choosing what to price—for example, the "regular" or "fancy" baby parakeet—can seem arbitrary. After consulting surveys that track consumer buying habits, the labor statistics bureau selects popular stores and item categories— say, women's tops. The price-taker then asks a store employee to help zero in on an item of the price-taker's choosing. They narrow to the size of the top, its style (short-sleeve, long-sleeve, tank, or turtleneck), and so on; items that generate the most revenue in a category have the best chance of getting picked.

Shoppers know that relying on employees for anything can be chancy. At a downtown Chicago department store (the government doesn't disclose names) price-taker Mary Ann Latter squints at a sale sign above an ivory shell blouse. "Save 45%–60% when you take an additional 30% off permanently reduced merchandise. Markdown taken at register," the sign says.

Confused, Ms. Latter asks a clerk to scan the item. There is a pause. "It's 30 percent off," she says, just before the lunch-hour rush.

"I know," Ms. Latter says, "but can you scan it just to make sure?" Under her breath, she mumbles, "So helpful."

Downstairs in the jewelry department, Ms. Latter tries to price the one 18-inch silver necklace left, but there is

The second problem with the consumer price index is the *introduction of new goods.* When a new good is introduced, consumers have more variety from which to choose. Greater variety, in turn, makes each dollar more valuable, so consumers need fewer dollars to maintain any given standard of living. Yet because the consumer price index is based on a fixed basket of goods, it does not reflect this change in the purchasing power of the dollar.

Again, let's consider an example. When VCRs were introduced, consumers could now watch their favorite movies at home. This new good increased consumers' well-being by expanding their consumption choices. A perfect cost-of-living index would reflect this change with a decrease in the cost of living. The consumer price index, however, did not decrease in response to the introduction of the VCR. Eventually, the Bureau of Labor Statistics did revise the basket of goods to include VCRs, and subsequently the index reflected changes in VCR prices. But the reduction in the cost of living associated with the initial introduction of the VCR never showed up in the index.

no tag. "Do I have to look it up now?" moans the employee behind the counter. Ms. Latter watches her wait on several customers, then asks again: "Could you find it?" The harried saleswoman throws on the counter a thick notebook with a dizzying array of jewelry sketches. Ms. Latter finally locates a silver weave that looks about right.

When the exact item can't be found, price-takers must substitute. That can be difficult. Consider a haircut: If the stylist leaves, his fill-in must have about the same experience; a newer stylist, for example, might charge less. This frigid winter afternoon, Ms. Latter needs to substitute a coat because clothing items rarely remain on the racks for more than a couple months. It must be a lightweight swing coat of less than half wool. After digging through heavy winter wear, trying to locate tags in three departments on two floors, she gives up. It is off season anyway, so she will have to wait months to choose a substitute.

Making it harder for price detectives to grasp the true cost of living is that the master list of 207 categories they price—called the market basket—is updated only once every ten years. Cellular

phones? Too new to be priced because they don't fit into any of the categories set up in the 1980s. They probably will be included when the new categories arrive in 1998.

Some changes within these categories are made every five years. So within "new cars," for example, if domestic autos overtake imports in a big way, price-takers might examine more Fords and fewer Toyotas. But that doesn't happen often enough, critics say. Ms. Latter, a city-dwelling Generation X'er, continually must price "Always Twenty-One" girdles, yet ignore the new, popular WonderBras behind her. . . .

Ms. Latter's colleague in suburban Chicago, Sheila Ward, must ignore the hoopla over Tickle Me Elmo and instead price a GI Joe Extreme doll with "painted, molded hair." Reliance on outdated goods, says Mrs. Ward, "would be one of the criticisms of us." She recalls a music store owner who became frustrated because she kept seeking prices on a guitar he could never imagine playing—much less selling. He finally threw her out of his shop, screaming, "The damned government! Is this what I'm paying taxes for?"

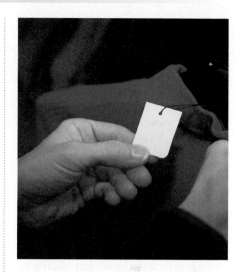

Price-takers can't do much about these problems. What they can do is interrogate. At a simple restaurant, Mrs. Ward asks if food portions have changed. The owner says they haven't. But she remembers that the price of bacon has been climbing, and asks again about his BLT. Suddenly, he recalls that he has cut the number of bacon slices from three to two. And that is a very different sandwich.

SOURCE: *The Wall Street Journal,* January 16, 1997, p. A1.

The third problem with the consumer price index is *unmeasured quality change.* If the quality of a good deteriorates from one year to the next, the value of a dollar falls, even if the price of the good stays the same. Similarly, if the quality rises from one year to the next, the value of a dollar rises. The Bureau of Labor Statistics does its best to account for quality change. When the quality of a good in the basket changes—for example, when a car model has more horsepower or gets better gas mileage from one year to the next—the Bureau adjusts the price of the good to account for the quality change. It is, in essence, trying to compute the price of a basket of goods of constant quality. Nonetheless, changes in quality remain a problem, because quality is so hard to measure.

There is still much debate among economists about how severe these measurement problems are and what should be done about them. The issue is important because many government programs use the consumer price index to adjust for changes in the overall level of prices. Recipients of Social Security, for instance, get annual increases in benefits that are tied to the consumer price

IN THE NEWS

The CPI

Commission

IN 1996 A COMMISSION OF PROMINENT economists appointed by Congress reported on the measurement problems in the consumer price index. In the following article, commission chairman Michael Boskin discusses their findings.

Prisoners of Faulty Statistics

BY MICHAEL J. BOSKIN

Just as subatomic particles are the basic building blocks of physics, so prices and quantities are the fundamental building blocks of the economy, the foundation upon which all analysis, theory, measurement, and policy rest. If prices or their rate of change, inflation, are not measured accurately, there will be cracks in the foundation. We will be prisoners of faulty statistics.

But measuring inflation accurately is central to almost every economic issue, from monetary policy to measuring economic progress to the cost and structure of indexed spending and taxes. Many private contracts, including the forthcoming indexed Treasury bonds, are explicitly tied to the consumer price index (CPI), and an even larger number calibrate informally. Financial markets price expected future inflation into asset prices. About one-third of federal budget outlays are annually automatically escalated by the change in the CPI, as are income tax brackets (but unfortunately not the definition of income).

Yesterday, the Congressional Advisory Commission on the Consumer Price Index, which I chair, released its final report. My four eminent economist colleagues and I concluded that changes in the consumer price index currently overstate the change in the cost of living by about 1.1 percentage points per year. That is, if inflation as measured by the percentage change in the consumer price index is running 3 percent, the true change in the cost of living is about 2 percent. This bias might seem small. But when compounded over time, the implications are enormous. For example, over a dozen years, the cumulative additional national debt from over-indexing the budget would amount to $1 trillion! . . .

The implications of overstating inflation for understanding economic progress are equally striking. Instead of falling by 13 percent, real hourly earnings have risen by 13 percent from 1973 to 1995. Certainly there has been a slowdown in wage growth, reflecting the productivity slowdown, but not a decline. Real median family income over the same period grew 36 percent, not the puny 4 percent in the official statistics that deflate by the CPI. The CPI component price indexes are also used as input into the national income accounts (NIA). While the Commerce Department's NIA methodology reduces the bias from the CPI, much remains and thus our measures of real economic growth and productivity gains are also understated substantially, by perhaps three-quarters of a percentage point per year.

The commission recommended that the president and the Congress explicitly decide whether they wish to continue the widespread substantial over-indexing

index. Some economists have suggested modifying these programs to correct for the measurement problems. For example, most studies conclude that the consumer price index overstates inflation by 0.5 to 2.0 percentage points per year. In response to these findings, Congress could change the Social Security program so that benefits increased every year by the measured inflation rate minus 1 percentage point. Such a change would provide a crude way of offsetting the measurement problems and, at the same time, reduce government spending by billions of dollars each year.

THE GDP DEFLATOR VERSUS THE CONSUMER PRICE INDEX

In the preceding chapter, we saw another measure of the overall level of prices in the economy—the GDP deflator. The GDP deflator is the ratio of nominal GDP to real GDP. Because nominal GDP is current output valued at current prices and in the budget. If the purpose of indexing is a full and accurate insulation from changes in the cost of living, no more and no less, they should pass legislation wholly or partly correcting the problem. . . .

But why does the CPI overstate actual inflation? The strength of the CPI is the underlying simplicity of its concept: pricing a fixed, but representative, market basket of goods and services over time. Its weakness follows from the same conception: the "fixed basket" becomes less and less representative over time as consumers respond to price changes and new choices.

Follow the actual behavior of consumers in the economy. Hop into your car and drive to a discount outlet, purchase a VCR for your child's birthday, swing by the supermarket where the price of beef has gone up substantially so you buy chicken instead. Return home, defrost the frozen vegetables in the microwave oven and turn on the television to watch the evening news. In this hour or two that reflects the everyday buying habits of millions of Americans, note the following: You drove on radial tires, which are far safer than bias-ply tires (and which last three to five times

longer, thus reducing maintenance costs); the VCR you purchased for $170, which would cost $200 at a local appliance store, has many more features and is far more reliable than the first generation, which cost about $1,000 two decades ago; by substituting chicken, you partially insulate your family from the rise in beef prices; the microwave oven did not exist 30 years ago; and your TV is color, likely to get 50 cable channels, has a much clearer picture, and is much more reliable than TVs were a generation ago (remember home visits from TV repairmen?).

The CPI uses a fixed market basket from 1982–1984, so it makes no account whatsoever for substitution among commodities. It prices within outlets, and hence fails to record the shift to lower price outlets as, at least partly, lowering prices. Many new products are brought into the CPI infrequently, usually at the time of the ten-year revisions; hence, VCRs and microwave ovens first appeared a decade after they were in widespread use, and after their prices fell 80 percent or more. This price decline, common in the product cycle, particularly for durable goods, never shows up in the CPI. Despite the efforts of the

Bureau of Labor Statistics (BLS) to account for quality changes, it is widely recognized that improvements in safety, durability, and energy efficiency are not fully reflected. . . .

In the first major external evaluation since the Stigler Commission in 1961, our commission recommended that the BLS replace the fixed-weight index with a cost-of-living index taking account of consumer substitution. Other recommendations, such as use of scanner data, would enable the BLS to get new products incorporated more quickly and to more fully adjust for quality change. The overriding theme of these suggestions is for the BLS to be in continual revision mode, rather than organizing itself for major revisions only once every 10 or 15 years. . . .

The commission's recommendations provide the BLS with an historic opportunity to make major improvements in the nation's price statistics, and the president and the Congress with an opportunity to get indexing right. The current measures are simply not accurate enough.

SOURCE: *The Wall Street Journal*, December 5, 1996, p. A20.

real GDP is current output valued at base-year prices, the GDP deflator reflects the current level of prices relative to the level of prices in the base year.

Economists and policymakers monitor both the GDP deflator and the consumer price index to gauge how quickly prices are rising. Usually, these two statistics tell a similar story. Yet there are two important differences that can cause them to diverge.

The first difference is that the GDP deflator reflects the prices of all goods and services *produced domestically*, whereas the consumer price index reflects the prices of all goods and services *bought by consumers*. For example, suppose that the price of an airplane produced by Boeing and sold to the Air Force rises. Even though the plane is part of GDP, it is not part of the basket of goods and services bought by a typical consumer. Thus, the price increase shows up in the GDP deflator but not in the consumer price index.

As another example, suppose that Volvo raises the price of its cars. Because Volvos are made in Sweden, the car is not part of U.S. GDP. But U.S. consumers do buy Volvos, and so the car is part of the typical consumer's basket of goods. Hence, a price increase in an imported consumption good, such as a Volvo, shows up in the consumer price index but not in the GDP deflator.

This first difference between the consumer price index and the GDP deflator is particularly important when the price of oil changes. Although the United States does produce some oil, much of the oil we use is imported from the Middle East. As a result, oil and oil products such as gasoline and heating oil are a much larger share of consumer spending than they are of GDP. When the price of oil rises, the consumer price index rises by much more than does the GDP deflator.

The second and more subtle difference between the GDP deflator and the consumer price index concerns how various prices are weighted to yield a single number for the overall level of prices. The consumer price index compares the price of a *fixed* basket of goods and services to the price of the basket in the base year. Only occasionally does the Bureau of Labor Statistics change the basket of goods. By contrast, the GDP deflator compares the price of *currently produced* goods and services to the price of the same goods and services in the base year. Thus, the group of goods and services used to compute the GDP deflator changes automatically over time. This difference is not important when all prices are changing proportionately. But if the prices of different goods and services are changing by varying amounts, the way we weight the various prices matters for the overall inflation rate.

Figure 23-2 shows the inflation rate as measured by both the GDP deflator and the consumer price index for each year since 1965. You can see that sometimes the two measures diverge. When they do diverge, it is possible to go behind these numbers and explain the divergence with the two differences we have discussed. The figure shows, however, that divergence between these two measures is the exception rather than the rule. In the late 1970s, both the GDP

Figure 23-2

TWO MEASURES OF INFLATION. This figure shows the inflation rate—the percentage change in the level of prices—as measured by the GDP deflator and the consumer price index using annual data since 1965. Notice that the two measures of inflation generally move together.

SOURCE: U.S. Department of Labor; U.S. Department of Commerce.

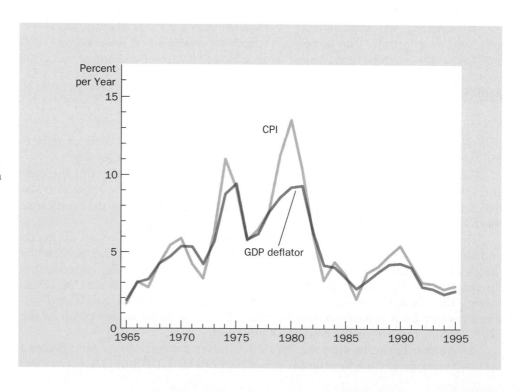

deflator and the consumer price index show high rates of inflation. In the late 1980s and early 1990s, both measures show low rates of inflation.

■ **QUICK QUIZ** Explain briefly what the consumer price index is trying to measure and how it is constructed.

CORRECTING ECONOMIC VARIABLES FOR THE EFFECTS OF INFLATION

The purpose of measuring the overall level of prices in the economy is to permit comparison between dollar figures from different points in time. Now that we know how price indexes are calculated, let's see how we might use such an index to compare a dollar figure from the past to a dollar figure in the present.

DOLLAR FIGURES FROM DIFFERENT TIMES

We first return to the issue of Babe Ruth's salary. Was his salary of $80,000 in 1931 high or low compared to the salaries of today's players?

To answer this question, we need to know the level of prices in 1931 and the level of prices today. Part of the increase in baseball salaries just compensates players for the higher level of prices today. To compare Ruth's salary to those of today's players, we need to inflate Ruth's salary to turn 1931 dollars into today's dollars. A price index determines the size of this inflation correction.

Government statistics give a price index of 8.7 for 1931 and 107.6 for 1995. (The base year is 1992.) Thus, the overall level of prices has risen by a factor of 12.4 (which equals 107.6/8.7). We can use these numbers to measure Ruth's salary in 1995 dollars. The calculation is:

$$\text{Salary in 1995 dollars} = \text{Salary in 1931 dollars} \times \frac{\text{Price level in 1995}}{\text{Price level in 1931}}$$

$$= \$80,000 \times \frac{107.6}{8.7}$$

$$= \$989,425.$$

AUDIO-VIDEO

"The price may seem a little high, but you have to remember that's in today's dollars."

We find that Babe Ruth's 1931 salary is equivalent to a salary today of just under $1 million. That is not a bad income, but it is somewhat less than the salary of the average baseball player today, and it is far less than the amount paid to today's baseball superstars. Baltimore Orioles shortstop Cal Ripken, for instance, was paid $5.4 million in 1995.

Let's also examine President Hoover's 1931 salary of $75,000. To translate that figure into 1995 dollars, we again multiply the ratio of the price levels in the two years. We find that Hoover's salary is equivalent to $75,000 × (107.6/8.7), or $927,586, in 1995 dollars. This is well above President Clinton's salary of $200,000. It seems that President Hoover did have a pretty good year after all.

IN THE NEWS

Mr. Index Goes

to Hollywood

WHAT WAS THE MOST POPULAR MOVIE OF all time? As the following article notes, answering this question requires an understanding of price indexes.

Winner and Still Champ

As if saving the world from invading aliens wasn't enough, *Independence*

"FRANKLY, MY DEAR, I DON'T CARE MUCH FOR THE EFFECTS OF INFLATION."

Day's Will Smith and company also conquered the box office. The action epic topped $100 million in under a week; the previous champ, 1993's *Jurassic Park*, took nine days to hit that mark. Some industry watchers expect *Independence Day* to draw more than $400 million domestically, breaking the record set by *E.T.* in the 1980s.

But those records are for dollars not adjusted for inflation. Exhibitor Relations, a Los Angeles firm that tracks box office receipts, used today's dollars to calculate the grosses of movies old and new. Its list indicates that *Independence Day*, even with a take of $400 million, will still fall far short of what Scarlett and Rhett accomplished more than a half century ago.

SOURCE: *U.S. News and World Report,* July 29, 1996, p. 8.

TITLE	YEAR OF RELEASE	ESTIMATED DOMESTIC GROSS IN 1996 DOLLARS
Gone with the Wind	1939	$859 million
Star Wars	1977	628
The Ten Commandments	1956	570
The Sound of Music	1965	568
Jaws	1975	557
E.T.	1982	552
Doctor Zhivago	1965	540
Jungle Book	1967	483
Snow White	1937	474
Ben-Hur	1959	468
101 Dalmatians	1961	458
The Exorcist	1973	410
The Sting	1973	397
Jurassic Park	1993	375
The Graduate	1967	372
The Godfather	1972	368
Return of the Jedi	1983	364
Fantasia	1940	361
The Empire Strikes Back	1980	361
Forrest Gump	1994	346

TOP 20 FILMS, ADJUSTED FOR INFLATION

INDEXATION

indexation

the automatic correction of a dollar amount for the effects of inflation by law or contract

As we have just seen, price indexes are used to correct for the effects of inflation when comparing dollar figures from different times. This type of correction shows up in many places in the economy. When some dollar amount is automatically corrected for inflation by law or contract, the amount is said to be **indexed** for inflation.

For example, many long-term contracts between firms and unions include partial or complete indexation of the wage to the consumer price index. Such a provision is called a cost-of-living allowance, or COLA. A COLA automatically raises the wage when the consumer price index rises.

Indexation is also a feature of many laws. Social Security benefits, for example, are adjusted every year to compensate the elderly for increases in prices. The brackets of the federal income tax—the income levels at which the tax rates change—are also indexed for inflation. There are, however, many ways in which the tax system is not indexed for inflation, even when perhaps it should be. We discuss these issues more fully when we discuss the costs of inflation later in this book.

REAL AND NOMINAL INTEREST RATES

Correcting economic variables for the effects of inflation is particularly important, and somewhat tricky, when we look at data on interest rates. When you deposit your savings in a bank account, you will earn interest on your deposit. Conversely, when you borrow from a bank to pay your tuition, you will pay interest on your student loan. Interest represents a payment in the future for a transfer of money in the past. As a result, interest rates always involve comparing amounts of money at different points in time. To fully understand interest rates, we need to know how to correct for the effects of inflation.

Let's consider an example. Suppose that Sally Saver deposits $1,000 in a bank account that pays an annual interest rate of 10 percent. After a year passes, Sally has accumulated $100 in interest. Sally then withdraws her $1,100. Is Sally $100 richer than she was when she made the deposit a year earlier?

The answer depends on what we mean by the word "richer." Sally does have $100 more than she had before. In other words, the number of dollars has risen by 10 percent. But if prices have risen at the same time, each dollar now buys less than it did a year ago. Thus, her purchasing power has not risen by 10 percent. If the inflation rate was 4 percent, then the amount of goods she can buy has increased by only 6 percent. And if the inflation rate was 15 percent, then the price of goods has increased proportionately more than the number of dollars in her account. In that case, Sally's purchasing power has actually fallen by 5 percent.

The interest rate that the bank pays is called the **nominal interest rate,** and the interest rate corrected for inflation is called the **real interest rate.** We can write the relationship among the nominal interest rate, the real interest rate, and inflation as follows:

$$\text{Real interest rate} = \text{Nominal interest rate} - \text{Inflation rate.}$$

The real interest rate is the difference between the nominal interest rate and the rate of inflation. The nominal interest rate tells you how fast the number of dollars in your bank account rises over time. The real interest rate tells you how fast the purchasing power of your bank account rises over time.

Figure 23-3 shows real and nominal interest rates since 1965. The nominal interest rate is the interest rate on three-month Treasury bills. The real interest rate is computed by subtracting inflation—the percentage change in the consumer price index—from this nominal interest rate.

nominal interest rate
the interest rate as usually reported without a correction for the effects of inflation

real interest rate
the interest rate corrected for the effects of inflation

Figure 23-3

REAL AND NOMINAL INTEREST RATES. This figure shows nominal and real interest rates using annual data since 1965. The nominal interest rate is the rate on a three-month Treasury bill. The real interest rate is the nominal interest rate minus the inflation rate as measured by the consumer price index. Notice that nominal and real interest rates often do not move together.

SOURCE: U.S. Department of Labor; U.S. Department of the Treasury.

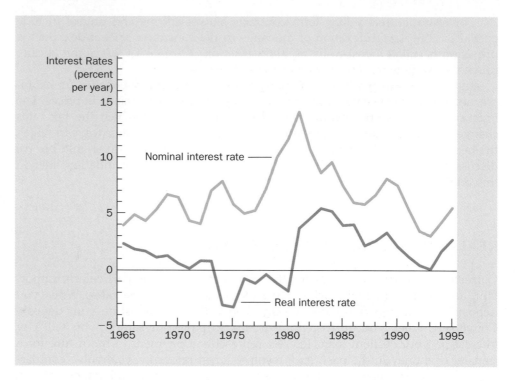

You can see that real and nominal interest rates do not always move together. For example, in the late 1970s, nominal interest rates were high. But since inflation was very high, real interest rates were low. Indeed, in some years, real interest rates were negative, for inflation eroded people's savings more quickly than nominal interest payments increased them. By contrast, in the late 1980s, nominal interest rates were low. But since inflation was also low, real interest rates were relatively high. In the coming chapters, when we study the causes and effects of changes in interest rates, it will be important for us to keep in mind the distinction between real and nominal interest rates.

QUICK QUIZ Henry Ford paid his workers $5 a day in 1914. If a price index was 11 in 1914 and 131 in 1996, how much is the Ford paycheck worth in 1996 dollars?

CONCLUSION

"A nickel ain't worth a dime anymore," baseball player Yogi Berra once quipped. Indeed, throughout recent history, the real values behind the nickel, the dime, and the dollar have not been stable. Persistent increases in the overall level of prices have been the norm. Such inflation reduces the purchasing power of each unit of money over time. When comparing dollar figures from different times, it is important to keep in mind that a dollar today is not the same as a dollar 20 years ago or, most likely, 20 years from now.

This chapter has discussed how economists measure the overall level of prices in the economy and how they use price indexes to correct economic variables for the effects of inflation. This analysis is only a starting point. We have not yet examined the causes and effects of inflation or how inflation interacts with other economic variables. To do that, we need to go beyond issues of measurement. Indeed, that is our next task. Having explained how economists measure macroeconomic quantities and prices in the past two chapters, we are now ready to develop the models that explain long-run and short-run movements in these variables.

Summary

- The consumer price index shows the cost of a basket of goods and services relative to the cost of the same basket in the base year. The index is used to measure the overall level of prices in the economy. The percentage change in the consumer price index measures the inflation rate.

- The consumer price index is an imperfect measure of the cost of living for three reasons. First, it does not take into account consumers' ability to substitute toward goods that become relatively cheaper over time. Second, it does not take into account increases in the purchasing power of the dollar due to the introduction of new goods. Third, it is distorted by unmeasured changes in the quality of goods and services. Because of these measurement problems, the CPI overstates annual inflation by about 1 percentage point.

- Although the GDP deflator also measures the overall level of prices in the economy, it differs from the consumer price index because it includes goods and services produced rather than goods and services consumed. As a result, imported goods affect the consumer price index but not the GDP deflator. In addition, while the consumer price index uses a fixed basket of goods, the GDP deflator automatically changes the group of goods and services over time as the composition of GDP changes.

- Dollar figures from different points in time do not represent a valid comparison of purchasing power. To compare a dollar figure from the past to a dollar figure today, the older figure should be inflated using a price index.

- Various laws and private contracts use price indexes to correct for the effects of inflation. The tax laws, however, are only partially indexed for inflation.

- A correction for inflation is especially important when looking at data on interest rates. The nominal interest rate is the interest rate usually reported; it is the rate at which the number of dollars in a savings account increases over time. By contrast, the real interest rate takes into account changes in the value of the dollar over time. The real interest rate equals the nominal interest rate minus the rate of inflation.

Key Concepts

consumer price index (CPI), p. 496
inflation rate, p. 499

producer price index, p. 499
indexation, p. 506

nominal interest rate, p. 507
real interest rate, p. 507

Questions for Review

1. Which do you think has a greater effect on the consumer price index: a 10 percent increase in the price of chicken or a 10 percent increase in the price of caviar? Why?

2. Describe the three problems that make the consumer price index an imperfect measure of the cost of living.

3. If the price of a Navy submarine rises, is the consumer price index or the GDP deflator affected more? Why?

4. Over a long period of time, the price of a candy bar rose from $0.10 to $0.60. Over the same period, the consumer price index rose from 150 to 300. Adjusted for overall

inflation, how much did the price of the candy bar change?

5. Explain the meaning of *nominal interest rate* and *real interest rate*. How are they related?

Problems and Applications

1. Suppose that people consume only three goods, as shown in this table:

	TENNIS BALLS	TENNIS RACQUETS	GATORADE
1998 price	$2	$40	$1
1998 quantity	100	10	200
1999 price	$2	$60	$2
1999 quantity	100	10	200

a. What is the percentage change in the price of each of the three goods? What is the percentage change in the overall price level?

b. Do tennis racquets become more or less expensive relative to Gatorade? Does the well-being of some people change relative to the well-being of others? Explain.

2. Suppose that the residents of Veggieland spend all of their income on cauliflower, broccoli, and carrots. In 1998 they buy 100 heads of cauliflower for $200, 50 bunches of broccoli for $75, and 500 carrots for $50. In 1999 they buy 75 heads of cauliflower for $225, 80 bunches of broccoli for $120, and 500 carrots for $100. If the base year is 1998, what is the CPI in both years? What is the inflation rate in 1999?

3. From 1947 to 1997 the consumer price index in the United States rose 637 percent. Use this fact to adjust each of the following 1947 prices for the effects of inflation. Which items cost less in 1997 than in 1947 after adjusting for inflation? Which items cost more?

ITEM	1947 PRICE	1997 PRICE
University of Iowa tuition	$130	$2,470
Gallon of gasoline	$0.23	$1.22
Three-minute phone call from New York to Los Angeles	$2.50	$0.45
One-day hospital stay in intensive care unit	$35	$2,300
McDonald's hamburger	$0.15	$0.59

4. Beginning in 1994, environmental regulations have required that gasoline contain a new additive to reduce air pollution. This requirement raised the cost of gasoline. The Bureau of Labor Statistics (BLS) decided that this increase in cost represented an improvement in quality.
    a. Given this decision, did the increased cost of gasoline raise the CPI?
    b. What is the argument in favor of the BLS's decision? What is the argument for a different decision?

5. Which of the problems in the construction of the CPI might be illustrated by each of the following situations? Explain.
    a. the invention of the Sony Walkman
    b. the introduction of air bags in cars
    c. increased personal computer purchases in response to a decline in their price
    d. more scoops of raisins in each package of Raisin Bran
    e. greater use of fuel-efficient cars after gasoline prices increase

6. *The New York Times* cost $0.15 in 1970 and $0.40 in 1990. The average wage in manufacturing was $3.35 per hour in 1970 and $10.82 in 1990.
    a. By what percentage did the price of a newspaper rise?
    b. By what percentage did the wage rise?
    c. In each year, how many minutes does a worker have to work to earn enough to buy a newspaper?
    d. Did workers' purchasing power in terms of newspapers rise or fall?

7. The chapter explains that Social Security benefits are increased each year in proportion to the increase in the CPI, even though most economists believe that the CPI overstates actual inflation.
    a. If the elderly consume the same market basket as other people, does Social Security provide the elderly with an improvement in their standard of living each year? Explain.
    b. In fact, the elderly consume more health care than younger people, and health care costs have risen

faster than overall inflation. What would you do to determine whether the elderly are actually better off from year to year?

8. Suppose that a borrower and a lender agree on the nominal interest rate to be paid on a loan. Then inflation turns out to be higher than they both expected.
   a. Is the real interest rate on this loan higher or lower than expected?
   b. Does the lender gain or lose from this unexpectedly high inflation? Does the borrower gain or lose?
   c. Inflation during the 1970s was much higher than most people expected when the decade began. How did this affect homeowners who obtained fixed-rate mortgages during the 1960s? How did it affect the banks that lent the money?

9. The chapter defines the real interest rate as the nominal interest rate less inflation. Because the U.S. tax code taxes nominal interest income, we can define the *after-tax* real interest rate as the nominal interest rate after taxes, less inflation.

   a. Suppose that the inflation rate is 0 percent, the nominal interest rate is 3 percent, and the tax rate is 33 percent. What is the real interest rate? What is the after-tax real interest rate? What is the effective tax rate on real interest income (the percentage reduction in real interest income due to taxes)?
   b. Now suppose that the inflation rate rises to 3 percent, and the nominal interest rate rises to 6 percent. What is the real interest rate now? What is the after-tax real interest rate? What is the effective tax rate on real interest income?
   c. Some economists argue that because of our tax system, inflation discourages saving. Use your answers to parts (a) and (b) to explain this view.

10. Income tax brackets were not indexed until 1985. When inflation pushed up people's nominal incomes during the 1970s, what do you think happened to real tax revenue? (Hint: This phenomenon was known as "bracket creep.")

IX

THE REAL ECONOMY
IN THE LONG RUN

24

PRODUCTION AND GROWTH

IN THIS CHAPTER YOU WILL

See how much economic growth differs around the world

Consider why productivity is the key determinant of a country's standard of living

Analyze the factors that determine a country's productivity

Examine how a country's policies influence its productivity growth

When you travel around the world, you see tremendous variation in the standard of living. The average person in a rich country, such as the United States, Japan, or Germany, has an income more than ten times as high as the average person in a poor country, such as India, Indonesia, or Nigeria. These large differences in income are reflected in large differences in the quality of life. Richer countries have more automobiles, more telephones, more televisions, better nutrition, safer housing, better health care, and longer life expectancy.

Even within a country, there are large changes in the standard of living over time. In the United States over the past century, average income as measured by real GDP per person has grown by about 2 percent per year. Although 2 percent might seem small, this rate of growth implies that average income doubles every 35 years. Because of this growth, average income today is about eight times as high as average income a century ago. As a result, the typical American enjoys much greater economic prosperity than did his or her parents, grandparents, and great-grandparents.

Growth rates vary substantially from country to country. In some East Asian countries, such as Hong Kong, Singapore, South Korea, and Taiwan, average income has risen about 7 percent per year in recent decades. At this rate, average income doubles every ten years. These countries have, in the length of one generation, gone from being among the poorest countries in the world to being among the richest. By contrast, in some African countries, such as Chad, Ethiopia, and Nigeria, average income has been stagnant for many years.

What explains these diverse experiences? How can the rich countries be sure to maintain their high standard of living? What policies should the poor countries pursue to promote more rapid growth in order to join the developed world? These are among the most important questions in macroeconomics. As economist Robert Lucas put it, "The consequences for human welfare in questions like these are simply staggering: Once one starts to think about them, it is hard to think about anything else."

In the previous two chapters we discussed how economists measure macroeconomic quantities and prices. In this chapter we start studying the forces that determine these variables. As we have seen, an economy's gross domestic product (GDP) measures both the total income earned in the economy and the total expenditure on the economy's output of goods and services. The level of real GDP is a good gauge of economic prosperity, and the growth of real GDP is a good gauge of economic progress. Here we focus on the long-run determinants of the level and growth of real GDP. Later in this book we will study the short-run fluctuations of real GDP around its long-run trend.

We proceed here in three steps. First, we examine international data on real GDP per person. These data will give you some sense of how much the level and growth of living standards vary around the world. Second, we examine the role of *productivity*—the amount of goods and services produced for each hour of a worker's time. In particular, we see that a nation's standard of living is determined by the productivity of its workers, and we consider the factors that determine a nation's productivity. Third, we consider the link between productivity and the economic policies that a nation pursues.

ECONOMIC GROWTH AROUND THE WORLD

As a starting point for our study of long-run growth, let's look at the experiences of some of the world's economies. Table 24-1 shows data on real GDP per person for 13 countries. For each country, the data cover about a century of history. The first and second columns of the table present the countries and time periods. (The time periods differ somewhat from country to country because of differences in data availability.) The third and fourth columns show real GDP per person about a century ago and for a recent year.

The data on real GDP per person show that living standards vary widely from country to country. Income per person in the United States, for instance, is about 10 times that in China and almost 30 times that in India. The poorest countries have average levels of income that have not been seen in the United States for many decades. The typical Mexican in 1987 had about as much real income as the typical American in 1870. The typical person in India in 1987 had about one-third the real income of a typical American a century ago.

The last column of the table shows each country's growth rate. The growth rate measures how rapidly real GDP per person grew in the typical year. In the United States, for example, real GDP per person was $2,244 in 1870 and $18,258 in 1990. The growth rate was 1.76 percent per year. This means that if real GDP per person, beginning at $2,244, were to increase by 1.76 percent for each of 120 years, it would end up at $18,258. Of course, real GDP per person did not actu-

COUNTRY	PERIOD	REAL GDP PER PERSON AT BEGINNING OF PERIOD[a]	REAL GDP PER PERSON AT END OF PERIOD[a]	GROWTH RATE (PER YEAR)
Japan	1890–1990	$ 842	$16,144	3.00%
Brazil	1900–1987	436	3,417	2.39
Canada	1870–1990	1,330	17,070	2.15
West Germany	1870–1990	1,223	14,288	2.07
United States	1870–1990	2,244	18,258	1.76
China	1900–1987	401	1,748	1.71
Mexico	1900–1987	649	2,667	1.64
United Kingdom	1870–1990	2,693	13,589	1.36
Argentina	1900–1987	1,284	3,302	1.09
Indonesia	1900–1987	499	1,200	1.01
Pakistan	1900–1987	413	885	0.88
India	1900–1987	378	662	0.65
Bangladesh	1900–1987	349	375	0.08

THE VARIETY OF GROWTH EXPERIENCES

Table 24-1

[a]Real GDP is measured in 1985 dollars.

SOURCE: Robert J. Barro and Xavier Sala-i-Martin, *Economic Growth* (New York: McGraw-Hill, 1995), tables 10.2 and 10.3; and author's calculations.

ally rise exactly 1.76 percent every year: There are short-run fluctuations around the long-run trend. The growth rate of 1.76 percent represents an average rate of growth for real GDP per person over many years.

The countries in Table 24-1 are ordered by their growth rate from the most to the least rapid. Japan tops the list, with a growth rate of 3.00 percent per year. A hundred years ago, Japan was not a rich country. Japan's average income was only somewhat higher than Mexico's, and it was well behind Argentina's. To put the issue another way, Japan's 1890 income was close to Pakistan's 1987 income. But because of its spectacular growth, Japan is today an economic superpower, with average income about the same as the United States. At the bottom of the list of countries is Bangladesh, which has experienced hardly any growth at all over the past century. The typical resident of Bangladesh lives in abject poverty similar to that experienced by his or her great-grandparents.

Because of differences in growth rates, the ranking of countries by income changes substantially over time. As we have seen, Japan is a country that has risen relative to others. Two countries that have fallen behind are the United Kingdom and Argentina. In 1870, the United Kingdom was the richest country in the world, with average income about 20 percent higher than that of the United States and about twice that of Canada. Today, average income in the United Kingdom is well below average income in its two former colonies. In 1900, Argentina had about three times the income of its South American neighbor Brazil. Today, Argentina is on par with Brazil.

These data show that the world's richest countries have no guarantee they will stay the richest and that the world's poorest countries are not doomed forever to remain in poverty. But what explains these changes over time? Why do

FYI

The Magic of Compounding and the Rule of 70

IT MAY BE TEMPTING TO DISmiss differences in growth rates as insignificant. If one country grows at 1 percent while another grows at 3 percent, so what? What difference can 2 percent make?

The answer is a big difference. Even growth rates that seem small when written in percentage terms seem large after they are compounded for many years. *Compounding* refers to the accumulation of a growth rate over a period of time.

Consider an example. Suppose that two college graduates—Jerry and Elaine—both take their first jobs at the age of twenty-two earning $30,000 a year. Jerry lives in an economy where all incomes grow at 1 percent per year, while Elaine lives in one where incomes grow at 3 percent per year. Straightforward calculations show what happens. Forty years later, when both are sixty-two years old, Jerry earns $45,000 a year, while Elaine earns $98,000. Because of that difference of 2 percentage points in the growth rate, Elaine's salary in old age is more than twice Jerry's.

An old rule of thumb, called the *rule of 70*, is helpful in understanding growth rates and the effects of compounding. According to the rule of 70, if some variable grows at a rate of x percent per year, then that variable doubles in approximately $70/x$ years. In Jerry's economy, incomes grow at 1 percent per year, so it takes about 70 years for incomes to double. In Elaine's economy, incomes grow at 3 percent per year, so it takes about 70/3, or 23, years for incomes to double.

The rule of 70 applies not only to a growing economy but also to a growing savings account. Here is an example: In 1791, Ben Franklin died and left $5,000 to be invested for a period of 200 years to benefit medical students and scientific research. If this money had earned 7 percent per year (which would, in fact, have been very possible to do), the investment would have doubled in value every 10 years. Over 200 years, it would have doubled 20 times. At the end of 200 years of compounding, the investment would have been worth $2^{20} \times$ $5,000, which is about $5 billion. (In fact, Franklin's $5,000 grew to only $2 million over 200 years because some of the money was spent along the way.)

As these examples show, growth rates compounded over many years can lead to some spectacular results. That is probably why Albert Einstein once called compounding "the greatest mathematical discovery of all time."

some countries zoom ahead while others lag behind? These are precisely the questions that we take up next.

QUICK QUIZ What is the approximate growth rate of real GDP per person in the United States? Name a country that has had faster growth and a country that has had slower growth.

PRODUCTIVITY: ITS ROLE AND DETERMINANTS

Explaining the large variation in living standards around the world is, in one sense, very easy. As we will see, the explanation can be summarized in a single word—*productivity*. But, in another sense, the international variation is deeply puzzling. To explain why incomes are so much higher in some countries than in others, we must look at the many factors that determine a nation's productivity.

WHY PRODUCTIVITY IS SO IMPORTANT

Let's begin our study of productivity and economic growth by developing a simple model based loosely on Daniel DeFoe's famous novel *Robinson Crusoe*. Robinson Crusoe, as you may recall, is a sailor stranded on a desert island. Because Crusoe lives alone, he catches his own fish, grows his own vegetables, and makes his own clothes. We can think of Crusoe's activities—his production and consumption of fish, vegetables, and clothing—as being a simple economy. By examining Crusoe's economy, we can learn some lessons that also apply to more complex and realistic economies.

What determines Crusoe's standard of living? The answer is obvious. If Crusoe is good at catching fish, growing vegetables, and making clothes, he lives well. If he is bad at doing these things, he lives poorly. Because Crusoe gets to consume only what he produces, his living standard is tied to his productive ability.

The term **productivity** refers to the quantity of goods and services that a worker can produce for each hour of work. In the case of Crusoe's economy, it is easy to see that productivity is the key determinant of living standards and that growth in productivity is the key determinant of growth in living standards. The more fish Crusoe can catch per hour, the more he eats at dinner. If Crusoe finds a better place to catch fish, his productivity rises. This increase in productivity makes Crusoe better off: He could eat the extra fish, or he could spend less time fishing and devote more time to making other goods he enjoys.

productivity
the amount of goods and services produced from each hour of a worker's time

The key role of productivity in determining living standards is as true for nations as it is for stranded sailors. Recall that an economy's gross domestic product (GDP) measures two things at once: the total income earned by everyone in the economy and the total expenditure on the economy's output of goods and services. The reason why GDP can measure these two things simultaneously is that, for the economy as a whole, they must be equal. Put simply, an economy's income is the economy's output.

Like Crusoe, a nation can enjoy a high standard of living only if it can produce a large quantity of goods and services. Americans live better than Nigerians because American workers are more productive than Nigerian workers. The Japanese have enjoyed more rapid growth in living standards than Argentineans because Japanese workers have experienced more rapidly growing productivity. Indeed, one of the *Ten Principles of Economics* in Chapter 1 is that a country's standard of living depends on its ability to produce goods and services.

Hence, to understand the large differences in living standards we observe across countries or over time, we must focus on the production of goods and services. But seeing the link between living standards and productivity is only the first step. It leads naturally to the next question: Why are some economies so much better at producing goods and services than others?

HOW PRODUCTIVITY IS DETERMINED

Although productivity is uniquely important in determining Robinson Crusoe's standard of living, many factors determine Crusoe's productivity. Crusoe will be better at catching fish, for instance, if he has more fishing poles, if he has been trained in the best fishing techniques, if his island has a plentiful fish supply, and if he has figured out the best places on his island to fish. Each of these determinants of Crusoe's productivity—which we can call *physical capital, human capital, natural resources,* and *technological knowledge*—has a counterpart in more complex and realistic economies. Let's consider each of these factors in turn.

Physical Capital Workers are more productive if they have tools with which to work. The stock of equipment and structures that are used to produce goods and services is called **physical capital,** or just *capital.* For example, when woodworkers make furniture, they use saws, lathes, and drill presses. More tools allow work to be done more quickly and more accurately. That is, a worker with only basic hand tools can make less furniture each week than a worker with sophisticated and specialized woodworking equipment.

As you may recall from Chapter 2, the inputs used to produce goods and services—labor, capital, and so on—are called the *factors of production.* An important feature of capital is that it is a *produced* factor of production. That is, capital is an input into the production process that in the past was an output from the production process. The woodworker uses a lathe to make the leg of a table. Earlier the lathe itself was the output of a firm that manufactures lathes. The lathe manufacturer in turn used other equipment to make its product. Thus, capital is a factor of production used to produce all kinds of goods and services, including more capital.

Human Capital A second determinant of productivity is human capital. **Human capital** is the economist's term for the knowledge and skills that workers acquire through education, training, and experience. Human capital includes the skills accumulated in early childhood programs, grade school, high school, college, and on-the-job training for adults in the labor force.

Although education, training, and experience are less tangible than lathes, bulldozers, and buildings, human capital is like physical capital in many ways. Like physical capital, human capital raises a nation's ability to produce goods and services. Also like physical capital, human capital is a produced factor of production. Producing human capital requires inputs in the form of teachers, libraries, and student time. Indeed, students can be viewed as "workers" who have the important job of producing the human capital that will be used in future production.

Natural Resources A third determinant of productivity is **natural resources.** Natural resources are inputs into production that are provided by nature, such as land, rivers, and mineral deposits. Natural resources take two forms: renewable and nonrenewable. A forest is an example of a renewable resource. When one tree is cut down, a seedling can be planted in its place to be harvested in the future. Oil is an example of a nonrenewable resource. Because oil is produced by nature over many thousands of years, there is only a limited supply. Once the supply of oil is depleted, it is impossible to create more.

Differences in natural resources are responsible for some of the differences in standards of living around the world. The historical success of the United States was driven in part by the large supply of land well suited for agriculture. Today, some countries in the Middle East, such as Kuwait and Saudi Arabia, are rich simply because they happen to be on top of some of the largest pools of oil in the world.

Although natural resources can be important, they are not necessary for an economy to be highly productive in producing goods and services. Japan, for

---

physical capital

the stock of equipment and structures that are used to produce goods and services

human capital

the knowledge and skills that workers acquire through education, training, and experience

natural resources

the inputs into the production of goods and services that are provided by nature, such as land, rivers, and mineral deposits instance, is one of the richest countries in the world, despite having few natural resources. International trade makes Japan's success possible. Japan imports many of the natural resources it needs, such as oil, and exports its manufactured goods to economies rich in natural resources.

CASE STUDY ARE NATURAL RESOURCES A LIMIT TO GROWTH?

The world's population is far larger today than it was a century ago, and many people are enjoying a much higher standard of living. A perennial debate concerns whether this growth in population and living standards can continue in the future.

Many commentators have argued that natural resources provide a limit to how much the world's economies can grow. At first, this argument might seem hard to ignore. If the world has only a fixed supply of nonrenewable natural resources, how can population, production, and living standards continue to grow over time? Eventually, won't supplies of oil and minerals start to run out? When these shortages start to occur, won't they stop economic growth and, perhaps, even force living standards to fall?

Despite the apparent appeal of such arguments, most economists are less concerned about such limits to growth than one might guess. They argue that technological progress often yields ways to avoid these limits. If we compare the economy today to the economy of the past, we see various ways in which the use of natural resources has improved. Modern cars have better gas mileage. New houses have better insulation and require less energy to heat and cool them. More efficient oil rigs waste less oil in the process of extraction. Recycling allows some nonrenewable resources to be reused. The development of alternative fuels, such as ethanol instead of gasoline, allows us to substitute renewable for nonrenewable resources.

Fifty years ago, some conservationists were concerned about the excessive use of tin and copper. At the time, these were crucial commodities: Tin was

What happens as these run dry?

IN THE NEWS

Computers and

Productivity

ONE DETERMINANT OF PRODUCTIVITY IS technological knowledge, and one recent advance in technological knowledge has been the computer revolution. As the following article describes, however, this revolution has not yet had the great impact on productivity that many people expected.

What Has the Computer Done for Us Lately?

BY LOUIS UCHITELLE

At the end of the nineteenth century, railroads and electric motors were ex-pected to transform America, making a young industrial economy far more productive than any seen before. And they did. At the end of the twentieth century, computers were supposed to perform the same miracle.

They haven't.

Computers do wonderful things. But in purely economic terms, their contribution has been less than a transforming force; they have failed to bring back the strong growth that characterized so many decades of the American century. By that standard, they have been a disappointment.

"It is a pipe dream to think that computers will lead us back to a promised land," said Alan Krueger, a Princeton University economist.

The issue is productivity. Those who look to computers for economic miracles, and there are many, insist that measuring their contribution only in dollars misses the less tangible improvement in quality that computers have made possible. But quality is often in the eyes of the beholders rather than in their wallets.

PRODUCTIVITY—OR TETRIS?

Through decades of invention and change, productivity has been measured as the amount of "output," in dollars, that comes from an hour of labor. A worker who makes 100 pencils in an hour, each valued at $0.50, produces $50 of output. And the more output from each of the nation's workers, the greater the national wealth.

Or, put more broadly, productivity is the amount of output in dollars that comes from various "inputs," not only a worker's labor, but the tools he or she uses to carry out that labor: a machine or a computer or a wrench or an air condi-

used to make many food containers, and copper was used to make telephone wire. Some people advocated mandatory recycling and rationing of tin and copper so that supplies would be available for future generations. Today, however, plastic has replaced tin as a material for making many food containers, and phone calls often travel over fiber-optic cables, which are made from sand. Technological progress has made once crucial natural resources less necessary.

But are all these efforts enough to permit continued economic growth? One way to answer this question is to look at the prices of natural resources. In a market economy, scarcity is reflected in market prices. If the world were running out of natural resources, then the prices of those resources would be rising over time. But, in fact, the opposite is more nearly true. The prices of most natural resources (adjusted for overall inflation) are stable or falling. It appears that our ability to conserve these resources is growing more rapidly than their supplies are dwindling. Market prices give no reason to believe that natural resources are a limit to economic growth.

tioner that makes work more comfortable in summer. People work faster or concentrate better, and that shows up quickly in tangible output.

By this definition, the output resulting from the computer revolution of the last 25 years has been disappointing. Computers have, of course, contributed to productivity and economic growth. But that contribution has failed to register in government statistics as the kind of robust catalyst that made the 1950s and 1960s such prosperous years.

If computers have fallen short of expectations, that would help explain an apparent paradox that has puzzled economists and policymakers for two decades: how rapid technological progress and a booming stock market took place during a period of sluggish economic performance—sluggish, that is, relative to earlier decades.

One possibility is that the statistics are wrong. A panel of economists came to this conclusion in a report to Congress last week, suggesting that growth has actually been quite robust but that this fact has been obscured by overstating the amount of output lost to inflation. This happened, the panel hinted, partly because the beneficial economic role of computers was not correctly taken into account. Some price increases that registered as inflation should really have registered as increases in output from computers.

But there is another explanation. Perhaps the computer is one of those inventions, like the lightbulb early in the century, that makes life much better without adding as much to tangible national wealth as appearances might suggest. That is because, while the lightbulb allowed factories to operate night shifts and students to study more easily, the measurable result was less impressive than the great improvement in the quality of life that the electric lightbulb made possible.

Given the computer's ubiquity and convenience, should the calculation of productivity and wealth be changed to give more dollar value to the conveniences the computer has wrought?

That kind of recalculation has not been done over generations of technological change, largely because convenience is too hard to quantify and translate into dollars. Too often, convenience increases consumption more than production. With computers, "most of the recent use has been on the consumption side," said Zvi Griliches, a Harvard economist. "The time you waste surfing the Internet is not an output."

Others take a broader view. Children using home computers for schoolwork—gathering data from the Internet, for example—become better students, they say. In time, that will translate into rising workplace skills and greater measurable output. But it hasn't yet, and standard practice dictates that the nation wait until it shows up in the numbers before proclaiming the computer's great contribution to productivity.

SOURCE: *The New York Times*, December 8, 1996, Week in Review, Section 4, pp. 1, 4.

Technological Knowledge   A fourth determinant of productivity is **technological knowledge**—the understanding of the best ways to produce goods and services. A hundred years ago, most Americans worked on farms, because farm technology required a high input of labor in order to feed the entire population. Today, thanks to advances in the technology of farming, a small fraction of the population can produce enough food to feed the entire country. This technological change made labor available to produce other goods and services.

Technological knowledge takes many forms. Some technology is common knowledge—after it becomes used by one person, everyone becomes aware of it. For example, once Henry Ford successfully introduced production in assembly lines, other car makers quickly followed suit. Other technology is proprietary—it is known only by the company that discovers it. Only the Coca-Cola Company, for instance, knows the secret recipe for making its famous soft drink. Still other technology is proprietary for a short time. When a drug company discovers a new drug, the patent system gives that company a temporary right to

technological knowledge
society's understanding of the best ways to produce goods and services

be the exclusive manufacturer of this particular drug. When the patent expires, however, other companies are allowed to make the drug. All these forms of technological knowledge are important for the economy's production of goods and services.

It is worthwhile to distinguish between technological knowledge and human capital. Although they are closely related, there is an important difference. Technological knowledge refers to society's understanding about how the world works. Human capital refers to the resources expended transmitting this understanding to the labor force. To use a relevant metaphor, knowledge is the quality of society's textbooks, whereas human capital is the amount of time that the population has devoted to reading them. Workers' productivity depends on both the quality of textbooks they have available and the amount of time they have spent studying them.

THE PRODUCTION FUNCTION

Economists often use a *production function* to describe the relationship between the quantity of inputs used in production and the quantity of output from production. For example, suppose Y denotes the quantity of output, L the quantity of labor, K the quantity of physical capital, H the quantity of human capital, and N the quantity of natural resources. Then we might write

$$Y = A \, F(L, K, H, N),$$

where $F(\ )$ is a function that shows how the inputs are combined to produce output. A is a variable that reflects the available production technology. As technology improves, A rises, so the economy produces more output from any given combination of inputs.

Many production functions have a property called *constant returns to scale*. If a production function has constant returns to scale, then a doubling of all the inputs causes the amount of output to double as well. Mathematically, we write that a production function has constant returns to scale if, for any positive number x,

$$xY = A \, F(xL, xK, xH, xN).$$

A doubling of all inputs is represented in this equation by $x = 2$. The right-hand side shows the inputs doubling, and the left-hand side shows output doubling. Production functions with constant returns to scale have an interesting implication. To see what it is, set $x = 1/L$. Then the equation above becomes

$$Y/L = A \, F(1, K/L, H/L, N/L).$$

Notice that Y/L is output per worker, which is a measure of productivity. This equation says that productivity depends on physical capital per worker (K/L), human capital per worker (H/L), and natural resources per worker (N/L). Productivity also depends on the state of technology, as reflected by the variable A. Thus, this equation provides a mathematical summary of the four determinants of productivity we have just discussed.

▌ QUICK QUIZ   List and describe four determinants of a country's
productivity.

ECONOMIC GROWTH AND PUBLIC POLICY

So far, we have determined that a society's standard of living depends on its
ability to produce goods and services and that its productivity depends on physical capital, human capital, natural resources, and technological knowledge. Let's
now turn to the question faced by policymakers around the world: What can
government policy do to raise productivity and living standards?

THE IMPORTANCE OF SAVING AND INVESTMENT

Because capital is a produced factor of production, a society can change the
amount of capital it has. If today the economy produces a large quantity of new
capital goods, then tomorrow it will have a larger stock of capital and be able
to produce more of all types of goods and services. Thus, one way to raise future
productivity is to invest more current resources in the production of capital.

One of the *Ten Principles of Economics* presented in Chapter 1 is that people
face tradeoffs. This principle is especially important when considering the accumulation of capital. Because resources are scarce, devoting more resources to pro
ducing capital requires devoting fewer resources to producing goods and services for current consumption. That is, for society to invest more in capital, it
must consume less and save more of its current income. The growth that arises
from capital accumulation is not a free lunch: It requires that society sacrifice
consumption of goods and services in the present in order to enjoy higher consumption in the future.

The next chapter examines in more detail how the economy's financial markets coordinate saving and investment. It also examines how government policies influence the amount of saving and investment that takes place. At this point
it is important to note that encouraging saving and investment is one way that
a government can encourage growth and, in the long run, raise the economy's
standard of living.

To see the importance of investment for economic growth, consider Figure
24-1, which displays data on 15 countries. Panel (a) shows each country's growth
rate over a 31-year period. The countries are ordered by their growth rates, from
most to least rapid. Panel (b) shows the percentage of GDP that each country
devotes to investment. The correlation between growth and investment, although
not perfect, is strong. Countries that devote a large share of GDP to investment,
such as Singapore and Japan, tend to have high growth rates. Countries that
devote a small share of GDP to investment, such as Rwanda and Bangladesh,
tend to have low growth rates. Studies that examine a more comprehensive list
of countries confirm this strong correlation between investment and growth.

There is, however, a problem in interpreting these data. As the appendix to
Chapter 2 discussed, a correlation between two variables does not establish

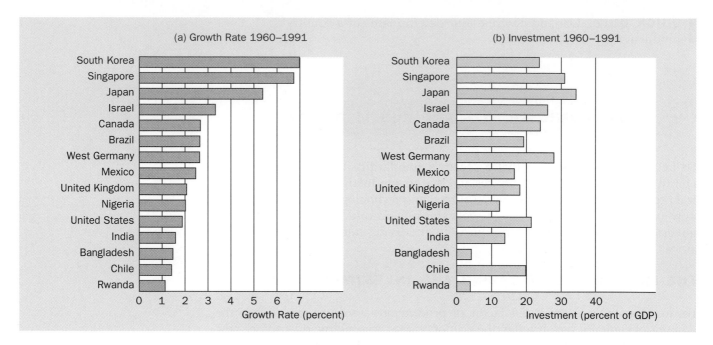

Figure 24-1

GROWTH AND INVESTMENT. Panel (a) shows the growth rate of GDP per person for 15 countries over the period 1960–1991. Panel (b) shows the percentage of GDP that each country devoted to investment over this period. The figure shows that investment and growth are positively correlated.

which variable is the cause and which is the effect. It is possible that high investment causes high growth, but it is also possible that high growth causes high investment. (Or, perhaps, high growth and high investment are both caused by a third variable that has been omitted from the analysis.) The data by themselves cannot tell us the direction of causation. Nonetheless, because capital accumulation affects productivity so clearly and directly, many economists interpret these data as showing that high investment leads to more rapid economic growth.

DIMINISHING RETURNS AND THE CATCH-UP EFFECT

Suppose that a government, convinced by the evidence in Figure 24-1, pursues policies that raise the nation's saving rate—the percentage of GDP devoted to saving rather than consumption. What happens? With the nation saving more, fewer resources are needed to make consumption goods, and more resources are available to make capital goods. As a result, the capital stock increases, leading to rising productivity and more rapid growth in GDP. But how long does this higher rate of growth last? Assuming that the saving rate remains at its new higher level, does the growth rate of GDP stay high indefinitely or only for a period of time?

diminishing returns

the property whereby the benefit from an extra unit of an input declines as the quantity of the input increases

The traditional view of the production process is that capital is subject to **diminishing returns:** As the stock of capital rises, the extra output produced from an additional unit of capital falls. In other words, when workers already have a large quantity of capital to use in producing goods and services, giving them an additional unit of capital increases their productivity only slightly. Because of diminishing returns, an increase in the saving rate leads to higher growth only for a while. As the higher saving rate allows more capital to be accumulated, the benefits from additional capital become smaller over time, and so growth slows down. *In the long run, the higher saving rate leads to a higher level of productivity and income, but not to higher growth in these variables.* Reaching this long run, however, can take quite a while. According to studies of international data on economic growth, increasing the saving rate can lead to substantially higher growth for a period of several decades.

The diminishing returns to capital has another important implication: Other things equal, it is easier for a country to grow fast if it starts out relatively poor. This effect of initial conditions on subsequent growth is sometimes called the **catch-up effect.** In poor countries, workers lack even the most rudimentary tools and, as a result, have low productivity. Small amounts of capital investment would substantially raise these workers' productivity. By contrast, workers in rich countries have large amounts of capital with which to work, and this partly explains their high productivity. Yet with the amount of capital per worker already so high, additional capital investment has a relatively small effect on productivity. Studies of international data on economic growth confirm this catch-up effect: Controlling for other variables, such as the percentage of GDP devoted to investment, poor countries do tend to grow faster than rich countries.

catch-up effect
the property whereby countries that start off poor tend to grow more rapidly than countries that start off rich

This catch-up effect can help explain some of the puzzling results in Figure 24-1. Over this 31-year period, the United States and South Korea devoted a similar share of GDP to investment. Yet the United States experienced only mediocre growth of about 2 percent, while Korea experienced spectacular growth of more than 6 percent. The explanation is the catch-up effect. In 1960, Korea had GDP per person less than one-tenth the U.S. level, in part because previous investment had been so low. With a small initial capital stock, the benefits to capital accumulation were much greater in Korea, and this gave Korea a higher subsequent growth rate.

This catch-up effect shows up in other aspects of life. When a school gives an end-of-year award to the "Most Improved" student, that student is usually one who began the year with relatively poor performance. Students who began the year not studying find improvement easier than students who always worked hard. Note that it is good to be "Most Improved," given the starting point, but it is even better to be "Best Student." Similarly, economic growth over the last several decades has been much more rapid in South Korea than in the United States, but GDP per person is still higher in the United States.

INVESTMENT FROM ABROAD

So far we have discussed how policies aimed at increasing a country's saving rate can increase investment and, thereby, long-term economic growth. Yet saving by domestic residents is not the only way for a country to invest in new capital. The other way is investment by foreigners.

Investment from abroad takes several forms. Ford Motor Company might build a car factory in Mexico. A capital investment that is owned and operated by a foreign entity is called *foreign direct investment.* Alternatively, an American might buy stock in a Mexican corporation (that is, buy a share in the ownership of the corporation); the Mexican corporation can use the proceeds from the stock sale to build a new factory. An investment that is financed with foreign money but operated by domestic residents is called *foreign portfolio investment.* In both cases, Americans provide the resources necessary to increase the stock of capital in Mexico. That is, American saving is being used to finance Mexican investment.

When foreigners invest in a country, they do so because they expect to earn a return on their investment. Ford's car factory increases the Mexican capital stock and, therefore, increases Mexican productivity and Mexican GDP. Yet Ford takes some of this additional income back to the United States in the form of profit. Similarly, when an American investor buys Mexican stock, the investor has a right to a portion of the profit that the Mexican corporation earns.

Investment from abroad, therefore, affects GDP and GNP differently. Recall that gross domestic product is the income earned within a country by both residents and nonresidents, whereas gross national product is the income earned by residents of a country both at home and abroad. When Ford opens its car factory in Mexico, some of the income the factory generates accrues to people who do not live in Mexico. As a result, this investment raises Mexico's GDP more than it raises Mexico's GNP.

Investment from abroad is one way for a country to grow. Even though some of the benefits from this investment flow back to the foreign owners, this investment does increase the economy's stock of capital, leading to higher productivity and higher wages. Moreover, investment from abroad is one way for poor countries to learn the state-of-the-art technologies developed and used in richer countries. For these reasons, many economists who advise governments in less developed economies advocate policies that encourage investment from abroad. Often this means removing restrictions that governments have imposed on foreign ownership of domestic capital.

An organization that tries to encourage the flow of investment to poor countries is the World Bank. This international organization obtains funds from the world's advanced countries, such as the United States, and uses these resources to make loans to less developed countries so that they can invest in roads, sewer systems, schools, and other types of capital. It also offers the countries advice about how the funds might best be used. The World Bank, together with its sister organization, the International Monetary Fund, was set up after World War II. One lesson from the war was that economic distress often leads to political turmoil, international tensions, and military conflict. Thus, every country has an interest in promoting economic prosperity around the world. The World Bank and the International Monetary Fund are aimed at achieving that common goal.

EDUCATION

Education—investment in human capital—is at least as important as investment in physical capital for a country's long-run economic success. In the United States, each year of schooling raises a person's wage on average by about 10 percent. In less developed countries, where human capital is especially scarce, the gap between the wages of educated and uneducated workers is even larger. Thus, one way in which government policy can enhance the standard of living is to provide good schools and to encourage the population to take advantage of them.

Investment in human capital, like investment in physical capital, has an opportunity cost. When students are in school, they forgo the wages they could

IN THE NEWS

The World Bank

AS THE FOLLOWING ARTICLE DESCRIBES, the World Bank encourages firms to invest in some of the world's poorest, and politically least stable, countries.

World Bank Focusing on Areas Shunned by Western Business

BY PAUL LEWIS

WASHINGTON—The World Bank announced a plan today to attract private investment to developing countries that Western businesses have largely shunned.

The agency's International Finance Corporation said it had selected 16 countries and regions either very poor or troubled by their social past as the focus of its efforts. It said it would send investment officers to the areas to generate business opportunities for local and foreign entrepreneurs. The areas include Albania, Bosnia and Herzegovina, Cambodia, Kazakstan, Uzbekistan, Mongolia, El Salvador, and the West Bank and Gaza.

At the same time, Jannik Lindbaek, the International Finance Corporation's executive vice president, said the agency had approved a record $3.2 billion in financing for 264 private investment projects in the developing world last year, a rise of 12 percent from 1994 and the fifth consecutive double-digit increase. Private industry invested $16.4 billion in the same projects, he added. "There is a continuing trend in favor of the private sector in the developing world," Mr. Lindbaek said.

The decision to set up shop in distressed countries as well as the overall increase in activities in the Third World are part of the development strategy that the World Bank's president, James D. Wolfensohn, has been pushing since he took over the United Nations agency in June 1995. Under his leadership, the World Bank has tried to compensate for declines in foreign aid from richer countries by stimulating private-sector investment in the developing world and spreading it around more evenly.

As part of that drive, the agency plans to offer foreign companies more generous guarantees against the political risks of investing in the developing world, such as unexpected government price controls or outright expropriations of property. It is also working with the International Monetary Fund on a plan for reducing the debts of the most highly indebted poor countries.

While official aid has stagnated at $55 billion to $65 billion annually in recent years, such private investment has nearly quadrupled to $167 billion last year from $44 billion in 1990.

SOURCE: *The New York Times,* September 19, 1996, p. D2.

---

have earned. In less developed countries, children often drop out of school at an early age, even though the benefit of additional schooling is very high, simply because their labor is needed to help support the family.

Some economists have argued that human capital is particularly important for economic growth because human capital conveys positive externalities. An *externality* is the effect of one person's actions on the well-being of a bystander. An educated person, for instance, might generate new ideas about how best to produce goods and services. If these ideas enter society's pool of knowledge, so everyone can use them, then the ideas are an external benefit of education. In this case, the return to schooling for society is even greater than the return for the individual. This argument would justify the large subsidies to human-capital investment that we observe in the form of public education.

One problem facing some poor countries is the *brain drain*—the emigration of many of the most highly educated workers to rich countries, where these workers can enjoy a higher standard of living. If human capital does have positive externalities, then this brain drain makes those people left behind poorer than they otherwise would be. This problem offers policymakers a dilemma. On the one hand, the United States and other rich countries have the best systems of higher education, and it would seem natural for poor countries to send their best students abroad to earn higher degrees. On the other hand, those students who have spent time abroad may choose not to return home, and this brain drain will reduce the poor nation's stock of human capital even further.

PROPERTY RIGHTS AND POLITICAL STABILITY

Another way in which policymakers can foster economic growth is by protecting property rights and promoting political stability. As we first noted when we discussed economic interdependence in Chapter 2, production in market economies arises from the interactions of millions of individuals and firms. When you buy a car, for instance, you are buying the output of a car dealer, a car manufacturer, a steel company, an iron ore mining company, and so on. This division of production among many firms allows the economy's factors of production to be used as effectively as possible. To achieve this outcome, the economy has to coordinate transactions among these firms, as well as between firms and consumers. Market economies achieve this coordination through market prices. That is, market prices are the instrument with which the invisible hand of the marketplace brings supply and demand into balance.

An important prerequisite for the price system to work is an economy-wide respect for *property rights*. Property rights refer to the ability of people to exercise authority over the resources they own. A mining company will not make the effort to mine iron ore if it expects the ore to be stolen. The company mines the ore only if it is confident that it will benefit from the ore's subsequent sale. For this reason, courts serve an important role in a market economy: They enforce property rights. Through the criminal justice system, the courts discourage direct theft. In addition, through the civil justice system, the courts ensure that buyers and sellers live up to their contracts.

Although those of us in developed countries tend to take property rights for granted, those living in less developed countries understand that lack of property rights can be a major problem. In many countries, the system of justice does not work well. Contracts are hard to enforce, and fraud often goes unpunished. In more extreme cases, the government not only fails to enforce property rights but actually infringes upon them. To do business in some countries, firms are expected to bribe powerful government officials. Such corruption impedes the coordinating power of markets. It also discourages domestic saving and investment from abroad.

One threat to property rights is political instability. When revolutions and coups are common, there is doubt about whether property rights will be respected in the future. If a revolutionary government might confiscate the capital of some businesses, as was often true after communist revolutions, domestic residents have less incentive to save, invest, and start new businesses. At the same time, foreigners have less incentive to invest in the country. Even the threat of revolution can act to depress a nation's standard of living.

Thus, economic prosperity depends in part on political prosperity. A country with an efficient court system, honest government officials, and a stable constitution will enjoy a higher economic standard of living than a country with a poor court system, corrupt officials, and frequent revolutions and coups.

CASE STUDY   WHAT CAUSES FAMINE?

A recurring problem facing the world's poorest countries is famine. Every few years, haunting pictures of starving people in an underdeveloped country show up on the nightly news. Such tragedies are surely among the most serious economic problems the world's nations face.

It is tempting to think that the problem of famine is simply due to excessive population. After all, if there were fewer people, then each person could get a larger share of the available food supply. Reducing population growth would seem to be the natural remedy for recurrent famine. It turns out, however, that this straightforward logic is not right.

In many cases, famine is caused not by an inadequate *supply* of food but by an inadequate *distribution* of food. That is, food is available, but it is not getting to the people who need it. The failure of distribution, in turn, is caused by political instability and poor enforcement of property rights. An example is the famine in Somalia in the early 1990s. Fighting among rival factions in the civil war there prevented trucks with food from reaching the hungry. Eventually, U.S. President George Bush sent American troops in an attempt to reestablish order and allow the available food to be distributed properly.

Somalia: Too many people was not the problem.

FREE TRADE

Some of the world's poorest countries have tried to achieve more rapid economic growth by pursuing *inward-oriented policies.* These policies are aimed at raising productivity and living standards within the country by avoiding interaction with the rest of the world. As we discussed in Chapter 9, domestic firms sometimes claim they need protection from foreign competition in order to compete and grow. This infant-industry argument, together with a general distrust of foreigners, has at times led policymakers in less developed countries to impose tariffs and other trade restrictions.

Most economists today believe that poor countries are better off pursuing *outward-oriented policies* that integrate these countries into the world economy. Chapters 3 and 9 showed how international trade can improve the economic

IN THE NEWS

*The Sachs Solution
to the African Problem*

ECONOMIST JEFFREY SACHS HAS BEEN A prominent adviser to governments seeking to reform their economies in order to promote more rapid economic growth. Over the past decade, Bolivia, Poland, and Russia have been among his many clients. Sachs has also been a critic of the World Bank and the International Monetary Fund (IMF), which are international policy organizations that dispense both advice and money to struggling countries. In the following article, Sachs discusses how the countries of Africa can escape their continuing poverty.

Growth in Africa: It Can Be Done

BY JEFFREY SACHS

In the old story, the peasant goes to the priest for advice on saving his dying chickens. The priest recommends prayer, but the chickens continue to die. The priest then recommends music for the chicken coop, but the deaths continue unabated. Pondering again, the priest recommends repainting the chicken coop in bright colors. Finally, all the chickens die. "What a shame," the priest tells the peasant. "I had so many more good ideas."

Since independence, African countries have looked to donor nations—often their former colonial rulers—and to the international finance institutions for guidance on growth. Indeed, since the onset of the African debt crises of the 1980s, the guidance has become a kind of economic receivership, with the policies of many African nations decided in a seemingly endless cycle of meetings with the IMF, the World Bank, donors, and creditors.

What a shame. So many good ideas, so few results. Output per head fell 0.7 percent between 1978 and 1987, and 0.6 percent during 1987–1994. Some growth is estimated for 1995 but only at 0.6 percent—far below the faster-growing developing countries. . . .

The IMF and World Bank would be absolved of shared responsibility for slow growth if Africa were structurally incapable of growth rates seen in other parts of the world or if the continent's low growth were an impenetrable mystery. But Africa's growth rates are not huge mysteries. The evidence on cross-country growth suggests that Africa's chronically low growth can be explained by standard economic variables linked to identifiable (and remediable) policies. . . .

Studies of cross-country growth show that per capita growth is related to:

♦ the initial income level of the country, with poorer countries tending to grow faster than richer countries;

♦ the extent of overall market orientation, including openness to trade, domestic market liberalization, private rather than state ownership, protection of private property rights, and low marginal tax rates;

♦ the national saving rate, which in turn is strongly affected by the government's own saving rate; and

♦ the geographic and resource structure of the economy. . . .

These four factors can account broadly for Africa's long-term growth predicament. While it should have grown faster than other developing areas because of relatively low income per head (and hence larger opportunity for "catch-up" growth), Africa grew more slowly. This was mainly because of much higher trade barriers; excessive tax rates; lower saving rates; and adverse structural conditions, including an unusually high incidence of inaccessibility to the sea (15 of 53 countries are landlocked). . . .

If the policies are largely to blame, why, then, were they adopted? The historical origins of Africa's antimarket orientation are not hard to discern. After almost a century of colonial depredations, African nations understandably if erro-

well-being of a country's citizens. Trade is, in some ways, a type of technology. When a country exports wheat and imports steel, the country benefits in the same way as if it had invented a technology for turning wheat into steel. A country that eliminates trade restrictions will, therefore, experience the same kind of economic growth that would occur after a major technological advance.

The adverse impact of inward orientation becomes clear when one considers the small size of many less developed economies. The total GDP of Argentina, neously viewed open trade and foreign capital as a threat to national sovereignty. As in Sukarno's Indonesia, Nehru's India, and Peron's Argentina, "self-sufficiency" and "state leadership," including state ownership of much of industry, became the guideposts of the economy. As a result, most of Africa went into a largely self-imposed economic exile. . . .

Adam Smith in 1755 famously remarked that "little else is requisite to carry a state to the highest degrees of opulence from the lowest barbarism, but peace, easy taxes, and tolerable administration of justice." A growth agenda need not be long and complex. Take his points in turn.

Peace, of course, is not so easily guaranteed, but the conditions for peace on the continent are better than today's ghastly headlines would suggest. Several of the large-scale conflicts that have ravaged the continent are over or nearly so. . . . The ongoing disasters, such as in Liberia, Rwanda and Somalia, would be better contained if the West were willing to provide modest support to African-based peacekeeping efforts.

"Easy taxes" are well within the ambit of the IMF and World Bank. But here, the IMF stands guilty of neglect, if not malfeasance. African nations need simple, low taxes, with modest revenue targets as a share of GDP. Easy taxes are most essential in international trade, since successful growth will depend, more than anything else, on economic in-

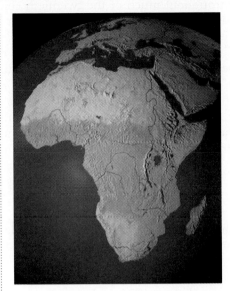

A CONTINENT WITH PROBLEMS

tegration with the rest of the world. Africa's largely self-imposed exile from world markets can end quickly by cutting import tariffs and ending export taxes on agricultural exports. Corporate tax rates should be cut from rates of 40 percent and higher now prevalent in Africa, to rates between 20 percent and 30 percent, as in the outward-oriented East Asian economies. . . .

Adam Smith spoke of a "tolerable" administration of justice, not perfect justice. Market liberalization is the primary key to strengthening the rule of law. Free trade, currency convertibility and automatic incorporation of business vastly reduce the scope for official corruption and allow the government to focus on

the real public goods—internal public order, the judicial system, basic public health and education, and monetary stability. . . .

All of this is possible only if the government itself has held its own spending to the necessary minimum. The Asian economies show how to function with government spending of 20 percent of GDP or less (China gets by with just 13 percent). Education can usefully absorb around 5 percent of GDP; health, another 3 percent; public administration, 2 percent; the army and police, 3 percent. Government investment spending can be held to 5 percent of GDP but only if the private sector is invited to provide infrastructure in telecommunications, port facilities, and power. . . .

This fiscal agenda excludes many popular areas for government spending. There is little room for transfers or social spending beyond education and health (though on my proposals, these would get a hefty 8 percent of GDP). Subsidies to publicly owned companies or marketing boards should be scrapped. Food and housing subsidies for urban workers cannot be financed. And, notably, interest payments on foreign debt are not budgeted for. This is because most bankrupt African states need a fresh start based on deep debt-reduction, which should be implemented in conjunction with far-reaching domestic reforms.

SOURCE: *Economist*, June 29, 1996, pp. 19–21.

for instance, is about that of Philadelphia. Imagine what would happen if the Philadelphia city council were to prohibit city residents from trading with people living outside the city limits. Without being able to take advantage of the gains from trade, Philadelphia would need to produce all the goods it consumes. It would also have to produce all its own capital goods, rather than importing state-of-the-art equipment from other cities. Living standards in Philadelphia would fall immediately, and the problem would likely only get worse over time.

This is precisely what happened when Argentina pursued inward-oriented policies throughout much of the twentieth century. By contrast, countries pursuing outward-oriented policies, such as South Korea, Singapore, and Taiwan, have enjoyed high rates of economic growth.

The amount that a nation trades with others is determined not only by government policy but also by geography. Countries with good natural seaports find trade easier than countries without this resource. It is not a coincidence that many of the world's major cities, such as New York, San Francisco, and Hong Kong, are located next to oceans. Similarly, because landlocked countries find international trade more difficult, they tend to have lower levels of income than countries with easy access to the world's waterways.

THE CONTROL OF POPULATION GROWTH

A country's productivity and living standard are determined in part by its population growth. Obviously, population is a key determinant of a country's labor force. It is no surprise, therefore, that countries with large populations (such as the United States and Japan) tend to produce greater GDP than countries with small populations (such as Luxembourg and the Netherlands). But *total* GDP is not a good measure of economic well-being. For policymakers concerned about living standards, GDP *per person* is more important, for it tells us the quantity of goods and services available for the typical individual in the economy.

How does growth in the number of people affect the amount of GDP per person? The answer is that high population growth reduces GDP per person. The reason is that rapid growth in the number of workers forces the other factors of production to be spread more thinly. In particular, when population growth is rapid, equipping each worker with a large quantity of capital is more difficult. A smaller quantity of capital per worker leads to lower productivity and lower GDP per worker.

This problem is most apparent in the case of human capital. Countries with high population growth have large numbers of school-age children. This places a larger burden on the educational system. It is not surprising, therefore, that educational attainment tends to be low in countries with high population growth.

The differences in population growth around the world are large. In developed countries, such as the United States and western Europe, the population has risen about 1 percent per year in recent decades, and it is expected to rise even more slowly in the future. By contrast, in many poor African countries, population growth is about 3 percent per year. At this rate, the population doubles every 23 years.

Reducing the rate of population growth is widely thought to be one way less developed countries can try to raise their standards of living. In some countries, this goal is accomplished directly with laws regulating the number of children families may have. China, for instance, allows only one child per family; couples who violate this rule are subject to substantial fines. In countries with greater freedom, the goal of reduced population growth is accomplished less directly by increasing awareness of birth control techniques.

The final way in which a country can influence population growth is to apply one of the *Ten Principles of Economics:* People respond to incentives. Bearing a child, like any decision, has an opportunity cost. When the opportunity cost rises, people will choose to have smaller families. In particular, women with the opportunity to receive good education and desirable employment tend to want fewer children than those with fewer opportunities outside the home. Hence, policies that foster equal treatment of women are one way for less developed economies to reduce the rate of population growth.

RESEARCH AND DEVELOPMENT

The primary reason that living standards are higher today than they were a century ago is that technological knowledge has advanced. The telephone, the transistor, the computer, and the internal combustion engine are among the thousands of innovations that have improved the ability to produce goods and services.

Although most technological advance comes from private research by firms and individual inventors, there is also a public interest in promoting these efforts. To a large extent, knowledge is a *public good:* Once one person discovers an idea, the idea enters society's pool of knowledge, and other people can freely use it. Just as government has a role in providing a public good such as national defense, it also has a role in encouraging the research and development of new technologies.

The U.S. government has long played a role in the creation and dissemination of technological knowledge. A century ago, the government sponsored research about farming methods and advised farmers how best to use their land. More recently, the U.S. government has, through the Air Force and NASA, supported aerospace research; as a result, the United States is a leading maker of rockets and planes. The government continues to encourage advances in knowledge with research grants from the National Science Foundation and the National Institutes of Health and with tax breaks for firms engaging in research and development.

Yet another way in which government policy encourages research is through the patent system. When a person or firm invents a new product, such as a new drug, the inventor can apply for a patent. If the product is deemed truly original, the government awards the patent, which gives the inventor the exclusive right to make the product for a specified number of years. In essence, the patent gives the inventor a property right over his invention, turning his new idea from a public good into a private good. By allowing inventors to profit from their inventions—even if only temporarily—the patent system enhances the incentive for individuals and firms to engage in research.

CASE STUDY   THE PRODUCTIVITY SLOWDOWN

From 1959 to 1973, productivity, as measured by output per hour worked in U.S. businesses, grew at a rate of 3.2 percent per year. From 1973 to 1994, productivity grew by only 1.3 percent per year. Not surprisingly, this slowdown in productivity growth has been reflected in reduced growth in real wages and family incomes. It is also reflected in a general sense of economic anxiety. Because it has accumulated over so many years, this fall in productivity growth of 1.9 percentage points has had a large effect on incomes. If this slowdown had not occurred, the income of the average American would today be about 50 percent higher.

The slowdown in economic growth has been one of the most important problems facing economic policymakers. Economists are often asked what caused the slowdown and what can be done to reverse it. Unfortunately, despite much research on these questions, the answers remain elusive.

Two facts are well established. First, the slowdown in productivity growth is a worldwide phenomenon. Sometime in the mid-1970s, economic growth slowed not only in the United States but also in other industrial countries, including Canada, France, Germany, Italy, Japan, and the United Kingdom. Although some of these countries have had more rapid growth than the United States, all of them have had slow growth compared to their own past experience. To explain the slowdown in U.S. growth, therefore, it seems necessary to look beyond our borders.

Second, the slowdown cannot be traced to those factors of production that are most easily measured. Economists can measure directly the quantity of physical capital that workers have available. They can also measure human capital in the form of years of schooling. It appears that the slowdown in productivity is not primarily attributable to reduced growth in these inputs.

Technology appears to be one of the few remaining culprits. That is, having ruled out most other explanations, many economists attribute the slowdown in economic growth to a slowdown in the creation of new ideas about how to produce goods and services. Because the quantity of "ideas" is hard to measure, this explanation is difficult to confirm or refute.

In some ways, it is odd to say that the last 20 years have been a period of slow technological progress. This period has witnessed the spread of computers across the economy—an historic technological revolution that has affected almost every industry and almost every firm. Yet, for some reason, this change has not yet been reflected in more rapid economic growth. As economist Robert Solow put it, "You can see the computer age everywhere but in the productivity statistics."

What does the future of economic growth hold? An optimistic scenario is that the computer revolution will rejuvenate economic growth once these new machines are integrated into the economy and their potential is fully understood. Economic historians note that the discovery of electricity took many decades to have a large impact on productivity and living standards because people had to figure out the best ways to use the new resource. Perhaps the computer revolution will have a similar delayed effect.

A more pessimistic scenario is that, after a period of rapid scientific and technological advance, we have entered a new phase of slower growth in knowledge, productivity, and incomes. Data from a longer span of history seem to support this conclusion. Figure 24-2 shows the average growth of real GDP per person in the developed world going back to 1870. The productivity slowdown is apparent in the last two entries: Around 1970, the growth rate slowed from 3.7 to 2.2 percent. But compared to earlier periods of history, the anomaly is not the slow growth of recent years but rather the rapid growth during the 1950s and 1960s. Perhaps the decades after World War II were a period of unusually rapid technological advance, and growth has slowed down simply because technological progress has returned to a more normal rate.

QUICK QUIZ   Describe three ways in which a government policymaker can try to raise the growth in living standards in a society. Are there any drawbacks to these policies?

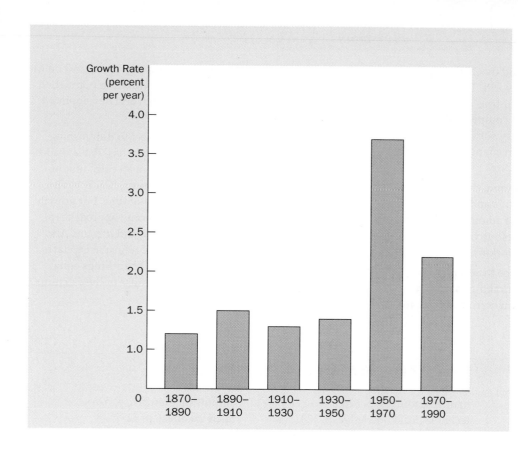

Figure 24-2

THE GROWTH IN REAL GDP PER
PERSON. This figure shows the
average growth rate of real GDP
per person for 16 advanced
economies, including the major
countries of Europe, Canada, the
United States, Japan, and
Australia. Notice that the growth
rate rose substantially after 1950
and then fell after 1970.

SOURCE: Robert J. Barro and Xavier Sala-i-
Martin, *Economic Growth* (New York:
McGraw-Hill, 1995), p. 6.

CONCLUSION: THE IMPORTANCE
OF LONG-RUN GROWTH

In this chapter we have discussed what determines the standard of living in
a nation and how policymakers can endeavor to raise the standard of living through policies that promote economic growth. Most of this chapter is
summarized in one of the *Ten Principles of Economics:* A country's standard of
living depends on its ability to produce goods and services. Policymakers who
want to encourage growth in standards of living must aim to increase their
nation's productive ability by encouraging rapid accumulation of the factors of
production and ensuring that these factors are employed as effectively as possible.

Economists differ in their views of the role of government in promoting economic growth. At the very least, government can lend support to the invisible
hand by maintaining property rights and political stability. More controversial
is whether government should target and subsidize specific industries that
might be especially important for technological progress. There is no doubt that
these issues are among the most important in economics. The success of one
generation's policymakers in learning and heeding the fundamental lessons
about economic growth determines what kind of world the next generation will
inherit.

Summary

◆ Economic prosperity, as measured by GDP per person, varies substantially around the world. The average income in the world's richest countries is more than ten times that in the world's poorest countries. Because growth rates of real GDP also vary substantially, the relative positions of countries can change dramatically over time.

◆ The standard of living in an economy depends on the economy's ability to produce goods and services. Productivity, in turn, depends on the amounts of physical capital, human capital, natural resources, and technological knowledge available to workers.

◆ Government policies can influence the economy's growth rate in many ways: encouraging saving and investment, encouraging investment from abroad, fostering education, maintaining property rights and political stability, allowing free trade, controlling population growth, and promoting the research and development of new technologies.

◆ The accumulation of capital is subject to diminishing returns: The more capital an economy has, the less additional output the economy gets from an extra unit of capital. Because of diminishing returns, higher saving leads to higher growth for a period of time, but growth eventually slows down as the economy approaches a higher level of capital, productivity, and income. Also because of diminishing returns, the return to capital is especially high in poor countries. Other things equal, these countries can grow faster because of the catch-up effect.

Key Concepts

productivity, p. 519
physical capital, p. 520
human capital, p. 520

natural resources, p. 520
technological knowledge, p. 523

diminishing returns, p. 526
catch-up effect, p. 527

Questions for Review

1. What two things does GDP measure? What does this dual meaning tell us about the determinants of the standard of living in a society?

2. List and describe four determinants of productivity.

3. In what way is a college degree a form of capital?

4. Explain how higher saving leads to a higher standard of living. What might deter a policymaker from trying to raise the rate of saving?

5. Does a higher rate of saving lead to higher growth temporarily or indefinitely?

6. Why would removing a trade restriction, such as a tariff, lead to more rapid economic growth?

7. How does the rate of population growth influence the level of GDP per person?

8. Describe two ways in which the U.S. government tries to encourage advances in technological knowledge.

Problems and Applications

1. Most countries, including the United States, import substantial amounts of goods and services from other countries. Yet the chapter says that a nation can enjoy a high standard of living only if it can produce a large quantity of goods and services itself. Can you reconcile these two facts?

2. List the capital inputs necessary to produce each of the following:
    a. cars
    b. high school educations
    c. plane travel
    d. fruits and vegetables

3. U.S. income per person today is roughly eight times what it was a century ago. Many other countries have also experienced significant growth over that period. What are some specific ways in which your standard of living differs from that of your great-grandparents?

4. The chapter discusses how employment has declined relative to output in the farm sector. Can you think of another sector of the economy where the same phenomenon has occurred more recently? Would you consider the change in employment in this sector to represent a success or a failure from the standpoint of society as a whole?

5. Suppose that society decided to reduce consumption and increase investment.
    a. How would this change affect economic growth?
    b. What groups in society would benefit from this change? What groups might be hurt?

6. Societies choose what share of their resources to devote to consumption and what share to devote to investment. Some of these decisions involve private spending; others involve government spending.
    a. Describe some forms of private spending that represent consumption, and some forms that represent investment.
    b. Describe some forms of government spending that represent consumption, and some forms that represent investment.

7. What is the opportunity cost of investing in capital? Do you think a country can "over-invest" in capital? What is the opportunity cost of investing in human capital? Do you think a country can "over-invest" in human capital? Explain.

8. Suppose that an auto company owned entirely by German citizens opens a new factory in South Carolina.
    a. What sort of foreign investment would this represent?
    b. What would be the effect of this investment on U.S. GDP? Would the effect on U.S. GNP be larger or smaller?

9. In the 1980s Japanese investors made significant direct and portfolio investments in the United States. At the time, many Americans were unhappy that this investment was occurring.
    a. In what way was it better for the United States to receive this Japanese investment than not to receive it?
    b. In what way would it have been better still for Americans to have done this investment?

10. In the countries of South Asia in 1992, only 56 young women were enrolled in secondary school for every 100 young men. Describe several ways in which greater educational opportunities for young women could lead to faster economic growth in these countries.

11. Suppose the government increased the number of years for which a patent lasts. What would be the effect of this change on the incentive to do research? Could this change produce a decline in the growth rate of GDP? Explain.

12. International data show a positive correlation between political stability and economic growth.
    a. Through what mechanism could political stability lead to strong economic growth?
    b. Through what mechanism could strong economic growth lead to political stability?

25

SAVING, INVESTMENT, AND THE FINANCIAL SYSTEM

IN THIS CHAPTER YOU WILL

Learn about some of the important financial institutions in the U.S. economy

Consider how the financial system is related to key macroeconomic variables

Develop a model of the supply and demand for loanable funds in financial markets

Use the loanable-funds model to analyze various government policies

Consider how government budget deficits affect the U.S. economy

Imagine that you have just graduated from college (with a degree in economics, of course) and you decide to start your own business—an economic forecasting firm. Before you make any money selling your forecasts, you have to incur substantial costs to set up your business. You have to buy computers with which to make your forecasts, as well as desks, chairs, and filing cabinets to furnish your new office. Each of these is a type of capital that your firm will use to produce and sell its services.

How do you obtain the funds to invest in these capital goods? Perhaps you are able to pay for them out of your past savings. More likely, however, like most entrepreneurs, you do not have enough money on your own to finance the start of your business. As a result, you have to get the money you need from other sources.

There are various ways for you to finance these capital investments. You could borrow the money, perhaps from a bank or from a friend or relative. In this case, you would promise not only to return the money at a later date but also to pay interest for the use of the money. Alternatively, you could convince someone to provide the money you need for your business in exchange for a share of your future profits, whatever they might happen to be. In either case, your investment in computers and office equipment is being financed by someone else's saving.

financial system

the group of institutions in the economy that help to match one person's saving with another person's investment

The **financial system** consists of those institutions in the economy that help to match one person's saving with another person's investment. As we discussed in the previous chapter, saving and investment are key ingredients to economic growth. When a country saves a large portion of its GDP, more resources are available for investment in capital, and higher capital raises a country's productivity and living standard. But that chapter did not explain how the economy coordinates saving and investment. At any time, some people want to save some of their income for the future, and others want to borrow in order to finance investments in new and growing businesses. What brings these two groups of people together? What ensures that the supply of funds from those who want to save balances the demand for funds from those who want to invest?

This chapter examines how the financial system works. First, we discuss the large variety of institutions that make up the financial system in our economy. Second, we discuss the relationship between the financial system and some key macroeconomic variables—notably saving and investment. Third, we develop a model of the supply and demand for funds in financial markets. In the model, the interest rate is the price that adjusts to balance supply and demand. The model shows how various government policies affect the interest rate and, thereby, society's allocation of scarce resources.

FINANCIAL INSTITUTIONS IN THE U.S. ECONOMY

At the broadest level, the financial system moves the economy's scarce resources from savers (people who spend less than they earn) to borrowers (people who spend more than they earn). Savers save for various reasons—to put a child through college in several years or to retire comfortably in several decades. Similarly, borrowers borrow for various reasons—to buy a house in which to live or to start a business with which to make a living. Savers supply their money to the financial system with the expectation that they will get it back with interest at a later date. Borrowers demand money from the financial system with the knowledge that they will be required to pay it back with interest at a later date.

The financial system is made up of various financial institutions that help coordinate savers and borrowers. As a prelude to analyzing the economic forces that drive the financial system, let's discuss the most important of these institutions. Financial institutions can be grouped into two categories—financial markets and financial intermediaries. We consider each category in turn.

FINANCIAL MARKETS

financial markets

financial institutions through which savers can directly provide funds to borrowers

Financial markets are the institutions through which a person who wants to save can directly supply funds to a person who wants to borrow. The two most important financial markets in our economy are the bond market and the stock market.

The Bond Market   When Intel, the giant maker of computer chips, wants to borrow to finance construction of a new factory, it can borrow directly from the public. It does this by selling bonds. A **bond** is a certificate of indebtedness that specifies the obligations of the borrower to the holder of the bond. Put simply, a bond is just an IOU. It identifies the time at which the loan will be repaid, called the *date of maturity,* and the rate of interest that will be paid periodically until the loan matures. The buyer of a bond gives his or her money to Intel in exchange for this promise of interest and eventual repayment of the amount borrowed (called the *principal*). The buyer can hold the bond until maturity or can sell the bond at an earlier date to someone else.

bond
a certificate of indebtedness

There are literally millions of different bonds in the U.S. economy. When large corporations, the federal government, or state and local governments need to borrow to finance the purchase of a new factory, a new jet fighter, or a new school, they usually do so by issuing bonds. If you look at *The Wall Street Journal* or the business section of your local newspaper, you will find a listing of the prices and interest rates on some of the most important bond issues. Although these bonds differ in many ways, three characteristics of bonds are most important.

The first characteristic is a bond's *term*—the length of time until the bond matures. Some bonds have short terms, such as a few months, while others have terms as long as 30 years. (The British government has even issued a bond that never matures, called a *perpetuity.* This bond pays interest forever, but the principal is never repaid.) The interest rate on a bond depends, in part, on its term. Long-term bonds are riskier than short-term bonds because holders of long-term bonds have to wait longer for repayment of principal. If a holder of a long-term bond needs his money earlier than the distant date of maturity, he has no choice but to sell the bond to someone else, perhaps at a reduced price. To compensate for this risk, long-term bonds usually pay higher interest rates than short term bonds.

The second important characteristic of a bond is its *credit risk*—the probability that the borrower will fail to pay some of the interest or principal. Such a failure to pay is called a *default.* Borrowers can (and sometimes do) default on their loans by declaring bankruptcy. When bond buyers perceive that the probability of default is high, they demand a higher interest rate to compensate them for this risk. Because the U.S. government is considered a safe credit risk, government bonds tend to pay low interest rates. By contrast, financially shaky corporations raise money by issuing *junk bonds,* which pay very high interest rates. Buyers of bonds can judge credit risk by checking with various private agencies, such as Standard & Poor's, which rate the credit risk of different bonds.

The third important characteristic of a bond is its *tax treatment*—the way in which the tax laws treat the interest earned on the bond. The interest on most bonds is taxable income, so that the bond owner has to pay a portion of the interest in income taxes. By contrast, when state and local governments issue bonds, called *municipal bonds,* the bond owners are not required to pay federal income tax on the interest income. Because of this tax advantage, bonds issued by state and local governments pay a lower interest rate than bonds issued by corporations or the federal government.

The Stock Market Another way for Intel to raise funds to build a new semiconductor factory is to sell stock in the company. **Stock** represents ownership in a firm and is, therefore, a claim to the profits that the firm makes. For example, if Intel sells a total of 1,000,000 shares of stock, then each share represents ownership of 1/1,000,000 of the business.

stock
a claim to partial ownership in a firm

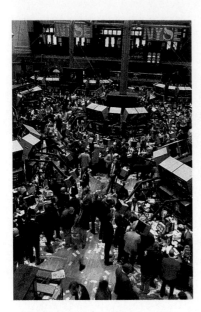

The New York Stock Exchange

The sale of stock to raise money is called *equity finance,* whereas the sale of bonds is called *debt finance.* Although corporations use both equity and debt finance to raise money for new investments, stocks and bonds are very different. The owner of shares of Intel stock is a part owner of Intel; the owner of an Intel bond is a creditor of the corporation. If Intel is very profitable, the stockholders enjoy the benefits of these profits, whereas the bondholders get only the interest on their bonds. And if Intel runs into financial difficulty, the bondholders are paid what they are due before stockholders receive anything at all. Compared to bonds, stocks offer the holder both higher risk and potentially higher return.

After a corporation issues stock by selling shares to the public, these shares trade among stockholders on organized stock exchanges. In these transactions, the corporation itself receives no money when its stock changes hands. The most important stock exchanges in the U.S. economy are the New York Stock Exchange, the American Stock Exchange, and NASDAQ (National Association of Securities Dealers Automated Quotation system). Most of the world's countries have their own stock exchanges on which the shares of local companies trade.

The prices at which shares trade on stock exchanges are determined by the supply and demand for the stock in these companies. Because stock represents ownership in a corporation, the demand for a stock (and thus its price) reflects people's perception of the corporation's future profitability. When people become optimistic about a company's future, they raise their demand for its stock and thereby bid up the price of a share of stock. Conversely, when people come to expect a company to have little profit or even losses, the price of a share falls.

Various stock indexes are available to monitor the overall level of stock prices. A *stock index* is computed as an average of a group of stock prices. The most famous stock index is the Dow Jones Industrial Average, which has been computed regularly since 1896. It is now based on the prices of the stocks of 30 major U.S. companies, such as General Motors, General Electric, Coca-Cola, AT&T, and IBM. Another well-known stock index is the Standard & Poor's 500 Index, which is based on the prices of 500 major companies. Because stock prices reflect expected profitability, these stock indexes are watched closely as possible indicators of future economic conditions.

FINANCIAL INTERMEDIARIES

financial intermediaries

financial institutions through which savers can indirectly provide funds to borrowers

Financial intermediaries are financial institutions through which savers can indirectly provide funds to borrowers. The term *intermediary* reflects the role of these institutions in standing between savers and borrowers. Here we consider two of the most important financial intermediaries—banks and mutual funds.

Banks   If the owner of a small grocery store wants to finance an expansion of his business, he probably takes a strategy quite different from Intel. Unlike Intel, a small grocer would find it difficult to raise funds in the bond and stock markets. Most buyers of stocks and bonds prefer to buy those issued by larger, more familiar companies. The small grocer, therefore, most likely finances his business expansion with a loan from a local bank.

Banks are the financial intermediaries with which people are most familiar. A primary job of banks is to take in deposits from people who want to save and use these deposits to make loans to people who want to borrow. Banks pay depositors interest on their deposits and charge borrowers slightly higher interest

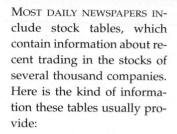

MOST DAILY NEWSPAPERS INclude stock tables, which contain information about recent trading in the stocks of several thousand companies. Here is the kind of information these tables usually provide:

◆ *Price.* The single most important piece of information about a stock is the price of a share. The newspaper usually presents several prices. The "last" or "closing" price is the price of the last transaction that occurred before the stock exchange closed the previous day. Many newspapers also give the "high" and "low" prices over the past day of trading and, sometimes, over the past year as well.

◆ *Volume.* Most newspapers present the number of shares sold during the past day of trading. This figure is called the *daily volume.*

◆ *Dividend.* Corporations pay out some of their profits to their stockholders; this amount is called the *dividend.* (Profits not paid out are called *retained earnings* and are used by the corporation for additional investment.) Newspapers often report the dividend paid over the previous year for each share of stock. They sometimes report the *dividend yield*, which is the dividend expressed as a percentage of the stock's price.

◆ *Price–earnings ratio.* A corporation's earnings, or profit, is the amount of revenue it receives for the sale of its products minus its costs of production as measured by its accountants. Some of the earnings are used to pay dividends; the rest is kept in the firm to make new investments. The price–earnings ratio, often called the P/E, is the price of a corporation's stock divided by the amount the corporation earned per share over the past year. Historically, the typical price–earnings ratio is about 15. A higher P/E indicates that a corporation's stock is expensive relative to its recent earnings; this might indicate either that people expect earnings to rise in the future or that the stock is overvalued. Conversely, a lower P/E indicates that a corporation's stock is cheap relative to its recent earnings; this might indicate either that people expect earnings to fall or that the stock is undervalued.

Why does the newspaper report all these data every day? Many people who invest their savings in stock follow these numbers closely when deciding which stocks to buy and sell. By contrast, other stockholders follow a buy-and-hold strategy: They buy the stock of well-run companies, hold it for long periods of time, and do not respond to the daily fluctuations reported in the paper.

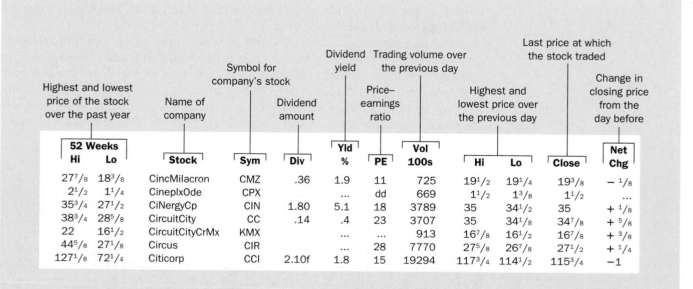

52 Weeks		Stock	Sym	Div	Yld %	PE	Vol 100s	Hi	Lo	Close	Net Chg
Hi	Lo										
27⁷/₈	18³/₈	CincMilacron	CMZ	.36	1.9	11	725	19¹/₂	19¹/₄	19³/₈	− ¹/₈
2¹/₂	1¹/₄	CineplxOde	CPX		...	dd	669	1¹/₂	1³/₈	1¹/₂	...
35³/₄	27¹/₂	CiNergyCp	CIN	1.80	5.1	18	3789	35	34¹/₂	35	+ ¹/₈
38³/₄	28⁵/₈	CircuitCity	CC	.14	.4	23	3707	35	34¹/₈	34⁷/₈	+ ⁵/₈
22	16¹/₂	CircuitCityCrMx	KMX		...	...	913	16⁷/₈	16¹/₂	16⁷/₈	+ ³/₈
44⁵/₈	27¹/₈	Circus	CIR		...	28	7770	27⁵/₈	26⁷/₈	27¹/₂	+ ¹/₄
127¹/₈	72¹/₄	Citicorp	CCI	2.10f	1.8	15	19294	117³/₄	114¹/₂	115³/₄	−1

Labels above the table:

- Highest and lowest price of the stock over the past year → **52 Weeks / Hi / Lo**
- Name of company → **Stock**
- Symbol for company's stock → **Sym**
- Dividend amount → **Div**
- Dividend yield → **Yld %**
- Price–earnings ratio → **PE**
- Trading volume over the previous day → **Vol 100s**
- Highest and lowest price over the previous day → **Hi / Lo**
- Last price at which the stock traded → **Close**
- Change in closing price from the day before → **Net Chg**

on their loans. The difference between these rates of interest covers the banks' costs and returns some profit to the owners of the banks.

Besides being financial intermediaries, banks play a second important role in the economy: They facilitate purchases of goods and services by allowing people to write checks against their deposits. In other words, banks help create a special asset that people can use as a *medium of exchange*. A medium of exchange is an item that people can easily use to engage in transactions. A bank's role in providing a medium of exchange distinguishes it from many other financial institutions. Stocks and bonds, like bank deposits, are a possible *store of value* for the wealth that people have accumulated in past saving, but access to this wealth is not as easy, cheap, and immediate as just writing a check. For now, we ignore this second role of banks, but we will return to it when we discuss the monetary system in a later chapter.

mutual fund

an institution that sells shares to the public and uses the proceeds to buy a portfolio of stocks and bonds

Mutual Funds   A financial intermediary of increasing importance in the U.S. economy is the mutual fund. A **mutual fund** is an institution that sells shares to the public and uses the proceeds to buy a selection, or *portfolio*, of various types of stocks, bonds, or both stocks and bonds. The shareholder of the mutual fund accepts all the risk and return associated with the portfolio. If the value of the portfolio rises, the shareholder benefits; if the value of the portfolio falls, the shareholder suffers the loss.

The primary advantage of mutual funds is that they allow people with small amounts of money to diversify. Buyers of stocks and bonds are well advised to heed the adage: Don't put all your eggs in one basket. Because the value of any single stock or bond is tied to the fortunes of one company, holding a single kind of stock or bond is very risky. By contrast, people who hold a diverse portfolio of stocks and bonds face less risk because they have only a small stake in each company. Mutual funds make this diversification easy. With only a few hundred dollars, a person can buy shares in a mutual fund and, indirectly, become the part owner or creditor of hundreds of major companies. For this service, the company operating the mutual fund charges shareholders a fee, usually between 0.5 and 2.0 percent of assets each year.

A second advantage claimed by mutual fund companies is that mutual funds give ordinary people access to the skills of professional money managers. The managers of most mutual funds pay close attention to the developments and prospects of the companies in which they buy stock. These managers buy the stock of those companies that they view as having a profitable future and sell the stock of companies with less promising prospects. This professional man-

ARLO AND JANIS by Jimmy Johnson

agement, it is argued, should increase the return that mutual fund depositors earn on their savings.

Financial economists, however, are often skeptical of this second argument. With thousands of money managers paying close attention to each company's prospects, the price of a company's stock is usually a good reflection of the company's true value. As a result, it is hard to "beat the market" by buying good stocks and selling bad ones. In fact, mutual funds called *index funds*, which buy all the stocks in a given stock index, perform somewhat better on average than mutual funds that take advantage of active management by professional money managers. The explanation for the superior performance of index funds is that they keep costs low by buying and selling very rarely and by not having to pay the salaries of the professional money managers.

SUMMING UP

The U.S. economy contains a large variety of financial institutions. In addition to the bond market, the stock market, banks, and mutual funds, there are also pension funds, credit unions, insurance companies, and even the local loan shark. These institutions differ in many ways. When analyzing the macroeconomic role of the financial system, however, it is more important to keep in mind the similarity of these institutions than the differences. These financial institutions all serve the same goal—directing the resources of savers into the hands of borrowers.

QUICK QUIZ What is stock? What is a bond? How are they different? How are they similar?

SAVING AND INVESTMENT IN THE NATIONAL INCOME ACCOUNTS

Events that occur within the financial system are central to understanding developments in the overall economy. As we have just seen, the institutions that make up this system—the bond market, the stock market, banks, and mutual funds—have the role of coordinating the economy's saving and investment. And as we saw in the previous chapter, saving and investment are important determinants of long-run growth in GDP and living standards. As a result, macroeconomists need to understand how financial markets work and how various events and policies affect them.

As a starting point for an analysis of financial markets, we discuss in this section the key macroeconomic variables that measure activity in these markets. Our emphasis here is not on behavior but on accounting. *Accounting* refers to how various numbers are defined and added up. A personal accountant might help an individual add up his income and expenses. A national income accountant does the same thing for the economy as a whole. The national income accounts include, in particular, GDP and the many related statistics.

The rules of national income accounting include several important identities. Recall that an *identity* is an equation that must be true because of the way the variables in the equation are defined. Identities are useful to keep in mind, for they clarify how different variables are related to one another. Here we consider some accounting identities that shed light on the macroeconomic role of financial markets.

SOME IMPORTANT IDENTITIES

Recall that gross domestic product (GDP) is both total income in an economy and the total expenditure on the economy's output of goods and services. GDP (denoted as Y) is divided into four components of expenditure: consumption (C), investment (I), government purchases (G), and net exports (NX). We write

$$Y = C + I + G + NX.$$

This equation is an identity because every dollar of expenditure that shows up on the left-hand side also shows up in one of the four components on the right-hand side. Because of the way each of the variables is defined and measured, this equation must always hold.

In this chapter, we simplify our analysis by assuming that the economy we are examining is closed. A *closed economy* is one that does not interact with other economies. In particular, a closed economy does not engage in international trade in goods and services, nor does it engage in international borrowing and lending. Of course, actual economies are *open economies*, that is, they interact with other economies around the world. (We will examine the macroeconomics of open economies later in this book.) Nonetheless, assuming a closed economy is a useful simplification with which we can learn some lessons that apply to all economies. Moreover, this assumption applies perfectly to the world economy (since interplanetary trade is not yet common).

Because a closed economy does not engage in international trade, imports and exports are exactly zero. Therefore, net exports (NX) are also zero. In this case, we can write

$$Y = C + I + G.$$

This equation states that GDP is the sum of consumption, investment, and government purchases. Each unit of output sold in a closed economy is consumed, invested, or bought by the government.

To see what this identity can tell us about financial markets, subtract C and G from both sides of this equation. We obtain

$$Y - C - G = I.$$

The left-hand side of this equation ($Y - C - G$) is the total income in the economy that remains after paying for consumption and government purchases: This amount is called **national saving,** or just **saving,** and is denoted S. Substituting S for $Y - C - G$, we can write the last equation as

$$S = I.$$

This equation states that saving equals investment.

national saving (saving)

the total income in the economy that remains after paying for consumption and government purchases

To understand the meaning of national saving, it is helpful to manipulate the definition a bit more. Let T denote the amount that the government collects from households in taxes minus the amount it pays back to households in the form of transfer payments (such as Social Security and welfare). We can then write national saving in either of two ways:

$$S = Y - C - G$$

or

$$S = (Y - T - C) + (T - G).$$

These equations are the same, since the two T's in the second equation cancel each other, but each reveals a different way of thinking about national saving. In particular, the second equation separates national saving into two pieces: private saving $(Y - T - C)$ and public saving $(T - G)$.

Consider each of these two pieces. **Private saving** is the amount of income that households have left after paying their taxes and paying for their consumption. In particular, because households receive income of Y, pay taxes of T, and spend C on consumption, private saving is $Y - T - C$. **Public saving** is the amount of tax revenue that the government has left after paying for its spending. The government receives T in tax revenue and spends G on goods and services. If T exceeds G, the government runs a **budget surplus** because it receives more money than it spends. This surplus of $T - G$ represents public saving. If the government spends more than it receives in tax revenue (as has been the case in recent U.S. history), then G is larger than T. In this case, the government runs a **budget deficit,** and public saving $T - G$ is a negative number.

Now consider how these accounting identities are related to financial markets. The equation $S = I$ reveals an important fact: *For the economy as a whole, saving must be equal to investment.* Yet this fact raises some important questions: What mechanisms lie behind this identity? What coordinates those people who are deciding how much to save and those people who are deciding how much to invest? The answer is the financial system. The bond market, the stock market, banks, mutual funds, and other financial markets and intermediaries stand between the two sides of the $S = I$ equation. They take in the nation's saving and direct it to the nation's investment.

private saving
the income that households have left after paying for taxes and consumption

public saving
the tax revenue that the government has left after paying for its spending

budget surplus
an excess of tax revenue over government spending

budget deficit
a shortfall of tax revenue from government spending

THE MEANING OF SAVING AND INVESTMENT

The terms *saving* and *investment* can sometimes be confusing. Most people use these terms casually and sometimes interchangeably. By contrast, the macroeconomists who put together the national income accounts use these terms carefully and distinctly.

Consider an example. Suppose that Larry earns more than he spends and deposits his unspent income in a bank or uses it to buy a bond or some stock from a corporation. Because Larry's income exceeds his consumption, he adds to the nation's saving. Larry might think of himself as "investing" his money, but a macroeconomist would call Larry's act saving rather than investment.

In the language of macroeconomics, investment refers to the purchase of new capital, such as equipment or buildings. When Moe borrows from the bank to build himself a new house, he adds to the nation's investment. Similarly, when the Curly Corporation sells some stock and uses the proceeds to build a new factory, it also adds to the nation's investment.

Although the accounting identity $S = I$ shows that saving and investment are equal for the economy as a whole, this does not have to be true for every individual household or firm. Larry's saving can be greater than his investment, and he can deposit the excess in a bank. Moe's saving can be less than his investment, and he can borrow the shortfall from a bank. Banks and other financial institutions make these individual differences between saving and investment possible by allowing one person's saving to finance another person's investment.

▌QUICK QUIZ   Define *private saving, public saving, national saving,* and *investment.* How are they related?

THE MARKET FOR LOANABLE FUNDS

Having discussed some of the important financial institutions in our economy and the macroeconomic role of these institutions, we are ready to build a model of financial markets. Our purpose in building this model is to explain how financial markets coordinate the economy's saving and investment. The model also gives us a tool with which we can analyze various government policies that influence saving and investment.

market for loanable funds
the market in which those who want to save supply funds and those who want to borrow to invest demand funds

To keep things simple, we assume that the economy has only one financial market, called the **market for loanable funds.** All savers go to this market to deposit their saving, and all borrowers go to this market to get their loans. In this market, there is one interest rate, which is both the return to saving and the cost of borrowing.

The assumption of a single financial market, of course, is not literally true. As we have seen, the economy has many types of financial institutions. But, as we discussed in Chapter 2, the art in building an economic model is simplifying the world in order to explain it. For our purposes here, we can ignore the diversity of financial institutions and assume that the economy has a single financial market.

SUPPLY AND DEMAND FOR LOANABLE FUNDS

The economy's market for loanable funds, like other markets in the economy, is governed by supply and demand. To understand how the market for loanable funds operates, therefore, we first look at the sources of supply and demand in that market.

The supply of loanable funds comes from those people who have some extra income they want to save and lend out. This lending can occur directly, such as when a household buys a bond from a firm, or it can occur indirectly, such as when a household makes a deposit in a bank which in turn uses the funds to make loans. In both cases, saving is the source of the supply of loanable funds.

The demand for loanable funds comes from households and firms who wish to borrow to make investments. This demand includes families taking out mortgages to buy homes. It also includes firms borrowing to buy new equipment or build factories. In both cases, investment is the source of the demand for loanable funds.

The interest rate is the price of a loan. It represents the amount that borrowers pay for loans and the amount that lenders receive on their saving. Because a high interest rate makes borrowing more expensive, the quantity of loanable funds demanded falls as the interest rate rises. Similarly, because a high interest rate makes saving more attractive, the quantity of loanable funds supplied rises as the interest rate rises. In other words, the demand curve for loanable funds slopes downward, and the supply curve for loanable funds slopes upward.

Figure 25-1 shows the interest rate that balances the supply and demand for loanable funds. In the equilibrium shown, the interest rate is 5 percent, and the quantity of loanable funds demanded and the quantity of loanable funds supplied both equal $1,200 billion. The adjustment of the interest rate to the equilibrium level occurs for the usual reasons. If the interest rate were lower than the equilibrium level, the quantity of loanable funds supplied would be less than the quantity of loanable funds demanded. The resulting shortage of loanable funds would encourage lenders to raise the interest rate they charge. Conversely, if the interest rate were higher than the equilibrium level, the quantity of loanable funds supplied would exceed the quantity of loanable funds demanded. As lenders competed for the scarce borrowers, interest rates would be driven down. In this way, the interest rate approaches the equilibrium level at which the supply and demand for loanable funds exactly balance.

Recall that economists distinguish between the real interest rate and the nominal interest rate. The nominal interest rate is the interest rate as usually reported—the monetary return to saving and cost of borrowing. The real interest

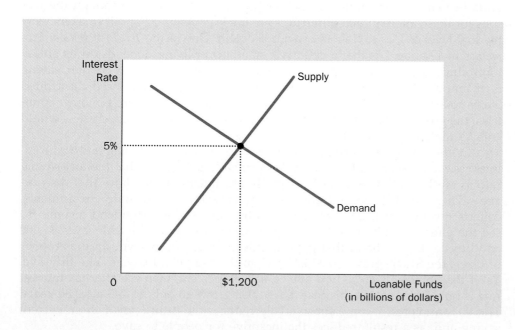

Figure 25-1

THE MARKET FOR LOANABLE FUNDS. The interest rate in the economy adjusts to balance the supply and demand for loanable funds. The supply of loanable funds comes from national saving, including both private saving and public saving. The demand for loanable funds comes from firms and households that want to borrow for purposes of investment. Here the equilibrium interest rate is 5 percent, and $1,200 billion of loanable funds are supplied and demanded.

rate is the nominal interest rate corrected for inflation; it equals the nominal interest rate minus the inflation rate. Because inflation erodes the value of money over time, the real interest rate more accurately reflects the real return to saving and cost of borrowing. Therefore, the supply and demand for loanable funds depend on the real (rather than nominal) interest rate, and the equilibrium in Figure 25-1 should be interpreted as determining the real interest rate in the economy. For the rest of this chapter, when you see the term *interest rate,* you should remember that we are talking about the real interest rate.

This model of the supply and demand for loanable funds shows that financial markets work much like other markets in the economy. In the market for milk, for instance, the price of milk adjusts so that the quantity of milk supplied balances the quantity of milk demanded. In this way, the invisible hand coordinates the behavior of dairy farmers and the behavior of milk drinkers. Once we realize that saving represents the supply of loanable funds and investment represents the demand, we can see how the invisible hand coordinates saving and investment. When the interest rate adjusts to balance supply and demand in the market for loanable funds, it coordinates the behavior of people who want to save (the suppliers of loanable funds) and the behavior of people who want to invest (the demanders of loanable funds).

We can now use this analysis of the market for loanable funds to examine various government policies that affect the economy's saving and investment. Because this model is just supply and demand in a particular market, we analyze any policy using the three steps discussed in Chapter 4. First, we decide whether the policy shifts the supply curve or the demand curve. Second, we determine the direction of the shift. Third, we use the supply-and-demand diagram to see how the equilibrium changes.

POLICY 1: TAXES AND SAVING

American families save a smaller fraction of their incomes than their counterparts in many other countries, such as Japan and Germany. Although the reasons for these international differences are unclear, many U.S. policymakers view the low level of U.S. saving as a major problem. One of the *Ten Principles of Economics* in Chapter 1 is that a country's standard of living depends on its ability to produce goods and services. And, as we discussed in the last chapter, saving is an important long-run determinant of a nation's productivity. If the United States could somehow raise its saving rate to the level that prevails in other countries, the growth rate of GDP would increase, and over time, U.S. citizens would enjoy a higher standard of living.

Another of the *Ten Principles of Economics* is that people respond to incentives. Many economists have used this principle to suggest that the low saving rate in the United States is at least partly attributable to tax laws that discourage saving. The U.S. federal government, as well as many state governments, collects revenue by taxing income, including interest and dividend income. To see the effects of this policy, consider a twenty-five-year-old who saves $1,000 and buys a 30-year bond that pays an interest rate of 9 percent. In the absence of taxes, the $1,000 grows to $13,268 when the individual reaches age fifty-five. Yet if that interest is taxed at a rate of, say, 33 percent, then the after-tax interest rate is only 6 percent. In this case, the $1,000 grows to only $5,743 after 30 years. The tax on interest income substantially reduces the future payoff from current saving and, as a result, reduces the incentive for people to save.

In response to this problem, many economists and lawmakers have proposed changing the tax code to encourage greater saving. In 1995, for instance, when Congressman Bill Archer became chairman of the powerful House Ways and Means Committee, he proposed replacing the current income tax with a consumption tax. Under a consumption tax, income that is saved would not be taxed until the saving is later spent; in essence, a consumption tax is like the sales taxes that many states now use to collect revenue. A more modest proposal is to expand eligibility for special accounts, such as Individual Retirement Accounts, that allow people to shelter some of their saving from taxation. Let's consider the effect of such a saving incentive on the market for loanable funds, as illustrated in Figure 25-2.

First, which curve would this policy affect? Because the tax change would alter the incentive for households to save *at any given interest rate*, it would affect the quantity of loanable funds supplied at each interest rate. Thus, the supply of loanable funds would shift. Because the tax change would not directly affect the amount that borrowers want to borrow at any given interest rate, the demand for loanable funds would be unchanged.

Second, which way would the supply curve shift? Because saving would be taxed less heavily than under current law, households would increase their saving by consuming a smaller fraction of their income. Households would use this additional saving to increase their deposits in banks or to buy more bonds. The supply of loanable funds would increase, and the supply curve would shift to the right from S_1 to S_2, as shown in Figure 25-2.

Finally, we can compare the old and new equilibria. In the figure, the increased supply of loanable funds reduces the interest rate from 5 percent to 4 percent. The lower interest rate raises the quantity of loanable funds demanded from $1,200 billion to $1,600 billion. That is, the shift in the supply curve moves the market equilibrium along the demand curve. With a lower cost of borrowing, households and firms are motivated to borrow more to finance greater

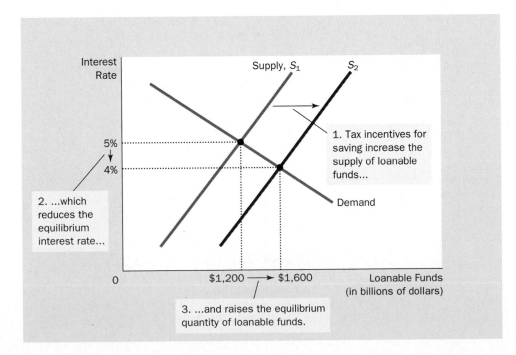

Figure 25-2

AN INCREASE IN THE SUPPLY OF LOANABLE FUNDS. A change in the tax laws to encourage Americans to save more would shift the supply of loanable funds to the right from S_1 to S_2. As a result, the equilibrium interest rate would fall, and the lower interest rate would stimulate investment. Here the equilibrium interest rate falls from 5 percent to 4 percent, and the equilibrium quantity of loanable funds saved and invested rises from $1,200 billion to $1,600 billion.

investment. Thus, *if a change in the tax laws encouraged greater saving, the result would be lower interest rates and greater investment.*

Although this analysis of the effects of increased saving is widely accepted among economists, there is less consensus about what kinds of tax changes should be enacted. Many economists endorse tax reform aimed at increasing saving in order to stimulate investment and growth. Yet others are skeptical that these tax changes would have much effect on national saving. These skeptics also doubt the equity of the proposed reforms. They argue that, in many cases, the benefits of the tax changes would accrue primarily to the wealthy, who are least in need of tax relief. We examine this debate more fully in the final chapter of this book.

POLICY 2: TAXES AND INVESTMENT

Suppose that Congress passed a law giving a tax reduction to any firm building a new factory. In essence, this is what Congress does when it institutes an *investment tax credit,* which it does from time to time. Let's consider the effect of such a law on the market for loanable funds, as illustrated in Figure 25-3.

First, would the law affect supply or demand? Because the tax credit would alter the incentive of firms to borrow and invest in new capital, it would alter the demand for loanable funds. By contrast, because the tax credit would not affect the amount that households save at any given interest rate, it would not affect the supply of loanable funds.

Second, which way would the demand curve shift? Because firms would have an incentive to increase investment at any interest rate, the quantity of loanable funds demanded would be higher at any given interest rate. Thus, the

Figure 25-3

AN INCREASE IN THE DEMAND FOR LOANABLE FUNDS. If the passage of an investment tax credit encouraged American firms to invest more, the demand for loanable funds would increase. As a result, the equilibrium interest rate would rise, and the higher interest rate would stimulate saving. Here, when the demand curve shifts from D_1 to D_2, the equilibrium interest rate rises from 5 percent to 6 percent, and the equilibrium quantity of loanable funds saved and invested rises from $1,200 billion to $1,400 billion.

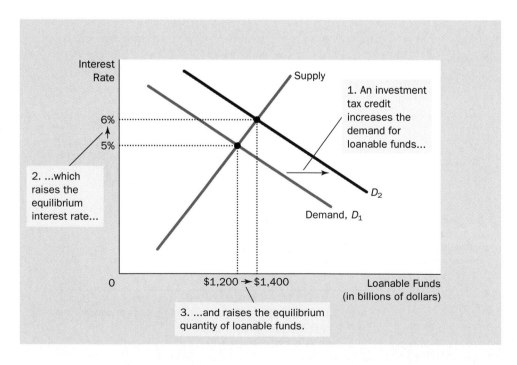

demand curve for loanable funds would shift to the right from D_1 to D_2, as shown in the figure.

Third, consider how the equilibrium would change. In Figure 25-3, the increased demand for loanable funds raises the interest rate from 5 percent to 6 percent, and the higher interest rate in turn increases the quantity of loanable funds supplied from $1,200 billion to $1,400 billion, as households respond by increasing the amount they save. This change in household behavior is represented here as a movement along the supply curve. Thus, *if a change in the tax laws encouraged greater investment, the result would be higher interest rates and greater saving.*

POLICY 3: GOVERNMENT BUDGET DEFICITS

One of the most pressing policy issues of the past decade has been the government budget deficit. When the government spends more than it receives in tax revenue, the shortfall is called the *budget deficit.* The accumulation of past budget deficits is called the *government debt.* In recent years, the U.S. federal government has run large budget deficits, resulting in a rapidly growing government debt. As a result, much public debate has centered on the effects of these deficits both on the allocation of the economy's scarce resources and on long-term economic growth.

We can analyze the effects of a budget deficit by following our three steps in the market for loanable funds, which is illustrated in Figure 25-4. First, which curve shifts when the budget deficit rises? Recall that national saving—the source of the supply of loanable funds—is composed of private saving and public saving. A change in the government budget deficit represents a change in public saving and, thereby, in the supply of loanable funds. Because the budget

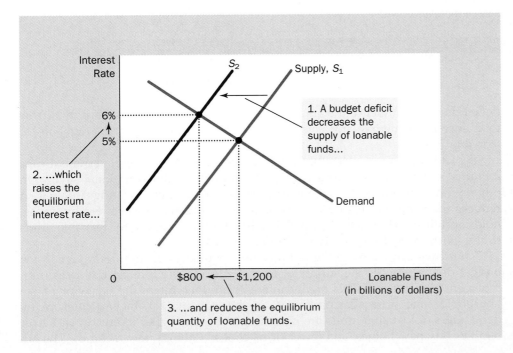

Figure 25-4

THE EFFECT OF A GOVERNMENT BUDGET DEFICIT. When the government spends more than it receives in tax revenue, the resulting budget deficit lowers national saving. The supply of loanable funds decreases, and the equilibrium interest rate rises. Thus, when the government borrows to finance its budget deficit, it crowds out households and firms who otherwise would borrow to finance investment. Here, when the supply shifts from S_1 to S_2, the equilibrium interest rate rises from 5 percent to 6 percent, and the equilibrium quantity of loanable funds saved and invested falls from $1,200 billion to $800 billion.

FYI

Ricardian Equivalence: An Alternative View of Government Budget Deficits

ALTHOUGH MOST ECONOMISTS accept the view that government budget deficits reduce national saving and crowd out investment, a small group questions this conclusion. They advance a theory called *Ricardian equivalence.* This view is named after the famous nineteenth-century economist David Ricardo, who first noted the theoretical argument (and who also raised doubts about whether it holds in practice).

The Ricardian argument runs as follows: Imagine that the government cuts taxes without changing its spending. As a result of the budget deficit, public saving falls. But if households save all of the tax cut, rather than spending some of it, private saving will rise by exactly the same amount that public saving falls. National saving, which is the sum of public and private saving, will not change. Neither will the supply of loanable funds nor the equilibrium interest rate. In fact, nothing will change (except for the division of national saving between public and private saving). The situation with the budget deficit is equivalent to the situation without it.

Why, you might ask, would households save all of the tax cut? According to the theory of Ricardian equivalence, when people see the government running a budget deficit, they understand that the government will need to raise their taxes in the future in order to pay off the debt that it is now accumulating. A tax cut and budget deficit does not reduce households' overall tax bill; it merely postpones it. In a sense, a tax cut financed by a budget deficit is more of a loan from the government than a gift. Because the policy does not make people any richer than they were, they should not use it to increase their spending. Instead, they should save the tax cut for the day when the loan comes due in the form of higher taxes.

Many economists dismiss Ricardian equivalence as idle speculation. Certainly, the large budget deficits in the United States since the early 1980s have not been accompanied by a rise in private saving, as the Ricardian theory suggests. In fact, the opposite is more nearly the case. As U.S. public saving fell, so did U.S. private saving.

The theory of Ricardian equivalence does, however, raise an intriguing question: If a rise in government debt requires higher taxes in the future, as surely it does, why aren't households saving in anticipation of these taxes? One possibility is that people are too short-sighted in their decisions to look ahead to the ramifications of current government policies. Another possibility is that they expect these taxes to fall not on themselves but on future generations of taxpayers. Indeed, many economists point to the redistribution of taxes across generations as an important aspect of a policy of government budget deficits.

---

deficit does not influence the amount that households and firms want to borrow to finance investment at any given interest rate, it does not alter the demand for loanable funds.

Second, which way does the supply curve shift? When the government runs a budget deficit, public saving is negative, and this reduces national saving. In other words, when the government borrows to finance its budget deficit, it reduces the supply of loanable funds available to finance investment by households and firms. Thus, a budget deficit shifts the supply curve for loanable funds to the left from S_1 to S_2, as shown in Figure 25-4.

Third, we can compare the old and new equilibria. In the figure, when the budget deficit reduces the supply of loanable funds, the interest rate rises from 5 percent to 6 percent. This higher interest rate then alters the behavior of the households and firms that participate in the loan market. In particular, many demanders of loanable funds are discouraged by the higher interest rate. Fewer families buy new homes, and fewer firms choose to build new factories. The fall in investment because of government borrowing is called **crowding out** and is represented in the figure by the movement along the demand curve from a quantity of $1,200 billion in loanable funds to a quantity of $800 billion. That is, when the government borrows to finance its budget deficit, it crowds out private borrowers who are trying to finance investment.

crowding out
a decrease in investment that results from government borrowing

Thus, the most basic lesson about budget deficits follows directly from their effects on the supply and demand for loanable funds: *When the government reduces national saving by running a budget deficit, the interest rate rises, and investment falls.* Because investment is important for long-run economic growth, government budget deficits reduce the economy's growth rate.

CASE STUDY GOVERNMENT DEBT AND DEFICITS IN THE UNITED STATES

Budget deficits have been a chronic problem for the U.S. economy since the early 1980s. When President Ronald Reagan took office in 1981, he was committed to smaller government and lower taxes. Yet he found reducing government spending to be more difficult politically than reducing taxes. The result was the beginning of a period of large budget deficits that continued not only through Reagan's time in office but also through George Bush's and (so far) Bill Clinton's.

Figure 25-5 shows the debt of the U.S. federal government expressed as a percentage of U.S. GDP. From the 1950s through the 1970s, the debt–GDP ratio declined. Although the government did run budget deficits during some of these years, the deficits were sufficiently small that the size of the government's debt grew less rapidly than the overall economy. Because GDP is a rough measure of the government's ability to raise tax revenue, a declining debt–GDP ratio indicates the economy is, in some sense, living within its means. By contrast, when the budget deficits ballooned in the early 1980s, the

"Our deficit-reduction plan is simple, but it will require a great deal of money."

Figure 25-5

THE U.S. GOVERNMENT DEBT. The debt of the U.S. federal government, expressed here as a percentage of GDP, was high after the large expenditures of World War II but then declined throughout the 1950s and 1960s. It began rising again in the early 1980s when Ronald Reagan's tax cuts were not accompanied by similar cuts in government spending.

SOURCE: U.S. Department of the Treasury; U.S. Department of Commerce.

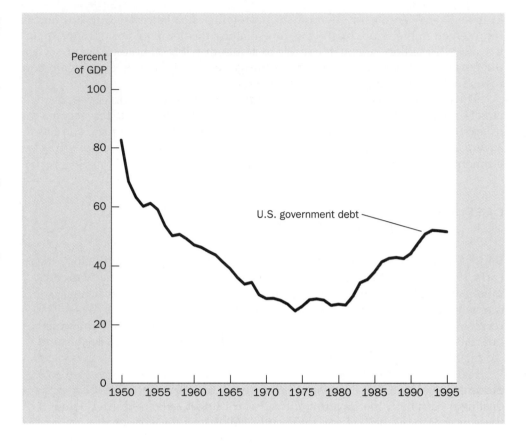

government debt started rising more rapidly than the overall economy. As a result, the debt–GDP ratio started to rise.

Table 25-1 shows the impact of this policy on various measures of saving. Beginning in the early 1980s, when the U.S. government began running massive budget deficits, public saving as a percentage of GDP fell by 2.4 percentage points. At the same time, private saving rates also fell slightly. National saving fell by about 2.9 percentage points.

As we saw in the previous chapter, national saving is a key ingredient in long-run economic growth. By using some of the private sector's saving to finance the budget deficit, the government pulls resources away from investment in new capital and, thereby, depresses the living standards of future generations. Policymakers from both political parties accept this basic argument and view persistent budget deficits as an important policy problem. When Bill Clinton moved into the Oval Office in 1993, deficit reduction was his first major goal. Similarly, when the Republicans took control of Congress in 1995, deficit reduction was high on their legislative agenda. Both of these efforts substantially reduced the size of the government budget deficit, but they did not completely eliminate it.

Why, if there is such unanimity, does the U.S. government continue to run budget deficits? Part of the answer is that there is disagreement about how to eliminate the deficit. President Clinton argued for tax increases, especially on more wealthy taxpayers, and for relatively modest reductions in spending. The Republicans in Congress are opposed to tax increases and, indeed, would

Table 25-1

SAVING IN THE U.S. ECONOMY

RATE OF:	SYMBOL	1960–1981	1982–1994	CHANGE
Public saving	$T - G$	0.8	-1.6	-2.4
Private saving	$Y - T - C$	16.1	15.7	-0.4
National saving	$Y - C - G$	16.9	14.0	-2.9

NOTE: The saving rates are gross nominal amounts expressed as a percentage of nominal GDP. Public and private saving have been adjusted for the effects of inflation: Only the real interest on the government debt is counted as expenditure by the government and income by the private sector.

SOURCE: U.S. Department of Commerce; and author's calculations.

like to cut some taxes in order to stimulate private saving. They would balance the budget through deeper cuts in government spending than President Clinton deems wise. In this way, disagreement over the details of deficit reduction, together with a general reluctance to make hard decisions, has allowed government budget deficits to persist.

Like most policy debates, the debate over the government budget deficit has many facets. We discuss more of these in the final chapter of this book. But the basic elements of this debate should already be clear. Whenever policymakers consider the government's budget deficit and its impact on the economy, foremost in their minds are saving, investment, and interest rates.

QUICK QUIZ If more Americans adopted a "live for today" approach to life, how would this affect saving, investment, and the interest rate?

CONCLUSION

"Neither a borrower nor a lender be," Polonius advises his son in Shakespeare's *Hamlet.* If everyone followed this advice, this chapter would have been unnecessary.

Few economists would agree with Polonius. In our economy, people borrow and lend often, and usually for good reason. You may borrow one day to start your own business or to buy a home. And people may lend to you in the hope that the interest you pay will allow them to enjoy a more prosperous retirement. The financial system has the job of coordinating all this borrowing and lending activity.

In many ways, financial markets are like other markets in the economy. The price of loanable funds—the interest rate—is governed by the forces of supply and demand, just as other prices in the economy are. And we can analyze shifts in supply or demand in financial markets as we do in other markets. One of the

IN THE NEWS

The Balanced

Budget

Amendment

IN RECENT YEARS, SOME MEMBERS OF Congress have advocated a constitutional amendment that would require the federal government to balance its budget. President Clinton, however, has opposed the amendment. In the following opinion column, economist Robert Eisner presents the case against it.

Balanced Budget: Bad Economics

BY ROBERT EISNER

Along with two Nobel laureates, Robert Solow of M.I.T. and James Tobin of Yale, I have been soliciting economists' en-

dorsements of a statement opposing a balanced budget amendment to the Constitution. We have initial support from 35 distinguished members of the profession, including seven other Nobel laureates. . . .

The problem is that the amendment would violate the principles of sound economics that many of us have been teaching for decades. Any good accountant—or informed investor—knows how difficult and arbitrary measures of "balance," the difference between profit and loss, can be for a company. What is a current expense, how fast do you depreciate, what do you amortize, how do you price inventories, when do you put in special charges, how do you handle pension funds, what do you do about "deferred" taxes? The issues are more complex—much more complex—for the federal government. . . .

Consider the handling of portfolio transactions. When an individual buys a stock or bond he hardly classifies that as a current expenditure that may put him into "deficit" or reduce his saving. By federal accounting it would. Thus, a few years ago, when the Treasury was financing the purchase of savings and

loans' assets, as part of the S&L bailout, the deficit soared, fueling further, misinformed warnings that the deficit was destroying national saving and hence jeopardizing our future. Then, when the government sold off the old S&L portfolios, our "deficit" miraculously came down.

Another problem: The federal government has no separate capital budget. If federal accounting were to be consistent with that of private business, it would include not current capital outlays but only depreciation charges on existing capital in its measure of surplus or deficit, the counterpart of a firm's profit-and-loss statement. But then how would we measure depreciation? How fast is our vast defense arsenal becoming obsolete? With the end of the Cold War, should we take a special charge and write off much of it? What also should be done about the increasing amounts of investment in intangible capital, in computer software, in research and development, in education and training, and in health?

These are just a few of the oddities of current federal accounting. One may wonder if the congressional supporters

Ten Principles of Economics introduced in Chapter 1 is that markets are usually a good way to organize economic activity. This principle applies to financial markets as well. When financial markets bring the supply and demand for loanable funds into balance, they help allocate the economy's scarce resources to their most efficient use.

In one way, however, financial markets are special. Financial markets, unlike most other markets, serve the important role of linking the present and the future. Those who supply loanable funds—savers—do so because they want to convert some of their current income into future purchasing power. Those who demand loanable funds—borrowers—do so because they want to invest today in order to have additional capital in the future to produce goods and services. Thus, well-functioning financial markets are important not only for current generations but also for future generations who will inherit many of the resulting benefits.

of a constitutional amendment intend to order that all accounting rules that would determine "balance" be kept in place. Would we set up commissions to revise them from time to time? Or would we leave it to the courts to determine which rules fit the "intent" of the amendment? . . .

As proposed in the last Congress, the amendment would allow federal borrowing only if approved by three-fifths majorities of all of the members, a very difficult hurdle. Many say, "I balance my checkbook, and state and local governments have balanced budget provisions in their constitutions, why can't the federal government be the same? Why must it borrow?" In fact, almost all of us borrow—to finance our homes, to send our children to college, and to buy cars and other durable goods. Businesses borrow—look at the corporate bond market. State and local governments generally have separate capital budgets; the constraints of balance apply only to current or operating budgets. They borrow for all kinds of capital investment. The balanced budget amendment would put only our federal government under that strict limitation to borrowing.

Finally, the amendment is ludicrous—perhaps fortunately—in its pretense of enforceability. In one section it declares, "Prior to each fiscal year, the President shall transmit to the Congress a proposed budget for the United States Government for that fiscal year, in which total outlays do not exceed total receipts." What would stop the president from simply estimating prospective receipts high enough to equal outlays? Given the general uncertainty and inaccuracy of such projections, this could be done with reasonable honesty.

Section 1 indeed declares, "Total outlays for any fiscal year shall not exceed total receipts for that year. . . . " But who can say what will actually happen to outlays or receipts? Suppose more people get sick and use more Medicare or Medicaid. Suppose there is a fall in income and tax revenues decline. This section might as well assert that the waves of the Atlantic Ocean shall not cross a certain line. What if they do? Do we put the president or Congress in jail?

On the matter of evasion, I should probably welcome passage of the amendment and set up a consulting firm to make millions by advising how to get

around it. One simple technique would be the sale of government assets, which under federal accounting would count as offsets to outlays. We could begin with our national parks, federal land in general, our oil reserves and all parts of the federally owned transportation infrastructure. . . . We could then go on to public buildings, including the Capitol and the White House, perhaps renting them back for current use. . . . Of course, eventually we would run out of public assets to sell. But by then perhaps, as with Prohibition, there would be sufficient awareness of the folly of it all for the amendment to be repealed.

SOURCE: *The Wall Street Journal*, January 22, 1997, p. A14.

Summary

◆ The U.S. financial system is made up of many types of financial institutions, such as the bond market, the stock market, banks, and mutual funds. All these institutions act to direct the resources of households who want to save some of their income into the hands of households and firms who want to borrow.

◆ National income accounting identities reveal some important relationships among macroeconomic variables. In particular, for a closed economy, national saving must equal investment. Financial institutions are the mechanism through which the economy matches one person's saving with another person's investment.

◆ The interest rate is determined by the supply and demand for loanable funds. The supply of loanable funds comes from households who want to save some of their income and lend it out. The demand for loanable funds comes from households and firms who want to borrow for investment. To analyze how any policy or event affects the interest rate, one must consider how it affects the supply and demand for loanable funds.

◆   National saving equals private saving plus public saving. A government budget deficit represents negative public saving and, therefore, reduces national saving and the supply of loanable funds available to finance investment. When a government budget deficit crowds out investment, it reduces the growth of productivity and GDP.

Key Concepts

financial system, p. 542
financial markets, p. 542
bond, p. 543
stock, p. 543
financial intermediaries, p. 544

mutual fund, p. 546
national saving (saving), p. 548
private saving, p. 549
public saving, p. 549

budget surplus, p. 549
budget deficit, p. 549
market for loanable funds, p. 550
crowding out, p. 557

Questions for Review

1. What is the role of the financial system? Name and describe two markets that are part of the financial system in our economy. Name and describe two financial intermediaries.

2. What is national saving? What is private saving? What is public saving? How are these three variables related?

3. What is investment? How is it related to national saving?

4. Describe a change in the tax code that might increase private saving. If this policy were implemented, how would it affect the market for loanable funds?

5. What is a government budget deficit? How does it affect interest rates, investment, and economic growth?

Problems and Applications

1. For each of the following pairs, which bond would you expect to pay a higher interest rate? Explain.
    a. a bond of the U.S. government or a bond of an Eastern European government
    b. a bond that repays the principal in year 2005 or a bond that repays the principal in year 2025
    c. a bond from Coca-Cola or a bond from a software company you run in your garage
    d. a bond issued by the federal government or a bond issued by New York State

2. The "yield curve" is a graph of the interest rates on bonds of different terms, with the term shown on the horizontal axis and the interest rate shown on the vertical axis.
    a. Based on the discussion in the chapter, would you expect the yield curve to be upward sloping or downward sloping?
    b. Using the business section of a recent newspaper, graph the yield curve for U.S. government bonds. Does the curve have the slope you expected?

3. Theodore Roosevelt once said, "There is no moral difference between gambling at cards or in lotteries or on the race track and gambling in the stock market." What social purpose do you think is served by the existence of the stock market?

4. Declines in stock prices are sometimes viewed as harbingers of future declines in real GDP. Why do you suppose that might be true?

5. The chapter explains that mutual funds allow people with small amounts of money to buy a diverse portfolio of stocks and bonds. What is the advantage of owning a diverse portfolio rather than holding stocks or bonds from a single company?

6. Many workers hold large amounts of stock issued by the firms at which they work. Why do you suppose companies encourage this behavior? Why might a person *not* want to hold stock in the company where he works?

7. Your roommate says that he buys stock only in companies that everyone believes will experience big increases in profits in the future. How do you suppose the price–earnings ratio of these companies compares to the price–earnings ratio of other companies? What might be the disadvantage of buying stock in these companies?

8. Explain the difference between saving and investment as defined by a macroeconomist. Which of the following situations represent investment? Saving? Explain.
    a. Your family takes out a mortgage and buys a new house.
    b. You use your $200 paycheck to buy stock in AT&T.
    c. Your roommate earns $100 and deposits it in her account at a bank.
    d. You borrow $1,000 from a bank to buy a car to use in your pizza delivery business.

9. Suppose that Intel is considering building a new chip-making factory.
    a. Assuming that Intel needs to borrow money in the bond market, why would an increase in interest rates affect Intel's decision about whether to build the factory?
    b. If Intel has enough of its own funds to finance the new factory without borrowing, would an increase in interest rates still affect Intel's decision about whether to build the factory? Explain.

10. Suppose the government borrows $20 billion more next year than this year.
    a. Use a supply-and-demand diagram to analyze this policy. Does the interest rate rise or fall?
    b. What happens to investment? To private saving? To public saving? To national saving? Compare the size of the changes to the $20 billion of extra government borrowing.

    c. How does the elasticity of supply of loanable funds affect the size of these changes? (Hint: See Chapter 5 to review the definition of elasticity.)
    d. How does the elasticity of demand for loanable funds affect the size of these changes?
    e. Suppose households believe that greater government borrowing today implies higher taxes to pay off the government debt in the future. What does this belief do to private saving and the supply of loanable funds today? Does it increase or decrease the effects you discussed in parts (a) and (b)?

11. Over the past ten years, new computer technology has enabled firms to reduce substantially the amount of inventories they hold for each dollar of sales. Illustrate the effect of this change on the market for loanable funds. (Hint: Expenditure on inventories is a type of investment.) What do you think has been the effect on investment in factories and equipment?

12. "Some economists worry that the aging populations of industrial countries are going to start running down their savings just when the investment appetite of emerging economies is growing" (*Economist,* May 6, 1995). Illustrate the effect of these phenomena on the world market for loanable funds.

13. This chapter explains that investment can be increased both by reducing taxes on private saving and by reducing the government budget deficit.
    a. Why is it difficult to implement both of these policies at the same time?
    b. What would you need to know about private saving in order to judge which of these two policies would be a more effective way to raise investment?

26

THE NATURAL RATE OF UNEMPLOYMENT

Losing a job can be the most distressing economic event in a person's life. Most people rely on their labor earnings to maintain their standard of living, and many people get from their work not only income but also a sense of personal accomplishment. A job loss means a lower living standard in the present, anxiety about the future, and reduced self-esteem. It is not surprising, therefore, that politicians campaigning for office often speak about how their proposed policies will help create jobs.

In the last two chapters we have seen some of the forces that determine the level and growth of a country's standard of living. A country that saves and invests a high fraction of its income, for instance, enjoys more rapid growth in its capital stock and its GDP than a similar country that saves and invests less. An even more obvious determinant of a country's standard of living is the amount of unemployment it typically experiences. People who would like to work but cannot find a job are not contributing to the economy's production of goods and services. Although some degree of unemployment is inevitable in a complex economy with thousands of firms and millions of workers, the amount of unemployment varies substantially over time and across countries. When a country keeps its workers as fully employed as possible, it achieves a higher level of GDP than it would if it left many of its workers standing idle.

This chapter begins our study of unemployment. The problem of unemployment is usefully divided into two categories—the long-run problem and the short-run problem. The economy's *natural rate of unemployment* refers to the amount of unemployment that the economy normally experiences. *Cyclical unemployment* refers to the year-to-year fluctuations in unemployment around its natural rate, and it is closely associated with the short-run ups and downs of economic activity. Cyclical unemployment has its own explanation, which we defer until we study short-run economic fluctuations later in this book. In this chapter we discuss the determinants of an economy's natural rate of unemployment. As we will see, the designation *natural* does not in any way imply that this rate of unemployment is desirable or inevitable. It merely means that this unemployment does not go away on its own even in the long run.

We begin the chapter by looking at some of the relevant facts that describe unemployment. In particular, we examine three questions: How does the government measure the economy's rate of unemployment? What problems arise in interpreting the unemployment data? How long are the unemployed typically without work?

We then turn to the reasons why economies always experience some unemployment and the ways in which policymakers can help the unemployed. We discuss four explanations for the economy's natural rate of unemployment: minimum-wage laws, unions, efficiency wages, and job search. As we will see, long-run unemployment does not arise from a single problem that has a single solution. Instead, it reflects a variety of related problems. As a result, there is no easy way for policymakers to reduce the economy's natural rate of unemployment and, at the same time, to alleviate the hardships experienced by the unemployed.

IDENTIFYING UNEMPLOYMENT

We begin this chapter by examining more precisely what the term *unemployment* means. We consider how the government measures unemployment, what problems arise in interpreting the unemployment data, and how long the typical spell of unemployment lasts.

HOW IS UNEMPLOYMENT MEASURED?

Measuring unemployment is the job of the Bureau of Labor Statistics (BLS), which is part of the Department of Labor. Every month the BLS produces data on unemployment and on other aspects of the labor market, such as types of employment, length of the average workweek, and the duration of unemployment. These data come from a regular survey of about 60,000 households, called the Current Population Survey.

Based on the answers to survey questions, the BLS places each adult (aged sixteen and older) in each surveyed household into one of three categories:

- Employed
- Unemployed
- Not in the labor force

A person is considered employed if he or she spent most of the previous week working at a paid job. A person is unemployed if he or she is on temporary lay-off, is looking for a job, or is waiting for the start date of a new job. A person who fits neither of the first two categories, such as a full-time student, home-maker, or retiree, is not in the labor force. Figure 26-1 shows this breakdown for 1995.

Once the BLS has placed all the individuals covered by the survey in a category, it computes various statistics to summarize the state of the labor market. The BLS defines the **labor force** as the sum of the employed and the unemployed:

labor force
the total number of workers, including both the employed and the unemployed

$$\text{Labor force} = \text{Number of employed} + \text{Number of unemployed}.$$

The BLS defines the **unemployment rate** as the percentage of the labor force that is unemployed:

unemployment rate
the percentage of the labor force that is unemployed

$$\text{Unemployment rate} = \frac{\text{Number of unemployed}}{\text{Labor force}} \times 100.$$

The BLS computes unemployment rates for the entire adult population and for more narrow groups—blacks, whites, men, women, and so on.

The BLS uses the same survey to produce data on labor-force participation. The **labor-force participation rate** measures the percentage of the total adult population of the United States that is in the labor force:

labor-force participation rate
the percentage of the adult population that is in the labor force

Figure 26-1

THE BREAKDOWN OF THE POPULATION IN 1995. The Bureau of Labor Statistics divides the adult population into three categories: employed, unemployed, and not in the labor force.

SOURCE: Bureau of Labor Statistics.

Adult population (198.6 million)

Employed (124.9 million)

Unemployed (7.4 million)

Not in labor force (66.3 million)

Labor force (132.3 million)

$$\text{Labor-force participation rate} = \frac{\text{Labor force}}{\text{Adult population}} \times 100.$$

This statistic tells us the fraction of the population that has chosen to participate in the labor market. The labor-force participation rate, like the unemployment rate, is computed both for the entire adult population and for more narrow groups.

To see how these data are computed, consider the figures for 1995. In that year, 124.9 million people were employed, and 7.4 million people were unemployed. The labor force was

$$\text{Labor force} = 124.9 + 7.4 = 132.3 \text{ million.}$$

The unemployment rate was

$$\text{Unemployment rate} = (7.4/132.3) \times 100 = 5.6\%.$$

Because the adult population was 198.6 million, the labor-force participation rate was

$$\text{Labor-force participation rate} = (132.3/198.6) \times 100 = 66.6\%.$$

Hence, in 1995, two-thirds of the U.S. adult population were participating in the labor market, and 5.6 percent of those labor-market participants were without work.

Table 26-1 shows the statistics on unemployment and labor-force participation for various groups within the U.S. population. Three comparisons are most

Table 26-1

THE LABOR-MARKET EXPERIENCES OF VARIOUS DEMOGRAPHIC GROUPS. This table shows the unemployment rate and the labor-force participation rate of various groups in the population for 1995.

DEMOGRAPHIC GROUP	UNEMPLOYMENT RATE	LABOR-FORCE PARTICIPATION RATE
ADULTS (AGES 16 AND OVER)		
Total	5.6%	66.6%
White, male	4.9	75.7
White, female	4.8	59.0
Black, male	10.6	69.0
Black, female	10.2	59.5
TEENAGERS (AGES 16–19)		
Total	17.3	53.5
White, male	15.6	58.5
White, female	13.4	55.5
Black, male	37.1	40.1
Black, female	34.3	39.8

SOURCE: Bureau of Labor Statistics.

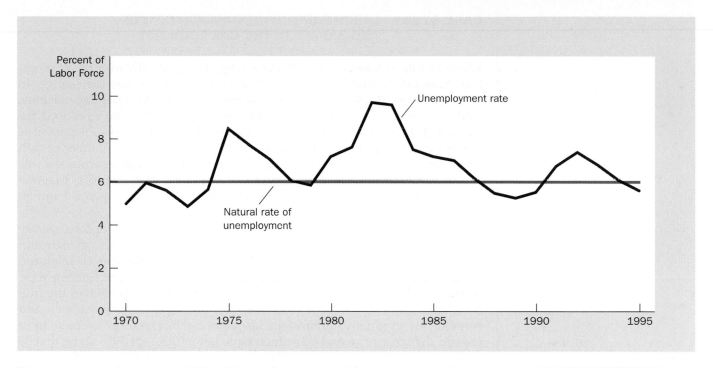

UNEMPLOYMENT RATE SINCE 1970. This graph uses annual data on the unemployment rate to show the fraction of the labor force without a job.

SOURCE: U.S. Department of Labor.

Figure 26-2

apparent. First, women have lower rates of labor-force participation than men, but once in the labor force, women have similar rates of unemployment. Second, blacks have somewhat lower rates of labor-force participation than whites, and they have much higher rates of unemployment. Third, teenagers have lower rates of labor-force participation and much higher rates of unemployment than the overall population. More generally, these data show that labor-market experiences vary widely among groups within the economy.

The BLS data on the labor market also allow economists and policymakers to monitor changes in the economy over time. Figure 26-2 shows the unemployment rate in the United States since 1970. The figure shows that the economy always has some unemployment and that the amount changes from year to year. The normal rate of unemployment around which the unemployment rate fluctuates is called the **natural rate of unemployment,** and the deviation of unemployment from its natural rate is called **cyclical unemployment.** In the figure, the natural rate is shown as a horizontal line at 6 percent, which is a rough estimate of the natural rate for the U.S. economy during this period. Later in this book we discuss short-run economic fluctuations, including the year-to-year fluctuations in unemployment around its natural rate. In the rest of this chapter, however, we ignore the short-run fluctuations and examine why unemployment is a chronic problem for market economies.

natural rate of unemployment
the normal rate of unemployment around which the unemployment rate fluctuates

cyclical unemployment
the deviation of unemployment from its natural rate

CASE STUDY   LABOR-FORCE PARTICIPATION OF MEN AND WOMEN IN THE U.S. ECONOMY

Women's role in American society has changed dramatically over the past century. Social commentators have pointed to many causes for this change. In part, it is attributable to new technologies, such as the washing machine, clothes dryer, refrigerator, freezer, and dishwasher, which have reduced the amount of time required to complete routine household tasks. In part, it is attributable to improved birth control, which has reduced the number of children born to the typical family. And, of course, this change in women's role is also partly attributable to changing political and social attitudes. Together these developments have had a profound impact on society in general and on the economy in particular.

Nowhere is that impact more obvious than in data on labor-force participation. Figure 26-3 shows the labor-force participation rates of men and women in the United States since 1950. Just after World War II, men and women had very different roles in society. Only 33 percent of women were working or looking for work, in contrast to 87 percent of men. Over the past several decades, the difference between the participation rates of men and women has gradually diminished, as growing numbers of women have entered the labor force and some men have left it. Data for 1995 show that 59 percent of women were in the labor force, in contrast to 75 percent of men. As measured by labor-force participation, men and women are now playing a more equal role in the economy.

The increase in women's labor-force participation is easy to understand, but the fall in men's may seem puzzling. There are several reasons for this decline. First, young men now stay in school longer than their fathers and grandfathers did. Second, older men now retire earlier and live longer. Third,

Figure 26-3

Labor-Force Participation Rates for Men and Women since 1950. Over the past several decades, women have entered the labor force, and men have left it.

Source: U.S. Department of Labor.

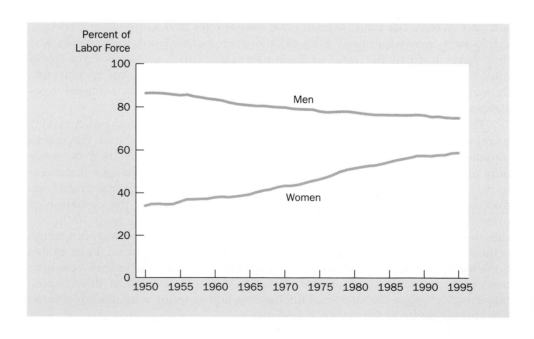

with more women employed, more fathers now stay at home to raise their children. Full-time students, retirees, and stay-at-home fathers are all counted as out of the labor force.

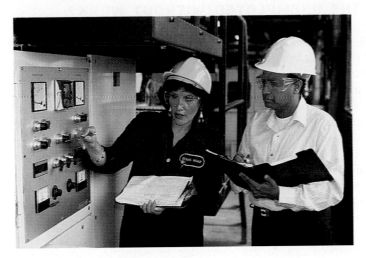

More women are working now than ever before.

IS UNEMPLOYMENT MEASURED CORRECTLY?

Measuring the amount of unemployment in the economy might seem straightforward. In fact, it is not. While it is easy to distinguish between a person with a full-time job and a person who is not working at all, it is much harder to distinguish between a person who is unemployed and a person who is not in the labor force.

Movements into and out of the labor force are, in fact, very common. More than one-third of the unemployed are recent entrants into the labor force. These entrants include young workers looking for their first jobs, such as recent college graduates. They also include, in greater numbers, older workers who had previously left the labor force but have now returned to look for work. Moreover, not all unemployment ends with the job seeker finding a job. Almost half of all spells of unemployment end when the unemployed person leaves the labor force.

Because people move into and out of the labor force so often, statistics on unemployment are difficult to interpret. On the one hand, some of those who report being unemployed may not, in fact, be trying hard to find a job. They may be calling themselves unemployed in order to qualify for one of the government programs that provide financial assistance for the unemployed. It would be more realistic to view some of these individuals as out of the labor force. On the other hand, some of those who report being out of the labor force may, in fact, want to work. These individuals may have tried to find a job but have given up after an unsuccessful search. Such individuals, called **discouraged workers,** do not show up in unemployment statistics, even though they are truly workers without jobs.

There is no easy way to fix the unemployment rate as reported by the BLS to make it a more reliable indicator of conditions in the labor market. In the end,

discouraged workers
individuals who would like to work but have given up looking for a job

it is best to view the reported unemployment rate as a useful but imperfect measure of joblessness.

HOW LONG ARE THE UNEMPLOYED WITHOUT WORK?

In judging how serious the problem of unemployment is, one question to consider is whether unemployment is typically a short-term or long-term condition. If unemployment is short-term, one might conclude that it is not a big problem. Workers may require a few weeks between jobs to find the openings that best suit their skills and tastes. Yet if unemployment is long-term, one might conclude that it is a serious problem. Workers unemployed for many months are more likely to suffer economic and psychological hardship.

Because the duration of unemployment can affect our view about how big a problem unemployment is, economists have devoted much energy to studying data on the duration of unemployment spells. In this work, they have uncovered a result that is important, subtle, and seemingly contradictory: *Most spells of unemployment are short, and most unemployment observed at any given time is long-term.*

To see how this statement can be true, consider an example. Suppose that you visited the government's unemployment office every week for a year to survey the unemployed. Each week you find that there are four unemployed workers. Three of these workers are the same individuals for the whole year, while the fourth person changes every week. Based on this experience, would you say that unemployment is typically short-term or long-term?

Some simple calculations help answer this question. In this example, you meet a total of 55 unemployed people; 52 of them are unemployed for 1 week, and 3 are unemployed for the full year. Thus, 52/55, or 95 percent, of unemployment spells end in 1 week. That is, most spells of unemployment are short. Yet consider the total amount of unemployment. The 3 people unemployed for 1 year (52 weeks) make up a total of 156 weeks of unemployment. Together with the 52 people unemployed for 1 week, this makes 208 weeks of unemployment. In this example, 156/208, or 75 percent, of unemployment is attributable to those individuals who are unemployed for a full year. Thus, most unemployment observed at any given time is long-term.

This subtle conclusion implies that economists and policymakers must be careful when interpreting data on unemployment and when designing policies to help the unemployed. Most people who become unemployed will soon find jobs. Yet most of the economy's unemployment problem is attributable to the relatively few workers who are jobless for long periods of time.

WHY IS THERE UNEMPLOYMENT?

We have discussed how the government measures the amount of unemployment, the problems that arise in interpreting unemployment statistics, and the findings of labor economists on the duration of unemployment. You should now have a good idea about what unemployment is.

This discussion, however, has not explained why economies experience unemployment. In most markets in the economy, prices adjust to bring quantity supplied and quantity demanded into balance. In an ideal labor market, wages would adjust to balance the quantity of labor supplied and the quantity of labor demanded. This adjustment of wages would ensure that all workers are always fully employed.

Of course, reality does not resemble this ideal. There are always some workers without jobs, even when the overall economy is doing well. In other words, the unemployment rate never falls to zero; instead, it fluctuates around the natural rate of unemployment. To understand this natural rate, we now examine four reasons why actual labor markets depart from the ideal of full employment: minimum-wage laws, unions, efficiency wages, and job search.

QUICK QUIZ How is the unemployment rate measured? ◆ How might the unemployment rate overstate the amount of joblessness? How might it understate it?

MINIMUM-WAGE LAWS

We begin by reviewing how unemployment arises from minimum-wage laws—a topic we first analyzed in Chapter 6. Although minimum wages are not the predominant reason for unemployment in our economy, they do have an important effect on certain groups with particularly high unemployment rates. Moreover, the analysis of minimum wages is a natural place to start because, as we will see, it can be used to understand some of the more common reasons for unemployment.

Figure 26-4 reviews the basic economics of a minimum wage. When a minimum-wage law forces the wage to remain above the level that balances supply

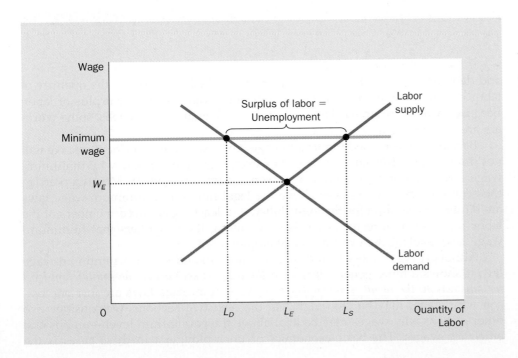

Figure 26-4

UNEMPLOYMENT FROM A WAGE ABOVE THE EQUILIBRIUM LEVEL. In this labor market, the wage at which supply and demand balance is W_E. At this equilibrium wage, the quantity of labor supplied and the quantity of labor demanded both equal L_E. By contrast, if the wage is forced to remain above the equilibrium level, perhaps because of a minimum-wage law, the quantity of labor supplied rises to L_S, and the quantity of labor demanded falls to L_D. The resulting excess supply of labor, $L_S - L_D$, represents unemployment.

IN THE NEWS

The

Minimum-Wage

Debate

IN 1996, AS THE PRESIDENTIAL CAMPAIGN was heating up, the minimum wage became a topic of debate. Most Democrats in Congress supported an increase in the minimum wage, while most Republicans opposed it. Eventually, an increase in the minimum wage was passed by Congress and signed by President Clinton. The following article describes some of the issues in this debate.

Thesis: Rise in Wages Will Hurt Teenage Group

BY ROBERT D. HERSHEY, JR.

At one time, Sidewinder Pumps Inc., in Lafayette, La., would hire a dozen or more young people to work each summer at minimum-wage jobs like weeding or expanding the parking lot—tasks that were not really essential to the company but that let it give teenagers a taste of what paid work is like.

When the federal minimum wage went up in the early 1990s, the company cut back to three or four summer workers. And this year, the prospect of another increase led the company to end this quarter-century tradition. "We don't have any part-timers," said Ernie George, a co-owner of Sidewinder.

As the Senate prepares to vote today on another round of increases, to $4.75, probably within a month of passage, and then to $5.15 next year, most of the incendiary political and economic debate has dissolved into an inconclu-

"IF THE GOVERNMENT RAISED MY WAGE, WOULD I STILL HAVE A JOB?"

sive statistical battle over whether the move will hurt more workers than it helps.

But some economists point to employment figures to argue that however lightly a higher minimum wage may weigh on the economy at large, in the past it has fallen heavily on teenagers,

and demand, it raises the quantity of labor supplied and reduces the quantity of labor demanded compared to the equilibrium level. There is a surplus of labor. Because there are more workers willing to work than there are jobs, some workers are unemployed.

Because we discussed minimum-wage laws extensively in Chapter 6, we will not discuss them further here. It is, however, important to note why minimum-wage laws are not a predominant reason for unemployment: Most workers in the economy have wages well above the legal minimum. Minimum-wage laws are binding most often for the least skilled and least experienced members of the labor force, such as teenagers. It is only among these workers that minimum-wage laws explain the existence of unemployment.

Although Figure 26-4 was drawn to show the effects of a minimum-wage law, it shows a more general lesson: *If the wage is kept above the equilibrium level for any reason, the result is unemployment.* Minimum-wage laws are just one reason why wages may be "too high." In the next two sections, we consider two other reasons why wages may be kept above the equilibrium level—unions and efficiency wages. The basic economics of unemployment in these cases is the especially black teenagers, and on adults with little education. These are groups often also pointed to as having the greatest need to learn basic job habits, such as the importance of showing up regularly and on time.

A look at what happened after the last round of increases—to $3.80 in April 1990 and to $4.25 in April 1991—shows how sharply the bottom end of the job market can contract, especially when this disincentive to hire workers coincides with an economic downturn.

While almost nobody argues that the higher minimum wage contributed significantly to the latest recession, which was ultimately determined to have lasted from July 1990 to March 1991, the higher wage does seem to have coincided with a marked worsening of the job market for the youngest and least skilled.

In March 1990, just before the federal government raised the minimum to $3.80 from $3.35, 47.1 percent of teenagers had jobs, but that promptly began a slide that carried it down to less than 43 percent a year later, when the $4.25 wage kicked in. The figure then tumbled to 39.8 percent by June 1992 before slowly recovering to 43.2 percent now.

"The timing of the drop in teenage employment is absolutely coincident with the increase in the minimum, whereas for other groups the recession's bite was delayed," declared Finis Welch, an economics professor at Texas A&M University and a prominent student of the subject. . . .

Those who support raising the minimum wage, which is paid more in the South than in other regions, contend that it will help millions of workers at the bottom of the economic ladder, allowing many to avoid welfare.

They join Labor Secretary Robert B. Reich in dismissing likely job loss as "negligible" and in denying any concentration of effects. "One never knows for particular groups," Mr. Reich said in an interview.

And Joseph E. Stiglitz, head of President Clinton's Council of Economic Advisers, insisted, "The evidence is just very ambiguous. . . ."

The idea that an increase in the minimum wage would cost jobs found a great deal of skepticism as well among a number of black teenagers working at such jobs yesterday in Silver Spring, Md. That danger appeared remote next to the tangible benefits they saw from what they considered a long-overdue increase.

"I know plenty of kids who are trying to save money for college and other things, so any increase in the minimum wage will be greatly appreciated," said Lamont Smith, who will begin college this fall.

A coworker chimed in: "I don't know what all the fuss is about. This increase can go a long way to helping me get to the next level."

SOURCE: *The New York Times*, July 9, 1996, pp. D1, D18.

same as that shown in Figure 26-4, but these explanations of unemployment can apply to many more of the economy's workers.

QUICK QUIZ Draw the supply curve and the demand curve for a labor market in which the wage is fixed above the equilibrium level. Show the quantity of labor supplied, the quantity demanded, and the amount of unemployment.

UNIONS AND COLLECTIVE BARGAINING

A **union** is a worker association that bargains with employers over wages and working conditions. Whereas only 16 percent of U.S. workers now belong to unions, unions played a much larger role in the U.S. labor market in the past. In

union
a worker association that bargains with employers over wages and working conditions

the 1940s and 1950s, when unions were at their peak, about a third of the U.S. labor force was unionized. Moreover, unions continue to play a large role in many European countries. In Sweden and Denmark, for instance, more than three-fourths of workers belong to unions.

THE ECONOMICS OF UNIONS

collective bargaining

the process by which unions and firms agree on the terms of employment

strike

the organized withdrawal of labor from a firm by a union

A union is a type of cartel. Like any cartel, a union is a group of sellers acting together in the hope of exerting their joint market power. Most workers in the economy discuss their wages, benefits, and working conditions with their employers as individuals. By contrast, workers in a union do so as a group. The process by which unions and firms agree on the terms of employment is called **collective bargaining.**

When a union bargains with a firm, it asks for higher wages, better benefits, and better working conditions than the firm would offer in the absence of a union. If the union and the firm do not reach agreement, the union can organize a withdrawal of labor from the firm, called a **strike.** Because a strike reduces production, sales, and profit, a firm facing a strike threat is likely to agree to pay higher wages than it otherwise would. Economists who study the effects of unions typically find that union workers earn about 10 to 20 percent more than similar workers who do not belong to unions.

When a union raises the wage above the equilibrium level, it raises the quantity of labor supplied and reduces the quantity of labor demanded, resulting in unemployment. Those workers who remain employed are better off, but those who were previously employed and are now unemployed at the higher wage are worse off. Indeed, unions are often thought to cause conflict between different groups of workers—between the *insiders* who benefit from high union wages and the *outsiders* who do not get the union jobs.

The outsiders can respond to their status in one of two ways. Some of them remain unemployed and wait for the chance to become insiders and earn the high union wage. Others take jobs in firms that are not unionized. Thus, when unions raise wages in one part of the economy, the supply of labor increases in other parts of the economy. This increase in labor supply, in turn, reduces wages in industries that are not unionized. In other words, workers in unions reap the benefit of collective bargaining, while workers not in unions bear some of the cost.

The role of unions in the economy depends in part on the laws that govern union organization and collective bargaining. Normally, explicit agreements among members of a cartel are illegal. If firms that sell a common product were to agree to set a high price for that product, the agreement would be a "conspiracy in restraint of trade." The government would prosecute these firms in civil and criminal court for violating the antitrust laws. By contrast, unions are exempt from these laws. The policymakers who wrote the antitrust laws believed that workers needed greater market power as they bargained with employers. Indeed, various laws are designed to encourage the formation of unions. In particular, the Wagner Act of 1935 prevents employers from interfering when workers try to organize unions and requires employers to bargain with unions in good faith. The National Labor Relations Board (NLRB) is the government agency that enforces workers' right to unionize.

Legislation affecting the market power of unions is a perennial topic of political debate. State lawmakers sometimes debate *right-to-work laws,* which give workers in a unionized firm the right to choose whether to join the union. In the absence of such laws, unions can insist during collective bargaining that firms make union membership a requirement for employment. In recent years, lawmakers in Washington have debated a proposed law that would prevent firms from hiring permanent replacements for workers who are on strike. This law would make strikes more costly for firms and, thereby, would increase the market power of unions. These and similar policy decisions will help determine the future of the union movement.

ARE UNIONS GOOD OR BAD FOR THE ECONOMY?

Economists disagree about whether unions are good or bad for the economy as a whole. Let's consider both sides of the debate.

Critics of unions argue that unions are merely a type of cartel. When unions raise wages above the level that would prevail in competitive markets, they reduce the quantity of labor demanded, cause some workers to be unemployed, and reduce the wages in the rest of the economy. The resulting allocation of labor is, critics argue, both inefficient and inequitable. It is inefficient because high union wages reduce employment in unionized firms below the efficient, competitive level. It is inequitable because some workers benefit at the expense of other workers.

Advocates of unions contend that unions are a necessary antidote to the market power of the firms that hire workers. The extreme case of this market power is the "company town," where a single firm does most of the hiring in a geographic region. In a company town, if workers do not accept the wages and working conditions that the firm offers, they have little choice but to move or stop working. In the absence of a union, therefore, the firm could use its market power to pay lower wages and offer worse working conditions than would prevail if it had to compete with other firms for the same workers. In this case, a union may balance the firm's market power and protect the workers from being at the mercy of the firm owners.

Advocates of unions also claim that unions are important for helping firms respond efficiently to workers' concerns. Whenever a worker takes a job, the worker and the firm must agree on many attributes of the job in addition to the wage: hours of work, overtime, vacations, sick leave, health benefits, promotion schedules, job security, and so on. By representing workers' views on these issues, unions allow firms to provide the right mix of job attributes. Even if unions have the adverse effect of pushing wages above the equilibrium level and causing unemployment, they have the benefit of helping firms keep a happy and productive workforce.

In the end, there is no consensus among economists about whether unions are good or bad for the economy. Like many institutions, their influence is probably beneficial in some circumstances and adverse in others.

QUICK QUIZ   How does a union in the auto industry affect wages and employment at General Motors and Ford? How does it affect wages and employment in other industries?

IN THE NEWS

The UAW's

Tradeoff

UNION NEGOTIATORS KNOW WELL THAT higher wages mean fewer jobs. The following article discusses a 1996 agreement with Ford Motor Company in which the United Auto Workers union accepted lower wages in exchange for some job guarantees.

New Approach for Auto Union in Ford Accord—The Deal: No Job Cuts but Less Pay for Some

BY KEITH BRADSHER

DETROIT—The new contract between the Ford Motor Company and the United Automobile Workers union addresses two issues that have haunted organized labor for more than a decade: layoffs and moves by companies to rely more on outside suppliers.

The new contract, reached Monday evening, requires Ford to guarantee a minimum number of union jobs, while adding incentives for the company to produce more auto parts itself.

All this runs counter to a trend in which Detroit's automakers have halved their workforces over the last 15 years partly by closing or selling parts factories, while buying more parts from nonunion suppliers.

In exchange for the employment guarantee, the UAW decided to let Ford pay permanently lower wages in any new auto parts businesses that it enters.

What remains unclear is whether the Ford deal will set a precedent for other companies, both inside and outside the auto industry. Only a tenth of the nation's private-sector workforce is unionized and there are few other industries where unions hold so much power.

The first test for the union will come quickly as it tries to impose similar settlements on the General Motors Corporation and the Chrysler Corporation. Analysts said GM in particular would be hard pressed to accept such a deal because the company was trying to cut its workforce and rely less on its own auto parts manufacturing operations.

And beyond the automakers, the Ford contract might have much weaker influence, even in those industries in which the UAW represents workers. For example, Caterpillar, Inc., a maker of heavy equipment, was able to hire replacement workers and continue doing business last year despite a UAW strike.

"I think that may be the model to look at, rather than Ford," said Sharon F. Canner, the vice president for human resources policy at the National Association of Manufacturers in Washington. . . .

The new arrangement could still run into problems. The UAW long resisted lower wages for auto parts workers, fearing friction between low-wage and high-wage workers in the same union. But that friction could now be limited given that the low-wage workers will be mainly in new Ford factories and may seldom meet high-wage workers.

In an interview on September 5, Alexander Trotman, Ford's chairman, chief executive, and president, said Ford would be more interested in entering new parts businesses if the union allowed lower wages. "To the degree that we can figure out how to make widgets much more effectively than we do today, it increases the likelihood we're going to make more of those widgets and even make widgets we're not making today," he said.

SOURCE: *The New York Times,* September 18, 1996, p. A1.

THE THEORY OF EFFICIENCY WAGES

efficiency wages

above-equilibrium wages paid by firms in order to increase worker productivity

A third reason why economies always experience some unemployment is suggested by the theory of **efficiency wages.** According to this theory, firms operate more efficiently if wages are above the equilibrium level. Therefore, it may be profitable for firms to keep wages high even in the presence of an excess supply of labor.

In some ways, the unemployment that arises from efficiency wages is similar to the unemployment that arises from minimum-wage laws and unions. In all three cases, unemployment is the result of wages above the level that balances the quantity of labor supplied and the quantity of labor demanded. Yet there is also an important difference. Minimum-wage laws and unions prevent firms from lowering wages in the presence of a surplus of workers. Efficiency-wage theory states that such a constraint on firms is unnecessary in many cases because firms may be better off keeping wages above the equilibrium level.

Why should firms want to keep wages high? In some ways, this decision seems odd, for wages are a large part of firms' costs. Normally, we expect profit-maximizing firms to want to keep costs—and therefore wages—as low as possible. The novel insight of efficiency-wage theory is that paying high wages might be profitable because they might raise the efficiency of a firm's workers.

There are several types of efficiency-wage theory. Each type suggests a different explanation for why firms may want to pay high wages. Let's now consider four of these types.

WORKER HEALTH

The first and simplest type of efficiency-wage theory emphasizes the link between wages and worker health. Better paid workers eat a more nutritious diet, and workers who eat a better diet are healthier and more productive. A firm may find it more profitable to pay high wages and have healthy, productive workers than to pay lower wages and have less healthy, less productive workers.

This type of efficiency-wage theory is not relevant for firms in rich countries such as the United States. In these countries, the equilibrium wages for most workers are well above the level needed for an adequate diet. Firms are not concerned that paying equilibrium wages would place their workers' health in jeopardy.

This type of efficiency-wage theory is more relevant for firms in less developed countries where inadequate nutrition is a more common problem. Unemployment is high in the cities of many poor African countries, for example. In these countries, firms may fear that cutting wages would, in fact, adversely influence their workers' health and productivity. In other words, concern over nutrition may explain why firms do not cut wages despite a surplus of labor.

WORKER TURNOVER

A second type of efficiency-wage theory emphasizes the link between wages and worker turnover. Workers quit jobs for many reasons—to take jobs in other firms, to move to other parts of the country, to leave the labor force, and so on. The frequency with which they quit depends on the entire set of incentives they face, including the benefits of leaving and the benefits of staying. The more a firm pays its workers, the less often its workers will choose to leave. Thus, a firm can reduce turnover among its workers by paying them a high wage.

Why do firms care about turnover? The reason is that it is costly for firms to hire and train new workers. Moreover, even after they are trained, newly hired workers are not as productive as experienced workers. Firms with higher turnover, therefore, will tend to have higher production costs. Firms may find it profitable to pay wages above the equilibrium level in order to reduce worker turnover.

WORKER EFFORT

A third type of efficiency-wage theory emphasizes the link between wages and worker effort. In many jobs, workers have some discretion over how hard to work. As a result, firms monitor the efforts of their workers, and workers caught shirking their responsibilities are fired. But not all shirkers are caught immediately because monitoring workers is costly and imperfect. A firm can respond to this problem by paying wages above the equilibrium level. High wages make workers more eager to keep their jobs and, thereby, give workers an incentive to put forward their best effort.

This particular type of efficiency-wage theory is similar to the old Marxist idea of the "reserve army of the unemployed." Marx thought that employers benefited from unemployment because the threat of unemployment helped to discipline those workers who had jobs. In the worker-effort variant of efficiency-wage theory, unemployment fills a similar role. If the wage were at the level that balanced supply and demand, workers would have less reason to work hard because if they were fired, they could quickly find new jobs at the same wage. Therefore, firms raise wages above the equilibrium level, causing unemployment and providing an incentive for workers not to shirk their responsibilities.

WORKER QUALITY

A fourth and final type of efficiency-wage theory emphasizes the link between wages and worker quality. When a firm hires new workers, it cannot perfectly gauge the quality of the applicants. By paying a high wage, the firm attracts a better pool of workers to apply for its jobs.

To see how this might work, consider a simple example. Waterwell Company owns one well and needs one worker to pump water from the well. Two workers, Bill and Ted, are interested in the job. Bill, a proficient worker, is willing to work for $10 per hour. Below that wage, he would rather start his own lawn-mowing business. Ted, a complete incompetent, is willing to work for anything above $2 per hour. Below that wage, he would rather sit on the beach. Economists say that Bill's *reservation wage*—the lowest wage he would accept— is $10, and Ted's reservation wage is $2.

DILBERT By Scott Adams

What wage should the firm set? If the firm were interested in minimizing labor costs, it would set the wage at $2 per hour. At this wage, the quantity of workers supplied (one) would balance the quantity demanded. Ted would take the job, and Bill would not apply for it. Yet suppose Waterwell knows that only

FYI

The Economics of Asymmetric Information

IN MANY SITUATIONS IN LIFE, information is asymmetric: One person in a transaction knows more about what is going on than the other person. This possibility raises a variety of interesting problems for economic theory. We have just seen some of these problems raised in the context of developing the theory of efficiency wages. These problems, however, go beyond the study of unemployment.

The worker-quality variant of efficiency-wage theory illustrates a general principle called *adverse selection*. Adverse selection arises when one person knows more about the attributes of a good than another and, as a result, the uninformed person runs the risk of being sold a good of low quality. In the worker-quality story, for instance, workers have better information about their own abilities than firms do. When a firm cuts the wage it pays, the selection of workers changes in a way that is adverse to the firm.

Adverse selection arises in many other circumstances. Here are two examples:

- Sellers of used cars know their cars' defects while buyers often do not. Because owners of the worst cars are more likely to sell them than are the owners of the best cars, car buyers are correctly apprehensive about getting a "lemon." As a result, many people avoid buying cars in the used car market.

- Buyers of health insurance know more about their own health problems than do insurance companies. Because people with greater hidden health problems are more likely to buy health insurance than are other people, the price of health insurance reflects the costs of a sicker-than-average person. As a result, people with average health problems are discouraged from buying health insurance.

In each case, the market for the product—used cars or health insurance—does not work as well as it might because of the problem of adverse selection.

Similarly, the worker-effort variant of efficiency-wage theory illustrates a general phenomenon called *moral hazard.* Moral hazard arises when one person, called the *agent*, is performing some task on behalf of another person, called the *principal.* Because the principal cannot perfectly monitor the agent's behavior, the agent tends to undertake less effort than the principal considers desirable. The term *moral hazard* refers to the risk of dishonest or otherwise inappropriate behavior by the agent. In such a situation, the principal tries various ways to encourage the agent to act more responsibly.

In an employment relationship, the firm is the principal and the worker is the agent. The moral-hazard problem is the temptation of imperfectly monitored workers to shirk their responsibilities. According to the worker-effort variant of efficiency-wage theory, the principal can encourage the agent not to shirk by paying a wage above the equilibrium level because then the agent has more to lose if caught shirking. In this way, high wages reduce the problem of moral hazard.

Moral hazard arises in many other situations. Here are some examples:

- A homeowner with fire insurance buys too few fire extinguishers. The reason is that the homeowner bears the cost of the extinguisher while the insurance company receives much of the benefit.

- A babysitter allows children to watch more television than the parents of the children prefer. The reason is that more educational activities require more energy from the babysitter, even though they are beneficial for the children.

- A family lives near a river with a high risk of flooding. The reason it continues to live there is that the family enjoys the scenic views, and the government will bear part of the cost when it provides disaster relief after a flood.

Can you identify the principal and the agent in each of these situations? How do you think the principal in each case might solve the problem of moral hazard?

one of these two applicants is competent, but it does not know whether it is Bill or Ted. If the firm hires the incompetent worker, he will damage the well, causing the firm huge losses. In this case, the firm has a better strategy than paying the equilibrium wage of $2 and hiring Ted. It can offer $10 per hour, inducing both Bill and Ted to apply for the job. By choosing randomly between these two applicants and turning the other away, the firm has a fifty-fifty chance of hiring the competent one. By contrast, if the firm offers any lower wage, it is sure to hire the incompetent worker.

This story illustrates a general phenomenon. When a firm has an excess supply of workers, it might seem profitable to reduce the wage it is offering. But by reducing the wage, the firm induces an adverse change in the mix of workers. In this case, at a wage of $10, Waterwell has two workers applying for one job. But if Waterwell responds to this excess supply by reducing the wage, the competent worker (who has better alternative opportunities) will not apply. Thus, it is profitable for the firm to pay a wage above the level that balances supply and demand.

CASE STUDY HENRY FORD AND THE VERY GENEROUS $5-A-DAY WAGE

Henry Ford was an industrial visionary. As founder of the Ford Motor Company, he was responsible for introducing modern techniques of production. Rather than building cars with small teams of skilled craftsmen, Ford built cars on assembly lines in which unskilled workers were taught to perform the same simple tasks over and over again. The output of this assembly process was the Model T Ford, one of the most famous early automobiles.

In 1914, Ford introduced another innovation: the $5 workday. This might not seem like much today, but back then $5 was about twice the going wage. It was also far above the wage that balanced supply and demand. When the new $5-a-day wage was announced, long lines of job seekers formed outside the Ford factories. The number of workers willing to work at this wage far exceeded the number of workers Ford needed.

Ford's high-wage policy had many of the effects predicted by efficiency-wage theory. Turnover fell, absenteeism fell, and productivity rose. Workers were so much more efficient that Ford's production costs were lower even though wages were higher. Thus, paying a wage above the equilibrium level was profitable for the firm. Henry Ford himself called the $5-a-day wage "one of the finest cost-cutting moves we ever made."

Historical accounts of this episode are also consistent with efficiency-wage theory. An historian of the early Ford Motor Company wrote, "Ford and his associates freely declared on many occasions that the high-wage policy turned out to be good business. By this they meant that it had improved the discipline of the workers, given them a more loyal interest in the institution, and raised their personal efficiency."

Why did it take Henry Ford to introduce this efficiency wage? Why were other firms not already taking advantage of this seemingly profitable business strategy? According to some analysts, Ford's decision was closely linked to his use of the assembly line. Workers organized in an assembly line are highly interdependent. If one worker is absent or works slowly, other workers are less able to complete their own tasks. Thus, while assembly lines made production more efficient, they also raised the importance of low worker turnover, high worker quality, and high worker effort. As a result, paying efficiency wages may have been a better strategy for the Ford Motor Company than for other businesses at the time.

An early Ford
assembly line

QUICK QUIZ Give four explanations for why firms might find it profitable to pay wages above the level that balances quantity of labor supplied and quantity of labor demanded.

JOB SEARCH

A fourth reason why economies always experience some unemployment, besides minimum-wage laws, unions, and efficiency wages, is job search. **Job search** is the process of matching workers with appropriate jobs. If all workers and all jobs were the same, so that all workers were equally well suited for all jobs, job search would not be a problem. Laid-off workers would quickly find new jobs that were well suited for them. But, in fact, workers differ in their tastes and skills, jobs differ in their attributes, and information about job candidates and job vacancies is disseminated slowly among the many firms and households in the economy.

The unemployment that arises because of job search is, in an important sense, different from the unemployment that arises because of minimum-wage laws, unions, and efficiency wages. In the previous three cases, the wage is above the equilibrium level, so the quantity of labor supplied exceeds the quantity of labor demanded; workers are unemployed because they are *waiting* for jobs to open up. By contrast, job search is not due to the failure of wages to balance labor supply and labor demand. When job search is the explanation for unemployment, workers are *searching* for the jobs that best suit them.

job search
the process by which workers find appropriate jobs given their tastes and skills

THE INEVITABILITY OF SEARCH UNEMPLOYMENT

Search unemployment is often the result of changes in the demand for labor among different firms. When consumers decide that they prefer Compaq over Dell computers, Compaq increases employment, and Dell lays off workers. The former Dell workers must now search for new jobs, and Compaq must decide which new workers to hire for the various jobs that have opened up. The result of this transition is temporary unemployment.

Similarly, because different regions of the country produce different goods, employment can rise in one region while it falls in another. Consider, for instance, what happens when the world price of oil falls. Oil-producing firms in Texas respond to the lower price by cutting back on production and employment. At the same time, cheaper gasoline stimulates car sales, so auto-producing firms in Michigan raise production and employment. Changes in the composition of demand among industries or regions are called *sectoral shifts*. Because it takes time for workers to search for jobs in the new sectors, sectoral shifts temporarily cause unemployment.

Search unemployment is inevitable simply because the economy is always changing. A century ago, the four industries with the largest employment in the United States were cotton goods, woolen goods, men's clothing, and lumber. Today, the four largest industries are autos, aircraft, communications, and electrical components. As this transition took place, jobs were created in some firms, and jobs were destroyed in others. The end result of this process has been higher productivity and higher living standards. But, along the way, workers in declining industries found themselves out of work and searching for new jobs.

PUBLIC POLICY AND JOB SEARCH

Even if some search unemployment is inevitable, public policy can nonetheless affect its prevalence. To the extent that policy can reduce the time it takes unemployed workers to find new jobs, it can reduce search unemployment.

Government programs try to facilitate job finding in various ways. One way is through government-run employment agencies, which give out information about job vacancies in order to match workers and jobs more quickly. Another way is through public training programs, which aim to ease the transition of workers from declining to growing industries and to help disadvantaged groups escape poverty. The federal government now spends more than $4 billion a year on job training programs, and President Clinton has advocated increased funding.

Critics of these programs question whether the government should get involved with the process of job search. They argue that it is better to let the private market match workers and jobs. In fact, most job search in our economy takes place without intervention by the government. Newspaper ads, job newsletters, college placement offices, headhunters, and word of mouth all help spread information about job openings and job candidates. Similarly, much worker education is done privately, either through schools or through on-the-job training. These critics contend that the government is no better—and most likely worse—at disseminating the right information to the right workers and deciding what kinds of worker training would be most valuable. They claim that these decisions are best made privately by workers and employers.

UNEMPLOYMENT INSURANCE

One government program that increases the amount of search unemployment, without intending to do so, is **unemployment insurance.** This program is designed to offer workers partial protection against job loss. The unemployed who quit their jobs, were fired for cause, or just entered the labor force are not eligible. Benefits are paid only to the unemployed who were laid off because their previous employers no longer needed their skills. Although the terms of the program vary over time and across states, a typical American worker covered by unemployment insurance receives 50 percent of his or her former wages for 26 weeks.

unemployment insurance
a government program that partially protects workers' incomes when they become unemployed

While unemployment insurance reduces the hardship of unemployment, it also increases the amount of unemployment. The explanation is based on one of the *Ten Principles of Economics* in Chapter 1: People respond to incentives. Because unemployment benefits stop when a worker takes a new job, the unemployed devote less effort to job search and are more likely to turn down unattractive job offers. In addition, because unemployment insurance makes unemployment less onerous, workers are less likely to seek guarantees of job security when they negotiate with employers over the terms of employment.

Many studies by labor economists have examined the incentive effects of unemployment insurance. One study examined an experiment run by the state of Illinois in 1985. When unemployed workers applied to collect unemployment insurance benefits, the state randomly selected some of them and offered each a $500 bonus if they found new jobs within 11 weeks. This group was then compared to a control group not offered the incentive. The average spell of unemployment for the group offered the bonus was 7 percent shorter than the average spell for the control group. This experiment shows that the design of the unemployment insurance system influences the effort that the unemployed devote to job search.

Several other studies examined search effort by following a group of workers over time. Unemployment insurance benefits, rather than lasting forever, usually run out after six months or a year. These studies found that when the unemployed become ineligible for benefits, the probability of their finding a new job rises markedly. Thus, receiving unemployment insurance benefits does reduce the search effort of the unemployed.

Even though unemployment insurance reduces search effort and raises unemployment, we should not necessarily conclude that the policy is a bad one. The program does achieve its primary goal of reducing the income uncertainty that workers face. In addition, when workers turn down unattractive job offers, they have the opportunity to look for jobs that better suit their tastes and skills. Some economists have argued that unemployment insurance improves the ability of the economy to match each worker with the most appropriate job.

The study of unemployment insurance shows that the unemployment rate is an imperfect measure of a nation's overall level of economic well-being. Most economists agree that eliminating unemployment insurance would reduce the amount of unemployment in the economy. Yet economists disagree on whether economic well-being would be enhanced or diminished by this change in policy.

QUICK QUIZ How would an increase in the world price of oil affect the amount of search unemployment? Is this unemployment undesirable? What public policies might affect the amount of unemployment caused by this price change?

CONCLUSION

In this chapter we discussed the measurement of unemployment and the reasons why economies always experience some degree of unemployment. We have seen how minimum-wage laws, unions, efficiency wages, and job search can all help explain why some workers do not have jobs. Which of these four explanations for the natural rate of unemployment are the most important for the U.S. economy and other economies around the world? Unfortunately, there is no easy way to tell. Economists therefore differ in which of these explanations of unemployment they consider most important.

Unemployment is not a simple problem with a simple solution. Instead, it has various explanations and is affected by various public policies. When Congress debates the minimum wage, the laws regulating collective bargaining, or unemployment insurance, one issue is always the impact of these policies on the economy's natural rate of unemployment.

Summary

◆ The unemployment rate is the percentage of those who would like to work but do not have jobs. The Bureau of Labor Statistics calculates this statistic monthly based on a survey of thousands of households.

◆ The unemployment rate is an imperfect measure of joblessness. Some people who call themselves unemployed may actually not want to work, and some people who would like to work have left the labor force after an unsuccessful search.

◆ In the U.S. economy, most people who become unemployed find work within a short period of time. Nonetheless, most unemployment observed at any given time is attributable to the few people who are unemployed for long periods of time.

◆ One reason why our economy always has some unemployment is minimum-wage laws. By raising the wage of unskilled and inexperienced workers above the equilibrium level, minimum-wage laws raise the quantity of labor supplied and reduce the quantity demanded. The resulting excess supply of labor represents unemployment.

◆ A second reason for unemployment is the market power of unions. When unions push the wages in unionized industries above the equilibrium level, they create an excess supply of labor.

◆ A third reason for unemployment is suggested by the theory of efficiency wages. According to this theory, firms find it profitable to pay wages above the equilibrium level. High wages can improve worker health, lower worker turnover, increase worker effort, and raise worker quality.

◆ A fourth reason for unemployment is the time it takes for workers to search for jobs that best suit their skills and tastes. Unemployment insurance is a government policy that, while protecting workers' incomes, increases the amount of search unemployment.

Key Concepts

labor force, p. 567
unemployment rate, p. 567
labor-force participation rate, p. 567
natural rate of unemployment, p. 569

cyclical unemployment, p. 569
discouraged workers, p. 571
union, p. 575
collective bargaining, p. 576

strike, p. 576
efficiency wages, p. 578
job search, p. 583
unemployment insurance, p. 585

Questions for Review

1. What are the three categories into which the Bureau of Labor Statistics divides everyone? How does it compute the labor force, the unemployment rate, and the labor-force participation rate?

2. Is unemployment typically short-term or long-term? Explain.

3. Are minimum-wage laws a better explanation for unemployment among teenagers or among college graduates? Why?

4. How do unions affect the natural rate of unemployment?

5. What claims do advocates of unions make to argue that unions are good for the economy?

6. Explain four ways in which a firm might increase its profits by raising the wages it pays.

7. Why is search unemployment inevitable? How might the government reduce the amount of search unemployment?

Problems and Applications

1. The Bureau of Labor Statistics announced that in November 1996, of all adult Americans, 127,587,000 were employed, 7,221,000 were unemployed, and 66,645,000 were not in the labor force. How big was the labor force? What was the labor-force participation rate? What was the unemployment rate?

2. As shown in Figure 26-3, the overall labor-force participation rate of men declined between 1970 and 1990. This overall decline reflects different patterns for different age groups, however, as shown in the following table.

	ALL MEN	MEN 16–24	MEN 25–54	MEN 55 AND OVER
1970	80%	69%	96%	56%
1990	76	72	93	40

Which group experienced the largest decline? Given this information, what factor may have played an important role in the decline in overall male labor-force participation over this period?

3. The labor-force participation rate of women increased sharply between 1970 and 1990, as shown in Figure 26-3. As with men, however, there were different patterns for different age groups, as shown in this table.

	ALL WOMEN	WOMEN 25–54	WOMEN 25–34	WOMEN 35–44	WOMEN 45–54
1970	43%	50%	45%	51%	54%
1990	58	74	74	77	71

Why do you think that younger women experienced a bigger increase in labor-force participation than older women?

4. In November 1994, the Bureau of Labor Statistics reported that total U.S. employment had increased by 2.6 million workers since January, but that the number of unemployed workers had declined by only 1.4 million over the same period. How are these numbers consistent with each other? Why might one expect a reduction in the number of people counted as unemployed to be smaller than the increase in the number of people employed?

5. Are the following workers more likely to experience short-term or long-term unemployment? Explain.
   a. a construction worker laid off because of bad weather
   b. a manufacturing worker who loses her job at a plant in an isolated area
   c. a stagecoach-industry worker laid off because of competition from railroads
   d. a short-order cook who loses his job when a new restaurant opens across the street
   e. an expert welder with little formal education who loses her job when the company installs automatic welding machinery

6. Using a diagram of the labor market, show the effect of an increase in the minimum wage on the wage paid to workers, the number of workers supplied, the number of workers demanded, and the amount of unemployment.

7. Do you think that firms in small towns or cities have more market power in hiring? Do you think that firms generally have more market power in hiring today than 50 years ago, or less? How do you think this change over time has affected the role of unions in the economy? Explain.

8. Consider an economy with two labor markets, neither of which is unionized. Now suppose a union is established in one market.
   a. Show the effect of the union on the market in which it is formed. In what sense is the quantity of labor employed in this market an inefficient quantity?
   b. Show the effect of the union on the nonunionized market. What happens to the equilibrium wage in this market?

9. It can be shown that an industry's demand for labor will become more elastic when the demand for the industry's product becomes more elastic. Let's consider the implications of this fact for the U.S. automobile industry and the auto workers' union (the UAW).
   a. What happened to the elasticity of demand for American cars when the Japanese developed a strong auto industry? What happened to the elasticity of demand for American auto workers? Explain.
   b. As the chapter explains, a union generally faces a tradeoff in deciding how much to raise wages, because a bigger increase is better for workers who remain employed but also results in a greater reduction in employment. How did the rise in auto imports from Japan affect the wage–employment tradeoff faced by the UAW?
   c. Do you think the growth of the Japanese auto industry increased or decreased the gap between the competitive wage and the wage chosen by the UAW? Explain.

10. Each of the following situations involves moral hazard. In each case, identify the principal and the agent, and explain why there is asymmetric information. How does the action described reduce the problem of moral hazard?
   a. Landlords require tenants to pay security deposits.
   b. Firms compensate top executives with options to buy company stock at a given price in the future.
   c. Car insurance companies offer discounts to customers who install antitheft devices in their cars.

11. Suppose that the Live-Long-and-Prosper Health Insurance Company charges $5,000 annually for a family insurance policy. The company's president suggests that the company raise the annual price to $6,000 in order to increase its profits. If the firm followed this suggestion, what economic problem might arise? Would the firm's pool of customers tend to become more or less healthy on average? Would the company's profits necessarily increase?

12. (This problem is challenging.) Suppose that Congress passes a law requiring employers to provide employees some benefit (such as health care) that raises the cost of an employee by $4 per hour.
   a. What effect does this employer mandate have on the demand for labor? (In answering this and the following questions, be quantitative when you can.)
   b. If employees place a value on this benefit exactly equal to its cost, what effect does this employer mandate have on the supply of labor?
   c. If the wage is free to balance supply and demand, how does this law affect the wage and the level of employment? Are employers better or worse off? Are employees better or worse off?
   d. If a minimum-wage law prevents the wage from balancing supply and demand, how does the employer mandate affect the wage, the level of employment, and the level of unemployment? Are employers better or worse off? Are employees better or worse off?
   e. Now suppose that workers do not value the mandated benefit at all. How does this alternative assumption change your answers to parts (b), (c), and (d) above?

X

MONEY AND PRICES IN
THE LONG RUN

27

THE MONETARY SYSTEM

IN THIS CHAPTER YOU WILL

Consider what money is and what functions money has in the economy

Learn what the Federal Reserve System is

Examine how the banking system helps determine the supply of money

See what tools the Federal Reserve uses to alter the supply of money

When you walk into a restaurant to buy a meal, you get something of value—a full stomach. To pay for this service, you might hand the restaurateur several worn-out pieces of greenish paper decorated with strange symbols, government buildings, and the portraits of famous dead Americans. Or you might hand him a single piece of paper with the name of a bank and your signature. Whether you pay by cash or check, the restaurateur is happy to work hard to satisfy your gastronomical desires in exchange for these pieces of paper, which, in and of themselves, are worthless.

To anyone who has lived in a modern economy, this social custom is not at all odd. Even though paper money has no intrinsic value, the restaurateur is confident that, in the future, some third person will accept it in exchange for something that the restaurateur does value. And that third person is confident that some fourth person will accept the money, with the knowledge that yet a fifth person will accept the money . . . and so on. To the restaurateur and to other people in our society, your cash or check represents a claim to goods and services in the future.

The social custom of using money for transactions is extraordinarily useful in a large, complex society. Imagine, for a moment, that there was no item in the economy widely accepted in exchange for goods and services. People would have to rely on *barter*—the exchange of one good or service for another—to obtain the things they need. To get your restaurant meal, for instance, you would have to offer the restaurateur something of immediate value. You could offer to wash some dishes, clean his car, or give him your family's secret recipe for meat loaf. An economy that relies on barter will have trouble allocating its scarce resources efficiently. In such an economy, trade is said to require the *double coincidence of wants*—the unlikely occurrence that two people each have a good or service that the other wants.

The existence of money makes trade easier. The restaurateur does not care whether you can produce a valuable good or service for him. He is happy to accept your money, knowing that other people will do the same for him. Such a convention allows trade to be roundabout. The restaurateur accepts your money and uses it topay his chef; the chef uses her paycheck to send her child to day care; the day care center uses this tuition to pay a teacher; and the teacher hires you to mow his lawn. As money flows from person to person in the economy, it facilitates production and trade, thereby allowing each person to specialize in what he or she does best and raising everyone's standard of living.

In this chapter we begin to examine the role of money in the economy. We discuss what money is, the various forms that money takes, how the banking system helps create money, and how the government controls the quantity of money in circulation. Because money is so important in the economy, we devote much effort in the rest of this book to learning how changes in the quantity of money affect various economic variables, including inflation, interest rates, production, and employment. Consistent with our long-run focus in the last three chapters, we will examine the long-run effects of changes in the quantity of money in the next chapter. The short-run effects of monetary changes are a more complex topic, which we will take up later in the book. This chapter provides the background for all of this further analysis.

THE MEANING OF MONEY

money

the set of assets in an economy that people regularly use to buy goods and services from other people

What is money? This might seem like an odd question. When you read that billionaire Bill Gates has a lot of money, you know what that means: He is so rich that he can buy almost anything he wants. In this sense, the term *money* is used to mean *wealth*.

Economists, however, use the word in a more specific sense: **Money** is the set of assets in the economy that people regularly use to buy goods and services from other people. The cash in your wallet is money because you can use it to buy a meal at a restaurant or a shirt at a clothing store. By contrast, if you happened to own most of Microsoft Corporation, as Bill Gates does, you would be wealthy, but this asset is not considered a form of money. You could not buy a meal or a shirt with this wealth without first obtaining some cash. According to the economist's definition, money includes only those few types of wealth that are regularly accepted by sellers in exchange for goods and services.

THE FUNCTIONS OF MONEY

Money has three functions in the economy: It is a *medium of exchange*, a *unit of account*, and a *store of value.* These three functions together distinguish money from other assets.

A **medium of exchange** is an item that buyers give to sellers when they purchase goods and services. When you buy a shirt at a clothing store, the store gives you the shirt, and you give the store your money. This transfer of money from buyer to seller allows the transaction to take place. When you walk into a store, you are confident that the store will accept your money for the items it is selling because money is the commonly accepted medium of exchange.

A **unit of account** is the yardstick people use to post prices and record debts. When you go shopping, you might observe that a shirt costs $20 and a hamburger costs $2. Even though it would be accurate to say that the price of a shirt is 10 hamburgers and the price of a hamburger is 1/10 of a shirt, prices are never quoted in this way. Similarly, if you take out a loan from a bank, the size of your future loan repayments will be measured in dollars, not in a quantity of goods and services. When we want to measure and record economic value, we use money as the unit of account.

A **store of value** is an item that people can use to transfer purchasing power from the present to the future. When a seller accepts money today in exchange for a good or service, that seller can hold the money and become a buyer of another good or service at another time. Of course, money is not the only store of value in the economy. A person can also transfer purchasing power from the present to the future by holding stocks, bonds, real estate, art, or even baseball cards. The term *wealth* is used to refer to the total of all stores of value, including both money and nonmonetary assets.

Economists use the term **liquidity** to describe the ease with which an asset can be converted into the economy's medium of exchange. Because money is the economy's medium of exchange, it is the most liquid asset available. Other assets vary widely in their liquidity. Most stocks and bonds can be sold easily with small cost, so they are relatively liquid assets. By contrast, selling a house, a Rembrandt painting, or a 1948 Joe Dimaggio baseball card requires more time and effort, so these assets are less liquid.

When people decide in what form to hold their wealth, they have to balance the liquidity of each possible asset against the asset's usefulness as a store of value. Money is the most liquid asset, but it is far from perfect as a store of value. When prices rise, the value of money falls. In other words, when goods and services become more expensive, each dollar in your wallet can buy less. This link between the price level and the value of money will turn out to be important for understanding how money affects the economy.

THE KINDS OF MONEY

When money takes the form of a commodity with intrinsic value, it is called **commodity money.** The term *intrinsic value* means that the item would have value even if it were not used as money. One example of commodity money is gold. Gold has intrinsic value because it is used in industry and in the making of jewelry. Although today we no longer use gold as money, historically gold has been a common form of money because it is relatively easy to carry, measure, and verify for impurities. When an economy uses gold as money (or uses paper money that is convertible into gold on demand), it is said to be operating under a *gold standard*.

Another example of commodity money is cigarettes. In prisoner-of-war camps during World War II, prisoners traded goods and services with one

medium of exchange
an item that buyers give to sellers when they want to purchase goods and services

unit of account
the yardstick people use to post prices and record debts

store of value
an item that people can use to transfer purchasing power from the present to the future

liquidity
the ease with which an asset can be converted into the economy's medium of exchange

commodity money
money that takes the form of a commodity with intrinsic value

IN THE NEWS

Money on the Island of Yap

THE ROLE OF SOCIAL CUSTOM IN THE monetary system is most apparent in foreign cultures with customs very different from our own. The following article describes the money on the island of Yap. As you read the article, ask yourself whether Yap is using a type of commodity money, a type of fiat money, or something in between.

Fixed Assets, or Why a Loan in Yap Is Hard to Roll Over

BY ART PINE

YAP, MICRONESIA—On this tiny South Pacific island, life is easy and the currency is hard.

Elsewhere, the world's troubled monetary system creaks along; floating exchange rates wreak havoc on currency markets, and devaluations are commonplace. But on Yap the currency is as solid as a rock. In fact, it *is* rock. Limestone to be precise.

For nearly 2,000 years the Yapese have used large stone wheels to pay for major purchases, such as land, canoes and permissions to marry. Yap is a U.S. trust territory, and the dollar is used in grocery stores and gas stations. But reliance on stone money, like the island's ancient caste system and the traditional dress of loincloths and grass skirts, continues.

Buying property with stones is "much easier than buying it with U.S. dollars," says John Chodad, who recently purchased a building lot with a 30-inch stone wheel. "We don't know the value of the U.S. dollar. . . ."

Stone wheels don't make good pocket money, so for small transactions, Yapese use other forms of currency, such as beer. Beer is proffered as payment for all sorts of odd jobs, including construction. The 10,000 people on Yap consume 40,000 to 50,000 cases a year, mostly of Budweiser. . . .

The people of Yap have been using stone money ever since a Yapese warrior named Anagumang first brought the huge stones from limestone caverns on neighboring Palau, some 1,500 to 2,000 years ago. Inspired by the moon, he fashioned the stone into large circles. The rest is history.

Yapese lean the stone wheels against their houses or prop up rows of them in village "banks." Most of the stones are 2 1/2 to 5 feet in diameter, but some are as much as 12 feet across. Each has a hole in the center so it can be slipped onto the trunk of a fallen betel nut tree and carried. It takes 20 men to lift some stones.

By custom, the stones are worthless when broken. You never hear people on Yap musing about wanting a piece of the rock. Rather than risk a broken stone—or back—Yapese tend to leave the larger stones where they are and make a mental accounting that the ownership has been transferred—much as

MONEY ON THE ISLAND OF YAP: NOT EXACTLY POCKET CHANGE

gold bars used in international transactions change hands without leaving the vaults of the New York Federal Reserve Bank. . . .

There are some decided advantages to using massive stones for money. They are immune to black-market trading, for one thing, and they pose formidable obstacles to pickpockets. In addition, there aren't any sterile debates about how to stabilize the Yapese monetary system. With only 6,600 stone wheels remaining on the island, the money supply stays put. . . .

Meanwhile, Yap's stone money may be about to take on international significance. Just yesterday, Washington received notice that Tosiho Nakayama, the president of Micronesia, plans to bring a stone disk when he visits the United States next month. It will be flown by Air Force jet.

Officials say Mr. Nakayama intends the stone as Micronesia's symbolic contribution toward reducing the U.S. budget deficit.

SOURCE: *The Wall Street Journal,* March 29, 1984, p. A1.

another using cigarettes as the store of value, unit of account, and medium of exchange. Similarly, as the Soviet Union was breaking up in the late 1980s, cigarettes started replacing the ruble as the preferred currency in Moscow. In both cases, even nonsmokers were happy to accept cigarettes in an exchange, knowing that they could use the cigarettes to buy other goods and services.

Money without intrinsic value is called **fiat money**. A *fiat* is simply an order or decree, and fiat money is established as money by government decree. For example, compare the paper dollars in your wallet (printed by the U.S. government) and the paper dollars from a game of Monopoly (printed by the Parker Brothers game company). Why can you use the first to pay your bill at a restaurant but not the second? The answer is that the U.S. government has decreed its dollars to be valid money. Each paper dollar in your wallet reads: "This note is legal tender for all debts, public and private."

Although the government is central to establishing and regulating a system of fiat money (such as by prosecuting counterfeiters), other factors are also required for the success of such a monetary system. To a large extent, the acceptance of fiat money depends as much on expectations and social convention as on government decree. The Soviet government in the 1980s never abandoned the ruble as the official currency. Yet the people of Moscow preferred to accept cigarettes (or even American dollars) in exchange for goods and services, because they were more confident that these alternative monies would be accepted by others in the future.

fiat money
money without intrinsic value that is used as money because of government decree

MONEY IN THE U.S. ECONOMY

As we will see, the quantity of money circulating in the economy, called the *money stock*, has a powerful influence on many economic variables. But before we consider why that is true, we need to ask a preliminary question: What is the quantity of money? In particular, suppose you were given the task of measuring how much money there is in the U.S. economy. What would you include in your measure?

The most obvious asset to include is **currency**—the paper bills and coins in the hands of the public. Currency is clearly the most widely accepted medium of exchange in our economy. There is no doubt that it is part of the money stock.

currency
the paper bills and coins in the hands of the public

Yet currency is not the only asset that you can use to buy goods and services. Many stores also accept personal checks. Wealth held in your checking account is almost as convenient for buying things as wealth held in your wallet. To measure the money stock, therefore, you might want to include **demand deposits**—balances in bank accounts that depositors can access on demand simply by writing a check.

demand deposits
balances in bank accounts that depositors can access on demand by writing a check

Once you start to consider balances in checking accounts as part of the money stock, you are led to consider the large variety of other accounts that people hold at banks and other financial institutions. Bank depositors usually cannot write checks against the balances in their savings accounts, but they can easily transfer funds from savings into checking accounts. In addition, depositors in money market mutual funds can often write checks against their balances. Thus, these other accounts should plausibly be part of the U.S. money stock.

In a complex economy such as ours, it is not easy to draw a line between assets that can be called "money" and assets that cannot. The coins in your

Table 27-1

TWO MEASURES OF THE MONEY
STOCK FOR THE U.S. ECONOMY

MEASURE	AMOUNT IN 1996	WHAT'S INCLUDED
M1	$1,117 billion	Currency Traveler's checks Demand deposits Other checkable deposits
M2	$3,737 billion	Everything in M1 Savings deposits Small time deposits Money market mutual funds A few minor categories

SOURCE: Federal Reserve.

pocket are clearly part of the money stock, and the Empire State Building clearly is not, but there are many assets in between these extremes for which the choice is less clear. Therefore, various measures of the money stock are available for the U.S. economy. Table 27-1 shows the two most important, designated M1 and M2. Each of these measures uses a slightly different criterion for distinguishing monetary and nonmonetary assets.

For our purposes in this book, we need not dwell on the differences between the various measures of money. The important point is that the money stock for the U.S. economy includes not just currency but also deposits in banks and other financial institutions that can be readily accessed and used to buy goods and services.

CASE STUDY   WHERE IS ALL THE CURRENCY?

One puzzle about the money stock of the U.S. economy concerns the amount of currency. In 1996 there was about $380 billion of currency outstanding. To put this number in perspective, we can divide it by 200 million, the number of adults (age sixteen and over) in the United States. This calculation implies that the average adult holds about $1,900 of currency. Most people are surprised to learn that our economy has so much currency because they carry far less than this in their wallets.

Who is holding all this currency? No one knows for sure, but there are two plausible explanations.

The first explanation is that much of the currency is being held abroad. In foreign countries without a stable monetary system, people often prefer U.S. dollars to domestic assets. It is, in fact, not unusual to see U.S. dollars being used overseas as the medium of exchange, unit of account, and store of value.

The second explanation is that much of the currency is being held by drug dealers, tax evaders, and other criminals. For most people in the U.S. economy, currency is not a particularly good way to hold wealth. Currency can be lost or stolen. Moreover, currency does not earn interest, whereas money in a

FYI

Credit Cards, Debit Cards, and Money

IT MIGHT SEEM NATURAL TO include credit cards as part of the economy's stock of money. After all, people use credit cards to make many of their purchases. Aren't credit cards, therefore, a medium of exchange?

Although at first this argument may seem persuasive, credit cards are excluded from all measures of the quantity of money. The reason is that credit cards are not really a method of payment but a method of *deferring* payment. When you buy a meal with a credit card, the bank that issued the card pays the restaurant what it is due. At a later date, you will have to repay the bank (perhaps with interest). When the time comes to pay your credit card bill, you will probably do so by writing a check against your checking account. The balance in this checking account is part of the economy's stock of money.

Notice that credit cards are very different from debit cards, which automatically withdraw funds from a bank

account to pay for items bought. Rather than allowing the user to postpone payment for a purchase, a debit card allows the user immediate access to deposits in a bank account. In this sense, a debit card is more similar to a check than to a credit card.

IS THIS MONEY?

The account balances that lie behind debit cards are included in measures of the quantity of money.

Even though credit cards are not considered a form of money, they are nonetheless important for analyzing the monetary system. People who have credit cards can pay many of their bills all at once at the end of the month, rather than sporadically as they make purchases. As a result, people who have credit cards probably hold less money on average than people who do not have credit cards. Thus, the introduction and increased popularity of credit cards may reduce the amount of money that people choose to hold.

bank account does. Thus, most people hold only small amounts of currency. By contrast, criminals may prefer not to hold their wealth in banks. A bank deposit would give police a paper trail with which to trace their illegal activities. For criminals, currency may be the best store of value available.

■ **QUICK QUIZ** List and describe the three functions of money.

THE FEDERAL RESERVE

Whenever an economy relies on a system of fiat money, as the U.S. economy does, some agency must be responsible for regulating the system. In the United States, that agency is the **Federal Reserve,** often simply called the **Fed.** If you look at the top of a dollar bill, you will see that it is called a "Federal Reserve Note." The Fed is an example of a **central bank**—an institution designed to oversee the banking system and regulate the quantity of money in the economy. Other major central banks around the world include the Bank of England, the Bank of Japan, and Germany's Bundesbank.

Federal Reserve (Fed)
the central bank of the United States

central bank
an institution designed to oversee the banking system and regulate the quantity of money in the economy

THE FED'S ORGANIZATION

The Federal Reserve was created in 1914 after a series of bank failures in 1907 convinced Congress that the United States needed a central bank to ensure the health of the nation's banking system. Today, the Fed is run by its Board of Governors, which has seven members appointed by the president and confirmed by the Senate. The governors have 14-year terms. Just as federal judges are given lifetime appointments to insulate them from politics, Fed governors are given long terms to give them independence from short-term political pressures when they formulate monetary policy.

Among the seven members of the Board of Governors, the most important is the chairman. The chairman directs the Fed staff, presides over board meetings, and testifies regularly about Fed policy in front of Congressional committees. The president appoints the chairman to a four-year term. As this book was going to press, the chairman of the Fed was Alan Greenspan.

The Federal Reserve System is made up of the Federal Reserve Board in Washington, D.C., and 12 regional Federal Reserve Banks located in major cities around the country. (If you look at any dollar bill, you can find the name of the regional bank that issued that dollar.) The presidents of the regional banks are chosen by each bank's board of directors, whose members are typically drawn from the local banking and business community.

The Fed has two related jobs. The first job is to regulate banks and ensure the health of the banking system. This task is largely the responsibility of the regional Federal Reserve Banks. In particular, the Fed monitors each bank's financial condition and helps to facilitate bank transactions by clearing checks. It also acts as a banker's bank. That is, the Fed makes loans to banks when banks themselves want to borrow. When financially troubled banks find themselves short of cash, the Fed acts as a *lender of last resort*—a lender to those who cannot borrow anywhere else—in order to maintain stability in the overall banking system.

The Fed's second and more important job is to control the quantity of money that is made available in the economy, called the **money supply.** Decisions by policymakers concerning the money supply constitute **monetary policy.** At the Federal Reserve, monetary policy is made by the Federal Open Market Committee.

money supply
the quantity of money available in the economy

monetary policy
the setting of the money supply by policymakers in the central bank

THE FEDERAL OPEN MARKET COMMITTEE

The Federal Open Market Committee (FOMC) is made up of the 7 members of the Board of Governors and 5 of the 12 regional bank presidents. (All 12 regional presidents attend each FOMC meeting, but only 5 get to vote. The 5 with voting rights rotate among the 12 regional presidents over time. The president of the New York Fed always gets a vote, however, because New York is the traditional financial center of the U.S. economy and because all Fed purchases and sales of government bonds are conducted at the New York Fed's trading desk.) The FOMC meets about every six weeks in Washington, D.C., in order to discuss the condition of the economy and consider changes in monetary policy.

Through the decisions of the FOMC, the Fed has the power to increase or decrease the number of dollars in the economy. In simple metaphorical terms, you can imagine the Fed printing up dollar bills and dropping them around the country by helicopter. Similarly, you can imagine the Fed using a giant vacuum cleaner to suck dollar bills out of people's wallets. Although in practice the Fed's methods for changing the money supply are more complex and subtle than this, the helicopter-vacuum metaphor is a good first approximation to the meaning of monetary policy.

We discuss later in this chapter how the Fed actually changes the money supply, but it is worth noting here that the Fed's primary tool is *open-market operations*—the purchase and sale of U.S. government bonds. (Recall that a U.S. government bond is a certificate of indebtedness of the federal government.) If the FOMC decides to increase the money supply, the Fed creates dollars and uses them to buy government bonds from the public in the nation's bond markets. After the purchase, these dollars are in the hands of the public. Thus, an open-market purchase of bonds by the Fed increases the money supply. Conversely, if the FOMC decides to decrease the money supply, the Fed sells government bonds from its portfolio to the public in the nation's bond markets. After the sale, the dollars it receives for the bonds are out of the hands of the public. Thus, an open-market sale of bonds by the Fed decreases the money supply.

The Fed is an important institution because changes in the money supply can profoundly affect the economy. One of the *Ten Principles of Economics* in Chapter 1 is that prices rise when the government prints too much money. Another of the *Ten Principles of Economics* is that society faces a short-run trade-off between inflation and unemployment. The power of the FOMC rests on these principles. For reasons we discuss more fully in the coming chapters, the FOMC's policy decisions have an important influence on the economy's rate of inflation in the long run and the economy's employment and production in the short run. Indeed, the chairman of the Federal Reserve has been called the second most powerful person in the United States.

QUICK QUIZ How does the Fed increase the supply of money in the economy?

BANKS AND THE MONEY SUPPLY

So far we have introduced the concept of "money" and discussed how the Federal Reserve controls the supply of money by buying and selling government bonds in open-market operations. Although this explanation of the money supply is correct, it is not complete. In particular, it omits the central role that banks play in the monetary system.

Recall that the amount of money you hold includes both currency (the bills in your wallet and coins in your pocket) and demand deposits (the balance in your checking account). Because demand deposits are held in banks, the behavior of banks can influence the quantity of demand deposits in the economy and, therefore, the money supply. This section examines how banks affect the money supply and how they complicate the Fed's job of controlling the money supply.

THE SIMPLE CASE OF 100-PERCENT-RESERVE BANKING

To see how banks influence the money supply, it is useful to imagine first a world without any banks at all. In this simple world, currency is the only form of money. To be concrete, let's suppose that the total quantity of currency is $100. The supply of money is, therefore, $100.

Now suppose that someone opens a bank, appropriately called First National Bank. First National Bank is only a depository institution. That is, the bank accepts deposits but does not make loans. The purpose of the bank is to give depositors a safe place to keep their money. Whenever a person deposits some money, the bank keeps the money in its vault until the depositor comes to withdraw it or writes a check against his or her balance. Deposits that banks have received but have not loaned out are called **reserves.** In this imaginary economy, all deposits are held as reserves, so this system is called *100-percent-reserve banking.*

We can express the financial position of First National Bank with a *T-account,* which is a simplified accounting statement that shows changes in a bank's assets and liabilities. Here is the T-account for First National Bank if the economy's entire $100 of money is deposited in the bank:

reserves

deposits that banks have received but have not loaned out

FIRST NATIONAL BANK

Assets		Liabilities	
Reserves	$100.00	Deposits	$100.00

On the left-hand side of the T-account are the bank's assets of $100 (the reserves it holds in its vaults). On the right-hand side of the T-account are the bank's liabilities of $100 (the amount it owes to its depositors). Notice that the assets and liabilities of First National Bank exactly balance.

Now consider the money supply in this imaginary economy. Before First National Bank opens, the money supply is the $100 of currency that people are holding. After the bank opens and people deposit their currency, the money supply is the $100 of demand deposits. (There is no longer any currency outstanding, for it is all in the bank vault.) Each deposit in the bank reduces currency and raises demand deposits by exactly the same amount, leaving the money supply unchanged. Thus, *if banks hold all deposits in reserve, banks do not influence the supply of money.*

MONEY CREATION WITH FRACTIONAL-RESERVE BANKING

Eventually, the bankers at First National Bank may start to reconsider their policy of 100-percent-reserve banking. Leaving all that money sitting idle in their vaults seems unnecessary. Why not use some of it to make loans? Families buying houses, firms building new factories, and students paying for college would all be happy to pay interest to borrow some of that money for a while. Of course, First National Bank has to keep some reserves so that currency is available if depositors want to make withdrawals. But if the flow of new deposits is roughly the same as the flow of withdrawals, First National needs to keep only a fraction of its deposits in reserve. Thus, First National adopts a system called **fractional-reserve banking.**

fractional-reserve banking

a banking system in which banks hold only a fraction of deposits as reserves

"I've heard a lot about money, and now I'd like to try some."

Let's suppose that First National decides to keep 10 percent of its deposits in reserve and to loan out the rest. We say that the **reserve ratio**—the fraction of total deposits that the bank holds as reserves—is 10 percent. Now let's look again at the bank's T-account:

reserve ratio
the fraction of deposits that banks hold as reserves

FIRST NATIONAL BANK

ASSETS		LIABILITIES	
Reserves	$10.00	Deposits	$100.00
Loans	90.00		

First National still has $100 in liabilities because making the loans did not alter the bank's obligation to its depositors. But now the bank has two kinds of assets: It has $10 of reserves in its vault, and it has loans of $90. (These loans are liabilities of the people taking out the loans but they are assets of the bank making the loans, because the borrowers will later repay the bank.) In total, First National's assets still equal its liabilities.

Once again consider the supply of money in the economy. Before First National makes any loans, the money supply is the $100 of deposits in the bank. Yet when First National makes these loans, the money supply increases. The depositors still have demand deposits totaling $100, but now the borrowers hold $90 in currency. The money supply (which equals currency plus demand deposits) equals $190. Thus, *when banks hold only a fraction of deposits in reserve, banks create money.*

At first, this creation of money by fractional-reserve banking may seem too good to be true because it appears that the bank has created money out of thin air. To make this creation of money seem less miraculous, note that when First National Bank loans out some of its reserves and creates money, it does not create any wealth. Loans from First National give the borrowers some currency and thus the ability to buy goods and services. Yet the borrowers are also taking on debts, so the loans do not make them any richer. In other words, as a bank creates the asset of money, it also creates a corresponding liability for its borrowers. At the end of this process of money creation, the economy is more liquid in the sense that there is more of the medium of exchange, but the economy is no wealthier than before.

THE MONEY MULTIPLIER

The creation of money does not stop with First National Bank. Suppose the borrower from First National uses the $90 to buy something from someone who then deposits the currency in Second National Bank. Here is the T-account for Second National Bank:

SECOND NATIONAL BANK

Assets		Liabilities	
Reserves	$ 9.00	Deposits	$90.00
Loans	81.00		

After the deposit, this bank has liabilities of $90. If Second National also has a reserve ratio of 10 percent, it keeps assets of $9 in reserve and makes $81 in loans. In this way, Second National Bank creates an additional $81 of money. If this $81 is eventually deposited in Third National Bank, which also has a reserve ratio of 10 percent, this bank keeps $8.10 in reserve and makes $72.90 in loans. Here is the T-account for Third National Bank:

THIRD NATIONAL BANK

Assets		Liabilities	
Reserves	$ 8.10	Deposits	$81.00
Loans	72.90		

The process goes on and on. Each time that money is deposited and a bank loan is made, more money is created.

How much money is eventually created in this economy? Let's add it up:

Original deposit	=	$ 100.00
First National lending	=	$ 90.00 [= .9 × $100.00]
Second National lending	=	$ 81.00 [= .9 × $90.00]
Third National lending	=	$ 72.90 [= .9 × $81.00]
•		•
•		•
•		•
Total money supply	=	$1,000.00

It turns out that even though this process of money creation can continue forever, it does not create an infinite amount of money. If you laboriously add the infinite sequence of numbers in the foregoing example, you find the $100 of reserves generates $1,000 of money. The amount of money the banking system generates with each dollar of reserves is called the **money multiplier.** In this imaginary economy, where the $100 of reserves generates $1,000 of money, the money multiplier is 10.

money multiplier

the amount of money the banking system generates with each dollar of reserves

What determines the size of the money multiplier? It turns out that the answer is simple: *The money multiplier is the reciprocal of the reserve ratio.* If R is the reserve ratio for all banks in the economy, then each dollar of reserves generates $1/R$ dollars of money. In our example, $R = 1/10$, so the money multiplier is 10.

This reciprocal formula for the money multiplier makes sense. If a bank holds $1,000 in deposits, then a reserve ratio of 1/10 (10 percent) means that the bank must hold $100 in reserves. The money multiplier just turns this idea around: If the banking system holds a total of $100 in reserves, it can have only $1,000 in deposits. Similarly, if the reserve ratio were 1/5 (20 percent), the banking system must have five times as much in deposits as in reserves, implying a money multiplier of 5. The higher the reserve ratio, the less of each deposit banks loan out, and the smaller the money multiplier. In the special case of 100-percent-reserve banking, the reserve ratio is 1, the money multiplier is 1, and banks do not create money.

THE FED'S TOOLS OF MONETARY CONTROL

As we have already discussed, the Federal Reserve is responsible for controlling the supply of money in the economy. Now that we understand how fractional-reserve banking works, we are in a better position to understand how the Fed carries out this job. Because banks create money in a system of fractional-reserve banking, the Fed's control of the money supply is indirect. When the Fed decides to change the money supply, it must consider how its actions will work through the banking system.

The Fed has three tools in its monetary toolbox: open-market operations, reserve requirements, and the discount rate. Let's discuss how the Fed uses each of these tools.

Open-Market Operations As we noted earlier, the Fed conducts **open-market operations** when it buys or sells government bonds from the public. To increase the money supply, the Fed instructs its bond traders at the New York Fed to buy bonds in the nation's bond markets. The dollars the Fed pays for the bonds increase the number of dollars in circulation. Some of these new dollars are held as currency, and some are deposited in banks. Each new dollar held as currency increases the money supply by exactly $1. Each new dollar deposited in a bank increases the money supply to an even greater extent because it increases reserves and, thereby, the amount of money that the banking system can create.

To reduce the money supply, the Fed does just the opposite: It sells government bonds to the public in the nation's bond markets. The public pays for these bonds with its holdings of currency and bank deposits, directly reducing the amount of money in circulation. In addition, as people make withdrawals from banks, banks find themselves with a smaller quantity of reserves. In response, banks reduce the amount of lending, and the process of money creation reverses itself.

Open-market operations are easy to conduct. In fact, the Fed's purchases and sales of government bonds in the nation's bond markets are similar to the transactions that any individual might undertake for his own portfolio. (Of course, when an individual buys or sells a bond, money changes hands, but the amount of money in circulation remains the same.) In addition, the Fed can use

open-market operations
the purchase and sale of U.S. government bonds by the Fed

open-market operations to change the money supply by a small or large amount on any day without major changes in laws or bank regulations. Therefore, open-market operations are the tool of monetary policy that the Fed uses most often.

Reserve Requirements   The Fed also influences the money supply with **reserve requirements,** which are regulations on the minimum amount of reserves that banks must hold against deposits. Reserve requirements influence how much money the banking system can create with each dollar of reserves. An increase in reserve requirements means that banks must hold more reserves and, therefore, can loan out less of each dollar that is deposited; as a result, it raises the reserve ratio, lowers the money multiplier, and decreases the money supply. Conversely, a decrease in reserve requirements lowers the reserve ratio, raises the money multiplier, and increases the money supply.

The Fed uses changes in reserve requirements only rarely because frequent changes would disrupt the business of banking. When the Fed increases reserve requirements, for instance, some banks find themselves short of reserves, even though they have seen no change in deposits. As a result, they have to curtail lending until they build their level of reserves to the new required level.

The Discount Rate   The last tool in the Fed's toolbox is the **discount rate,** the interest rate on the loans that the Fed makes to banks. A bank borrows from the Fed when it has too few reserves to meet reserve requirements. This might occur because the bank made too many loans or because it has experienced recent withdrawals. When the Fed makes such a loan to a bank, the banking system has more reserves than it otherwise would, and these additional reserves allow the banking system to create more money.

The Fed can alter the money supply by changing the discount rate. A higher discount rate discourages banks from borrowing reserves from the Fed. Thus, an increase in the discount rate reduces the quantity of reserves in the banking system, which in turn reduces the money supply. Conversely, a lower discount rate encourages bank borrowing from the Fed, increases the quantity of reserves, and increases the money supply.

The Fed uses discount lending not only to control the money supply but also to help financial institutions when they are in trouble. For example, in 1984, rumors circulated that Continental Illinois National Bank had made a large number of bad loans, and these rumors induced many depositors to withdraw their deposits. As part of an effort to save the bank, the Fed acted as a lender of last resort and loaned Continental Illinois more than $5 billion. Similarly, when the stock market crashed on October 19, 1987, many Wall Street brokerage firms found themselves temporarily in need of funds to finance the high volume of stock trading. The next morning, before the stock market opened, Fed Chairman Alan Greenspan announced the Fed's "readiness to serve as a source of liquidity to support the economic and financial system." Many economists believe that Greenspan's reaction to the stock crash was an important reason why it had so few repercussions.

PROBLEMS IN CONTROLLING THE MONEY SUPPLY

The Fed's three tools—open-market operations, reserve requirements, and the discount rate—have powerful effects on the money supply. Yet the Fed's control of the money supply is not precise. The Fed must wrestle with two problems,

reserve requirements

regulations on the minimum amount of reserves that banks must hold against deposits

discount rate

the interest rate on the loans that the Fed makes to banks each of which arises because much of the money supply is created by our system of fractional-reserve banking.

The first problem is that the Fed does not control the amount of money that households choose to hold as deposits in banks. The more money that households deposit, the more reserves banks have, and the more money the banking system can create. And the less money that households deposit, the less reserves banks have, and the less money the banking system can create. To see why this is a problem, suppose that one day people begin to lose confidence in the banking system and, therefore, decide to withdraw deposits and hold more currency. When this happens, the banking system loses reserves and creates less money. The money supply falls, even without any Fed action.

The second problem of monetary control is that the Fed does not control the amount that bankers choose to lend. Once money is deposited in a bank, it creates more money only when the bank loans it out. Yet banks can choose to hold reserves above what the Fed requires, called *excess reserves*. To see why excess reserves complicate control of the money supply, suppose that one day bankers become more cautious about economic conditions and decide to make fewer loans and hold greater reserves. In this case, the banking system creates less money than it otherwise would. Because of the bankers' decision, the money supply falls.

Hence, in a system of fractional-reserve banking, the amount of money in the economy depends in part on the behavior of depositors and bankers. Because the Fed cannot control or perfectly predict this behavior, it cannot perfectly control the money supply. Yet, if the Fed is vigilant, these problems need not be large. The Fed collects data on deposits and reserves from banks every week, so it is quickly aware of any changes in depositor or banker behavior. It can, therefore, respond to these changes and keep the money supply close to whatever level it chooses.

CASE STUDY BANK RUNS AND THE MONEY SUPPLY

Although you have probably never witnessed a bank run in real life, you may have seen one depicted in movies such as *Mary Poppins* or *It's a Wonderful Life*. A bank run occurs when depositors suspect that a bank may go bankrupt and, therefore, "run" to the bank to withdraw their deposits.

Bank runs are a problem for banks under fractional-reserve banking. Because a bank holds only a fraction of its deposits in reserve, it cannot satisfy withdrawal requests from all depositors. Even if the bank is in fact *solvent* (meaning that its assets exceed its liabilities), it will not have enough cash on hand to allow all depositors immediate access to all of their money. When a run occurs, the bank is forced to close its doors until some bank loans are repaid or until some lender of last resort (such as the Fed) provides it with the currency it needs to satisfy depositors.

Bank runs complicate the control of the money supply. An important example of this problem occurred during the Great Depression in the early 1930s. After a wave of bank runs and bank closings, households and bankers became more cautious. Households withdrew their deposits from banks, preferring to hold their money in the form of currency. This decision reversed the process of money creation, as bankers responded to falling reserves by reducing bank loans. At the same time, bankers increased their reserve ratios so that they would have enough cash on hand to meet their depositors' demands in any future bank runs. The higher reserve ratio reduced the money multiplier, which also reduced the money supply. From 1929 to 1933, the money supply fell by 28 percent, even without the Federal Reserve taking any deliberate contractionary action. Many economists point to this massive fall in the money supply to explain the high unemployment and falling prices that prevailed during this period. (In future chapters we examine the mechanisms by which changes in the money supply affect unemployment and prices.)

Today, bank runs are not a major problem for the banking system or the Fed. The federal government now guarantees the safety of deposits at most banks, primarily through the Federal Deposit Insurance Corporation (FDIC). Depositors do not run on their banks because they are confident that, even if their bank goes bankrupt, the FDIC will make good on the deposits. As a result, most people see bank runs only in the movies.

A Not-So-Wonderful Bank Run

■ **QUICK QUIZ**   Describe how banks create money.

CONCLUSION

Several years ago, a book made the best-seller list with the title *Secrets of the Temple: How the Federal Reserve Runs the Country*. Although no doubt an exaggeration, this title did highlight the important role of the monetary system in our daily lives. Whenever we buy or sell anything, we are relying on the extraordinarily useful social convention called "money." Now that we know what money is and what determines its supply, we can discuss how changes in the quantity of money affect the economy. We begin to address that topic in the next chapter.

Summary

◆ The term *money* refers to assets that people regularly use to buy goods and services.

◆ Money serves three functions. As a medium of exchange, it provides the item used to make transactions. As a unit of account, it provides the way in which prices and other economic values are recorded. As a store of value, it provides a way of transferring purchasing power from the present to the future.

◆ Commodity money, such as gold, is money that has intrinsic value: It would be valued even if it were not used as money. Fiat money, such as paper dollars, is money without intrinsic value: It would be worthless if it were not used as money.

◆ In the U.S. economy, money takes the form of currency and various types of bank deposits, such as checking accounts.

◆ The Federal Reserve, the central bank of the United States, is responsible for regulating the U.S. monetary system. The Fed controls the money supply primarily through open-market operations: The purchase of government bonds increases the money supply, and the sale of government bonds decreases the money supply. The Fed can also alter the money supply by changing reserve requirements or the discount rate.

◆ When banks loan out some of their deposits, they increase the quantity of money in the economy. Because of this role of banks in determining the money supply, the Fed's control of the money supply is imperfect.

Key Concepts

money, p. 592
medium of exchange, p. 593
unit of account, p. 593
store of value, p. 593
liquidity, p. 593
commodity money, p. 593
fiat money, p. 595

currency, p. 595
demand deposits, p. 595
Federal Reserve (Fed), p. 597
central bank, p. 597
money supply, p. 598
monetary policy, p. 598
reserves, p. 600

fractional-reserve banking, p. 600
reserve ratio, p.601
money multiplier, p. 602
open-market operations, p. 603
reserve requirements, p. 604
discount rate, p. 604

Questions for Review

1. What distinguishes money from other assets in the economy?

2. What is commodity money? What is fiat money? Which kind do we use?

3. What are demand deposits, and why should they be included in the stock of money?

4. If the Fed wants to increase the money supply with open-market operations, what does it do?

5. What is the discount rate? What happens to the money supply when the Fed raises the discount rate?

6. What are reserve requirements? What happens to the money supply when the Fed raises reserve requirements?

7. Why can't the Fed control the money supply perfectly?

Problems and Applications

1. Which of the following are money in the U.S. economy? Which are not? Explain your answers by discussing each of the three functions of money.
   a. a U.S. penny
   b. a Mexican peso
   c. a Picasso painting
   d. a plastic credit card

2. Every month *Yankee* magazine includes a "Swopper's [sic] Column" of offers to barter goods and services.

Here is a recent example: "Will swop custom-designed wedding gown and up to 6 bridesmaids' gowns for 2 round-trip plane tickets and 3 nights' lodging in the countryside of England."
   a. Why would it be difficult to run our economy using a "Swopper's Column" instead of money?
   b. In light of your answer to part (a), why might the *Yankee* "Swopper's Column" exist?

3. What characteristics of an asset make it useful as a medium of exchange? As a store of value?

4. Consider how the following situations would affect the economy's monetary system.
   a. Suppose that the people on Yap discovered an easy way to make limestone wheels. How would this development affect the usefulness of stone wheels as money? Explain.
   b. Suppose that someone in the United States discovered an easy way to counterfeit $100 bills. How would this development affect the U.S. monetary system? Explain.

5. Your uncle repays a $100 loan from Tenth National Bank by writing a $100 check from his TNB checking account. Use T-accounts to show the effect of this transaction on your uncle and on TNB. Has your uncle's wealth changed? Explain.

6. Beleaguered State Bank (BSB) holds $250 million in deposits and maintains a reserve ratio of 10 percent.
   a. Show a T-account for BSB.
   b. Now suppose that BSB's largest depositor withdraws $10 million from her account in cash. If BSB decides to restore its reserve ratio by reducing the amount of loans outstanding, show its new T-account.
   c. Explain what effect BSB's action will have on other banks.
   d. Why might it be difficult for BSB to take the action described in part (b)? Discuss another way for BSB to return to its original reserve ratio.

7. You take $100 you had kept under your pillow and deposit it in your bank account. If this $100 stays in the banking system as reserves and if banks hold reserves equal to 10 percent of deposits, by how much does the total amount of deposits in the banking system increase? By how much does the money supply increase?

8. The Federal Reserve conducts a $10 million open-market purchase of government bonds. If the required reserve ratio is 10 percent, what is the largest possible increase in the money supply that could result? Explain. What is the smallest possible increase? Explain.

9. Suppose that the T-account for First National Bank is as follows:

ASSETS		LIABILITIES	
Reserves	$100,000	Deposits	$500,000
Loans	400,000		

a. If the Fed requires banks to hold 5 percent of deposits as reserves, how much in excess reserves does First National now hold?
b. Assume that all other banks hold only the required amount of reserves. If First National decides to reduce its reserves to only the required amount, by how much would the economy's money supply increase?

10. Suppose that the reserve requirement for checking deposits is 10 percent and that banks do not hold any excess reserves.
    a. If the Fed sells $1 million of government bonds, what is the effect on the economy's reserves and money supply?
    b. Now suppose the Fed lowers the reserve requirement to 5 percent, but banks choose to hold another 5 percent of deposits as excess reserves. Why might banks do so? What is the overall change in the money multiplier and the money supply as a result of these actions?

11. Assume that the banking system has total reserves of $100 billion. Assume also that required reserves are 10 percent of checking deposits, and that banks hold no excess reserves and households hold no currency.
    a. What is the money multiplier? What is the money supply?
    b. If the Fed now raises required reserves to 20 percent of deposits, what is the change in reserves and the change in the money supply?

12. (This problem is challenging.) The economy of Elmendyn contains 2,000 $1 bills.
    a. If people hold all money as currency, what is the quantity of money?
    b. If people hold all money as demand deposits and banks maintain 100 percent reserves, what is the quantity of money?
    c. If people hold equal amounts of currency and demand deposits and banks maintain 100 percent reserves, what is the quantity of money?
    d. If people hold all money as demand deposits and banks maintain a reserve ratio of 10 percent, what is the quantity of money?
    e. If people hold equal amounts of currency and demand deposits and banks maintain a reserve ratio of 10 percent, what is the quantity of money?

28

INFLATION:

ITS CAUSES AND COSTS

**IN THIS CHAPTER
YOU WILL**

*See why inflation results
from rapid growth in the
money supply*

*Learn the meaning of the
classical dichotomy and
monetary neutrality*

*See why some countries
print so much money
that they experience
hyperinflation*

*Examine how the
nominal interest
rate responds to the
inflation rate*

*Consider the various
costs that inflation
imposes on society*

Although today you need a dollar or two to buy yourself an ice-cream cone, life was very different 60 years ago. In one Trenton, New Jersey, candy store (run, incidentally, by this author's grandmother in the 1930s), ice-cream cones came in two sizes. A cone with a small scoop of ice cream cost three cents. Hungry customers could buy a large scoop for a nickel.

You are probably not surprised at the increase in the price of ice cream. In our economy, most prices tend to rise over time. This increase in the overall level of prices is called *inflation*. Earlier in the book we examined how economists measure the inflation rate as the percentage change in the consumer price index, the GDP deflator, or some other index of the overall price level. These price indexes show that, over the past 60 years, prices have risen on average about 5 percent per year. Accumulated over so many years, a 5 percent annual inflation rate leads to an 18-fold increase in the price level.

Inflation may seem natural and inevitable to a person who grew up in the United States during the second half of the twentieth century, but in fact it is not inevitable at all. There were long periods in the nineteenth century during which most prices fell—a phenomenon called *deflation*. The average level of prices in the U.S. economy was 23 percent lower in 1896 than in 1880, and this deflation was a major issue in the presidential election of 1896. Farmers, who had accumulated large debts, were suffering when the fall in crop prices reduced their incomes and thus their ability to pay off their debts. They advocated government policies to reverse the deflation.

Although inflation has been the norm in more recent history, there has been substantial variation in the rate at which prices rise. From 1990 to 1996, prices rose at an average rate of about 3 percent per year. By contrast, in the 1970s, prices rose by 7 percent per year, which meant a doubling of the price level over the decade. The public often views such high rates of inflation as a major economic problem. In fact, when President Jimmy Carter ran for reelection in 1980, challenger Ronald Reagan pointed to high inflation as one of the failures of Carter's economic policy.

International data show an even broader range of inflation experiences. Germany after World War I experienced a spectacular example of inflation. The price of a newspaper rose from 0.3 marks in January 1921 to 70,000,000 marks less than two years later. Other prices rose by similar amounts. An extraordinarily high rate of inflation such as this is called a *hyperinflation*. The German hyperinflation had such an adverse effect on the German economy that it is often viewed as one contributor to the rise of Nazism and, as a result, World War II. Over the past 50 years, with this episode still in mind, German policymakers have been extraordinarily averse to inflation, and Germany has had much lower inflation than the United States.

What determines whether an economy experiences inflation and, if so, how much? This chapter answers this question by developing the *quantity theory of money.* Chapter 1 summarized this theory as one of the *Ten Principles of Economics:* Prices rise when the government prints too much money. This insight has a long and venerable tradition among economists. The quantity theory was discussed by the famous eighteenth-century philosopher David Hume and has been advocated more recently by the prominent economist Milton Friedman. This theory of inflation can explain both moderate inflations, such as those we have experienced in the United States, and hyperinflations, such as those experienced in interwar Germany and, more recently, in some Latin American countries.

After developing a theory of inflation, we turn to a related question: Why is inflation a problem? At first glance, the answer to this question may seem obvious: Inflation is a problem because people don't like it. In the 1970s, when the United States experienced a relatively high rate of inflation, opinion polls placed inflation as the most important issue facing the nation. President Ford echoed this sentiment in 1974 when he called inflation "public enemy number one." Ford briefly wore a "WIN" button on his lapel—for Whip Inflation Now.

But what, exactly, are the costs that inflation imposes on a society? The answer may surprise you. Identifying the various costs of inflation is not as straightforward as it first appears. As a result, although all economists decry hyperinflation, some economists argue that the costs of moderate inflation are not nearly as large as the general public believes.

THE CAUSES OF INFLATION

We begin our study of inflation by developing the quantity theory of money. Most economists rely on this theory for explaining the long-run determinants of the price level and the inflation rate.

THE LEVEL OF PRICES AND THE VALUE OF MONEY

Suppose we observe over some period of time the price of an ice-cream cone rising from a nickel to a dollar. What conclusion should we draw from the fact that people are willing to give up so much more money in exchange for a cone? It is possible that people have come to enjoy ice cream more (perhaps because some chemist has developed a miraculous new flavor). Yet that is probably not the case. It is more likely that people's enjoyment of ice cream has stayed roughly the same and that, over time, the money used to buy ice cream has become less valuable. Indeed, the first insight about inflation is that it is more about the value of money than about the value of goods.

This insight helps point the way toward a theory of inflation. When the consumer price index and other measures of the price level rise, commentators are often tempted to look at the many individual prices that make up these price indexes: "The CPI rose by 3 percent last month, led by a 20 percent rise in the price of coffee and a 30 percent rise in the price of heating oil." Although this approach does contain some interesting information about what's happening in the economy, it also misses a key point: Inflation is an economy-wide phenomenon that concerns, first and foremost, the value of the economy's medium of exchange.

The economy's overall price level can be viewed in two ways. So far, we have viewed the price level as the price of a basket of goods and services. When the price level rises, people have to pay more for the goods and services they buy. Alternatively, we can view the price level as a measure of the value of money. A rise in the price level means a lower value of money because each dollar in your wallet now buys a smaller quantity of goods and services.

*"So what's it going to be? The same size as last year
or the same price as last year?"*

It may help to express these ideas mathematically. Suppose P is the price level as measured, for instance, by the consumer price index or the GDP deflator. Then P measures the number of dollars needed to buy a basket of goods and services. Now turn this idea around: The quantity of goods and services that can be bought with \$1 equals $1/P$. In other words, if P is the price of goods and services measured in terms of money, $1/P$ is the value of money measured in terms of goods and services. Thus, when the overall price level rises, the value of money falls.

MONEY SUPPLY, MONEY DEMAND, AND MONETARY EQUILIBRIUM

What determines the value of money? The answer to this question, like many in economics, is supply and demand. Just as the supply and demand for bananas determines the price of bananas, the supply and demand for money determines the value of money. Thus, our next step in developing the quantity theory of money is to consider the determinants of money supply and money demand.

First consider money supply. In the last chapter we discussed how the Federal Reserve, together with the banking system, determines the supply of money. Through open-market operations, the Fed can change the quantity of reserves available to banks, which in turn influences the quantity of money that the banking system can create. For our purposes in this chapter, we ignore most of the complications introduced by the banking system and simply take the quantity of money supplied as a policy variable that the Fed controls directly.

Now consider money demand. There are many determinants of the quantity of money demanded, just as there are many determinants of the quantity demanded of other goods and services. How much money people choose to hold in their wallets, for instance, depends on how much they rely on credit cards and on whether an automatic teller machine is easy to find. And, as we will emphasize in a later chapter, the quantity of money demanded depends on the interest rate that a person could earn by using the money to buy an interest-bearing bond rather than leaving it in a wallet or low-interest checking account.

Although many variables affect the demand for money, one variable stands out in importance: the average level of prices in the economy. People hold money because it is the medium of exchange. Unlike other assets, such as bonds or stocks, people can use money to buy the goods and services on their shopping lists. How much money they choose to hold for this purpose depends on the prices of those goods and services. The higher prices are, the more money the typical transaction requires, and the more money people will choose to hold in their wallets and checking accounts. That is, a higher price level (a lower value of money) increases the quantity of money demanded.

What ensures that the quantity of money the Fed supplies balances the quantity of money people demand? The answer, it turns out, depends on the time horizon being considered. Later in this book we will examine the short-run answer, and we will see that interest rates play a key role. In the long run, however, the answer is different and much simpler. *In the long run, the overall level of prices adjusts to the level at which the demand for money equals the supply.* If the price level is above the equilibrium level, people will want to hold more money than the Fed has created, so the price level must fall to balance supply and demand. If the price level is below the equilibrium level, people will want to hold less

Figure 28-1

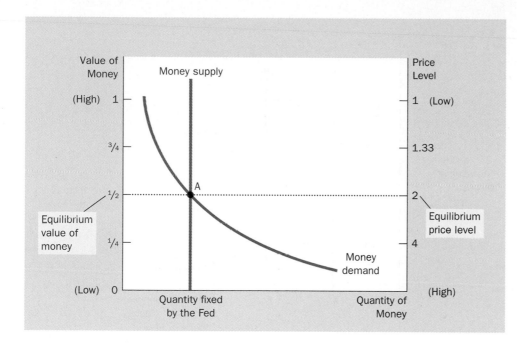

How the Supply and Demand for Money Determine the Equilibrium Price Level. The horizontal axis shows the quantity of money. The left vertical axis shows the value of money, and the right vertical axis shows the price level. The supply curve for money is vertical because the quantity of money supplied is fixed by the Fed. The demand curve for money is downward sloping because people want to hold a larger quantity of money when each dollar buys less. At the equilibrium, point A, the value of money (on the left axis) and the price level (on the right axis) have adjusted to bring the quantity of money supplied and the quantity of money demanded into balance.

money than the Fed has created, and the price level must rise to balance supply and demand. At the equilibrium price level, the quantity of money that people want to hold exactly balances the quantity of money supplied by the Fed.

Figure 28-1 illustrates these ideas. The horizontal axis of this graph shows the quantity of money. The left-hand vertical axis shows the value of money, and the right-hand vertical axis shows the price level. Notice that the price-level axis is inverted: When the value of money is high (as measured on the left axis), the price level is low (as measured on the right axis). The supply curve for money in this figure is vertical, indicating that the Fed has fixed the quantity of money available. The demand curve for money is downward sloping, indicating that when the value of money is low, people demand a larger quantity of it to buy goods and services. At the equilibrium, shown in the figure as point A, the quantity of money demanded balances the quantity of money supplied. This equilibrium of money supply and money demand determines the value of money and the price level.

THE EFFECTS OF A MONETARY INJECTION

Let's now consider the effects of a change in monetary policy. To do so, imagine that the economy is in equilibrium and then, suddenly, the Fed doubles the supply of money by printing some dollar bills and dropping them around the country from helicopters. (Or, less dramatically and more realistically, the Fed could inject money into the economy by buying some government bonds from the public in open-market operations.) What happens after such a monetary injection? How does the new equilibrium compare to the old one?

Figure 28-2 shows what happens. The monetary injection shifts the supply curve to the right from MS_1 to MS_2, and the equilibrium moves from point A to point B. As a result, the value of money (shown on the left axis) decreases from

Figure 28-2

AN INCREASE IN THE MONEY
SUPPLY. When the Fed increases
the supply of money, the money
supply curve shifts from MS_1 to
MS_2. The value of money (on the
left axis) and the price level (on
the right axis) adjust to bring
supply and demand back into
balance. The equilibrium moves
from point A to point B. Thus,
when an increase in the money
supply makes dollars more plentiful, the price level increases,
making each dollar less valuable.

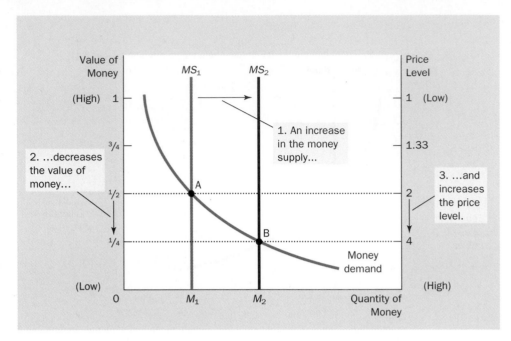

1/2 to 1/4, and the equilibrium price level (shown on the right axis) increases
from 2 to 4. In other words, when an increase in the money supply makes dollars more plentiful, the result is an increase in the price level that makes each
dollar less valuable.

This explanation of how the price level is determined and why it might
change over time is called the **quantity theory of money.** According to the quantity theory, the quantity of money available in the economy determines the value
of money, and growth in the quantity of money is the primary cause of inflation.
As economist Milton Friedman once put it, "Inflation is always and everywhere
a monetary phenomenon."

quantity theory of money

a theory asserting that the quantity
of money available determines the
price level and that the growth rate
in the quantity of money available
determines the inflation rate

A BRIEF LOOK AT THE ADJUSTMENT PROCESS

So far we have compared the old equilibrium and the new equilibrium after an
injection of money. How does the economy get from the old to the new equilibrium? A complete answer to this question requires an understanding of short-
run fluctuations in the economy, which we examine later in this book. Yet, even
now, it is instructive to consider briefly the adjustment process that occurs after
a change in money supply.

The immediate effect of a monetary injection is to create an excess supply of
money. Before the injection, the economy was in equilibrium (point A in Figure
28-2). At the prevailing price level, people had exactly as much money as they
wanted. But after the helicopters drop the new money and people pick it up off
the streets, people have more dollars in their wallets than they want. At the prevailing price level, the quantity of money supplied now exceeds the quantity
demanded.

People try to get rid of this excess supply of money in various ways. They
might buy goods and services with their excess holdings of money. Or they
might use this excess money to make loans to others by buying bonds or by

depositing the money in a bank savings account. These loans allow other people to buy goods and services. In either case, the injection of money increases the demand for goods and services.

Because the economy's ability to produce goods and services has not changed, this greater demand for goods and services causes the prices of goods and services to increase. The increase in the price level, in turn, increases the quantity of money demanded. Eventually, the economy reaches a new equilibrium (point B in Figure 28-2) at which the quantity of money demanded again equals the quantity of money supplied. In this way, the overall price level for goods and services adjusts to bring money supply and money demand into balance.

THE CLASSICAL DICHOTOMY AND MONETARY NEUTRALITY

We have seen how changes in the money supply lead to changes in the average level of prices of goods and services. How do these monetary changes affect other important macroeconomic variables, such as production, employment, real wages, and real interest rates? This question has long intrigued economists. Indeed, the great philosopher David Hume wrote about it in the eighteenth century. The answer we give today owes much to Hume's analysis.

Hume and his contemporaries suggested that all economic variables should be divided into two groups. The first group consists of **nominal variables**—variables measured in monetary units. The second group consists of **real variables**—variables measured in physical units. For example, the price of corn is a nominal variable because it is measured in dollars, whereas the amount of corn produced is a real variable because it is measured in pounds. Similarly, nominal GDP is a nominal variable because it measures the dollar value of the economy's output of goods and services, while real GDP is a real variable because it measures the total quantity of goods and services produced.

Although prices quoted in terms of money are nominal variables, *relative* prices are real variables. For instance, the price of corn and the price of wheat are both nominal variables, but the price of corn relative to the price of wheat is a real variable because it is measured in pounds of wheat per pound of corn. Similarly, the real wage (the dollar wage adjusted for inflation) is a real variable because it measures the rate at which the economy exchanges goods and services for each unit of labor. The real interest rate (the nominal interest rate adjusted for inflation) is a real variable because it measures the rate at which the economy exchanges goods and services produced today for goods and services produced in the future.

This division of variables into these two groups is called the **classical dichotomy.** Hume suggested that the classical dichotomy is useful in analyzing the economy because different forces influence real and nominal variables. In particular, he argued, nominal variables are heavily influenced by developments in the economy's monetary system, whereas the monetary system is largely irrelevant for understanding the determinants of important real variables.

Notice that Hume's idea was implicit in our earlier discussions of the real economy in the long run. In previous chapters, we examined how real GDP, saving, investment, real interest rates, and unemployment are determined without any mention of the existence of money. As explained in that analysis, the economy's production of goods and services depends on productivity and factor supplies, the real interest rate adjusts to balance the supply and demand for loanable

nominal variables
variables measured in monetary units

real variables
variables measured in physical units

classical dichotomy
the theoretical separation of nominal and real variables

funds, the real wage adjusts to balance the supply and demand for labor, and unemployment results when the real wage is for some reason kept above its equilibrium level. These important conclusions have nothing to do with the quantity of money supplied.

Changes in the supply of money, according to Hume, affect nominal variables but not real variables. When the central bank doubles the money supply, the price level doubles, the dollar wage doubles, and all other dollar values double. Real variables, such as production, employment, real wages, and real interest rates, are unchanged. This irrelevance of monetary changes for real variables is called **monetary neutrality.**

monetary neutrality

the proposition that changes in the money supply do not affect real variables

An analogy sheds light on the meaning of monetary neutrality. Recall that, as the unit of account, money is the yardstick we use to measure economic transactions. When a central bank doubles the money supply, all prices double, and the value of the unit of account falls by half. A similar change would occur if the government were to reduce the length of the yard from 36 to 18 inches: As a result of the new unit of measurement, all *measured* distances (nominal variables) would double, but the *actual* distances (real variables) would remain the same. The dollar, like the yard, is merely a unit of measurement, so a change in its value should not have important real effects.

Is this conclusion of monetary neutrality a realistic description of the world in which we live? The answer is: not completely. A change in the length of the yard from 36 to 18 inches would not matter much in the long run, but in the short run it would certainly lead to confusion and various mistakes. Similarly, most economists today believe that over short periods of time—within the span of a year or two—there is reason to think that monetary changes do have important effects on real variables. Hume himself also doubted that monetary neutrality would apply in the short run. (We will turn to the study of short-run nonneutrality in a later chapter, and this topic will shed light on the reasons why the Fed changes the supply of money over time.)

Yet most economists today accept Hume's conclusion as a description of the economy in the long run. Over the course of a decade, for instance, monetary changes have important effects on nominal variables but only negligible effects on real variables. When studying long-run changes in the economy, the neutrality of money offers a good description of how the world works.

VELOCITY AND THE QUANTITY EQUATION

We can obtain another perspective on the quantity theory of money by considering the following question: How many times per year is the typical dollar bill used to pay for a newly produced good or service? The answer to this question is given by a variable called the **velocity of money.** In physics, the term *velocity* refers to the speed at which an object travels. In economics, the velocity of money refers to the speed at which the typical dollar bill travels around the economy from wallet to wallet.

velocity of money

the rate at which money changes hands

To calculate the velocity of money, we divide the nominal value of output (nominal GDP) by the quantity of money. If P is the price level (the GDP deflator), Y the quantity of output (real GDP), and M the quantity of money, then velocity is

$$V = (P \times Y)/M.$$

To see why this makes sense, imagine a simple economy that produces only pizza. Suppose that the economy produces 100 pizzas in a year, that a pizza sells for $10, and that the quantity of money in the economy is $50. Then the velocity of money is

$$V = (\$10 \times 100)/\$50$$
$$= 20.$$

In this economy, people spend a total of $1,000 per year on pizza. For this $1,000 of spending to take place with only $50 of money, each dollar bill must change hands 20 times per year.

With slight algebraic rearrangement, this equation can be rewritten as

$$M \times V = P \times Y.$$

This equation states that the quantity of money *(M)* times the velocity of money *(V)* equals the price of output *(P)* times the amount of output *(Y)*. It is called the **quantity equation** because it relates the quantity of money *(M)* to the nominal value of output *(P × Y)*. The quantity equation shows that an increase in the quantity of money in an economy must be reflected in one of the other three variables: The price level must rise, the quantity of output must rise, or the velocity of money must fall.

In many cases, it turns out that the velocity of money is relatively stable. For example, Figure 28-3 shows nominal GDP, the quantity of money (as measured by M2), and the velocity of money for the U.S. economy since 1960. Although the velocity of money is not exactly constant, it has not changed dramatically. By contrast, the money supply and nominal GDP during this period have increased more than tenfold. Thus, for some purposes, the assumption of constant velocity may be a good approximation.

quantity equation
the equation M × V = P × Y, *which relates the quantity of money, the velocity of money, and the dollar value of the economy's output of goods and services*

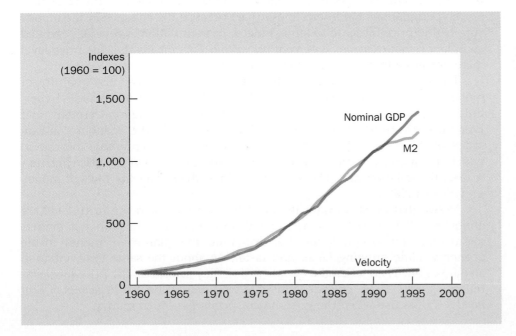

Figure 28-3

NOMINAL GDP, THE QUANTITY OF MONEY, AND THE VELOCITY OF MONEY. This figure shows the nominal value of output as measured by nominal GDP, the quantity of money as measured by M2, and the velocity of money as measured by their ratio. For comparability, all three series have been scaled to equal 100 in 1960. Notice that nominal GDP and the quantity of money have grown dramatically over this period, while velocity has been relatively stable.

SOURCE: U.S. Department of Commerce; Federal Reserve Board.

We now have all the elements necessary to explain the equilibrium price level and inflation rate. Here they are:

1. The velocity of money is relatively stable over time.
2. Because velocity is stable, when the Fed changes the quantity of money (*M*), it causes proportionate changes in the nominal value of output (*P* × *Y*).
3. The economy's output of goods and services (*Y*) is primarily determined by factor supplies and the available technology. In particular, because money is neutral, money does not affect output.
4. With output (*Y*) determined by factor supplies and technology, when the Fed alters the money supply (*M*) and induces parallel changes in the nominal value of output (*P* × *Y*), these changes are reflected in changes in the price level (*P*).
5. Therefore, when the Fed increases the money supply rapidly, the result is a high rate of inflation.

These five steps are the essence of the quantity theory of money.

CASE STUDY   MONEY AND PRICES DURING FOUR HYPERINFLATIONS

Although earthquakes can wreak havoc on a society, they have the beneficial by-product of providing much useful data for seismologists. These data can shed light on alternative theories and, thereby, help society predict and deal with future threats. Similarly, hyperinflations offer monetary economists a natural experiment they can use to study the effects of money on the economy.

Hyperinflations are interesting in part because the changes in the money supply and price level are so large. Indeed, hyperinflation is generally defined as inflation that exceeds 50 percent *per month*. This means that the price level increases more than 100-fold over the course of a year.

The data on hyperinflation show a clear link between the quantity of money and the price level. Figure 28-4 graphs data from four classic hyperinflations that occurred during the 1920s in Austria, Hungary, Germany, and Poland. Each graph shows the quantity of money in the economy and an index of the price level. The slope of the money line represents the rate at which the quantity of money was growing, and the slope of the price line represents the inflation rate. The steeper the lines, the higher the rates of money growth or inflation.

Notice that in each graph the quantity of money and the price level are almost parallel. In each instance, growth in the quantity of money is moderate at first, and so is inflation. But over time, the quantity of money in the economy starts growing faster and faster. At about the same time, inflation also takes off. Then when the quantity of money stabilizes, the price level stabilizes as well. These episodes illustrate well one of the *Ten Principles of Economics:* Prices rise when the government prints too much money.

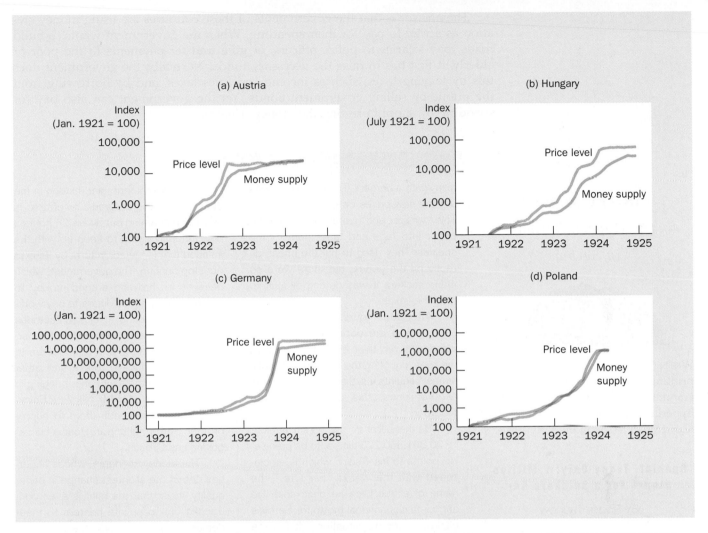

MONEY AND PRICES DURING FOUR HYPERINFLATIONS. This figure shows the quantity of money and the price level during four hyperinflations. (Note that these variables are graphed on *logarithmic* scales. This means that equal vertical distances on the graph represent equal *percentage* changes in the variable.) In each case, the quantity of money and the price level move closely together. The strong association between these two variables is consistent with the quantity theory of money, which states that growth in the money supply is the primary cause of inflation.

Figure 28-4

SOURCE: Adapted from Thomas J. Sargent, "The End of Four Big Inflations," in Robert Hall, ed., *Inflation*, Chicago: University of Chicago Press, 1983, 41–93.

THE INFLATION TAX

If inflation is so easy to explain, why do countries experience hyperinflation? That is, why do the central banks of these countries choose to print so much money that its value is certain to fall rapidly over time?

The answer is that the governments of these countries are using money creation as a way to pay for their spending. When the government wants to build roads, pay salaries to police officers, or give transfer payments to the poor or elderly, it first has to raise the necessary funds. Normally, the government does this by levying taxes, such as income and sales taxes, and by borrowing from the public by selling government bonds. Yet the government can also pay for spending by simply printing the money it needs.

IN THE NEWS

The Hyperinflation

in Serbia

WHENEVER GOVERNMENTS TURN TO THE printing press to finance substantial amounts of spending, the result is hyperinflation. Residents of Serbia learned that lesson in the early 1990s.

Special, Today Only: 6 Million Dinars for a Snickers Bar

BY ROGER THUROW

BELGRADE, YUGOSLAVIA—At the Luna boutique, a Snickers bar costs 6 million dinars. Or at least it does until manager Tihomir Nikolic reads the overnight fax from his boss.

"Raise prices 99 percent," the document tersely orders. It would be an even 100 percent except that the computers at the boutique, which would be considered a dime store in other parts of the world, can't handle three-digit changes.

So for the second time in three days, Mr. Nikolic sets about raising prices. He jams a mop across the door frame to keep customers from getting away with a bargain. The computer spits out the new prices on perforated paper. The manager and two assistants rip the paper into tags and tape them to the shelves. They used to put the prices directly on the goods, but there were so many stickers it was getting difficult to read the labels.

After four hours, the mop is removed from the door. The customers wander in, rub their eyes and squint at the tags, counting the zeros. Mr. Nikolic himself squints as the computer prints another price, this one for a video recorder.

"Is that billions?" he asks himself. It is: 20,391,560,223 dinars, to be precise. He points to his T-shirt, which is emblazoned with the words "Far Out," the name of a fruit juice he once sold. He suggests it is an ideal motto for Serbia's bizarre economic situation. "It fits the craziness," he says.

How else would you describe it? Since the international community imposed economic sanctions, the inflation rate has been at least 10 percent *daily.* This translates to an annual rate in the quadrillions—so high as to be meaningless. In Serbia, one U.S. dollar will get you 10 million dinars at the Hyatt hotel, 12 million from the shady money changers on Republic Square, and 17 million from a bank run by Belgrade's underworld. Serbs complain that the dinar is as worthless as toilet paper. But for the moment, at least, there is plenty of toilet paper to go around.

The government mint, hidden in the park behind the Belgrade racetrack, is said to be churning out dinars 24 hours a day, furiously trying to keep up with the inflation that is fueled, in turn, by its own nonstop printing. The government, which believes in throwing around money to damp dissent, needs dinars to pay workers for not working at closed factories and offices. It needs them to buy the harvest from the farmers. It needs them to finance its smuggling forays and other ways to evade the sanctions, bringing in everything from oil to Mr. Nikolic's Snickers bars. It also needs them to supply brother Serbs fighting in Bosnia-Herzegovina and Croatia.

The money changers, whose fingertips detect the slightest change in paper quality, insist that the mint is even contracting out to private printers to meet demand.

"We're experts. They can't fool us," says one of the changers as he hands over 800 million worth of 5-million-dinar bills. "These," he notes confidently, "are fresh from the mint." He says he got them from a private bank, which got them from the central bank, which got them from the mint—an unholy circuit linking the black market with the Finance Ministry. "It's collective lunacy," the money changer says, laughing wickedly.

SOURCE: *The Wall Street Journal,* August 4, 1993, p. A1.

When the government raises revenue by printing money, it is said to levy an **inflation tax.** The inflation tax is not exactly like other taxes, however, because no one receives a bill from the government for this tax. Instead, the inflation tax is more subtle. When the government prints money, the price level rises, and the dollars in your wallet are less valuable. Thus, *the inflation tax is like a tax on everyone who holds money.*

inflation tax
the revenue the government raises by creating money

The importance of the inflation tax varies from country to country and over time. In the United States in recent years, the inflation tax has been a trivial source of revenue: It has accounted for less than 3 percent of government revenue. During the 1770s, however, the Continental Congress of the fledgling United States relied heavily on the inflation tax to pay for military spending. Because the new government had a limited ability to raise funds through regular taxes or borrowing, printing continental dollars was the easiest way to pay the American soldiers. As the quantity theory predicts, the result was a high rate of inflation: Prices measured in terms of the continental dollar rose more than 100-fold over a few years.

Almost all hyperinflations follow the same pattern as the hyperinflation during the American Revolution. The government has high spending, inadequate tax revenue, and limited ability to borrow. As a result, it turns to the printing press to pay for its spending. The massive increases in the quantity of money lead to massive inflation. The inflation ends when the government institutes fiscal reforms—such as cuts in government spending—that eliminate the need for the inflation tax.

THE FISHER EFFECT

According to the principle of monetary neutrality, an increase in the rate of money growth raises the rate of inflation but does not affect any real variable. An important application of this principle concerns the effect of money on interest rates. Interest rates are important variables for macroeconomists to understand because they link the economy of the present and the economy of the future through their effects on saving and investment.

To understand the relationship between money, inflation, and interest rates, recall the distinction between the nominal interest rate and the real interest rate. The *nominal interest rate* is the interest rate you hear about at your bank. If you have a savings account, for instance, the nominal interest rate tells you how fast the number of dollars in your account will rise over time. The *real interest rate* corrects the nominal interest rate for the effect of inflation in order to tell you how fast the purchasing power of your savings account will rise over time. The real interest rate is the nominal interest rate minus the inflation rate:

$$\text{Real interest rate} = \text{Nominal interest rate} - \text{Inflation rate.}$$

For example, if the bank posts a nominal interest rate of 7 percent per year and the inflation rate is 3 percent per year, then the real value of the deposits grows by 4 percent per year.

We can rewrite this equation to show that the nominal interest rate is the sum of the real interest rate and the inflation rate:

$$\text{Nominal interest rate} = \text{Real interest rate} + \text{Inflation rate}.$$

This way of looking at the nominal interest rate is useful because different economic forces determine each of the two terms on the right-hand side of this equation. As we discussed in an earlier chapter, the supply and demand for loanable funds determines the real interest rate. And, according to the quantity theory of money, growth in the money supply determines the inflation rate.

Let's now consider how the growth in the money supply affects interest rates. In the long run over which money is neutral, a change in money growth should not affect the real interest rate. The real interest rate is, after all, a real variable. For the real interest rate not to be affected, the nominal interest rate must adjust one-for-one to changes in the inflation rate. Thus, *when the Fed increases the rate of money growth, the result is both a higher inflation rate and a higher nominal interest rate.* This adjustment of the nominal interest rate to the inflation rate is called the **Fisher effect,** after economist Irving Fisher (1867–1947), who first studied it.

The Fisher effect is, in fact, crucial for understanding changes over time in the nominal interest rate. Figure 28-5 shows the nominal interest rate and the inflation rate in the U.S. economy since 1950. The close association between these two variables is clear. The nominal interest rate rose from the 1950s through the 1970s because inflation was also rising during this time. Similarly, the nominal interest rate fell from the early 1980s through the mid-1990s because the Fed finally got inflation under control.

Fisher effect

the one-for-one adjustment of the nominal interest rate to the inflation rate

QUICK QUIZ   The government of a country increases the growth rate of the money supply from 5 percent per year to 50 percent per year. What happens to prices? What happens to nominal interest rates? Why might the government be doing this?

Figure 28-5

THE NOMINAL INTEREST RATE AND THE INFLATION RATE. This figure uses annual data since 1950 to show the nominal interest rate on three-month Treasury bills and the inflation rate as measured by the consumer price index. The close association between these two variables is evidence for the Fisher effect: When the inflation rate rises, so does the nominal interest rate.

SOURCE: U.S. Department of Treasury; U.S. Department of Labor.

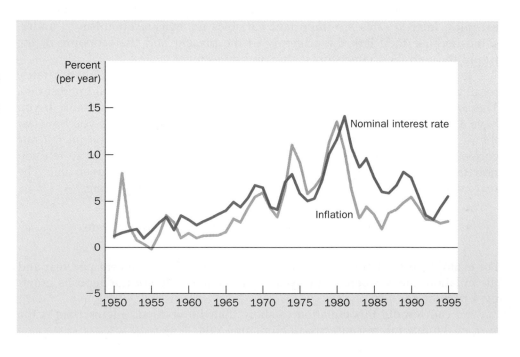

THE COSTS OF INFLATION

In the late 1970s, when the U.S. inflation rate reached about 10 percent per year, inflation dominated debates over economic policy. And even though inflation was low during the first half of the 1990s, inflation remained a closely watched macroeconomic variable. One 1996 study found that *inflation* was the economic term mentioned most often in U.S. newspapers (far ahead of second-place finisher *unemployment* and third-place finisher *productivity*).

Inflation is closely watched and widely discussed because it is thought to be a serious economic problem. But is that true? And if so, why?

A FALL IN PURCHASING POWER? THE INFLATION FALLACY

If you ask the typical person why inflation is bad, he will tell you that the answer is obvious: Inflation robs him of the purchasing power of his hard-earned dollars. When prices rise, each dollar of income buys fewer goods and services. Thus, it might seem that inflation directly lowers living standards.

Yet further thought reveals a fallacy in this answer. When prices rise, buyers of goods and services do pay more for what they buy. At the same time, however, sellers of goods and services get more for what they sell. Because most people earn their incomes by selling their services, such as their labor, inflation in incomes goes hand in hand with inflation in prices. Thus, *inflation does not in itself reduce people's real purchasing power.*

People believe the inflation fallacy because they do not appreciate the principle of monetary neutrality. A worker who receives an annual raise of 10 percent tends to view that raise as a reward for her own talent and effort. When an inflation rate of 6 percent reduces the real value of that raise to only 4 percent, the worker might feel that she has been cheated of what is rightfully her due. In fact, as we discussed in previous chapters, real incomes are determined by real variables, such as physical capital, human capital, natural resources, and the available production technology. Nominal incomes are determined by those factors and the overall price level. If the Fed were to lower the inflation rate from 6 percent to zero, our worker's annual raise would fall from 10 percent to 4 percent. She might feel less robbed by inflation, but her real income would not rise more quickly.

But if nominal incomes tend to keep pace with rising prices, why then is inflation a problem? It turns out that there is no single answer to this question. Instead, economists have identified several costs of inflation. Each of these costs shows some way in which persistent growth in the money supply does, in fact, have some effect on real variables.

SHOELEATHER COSTS

As we have discussed, inflation is like a tax on the holders of money. The tax itself is not a cost to society: It is only a transfer of resources from households to the government. Yet, as we first saw in Chapter 8, most taxes give people an incentive to alter their behavior to avoid paying the tax, and this distortion of incentives causes deadweight losses for society as a whole. Like other taxes, the inflation tax also causes deadweight losses, as people waste scarce resources trying to avoid it.

How can a person avoid paying the inflation tax? Because inflation erodes the real value of the money in your wallet, you can avoid the inflation tax by holding less money. One way to do this is to go to the bank more often. For example, rather than withdrawing $200 every four weeks, you might withdraw $50 once a week. By making more frequent trips to the bank, you can keep more of your wealth in your interest-bearing savings account and less in your wallet, where inflation erodes its value.

shoeleather costs

the resources wasted when inflation encourages people to reduce their money holdings

The cost of reducing your money holdings is called the **shoeleather cost** of inflation because making more frequent trips to the bank causes your shoes to wear out more quickly. Of course, this term is not to be taken literally: The actual cost of reducing your money holdings is not the wear and tear on your shoes but the time and convenience you must sacrifice to keep less money on hand than you would if there were no inflation.

The shoeleather costs of inflation may seem trivial. And, in fact, they are in the U.S. economy, which has had only moderate inflation in recent years. But this cost is magnified in countries experiencing hyperinflation. Here is a description of one person's experience in Bolivia during its hyperinflation (as reported in the August 13, 1985, issue of *The Wall Street Journal*, p. 1):

> When Edgar Miranda gets his monthly teacher's pay of 25 million pesos, he hasn't a moment to lose. Every hour, pesos drop in value. So, while his wife rushes to market to lay in a month's supply of rice and noodles, he is off with the rest of the pesos to change them into black-market dollars.
>
> Mr. Miranda is practicing the First Rule of Survival amid the most out-of-control inflation in the world today. Bolivia is a case study of how runaway inflation undermines a society. Price increases are so huge that the figures build up almost beyond comprehension. In one six-month period, for example, prices soared at an annual rate of 38,000 percent. By official count, however, last year's inflation reached 2,000 percent, and this year's is expected to hit 8,000 percent—though other estimates range many times higher. In any event, Bolivia's rate dwarfs Israel's 370 percent and Argentina's 1,100 percent—two other cases of severe inflation.
>
> It is easier to comprehend what happens to the thirty-eight-year-old Mr. Miranda's pay if he doesn't quickly change it into dollars. The day he was paid 25 million pesos, a dollar cost 500,000 pesos. So he received $50. Just days later, with the rate at 900,000 pesos, he would have received $27.

As this story shows, the shoeleather costs of inflation can be substantial. With the high inflation rate, Mr. Miranda does not have the luxury of holding the local money as a store of value. Instead, he is forced to convert his pesos quickly into goods or into U.S. dollars, which offer a more stable store of value. The time and effort that Mr. Miranda expends to reduce his money holdings are a waste of resources. If the monetary authority pursued a low-inflation policy, Mr. Miranda would be happy to hold pesos, and he could put his time and effort to more productive use. In fact, shortly after this article was written, the Bolivian inflation rate was reduced substantially with more restrictive monetary policy.

MENU COSTS

Most firms do not change the prices of their products every day. Instead, firms often announce prices and leave them unchanged for weeks, months, or even years. One survey found that the typical U.S. firm changes its prices about once a year.

Firms change prices infrequently because there are costs of changing prices. Costs of price adjustment are called **menu costs,** a term derived from a restaurant's cost of printing a new menu. Menu costs include the cost of printing new price lists and catalogs, the cost of sending these new price lists and catalogs to dealers and customers, the cost of advertising the new prices, the cost of deciding on new prices, and even the cost of dealing with customer annoyance over price changes.

menu costs

the costs of changing prices

Inflation increases the menu costs that firms must bear. In the current U.S. economy, with its low inflation rate, annual price adjustment is an appropriate business strategy for many firms. But when high inflation makes firms' costs rise rapidly, annual price adjustment is impractical. During hyperinflations, for example, firms must change their prices daily or even more often just to keep up with all the other prices in the economy.

RELATIVE-PRICE VARIABILITY AND THE MISALLOCATION OF RESOURCES

Suppose that the Eatabit Eatery prints a new menu with new prices every January and then leaves its prices unchanged for the rest of the year. If there is no inflation, Eatabit's relative prices—the prices of its meals compared to other prices in the economy—would be constant over the course of the year. By contrast, if the inflation rate is 12 percent per year, Eatabit's relative prices will automatically fall by 1 percent each month. The restaurant's prices will be relatively high in the early months of the year, just after it has printed a new menu, and relatively low in the later months. And the higher the inflation rate, the greater is this automatic variability. Thus, because prices change only once in a while, inflation causes relative prices to vary more than they otherwise would.

Why does this matter? The reason is that market economies rely on relative prices to allocate scarce resources. Consumers decide what to buy by comparing the quality and prices of various goods and services. Through these decisions, they determine how the scarce factors of production are allocated among industries and firms. When inflation distorts relative prices, consumer decisions are distorted, and markets are less able to allocate resources to their best use.

INFLATION-INDUCED TAX DISTORTIONS

Almost all taxes distort incentives, cause people to alter their behavior, and lead to a less efficient allocation of the economy's resources. Many taxes, however, become even more problematic in the presence of inflation. The reason is that lawmakers often fail to take inflation into account when writing the tax laws.

Economists who have studied the tax code conclude that inflation tends to raise the tax burden on income earned from savings.

One example of how inflation discourages saving is the tax treatment of *capital gains*—the profits made by selling an asset for more than its purchase price. Suppose that in 1980 you used some of your savings to buy stock in Microsoft Corporation for $10 and that in 1995 you sold the stock for $50. According to the tax law, you have earned a capital gain of $40, which you must include in your income when computing how much income tax you owe. But suppose the overall price level doubled from 1980 to 1995. In this case, the $10 you invested in 1980 is equivalent (in terms of purchasing power) to $20 in 1995. When you sell your stock for $50, you have a real gain (an increase in purchasing power) of only $30. The tax code, however, does not take account of inflation and assesses you a tax on a gain of $40. Thus, inflation exaggerates the size of capital gains and inadvertently increases the tax burden on this type of income.

Another example is the tax treatment of interest income. The income tax treats the *nominal* interest earned on savings as income, even though part of the nominal interest rate merely compensates for inflation. To see the effects of this policy, consider the numerical example in Table 28-1. The table compares two economies, both of which tax interest income at a rate of 25 percent. In Economy 1, inflation is zero, and the nominal and real interest rates are both 4 percent. In this case, the 25 percent tax on interest income reduces the real interest rate from 4 percent to 3 percent. In Economy 2, the real interest rate is again 4 percent, but the inflation rate is 8 percent. As a result of the Fisher effect, the nominal interest rate is 12 percent. Because the income tax treats this entire 12 percent interest as income, the government takes 25 percent of it, leaving an after-tax nominal interest rate of only 9 percent and an after-tax real interest rate of only 1 percent. In this case, the 25 percent tax on interest income reduces the real interest rate from 4 percent to 1 percent. Because the after-tax real interest rate provides the incentive to save, saving is much less attractive in the economy with inflation (Economy 2) than in the economy with stable prices (Economy 1).

Table 28-1		

HOW INFLATION RAISES THE TAX BURDEN ON SAVING. In the presence of zero inflation, a 25 percent tax on interest income reduces the real interest rate from 4 percent to 3 percent. In the presence of 8 percent inflation, the same tax reduces the real interest rate from 4 percent to 1 percent.

	ECONOMY 1 (PRICE STABILITY)	ECONOMY 2 (INFLATION)
Real interest rate	4%	4%
Inflation rate	0	8
Nominal interest rate (real interest rate + inflation rate)	4	12
Reduced interest due to 25 percent tax (.25 × nominal interest rate)	1	3
After-tax nominal interest rate (.75 × nominal interest rate)	3	9
After-tax real interest rate (after-tax nominal interest rate − inflation rate)	3	1

The taxes on nominal capital gains and on nominal interest income are two examples of how the tax code interacts with inflation. There are many others. Because of these inflation-induced tax changes, higher inflation tends to discourage people from saving. Recall that the economy's saving provides the resources for investment, which in turn is a key ingredient to long-run economic growth. Thus, when inflation raises the tax burden on saving, it tends to depress the economy's long-run growth rate. There is, however, no consensus among economists about the size of this effect.

One solution to this problem, other than eliminating inflation, is to index the tax system. That is, the tax laws could be rewritten to take account of the effects of inflation. In the case of capital gains, for example, the tax code could adjust the purchase price using a price index and assess the tax only on the real gain. In the case of interest income, the government could tax only real interest income by excluding that portion of the interest income that merely compensates for inflation. To some extent, the tax laws have moved in the direction of indexation. For example, the income levels at which income tax rates change are adjusted automatically each year based on changes in the consumer price index. Yet many other aspects of the tax laws—such as the tax treatment of capital gains and interest income—are not indexed.

In an ideal world, the tax laws would be written so that inflation would not alter anyone's real tax liability. In the world in which we live, however, tax laws are far from perfect. More complete indexation would probably be desirable, but it would further complicate a tax code that many people already consider too complex.

CONFUSION AND INCONVENIENCE

Imagine that we took a poll and asked people the following question: "This year the yard is 36 inches. How long do you think it should be next year?" Assuming we could get people to take us seriously, they would tell us that the yard should stay the same length—36 inches. Anything else would just complicate life needlessly.

What does this finding have to do with inflation? Recall that money, as the economy's unit of account, is what we use to quote prices and record debts. In other words, money is the yardstick with which we measure economic transactions. The job of the Federal Reserve is a bit like the job of the Bureau of Standards—to ensure the reliability of a commonly used unit of measurement. When the Fed increases the money supply and creates inflation, it erodes the real value of the unit of account.

It is difficult to judge the costs of the confusion and inconvenience that arise from inflation. Earlier we discussed how the tax code incorrectly measures real incomes in the presence of inflation. Similarly, accountants incorrectly measure firms' earnings when prices are rising over time. Because inflation causes dollars at different times to have different real values, computing a firm's profit—the difference between its revenue and costs—is more complicated in an economy with inflation. Therefore, to some extent, inflation makes investors less able to sort out successful from unsuccessful firms, which in turn impedes financial markets in their role of allocating the economy's saving to alternative types of investment.

A SPECIAL COST OF UNEXPECTED INFLATION: ARBITRARY REDISTRIBUTIONS OF WEALTH

So far, the costs of inflation we have discussed occur even if inflation is steady and predictable. Inflation has an additional cost, however, when it comes as a surprise. Unexpected inflation redistributes wealth among the population in a way that has nothing to do with either merit or need. These redistributions occur because many loans in the economy are specified in terms of the unit of account—money.

Consider an example. Suppose that Sam Student takes out a $20,000 loan at a 7 percent interest rate from Bigbank to attend college. In ten years, the loan will come due. After his debt has compounded for ten years at 7 percent, Sam will owe Bigbank $40,000. The real value of this debt will depend on inflation over the decade. If Sam is lucky, the economy will have a hyperinflation. In this case, wages and prices will rise so high that Sam will be able to pay the $40,000 debt out of pocket change. By contrast, if the economy goes through a major deflation, then wages and prices will fall, and Sam will find the $40,000 debt a greater burden than he anticipated.

IN THE NEWS

How to Protect Your Savings from Inflation

AS WE HAVE SEEN, UNEXPECTED CHANGES in the price level redistribute wealth among debtors and creditors. This would no longer be true, however, if debt contracts were written in real, rather than nominal, terms. In early 1997, the U.S. Treasury Department issued, for the first time, bonds with a return indexed to the price level. In the following opinion column, two prominent financial economists discuss the merits of this policy.

Inflation Fighters for the Long Term

BY JOHN Y. CAMPBELL AND ROBERT J. SHILLER

Treasury Secretary Robert Rubin announced on Thursday that the government plans to issue inflation-indexed bonds—that is, bonds whose interest and principal payments are adjusted upward for inflation, guaranteeing their real purchasing power in the future.

This is a historic moment. Economists have been advocating such bonds for many long and frustrating years. Index bonds were first called for in 1822 by the economist Joseph Lowe. In the 1870s, they were championed by the British economist William Stanley Jevons. In the early part of this century, the legendary Irving Fisher made a career of advocating them.

In recent decades, economists of every political stripe—from Milton Fried-

man to James Tobin, Alan Blinder to Alan Greenspan—have supported them. Yet, because there was little public clamor for such an investment, the government never issued indexed bonds.

Let's hope this lack of interest does not continue now that they will become available. The success of the indexed bonds depends on whether the public understands them—and buys them. Until now, inflation has made government bonds a risky investment. In 1966, when the inflation rate was only 3 percent, if someone had bought a 30-year government bond yielding 5 percent, he would have expected that by now his investment would be worth 180 percent of its original value. However, after years of higher-than-expected inflation, the investment is worth only 85 percent of its original value.

Because inflation has been modest in recent years, many people today are not worried about how it will affect their savings. This complacency is dangerous:

This example shows that unexpected changes in prices redistribute wealth among debtors and creditors. A hyperinflation enriches Sam at the expense of Bigbank because it diminishes the real value of the debt; Sam can repay the loan in less valuable dollars than he anticipated. Deflation enriches Bigbank at Sam's expense because it increases the real value of the debt; in this case, Sam has to repay the loan in more valuable dollars than he anticipated. If inflation were predictable, then Bigbank and Sam could take inflation into account when setting the nominal interest rate. (Recall the Fisher effect.) But if inflation is hard to predict, it imposes risk on Sam and Bigbank that both would prefer to avoid.

This cost of unexpected inflation is important to consider together with another fact: Inflation is especially volatile and uncertain when the average rate of inflation is high. This is seen most simply by examining the experience of different countries. Countries with low average inflation, such as Germany in the late twentieth century, tend to have stable inflation. Countries with high average inflation, such as many countries in Latin America, tend also to have unstable inflation. There are no known examples of economies with high, stable inflation. This relationship between the level and volatility of inflation points to another cost of inflation. If a country pursues a high-inflation monetary policy,

Even a low rate of inflation can seriously erode savings over long periods of time.

Imagine that you retire today with a pension invested in Treasury bonds that pay a fixed $10,000 each year, regardless of inflation. If there is no inflation, in 20 years the pension will have the same purchasing power that it does today. But if there is an inflation rate of only 3 percent per year, in 20 years your pension will be worth only $5,540 in today's dollars. Five percent inflation over 20 years will cut your purchasing power to $3,770, and 10 percent will reduce it to a pitiful $1,390. Which of these scenarios is likely? No one knows. Inflation ultimately depends on the people who are elected and appointed as guardians of our money supply.

At a time when Americans are living longer and planning for several decades of retirement, the insidious effects of inflation should be of serious concern. For this reason alone, the creation of inflation-indexed bonds, with their guarantee of a safe return over long periods of time, is a welcome development.

No other investment offers this kind of safety. Conventional government bonds make payments that are fixed in dollar terms; but investors should be concerned about purchasing power, not about the number of dollars they receive. Money market funds make dollar payments that increase with inflation to some degree, since short-term interest rates tend to rise with inflation. But many other factors also influence interest rates, so the real income from a money market fund is not secure.

The stock market offers a high rate of return on average, but it can fall as well as rise. Investors should remember the bear market of the 1970s as well as the bull market of the 1980s and 1990s.

Inflation-indexed government bonds have been issued in Britain for 15 years, in Canada for 5 years, and in many other countries, including Australia, New Zealand, and Sweden. In Britain, which has the world's largest indexed-bond market, the bonds have offered a yield 3 to 4 percent higher than the rate of inflation. In the United States, a safe long-term return of this sort should make indexed bonds an important part of retirement savings.

We expect that financial institutions will take advantage of the new inflation-indexed bonds and offer innovative new products. Indexed-bond funds will probably appear first, but indexed annuities and even indexed mortgages—monthly payments would be adjusted for inflation—should also become available.

Although the Clinton administration may not get much credit for it today, the decision to issue inflation-indexed bonds is an accomplishment that historians decades hence will single out for special recognition.

SOURCE: *The New York Times*, May 18, 1996, Section 1, p. 19.

it will have to bear not only the costs of high expected inflation but also the arbitrary redistributions of wealth associated with unexpected inflation.

CASE STUDY   *THE WIZARD OF OZ* AND THE FREE-SILVER DEBATE

As a child, you probably saw the movie *The Wizard of Oz*, based on a children's book written in 1900. The movie and book tell the story of a young girl, Dorothy, who finds herself lost in a strange land far from home. You probably did not know, however, that the story is actually an allegory about U.S. monetary policy in the late nineteenth century.

From 1880 to 1896, the price level in the U.S. economy fell by 23 percent. Because this event was unanticipated, it led to a major redistribution of wealth. Most farmers in the western part of the country were debtors. Their creditors were the bankers in the east. When the price level fell, it caused the real value of these debts to rise, which enriched the banks at the expense of the farmers.

According to populist politicians of the time, the solution to the farmers' problem was the free coinage of silver. During this period, the United States was operating with a gold standard. The quantity of gold determined the money supply and, thereby, the price level. The free-silver advocates wanted silver, as well as gold, to be used as money. If adopted, this proposal would have increased the money supply, pushed up the price level, and reduced the real burden of the farmers' debts.

The debate over silver was heated, and it was central to the politics of the 1890s. A common election slogan of the populists was "We Are Mortgaged. All But Our Votes." One prominent advocate of free silver was William Jennings Bryan, the Democratic nominee for president in 1896. He is remembered in part for a speech at the Democratic party's nominating convention in which he said, "You shall not press down upon the brow of labor this crown of thorns. You shall not crucify mankind upon a cross of gold." Rarely since then have politicians waxed so poetic about alternative approaches to monetary policy. Nonetheless, Bryan lost the election to Republican William McKinley, and the United States remained on the gold standard.

L. Frank Baum, the author of *The Wizard of Oz*, was a midwestern journalist. When he sat down to write a story for children, he made the characters represent protagonists in the major political battle of his time. Although modern commentators on the story differ somewhat in the interpretation they assign to each character, there is no doubt that the story highlights the debate over monetary policy. Here is how economic historian Hugh Rockoff, writing in the August 1990 issue of the *Journal of Political Economy*, interprets the story:

DOROTHY:	Traditional American values
TOTO:	Prohibitionist party, also called the Teetotalers
SCARECROW:	Farmers
TIN WOODSMAN:	Industrial workers
COWARDLY LION:	William Jennings Bryan
MUNCHKINS:	Citizens of the east

WICKED WITCH OF THE EAST: Grover Cleveland
WICKED WITCH OF THE WEST: William McKinley
WIZARD: Marcus Alonzo Hanna, chairman of the Republican party
OZ: Abbreviation for ounce of gold
YELLOW BRICK ROAD: Gold standard

In the end of Baum's story, Dorothy does find her way home, but it is not by just following the yellow brick road. After a long and perilous journey, she learns that the wizard is incapable of helping her or her friends. Instead, Dorothy finally discovers the magical power of her *silver* slippers. (When *The Wizard of Oz* was made into a movie in 1939, Dorothy's slippers were changed from silver to ruby. Apparently, the Hollywood filmmakers were not aware that they were telling a story about nineteenth-century monetary policy.)

Although the populists lost the debate over the free coinage of silver, they did eventually get the monetary expansion and inflation that they wanted. In 1898 prospectors discovered gold near the Klondike River in Alaska. Increased supplies of gold also arrived from the Canadian Yukon and the gold mines of South Africa. As a result, the money supply and the price level started to rise in the United States and other countries operating on the gold standard. Within 15 years, prices in the United States were back to the levels that had prevailed in the 1880s, and farmers were better able to handle their debts.

An early debate over monetary policy

■ **QUICK QUIZ** List and describe six costs of inflation.

CONCLUSION

This chapter discussed the causes and costs of inflation. The primary cause of inflation is simply growth in the quantity of money. When the central bank creates money in large quantities, the value of money falls quickly over time. To maintain stable prices, the central bank must maintain strict control over the money supply.

The costs of inflation are more subtle. They include shoeleather costs, menu costs, increased variability of relative prices, unintended changes in tax liabilities, confusion and inconvenience, and arbitrary redistributions of wealth. Are these costs, in total, large or small? All economists agree that they become huge during hyperinflation. But their size for moderate inflation—when prices rise by less than 10 percent per year—is more open to debate.

Although this chapter presented many of the most important lessons about inflation, the discussion is incomplete. When the Fed reduces the rate of money growth, prices rise less rapidly, as the quantity theory suggests. Yet as the economy makes the transition to this lower inflation rate, the change in monetary policy will have disruptive effects on production and employment. That is, even though monetary policy is neutral in the long run, it has profound effects on real variables in the short run. Later in this book we will examine the reasons for short-run monetary nonneutrality in order to enhance our understanding of the causes and costs of inflation.

Summary

- The overall level of prices in an economy adjusts to bring money supply and money demand into balance. When the central bank increases the supply of money, it causes the price level to rise. Persistent growth in the quantity of money supplied leads to continuing inflation.

- The principle of monetary neutrality asserts that changes in the quantity of money influence nominal variables but not real variables. Most economists believe that monetary neutrality approximately describes the behavior of the economy in the long run.

- A government can pay for some of its spending simply by printing money. When countries rely heavily on this "inflation tax," the result is hyperinflation.

- One application of the principle of monetary neutrality is the Fisher effect. According to the Fisher effect, when the inflation rate rises, the nominal interest rate rises by the same amount, so that the real interest rate remains the same.

- Many people think that inflation makes them poorer because it raises the cost of what they buy. This view is a fallacy, however, because inflation also raises nominal incomes.

- Economists have identified six costs of inflation: shoeleather costs associated with reduced money holdings, menu costs associated with more frequent adjustment of prices, increased variability of relative prices, unintended changes in tax liabilities due to nonindexation of the tax code, confusion and inconvenience resulting from a changing unit of account, and arbitrary redistributions of wealth between debtors and creditors. Many of these costs are large during hyperinflation, but the size of these costs for moderate inflation is less clear.

Key Concepts

quantity theory of money, p. 614
nominal variables, p. 615
real variables, p. 615
classical dichotomy, p. 615

monetary neutrality, p. 616
velocity of money, p. 616
quantity equation, p. 617
inflation tax, p. 621

Fisher effect, p. 622
shoeleather costs, p. 624
menu costs, p. 625

Questions for Review

1. Explain how an increase in the price level affects the real value of money.

2. According to the quantity theory of money, what is the effect of an increase in the quantity of money?

3. Explain the difference between nominal and real variables, and give two examples of each. According to the principle of monetary neutrality, which variables are affected by changes in the quantity of money?

4. In what sense is inflation like a tax? How does thinking about inflation as a tax help explain hyperinflation?

5. According to the Fisher effect, how does an increase in the inflation rate affect the real interest rate and the nominal interest rate?

6. What are the costs of inflation? Which of these costs do you think are most important for the U.S. economy?

7. If inflation is less than expected, who benefits—debtors or creditors? Explain.

Problems and Applications

1. It is often suggested that the Federal Reserve try to reduce the U.S. inflation rate to zero. If we assume that velocity is constant, does this zero-inflation goal require that the rate of money growth equal zero? If yes, explain why. If no, explain what the rate of money growth should equal.

2. The chapter preceding this one showed that there are several different measures of the money stock, with the larger measures including more types of assets than the smaller ones. How can the quantity equation hold for all of these measures? How can the quantity theory of money hold for all of these measures?

3. The economist John Maynard Keynes wrote: "Lenin is said to have declared that the best way to destroy the capitalist system was to debauch the currency. By a continuing process of inflation, governments can confiscate, secretly and unobserved, an important part of the wealth of their citizens." Justify Lenin's assertion.

4. Suppose that a country's inflation rate increases sharply. What happens to the inflation tax on the holders of money? Why is wealth that is held in savings accounts *not* subject to a change in the inflation tax? Can you think of any way in which holders of savings accounts are hurt by the increase in the inflation rate?

5. Hyperinflations are extremely rare in countries whose central banks are independent of the rest of the government. Why might this be so?

6. The dollars printed by the Continental Congress during the 1770s were called "continental dollars," or just "con-tinentals." A popular expression after the Revolutionary War was "It ain't worth a continental." Explain what this expression meant, and why.

7. Suppose that Bob is a bean farmer and Rita is a rice farmer. Bob and Rita are the only people in the economy, and both always consume equal amounts of rice and beans. In 1995 the price of beans was $1 and the price of rice was $3.
   a. Suppose that in 1996 the price of beans was $2 and the price of rice was $6. What was inflation? Was Bob better off, worse off, or unaffected by the changes in prices? What about Rita?
   b. Now suppose that in 1996 the price of beans was $2 and the price of rice was $4. What was inflation? Was Bob better off, worse off, or unaffected by the changes in prices? What about Rita?
   c. Finally, suppose that in 1996 the price of beans was $2 and the price of rice was $1.50. What was inflation? Was Bob better off, worse off, or unaffected by the changes in prices? What about Rita?

8. What are your shoeleather costs of going to the bank? How might you measure these costs in dollars? How do you think the shoeleather costs of your college president differ from your own?

9. Recall that money serves three functions in the economy. What are those functions? How does inflation affect the ability of money to serve each of these functions?

10. Suppose that Americans expect inflation to equal 3 percent in 1997, but in fact prices rise by 5 percent. How

would this unexpectedly high inflation rate help or hurt the following?

a. the federal government
b. a homeowner with a fixed-rate mortgage
c. a union worker in the second year of a labor contract
d. a college that has invested some of its endowment in Treasury bonds

11. Explain one harm associated with unexpected inflation that is *not* associated with expected inflation. Then explain one harm associated with both expected and unexpected inflation.

12. Explain whether the following statements are true, false, or uncertain.

a. "Inflation hurts borrowers and helps lenders, because borrowers must pay a higher rate of interest."
b. "If prices change in a way that leaves the overall price level unchanged, then no one is made better or worse off."
c. "Inflation does not reduce the purchasing power of most workers."

XI

THE MACROECONOMICS OF
OPEN ECONOMIES

29

OPEN-ECONOMY
MACROECONOMICS:
BASIC CONCEPTS

When you graduate from college and decide to buy a car, you may compare the latest models offered by Ford and Toyota. When you take your next vacation, you may consider spending it on a beach in Florida or in Mexico. When you get a job and begin to save for your retirement, you may choose between a mutual fund that buys stock in U.S. companies and one that buys stock in foreign companies. In all of these cases, you will be participating not just in the U.S. economy but in economies around the world.

There are clear benefits to being open to international trade: Trade allows people to produce what they produce best and to consume the great variety of goods and services produced around the world. Indeed, one of the *Ten Principles of Economics* highlighted in Chapter 1 is that trade can make everyone better off. Chapters 3 and 9 examined the gains from trade more fully. We learned that international trade can raise living standards in all countries by allowing each country to specialize in producing those goods and services in which it has a comparative advantage.

So far our development of macroeconomics has largely ignored the economy's interaction with other economies around the world. For most questions in macroeconomics, international issues are peripheral. Earlier in this book, for instance, when we discussed the natural rate of unemployment and the causes

Learn how net exports measure the international flow of goods and services

Learn how net foreign investment measures the international flow of capital

Consider why net exports must always equal net foreign investment

See how saving, domestic investment, and net foreign investment are related

Learn the meaning of the nominal exchange rate and the real exchange rate

Examine purchasing-power parity as a theory of how exchange rates are determined

closed economy
an economy that does not interact with other economies in the world

open economy
an economy that interacts freely with other economies around the world

of inflation, the effects of international trade could safely be ignored. Indeed, to keep their analysis simple, macroeconomists often assume a **closed economy**—an economy that does not interact with other economies.

Yet some new macroeconomic issues do arise in an **open economy**—an economy that interacts freely with other economies around the world. This chapter and the next one, therefore, provide an introduction to open-economy macroeconomics. We begin in this chapter by discussing the key macroeconomic variables that describe an open economy's interactions in world markets. You may have noticed mention of these variables—exports, imports, the trade balance, and exchange rates—when reading the newspaper or watching the nightly news. Our first job is to understand what these data mean. In the next chapter we develop a model to explain how these variables are determined and how they are affected by various government policies.

THE INTERNATIONAL FLOWS OF GOODS AND CAPITAL

An open economy interacts with other economies in two ways: It buys and sells goods and services in world product markets, and it buys and sells capital assets in world financial markets. Here we discuss these two activities and the close relationship between them.

THE FLOW OF GOODS: EXPORTS, IMPORTS, AND NET EXPORTS

exports
goods and services that are produced domestically and sold abroad

imports
goods and services that are produced abroad and sold domestically

As we first noted in Chapter 3, **exports** are domestically produced goods and services that are sold abroad, and **imports** are foreign-produced goods and services that are sold domestically. When Boeing, the U.S. aircraft manufacturer, builds a plane and sells it to Air France, the sale is an export for the United States

"But we're not just talking about buying a car—we're talking about confronting this country's trade deficit with Japan."

and an import for France. When Volvo, the Swedish car manufacturer, makes a car and sells it to a U.S. resident, the sale is an import for the United States and an export for Sweden.

The **net exports** of any country are the value of its exports minus the value of its imports. The Boeing sale raises U.S. net exports, and the Volvo sale reduces U.S. net exports. Because net exports tell us whether a country is, in total, a seller or a buyer in world markets for goods and services, net exports are also called the **trade balance.** If net exports are positive, exports are greater than imports, indicating that the country sells more goods and services abroad than it buys from other countries. In this case, the country is said to run a **trade surplus.** If net exports are negative, exports are less than imports, indicating that the country sells fewer goods and services abroad than it buys from other countries. In this case, the country is said to run a **trade deficit.** If net exports are zero, its exports and imports are exactly equal, and the country is said to have **balanced trade.**

In the next chapter we develop a theory that explains an economy's trade balance, but even at this early stage it is easy to think of many factors that might influence a country's exports, imports, and net exports. Those factors include the following:

◆ The tastes of consumers for domestic and foreign goods

◆ The prices of goods at home and abroad

◆ The exchange rates at which people can use domestic currency to buy foreign currencies

◆ The cost of transporting goods from country to country

◆ The policies of the government toward international trade

As these variables change over time, so does the amount of international trade.

net exports
the value of a nation's exports minus the value of its imports, also called the trade balance

trade balance
the value of a nation's exports minus the value of its imports, also called net exports

trade surplus
an excess of exports over imports

trade deficit
an excess of imports over exports

balanced trade
a situation in which exports equal imports

CASE STUDY   THE INCREASING OPENNESS OF THE U.S. ECONOMY

Perhaps the most dramatic change in the U.S. economy over the past four decades has been the increasing importance of international trade and finance. This change is illustrated in Figure 29-1, which shows the total value of goods and services exported to other countries and imported from other countries expressed as a percentage of gross domestic product. In the 1950s exports of goods and services averaged less than 5 percent of GDP. Today they are twice that level and still rising. Imports of goods and services have risen by a similar amount.

This increase in international trade is partly due to improvements in transportation. In 1950 the average merchant ship carried less than 10,000 tons of cargo; today, many ships carry more than 100,000 tons. The long-distance jet was introduced in 1958, and the wide-body jet in 1967, making air transport far cheaper. Because of these developments, goods that once had to be produced locally can now be traded around the world. Cut flowers, for instance, are now grown in Israel and flown to the United States to be sold. Fresh fruits and vegetables that can grow only in summer can now be consumed in winter as well, because they can be shipped to the United States from countries in the southern hemisphere.

Figure 29-1

THE INTERNATIONALIZATION OF THE U.S. ECONOMY. This figure shows exports and imports of the U.S. economy as a percentage of U.S. gross domestic product since 1950. The substantial increases over time show the increasing importance of international trade and finance.

SOURCE: U.S. Department of Commerce.

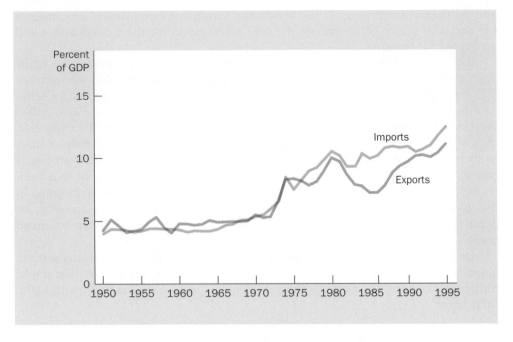

The increase in international trade has also been influenced by advances in telecommunications, which have allowed businesses to reach overseas customers more easily. For example, the first transatlantic telephone cable was not laid until 1956. As recently as 1966, the technology allowed only 138 simultaneous conversations between North America and Europe. Today, communications satellites permit more than 1 million conversations to occur at the same time.

Technological progress has also fostered international trade by changing the kinds of goods that economies produce. When bulky raw materials (such as steel) and perishable goods (such as foodstuffs) were a large part of the world's output, transporting goods was often costly and sometimes impossible. By contrast, goods produced with modern technology are often light and easy to transport. Consumer electronics, for instance, have low weight for

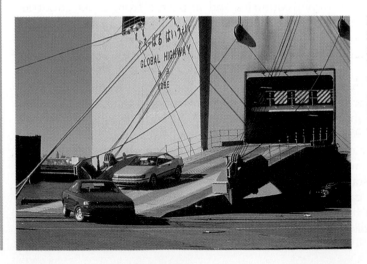

International trade is increasingly important for the U.S. economy. Here, workers in Baltimore drive newly imported cars off a Japanese cargo ship.

every dollar of value, which makes them easy to produce in one country and sell in another. An even more extreme example is the film industry. Once a studio in Hollywood makes a movie, it can send copies of the film around the world at almost zero cost. And, indeed, movies are a major export of the United States.

The government's trade policies have also been a factor in increasing international trade. As we discussed in Chapters 3 and 9, economists have long believed that free trade between countries is mutually beneficial. Over time, policymakers around the world have come to accept these conclusions. International agreements, such as the North American Free Trade Agreement (NAFTA) and the General Agreement on Tariffs and Trade (GATT), have gradually lowered trade barriers, such as tariffs and import quotas. The pattern of increasing trade illustrated in Figure 29-1 is a phenomenon that most economists and policymakers endorse and encourage.

THE FLOW OF CAPITAL: NET FOREIGN INVESTMENT

So far we have been discussing how residents of an open economy participate in world markets for goods and services. In addition, residents of an open economy participate in world financial markets. A U.S. resident with $20,000 could use that money to buy a car from Toyota, but he could instead use that money to buy stock in the Toyota corporation. The first transaction would represent a flow of goods, whereas the second would represent a flow of capital.

The term **net foreign investment** refers to the purchase of foreign assets by domestic residents minus the purchase of domestic assets by foreigners. When a U.S. resident buys stock in Telmex, the Mexican phone company, the purchase raises U.S. net foreign investment. When a Japanese resident buys a bond issued by the U.S. government, the purchase reduces U.S. net foreign investment.

net foreign investment
the purchase of foreign assets by domestic residents minus the purchase of domestic assets by foreigners

Recall that foreign investment takes two forms. If McDonald's opens up a fast-food outlet in Russia, that is an example of *foreign direct investment.* Alternatively, if an American buys stock in a Russian corporation, that is an example of *foreign portfolio investment.* In the first case, the American owner is actively managing the investment, whereas in the second case the American owner has a more passive role. In both cases, U.S. residents are buying assets located in another country, so both purchases increase U.S. net foreign investment.

We develop a theory to explain net foreign investment in the next chapter. Here, let's consider briefly some of the more important variables that influence net foreign investment, as follows:

◆ The real interest rates being paid on foreign assets
◆ The real interest rates being paid on domestic assets
◆ The perceived economic and political risks of holding assets abroad
◆ The government policies that affect foreign ownership of domestic assets

For example, consider U.S. investors deciding whether to buy Mexican government bonds or U.S. government bonds. (Recall that a bond is, in effect, an IOU of the issuer.) To make this decision, U.S. investors compare the real interest rates offered on the two bonds. The higher a bond's real interest rate, the more attractive it is. While making this comparison, however, U.S. investors must also take

IN THE NEWS

Capital Flows

to Russia

WITH ITS RECENT CONVERSION TO CAPI-talism, Russia has started to attract capital from investors around the world.

Foreign Buyers Look to Russia: Despite Risks, Investors Coming Up with the Cash

BY DAVID HOFFMAN

MOSCOW—Seen from the inside, the Russian economy looks frighteningly unstable: millions of workers unpaid for months, rampant tax evasion, industry stuck in a depression-sized slump, unchecked corruption and crime, economic power concentrated among wealthy clans, two-thirds of the country's banks considered shaky.

But from the outside, the view of Russia is brighter. Five years into the transition to a free-market economy and democracy, Russia has made a surprising debut on international capital markets that seems to ignore the chaos at home.

Twice in recent weeks, foreign investors have elbowed each other aside to sink their cash into Russia. In October, they snapped up $429 million worth of shares in Russia's natural gas monopoly, Gazprom, despite warnings of the risk. Last week foreign investors hurried again to invest $1 billion in Russia—this time in the state itself, the first sale of Russian bonds since 1917.

The demand for five-year Eurobonds—bonds sold only outside Russia and denominated in Western currency, such as dollars, rather than unconvertible rubles—far exceeded Russia's expectations and will provide a fresh injection of cash to the government's ailing budget. The bond sales came after a two-week, 14-city tour by senior policymakers to tout Russia's return to international capital markets. American investors picked up 41 percent of the bonds, Europeans 30 percent, and South Koreans 29 percent. . . .

"We can say that the world believes in the future of Russia," Finance Minister Alexander Livshits exulted, "and all that is left is that we have to believe in ourselves."

There are several explanations for why Russia has attracted foreign investors when its domestic economic woes are so serious. According to analysts, investors are looking beyond today's turmoil to the long-term picture, including the prospects for continued reform.

In a rating of the Russian Eurobond issued in October, Moody's Investors Service said the bonds represent "uncertainty," but also noted that Russia has a huge export potential and that its political institutions have stabilized.

At the same time, the Russian government took other steps to reassure investors. It successfully renegotiated a rescheduling of Soviet-era debt with the Paris Club of government creditors and the London Club of commercial banks.

Another factor attracting foreign investors is Russia's high bond yields. Five-year Eurobonds carried a 9.25 percent interest rate; the current rate paid on 5-year U.S. Treasury bonds is slightly less than 6 percent. "A lot of money out there just can't wait for higher yields . . . ," one economist said.

SOURCE: *Boston Globe*, November 28, 1996, p. B21.

into account the risk that one of these governments might *default* on its debt (that is, not pay interest or principal when it is due), as well as any restrictions that the Mexican government has imposed, or might impose in the future, on foreign investors in Mexico.

THE EQUALITY OF NET EXPORTS AND NET FOREIGN INVESTMENT

We have seen that an open economy interacts with the rest of the world in two ways—in world markets for goods and services and in world financial markets. Net exports and net foreign investment each measure a type of imbalance in these markets. Net exports measure an imbalance between a country's exports and its imports. Net foreign investment measures an imbalance between the amount of foreign assets bought by domestic residents and the amount of domestic assets bought by foreigners.

An important but subtle fact of accounting states that, for an economy as a whole, these two imbalances must offset each other. That is, net foreign investment *(NFI)* always equals net exports *(NX)*:

$$NFI = NX.$$

This equation holds because every transaction that affects one side of this equation must also affect the other side by exactly the same amount. This equation is an *identity*—an equation that must hold by the way the variables in the equation are defined and measured.

To see why this accounting identity is true, consider an example. Suppose that Boeing, the U.S. aircraft maker, sells some planes to a Japanese airline. In this sale, a U.S. company gives planes to a Japanese company, and a Japanese company gives yen to a U.S company. Notice that two things have occurred simultaneously. The United States has sold to a foreigner some of its output (the planes), and this sale increases U.S. net exports. In addition, the United States has acquired some foreign assets (the yen), and this acquisition increases U.S. net foreign investment.

Although Boeing most likely will not hold onto the yen it has acquired in this sale, any subsequent transaction will preserve the equality of net exports and net foreign investment. For example, Boeing may exchange its yen for dollars with a U.S. mutual fund that wants the yen to buy stock in Sony Corporation, the Japanese maker of consumer electronics. In this case, Boeing's net export of planes equals the mutual fund's net foreign investment in Sony stock. Hence, *NX* and *NFI* rise by an equal amount.

Alternatively, Boeing may exchange its yen for dollars with another U.S. company that wants to buy computers from Toshiba, the Japanese computer maker. In this case, U.S. imports (of computers) exactly offset U.S. exports (of planes). The sales by Boeing and Toshiba together affect neither U.S. net exports nor U.S. net foreign investment. That is, *NX* and *NFI* are the same as they were before these transactions took place.

The equality of net exports and net foreign investment follows from the fact that every international transaction is an exchange. When a seller country transfers a good or service to a buyer country, the buyer country gives up some asset to pay for this good or service. The value of that asset equals the value of the good or service sold. When we add everything up, the net value of goods and services sold by a country *(NX)* must equal the net value of assets acquired *(NFI)*. The international flow of goods and services and the international flow of capital are two sides of the same coin.

SAVING, INVESTMENT, AND THEIR RELATIONSHIP TO THE INTERNATIONAL FLOWS

A nation's saving and investment are, as we have seen in previous chapters, crucial to its long-run economic growth. Let's therefore consider how these variables are related to the international flows of goods and capital, as measured by net exports and net foreign investment. We can do this most easily with the help of some simple mathematics.

trial countries with insufficient funds
for their own capital accumulation?
Some people fear that both of these outcomes might occur. But an accounting
identity, and economist Paul Krugman,
tell us not to worry.

Fantasy Economics

BY PAUL KRUGMAN

Reports by international organizations
are usually greeted with well deserved
yawns. Occasionally, however, such a
report is a leading indicator of a sea
change in opinion.

A few weeks ago, the World Economic Forum—which every year draws
an unmatched assemblage of the world's
political and business elite to its conference in Davos, Switzerland—released
its annual report on international competitiveness. The report made headlines
because it demoted Japan and declared
America the world's most competitive
economy.

The revealing part of the report,
however, is not its more or less meaningless competitiveness rankings but its
introduction, which offers what seems to
be a very clear vision of the global economic future.

That vision, shared by many powerful people, is compelling and alarming. It
is also nonsense. And the fact that this
nonsense is being taken seriously by
many people who believe themselves to
be sophisticated about economics is itself an ominous portent for the world
economy.

The report finds that the spread of
modern technology to newly industrializing nations is deindustrializing high-wage
nations: Capital is flowing to the Third
World and low-cost producers in these
countries are flooding world markets
with cheap manufactured goods.

The report predicts that these
trends will accelerate, that service jobs
will soon begin to follow the lost jobs in
manufacturing and that the future of the
high-wage nations offers a bleak choice

As you may recall, the term *net exports* first appeared earlier in the book when we discussed the components of gross domestic product. The economy's gross domestic product *(Y)* is divided among four components: consumption *(C)*, investment *(I)*, government purchases *(G)*, and net exports *(NX)*. We write this as

$$Y = C + I + G + NX.$$

Total expenditure on the economy's output is the sum of expenditure on consumption, investment, government purchases, and net exports. Because each dollar of expenditure is placed into one of these four components, this equation is an accounting identity: It must be true because of the way the variables are defined and measured.

Recall that national saving is the income of the nation that is left after paying for current consumption and government purchases. National saving *(S)* equals $Y - C - G$. If we rearrange the above equation to reflect this fact, we obtain:

between declining wages and rising unemployment.

This vision resonates with many people. Yet as a description of what has actually happened in recent years, it is almost completely untrue.

Rapidly growing Third World economies have indeed increased their exports of manufactured goods. But today these exports absorb only about 1 percent of First World income. Moreover, Third World nations have also increased their imports.

Overall, the effect of Third World growth on the number of industrial jobs in Western nations has been minimal: Growing exports to the newly industrializing countries have created about as many jobs as growing imports have displaced.

What about capital flows? The numbers sound impressive. Last year, $24 billion flowed to Mexico, $11 billion to China. The total movement of capital from advanced to developing nations was about $60 billion. But though this

sounds like a lot, it is pocket change in a world economy that invests more than $4 trillion a year.

In other words, if the vision of a Western economy battered by low-wage competition is meant to describe today's world, it is a fantasy with hardly any basis in reality.

Even if the vision does not describe the present, might it describe the future? Well, growing exports of manufactured goods from South to North will lead to a net loss of northern industrial jobs only if they are not matched by growth in exports from North to South.

The authors of the report evidently envision a future of large-scale Third World trade surpluses. But it is an unavoidable fact of accounting that a country that runs a trade surplus must also be a net investor in other countries. So large-scale deindustrialization can take place only if low-wage nations are major exporters of capital to high-wage nations. This seems unlikely. In any case, it contradicts the rest of the story, which

predicts huge capital flows into low-wage nations.

Thus, the vision offered by the world competitiveness report conflicts not only with the facts but with itself. Yet it is a vision that a growing number of the world's most influential men and women seem to share. That is a dangerous trend.

Not everyone who worries about low-wage competition is a protectionist. Indeed, the authors of the world competitiveness report would surely claim to be champions of free trade. Nonetheless, the fact that such ideas have become respectable—that much would-be sophisticated opinion apparently now agrees with Ross Perot about the "great sucking sound" from the South—suggests that the intellectual consensus that has kept world trade relatively free, and that has allowed hundreds of millions of people in the Third World to get their first taste of prosperity, may be unraveling.

SOURCE: *The New York Times,* September 26, 1994, p. A17.

$$Y - C - G = I + NX$$
$$S = I + NX.$$

Because net exports *(NX)* also equal net foreign investment *(NFI)*, we can also write this equation as

$$S \quad = \quad I \quad + \quad NFI$$

$$\text{Saving} = \frac{\text{Domestic}}{\text{investment}} + \frac{\text{Net foreign}}{\text{investment}}.$$

This equation shows that a nation's saving must equal its domestic investment plus its net foreign investment. In other words, when U.S. citizens save a dollar of their income for the future, that dollar can be used to finance accumulation of domestic capital or it can be used to finance the purchase of capital abroad.

This equation should look somewhat familiar. Earlier in the book, when we analyzed the role of the financial system, we considered this identity for the special case of a closed economy. In a closed economy, net foreign investment is zero

(NFI = 0), so saving equals investment (S = I). By contrast, an open economy has two uses for its saving: domestic investment and net foreign investment.

As before, we can view the financial system as standing between the two sides of this identity. For example, suppose the Smith family decides to save some of its income for retirement. This decision contributes to national saving, the left-hand side of our equation. If the Smiths deposit their saving in a mutual fund, the mutual fund may use some of the deposit to buy stock issued by General Motors, which uses the proceeds to build a factory in Ohio. In addition, the mutual fund may use some of the Smiths' deposit to buy stock issued by Toyota, which uses the proceeds to build a factory in Osaka. These transactions show up on the right-hand side of the equation. From the standpoint of U.S. accounting, the General Motors expenditure on a new factory is domestic investment, and the purchase of Toyota stock by a U.S. resident is net foreign investment. Thus, all saving in the U.S. economy shows up as investment in the U.S. economy or as U.S. net foreign investment.

CASE STUDY   SAVING, INVESTMENT, AND NET FOREIGN INVESTMENT OF THE UNITED STATES

Let's see what these macroeconomic accounting identities tell us about the U.S. economy. Panel (a) of Figure 29-2 shows national saving and domestic investment for the U.S. economy as a percentage of GDP since 1965. Panel (b) shows net foreign investment as a percentage of GDP. Notice that, as the identities require, domestic investment plus net foreign investment always equals national saving.

The figure shows a dramatic change beginning in the early 1980s. Before 1980, national saving and domestic investment were very close, and so net foreign investment was small. After 1980, however, national saving fell dramatically. (This decline was due in part to increased government budget deficits and in part to a fall in private saving.) Yet the U.S. economy did not experience a similar fall in domestic investment. As a result, net foreign investment became a large negative number, indicating that foreigners were buying more assets in the United States than Americans were buying abroad. Because net exports must equal net foreign investment, net exports were also negative. In other words, the United States ran a trade deficit: Imports of goods and services exceeded exports. In 1995, the trade deficit was just over $100 billion.

Are these trade deficits a problem for the U.S. economy? Most economists argue that they are not a problem in themselves, but perhaps are a symptom of a problem—reduced national saving. Reduced national saving is potentially a problem because it means that the nation is putting away less to provide for its future. Once national saving has fallen, however, there is no reason to deplore the resulting trade deficits. If national saving fell without inducing a trade deficit, investment in the United States would have to fall. This fall in investment, in turn, would adversely affect the growth in the capital stock, labor productivity, and real wages. In other words, given the fact that U.S. citizens are not saving much, it is better to have foreigners invest in the U.S. economy than no one at all.

█ QUICK QUIZ   Define *net exports* and *net foreign investment*. Explain how they are related.

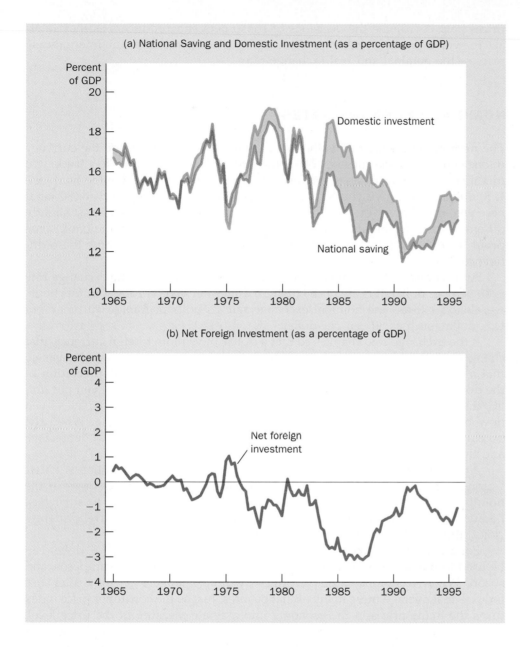

Figure 29-2

NATIONAL SAVING, DOMESTIC INVESTMENT, AND NET FOREIGN INVESTMENT. Panel (a) shows national saving and domestic investment as a percentage of GDP. Panel (b) shows net foreign investment as a percentage of GDP. You can see from the figure that national saving has been lower since 1980 than it was before 1980. This fall in national saving has been reflected primarily in reduced net foreign investment rather than in reduced domestic investment.

SOURCE: U.S. Department of Commerce.

THE PRICES FOR INTERNATIONAL TRANSACTIONS: REAL AND NOMINAL EXCHANGE RATES

So far we have discussed measures of the flow of goods and services and the flow of capital across a nation's border. In addition to these quantity variables, macroeconomists also study variables that measure the prices at which these international transactions take place. Just as the price in any market serves the important role of coordinating buyers and sellers in that market, international prices help coordinate the decisions of consumers and producers as they interact in world markets. Here we discuss the two most important international prices—the nominal and real exchange rates.

NOMINAL EXCHANGE RATES

nominal exchange rate

the rate at which a person can trade the currency of one country for the currency of another

The **nominal exchange rate** is the rate at which a person can trade the currency of one country for the currency of another. For example, if you go to a bank, you might see a posted exchange rate of 80 yen per dollar. If you give the bank one U.S. dollar, it will give you 80 Japanese yen; and if you give the bank 80 Japanese yen, it will give you one U.S. dollar. (In actuality, the bank will post slightly different prices for buying and selling yen. The difference gives the bank some profit for offering this service. For our purposes here, we can ignore these differences.)

An exchange rate can always be expressed in two ways. If the exchange rate is 80 yen per dollar, it is also 1/80 (0.0125) dollar per yen. Throughout this book, we always express the nominal exchange rate as units of foreign currency per U.S. dollar, such as 80 yen per dollar.

appreciation

an increase in the value of a currency as measured by the amount of foreign currency it can buy

depreciation

a decrease in the value of a currency as measured by the amount of foreign currency it can buy

If the exchange rate changes so that a dollar buys more foreign currency, that change is called an **appreciation** of the dollar. If the exchange rate changes so that a dollar buys less foreign currency, that change is called a **depreciation** of the dollar. For example, when the exchange rate rises from 80 to 90 yen per dollar, the dollar is said to appreciate. At the same time, because a Japanese yen now buys less of the U.S. currency, the yen is said to depreciate. When the exchange rate falls from 80 to 70 yen per dollar, the dollar is said to depreciate, and the yen is said to appreciate.

At times you may have heard the media report that the dollar is either "strong" or "weak." These descriptions usually refer to recent changes in the nominal exchange rate. When a currency appreciates, it is said to *strengthen* because it can then buy more foreign currency. Similarly, when a currency depreciates, it is said to *weaken*.

For any country, there are many nominal exchange rates. The U.S. dollar can be used to buy Japanese yen, British pounds, French francs, Mexican pesos, and so on. When economists study changes in the exchange rate, they often use indexes that average these many exchange rates. Just as the consumer price index turns the many prices in the economy into a single measure of the price level, an exchange rate index turns these many exchange rates into a single measure of the international value of the currency. So when economists talk about the dollar appreciating or depreciating, they often are referring to an exchange rate index that takes into account many individual exchange rates.

REAL EXCHANGE RATES

real exchange rate

the rate at which a person can trade the goods and services of one country for the goods and services of another

The **real exchange rate** is the rate at which a person can trade the goods and services of one country for the goods and services of another. For example, suppose that you go shopping and find that a case of German beer is twice as expensive as a case of American beer. We would then say that the real exchange rate is 1/2 case of German beer per case of American beer. Notice that, like the nominal exchange rate, the real exchange rate is expressed as units of the foreign item per unit of the domestic item. But in this instance the item is a good rather than a currency.

Real and nominal exchange rates are closely related. To see how, consider an example. Suppose that a bushel of American rice sells for $100, and a bushel of Japanese rice sells for 16,000 yen. What is the real exchange rate between American and Japanese rice? To answer this question, we must first use the nominal exchange rate to convert the prices into a common currency. If the nominal exchange rate is 80 yen per dollar, then a price for American rice of $100 per bushel is equivalent to 8,000 yen per bushel. American rice is half as expensive as Japanese rice. The real exchange rate is 1/2 bushel of Japanese rice per bushel of American rice.

We can summarize this calculation for the real exchange rate with the following formula:

$$\text{Real exchange rate} = \frac{\text{Nominal exchange rate} \times \text{Domestic price}}{\text{Foreign price}}.$$

Using the numbers in our example, the formula applies as follows:

$$\text{Real exchange rate} = \frac{(80 \text{ yen per dollar}) \times (\$100 \text{ per bushel of American rice})}{16,000 \text{ yen per bushel of Japanese rice}}$$

$$= \frac{8,000 \text{ yen per bushel of American rice}}{16,000 \text{ yen per bushel of Japanese rice}}$$

$$= 1/2 \text{ bushel of Japanese rice per bushel of American rice.}$$

Thus, the real exchange rate depends on the nominal exchange rate and on the prices of goods in the two countries measured in the local currencies.

Why does the real exchange rate matter? As you might guess, the real exchange rate is a key determinant of how much a country exports and imports. When Uncle Ben's, Inc., is deciding whether to buy U.S. rice or Japanese rice to put into its boxes, for example, it will ask which rice is cheaper. The real exchange rate gives the answer. As another example, imagine that you are deciding whether to take a seaside vacation in Miami, Florida, or in Cancun, Mexico. You might ask your travel agent the price of a hotel room in Miami (measured in dollars), the price of a hotel room in Cancun (measured in pesos), and the exchange rate between pesos and dollars. If you decide where to vacation by comparing costs, you are basing your decision on the real exchange rate.

When studying an economy as a whole, macroeconomists focus on overall prices rather than the prices of individual items. That is, to measure the real exchange rate, they use price indexes, such as the consumer price index. By using a price index for the United States (P), a price index for prices abroad (P^*), and the nominal exchange rate between the U.S. dollar and foreign currencies (e), we can compute the overall real exchange rate between the United States and other countries as follows:

$$\text{Real exchange rate} = (e \times P)/P^*.$$

This real exchange rate measures the price of a basket of goods and services available domestically relative to a basket of goods and services available abroad.

IN THE NEWS

A Dollar

Depreciation and

an Export Boom

WHEN THE DOLLAR DEPRECIATES, U.S. goods become less expensive relative to foreign goods, and this tends to stimulate U.S. exports. The following article from 1992, when the U.S. dollar was weak, describes how this works in practice.

Weak Dollar Makes U.S. World's Bargain Bazaar

BY SYLVIA NASAR

The declining dollar has turned the world's wealthiest economy into the Filene's basement of industrial countries. Despite its rebound during the European currency crisis, the dollar, which fell to record lows this summer, remains extraordinarily weak by historical standards.

To the Swiss businessman just off the Concorde, the $120 tab for a room at the Plaza looks like the lunch check back home. To the teenager from Paris, the $9 sticker on the tape at Tower Records and the $30 tag on a pair of Levi 501's read like big signs that say buy one, get one free.

Life in the United States may not seem like a bargain to the many Americans whose incomes have been pinched by nearly four years of economic stagnation. But in fact, the weakling dollar has made the United States the least expensive rich country for people to visit and shop, and for businesses to manufacture their products.

The image of the United States as the world's bargain bazaar might suggest a kind of place where tourists flock for cut-rate vacations and where labor is cheap, living standards are low, and products and services lack sophistication and quality.

But the United States is hardly a Third World nation. Its citizens still enjoy the highest standard of living and are the world's most productive workers. Their pay, measured in terms of the goods and services it can buy in the United States as opposed to foreign countries, is higher than in Canada, Germany, or Japan. . . .

Think of a low dollar as a special promotion of American-made products and services—not a "going out of business" sale. Still, bargains clearly abound. For example, a $50 bunch of lilies ordered through Calyx and Corolla set a Japanese suitor back nearly 7,000 yen a year ago when it took 137 yen to buy a dollar. The same bunch costs him just 6,000 yen now, one reason the San Francisco flower mail-order house is doing a brisk overseas business.

One measure of how cheap the dollar became even before its latest bout of weakness, according to Michael Roberts at the Organization for Economic Cooperation and Development in Paris, is that it took just $100 in May of this year to buy the same basket of consumer goods and services in the United States that cost $170 in Sweden and $128 in Germany.

Despite economic troubles in many other rich countries, many travelers are

As we will see more fully in the next chapter, a country's real exchange rate is a key determinant of its net exports of goods and services. A depreciation (fall) in the U.S. real exchange rate means that U.S. goods have become cheaper relative to foreign goods. This change encourages consumers both at home and abroad to buy more U.S. goods and fewer goods from other countries. As a result, U.S. exports rise, and U.S. imports fall, and both of these changes raise U.S. net exports. Conversely, an appreciation (rise) in the U.S. real exchange rate means that U.S. goods have become more expensive compared to foreign goods, so U.S. net exports fall.

QUICK QUIZ Define *nominal exchange rate* and *real exchange rate,* and explain how they are related. ◆ If the nominal exchange rate goes from 100 to 120 yen per dollar, has the dollar appreciated or depreciated?

taking advantage of the bargains here. More than 1.5 million Germans, 8 percent more than last year, are expected by the United States Tourism and Travel Agency this year, along with 3.4 million Japanese. . . .

For foreigners in strong-currency countries, coming here is almost cheaper than staying at home. The weekend rate at the Hyatt Regency Chicago, for example, is $89 for a double per night, half the rate of comparable hotels in Munich, London, or Rome. A Big Mac is one-third to one-half cheaper here. A movie ticket is one-fifth to one-half as much.

Or take that classic, a trip to Disney World. For a Frankfurt family, a week in Orlando could easily cost less than a visit to Euro Disney. As it turns out, one-third more foreign tourists than last year have arrived at Orlando International Airport.

In addition to shaking hands with Mickey, tourists from abroad are definitely doing more shopping. Japanese tourists are crowding the counters at Tiffany's, where clerks are familiar with Japanese ring sizes. And computer-literate Germans are buying laptops—avail-

able here at 20 to 30 percent below current retail prices in Germany.

Alert American entrepreneurs are looking for ways to capitalize on the trend. For example, Rex Fritchi, a Chicago travel agent, and Swissair are talking about offering a weekend shopping package this winter to enable Europeans to share the pleasures of off-price shopping at Gurnee Mall, a large mall outside the city. "We could fill up plane loads just coming over to buy bed sheets, shirts, socks, and underwear," he said.

Some Europeans and Japanese are ordering directly from American catalogue emporiums. One of the most popular catalogues, L. L. Bean, the woodsy Maine clothier, has had to expand the number of customer service representatives who handle foreign orders to 60, from 12. Orders are up 50 to 100 percent this year over last, said Richard Leslie, director of international marketing.

The cheaper dollar also makes conventional American exports like aircraft, chemicals, and machinery cheaper, especially in Europe. A Bureau of Labor Statistics index of prices of exports in various countries shows that prices of imports to the United States have risen about 40 percent more in dollars than prices of American exports.

"Every day the dollar gets weaker I'm very happy," said Andreas Barth, senior vice president at Compaq Computer's European division in Munich. "The Europeans are unhappy because it decreases the competitive position of their exports."

SOURCE: *The New York Times,* September 28, 1992, p. A1.

A FIRST THEORY OF EXCHANGE-RATE DETERMINATION: PURCHASING-POWER PARITY

Exchange rates vary substantially over time. In 1970, a U.S. dollar could be used to buy 3.65 German marks or 627 Italian lira. In 1995, a U.S dollar bought 1.43 German marks or 1,629 Italian lira. In other words, over this period the value of the dollar fell by more than half compared to the mark, while it more than doubled compared to the lira.

What explains these large changes? Economists have developed many models to explain how exchange rates are determined, each emphasizing some of the many forces at work. Here we develop the simplest theory of exchange rates, called **purchasing-power parity.** This theory states that a unit of any given

purchasing-power parity
a theory of exchange rates whereby a unit of any given currency should be able to buy the same quantity of goods in all countries

currency should be able to buy the same quantity of goods in all countries. Many economists believe that purchasing-power parity describes the forces that determine exchange rates in the long run. We now consider the logic on which this long-run theory of exchange rates is based, as well as the theory's implications and limitations.

THE BASIC LOGIC OF PURCHASING-POWER PARITY

The theory of purchasing-power parity is based on a principle called the *law of one price*. This law asserts that a good must sell for the same price in all locations. Otherwise, there would be opportunities for profit left unexploited. For example, suppose that coffee beans sold for less in Seattle than in Boston. A person could buy coffee in Seattle for, say, $4 a pound and then sell it in Boston for $5 a pound, making a profit of $1 per pound from the difference in price. The process of taking advantage of differences in prices in different markets is called *arbitrage*. In our example, as people took advantage of this arbitrage opportunity, they would increase the demand for coffee in Seattle and increase the supply in Boston. The price of coffee would rise in Seattle (in response to greater demand) and fall in Boston (in response to greater supply). This process would continue until, eventually, the prices were the same in the two markets.

Now consider how the law of one price applies to the international marketplace. If a dollar (or any other currency) could buy more coffee in the United States than in Japan, international traders could profit by buying coffee in the United States and selling it in Japan. This export of coffee from the United States to Japan would drive up the U.S. price of coffee and drive down the Japanese price. Conversely, if a dollar could buy more coffee in Japan than in the United States, traders could buy coffee in Japan and sell it in the United States. This import of coffee into the United States from Japan would drive down the U.S. price of coffee and drive up the Japanese price. In the end, the law of one price tells us that a dollar must buy the same amount of coffee in all countries.

This logic leads us to the theory of purchasing-power parity. According to this theory, a currency must have the same purchasing power in all countries. That is, a U.S. dollar must buy the same quantity of goods in the United States and Japan, and a Japanese yen must buy the same quantity of goods in Japan and the United States. Indeed, the name of this theory describes it well. *Parity* means equality, and *purchasing power* refers to the value of money. *Purchasing-power parity* states that a unit of all currencies must have the same real value in every country.

IMPLICATIONS OF PURCHASING-POWER PARITY

What does the theory of purchasing-power parity say about exchange rates? It tells us that the nominal exchange rate between the currencies of two countries depends on the price levels in those countries. If a dollar buys the same quantity of goods in the United States (where prices are measured in dollars) as in Japan (where prices are measured in yen), then the number of yen per dollar must reflect the prices of goods in the United States and Japan. For example, if a pound of coffee costs 500 yen in Japan and $5 in the United States, then the nominal exchange rate must be 100 yen per dollar (500 yen/$5 = 100 yen per dollar). Otherwise, the purchasing power of the dollar would not be the same in the two countries.

To see more fully how this works, it is helpful to use just a bit of mathematics. Suppose that P is the price level in the United States (measured in dollars), P^* is the price level in Japan (measured in yen), and e is the nominal exchange rate (the number of yen a dollar can buy). Now consider the quantity of goods a dollar can buy at home and abroad. At home, the price level is P, so the purchasing power of $1 at home is $1/P$. Abroad, a dollar can be exchanged into e units of foreign currency, which in turn have purchasing power e/P^*. For the purchasing power of a dollar to be the same in the two countries, it must be the case that

$$1/P = e/P^*.$$

With rearrangement, this equation becomes

$$1 = eP/P^*.$$

Notice that the left-hand side of this equation is a constant, and the right-hand side is the real exchange rate. Thus, *if the purchasing power of the dollar is always the same at home and abroad, then the real exchange rate—the relative price of domestic and foreign goods—cannot change.* To see the implication of this analysis for the nominal exchange rate, we can rearrange the last equation to solve for the nominal exchange rate:

$$e = P^*/P.$$

That is, the nominal exchange rate equals the ratio of the foreign price level (measured in units of the foreign currency) to the domestic price level (measured in units of the domestic currency). *According to the theory of purchasing-power parity, the nominal exchange rate between the currencies of two countries must reflect the different price levels in those countries.*

A key implication of this theory is that nominal exchange rates change when price levels change. As we saw in the preceding chapter, the price level in any country adjusts to bring the quantity of money supplied and the quantity of money demanded into balance. Because the nominal exchange rate depends on the price levels, it also depends on the money supply and money demand in each country. When a central bank in any country increases the money supply and causes the price level to rise, it also causes that country's currency to depreciate relative to other currencies in the world. In other words, when the central bank prints large quantities of money, that money loses value both in terms of the goods and services it can buy and in terms of the amount of other currencies it can buy.

We can now answer the question that began this section: Why has the U.S. dollar lost value compared to the German mark and gained value compared to the Italian lira? The answer is that Germany has pursued a less inflationary monetary policy than the United States, and Italy has pursued a more inflationary monetary policy. From 1970 to 1995, inflation in the United States was 5.6 percent per year. By contrast, inflation was 3.7 percent in Germany, and 10.5 percent in Italy. As U.S. prices rose relative to German prices, the value of the dollar fell relative to the mark. Similarly, as U.S. prices fell relative to Italian prices, the value of the dollar rose relative to the lira.

CASE STUDY   THE NOMINAL EXCHANGE RATE DURING A HYPERINFLATION

Macroeconomists cannot conduct controlled experiments. Instead, they must glean what they can from the natural experiments that history gives them. One natural experiment is hyperinflation—the high inflation that arises when a government turns to the printing press to pay for large amounts of government spending. Because hyperinflations are so extreme, they illustrate some basic economic principles with clarity.

Consider the German hyperinflation of the early 1920s. Figure 29-3 shows the German money supply, the German price level, and the nominal exchange rate (measured as U.S. cents per German mark) for that period. Notice that these series move closely together. When the supply of money starts growing quickly, the price level also takes off, and the German mark depreciates. When the money supply stabilizes, so does the price level and the exchange rate.

The pattern shown in this figure appears during every hyperinflation. It leaves no doubt that there is a fundamental link among money, prices, and the nominal exchange rate. The quantity theory of money discussed in the

Figure 29-3

MONEY, PRICES, AND THE NOMINAL EXCHANGE RATE DURING THE GERMAN HYPERINFLATION. This figure shows the money supply, the price level, and the exchange rate (measured as U.S. cents per mark) for the German hyperinflation from January 1921 to December 1924. Notice how similarly these three variables move. When the quantity of money started growing quickly, the price level followed, and the mark depreciated relative to the dollar. When the German central bank stabilized the money supply, the price level and exchange rate stabilized as well.

SOURCE: Adapted from Thomas J. Sargent, "The End of Four Big Inflations," in Robert Hall, ed., *Inflation,* Chicago: University of Chicago Press, 1983, 41–93.

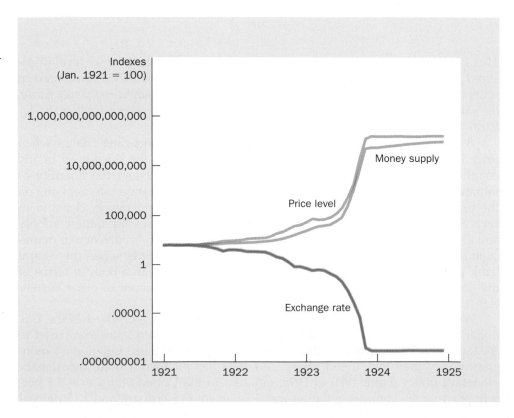

previous chapter explains how the money supply affects the price level. The theory of purchasing-power parity discussed here explains how the price level affects the nominal exchange rate.

LIMITATIONS OF PURCHASING-POWER PARITY

Purchasing-power parity provides a simple model of how exchange rates are determined. For understanding many economic phenomena, the theory works well. In particular, it can explain many long-term trends, such as the depreciation of the U.S. dollar against the German mark and the appreciation of the U.S. dollar against the Italian lira. It can also explain the major changes in exchange rates that occur during hyperinflations.

Yet the theory of purchasing-power parity is not completely accurate. That is, exchange rates do not always move to ensure that a dollar has the same real value in all countries all the time. There are two reasons why the theory of purchasing-power parity does not always hold in practice.

The first reason is that many goods are not easily traded. Imagine, for instance, that haircuts are more expensive in Paris than in New York. International travelers might avoid getting their haircuts in Paris, and some haircutters might move from New York to Paris. Yet such arbitrage would probably be too limited to eliminate the differences in prices. Thus, the deviation from purchasing-power parity might persist, and a dollar (or franc) would continue to buy less of a haircut in Paris than in New York.

The second reason that purchasing-power parity does not always hold is that even tradable goods are not always perfect substitutes when they are produced in different countries. For example, some consumers prefer German beer, and others prefer American beer. Moreover, consumer tastes for beer change over time. If German beer suddenly becomes more popular, the increase in demand will drive up the price of German beer. As a result, a dollar (or a mark) might then buy more beer in the United States than in Germany. But despite this difference in prices in the two markets, there might be no opportunity for profitable arbitrage because consumers do not view the two beers as equivalent.

Thus, both because some goods are not tradable and because some tradable goods are not perfect substitutes with their foreign counterparts, purchasing-power parity is not a perfect theory of exchange-rate determination. For these reasons, real exchange rates do in fact fluctuate over time. Nonetheless, the theory of purchasing-power parity does provide a useful first step in understanding exchange rates. The basic logic is persuasive: As the real exchange rate drifts from the level predicted by purchasing-power parity, people have greater incentive to move goods across national borders. Even if the forces of purchasing-power parity do not completely fix the real exchange rate, they do provide a reason to expect that changes in the real exchange rate are most often small or temporary. As a result, large and persistent movements in nominal exchange rates typically reflect changes in price levels at home and abroad.

QUICK QUIZ Over the past 20 years, Spain has had high inflation, and Japan has had low inflation. What do you predict has happened to the number of Spanish pesetas a person can buy with a Japanese yen?

CONCLUSION

The purpose of this chapter has been to develop some basic concepts that macroeconomists use to study open economies. You should now understand why a nation's net exports must equal its net foreign investment, and why national saving must equal domestic investment plus net foreign investment. You should also understand the meaning of the nominal and real exchange rates, as well as the implications and limitations of purchasing-power parity as a theory of how exchange rates are determined.

The macroeconomic variables defined here offer a starting point for analyzing an open economy's interactions with the rest of the world. In the next chapter we develop a model that can explain what determines these variables. We can then discuss how various events and policies affect a country's trade balance and the rate at which nations make exchanges in world markets.

Summary

◆ Net exports are the value of domestic goods and services sold abroad minus the value of foreign goods and services sold domestically. Net foreign investment is the acquisition of foreign assets by domestic residents minus the acquisition of domestic assets by foreigners. Because every international transaction involves an exchange of an asset for a good or service, an economy's net foreign investment always equals its net exports.

◆ An economy's saving can be used either to finance investment at home or to buy assets abroad. Thus, national saving equals domestic investment plus net foreign investment.

◆ The nominal exchange rate is the relative price of the currency of two countries, and the real exchange rate is the relative price of the goods and services of two coun-

tries. When the nominal exchange rate changes so that each dollar buys more foreign currency, the dollar is said to *appreciate* or *strengthen*. When the nominal exchange rate changes so that each dollar buys less foreign currency, the dollar is said to *depreciate* or *weaken*.

◆ According to the theory of purchasing-power parity, a dollar (or a unit of any other currency) should be able to buy the same quantity of goods in all countries. This theory implies that the nominal exchange rate between the currencies of two countries should reflect the price levels in those countries. As a result, countries with relatively high inflation should have depreciating currencies, and countries with relatively low inflation should have appreciating currencies.

Key Concepts

closed economy, p. 638
open economy, p. 638
exports, p. 638
imports, p. 638
net exports, p. 639

trade balance, p. 639
trade surplus, p. 639
trade deficit, p. 639
balanced trade, p. 639
net foreign investment, p. 641

nominal exchange rate, p. 648
appreciation, p. 648
depreciation, p. 648
real exchange rate, p. 648
purchasing-power parity, p. 651

Questions for Review

1. Define net exports and net foreign investment. Explain how and why they are related.

2. Explain the relationship among saving, investment, and net foreign investment.

3. If a Japanese car costs 500,000 yen, if a similar American car costs $10,000, and if a dollar can buy 100 yen, what is the nominal and real exchange rate?

4. Describe the economic logic behind the theory of purchasing-power parity.

5. If the Fed started printing large quantities of U.S. dollars, what would happen to the number of Japanese yen a dollar could buy?

Problems and Applications

1. How would the following transactions affect U.S. exports, imports, and net exports?
   a. An American art professor spends the summer touring museums in Europe.
   b. Students in Paris flock to see the latest Arnold Schwarzenegger movie.
   c. Your uncle buys a new Volvo.
   d. The student bookstore at Oxford University sells a pair of Levi's 501 jeans.
   e. A Canadian citizen shops at a store in northern Vermont to avoid Canadian sales taxes.

2. Suggest some specific reasons why each of the following products is traded internationally more today than in the past:
   a. wheat
   b. banking services
   c. computer software
   d. automobiles

3. How would the following transactions affect U.S. net foreign investment? Also, state whether each involves direct investment or portfolio investment.
   a. An American cellular phone company establishes an office in the Czech Republic.
   b. Harrod's of London sells stock to the General Electric pension fund.
   c. Honda expands its factory in Marysville, Ohio.
   d. A Fidelity mutual fund sells its Volkswagen stock to a French investor.

4. Holding national saving constant, does an increase in net foreign investment increase, decrease, or have no effect on a country's accumulation of domestic capital?

5. The business section of most major newspapers contains a table showing U.S. exchange rates. Find such a table and use it to answer the following questions.
   a. Does this table show nominal or real exchange rates? Explain.
   b. What are the exchange rates between the United States and Germany and between the United States and Japan? Calculate the exchange rate between Germany and Japan.

   c. If U.S. inflation exceeds German inflation over the next year, would you expect the dollar to appreciate or depreciate relative to the German mark?

6. Would each of the following groups be happy or unhappy if the U.S. dollar appreciated? Explain.
   a. Dutch pension funds holding U.S. government bonds
   b. U.S. manufacturing industries
   c. Australian tourists planning a trip to the United States
   d. An American firm trying to purchase property overseas

7. What is happening to the U.S. real exchange rate in each of the following situations? Explain.
   a. The U.S. nominal exchange rate is unchanged, but prices rise faster in the United States than abroad.
   b. The U.S. nominal exchange rate is unchanged, but prices rise faster abroad than in the United States.
   c. The U.S. nominal exchange rate declines, and prices are unchanged in the United States and abroad.
   d. The U.S. nominal exchange rate declines, and prices rise faster abroad than in the United States.

8. List three goods for which the law of one price is likely to hold, and three goods for which it is not. Justify your choices.

9. A can of soda costs $0.75 in the United States and 3 francs in France. What would the franc–dollar exchange rate be if purchasing-power parity holds?

10. Assume that American rice sells for $100 per bushel, Japanese rice sells for 16,000 yen per bushel, and the nominal exchange rate is 80 yen per dollar.
   a. Explain how you could make a profit from this situation. What would be your profit per bushel of rice? If other people exploit the same opportunity, what would happen to the price of rice in Japan and the price of rice in the United States?
   b. Suppose that rice is the only commodity in the world. What would happen to the real exchange rate between the United States and Japan?

11. *The Economist,* an international newsmagazine, regularly collects data on the price of a McDonald's Big Mac hamburger in different countries, in order to examine the theory of purchasing-power parity.

    a. Why might the Big Mac be a good product to use for this purpose?

    b. Based on the Big Mac data, purchasing-power parity appears to hold roughly across some countries, though not across others. Why might the assumptions underlying the theory of purchasing-power parity not hold exactly for Big Macs?

30

A MACROECONOMIC THEORY
OF THE OPEN ECONOMY

**IN THIS CHAPTER
YOU WILL**

*Build a model to explain
an open economy's trade
balance and exchange rate*

*Use the model to analyze
the effects of government
budget deficits*

*Use the model to analyze
the macroeconomic effects
of trade policies*

*Use the model to analyze
political instability and
capital flight*

Over the past decade, the United States has persistently imported more goods and services than it has exported. That is, U.S. net exports have been negative. Although economists debate whether these trade deficits are a problem for the U.S. economy, the nation's business community has a strong opinion. Many business leaders claim that the trade deficits reflect unfair competition: Foreign firms are allowed to sell their products in U.S. markets, they contend, while foreign governments impede U.S. firms from selling U.S. products abroad.

Imagine that you are the president and you want to end these trade deficits. What should you do? Should you try to limit imports, perhaps by imposing a quota on the import of cars from Japan? Or should you try to influence the nation's trade deficit in some other way?

To understand what factors determine a country's trade balance and how government policies can affect it, we need a macroeconomic theory of the open economy. The preceding chapter introduced some of the key macroeconomic variables that describe an economy's relationship with other economies—including net exports, net foreign investment, and the real and nominal exchange rates. This chapter develops a model that shows what forces determine these variables and how these variables are related to one another.

To develop this macroeconomic model of an open economy, we build on our previous analysis in two important ways. First, the model takes the economy's GDP as given. The economy's output of goods and services, as measured by real GDP, is assumed to be determined by the supplies of the factors of production and by the available production technology that turns these inputs into output.

Second, the model takes the economy's price level as given. The price level is assumed to adjust to bring the supply and demand for money into balance. In other words, this chapter takes as a starting point the lessons learned in previous chapters about the determination of the economy's output and price level.

The goal of the model in this chapter is to highlight those forces that determine the economy's trade balance and exchange rate. In one sense, the model is simple: It merely applies the tools of supply and demand to an open economy. Yet the model is also more complicated than others we have seen because it involves looking simultaneously at two related markets—the market for loanable funds and the market for foreign-currency exchange. After we develop this model of the open economy, we use it to examine how various events and policies affect the economy's trade balance and exchange rate. We will then be able to determine the government policies that are most likely to reverse the trade deficits that the U.S. economy has experienced over the past decade.

SUPPLY AND DEMAND FOR LOANABLE FUNDS AND FOR FOREIGN-CURRENCY EXCHANGE

To understand the forces at work in an open economy, we focus on supply and demand in two markets. The first is the market for loanable funds, which coordinates the economy's saving and investment (including its net foreign investment). The second is the market for foreign-currency exchange, which coordinates people who want to exchange the domestic currency for the currency of other countries. In this section we discuss supply and demand in each of these markets. In the next section we put these markets together to explain the overall equilibrium for an open economy.

THE MARKET FOR LOANABLE FUNDS

When we first analyzed the role of the financial system earlier in this book, we made the simplifying assumption that the financial system consists of only one market, called the *market for loanable funds.* All savers go to this market to deposit their saving, and all borrowers go to this market to get their loans. In this market, there is one interest rate, which is both the return to saving and the cost of borrowing.

To understand the market for loanable funds in an open economy, the place to start is the identity discussed in the preceding chapter:

$$S \quad = \quad I \quad + \quad NFI$$

Saving = Domestic investment + Net foreign investment.

Whenever a nation saves a dollar of its income, it can use that dollar to finance the purchase of domestic capital or to finance the purchase of an asset abroad. The two sides of this identity represent the two sides of the market for loanable funds. The supply of loanable funds comes from national saving (*S*). The demand for loanable funds comes from domestic investment (*I*) and net foreign investment *(NFI)*. Note that the purchase of a capital asset adds to the demand for loanable funds, regardless of whether that asset is located at home or abroad. Because net foreign investment can be either positive or negative, it can either add to or subtract from the demand for loanable funds that arises from domestic investment.

As we learned in our earlier discussion of the market for loanable funds, the quantity of loanable funds supplied and the quantity of loanable funds demanded depend on the real interest rate. A higher real interest rate encourages people to save and, therefore, raises the quantity of loanable funds supplied. A higher interest rate also makes borrowing to finance capital projects more costly; thus, it discourages investment and reduces the quantity of loanable funds demanded.

In addition to influencing national saving and domestic investment, the real interest rate in a country affects that country's net foreign investment. To see why, consider two mutual funds—one in the United States and one in Germany—deciding whether to buy a U.S. government bond or a German government bond. The mutual funds would make this decision in part by comparing the real interest rates in the United States and Germany. When the U.S. real interest rate rises, the U.S. bond becomes more attractive to both mutual funds. Thus, an increase in the U.S. real interest rate discourages Americans from buying foreign assets and encourages foreigners to buy U.S. assets. For both reasons, a high U.S. real interest rate reduces U.S. net foreign investment.

We represent the market for loanable funds on the familiar supply-and-demand diagram in Figure 30-1. As in our earlier analysis of the financial system, the supply curve slopes upward because a higher interest rate increases the quantity of loanable funds supplied, and the demand curve slopes downward because a higher interest rate decreases the quantity of loanable funds demanded. Unlike the situation in our previous discussion, however, the

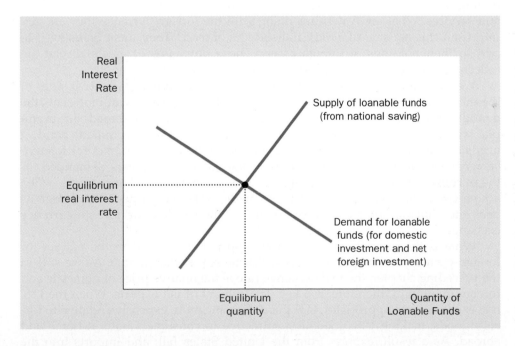

Figure 30-1

THE MARKET FOR LOANABLE FUNDS. The interest rate in an open economy, as in a closed economy, is determined by the supply and demand for loanable funds. National saving is the source of the supply of loanable funds. Domestic investment and net foreign investment are the sources of the demand for loanable funds. At the equilibrium interest rate, the amount that people want to save exactly balances the amount that people want to borrow for the purpose of buying domestic capital and foreign assets.

Real Interest Rate

Supply of loanable funds (from national saving)

Equilibrium real interest rate

Demand for loanable funds (for domestic investment and net foreign investment)

Equilibrium quantity

Quantity of Loanable Funds

demand side of the market now represents the behavior of both domestic investment and net foreign investment. That is, in an open economy, the demand for loanable funds comes not only from those who want to borrow funds to buy domestic capital goods but also from those who want to borrow funds to buy foreign assets.

The interest rate adjusts to bring the supply and demand for loanable funds into balance. If the interest rate were below the equilibrium level, the quantity of loanable funds supplied would be less than the quantity demanded. The resulting shortage of loanable funds would push the interest rate upward. Conversely, if the interest rate were above the equilibrium level, the quantity of loanable funds supplied would exceed the quantity demanded. The surplus of loanable funds would drive the interest rate downward. At the equilibrium interest rate, the supply of loanable funds exactly balances the demand. That is, *at the equilibrium interest rate, the amount that people want to save exactly balances the desired quantities of domestic investment and net foreign investment.*

THE MARKET FOR FOREIGN-CURRENCY EXCHANGE

The second market in our model of the open economy is the market for foreign-currency exchange. Participants in this market trade U.S. dollars in exchange for foreign currencies. To understand the market for foreign-currency exchange, we begin with another identity from the last chapter:

$$NFI = NX$$
Net foreign investment = Net exports.

This identity states that the imbalance between the purchase and sale of capital assets abroad *(NFI)* equals the imbalance between exports and imports of goods and services *(NX)*. When net exports are positive, for instance, foreigners are buying more U.S. goods and services than Americans are buying foreign goods and services. What are Americans doing with the foreign currency they are getting from this net sale of goods and services abroad? They must be using it to add to their holdings of foreign assets. These purchases of assets abroad are reflected in a positive value of net foreign investment.

We can view the two sides of this identity as representing the two sides of the market for foreign-currency exchange. Net foreign investment represents the quantity of dollars supplied for the purpose of buying assets abroad. For example, when a U.S. mutual fund wants to buy a Japanese government bond, it needs to change dollars into yen, so it supplies dollars in the market for foreign-currency exchange. Net exports represent the quantity of dollars demanded for the purpose of buying U.S. net exports of goods and services. For example, when a Japanese airline wants to buy a plane made by Boeing, it needs to change its yen into dollars, so it demands dollars in the market for foreign-currency exchange.

What is the price that balances the supply and demand in the market for foreign-currency exchange? The answer is the real exchange rate. As we saw in the preceding chapter, the real exchange rate is the relative price of domestic and foreign goods and, therefore, is a key determinant of net exports. When the U.S. real exchange rate appreciates, U.S. goods become more expensive relative to foreign goods, making U.S. goods less attractive to consumers both at home and abroad. As a result, exports from the United States fall, and imports into the

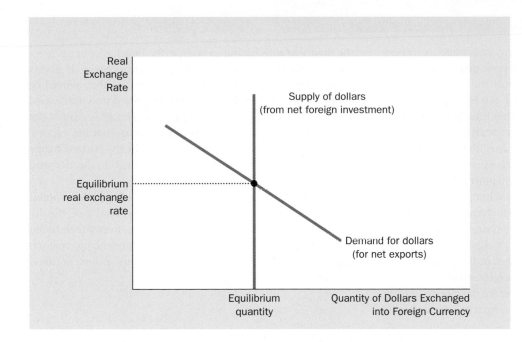

Figure 30-2

THE MARKET FOR FOREIGN-CURRENCY EXCHANGE. The real exchange rate is determined by the supply and demand for foreign-currency exchange. The supply of dollars to be exchanged into foreign currency comes from net foreign investment. Because net foreign investment does not depend on the real exchange rate, the supply curve is vertical. The demand for dollars comes from net exports. Because a lower real exchange rate stimulates net exports (and thus increases the quantity of dollars demanded to pay for these net exports), the demand curve is downward sloping. At the equilibrium real exchange rate, the number of dollars people supply to buy foreign assets exactly balances the number of dollars people demand to buy net exports.

United States rise. For both reasons, net exports fall. Hence, an appreciation of the real exchange rate reduces the quantity of dollars demanded in the market for foreign-currency exchange.

Figure 30-2 shows supply and demand in the market for foreign-currency exchange. The demand curve slopes downward for the reason we just discussed: A higher real exchange rate makes U.S. goods more expensive and reduces the quantity of dollars demanded to buy those goods. The supply curve is vertical because the quantity of dollars supplied for net foreign investment does not depend on the real exchange rate. (As discussed earlier, net foreign investment depends on the real interest rate. When discussing the market for foreign-currency exchange, we take the real interest rate and net foreign investment as given.)

The real exchange rate adjusts to balance the supply and demand for dollars just as the price of any good adjusts to balance supply and demand for that good. If the real exchange rate were below the equilibrium level, the quantity of dollars supplied would be less than the quantity demanded. The resulting shortage of dollars would push the value of the dollar upward. Conversely, if the real exchange rate were above the equilibrium level, the quantity of dollars supplied would exceed the quantity demanded. The surplus of dollars would drive the value of the dollar downward. *At the equilibrium real exchange rate, the demand for dollars to buy net exports exactly balances the supply of dollars to be exchanged into foreign currency to buy assets abroad.*

At this point, it is worth noting that the division of transactions between "supply" and "demand" in this model is somewhat artificial. In our model, net exports are the source of the demand for dollars, and net foreign investment is the source of the supply. Thus, when a U.S. resident imports a car made in Japan, our model treats that transaction as a decrease in the quantity of dollars demanded (because net exports fall) rather than an increase in the quantity of dollars supplied. Similarly, when a Japanese citizen buys a U.S. government

IN THE PRECEDING CHAPTER we developed a simple theory of the exchange rate called *purchasing-power parity*. This theory asserts that a dollar (or any other currency) must buy the same quantity of goods and services in every country. As a result, the real exchange rate is fixed, and all changes in the nominal exchange rate between two currencies reflect changes in the price levels in the two countries.

How is the model of the exchange rate developed here related to the theory of purchasing-power parity? According to the theory of purchasing-power parity, international trade responds quickly to international price differences. If goods were cheaper in one country than in another, they would be exported from the first country and imported into the second until the price differential disappeared. In other words, the theory of purchasing-power parity assumes that net exports are highly responsive to small changes in the real exchange rate. If net exports were in fact so responsive, the demand curve in Figure 30-2 would be horizontal.

Thus, the theory of purchasing-power parity is a special case of the model considered here. In that special case, the demand curve for foreign-currency exchange, rather than being downward sloping, is horizontal at the level of the real exchange rate that ensures parity of purchasing power at home and abroad.

bond, our model treats that transaction as a decrease in the quantity of dollars supplied (because net foreign investment falls) rather than an increase in the quantity of dollars demanded. This use of language may seem somewhat unnatural at first, but it will prove useful when analyzing the effects of various policies.

QUICK QUIZ Describe the sources of supply and demand in the market for loanable funds and the market for foreign-currency exchange.

EQUILIBRIUM IN THE OPEN ECONOMY

So far we have discussed supply and demand in two markets—the market for loanable funds and the market for foreign-currency exchange. Let's now consider how these markets are related to each other.

NET FOREIGN INVESTMENT: THE LINK BETWEEN THE TWO MARKETS

We begin by recapping what we've learned so far in this chapter. We have been discussing how the economy coordinates four important macroeconomic variables: national saving *(S)*, domestic investment *(I)*, net foreign investment *(NFI)*, and net exports *(NX)*. Keep in mind the following identities:

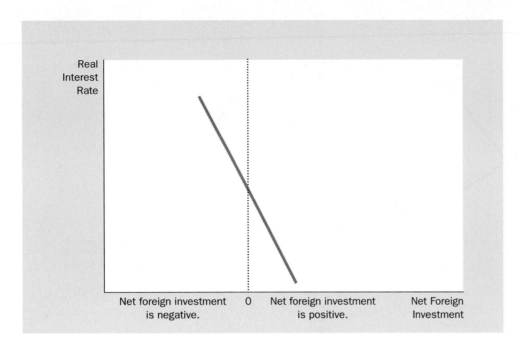

Figure 30-3

HOW NET FOREIGN INVESTMENT DEPENDS ON THE INTEREST RATE. Because a higher domestic real interest rate makes domestic assets more attractive, it reduces net foreign investment. Note the position of zero on the horizontal axis: Net foreign investment can be either positive or negative.

$$S = I + NFI$$

and

$$NFI = NX.$$

In the market for loanable funds, supply comes from national saving, demand comes from domestic investment and net foreign investment, and the real interest rate balances supply and demand. In the market for foreign-currency exchange, supply comes from net foreign investment, demand comes from net exports, and the real exchange rate balances supply and demand.

Net foreign investment is the variable that links these two markets. In the market for loanable funds, net foreign investment is a piece of demand. A person who wants to buy an asset abroad must finance this purchase by borrowing in the market for loanable funds. In the market for foreign-currency exchange, net foreign investment is the source of supply. A person who wants to buy an asset in another country must supply dollars in order to exchange them for the currency of that country.

The key determinant of net foreign investment, as we have discussed, is the real interest rate. When the U.S. interest rate is high, owning U.S. assets is more attractive, and U.S. net foreign investment is low. Figure 30-3 shows this negative relationship between the interest rate and net foreign investment. This net-foreign-investment curve is the link between the market for loanable funds and the market for foreign-currency exchange.

SIMULTANEOUS EQUILIBRIUM IN TWO MARKETS

We can now put all the pieces of our model together in Figure 30-4. This figure shows how the market for loanable funds and the market for foreign-currency

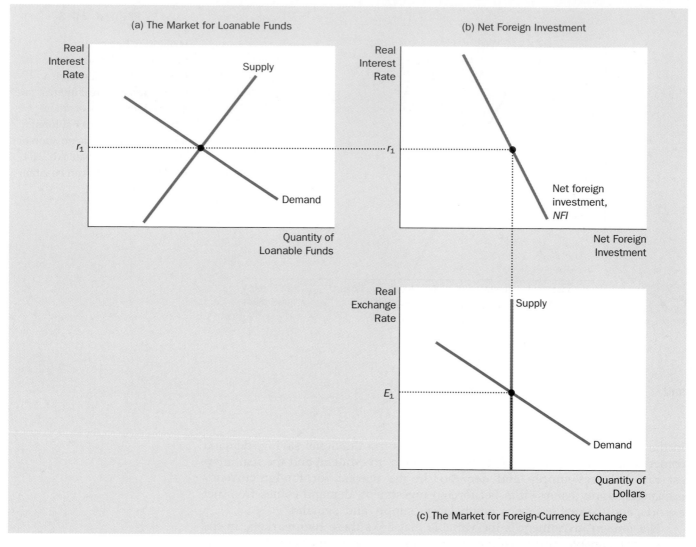

Figure 30-4

THE REAL EQUILIBRIUM IN AN OPEN ECONOMY. In panel (a), the supply and demand for loanable funds determine the real interest rate. In panel (b), the interest rate determines net foreign investment, which provides the supply of dollars in the market for foreign-currency exchange. In panel (c), the supply and demand for dollars in the market for foreign-currency exchange determine the real exchange rate.

exchange jointly determine the important macroeconomic variables of an open economy.

Panel (a) of the figure shows the market for loanable funds (taken from Figure 30-1). As before, national saving is the source of the supply of loanable funds. Domestic investment and net foreign investment are the source of the demand for loanable funds. The equilibrium real interest rate (r_1) brings the quantity of loanable funds supplied and the quantity of loanable funds demanded into balance.

FYI

The Classical Dichotomy Once Again

THE MACROECONOMIC THE-ory of the open economy that we have just developed is "classical." This term has two related meanings. First, the theory harkens back to themes emphasized by econ-omists of centuries past. Sec-ond, and more important, the theory uses the classical di-chotomy and the assumption of monetary neutrality. Recall that the classical dichotomy is the theoretical separation of real and nominal variables. Our model of the open economy is written completely in terms of real variables, including quantities (saving, invest-ment, net foreign investment, and net exports) and relative prices (the real interest rate and the real exchange rate). The model explains these real variables without including a role for money.

How do changes in the money supply affect the econ-omy? The answer is the same as in our analysis in previous chapters. Classical theory posits that the price level adjusts to balance money supply and money demand. If the central bank doubles the money supply, the price level doubles. If the central bank follows a policy of persistent growth in the money supply, the result is persistent inflation.

To ensure that real variables are not affected by monetary changes, all nominal variables must adjust to these changes. In particular, if the real exchange rate is not affected by mon-etary changes, then the nominal exchange rate (measured in units of foreign currency per dollar) must fall as the domestic price level rises. We first saw this effect of inflation on nomi-nal exchange rates in the preceding chapter when we dis-cussed the theory of purchasing-power parity. Nothing we have said about the open economy in this chapter alters these conclusions.

Recall that the assumption of monetary neutrality is best viewed as applying over the long run. To fully understand year-to-year changes in the economy, we need to incorporate reasons for short-run monetary nonneutrality. We cover that topic beginning in the next chapter. Throughout this chapter, we maintain the assumption of monetary neutrality in order to understand the implications of this classical model.

Panel (b) of the figure shows net foreign investment (taken from Figure 30-3). It shows how the interest rate from panel (a) determines net foreign invest-ment. A higher interest rate at home makes domestic assets more attractive, and this in turn reduces net foreign investment. Therefore, the net-foreign-investment curve in panel (b) slopes downward.

Panel (c) of the figure shows the market for foreign-currency exchange (taken from Figure 30-2). Because net foreign investment must be paid for with foreign currency, the quantity of net foreign investment from panel (b) determines the supply of dollars to be exchanged into foreign currencies. The real exchange rate does not affect net foreign investment, so the supply curve is vertical. The demand for dollars comes from net exports. Because a depreciation of the real exchange rate increases net exports, the demand curve for foreign-currency exchange slopes downward. The equilibrium real exchange rate (E_1) brings into balance the quantity of dollars supplied and the quantity of dollars demanded in the market for foreign-currency exchange.

The two markets shown in Figure 30-4 determine two relative prices—the real interest rate and the real exchange rate. The real interest rate determined in panel (a) is the price of goods and services in the present relative to goods and services in the future. The real exchange rate determined in panel (c) is the price of domestic goods and services relative to foreign goods and services. These two relative prices adjust simultaneously to balance supply and demand in these two markets. As they do so, they determine national saving, domestic investment, net foreign investment, and net exports. In a moment, we will use this model to see how all these variables change when some policy or event causes one of these curves to shift.

QUICK QUIZ   In the model of the open economy just developed, two markets determine two relative prices. What are the markets? What are the two relative prices?

HOW POLICIES AND EVENTS AFFECT AN OPEN ECONOMY

Having developed a model to explain how key macroeconomic variables are determined in an open economy, we can now use the model to analyze how changes in policy and other events alter the economy's equilibrium. As we proceed, keep in mind that our model is just supply and demand in two markets—the market for loanable funds and the market for foreign-currency exchange. When using the model to analyze any event, we can apply the three steps outlined in Chapter 4. First, we determine which of the supply and demand curves the event affects. Second, we determine which way the curves shift. Third, we use the supply-and-demand diagrams to examine how these shifts alter the economy's equilibrium.

GOVERNMENT BUDGET DEFICITS

When we first discussed the supply and demand for loanable funds earlier in the book, we examined the effects of government budget deficits, which occur when government spending exceeds government revenue. Because a government budget deficit represents *negative* public saving, it reduces national saving (the sum of public and private saving). Thus, a government budget deficit reduces the supply of loanable funds, drives up the interest rate, and crowds out investment.

Now let's consider the effects of a budget deficit in an open economy. First, which curve in our model shifts? As in a closed economy, the initial impact of the budget deficit is on national saving and, therefore, on the supply curve for loanable funds. Second, which way does this supply curve shift? Again as in a closed economy, a budget deficit represents *negative* public saving, so it reduces national saving and shifts the supply curve for loanable funds to the left. This is shown as the shift from S_1 to S_2 in panel (a) of Figure 30-5.

Our third and final step is to compare the old and new equilibria. Panel (a) shows the impact of a U.S. budget deficit on the U.S. market for loanable funds. With fewer funds available for borrowers in U.S. financial markets, the interest rate rises from r_1 to r_2 to balance supply and demand. Faced with a higher interest rate, borrowers in the market for loanable funds choose to borrow less. This change is represented in the figure as the movement from point A to point B along the demand curve for loanable funds. In particular, households and firms reduce their purchases of capital goods. As in a closed economy, budget deficits crowd out domestic investment.

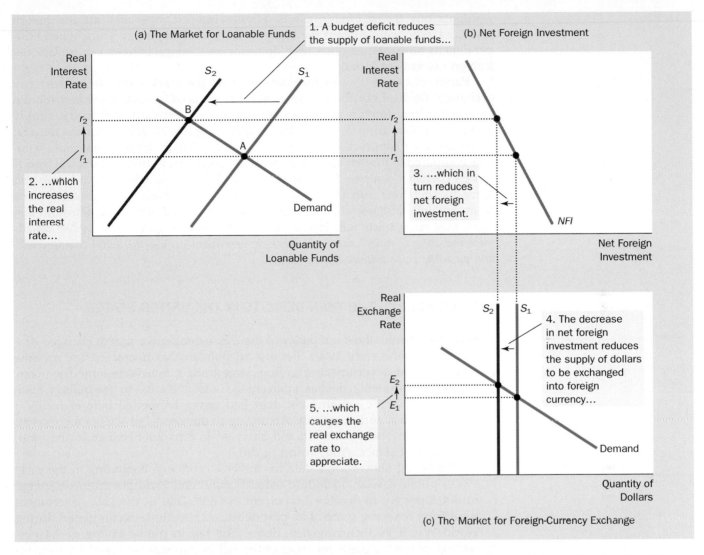

THE EFFECTS OF A GOVERNMENT BUDGET DEFICIT. When the government runs a budget deficit, it reduces the supply of loanable funds from S_1 to S_2 in panel (a). The interest rate rises from r_1 to r_2 to balance the supply and demand for loanable funds. In panel (b), the higher interest rate reduces net foreign investment. Reduced net foreign investment, in turn, reduces the supply of dollars in the market for foreign-currency exchange from S_1 to S_2 in panel (c). This fall in the supply of dollars causes the real exchange rate to appreciate from E_1 to E_2. The appreciation of the exchange rate pushes the trade balance toward deficit.

Figure 30-5

In an open economy, however, the reduced supply for loanable funds has additional effects. Panel (b) shows that the increase in the interest rate from r_1 to r_2 reduces net foreign investment. [This fall in net foreign investment is also part of the decrease in the quantity of loanable funds demanded in the movement from point A to point B in panel (a).] Because saving kept at home now earns higher rates of return, investing abroad is less attractive, and domestic residents buy fewer foreign assets. Higher interest rates also attract foreign investors, who want to earn the higher returns on U.S. assets. Thus, when budget deficits raise interest rates, both domestic and foreign behavior cause U.S. net foreign investment to fall.

Panel (c) shows how budget deficits affect the market for foreign-currency exchange. Because net foreign investment is reduced, people need less foreign currency to buy foreign assets, and this induces a leftward shift in the supply curve for dollars from S_1 to S_2. The reduced supply of dollars causes the real exchange rate to appreciate from E_1 to E_2. That is, the dollar becomes more valuable compared to foreign currencies. This appreciation, in turn, makes U.S. goods more expensive compared to foreign goods. Because people both at home and abroad switch their purchases away from the more expensive U.S. goods, exports from the United States fall, and imports into the United States rise. For both reasons, U.S. net exports fall. Hence, *in an open economy, government budget deficits raise real interest rates, crowd out domestic investment, cause the dollar to appreciate, and push the trade balance toward deficit.*

CASE STUDY   THE TWIN DEFICITS IN THE UNITED STATES

As we have seen, the fiscal policy of the U.S. federal government changed dramatically in the early 1980s. Because of policies that decreased tax revenue and increased government spending, large budget deficits became the norm, and the government's debt as a percentage of GDP started to rise quickly. Such a large rise in the government debt had never happened before during a period of peace and prosperity. According to our model of the open economy, this change in fiscal policy should have led to a parallel change in the economy's trade balance. And, in fact, it did.

Table 30-1 shows some data for the U.S. economy. Beginning in the early 1980s, public saving (including federal, state, and local governments) went from 0.8 percent to *negative* 1.6 percent of GDP. That is, the U.S. government went from repaying some of its past debts, such as those accumulated during World War II, to incurring new debts. The fall in public saving of 2.4 percentage points accounts for most of the fall in national saving of 2.9 percentage points during this period.

Table 30-1

THE TWIN DEFICITS IN THE UNITED STATES. This table shows public saving, private saving, national saving, domestic investment, and net foreign investment as a percentage of GDP. Note that negative values for public saving represent a budget deficit and negative values for net foreign investment represent a trade deficit.

	1960–1981	1982–1994	CHANGE
Public saving	0.8%	−1.6%	−2.4%
Private saving	16.1	15.7	−0.4
National saving	16.9	14.0	−2.9
Domestic investment	16.5	15.7	−0.8
Net foreign investment	0.3	−1.7	−2.0

SOURCE: U.S. Department of Commerce; and author's calculations. All data are gross nominal magnitudes as a percentage of nominal GDP. Public and private saving have been adjusted for the effects of inflation: Only the real interest on the national debt is counted as expenditure by the government and income by the private sector. The numbers in the table may not satisfy the accounting identities exactly because of rounding.

In our model, reduced national saving means that a smaller supply of loanable funds is available for domestic investment and net foreign investment. In the United States, the fall in national saving has been associated with a fall in domestic investment of only 0.8 percentage points. In other words, the crowding out of domestic investment has been relatively modest. Because the fall in national saving had such a small effect on domestic investment, it must have had a large effect on net foreign investment. In fact, U.S. net foreign investment went from a small positive number to a large negative one, a fall of 2.0 percentage points.

Negative net foreign investment means that the United States is selling some of its assets to foreigners on world financial markets. In 1981, the U.S. stock of net foreign assets was about 12.3 percent of GDP. That is, Americans owned more assets abroad than foreigners owned in the United States. Over time, with negative values of net foreign investment, this situation reversed itself. In 1993, the U.S. stock of net foreign assets was *negative* 8.8 percent of GDP, indicating that foreigners owned more assets in the United States than Americans owned abroad. The world's largest and richest economy went from being a creditor in world financial markets to being a debtor.

Because $NFI = NX$, negative net foreign investment must be accompanied by negative net exports. And, indeed, the United States did run a trade deficit throughout the recent period. This simultaneous switch in the early 1980s from budget surplus and trade surplus to budget deficit and trade deficit is, from the standpoint of our model, hardly a surprise. Because they are so closely related, the budget and trade deficits are sometimes called the *twin deficits.*

TRADE POLICY

A **trade policy** is a government policy that directly influences the quantity of goods and services that a country imports or exports. As we saw in Chapter 9, trade policy takes various forms. One common trade policy is a *tariff,* a tax on imported goods. Another is an *import quota,* a limit on the quantity of a good that can be produced abroad and sold domestically. Trade policies are common throughout the world, although sometimes they are disguised. For example, the U.S. government has often pressured Japanese automakers to reduce the number of cars they sell in the United States. These so-called "voluntary export restrictions" are not really voluntary and, in essence, are a form of import quota.

trade policy
a government policy that directly influences the quantity of goods and services that a country imports or exports

Let's consider the macroeconomic impact of trade policy. Suppose that the U.S. auto industry, concerned about competition from Japanese automakers, convinces the U.S. government to impose a quota on the number of cars that can be imported from Japan. In making their case, lobbyists for the auto industry assert that the trade restriction would shrink the size of the U.S. trade deficit. Are they right? Our model, as illustrated in Figure 30-6, offers an answer.

The first step in analyzing the trade policy is to determine which curve shifts. The initial impact of the import restriction is, not surprisingly, on imports. Because net exports equal exports minus imports, the policy also affects net exports. And because net exports are the source of demand for dollars in the market for foreign-currency exchange, the policy affects the demand curve in this market.

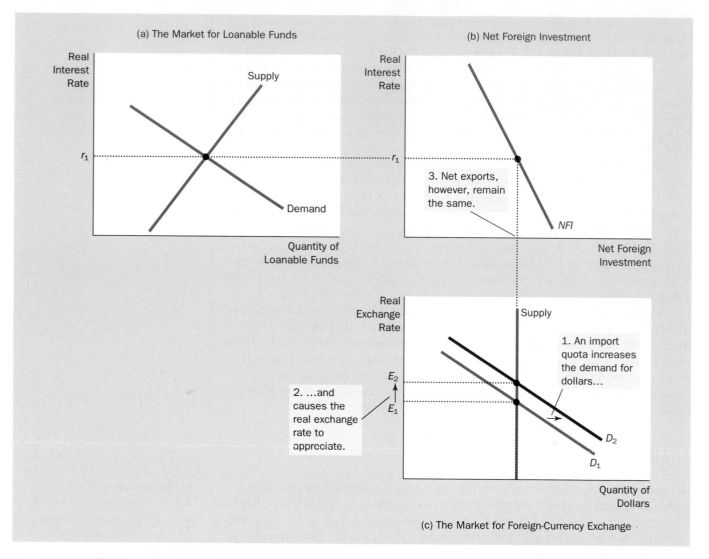

(a) The Market for Loanable Funds

(b) Net Foreign Investment

3. Net exports, however, remain the same.

2. ...and causes the real exchange rate to appreciate.

1. An import quota increases the demand for dollars...

(c) The Market for Foreign-Currency Exchange

Figure 30-6

THE EFFECTS OF AN IMPORT QUOTA. When the U.S. government imposes a quota on the import of Japanese cars, nothing happens in the market for loanable funds in panel (a) or to net foreign investment in panel (b). The only effect is a rise in net exports (exports minus imports) for any given real exchange rate. As a result, the demand for dollars in the market for foreign-currency exchange rises, as shown by the shift from D_1 to D_2 in panel (c). This increase in the demand for dollars causes the value of the dollar to appreciate from E_1 to E_2. This appreciation of the dollar tends to reduce net exports, offsetting the direct effect of the import quota on the trade balance.

The second step is to determine which way this demand curve shifts. Because the quota restricts the number of Japanese cars sold in the United States, it reduces imports at any given real exchange rate. Net exports, which equal exports minus imports, will therefore *rise* for any given real exchange rate. Because foreigners need dollars to buy U.S. net exports, there is an increased demand for dollars in the market for foreign-currency exchange. This increase in the demand for dollars is shown in panel (c) as the shift from D_1 to D_2.

The third step is to compare the old and new equilibria. As we can see in panel (c), the increase in the demand for dollars causes the real exchange rate to appreciate from E_1 to E_2. Because nothing has happened in the market for loanable funds in panel (a), there is no change in the interest rate. There is also no change in net foreign investment, shown in panel (b). And because there is no change in net foreign investment, there can be no change in net exports, even though the import quota has reduced imports.

The reason why net exports can stay the same while imports fall is explained by the change in the real exchange rate: When the dollar appreciates in value in the market for foreign-currency exchange, domestic goods become more expensive relative to foreign goods. This appreciation encourages imports and discourages exports—and both of these changes work to offset the direct increase in net exports due to the import quota. In the end, an import quota reduces both imports and exports, but net exports (exports minus imports) are unchanged.

We have thus come to a surprising implication: *Trade policies do not affect the trade balance.* That is, policies that directly influence exports or imports do not alter net exports. This conclusion seems less surprising if one recalls the accounting identity:

$$NX = NFI = S - I.$$

Net exports equal net foreign investment, which equals national saving minus domestic investment. Trade policies do not alter the trade balance because they do not alter national saving or domestic investment. For given levels of national saving and domestic investment, the real exchange rate adjusts to keep the trade balance the same, regardless of the trade policies the government puts in place.

Although trade policies do not affect a country's overall trade balance, these policies do affect specific firms, industries, and countries. When the U.S. government imposes an import quota on Japanese cars, General Motors has less competition from abroad and will sell more cars. At the same time, because the dollar has appreciated in value, Boeing, the U.S. aircraft maker, will find it harder to compete with Airbus, the European aircraft maker. U.S. exports of aircraft will fall, and U.S. imports of aircraft will rise. In this case, the import quota on Japanese cars will increase net exports of cars and decrease net exports of planes. In addition, it will increase net exports from the United States to Japan and decrease net exports from the United States to Europe. The overall trade balance of the U.S. economy, however, stays the same.

The effects of trade policies are, therefore, more microeconomic than macroeconomic. Although advocates of trade policies sometimes claim (incorrectly) that these policies can alter a country's balance of trade, they are usually more motivated by concerns about particular firms or industries. One should not be surprised, for instance, to hear an executive from General Motors advocating import quotas for Japanese cars. Economists almost always oppose such trade policies. As we saw in Chapters 3 and 9, free trade allows economies to specialize in doing what they do best, making residents of all countries better off. Trade restrictions interfere with these gains from trade and, thus, reduce overall economic well-being.

POLITICAL INSTABILITY AND CAPITAL FLIGHT

In 1994 political instability in Mexico, including the assassination of a prominent political leader, made world financial markets nervous. People began to view

capital flight

a large and sudden reduction in the demand for assets located in a country

Mexico as a much less stable country than they had previously thought. They decided to pull some of their assets out of Mexico in order to move these funds to the United States and other "safe havens." Such a large and sudden movement of funds out of a country is called **capital flight.** To see the implications of capital flight for the Mexican economy, we again follow our three steps for analyzing a change in equilibrium, but this time we apply our model of the open economy from the perspective of Mexico rather than the United States.

Consider first which curves in our model capital flight affects. When investors around the world observe political problems in Mexico, they decide to sell some of their Mexican assets and use the proceeds to buy U.S. assets. This act increases Mexican net foreign investment and, therefore, affects both markets in our model. Most obviously, it affects the net-foreign-investment curve, and this in turn influences the supply of pesos in the market for foreign-currency exchange. In addition, because the demand for loanable funds comes from both domestic investment and net foreign investment, capital flight affects the demand curve in the market for loanable funds.

Now consider which way these curves shift. When net foreign investment increases, there is greater demand for loanable funds to finance these purchases. Thus, as panel (a) of Figure 30-7 shows, the demand curve for loanable funds shifts to the right from D_1 to D_2. In addition, because net foreign investment is higher for any interest rate, the net-foreign-investment curve also shifts to the right from NFI_1 to NFI_2, as in panel (b).

To see the effects of capital flight on the economy, we compare the old and new equilibria. Panel (a) of Figure 30-7 shows that the increased demand for loanable funds causes the interest rate in Mexico to rise from r_1 to r_2. Panel (b) shows that Mexican net foreign investment increases. (Although the rise in the interest rate does make Mexican assets more attractive, this only partly offsets the impact of capital flight on net foreign investment.) Panel (c) shows that the increase in net foreign investment raises the supply of pesos in the market for foreign-currency exchange from S_1 to S_2. That is, as people try to get out of Mexican assets, there is a large supply of pesos to be converted into dollars. This increase in supply causes the peso to depreciate from E_1 to E_2. Thus, *capital flight from Mexico increases Mexican interest rates and decreases the value of the Mexican peso in the market for foreign-currency exchange.* This is exactly what was observed in 1994. From November 1994 to March 1995, the interest rate on short-term Mexican government bonds rose from 14 percent to 70 percent, and the peso depreciated in value from 29 to 15 U.S. cents per peso.

Although capital flight has its largest impact on the country from which capital is fleeing, it also affects other countries. When capital flows out of Mexico into the United States, for instance, it has the opposite effect on the U.S. economy as it has on the Mexican economy. In particular, the rise in Mexican net foreign investment coincides with a fall in U.S. net foreign investment. As the peso depreciates in value and Mexican interest rates rise, the dollar appreciates in value and U.S. interest rates fall. The size of this impact on the U.S. economy is small, however, because the economy of the United States is so large compared to that of Mexico.

Could the events that occurred in Mexico ever happen in the United States? Although the U.S. economy has long been viewed as a safe economy in which to invest, political developments in the United States have at times induced small amounts of capital flight. For example, the September 22, 1995, issue of *The New York Times* reported that on the previous day, "House Speaker Newt Gingrich

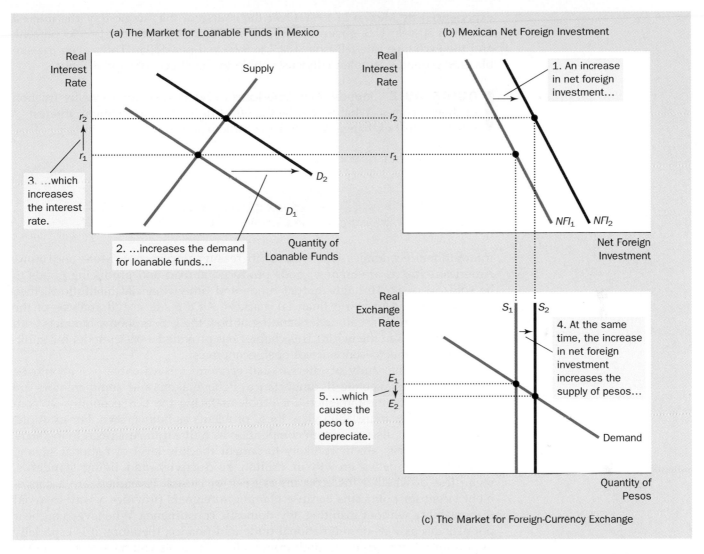

THE EFFECTS OF CAPITAL FLIGHT. If people in Mexico decide that Mexico is a risky place to keep their savings, they will move their capital to safer havens such as the United States, resulting in an increase in Mexican net foreign investment. Consequently, the demand for loanable funds in Mexico rises from D_1 to D_2, as shown in panel (a), and this drives up the Mexican real interest rate from r_1 to r_2. Because net foreign investment is higher for any interest rate, that curve also shifts to the right from NFI_1 to NFI_2 in panel (b). At the same time, in the market for foreign-currency exchange, the supply of pesos rises from S_1 to S_2, as shown in panel (c). This increase in the supply of pesos causes the peso to depreciate from E_1 to E_2, so the peso becomes less valuable compared to other currencies.

Figure 30-7

threatened to send the United States into default on its debt for the first time in the nation's history, to force the Clinton administration to balance the budget on Republican terms" (p. A1). Even though most people believed such a default was unlikely, the effect of the announcement was, in a small way, similar to that experienced by Mexico in 1994. Over the course of that single day, the interest rate on a 30-year U.S. government bond rose from 6.46 percent to 6.55 percent, and the exchange rate fell from 102.7 to 99.0 yen per dollar. Thus, even the stable U.S. economy is potentially susceptible to the effects of capital flight.

QUICK QUIZ   Suppose that Americans decided to spend a smaller fraction of their incomes. What would be the effect on saving, investment, interest rates, the real exchange rate, and the trade balance?

CONCLUSION

International economics is a topic of increasing importance. More and more, American citizens are buying goods produced abroad and producing goods to be sold overseas. Through mutual funds and other financial institutions, they borrow and lend in world financial markets. As a result, a full analysis of the U.S. economy requires an understanding of how the U.S. economy interacts with other economies in the world. This chapter has provided a basic model for thinking about the macroeconomics of open economies.

Although the study of international economics is valuable, we should be careful not to exaggerate its importance. Policymakers and commentators are often quick to blame foreigners for problems facing the U.S. economy. By contrast, economists more often view these problems as homegrown. For example, politicians often discuss foreign competition as a threat to American living standards. Economists are more likely to lament the low level of national saving. Low saving impedes growth in capital, productivity, and living standards, regardless of whether the economy is open or closed. Foreigners are a convenient target for politicians because blaming foreigners provides a way to avoid responsibility without insulting any domestic constituency. Whenever you hear popular discussions of international trade and finance, therefore, it is especially important to try to separate myth from reality. The tools you have learned in the past two chapters should help in that endeavor.

Summary

◆ To analyze the macroeconomics of open economies, two markets are central—the market for loanable funds and the market for foreign-currency exchange. In the market for loanable funds, the interest rate adjusts to balance the supply of loanable funds (from national saving) and the demand for loanable funds (from domestic investment and net foreign investment). In the market for foreign-currency exchange, the real exchange rate adjusts to balance the supply of dollars (for net foreign investment) and the demand for dollars (for net exports). Because net foreign investment is part of the demand for loanable funds and provides the supply of

dollars for foreign-currency exchange, it is the variable that connects these two markets.

◆ A policy that reduces national saving, such as a government budget deficit, reduces the supply of loanable funds and drives up the interest rate. The higher interest rate reduces net foreign investment, which reduces the supply of dollars in the market for foreign-currency exchange. The dollar appreciates, and net exports fall.

◆ Although restrictive trade policies, such as a tariff or quota on imports, are sometimes advocated as a way to alter the trade balance, they do not necessarily have that effect. A trade restriction increases net exports for a given exchange rate and, therefore, increases the demand for dollars in the market for foreign-currency exchange. As a result, the dollar appreciates in value, making domestic goods more expensive relative to foreign goods. This appreciation offsets the initial impact of the trade restriction on net exports.

◆ When investors change their attitudes about holding assets of a country, the ramifications for the country's economy can be profound. In particular, political instability can lead to capital flight, which tends to increase interest rates and cause the currency to depreciate.

Key Concepts

trade policy, p. 671

capital flight, p. 674

Questions for Review

1. Describe supply and demand in the market for loanable funds and the market for foreign-currency exchange. How are these markets linked?

2. Why are budget deficits and trade deficits sometimes called the twin deficits?

3. Suppose that a union of textile workers encourages people to buy only American-made clothes. What would this policy do to the trade balance and the real exchange rate? What is the impact on the textile industry? What is the impact on the auto industry?

4. Suppose that Congress passes an investment tax credit, which subsidizes domestic investment. How does this policy affect saving, domestic investment, net foreign investment, the interest rate, the exchange rate, and the trade balance?

Problems and Applications

1. Japan generally runs a significant trade surplus. Do you think this is most related to high foreign demand for Japanese goods, low Japanese demand for foreign goods, a high Japanese saving rate relative to Japanese investment, or structural barriers against imports into Japan? Explain your answer.

2. How would an increase in foreigners' income affect the U.S. net exports curve? How would this affect the value of the dollar in the market for foreign-currency exchange?

3. An article in *The New York Times* (Apr. 14, 1995) regarding a continued decline in the value of the dollar reported that "the president was clearly determined to signal that the United States remains solidly on a course of deficit reduction, which should make the dollar more attractive to investors." Would deficit reduction in fact raise the value of the dollar? Explain.

4. A column in *The New York Times* (Apr. 30, 1995) was entitled "Save the Dollar: Encourage Saving." What would be the effect of increased saving on the value of the dollar? Do you think this was what the columnist had in mind?

5. The chapter explains that the rise in the U.S. trade deficit during the 1980s was due largely to the rise in the U.S. budget deficit. On the other hand, the popular press sometimes claims that the increased trade deficit resulted from a decline in the quality of U.S. products relative to foreign products.
   a. Assume that U.S. products did decline in relative quality during the 1980s. How did this affect net exports *at any given exchange rate*?
   b. Use a three-panel diagram to show the effect of this shift in net exports on the U.S. real exchange rate and trade balance.
   c. Is the claim in the popular press consistent with the model in this chapter? Does a decline in the quality of U.S. products have any effect on our standard of living? (Hint: When we sell our goods to foreigners, what do we receive in return?)

6. In response to an article about trade policy in *The New Republic* (Apr. 1, 1991), an economist wrote: "One of the benefits of the United States removing its trade restrictions [is] the gain to U.S. industries that produce goods for export. Export industries would find it easier to sell

their goods abroad—even if other countries didn't follow our example and reduce their trade barriers." Explain in words why U.S. *export* industries would benefit from a reduction in restrictions on *imports* to the United States.

7. Suppose the French suddenly develop a strong taste for California wines. Answer the following questions in words and using a diagram.
   a. What happens to the demand for dollars in the market for foreign-currency exchange?
   b. What happens to the value of dollars in the market for foreign-currency exchange?
   c. What happens to the quantity of net exports?

8. A senator renounces her past support for protectionism: "The U.S. trade deficit must be reduced, but import quotas only annoy our trading partners. If we subsidize U.S. exports instead, we can reduce the deficit by increasing our competitiveness." Using a three-panel diagram, show the effect of an export subsidy on net exports and the real exchange rate. Do you agree with the senator?

9. Suppose that real interest rates increase across Europe. Explain how this will affect U.S. net foreign investment. Then explain how this change will affect U.S. net exports by using a formula from the chapter and by using a diagram. What will happen to the U.S. real exchange rate?

10. Suppose that Americans decide to increase their saving.
    a. If the elasticity of U.S. net foreign investment with respect to the real interest rate is very high, will this increase in private saving have a large or small effect on U.S. domestic investment?
    b. If the elasticity of U.S. exports with respect to the real exchange rate is very low, will this increase in private saving have a large or small effect on the U.S. real exchange rate?

11. Suppose that Europeans suddenly become very interested in investing in Canada.
    a. What happens to Canadian net foreign investment?
    b. What effect does this have on Canadian private saving and Canadian domestic investment?
    c. What is the long-run effect on the Canadian capital stock?

12. Over the past decade, some of Japanese saving has been used to finance American investment. That is, American net foreign investment in Japan has been negative.
    a. If the Japanese decided they no longer wanted to buy U.S. assets, what would happen in the U.S. market for loanable funds? In particular, what would happen to U.S. interest rates, U.S. saving, and U.S. investment?
    b. What would happen in the market for foreign-currency exchange? In particular, what would happen to the value of the dollar and the U.S. balance of trade?

13. (This problem is challenging.) Most models of open economies show that a decline in national saving leads to a decline in net foreign investment and thus in net exports. Thus, the case study in this chapter referred to the U.S. budget deficit and U.S. trade deficit as "twins." At the same time, economists have found that national saving has equaled domestic investment over long time periods in virtually every country.
    a. In what way does this fact seem to contradict the models?
    b. Suppose that investors are unwilling to accumulate too many assets from a single foreign country. How does this behavior help to reconcile the fact and the models?
    c. If investors are unwilling to accumulate too many assets from the United States, what would happen to the U.S. trade deficit over time even if the U.S. budget deficit remains large?

XII

SHORT-RUN ECONOMIC FLUCTUATIONS

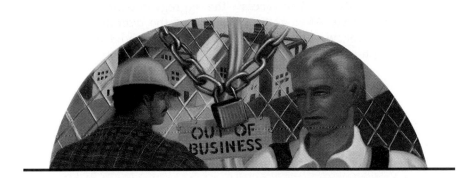

31

AGGREGATE DEMAND AND AGGREGATE SUPPLY

Economic activity fluctuates from year to year. In most years, the production of goods and services rises. Because of increases in the labor force, increases in the capital stock, and advances in technological knowledge, the economy can produce more and more over time. This growth allows everyone to enjoy a higher standard of living. On average over the past 50 years, the production of the U.S. economy as measured by real GDP has grown by about 3 percent per year.

In some years, however, this normal growth does not occur. Firms find themselves unable to sell all of the goods and services they have to offer, so they cut back on production. Workers are laid off, unemployment rises, and factories are left idle. With the economy producing fewer goods and services, real GDP and other measures of income fall. Such a period of falling incomes and rising

recession

a period of declining real incomes and rising unemployment

depression

a severe recession

unemployment is called a **recession** if it is relatively mild and a **depression** if it is more severe.

What causes short-run fluctuations in economic activity? What, if anything, can public policy do to prevent periods of falling incomes and rising unemployment? When recessions and depressions do occur, how can policymakers reduce their length and severity? These are the questions that we take up in this and the next two chapters.

The variables that we study in the coming chapters are largely those we have already seen. They include GDP, unemployment, interest rates, exchange rates, and the price level. Also familiar are the policy instruments of government spending, taxes, and the money supply. What differs in the next few chapters is the time horizon of our analysis. Our focus in the previous seven chapters has been on the behavior of the economy in the long run. Our focus now is on the economy's short-run fluctuations around its long-run trend.

Although there remains some debate among economists about how to analyze short-run fluctuations, most economists use the *model of aggregate demand and aggregate supply*. Learning how to use this model for analyzing the short-run effects of various events and policies is the primary task ahead. This chapter introduces the model's two key pieces—the aggregate-demand curve and the aggregate-supply curve. After getting a sense of the overall structure of the model in this chapter, we examine the pieces of the model in more detail in the next two chapters.

THREE KEY FACTS ABOUT ECONOMIC FLUCTUATIONS

Short-run fluctuations in economic activity occur in all countries. As a starting point for understanding these year-to-year fluctuations, let's discuss some of their most important properties.

FACT 1: ECONOMIC FLUCTUATIONS ARE IRREGULAR AND UNPREDICTABLE

Fluctuations in the economy are often called *the business cycle*. As this term suggests, economic fluctuations correspond to changes in business conditions. When real GDP grows rapidly, business is good. Firms find that customers are plentiful and that profits are growing. On the other hand, when real GDP falls, businesses have trouble. In recessions, most firms experience declining sales and profits.

The term *business cycle* is somewhat misleading, however, because it seems to suggest that economic fluctuations follow a regular, predictable pattern. In fact, economic fluctuations are not at all regular, and they are almost impossible to predict with much accuracy. Panel (a) of Figure 31-1 shows the real GDP of the U.S. economy since 1965. The shaded areas represent times of recession. As the figure shows, recessions do not come at regular intervals. Sometimes recessions are close together, such as the recessions of 1980 and 1982. Sometimes the economy goes many years without a recession.

(a) Real GDP

Figure 31-1

A Look at Short-Run Economic Fluctuations. This figure shows real GDP in panel (a), investment spending in panel (b), and unemployment in panel (c) for the U.S. economy using quarterly data since 1965. Recessions are shown as the shaded areas. Notice that real GDP and investment spending decline during recessions, while unemployment rises.

Source: U.S. Department of Commerce; U.S. Department of Labor.

(b) Investment Spending

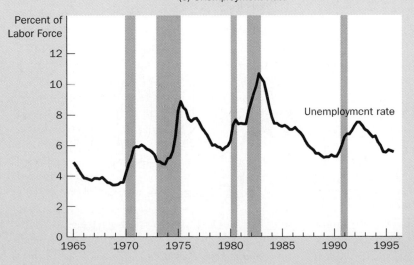

(c) Unemployment Rate

FACT 2: MOST MACROECONOMIC QUANTITIES FLUCTUATE TOGETHER

Real GDP is the variable that is most commonly used to monitor short-run changes in the economy because it is the most comprehensive measure of economic activity. Real GDP measures the value of all final goods and services produced within a given period of time. It also measures the total income (adjusted for inflation) of everyone in the economy.

It turns out, however, that for monitoring short-run fluctuations, it does not really matter which measure of economic activity one looks at. Most macroeconomic variables that measure some type of income, spending, or production fluctuate closely together. When real GDP falls in a recession, so do personal income, corporate profits, consumer spending, investment spending, industrial production, retail sales, home sales, auto sales, and so on. Because recessions are economy-wide phenomena, they show up in many sources of macroeconomic data.

Although many macroeconomic variables fluctuate together, they fluctuate by different amounts. In particular, as panel (b) of Figure 31-1 shows, investment spending varies greatly over the business cycle. Even though investment averages about one-seventh of GDP, declines in investment account for about two-thirds of the declines in GDP during recessions. In other words, when economic conditions deteriorate, much of the decline is attributable to reductions in spending on new factories, housing, and inventories.

FACT 3: AS OUTPUT FALLS, UNEMPLOYMENT RISES

Changes in the economy's output of goods and services are strongly correlated with changes in the economy's utilization of its labor force. In other words, when real GDP declines, the rate of unemployment rises. This fact is hardly surpris-

"You're fired. Pass it on."

FYI

Okun's Law

WHEN THE REAL GDP OF the economy fluctuates, how much does unemployment typically change? Economists answer this question with *Okun's law*. This law can be described with the following equation:

Change in unemployment rate = −1/2 × (Percent change in real GDP minus 3 percent).

According to this equation, when real GDP grows at its average rate of 3 percent, the unemployment rate remains unchanged. When the economy expands more rapidly than 3 percent, the unemployment rate falls by about half as much. For example, if real GDP grows by 5 percent from one year to the next (2 percent higher than normal), Okun's law predicts a fall in the unemployment rate of 1 percentage point. When real GDP falls, or rises by less than 3 percent, the unemploy-

ment rate rises. For example, if real GDP falls by 1 percent from one year to the next, as it might during a recession, Okun's law predicts a rise in unemployment of 2 percentage points.

Okun's law is named for economist Arthur Okun, who first studied the link between fluctuations in real GDP and fluctuations in unemployment for the U.S. economy. Okun did not claim his law to be a fundamental truth of economic theory. The law is, instead, a simple description of U.S. data on real GDP and unemployment. When economists look at data from other countries, they find that the numbers in the formula for Okun's law differ somewhat. Nonetheless, in all countries, there is a strong correlation between changes in GDP and changes in unemployment.

As we study economic fluctuations in the next few chapters, we should keep Okun's law in mind. This law reminds us that the business cycle concerns related movements in the quantity of goods and services that the economy is producing (as measured by real GDP) and the number of people who cannot find jobs (as measured by the unemployment rate).

ing: When firms choose to produce a smaller quantity of goods and services, they lay off workers, expanding the pool of unemployed.

Panel (c) of Figure 31-1 shows the unemployment rate in the U.S. economy since 1965. Once again, recessions are shown as the shaded areas in the figure. The figure shows clearly the impact of recessions on unemployment. In each of the recessions, the unemployment rate rises substantially. When the recession ends and real GDP starts to expand, the unemployment rate gradually declines. The unemployment rate never approaches zero; instead, it fluctuates around its natural rate of about 5 to 6 percent.

QUICK QUIZ List and discuss three key facts about economic fluctuations.

EXPLAINING SHORT-RUN ECONOMIC FLUCTUATIONS

Describing the regular patterns that economies experience as they fluctuate over time is easy. Explaining what causes these fluctuations is more difficult. Indeed, compared to the topics we have studied in previous chapters, the theory of economic fluctuations remains controversial. In this and the next two chapters, we develop the model that most economists use to explain short-run fluctuations in economic activity.

HOW THE SHORT RUN DIFFERS FROM THE LONG RUN

In previous chapters we developed theories to explain what determines most important macroeconomic variables. Chapter 24 explained the level and growth of productivity and real GDP. Chapter 25 explained how the real interest rate adjusts to balance saving and investment. Chapter 26 explained the various causes of unemployment. Chapters 27 and 28 explained the monetary system and how changes in the money supply affect the price level, the inflation rate, and the nominal interest rate. Chapters 29 and 30 extended this analysis to open economies in order to explain the trade balance and the exchange rate.

All of this previous analysis was based on two related ideas—the classical dichotomy and monetary neutrality. Recall that the classical dichotomy is the separation of variables into real variables (those that measure quantities or relative prices) and nominal variables (those measured in terms of money). According to classical macroeconomic theory, changes in the money supply affect nominal variables but not real variables. As a result of this monetary neutrality, Chapters 24, 25, and 26 were able to examine the determinants of real variables (real GDP, the real interest rate, and unemployment) without introducing nominal variables (the money supply and the price level).

Do these assumptions of classical macroeconomic theory apply to the world in which we live? The answer to this question is of central importance to understanding how the economy works: *Most economists believe that classical theory describes the world in the long run but not in the short run.* Beyond a period of several years, changes in the money supply affect prices and other nominal variables but do not affect real GDP, unemployment, or other real variables. When studying year-to-year changes in the economy, however, the assumption of monetary neutrality is no longer appropriate. Most economists believe that, in the short run, real and nominal variables are highly intertwined.

To understand the economy in the short run, therefore, we need a new model. To build this new model, we rely on many of the tools we have developed in previous chapters, but we have to abandon the classical dichotomy and the neutrality of money.

THE BASIC MODEL OF ECONOMIC FLUCTUATIONS

Our model of short-run economic fluctuations focuses on two variables. The first variable is the economy's output of goods and services, as measured by real GDP. The second variable is the overall price level, as measured by the CPI or the GDP deflator. Notice that output is a real variable, whereas the price level is a nominal variable. Hence, by focusing on the relationship between these two variables, we are highlighting the breakdown of the classical dichotomy.

model of aggregate demand and aggregate supply
the model that most economists use to explain short-run fluctuations in economic activity around its long-run trend

Just as we analyze an individual market with a market demand curve and a market supply curve, we analyze fluctuations in the economy as a whole with the **model of aggregate demand and aggregate supply.** This model is illustrated

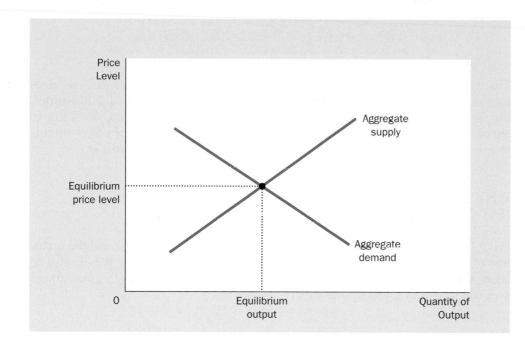

Figure 31-2

AGGREGATE DEMAND AND AGGREGATE SUPPLY. Economists use the model of aggregate demand and aggregate supply to analyze economic fluctuations. On the vertical axis is the overall level of prices. On the horizontal axis is the economy's total output of goods and services. Output and the price level adjust to the point at which the aggregate-supply and aggregate-demand curves intersect.

in Figure 31-2. On the vertical axis is the overall price level in the economy. On the horizontal axis is the overall quantity of goods and services. The **aggregate-demand curve** shows the quantity of goods and services that households, firms, and the government want to buy at any price level. The **aggregate-supply curve** shows the quantity of goods and services that firms produce and sell at any price level. According to this model, the price level and the quantity of output adjust to bring aggregate demand and aggregate supply into balance.

It may be tempting to view the model of aggregate demand and aggregate supply as nothing more than a large version of the model of market demand and market supply, which we introduced in Chapter 4. Yet in fact this model is quite different. When we consider demand and supply in a particular market—ice cream, for instance—the behavior of buyers and sellers depends on the ability of resources to move from one market to another. When the price of ice cream rises, the quantity demanded falls because buyers will use their incomes to buy products other than ice cream. Similarly, a higher price of ice cream raises the quantity supplied because firms that produce ice cream can increase production by hiring workers away from other parts of the economy. This *microeconomic* substitution from one market to another is impossible when we are analyzing the economy as a whole. After all, the quantity that our model is trying to explain—real GDP—includes the quantities produced in all of the economy's markets. To understand why the aggregate-demand curve is downward sloping and why the aggregate-supply curve is upward sloping, we need a *macroeconomic* theory. Developing such a theory is our next task.

aggregate-demand curve
a curve that shows the quantity of goods and services that households, firms, and the government want to buy at any price level

aggregate-supply curve
a curve that shows the quantity of goods and services that firms choose to produce and sell at any price level

QUICK QUIZ How does the economy's behavior in the short run differ from its behavior in the long run? ◆ Draw the model of aggregate demand and aggregate supply. What variables are on the two axes?

THE AGGREGATE-DEMAND CURVE

The aggregate-demand curve tells us the quantity of all goods and services demanded in the economy at any given price level. As Figure 31-3 illustrates, the aggregate-demand curve is downward sloping. This means that, other things equal, a fall in the economy's overall level of prices (from, say, P_1 to P_2) tends to raise the quantity of goods and services demanded (from Y_1 to Y_2).

WHY THE AGGREGATE-DEMAND CURVE IS DOWNWARD SLOPING

What lies behind this negative relationship between the price level and the quantity of goods and services demanded? To answer this question, it is useful to recall that GDP (Y) is the sum of consumption (C), investment (I), government purchases (G), and net exports (NX):

$$Y = C + I + G + NX.$$

Each of these four components contributes to the aggregate demand for goods and services. Government spending is assumed to be a fixed policy variable, but the other three components of spending—consumption, investment, and net exports—depend on economic conditions and, in particular, on the price level. To understand the downward slope of the aggregate-demand curve, therefore, we must examine how the price level affects the quantity of goods and services demanded for consumption, investment, and net exports.

Figure 31-3

THE AGGREGATE-DEMAND CURVE. A fall in the price level from P_1 to P_2 increases the quantity of goods and services demanded from Y_1 to Y_2. There are three reasons for this negative relationship. As the price level falls, real wealth rises, interest rates fall, and the exchange rate depreciates. These effects stimulate spending on consumption, investment, and net exports. Increased spending on these components of output means a larger quantity of goods and services demanded.

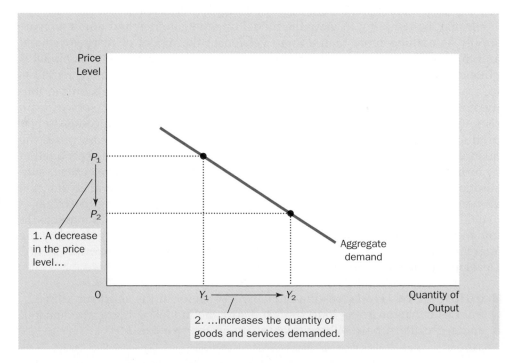

Pigou's Wealth Effect   Consider the money that you hold in your wallet and your bank account. The nominal value of this money is fixed, but its real value is not. When prices fall, these dollars are more valuable because then they can be used to buy more goods and services. Thus, *a decrease in the price level makes consumers feel more wealthy, which in turn encourages them to spend more. The increase in consumer spending means a larger quantity of goods and services demanded.* This wealth effect was emphasized by economist Arthur Pigou (1877–1959), and it is sometimes called the *Pigou effect.*

Keynes's Interest-Rate Effect   As we discussed in Chapter 28, the price level is one determinant of the quantity of money demanded. The lower the price level, the less money households need to hold to buy the goods and services they want. When the price level falls, therefore, households try to reduce their holdings of money by lending some of it out. For instance, a household might use its excess money to buy interest-bearing bonds. Or it might deposit its excess money in an interest-bearing savings account, and the bank would use these funds to make more loans. In either case, as households try to convert some of their money into interest-bearing assets, they drive down interest rates. Lower interest rates, in turn, encourage borrowing by firms that want to invest in new plants and equipment and by households who want to invest in new housing. Thus, *a lower price level reduces the interest rate, encourages greater spending on investment goods, and thereby increases the quantity of goods and services demanded.* This interest-rate effect was emphasized by the famous economist John Maynard Keynes (1883–1946), and it is sometimes called the *Keynes effect.*

Mundell–Fleming's Exchange-Rate Effect   As we have just discussed, a lower price level in the United States lowers the U.S. interest rate. In response, some U.S. investors will seek higher returns by investing abroad. For instance, as the interest rate on U.S. government bonds falls, a mutual fund might sell U.S. government bonds in order to buy German government bonds. As the mutual fund tries to move assets overseas, it increases the supply of dollars in the market for foreign-currency exchange. The increased supply of dollars causes the dollar to depreciate relative to other currencies. (That is, each dollar buys fewer units of foreign currencies.) As a result of this depreciation, foreign goods become more expensive relative to domestic goods, and this change in relative prices increases U.S. exports of goods and services and decreases U.S. imports of goods and services. Net exports, which equal exports minus imports, also increase. Thus, *when a fall in the U.S. price level causes U.S. interest rates to fall, the real exchange rate depreciates, and this depreciation stimulates U.S. net exports and thereby increases the quantity of goods and services demanded.* This exchange-rate effect was emphasized by economists Robert Mundell and Marcus Fleming.

Summary   There are, therefore, three distinct but related reasons why a fall in the price level increases the quantity of goods and services demanded: (1) Consumers feel wealthier, which stimulates the demand for consumption goods. (2) Interest rates fall, which stimulates the demand for investment goods. (3) The exchange rate depreciates, which stimulates the demand for net exports. For all three reasons, the aggregate-demand curve slopes downward.

It is important to keep in mind that the aggregate-demand curve (like all demand curves) is drawn holding "other things equal." In particular, our three explanations of the downward-sloping aggregate-demand curve assume that the money supply is fixed. That is, we have been considering how a change in the price level affects the demand for goods and services, holding the amount of money in the economy constant. As we will see, a change in the quantity of money shifts the aggregate-demand curve. At this point, just keep in mind that the aggregate-demand curve is drawn for a given quantity of money.

WHY THE AGGREGATE-DEMAND CURVE MIGHT SHIFT

The downward slope of the aggregate-demand curve shows that a fall in the price level raises the overall quantity of goods and services demanded. Many other factors beyond the price level, however, affect the quantity of goods and services demanded. When one of these other factors changes, the aggregate-demand curve shifts.

There are many possible examples of events that shift aggregate demand. Here are a few:

◆ Americans suddenly become more concerned about saving for retirement and, as a result, reduce their current consumption. Because the quantity of goods and services demanded at any price level is lower, the aggregate-demand curve shifts to the left.

◆ The computer industry introduces a faster line of computers, and many firms decide to invest in new computer systems. Because the quantity of goods and services demanded at any price level is higher, the aggregate-demand curve shifts to the right.

◆ Congress decides that, with the end of the Cold War, it will reduce purchases of new weapon systems. Because the quantity of goods and services demanded at any price level is lower, the aggregate-demand curve shifts to the left.

◆ The Federal Reserve expands the money supply by printing dollar bills and dropping them by helicopter around the country. After people pick up these dollars, they spend some of them. Because the quantity of goods and services demanded at any price level is higher, the aggregate-demand curve shifts to the right.

The shifts in the aggregate-demand curve in the first two examples arise from changes in spending plans by consumers or firms. The shifts in the last two examples arise from changes in fiscal or monetary policy. In fact, shifts in aggregate demand sometimes come from private behavior and sometimes come from public policy.

In the next chapter we examine the aggregate-demand curve in more detail. There we examine, in particular, how the tools of monetary and fiscal policy can shift aggregate demand. At this point, however, you should have some idea about why the aggregate-demand curve slopes downward and what kinds of events and policies can shift this curve.

QUICK QUIZ Explain the three reasons why the aggregate-demand curve slopes downward. ◆ Give an example of an event that would shift the aggregate-demand curve. Which way would this event shift the curve?

THE AGGREGATE-SUPPLY CURVE

The aggregate-supply curve tells us the quantity of goods and services that firms produce and sell at any given price level. The relationship between the price level and the quantity supplied depends on the time horizon. *In the long run, the aggregate-supply curve is vertical, whereas in the short run, the aggregate-supply curve is upward sloping.* To understand short-run economic fluctuations, and how the short-run behavior of the economy deviates from its long-run behavior, we need to examine both the long-run aggregate-supply curve and the short-run aggregate-supply curve.

WHY THE AGGREGATE-SUPPLY CURVE IS VERTICAL IN THE LONG RUN

What determines the quantity of goods and services supplied in the long run? We implicitly answered this question earlier in the book when we analyzed the process of economic growth. *In the long run, an economy's supply of goods and services depends on its supplies of capital and labor and on the available production technology used to turn capital and labor into goods and services.* Because the price level does not affect these long-run determinants of real GDP, the long-run aggregate-supply curve is vertical, as in Figure 31-4. In other words, the economy's capital, labor, and technology determine the quantity of goods and services supplied, and the quantity supplied is the same regardless of what the price level happens to be.

The vertical long-run aggregate-supply curve is, in essence, just an application of the classical dichotomy and monetary neutrality. As we have already discussed, classical macroeconomic theory is based on the assumption that real

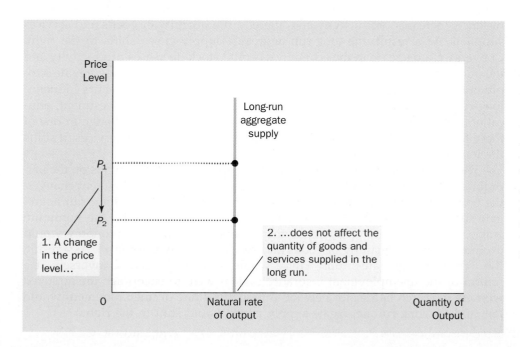

Figure 31-4

THE LONG-RUN AGGREGATE-SUPPLY CURVE. In the long run, the quantity of output supplied depends on the economy's quantities of capital and labor and on the technology for turning these inputs into output. The quantity supplied does not depend on the overall price level. As a result, the long-run aggregate-supply curve is vertical at the natural rate of output.

variables do not depend on nominal variables. The long-run aggregate-supply curve is consistent with this idea because it implies that the quantity of output (a real variable) does not depend on the level of prices (a nominal variable). As noted earlier, most economists believe that this principle works well when studying the economy over a period of many years, but not when studying year-to-year changes. Thus, the aggregate-supply curve is vertical only in the long run.

One might wonder why supply curves for specific goods and services can be upward sloping if the long-run aggregate-supply curve is vertical. The reason is that the supply of specific goods and services depends on *relative prices*—the prices of those goods and services compared to other prices in the economy. For example, when the price of ice cream rises, suppliers of ice cream increase their production, taking labor, milk, chocolate, and other inputs away from the production of other goods, such as frozen yogurt. By contrast, the economy's overall production of goods and services is limited by its capital, labor, and technology. Thus, when all prices in the economy rise together, there is no change in the overall quantity of goods and services supplied.

WHY THE LONG-RUN AGGREGATE-SUPPLY CURVE MIGHT SHIFT

The position of the long-run aggregate-supply curve shows the quantity of goods and services predicted by classical macroeconomic theory. This level of production is sometimes called *potential output* or *full-employment output*. These terms are somewhat misleading, however, because in the short run output can either fall below or rise above this level. To be more accurate, we will call this level of output the *natural rate of output* because it shows what the economy produces when unemployment is at its natural, or normal, rate. The natural rate of output is the level of production toward which the economy gravitates in the long run.

Any change in the economy that alters the natural rate of output shifts the long-run aggregate-supply curve. An increase in the economy's capital stock, for instance, increases productivity and, thereby, the quantity of goods and services supplied. As a result, the long-run aggregate-supply curve shifts to the right. Conversely, a decrease in the economy's capital stock decreases productivity and the quantity of goods and services supplied, shifting the long-run aggregate-supply curve to the left. As we have previously discussed, many factors influence long-run economic growth, including policies toward saving, investment, education, technology, international trade, and so on. Whenever a change in one of these factors alters the economy's ability to produce goods and services, it shifts the long-run aggregate-supply curve.

The position of the long-run aggregate-supply curve also depends on the natural rate of unemployment. That is, if the natural rate of unemployment changes, the economy's natural rate of output changes as well, and the long-run aggregate-supply curve shifts. For example, if Congress were to raise the minimum wage, the natural rate of unemployment would rise, and the economy would produce a smaller quantity of goods and services for any price level. As a result, the long-run aggregate-supply curve would shift to the left. Conversely, if a reform of the unemployment insurance system were to encourage unemployed workers to search harder for new jobs, the natural rate of unemployment would fall, and the long-run aggregate-supply curve would shift to the right.

In sum, the long-run aggregate-supply curve merely provides a new way of describing the classical model of the economy we developed in previous chapters. Any policy or event that raised real GDP in previous chapters can now be viewed as increasing the quantity of goods and services supplied and shifting the long-run aggregate-supply curve to the right. Similarly, any policy or event that lowered real GDP in previous chapters can now be viewed as decreasing the quantity of goods and services supplied and shifting the long-run aggregate-supply curve to the left.

WHY THE AGGREGATE-SUPPLY CURVE IS UPWARD SLOPING IN THE SHORT RUN

Although the model of aggregate demand and aggregate supply can be used to describe the economy in the long run, the model is designed to analyze short-run deviations from this long-run equilibrium. The key difference between the short run and the long run is the behavior of aggregate supply. In the short run, the aggregate-supply curve is upward sloping, as in Figure 31-5. That is, over a period of a year or two, an increase in the overall level of prices in the economy tends to raise the quantity of goods and services supplied, and a decrease in the level of prices tends to reduce the quantity of goods and services supplied.

What causes this positive relationship between the price level and output? Macroeconomists have proposed three theories for the upward slope of the short-run aggregate-supply curve. In each theory, a specific market imperfection causes the supply side of the economy to behave differently in the short run than in the long run. Although each of the following theories will differ in detail, they share a common theme: The quantity of output supplied deviates from its long-run, or "natural," level when the price level deviates from the price level that people expected. When the price level rises above the expected level, output rises above

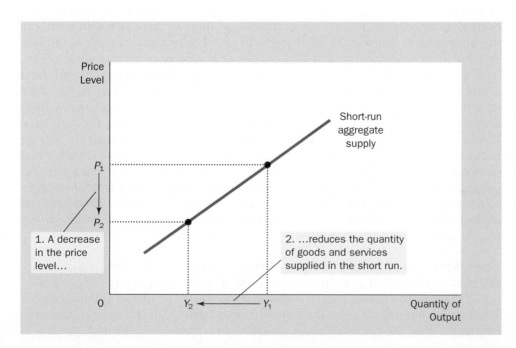

Figure 31-5

THE SHORT-RUN AGGREGATE-SUPPLY CURVE. In the short run, a fall in the price level from P_1 to P_2 reduces the quantity of output supplied from Y_1 to Y_2. This positive relationship could be due to misperceptions, sticky wages, or sticky prices. Over time, perceptions, wages, and prices adjust, so this positive relationship is only temporary.

its natural rate, and when the price level falls below the expected level, output falls below its natural rate.

The New Classical Misperceptions Theory   One theory of the short-run aggregate-supply curve, which is based on the work of economists Milton Friedman and Robert Lucas, is the new classical misperceptions theory. According to this theory, changes in the overall price level can temporarily mislead suppliers about what is happening in the markets in which they sell their output. As a result of these short-run misperceptions, suppliers respond to changes in the level of prices, and this response leads to an upward-sloping aggregate-supply curve.

To see how this might work, suppose the overall price level falls below the level that people expected. When suppliers see the prices of their products fall, they may mistakenly believe that their *relative* prices have fallen. For example, wheat farmers may notice a fall in the price of wheat before they notice a fall in the prices of the many items they buy as consumers. They may infer from this observation that the reward to producing wheat is temporarily low, and they may respond by reducing the quantity of wheat they supply. Similarly, workers may notice a fall in their nominal wages before they notice a fall in the prices of the goods they buy. They may infer that the reward to working is temporarily low and respond by reducing the quantity of labor they supply. In both cases, *a lower price level causes misperceptions about relative prices, and these misperceptions induce suppliers to respond to the lower price level by decreasing the quantity of goods and services supplied.*

The Keynesian Sticky-Wage Theory   Another explanation of the upward slope of the short-run aggregate-supply curve is based on the work of John Maynard Keynes. According to Keynes and many of his followers, the short-run aggregate-supply curve slopes upward because nominal wages are slow to adjust, or "sticky," in the short run. To some extent, the slow adjustment of nominal wages is attributable to long-term contracts between workers and firms that fix nominal wages, sometimes for as long as three years. In addition, this slow adjustment may be attributable to social norms and notions of fairness that influence wage setting and that change only slowly over time.

To see what sticky nominal wages mean for aggregate supply, imagine that a firm has agreed in advance to pay its workers a certain nominal wage based on what it expected the price level to be. If the price level P falls below the level that was expected and the nominal wage remains stuck at W, then the real wage W/P rises above the level the firm planned to pay. Because wages are a large part of a firm's production costs, a higher real wage means that the firm's real costs have risen. The firm responds to these higher costs by hiring less labor and producing a smaller quantity of goods and services. In other words, *because wages do not adjust immediately to the price level, a lower price level makes employment and production less profitable, which induces firms to reduce the quantity of goods and services supplied.*

The New Keynesian Sticky-Price Theory   Recently, some economists have advocated a third theory of the short-run aggregate-supply curve, called the new Keynesian theory. As we just discussed, Keynes originally emphasized that nominal wages adjust slowly over time. New Keynesian theorists emphasize that the prices of some goods and services also adjust sluggishly in response to changing economic conditions. This slow adjustment of prices occurs in part because there are costs to adjusting prices, called *menu costs.* These menu costs include the cost of printing and distributing catalogs and the time required to change price tags. As a result of these costs, prices as well as wages may be sticky in the short run.

To see the implications of sticky prices for aggregate supply, suppose that each firm in the economy announces its prices in advance based on the economic conditions it expects to prevail. Then, after prices are announced, the economy experiences an unexpected contraction in the money supply, which (as we have learned) will reduce the overall price level in the long run. Although some firms reduce their prices immediately in response to changing economic conditions, other firms may not want to incur additional menu costs and, therefore, may temporarily lag behind. Because these lagging firms have prices that are too high, their sales decline. Declining sales, in turn, cause these firms to cut back on production and employment. In other words, *because not all prices adjust instantly to changing conditions, an unexpected fall in the price level leaves some firms with higher-than-desired prices, and these higher-than-desired prices depress sales and induce firms to reduce the quantity of goods and services they produce.*

Summary Thus, there are three alternative explanations for the upward slope of the short-run aggregate-supply curve: (1) misperceptions, (2) sticky wages, and (3) sticky prices. Economists debate which of these theories is correct. For our purposes in this book, however, the similarities of the theories are more important than the differences. All three theories suggest that output deviates from its natural rate when the price level deviates from the price level that people expected.

Notice that each of these three theories of short-run aggregate supply emphasizes a problem that is likely to be only temporary. Whether the upward slope of the aggregate-supply curve is attributable to misperceptions, sticky wages, or sticky prices, these conditions will not persist forever. Eventually, as people adjust their expectations, misperceptions are corrected, nominal wages adjust, and prices become unstuck. In the long run, therefore, the aggregate-supply curve is vertical rather than upward sloping.

WHY THE SHORT-RUN AGGREGATE-SUPPLY CURVE MIGHT SHIFT

The short-run aggregate-supply curve tells us the quantity of goods and services supplied in the short run for any given level of prices. Many events that shift the long-run aggregate-supply curve shift the short-run aggregate-supply curve as well. For example, when an increase in the economy's capital stock increases productivity, both the long-run and short-run aggregate-supply curves shift to the right. When an increase in the minimum wage raises the natural rate of unemployment, both the long-run and short-run aggregate-supply curves shift to the left.

There is, however, an important new variable that affects the position of the short-run aggregate-supply curve: people's expectation of the price level. As we have discussed, the quantity of goods and services supplied depends, in the short run, on misperceptions, sticky wages, and sticky prices. Yet perceptions, wages, and prices are set on the basis of expectations of the price level. For example, when people expect the price level to be high, they will tend to set wages high. High wages tend to raise firms' costs and, for any given actual price level, reduce the quantity of goods and services that firms supply. *Thus, a higher expected price level decreases the quantity of goods and services supplied and shifts the short-run aggregate-supply curve to the left. Conversely, a lower expected price level increases the quantity of goods and services supplied and shifts the short-run aggregate-supply curve to the right.*

As we will see, this influence of expectations on the position of the short-run aggregate-supply curve reconciles the economy's behavior in the short run with its behavior in the long run. In the short run, expectations are fixed, and the economy finds itself at the intersection of the aggregate-demand curve and the short-run aggregate-supply curve. In the long run, expectations adjust, and the short-run aggregate-supply curve shifts. This shift ensures that the economy eventually finds itself at the intersection of the aggregate-demand curve and the long-run aggregate-supply curve.

QUICK QUIZ Explain why the long-run aggregate-supply curve is vertical. ◆ Explain three theories for why the short-run aggregate-supply curve is upward sloping.

TWO CAUSES OF RECESSION

Now that we have introduced the model of aggregate demand and aggregate supply, we have the basic tools we need to analyze short-run fluctuations in economic activity. In the next two chapters we will refine our understanding of how to use these tools. But even now we can use what we have learned about aggregate demand and aggregate supply to examine the two basic causes of recession.

Figure 31-6 shows an economy in long-run equilibrium. Equilibrium output and the price level are determined by the intersection of the aggregate-demand curve and the long-run aggregate-supply curve, shown as point A in the figure. At this point, output is at its natural rate. The short-run aggregate-supply curve passes through this point as well, indicating that perceptions, wages, and prices have fully adjusted to this long-run equilibrium. That is, when an economy is in its long-run equilibrium, perceptions, wages, and prices must have adjusted so that the intersection of aggregate demand with short-run aggregate supply is the same as the intersection of aggregate demand with long-run aggregate supply.

THE EFFECTS OF A SHIFT IN AGGREGATE DEMAND

Suppose that for some reason a wave of pessimism suddenly overtakes the economy. The cause might be a scandal in the White House, a crash in the stock market, or the outbreak of a war overseas. Because of this event, many people lose confidence in the future and alter their plans. Households cut back on their spending and delay major purchases, and firms put off buying new equipment.

What is the impact of such a wave of pessimism on the economy? Such an event reduces the aggregate demand for goods and services. That is, for any

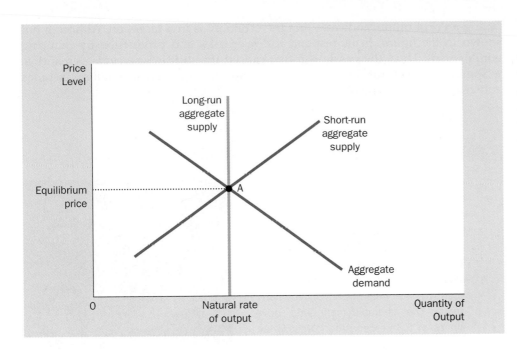

Figure 31-6

THE LONG-RUN EQUILIBRIUM. The long-run equilibrium of the economy is found where the aggregate-demand curve crosses the long-run aggregate-supply curve (point A). When the economy reaches this long-run equilibrium, perceptions, wages, and prices will have adjusted so that the short-run aggregate-supply curve crosses this point as well.

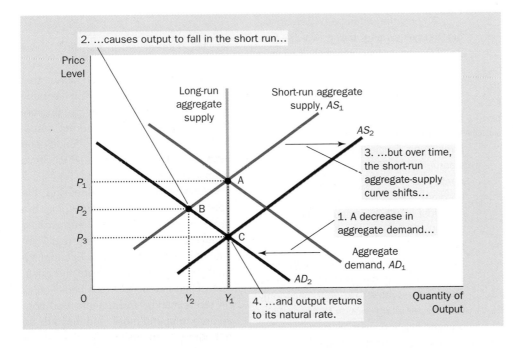

Figure 31-7

A CONTRACTION IN AGGREGATE DEMAND. A fall in aggregate demand, which might be due to a wave of pessimism in the economy, is represented with a leftward shift in the aggregate-demand curve from AD_1 to AD_2. The economy moves from point A to point B. Output falls from Y_1 to Y_2, and the price level falls from P_1 to P_2. Over time, as perceptions, wages, and prices adjust, the short-run aggregate-supply curve shifts to the right from AS_1 to AS_2, and the economy reaches point C, where the new aggregate-demand curve crosses the long-run aggregate-supply curve. The price level falls to P_3, and output returns to its natural rate, Y_1.

given price level, households and firms now want to buy a smaller quantity of goods and services. As Figure 31-7 shows, the aggregate-demand curve shifts to the left from AD_1 to AD_2.

In this figure we can examine the effects of the fall in aggregate demand. In the short run, the economy moves along the initial short-run aggregate-supply curve AS_1, going from point A to point B. As the economy moves from point A to point B, output falls from Y_1 to Y_2, and the price level falls from P_1 to P_2. The falling level of output indicates that the economy is in a recession. Although not shown in the figure, firms respond to lower sales and production by reducing employment. Thus, the pessimism that caused the shift in aggregate demand is, to some extent, self-fulfilling: Pessimism about the future leads to falling incomes and rising unemployment.

IN THE NEWS

How Consumers Shift

Aggregate Demand

AS WE HAVE SEEN, WHEN PEOPLE CHANGE their perceptions and spending, they shift the aggregate-demand curve and cause short-run fluctuations in the economy. According to the following article, such a shift occurred in 1996, just as the presidential campaign was getting under way.

Consumers Get the Credit for Expanding Economy

BY RICHARD W. STEVENSON

WASHINGTON—President Clinton claims the credit for himself, and analysts cite an array of other possible factors, but the most important source of the economy's remarkable resilience and vibrancy this year appears to be the consumer.

For most of this year, Americans have spent prodigiously on homes, cars, refrigerators, and dinners out, carrying forward an aging economic expansion that as recently as January seemed in danger of expiring. In the process, they have largely ignored warning signs that they are becoming overextended.

The consumer spending spree was a major force in the surprisingly robust economic data released Friday, economists said. The Labor Department estimated that the economy created 239,000 jobs in June, far more than expected, making that month the fifth consecutive one with strong employment gains. The unemployment rate now stands at 5.3 percent, the lowest in six years, and economic growth is so rapid that it has revived fears of inflation.

Among the industries showing the biggest gains was retailing, which added 75,000 jobs in June, nearly half of them in what the government classifies as eating and drinking places. Job growth was also strong at car dealers, gas stations, hotels, and stores selling building materials, garden supplies, and home furnishings. Employment in construction was up by 23,000, reflecting in part the continued upward strength of home building.

Just how long consumers can carry on with their free-spending ways, however, remains an open question and one that is critical to policymakers at the Federal Reserve as they decide whether to raise interest rates to keep the economy from accelerating enough to generate increased inflation.

Some economists believe that consumers have amassed so much debt that they will be forced to rein in their spending for the rest of the year, resulting in a slackening of economic growth. Credit card delinquencies in the first quarter were at their highest level since 1981, and personal bankruptcies were

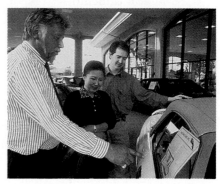

CONSUMERS: AGGREGATE-DEMAND SHIFTERS

up 15 percent from the first three months of 1995. . . .

Most economists also agree that the surge in spending this year has been driven in large part by temporary factors—including low interest rates, higher-than-expected tax refunds, and rebates from automakers—that have been reversed or phased out. . . .

One wild card in assessing the course of consumer spending is the stock market, which has been making relatively affluent consumers feel flush with its continued boom. Economists have grappled for years with the question of the extent to which paper gains on stock market investments lead consumers to spend more, and they still do not agree on an answer. But they said it was relatively clear that the bull market of recent years—and the fact that more and more Americans invest in the market through retirement plans and mutual funds—has provided some impetus to consumers to spend more.

SOURCE: *The New York Times,* July 8, 1996, p. D3.

What should policymakers do when faced with such a recession? One possibility is to take action to increase aggregate demand. As we noted earlier, an increase in government spending or an increase in the money supply would increase the quantity of goods and services demanded at any price and, therefore, would shift the aggregate-demand curve to the right. If policymakers can act with sufficient speed and precision, they can offset the initial shift in aggregate demand, return the aggregate-demand curve back to AD_1, and bring the economy back to point A. (The next chapter discusses in more detail the ways in which monetary and fiscal policy influence aggregate demand, as well as some of the practical difficulties in using these policy instruments.)

Even without action by policymakers, the recession eventually remedies itself. Over time, people correct the misperceptions, sticky wages, and sticky prices that cause aggregate supply to slope upward in the short run. In particular, as expectations of the price level fall, perceptions, wages, and prices are adjusted, and the short-run aggregate-supply curve shifts to the right from AS_1 to AS_2 in Figure 31-7. In the long run, the economy approaches point C, where the new aggregate-demand curve (AD_2) crosses the long-run aggregate-supply curve.

In the new long-run equilibrium, point C, output is back to its natural rate. Even though the wave of pessimism has reduced aggregate demand, the price level has fallen sufficiently (to P_3) to offset the shift in the aggregate-demand curve. Thus, in the long run, the shift in aggregate demand is reflected fully in the price level and not at all in the level of output. In other words, the long-run effect of a shift in aggregate demand is a nominal change (the price level is lower) but not a real change (output is the same).

To sum up, this story about shifts in aggregate demand has two important implications:

◆ In the short run, shifts in aggregate demand cause fluctuations in the economy's output of goods and services.

◆ In the long run, shifts in aggregate demand affect the overall price level but do not affect output.

THE EFFECTS OF A SHIFT IN AGGREGATE SUPPLY

Imagine once again an economy in its long-run equilibrium. Now suppose that suddenly some firms experience an increase in their costs of production. For example, bad weather in farm states might destroy some crops, driving up the cost of producing food products. Or a war in the Middle East might interrupt the shipping of crude oil, driving up the cost of producing oil products.

What is the macroeconomic impact of such an increase in production costs? For any given price level, firms now want to supply a smaller quantity of goods and services. Thus, as Figure 31-8 shows, the short-run aggregate-supply curve shifts to the left from AS_1 to AS_2. (Depending on the event, the long-run aggregate-supply curve might also shift. To keep things simple, however, we will assume that it does not.)

In this figure we can trace the effects of the leftward shift in aggregate supply. In the short run, the economy moves along the existing aggregate-demand curve, going from point A to point B. The output of the economy falls from Y_1 to Y_2, and the price level rises from P_1 to P_2. Because the economy is experiencing

Figure 31-8

AN ADVERSE SHIFT IN AGGREGATE SUPPLY. When some event increases firms' costs, the short-run aggregate-supply curve shifts to the left from AS_1 to AS_2. The economy moves from point A to point B. The result is stagflation: Output falls from Y_1 to Y_2, and the price level rises from P_1 to P_2.

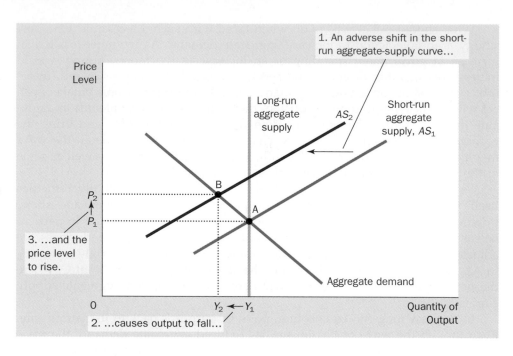

Figure 31-8

stagflation

a period of falling output and rising prices

both *stagnation* (falling output) and *inflation* (rising prices), such an event is sometimes called **stagflation.**

What should policymakers do when faced with stagflation? As we will discuss more fully later in this book, there are no easy choices. One possibility is to do nothing. In this case, the output of goods and services remains depressed at Y_2 for a while. Eventually, however, the recession will remedy itself as perceptions, wages, and prices adjust to the higher production costs. A period of low output and high unemployment, for instance, puts downward pressure on workers' wages. Lower wages, in turn, increase the quantity of output supplied. Over time, as the short-run aggregate-supply curve shifts back toward AS_1, the price level falls, and the quantity of output approaches its natural rate. In the long run, the economy returns to point A, where the aggregate-demand curve crosses the long-run aggregate-supply curve.

Alternatively, policymakers who control monetary and fiscal policy might attempt to offset some of the effects of the shift in the short-run aggregate-supply curve by shifting the aggregate-demand curve. This possibility is shown in Figure 31-9. In this case, changes in policy shift the aggregate-demand curve to the right from AD_1 to AD_2—exactly enough to prevent the shift in aggregate supply from affecting output. The economy moves directly from point A to point C. Output remains at its natural rate, and the price level rises from P_1 to P_3. In this case, policymakers are said to *accommodate* the shift in aggregate supply because they allow the increase in costs to affect the level of prices permanently.

To sum up, this story about shifts in aggregate supply has two important implications:

◆ Shifts in aggregate supply can cause stagflation—a combination of recession (falling output) and inflation (rising prices).

◆ Policymakers who can influence aggregate demand cannot offset both of these adverse effects simultaneously.

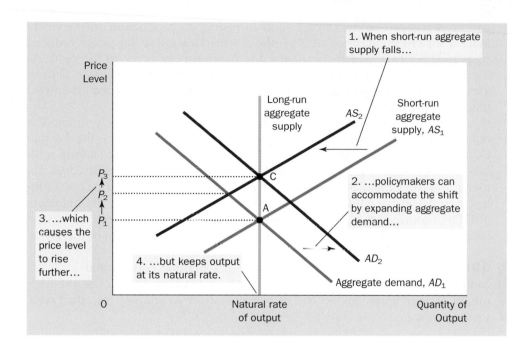

Figure 31-9

ACCOMMODATING AN ADVERSE SHIFT IN AGGREGATE SUPPLY. Faced with an adverse shift in aggregate supply from AS_1 to AS_2, policymakers who can influence aggregate demand might try to shift the aggregate-demand curve to the right from AD_1 to AD_2. The economy would move from point A to point C. This policy would prevent the supply shift from reducing output in the short run, but the price level would permanently rise from P_1 to P_3.

CASE STUDY   OIL AND THE ECONOMY

Some of the largest economic fluctuations in the U.S. economy have originated in the oil fields of the Middle East. Crude oil is a key input into the production of many goods and services, and much of the world's oil comes from Saudi Arabia, Kuwait, and other Middle Eastern countries. When some event (usually political in origin) reduces the supply of crude oil flowing from this region, the price of oil rises around the world. U.S. firms that produce gasoline, tires, and many other products experience rising costs. The result is a leftward shift in the aggregate-supply curve, which in turn leads to stagflation.

The first episode of this sort occurred in the mid-1970s. The countries with large oil reserves got together as members of OPEC, the Organization of Petroleum Exporting Countries. OPEC was a *cartel*—a group of sellers that attempts to thwart competition and reduce production in order to raise prices. And, indeed, oil prices rose substantially. From 1973 to 1975, oil approximately doubled in price. Oil-importing countries around the world experienced simultaneous inflation and recession. In the United States, the inflation rate as measured by the CPI exceeded 10 percent for the first time in decades. Unemployment rose from 4.9 percent in 1973 to 8.5 percent in 1975.

Almost the same thing happened again a few years later. In the late 1970s, the OPEC countries again restricted the supply of oil in order to raise the price. From 1978 to 1981, the price of oil more than doubled. Once again, the result was stagflation. Inflation, which had subsided somewhat after the first OPEC event, again rose above 10 percent per year. Unemployment rose from about 6 percent in 1978 and 1979 to about 10 percent a few years later.

The world market for oil can also be a source of favorable shifts in aggregate supply. In 1986 squabbling broke out among members of OPEC. Member

Changes in Middle East oil production are one source of U.S. economic fluctuations.

countries reneged on their agreements to restrict oil production. In the world market for crude oil, prices fell by about half. This fall in oil prices reduced costs to U.S. firms, which shifted the aggregate-supply curve to the right. As a result, the U.S. economy experienced the opposite of stagflation: Output grew rapidly, unemployment fell, and the inflation rate reached its lowest level in many years.

In recent years, the world market for oil has been relatively quiet. The only exception has been a brief period during 1990, just before the Persian Gulf War, when oil prices temporarily spiked up out of fear that a long military conflict might disrupt oil production. Yet this recent tranquillity does not mean that the United States no longer needs to worry about oil prices. Political troubles in the Middle East (or greater cooperation among the members of OPEC) could always send oil prices higher. The macroeconomic result of a large rise in oil prices would most likely resemble the stagflation of the 1970s.

QUICK QUIZ   Suppose that the election of a popular presidential candidate suddenly increases people's confidence in the future. Use the model of aggregate demand and aggregate supply to analyze the effect on the economy.

CONCLUSION: THE ORIGINS OF AGGREGATE DEMAND AND AGGREGATE SUPPLY

This chapter has achieved two goals. First, we have discussed some of the important facts about short-run fluctuations in economic activity. Second, we have introduced a basic model to explain those fluctuations, called the model of aggregate demand and aggregate supply. In the next two chapters we look at each piece of this model in more detail in order to understand more fully what causes fluctuations in the economy and how policymakers might respond to these fluctuations.

Now that we have a preliminary understanding of this model, it is worthwhile to step back from it and consider its history. How did this model of short-run fluctuations develop? The answer is that this model is, to a large extent, a by-product of the Great Depression of the 1930s. During this period, the U.S. economy and most other major economies around the world experienced a deep downturn in economic activity. In the United States, real GDP fell by 30 percent from 1929 to 1933, and unemployment rose from 3 percent to 25 percent. Economists and policymakers at the time were puzzled about what had caused this event and were uncertain about how to deal with it.

In 1936, economist John Maynard Keynes published a book titled *The General Theory of Employment, Interest, and Money*, which attempted to explain short-run economic fluctuations in general and the Great Depression in particular. Keynes's primary message was that recessions and depressions can occur because of inadequate aggregate demand for goods and services. Keynes had long been a critic of classical economic theory—the theory we examined in Chapters 24 through 30—because it could explain only the long-run effects of policies. A few years before offering *The General Theory*, Keynes had written the following about classical economics:

The long run is a misleading guide to current affairs. In the long run we are all dead. Economists set themselves too easy, too useless a task if in tempestuous seasons they can only tell us when the storm is long past, the ocean will be flat.

Keynes's message was aimed at policymakers as well as economists. As the world's economies suffered with high unemployment, Keynes advocated policies to increase aggregate demand, including government spending on public works. In the next chapter we examine in detail how policymakers can try to use the tools of monetary and fiscal policy to influence aggregate demand. The analysis in the next chapter, as well as in this one, owes much to the legacy of John Maynard Keynes.

Summary

- All societies experience short-run economic fluctuations around long-run trends. These fluctuations are irregular and largely unpredictable. When recessions do occur, real GDP and other measures of income, spending, and production fall, and unemployment rises.

- Economists analyze short-run economic fluctuations using the model of aggregate demand and aggregate supply. According to this model, the output of goods and services and the overall level of prices adjust to balance aggregate demand and aggregate supply.

- The aggregate-demand curve slopes downward for three reasons. First, a lower price level raises the real value of households' money holdings, which stimulates consumer spending. Second, a lower price level reduces the quantity of money households demand; as households try to convert money into interest-bearing assets, interest rates fall, which stimulates investment spending. Third, as a lower price level reduces interest rates, the dollar depreciates in the market for foreign-currency exchange, which stimulates net exports.

- The long-run aggregate-supply curve is vertical. In the long run, the quantity of goods and services supplied depends on the economy's labor, capital, and technology, but not on the overall level of prices.

- The short-run aggregate-supply curve is upward sloping. There are three theories to explain short-run aggre-

gate supply. According to the new classical misperceptions theory, an unexpected fall in the price level leads suppliers to mistakenly believe that their relative prices have fallen, which induces them to reduce production. According to the Keynesian sticky-wage theory, an unexpected fall in the price level temporarily raises real wages, which induces firms to reduce employment and production. According to the new Keynesian sticky-price theory, an unexpected fall in the price level leaves some firms with prices that are temporarily too high, which reduces their sales and causes them to cut back production.

- One possible cause of recession is a fall in aggregate demand. When the aggregate-demand curve shifts to the left, output and prices fall in the short run. Over time, as perceptions, wages, and prices adjust, the short-run aggregate-supply curve shifts to the right, and the economy returns to its natural rate of output at a new, lower price level.

- A second possible cause of recession is an adverse change in aggregate supply. When the aggregate-supply curve shifts to the left, the short-run effect is falling output and rising prices—a combination called stagflation. Over time, as perceptions, wages, and prices adjust, the price level falls back to its original level, and output recovers.

Key Concepts

recession, p. 682
depression, p. 682

model of aggregate demand and
    aggregate supply, p. 686
aggregate-demand curve, p. 687

aggregate-supply curve, p. 687
stagflation, p. 700

Questions for Review

1. Draw a diagram with aggregate demand, short-run aggregate supply, and long-run aggregate supply. Be careful to label the axes correctly.

2. List and explain the three reasons why the aggregate-demand curve is downward sloping.

3. Explain why the long-run aggregate-supply curve is vertical.

4. List and explain the three theories for why the short-run aggregate-supply curve is upward sloping.

5. What might shift the aggregate-demand curve to the left? Use the model of aggregate demand and aggregate supply to trace through the effects of such a shift.

6. What might shift the aggregate-supply curve to the left? Use the model of aggregate demand and aggregate supply to trace through the effects of such a shift.

Problems and Applications

1. Why do you think that investment is more variable over the business cycle than consumer spending? Which category of consumer spending do you think would be most volatile: durable goods (such as furniture and car purchases), nondurable goods (such as food and clothing), or services (such as haircuts and medical care)? Why?

2. Suppose that the economy is undergoing a recession because of a fall in aggregate demand.
   a. Using an aggregate-demand/aggregate-supply diagram, depict the current state of the economy.
   b. If real GDP is now 1 percent below last year's value, how does the unemployment rate compare to last year's rate? (Hint: Review Okun's law.)
   c. "Capacity utilization" is a measure of how intensively the capital stock is being used. In a recession, is capacity utilization above or below its long-run average? Explain.

3. Explain whether each of the following events will increase, decrease, or have no effect on long-run aggregate supply.
   a. The United States experiences a wave of immigration.
   b. The United Auto Workers union wins an unexpectedly high wage increase in its new contract.
   c. Intel invents a new and more powerful computer chip.
   d. A severe hurricane damages factories along the east coast.

4. In Figure 31-7, how does the unemployment rate at points B and C compare to the unemployment rate at point A? Under the sticky-wage explanation of the short-run aggregate-supply curve, how does the real wage at points B and C compare to the real wage at point A?

5. Explain why the following statements are false.
   a. "The aggregate-demand curve slopes downward because it is the horizontal sum of the demand curves for individual goods."
   b. "The long-run aggregate-supply curve is vertical because economic forces do not affect long-run aggregate supply."
   c. "If firms adjusted their prices every day, then the short-run aggregate-supply curve would be horizontal."
   d. "Whenever the economy enters a recession, its long-run aggregate-supply curve shifts to the left."

6. For each of the three theories for the upward slope of the short-run aggregate-supply curve, carefully explain the following:
   a. how the economy recovers from a recession and returns to its long-run equilibrium without any policy intervention.
   b. what determines the speed of that recovery.

7. Suppose that the economy is currently in a recession. If policymakers take no action, how will the economy evolve over time? Explain in words and using an aggregate-demand/aggregate-supply diagram.

8. Suppose workers and firms suddenly believe that inflation will be quite high over the coming year. Suppose also that the economy begins in long-run equilibrium, and the aggregate-demand curve does not shift.
   a. What happens to nominal wages? What happens to real wages?

b. Using an aggregate-demand/aggregate-supply diagram, show the effect of the change in expectations on both the short-run and long-run levels of prices and output.

c. Were the expectations of high inflation accurate? Explain.

9. The chapter explains that the economy will eventually recover from a recession even without action by policymakers. Why might policymakers nevertheless want to take some action?

10. Explain whether each of the following events shifts the short-run aggregate-supply curve, the aggregate-demand curve, both, or neither. For each event that does shift a curve, use a diagram to illustrate the effect on the economy.

a. Households decide to save a larger share of their income.

b. Florida orange groves suffer a prolonged period of below-freezing temperatures.

c. The birthrate shoots up nine months after a severe winter blizzard.

11. Suppose that firms become very optimistic about future business conditions and invest heavily in new capital equipment.

a. Use an aggregate-demand/aggregate-supply diagram to show the short-run effect of this optimism on the economy. Label the new levels of prices and real output. Explain in words why the aggregate quantity of output *supplied* changes.

b. Use the diagram from part (a) to show the new long-run equilibrium of the economy. (For now, assume there is no change in the long-run aggregate-supply curve.) Explain in words why the aggregate quantity of output *demanded* changes between the short run and the long run.

c. How might the investment boom affect the long-run aggregate-supply curve? Explain.

12. Assume that the economy begins in long-run equilibrium, and households decide to hold higher money balances than they did before.

a. What happens to the interest rate? Explain.

b. What happens to the quantity of investment demanded? Explain.

c. What happens to the value of the dollar? Explain.

d. What happens to the quantity of net exports demanded? Explain.

e. What happens to aggregate demand? Explain.

32

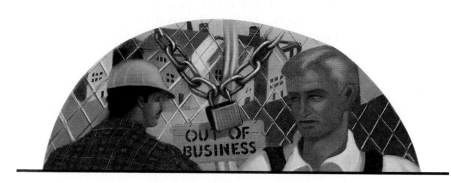

THE INFLUENCE OF MONETARY
AND FISCAL POLICY ON
AGGREGATE DEMAND

**IN THIS CHAPTER
YOU WILL**

*Learn the theory of
liquidity preference as a
short-run theory of the
interest rate*

*Analyze how monetary
policy affects interest
rates and aggregate
demand*

*Analyze how fiscal policy
affects interest rates and
aggregate demand*

*Discuss the debate over
whether policymakers
should try to stabilize the
economy*

*Reconsider how the
economy behaves
differently in the short
run and in the long run*

Imagine that you are a member of the Federal Open Market Committee, which sets monetary policy. You observe that the president and Congress have agreed to cut government spending in order to eliminate the budget deficit. How should the Fed respond to this change in fiscal policy? Should it expand the money supply, contract the money supply, or leave the money supply the same?

To answer this question, you need to consider the impact of monetary and fiscal policy on the economy. In the preceding chapter we saw how to explain short-run economic fluctuations using the model of aggregate demand and aggregate supply. When the aggregate-demand curve or the aggregate-supply curve shifts, the result is fluctuations in the economy's overall output of goods and services and in its overall level of prices. As we noted in the previous chapter, monetary and fiscal policy can each influence aggregate demand. Thus, a change in one of these policies can lead to short-run fluctuations in output and prices. Policymakers will want to anticipate this effect and, perhaps, adjust the other policy in response.

In this chapter we examine in more detail how the government's tools of monetary and fiscal policy influence the position of the aggregate-demand curve. We have previously discussed the long-run effects of these policies. In Chapters 24 and 25 we saw how fiscal policy affects saving, investment, and long-run economic growth. In Chapters 27 and 28 we saw how the Fed controls the money supply and how the money supply affects the price level in the long run. We now see how these policy tools can shift the aggregate-demand curve and, in doing so, affect short-run economic fluctuations.

As we have already learned, many factors influence aggregate demand besides monetary and fiscal policy. In particular, desired spending by households and firms determines the overall demand for goods and services. When desired spending changes, aggregate demand shifts. If policymakers do not respond, such shifts in aggregate demand cause short-run fluctuations in output and employment. As a result, monetary and fiscal policymakers sometimes use the policy levers at their disposal to try to offset these shifts in aggregate demand and thereby stabilize the economy. Here we discuss the theory behind these policy actions and some of the difficulties that arise in using this theory in practice.

HOW MONETARY POLICY INFLUENCES AGGREGATE DEMAND

The aggregate-demand curve shows the quantity of goods and services demanded for any price level. As you may recall from the preceding chapter, the aggregate-demand curve slopes downward for three reasons:

◆ *Pigou's wealth effect:* A lower price level raises the real value of households' money holdings, and higher real wealth stimulates consumer spending.

◆ *Keynes's interest-rate effect:* A lower price level lowers the interest rate as people try to lend out their excess money holdings, and the lower interest rate stimulates investment spending.

◆ *Mundell–Fleming's exchange-rate effect:* When a lower price level lowers the interest rate, investors move some of their funds overseas and cause the domestic currency to depreciate relative to foreign currencies. This depreciation makes domestic goods cheaper compared to foreign goods and, therefore, stimulates net exports.

These three effects should not be viewed as alternative theories. Instead, they occur simultaneously to increase the quantity of goods and services demanded when the price level falls.

Although all three effects work together in explaining the downward slope of the aggregate-demand curve, they are not of equal importance. Because money holdings are a small part of household wealth, Pigou's wealth effect is the least important of the three. In addition, because exports and imports represent only a small fraction of U.S. GDP, Mundell–Fleming's exchange-rate effect is not very large for the U.S. economy. (This effect is much more important for smaller countries because smaller countries typically export and import a higher fraction of their GDP.) For the U.S. economy, the most important reason for the downward slope of the aggregate-demand curve is Keynes's interest-rate effect.

To understand how policy influences aggregate demand, therefore, we examine Keynes's interest-rate effect in more detail. Here we develop Keynes's theory of how the interest rate is determined, called the **theory of liquidity pref-erence.** After we develop this theory, we use it to understand the downward slope of the aggregate-demand curve and how monetary policy shifts this curve. By shedding new light on the aggregate-demand curve, the theory of liquidity preference expands our understanding of short-run economic fluctuations.

theory of liquidity preference
Keynes's theory that the interest rate adjusts to bring money supply and money demand into balance

THE THEORY OF LIQUIDITY PREFERENCE

In his classic book *The General Theory of Employment, Interest, and Money,* Keynes proposed the theory of liquidity preference to explain what factors determine the economy's interest rate. The theory is, in essence, just an application of supply and demand. According to Keynes, the interest rate adjusts to balance the supply and demand for money. Let's therefore consider the supply and demand for money and how each depends on the interest rate.

Money Supply   The first piece of the theory of liquidity preference is the supply of money. As we first discussed in Chapter 27, the money supply in the U.S. economy is controlled by the Federal Reserve. The Fed alters the money supply primarily by changing the quantity of reserves in the banking system through the purchase and sale of government bonds in open-market operations. When the Fed buys government bonds, the dollars it pays for the bonds are typically deposited in banks, and these dollars are added to bank reserves. When the Fed sells government bonds, the dollars it receives for the bonds are withdrawn from the banking system, and bank reserves fall. These changes in bank reserves, in turn, lead to changes in banks' ability to make loans and create money. In addition to these open-market operations, the Fed can alter the money supply by changing reserve requirements (the amount of reserves banks must hold against deposits) or the discount rate (the interest rate at which banks can borrow reserves from the Fed).

These details of monetary control are important for the implementation of Fed policy, but they are not crucial in this chapter. Our goal here is to examine how changes in the money supply affect the aggregate demand for goods and services. For this purpose, we can ignore the details of how Fed policy is implemented and simply assume that the Fed controls the money supply directly. In other words, the quantity of money supplied in the economy is fixed at whatever level the Fed decides to set it.

Because the quantity of money supplied is fixed by Fed policy, it does not depend on other economic variables. In particular, it does not depend on the interest rate. Once the Fed has made its policy decision, the quantity of money supplied is the same, regardless of the prevailing interest rate. We represent a fixed money supply with a vertical supply curve, as in Figure 32-1.

Money Demand   The second piece of the theory of liquidity preference is the demand for money. As a starting point for understanding money demand, recall that any asset's *liquidity* refers to the ease with which that asset is converted into the economy's medium of exchange. Money is the economy's medium of exchange, so it is by definition the most liquid asset available. The liquidity of money explains the demand for it: People choose to hold money

Figure 32-1

THE SUPPLY OF MONEY. The supply of money in an economy is fixed by the central bank, which in the United States is the Federal Reserve. Because the quantity of money supplied does not depend on the interest rate, the supply curve is vertical.

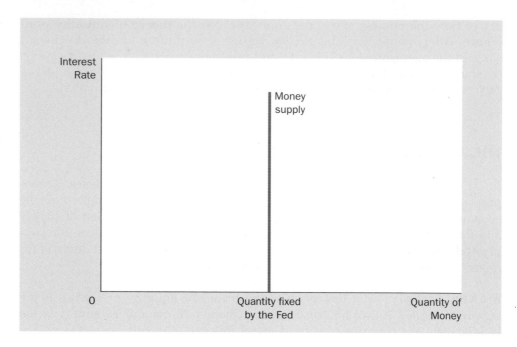

instead of other assets that offer higher rates of return because money can be used to buy goods and services.

Although there are many determinants of the quantity of money demanded, the theory of liquidity preference emphasizes that one of the most important is the interest rate. The reason is that the interest rate is the opportunity cost of holding money. That is, when you hold wealth as cash in your wallet, instead of as an interest-bearing bond, you lose the interest you could have earned. An increase in the interest rate raises the cost of holding money and, as a result, reduces the quantity of money demanded. Thus, as shown in Figure 32-2, the money-demand curve is downward sloping.

Equilibrium in the Money Market   According to the theory of liquidity preference, the interest rate adjusts to balance the supply and demand for money. This is shown in Figure 32-3. There is one interest rate, called the *equilibrium interest rate*, at which the quantity of money demanded exactly balances the quantity of money supplied. If the interest rate is at any other level, people will try to adjust their portfolios of assets and, as a result, drive the interest rate toward the equilibrium.

For example, suppose that the interest rate is above the equilibrium level, such as r_1 in Figure 32-3. In this case, the quantity of money that people want to hold, M_1^d, is less than the quantity of money that the Fed has supplied. Those people who are holding the excess supply of money will try to get rid of it by buying interest-bearing bonds or by depositing it in an interest-bearing bank account. Because bond issuers and banks prefer to pay lower interest rates, they respond to this excess supply of money by lowering the interest rates they offer. As the interest rate falls, people become more willing to hold money until, at the equilibrium interest rate, people are happy to hold exactly the amount of money the Fed has supplied.

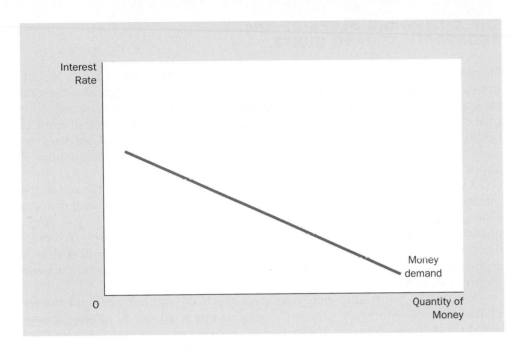

Figure 32-2

THE DEMAND FOR MONEY. Because the interest rate measures the opportunity cost of holding non-interest-bearing money instead of interest-bearing bonds, an increase in the interest rate reduces the quantity of money demanded. A downward-sloping demand curve represents this negative relationship.

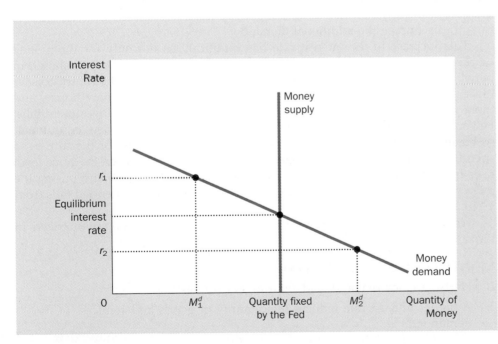

Figure 32-3

EQUILIBRIUM IN THE MONEY MARKET. According to the theory of liquidity preference, the interest rate adjusts to bring the quantity of money supplied and the quantity of money demanded into balance. If the interest rate is above the equilibrium level (such as at r_1), the quantity of money people want to hold (M_1^d) is less than the quantity the Fed has created, and this excess supply of money puts downward pressure on the interest rate. Conversely, if the interest rate is below the equilibrium level (such as at r_2), the quantity of money people want to hold (M_2^d) is greater than the quantity the Fed has created, and this excess demand for money puts upward pressure on the interest rate. Thus, the forces of supply and demand in the market for money push the interest rate toward the equilibrium interest rate, at which people are content holding the quantity of money the Fed has created.

Conversely, at interest rates below the equilibrium level, such as r_2 in Figure 32-3, the quantity of money that people want to hold, M_2^d, is greater than the quantity of money that the Fed has supplied. As a result, people try to increase their holdings of money by reducing their holdings of bonds and other interest-bearing assets. As people cut back on their holdings of bonds, bond issuers find that they have to offer higher interest rates in order to attract buyers. Thus, the interest rate rises and approaches the equilibrium level.

THE DOWNWARD SLOPE OF THE AGGREGATE-DEMAND CURVE

Having seen how the theory of liquidity preference explains the economy's equilibrium interest rate, we now consider its implications for the aggregate demand for goods and services. We first use the model to explain the downward slope of the aggregate-demand curve. In particular, suppose that the overall level of prices in the economy rises. What happens to the interest rate that balances the supply and demand for money, and how does that change affect the quantity of goods and services demanded?

As we discussed in Chapter 28, the price level is one determinant of the quantity of money demanded. At higher prices, more money is exchanged every time a good or service is sold. As a result, people will choose to hold a larger quantity of money. That is, a higher price level increases the quantity of money demanded for any given interest rate. Thus, as panel (a) of Figure 32-4 shows, an increase in the price level from P_1 to P_2 shifts the money-demand curve to the right from MD_1 to MD_2.

Notice how this shift in money demand affects the equilibrium in the money market. For a fixed money supply, the interest rate must rise to balance money supply and money demand. The higher price level has increased the amount of money people want to hold and shifted the demand curve to the right. Yet the quantity of money supplied is unchanged, so the interest rate must rise from r_1 to r_2 to discourage the additional demand.

This increase in the interest rate has ramifications not only for the money market but also for the quantity of goods and services demanded, as shown in panel (b). At a higher interest rate, the cost of borrowing and the return to saving are greater. Fewer households choose to borrow to buy a new house, and those who do buy smaller houses, so the demand for residential investment falls. Fewer firms choose to borrow to build new factories and buy new equipment, so business investment falls. Households choose to save more for the future, so spending on consumption goods falls. For all these reasons, when the price level rises from P_1 to P_2, increasing money demand from MD_1 to MD_2 and raising the interest rate from r_1 to r_2, the quantity of goods and services demanded falls from Y_1 to Y_2.

Hence, this analysis of Keynes's interest-rate effect can be summarized in three steps:

1. A higher price level raises money demand.
2. Higher money demand leads to a higher interest rate.
3. A higher interest rate reduces the quantity of goods and services demanded.

The end result of this analysis is a negative relationship between the price level and the quantity of goods and services demanded. This relationship is illustrated with a downward-sloping aggregate-demand curve.

CHANGES IN THE MONEY SUPPLY

So far we have used the theory of liquidity preference merely to explain more fully the downward slope of the aggregate-demand curve. The theory is useful,

Figure 32-4

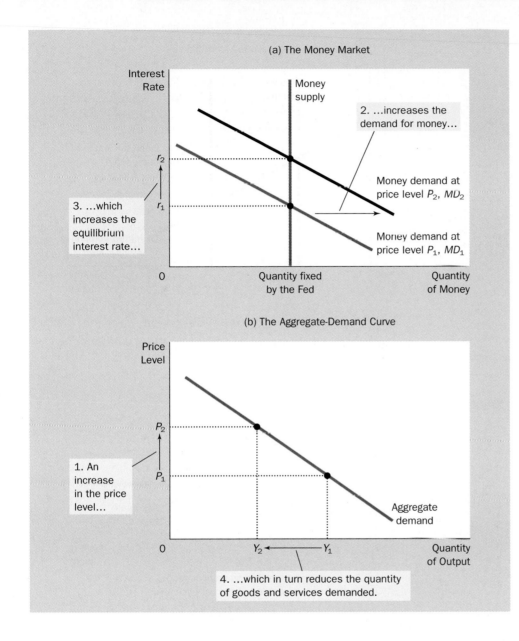

(a) The Money Market

Interest Rate

Money supply

2. ...increases the demand for money...

r_2

Money demand at price level P_2, MD_2

3. ...which increases the equilibrium interest rate...

r_1

Money demand at price level P_1, MD_1

0

Quantity fixed by the Fed

Quantity of Money

(b) The Aggregate-Demand Curve

Price Level

P_2

1. An increase in the price level...

P_1

Aggregate demand

0

$Y_2 \leftarrow Y_1$

Quantity of Output

4. ...which in turn reduces the quantity of goods and services demanded.

THE MONEY MARKET AND THE SLOPE OF THE AGGREGATE-DEMAND CURVE. An increase in the price level from P_1 to P_2 shifts the money-demand curve to the right, as in panel (a). This increase in money demand causes the interest rate to rise from r_1 to r_2. Because the interest rate is the cost of borrowing, the increase in the interest rate reduces the quantity of goods and services demanded from Y_1 to Y_2. This negative relationship between the price level and quantity demanded is represented with a downward-sloping aggregate-demand curve, as in panel (b).

however, because it also sheds light on how the Fed shifts the aggregate-demand curve when it changes monetary policy. Suppose that the Fed increases the money supply by buying government bonds in open-market operations. And suppose that the price level does not, in the short run, respond at all to this monetary injection. How does this monetary injection affect the equilibrium interest rate and the aggregate-demand curve?

As panel (a) of Figure 32-5 shows, an increase in the money supply shifts the money-supply curve to the right from MS_1 to MS_2. Because the money-demand curve has not changed, the interest rate falls from r_1 to r_2 to balance money supply and money demand. That is, the interest rate must fall to induce people to hold the additional money the Fed has created.

Figure 32-5

A MONETARY INJECTION. In panel (a), an increase in the money supply from MS_1 to MS_2 reduces the equilibrium interest rate from r_1 to r_2. Because the interest rate is the cost of borrowing, the fall in the interest rate raises the quantity of goods and services demanded at a given price level from Y_1 to Y_2. Thus, in panel (b), the aggregate-demand curve shifts to the right from AD_1 to AD_2.

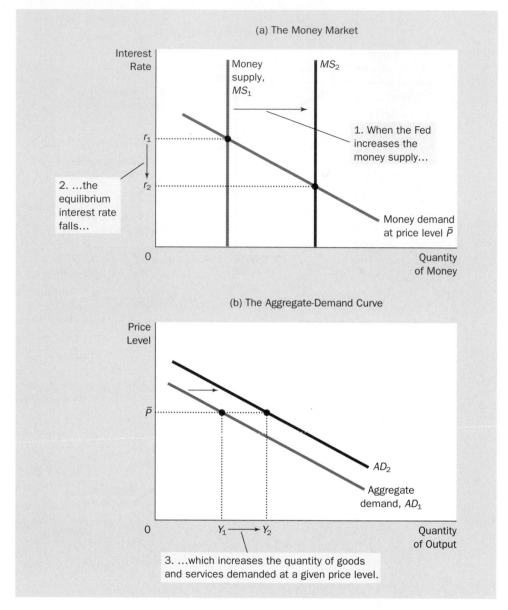

(a) The Money Market

1. When the Fed increases the money supply...

2. ...the equilibrium interest rate falls...

(b) The Aggregate-Demand Curve

3. ...which increases the quantity of goods and services demanded at a given price level.

Once again, the interest rate influences the quantity of goods and services demanded, as shown in panel (b) of Figure 32-5. The lower interest rate reduces the cost of borrowing and the return to saving. Households buy more and larger houses, stimulating the demand for residential investment. Firms spend more on new factories and new equipment, stimulating business investment. Households save less and spend more on consumption goods. For all of these reasons, the quantity of goods and services demanded at the given price level, $\bar{P}$, rises from Y_1 to Y_2.

To sum up: *A monetary injection by the Fed increases the money supply. For any given price level, a higher money supply leads to a lower interest rate, which in turn increases the quantity of goods and services demanded. Thus, a monetary injection shifts the aggregate-demand curve to the right.*

INTEREST-RATE TARGETS AND FED POLICY

How does the Federal Reserve affect the economy? Our discussion here and earlier in the book has treated the money supply as the Fed's policy instrument. When the Fed buys government bonds in open-market operations, it increases the money supply and expands aggregate demand. When the Fed sells government bonds in open-market operations, it decreases the money supply and contracts aggregate demand.

Often discussions of Fed policy treat the interest rate, rather than the money supply, as the Fed's policy instrument. Indeed, in recent years, the Federal Reserve has conducted policy by setting a target for the *federal funds rate*—the interest rate that banks charge one another for short-term loans. This target is reevaluated every six weeks at meetings of the Federal Open Market Committee (FOMC). The FOMC has chosen to set a target for the federal funds rate (rather than for the money supply, as it has done at times in the past) in part because the money supply is hard to measure with sufficient precision.

The Fed's decision to target an interest rate does not fundamentally alter our analysis of monetary policy. The theory of liquidity preference illustrates an important principle: *Monetary policy can be described either in terms of the money supply or in terms of the interest rate.* When the FOMC sets a target for the federal funds rate of, say, 6 percent, the Fed's bond traders are told: "Conduct open-market operations to ensure that the equilibrium interest rate equals 6 percent." That is, when the Fed sets a target for the interest rate, it commits itself to adjusting the money supply in order to make the equilibrium in the money market hit that target.

Similarly, changes in monetary policy can be viewed either in terms of a changing target for the interest rate or in terms of a change in the money supply. When the FOMC lowers the target for the federal funds rate, the Fed's bond

*"Ray Brown on bass, Elvin Jones on drums, and
Alan Greenspan on interest rates."*

traders buy government bonds, and this purchase increases the money supply and lowers the equilibrium interest rate. When the FOMC raises the target, the bond traders sell government bonds, and this sale decreases the money supply and raises the equilibrium interest rate. Thus, a change in monetary policy that aims to expand aggregate demand can be described either as increasing the money supply or as lowering the interest rate. A change in policy that aims to contract aggregate demand can be described either as decreasing the money supply or as raising the interest rate.

> **QUICK QUIZ**   Use the theory of liquidity preference to explain how a decrease in the money supply affects the equilibrium interest rate. How does this change in monetary policy affect the aggregate-demand curve?

HOW FISCAL POLICY INFLUENCES AGGREGATE DEMAND

The government can influence the behavior of the economy not only with monetary policy but also with fiscal policy. Fiscal policy refers to the government's choices regarding the overall level of government purchases or taxes. Earlier in the book we examined how fiscal policy influences saving, investment, and growth in the long run. In the short run, however, the primary effect of fiscal policy is on the aggregate demand for goods and services.

CHANGES IN GOVERNMENT PURCHASES

When the government changes its own purchases of goods and services, it shifts the aggregate-demand curve directly. Suppose, for instance, that the U.S. Department of Defense places a $20 billion order for new fighter planes with McDonnell Douglas, the large defense contractor. This order raises the demand for the output produced by McDonnell Douglas, which induces the company to hire more workers and increase production. Because McDonnell Douglas is part of the economy, the increase in the demand for McDonnell Douglas planes is reflected in an increase in the aggregate demand for goods and services. The aggregate-demand curve shifts to the right.

By how much does this $20 billion order from the government shift the aggregate-demand curve? At first, one might guess that the aggregate-demand curve shifts to the right by exactly $20 billion. It turns out, however, that this is not right. There are two macroeconomic effects that make the size of the shift in aggregate demand differ from the change in government purchases. The first—the multiplier effect—suggests that the shift in aggregate demand could be *larger* than $20 billion. The second—the crowding-out effect—suggests that the shift in aggregate demand could be *smaller* than $20 billion. We now discuss each of these effects in turn.

THE MULTIPLIER EFFECT

When the government buys $20 billion of goods from McDonnell Douglas, that purchase has repercussions. The immediate impact of the higher demand from the government is to raise employment and profits at McDonnell Douglas. But as the workers see higher earnings and the firm owners see higher profits, they respond to this increase in income by raising their own spending on consumer goods. As a result, the government purchase from McDonnell Douglas raises the demand for the products of many other firms in the economy as well. Because each dollar spent by the government can raise the aggregate demand for goods and services by more than a dollar, government purchases are said to have a **multiplier effect** on aggregate demand.

This multiplier effect continues even after this first round. When consumer spending rises, the firms that produce these consumer goods hire more people and experience higher profits. Higher earnings and profits stimulate consumer spending once again, and so on. Thus, there is positive feedback as higher demand leads to higher income, which in turn leads to even higher demand. Once all these effects are added together, the total impact on the quantity of goods and services demanded can be much larger than the initial impulse from higher government spending.

Figure 32-6 illustrates the multiplier effect. The increase in government purchases of $20 billion initially shifts the aggregate-demand curve to the right from AD_1 to AD_2, by exactly $20 billion. But when consumers respond by increasing their spending, the aggregate-demand curve shifts still further to AD_3.

This multiplier effect arising from the response of consumer spending can be strengthened by the response of investment to higher levels of demand. For instance, McDonnell Douglas might respond to the higher demand for planes by

multiplier effect
the additional shifts in aggregate demand that result when expansionary fiscal policy increases income and thereby increases consumer spending

Figure 32-6

THE MULTIPLIER EFFECT. An increase in government purchases of $20 billion can shift the aggregate-demand curve to the right by more than $20 billion. This multiplier effect arises because increases in aggregate income stimulate additional spending by consumers.

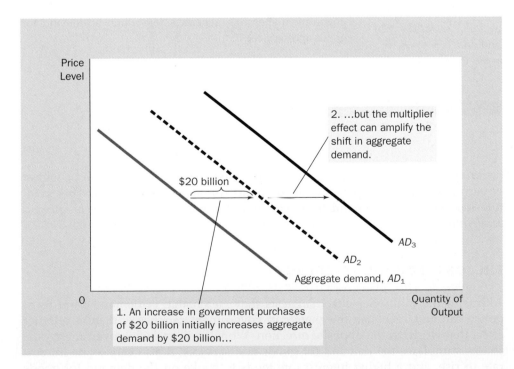

2. ...but the multiplier effect can amplify the shift in aggregate demand.

$20 billion

AD_3

AD_2

Aggregate demand, AD_1

Price Level

Quantity of Output

1. An increase in government purchases of $20 billion initially increases aggregate demand by $20 billion...

FYI

A Formula for the Government-Purchases Multiplier

A LITTLE HIGH SCHOOL ALGE-bra permits us to derive a formula for the size of the multiplier effect that arises from consumer spending. An important number in this formula is the *marginal propensity to consume (MPC)*—the fraction of extra income that a household consumes rather than saves. For example, suppose that the marginal propensity to consume is 3/4. This means that for every extra dollar that a household earns, the household saves $0.25 and spends $0.75. With an *MPC* of 3/4, when the workers and owners of McDonnell Douglas earn $20 billion from the government contract, they increase their consumer spending by 3/4 × $20 billion, or $15 billion.

To gauge the impact on aggregate demand of a change in government purchases, we follow the effects step-by-step. The process begins when the government spends $20 billion, which implies that income (earnings and profits) also rises by this amount. This increase in income in turn raises consumer spending by *MPC* × $20 billion, which in turn raises the income for the workers and owners of the firms that produce the consumption goods. This second increase in income again raises consumer spending, this time by *MPC* × (*MPC* × $20 billion). These feedback effects go on and on.

To find the total impact on the demand for goods and services, we add up all these effects:

Change in government purchases	=	$20 billion
First change in consumption	=	MPC × $20 billion
Second change in consumption	=	MPC^2 × $20 billion
Third change in consumption	=	MPC^3 × $20 billion
•		•
•		•
•		•

Total change in demand =
$$(1 + MPC + MPC^2 + MPC^3 + \ldots) \times \$20 \text{ billion.}$$

Here, "..." represents an infinite number of similar terms. We say that the government-purchases multiplier is

$$\text{Multiplier} = 1 + MPC + MPC^2 + MPC^3 + \ldots.$$

This multiplier tells us the demand for goods and services that each dollar of government purchases generates.

To simplify this equation for the multiplier, recall from math class that this expression is an infinite geometric series. For x between -1 and $+1$,

$$1 + x + x^2 + x^3 + \ldots = 1/(1 - x).$$

In our case, $x = MPC$. Thus,

$$\text{Multiplier} = 1/(1 - MPC).$$

For example, if *MPC* is 3/4, the government-purchases multiplier is $1/(1 - 3/4)$, which is 4. In this case, the $20 billion of government spending generates $80 billion of demand for goods and services.

deciding to buy more equipment or build another plant. In this case, higher government demand spurs higher demand for investment goods. This positive feedback from demand to investment is sometimes called the *investment accelerator*.

THE CROWDING-OUT EFFECT

Although the multiplier effect suggests that the change in demand from fiscal policy can be larger than the change in government purchases, there is another effect that works in the opposite direction. While an increase in government purchases stimulates the demand for goods and services, it also causes the interest rate to rise, and a higher interest rate tends to choke off the demand for goods and services. The reduction in demand that results when a fiscal expansion raises the interest rate is called the **crowding-out effect.**

To see why crowding out occurs, let's consider once again what happens when the government buys $20 billion of planes from McDonnell Douglas. As we have discussed, this increase in demand raises the incomes of the workers and owners of this firm (and, because of the multiplier effect, of other firms as well). As incomes rise, households plan to buy more goods and services and, as a result, choose to hold more of their wealth in liquid form. That is, the increase in income caused by the fiscal expansion raises the demand for money.

The effect of the increase in money demand is shown in panel (a) of Figure 32-7. Because the Fed has not changed the money supply, the vertical supply curve remains the same. When the higher level of income shifts the money-demand curve to the right from MD_1 to MD_2, the interest rate must rise from r_1 to r_2 in order to keep supply and demand in balance.

crowding-out effect
the offset in aggregate demand that results when expansionary fiscal policy raises the interest rate and thereby reduces investment spending

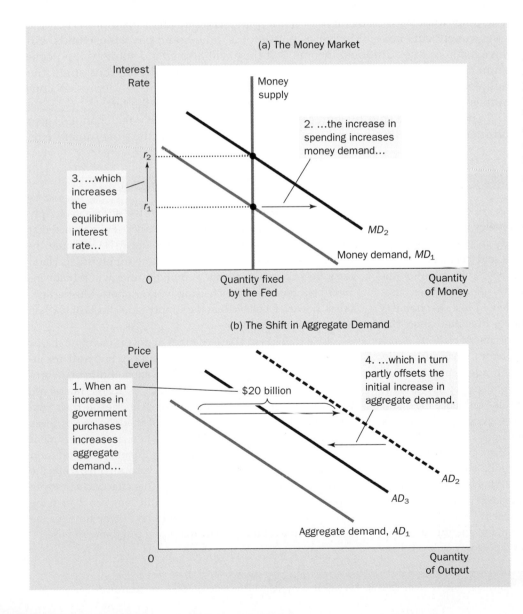

Figure 32-7

THE CROWDING-OUT EFFECT. Panel (a) shows the money market. When the government increases its purchases of goods and services, the resulting increase in income raises the demand for money from MD_1 to MD_2, and this causes the equilibrium interest rate to rise from r_1 to r_2. Panel (b) shows the effects on aggregate demand. The initial impact of the increase in government purchases shifts the aggregate-demand curve from AD_1 to AD_2. Yet, because the interest rate is the cost of borrowing, the increase in the interest rate tends to reduce the quantity of goods and services demanded, particularly for investment goods. This crowding out of investment partially offsets the impact of the fiscal expansion on aggregate demand. In the end, the aggregate-demand curve shifts only to AD_3.

The increase in the interest rate, in turn, reduces the quantity of goods and services demanded. In particular, because borrowing is more expensive, the demand for residential and business investment goods declines. That is, as the increase in government purchases increases the demand for goods and services, it may also crowd out investment. This crowding-out effect partially offsets the impact of government purchases on aggregate demand, as illustrated in panel (b) of Figure 32-7. The initial impact of the increase in government purchases is to shift the aggregate-demand curve from AD_1 to AD_2, but once crowding out takes place, the aggregate-demand curve drops back to AD_3.

To sum up: *When the government increases its purchases by $20 billion, the aggregate demand for goods and services could rise by more or less than $20 billion, depending on whether the multiplier effect or the crowding-out effect is larger.*

CHANGES IN TAXES

The other important instrument of fiscal policy is the level of taxation. When the government cuts taxes, it increases households' take-home pay. Households will save some of this additional income, but they will also spend some of it on consumer goods. Because it increases consumer spending, the tax cut shifts the aggregate-demand curve to the right. Similarly, a tax increase depresses consumer spending and shifts the aggregate-demand curve to the left.

The size of the shift in aggregate demand resulting from a tax change is also affected by the multiplier and crowding-out effects. When the government cuts

FYI

How Fiscal Policy Might Affect Aggregate Supply

So far our discussion of fiscal policy has stressed how changes in government purchases and changes in taxes influence the quantity of goods and services demanded. Most economists believe that the short-run macroeconomic effects of fiscal policy work primarily through aggregate demand. Yet fiscal policy can potentially also influence the quantity of goods and services supplied.

For instance, consider the effects of tax changes on aggregate supply. One of the *Ten Principles of Economics* in Chapter 1 is that people respond to incentives. When government policymakers cut tax rates, workers get to keep more of each dollar they earn, so they have a greater incentive to work and to produce goods and services. As a result, the quantity of goods and services supplied is greater at any given price level. This is represented by a rightward shift in the aggregate-supply curve. Some economists, called *supply-siders,* have argued that the influence of tax cuts on aggregate supply is very large. Indeed, as we discussed in Chapter 8, some supply-siders claim the influence is so large that a cut in tax rates will actually increase tax revenue by increasing worker effort. Most economists, however, believe that the supply-side effects of tax cuts are much smaller.

Like changes in taxes, changes in government purchases can also potentially affect aggregate supply. Suppose, for instance, that the government increases expenditure on a form of government-provided capital, such as roads. Roads are used by private businesses to make deliveries to their customers; an increase in the quantity of roads increases these businesses' productivity. Hence, when the government spends more on roads, it increases the quantity of goods and services supplied at any given price level and, thus, shifts the aggregate-supply curve to the right. This effect on aggregate supply is probably more important in the long run than in the short run, however, because it would take some time for the government to build the new roads and put them into use.

taxes and stimulates consumer spending, earnings and profits rise, which further stimulates consumer spending. This is the multiplier effect. At the same time, higher income leads to higher money demand, which tends to raise interest rates. Higher interest rates make borrowing more costly, which reduces investment spending. This is the crowding-out effect. Depending on the size of the multiplier and crowding-out effects, the shift in aggregate demand could be larger or smaller than the tax change that causes it.

In addition to the multiplier and crowding-out effects, there is another important determinant of the size of the shift in aggregate demand that results from a tax change: households' perceptions about whether the tax change is permanent or temporary. For example, suppose that the government announces a tax cut of $1,000 per household. In deciding how much of this $1,000 to spend, households must ask themselves how long this extra income will last. If households expect the tax cut to be permanent, they will view it as adding substantially to their financial resources and, therefore, increase their spending by a large amount. In this case, the tax cut will have a large impact on aggregate demand. By contrast, if households expect the tax change to be temporary, they will view it as adding only slightly to their financial resources and, therefore, will increase their spending by only a small amount. In this case, the tax cut will have a small impact on aggregate demand.

An extreme example of a temporary tax cut was the one announced in 1992. In that year, President George Bush faced a lingering recession and an upcoming reelection campaign. He responded to these circumstances by announcing a reduction in the amount of income tax that the federal government was withholding from workers' paychecks. Because legislated income tax rates did not change, however, every dollar of reduced withholding in 1992 meant an extra dollar of taxes due on April 15, 1993, when income tax returns for 1992 were to be filed. Thus, Bush's "tax cut" actually represented only a short-term loan from the government. Not surprisingly, the impact of the policy on consumer spending and aggregate demand was relatively small.

QUICK QUIZ   Suppose that the government reduces spending on highway construction by $10 billion. Which way does the aggregate-demand curve shift? Explain why the shift might be larger than $10 billion. Explain why the shift might be smaller than $10 billion.

USING POLICY TO STABILIZE THE ECONOMY

We have seen how monetary and fiscal policy can affect the economy's aggregate demand for goods and services. These theoretical insights raise an important policy question: Should policymakers use these instruments in order to control aggregate demand and stabilize the economy? If so, when? If not, why not?

THE CASE FOR ACTIVE STABILIZATION POLICY

Let's return to the question that began this chapter: When the president and Congress cut government spending to eliminate the budget deficit, how should the

Federal Reserve respond? As we have seen, government spending is one determinant of the position of the aggregate-demand curve. When the government cuts spending, aggregate demand will fall, which will depress production and employment in the short run. If the Federal Reserve wants to prevent this adverse effect of the fiscal policy, it can act to expand aggregate demand by increasing the money supply. A monetary expansion would reduce interest rates and stimulate consumption and investment spending. If monetary policy responds appropriately, the combined change in monetary and fiscal policy leaves the aggregate demand for goods and services unaffected.

This analysis is exactly the sort followed by members of the Federal Open Market Committee. They know that monetary policy is an important determinant of aggregate demand. They also know that there are other important determinants as well, including fiscal policy set by the president and Congress. As a result, the Fed's Open Market Committee watches the debates over fiscal policy with a keen eye.

This response of monetary policy to the change in fiscal policy is an example of a more general phenomenon: the use of policy instruments to stabilize aggregate demand and, as a result, production and employment. Economic stabilization has been an explicit goal of U.S. policy since the Employment Act of 1946. This act states that "it is the continuing policy and responsibility of the federal government to . . . promote full employment and production." In essence, the government has chosen to hold itself accountable for short-run macroeconomic performance.

The Employment Act has two implications. The first, more modest, implication is that the government should avoid being a cause of economic fluctuations. Thus, most economists advise against large and sudden changes in monetary and fiscal policy, for such changes are likely to cause fluctuations in aggregate demand. Moreover, when large changes do occur, it is important that monetary and fiscal policymakers be aware and respond to the other's actions.

The second, more ambitious, implication of the Employment Act is that the government should respond to changes in the private economy in order to stabilize aggregate demand. The act was passed not long after the publication of John Maynard Keynes's *The General Theory of Employment, Interest, and Money*. As we discussed in the preceding chapter, *The General Theory* has been one of the most influential books ever written about economics. In it, Keynes emphasized the key role of aggregate demand in explaining short-run economic fluctuations. Keynes claimed that the government should actively stimulate aggregate demand when aggregate demand appeared insufficient to maintain production at its full-employment level.

Keynes (and his many followers) argued that aggregate demand fluctuates because of largely irrational waves of pessimism and optimism. He used the term *animal spirits* to refer to these arbitrary changes in attitude. When pessimism reigns, households reduce consumption spending, and firms reduce investment spending. The result is reduced aggregate demand, lower production, and higher unemployment. Conversely, when optimism reigns, households and firms increase spending. The result is higher aggregate demand, higher production, and inflationary pressure. Notice that these changes in attitude are, to some extent, self-fulfilling.

In principle, the government can adjust its monetary and fiscal policy in response to these waves of optimism and pessimism and, thereby, stabilize aggregate demand. For example, when people are excessively pessimistic, the

Fed can expand the money supply; when they are excessively optimistic, it can contract the money supply. William McChesney Martin, former Fed chairman, described this view of monetary policy very simply: "The Federal Reserve's job is to take away the punch bowl just as the party gets going."

CASE STUDY KEYNESIANS IN THE WHITE HOUSE

When a reporter in 1961 asked President John F. Kennedy why he advocated a tax cut, Kennedy replied, "To stimulate the economy. Don't you remember your Economics 101?" Kennedy's policy was, in fact, based on the analysis of taxes we have developed in this chapter. His goal was to increase aggregate demand in order to stimulate production and employment.

In choosing this policy, Kennedy was relying on his team of economic advisers. This team included such prominent economists as James Tobin and Robert Solow, who later would win Nobel prizes for their contributions to economics. As students in the 1940s, these economists had closely studied John Maynard Keynes's *General Theory*, which then was only a few years old. When the Kennedy advisers proposed cutting taxes, they were putting Keynes's ideas into action.

Although tax changes can have a potent influence on aggregate demand, they have other effects as well. In particular, by changing the incentives that people face, taxes can alter the aggregate supply of goods and services. Part of the Kennedy proposal was an investment tax credit, which gives a tax break to firms that invest in new capital. Higher investment would not only stimulate aggregate demand immediately but would also increase the economy's productive capacity over time. Thus, the short-run goal of increasing production through higher aggregate demand was coupled with a long-run goal of increasing production through higher aggregate supply. And, indeed, when the tax cut Kennedy proposed was finally enacted in 1964, it helped usher in a period of robust economic growth.

Since the 1964 tax cut, policymakers have from time to time proposed using fiscal policy as a tool for controlling aggregate demand. As we discussed earlier, President Bush attempted to speed recovery from a recession by reducing tax withholding. Similarly, when President Clinton moved into the Oval Office in 1993, one of his first proposals was a "stimulus package" of increased government spending. His announced goal was to help the economy recover

A visionary and two disciples

John Maynard Keynes   John F. Kennedy   Bill Clinton

more quickly from the recession the U.S. economy had just experienced. In the end, however, the stimulus package was defeated. Many in Congress (and many economists) considered the Clinton proposal too late to be of much help. Moreover, deficit reduction to encourage long-run economic growth was considered a higher priority than a short-run expansion in aggregate demand.

THE CASE AGAINST ACTIVE STABILIZATION POLICY

Some economists argue that the government should avoid using monetary and fiscal policy to try to stabilize the economy. They claim that these policy instruments should be set to achieve long-run goals, such as rapid economic growth and low inflation, and that the economy should be left to deal with short-run fluctuations on its own. Although these economists may admit that monetary and fiscal policy can stabilize the economy in theory, they doubt whether it can do so in practice.

IN THE NEWS

The Independence

of the

Federal Reserve

CLOSELY RELATED TO THE QUESTION OF whether monetary and fiscal policy should be used to stabilize the economy is the question of who should set monetary and fiscal policy. In the United States, monetary policy is made by a central bank that operates free of most political pressures. As the following opinion column discusses, however, some members of Congress have recently advocated legislation to reduce the Fed's independence.

Don't Tread on the Fed

BY MARTIN AND KATHLEEN FELDSTEIN

We and most other economists give very high marks to the Federal Reserve for the way it has managed monetary policy in recent years. Fed officials have very successfully carried out their responsibility to reduce the rate of inflation and have done so without interrupting the economic expansion that began back in 1991.

Despite that excellent record, there are influential figures in Congress who are planning to introduce legislation that would weaken the Federal Reserve's ability to continue to make sound monetary policy decisions. That legislation would give Congress and the president more influence over Federal Reserve policy, making monetary policy responsive to political pressures. If that happened, the risk of higher inflation and of increased cyclical volatility would become much greater.

To achieve the good economic performance of the past five years, the Fed had to raise interest rates several times in 1994 and, more recently, has had to avoid political calls for easier money to speed up the pace of economic activity. Looking ahead, the economy may slow in the next year. If it does, you can expect to hear members of Congress and maybe the White House urging the Fed to lower interest rates in order to maintain economic momentum. But we're betting that, even if the economy does slow, the inflationary pressures are building and will force the Fed to raise interest rates by early in the new year.

If the Fed does raise interest rates in order to prevent a rise in inflation, the increased political pressure on the Fed may find popular support. There is always public resistance to higher interest rates, which make borrowing more expensive for both businesses and homeowners. Moreover, the purpose of higher interest rates would be to slow the growth of spending in order to prevent an overheating of demand. That too

The primary argument against active monetary and fiscal policy is that these policies affect the economy with a substantial lag. As we have seen, monetary policy works by changing interest rates, which in turn influence investment spending. But many firms make investment plans far in advance. Thus, changes in monetary policy are thought to take at least six months to have much effect on output and employment, and these effects can last for several years. Critics of stabilization policy argue that because of this lag, the Fed should not try to fine-tune the economy. They claim that the Fed often reacts too late to changing economic conditions and, as a result, ends up being a cause rather than a cure of economic fluctuations. They advocate a passive monetary policy, such as low and steady growth in the money supply.

Fiscal policy also works with a lag, but unlike the lag in monetary policy, the lag in fiscal policy is largely attributable to the political process. In the United States, most changes in government spending and taxes must go through congressional committees in both the House and the Senate, be passed by both legislative bodies, and then be signed by the president. Completing this process can take months and, in some cases, years. By the time the change in fiscal policy is

will meet popular opposition. It is, in part, because good economic policy is not always popular in the short run that it is important for the Fed to be sheltered from short-run political pressures.

The Fed is an independent agency that reports to Congress but doesn't take orders from anyone. Monetary policy and short-term interest rates are determined by the Federal Open Market Committee (the FOMC), which consists of the 7 governors of the Fed plus the 12 presidents of the regional Federal Reserve Banks. The regional presidents vote on an alternating basis but all participate in the deliberations.

A key to the independence of the Fed's actions lies in the manner that appointments are made within the system. Although the 7 Federal Reserve governors are appointed by the president and confirmed by the Senate, each of the 12 Federal Reserve presidents is selected by the local board of a regional Federal Reserve Bank rather than being responsive to Washington. These regional presidents often serve for many years. Fre-

quently they are long-term employees of the Federal Reserve system who have risen through the ranks. And many are professional economists with expertise in monetary economics. But whatever their backgrounds, they are not political appointees or friends of elected politicians. Their allegiance is to the goal of sound monetary policy, including both macroeconomic performance and supervision of the banking system.

The latest challenge to Fed independence would be to deny these Federal Reserve presidents the power to vote on monetary policy. This bad idea, explicitly proposed by Senator Paul Sarbanes, a powerful Democrat on the Senate Banking Committee, would mean shifting all of the authority to the 7 governors. Because at least one governor's term ends every two years, a president who spends eight years in the White House would be able to appoint a majority of the Board of Governors and could thus control monetary policy. An alternative bad idea, proposed by Representative Henry Gonzalez, a key Democrat on the House

Banking Committee, would take away the independence of the Fed by having the regional Fed presidents appointed by the president subject to Senate confirmation.

Either approach would inevitably mean more politicalization of Federal Reserve policy. In an economy that is starting to overheat, the temptation would be to resist raising interest rates and to risk an acceleration of inflation. In the long run, that would mean volatile interest rates and less stability in the overall economy.

Ironically, such a move toward cutting the independence of the Federal Reserve is just counter to developments in other countries. Experience around the world has confirmed that the independence of central banks such as our Fed is the key to sound monetary policy. It would be a serious mistake for the United States to move in the opposite direction.

SOURCE: *Boston Globe*, November 12, 1996, p. D4.

passed and ready to implement, the condition of the economy may well have changed.

These lags in monetary and fiscal policy are a problem in part because economic forecasting is so imprecise. If forecasters could accurately predict the condition of the economy a year in advance, then monetary and fiscal policymakers could look ahead when making policy decisions. In this case, policymakers could stabilize the economy, despite the lags they face. In practice, however, recessions and depressions arrive without much advance warning. The best policymakers can do at any time is to respond to economic changes as they occur.

AUTOMATIC STABILIZERS

automatic stabilizers

changes in fiscal policy that stimulate aggregate demand when the economy goes into a recession without policymakers having to take any deliberate action

All economists—both advocates and critics of stabilization policy—agree that the lags in the implementation of policy render policy less useful as a tool for short-run stabilization. The economy would be more stable, therefore, if policymakers could find a way to avoid some of these lags. In fact, they have. **Automatic stabilizers** are changes in fiscal policy that stimulate aggregate demand when the economy goes into a recession without policymakers having to take any deliberate action.

The most important automatic stabilizer is the tax system. When the economy goes into a recession, the amount of taxes collected by the government falls automatically because almost all taxes are closely tied to economic activity. The personal income tax depends on households' incomes, the payroll tax depends on workers' earnings, and the corporate income tax depends on firms' profits. Because incomes, earnings, and profits all fall in a recession, the government's tax revenue falls as well. This automatic tax cut stimulates aggregate demand and, thereby, reduces the magnitude of economic fluctuations.

Government spending also acts as an automatic stabilizer. In particular, when the economy goes into a recession and workers are laid off, more people apply for unemployment insurance benefits, welfare benefits, and other forms of income support. This automatic increase in government spending stimulates aggregate demand at exactly the time when aggregate demand is insufficient to maintain full employment. Indeed, when the unemployment insurance system was first enacted in the 1930s, economists who advocated this policy did so in part because of its power as an automatic stabilizer.

The automatic stabilizers in the U.S. economy are not sufficiently strong to prevent recessions completely. Nonetheless, without these automatic stabilizers, output and employment would probably be more volatile than they are. For this reason, many economists oppose a constitutional amendment that would require the federal government always to run a balanced budget, as some politicians have proposed. When the economy goes into a recession, taxes fall, government spending rises, and the government's budget moves toward deficit. If the government faced a strict balanced-budget rule, it would be forced to look for ways to raise taxes or cut spending in a recession. In other words, a strict balanced-budget rule would eliminate the automatic stabilizers inherent in our current system of taxes and government spending.

QUICK QUIZ Suppose firms become pessimistic about the future. What happens to aggregate demand? If the Fed wants to stabilize aggregate demand, how should it alter the money supply? If it does this, what happens to the interest rate?

THE ECONOMY IN THE LONG RUN
AND THE SHORT RUN

At this point, we should pause and reflect on a seemingly awkward embarrassment of riches. It might appear as if we now have two theories for how interest rates are determined. Chapter 25 said that the interest rate adjusts to balance the supply and demand for loanable funds (that is, national saving and desired investment). By contrast, this chapter said that the interest rate adjusts to balance the supply and demand for money. Which of these theories is right? The answer is, both.

To understand how this can be true, we must consider the differences between the long-run and short-run behavior of the economy. Three macroeconomic variables are of central importance: the economy's output of goods and services, the interest rate, and the price level. According to the classical macroeconomic theory we developed in Chapters 24, 25, and 28, these variables are determined as follows:

1. *Output* is determined by the supplies of capital and labor and the available production technology for turning capital and labor into output.

2. For any given level of output, the *interest rate* adjusts to balance the supply and demand for loanable funds.

3. The *price level* adjusts to balance the supply and demand for money. Changes in the supply of money lead to proportionate changes in the price level.

These are three of the essential propositions of classical economic theory. Most economists believe that these propositions do a good job of describing how the economy works *in the long run.*

Yet these propositions do not hold in the short run. As we discussed in the preceding chapter, many prices are slow to adjust to changes in the money supply. As a result, the overall price level cannot, by itself, balance the supply and demand for money in the short run. This price inflexibility forces the interest rate to move in order to bring the money market into equilibrium. These changes in the interest rate, in turn, affect the aggregate demand for goods and services. As aggregate demand fluctuates, the economy's output of goods and services moves away from the level determined by factor supplies and technology.

For thinking about the economy in the short run, then, it is best to reverse the order of analysis:

1. The *price level* is stuck at some level and, in the short run, is relatively unresponsive to changing economic conditions.

2. For any given price level, the *interest rate* adjusts to balance the supply and demand for money.

3. The level of *output* responds to changes in the aggregate demand for goods and services, which is in part determined by the interest rate that balances the money market.

Figure 32-8 summarizes these propositions and highlights the differences between the economy in the long run and the economy in the short run.

Figure 32-8

How Long-Run and Short-Run Macroeconomic Theories Differ. This figure illustrates the differences between the long-run and short-run behavior of the economy. In the long run, the interest rate and price level adjust to accommodate a fixed level of output. In the short run, the interest rate and output adjust to accommodate a predetermined level of prices.

(a) The Long Run

Output is fixed by factor supplies and technology. → Interest rate balances supply and demand for loanable funds. → Price level balances supply and demand for money.

(b) The Short Run

Price level is predetermined (sticky). → Interest rate balances supply and demand for money. → Output responds to changes in aggregate demand.

FYI

The Long Run and the Short Run: An Algebraic Explanation

A FEW MATHEMATICALLY INclined readers might find the following algebraic explanation helpful for clarifying the difference between the economy's behavior in the long run and its behavior in the short run. If you are not so inclined, just skip this box.

We can view the economy as described by two key markets: the money market and the goods market. Supply and demand in the money market are described by the equation

$$M = L(r)P,$$

where M is the money supply, P the price level, and r the interest rate. $L(r)$ is a function showing how money demand responds to the interest rate. This is called the *LM* (liquidity–money) equation. Supply and demand in the goods market are described by the equation

$$Y = C + I(r) + G,$$

where Y is output, C consumption, I investment, and G government purchases. (For simplicity, we assume here a closed economy, so net exports do not enter this equation.) Note that national saving, $Y - C - G$, represents the supply of loanable funds, and investment, $I(r)$, represents the demand for loanable funds, which depends on the interest rate. This is called the *IS* (investment–saving) equation. The *IS* and *LM* equations together describe two relationships among three variables: output Y, the interest rate r, and the price level P.

Now let's compare the long run and short run. Over both time horizons, the *IS* and the *LM* equations must be satisfied to ensure equilibrium in both the goods market and the money market. But different variables move to maintain equilibrium in the long run and the short run. Here is the difference:

◆ In the long run, output Y is determined by factor supplies and technology. Given the fixed level of output, the interest rate r adjusts to satisfy the *IS* equation. Given this interest rate, the price level P adjusts to satisfy the *LM* equation.

◆ In the short run, the price level P is stuck at a level set in the past. Given the fixed price level, the interest rate r adjusts to satisfy the *LM* equation. Given this interest rate, the level of output Y adjusts to satisfy the *IS* equation.

The long-run case corresponds to our analysis in Chapters 24, 25, and 28. The short-run case corresponds to our analysis of monetary and fiscal policy in this chapter.

Thus, the different theories of the interest rate are useful for different purposes. When thinking about the long-run determinants of interest rates, it is best to keep in mind the loanable-funds theory. This theory highlights the importance of an economy's saving propensities and investment opportunities. By contrast, when thinking about the short-run determinants of interest rates, it is best to keep in mind the liquidity-preference theory. This theory highlights the importance of monetary policy.

QUICK QUIZ   Explain the difference between long-run and short-run macroeconomic analysis. ◆ What theory of the interest rate is best for analyzing the economy in the long run? What theory is best for analyzing the economy in the short run?

CONCLUSION

Before policymakers make any change in policy, they need to consider all the effects of their decisions. Earlier in the book we examined classical models of the economy, which describe the long-run effects of monetary and fiscal policy. There we saw how fiscal policy influences saving, investment, the trade balance, and long-run growth, and how monetary policy influences the price level and the inflation rate.

In this chapter we examined the short-run effects of monetary and fiscal policy. We saw how these policy instruments can change the aggregate demand for goods and services and, thereby, alter the economy's production and employment in the short run. When Congress reduces government spending in order to balance the budget, it needs to consider both the long-run effects on saving and growth and the short-run effects on aggregate demand and employment. When the Fed reduces the growth rate of the money supply, it must take into account the long-run effect on inflation as well as the short-run effect on production. In the next chapter we discuss the transition between the short run and the long run more fully, and we see that policymakers often face a tradeoff between long-run and short-run goals.

Summary

◆ In developing a theory of short-run economic fluctuations, Keynes proposed the theory of liquidity preference to explain the determinants of the interest rate. According to this theory, the interest rate adjusts to balance the supply and demand for money.

◆ An increase in the price level raises money demand and increases the interest rate that brings the money market into equilibrium. Because the interest rate represents the cost of borrowing, a higher interest rate reduces investment and, thereby, the quantity of goods and services demanded. The downward-sloping aggregate-demand curve expresses this negative relationship between the price level and the quantity demanded.

◆ Policymakers can influence aggregate demand with monetary policy. An increase in the money supply reduces the equilibrium interest rate for any given price level. Because a lower interest rate stimulates investment spending, the aggregate-demand curve shifts to the right. Conversely, a decrease in the money supply raises the equilibrium interest rate for any given price level and shifts the aggregate-demand curve to the left.

◆ Policymakers can also influence aggregate demand with fiscal policy. An increase in government purchases or a cut in taxes shifts the aggregate-demand curve to the right. A decrease in government purchases or an increase in taxes shifts the aggregate-demand curve to the left.

◆ When the government alters spending or taxes, the resulting shift in aggregate demand can be larger or smaller than the fiscal change. The multiplier effect tends to amplify the effects of fiscal policy on aggregate demand. The crowding-out effect tends to dampen the effects of fiscal policy on aggregate demand.

◆ Because monetary and fiscal policy can influence aggregate demand, the government sometimes uses these policy instruments in an attempt to stabilize the economy. Economists disagree about how active the government should be in this effort. According to advocates of active stabilization policy, changes in attitudes by households and firms shift aggregate demand; if the government does not respond, the result is undesirable and unnecessary fluctuations in output and employment. According to critics of active stabilization policy, monetary and fiscal policy work with such long lags that attempts at stabilizing the economy often end up being destabilizing.

◆ The effects of monetary and fiscal policy depend on the time horizon. The aggregate-demand effects on output emphasized in this chapter only hold in the short run, over which prices are sticky. In the long run, output is determined by factor supplies and technology.

Key Concepts

theory of liquidity preference, p. 709   crowding-out effect, p. 719   automatic stabilizers, p. 726
multiplier effect, p. 717

Questions for Review

1. What is the theory of liquidity preference? How does it help explain the downward slope of the aggregate-demand curve?

2. Use the theory of liquidity preference to explain how a decrease in the money supply affects the aggregate-demand curve.

3. The government spends $3 billion to buy police cars. Explain why aggregate demand might increase by more than $3 billion. Explain why aggregate demand might increase by less than $3 billion.

4. Suppose that survey measures of consumer confidence indicate a wave of pessimism is sweeping the country. If policymakers do nothing, what will happen to aggregate demand? What should the Fed do if it wants to stabilize aggregate demand? If the Fed does nothing, what might Congress do to stabilize aggregate demand?

5. Give an example of a government policy that acts as an automatic stabilizer. Explain why this policy has this effect.

6. Why do changes in monetary policy have different effects over different time horizons?

Problems and Applications

1. Explain how each of the following developments would affect the supply of money, the demand for money, and the interest rate. Illustrate your answers with diagrams.
   a. A wave of optimism boosts business investment.
   b. The Federal Reserve reduces reserve requirements.
   c. An increase in oil prices shifts the short-run aggregate-supply curve upward.
   d. Households decide to hold more money to use for holiday shopping.

2. Suppose banks install automatic teller machines on every block and, by making cash readily available, reduce the amount of money people want to hold.
   a. Assume the Fed does not change the money supply. According to the theory of liquidity preference, what

happens to the interest rate? What happens to aggregate demand?

b. If the Fed wants to stabilize aggregate demand, how should it respond?

3. Consider two policies—a tax cut that will last for only one year, and a tax cut that is expected to be permanent. Which policy will stimulate greater spending by consumers? Which policy will have the greater impact on aggregate demand? Explain.

4. The interest rate in the United States fell sharply during 1991. Many observers believed this decline showed that monetary policy was quite expansionary during the year. Could this conclusion be incorrect? (Hint: The United States hit the trough of a recession in 1991.)

5. In the early 1980s, new legislation allowed banks to pay interest on checking deposits, which they could not do previously.
   a. If we define money to include checking deposits, what effect did this legislation have on money demand? Explain.
   b. If the Federal Reserve had maintained a constant money supply in the face of this change, what would have happened to the interest rate? What would have happened to aggregate demand and aggregate output?
   c. If the Federal Reserve had maintained a constant market interest rate (the interest rate on nonmonetary assets) in the face of this change, what change in the money supply would have been necessary? What would have happened to aggregate demand and aggregate output?

6. This chapter explains that expansionary monetary policy reduces the interest rate and thus stimulates demand for consumption and investment goods. Explain how such a policy also stimulates the demand for net exports.

7. Suppose economists observe that an increase in government spending of $10 billion raises the total demand for goods and services by $30 billion.
   a. If these economists ignore the possibility of crowding out, what would they estimate the marginal propensity to consume (MPC) to be?
   b. Now suppose the economists allow for crowding out. Would their new estimate of the MPC be larger or smaller than their initial one?

8. Suppose the government reduces taxes by $20 billion, that there is no crowding out, and that the marginal propensity to consume is 3/4.

a. What is the initial effect of the tax reduction on aggregate demand?

b. What additional effects follow this initial effect? What is the total effect of the tax cut on aggregate demand?

c. How does the total effect of this $20 billion tax cut compare to the total effect of a $20 billion increase in government purchases? Why?

9. Suppose consumers suddenly become more optimistic about their future incomes and decide to purchase $30 billion of additional goods and services. Will this change have a "multiplied" effect on total output? Explain.

10. Suppose government spending increases. Would the effect on aggregate demand be larger if the Federal Reserve took no action in response, or if the Fed were committed to maintaining a fixed interest rate? Explain.

11. In which of the following circumstances is expansionary fiscal policy more likely to lead to a short-run increase in investment? Explain.
    a. when the investment accelerator is large, or when it is small?
    b. when the interest sensitivity of investment is large, or when it is small?

12. Assume the economy is in a recession. Explain how each of the following policies would affect consumption and investment. In each case, indicate any direct effects, any effects resulting from changes in total output, any effects resulting from changes in the interest rate, and the overall effect. If there are conflicting effects making the answer ambiguous, say so.
    a. an increase in government spending
    b. a reduction in taxes
    c. an expansion of the money supply

13. For various reasons, fiscal policy changes automatically when output and employment fluctuate.
    a. Explain why tax revenue changes when the economy goes into a recession.
    b. Explain why government spending changes when the economy goes into a recession.
    c. If the government were to operate under a strict balanced-budget rule, what would it have to do in a recession? Would that make the recession more or less severe?

14. In response to an increase in the money supply, would the following things be smaller, larger, or no different in the long run than in the short run?
    a. consumer expenditures
    b. the price level

c. the interest rate

d. aggregate output

15. Suppose that the Federal Reserve decides to expand the money supply.

    a. What is the effect of this policy on the interest rate in the short run? Illustrate your answer with an appropriate diagram.

    b. What is the effect of this policy on the interest rate in the long run? How do you know?

    c. What characteristic of the economy makes the short-run effect of monetary policy on the interest rate different from the long-run effect?

33

THE SHORT-RUN TRADEOFF BETWEEN INFLATION AND UNEMPLOYMENT

IN THIS CHAPTER YOU WILL

Learn why policymakers face a short-run tradeoff between inflation and unemployment

Consider why the inflation–unemployment tradeoff disappears in the long run

See how supply shocks can shift the inflation–unemployment tradeoff

Consider the short-run cost of reducing the rate of inflation

See how policymakers' credibility might affect the cost of reducing inflation

Two closely watched indicators of economic performance are inflation and unemployment. When the Bureau of Labor Statistics releases data on these variables each month, policymakers are eager to hear the news. Some commentators have added together the inflation rate and the unemployment rate to produce a *misery index*, which purports to measure the health of the economy.

How are these two measures of economic performance related to each other? Earlier in the book we discussed the long-run determinants of unemployment and the long-run determinants of inflation. We saw that the natural rate of unemployment depends on various features of the labor market, such as minimum-wage laws, the market power of unions, the role of efficiency wages, and the effectiveness of job search. By contrast, the inflation rate depends primarily on growth in the quantity of money, which the central bank controls. In the long run, therefore, inflation and unemployment are largely unrelated problems.

In the short run, just the opposite is true. One of the *Ten Principles of Economics* discussed in Chapter 1 is that society faces a short-run tradeoff between inflation and unemployment. If monetary and fiscal policymakers expand aggregate demand, they can lower unemployment in the short run, but only at the cost of higher inflation. If they contract aggregate demand, they can lower inflation, but only at the cost of temporarily higher unemployment.

In this chapter we examine this tradeoff more closely. The relationship between inflation and unemployment is a topic that has attracted the attention

733

of some of the most important economists of the last half century. The best way to understand this relationship is to see how thinking about it has evolved over time. As we will see, the history of thought regarding inflation and unemployment since the 1950s is inextricably connected to the history of the U.S. economy. These two histories will show why the tradeoff between inflation and unemployment holds in the short run, why it does not hold in the long run, and what issues it raises for economic policymakers.

THE PHILLIPS CURVE

The short-run relationship between inflation and unemployment is often called the *Phillips curve*. We begin our story with the discovery of the Phillips curve and its migration to America.

ORIGINS OF THE PHILLIPS CURVE

In 1958, economist A. W. Phillips published an article in the British journal *Economica* that would make him famous. The article was titled "The Relationship between Unemployment and the Rate of Change of Money Wages in the United Kingdom, 1861–1957." In it, Phillips showed a negative correlation between the rate of unemployment and the rate of inflation. That is, Phillips showed that years with low unemployment tend to have high inflation, and years with high unemployment tend to have low inflation. (Phillips examined inflation in nominal wages rather than inflation in prices, but for our purposes that distinction is not important. These two measures of inflation usually move together.) Phillips concluded that two important macroeconomic variables—inflation and unemployment—were linked in a way that economists had not previously appreciated.

Although Phillips's discovery was based on data for the United Kingdom, researchers quickly extended his finding to other countries. Two years after Phillips published his article, economists Paul Samuelson and Robert Solow published an article in the *American Economic Review* called "Analytics of Anti-Inflation Policy" in which they showed a similar negative correlation between inflation and unemployment in data for the United States. They reasoned that this correlation arose because low unemployment was associated with high aggregate demand and because high demand puts upward pressure on wages and prices throughout the economy. Samuelson and Solow dubbed the negative association between inflation and unemployment the **Phillips curve.** Figure 33-1 shows an example of a Phillips curve like the one found by Samuelson and Solow.

As the title of their paper suggests, Samuelson and Solow were interested in the Phillips curve because they believed that it held important lessons for policymakers. In particular, they suggested that the Phillips curve offers policymakers a menu of possible economic outcomes. By altering monetary and fiscal policy to influence aggregate demand, policymakers could choose any point on this curve. Point A offers high unemployment and low inflation. Point B offers low

Phillips curve

a curve that shows the short-run tradeoff between inflation and unemployment

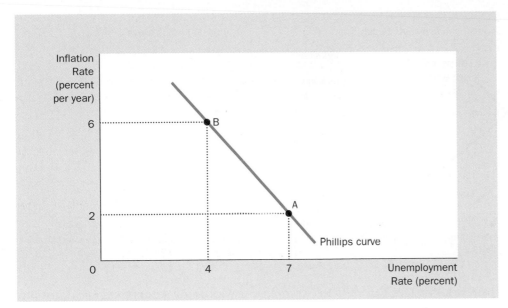

Figure 33-1

THE PHILLIPS CURVE. The Phillips curve illustrates a negative association between the inflation rate and the unemployment rate. At point A, inflation is low and unemployment is high. At point B, inflation is high and unemployment is low.

unemployment and high inflation. Policymakers might prefer both low inflation and low unemployment, but the historical data as summarized by the Phillips curve indicates that this combination is impossible. According to Samuelson and Solow, policymakers face a tradeoff between inflation and unemployment, and the Phillips curve illustrates that tradeoff.

AGGREGATE DEMAND, AGGREGATE SUPPLY, AND THE PHILLIPS CURVE

The model of aggregate demand and aggregate supply provides an easy explanation for the menu of possible outcomes described by the Phillips curve. *The Phillips curve simply shows the combinations of inflation and unemployment that arise in the short run as shifts in the aggregate-demand curve move the economy along the short-run aggregate-supply curve.* As we discussed in Chapter 31, the greater the aggregate demand for goods and services, the greater the economy's output and the higher the overall price level. Okun's law tells us that greater output means a lower rate of unemployment. In addition, because the previous year's price level is already given, the higher the price level in the current year, the higher the rate of inflation. Thus, an increase in aggregate demand moves the economy along the Phillips curve to a point with lower unemployment and higher inflation.

To see how this works, let's consider an example. To keep the numbers simple, imagine that the price level (as measured, for instance, by the consumer price index) equals 100 in the year 2000. Figure 33-2 shows two possible outcomes that might occur in year 2001. Panel (a) shows the two outcomes using the model of aggregate demand and aggregate supply. Panel (b) illustrates the same two outcomes using the Phillips curve.

In panel (a) of the figure, we can see the implications for output and the price level in the year 2001. If the aggregate demand for goods and services is

Figure 33-2

How the Phillips Curve Is Related to the Model of Aggregate Demand and Aggregate Supply. This figure assumes a price level of 100 for the year 2000 and charts possible outcomes for the year 2001. Panel (a) shows the model of aggregate demand and aggregate supply. If aggregate demand is low, the economy is at point A; output is low (7,500), and the price level is low (102). If aggregate demand is high, the economy is at point B; output is high (8,000), and the price level is high (106). Panel (b) shows the implications for the Phillips curve. Point A, which arises when aggregate demand is low, has high unemployment (7 percent) and low inflation (2 percent). Point B, which arises when aggregate demand is high, has low unemployment (4 percent) and high inflation (6 percent).

relatively low, the economy experiences outcome A. The economy produces output of 7,500, and the price level is 102. By contrast, if aggregate demand is relatively high, the economy experiences outcome B. Output is 8,000, and the price level is 106. Thus, higher aggregate demand moves the economy to an equilibrium with higher output and a higher price level.

In panel (b) of the figure, we can see what these two possible outcomes mean for unemployment and inflation. Because firms need more workers when they produce a greater output of goods and services, unemployment is lower in outcome B than in outcome A. In this example, when output rises from 7,500 to 8,000, unemployment falls from 7 percent to 4 percent. Moreover, because the price level is higher at outcome B than at outcome A, the inflation rate (the percentage change in the price level from the previous year) is also higher. In particular, since the price level was 100 in year 2000, outcome A has an inflation rate of 2 percent, and outcome B has an inflation rate of 6 percent. Thus, we can compare the two possible outcomes for the economy either in terms of output and the price level (using the model of aggregate demand and aggregate supply) or in terms of unemployment and inflation (using the Phillips curve).

As we saw in the preceding chapter, monetary and fiscal policy can shift the aggregate-demand curve. Therefore, monetary and fiscal policy can move the economy along the Phillips curve. Increases in the money supply, increases in

IN THE NEWS

The Effects of Low Unemployment

ACCORDING TO THE PHILLIPS CURVE, when unemployment falls to low levels, wages and prices start to rise more quickly. The following article illustrates this link between labor-market conditions and inflation.

Tighter Labor Market Widens Inflation Fears

BY ROBERT D. HERSHEY, JR.

REMINGTON, VA.—Trinity Packaging's plant here recently hired a young man for a hot, entry-level job feeding plastic scrap onto a conveyor belt. The pay was OK for unskilled labor—a good $3 or so above the federal minimum of $4.25 an hour—but the new worker lasted only one shift.

"He worked Friday night and then just told the supervisor that this work's too hard—and we haven't seen him since," said Pat Roe, a personnel director for the Trinity Packaging Corporation, a producer of plastic bags for supermarkets and other users. "Three years ago he'd have probably stuck it out."

This is just one of the many examples of how a growing number of companies these days are facing something they have not seen for many years: a tight labor market in which many workers can be much more choosy about their job. Breaking a sweat can be reason enough to quit in search of better opportunities.

"This summer's been extremely difficult, with unemployment so low," said Eleanor J. Brown, proprietor of a small temporary-help agency in nearby Culpeper, which supplies workers to Trinity Packaging. "It's hard to find, especially, industrial workers and laborers."

From iron mines near Lake Superior to retailers close to Puget Sound to construction contractors around Atlanta, a wide range of employers in many parts of the country are grappling with an inability to fill their ranks with qualified workers. These areas of virtually full employment hold important implications for household incomes, financial markets, and political campaigns as well as business profitability itself.

So far, the tightening labor market has generated only scattered—and in most cases modest—pay increases. Most companies, unable to pass on higher costs by raising prices because of intense competition from foreign and domestic rivals, are working even harder to keep a lid on labor costs, in part by adopting novel ways of coupling pay to profits.

"The overriding need is for expense control," said Kenneth T. Mayland, chief financial economist at Keycorp, a Cleveland bank, "at a time when revenue growth is constrained."

But with unemployment already at a low 5.5 percent and the economy looking stronger than expected this summer, more analysts are worried that it may be only a matter of time before wage pressures begin to build again as they did in the late 1980s. . . .

The labor shortages are widespread and include both skilled and unskilled jobs. Among the hardest occupations to fill are computer analyst and programmer, aerospace engineer, construction trades worker, and various types of salespeople. But even fast-food establishments in the St. Louis area and elsewhere have resorted to signing bonuses as well as premium pay and more generous benefits to attract applicants. . . .

So far, upward pressure on pay is relatively modest, a phenomenon that economists say is surprising in light of an uninterrupted business expansion that is now five and a half years old.

"We have less wage pressure than, historically, anyone would have guessed," said Stuart G. Hoffman, chief economist at PNC Bank in Pittsburgh.

But wages have already crept up a bit and could accelerate even if the economy slackens from its recent rapid growth pace. And if the economy maintains significant momentum, some analysts say, all bets are off. If growth continues another six months at above 2.5 percent or so, Mark Zandi, chief economist for Regional Financial Associates, said, "we'll be looking at wage inflation right square in the eye. . . ."

One worker who has taken advantage of the current environment is Clyde Long, a thirty-year-old who switched jobs to join Trinity Packaging in May. He had been working about two miles away at Ross Industries, which makes food-processing equipment, and quit without having anything else lined up.

In a week, Mr. Long had hired on at Trinity where, as a press operator, he now earns $8.55 an hour—$1.25 more than at his old job—with better benefits and training as well. "It's a whole lot better here," he said.

SOURCE: *The New York Times,* September 5, 1996, p. D1.

government spending, or cuts in taxes shift the aggregate-demand curve to the right and move the economy to a point on the Phillips curve with lower unemployment and higher inflation. Decreases in the money supply, cuts in government spending, or increases in taxes shift the aggregate-demand curve to the left and move the economy to a point on the Phillips curve with lower inflation and higher unemployment. In this sense, the Phillips curve offers policymakers a menu of combinations of inflation and unemployment.

QUICK QUIZ   Draw the Phillips curve. Use the model of aggregate demand and aggregate supply to show how policy can move the economy from a point on this curve with high inflation to a point with low inflation.

SHIFTS IN THE PHILLIPS CURVE: THE ROLE OF EXPECTATIONS

The Phillips curve seems to offer policymakers a menu of possible inflation–unemployment outcomes. But does this menu remain stable over time? Is the Phillips curve a relationship on which policymakers can rely? These are the questions that economists took up in the late 1960s, shortly after Samuelson and Solow had introduced the Phillips curve into the macroeconomic policy debate.

THE LONG-RUN PHILLIPS CURVE

In 1968 economist Milton Friedman published a paper in the *American Economic Review,* based on an address he had recently given as president of the American Economic Association. The paper was titled "The Role of Monetary Policy." It contained sections on "What Monetary Policy Can Do" and "What Monetary Policy Cannot Do." Friedman argued that one thing monetary policy cannot do, other than for only a short time, is pick a combination of inflation and unemployment on the Phillips curve. At about the same time, another economist, Edmund Phelps, also published a paper denying the existence of a long-run tradeoff between inflation and unemployment.

Friedman and Phelps reasoned from classical principles of macroeconomics, which we discussed in Chapters 24 through 30. Recall that classical theory points to growth in the quantity of money as the primary determinant of inflation. But classical theory also states that monetary growth does not have real effects—it merely alters all prices and nominal incomes proportionately. In particular, monetary growth does not influence those factors that determine the economy's unemployment rate, such as the market power of unions, the role of efficiency wages, or the process of job search. Friedman and Phelps concluded that there is no reason to think the rate of inflation would, *in the long run,* be related to the rate of unemployment.

Here, in his own words, is Friedman's view about what the Fed can hope to accomplish in the long run:

The monetary authority controls nominal quantities—directly, the quantity of its own liabilities [currency plus bank reserves]. In principle, it can use this control to peg a nominal quantity—an exchange rate, the price level, the nominal level of national income, the quantity of money by one definition or another—or to peg the change in a nominal quantity—the rate of inflation or deflation, the rate of growth or decline in nominal national income, the rate of growth of the quantity of money. It cannot use its control over nominal quantities to peg a real quantity—the real rate of interest, the rate of unemployment, the level of real national income, the real quantity of money, the rate of growth of real national income, or the rate of growth of the real quantity of money.

These views have important implications for the Phillips curve. In particular, they imply that monetary policymakers face a long-run Phillips curve that is vertical, as in Figure 33-3. If the Fed increases the money supply slowly, the inflation rate is low, and the economy finds itself at point A. If the Fed increases the money supply quickly, the inflation rate is high, and the economy finds itself at point B. In either case, the unemployment rate tends toward its normal level, called the *natural rate of unemployment*. The vertical long-run Phillips curve illustrates the conclusion that unemployment does not depend on money growth and inflation in the long run.

The vertical long-run Phillips curve is, in essence, one expression of the classical idea of monetary neutrality. As you may recall, we expressed this idea in Chapter 31 with a vertical long-run aggregate-supply curve. Indeed, as Figure 33-4 illustrates, the vertical long-run Phillips curve and the vertical long-run aggregate-supply curve are two sides of the same coin. In panel (a) of this figure, an increase in the money supply shifts the aggregate-demand curve to the right from AD_1 to AD_2. As a result of this shift, the long-run equilibrium moves from point A to point B. The price level rises from P_1 to P_2, but because the aggregate-supply curve is vertical, output remains the same. In panel (b), more rapid growth in the money supply raises the inflation rate by moving the economy

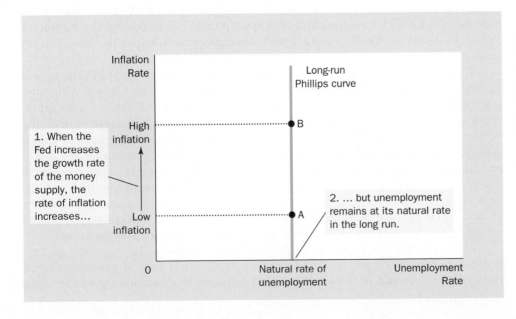

1. When the Fed increases the growth rate of the money supply, the rate of inflation increases...

2. ... but unemployment remains at its natural rate in the long run.

Figure 33-3

THE LONG-RUN PHILLIPS CURVE. According to Friedman and Phelps, there is no tradeoff between inflation and unemployment in the long run. Growth in the money supply determines the inflation rate. Regardless of the inflation rate, the unemployment rate gravitates toward its natural rate. As a result, the long-run Phillips curve is vertical.

(a) The Model of Aggregate Demand and Aggregate Supply

(b) The Phillips Curve

Price Level

Long-run aggregate supply

1. An increase in the money supply increases aggregate demand...

2. ...raises the price level...

P_2

B

P_1

A

AD_2

Aggregate demand, AD_1

0   Natural rate of output   Quantity of Output

Inflation Rate

Long-run Phillips curve

3. ...and increases the inflation rate...

B

A

0   Natural rate of unemployment   Unemployment Rate

4. ...but leaves output and unemployment at their natural rates.

Figure 33-4   HOW THE LONG-RUN PHILLIPS CURVE IS RELATED TO THE MODEL OF AGGREGATE DEMAND AND AGGREGATE SUPPLY. Panel (a) shows the model of aggregate demand and aggregate supply with a vertical aggregate-supply curve. When expansionary monetary policy shifts the aggregate-demand curve to the right from AD_1 to AD_2, the equilibrium moves from point A to point B. The price level rises from P_1 to P_2, while output remains the same. Panel (b) shows the long-run Phillips curve, which is vertical at the natural rate of unemployment. Expansionary monetary policy moves the economy from lower inflation (point A) to higher inflation (point B) without changing the rate of unemployment.

from point A to point B. But because the Phillips curve is vertical, the rate of unemployment is the same at these two points. Thus, the vertical long-run aggregate-supply curve and the vertical long-run Phillips curve both imply that monetary policy influences nominal variables (the price level and the inflation rate) but not real variables (output and unemployment). Regardless of the monetary policy pursued by the Fed, output and unemployment are, in the long run, at their natural rates.

What is so "natural" about the natural rate of unemployment? Friedman and Phelps used this adjective to describe the unemployment rate toward which the economy tends to gravitate in the long run. Yet the natural rate of unemployment is not necessarily the socially desirable rate of unemployment. Nor is the natural rate of unemployment constant over time. For example, suppose that a newly formed union uses its market power to raise the real wages of some workers above the equilibrium level. The result is an excess supply of workers and, therefore, a higher natural rate of unemployment. This unemployment is "natural" not because it is good but because it is beyond the influence of monetary policy. More rapid money growth would not reduce the market power of the union or the level of unemployment; it would lead only to more inflation.

Although monetary policy cannot influence the natural rate of unemployment, other types of policy can. To reduce the natural rate of unemployment, policymakers should look to policies that improve the functioning of the labor market. Earlier in the book we discussed how various labor-market policies, such as minimum-wage laws, collective-bargaining laws, unemployment insurance, and job-training programs, affect the natural rate of unemployment. A policy change that reduced the natural rate of unemployment would shift the long-run Phillips curve to the left. In addition, because lower unemployment means more workers are producing goods and services, the quantity of goods and services supplied would be larger at any given price level, and the long-run aggregate-supply curve would shift to the right. The economy could then enjoy lower unemployment and higher output for any given rate of money growth and inflation.

EXPECTATIONS AND THE SHORT-RUN PHILLIPS CURVE

At first, the denial by Friedman and Phelps of a long-run tradeoff between inflation and unemployment might not seem persuasive. Their argument was based on an appeal to *theory*. By contrast, the negative correlation between inflation and unemployment documented by Phillips, Samuelson, and Solow was based on *data*. Why should anyone believe that policymakers faced a vertical Phillips curve when the world seemed to offer a downward-sloping one? Shouldn't the findings of Phillips, Samuelson, and Solow lead us to reject the classical conclusion of monetary neutrality?

Friedman and Phelps were well aware of these questions, and they offered a way to reconcile classical macroeconomic theory with the finding of a downward-sloping Phillips curve in data from the United Kingdom and the United States. They claimed that a negative relationship between inflation and unemployment holds in the short run but that it cannot be used by policymakers in the long run. In other words, policymakers can pursue expansionary monetary policy to achieve lower unemployment for a while, but eventually unemployment returns to its natural rate, and more expansionary monetary policy leads only to higher inflation.

Friedman and Phelps reasoned as we did in Chapter 31 when we explained the difference between the short-run and long-run aggregate-supply curves. (In fact, the discussion in that chapter drew heavily on the legacy of Friedman and Phelps.) As you may recall, the short-run aggregate-supply curve is upward sloping, indicating that an increase in the price level raises the quantity of goods and services that firms supply. By contrast, the long-run aggregate-supply curve is vertical, indicating that the price level does not influence quantity supplied in the long run. Chapter 31 presented three theories to explain the upward slope of the short-run aggregate-supply curve: misperceptions about relative prices, sticky wages, and sticky prices. Because perceptions, wages, and prices adjust to changing economic conditions over time, the positive relationship between the price level and quantity supplied applies in the short run but not in the long run. Friedman and Phelps applied this same logic to the Phillips curve. Just as the aggregate-supply curve slopes upward only in the short run, the tradeoff between inflation and unemployment holds only in the short run. And just as the long-run aggregate-supply curve is vertical, the long-run Phillips curve is also vertical.

To help explain the short-run and long-run relationship between inflation and unemployment, Friedman and Phelps introduced a new variable into the analysis: *expected inflation*. Expected inflation measures how much people expect the overall price level to change. As we discussed in Chapter 31, the expected price level affects the perceptions of relative prices that people form and the wages and prices that they set. As a result, expected inflation is one factor that determines the position of the short-run aggregate-supply curve. In the short run, the Fed can take expected inflation (and thus the short-run aggregate-supply curve) as already determined. When the money supply changes, the aggregate-demand curve shifts, and the economy moves along a given short-run aggregate-supply curve. In the short run, therefore, monetary changes lead to unexpected fluctuations in output, prices, unemployment, and inflation. In this way, Friedman and Phelps explained the Phillips curve that Phillips, Samuelson, and Solow had documented.

Yet the Fed's ability to create unexpected inflation by increasing the money supply exists only in the short run. In the long run, people come to expect whatever inflation rate the Fed chooses to produce. Because perceptions, wages, and prices will eventually adjust to the inflation rate, the long-run aggregate-supply curve is vertical. In this case, changes in aggregate demand, such as those due to changes in the money supply, do not affect the economy's output of goods and services. Thus, Friedman and Phelps concluded that unemployment returns to its natural rate in the long run.

The analysis of Friedman and Phelps can be summarized in the following equation:

$$\text{Unemployment rate} = \text{Natural rate of unemployment} - a\left(\text{Actual inflation} - \text{Expected inflation}\right).$$

This equation relates the unemployment rate to the natural rate of unemployment, actual inflation, and expected inflation. In the short run, expected inflation is already given. As a result, higher actual inflation is associated with lower unemployment. (How much unemployment responds to unexpected inflation is determined by the size of a, a number that in turn depends on the slope of the short-run aggregate-supply curve.) In the long run, however, people come to expect whatever inflation the Fed produces. Thus, actual inflation equals expected inflation, and unemployment is at its natural rate.

According to Friedman and Phelps, it is dangerous to view the Phillips curve as a menu of options available to policymakers. To see why, imagine an economy at its natural rate of unemployment with low inflation and low expected inflation, shown in Figure 33-5 as point A. Now suppose that policymakers try to take advantage of the tradeoff between inflation and unemployment by using monetary or fiscal policy to expand aggregate demand. In the short run when expected inflation is given, the economy goes from point A to point B. Unemployment falls below its natural rate, and inflation rises above expected inflation. Over time, people get used to this higher inflation rate, and they raise their expectations of inflation. When expected inflation rises, the short-run tradeoff between inflation and unemployment shifts upward. The economy ends up at point C, with higher inflation than at point A but with the same level of unemployment.

Thus, Friedman and Phelps concluded that policymakers do face a tradeoff between inflation and unemployment, but only a temporary one. If policymakers use this tradeoff, they lose it.

Figure 33-5

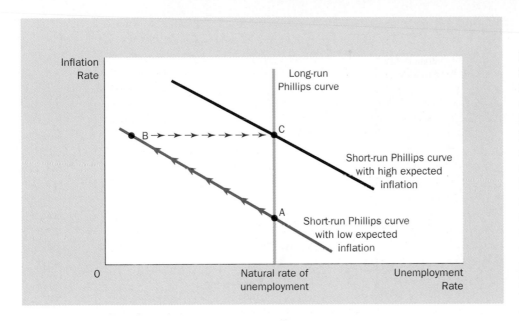

HOW EXPECTED INFLATION SHIFTS THE SHORT-RUN PHILLIPS CURVE. The higher the expected rate of inflation, the higher the short-run tradeoff between inflation and unemployment. At point A, expected inflation and actual inflation are both low, and unemployment is at its natural rate. If the Fed pursues an expansionary monetary policy, the economy moves from point A to point B in the short run. At point B, expected inflation is still low, but actual inflation is high. Unemployment is below its natural rate. In the long run, expected inflation rises, and the economy moves to point C. At point C, expected inflation and actual inflation are both high, and unemployment is back to its natural rate.

THE NATURAL EXPERIMENT FOR THE NATURAL-RATE HYPOTHESIS

Friedman and Phelps had made a bold prediction in 1968: If policymakers try to take advantage of the Phillips curve by choosing higher inflation in order to reduce unemployment, they will succeed at reducing unemployment only temporarily. This view—that unemployment eventually returns to its natural rate, regardless of the rate of inflation—is called the **natural-rate hypothesis.** A few years after Friedman and Phelps proposed this hypothesis, monetary and fiscal policymakers inadvertently created a natural experiment to test it. Their laboratory was the U.S. economy.

Before we see the outcome of this test, however, let's look at the data that Friedman and Phelps had when they made their prediction in 1968. Figure 33-6 shows the unemployment rate and the inflation rate for the period from 1961 to 1968. These data trace out a Phillips curve. As inflation rose over these eight years, unemployment fell. The economic data from this era seemed to confirm the tradeoff between inflation and unemployment.

The apparent success of the Phillips curve in the 1960s made the prediction of Friedman and Phelps all the more bold. In 1958 Phillips had suggested a negative association between inflation and unemployment. In 1960 Samuelson and Solow had showed it in U.S. data. Another decade of data had confirmed the relationship. To some economists at the time, it seemed ridiculous to claim that the Phillips curve would break down once policymakers tried to use it.

But, in fact, that is exactly what happened. Beginning in the late 1960s, the government followed policies that expanded the aggregate demand for goods and services. In part, this expansion was due to fiscal policy: Government spending rose as the Vietnam War heated up. In part, it was due to monetary policy: Because the Fed was trying to hold down interest rates in the face of expansionary fiscal policy, the quantity of money (as measured by M2) rose about 13 percent per year during the period from 1970 to 1972, compared to 7 percent per

natural-rate hypothesis
the claim that unemployment eventually returns to its normal, or natural, rate, regardless of the rate of inflation

Figure 33-6

THE PHILLIPS CURVE IN THE 1960s. This figure uses annual data from 1961 to 1968 on the unemployment rate and on the inflation rate (as measured by the GDP deflator) to show the negative relationship between inflation and unemployment.

SOURCE: U.S. Department of Labor, U.S. Department of Commerce.

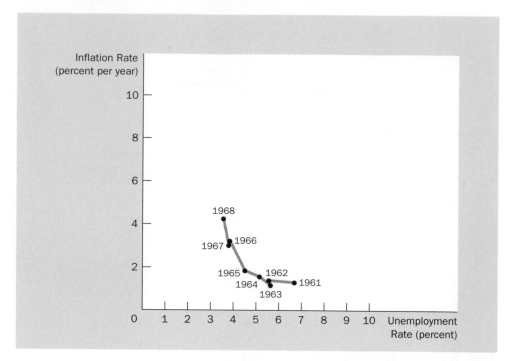

Figure 33-7

THE BREAKDOWN OF THE PHILLIPS CURVE. This figure shows annual data from 1961 to 1973 on the unemployment rate and on the inflation rate (as measured by the GDP deflator). Notice that the Phillips curve of the 1960s breaks down in the early 1970s.

SOURCE: U.S. Department of Labor, U.S. Department of Commerce.

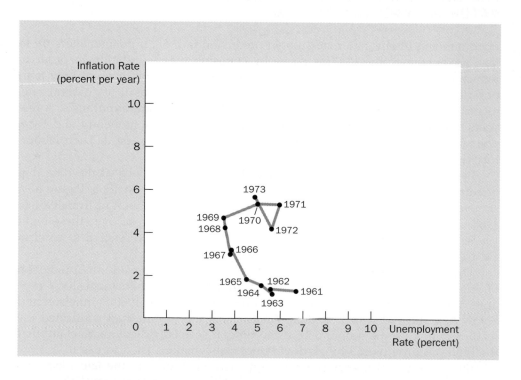

year in the early 1960s. As a result, inflation stayed high (about 5 to 6 percent per year in the late 1960s and early 1970s, compared to about 1 to 2 percent per year in the early 1960s). But, as Friedman and Phelps had predicted, unemployment did not stay low.

Figure 33-7 shows the history of inflation and unemployment from 1961 to 1973. Notice that the simple negative relationship between these two variables started to break down around 1970. In particular, as inflation remained high in the early 1970s, people's expectations of inflation caught up with reality, and the unemployment rate reverted to the 5 percent to 6 percent range that had prevailed in the early 1960s. By 1973, policymakers had learned that Friedman and Phelps were right: There is no tradeoff between inflation and unemployment in the long run.

▌**QUICK QUIZ**   Draw the short-run Phillips curve and the long-run Phillips curve. Explain why they are different.

SHIFTS IN THE PHILLIPS CURVE: THE ROLE OF SUPPLY SHOCKS

Friedman and Phelps had suggested in 1968 that changes in expected inflation shift the short-run Phillips curve, and the experience of the early 1970s convinced most economists that Friedman and Phelps were right. Within a few years, however, the economics profession would turn its attention to a different source of shifts in the short-run Phillips curve: shocks to aggregate supply.

This time, the shift in focus came not from two American economics professors but from a group of Arab sheiks. In 1974, the Organization of Petroleum Exporting Countries (OPEC) began to exert its market power as a cartel in the world oil market in order to increase its members' profits. The countries of OPEC, such as Saudi Arabia, Kuwait, and Iraq, restricted the amount of crude oil they pumped and sold on world markets. Within a few years, this reduction in supply caused the price of oil to almost double.

As we first discussed in Chapter 31, this OPEC price increase had major macroeconomic effects. Because an increase in the price of oil raises the cost of producing many goods and services, it reduces the quantity of goods and services supplied at any given price level. As panel (a) of Figure 33-8 shows, this reduction in supply is represented by the leftward shift in the aggregate-supply curve from AS_1 to AS_2. The price level rises from P_1 to P_2, and output falls from Y_1 to Y_2. The result is called *stagflation*.

This shift in aggregate supply is associated with a similar shift in the short-run Phillips curve, shown in panel (b). Because firms need fewer workers to produce the smaller output, employment falls and unemployment rises. Because the price level is higher, the inflation rate—the percentage change in the price level from the previous year—is also higher. Thus, the shift in aggregate supply leads to higher unemployment and higher inflation. The short-run tradeoff between inflation and unemployment shifts to the right from PC_1 to PC_2.

Confronted with an adverse shift in aggregate supply, policymakers face a difficult choice. If they contract aggregate demand to fight inflation, they will raise unemployment further. If they expand aggregate demand to fight unemployment, they will raise inflation further. In other words, policymakers face a less favorable tradeoff between inflation and unemployment than they did before the shift in aggregate supply: They have to live with a higher rate of inflation for a given rate of unemployment, a higher rate of unemployment for a given rate of inflation, or some combination of higher unemployment and higher inflation.

Figure 33-8

AN ADVERSE SHOCK TO AGGREGATE SUPPLY. Panel (a) shows the model of aggregate demand and aggregate supply. When the aggregate-supply curve shifts to the left from AS_1 to AS_2, the equilibrium moves from point A to point B. Output falls from Y_1 to Y_2, and the price level rises from P_1 to P_2. Panel (b) shows the short-run tradeoff between inflation and unemployment. The adverse shift in aggregate supply moves the economy from a point with lower unemployment and lower inflation (point A) to a point with higher unemployment and higher inflation (point B). The short-run Phillips curve shifts to the right from PC_1 to PC_2. Policymakers now face a worse tradeoff between inflation and unemployment.

An important question is whether this adverse shift in the Phillips curve is temporary or permanent. The answer depends on how people adjust their expectations of inflation. If people view the event as a temporary aberration, expected inflation does not change, and the Phillips curve will soon revert to its former position. But if people view the shock as leading to a new era of higher inflation, then expected inflation rises, and the Phillips curve remains at its new, less desirable position.

In the United States during the 1970s, expected inflation did rise substantially. This rise in expected inflation is partly attributable to the decision of the Fed to accommodate the supply shock with higher money growth. (As we saw in Chapter 31, policymakers are said to *accommodate* an adverse supply shock when they respond to it by increasing aggregate demand.) Because of this policy decision, the recession that resulted from the supply shock was smaller than it otherwise might have been, but the U.S. economy faced an unfavorable tradeoff between inflation and unemployment for many years. The problem was compounded in 1979, when OPEC once again started to exert its market power, more than doubling the price of oil. Figure 33-9 shows inflation and unemployment in the U.S. economy during this period.

In 1980, after two OPEC supply shocks, the U.S. economy had an inflation rate of more than 9 percent and an unemployment rate of about 7 percent. This combination of inflation and unemployment was not at all near the tradeoff that seemed possible in the 1960s. (In the 1960s, the Phillips curve suggested that an unemployment rate of 7 percent would be associated with an inflation rate of

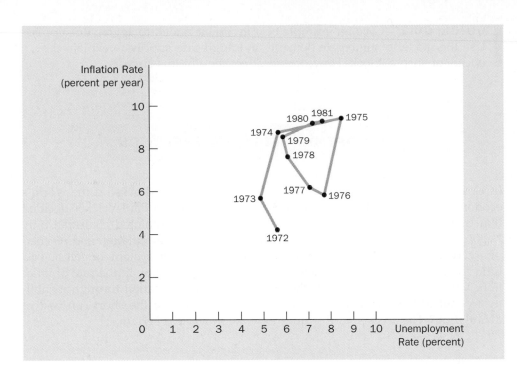

Figure 33-9

THE SUPPLY SHOCKS OF THE 1970s. This figure shows annual data from 1972 to 1981 on the unemployment rate and on the inflation rate (as measured by the GDP deflator). In the periods 1973–1975 and 1978–1981, increases in world oil prices led to higher inflation and higher unemployment.

SOURCE: U.S. Department of Labor, U.S. Department of Commerce.

only 1 percent. Inflation of more than 9 percent was unthinkable.) With the misery index in 1980 near an historic high, the public was widely dissatisfied with macroeconomic performance. Largely because of this dissatisfaction, President Jimmy Carter lost his bid for reelection in November 1980 and was replaced by Ronald Reagan. Something had to be done, and soon it would be.

"Remember the good old days when all the economy
needed was a little fine-tuning?"

QUICK QUIZ   Give an example of a favorable shock to aggregate supply. Use the model of aggregate demand and aggregate supply to explain the effects of such a shock. How does it affect the Phillips curve?

THE COST OF REDUCING INFLATION

When Paul Volcker became Fed chairman, inflation was widely viewed as one of the nation's foremost problems.

In October 1979, as OPEC was imposing adverse supply shocks on the world's economies for the second time in a decade, Fed Chairman Paul Volcker decided that the time for action had come. Volcker had been appointed chairman only two months earlier, and he had taken the job knowing that inflation had reached unacceptable levels. As guardian of the nation's monetary system, he felt he had little choice but to pursue a policy of *disinflation*—a reduction in the rate of inflation. Volcker had no doubt that the Fed could reduce inflation through its ability to control the quantity of money. But what would be the short-run cost of disinflation? The answer to this question was much less certain.

THE SACRIFICE RATIO

To reduce the inflation rate, the Fed has to pursue contractionary monetary policy. Figure 33-10 shows some of the effects of such a decision. When the Fed slows the rate of money growth, it contracts aggregate demand. The fall in aggregate demand, in turn, reduces the quantity of goods and services that firms produce, and this fall in production leads to a fall in employment. The economy begins at point A in the figure and moves along the short-run Phillips curve to point B, which has lower inflation and higher unemployment. Over time, as peo-

Figure 33-10

DISINFLATIONARY MONETARY POLICY IN THE SHORT RUN AND LONG RUN. When the Fed pursues contractionary monetary policy to reduce inflation, the economy moves along a short-run Phillips curve from point A to point B. Over time, expected inflation falls, and the short-run Phillips curve shifts downward. When the economy reaches point C, unemployment is back at its natural rate.

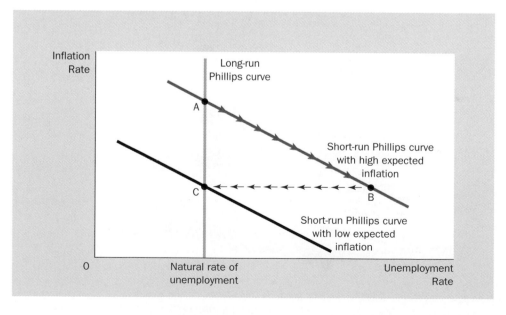

ple come to understand that prices are rising more slowly, expected inflation falls, and the short-run Phillips curve shifts downward. The economy moves from point B to point C. Inflation is lower, and unemployment is back at its natural rate.

Thus, if an economy is to reduce inflation, it must endure a period of high unemployment and low output. In Figure 33-10, this cost is represented by the movement of the economy through point B as it travels from point A to point C. The size of this cost depends on the slope of the Phillips curve and how quickly expectations of inflation adjust to the new monetary policy.

Many studies have examined the data on inflation and unemployment in order to estimate the cost of reducing inflation. The findings of these studies are often summarized in a statistic called the **sacrifice ratio.** The sacrifice ratio is the number of percentage points of annual output lost in the process of reducing inflation by 1 percentage point. A typical estimate of the sacrifice ratio is 5. That is, for each percentage point that inflation is reduced, 5 percent of annual output must be sacrificed in the transition.

Such estimates surely must have made Paul Volcker apprehensive as he confronted the task of reducing inflation. Inflation was running at almost 10 percent per year. To reach moderate inflation of, say, 4 percent per year would mean reducing inflation by 6 percentage points. If each percentage point cost 5 percent of the economy's annual output, then reducing inflation by 6 percentage points would require sacrificing 30 percent of annual output.

According to studies of the Phillips curve and the cost of disinflation, this sacrifice could be paid in various ways. An immediate reduction in inflation would depress output by 30 percent for a single year, but that outcome was surely too harsh even for an inflation hawk like Paul Volcker. It would be better, many argued, to spread out the cost over several years. If the reduction in inflation took place over 5 years, for instance, then output would have to average only 6 percent below trend during that period to add up to a sacrifice of 30 percent. An even more gradual approach would be to reduce inflation slowly over a decade, so that output would have to be only 3 percent below trend. Whatever path was chosen, however, it seemed that reducing inflation would not be easy.

sacrifice ratio
the number of percentage points of annual output lost in the process of reducing inflation by 1 percentage point

RATIONAL EXPECTATIONS AND THE POSSIBILITY OF COSTLESS DISINFLATION

Just as Paul Volcker was pondering how costly reducing inflation might be, a group of economics professors was leading an intellectual revolution that would challenge the conventional wisdom on the sacrifice ratio. This group included such prominent economists as Robert Lucas, Thomas Sargent, and Robert Barro. Their revolution was based on a new approach to economic theory and policy called **rational expectations.** According to the theory of rational expectations, people optimally use all the information they have, including information about government policies, when forecasting the future.

This new approach has had profound implications for many areas of macroeconomics, but none is more important than its application to the tradeoff between inflation and unemployment. As Friedman and Phelps had first emphasized, expected inflation is an important variable that explains why there is a tradeoff between inflation and unemployment in the short run but not in the

rational expectations
the theory according to which people optimally use all the information they have, including information about government policies, when forecasting the future

long run. How quickly the short-run tradeoff disappears depends on how quickly expectations adjust. Proponents of rational expectations built on the Friedman–Phelps analysis to argue that when economic policies change, people adjust their expectations of inflation accordingly. Studies of inflation and unemployment that tried to estimate the sacrifice ratio had failed to take account of the direct effect of the policy regime on expectations. As a result, estimates of the sacrifice ratio were, according to the rational-expectations theorists, unreliable guides for policy.

In a 1981 paper titled "The End of Four Big Inflations," Thomas Sargent described this new view as follows:

> An alternative "rational expectations" view denies that there is any inherent momentum to the present process of inflation. This view maintains that firms and workers have now come to expect high rates of inflation in the future and that they strike inflationary bargains in light of these expectations. However, it is held that people expect high rates of inflation in the future precisely because the government's current and prospective monetary and fiscal policies warrant those expectations. . . . An implication of this view is that inflation can be stopped much more quickly than advocates of the "momentum" view have indicated and that their estimates of the length of time and the costs of stopping inflation in terms of foregone output are erroneous. . . . This is not to say that it would be easy to eradicate inflation. On the contrary, it would require more than a few temporary restrictive fiscal and monetary actions. It would require a change in the policy regime. . . . How costly such a move would be in terms of foregone output and how long it would be in taking effect would depend partly on how resolute and evident the government's commitment was.

According to Sargent, the sacrifice ratio could be much smaller than suggested by previous estimates. Indeed, in the most extreme case, it could be zero. If the government made a credible commitment to a policy of low inflation, people would be rational enough to lower their expectations of inflation immediately. The short-run Phillips curve would shift downward, and the economy would reach low inflation quickly without the cost of temporarily high unemployment and low output.

THE VOLCKER DISINFLATION

As we have seen, when Paul Volcker faced the prospect of reducing inflation from its peak of about 10 percent, the economics profession offered two conflicting predictions. One group of economists offered estimates of the sacrifice ratio and concluded that reducing inflation would have great cost in terms of lost output and high unemployment. Another group offered the theory of rational expectations and concluded that reducing inflation could be much less costly and, perhaps, could even have no cost at all. Who was right?

Figure 33-11 shows inflation and unemployment during this period. As you can see, Volcker did succeed at reducing inflation. Inflation came down from almost 10 percent in 1981 and 1982 to about 4 percent in 1983 and 1984. Credit for this reduction in inflation goes completely to monetary policy. Fiscal policy at this time was acting in the opposite direction: The increases in the budget deficit during the Reagan administration were expanding aggregate demand,

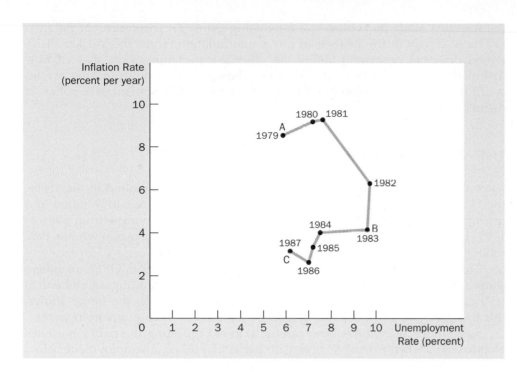

Figure 33-11

THE VOLCKER DISINFLATION.
This figure shows annual data
from 1979 to 1987 on the unemployment rate and on the inflation rate (as measured by the
GDP deflator). The reduction in
inflation during this period came
at the cost of very high unemployment in 1982 and 1983. Note
that the points labeled A, B, and
C in this figure correspond
roughly to the points in Figure
33-10.

SOURCE: U.S. Department of Labor, U.S.
Department of Commerce.

which tends to raise inflation. The fall in inflation from 1981 to 1984 is attributable to the tough anti-inflation policies of Fed Chairman Paul Volcker.

The figure shows that the Volcker disinflation did come at the cost of high
unemployment. In 1982 and 1983, the unemployment rate was about 10 percent.
At the same time, the production of goods and services as measured by real GDP
was well below its trend level. (See Figure 31-1 in Chapter 31.) The Volcker disinflation produced the deepest recession in the United States since the Great
Depression of the 1930s.

Does this experience refute the possibility of costless disinflation as suggested by the rational-expectations theorists? Some economists have argued that
the answer to this question is a resounding yes. Indeed, the pattern of disinflation shown in Figure 33-11 is very similar to the pattern predicted in Figure 33-
10. To make the transition from high inflation (point A in both figures) to low
inflation (point C), the economy had to experience a painful period of high
unemployment (point B).

Yet there are two reasons not to reject the conclusions of the rational-expectations theorists so quickly. First, even though the Volcker disinflation did impose
a cost of temporarily high unemployment, the cost was not as large as many
economists had predicted. Most estimates of the sacrifice ratio based on the Volcker disinflation are smaller than estimates that had been obtained from previous data. Perhaps Volcker's tough stand on inflation did have some direct effect
on expectations, as the rational-expectations theorists claimed.

Second, and more important, even though Volcker announced that he would
aim monetary policy to lower inflation, much of the public did not believe him.
Because few people thought Volcker would reduce inflation as quickly as he did,
expected inflation did not fall, and the short-run Phillips curve did not shift
down as quickly as it might have. Some evidence for this hypothesis comes from

the forecasts made by commercial forecasting firms: Their forecasts of inflation fell more slowly in the 1980s than did actual inflation. Thus, the Volcker disinflation does not necessarily refute the rational-expectations view that credible disinflation can be costless. It does show, however, that policymakers cannot count on people immediately believing them when they announce a policy of disinflation.

THE GREENSPAN ERA

Since the OPEC inflation of the 1970s and the Volcker disinflation of the 1980s, the U.S. economy has experienced relatively mild fluctuations in inflation and unemployment. Figure 33-12 shows inflation and unemployment from 1984 to 1995. This period is called the Greenspan era, after Alan Greenspan who in 1987 followed Paul Volcker as chairman of the Federal Reserve.

This period began with a favorable supply shock. In 1986, OPEC members started arguing over production levels, and their long-standing agreement to restrict supply broke down. Oil prices fell by about half. As the figure shows, this favorable supply shock led to falling inflation and falling unemployment.

Since then, the Fed has been careful to avoid repeating the policy mistakes of the 1960s, when excessive aggregate demand pushed unemployment below the natural rate and raised inflation. Unemployment has stayed relatively close to 6 percent, which many economists estimate to be the natural rate for the U.S. economy. When unemployment fell and inflation rose in 1989 and 1990, the Fed contracted aggregate demand, leading to a small recession in 1991 and 1992. Unemployment then rose above the natural rate, and inflation fell. The economy gradually recovered from this recession in the mid-1990s, and inflation stabilized at about 3 percent.

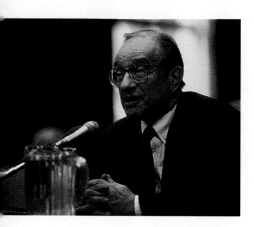

Fed Chairman Alan Greenspan testifies regularly before congressional committees.

Figure 33-12

THE GREENSPAN ERA. This figure shows annual data from 1984 to 1995 on the unemployment rate and on the inflation rate (as measured by the GDP deflator). During most of this period, Alan Greenspan has been chairman of the Federal Reserve. Fluctuations in inflation and unemployment have been relatively small.

SOURCE: U.S. Department of Labor, U.S. Department of Commerce.

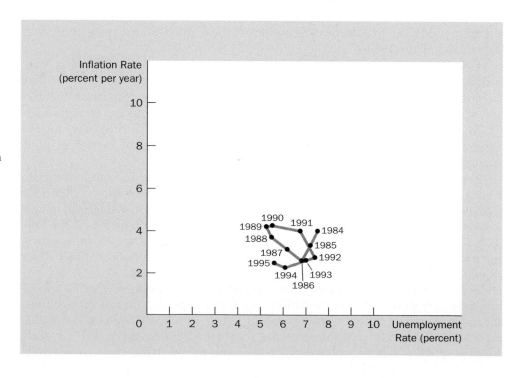

What does the future hold? Macroeconomists are notoriously bad at forecasting, but several lessons of the past are clear. First, as long as the Fed remains vigilant in its control over the money supply and, thereby, aggregate demand, there is no reason to allow inflation to heat up needlessly, as it did in the late

IN THE NEWS

Unemployment and Its Natural Rate

As the presidential election of 1996 neared, the unemployment rate fell to 5.1 percent, its lowest level in years. The Fed faced a difficult question: Was this rate of unemployment below the natural rate?

Trying to Figure Out How Low Unemployment Figures Can Go

By Richard W. Stevenson

Washington—Beyond the clear political gain it represents for President Clinton, the decline in unemployment to its lowest level in seven years has focused added attention on an issue that increasingly dominates policy debates and financial markets: whether the economy has changed so fundamentally in recent years that it can accommodate a lower rate of unemployment, and the resulting wage increases, without reigniting inflation.

Over the last two years, as the unemployment rate edged below 6 percent and slid gradually down to its current level of 5.1 percent, economists have had to reassess one of their most widely accepted assumptions: that the natural rate of unemployment was a little more than 6 percent. Below that rate, the assumption held, labor markets would become so tight that wages would surge, sending prices upward.

As unemployment has fallen below that level, the Federal Reserve and the bond markets have strained mightily to detect the expected signs of inflation, and have so far found almost nothing. While wages have been creeping up, most companies have reported an inability to push through price increases to customers, keeping inflation quiescent.

The resulting economic mix—low unemployment, low inflation, steady growth, and signs that wages might be edging up after a long period of stagnation could not be more ideal for Mr. Clinton as he confronts a Republican nominee, Bob Dole, who has built his campaign on the argument that the nation is being shortchanged economically.

Indeed, the economic gods have smiled on Mr. Clinton since 1992, when it was George Bush's bad fortune to preside over an economy that came out of recession in a slow and faltering way. While unemployment generally drifted upward throughout Mr. Bush's presidency, it has moved down during Mr. Clinton's term.

Whether Mr. Clinton deserves any credit for the economic record of the last three years and eight months is a matter of intense partisan debate, and Mr. Clinton could remain vulnerable to widespread if dissipating economic anxiety and resentment about stagnant wages and job insecurity. But Mr. Clinton is maintaining his big lead in the polls, and the unemployment report will make it that much harder for Mr. Dole to get a hearing for his argument that the nation needs to improve its long-run economic performance. . . .

Although the Fed has indicated that it is leaning toward raising rates if the economy does not show signs of cooling off, Fed officials over the last week have said they remain undecided whether they need to act, and if so, by how much they will need to raise rates.

Clinton administration officials stuck today to their position that they do not comment on the Fed's monetary policy. But they said they saw no signs of inflation, and left little doubt that they would view any rate increase before the election as unjustified, even though it takes months before higher rates begin working to slow the economy.

They also argued that the Fed should continue to engage in what has amounted to an experiment in determining just how low unemployment can go before signs of inflation emerge. Despite its reputation for taking a hard line on inflation, the Fed, in the view of some analysts, has been remarkably restrained in allowing unemployment to go so low and economic growth to remain so strong without raising rates.

"In the presence of such strong stability in the economy, it should be possible at low cost to reverse any slight overheating," said Joseph E. Stiglitz, the chairman of the president's Council of Economic Advisers.

Source: *The New York Times*, September 7, 1996, p. 35.

1960s. Second, the possibility always exists for the economy to experience adverse shocks to aggregate supply, as it did in the 1970s. If that unfortunate development occurs, policymakers will have little choice but to confront a less desirable tradeoff between inflation and unemployment.

QUICK QUIZ   What is the sacrifice ratio? How might the credibility of the Fed's commitment to reduce inflation affect the sacrifice ratio?

CONCLUSION

This chapter has examined how economists' thinking about inflation and unemployment has evolved over time. We have discussed the ideas of many of the best economists of the twentieth century: from the Phillips curve of Phillips, Samuelson, and Solow, to the natural-rate hypothesis of Friedman and Phelps, to the rational-expectations theory of Lucas, Sargent, and Barro. Four of this group have already won Nobel prizes for their work in economics, and more are likely to be so honored in the years to come.

Although the tradeoff between inflation and unemployment has generated much intellectual turmoil over the past 40 years, certain principles have developed that today command consensus. Here is how Milton Friedman expressed the relationship between inflation and unemployment in 1968:

> There is always a temporary tradeoff between inflation and unemployment; there is no permanent tradeoff. The temporary tradeoff comes not from inflation per se, but from unanticipated inflation, which generally means, from a rising rate of inflation. The widespread belief that there is a permanent tradeoff is a sophisticated version of the confusion between "high" and "rising" that we all recognize in simpler forms. A rising rate of inflation may reduce unemployment, a high rate will not.
>
> But how long, you will say, is "temporary"? . . . I can at most venture a personal judgment, based on some examination of the historical evidence, that the initial effects of a higher and unanticipated rate of inflation last for something like two to five years.

Today, about 30 years later, this statement still summarizes the view of most macroeconomists.

Summary

◆   The Phillips curve describes a negative relationship between inflation and unemployment. By expanding aggregate demand, policymakers can choose a point on the Phillips curve with higher inflation and lower unemployment. By contracting aggregate demand, policymakers can choose a point on the Phillips curve with lower inflation and higher unemployment.

◆   The tradeoff between inflation and unemployment described by the Phillips curve holds only in the short run. In the long run, expected inflation adjusts to changes in actual inflation, and the short-run Phillips curve shifts. As a result, the long-run Phillips curve is vertical at the natural rate of unemployment.

◆ The short-run Phillips curve also shifts because of shocks to aggregate supply. An adverse supply shock, such as the increase in world oil prices during the 1970s, gives policymakers a less favorable tradeoff between inflation and unemployment. That is, after an adverse supply shock, policymakers have to accept a higher rate of inflation for any given rate of unemployment, or a higher rate of unemployment for any given rate of inflation.

◆ When the Fed contracts monetary growth to reduce inflation, it moves the economy along the short-run Phillips curve, which results in temporarily high unemployment. The cost of disinflation depends on how quickly expectations of inflation fall. Some economists argue that a credible commitment to low inflation can reduce the cost of disinflation by inducing a quick adjustment of expectations.

Key Concepts

Phillips curve, p. 734
natural-rate hypothesis, p. 743

sacrifice ratio, p. 749

rational expectations, p. 749

Questions for Review

1. Draw the short-run tradeoff between inflation and unemployment. How might the Fed move the economy from one point on this curve to another?

2. Draw the long-run tradeoff between inflation and unemployment. Explain how the short-run and long-run tradeoffs are related.

3. Why might the natural rate of unemployment differ across countries?

4. Suppose a drought destroys farm crops and drives up the price of food. What is the effect on the short-run tradeoff between inflation and unemployment?

5. The Fed decides to reduce inflation. Use the Phillips curve to show the short-run and long-run effects of this policy. How might the short-run costs be reduced?

Problems and Applications

1. Suppose the natural rate of unemployment is 6 percent. On one graph, draw two Phillips curves that can be used to describe the four situations listed here. Label the point that shows the position of the economy in each case:
   a. Actual inflation is 5 percent and expected inflation is 3 percent.
   b. Actual inflation is 3 percent and expected inflation is 5 percent.
   c. Actual inflation is 5 percent and expected inflation is 5 percent.
   d. Actual inflation is 3 percent and expected inflation is 3 percent.

2. Illustrate the effects of the following developments on both the short-run and long-run Phillips curves. Give the economic reasoning underlying your answers.
   a. a rise in the natural rate of unemployment
   b. a decline in the price of imported oil

   c. a rise in government spending
   d. a decline in expected inflation

3. Suppose that reduced consumer spending causes a recession.
   a. Illustrate the changes in the economy using both an aggregate-supply/aggregate-demand diagram and a Phillips-curve diagram.
   b. What will happen in the long run if expected inflation is unchanged? What will happen in the long run if expected inflation changes in the same direction that actual inflation changes in the short run? Illustrate your answers using your diagrams from part (a).

4. Suppose the economy is in a long-run equilibrium.
   a. Draw the economy's short-run and long-run Phillips curves.
   b. Suppose a wave of business pessimism reduces aggregate demand. Show the effect of this shock on

your diagram from part (a). If the Fed undertakes expansionary monetary policy, can it return the economy to its original inflation rate and original unemployment rate?

c. Now suppose the economy is back in long-run equilibrium, and then the price of imported oil rises. Show the effect of this shock with a new diagram like that in part (a). If the Fed undertakes expansionary monetary policy, can it return the economy to its original inflation rate and original unemployment rate? If the Fed undertakes contractionary monetary policy, can it return the economy to its original inflation rate and original unemployment rate? Explain why this situation differs from that in part (b).

5. Suppose the Federal Reserve believed that the natural rate of unemployment was 6 percent when the actual natural rate was 5.5 percent. If the Fed based its policy decisions on its belief, what would happen to the economy?

6. Suppose the Federal Reserve announced that it would pursue contractionary monetary policy in order to reduce the inflation rate. Would the following conditions make the ensuing recession more or less severe? Explain.

a. Wage contracts have short durations.

b. There is little confidence in the Fed's determination to reduce inflation.

c. Expectations of inflation adjust quickly to actual inflation.

7. Some economists believe that the short-run Phillips curve is relatively steep and shifts quickly in response to changes in the economy. Would these economists be more or less likely to favor contractionary policy in order to reduce inflation than economists who had the opposite views?

8. According to one version of Okun's law (discussed in Chapter 31), when real GDP is 1 percent below its trend level, the unemployment rate is half a percentage point above its natural rate. If the sacrifice ratio in the United States is 5, the natural rate of unemployment is 6 percent, and the Federal Reserve wants to reduce inflation by 2 percent, what rate of unemployment would be necessary for the Fed to reach its goal in 5 years?

9. Imagine an economy in which all wages are set in three-year contracts. In this world, the Fed announces a disinflationary change in monetary policy to begin immediately. Everyone in the economy believes the Fed's announcement. Would this disinflation be costless? Why or why not? What might the Fed do to reduce the cost of disinflation?

10. Given the unpopularity of inflation, why don't elected leaders always support efforts to reduce inflation? Economists believe that countries can reduce the cost of disinflation by letting their central banks make decisions about monetary policy without interference from politicians. Why might this be so?

XIII

FINAL THOUGHTS

34

FIVE DEBATES OVER
MACROECONOMIC POLICY

It is hard to open up the newspaper without finding some politician or editorial writer advocating a change in economic policy. The president should cut government spending to reduce the budget deficit, or he should stop worrying about the budget deficit. The Federal Reserve should cut interest rates to stimulate a flagging economy, or it should avoid such moves in order not to risk higher inflation. The Congress should reform the tax system to promote faster economic growth, or it should reform the tax system to achieve a more equal distribution of income. Economic issues are central to the continuing political debate in the United States and other countries around the world. It is no surprise that when Bill Clinton first ran for president in 1992, his chief strategist posted a sign to remind the staff of the central campaign issue: "The economy, stupid."

The previous dozen chapters have developed the tools that economists use when analyzing the behavior of the economy as a whole and the impact of policies on the economy. This final chapter presents both sides in five leading debates over macroeconomic policy. The knowledge you have accumulated in this course provides the background with which we can discuss these important, unsettled issues. It should help you choose a side in these debates or, at least, help you see why choosing a side is so difficult.

RESOLVED: MONETARY AND FISCAL POLICYMAKERS SHOULD TRY TO STABILIZE THE ECONOMY

In Chapters 31, 32, and 33, we saw how changes in aggregate demand and aggregate supply can lead to short-run fluctuations in production and employment. We also saw how monetary and fiscal policy can shift aggregate demand and, thereby, influence these fluctuations. But even if policymakers *can* influence short-run economic fluctuations, does that mean they *should*? Our first debate concerns whether monetary and fiscal policymakers should use the tools at their disposal in an attempt to smooth the ups and downs of the business cycle.

PRO: POLICYMAKERS SHOULD TRY TO STABILIZE THE ECONOMY

Left on their own, economies tend to fluctuate. When households and firms become pessimistic, for instance, they cut back on spending, and this reduces the aggregate demand for goods and services. The fall in aggregate demand, in turn, reduces the production of goods and services. Firms lay off workers, and the unemployment rate rises. Real GDP and other measures of income fall. Rising unemployment and falling income help confirm the pessimism that initially generated the economic downturn.

Such a recession has no benefit for society—it represents a sheer waste of resources. Workers who become unemployed because of inadequate aggregate demand would rather be working. Business owners whose factories are left idle during a recession would rather be producing valuable goods and services and selling them at a profit.

There is no reason for society to suffer through the booms and busts of the business cycle. The development of macroeconomic theory has shown policymakers how to reduce the severity of economic fluctuations. By "leaning against the wind" of economic change, monetary and fiscal policy can stabilize aggregate demand and, thereby, production and employment. When aggregate demand is inadequate to ensure full employment, policymakers should boost government spending, cut taxes, and expand the money supply. When aggregate demand is excessive, risking higher inflation, policymakers should cut government spending, raise taxes, and reduce the money supply. Such policy actions put macroeconomic theory to its best use by leading to a more stable economy, which benefits everyone.

CON: POLICYMAKERS SHOULD NOT TRY TO STABILIZE THE ECONOMY

Although monetary and fiscal policy can be used to stabilize the economy in theory, there are substantial obstacles to the use of such policies in practice.

One problem is that monetary and fiscal policy do not affect the economy immediately but instead work with a substantial lag. Monetary policy affects aggregate demand by changing interest rates, which in turn affects spending, especially residential and business investment. But many households and firms set their spending plans in advance. As a result, it takes time for changes in interest rates to alter the aggregate demand for goods and services. Many studies indicate that changes in monetary policy have little effect on aggregate demand until about six months after the change is made.

Fiscal policy works with a lag because of the long political process that governs changes in spending and taxes. To make any change in fiscal policy, a bill must go through congressional committees, pass both the House and the Senate, and be signed by the president. It can take years to propose, pass, and implement a major change in fiscal policy.

Because of these long lags, policymakers who want to stabilize the economy need to look ahead to economic conditions that are likely to prevail when their actions will take effect. Unfortunately, economic forecasting is highly imprecise, in part because macroeconomics is such a primitive science and in part because the shocks that cause economic fluctuations are intrinsically unpredictable. Thus, when policymakers change monetary or fiscal policy, they must rely on educated guesses about future economic conditions.

All too often, policymakers trying to stabilize the economy do just the opposite. Economic conditions can easily change between the time when a policy action begins and when it takes effect. Because of this, policymakers can inadvertently exacerbate rather than mitigate the magnitude of economic fluctuations. Some economists have claimed that many of the major economic fluctuations in history, including the Great Depression of the 1930s, can be traced to destabilizing policy actions.

One of the first rules taught to physicians is "do no harm." The human body has natural restorative powers. Confronted with a sick patient and an uncertain diagnosis, often a doctor should do nothing but leave the patient's body to its own devices. Intervening in the absence of reliable knowledge merely risks making matters worse.

The same can be said about treating an ailing economy. It might be desirable if policymakers could eliminate all economic fluctuations, but that is not a realistic goal given the limits of macroeconomic knowledge and the inherent unpredictability of world events. Economic policymakers should refrain from intervening often with monetary and fiscal policy and be content if they do no harm.

▌ QUICK QUIZ Explain why monetary and fiscal policy work with a lag. Why do these lags matter in the choice between active and passive policy?

RESOLVED: MONETARY POLICY SHOULD BE MADE BY RULE RATHER THAN BY DISCRETION

As we first discussed in Chapter 27, the Federal Open Market Committee sets monetary policy in the United States. The committee meets about every six weeks to evaluate the state of the economy. Based on this evaluation and forecasts of future economic conditions, it chooses whether to raise, lower, or leave unchanged the level of short-term interest rates. The Fed then adjusts the money supply to reach that interest-rate target until the next meeting, when the target is reevaluated.

The Federal Open Market Committee operates with almost complete discretion over how to conduct monetary policy. The laws that created the Fed give the institution only vague recommendations about what goals it should pursue. And they do not tell the Fed how to pursue whatever goals it might choose. Once members are appointed to the Federal Open Market Committee, they have little mandate but to "do the right thing."

Some economists are critical of this institutional design. Our second debate over macroeconomic policy, therefore, focuses on whether the Federal Reserve should have its discretionary powers reduced and, instead, be committed to following a rule in how it conducts monetary policy.

PRO: MONETARY POLICY SHOULD BE MADE BY RULE

Discretion in the conduct of monetary policy has two problems. The first is that it does not limit incompetence and abuse of power. When the government sends police into a community to maintain civic order, it gives them strict guidelines about how to carry out their job. Because police have great power, allowing them to exercise that power in whatever way they want would be dangerous. Yet when the government gives central bankers the authority to maintain economic order, it gives them no guidelines. Monetary policymakers are allowed undisciplined discretion.

As an example of abuse of power, central bankers are sometimes tempted to use monetary policy to affect the outcome of elections. Suppose that the vote for the incumbent president is based on economic conditions at the time he is up for reelection. A central banker sympathetic to the incumbent might be tempted to pursue expansionary policies just before the election to stimulate production and employment, knowing that the resulting inflation will not show up until after the election. Thus, to the extent that central bankers ally themselves with politicians, discretionary policy can lead to economic fluctuations that reflect the electoral calendar. Economists call such fluctuations the *political business cycle*.

The second, more subtle, problem with discretionary monetary policy is that it might lead to more inflation than is desirable. Central bankers, knowing that there is no long-run tradeoff between inflation and unemployment, often announce that their goal is zero inflation. Yet they rarely achieve price stability. Why? Perhaps it is because, once the public forms expectations of inflation, policymakers face a short-run tradeoff between inflation and unemployment. They are tempted to renege on their announcement of price stability in order to achieve lower unemployment. This discrepancy between announcements (what policymakers *say* they are going to do) and actions (what they subsequently in fact do) is called the *time inconsistency of policy*. Because policymakers are so often time inconsistent, people are skeptical when central bankers announce their intentions to reduce the rate of inflation. As a result, people always expect more inflation than monetary policymakers claim they are trying to achieve. Higher expectations of inflation, in turn, shift the short-run Phillips curve upward, making the short-run tradeoff between inflation and unemployment less favorable than it otherwise might be.

One way to avoid these two problems with discretionary policy is to commit the central bank to a policy rule. For example, suppose that Congress passed a law requiring the Fed to increase the money supply by exactly 3 percent per year. (Why 3 percent? Because real GDP grows on average about 3 percent per year and because money demand grows with real GDP, 3 percent growth in the money supply is roughly the rate necessary to produce long-run price stability.) Such a law would eliminate incompetence and abuse of power on the part of the Fed, and it would make the political business cycle impossible. In addition, policy could no longer be time inconsistent. People would now believe the Fed's announcement of low inflation because the Fed would be legally required to pursue a low-inflation monetary policy. With low expected inflation, the economy would face a more favorable short-run tradeoff between inflation and unemployment.

Other rules for monetary policy are also possible. A more active rule might allow some feedback from the state of the economy to changes in monetary policy. For example, a more active rule might require the Fed to increase monetary growth by 1 percentage point for every percentage point that unemployment rises above its natural rate. Regardless of the precise form of the rule, committing the Fed to some rule would yield advantages by limiting incompetence, abuse of power, and time inconsistency in the conduct of monetary policy.

CON: MONETARY POLICY SHOULD NOT BE MADE BY RULE

Although there may be pitfalls with discretionary monetary policy, there is also an important advantage to it: flexibility. The Fed has to confront various circumstances, not all of which can be foreseen. In the 1930s banks failed in record numbers. In the 1970s the price of oil skyrocketed around the world. In October 1987 the stock market fell by 22 percent in a single day. The Fed must decide how to respond to these shocks to the economy. A designer of a policy rule could not possibly consider all the contingencies and specify in advance the right policy response. It is better to appoint good people to conduct monetary policy and then give them the freedom to do the best they can.

Moreover, the alleged problems with discretion are largely hypothetical. The practical importance of the political business cycle, for instance, is far from clear. In some cases, just the opposite seems to occur. For example, President Jimmy Carter appointed Paul Volcker to head the Federal Reserve in 1979. Nonetheless, in October of that year Volcker moved to contract monetary policy in order to combat the high rate of inflation that he had inherited from his predecessor. The predictable result of Volcker's decision was a recession, and the predictable result of the recession was a decline in Carter's popularity. Rather than using monetary policy to help the president who had appointed him, Volcker helped to ensure Carter's defeat by Ronald Reagan in the November 1980 election.

The practical importance of time inconsistency is also far from clear. Although most people are skeptical of central-bank announcements, central bankers can achieve credibility over time by backing up their words with actions. In the 1990s, the Fed has achieved and maintained a low rate of inflation, despite the ever-present temptation to take advantage of the short-run tradeoff between inflation and unemployment. This experience shows that low inflation does not require that the Fed be committed to a policy rule.

Any attempt to replace discretion with a rule must confront the difficult task of specifying a precise rule. Despite much research examining the costs and benefits of alternative rules, economists have not reached a consensus about what a good rule would be. Until there is a consensus, society has little choice but to give central bankers discretion to conduct monetary policy as they see fit.

❚ QUICK QUIZ Give an example of a monetary policy rule. Why might your rule be better than discretionary policy? Why might it be worse?

RESOLVED: THE CENTRAL BANK SHOULD AIM FOR ZERO INFLATION

One of the *Ten Principles of Economics* discussed in Chapter 1, and developed more fully in Chapter 28, is that prices rise when the government prints too much money. Another of the *Ten Principles of Economics* discussed in Chapter 1, and developed more fully in Chapter 33, is that society faces a short-run tradeoff between inflation and unemployment. Put together, these two principles raise a question for policymakers: How much inflation should the central bank be willing to tolerate? Our third debate is whether zero is the right target for the inflation rate.

PRO: THE CENTRAL BANK SHOULD AIM FOR ZERO INFLATION

Inflation confers no benefit to society, but it does impose several real costs. As we discussed in Chapter 28, economists have identified six costs of inflation:

◆ Shoeleather costs associated with reduced money holdings
◆ Menu costs associated with more frequent adjustment of prices
◆ Increased variability of relative prices

◆ Unintended changes in tax liabilities due to nonindexation of the tax code

◆ Confusion and inconvenience resulting from a changing unit of account

◆ Arbitrary redistributions of wealth associated with dollar-denominated debts

Some economists argue that these costs are small, at least for moderate rates of inflation, such as the 3 percent inflation experienced in the United States during the first half of the 1990s. But other economists claim these costs can be substantial, even for moderate inflation. Moreover, there is no doubt that the public dislikes inflation. When inflation heats up, opinion polls identify inflation as one of the nation's leading problems.

Of course, the benefits of zero inflation have to be weighed against the costs of achieving it. Reducing inflation usually requires a period of high unemployment and low output, as illustrated by the short-run Phillips curve. But this disinflationary recession is only temporary. Once people come to understand that policymakers are aiming for zero inflation, expectations of inflation will fall, which improves the short-run tradeoff. Because expectations adjust, there is no tradeoff between inflation and unemployment in the long run.

Reducing inflation is, therefore, a policy with temporary costs and permanent benefits. That is, once the disinflationary recession is over, the benefits of zero inflation would persist into the future. If policymakers are farsighted, they should be willing to incur the temporary costs for the permanent benefits. This is precisely the calculation made by Paul Volcker in the early 1980s, when he reduced inflation from about 10 percent in 1980 to about 4 percent in 1983. Today Volcker is considered a hero among central bankers.

Moreover, the costs of reducing inflation need not be as large as some economists claim. If the Fed announces a credible commitment to zero inflation, it can directly influence expectations of inflation. Such a change in expectations can improve the short-run tradeoff between inflation and unemployment, allowing the economy to reach lower inflation at a reduced cost. The key to this strategy is credibility: People must believe that the Fed is actually going to carry through on its announced policy. Congress could help in this regard by passing legislation that made price stability the Fed's primary goal. Such a law would make it less costly to achieve zero inflation without reducing any of the resulting benefits.

One advantage of a zero-inflation target is that zero provides a more natural focal point for policymakers than any other number. Suppose, for instance, that the Fed were to announce that it would keep inflation at 3 percent—the rate experienced during the first half of the 1990s. Would the Fed really stick to that 3 percent target? If events inadvertently pushed inflation up to 4 or 5 percent, why wouldn't they just raise the target? There is, after all, nothing special about the number three. By contrast, zero is the only number for the inflation rate at which the Fed can claim that it achieved price stability and fully eliminated the costs of inflation.

CON: THE CENTRAL BANK SHOULD NOT AIM FOR ZERO INFLATION

Although price stability may be desirable, the benefits of zero inflation compared to moderate inflation are small, whereas the costs of reaching zero inflation are large. Estimates of the sacrifice ratio suggest that reducing inflation by

1 percentage point requires giving up about 5 percent of one year's output. Reducing inflation from, say, 4 percent to zero requires a loss of 20 percent of a year's output. At the current level of gross domestic product of about $7 trillion, this cost translates into $1.4 trillion of lost output, which is about $5,000 per person. Although people might dislike inflation, it is not at all clear that they would (or should) be willing to pay this much to get rid of it.

The social costs of disinflation are even larger than this $5,000 figure suggests, for the lost income is not spread equitably over the population. When the economy goes into recession, all incomes do not fall proportionately. Instead, the fall in aggregate income is concentrated on those workers who lose their jobs. The vulnerable workers are often those with the least skills and experience. Hence, much of the cost of reducing inflation is borne by those who can least afford to pay it.

Although economists can list several costs of inflation, there is no professional consensus that these costs are substantial. The shoeleather costs, menu costs, and others that economists have identified do not seem great, at least for moderate rates of inflation. It is true that the public dislikes inflation, but the public may be misled into believing the inflation fallacy—the view that inflation erodes living standards. Economists understand that living standards depend on productivity, not monetary policy. Because inflation in nominal incomes goes hand in hand with inflation in prices, reducing inflation would not cause real incomes to rise more rapidly.

Moreover, policymakers can reduce many of the costs of inflation without actually reducing inflation. They can eliminate the problems associated with the nonindexed tax system by rewriting the tax laws to take account of the effects of inflation. They can also reduce the arbitrary redistributions of wealth between creditors and debtors caused by unexpected inflation by issuing indexed government bonds, as in fact the Clinton administration did in 1997. Such an act insulates holders of government debt from inflation. In addition, by setting an example, it might encourage private borrowers and lenders to write debt contracts indexed for inflation.

Reducing inflation might be desirable if it could be done at no cost, as some economists argue is possible. Yet this trick seems hard to carry out in practice. When economies reduce their rate of inflation, they almost always experience a period of high unemployment and low output. It is risky to believe that the central bank could achieve credibility so quickly as to make disinflation painless.

Indeed, a disinflationary recession can potentially leave permanent scars on the economy. Firms in all industries reduce their spending on new plants and equipment substantially during recessions, making investment the most volatile component of GDP. Even after the recession is over, the smaller stock of capital reduces productivity, incomes, and living standards below the levels they otherwise would have achieved. In addition, when workers become unemployed in recessions, they lose valuable job skills. Even after the economy has recovered, their value as workers is diminished. Some economists have argued that the high unemployment in many European economies during the past decade is the aftermath of the disinflations of the 1980s.

Why should policymakers put the economy through a costly, inequitable disinflationary recession to achieve zero inflation, which may have only modest benefits? Economist Alan Blinder, whom Bill Clinton appointed to be vice chairman of the Federal Reserve, argued forcefully in his book *Hard Heads, Soft Hearts* that policymakers should not make this choice:

The costs that attend the low and moderate inflation rates experienced in the United States and in other industrial countries appear to be quite modest— more like a bad cold than a cancer on society. . . . As rational individuals, we do not volunteer for a lobotomy to cure a head cold. Yet, as a collectivity, we routinely prescribe the economic equivalent of lobotomy (high unemployment) as a cure for the inflationary cold.

Blinder concludes that it is better to learn to live with moderate inflation.

QUICK QUIZ Explain the costs and benefits of reducing inflation to zero. Which are temporary and which are permanent?

RESOLVED: THE GOVERNMENT SHOULD BALANCE ITS BUDGET

Perhaps the most persistent macroeconomic debate in recent years has been over the federal government's budget deficit. As you may recall, a budget deficit is an excess of government spending over government revenue. The government finances a budget deficit by issuing government debt. When we studied financial markets in Chapter 25, we saw how budget deficits affect saving, investment, and interest rates. But how big a problem are budget deficits? Our fourth debate concerns whether fiscal policymakers should make balancing the government's budget a high priority.

PRO: THE GOVERNMENT SHOULD BALANCE ITS BUDGET

Since the early 1980s, the U.S. government has spent substantially more than it has received in tax revenue. Because of these budget deficits, the debt of the federal government rose from $710 billion in 1980 to $3.6 trillion in 1995. If we divide today's debt by the size of the population, we learn that each person's share of the government debt is about $14,000.

The most direct effect of the government debt is to place a burden on future generations of taxpayers. When these debts and accumulated interest come due, future taxpayers will face a difficult choice. They can pay higher taxes, enjoy less government spending, or both, in order to make resources available to pay off the debt and accumulated interest. Or they can delay the day of reckoning and put the government into even deeper debt by borrowing once again to pay off the old debt and interest. In essence, when the government runs a budget deficit, it allows current taxpayers to pass the bill for some of their government spending on to future taxpayers. Inheriting such a large debt cannot help but lower the living standard of future generations.

In addition to this direct effect, budget deficits also have various macroeconomic effects. Because budget deficits represent *negative* public saving, they lower national saving (the sum of private and public saving). Reduced national saving causes real interest rates to rise and investment to fall. Reduced investment leads over time to a smaller stock of capital. A lower capital stock reduces labor productivity, real wages, and the economy's production of goods and services. Thus, when the government increases its debt, future generations are born into an economy with lower incomes as well as higher taxes.

There are, nevertheless, situations in which running a budget deficit is justifiable. Throughout history, the most common cause of increased government debt is war. When a military conflict raises government spending temporarily, it is reasonable to finance this extra spending by borrowing. Otherwise, taxes during wartime would have to rise precipitously. Such high tax rates would greatly distort the incentives faced by those who are taxed, leading to large deadweight losses. In addition, such high tax rates would be unfair to current generations of taxpayers, who already have to make the sacrifice of fighting the war.

Similarly, it is reasonable to allow a budget deficit during a temporary downturn in economic activity. When the economy goes into a recession, tax revenue falls automatically, because the income tax and the payroll tax are levied on measures of income. If the government tried to balance its budget during a recession, it would have to raise taxes or cut spending at a time of high unemployment. Such a policy would tend to depress aggregate demand at precisely the time it needed to be stimulated and, therefore, would tend to increase the magnitude of economic fluctuations.

Recent budget deficits, however, cannot be justified by appealing to war or recession. Since the early 1980s, the United States has avoided major military conflict and major economic downturn. Nonetheless, the government has consistently run a budget deficit, largely because the president and Congress have found it easier to increase government spending than to increase taxes. As a result, government debt as a percentage of annual gross domestic product increased from 26 percent in 1980 to 51 percent in 1995. It is hard to see any rationale for this policy. Although the government need not commit itself to a balanced budget as an inflexible rule, a balanced budget should be the normal state of affairs. If the U.S. government had been operating with a balanced budget since 1980, today's college graduates would be entering an economy that promised them greater economic prosperity.

CON: THE GOVERNMENT SHOULD NOT BALANCE ITS BUDGET

The problem of the budget deficit is often exaggerated. Although government debt does represent a tax burden on younger generations, it is not large compared to the average person's lifetime income. The debt of the U.S. federal government is about $14,000 per person. A person who works 40 years for $25,000 a year will earn $1 million over his lifetime. His share of the government debt represents less than 2 percent of his lifetime resources.

Moreover, it is misleading to view the effects of budget deficits in isolation. The budget deficit is just one piece of a large picture of how the government chooses to raise and spend money. In making these decisions over fiscal policy, policymakers affect different generations of taxpayers in many ways. The budget deficit should be considered together with these other policies.

For example, suppose the government reduces the budget deficit by cutting spending on education. Does this change in policy make young generations better off? The government debt will be smaller when they enter the labor force, which means a smaller tax burden. Yet if they are less well educated, their productivity and incomes will be lower. Many estimates of the return to schooling (the increase in a worker's wage that results from an additional year in school) find that it is quite large. Reducing the budget deficit by cutting education spending could, all things considered, make future generations worse off.

Single-minded concern about the budget deficit is also dangerous because it draws attention away from various other policies that redistribute income across generations. For example, in the 1960s and 1970s, the U.S. federal government raised Social Security benefits for the elderly. It financed this higher spending by increasing the payroll tax on the working-age population. This policy redistributed income away from younger generations toward older generations, even though it did not affect the budget deficit. Thus, the budget deficit is only a small piece of the larger issue of how government policy affects the welfare of different generations.

To some extent, the adverse effects of government budget deficits can be reversed by forward-looking parents. Suppose a parent is worried about the impact of the government debt on his children. The parent can offset the impact simply by saving and leaving a larger bequest. The bequest would enhance the children's ability to bear the burden of future taxes. Some economists claim that people do in fact behave this way. If this were true, higher private saving by parents would offset the public dissaving of budget deficits, and deficits would not affect the economy. (As Chapter 25 noted, this theory is called *Ricardian equivalence*.) Most economists doubt that parents are so farsighted, but some people probably do act this way, and anyone could. Deficits give people the opportunity to consume at the expense of their children, but deficits do not require them to do so. If the government debt were actually a great problem facing future generations, some parents would help to solve it.

Critics of budget deficits sometimes assert that the government debt cannot continue to rise forever, but in fact it can. Just as a bank evaluating a loan application would compare a person's debts to his income, we should judge the burden of the government debt relative to the size of the nation's income. Population growth and technological progress cause the total income of the U.S. economy to grow over time. As a result, the nation's ability to pay the interest on the government debt grows over time as well. As long as the government debt grows more slowly than the nation's income, there is nothing to prevent the government debt from growing forever.

Some numbers can put the budget deficit into perspective. The real output of the U.S. economy grows on average about 3 percent per year. If the inflation rate is 4 percent per year, then nominal income grows at a rate of 7 percent per year. The government debt, therefore, can rise by 7 percent per year without increasing the ratio of debt to income. In 1995 the federal government debt was $3,603 billion; 7 percent of this figure is $252 billion. As long as the federal budget deficit is smaller than $252 billion, as it has been in recent years, the policy is sustainable. There will never be any day of reckoning that forces budget deficits to end or the economy to collapse.

▌ QUICK QUIZ Explain how a budget deficit makes future generations worse off. Explain how reducing the budget deficit might make future generations worse off.

RESOLVED: THE TAX LAWS SHOULD BE REFORMED TO ENCOURAGE SAVING

A nation's standard of living depends on its ability to produce goods and services. This was one of the *Ten Principles of Economics* in Chapter 1. As we saw in Chapter 24, a nation's productive capability, in turn, is determined largely by how much it saves and invests for the future. Our fifth debate is whether policymakers should reform the tax laws in order to encourage greater saving and investment.

PRO: THE TAX LAWS SHOULD BE REFORMED TO ENCOURAGE SAVING

A nation's saving rate is a key determinant of its long-run economic prosperity. When the saving rate is higher, more resources are available for investment in new plant and equipment. A larger stock of plant and equipment, in turn, raises labor productivity, wages, and incomes. It is, therefore, no surprise that international data show a strong correlation between national saving rates and measures of economic well-being.

Another of the *Ten Principles of Economics* presented in Chapter 1 is that people respond to incentives. This lesson should apply to people's decisions about how much to save. If a nation's laws make saving attractive, people will save a higher fraction of their incomes, and this higher saving will lead to a more prosperous future.

Unfortunately, the U.S. tax system discourages saving by taxing the return to saving quite heavily. For example, consider a twenty-five-year-old worker who saves $1,000 of her income in order to have a more comfortable retirement at the age of seventy. If she buys a bond that pays an interest rate of 10 percent, the $1,000 will accumulate at the end of 45 years to $72,900 in the absence of taxes on interest. But suppose she faces a marginal tax rate on interest income of 40 percent, which is typical of many workers once federal and state income taxes are added together. In this case, her after-tax interest rate is only 6 percent, and the $1,000 will accumulate at the end of 45 years to only $13,800. That is, accumulated over this long span of time, the tax rate on interest income reduces the benefit of saving $1,000 from $72,900 to $13,800—or by about 80 percent.

The tax code further discourages saving by taxing some forms of capital income twice. Suppose a person uses some of his saving to buy stock in a corporation. When the corporation earns a profit from its capital investments, it first pays tax on this profit in the form of the corporate income tax. If the corporation pays out the rest of the profit to the stockholder in the form of dividends, the stockholder pays tax on this income a second time in the form of the individual income tax. This double taxation substantially reduces the return to the stockholder, thereby reducing the incentive to save.

The tax laws again discourage saving if a person wants to leave his accumulated wealth to his children (or anyone else) rather than consuming it during his lifetime. The inheritance tax exempts the first $600,000 that a person leaves at his death, but it taxes amounts above that at rates that range as high as 55 percent. To a large extent, concern about national saving is motivated by a desire to ensure economic prosperity for future generations. It is odd, therefore, that the tax laws discourage the most direct way in which one generation can help the next.

In addition to the tax code, many other policies and institutions in our society reduce the incentive for households to save. Some government benefits, such as welfare and Medicaid, are means-tested; that is, the benefits are reduced for those who in the past have been prudent enough to save some of their income. Colleges and universities grant financial aid as a function of the wealth of the students and their parents. Such a policy is like a tax on wealth and, as such, discourages students and parents from saving.

There are various ways in which the tax code could provide an incentive to save, or at least reduce the disincentive that households now face. Already the tax laws give preferential treatment to some types of retirement saving. When a taxpayer puts income into an Individual Retirement Account (IRA), for instance, that income and the interest it earns are not taxed until the funds are withdrawn at retirement. The tax code gives a similar tax advantage to retirement accounts that go by other names, such as 401(k), 403(b), Keogh, and profit-sharing plans. There are, however, limits to who is eligible to use these plans and, for those who are eligible, limits on the amount that can be put in them. Moreover, because there are penalties for withdrawal before retirement age, these retirement plans provide little incentive for other types of saving, such as saving to buy a house or pay for college. A small step to encourage greater saving would be to expand the ability of households to use such tax-advantaged savings accounts.

A more comprehensive approach would be to reconsider the entire basis by which the government collects revenue. The centerpiece of the U.S. tax system is the income tax. A dollar earned is taxed the same whether it is spent or saved. An alternative advocated by many economists is a consumption tax. Under a consumption tax, a household pays taxes only on the basis of what it spends. Income that is saved is exempt from taxation until the saving is later withdrawn and spent on consumption goods. In essence, a consumption tax puts all saving automatically into a tax-advantaged savings account, much like an IRA. A switch from income to consumption taxation would greatly increase the incentive to save.

CON: THE TAX LAWS SHOULD NOT BE REFORMED TO ENCOURAGE SAVING

Although increasing saving may be desirable, it is not the only goal of tax policy. Policymakers also must be sure to distribute the tax burden fairly. The problem with proposals to increase the incentive to save is that they increase the tax burden on those who can least afford it.

It is an undeniable fact that high-income households save a higher fraction of their income than low-income households. As a result, any tax change that favors people who save will also tend to favor people with high income. Policies such as tax-advantaged retirement accounts may seem appealing, but they lead to a less egalitarian society. By reducing the tax burden on the wealthy who can take advantage of these accounts, they force the government to raise the tax burden on the poor.

Moreover, it is not clear if tax policies designed to encourage saving are effective at achieving that goal. Many studies have found that saving is relatively inelastic—that is, the amount of saving is not very sensitive to the rate of return on saving. If this is indeed the case, then tax provisions that raise the effective return by reducing the taxation of capital income will further enrich the wealthy without inducing them to save more than they otherwise would.

From the standpoint of economic theory, it is not clear whether a higher rate of return would increase saving. The outcome depends on the relative size of two conflicting effects, called the *substitution effect* and the *income effect*. On the one hand, a higher rate of return raises the benefit of saving: Each dollar saved today produces more consumption in the future. This substitution effect tends to raise saving. On the other hand, a higher rate of return lowers the need for saving: A household has to save less to achieve any target level of consumption in the future. This income effect tends to reduce saving. If the substitution and income effects approximately cancel each other, as some studies suggest, then saving will not change when lower taxation of capital income raises the rate of return.

There are other ways to raise national saving than by giving tax breaks to the rich. National saving is the sum of private and public saving. Instead of trying to alter the tax code to encourage greater private saving, policymakers can simply raise public saving by reducing the budget deficit. Reducing the budget deficit, perhaps by raising taxes on the wealthy, offers a direct way of raising national saving and increasing prosperity for future generations.

Indeed, once public saving is taken into account, it seems that tax provisions to encourage saving might backfire. Tax changes that reduce the taxation of capital income reduce government revenue and, thereby, increase the budget deficit. To increase national saving, such a change in the tax code must stimulate private saving by more than it increases the budget deficit. If this is not the case, so-called saving incentives can potentially make matters worse.

QUICK QUIZ   Give three examples of how our society discourages saving. What are the drawbacks of eliminating these disincentives?

CONCLUSION

This chapter has considered five debates over macroeconomic policy. For each, it began with a controversial proposition and then offered the arguments pro and con. If you find it hard to choose a side in these debates, you may find some comfort in the fact that you are not alone. The study of economics does not always make it easy to choose among alternative policies. Indeed, by clarifying the inevitable tradeoffs that policymakers face, it can make the choice more difficult.

Difficult choices, however, have no right to seem easy. When you hear politicians or commentators proposing something that sounds too good to be true, it probably is. If they sound like they are offering you a free lunch, you should look for the hidden price tag. Few if any policies come with benefits but no costs. By helping you see through the fog of rhetoric so common in political discourse, the study of economics should make you a better participant in our national debates.

Summary

- Advocates of active monetary and fiscal policy view the economy as inherently unstable and believe that policy can manage aggregate demand in order to offset the inherent instability. Critics of active monetary and fiscal policy emphasize that policy affects the economy with a lag and that our ability to forecast future economic conditions is quite bad. As a result, attempts to stabilize the economy can end up being destabilizing.

- Advocates of rules for monetary policy argue that discretionary policy can suffer from incompetence, abuse of power, and time inconsistency. Critics of rules for monetary policy argue that discretionary policy is more flexible in responding to changing economic circumstances.

- Advocates of a zero-inflation target emphasize that inflation has many costs and few if any benefits. Moreover, the cost of eliminating inflation—depressed output and employment—is only temporary. Even this cost can be reduced if the central bank announces a credible plan to reduce inflation, thereby directly lowering expectations of inflation. Critics of a zero-inflation target claim that moderate inflation imposes only small costs on society, whereas the recession necessary to reduce inflation is quite costly.

- Advocates of a balanced government budget argue that budget deficits impose an unjustifiable burden on future generations by raising their taxes and lowering their incomes. Critics of a balanced government budget argue that the deficit is only one small piece of fiscal policy. Single-minded concern about the budget deficit can obscure the many ways in which policy, including various spending programs, affects different generations.

- Advocates of tax incentives for saving point out that our society discourages saving in many ways, such as by heavily taxing the income from capital and by reducing benefits for those who have accumulated wealth. They endorse reforming the tax laws to encourage saving, perhaps by switching from an income tax to a consumption tax. Critics of tax incentives for saving argue that many proposed changes to stimulate saving would primarily benefit the wealthy, who do not need a tax break. They also argue that such changes might have only a small effect on private saving. Raising public saving by eliminating the government's budget deficit would provide a more direct and equitable way to increase national saving.

Questions for Review

1. What causes the lags in the effect of monetary and fiscal policy on aggregate demand? What are the implications of these lags for the debate over active versus passive policy?

2. What might motivate a central banker to cause a political business cycle? What does the political business cycle imply for the debate over policy rules?

3. Explain how credibility might affect the cost of reducing inflation.

4. Why are some economists against a target of zero inflation?

5. Explain two ways in which a government budget deficit hurts a future worker.

6. What are two situations in which a budget deficit is justifiable?

7. Give an example of how the government might hurt young generations, even while reducing the government debt they inherit.

8. Some economists say that the government can continue running a budget deficit forever. How is that possible?

9. Some income from capital is taxed twice. Explain.

10. Give an example, other than tax policy, of how our society discourages saving.

11. What adverse effect might be caused by tax incentives to raise saving?

Problems and Applications

1. The chapter suggests that the economy, like the human body, has "natural restorative powers."
   a. Illustrate the short-run effect of a fall in aggregate demand using an aggregate-demand/aggregate-supply diagram. What happens to total output, income, and employment?
   b. If the government does not use stabilization policy, what happens to the economy over time? Illustrate on your diagram. Does this adjustment generally occur in a matter of months or a matter of years?
   c. Does the economy restore itself? How quickly do the economy's restorative powers work?

2. Policymakers who want to stabilize the economy must decide how much to change the money supply, government spending, or taxes. Why is it difficult for policymakers to choose the appropriate strength of their actions?

3. Suppose that people suddenly wanted to hold more money balances.
   a. What would be the effect of this change on the economy if the Federal Reserve followed a rule of increasing the money supply by 3 percent per year? Illustrate your answer with a money market diagram and an aggregate-demand/aggregate-supply diagram.
   b. What would be the effect of this change on the economy if the Fed followed a rule of increasing the money supply by 3 percent per year *plus* 1 percentage point for every percentage point that unemployment rises above its normal level? Illustrate your answer.
   c. Which of the foregoing rules better stabilizes the economy? Would it help to allow the Fed to respond to predicted unemployment instead of current unemployment? Explain.

4. The problem of time inconsistency applies to fiscal policy as well as to monetary policy. Suppose the government announced a reduction in taxes on income from capital investments, like new factories.
   a. If investors believed that capital taxes would remain low, how would the government's action affect the level of investment?
   b. After investors have responded to the announced tax reduction, does the government have an incentive to renege on its policy? Explain.
   c. Given your answer to part (b), would investors believe the government's announcement? What can the government do to increase the credibility of announced policy changes?
   d. Explain why this situation is similar to the time inconsistency problem faced by monetary policymakers.

5. Chapter 2 explains the difference between positive analysis and normative analysis. In the debate about whether the central bank should aim for zero inflation, which areas of disagreement involve positive statements and which involve normative judgments?

6. Why are the benefits of reducing inflation permanent and the costs temporary? Why are the costs of increasing inflation permanent and the benefits temporary? Use Phillips-curve diagrams in your answer.

7. Explain how each of the following policies redistributes income across generations. Is the redistribution from young to old, or from old to young?
   a. an increase in the budget deficit
   b. more generous subsidies for education loans
   c. greater investments in highways and bridges
   d. indexation of Social Security benefits to inflation

8. Surveys suggest that most people are opposed to budget deficits, but these same people elect representatives who pass budgets with significant deficits anyway. Why might the opposition to budget deficits be stronger in principle than in practice?

9. The chapter says that budget deficits reduce the income of future generations, but can boost output and income during a recession. Explain how both of these statements can be true.

10. The chapter says that tax changes that encourage saving will tend to favor people with high incomes. If the government cut taxes on capital income, what could it do at the same time to avoid redistributing income?

11. What is the fundamental tradeoff that society faces if it chooses to save more?

12. Suppose the government reduced the tax rate on income from savings.
    a. Who would benefit from this tax reduction most directly?
    b. What would happen to the capital stock over time? What would happen to the capital available to each worker? What would happen to productivity? What would happen to wages?

c. In light of your answer to part (b), who might benefit from this tax reduction in the long run?

13. For several of the policy debates discussed in this chapter, the costs of certain choices are borne primarily by a narrow segment of the population.

a. Give several examples, and explain why the costs are unevenly distributed.

b. How does the uneven distribution of costs affect your view of these debates?

GLOSSARY

ability-to-pay principle—the idea that taxes should be levied on a person according to how well that person can shoulder the burden

absolute advantage—the comparison among producers of a good according to their productivity

aggregate-demand curve—a curve that shows the quantity of goods and services that households, firms, and the government want to buy at any price level

aggregate-supply curve—a curve that shows the quantity of goods and services that firms choose to produce and sell at any price level

appreciation—an increase in the value of a currency as measured by the amount of foreign currency it can buy

automatic stabilizers—changes in fiscal policy that stimulate aggregate demand when the economy goes into a recession without policymakers having to take any deliberate action

average fixed cost—fixed costs divided by the quantity of output

average revenue—total revenue divided by the quantity sold

average tax rate—total taxes paid divided by total income

average total cost—total cost divided by the quantity of output

average variable cost—variable costs divided by the quantity of output

balanced trade—a situation in which exports equal imports

benefits principle—the idea that people should pay taxes based on the benefits they receive from government services

bond—a certificate of indebtedness.

budget constraint—the limit on the consumption bundles that a consumer can afford

budget deficit—a shortfall of tax revenue from government spending

budget surplus—an excess of tax revenue over government spending

capital—the equipment and structures used to produce goods and services

capital flight—a large and sudden reduction in the demand for assets located in a country

cartel—a group of firms acting in unison

catch-up effect—the property whereby countries that start off poor tend to grow more rapidly than countries that start off rich

central bank—an institution designed to oversee the banking system and regulate the quantity of money in the economy

ceteris paribus—a Latin phrase, translated as "other things being equal," used as a reminder that all variables other than the ones being studied are assumed to be constant

circular-flow diagram—a visual model of the economy that shows how dollars flow through markets among households and firms

classical dichotomy—the theoretical separation of nominal and real variables

closed economy—an economy that does not interact with other economies in the world

Coase theorem—the proposition that if private parties can bargain without cost over the allocation of resources, they can solve the problem of externalities on their own

collective bargaining—the process by which unions and firms agree on the terms of employment

collusion—an agreement among firms in a market about quantities to produce or prices to charge

commodity money—money that takes the form of a commodity with intrinsic value

common resources—goods that are rival but not excludable

comparable worth—a doctrine according to which jobs deemed comparable should be paid the same wage

comparative advantage—the comparison among producers of a good according to their opportunity cost

compensating differential—a difference in wages that arises to offset the nonmonetary characteristics of different jobs

competitive market—a market in which there are many buyers and many sellers so that each has a negligible impact on the market price

complements—two goods for which an increase in the price of one good leads to a decrease in the demand for the other good

constant returns to scale—the property whereby long-run average total cost stays the same as the quantity of output changes

consumer price index (CPI)—a measure of the overall cost of the goods and services bought by a typical consumer

consumer surplus—a buyer's willingness to pay minus the amount the buyer actually pays

consumption—spending by households on goods and services, with the exception of purchases of new housing

cost—the value of everything a seller must give up to produce a good

cost–benefit analysis—a study that compares the costs and benefits to society of providing a public good

crowding out—a decrease in investment that results from government borrowing

crowding-out effect—the offset in aggregate demand that results when expansionary fiscal policy raises the interest rate and thereby reduces investment spending

currency—the paper bills and coins in the hands of the public

cyclical unemployment—the deviation of unemployment from its natural rate

deadweight loss—the reduction in total surplus that results from a market distortion, such as a tax or monoploy price.

demand curve—a graph of the relationship between the price of a good and the quantity demanded

demand deposits—balances in bank accounts that depositors can access on demand by writing a check

demand schedule—a table that shows the relationship between the price of a good and the quantity demanded

depreciation—a decrease in the value of a currency as measured by the amount of foreign currency it can buy

depression—a severe recession

diminishing marginal product—the property whereby the marginal product of an input declines as the quantity of the input increases

diminishing returns (also known as diminishing marginal product)—the property whereby the benefit from an extra unit of an input declines as the quantity of the input increases

discount rate—the interest rate on the loans that the Fed makes to banks

discouraged workers—individuals who would like to work but have given up looking for a job

discrimination—the offering of different opportunities to similar individuals who differ only by race, ethnic group, sex, age, or other personal characteristics

diseconomies of scale—the property whereby long-run average total cost rises as the quantity of output increases

dominant strategy—a strategy that is best for a player in a game regardless of the strategies chosen by the other players

economics—the study of how society manages its scarce resources

economies of scale—the property whereby long-run average total cost falls as the quantity of output increases

efficiency—the property of society getting the most it can from its scarce resources

efficiency wages—above-equilibrium wages paid by firms in order to increase worker productivity

efficient scale—the quantity of output that minimizes average total cost

elasticity—a measure of the responsiveness of quantity demanded or quantity supplied to one of its determinants

equilibrium—a situation in which supply and demand have been brought into balance

equilibrium price—the price that balances supply and demand

equilibrium quantity—the quantity supplied and the quantity demanded when the price has adjusted to balance supply and demand

equity—the property of distributing economic prosperity fairly among the members of society

excess demand—a situation in which quantity demanded is greater than quantity supplied

excess supply—a situation in which quantity supplied is greater than quantity demanded

excludability—the property of a good whereby a person can be prevented from using it

exports—goods and services produced domestically and sold abroad

externality—the impact of one person's actions on the well-being of a bystander

factors of production—the inputs used to produce goods and services

Federal Reserve (Fed)—the central bank of the United States

fiat money—money without intrinsic value that is used as money because of government decree

financial intermediaries—financial institutions through which savers can indirectly provide funds to borrowers

financial markets—financial institutions through which savers can directly provide funds to borrowers

financial system—the group of institutions in the economy that help to match one person's saving with another person's investment

Fisher effect—the one-for-one adjustment of the nominal interest rate to the inflation rate

fixed costs—costs that do not vary with the quantity of output produced

fractional-reserve banking—a banking system in which banks hold only a fraction of deposits as reserves

free rider—a person who receives the benefit of a good but avoids paying for it

game theory—the study of how people behave in strategic situations

GDP deflator—a measure of the price level calculated as the ratio of nominal GDP to real GDP times 100

Giffen good—a good for which an increase in the price raises the quantity demanded

government purchases—spending on goods and services by local, state, and federal governments

gross domestic product (GDP)—the market value of all final goods and services produced within a country in a given period of time

gross national product (GNP)—the market value of all final goods and services produced by permanent residents of a nation within a given period of time

horizontal equity—the idea that taxpayers with similar abilities to pay taxes should pay the same amount

human capital—the knowledge and skills that workers acquire through education, training, and experience

import quota—a limit on the quantity of a good that can be produced abroad and sold domestically

imports—goods and services produced abroad and sold domestically

in-kind transfers—transfers to the poor given in the form of goods and services rather than cash

income effect—the change in consumption that results when a price change moves the consumer to a higher or lower indifference curve

income elasticity of demand—a measure of how much the quantity demanded of a good responds to a change in consumers' income, computed as the percentage change in quantity demanded divided by the percentage change in income

indexation—the automatic correction of a dollar amount for the effects of inflation by law or contract

indifference curve—a curve that shows consumption bundles that give the consumer the same level of satisfaction

inferior good—a good for which, other things being equal, an increase in income leads to a decrease in quantity demanded

inflation—an increase in the overall level of prices in the economy

inflation rate—the percentage change in the price index from the preceding period

inflation tax—the revenue the government raises by creating money

internalizing an externality—altering incentives so that people take account of the external effects of their actions

investment—spending on capital equipment, inventories, and structures, including household purchases of new housing

job search—the process by which workers find appropriate jobs given their tastes and skills

labor force—the total number of workers, including both the employed and the unemployed

labor-force participation rate—the percentage of the adult population that is in the labor force

law of demand—the claim that, other things being equal, the quantity demanded of a good falls when the price of the good rises

law of supply—the claim that, other things being equal, the quantity supplied of a good rises when the price of the good rises

law of supply and demand—the claim that the price of any good adjusts to bring the supply and demand for that good into balance

liberalism—the political philosophy according to which the government should choose policies deemed to be just, as evaluated by an impartial observer behind a "veil of ignorance"

libertarianism—the political philosophy according to which the government should punish crimes and enforce voluntary agreements but not redistribute income

life cycle—the regular pattern of income variation over a person's life

liquidity—the ease with which an asset can be converted into the economy's medium of exchange

lump-sum tax—a tax that is the same amount for every person

macroeconomics—the study of economy-wide phenomena, including inflation, unemployment, and economic growth

marginal changes—small incremental adjustments to a plan of action

marginal cost—the increase in total cost that arises from an extra unit of production

marginal product—the increase in output that arises from an additional unit of input

marginal product of labor—the increase in the amount of output from an additional unit of labor

marginal rate of substitution—the rate at which a consumer is willing to trade one good for another

marginal revenue—the change in total revenue from an additional unit sold

marginal tax rate—the extra taxes paid on an additional dollar of income

market—a group of buyers and sellers of a particular good or service

market economy—an economy that allocates resources through the decentralized decisions of many firms and households as they interact in markets for goods and services

market failure—a situation in which a market left on its own fails to allocate resources efficiently

market for loanable funds—the market in which those who want to save supply funds and those who want to borrow to invest demand funds

market power—the ability of a single economic actor (or small group of actors) to have a substantial influence on market prices

maximin criterion—the claim that the government should aim to maximize the well-being of the worst-off person in society

medium of exchange—an item that buyers give to sellers when they want to purchase goods and services

menu costs—the costs of changing prices

microeconomics—the study of how households and firms make decisions and how they interact in markets

model of aggregate demand and aggregate supply—the model that most economists use to explain short-run fluctuations in economic activity around its long-run trend

monetary neutrality—the proposition that changes in the money supply do not affect real variables

monetary policy—the setting of the money supply by policymakers in the central bank

money—the set of assets in an economy that people regularly use to buy goods and services from other people

money multiplier—the amount of money the banking system generates with each dollar of reserves

money supply—the quantity of money available in the economy

monopolistic competition—a market structure in which many firms sell products that are similar but not identical

monopoly—a firm that is the sole seller of a product without close substitutes

multiplier effect—the additional shifts in aggregate demand that result when expansionary fiscal policy increases income and thereby increases consumer spending

mutual fund—an institution that sells shares to the public and uses the proceeds to buy a portfolio of stocks and bonds

Nash equilibrium—a situation in which economic actors interacting with one another each choose their best strategy given the strategies that all the other actors have chosen

national saving (saving)—the total income in the economy that remains after paying for consumption and government purchases

natural monopoly—a monopoly that arises because a single firm can supply a good or service to an entire market at a smaller cost than could two or more firms

natural rate of unemployment—the normal rate of unemployment around which the unemployment rate fluctuates

natural resources—the inputs into the production of goods and services that are provided by nature, such as land, rivers, and mineral deposits

natural-rate hypothesis—the claim that unemployment eventually returns to its normal, or natural, rate, regardless of the rate of inflation

negative income tax—a tax system that collects revenue from high-income households and gives transfers to low-income households

net exports—spending on domestically produced goods by foreigners (exports) minus spending on foreign goods by domestic residents (imports)

net foreign investment—the purchase of foreign assets by domestic residents minus the purchase of domestic assets by foreigners

nominal GDP—the production of goods and services valued at current prices

nominal exchange rate—the rate at which a person can trade the currency of one country for the currency of another

nominal interest rate—the interest rate as usually reported without a correction for the effects of inflation

nominal variables—variables measured in monetary units

normal good—a good for which, other things being equal, an increase in income leads to an increase in quantity demanded

normative statements—claims that attempt to prescribe how the world should be

oligopoly—a market structure in which only a few sellers offer similar or identical products

open economy—an economy that interacts freely with other economies around the world

open-market operations—the purchase and sale of U.S. government bonds by the Fed

opportunity cost—whatever must be given up to obtain some item

perfect complements—two goods with right-angle indifference curves

perfect substitutes—two goods with straight-line indifference curves

permanent income—a person's normal income

Phillips curve—a curve that shows the short-run tradeoff between inflation and unemployment

physical capital—the stock of equipment and structures that are used to produce goods and services

Pigovian tax—a tax enacted to correct the effects of a negative externality

positive statements—claims that attempt to describe the world as it is

poverty line—an absolute level of income set by the federal government for each family size below which a family is deemed to be in poverty

poverty rate—the percentage of the population whose family income falls below an absolute level called the poverty line

price ceiling—a legal maximum on the price at which a good can be sold

price discrimination—the business practice of selling the same good at different prices to different customers

price elasticity of demand—a measure of how much the quantity demanded of a good responds to a change in the price of that good, computed as the percentage change in quantity demanded divided by the percentage change in price

price elasticity of supply—a measure of how much the quantity supplied of a good responds to a change in the price of that good, computed as the percentage change in quantity supplied divided by the percentage change in price

price floor—a legal minimum on the price at which a good can be sold

prisoners' dilemma—a particular "game" between two captured prisoners that illustrates why cooperation is difficult to maintain even when it is mutually beneficial

private goods—goods that are both excludable and rival

private saving—the income that households have left after paying for taxes and consumption

producer price index—a measure of the cost of a basket of goods and services bought by firms

producer surplus—the amount a seller is paid for a good minus the seller's cost

production function—the relationship between quantity of inputs used to make a good and the quantity of output of that good

production possibilities frontier—a graph that shows the various combinations of output that the economy can possibly produce given the available factors of production and the available production technology

productivity—the quantity of goods and services produced from each hour of a worker's time

profit—total revenue minus total cost

progressive tax—a tax for which high-income taxpayers pay a larger fraction of their income than do low-income taxpayers

proportional tax—a tax for which high-income and low-income taxpayers pay the same fraction of income

public goods—goods that are neither excludable nor rival

public saving—the tax revenue that the government has left after paying for its spending

purchasing-power parity—a theory of exchange rates whereby a unit of any given currency should be able to buy the same quantity of goods in all countries

quantity demanded—the amount of a good that buyers are willing and able to purchase

quantity equation—the equation $M \times V = P \times Y$, which relates the quantity of money, the velocity of money, and the dollar value of the economy's output of goods and services

quantity supplied—the amount of a good that sellers are willing and able to sell

quantity theory of money—a theory asserting that the quantity of money available determines the price level and that the growth rate in the quantity of money available determines the inflation rate

rational expectations—the theory according to which people optimally use all the information they have, including information about government policies, when forecasting the future

real GDP—the production of goods and services valued at constant prices

real exchange rate—the rate at which a person can trade the goods and services of one country for the goods and services of another

real interest rate—the interest rate corrected for the effects of inflation

real variables—variables measured in physical units

recession—a period of declining real incomes and rising unemployment

regressive tax—a tax for which high-income taxpayers pay a smaller fraction of their income than do low-income taxpayers

reserve ratio—the fraction of deposits that banks hold as reserves

reserve requirements—regulations on the minimum amount of reserves that banks must hold against deposits

reserves—deposits that banks have received but have not loaned out

rivalness—the property of a good whereby one person's use diminishes other people's use

sacrifice ratio—the number of percentage points of annual output lost in the process of reducing inflation by 1 percentage point

scarcity—the limited nature of society's resources

shoeleather costs—the resources wasted when inflation encourages people to reduce their money holdings

stagflation—a period of falling output and rising prices

stock—a claim to partial ownership in a firm

store of value—an item that people can use to transfer purchasing power from the present to the future

strike—the organized withdrawal of labor from a firm by a union

substitutes—two goods for which an increase in the price of one good leads to an increase in the demand for the other good

substitution effect—the change in consumption that results when a price change moves the consumer along a given indifference curve to a point with a new marginal rate of substitution

supply curve—a graph of the relationship between the price of a good and the quantity supplied

supply schedule—a table that shows the relationship between the price of a good and the quantity supplied

tariff—a tax on goods produced abroad and sold domestically

tax incidence—the study of who bears the burden of taxation

technological knowledge—society's understanding of the best ways to produce goods and services

theory of liquidity preference—Keynes's theory that the interest rate adjusts to bring money supply and money demand into balance

total cost—the amount a firm pays to buy the inputs into production

total revenue (for a firm)—the amount a firm receives for the sale of its output

total revenue (in a market)—the amount paid by buyers and received by sellers of a good, computed as the price of the good times the quantity sold

trade balance—the value of a nation's exports minus the value of its imports, also called net exports

trade deficit—an excess of imports over exports

trade policy—a government policy that directly influences the quantity of goods and services that a country imports or exports

trade surplus—an excess of exports over imports

Tragedy of the Commons—a parable that illustrates why common resources get used more than is desirable from the standpoint of society as a whole

transaction costs—the costs that parties incur in the process of agreeing and following through on a bargain

unemployment insurance—a government program that partially protects workers' incomes when they become unemployed

unemployment rate—the percentage of the labor force that is unemployed

union—a worker association that bargains with employers over wages and working conditions

unit of account—the yardstick people use to post prices and record debts

utilitarianism—the political philosophy according to which the government should choose policies to maximize the total utility of everyone in society

utility—a measure of happiness or satisfaction

value of the marginal product—the marginal product of an input times the price of the output

variable costs—costs that vary with the quantity of output produced

velocity of money—the rate at which money changes hands

vertical equity—the idea that taxpayers with a greater ability to pay taxes should pay larger amounts

welfare—government programs that supplement the incomes of the needy

welfare economics—the study of how the allocation of resources affects economic well-being

willingness to pay—the maximum amount that a buyer will pay for a good

world price—the price of a good that prevails in the world market for that good

CREDITS

Photos and Cartoons

P. 6 © Al Tieleman/Sports Illustrated

P. 8 Reprinted by permission of The Wall Street Journal © 1990 Dow Jones and Company, Inc. All rights reserved worldwide.

P. 12 © 1978 Stayskal and The Chicago Tribune

P. 18 Drawing by Handelsman; © 1986 The New Yorker Magazine, Inc.

P. 27 Drawing by Stevenson; © 1981 The New Yorker Magazine, Inc.

P. 54 Corbis-Bettmann

P. 69 © Michael Newman/Photo Edit

P. 78 © 1995 The Washington Post

P. 84 Drawing by Robert Day; © 1972 The New Yorker Magazine, Inc.

P. 96 © Swanson/Gamma Liaison

P. 104 © Gary Trudeau and Universal Press Syndicate. Reprinted with permission.

P. 127 © Roger Markham-Smith/International Stock

P. 145 Corbis-Bettmann

P. 148 © Robert Ginn/Photo Edit

P. 149 Drawing by Dana Fradon; © 1992 The New Yorker Magazine, Inc.

P. 156 Drawing by Handelsman; © 1970 The New Yorker Magazine, Inc.

P. 163 (top) © 1991 Alon Reininger/Contact Press Images

P. 163 (bottom) Corbis-Bettmann

P. 187 Berry's World, © Berry's World reprinted by permission of Newspaper Enterprises Association.

P. 190 © Donald L. Miller/International Stock

P. 203 Drawing by Handelsman; © 1970 The New Yorker Magazine, Inc.

P. 205 © Mark Richards/Photo Edit

P. 208 © Tony Freeman/Photo Edit

P. 215 © Bruce Fier/Gamma Liaison

P. 223 Drawing by Dana Fradon; © 1989 The New Yorker Magazine, Inc.

P. 224 © Bill Truslow/Gamma Liaison

P. 226 © Leverett Bradley/Gamma Liaison

P. 230 © Robert Brenner/Photo Edit

P. 233 © Daniel Nichols/Gamma Liaison

P. 244 © Berry's World, Berry's World reprinted by permission of Newspaper Enterprises Association.

P. 245 (left) © Bill Pudliano/Gamma Liaison

P. 245 (right) Hal Kem/International Stock

P. 253 Drawing by Levin; © 1993 The New Yorker Magazine, Inc.

P. 254 © Frank Fisher/Gamma Liaison

P. 291 © D. Young-Wolff/Photo Edit

P. 296 © 1997 by North American Syndicate, Inc. World rights reserved. Printed with special permission of North American Syndicate, Inc.

P. 314 © Michael Newman/Photo Edit

P. 320 © 1998 by Sydney Harris

P. 324 © 1993 Copyright Photo Disc, Inc.

P. 328 William Hamilton's cartoon is reprinted courtesy of Chronicle Features, San Francisco, California.

P. 330 Richard Mackson/Sports Illustrated © Time, Inc.

P. 344 © Gamma Liaison

P. 357 © Eric Sander/Gamma Liaison

P. 366 © 1998 by Sydney Harris

P. 374 © 1998 by Sydney Harris

P. 376 TM and © Warner Bros., 1997

P. 397 Corbis-Bettmann

P. 402 Drawing by Dana Fradon; © 1985 The New Yorker Magazine, Inc.

P. 406 Warner Brothers/The Kobal Collection

P. 408 © David Young-Wolff/Photo Edit

P. 414 Joe Marquette/AP Wide World Photos

P. 422 Drawing by Mankoff; © 1989 The New Yorker Magazine, Inc.

P. 425 © Mark Reinstein/FPG International

P. 466 © David Boe/UPI/Corbis-Bettmann

P. 501 © 1993 Copyright Photo Disc

P. 505 Reprinted by permission of The Wall Street Journal © 1990 Dow Jones and Company, Inc. All rights reserved worldwide.

P. 506 The Kobal Collection

P. 521 © Michael Newman/Photo Edit

P. 522 © Jeff Greenberg/Photo Edit

P. 531 © Steve Lehman/SABA

P. 533 Andomeda Interactive

P. 544 © J. P. Laffont/Sygma

P. 546 Arlo & Janis reprinted by permission of Newspaper Enterprises Association, Inc.

P. 557 Drawing by Robert Weber; © 1989 The New Yorker Magazine, Inc.

P. 561 © 1993 Copyright Photo Disc

P. 571 © Jeff Greenberg/Photo Edit

P. 574 © R. Maiman/Sygma

P. 580 Reprinted by permission of United Features Syndicate

P. 583 UPI/Corbis-Bettmann

P. 594 Reprinted by permission of The Wall Street Journal © 1984 Dow Jones and Company, Inc. All rights reserved worldwide.

P. 597 © Tony Freeman/Photo Edit

P. 601 Drawing by M. Stevens; © 1989 The New Yorker Magazine, Inc.

P. 606 The Kobal Collection

P. 611 Drawing by Modell; © 1978 The New Yorker Magazine, Inc.

P. 631 The Kobal Collection

P. 638 Drawing by Mort Gerberg; © 1992 The New Yorker Magazine, Inc.

P. 640 © Paul Conklin/Photo Edit

P. 651 Digital Stock

INDEX

SUGGESTIONS FOR SUMMER READING

*If you enjoyed the economics course you have just finished,
you might like reading more about economic issues in the following books.*

■ **GETTING IT RIGHT: MARKETS AND CHOICES IN A FREE SOCIETY,** Robert J. Barro, Cambridge, Mass.: MIT Press, 1996. In this collection of essays based on his *Wall Street Journal* columns, conservative economist Robert Barro offers his view about the workings of the economy and the proper scope of economic policy.

■ **HARD HEADS, SOFT HEARTS: TOUGH-MINDED ECONOMICS FOR A JUST SOCIETY,** Alan S. Blinder, Reading, Mass.: Addison-Wesley, 1987. How should government policymakers balance economic efficiency and social compassion? Alan Blinder, who has served as an economic adviser to President Clinton, offers his answers in this wide-ranging book.

■ **NEW IDEAS FROM DEAD ECONOMISTS,** Todd G. Buchholz, New York: Penguin Books, 1989. This amusing book provides an overview of the history of economic thought.

■ **THINKING STRATEGICALLY: A COMPETITIVE EDGE IN BUSINESS, POLITICS, AND EVERYDAY LIFE,** Avinash Dixit and Barry Nalebuff, New York: Norton, 1991. This introduction to game theory discusses how all people—from corporate executives to arrested criminals—should and do make strategic decisions that affect themselves and others.

■ **THE WINNER-TAKE-ALL SOCIETY: HOW MORE AND MORE AMERICANS COMPETE FOR FEWER AND BIGGER PRIZES, ENCOURAGING ECONOMIC WASTE, INCOME INEQUALITY, AND AN IMPOVERISHED CULTURAL LIFE,** Robert H. Frank and Philip J. Cook, New York: The Free Press, 1995. This book examines some of the reasons for, and the effects of, increasing inequality of incomes in the United States.

■ **DAY OF RECKONING: THE CONSEQUENCES OF AMERICAN ECONOMIC POLICY UNDER REAGAN AND AFTER,** Benjamin Friedman, New York: Random House, 1988. Benjamin Friedman presents an uncompromising critique of the large increase in government debt that began during the first Reagan administration.